P9-BYB-079

HUMAN SEXUALITY

IN A WORLD

OF DIVERSITY

UMAN SEXUALITY IN A WORLD OF DIVERSITY

THIRD EDITION

Spencer A. Rathus
St. John's University

Jeffrey S. Nevid
St. John's University

Lois Fichner-Rathus
The College of New Jersey

ALLYN AND BACON

Boston
London
Toronto
Sydney
Tokyo
Singapore

Vice President and Editor-in-Chief, Social Sciences: Sean W. Wakely
Senior Editor: Carolyn Merrill
Editorial Assistant: Alyssa Dorrie
Marketing Manager: Joyce Nilsen
Production Administrator: Deborah Brown
Editorial/Production Services: Colophon
Text Designer: Melinda Grosser for *Silk*
Cover Administrator: Linda Knowles
Cover Designer: Studio Nine
Composition Buyer: Linda Cox
Manufacturing Buyer: Megan Cochran
Photo Researcher: Laurie Frankenthaler

Copyright © 1997, 1995, 1993 by Allyn & Bacon
A Viacom Company
160 Gould Street
Needham Heights, MA 02194-2130
Internet: www.abcon.com
America Online: Keyword: College Online

All rights reserved. No part of the material protected by this copyright notice may be reproduced or utilized in any form by any means, electronic or mechanical, including photocopying, recording, or by any information storage and retrieval system, without the written permission of the copyright owner.

Library of Congress Cataloging-in-Publication Data

Rathus, Spencer A.
    Human sexuality in a world of diversity / Spencer A. Rathus,
Jeffrey S. Nevid, Lois Fichner-Rathus.   3rd ed.
      p. cm.
    Nevid's name appears first on the previous edition.
    Includes bibliographical references and index.
    ISBN 0-205-20018-4
    1. Sex. I. Nevid, Jeffrey S. II. Fichner-Rathus, Lois, 1953-
HQ21.R23   1996
306.7--dc 20   96-18060
                                      CIP

Printed in the United States of America

10 9 8 7 6 5 4 3 2   01 00 99 98 97

Photo Credits: **Chapter 1:** p. 9, Lou Jones; p. 12, Ali Meyer/The Bridgeman Library Ltd.; p. 13, Art Resource; p. 16, Corbis-Bettman; p. 17 (left), North Wind Picture Archives; p. 17 (right), The Bridgeman Library Ltd.; p. 21, Dan Habib/Impact Visuals; p. 24, Wolfgang Kaehler; p. 26, National Library of Medicine. **Chapter 2:** p. 39, Courtesy of Farrall Instruments; p. 44, Reprinted by permission of the Kinsey Institute for Research in Sex, Gender, and Reproduction; p. 48 (left), Bob Daemmrich/The Image Works; p. 48 (right), John Eastcott/Yva Momatiuk/Photo Researchers; p. 49, Steve McCurry/Magnum Photos; p. 51, Elliott Erwitt/Magnum Photos. **Chapter 3:** p. 66, Catherine Leroy/SIPA Press; p. 75, John Giannicchi/Photo Researchers Science Source; p. 79, Susan Van Etten/The Picture Cube; p. 82, Lynn Johnson/Black Star; p. 91, Corbis-Bettmann; p. 93, Shumsky/The Image Works; p. 98, Robert Harbison. **Chapter 4:** p. 109, Skjold/ The Image Works; p. 110 (top), Professor P. Motta/Dept. of Anatomy/Rome University/Science Photo Library/Photo Researchers; p. 110 (bottom), Dr. Rom Verna/Phototake; p. 114, Charles Gupton/Stock, Boston. **Chapter 5:** p. 127, Willie Hill, Jr./The Image Works; p. 129, Willie Hill, Jr./The Image Works; p. 133, A. Farnsworth/The Image Works; p. 137, Douglas Mason/Woodfin Camp & Associates. **Chapter 6:** p. 158, from *Sex Errors of the Body* © Dr. John Money; p. 159 (both), from *Sex Errors of the Body* © Dr. John Money; p. 161 (both), AP/Wide World Photos; p. 165, M. Edrington/The Image Works; p. 167, Bob Daemmrich/The Image Works; p. 168, AP/Wide World Photos; p. 171, Bob Krist/Black Star; p. 176 (left), Kolvoord/The Image Works; p. 176 (right), Elizabeth Crews/The Image Works. **Chapter 7:** p. 188 (top left), Adam Wolfitt/Woodfin Camp & Associates; p. 188 (top middle), Archive Photos/Lee; p. 188 (top right), Claus Meyer/Black Star; p. 188 (bottom left), Mitch Kezar/Black Star; p. 188 (bottom right), Nicholas DeVore III/Photographers Aspen; p. 189, Guy Marineau/Black Star; p. 190 (both), D. Perrett, K. May & S. Yoshikawa, University of St. Andrews/Science Photo Library/Photo Researchers; p. 195, Paul Fusco/Magnum Photos; Page 204, Roy Morsch/The Stock Market. **Chapter 8:** p. 212, Douglas Mason/Woodfin Camp & Associates; p. 218, Catherine Karnow/Woodfin Camp & Associates; p. 219, Fritz Hoffman/JB Pictures; p. 220, Nicholas DeVore III/Photographers Aspen; p. 224, Robert Harbison.

Photo credits continue on page 713 which constitutes a continuation of the copyright page.

Brief Contents

Contents

16 Sexually Transmitted Diseases   *471*

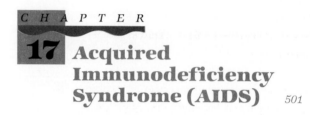

17 Acquired Immunodeficiency Syndrome (AIDS)   *501*

CHAPTER

21 Making Responsible Sexual Decisions— An Epilogue *629*

Preface

*There are more things in heaven and earth, Horatio,
Than are dreamt of in your philosophy.*

Shakespeare, *Hamlet*

There are, indeed, more kinds of people in this world and more ways in which people experience their sexuality than most of us might imagine. Human sexuality may be closely related to human biology, but it is also interwoven in the cultural fabric of society. To this end, the third edition of *Human Sexuality in a World of Diversity* provides a multicultural perspective; that is, a perspective of human sexuality from historical, biological, psychological, cultural, and sociological points of view. In this text students learn to examine a broad view of sexual experience and to examine the latest scientific findings in the field at the same time.

The text covers the core topics in the field of human sexuality including sexual anatomy and physiology, sexual arousal and response, gender roles, attraction, love, intimate relationships, sexual communication, sexual techniques, sexual orientation, conception, birth control, prenatal development, childbirth, sexual behavior across the life span, sexual dysfunction and sex therapy, sexually transmitted diseases, atypical variations in sexual behavior, sexual coercion, and commercial sex.

The text is written in a style intended to capture student interest and one that is sensitive to students' experience and background as well as at a level that students will find compelling and accessible, but not oversimplified or patronizing. The selective use of humor and author asides build interest and enliven descriptions.

Themes of the Text

The four main themes that thread throughout *Human Sexuality in a World of Diversity* are the rich diversity found in gender roles, sexual attitudes, and sexual behaviors; critical thinking as a tool for learning and taking action; sexually responsible decision making; and sexual health.

Diversity

Colleges and universities are in the business of broadening students' perspectives to enable them to appreciate and understand human diversity.

The United States is a nation of hundreds of different ethnic and religious groups, many of whom endorse culturally distinct beliefs about appropriate gender roles for men and women and sexual practices and customs. Diversity is even broader within the global village of the the world's nearly 200 nations and those nation's own distinctive subcultures. *Human Sexuality in a World of Diversity, Third Edition,* incorporates a multicultural, multiethnic perspective that reflects the diversity of sexual experience in our own society and around the world. This diversity is reflected in customs and beliefs of social roles and sexual conduct in light of cultural traditions and standards.

Critical Thinking

As we approach the next century in a closer knit world, colleges and universities are encouraging students to become critical thinkers and to take a stand on their place in the world. However, today's students are so inundated with data about gender, sexuality, and behavior that it is often difficult to sort out truth from fiction. Not only are politicians, theologians, and community leaders speaking openly about gender- and sex-related attitudes, but radio, television, and the press provide continuous commentary about gender roles and issues concerning human sexuality.

This text asks students to question information that is presented in print or is part of the daily media and culture. A critical thinking approach in the subject matter of sexuality requires thoughtful and sensitive analysis and a willingness to challenge conventional wisdom and common knowledge that is easily taken for granted. It means scrutinizing definitions of terms, premises of assumptions, and the logic of arguments.

The book raises questions through self-scoring questionnaires and a reflections section, new to this edition, which stimulate analysis and evaluation of beliefs and attitudes in light of the ongoing scientific record in the study of sexuality.

Responsible Sexual Decision Making

In addition, students are encouraged to make responsible sexual decisions and to be cognizant of psychological and physical dangers in "going with the flow" or being passive about their sexuality. Students' sexual decisions are ultimately private matters, and we encourage students to actively make their own sexual decisions but on the basis of accurate information. The text assists in breaking down the steps towards making responsible decisions, such as how to decide whom to date, how and when to become sexually intimate, whether to practice contraception and which methods to use, and how to protect against AIDS and other sexually transmitted diseases (STDs).

The new Reflections sections in each chapter and the epilogue, "Making Responsible Sexual Decisions," help in clarifying each person's sexual values. The epilogue examines the major ethical systems that are used in moral reasoning and provides a decision-making model that will help students weigh the pluses and minuses of the choices they face.

Sexual Health

Human Sexuality in a World of Diversity places a strong emphasis on issues relating to sexual health including extensive coverage of HIV/AIDS and other STDs, innovations in contraception and reproductive technologies, breast cancer, menstrual distress, diseases that affect the reproductive tracts, sex and disabilities, and sex and the later years. The text encourages students to take an active role in health promotion. For example, it includes exercises and features that teach breast and testes examination for abnormalities, how to reduce the risk of HIV infection, and how to cope with menstrual discomfort. The text also thoroughly covers problems of dysfunction in sexual behavior and practices.

Features of the Text

A World of Diversity highlights the rich variety of human sexual customs around the world. This feature, which occurs in every chapter, helps students understand that partners who may not share the same ethnic or religious heritage may feel differently than they do about sexual intimacy. Concepts that are covered in this feature include: sexual permissiveness, AIDS and motherhood, premarital intercourse for teens and different ethnic groups, abortion in Asia, rape in societies that are rape-prone and rape-free, to name a few.

A Closer Look boxes provide indepth discussions of particular sex-related topics from the authors' files, including social issues such as the debate about public school policy regarding contraceptives; an essay on art, pornography, and censorship; transvestism; and many more.

What Do You Say Now? features are carefully constructed applications that place students in a realistic setting and allow them to compare their answers with answers suggested by the authors. As such, students may examine their attitudes but also project new ways of handling demanding situations. Worded as active dialogues, these features cover topics such as date-seeking skills, talking to partners, children, and friends about contraception, sex, STDs, and sexual pressure lines.

Self-Scoring **Questionnaires** help students examine their own behaviors and attitudes about love, abortion, and STDs.

Learning Aids

The text is organized to maximize learning and critical thinking in a multicultural setting, as has been noted, and each chapter includes an initial chapter outline; glossary terms boldfaced in the text and defined in the margin, often with a cultural or word origin reference; a wide variety of illustrations, anatomicals, and photographs; and a complete summing up organized by major chapter heads. A prominent organizing feature is **Truth or Fiction,** statements of common misunderstandings regarding human sexuality, which appear on the outline page. **Truth or Fiction Revisited** sections follow throughout the text providing feedback as to the accuracy of the statements.

New to the Third Edition

This edition is thoroughly updated with hundreds of new references, a new feature, and many new feature topics.

Reflections Sections

New to this edition are the **Reflections** sections which are found at the end of every major section of each chapter. The significance of the section for students points to the value of the activity of reflecting; that is, thinking about things or images that a person has some knowledge of. Reflecting on ideas raised in this textbook helps students accomplish four goals:

1. Effective learning. Reflecting makes new material more meaningful and easier to remember. Reflecting requires students to put ideas into their heads in their own words and to actively acquire information. These sections also act as interim summaries.

2. Critical thinking. Reflecting encourages students to analyze the definitions of terms, evaluate the adequacy of research methods, and examine the logic of arguments.
3. Values clarification. Reflecting enables students to identify and evaluate their own values concerning human sexuality. Students will find they are better able to understand where they are coming from, their opinions, and their feelings.
4. Applications to Students' Lives. Reflecting enhances the likelihood that students will be able to apply text material to their own lives.

The NHSLS (National Health and Social Life Survey) Study

Particularly noteworthy in this edition is the inclusion of the results of the NHSLS (National Health and Social Life Survey) study, which was conducted by a research group headed by Edward O. Laumann at the University of Chicago. The NHSLS study was originally designed to be supported by government funds, but government ambivalence about a sex survey forced the research team to obtain funding from private sources. We elaborate on the sampling techniques of the NHSLS study in Chapter 2, and many of the study results are reported in several other chapters. This study may be the most valid large-scale study on human sexuality since Kinsey's day. The data indicate two important values not covered by most previous surveys and not covered in previous editions of this text.

1. The NHSLS study samples African Americans and Hispanic Americans in large numbers. These data permit valid ethnic comparisons in sexual behavior and sex-related behavior which we have shown in Tables 1.3, 9.2, 14.4, and 15.2.
2. The NHSLS study suggests that many earlier studies, including some which have served as marker studies throughout the 1970s and 1980s, may have yielded highly skewed results through sampling bias. In short, the NHSLS study suggests that Americans are more faithful and somewhat less sexually active than other surveys and the popular media would suggest.

Acquired Immunodeficiency Syndrome (AIDS)— Chapter 17

The AIDS chapter has been updated for this edition. All statistics and current events are updated to reveal the most recent trends. The most recent data on prevalence, diagnosis, and innovations in the treatment of HIV disease and AIDS are also noted. As in the previous editions, we strongly note that sexually transmitted diseases, such as chlamydia and genital warts, are less deadly than AIDS but represent much wider threats, especially among the college population.

Research Methods Chapter 2

The chapter on research methods has been extensively revised to permit us to:

- Discuss sampling separately as it applies to all research methods, not merely in the context of surveys.
- Reevaluate our discussion of historic surveys based on the finding of the NHSLS study.
- Present a more detailed discussion of the difference between correlation and causation as found in correlational studies versus experimental studies. This distinction is now made clearer in the text through the use of new figures. These new figures illustrate how alternate explanations of correlational data are possible.

Expanded Features

In addition to the previous editions' feature topics, the A World of Diversity and A Closer Look features have been expanded to reflect recent events and current research. For instance, gender issues regarding working women and Japanese women in a state of rebellion are included in A World of Diversity, and the effects of Cyberspace on dating and murder of abortion doctors are covered in A Closer Look.

Acknowledgments

The authors owe a great debt of gratitude to the many researchers and scholars whose contributions to the body of knowledge in the field of human sexuality are presented in these pages. Underscoring the interdisciplinary nature of the field, we have drawn upon the work of scholars in such fields as psychology, sociology, medicine, anthropology, theology, and philosophy, to name a few. We are also indebted to the many researchers who have generously allowed us to quote from their work and reprint tabular material representing their findings. We also wish to thank our professional colleagues who reviewed this text at various stages in its development.

We also wish to thank our professional colleagues who served as reviewers for the first and second editions: Richard Archer, Southwest Texas State University; Elaine Baker, Marshall University; Judith Baker, Texas Women's

University; Kenneth Beausang, Black Hawk College; Larry Bell, Northeastern University; Thomas Billimek, San Antonio College; Barry R. Burkhart, Auburn University; Jean Byrne, Kent State University; Willie A. Campbell, South Suburban College; Mona Coates, Orange Coast College; Clive Davis, Syracuse University; Linda DeVillers, Chaffey College; Beverly Drinnin, Des Moines Area Community College; Vera Dunwoody, Chaffey College; Katherine Ellison, Montclair College; Basil Fiorito, California Polytechnic State University; Julio R. Garcia, Southwestern College; Michael Gonzalez, University Psychological Associates; Ralph Hammond, University of Arkansas at Little Rock; Richard J. Hardy, Central Michigan University; Robert Holdsambeck, Allan Hancock College; Karen Huffman, Palomar College; David Johnson, University of Southern Alabama; Vicki Krenz, California State University, Fresno; R. Martin Lobdell, Pierce College; John T. Long, San Antonio College; Deborah McDonald, New Mexico State College; Gilbert Meyer, Illinois Valley Community College; Gregory D. Murrow, Edinboro University of Pennsylvania; Robert Pollack, University of Georgia; Daphne Long Rankin, Virginia Commonwealth University; Jane Ellen Smith, University of New Mexico; Tom Springer, Louisiana Tech University; Marlene Tufts, Clackamus Community College; Mary Ann Watson, Metro State College of Denver; Charles Weichert, San Antonio College; Paul Zelhart, East Texas State University.

We would like to single out the contributions of one reviewer and editor, Beverly Drinnin, as we did in the first and second editions. Professor Drinnin has added a wealth of knowledge to our study of human sexuality, helped us sharpen our writing style and approach, and has again written the annotations for the teacher's edition of the third edition as well as the Instructor's Manual and Study Guide.

We are also thankful to the many professionals at Allyn and Bacon who encouraged and supported us and helped steer our course through the three editions of this text, including the development and production of the text. We particularly want to thank Melinda Grosser who has now designed all three editions of the interior text; perhaps, this edition is more stunning than the first and second editions.

S.A.R.
Short Hills, New Jersey

J.S.N.
New York, New York

L.F.-R.
Short Hills, New Jersey

About the Authors

Spencer A. Rathus received his Ph.D. in psychology from SUNY Albany. A member of the psychology faculty of St. John's University, he has also engaged in clinical practice and published numerous articles in scientific journals on topics such as orgasm disorders in women and men, atypical variations in sexual behavior, and assessment of deviant behavior. Dr. Rathus is also the author of the Rathus Assertiveness Schedule and of several books, including *Psychology, Essentials of Psychology,* and *Understanding Child Development.* He has coauthored *AIDS—What Every Student Needs to Know* with Susan Boushn; coauthored *The Right Start* with Lois Fichner-Rathus; and coauthored *Behavior Therapy* and *Adjustment and Growth,* with Jeffrey S. Nevid and *Abnormal Psychology in a Changing World* with Jeffrey S. Nevid and Beverly Greene.

Jeffrey S. Nevid is a Professor of Psychology at St. John's University in New York, where he also directs the Doctoral Program in Clinical Psychology. He received his Ph.D. in Clinical Psychology from SUNY Albany and holds a Diplomate in Clinical Psychology from the American Board of Professional Psychology. Dr. Nevid has been awarded several research grants to support his research on health interventions and has published numerous research articles in scientific journals on such topics as attitudes toward homosexuality, sexual attraction, assessment of sex offenders, and health psychology. He has authored the books *Adjustment and Growth* and *Behavior Therapy* with Spencer A. Rathus, *Abnormal Psychology in a Changing World* with Spencer A. Rathus and Beverly Greene, and *A Student's Guide to AIDS and Other Sexually Transmitted Diseases, 201 Things You Should Know About AIDS and Other Sexually Transmitted Diseases,* and *Choices.*

Lois Fichner-Rathus is an Associate Professor of Art at Trenton State College. She received her Ph.D. in History, Theory, and Criticism of Art from Massachusetts Institute of Technology. She has published numerous articles in professional journals and has authored several exhibition catalogues. She has received grants to curate several exhibitions of art by women artists and by artists of color; has served as Coordinator of the Women's Studies program at Trenton State College; and has worked to integrate gender, race, and social-class issues in the college curriculum. She is author of *Understanding Art* and coauthor, with Spencer A. Rathus, of *The Right Start.*

Dedicated with love to our children,
Taylor Lane Rathus and Michael Zev Nevid,
who were born during the time that
the first edition of this book was being written.

Taylor Lane Rathus
November 3, 1990

Michael Zev Nevid
January 17, 1991

HUMAN SEXUALITY
IN A WORLD
OF DIVERSITY

CHAPTER 1

Henri Matisse, *Icarus,* Plate 8 from *Jazz.* The Metropolitan Museum of Art, Gift of Lila Acheson Wallace, 1983. © 1996 Succession H. Matisse/ Artist Rights Society (ARS), New York. © 1985 by The Metropolitan Museum of Art.

What Is Human Sexuality?

Truth OR Fiction?

_T_ Ancient civilizations worshipped women's ability to bear children and perpetuate the species.

_T_ In ancient Greece, a mature man would take a sexual interest in an adolescent boy, often with the blessing of the boy's parents.

_F_ The production of illustrated sex manuals originated in modern times.

_T_ The graham cracker came into being as a means for helping young men control their sexual appetites.

_T_ Some African kings were literally the "fathers of their countries." That is, they had hundreds of wives and thousands of children.

_T_ Trobrianders consider their children old enough to engage in sexual intercourse when they are . . . old enough.

_T_ In our dreams, airplanes, bullets, snakes, sticks, and similar objects symbolize the male genitals.

We are about to embark on the study of human sexuality. But why, you may wonder, do we need to *study* human sexuality? Isn't sex something to *do* rather than to *talk about?* Isn't sex a natural function? Don't we learn what we need to know from personal experience or from our parents or our friends?

Yes, we can learn how our bodies respond to sexual stimulation—what turns us on and what turns us off—through personal experience. Personal experience teaches us little, however, about the biological processes that bring about sexual response and orgasm. Nor does experience inform us about the variations in sexual behavior that exist around the world, or in the neighborhood. Experience does not prepare us to recognize the signs of sexually transmitted diseases or to evaluate the risks of pregnancy. Nor does experience help us deal with most sexual problems or dysfunctions. What of our parents? What many of us learned about sex from our parents can probably be summarized in a single word: "Don't." The information we received from our friends was probably riddled with fabrication, exaggeration, and folklore. Yes, many young people today do receive accurate information through sex-education courses in the schools, which is all the more important now that the specter of AIDS hangs over every sexual decision.

There is also something of a myth in our culture that love conquers all—that love is all we need to achieve and sustain satisfying and healthy relationships. Yet, how likely are we to establish healthy and mutually satisfying relationships without some formal knowledge of our own and our partner's sexuality? Without some knowledge of the biology of how our bodies function? Without some awareness of the psychological aspects of our sexuality? In a scientific vacuum?

Concerns about AIDS and unwanted teenage pregnancies have focused greater attention today on the importance of sex education. Many children receive some form of sex education as early as elementary school. Courses on human sexuality, rarely offered as recently as the 1950s, are now routine on college campuses across the United States and Canada. You may know more about human sexuality than your parents or grandparents did at your age, or do today. But how much do you really know? What, for example, happens inside your body when you are sexually stimulated? What causes erection or vaginal lubrication? Can people who are paralyzed from the neck down become erect or lubricated? What do we know of the factors that determine a person's sexual orientation? What are the causes of sexual dysfunctions? How do our sexual responsiveness and interests change as we age? Why does the United States have the highest incidence of rape in the industrialized world? Can you contract a sexually transmitted disease and not know that you have it until you wind up sterile? Can you infect others without having any symptoms yourself?

These are just a few of the issues we will explore in this book. Much of the information we present was discovered in recent years. It is almost as new to us as it may be to you. We also expect to debunk some common but erroneous ideas about sex that you may have picked up before you began this course. Before we proceed further, let us define our subject.

What Is Human Sexuality?

Gender
One's personal, social, and legal status as male or female.

What *is* human sexuality? This is not a trick question. Consider the meaning, or rather meanings, of the word *sex*. The word derives from Latin roots meaning "to cut or divide," signifying the division of organisms into male and female genders. One use of the term *sex*, then, refers to our **gender,** or state of being male or female. The word *sex* (or *sexual*)

Coitus
(co-it-us or co-EET-us). Sexual intercourse.

Erotic
Arousing sexual feelings or desires. (From the Greek word for love, *eros*.)

Gender identity
One's personal experience of being male or female.

Gender roles
Complex clusters of ways in which males and females are expected to behave within a given culture.

Foreplay
Mutual sexual stimulation that precedes sexual intercourse.

Human sexuality
The ways in which we experience and express ourselves as sexual beings.

Values
The qualities in life that are deemed important or unimportant, right or wrong, desirable or undesirable.

is also used to refer to anatomic structures, called sex (or sexual) organs, that play a role in reproduction or sexual pleasure. We may also speak of sex when referring to physical activities involving our sex organs for purposes of reproduction or pleasure: masturbation, hugging, kissing, **coitus,** and so on. Sex also relates to **erotic** feelings, experiences, or desires, such as sexual fantasies and thoughts, sexual urges, or feelings of sexual attraction to another person.

We usually make our usage of the term *sex* clear enough in our everyday speech. When we ask about the sex of a newborn, we are referring to anatomic sex. When we talk of "having sex" (a rather ugly phrase, since it implies that we engage in sexual activity as we "have" a ham sandwich), we generally mean the physical expression of erotic feelings.

The terms *sex organs* or *sexual organs* may be used in different ways. Sometimes the terms are used to refer to those organs required for, and involved directly in, reproduction. These include the penis and testes in men, and the vagina, uterus, and ovaries in women. The terms *sex organs* and *sexual organs* are also sometimes used to refer to organs or structures that are eroticized, even though they may play no direct role in reproduction (such as the clitoris or the breasts). Let us define sex (or sexual) organs as bodily structures that can be eroticized (such as the clitoris or the breasts) or that play a role in reproduction (such as the testes in the man and the uterus in the woman). They can also perform both functions, of course, as do the penis in the man and the vagina in the woman. We will use the term *gender* in this text to refer to the state of being male or female, as in **gender identity** and **gender roles.**

The term *sexual behavior* refers to activities that involve the body in the expression of erotic or affectionate feelings. This description of sexual behavior includes but is not limited to behavior involving reproduction. *Masturbation,* for example, is sexual behavior that is performed for pleasure, not reproduction. Kissing, hugging, manual manipulation of the genitals, and oral–genital contact are all sexual behaviors that can provide sensual stimulation, even though they do not directly lead to reproduction. They may also be used as forms of **foreplay,** which leads to coitus, which can lead to reproduction.

We can now define **human sexuality** as the ways in which we experience and express ourselves as sexual beings. Our awareness of ourselves as females or males is part of our sexuality, as is the capacity we have for erotic experiences and responses. Our sexuality is an essential part of ourselves, whether or not we ever engage in sexual intercourse or sexual fantasy, or even if we lose sensation in our genitals because of injury.

The Study of Human Sexuality

The study of human sexuality is an interdisciplinary enterprise that draws upon the scientific expertise of anthropologists, biologists, medical researchers, sociologists, and psychologists, to name but a few of the professional groups involved in the field. No other area of study draws on so many disciplines. These disciplines all have contributions to make, since sexual behavior reflects our biological capabilities, our psychological characteristics, and social and cultural influences. Biologists inform us about the physiological mechanisms of sexual arousal and response. Medical science teaches us about sexually transmitted diseases and the biological bases of sexual dysfunctions. Psychologists examine how our sexual behavior and attitudes are shaped by perception, learning, thought, motivation and emotion, and personality. Sociocultural theorists consider the sociocultural contexts of sexual behavior. For example, they examine relationships between sexual behavior and religion, race, and social class. Anthropologists focus on cross-cultural similarities and differences in sexual behavior. Scientists from many disciplines explore parallels between the sexual behavior of humans and other animals.

Science provides us with information, but it cannot make sexual decisions for us. Our **values** come into play in determining our sexual choices and behavior. The Declaration of Independence endorsed the fundamental values of "life, liberty, and the pursuit of happiness"—not a bad beginning. Our religious traditions also play a prominent role in shaping our values. Our study of human sexuality will thus consider how religious teachings shape sexual values.

Sexuality and Values

Our society is pluralistic. It embraces a wide range of sexual attitudes and values. Some readers may be liberal in their sexual views and behavior. Others may be conservative or traditional. Some will be staunchly pro-choice on abortion, others adamantly pro-life. Some will approve of premarital sex for couples who are dating casually. Others will hold the line at emotional commitment. Still others will believe that people should wait until marriage.

Since we encourage you through the course of this text to explore your own values about the issues we discuss, let us reveal two values that guided *our* writing:

1. *Sexual knowledge and critical thinking skills are of value because they allow us to make informed sexual decisions.* We hope that readers will confirm our belief. Having agreed on this much, your authors admit that they hold different values about a number of the issues we discuss. Therefore, we—your authors—do not try to persuade readers to adopt a particular stance concerning specific issues raised in the textbook. We present opposing points of view on controversial matters such as abortion and the distribution of condoms in schools. We hope that readers will critically consider their preconceptions and that the views that they form will be their own.
2. *Students should take an active role in enhancing their health.* In the course of this text, we will urge you, for example, to examine your bodies for possible abnormalities, to see your physician when you have questions about painful menstruation or other physical complaints, to become sensitive to the signs of sexually transmitted diseases, to get good prenatal care, and so forth.

People's sexual attitudes, experiences, and behaviors are shaped to a large extent by their cultural traditions and beliefs. Because our world consists of diverse peoples and cultures, the study of human sexuality is really the study of human sexuali*ties*. In this book we highlight the many ways in which people experience their sexuality. We preview some of the findings of our review of sexuality in this chapter's A World of Diversity feature.

～ *Reflections* ～

A reflection is literally the image or likeness of a thing. In psychological terms, reflecting on things means *relating* them to things you already know (Willoughby et al., 1994). Things you know about already include your own experiences and the subject matter from other courses. Reflecting on the images and ideas raised in this textbook will help you accomplish four goals:

▪ *Effective learning.* Reflecting on the material in this textbook will make it more meaningful and easy to remember (DeAngelis, 1994; Woloshyn et al., 1994). As noted by psychologist Wilbert McKeachie, "The research shows that if students are going to remember something, they have to think about it. They need to put it in their own heads in their own words, not just sit back passively and absorb it" (1994, p. 39).

▪ *Critical thinking.* Reflecting on the material will encourage you to analyze the definitions of terms, evaluate the adequacy of research methods, and examine the logic of arguments.

▪ *Values clarification.* Reflecting will enable you to identify and evaluate your values on matters relating to human sexuality.

▪ *Application of the material in the textbook to your own life.* Reflecting on the subject matter also enhances the likelihood that you will be able to *apply* it to your own life (Kintsch, 1994).

The Reflections questions in each major section will help you accomplish these goals. For example, now that you have read the section What Is Human Sexuality?, reflect on the following questions:

- Why do we need to study human sexuality?
- What are the meanings of the word *sex?* What is the meaning of *gender?* Why is it important to differentiate between the two?
- How is the study of human sexuality enriched by exploring the variety of sexual expression found worldwide?

Thinking Critically About Human Sexuality

We are inundated with so much information about sex that it is difficult to separate truth from fiction. Newspapers, TV shows, and popular books and magazines contain one feature after another about sex. Many of them contradict one another, contain half-truths, or draw misleading or unsubstantiated conclusions. A scientific approach to human sexuality encourages people to think critically about the false claims and findings that are presented as truths.

Sad to say, most of us take certain "truths" for granted. We tend to assume that authority figures like doctors and government officials provide us with factual information and are qualified to make decisions that affect our lives. When two doctors disagree on the need for a hysterectomy, however, or two officials disagree as to whether condoms should be distributed in public schools, we wonder how both can be correct. Critical thinkers never say, "This is true because so-and-so says that it is true."

To help students evaluate claims, arguments, and widely held beliefs, most colleges encourage *critical thinking.* Critical thinking has several features. One aspect of critical thinking is skepticism—not taking things for granted. It means being skeptical of things that are presented in print, uttered by authority figures or celebrities, or passed along by friends. Another aspect of critical thinking is thoughtful analysis and probing of claims and arguments. Critical thinking requires willingness to challenge the conventional wisdom and common knowledge that many of us take for granted. It means scrutinizing definitions of terms and evaluating the premises of arguments and their logic. It also means finding *reasons* to support your beliefs, rather than relying on feelings. When people think critically, they maintain open minds. They suspend their beliefs until they have obtained and evaluated the evidence.

Throughout the book we raise issues that demand critical thinking. These issues may stimulate you to analyze and evaluate your beliefs and attitudes about sex in the light of scientific evidence. For example, upon reading Chapter 10 you may wish to reconsider your beliefs on whether or not gay males and lesbians *choose* their sexual orientation. Upon reading Chapter 4 you may reexamine folklore that suggests that sexual activity impairs a man's athletic performance on the following day. The discussion of abortion in Chapter 12 will encourage you to consider exactly when we begin to be *human*. When you read Chapters 13 and 17, you will face the question of whether or not schools should provide students with contraceptives.

Some Features of Critical Thinking

Critical thinkers maintain a healthy skepticism. They examine definitions of terms, weigh premises, consider evidence, and decide whether arguments are valid and logical. Here are suggestions for critical thinking:

1. *Be skeptical.* Politicians, religious leaders, and other authority figures attempt to convince you of their points of view. Even researchers and authors may hold certain biases. Have the attitude that you will accept nothing as true—including the comments of the authors of this text—until you have personally weighed the evidence.

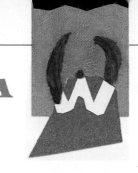 

A WORLD OF DIVERSITY

AROUND THE WORLD IN EIGHTY WAYS—A PREVIEW

Like other aspects of human behavior, sexual beliefs and behaviors vary widely around the world. The United States alone is a nation of hundreds of different ethnic and religious groups, which vary in their sexual customs, attitudes, and beliefs. This diversity extends to the entire "global village" of the world's nearly 200 nations and to each nation's own distinctive subcultures.

The World of Diversity features that appear throughout this text explore the rich variety of sexual expression found worldwide. Seeing sexuality in contexts other than our own can help us understand the role of a culture's beliefs, values, and attitudes on our own and others' expressions of sexuality. It can help us understand why our partners, who may not share the same ethnic or religious heritage, may have different beliefs about sexual intimacy. Exploring diversity can also help us understand cultural differences related to gender, sexual orientation, sexual attraction, sexual jealousy, premarital sex, teenage pregnancy, and risks of sexually transmitted diseases.

People in some societies believe, for instance, that a brother and sister who eat at the same table are engaging in a mildly erotic type of act. The practice is therefore forbidden (Davenport, 1977). In contemporary Islamic societies, female sexuality is often viewed as dangerous. If women's behavior and attire are not kept under strict control, they can be "fatal attractions" for men (Kammeyer et al., 1990). What is sexually arousing, too, varies from culture to culture. Among the Abkhasians in the southern part of what used to be the Soviet Union, men regard the female armpit as highly arousing. A woman's armpits are, therefore, a sight for her husband alone (Kammeyer et al., 1990).

Of course, one glaring reason for today's heightened interest in understanding sexuality in a broader perspective is the worldwide AIDS epidemic. Any effort to end this scourge requires that we open our eyes to cultural attitudes and traditions that may increase the risk of transmission of the disease.

If we take a quick tour of the world of diversity within our own borders and beyond, we find that:

- Kissing is practiced nearly universally as a form of petting in the United States, but it is unpopular in Japan and unknown among some cultures in Africa and South America (see Chapter 9).
- Some societies encourage sexual experimentation and even sexual intercourse among children and adolescents, while others punish any form of childhood sexual play (see Chapter 13).

- Marital fidelity is a prominent value in Western culture, but among some people of the Arctic it is considered hospitable for a man to offer his wife to a visiting tribesman (see Chapter 14).
- In the United States, there remains a tendency to blame the victims of crimes—especially rape victims—rather than the perpetrators. In the strongly patriarchal society of Islamic Pakistan, however, the so-called Hudood Ordinance has actually resulted in *prison sentences* for some women who have brought rape charges against men. Hudood, you see, grants more credibility to the testimony of men than to that of women. An accused man may claim that any sexual contact between himself and the woman making the accusations was consensual, and the court will be inclined to believe him. Women too are also frequently prevented from testifying in court. The result has been that some women who bring charges of rape are sometimes prosecuted for adultery and jailed if found guilty, while their assailants go free (Schork, 1990).
- Sex was typically considered "indecent and unmentionable" in Russia, according to Kon (1995), "a subject only for the degenerate underground." However,

2. *Examine definitions of terms.* Some statements are true when a term is defined in one way but not true when it is defined in another. Consider the statement "Love is blind." If love is defined as head-over-heels infatuation, there may be substance to the statement. Infatuated people tend to idealize loved ones and overlook their faults. If love is defined as deep caring and commitment involving a more realistic (if still somewhat slanted) appraisal of the loved one, however, then love is not so much blind as a bit nearsighted.

3. *Examine the assumptions or premises of arguments.* Consider the statement "Abortion is murder." *Webster's New World Dictionary* defines murder as "the unlawful and ma-

since the collapse of the Soviet Union, sex has apparently been escaping into the mainstream of Russian life. In today's Russia, newspapers and television regularly cover prostitution and pornography as well as the traditional bus accidents (Schillinger, 1995). As sex has grabbed the Russian imagination, the incidences of premarital sex and rape are also apparently on the rise (Kon, 1995).

- Although U.S. government officials may occasionally voice public condemnation of premarital sexual relations, the majority of people in the United States engage in them without fear of government reprisal. In China, however, where the results of a national survey (see Chapter 2) showed that about half of the population engages in premarital relations, a male college student was expelled from a Beijing university when it became known that he had engaged in premarital sexual relations (Southerland, 1990). Other students report that the punishment was typical.
- Perhaps in response to feelings of guilt or remorse, many Japanese women who have abortions place miniature stone statues known as *mizuko-jizo* in Buddhist temples in memory of their aborted fetuses (see Chapter 12). They sometimes decorate the statues with bibs or little hats and surround them with little stuffed animals, baby food, and pacifiers—all in the belief that it keeps the souls of their aborted fetuses warm and entertained (Bumiller, 1990).
- The United States has its romantic Valentine's Day, but Japan has a blatantly erotic day: Christmas Eve. (Yes, Christmas Eve.) Whereas Christmas Eve is a time of religious devotion in many Western nations, it has become a time of sexual devotion in Japan. On Christmas Eve every single person must have a date—one that includes an overnight visit (Reid, 1990). The cost of a typical Christmas Eve date exceeds $1,000. Where do Tokyo singles like to go before their overnight visits? Tokyo Disneyland (see Chapter 14).
- We elaborate on such topics and issues concerning sexual diversity in subsequent chapters.

Kissing. Kissing is a nearly universal form of light petting in the United States, but it is unpopular in Japan and unknown in many African and South American cultures.

licious or premeditated killing of one human being by another." The statement can be true, according to this dictionary, only if the victim is held to be a human being (and if the act is unlawful and either malicious or premeditated). Pro-life advocates argue that embryos and fetuses are human beings. Pro-choice advocates claim that they are not, at least not until they are capable of surviving on their own. So the argument that abortion is murder would rest in part on the assumption that the embryo or fetus is a human being.

4. *Be cautious in drawing conclusions from evidence.* In Chapter 14 we shall discuss research findings that show that married people who cohabited before marriage are more

likely to eventually get divorced than are those who didn't cohabit first. It may seem at first glance that cohabitation is a *cause* of divorce. However, married couples who cohabit before marriage may differ from those who do not in ways other than choosing cohabitation—which brings us to our next suggestion for critical thinking.

5. *Consider alternative interpretations of research evidence.* For example, cohabitors who later get married may be more likely to eventually get divorced because they are more liberal and less traditional than married couples who did not cohabit before marriage. Eventual divorce would then be *connected* with cohabitation but would not be *caused* by cohabitation.

6. *Consider the kinds of evidence upon which conclusions are based.* Some conclusions, even seemingly "scientific" conclusions, are based on anecdotes and personal endorsements. They are not founded on sound research.

7. *Do not oversimplify.* Consider the statement "Homosexuality is inborn." There is some evidence that sexual orientation may involve inborn biological predispositions, such as genetic influences. However, biology is not destiny in human sexuality. Gay male, lesbian, and heterosexual sexual orientations appear to develop as the result of a complex interaction of biological and environmental factors.

8. *Do not overgeneralize.* Consider the belief that gay males are effeminate and lesbians are masculine. Yes, some gay males and lesbians fit these stereotypes. However, many do not. Overgeneralizing makes us vulnerable to accepting stereotypes.

～ *Reflections* ～

■ Why is critical thinking an important aspect of your education? Why is critical thinking essential to the study of human sexuality?

■ Why is skepticism at the heart of critical thinking?

■ A friend of yours insists that something is true because a noted sex researcher, his minister, or this textbook claims that it is true. Would a critical thinker accept your friend's argument as proof? Why, or why not?

Perspectives on Human Sexuality

Human sexuality is a complex topic. No single theory or perspective can capture all its nuances. In this book we explore human sexuality from many perspectives. In this section we introduce a number of perspectives—historical, biological, cross-species, cross-cultural, psychological, and sociocultural. We will draw on them in subsequent chapters.

The Historical Perspective

History places our sexual behavior in context. It informs us as to whether our sexual behavior reflects trends that have been with us through the millennia or the customs of a particular culture and era.

Our reading of history shows little evidence of universal sexual trends. Attitudes and behaviors vary extensively from one time and place to another. Contemporary U.S. society may be permissive when compared to the Victorian and postwar eras. Yet it looks staid when compared to the sexual excesses of some ancient societies, most notably the ruling class of ancient Rome.

History also involves the study of religious traditions. Religions provide explanations for natural events based on the existence of a supreme being or beings or on supernatural forces. Beliefs about the supernatural provide foundations for moral and ethical behavior. Religions have thus been major influences on sexual values and behavior. Yet the traditions and religions of diverse cultures have cast sexual behavior in different lights.

The rise of science since the Age of Enlightenment in the eighteenth century has also profoundly affected contemporary views of human sexuality. Let us trace some historical changes in attitudes toward sexuality. We begin by turning the clock back 20,000 or 30,000 years, to the days before written records were kept—that is, to *pre*history.

Prehistoric Sexuality: From Female Idols to Phallic Worship

Information about life among our Stone Age ancestors is drawn largely from cave drawings, stone artifacts, and the customs of modern-day preliterate peoples whose existence may have changed little over the millennia. From such sources, historians and anthropologists infer a prehistoric division of labor. By and large, men hunted for game. Women tended to remain close to home. They nurtured children and gathered edible plants and nuts, and crabs and other marine life that wandered along the shore or swam in shallow waters.

Art produced in the Stone Age, some 20,000 years ago, suggests the worship of women's ability to bear children and perpetuate the species (Fichner-Rathus, 1995). Primitive statues and cave drawings portray women with large, pendulous breasts, rounded hips, and prominent sex organs. Most theorists regard the figurines as fertility symbols.

Truth **OR** *Fiction?*
R E V I S I T E D

It is true that ancient civilizations worshipped women's ability to bear children and perpetuate the species. Stone Age art suggests that people did worship women's ability to bear children and perpetuate the species. Primitive statues and cave drawings portraying women are regarded as fertility symbols. ■

Emphasis on the female reproductive role may also have signified ignorance of the male's contribution to reproduction.

As the ice sheets of the last ice age retreated (about 11,000 B.C.) and the climate warmed, human societies turned agrarian. Hunters and gatherers became farmers and herders. Villages sprang up around fields. Men tended the livestock. Women became farmers, supplementing their plant-gathering skills with expertise in cultivation. As people grew aware of the male role in reproduction, **phallic worship** sprang into being. Knowledge of paternity is believed to have developed around 9000 B.C., which is about the time that people shifted from being hunters and gatherers to being farmers and shepherds. The male's role in reproduction may seem obvious enough to us. However, uninformed people might not have connected childbirth to a sexual act that predated the most visible signs of pregnancy by months. Knowledge of paternity may have been a side benefit of the herding of livestock:

> For the first time, [people were] watching the same individual animals every day, all the year around, and [they] could scarcely fail to note the relatively constant length of the interval that elapsed between a ram servicing a ewe and the ewe dropping her lambs.
>
> (Tannahill, 1980, p. 46)

Of course, prehistoric people did not keep records that might help us to confirm this explanation. Had they done so, they would not have been *pre*historic.

In any event, the penis was glorified in art as a plough, an ax, or a sword. **Phallic symbols** played roles in religious ceremonies in ancient Egypt. Ancient Greek art revered phalluses, rendering them sometimes as rings and sometimes as necklaces. Some phalluses were given wings, suggesting the power ascribed to them. In ancient Rome, a large phallus was carried like a float in a parade honoring Venus, the goddess of love.

The **incest taboo** may have been the first human taboo (Tannahill, 1980). All human societies apparently have some form of incest taboo (Ember & Ember, 1990). Societies have varied in terms of the strictness of the taboo, however. Brother–sister marriages were permitted among the presumably divine rulers of ancient Egypt and among the royal families of the Incas and of Hawaii, even though they were generally prohibited among commoners. Father–daughter marriages were permitted among the aristocracy and royalty of ancient Egypt. Incestuous relationships in these royal blood lines may have ensured that wealth and power, as well as "divinity," would be kept in the family. Many societies, even today, permit marriages between some blood relatives, such as first cousins.

Phallic worship
Worship of the penis as a symbol of generative power.

Phallic symbols
Images of the penis.

Incest taboo
The prohibition against intercourse and reproduction among close blood relatives.

Polygamy
The practice of having two or more spouses at the same time. (From the Greek roots meaning "many" [*poly-*] and "marriage" [*gamos*].)

Monogamy
The practice of having one spouse. (From the Greek *mono-*, meaning "single" or "alone.")

The Ancient Hebrews　The ancient Hebrews viewed sex, at least sex in marriage, as a fulfilling experience intended to fulfill the divine injunction to "be fruitful and multiply." The emphasis on the procreative function of sex led to some interesting social customs. For example, childlessness and the development of a repulsive abnormality, such as a boil, were grounds for divorce. After all, repulsiveness would dampen the mate's enthusiasm for reproducing. Male–male and female–female sexual behavior were strongly condemned, as it was believed to represent a threat to the perpetuation of the family. Adultery, too, was condemned—at least for a woman. Although the Hebrew Bible (called the Old Testament in the Christian faith) permitted **polygamy,** it expressed a clear preference for **monogamy**—"one man, one wife." As a contemporary Jewish writer notes, "Indeed, the most obvious evidence of the [Bible's] preference for monogamy is that the first human beings God created were Adam and Eve, not Adam, Eve, and Joan" (Telushkin, 1991, p. 178). In any event, the vast majority of the Hebrews were monogamous.

The ancient Hebrews approved of sex within marriage not simply for procreation but also for mutual pleasure and fulfillment. They believed that the expression of sexual needs and desires helped strengthen marital bonds and solidify the family. Jewish law even legislated the minimum frequency of marital relations, which varied according to the man's profession and the amount of time he spent at home:

> Every day for those who have no occupation, twice a week for laborers, once a week for ass-drivers; once every thirty days for camel drivers; and once every six months for sailors. (Mishna Ketubot 5:6; Ketubot 62b–63b; quoted in Telushkin, 1991, p. 616)

What of the feminine gender role among the ancient Hebrews? Women were to be good wives and mothers. What *is* a "good wife"? According to the Book of Proverbs, a good wife rises before dawn to tend to her family's needs, brings home the food, instructs the servants, tends the vineyards, makes the clothes, keeps the ledger, helps the needy, and works well into the night. For all this, among the Ancient Hebrews, a wife was considered the property of her husband. If she offended him, she could be divorced on a whim (although they almost never were). A wife could also be stoned to death for adultery. She might also have had to share her husband with his secondary wives and concubines. Men who committed adultery by consorting with the wives of other men were considered to have violated the property rights of the other men. Although they were subject to harsh penalties for violation of property rights, they would not be put to death.

The Venus of Willendorf. Anthropologists believe that the Venus is an ancient fertility symbol.

Bisexual
Sexually responsive to either gender. (From the Latin *bi-*, meaning "two.")

The Ancient Greeks　The classical or golden age of ancient Greece lasted for about 200 years, from about 500 B.C. to 300 B.C. Within this relatively short span lived the philosophers Socrates, Plato, and Aristotle; the playwrights Aristophanes, Aeschylus, and Sophocles; the natural scientist Archimedes; and the lawgiver Solon. Like the Hebrews, the Greeks valued family life. But the Greeks did not cement family ties by limiting sexual interests to marriage—at least not male sexual interests. The Greeks expressed sexual interests openly. They admired the well-developed body, male or female, and enjoyed nude wrestling among men in the arena. The female ideal was slender compared with the earth mother ideals of prehistory. She epitomized graceful sensuality, not reproduction. Erotic encounters and off-color jokes characterized the plays of Aristophanes and other playwrights. The Greeks held that the healthy mind must dwell in a healthy body. They cultivated muscle and movement along with mind.

The Greeks viewed their gods—Zeus, god of gods; Apollo, who inspired art and music; Aphrodite, the goddess of carnal love whose name is the basis of the word *aphrodisiac;* and others—as voracious seekers of sexual variety. Not only were they believed to have sexual adventures among themselves, but they were also thought to have seduced mortals.

Three aspects of Greek sexuality are of particular interest to our study of sexual practices in the ancient world: male–male sexual behavior, pederasty, and prostitution. The Greeks viewed men and women as **bisexual.** One of their heroes was Heracles (Hercules). Heracles is said to have ravished 50 virgins in a night. Nevertheless, he also had affairs with men, including "sweet Hylas, he of the curling locks" (Tannahill, 1980, p. 85).

Male–male *sex* was deemed normal. However, only a few male–male *relationships*, such as relationships between soldiers and between adolescents and older men, received the stamp of social approval. Male–male sexual behavior was tolerated so long as it did not threaten the institution of the family. Exclusive male–male sexual behavior was therefore discouraged. Some Greeks idealized romantic love between men, of the sort that bound Achilles to Patroclus in Homer's *Iliad*. The warrior Achilles could not be moved to fight the Trojans by love of country or the pleas of his king. He sprang into action, however, when the enemy slew his lover Patroclus.

Pederasty means love of boys. Greek men might take on an adolescent male as a lover and pupil. Sex between men and prepubescent boys was illegal, however. Families were generally pleased if their adolescent sons attracted socially prominent mentors. Pederasty did not impede the boy's future male–female functioning, since the pederast himself was usually married, and Greeks believed people equally capable of male–female and male–male sexual activity.

Truth OR Fiction?

REVISITED

It is true that in ancient Greece, a mature man would take a sexual interest in an adolescent boy, often with the blessing of the boy's parents. The Greeks viewed people as naturally bisexual. ■

Not all Greeks approved of pederasty, however. Aristotle, for one, considered it depraved.

Prostitution flourished at every level of society. Prostitutes ranged from refined **courtesans** to **concubines,** who were usually slaves. Courtesans were similar to the geisha girls of Japan. They could play musical instruments, dance, engage in witty repartee, or discuss the latest political crisis. They were also skilled in the arts of love. No social stigma was attached to visiting a courtesan. Their clients included philosophers, playwrights, politicians, generals, and the very affluent. At the lower rungs of society were streetwalkers and prostitutes who lived in tawdry brothels. They were not hard to find. A wooden or painted penis invariably stood by the door.

Women in general held a low social status in society. The women of Athens had no more legal or political rights than slaves. They were subject to the authority of their male next-of-kin before marriage and to their husbands afterwards. They received no formal education and were consigned most of the time to women's quarters in their homes. They were chaperoned when they ventured out of doors. A husband could divorce his wife without cause and was obligated to do so if she committed adultery. A wife, however, could divorce her husband only under extreme circumstances, which did not include adultery or

Pederasty
Sexual love of boys. (From the Greek *paidos*, meaning "boy.")

Courtesan
A prostitute—especially the mistress of a noble or wealthy man. (From Italian roots meaning "court lady.")

Concubine
A secondary wife, usually of inferior legal and social status. (From Latin roots meaning "lying with.")

Male–Male Relationships. In ancient Greece, people were seen as bisexual and sexual relationships between adolescent boys and adult men (pederasty) were commonplace.

pederasty. The legal and social rights of women in ancient Athens were similar to those of their contemporaries in Babylonia and Egypt, and among the ancient Hebrews. All in all, the women of the ancient world were treated as *chattels*—property.

Bestiality
Sexual relations between a person and an animal.

Sadism
The practice of achieving sexual gratification through hurting or humiliating others.

Fellatio
A sexual activity involving oral contact with the penis.

Cunnilingus
A sexual activity involving oral contact with the female genitals.

Fornication
Sexual intercourse between people who are not married to one another. (If one of the partners is married, the act may be labeled *adultery*.)

The Ancient Romans   Much is made of the sexual excesses of the Roman emperors and ruling families. Julius Caesar is reputed to have been bisexual—"a man to every woman and a woman to every man." Other emperors, like Caligula, sponsored orgies at which guests engaged in a wide variety of sexual practices, including in some cases **bestiality** and **sadism.** These sexual excesses were found more often among the upper classes of palace society than among average Romans, however. Unlike their counterparts in ancient Greece, Romans viewed male–male sexual behavior as a threat to the integrity of the Roman family and to the position of the Roman woman. Thus, it was not held in favor.

Western society traces the roots of many of its sexual terms to Roman culture, as indicated by their Latin roots. **Fellatio,** for example, derives from the Latin *fellare,* meaning "to suck." **Cunnilingus** derives from *cunnus,* meaning "vulva," and *lingere,* "to lick." **Fornication** derives from *fornix,* an arch or vault. The term stems from Roman streetwalkers' practice of serving their customers in the shadows of archways near public buildings such as stadiums and theaters.

The family was viewed as the source of strength of the Roman Empire. Although Roman women were more likely than their Greek counterparts to share their husbands' social lives, they still were considered to be the property of their husbands.

The Early Christians   Christianity emerged within the Roman Empire during the centuries following the death of Christ. According to the Christian Bible's New Testament, Jesus taught that love and tolerance are paramount in human relations, and that God is forgiving. Little is known about Jesus' views on sex, however. Early Christian views on sexuality were largely shaped by Saint Paul and the church fathers in the first century and by Saint Augustine in the latter part of the fourth century. Adultery and fornication were rampant among the upper classes of Rome during this era. It was against this backdrop of sexual decadence that the early Christian leaders began to associate sexuality with sin.

In replacing the pagan values of Rome, the early Christians, like the Hebrews, sought to restrict sex to the marriage bed. They saw temptations of the flesh as distractions from spiritual devotion to God. Paul preached that celibacy was closer to the Christian ideal than marriage. He recognized that not everyone could achieve celibacy, however, so he said that it was "better to marry than to burn" (with passion, that is). Marriage was no sin, but it was spiritually inferior to celibacy.

Christians, like Jews before them, demanded virginity of brides. Masturbation and prostitution were condemned as sinful. Early Christians taught that men should love their wives with restraint, not passion. The goal of procreation should govern sexual behavior—the intellect should rule the flesh. Divorce was outlawed. Unhappiness with one's spouse might reflect sexual, thus sinful, restlessness. Dissolving a marriage might also jeopardize the tight social structure that supported the church.

Over subsequent centuries, Christian leaders took an even more negative view of sexuality. Particularly influential were the ideas of Saint Augustine (A.D. 353–430), who associated sexual lust with the original sin of Adam and Eve in the Garden of Eden. According to Augustine, lust had transformed the innocent procreative instinct, instilled in humanity by God, into sin. Following their fall from grace, Adam and Eve cloaked their nakedness with fig leaves. Shame had entered the picture. To Augustine, lust and shame were passed down from Adam and Eve through the generations. Lust made any sexual expression, even intercourse in marriage, inherently evil and wicked. Only through celibacy, according to Augustine, could men and women attain a state of grace.

Nonprocreative sexual activity was deemed most sinful. Masturbation, male–male sexual behavior, female–female sexual behavior, oral–genital contact, anal intercourse—all were viewed as abominations in the eyes of God. To the Jews, sex was a natural and pleasurable function, so long as it was practiced within marriage. There was no sin attached to sexual pleasure. To the early Christians, however, sexual pleasure, even within marriage, was stained by the original sin of Adam and Eve. Marital sex was deemed somewhat less sinful when practiced for procreation and without passion.

Sexuality and the Eastern Religions   An appreciation of the religious traditions of the Middle East and Far East can broaden our perspective of the history of sexual customs and practices. Islam, the dominant religion in the Middle East, was founded by the Prophet Muhammad. Muhammad was born in Mecca, in what is now Saudi Arabia, in about A.D. 570. The Islamic tradition treasures marriage and sexual fulfillment in marriage. Premarital intercourse invites shame and social condemnation. In some fundamentalist Islamic states, it incurs the death penalty.

The family is the backbone of Islamic society. Celibacy is frowned upon (Ahmed, 1991). Muhammad decreed that marriage represents the only road to virtue (Minai, 1981). Islamic tradition permits a sexual double standard, however. Men may take up to four wives, but women are permitted only one husband. Public social interactions between men and women are severely restricted in Islamic societies. In traditional Islamic cultures, social dancing between the genders is shunned. Women in most traditional Islamic societies are expected to keep their heads and faces veiled in public and to avoid all contact, even a handshake, with men other than their husbands.

In the cultures of the Far East, sexuality was akin to spirituality. To the Taoist masters of China, who influenced Chinese culture for millennia, sex was anything but sinful. Rather, they taught that sex was a sacred duty. It was a form of worship that was believed to lead toward immortality. Sex was to be performed well and often if one was to achieve harmony with nature.

The Chinese culture was the first to produce a detailed sex manual, which came into use about 200 years before the birth of Jesus. The manual helped educate men and women in the art of lovemaking. The man was expected to extend intercourse as long as possible, thereby absorbing more of his wife's natural essence, or *yin*. Yin would enhance his own masculine essence, or *yang*. Moreover, he was expected to help bring his partner to orgasm so as to increase the flow of energy that he might absorb. (Her pleasure was incidental or secondary.)

Taoists believed that it was wasteful for a man to "spill his seed." Masturbation, acceptable for women, was ruled out for men. Sexual practices such as anal intercourse and oral–genital contact (fellatio and cunnilingus) were permissible, so long as the man did not squander *yang* through wasteful ejaculation. Another parallel to Western cultures was the role accorded women in traditional Chinese society. The "good wife," like her Western counterparts, was limited largely to the domestic roles of child rearing and homemaking.

Perhaps no culture has cultivated sexual pleasure as a spiritual ideal to the extent of the ancient Hindus of India. From the fifth century onward, temples show sculptures of gods, heavenly nymphs, and ordinary people in erotic poses (Gupta, 1994). Hindu sexual practices were codified in a sex manual, the *Kama Sutra*. The *Kama Sutra* illustrates sexual positions, some of which would challenge a contortionist. It holds recipes for alleged aphrodisiacs, ways of making love, and so on. This manual remains the most influential sex manual ever produced. It is believed to have been written by the Hindu sage Vatsyayana sometime between the third and fifth centuries A.D., at about the time that Christianity was taking shape in the West as an organized religion.

T r u t h **OR** *Fiction?*
R E V I S I T E D

It is not true that the production of illustrated sex manuals originated in modern times. Actually, the most influential sex manual ever produced was written and illustrated—profusely!—in ancient India. ■

In its graphic representations of sexual positions and practices, the *Kama Sutra* reflected the Hindu belief that sex was a religious duty, not a source of shame or guilt. In the Hindu doctrine of *karma* (the passage or transmigration of souls from one place to another), sexual fulfillment was regarded as one way to become reincarnated at a higher level of existence.

All in all, early Indian culture viewed sex as virtuous and natural. Indian society grew more restrictive toward sexuality after about A.D. 1000, however (Tannahill, 1980).

An Illustration from the *Kama Sutra*. The *Kama Sutra*, an Indian sex manual believed to have been written sometime between the third and fifth centuries A.D., contained graphic illustrations of sexual techniques and practices.

The Middle Ages   The Middle Ages, sometimes called medieval times, span the millennium of Western history from about A.D. 476 to A.D. 1450. These years are sometimes termed the Dark Ages because some historians have depicted them as an era of cultural and intellectual decay and stagnation. The Roman Catholic Church continued to grow in influence. Its attitudes toward sexuality, largely unchanged since the time of Augustine, dominated medieval thought. Some cross-currents of change crept across medieval Europe, however, especially in the social standing of women. The Roman Catholic Church had long regarded all women as being tainted by the sin of Eve, whom it blamed for humankind's downfall in the Garden of Eden. In the Eastern church of Constantinople, the cult of the Virgin Mary flourished. The ideal of womanhood was in the image of Mary: good, gracious, loving, and saintly.

Imported by the Crusaders and others who returned from the East, the cult of the Virgin Mary swept European Christendom and helped elevate the status of women. Hundreds of new abbeys were founded across Europe. Their monks were devoted to the Virgin. They erected chapels in their churches in her honor and wore white in tribute to her purity.

Two conflicting concepts of women thus dominated medieval thought: one, *woman as Eve,* the temptress; the other, *woman as Mary,* virtuous and pure. Contemporary Western images of women still show the schism between the good girl and the bad girl—the Madonna and the whore. Part of the fascination of the rock star Madonna is that she combines the name of the Virgin Mary and crucifixes with an open display of undergarments and simulated lovemaking on the stage and in her videos. Note the Western double standard: An unmarried, sexually active woman runs the risk of being branded a "slut." An unmarried, sexually active man is likely to receive more complimentary labels such as "stud," "playboy," or "ladies' man." Society has generally been more accepting of men's sexuality than women's.

Among the upper classes of medieval times, a concept of courtly love also emerged. It was part chivalry and part romance novel. Troubadours of the twelfth and thirteenth centuries sang of pure and ennobling love that burned brightly but remained unconsummated. Their verses often depicted the chaste love between a married lady of the court and a handsome suitor of lower rank who sought her favor through heroic deeds.

The Protestant Reformation   During the Reformation, Martin Luther (1483–1546) and other Christian reformers such as John Calvin (1509–1564) split off from the Roman Catholic Church and formed their own sects, which led to the development of the modern Protestant denominations of western Europe (and later, the New World). Luther disputed many Roman Catholic doctrines on sexuality. He believed that priests should be

Conflicting Views of Women. Two conflicting concepts of women dominated medieval thought. One was of woman as Eve, the temptress. The other was of woman as the Virgin Mary, virtuous and pure. Contemporary Western images of women still show the schism between the Madonna and the whore.

allowed to marry and rear children. To Luther, marriage was as much a part of human nature as eating or drinking (Tannahill, 1980). Calvin rejected the Roman church's position that sex in marriage was permissible only for the purpose of procreation. To Calvin, sexual expression in marriage fulfilled other legitimate roles, such as strengthening the marriage bond and helping to relieve the stresses of everyday life. The Protestant Reformation encouraged a more accepting view of sexuality, although it maintained strict adherence to the belief that sex was permissible only in the context of marriage. Stern penalties were meted out for premarital and extramarital sex. The Puritans, one of the earliest Protestant sects to settle in America, subjected fornicators to flogging and sent parents to the pillory or the stocks if their children were born too soon after the wedding date. Adulterers, too, were flogged and sometimes branded. Remember the scarlet A that the adulteress Hester Prynne was compelled to wear in Nathaniel Hawthorne's novel *The Scarlet Letter*?

Shaping the Present: From Repression to Revolution to Reaction
Early settlers brought to the New World the religious teachings that had dominated Western thought and culture for centuries. Whatever their differences, each religion stressed the ideal of family life and viewed sex outside of marriage as immoral or sinful. A woman's place, by and large, was in the home and in the fields. Not until 1833, when Oberlin opened its doors to women, were women permitted to attend college in the United States. Not until the twentieth century did women gain the right to vote.

In this century, social change has swept through Western culture at a sometimes dizzying pace. Sexual behaviors and attitudes that would have been unthinkable a couple of generations ago—such as cohabitation ("living together")—have become commonplace. The social barriers that had restricted women's roles have largely broken down.

The middle and later parts of the nineteenth century are generally called the Victorian period, named after Queen Victoria of England. Victoria assumed the throne in 1837 and ruled until her death in 1901. Her name has become virtually synonymous with sexual repression. Victorian society in Europe and the United States, on the surface at least, was prim and proper. Sex was not discussed in polite society. Even the legs of pianos were draped with cloth for the sake of modesty. Many women viewed sex as a marital duty to be performed for procreation or to satisfy their husbands' cravings. Consider the following quotation:

> I am happy now that Charles calls on my bed chamber less frequently than of old. As it is, I now endure but two calls a week and when I hear his steps outside my door I lie down on my bed, close my eyes, open my legs and think of England.

(Attributed to Alice, Lady Hillingdon, wife of the second Baron Hillingdon)

Women were assumed not to experience sexual desires or pleasures. "I would say," observed Dr. William Acton (1814–1875), an influential English physician, in 1857, "that the majority of women (happily for society) are not much troubled with sexual feeling of any kind." Women, thought Acton, were born with a sort of *sexual anesthesia.*

It was widely believed among medical authorities in England and the United States that sex drains the man of his natural vitality. Physicians thus recommended that intercourse be practiced infrequently, perhaps once a month or so. The Reverend Sylvester Graham (1794–1851) preached that ejaculation deprived men of the "vital fluids" they need to maintain health and vitality. Graham believed that the loss of an ounce of semen was equal to the loss of several ounces of blood. Each time a man ejaculated, in Graham's view, he risked his physical health. Graham preached against "wasting the seed" by masturbation or frequent marital intercourse. (How frequent was frequent? In Graham's view, intercourse more than once a month could dangerously deplete the man's vital energies.) Graham recommended that young men control their sexual appetites by adopting a diet of simple foods based on whole-grain flours. To this day, his name is identified with a type of cracker he developed for this purpose in the 1830s, the graham cracker, derived from unbolted wheat (graham flour).

Truth OR Fiction?
R E V I S I T E D

It is true that the graham cracker came into being as a means for helping young men control their sexual appetites. Graham believed that a diet based on whole-grain flours was a key to self-control. ■

It appears, though, that the actual behavior of Victorians was not as repressed as advertised. Despite the belief in female sexual anesthesia, Victorian women, as women before and after them, certainly did experience sexual pleasure and orgasm. One piece of evidence was provided by an early sex survey conducted in 1892 by a female physician, Celia Duel Mosher. Though her sample was small and nonrandom, 35 of the 44 women who responded admitted to desiring sexual intercourse. And 34 of them reported experiencing orgasm. Women's diaries of the time also contained accounts of passionate and sexually fulfilling love affairs (Gay, 1984).

Prostitution also flourished during the Victorian era. Men apparently thought that they were doing their wives a favor by looking elsewhere. Accurate statistics are hard to come by, but there may have been as many as 1 prostitute for every 12 London men during the nineteenth century; in Vienna, perhaps 1 for every 7 men.

The Foundations of the Scientific Study of Sexuality Against this backdrop of sexual repression, scientists and scholars first began to approach sexuality as an area of legitimate scientific study. An early important contributor to the science of human sexuality was the English physician Havelock Ellis (1859–1939). Ellis compiled a veritable encyclopedia of sexuality: a series of volumes published between 1897 and 1910, entitled *Studies in the Psychology of Sex.* Ellis drew information from various sources, including case histories, anthropological findings, and medical knowledge. He challenged the prevailing view by arguing that sexual desires in women were natural and healthy. He promoted the view that many sexual problems had psychological rather than physical causes. He also promoted acceptance of the view that a gay male or lesbian sexual orientation was a naturally occurring variation within the spectrum of normal sexuality, and not an aberration. Presaging some contemporary views, Ellis treated gay male and lesbian sexual orientations as inborn dispositions, not as vices or character flaws.

Sexologist
A person who engages in the scientific study of sexual behavior.

Another influential **sexologist,** the German psychiatrist Richard von Krafft-Ebing (1840–1902), described more than 200 case histories of individuals with various sexual deviations in his book *Psychopathia Sexualis*. His writings contain vivid descriptions of deviations ranging from sadomasochism (sexual gratification through inflicting or receiving pain) and bestiality (sex with animals) to yet more bizarre and frightening forms, such as necrophilia (intercourse with dead people). Krafft-Ebing viewed sexual deviations as mental diseases that could be studied and perhaps treated by medical science.

At about the same time, a Viennese physician, Sigmund Freud (1856–1939), was developing a theory of personality that has had an enormous influence on modern culture and science. Freud believed that the sex drive is our principal motivating force.

Alfred Kinsey (1894–1956), an Indiana University zoologist, conducted the first large-scale studies of sexual behavior in the 1930s and 1940s. It was then that sex research became recognized as a field of scientific study in its own right. In 1938 Kinsey had been asked to teach a course on marriage. When researching the course, Kinsey discovered that little was known about sexual practices in American society. He soon embarked upon an ambitious research project. Detailed personal interviews with nearly 12,000 people across the United States were conducted. The results of his surveys were published in two volumes, *Sexual Behavior in the Human Male* (1948) and *Sexual Behavior in the Human Female* (1953). They comprised the first scientific attempts to provide a comprehensive picture of sexual behavior in the United States.

These books made for rather dry reading and were filled with statistical tables rather than racy pictures or vignettes. Nevertheless, they became best-sellers. They exploded on a public that had not yet learned to discuss sex openly. Their publication—especially the book on female sexual behavior—unleashed a torrent of criticism. Kinsey's work had some methodological flaws, but much of the criticism branded it immoral and obscene. *The New York Times* refused to run advertisements for the 1948 volume on male sexuality. Many newspapers refused to report the results of his survey on female sexuality. A congressional committee in the 1950s went so far as to claim that Kinsey's work undermined the moral fiber of the nation, rendering it more vulnerable to a Communist takeover (Gebhard, 1976).

Kinsey died in 1956. His death may have been hastened by the emotional toll he suffered because of the public's reaction to his work (Gagnon, 1990). Even so, Kinsey and his colleagues made sex research a scientifically respectable field of study. They helped lay the groundwork for greater openness in discussing sexual behavior.

The Path to the Present: Sexuality in the Twentieth Century

Victorian attitudes toward sexuality dominated society's view of sexuality well into the middle of the twentieth century. The belief that women did not desire sex was something of a self-fulfilling prophecy. That is, couples who held this belief may not have sought ways of enhancing the woman's sexual pleasure. Women were expected to remain virgins until marriage, although society gave tacit permission to men to sow their wild oats. Men were permitted to seek sex with prostitutes or "loose" women, or at least others looked the other way when they did.

Although steamy passages were found in early twentieth-century writings like D. H. Lawrence's *Lady Chatterley's Lover,* the most explicit sexual contact permitted in the films of the 1930s and 1940s was a discreet kiss. Open-mouth kissing was not allowed. No public forums featured sexual exotica or discussed sex openly. Nor was human sexuality widely taught in public schools, colleges, or even medical schools. By and large, sex remained shrouded in ignorance and secrecy.

The Sexual Revolution   The period of the mid-1960s to the mid-1970s is often referred to as the *sexual revolution*. Dramatic changes occurred in U.S. sexual attitudes and practices during the "Swinging Sixties." When folksinger Bob Dylan sang "The Times They Are A-Changin'," our society was on the threshold of major social upheaval, not only in sexual behavior, but also in science, politics, fashion, music, art, and cinema. The so-called Woodstock generation, disheartened by commercialism and the Vietnam War, tuned in (to rock music on the radio), turned on (to drugs), and dropped out (of mainstream society). The heat was on between the hippies and the hardhats. Long hair became the mane of men. Bell-bottomed jeans flared out. Films became sexually explicit. Critics seriously contemplated whether the pornography classic *Deep Throat* had deep social implications. Hard rock music bellowed the message of rebellion and revolution.

No single event marked the onset of the sexual revolution. There was no charge up a sexual Bunker Hill. Social movements often gain momentum from a timely interplay of scientific, social, political, and economic forces. The war (in Vietnam), the bomb (fear of the nuclear bomb), the pill (the introduction of the birth-control pill), and the tube (TV, that is) were four such forces. The pill ended the risk of unwanted pregnancy for young people. It permitted them to engage in recreational or casual sex, rather than procreative sex (Asbell, 1995). Pop psychology movements, like the Human Potential Movement of the 1960s and 1970s (the "Me Decade"), spread the message that people should get in touch with and express their genuine feelings, including their sexual feelings. "Doing your own thing" became one catchphrase. "If it feels right, go with it" became another. The lamp was rubbed. Out popped the sexual genie.

The sexual revolution was tied to social permissiveness and political liberalism. In part reflecting the times, in part acting the catalyst, the media dealt openly with sex. Popular books encouraged people to explore their sexuality. Film scenes of lovemaking became so commonplace that the movie rating system was introduced to alert parents. Protests against the Vietnam War and racial discrimination spilled over into broader protests against conventional morality and hypocrisy. Traditional prohibitions against drugs, casual sex, even group sex crumbled suddenly.

Some of the alternative lifestyles that preoccupied the media in the 1960s and 1970s have fallen by the wayside. We no longer hear much about mate-swapping (also called *swinging*) or "open marriages." Casual sex may also be on the wane—in part because of fear of AIDS, in part as a pendulum swing back toward commitment and romance. Many singles' bars, where the phrase "Your place or mine?" became popular, have closed or been turned into "health bars."

Yet if the pendulum has swung partway back, the incidence of premarital sex among teenagers, especially younger teens, appears headed in the opposite direction. More teenagers are sexually active today, and at younger ages (Barringer, 1990; Brooks-Gunn & Furstenberg, 1989; Zeman, 1990). In addition to premarital sex, two other features of the sexual revolution have become permanent parts of our social fabric: the liberation of female sexuality and a greater willingness to discuss sex openly.

What, then, does history tell us about sex? Is there a universal standard for defining sexual values, or are there many standards? All societies have some form of an incest taboo. Most societies have placed a value on procreative sex within the context of an enduring relationship. The societal value of an enduring social, economic, and intimate relationship—usually in the form of marriage—lies in the roles it serves in providing security for children, maintaining or increasing the population, and ensuring the orderly transfer of property from generation to generation.

Other sexual practices—masturbation, promiscuous sex, male–male sexual behavior, female–female sexual behavior, prostitution, polygamy, and so on—have been condemned in some societies, tolerated by others, and encouraged by still others. Some societies have looked with favor upon nonprocreative sex, at least within the context of marriage. Others have condemned it. Some historians argue that the pagan "degradations" of Rome led to its demise—that otherwise a "purer" Rome might still bestride the earth. They warn that the "excesses" of our own sexual revolution may also bring us down. Rome, however, also suffered from the administrative difficulties of tending to a far-flung empire. Rome was also besieged by "barbarians" in the outposts and, eventually, at the city gates. In fact, the civilizations of ancient Greece and Rome maintained their prominence for hundreds of years. When we consider their contributions to Western art, philosophical thought, and the languages we speak, we may question whether they fell at all.

Are Today's Young People More or Less Liberal in the Expression of Their Sexuality than People in Earlier Generations? Today the threat of AIDS hangs over every sexual encounter. While many young people today are selective in their choice of partners and take precautions to make sex safer, more teenagers are engaging in sexual activity, and at younger ages, than in previous generations.

The Biological Perspective

The biological perspective focuses on the roles of genes, hormones, the nervous system, and other biological factors in human sexuality. Sex, after all, serves the biological function of reproduction. We are biologically endowed with anatomic structures and physiological capabilities that make sexual behavior possible—and, for most people, pleasurable.

Study of the biology of sex informs us about the mechanisms of reproduction. It informs us of the physiological mechanisms of sexual arousal and response. By studying the biology of sex, we learn that erection occurs when the penis becomes engorged with blood. We learn that vaginal lubrication is the result of a "sweating" action of the vaginal walls. We learn that orgasm is a spinal reflex as well as a psychological event.

Biological researchers have made major strides in assisting infertile couples to conceive through laboratory-based methods of fertilization. "Test-tube babies" have been conceived in laboratory dishes and inserted into their mothers' uteruses, where they have developed to term. In some cases in which women cannot provide egg cells of their own, other women have donated egg cells that are fertilized by the father's sperm and then inserted into the mother's uterus.

Knowledge of biology has furthered our understanding of sexuality and our ability to overcome sexual problems. To what extent does biology govern sexual behavior? Is sex controlled by biological instincts? Or are psychosocial factors, such as culture, experience, and decision-making ability more important? Although the sexuality of other species is largely governed by biological processes, culture and experience play vital roles—and in many cases, the key roles—in human sexuality. *Human* sexuality involves a complex interaction of biological and psychosocial factors. Biology indicates what is possible, and often, what is pleasurable or painful. Biology is not destiny, however. It does not imply what is proper and improper or determine the sexual decisions that we make. Religious tradition, cultural and personal values, and learning and experience guide these decisions.

The Cross-Species Perspective

Analogue
Something that is similar or comparable to something else.

The study of other animal species places human behavior in broader context. A surprising variety of sexual behaviors exists among nonhumans. There are animal examples, or **analogues,** of human male–male sexual behavior, female–female sexual behavior, oral–genital contact, and oral–oral behavior (i.e., kissing). Foreplay is also well known in

Copulation

Sexual intercourse. (From the Latin *copulare*, meaning "to unite" or "to couple.")

Evolution

The development of a species to its present state, which is believed to involve adaptations to its environment.

Natural selection

The evolutionary process by which adaptive traits enable members of a species to survive to reproductive age and transmit these traits to future generations.

Genes

The basic units of heredity, which consist of chromosomal segments of DNA.

Chromosomes

The rodlike structures that reside in the nucleus of every living cell and carry the genetic code in the form of genes.

DNA

Deoxyribonucleic acid—the chemical substance whose molecules make up genes and chromosomes.

Mutations

Random changes in the molecular structure of DNA.

the animal world. Turtles massage their mates' heads with their claws. Male mice nibble at their partner's necks. Most mammals use only a rear-entry position for **copulation,** but some animals, such as apes, use a variety of coital positions.

We even find analogues of deviant forms of sexual behavior, such as rape, in the animal world. We should be careful about drawing a connection between human rape and animal analogues, however. Human (perhaps we should say *in*human) rape is often motivated by the desire to punish and humiliate the victim, a motive that may be entirely absent in the forced copulations among other animals that resemble rape among humans.

Cross-species research reveals an interesting pattern. Sexual behavior among "higher" mammals, such as primates, is less directly controlled by instinct than it is among the "lower" species, such as birds, fish, or lower mammals. Experience and learning play more important roles in sexuality as we travel up the evolutionary ladder.

Species vary not only in their physical characteristics but also in their social behavior, including their mating behavior. Scientists look to the process of **evolution** to help explain such variability. What is evolution? How might the sexual behavior of various species, including our own, be influenced by evolutionary forces?

The English naturalist Charles Darwin (1809–1882), the founder of the modern theory of evolution, believed that animal and plant species were not created independently, but evolved from other life-forms. The mechanism by which species evolved was **natural selection,** or in the vernacular, "survival of the fittest." In each species, some individuals are better adapted to their environments than others. Better-adapted members are more likely to survive to reproduce. Therefore, they are also more likely to transmit their traits to succeeding generations. As the generations pass, a greater proportion of the species population carries the traits of the fittest members. Fitness, in the evolutionary sense, means reproductive success—the ability to produce surviving offspring. The fittest members of a species produce the greatest number of surviving offspring. They are not necessarily the strongest or fleetest of foot, although these traits may be adaptive in some environments and so enhance reproductive success.

Over time, natural selection favors traits that contribute to survival and reproduction. When environmental conditions change, natural selection favors those members of a species who possess traits that help them adapt. These forms of the species proliferate, eventually replacing forms that fail to survive and reproduce. Species that lack forms that possess adaptive traits will eventually become extinct and be replaced by species that are better suited to their environmental conditions.

Darwin was too early—the technology of his day did not allow him to find the mechanisms that transmit traits from generation to generation. Nor could he explain how a species evolved from one form to another. Not until the discovery of the principles of genetic inheritance by the Austrian monk Gregor Mendel (1822–1884) did the pieces of the puzzle of evolution begin to fall into place. Mendel discovered that traits are transmitted by units of heredity that we now call **genes.** Traits are determined by the combinations of genes that offspring inherit from their parents.

We now understand that genes are segments of **chromosomes,** which are composed of **DNA.** The chemical structure of genes provides genetic instructions. Each human cell normally contains a complement of 46 chromosomes, which are arranged in 23 pairs. Each human chromosome consists of more than 1,000 genes. A child normally inherits one member of each pair of chromosomes from each parent. So each offspring inherits 50% of his or her genes from each parent. The particular combinations of genes that one inherits from one's parents account for whether one has blue eyes or brown eyes, light or dark hair, and a wide range of other characteristics.

New variations in species are introduced through random genetic changes called **mutations.** Mutations occur randomly but are subject to natural selection. That is, some mutations are adaptive in that they enhance reproductive success. As a result, these adaptive mutations are more likely to be retained and to proliferate in a species. As more members of the species possess a variety of these adaptive traits, the species as a whole changes in form. Most mutations are not adaptive, however, and quickly disappear from the genetic pool.

Sociobiology
The theory that dispositions toward behavior patterns that enhance reproductive success may be genetically transmitted.

In recent years, some theorists have suggested that there is a genetic basis to social behavior, including sexual behavior, among humans and other animals. This theory, called **sociobiology,** proposes that dispositions toward *behavior patterns* that enhance reproductive success—as well as physical traits that do so—may be genetically transmitted. If so, we may carry traits that helped our prehistoric ancestors survive and reproduce successfully, even if these traits are no longer adaptive in modern culture. "Modern culture"—dating, say, from classical Greece—is but a moment in the lifetime of our species.

There is a tendency to think of adaptive traits as somehow more "worthy," "good," or "admirable" than less adaptive traits. Evolution is not a moralistic enterprise, however. A trait either does or does not enhance reproductive success. It is not in itself good or bad. It may be adaptive for the female of a species to eat the male after mating. "Dad" then literally nourishes his offspring during the period of gestation. In evolutionary terms, his personal sacrifice is adaptive if it increases the chances that the offspring will survive and carry his genes. In other species, it may be adaptive for fathers to "love them and leave them"—that is, to mate with as many females as possible and abruptly abandon them to "plant their seed" elsewhere.

Sociobiologists are interested in sexual behavior because it is so interwoven with reproductive success. They seek common sexual themes across cultures in the belief that common themes may represent traits that helped our ancestors survive and became part of the human genetic endowment. For example, there is considerable cross-cultural evidence that men are more promiscuous than women and have "spread their seed" widely.

T r u t h **OR** *Fiction?*
R E V I S I T E D

It is true that some African kings were literally the "fathers of their countries." They did have hundreds of wives and thousands of children. Some sociobiologists assert that male promiscuity is genetically determined. ■

Some sociobiologists argue that men are naturally more promiscuous because they are the genetic heirs of ancestors whose reproductive success increased in relation to the number of women they were able to impregnate (Symons, 1979). Women, by contrast, can produce only a few offspring in their lifetimes. Thus, the theory goes, they have to be more selective with respect to their mating partners. Women's reproductive success is enhanced by mating with the fittest males—not with any Tom, Dick, or Harry who happens by. From this perspective, the male's "roving eye" and the female's selectivity are embedded in their genes (Townsend, 1995).

To some sociobiologists, human beings are like marionettes on strings being tugged by invisible puppet masters—their genes. Genes govern the biological processes of sexual maturation and the production of sex hormones. Hormones, in turn, are largely responsible for regulating the sexual behavior of other animal species. Extending the sociobiological model to human behavior sparks considerable controversy, however. Critics contend that human behavior largely reflects learning and personal choice, not heredity.

Critics also claim that sociobiology is largely conjectural. No one, for example, has yet discovered a gene for promiscuity. There is no direct evidence that either male promiscuity or female selectivity is genetically determined. Critics also point to examples of cultural diversity as evidence that culture and experience, not genetics, play the pivotal role in human behavior. Nor is cross-cultural similarity in sexual practices necessarily proof of a common genetic factor. Different cultures may adopt similar customs because such customs serve a similar function. For example, marriage exists in some form in every human society. Perhaps marriage serves similar functions in various cultures, such as in regulating the availability of sexual partners and providing an economic and social arrangement that will provide for the care of offspring. All in all, the evidence is far from clear (or compelling) for regarding human social and sexual behavior as direct products of our genes.

The Cross-Cultural Perspective

The cross-cultural perspective, like the historical perspective, provides insight into the ways in which cultural beliefs affect sexual behavior and people's sense of morality. Unlike historians, who are limited in their sources to the eyewitness accounts of others and

Village Life. Anthropologists study sexual customs among preliterate societies to learn about the similarities and differences across cultures.

the shards of information that can be gleaned from fading relics, anthropologists can observe other cultures firsthand. Interest in the cross-cultural perspective on sexuality was spurred by the early-twentieth-century work of the anthropologists Margaret Mead (1901–1978) and Bronislaw Malinowski (1884–1942).

In *Sex and Temperament in Three Primitive Societies* (1935), Mead laid the groundwork for recent psychological and sociological research challenging gender-role stereotypes. In most cultures characterized by a gender division of labor, men typically go to business or to the hunt, and—when necessary—to war. In such cultures, men are perceived as strong, active, independent, and logical. Women are viewed as passive, dependent, nurturant, and emotional. Mead concluded that these stereotypes are not inherent in our genetic heritage. Rather, they are acquired through cultural expectations and socialization. That is, men and women learn to behave in ways that are expected of them in their particular culture.

Malinowski lived on the Trobriand island of Boyawa in the South Pacific during World War I. There he gathered data on two societies of the South Pacific, the Trobrianders and the Amphett islanders. The Amphett islanders maintained strict sexual prohibitions, whereas the Trobrianders enjoyed greater freedom. Trobrianders, for example, encouraged their children to masturbate. Boys and girls were expected to begin to engage in intercourse when they were biologically old enough. According to custom, they would pair off, exchange a coconut, a bit of betel nut, a few beads, or some fruit from the bush. Then they would go off together and engage in intercourse (Malinowski, 1929, p. 488). Adolescents were expected to have multiple sex partners until they married.

Truth OR *Fiction?*
R E V I S I T E D

It is true that Trobrianders consider their children old enough to engage in sexual intercourse when they are . . . old enough. In traditional Trobriand society, children were encouraged by their elders to engage in sexual intercourse when they were biologically mature enough to do so. ■

Malinowski found the Trobrianders less anxiety-ridden than the Amphett islanders. He attributed the difference to their sexual freedom, thus making an early plea to relax prohibitions in Western societies. Even sexually permissive cultures like that of the Trobrianders, however, placed limits on sexual freedom. They frowned on extramarital relationships, for example. Other cultures, however, like that of the Toda of southern India, consider it immoral for a husband to restrict his wife's extramarital relations (Howard, 1989). Chukchee men of Arctic Siberia often exchange their wives with their friends.

Cross-Cultural Commonalities and Differences in Sexual Behavior

In 1951, Clellan Ford, an anthropologist, and Frank Beach, a psychologist, reviewed sexual behavior in preliterate societies around the world, as well as in other animals. They found great variety in sexual customs and beliefs among the almost 200 societies they studied. They also found some common threads, although there were exceptions to each. Although Ford and Beach's work is almost half a century old, it remains a valuable source of information about cross-cultural and cross-species patterns in sexuality (Frayser, 1985). Throughout the text, our discussion of cross-cultural patterns in sexuality is guided by their work and by more recent cross-cultural studies conducted by Gwen Broude and Sarah Greene (1976) and by Suzanne Frayser (1985), among others.

Ford and Beach reported that kissing was quite common across the cultures they studied, although not universal. The Thonga of Africa were one society that did not practice kissing. Upon witnessing two European visitors kissing each other, members of the tribe commented that they could not understand why Europeans "ate" each other's saliva and dirt. The frequency of sexual intercourse also varies from culture to culture, but intercourse is relatively more frequent among young people everywhere.

Societies differ in their attitudes toward childhood masturbation. Some societies, such as the Hopi Native Americans of the southwest United States, ignore it. Trobrianders encourage children to stimulate themselves. Other societies condemn it. The people of the Pacific island of East Bay discourage children from touching their genitals and may subject them to ridicule or scolding (Davenport, 1965).

Although all cultures place some prohibitions on incestuous relationships, intercourse between brother and sister has been viewed as natural and desirable in some cultures, such as that of the Dahomey of West Africa (Stephens, 1982). The acceptability of incestuous relations has also varied in some cultures according to social class. In some societies incestuous marriages were permitted among the ruling classes. Virtually all cultures have strict incest taboos, however. Ford and Beach reported that marriage was even taboo between people speaking the same dialect in one Australian tribe—a prohibition that did not enhance marital communication.

Polygyny
A form of marriage in which a man has two or more wives. (From the Greek *gyne*, meaning "woman.")

Polyandry
A form of marriage in which a woman has two or more husbands. (From the Greek *andros*, meaning "man" or "male.")

Eighty-four percent of Ford and Beach's (1951) preliterate cultures practiced polygamy. The researchers concluded that monogamy was relatively uncommon. More common is the form of polygamy called **polygyny,** in which men are permitted to have more than one wife. Similarly, Frayser (1985) found that polygyny was practiced by the great majority (82%) of societies in her cross-cultural sample. In many cultures, the number of wives a man has is an emblem of his wealth and status. The cultures studied in Ford and Beach's and Frayser's cross-cultural samples typically had few members, however. Monogamy, which is the custom in the more populous, technologically advanced cultures, is thus more prevalent worldwide. Even in polygynous cultures, the numbers of people who are monogamously married are greater than those who are married polygamously. Few societies have the oversupply of women that universal polygyny would entail (Ember & Ember, 1990). Rarer still is **polyandry,** a practice that permits women to have more than one husband. Frayser (1985) found polyandry in only 2% of societies she studied. In fraternal polyandry, the most common form of polyandry, two or more brothers share a wife, and all live together in the same household. The wife "visits" each brother according to a schedule arranged by the men (Ember & Ember, 1990).

Polygyny has a long tradition in Western culture. King Solomon was reputed to have 700 wives. Polygyny was practiced in the nineteenth-century United States by an early leader of the Mormon church, Brigham Young, and by some of his followers. It has since been banned by the Mormon church as well as by state laws, although it is still practiced in some disenfranchised Mormon communities.

The cross-cultural perspective illustrates the importance of learning in human sexual behavior. Societies differ widely in their sexual attitudes, customs, and practices. The members of all human societies share the same anatomic structures and physiological capacities for sexual pleasure, however. The same hormones flow through their arteries. Yet their sexual practices, and the pleasure they reap or fail to attain, may set them apart. Were human sexuality completely or predominantly determined by biology, we would not find such diversity.

Although sexual practices vary widely across cultures, there are some universal patterns. For one, all societies regulate sexual behavior in some fashion. No society allows un-

Ethnocentric

Adjectival form of the noun *ethnocentrism*, meaning the tendency to view other groups or cultures according to the standards of one's own. (From the Greek *ethnos* meaning "race," "culture," or "people," and *kentric*, meaning "center.")

Sigmund Freud

Psychoanalysis

The theory of personality originated by Sigmund Freud, which proposes that human behavior represents the outcome of clashing inner forces.

Id

In Freud's theory, the mental structure that is present at birth, embodies physiological drives, and is fully unconscious.

Ego

In Freud's theory, the second mental structure to develop, which is characterized by self-awareness, planning, and delay of gratification.

Truth  Fiction?
R E V I S I T E D

bounded sexual freedom. There is usually some societal control over the acceptability of sexual and marital partners, and extramarital relations. Nearly all societies have some form of an incest taboo. Nevertheless, cross-cultural comparisons show evidence of great variety. What is considered natural, normal, or moral in one culture may be deemed unnatural, abnormal, or immoral in another.

Yet people often apply an **ethnocentric** standard when judging other cultures. That is, they tend to treat the standards of their own cultures as the norm by which to judge other peoples. Cross-cultural information helps us to appreciate the relativity of the concept of normalcy and to recognize the cultural contexts of sexual behavior. When we consider the historical and cross-cultural perspectives, we come to appreciate that our behavior exists in the context both of our own culture and our own time.

Psychological Perspectives

Psychological perspectives focus on the many psychological influences—perception, learning, motivation, emotion, personality, and so on—that affect our sexual behavior and our experience of ourselves as female or male. Some psychological theorists, such as Sigmund Freud, focus on the motivational role of sex in human personality. Others focus on how our experiences and mental representations of the world affect our sexual behavior.

Sigmund Freud and Psychoanalytic Theory

Sigmund Freud, a Viennese physician, formulated a grand theory of personality termed **psychoanalysis.** Freud believed that we are all born with biologically based sex drives. These drives must be channeled through socially approved outlets if family and social life are to carry on without undue conflict. He hypothesized that conflicts between sexuality and society become internalized in the form of an inner conflict between two opposing parts of the personality—the **id,** which is the repository of biologically based drives or "instincts" (such as hunger, thirst, elimination, sex, and aggression) and the **ego,** which represents reason and good sense. The ego seeks socially appropriate outlets for satisfying the basic drives that arise from the id. Your id, for example, prompts you to feel sexual urges. Your ego attempts to find ways of satisfying those urges without incurring condemnation from others or from your own moral conscience, which Freud called the **superego.** How these internal conflicts are resolved, in Freud's view, largely determines our ability to love, work, and lead well-adjusted lives.

Freud proposed that the mind operates on conscious and unconscious levels. The conscious level corresponds to our state of present awareness. The **unconscious mind** refers to the darker reaches of the mind that lie outside our direct awareness. The ego shields the conscious mind from awareness of our baser sexual and aggressive urges by means of **defense mechanisms** such as **repression,** or motivated forgetting. Examples of defense mechanisms are shown in Table 1.1 on page 27.

Although many sexual ideas and impulses are banished to the unconscious, they continue to seek expression. One avenue of expression is the dream, through which sexual impulses may be perceived in disguised, or symbolic, form. The therapists and scholars who follow in the Freudian tradition are quite interested in analyzing dreams, and the dream objects listed in Table 1.2 on page 28 are often considered sexual symbols. Freud himself maintained a bit of skepticism about the import of dream symbols, however. He once remarked, "Sometimes a cigar is just a cigar."

To a psychoanalyst, dreams of airplanes, bullets, snakes, sticks, and similar objects may indeed symbolize the male genitals. Even Freud had to admit, however, that "sometimes a cigar is just a cigar"! ■

Freud introduced us to new and controversial ideas about ourselves as sexual beings. For example, he originated the concept of **erogenous zones**—the idea that many parts of the body, not just the genitals, are responsive to sexual stimulation.

TABLE 1.1 Defense mechanisms, according to psychoanalytic theory

Mechanism	Definition	Examples
Repression	Ejecting unacceptable impulses and memories from consciousness.	Repressing incestuous impulses toward one's parents or one's children.
Denial	Not perceiving a threatening event.	A person is overwhelmed by sexual passion and engages in sexual relations with a stranger, thinking, "There's no chance I'll get AIDS."
Projection	Attributing one's own unacceptable impulses to others.	A sexually repressed person assumes that others are making sexual advances toward him or her.
Rationalization	Finding an apparently logical reason for unacceptable behavior.	The Victorian husband rationalizes a visit to a prostitute by telling himself that he is sparing his wife an odious chore. The prostitute rationalizes her behavior, in turn, by arguing that she would be out of business if wives were properly performing their duty. The rapist rationalizes his aggression by claiming that the victim should not have been wearing a miniskirt.
Reaction formation	Expressing emotions and ideas that contradict one's genuine emotions and ideas as a way of keeping them repressed.	A sexually repressed individual goes on a campaign against revealing clothing or local news outlets that distribute the swimsuit edition of *Sports Illustrated*.
Intellectualization	Perceiving threatening events and emotional conflicts in emotionless, theoretical terms.	A physician examines an attractive person without regarding him or her as sexually stimulating.
Sublimation	Redirecting basic impulses from sexual objects or activities to socially approved cultural or creative activities.	Writing novels, building cities, drawing or painting nudes, advancing biological science.

Superego
In Freud's theory, the third mental structure, which functions as a moral guardian and sets forth high standards for behavior.

Unconscious mind
Those parts or contents of the mind that lie outside of conscious awareness.

Defense mechanisms
In psychoanalytic theory, automatic processes that protect the ego from anxiety by disguising or ejecting unacceptable ideas and urges.

One of Freud's most controversial beliefs was that children normally harbor erotic interests. He believed that the suckling of the infant in the oral stage was an erotic act. So too was anal bodily experimentation through which children learn to experience pleasure in the control of their sphincter muscles and the processes of elimination. He theorized that it was normal for children to progress through stages of development in which the erotic interest shifts from one erogenous zone to another, as, for example, from the mouth or oral cavity to the anal cavity. According to his theory of **psychosexual development,** children undergo five stages of development: oral, anal, phallic, latency, and genital, which are named according to the predominant erogenous zones of each stage. Each stage gives rise to certain kinds of conflicts. Moreover, inadequate or excessive gratification in any stage can lead to **fixation** in that stage and the development of traits and sexual preferences characteristic of that stage. (Parents who seek to rear their children according to psychoanalytic theory have been frustrated in that Freud never specified the proper amount of gratification in any stage or how to provide it.)

Freud believed that it was normal for children to develop erotic feelings toward the parent of the other gender during the phallic stage. These incestuous urges lead to conflict with the parent of the same gender. In later chapters we shall see that these developments, which Freud termed the **Oedipus complex,** have profound implications for the assumption of gender roles and sexual orientation.

Repression
The automatic ejection of anxiety-evoking ideas from consciousness.

Erogenous zones
Parts of the body, including but not limited to the sex organs, that are responsive to sexual stimulation.

Psychosexual development
In psychoanalytic theory, the process by which sexual feelings shift from one erogenous zone to another as a human being matures.

Fixation
In psychoanalytic theory, arrested development, which includes attachment to objects of an earlier stage of psychosexual development.

Oedipus complex
In psychoanalytic theory, a conflict of the phallic stage in which the boy wishes to possess his mother sexually and perceives his father as a rival in love. (The analogous conflict for girls is the *Electra complex.*)

TABLE 1.2 Dream symbols in psychoanalytic theory*

Symbols for the Male Genital Organs

airplanes	fish	neckties	tools	weapons
bullets	hands	poles	trains	
feet	hoses	snakes	trees	
fire	knives	sticks	umbrellas	

Symbols for the Female Genital Organs

bottles	caves	doors	ovens	ships
boxes	chests	hats	pockets	tunnels
cases	closets	jars	pots	

Symbols for Sexual Intercourse

climbing a ladder	flying in an airplane
climbing a staircase	riding a horse
crossing a bridge	riding an elevator
driving an automobile	riding a roller coaster
entering a room	walking into a tunnel or down a hall

Symbols for the Breasts

apples	peaches

*Freud theorized that the content of dreams symbolized urges, wishes, and objects of fantasy that we would censor in the waking state.
Source: Adapted from Rathus, S. A. (1996). *Psychology in the New Millennium,* 6th ed. Ft. Worth: Harcourt Brace.

Learning Theories   To what extent does sexual behavior reflect experience? Would you hold the same sexual attitudes and do the same things if you had been reared in another culture? We think not. Even within the same society, family and personal experiences can shape unique sexual attitudes and behaviors. Whereas psychoanalytic theory plumbs the depths of the unconscious, learning theorists focus on environmental factors that shape behavior.

Behaviorists
Learning theorists who argue that a scientific approach to understanding behavior must refer only to observable and measurable behaviors.

Behaviorists such as John B. Watson (1878–1958) and B. F. Skinner (1904–1990) emphasized the importance of rewards and punishments in the learning process. In psychology, events (such as rewards) that increase the frequency or likelihood of behavior are termed reinforcements. Children left to explore their bodies without parental condemnation will learn what feels good and tend to repeat it. The Trobriand child who is rewarded for masturbation and premarital coitus through parental praise and encouragement will be more likely to repeat these behaviors (at least openly!) than the child in a more sexually restrictive culture, who is punished for the same behavior. When sexual behavior (like masturbation) feels good, but parents connect it with feelings of guilt and shame, the child is placed in conflict and may vacillate between masturbating and swearing off it.

Of course parental punishment does not necessarily eliminate childhood masturbation. Nor has it stemmed the rising rate of teenage pregnancy in our society. Punishment tends to suppress behavior in circumstances in which it is expected to occur. People can learn to engage in prohibited behavior secretly, however. Still, if we as young children are severely punished for sexual exploration, we may come to associate sexual stimulation *in general* with feelings of guilt or anxiety. Such early learning experiences can set the stage for sexual dysfunctions in adulthood.

Social-learning theorists also use the concepts of reward and punishment, but they emphasize the importance of cognitive activity (anticipations, thoughts, plans, and so on) and learning by observation. Observational learning, or **modeling,** refers to acquiring knowledge and skills through observing others. Observational learning involves more than direct observation of other people. It includes seeing models in films or on television, hearing about them, and reading about them. According to social-learning theory, children acquire the gender roles deemed appropriate in a society through reinforcement of gender-appropriate behavior and through observing the gender-role behavior of their parents, their peers, and other models on television, in films, in books, and so on.

Psychological theories shed light on the ways in which sexuality is influenced by rewards, punishments, and mental processes such as fantasy, thoughts, attitudes, and expectations. Sigmund Freud helped bring sexuality within the province of scientific investigation. He also helped make it possible for people to recognize and talk about the importance of sexuality in their lives. Critics contend, however, that he may have placed too much emphasis on sexual motivation in determining behavior and on the role of unconscious processes.

The psychological perspective has much to offer to our understanding of human sexuality. Psychological factors affect every dimension of our sexuality. Those who harbor excessive guilt or anxiety over sexual activity may have difficulty enjoying sex or responding adequately to sexual stimulation. Even our basic gender identity is largely shaped by psychological factors, such as the experience in a given society of being reared as a girl or as a boy.

Sociocultural Perspectives

Sexual behavior is determined not only by biological and psychological factors, but also by social factors. Social factors contribute to the shaping of our sexual attitudes, beliefs, and behavior. Whereas anthropologists contribute to our understanding of cross-cultural variance in sexuality, sociocultural theorists focus on differences in sexuality among the subgroups of a society, as defined, for example, by differences in religion, race/ethnicity, country of origin, socioeconomic status, marital status, age, educational level, and gender. Such a society is the United States.

Consider the issue of the numbers of sex partners people have. Table 1.3 on page 30 reports the results of a national survey concerning the number of sex partners people report having since the age of 18. It considers the factors of gender, age, marital status, level of education, religion, and race/ethnicity (Laumann et al., 1994).

Consider gender. Males, according to the survey, report having greater numbers of sex partners than females do. For example, 1 male in 3 (33%) reports having 11 or more sex partners since the age of 18, as compared with fewer than 1 woman in 10 (9.2%). Throughout the text, we shall be focusing on gender differences and why men seem generally more likely than women to seek a wide range of sexual experience.

Concerning age, the numbers of sex partners appear to rise with age into the 40s. As people gain in years, they have had more opportunity to accumulate life experiences, including sexual experiences. But then the numbers of partners fall off among respondents in their 50s. Older respondents entered adulthood prior to the sexual revolution and were thus generally exposed to more conservative sexual attitudes. We shall find this sort of age difference, or age gradient, throughout the text as well.

Level of education is also connected with sexual behavior. Generally speaking, it would appear that education is something of a liberalizing influence. Therefore, it is not

Social-learning theory
A cognitively oriented learning theory in which observational learning, values, and expectations play key roles in determining behavior.

Modeling
Acquiring knowledge and skills by observing others.

TABLE 1.3 Number of sex partners since age 18 as found in the NHSLS* study

Social Characteristics	Number of Sex Partners (%)					
	0	1	2–4	5–10	11–20	21+
Gender						
Male	3.4	19.5	20.9	23.3	16.3	16.6
Female	2.5	31.5	36.4	20.4	6.0	3.2
Age						
18–24	7.8	32.1	34.1	15.4	7.8	2.8
25–29	2.2	25.3	31.3	22.2	9.9	9.0
30–34	3.1	21.3	29.3	25.2	10.8	10.3
35–39	1.7	18.9	29.7	24.9	14.0	10.8
40–44	0.7	21.9	27.6	24.2	13.7	12.0
45–49	2.0	25.7	23.8	25.1	9.6	13.9
50–54	2.4	33.9	27.8	18.0	9.0	9.0
55–59	1.3	40.0	28.3	15.2	8.3	7.0
Marital Status						
Never married (not cohabiting)	12.3	14.8	28.6	20.6	12.1	11.6
Never married (cohabiting)	0.0	24.6	37.3	15.7	9.7	12.7
Married	0.0	37.1	28.0	19.4	8.7	6.8
Education						
Less than high school	4.2	26.7	36.0	18.6	8.8	5.8
High school graduate	3.4	30.2	29.1	20.0	9.8	7.4
Some college	2.1	23.9	29.4	23.3	11.9	9.3
College graduate	2.1	24.1	25.8	23.9	11.1	13.0
Advanced degree	3.5	24.6	26.3	22.8	9.6	13.2
Religion						
None	2.6	16.2	29.0	20.3	15.9	15.9
Liberal, moderate Protestant	2.3	22.8	31.2	23.0	12.4	8.3
Conservative Protestant	2.9	29.8	30.4	20.4	9.5	7.0
Catholic	3.8	27.2	29.2	22.7	8.1	9.1
Jewish†	0.0	24.1	13.0	29.6	16.7	16.7
Race/Ethnicity						
White (non-Hispanic)	3.0	26.2	28.9	22.0	10.9	9.1
African American	2.2	18.0	34.2	24.1	11.0	10.5
Hispanic American	3.2	35.6	27.1	17.4	8.2	8.5
Asian American†	6.2	46.2	24.6	13.8	6.2	3.1
Native American†	5.0	27.5	35.0	22.5	5.0	5.0

*National Health and Social Life Survey, conducted by a research team centered at the University of Chicago.
†These sample sizes are quite small.
Source: Adapted from Laumann, E. O., Gagnon, J. H., Michael, R. T., & Michaels, S. (1994). *The Social Organization of Sexuality: Sexual Practices in the United States.* Chicago: University of Chicago Press, Table 5.1C, p. 179.

surprising that people with some college education, or who have completed college, are likely to have more sex partners than those who attended only grade school or high school. We shall see that the effect of education is quite pronounced in the practices of oral and anal sex, as described in Chapter 9.

If education is a liberating influence on sexuality, conservative religious experience would appear to be a restraining factor. In Table 1.3, those who report no religion and liberal Protestants (e.g., Methodists, Lutherans, Presbyterians, Episcopalians, and United Church of Christ) report higher numbers of sex partners than do Catholics and conservative Protestants (e.g., members of Baptist churches, Pentecostal churches, Churches of Christ, and Assemblies of God). Results for Jews are obscured by a small sample size. Research in general would suggest that Orthodox Judaism is a restraining factor on sexual behavior, as compared to more liberal branches of Judaism.

The factor of ethnicity is also connected with sexual behavior. Throughout the text, our coverage of diversity will address differences between non-Hispanic White Americans, African Americans, Hispanic Americans, Asian Americans, and Native Americans. The research findings listed in Table 1.3 suggest that White (non-Hispanic Americans) and African Americans have the highest numbers of sex partners. Hispanic Americans are mostly Catholic, and Catholicism, as noted, provides something of a restraint on sexual behavior. Asian Americans would appear to be the most sexually restrained ethnic group. However, as noted in the footnote to the table, the sample sizes of Asian Americans and Native Americans are relatively small.

The sociocultural perspective informs us of the relationship between sexuality and one's social group within a society. Sociocultural theorists view sexual behavior as occurring within a particular sociocultural system. They study the ways in which the values, beliefs, and norms of a group influence the sexual behavior of its members. To a certain extent, we share attitudes and behavior patterns with people from similar backgrounds— for example, people with the same ethnic identity. Even so, not all Protestants or all members of a given ethnic group act or think alike.

Gender Roles   Sociocultural theorists also study gender roles. In Western cultures, men have traditionally been expected to be the breadwinners, whereas women have been expected to remain in the home and rear the children. Traditional gender roles also define sexual relations. Men, by this standard, are expected to be assertive; women, compliant. Men are to initiate romantic overtures. Women are to perform a "gatekeeping" role and determine which advances they will accept. Today, many of these traditions are falling by the wayside. Most women today are members of the workforce. Many are pursuing careers in traditionally male domains, such as law, medicine, and engineering. Some women command naval vessels. Others pilot military helicopters. Yet even women who become presidents and vice presidents of corporations are still burdened with the bulk of household chores (Rogan, 1984). Sexual practices are also changing to some degree. More women today initiate dates and sexual interactions than was the case in past generations.

Multiple Perspectives on Human Sexuality

Given the complexity and range of human sexual behavior, we need to consider multiple perspectives to understand sexuality. Each perspective—historical, biological, cross-species, cross-cultural, psychological, and sociocultural—has something to offer to this enterprise. Let us venture a few conclusions based on our overview of these perspectives. First, human sexuality appears to reflect a combination of biological, social, cultural, sociocultural, and psychological factors that interact in complex ways, perhaps in combinations that are unique for each individual. Second, there are few universal patterns of sexual behavior, and views on what is right and wrong show great diversity. Third, although our own cultural values and beliefs may be deeply meaningful to us, they may not indicate what is normal, natural, or moral in terms of sexual behavior. The complexity of human sexuality—complexity that causes it to remain somewhat baffling to scientists—adds to the wonder and richness of our sexual experience.

What is the relationship between our religious backgrounds and our judgments as to what kinds of sexual behavior are right and wrong? How have people from different cultures and different historical periods viewed human sexuality?

Why is it important to understand the biological aspects of human sexuality? After all, isn't sex a "natural function"?

How does the sociocultural perspective enhance our understanding of human sexuality?

Summing Up

What Is Human Sexuality?

The term *human sexuality* refers to matters of gender, sexual behavior, sexual feelings, and the biology of sex. Human sexuality concerns the ways in which we experience and express ourselves as sexual beings.

The Study of Human Sexuality The study of human sexuality draws upon the expertise of anthropologists, biologists, medical researchers, sociologists, psychologists, and other scientists.

Sexuality and Values Our pluralistic society embraces a wide range of sexual attitudes and values.

Thinking Critically About Human Sexuality

The text encourages critical thinking to help students evaluate claims, arguments, and widely held beliefs. Critical thinking encourages thoughtful analysis and probing of arguments, willingness to challenge conventional wisdom and common knowledge, and maintaining open minds.

Some Features of Critical Thinking The text enumerates several features of critical thinking. These include being skeptical, examining definitions of terms, examining the assumptions or premises of arguments, being cautious in drawing conclusions from evidence, considering alternative interpretations of evidence, and avoiding oversimplification and overgeneralization.

Perspectives on Human Sexuality

Human sexuality is a complex field, and no single theory or perspective can capture all its nuances. The text offers diverse perspectives on sexuality:

The Historical Perspective History places our sexual behavior in the context of time. History shows little evidence of universal sexual trends. There is evidence of prehistoric worship of generative power in women and men. Jews and Christians have emphasized the role of sex as a means of propagation and have generally restricted sex to the context of family life. The ancient Greeks and Romans dwelled in male-oriented societies that viewed women as chattel. Some Eastern civilizations have equated sexual pleasure with religious experience and have developed sex manuals. Repressive Victorian sexual attitudes gave way to the sexual revolution of the 1960s and 1970s in the West.

The Biological Perspective The biological perspective focuses on the role of biological processes, such as genetic, hormonal, vascular, and neural factors, in explaining human sexual behavior. Knowledge of biology helps us understand how our bodies respond to sexual stimulation and enhances our sexual health.

The Cross-Species Perspective The study of other animal species reveals a surprising variety of sexual behaviors among nonhumans. There are, for example, animal analogues of male–male sexual behavior, female–female sexual behavior, oral sex, foreplay, and rape. Still, we must be cautious in generalizing from lower animals to humans. We find that experience and learning play more important roles in sexuality as we travel up the evolutionary ladder. Sociobiological theory proposes that dispositions toward behavior patterns that enhance reproductive success—as well as physical traits that do so—may be genetically transmitted.

The Cross-Cultural Perspective This perspective, like the historical perspective, provides insight into the ways in which cultural beliefs affect sexual behavior and people's sense of morality. Anthropologists observe other cultures firsthand when possible. Cross-cultural evidence challenges the notion of the universality of gender-role stereotypes. All cultures apparently place some limits on sexual freedom (and almost all cultures place some prohibitions on incestuous relationships), but some cultures are more sexually permissive than others.

Psychological Perspectives Psychological perspectives focus on the psychological factors of perception, learning, motivation, emotion, personality, and so on that affect gender and sexual behavior in the individual. Sigmund Freud formulated the theory of psychoanalysis, which proposes that biologically based sex drives come into conflict with social codes. Erogenous zones shift through the process of psychosexual development, and defense mechanisms keep threatening ideas and impulses out of conscious awareness. Learning theorists focus on the roles of rewards, punishments, and modeling in sexual behavior.

Sociocultural Perspectives Sociocultural theorists focus on differences in sexuality among the groups within a society, as defined, for example, by differences in religion, race, country of origin, socioeconomic status, age, educational level, and gender.

Multiple Perspectives on Human Sexuality Given the complexity and range of human sexual behavior, we need to consider multiple perspectives to understand human sexuality.

HAPTER 2

Henri Matisse, *The Snail,* 1953. Tate Gallery, London/Art Resource, NY. © 1996
Succession H. Matisse/Artist Rights Society (ARS), New York.

Research Methods

Truth OR Fiction?

_T_ You could study the sexual behavior of millions of Americans and still not obtain an accurate picture of the sexual behavior of the general U.S. population.

_F_ Researchers can overcome refusal of some people to participate in a study of sexual behavior by recruiting larger numbers of volunteers.

_T_ Case studies have been carried out on people who are dead.

_T_ Residents of China are more likely than people in the United States to approve of extramarital affairs.

_T_ Some sex researchers have engaged in "swinging" with the people they have studied.

_T_ Masters and Johnson created a transparent artificial penis containing photographic equipment to study female sexual response.

_T_ Regular churchgoers report higher levels of sexual satisfaction.

ave you ever wondered about questions such as these: Are my sexual interests and behavior patterns unique or shared by many others? Does alcohol stimulate or dampen sexual response? Why do people engage in male–male or female–female sexual behavior? How do people contract AIDS? Does pornography cause rape?

You may have thought of such questions. You may even have expressed opinions on them. But scientists insist that opinions about behavior, including sexual behavior, be supported by evidence. Evidence, in turn, must be based upon careful observations in the laboratory or in the field.

In this chapter we explore the methods that scientists use to study human sexuality. We then focus on ethical issues in research on sex. Researchers in all behavioral sciences confront ethical problems, but the problems are heightened in sex research. After all, the field of human sexuality touches on some of the most personal and intimate experiences of our lives.

A Scientific Approach to Human Sexuality

Empirical

Derived from or based on observation and experimentation.

Scientists and researchers who study human sexuality take an **empirical** approach. They base their knowledge on research evidence, rather than on intuition, faith, or superstition. Scientists' and other people's intuitions or religious beliefs may suggest topics to be studied scientifically. Yet once the topics are selected, answers are sought on the basis of the scientific method.

The Scientific Method

Critical thinking and the scientific approach share the hallmark of skepticism. As skeptics, scientists question prevailing assumptions and theories about sexual behavior. They are willing to dispute the assertions of authority figures such as political and religious leaders—even other scientists. Scientists also recognize that they cannot gain perfect knowledge. One era's "truths" may become another era's ancient myths and fallacies. Scientists are involved in the continuous quest for truth, but they do not see themselves as experiencing revelations or defining final truths.

The *scientific method* is a systematic way of gathering scientific evidence and testing assumptions through research. It has a number of elements:

1. *Formulating a research question.* Does alcohol inspire or impair sexual response? Scientists formulate research questions on the basis of their observations of, or theories about, events or behavior. They then seek answers to such questions by conducting empirical research.

Hypothesis

A precise prediction about behavior that is tested through research.

2. *Framing the research question in the form of a hypothesis.* Experiments are usually undertaken with a **hypothesis** in mind—a precise prediction about behavior that is often derived from theory. A hypothesis is tested through research. For instance, a scientist might theorize that alcohol enhances sexual responsiveness either by directly stimulating sexual response or by reducing feelings of guilt associated with sex. He or she might then hypothesize that an intervention (called, in experimental terms, a "treatment"), such as drinking alcohol in a laboratory setting, will lead to heightened sexual arousal in the presence of erotic stimuli (such as sexually explicit films). Hypotheses, then, can be considered educated guesses that anticipate the results of an experiment in advance.

3. *Testing the hypothesis.* Scientists then test hypotheses through carefully controlled observation and experimentation. A specific hypothesis about alcohol and sexual arousal—that alcohol either increases or decreases sexual responsiveness—might be tested by administering a certain amount of alcohol to one group of people and then comparing their level of sexual arousal following specific types of sexual stimulation (such as exposure to sexually explicit films) to the level of sexual arousal of another group of people who were shown the films but not given any alcohol.

4. *Drawing conclusions.* Scientists then draw conclusions or inferences about the correctness of their hypotheses, based on their analyses of the results of their studies. If the results of well-designed research studies fail to bear out certain hypotheses, scientists can revise the theories that served as the frameworks for the hypotheses. Research findings often lead scientists to modify their theories, and in turn, generate new hypotheses that can be tested in further research.

Some investigators include the publication of results in professional journals as part and parcel of the scientific method. Publication shares scientific knowledge with the public at large and also exposes research methods to evaluation by the scientific community. In this way, results can be interpreted in terms of potential flaws in methodology.

Goals and Methods of the Science of Human Sexuality

The goals of the science of human sexuality are congruent with those of other sciences: to describe, explain, predict, and control the events (in this case, the sexual behaviors) that are of interest. Let us discuss some of the general goals of science and how they relate to the study of human sexuality as a science.

Description is a basic objective of science. To understand sexual behavior, for example, we must first be able to describe it. So description of behavior precedes understanding. Scientists attempt to be clear, unbiased, and precise in their descriptions of events and behavior. The scientific approach to human sexuality describes sexual behavior through techniques as varied as the field study, the survey, the individual case study, and the laboratory experiment.

To underscore the importance of the need for unbiased description, consider the name of a tropical fish that will be familiar to many readers: the kissing gourami. These small, flat fish—particularly the males—approach each other frontally and press their open mouths against one another. Yet the term *kissing gourami* may well be something of a misnomer if the word "kissing" is meant to imply affection. Prolonged observations of the fish suggest that it is more likely that kissing in gouramis is a test of strength. More powerful "kissers" apparently achieve positions of social dominance that are connected with privileges in feeding and mating.

Inference
Conclusion or opinion.

Anthropomorphism
The attributing of human characteristics to an animal.

The error in describing the behavior of gouramis as "kissing" involves confusing **inference** with description. It is, in fact, an **anthropomorphic** inference, in that it involves applying human standards to explain animal behavior. One of the great challenges to scientists is the separation of description from inference.

Inference, like description, is crucial to science. Inference allows us to move from observations or descriptions of particular events or behavior to general principles that can be woven into models and theories that help explain them, such as the psychoanalytic and learning theories or models. Without a means for organizing our descriptions of events and behavior in terms of models and theories, we would be left with nothing more than a buzzing confusion of disconnected observations. Scientists need to distinguish between *description* and *inference,* however—to recognize when they jump from a description of events to an inference based on an interpretation of those events. For example, one does not *describe* a person's sexual behavior as "deviant." Rather, one *labels* or *classifies* it as deviant when one believes it to deviate from a certain norm. But what is deviant in one culture may be normal in another. Incestuous relationships between brothers and sisters are permitted among the Dahomey of West Africa (Stephens, 1982). The same behavior is

Variables
Quantities or qualities that vary or may vary.

Demographic
Concerning the vital statistics (density, race, age, etc.) of human populations.

considered deviant in our own culture and virtually all others. Even within the same larger culture, behavior may be deviant by the standards of some subcultures and not by others.

Researchers attempt to relate their observations to other factors, or **variables,** that can help explain them. For example, researchers may attempt to explain variations in the frequency of coitus by relating—or *correlating*—coitus with **demographic** variables such as age, religious or social background, or cultural expectations. The variables that are commonly used to explain sexual behavior include biological (age, health), psychological (anxieties, skills), and sociological (educational level, socioeconomic status, ethnicity) ones. Explanations of behavior can involve reference to many variables, even those that cannot be measured directly, such as unconscious motivation. Relationships among variables may be tied together into theories of behavior. For example, psychoanalytic theory emphasizes the role of unconscious forces in determining behavior. Learning theories focus on how variables such as rewards, punishments, and expectations shape behavior.

Theories provide frameworks within which scientists can explain what they observe and make predictions. It is not sufficient for theories to help us make sense of events that have already occurred. Theories must also allow us to make predictions. One test of the soundness of psychoanalytic and learning theories is whether or not they allow us to predict behavior. Prediction requires discovering variables that anticipate events. Geologists seek clues in the forces that affect the earth to forecast events such as earthquakes and volcanic eruptions. Sex researchers study factors that may predict various types of sexual behavior. Some researchers, for example, have examined childhood interests and behavior patterns that may predict the development of a gay male or lesbian sexual orientation. Others have explored factors, such as the age at which dating begins and the quality of the relationships between teens and their parents, that may predict the likelihood of premarital intercourse during adolescence.

The notion of controlling human behavior of any kind—especially sexual behavior—is controversial and misunderstood. Behavioral scientists and health practitioners are generally committed to preserving the dignity of the individual. If people are to have dignity, they must be free to make their own decisions. Within this context, *controlling behavior* does not mean coercing people to do the bidding of others. Rather, it means drawing upon scientific knowledge to help people create their own goals and marshal their resources to meet them. Reputable scientists are held to ethical and professional standards that ban the use of harmful techniques in research or practice and that safeguard the rights of participants in research.

The science of human sexuality does not tell people how they *ought* to behave. It does not attempt to limit or expand their variety of sexual activities. Rather, it furnishes information that people may use to help themselves or others make decisions about their own behavior. For instance, the science of human sexuality provides information that increases the chances that a couple who are having difficulty becoming pregnant will be able to conceive. At the same time, it develops and evaluates means of birth control that can be used to help couples regulate their reproductive choices. The science of human sexuality also seeks to develop techniques that can help people overcome sexual dysfunctions and enhance the gratification they find in sexual relations. "Control" also takes the form of enabling couples to give and receive more sexual pleasure, of enhancing fetal health, and of preventing and curing sexually transmitted diseases.

Operational Definitions

How do we study concepts such as sexual satisfaction or an even broader concept, marital satisfaction? One of the requirements in sex research, as in other types of research, is specification of the definitions of the concepts, or "constructs," of interest. Different investigators may define marital satisfaction or sexual satisfaction in different ways. They may be studying different events although they may use the same terms.

What, for example, is sexual arousal? Many studies seek to assess the effects of various stimuli (such as sexually explicit material) on sexual arousal, but sexual arousal can mean several things. It can mean the *subjective* "feeling" that one is sexually aroused. It

38 ∼ CHAPTER 2   RESEARCH METHODS

PHYSIOLOGICAL MEASURES OF SEXUAL AROUSAL

Scientific studies depend on the ability to measure the phenomena of interest. The phenomena of sexual arousal may be measured by different means, such as self-report and physiological measures. Self-report measures of sexual arousal are considered *subjective*. They ask people to give their impressions of the level of their sexual arousal at a given time, such as by circling their response on a ten-point scale that ranges from zero, "not at all aroused," to ten, "extremely aroused." Physiological devices measure the degree of vasocongestion that builds up in the genitals during sexual arousal. (Vasocongestion—that is, congestion with blood—leads to erection in men and vaginal lubrication in women.) In men, vasocongestion is frequently measured by a **penile strain gauge.** This device is worn under the man's clothing. It is fitted around the penis and measures his erectile response by

recording changes in the circumference of the penis. The device is sensitive to small changes in circumference that may not be noticed (and thus not reported) by the man.

Physiological measurement of sexual arousal in women is most often accomplished by means of a **vaginal photoplethysmograph.** The vaginal photoplethysmograph is a tampon-shaped probe with a light and a photocell in its tip. It is inserted in the vagina and indicates the level of blood congestion by means of measuring the amount of light reflected from the vaginal walls. The more light that is absorbed by the vaginal walls, the less that is reflected. Less reflected light indicates greater vasocongestion.

Sex researchers sometimes measure sexual arousal in response to stimuli such as erotic films or audio-taped dramatizations of erotic scenes. What happens when physiological de-

vices give a different impression of sexual arousal than those offered by self-report? Objectively (physiologically) measured sexual arousal does not always agree with subjective feelings of sexual arousal, as measured by self-report. For example, a person may say that he or she is relatively unaroused while the physiological measures suggest otherwise. Which is the *truer* measure of arousal, the person's subjective reports or the levels shown on the objective instruments?

Discrepancies across measures suggest that people may be sexually aroused (as measured by physiological indicators) but psychologically unprepared to recognize it or unwilling to admit it. In the real world of human relationships, sexual arousal has psychological as well as physiological aspects. The reflexes of erection and vaginal lubrication do not necessarily translate into "Yes."

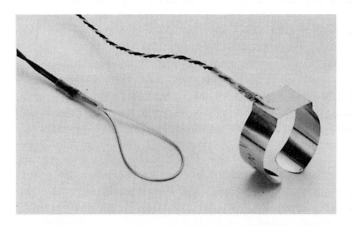 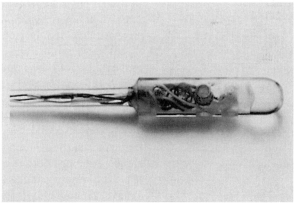

The Penile Strain Gauge and the Vaginal Photoplethysmograph. These devices measure vasocongestion in the genitals of men and women, providing an objective measure of their level of sexual arousal. Can you think of other aspects of sexual arousal?

Penile strain gauge
A device for measuring sexual arousal in men in terms of changes in the circumference of the penis.

can mean one's self-report of genital sensations. It may refer to direct physiological measures of blood congestion (**vasocongestion**) in the genitals. We further explore the measurement of sexual arousal in the nearby Closer Look feature.

The **operational definition** of a construct links its meaning to the methods used to measure it. In some studies reported in this book, sexual arousal is operationally defined as vasocongestion. In others, it is operationally defined as self-report of sexual interest or

Vaginal photoplethysmograph
A tampon-shaped probe that is inserted in the vagina and suggests the level of vasocongestion by measuring the light reflected from the vaginal walls.

Vasocongestion
Congestion from the flow of blood. (From the Latin *vas*, meaning "vessel.")

Operational definition
A definition of a construct or variable in terms of the methods used to measure it.

genital sensations. In still others, a combination of measures is used. It is important to recognize that our ability to generalize the results of research is limited by the operational definitions of the variables. That is, we may be able to generalize only to instances that define terms in the same way.

~ *Reflections* ~

What is the scientific method? Why do scholars of human sexuality use it?

Does the science of human sexuality aim to tell people how they *ought* to behave? Why, or why not?

Do you believe that scientists should be permitted to use instruments such as the penile strain gauge or vaginal photoplethysmograph in their research? Why, or why not?

Let us now examine the ways in which scientists study human sexuality. The first thing scientists do is to identify *whom* or *what* they will study, which brings us to the topic of sampling.

Populations and Samples: Representing the World of Diversity

Population
A complete group of organisms or events.

Sample
Part of a population.

Generalize
To go from the particular to the general.

Researchers undertake to learn about **populations.** Populations are complete groups of people or animals. Many researchers have attempted to learn about people in the United States, for example. (In 1996, there were about 270 million of them—a sizable population.) Other researchers may identify American adults, or American adolescents, as their population. Still other researchers attempt to compare the sexual behavior of African Americans to that of Hispanic Americans and other Americans. These are termed the *populations of interest,* or *target populations.* These target populations are all sizable. It would be expensive, difficult, and, in fact, all but impossible to study every individual in them.

Because of the impossibility of studying all members of a population, scientists select individuals from the population and study them. The individuals who participate in research are said to comprise a **sample.** However, we cannot truly learn about the population of interest unless the sample *represents* that population. A *representative sample* is a research sample of participants who accurately represent the population of interest.

If you wished to learn about dating practices at your college or university, the population of interest would be the total student population. If you were to select your research sample from one dormitory or class, it would probably not be a representative sample (unless the dormitory or class contained a true cross-section of the entire student body). If our samples do not represent the target populations, we cannot extend or **generalize** the results of our research to the populations of interest. If we wished to study the sexual behavior of Asian Americans, our population would consist of *all* Asian Americans. If we used only Asian American college students as our sample, we could not generalize our findings to all Asian Americans. Our sample would not *represent* all Asian Americans.

In a perfect world, research into populations would include every member of the target populations. Then we would know that our findings applied to these populations. Including all people in the United States in a study of sexual behavior would be impossible. We cannot even find all people in the United States when we conduct the census each decade. Sex research would undoubtedly cause many more people to refuse to participate than would a simple counting of noses. Sampling a part of a target population makes research practical and possible—if imperfect.

Sampling Methods

Random sample

A sample in which every member of a population has an equal chance of participating.

Probability sample

A sample in which the probability of inclusion in the sample of any particular member is known.

Since we cannot sample every member of a population, we need to select samples that represent that population. One way of acquiring a representative sample is through random sampling. A **random sample** is one in which every member of the target population has an equal chance of participating. A random sample is a type of **probability sample.** Statisticians use the term *probability sample* to describe samples in which we know the probability of any particular member's being included in the sample.

Now and then magazine editors boast that they have surveyed samples of 20,000 or 30,000 readers, but size alone does not mean that a sample is representative. As an example, the *Literary Digest* magazine polled thousands of voters by telephone to predict the outcome of the 1936 presidential election. Based on the survey, the magazine predicted that Alfred Landon would defeat Franklin D. Roosevelt, but Roosevelt won by a landslide of nearly 11 million votes. The problem was that the election was held during the Great Depression, when only relatively affluent people could afford telephones. Those who could afford phones were also more likely to be Republicans and to vote for the Republican candidate, Landon. Thus, the *Digest* poll, although large, was biased. A sample of 30 million voters will not provide an accurate picture if it is biased.

T r u t h OR *Fiction?*
R E V I S I T E D

It is true that you could study millions of people in the United States and still not obtain an accurate picture of the sexual behavior of the general U.S. population. A sample of many millions might not represent the U.S. population. Sample size alone does not guarantee that the sample's members have been selected in an unbiased manner. ∎

Stratified random sample

A random sample in which known subgroups in a population are represented in proportion to their numbers in the population.

Researchers overcome biased sampling by drawing *random* or *stratified random* samples of populations. In a random sample, every member of a population has an equal chance of participating. In a **stratified random sample,** known subgroups of a population are represented in proportion to their numbers in the population. For instance, about 12% of the U.S. population is African American. Researchers could therefore decide that 12% of their sample must be African American if they are to represent all people in the United States. The randomness of the sample would be preserved since the members of the subgroups would be selected randomly from their particular subgroups. In practical terms, however, a reasonably large *random* sample with no prior stratification will turn out to be reasonably well stratified in the end. Put it another way: If you blindfold yourself, shake up a jar of jelly beans, and take out a scoopful, the proportions of the different colors of beans in the scoop are likely to approximate the proportions of those colors in the entire jar.

Random samples can be hard to come by, especially when it comes to asking people about their sexual attitudes or behavior. For instance, the Playboy Foundation (Hunt, 1974) sampled people listed in telephone directories in various cities in the United States in the early 1970s. Most people at the time had phones, yet the sample could not have included the very poor who may not have been able to afford to keep a phone, those who had unlisted numbers, and college students without private phones.

Another problem is that sexual research is almost invariably conducted with people who volunteer to participate. Volunteers may differ from people who refuse to participate. For example, volunteers tend to be more open about their sexuality than the general population. They may even tend to exaggerate behaviors that others might consider deviant or abnormal.

Volunteer bias

A slanting of research data that is caused by the characteristics of individuals who volunteer to participate, such as willingness to discuss intimate behavior.

The problem of a **volunteer bias** is a thorny one for sex researchers, since the refusal of people who have been randomly selected to participate in the survey can ruin the representativeness of the sample. Since it would be unethical to coerce people to participate in a study on sexual behavior (or any other type of study), researchers must use samples of volunteers, rather than true random samples. A low response rate to a voluntary survey is an indication that the responses obtained may not be representative of the original sample (Biggar & Melbye, 1992). They may reflect only the type of people who chose to participate.

It is not true that researchers can overcome refusal of some people to participate by recruiting larger numbers of volunteers. Volunteers differ from people who refuse to participate. Therefore, volunteers do not *represent* the entire population. ■

In some cases, as in the Janus and Janus (1993) survey, samples are *samples of convenience.* They consist of individuals who happen to be available to the researcher and who share some characteristics with the target population, perhaps religious background or sexual orientation. Still, they may not truly represent the target group. Convenience samples often consist of White, middle-class college students who volunteer for studies conducted at their schools. They may not be (and probably are not) representative of students in general. They do not even represent the general student population at their own school. Random samples of gay males or lesbians are perhaps the most difficult to come by. The social stigma attached to their sexual orientations may discourage gay males and lesbians from disclosing them.

～ *Reflections* ～

■ To what "target populations" do you belong? How could researchers obtain representative samples of these populations?

■ If you were asked to participate in a survey on sexual behavior, would you? Why, or why not? Why do you think many people are reluctant to participate in such surveys? What kinds of assurances might you seek from a researcher?

Methods of Observation

Once scientists have chosen those they will study, they observe them. In this section, we consider several methods of observation: the case-study method, the survey method, naturalistic observation, ethnographic observation, participant observation, and laboratory observation.

The Case-Study Method

Case study
A carefully drawn, in-depth biography of an individual or a small group of individuals that may be obtained through interviews, questionnaires, and historical records.

A **case study** is a carefully drawn, in-depth biography of an individual or a small group. The focus is on understanding one or several individuals as fully as possible by unraveling the interplay of various factors in their backgrounds. In most case studies, the researcher comes to know the individual or group through interviews or other contacts conducted over a prolonged period of time. The interviewing pattern tends to build upon itself with a good deal of freedom, as opposed to the one-shot, standardized set of questions used in survey questionnaires.

Researchers may also conduct case studies by interviewing people who have known the individuals or by examining public records. Sigmund Freud, for example, drew upon historical records in his case study of the Renaissance inventor and painter Leonardo da Vinci. Freud concluded that Leonardo's artistic productions represented the sublimating, or channeling, of male–male sexual impulses.

It is true that case studies have been carried out on people who are dead. Such case studies rely on historical records rather than interviews with the individuals themselves or their contemporaries. ■

Reports of innovative treatments for sexual dysfunctions usually appear as well-described case studies. A clinician typically reports the background of the client in depth, describes the treatment, reports the apparent outcomes, and suggests factors that might have contributed to the treatment's success or failure. In writing a treatment case study, the therapist attempts to provide information that may be of help to therapists who treat clients with similar problems. Case studies or "multiple case studies" (reports concerning a few individuals) that hold promise may be subjected to controlled investigation—ideally, to experimental studies involving treatment and control groups.

Limitations of the Case-Study Method   Despite the richness of material that may be derived from the case-study approach, it is not as rigorous a research design as an experiment. People often have gaps in memory, especially concerning childhood events. The potential for observer bias is also a prominent concern. Clinicians and interviewers may unintentionally guide people into saying what they expect to hear. Then, too, researchers may inadvertently color people's reports when they jot them down—shape them subtly in ways that reflect their own views.

Remember that clinicians who test a treatment method with a single client (or with a few clients) through a course of therapy are manipulating an independent variable (the treatment) with one or more people who are unlikely to represent the general population. For one thing, the clients have sought (or been placed in) professional treatment. In a case study, we cannot be certain whether treatment outcomes are due to the treatment methods, giving clients hope that they will get better, having clients talk about their problems, or even improvement that comes about naturally as a result of time. We will see that the experiment allows us to eliminate such rival explanations.

The Survey Method

Survey
A detailed study of a sample obtained by means such as interviews and questionnaires.

Surveys typically gather information about behavior through questionnaires or interviews. Researchers may interview or administer questionnaires to thousands of people from particular population groups to learn about their sexual behavior and attitudes. Interviews such as those used by Kinsey and his colleagues (1948, 1953) have the advantages of face-to-face contact and of giving the interviewer the opportunity to *probe*—that is, to follow up on answers that seem to lead toward useful information. A skilled interviewer may be able to set a respondent at ease and establish a sense of trust or *rapport* that encourages self-disclosure. On the other hand, unskilled interviewing may cause respondents to conceal information.

Questionnaires are inexpensive when compared to interviews. The major expenses in using questionnaires involve printing and distribution. Questionnaires can be administered to groups of people at once, and respondents can return them unsigned, so that they are anonymous. Anonymity may encourage respondents to disclose intimate information. Questionnaires, of course, can be used only by people who can read and record their responses. Interviews can be used even with people who cannot read or write. But interviewers must be trained, sometimes extensively, and then paid for their time.

Some of the major surveys described in this book were conducted by Kinsey and his colleagues (1948, 1953), the Playboy Foundation (Hunt, 1974), Bell and his colleagues (1978, 1981), Coles and Stokes (1985), Wyatt and her colleagues (Wyatt, 1985, 1989; Wyatt et al., 1988a, 1988b), researchers at the Battelle Memorial Institute of Seattle (Billy et al., 1993; Tanfer et al., 1993), Janus and Janus (1993), and the University of Chicago group (Laumann et al., 1994). The book also discusses surveys conducted by popular magazines such as *Redbook*. By and large, these surveys have reported the incidence and frequency of sexual activities among men and women, both married and single; male–female, male–male, and female–female sexual activity; and sexual behaviors of adolescents, adults, and older people.

Many of these surveys have *something* to offer to our understanding of human sexuality, but some are more methodologically sound than others. None represents the U.S. population at large, however. Most people consider their sexuality to be among the most intimate, *private* aspects of their lives. People who willingly agree to be polled as to their political preferences may resist participation in surveys concerning their sexual behavior. As a result, it is difficult, if not impossible, for researchers to recruit a truly representative

Alfred Kinsey. Kinsey and his colleagues conducted the first large-scale scientific study of sexual behavior in the United States.

sample of the population. Bear in mind, then, that survey results provide, at best, an approximation of the sexual attitudes, beliefs, and behaviors of the U.S. population.

Let us review the sampling techniques of some of the major studies of human sexuality. Throughout the book we shall reconsider the findings of these surveys, especially those that shed light on the changes that have occurred between Kinsey's surveys and the present. But for now let us focus on the methods used by Kinsey and others to survey sexual behavior patterns in the United States.

The Kinsey Reports   Kinsey and his colleagues (1948, 1953) interviewed 5,300 males and 5,940 females in the United States between 1938 and 1949. They asked a wide array of questions on various types of sexual experiences, including masturbation, oral sex, and coitus that occurred before, during, and outside of marriage. The survey was a reasonable method for obtaining these data, since Kinsey was interested in studying the frequencies of various sexual behaviors, rather than their underlying causes. For obvious reasons Kinsey could not use more direct observational methods, such as sending his researchers to peer through bedroom windows. Kinsey chose not to try to obtain a random sample. He believed that a high refusal rate would wreck the chances of accurately representing the general population. Instead, he adopted a *group sampling* approach. He recruited study participants from the organizations and community groups to which they belonged, such as college fraternities and sororities. He contacted representatives of groups in diverse communities and tried to persuade them to secure the cooperation of fellow group members. If he showed these individuals that they would not be subjected to embarrassment or discomfort, Kinsey hoped that they would persuade other members to participate. Kinsey understood that the groups he solicited were not necessarily representative of the general population. He believed, however, that his sampling approach was dictated by practical constraints. Even so, he made an attempt to sample as broadly as possible from the groups he solicited. In some cases he obtained full participation. In other cases he obtained a large enough proportion of the group membership to help ensure representativeness, at least of the group.

Still, Kinsey's samples did not represent the general population. People of color, people in rural areas, older people, the poor, and Catholics and Jews were all underrepresented in his samples. Statisticians who have reviewed Kinsey's methods have concluded that there were systematic biases in his sampling methods, but that it would have been impossible to obtain a true probability sample from the general population (see, e.g., Cochran et al., 1953). There is thus no way of knowing whether or not Kinsey's results accurately mirrored the U.S. population at the time. In Chapter 10 we shall see that his estimate that 37% of the male population had reached orgasm at least once through male–male sexual activity was probably too high. The *relationships* Kinsey uncovered, however, such as the positive link between level of education and participation in oral sex, may be more generalizable (see Chapter 9).

To his credit, Kinsey took measures to instill candor in the people he interviewed. For one, study participants were assured of the confidentiality of their records. For another, Kinsey's interviewers were trained to conduct the interviews in an objective and matter-of-fact style. To reduce the tendency to slant responses in a socially desirable direction, participants were reassured that the interviewers were not passing judgment on them. Interviewers were trained not to show emotional reactions that the people they interviewed could interpret as signs of disapproval (they maintained a "calm and steady eye" and a constant tone of voice).

Kinsey also checked the **reliability** of his data by evaluating the consistency of the responses given by several hundred interviewees who were reexamined after at least 18 months. Their reports of the **incidence** of sexual activities (for example, whether or not they had ever engaged in premarital or extramarital coitus) were highly reliable. That is, participants tended to give the same answers on both occasions. But reports of the **frequency** of sexual activities (such as the number of times one has masturbated to orgasm or the frequency of coitus in marriage) were less consistent. People do tend to find it more difficult to compute the frequencies of their activities than to answer whether or not they have ever engaged in them.

Reliability
The consistency or accuracy of a measure.

Incidence
A measure of the occurrence or the degree of occurrence of an event.

Frequency
The number of times an action is repeated within a given period.

Validity
With respect to tests, the degree to which a particular test measures the constructs or traits it purports to measure.

Kinsey recognized that consistency of responses across time—or *retakes,* as he called them—did not guarantee their **validity.** That is, the retakes did not show whether the reported behaviors had some basis in fact. He could not validate self-reports directly, as one might validate reports that one is drug-free by means of urine analysis. He could not send his investigators to peer through bedroom windows, so he had to use indirect means to validate the data. One indirect measure was comparison of the reports of husbands and wives, for example, with respect to the *incidence* of oral–genital sex or the *frequency* of intercourse. There was a remarkable consistency in the reports of 706 pairs of spouses; this lends support to the view that their self-reports were accurate. (It is possible, but highly unlikely, that spouses colluded to misrepresent their behavior.)

The NHSLS Study   The National Health and Social Life Survey was intended to provide general information about sexual behavior in the United States, and also specific information that might be used to predict and prevent the spread of AIDS. It was conducted by Edward O. Laumann of the University of Chicago and three colleagues—John H. Gagnon, Robert T. Michael, and Stuart Michaels—in the 1990s and published as *The Social Organization of Sexuality: Sexual Practices in the United States* in 1994. A companion volume authored by Michael, Gagnon, Laumann, and Gina Kolata—a *New York Times* science reporter—was also published: *Sex in America: A Definitive Survey. Sex in America* is a bit less technical in presentation but also offers some interesting data not found in the other version. The NHSLS study was to be originally supported by government funds, but government ambivalence about conducting a sex survey forced the research team to obtain funding from private sources.

The sample included 3,432 people. Of this number, 3,159 were drawn from English-speaking adults living in households (not dormitories, prisons, and so forth), ages 18 to 59. The other 273 were purposely obtained by oversampling African American and Hispanic American households, so that more information could be obtained about these ethnic groups. Although the sample probably represents the overall U.S. population quite well (or at least those of ages 18–59), there may be too few Asian Americans, Native Americans, and Jews to offer much information about these groups.

The researchers identified samples of households in geographic areas—by addresses, not names. They sent a letter to each household, describing the purpose and methods of the study, and an interviewer visited each household one week later. The people targeted were assured that the purposes of the study were important and that the identities of participants would be kept confidential. Incentives of up to $100 were offered for cooperating. A high completion rate of close to 80% was obtained in this way. All in all, the NHSLS study could be the only one since Kinsey's day that offers a reasonably accurate picture of the sexual practices of the general population of the United States.

The Playboy Foundation Survey   A survey of sexual practices in the 1970s was commissioned by the Playboy Foundation. The results were reported by Morton Hunt in his 1974 book, *Sexual Behavior in the 1970's.* The *Playboy survey,* or *Hunt survey,* as it is sometimes called, sought to examine the changes in sexual behavior in the United States between Kinsey's time and the early 1970s.

The *Playboy* sample was drawn randomly from phone book listings in 24 U.S. cities. People were asked to participate in small group discussions focusing on trends in sexual practices in the United States. They were not told that they would also be completing a questionnaire, an approach that has raised ethical concerns. That is, the participants were not fully informed about their role in the study when they agreed to participate. (Interestingly, though, none of 2,026 people who participated in the group meetings refused to complete the questionnaires.) The phone sampling method was supplemented by an additional sample of young people, who were likely to have been underrepresented in telephone directories. But even with these additional people, rural people and inmates of prisons and mental hospitals remained underrepresented.

Because the Playboy Foundation did not sample rural people and selected only 24 urban centers, the study's participants do not represent the general U.S. population at the time. Hunt argues, perhaps with some justification, that the final sample of 2,026 is stratified properly as to the ages and races of urban residents across a diverse sample of U.S. cities. The major flaw in the method, however, is that 80% of the people contacted refused to participate. The final 2,026 were clearly willing to volunteer to participate in discussion groups and to then complete a sex questionnaire. We suspect that they were more open and frank about sexual issues than the population at large.

The Janus Report   Another nationwide survey of sexual behavior in the United States was conducted from 1988 to 1992 by a husband-and-wife team, Samuel and Cynthia Janus (1993). *The Janus Report on Sexual Behavior* was based on a survey of 2,765 people of age 18 years or older (1,347 men and 1,418 women) who anonymously completed written questionnaires assessing a wide range of sexual behaviors and attitudes. In-depth interviews were also conducted with a subset of the larger sample.

The Janus sample, like the Kinsey sample before it, was not randomly selected from the general population. Rather, the Januses assembled a team of researchers from every region of the contiguous 48 states, who then made contact with groups of potential respondents. In all, the survey team distributed 4,550 questionnaires in various sites across the country. Satisfactorily completed questionnaires (those with few missing responses) were returned from 2,765 respondents, representing a return rate of only 61%. The surveyists attempted to construct a sample that represented a fairly typical cross-section of the U.S. population with respect to characteristics such as age, gender, income, and educational background. Although the findings may offer some insights into contemporary sexuality in American society, we have no assurance that the sample truly represented the general population. People who respond to sex surveys may not only be more open about discussing their sexuality than the general population. They may also hold more permissive views about sex.

The Magazine Surveys   Major readership surveys have also been conducted by popular magazines, such as *Psychology Today, Redbook, Ladies' Home Journal, McCall's, Cosmopolitan,* and even *Consumer Reports.* Although these surveys all offer some useful information and may be commended for attaining large samples (ranging from 20,000 to 106,000!), their sampling techniques are inherently unscientific and biased. Each sample represents, at best, the readers of the magazine in which the questionnaire appeared. Moreover, we learn only about readers who volunteered to respond to these questionnaires. They likely differed in important ways from the majority of readers who failed to respond. Finally, readers of these magazines are more affluent than the public at large, and readers of *Cosmopolitan, Psychology Today,* and even *Redbook* tend to be more liberal. So the samples may represent only those readers who were willing to complete and mail in the surveys.

A nonacademic researcher, Shere Hite, published several popular—perhaps we should say "notorious"—books on sexual behavior in men and women. Her samples for her 1976 book on female sexuality, *The Hite Report,* and her 1981 book on male sexuality, *The Hite Report on Male Sexuality,* were gleaned from people who completed questionnaires received in direct mailings, printed in sexually explicit magazines like *Penthouse,* and made available through other outlets, including some churches. Her final samples of some 3,000 women, in the 1976 report, and 7,000 men, in the 1981 book, may seem large. However, they actually represent small return rates of 3% and 6%, respectively. For these reasons, among others, the "Hite reports" cannot be considered scientific studies.

Laumann and his colleagues (1994) are particularly harsh in their judgment of such surveys. They write that "such studies, in sum, produce junk statistics of no value whatsoever in making valid and reliable population projections" (p. 45).

Surveys of Specific Populations   The Kinsey and NHSLS studies were broad based. They queried men and women from different localities, socioeconomic strata, and age groups. Magazine surveys tend to recruit people more narrowly, as defined by reader characteristics. In some cases, however, researchers have focused their efforts on particular populations, such as adolescents, older people, people from particular racial/ethnic groups, and gay men and lesbians.

In recent years, large-scale studies in the United States and other countries have been conducted to acquire information concerning sexual practices that might prove useful in the fight against AIDS (Adler, 1993). In the United States, for example, researchers from the Battelle Memorial Institute of Seattle interviewed a nationally representative sample of 3,321 men between the ages of 20 and 39 in order to determine the prevalence of unsafe sexual practices among young adult men (Billy et al., 1993; Tanfer et al., 1993).

In later chapters we shall discuss some of the findings from these various surveys. In this chapter's World of Diversity feature, we consider some survey findings concerning Native Americans, African Americans, and people in China.

The Kinsey Institute Reports on Gay People: 1978 and 1981

These reports by the Indiana University Institute for Sex Research, also called the Kinsey Institute, were based on a sample of 979 gay people from the San Francisco area and a reference group of 477 people matched for age, race, and educational and occupational achievements (Bell & Weinberg, 1978; Bell et al., 1981). In their 1978 book, *Homosexualities,* researchers Alan Bell and Martin Weinberg recognized that their findings could not necessarily be extended to gay people who lived in other cities or sections of the country. Indeed, they acknowledged that their sample might not even represent gay people in San Francisco. It consisted of people who had "come out of the closet" to join gay rights organizations, who attended gay bars and baths, and so forth. Nevertheless, these reports have provided wide-ranging information on parent–child relationships and sexual orientation and on the diversity of lifestyles among gay people (see Chapter 10).

Limitations of the Survey Method

The Kinsey studies may be criticized because the interviewers were all men. Women respondents might have felt more free to open up to female interviewers. Gender of the interviewer can have an impact on a respondent's willingness to disclose sensitive material. A recent investigation in the Asian country of Nepal, for example, showed that male interviewers generally elicited an underreporting of some sensitive aspects of sexual activity (Axinn, 1991). Problems in obtaining reliable estimates may also occur when interviewers and respondents are of different racial or socioeconomic backgrounds.

Yet another limitation of all surveys is that they require self-reports of respondents' behaviors. But self-reports are subject to inaccuracies or biases because of factors such as faulty memories of sexual behavior; tendencies to distort or conceal information because of embarrassment, shame, or guilt; or attempts to present a socially favorable image of oneself. Survey data may also be drawn from haphazard or nonrepresentative samples and thus not represent the target population. Let us consider several weaknesses of the survey method.

Volunteer Bias

Many people refuse to participate in surveys. Samples are thus biased by large numbers of volunteers. Volunteers are in general willing to take the time to participate. In the case of sex surveys, they also tend to be more sexually permissive and liberal-minded than nonvolunteers. The results of a survey based on a volunteer sample thus may not accurately reflect the population at large.

Faulty Estimation

Respondents may recall their behavior inaccurately or purposely misrepresent it. People may not recall the age at which they first engaged in petting or masturbated to orgasm. People may have difficulty recalling or calculating the frequencies of certain behaviors, such as the weekly frequency of marital intercourse ("Well, let's see, this week I think it was four times, but last week only two times, and I can't remember the week before that"). Kinsey and Hunt speculated that people who desire more frequent sex tend to underestimate the frequency of marital coitus, whereas people who want less frequent sex tend to overestimate it.

Social desirability
A response bias to a questionnaire or interview in which the person provides a socially acceptable response.

Social-Desirability Response Bias

Even people who consent to participate in surveys of sexual behavior may feel pressured to answer questions in the direction of **social desirability.** Some respondents, that is, try to ingratiate themselves with their

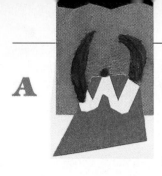

SURVEYS OF THE SEXUAL BEHAVIOR OF DIVERSE POPULATIONS

Questions abound about the sexual behavior of Native Americans and African Americans. Kinsey did not survey Native Americans. Nor did Hunt, Wyatt, or other leading researchers. The 1982 government survey known as the National Survey of Family Growth (NSFG), which surveyed the reproductive behavior of more than 7,500 women nationwide, included only 83 Native American women in the sample, far too few to be a meaningful indicator of general patterns (Warren et al., 1990). The number of Native Americans in the NHSLS study was in the 40's (Laumann et al., 1994).

Kinsey obtained some data on the sexual behavior of African Americans but did not report it in his surveys because African Americans were clearly underrepresented in his samples. However, more recent studies by Gail Wyatt and the NHSLS group have reported some useful information.

It is interesting to compare results of these surveys with similar surveys in different countries and cultures, such as China. China was never a particularly prudish country. China's tradition of concubines and prostitution predates the birth of Jesus. After the Communists came into power in 1949, China transformed into a fairly puritanical society. Now, according to a Shanghai-based sociologist Liu Dalin, since China's opening to the outside world in the 1970s, the times have changed again.

The Billings Indian Health Service Survey

In one of the first efforts to survey the reproductive and health behavior of Native Americans, the Billings (Montana) Indian Health Service office surveyed 232 Native American women in the Billings area, ages 15 to 49. Half of the women lived on the Blackfeet Reservation. The other half lived off the reservation in nearby Great Falls (Warren et al., 1990). Surveys were conducted in 1987. The results were compared to data on White and African American women obtained from the 1982 NSFG survey. Nearly 40% of the Native American households did not have telephones. Therefore, a face-to-face interview format was adopted. Virtually all of the women interviewed on the Blackfeet Reservation were Blackfeet, but a variety of tribes were represented among interviewees living in Great Falls, including Chippewa–Cree, Little Shell, Assiniboine, and Chippewa, as well as Blackfeet.

Slightly more than half of the Native American women and African American women reported having engaged in sexual intercourse by the age of 17, as compared to 28% of the White women. Native American women bore an average of 3.4 to 4.0 children. This figure exceeded the average among White women (2.7 children) but was similar to the average among African Americans (3.4). The percentage of last pregnancies that were unplanned was similar for off-reservation Native American women (64%) and African American women (61%) but higher than that for White women (44.6%). Native American women living on the reservation showed an intermediate level (51.2%) of unplanned last pregnancies. Reservation women were more likely than White women to use contraception (79% versus 69%). The percentage of off-reservation Native American women who used contraception was lower, 58%—a figure that was similar to the level of contraceptive use among African American women (60%). Although female sterilization was the most commonly used contraceptive method among all three groups, its incidence was higher among Native Americans (more than 30%) than among White Americans (16%) or African Americans (21%).

Overall, the survey underscores the similarities in reproductive patterns between Native American women living off the reservation and African American women in the larger community. Both groups tended to initiate intercourse at an early age, have a high number of unplanned pregnancies, and make only moderate use of contraception. The reproductive patterns they shared may reflect the plight of economically disadvantaged groups in the United States. Native American women living on the reservation showed reproductive patterns different from those of African Americans and White Americans, and even from those of the urbanized, off-reservation Native American sample. Perhaps their reproductive behavior

Native American Women. Research shows that the reproductive behavior of Native American women in urban areas is more similar to that of other U.S. minorities than to that of Native Americans living on reservations.

adheres more closely to traditional cultural norms than does that of Native American women living off the reservation who may be attempting to assimilate into the larger community.

The Wyatt Survey on African American and White Women in Los Angeles

In the 1980s, UCLA researcher Gail Wyatt and her colleagues (Wyatt, 1985, 1989; Wyatt et al., 1988a, 1988b) examined the sexual behavior of a sample of 122 White and 126 African American women in Los Angeles County. The women ranged in age from 18 to 36 years. Women in the study were sampled randomly from telephone listings. People who agreed to participate were selected to balance the sample with respect to demographic characteristics such as age, education, number of children, and marital status. One in three prospective participants refused to cooperate. The participants were interviewed in Kinsey-style, face-to-face interviews that lasted for three to eight hours.

Because Wyatt and Kinsey used similar means to obtain data, direct comparisons can be made between their studies. Wyatt used statistical adjustments to control for differences in the sociodemographic characteristics (age, education, social class) between her samples and Kinsey's to enable comparisons between the two.

Wyatt's work is important for several reasons. It addresses changes in sexual behavior that have taken place in U.S. society since Kinsey's day. It focuses on social issues that have become prominent, such as sexual abuse in childhood. It also is one of the few detailed studies of sexual behavior among African American women.

One of the striking differences between Kinsey's data and Wyatt's was that women in her 1980s sample—African American and White—engaged in intercourse for the first time at earlier ages than was the case in Kinsey's sample. Kinsey reported that by the age of 20, about one in five women had engaged in premarital coitus. By contrast, Wyatt reported that 98% of the people in her study (African American and White) had experienced premarital intercourse by that age (Wyatt,

1989). When social class differences were taken into consideration, the ages of first intercourse for African American and White women in Wyatt's sample were quite similar.

Wyatt's research was limited to Los Angeles and may not represent the general U.S. population. Kinsey's sample was also geographically skewed. The Northeast was overrepresented although he included respondents from other regions.

Let us also note the refusal rate in Wyatt's study. Wyatt was more successful in obtaining cooperation than the *Playboy* survey takers (67% of the people contacted agreed to participate, versus 20% for *Playboy*). Nonetheless, Wyatt's 33% refusal rate may have compromised representativeness. Also, to control for demographic differences between White and African American women, Wyatt limited the pool of cooperating individuals to demographically comparable women. Her sample of African American women did match the demographic characteristics of the larger population of African American women in Los Angeles County. However, her White sample did not match the population characteristics for White women in the county. It contained a greater proportion of White women from lower-income families. These kinds of trade-offs can occur when researchers attempt to control for demographic differences.

The Liu Report: Sexual Behavior in China

Liu interviewed 23,000 Chinese over a period of 18 months (Southerland, 1990). China's "Kinsey Report" was the first nationwide sex survey ever conducted in China. It polled twice as many people as Kinsey and his colleagues did. Participants included students, professionals, peasants, even convicted sex offenders drawn from 3 major cities and 12 provinces. The researchers encountered problems—lack of funds, illiteracy, and reluctance to reveal intimate sexual information.

Here are some of Liu's findings:
- Chinese youth today are reaching sexual maturity about a year earlier than their grandparents

Sex in Contemporary China. Based on 23,000 interviews, Liu reported that about 50 percent of young people in cities and on farms engage in premarital intercourse.

did, partly because of improved nutrition.
- About 50% of young people in cities and on farms report engaging in premarital intercourse.
- About 14% of the women living in large cities said they engaged in extramarital sex. Overall, 69% of the respondents approved of such affairs, a larger approval rate than is found in the United States, where the majority of respondents disapprove of affairs (Blumstein & Schwartz, 1990; Hunt, 1974).
- Many Chinese couples use very little foreplay. 44% of urban wives and 37% of rural wives reported at least some pain during intercourse due to insufficient vaginal lubrication.
- Women are more likely than men to initiate divorces. Three out of five divorces are sought by women.

Truth **OR** *Fiction?*
R E V I S I T E D

It does appear from the results of the Liu survey that the Chinese are more likely to approve of extramarital affairs than are people in the United States. ■

interviewers by offering what they believe to be socially desirable answers. Although some respondents may readily divulge information concerning the frequency of marital coitus, they may deny experiences involving prohibited activities such as child molestation, voyeurism, or coerced sexual activity. (People who engage in these proscribed activities may also be more likely to decline to participate in sex surveys.)

Some people may not divulge sensitive information for fear of disapproval by the interviewer. Others may fear criminal prosecution. Even though interviewers may insist that they are nonjudgmental and that study participants will remain anonymous, respondents may fear that their identities may be uncovered someday.

Exaggeration   For some respondents, the "socially desirable" response is exaggeration. In our culture, men may tend to exaggerate their sexual exploits. Women may tend to play them down (Havemann & Lehtinen, 1990). Males and "liberated" females may fear that the interviewer will think less of them for reporting only infrequent sexual contacts, or for sounding too "straight." Some respondents falsify their attitudes and exaggerate the bizarreness of their behavior, perhaps to draw attention to themselves, perhaps to foul up the results.

Denial   Another source of bias in sex survey research is denial. People may deny, even to themselves, sexual feelings or experiences that might elicit anxiety if they were acknowledged, such as male–male or female–female fantasies or feelings.

Differences in Meanings of Terms   Survey respondents can respond only to the questions posed by interviewers or questionnaires. A word or phrase may mean different things to different people, however. One person asked whether he or she has engaged in French kissing may think of deep, open-mouthed tongue kissing (the generally accepted meaning of the term). To another, the term may denote a prolonged but gentle kiss on the lips. To some people, the term "sexual satisfaction" may denote an intense orgasm. To others, it signifies the pleasure of sharing physical intimacy with a loved one. To the extent that people interpret the same terms on sex surveys differently, they may differ in their responses because of differences in semantics, not because of differences in behavior.

You might think that these problems would render the survey method useless as a means of learning about human sexuality. Actually, carefully conceived and executed surveys offer many insights into sexual attitudes and practices. In many cases they are the only available means. Before Kinsey we had little information about the sexual practices of people in our society.

The Naturalistic-Observation Method

Naturalistic observation
A method in which organisms are observed in their natural environments.

In **naturalistic observation,** also called the *field study,* scientists directly observe the behavior of animals and humans where it happens. Anthropologists, for example, have lived among preliterate societies and reported on their social and sexual customs. Other disciplines, too, have adopted methods of naturalistic observation in their research on human sexuality. Sociologists have observed the street life of prostitutes. Psychologists have observed patterns of nonverbal communication and body language between couples in dating situations.

Scientists take precautions to keep their naturalistic observations *unobtrusive.* They try not to influence the behavior of the individuals they study. Over the years, naturalistic observers have been placed in ethical dilemmas. They have allowed sick or injured animals to die, rather than intervene, when medical assistance could have saved them. They have allowed substance abuse and illicit sexual behavior to go unreported to authorities. The ethical trade-off is that unobtrusive observation may yield data that will benefit large numbers of people—the greatest good for the greatest number.

Ethnography
The branch of anthropology that deals descriptively with specific cultures, especially preliterate societies.

The Ethnographic-Observation Method

Anthropologists have lived among societies of people in the four corners of the earth in order to observe and study human diversity. Margaret Mead (1935) reported on the social and sexual customs of various peoples of New Guinea. Bronislaw Malinowski (1929) studied the Trobriand islanders, among other peoples. Ford and Beach's (1951) account of sexual practices around the world and in nonhuman species remains to this date a classic study of cross-cultural and cross-species comparisons. **Ethnographic** research has provided us with data concerning sexual behaviors and customs that occur widely across cultures and those that are limited to one or few cultures. Ethnographers are trained to be keen observers, but direct observation has its limits in the study of sexual behavior. Sexual activities are most commonly performed away from the watchful eyes of others, especially from those of visitors from other cultures. Ethnographers may thus have to rely on methods such as personal interviewing to learn more about sexual customs.

The Participant-Observation Method

Participant observation
A method in which observers interact with the people they study as they collect data.

Swinging
Partner- or mate-swapping.

In **participant observation,** the investigators learn about people's behavior by directly interacting with them. Participant observation has been used in studies of male–male sexual behavior and mate-swapping. In effect, participation has been the "price of admission" for observation.

Investigators of mate-swapping, or **swinging,** have contacted swinging couples through newsletter ads and other sources and presented themselves as "baby swingers" (novices) seeking sexual relations (Bartell, 1970; Palson & Palson, 1972). Thus, some investigators may have deceived the people they studied. In some cases, however, as in Bartell's study, individuals were informed that the investigator was conducting research after he was admitted to the party. In some cases, researchers have engaged in coitus with study participants during "swinging parties," which raises questions about how far one should go "for the sake of science."

T r u t h ◆ OR ◆ *Fiction?*
R E V I S I T E D

It is true that some sex researchers have engaged in "swinging" with the people they studied. But this is a rare occurrence, and the ethics of this research method have been questioned. ■

Sampling biases are another concern. There is no way of knowing whether the swingers who were contacted by newspaper ads were typical of swingers in general. The sampling methods also limited the investigations to active swingers and excluded people who had once "swung" but no longer did so.

The Laboratory-Observation Method

William Masters and Virginia Johnson. Masters and Johnson pioneered the physiological measurement of sexual response in a laboratory setting.

In *Human Sexual Response* (1966), William Masters and Virginia Johnson were among the first to report direct laboratory observations of individuals and couples engaged in sexual acts. In all, 694 people (312 men and 382 women) participated in the research. The women ranged from 18 to 78 in age; the men, from 21 to 80. There were 276 married couples, 106 single women, and 36 single men. The married couples engaged in intercourse and other forms of mutual stimulation, such as manual and oral stimulation of the genitals. The unmarried people participated in studies that did not require intercourse, such as measurement of female sexual arousal to insertion of a penis-shaped probe and male ejaculation during masturbation. Masters and Johnson performed similar laboratory observations of sexual response among gay people for their 1979 book, *Homosexuality in Perspective*.

Direct laboratory observation of biological processes was not invented by Masters and Johnson. However, they were confronting a society that was still unprepared to speak openly of sex, let alone to observe people engaged in sexual activity in the laboratory. Masters and Johnson were accused of immorality, voyeurism, and an assortment of other evils. Nevertheless, their methods offered the first reliable set of data on what happens to the body during sexual response. Their instruments permitted them to directly measure vasocongestion (blood flow to the genitals), myotonia (muscle tension), and other physiological responses. Perhaps their most controversial device was a "coition machine." This was a transparent artificial penis outfitted with photographic equipment. It enabled them to study changes in women's internal sexual organs as they became sexually aroused. From these studies, Masters and Johnson observed that it is useful to divide sexual response into four stages (their "sexual response cycle").

Truth **OR** *Fiction?*

R E V I S I T E D

It is true that Masters and Johnson created a transparent artificial penis ("coition machine") containing photographic equipment to study female sexual response. ■

Researchers have since developed more sophisticated physiological methods of measuring sexual arousal and response. Masters and Johnson's laboratory method is now used, with some variations but with less controversy, in research centers across the country (Rosen & Beck, 1988).

Observer effect
A distortion of individuals' behavior caused by the act of observation.

Limitations of Observational Research   One of the basic problems with naturalistic observation is the possibility that the behavior under study may be *reactive* to the measurement itself. This source of bias is referred to as the **observer effect.**

The ethnographer who studies a particular culture or subgroup within a culture may unwittingly alter the behavior of the members of the group by focusing attention on some facets of their behavior. Falling prey to social desirability, some people may "straighten out their act" while the ethnographer is present. Other people may try to impress the ethnographer by acting in ways that are more aggressive or sexually provocative than usual. In either case, people supply distorted or biased information. Ethnographers must corroborate self-reported information by using multiple sources. They must also consider whether their own behavior is more obtrusive than they think.

Observer bias can distort researchers' perceptions of the behaviors they observe. Observers who hold rigid sexual attitudes may be relatively unwilling to examine sexual activities that they consider to be offensive or objectionable. They may unwittingly (or intentionally) slant interviews in a way that presents a "sanitized" view of the behavior of those they study, or exaggerate or "sensationalize" certain sexual practices to conform to their preconceptions of the sexual behavior of the people they study.

The method of laboratory observation used by Masters and Johnson may be even more subject to distortion. Unlike animals, which naturalists may observe unobtrusively from afar, people who participate in laboratory observation know that they are being observed and that their responses are being measured. The problem of volunteer bias, troublesome for sex surveys, is even thornier in laboratory observation. How many of us would assent to performing sexual activities in the laboratory while we were connected to physiological monitoring equipment in full view of researchers? Some of the women observed by Masters and Johnson were patients of Dr. Masters who felt indebted to him and agreed to participate. Many were able to persuade their husbands to participate as well. Some were medical students and graduate students who may have been motivated to earn extra money (participants were paid for their time) as well as by scientific curiosity.

Another methodological concern of the Masters and Johnson approach is that observing people engaged in sexual activities may in itself alter their responses. People may not respond publicly in the same way that they would in private. Perhaps sexual response in the laboratory bears little relationship to sexual response in the bedroom. The physiological monitoring equipment may also alter their natural responses. With these constraints in mind, it is perhaps remarkable that the people studied by Masters and Johnson were able to become sexually aroused and reach orgasm.

~ *Reflections* ~

▪ Consider your own knowledge of other people. Could you say you have ever conducted a case study on anyone? What were the limitations of your "research"?

How do the volunteer bias and social desirability response sets invalidate the results of many surveys? How did the Kinsey group, Morton Hunt, Shere Hite, and the University of Chicago group sample their target populations? Are the results of each survey believable? Why, or why not?

What are your own feelings about the methods of laboratory observation used by Masters and Johnson? Why?

The Correlational Method

What are the relationships between age and frequency of coitus among married couples? What is the connection between socioeconomic status and teenage pregnancy? In each case, two variables are being related to one another: age and frequency of coitus, and socioeconomic status and rates of teenage pregnancy. Correlational research describes the relationship between variables such as these.

A **correlation** is a statistical measure of the relationship between two variables. In correlational studies, two or more variables are related, or linked to, one another by statistical means. The strength and direction (positive or negative) of the relationship between any two variables is expressed with a statistic called a **correlation coefficient.**

Research has shown relationships (correlations) between marital satisfaction and a host of variables: communication skills, shared values, flexibility, frequency of social interactions with friends, and churchgoing, to name a few. Although such research may give us an idea of the factors associated with marital satisfaction, the experimenters have not manipulated the variables of interest. For this reason we cannot say which, if any, of the factors is causally related to marital happiness. Consider the relationship between churchgoing and marital happiness. Couples who attend church more frequently report higher rates of marital satisfaction (Wilson & Filsinger, 1986). It is possible that churchgoing stabilizes marriages. It is also possible that people who attend church regularly are more stable and committed to marriage in the first place.

Correlation

A statistical measure of the relationship between two variables.

Correlation coefficient

A statistic that expresses the strength and direction (positive or negative) of the relationship between two variables.

T r u t h OR *Fiction?*
R E V I S I T E D

It is true that regular churchgoers report higher levels of sexual satisfaction. We cannot say, however, that churchgoing is causally related to marital satisfaction. ■

Correlations may be *positive* or *negative.* Two variables are positively correlated if one increases as the other increases. Frequency of intercourse, for example, has been found to be positively correlated with sexual satisfaction (Blumstein & Schwartz, 1983). That is, married couples who engage in coitus more frequently report higher levels of sexual satisfaction. However, the experimenters did not manipulate the variables. Therefore, we cannot conclude that sexual satisfaction *causes* high coital frequency. It could also be that frequent coitus contributes to greater sexual satisfaction. It is also possible that there is no causal relationship between the variables. Perhaps both coital frequency and sexual satisfaction are affected by other factors, such as communication ability, general marital satisfaction, general health, and so on (see Figure 2.1 on page 54). Similarly, height and weight are positively correlated but do not cause each other. Other factors that we label the growth process contribute to both.

Limitations of the Correlational Method

Correlation is not causation. Many variables are correlated but not causally related to one another.

Although correlations do not show cause and effect, they can be used to make predictions. For example, we can predict that people who were sexually traumatized as children are more likely to encounter psychological problems later on. They find it more difficult to establish intimate relationships in adulthood. However, we cannot demonstrate that sexual trauma directly causes these problems. Although correlation does not provide causal

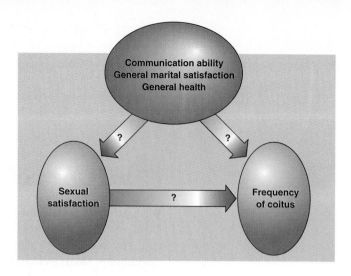

Figure 2.1. What Is the Relationship Between Frequency of Intercourse and Sexual Satisfaction?
Married couples who engage in coitus more frequently report higher levels of sexual satisfaction, but why? Since researchers have not manipulated the variables, we cannot conclude that sexual satisfaction *causes* high coital frequency. Nor can we say that frequent coitus causes greater sexual satisfaction. Perhaps both variables are affected by other factors, such as communication ability, general marital satisfaction, and general health.

knowledge, it permits us to anticipate the needs of victims of sexual assault for treatment services. Knowledge of correlational relationships may also lead to controlled experiments that more directly address questions of cause and effect.

⁓ *Reflections* ⁓

▪ Couples who attend church more frequently report higher rates of marital satisfaction. Can you suggest three possible cause–effect connections between churchgoing and marital satisfaction?

▪ Here is another relationship between two variables: Men who are married live longer. (True.) It is possible that marriage "causes" longevity, but can you think of other possible reasons for the relationship?

Experiment
A scientific method that seeks to confirm cause-and-effect relationships by manipulating independent variables and observing their effects on dependent variables.

Treatment
In experiments, an intervention that is administered to participants (e.g., a test, a drug, or a sex education program) so that its effects may be observed.

Independent variable
A condition in a scientific study that is manipulated so that its effects may be observed.

Dependent variables
The measured results of an experiment, which are believed to be a function of the independent variables.

The Experimental Method

The best (if not always feasible) method for studying *cause-and-effect* relationships is the **experiment.** Experiments permit scientists to draw conclusions about cause-and-effect relationships because the experimenter is able to control or manipulate the factors or variables of interest directly and to observe their effects.

In an experiment on the effects of alcohol on sexual arousal, for example, a group of participants would receive an intervention, called a **treatment,** such as a dose of alcohol. (In other experiments, the intervention or treatment might involve the administration of a drug, exposure to violent pornography, a program of sex education, etc.). They would then be carefully observed to learn whether this treatment made a difference in their behavior—in this case, their sexual arousal.

Aspects of the Experimental Method

Independent and Dependent Variables   In an experiment, the variables (treatments) that are hypothesized to have a causal effect are manipulated or controlled by the researcher. Consider an experiment designed to determine whether or not alcohol stimulates sexual arousal. The design might involve giving one group of participants a certain dosage of alcohol, and then measuring its effects. In such an experimental arrangement, the dosage of alcohol is considered an **independent variable,** whose presence and quantity is manipulated by the researchers. The measured results are called **dependent variables,**

since changes in their values are believed to depend on the independent variable or variables. In this experiment, measures of sexual arousal would be the dependent variables. Dependent variables are outcomes; they are observed and measured by the researchers, but not manipulated. Sexual arousal might be measured by means such as physiological measurement (gauging the degree of penile erection in the male, for example) or self-report (asking participants to rate their sexual arousal on a rating scale).

In a study of the effects of sex education on teenage pregnancy, sex education would be the independent variable. The incidence of teenage pregnancy would be the dependent variable. Researchers would administer the experimental treatment (sex education) and track the participants for a period of time to determine their pregnancy rates. But how would experimenters know whether or not the treatment had made a difference in the pregnancy rate? One way would be to compare the pregnancy rate among people in experiments to rates found in public records. It could be argued, however, that the individuals in the experiment differed in other ways (besides having received sex education) from the people whose records were kept in the public documents, that the records were made at a different time, and so forth. So experimenters would prefer to compare the pregnancy rates of people in experimental groups with those of people in control groups.

Experimental group
A group of study participants who receive a treatment.

Control group
A group of study participants who do not receive the experimental treatment. However, other conditions are held comparable to those of individuals in the experimental group.

Selection factor
A bias that may operate in research when people are allowed to determine whether or not they will receive a treatment.

Experimental and Control Groups   Well-designed experiments randomly assign people or animals to experimental and control groups. Participants in **experimental groups** receive the treatment. Participants in **control groups** do not. Every effort is made to hold all other conditions constant for both groups. By using random assignment and holding other conditions constant, researchers can be reasonably confident that the independent variable (treatment), and not extraneous factors (such as the temperature of the room in which the treatment was administered or differences between the participants in the experimental and control groups), brought about the results.

Why Is Random Assignment Important?   Why do experimenters assign individuals at random to experimental and control groups whenever possible? Consider a study conducted to determine the effects of alcohol on sexual arousal in response to sexually explicit material, such as X-rated films. If we permitted study participants to choose whether or not they would drink alcohol, we might not know if it was the alcohol itself that accounted for the results. Some other factor, called a **selection factor,** might discriminate between people who would or would not choose to drink alcohol. One difference might be that people who chose to drink might also have more permissive attitudes toward sexually explicit material than the others. Their permissiveness rather than the alcohol could affect their sexual responsiveness to these stimuli. If this were the case, experimental outcomes might reflect the effects of the selection factor rather than the alcohol.

Experimentation with Animals   Researchers frequently undertake studies with other animal species that would be impractical or unethical with people. For example, it may be hypothesized that prenatal sexual hormones "feminize" or "masculinize" the brain to give rise to gender-typed behaviors or predispose the individual to a heterosexual, gay male, or lesbian sexual orientation (see Chapters 6 and 10). The ideal method for examining these hypotheses would be to alter the balance of sex hormones systematically at various stages of fetal development and then monitor individuals' behavior in subsequent years. However, neither parents nor researchers would be willing to risk the well-being of children through such an experiment. Therefore, studies of this kind have been conducted on animals to try to shed some light on similar processes in people.

To the extent that we share physiological processes with animals, experiments with other species may inform us about ourselves. Because of their physiological similarities to people, rats and monkeys are commonly used in laboratory experiments. Unfortunately— or fortunately?—these animals are more similar to humans biologically than psychologically. Thus, we may make some generalizations from them to people concerning the effects of drugs and other biochemical treatments. We cannot, however, assume that their responses provide much of a clue to higher cognitive processes, such as thinking and reasoning. Nor can we claim that *pair bonding* between animals is equivalent to human marriage, or that (apparently) affectionate displays between animals are the equivalent of romantic love between people.

Limitations of the Experimental Method Although scientists agree that the experimental method provides the strongest evidence of cause-and-effect relationships, experimenters cannot manipulate many variables of interest directly. We may suspect that sexual trauma in the form of rape or sexual assault is a causal factor in the development of psychological or emotional problems (see Chapter 19). However, we would not expose people to sexual trauma to observe its effects. In the absence of a direct manipulation of the presumed causal factor (rape), we cannot be sure that adjustment problems in rape victims are directly attributable to rape itself, especially when they occur years later. Other factors may be involved, such as insensitive treatment of rape victims by their families or by representatives of the criminal justice system.

Nor can we conduct experiments to determine the effects of cohabitation on college students. We cannot assign an experimental group to cohabitation and a control group to separate living quarters. We can compare only groups of students who have chosen to cohabit to groups who have not. Our research may thus inform us that cohabitors have certain problems (for example, jealousy), but it cannot show that these problems are caused by cohabiting (see Chapter 14). Cohabitors and noncohabitors may differ on other factors that give rise to these differences in adjustment.

Similarly, we cannot conduct experiments to determine the effects of pornography on children and adolescents. Societal prohibitions and ethical standards preclude experimenters from exposing children or adolescents to erotic materials. Researchers must use other approaches, such as the correlational method, to study variables that cannot be manipulated.

~ *Reflections* ~

What would researchers have to do to run true experiments on the effects of cohabitation on college students or on the effects of pornography on children? Could such experiments be run? Why, or why not?

To run a true experiment on the effect of a new drug on people with AIDS, some people with AIDS would have to be assigned to a control group. To control for the effects of expectations, they might be told they are being given the real drug when they are really receiving "sugar pills" that look like the real thing. Can researchers justify withholding the real drug from people in the control group? What do you think?

Ethics in Sex Research

Sex researchers are required to protect the people being studied. This means that people will not be subjected to physical or psychological harm and will participate of their own free will.

In colleges, universities, hospitals, and research institutions, ethics review committees help researchers weigh the potential harm of administering the independent variables and review proposed studies in light of ethical guidelines. If the committee finds fault with a proposal, it may advise the researcher on how to modify the research design to comply with ethical standards and will withhold approval until the proposal has been so modified.

Pain and Stress

Individuals may be harmed if they are exposed to pain or placed in stressful situations. For this reason many potentially informative or useful studies have not been done. Researchers have not exposed children to erotic materials in order to determine the effects. Researchers have not exposed human fetuses to male or female sex hormones to learn whether they create fundamental predispositions toward tomboyishness, gay male and lesbian sexual orientations, career choices, and other variables of interest.

Sex researchers *have* studied children born to mothers who were given certain sex hormones to help maintain their pregnancies (see Chapter 6). But these treatments were standard medical procedures that were undertaken to help the women and their fetuses. The availability of these cases has made it possible for scientists to examine the effects on later gender-role behavior and sexual behavior of prenatal exposure to these hormones. But the investigators did not administer these treatments to the pregnant women for purposes of research.

When considering a study that poses a risk of harm, ethics review committees weigh the potential harm in light of the potential benefits to the participants, to science, and to society in general. Ethical standards require that research be conducted only when the expected benefits of the research outweigh the anticipated risks, when the experimenter attempts to minimize risks, and when the experimenter ensures that the pain and stress experienced by participants is neither excessive nor lasting. Moreover, participants are given general information about the stress or pain they may encounter before the study begins. Thus, they can decide whether or not they wish to participate and can prepare themselves.

Confidentiality

Sex researchers must keep the identities and responses of participants confidential to protect them from possible harm or embarrassment. Some participants may confide legally incriminating information to researchers, such as reports of illegal sexual activities. Some people might suffer harm or embarrassment if it were even known that they had participated in sex research.

Researchers can do many things to ensure the confidentiality of participants. They can make questionnaires anonymous. Interviewers may not be given the identities of interviewees. In reports of research, enough information about participants' backgrounds can be given to make the studies useful (size of city of origin, region of country, religion, age group, race, educational level, and so on) without divulging their identities. Once the need for follow-up has passed and the results have been fully analyzed, the names and addresses of participants and their records can be destroyed. If names and addresses are maintained, researchers can code them, keep them under lock and key, and spread the keys among several people, so that no one person has enough information to divulge an individual's sexual behavior.

Informed Consent

Informed consent
The term used by researchers to indicate that people have agreed to participate in research after receiving information about the purposes and nature of the study, and its potential risks and benefits.

The principle of **informed consent** requires that people freely agree to participate after being given enough information about the procedures and purposes of the research, and its risks and benefits, to make an informed decision. Information must be presented in a manner that potential participants can understand. People may not be coerced to participate. Once the study has begun, they must be free to withdraw at any time without penalty. In some cases, people may be told that some information about the study must be withheld until it is completed. This is especially so when deception is involved.

The Use of Deception

Ethical conflicts may emerge when experiments require that participants not know all about their purposes and methods. For example, in experiments on the effects of violent pornography on aggression against women, participants may be misled into believing that they are administering electric shocks to women (who are actually confederates of the experimenter), even though no shocks are actually delivered. The experimenter seeks to determine participants' willingness to hurt women following exposure to aggressive erotic films. Such studies could not be carried out if participants knew that no shocks would actually be delivered. In studies that involve deception, researchers must demonstrate that the effects of the treatment are not seriously harmful or prolonged and that the benefits of the information obtained outweigh the risks.

Debriefing

Debriefing
Information about a completed procedure that helps avert potential harm to participants.

Professional organizations like the American Psychological Association require that participants who are deceived receive a **debriefing** afterward to reduce potential harm. For example, people who are led to believe they have shocked other people are informed that they did not actually administer shocks and that their "victims" were in league with the experimenter. It is explained that deception was necessary to carry out the experiment, and that their behavior was understandable under the circumstances.

Relatively few scientific studies of human sexuality have required painful or stress-inducing treatments or deception. The vast majority of studies pose no harm to participants and are straightforward in purpose.

Research is the backbone of human sexuality as a science. This textbook focuses on scientific findings that can illuminate our understanding of sexuality, help enhance sexual experience, prevent and treat sexually transmitted diseases, and build more rewarding relationships.

~ Reflections ~

What standards do ethics review committees use to determine whether or not proposed research is ethical? Do you agree with these standards? Why, or why not?

Does any of the research discussed in the first two chapters of this book strike you as being unethical? Why? Would the researchers have been able to change their methods to agree with your standards of ethics? If so, how?

Summing Up

A Scientific Approach to Human Sexuality

Scientists insist that assumptions about sexual behavior be supported by evidence. Evidence is based on careful observations in the laboratory or in the field.

The Scientific Method The scientific method is a systematic way of gathering scientific evidence and testing assumptions through empirical research. It entails formulating a research question, framing a hypothesis, testing the hypothesis, and drawing conclusions about the hypothesis.

Goals and Methods of the Science of Human Sexuality The goals of the science of human sexuality are to describe, explain, predict, and control sexual behaviors. People often confuse description with inference. Inferences are woven into theories, when possible.

Operational Definitions The operational definition of a construct is linked to the methods used to measure it, enabling diverse researchers to understand what is being measured.

Populations and Samples: Representing the World of Diversity

Research samples should accurately represent the population of interest. Representative samples are usually obtained through random sampling.

Methods of Observation

The Case-Study Method Case studies are carefully drawn biographies of individuals or small groups that focus on unraveling the interplay of various factors in individuals' backgrounds.

The Survey Method Surveys typically gather information about behavior through interviews or questionnaires administered to large samples of people. Use of volunteers and the tendency of respondents to offer socially desirable responses are sources of bias in surveys.

The Naturalistic-Observation Method In naturalistic observation, scientists directly observe the behavior of animals and humans where it happens—in the "field." The scientists remain unobtrusive.

The Ethnographic-Observation Method Ethnographic research has provided us with data concerning sexual behaviors and customs that occur widely across cultures and those that are limited to one or few cultures.

The Participant-Observation Method In participant observation, investigators learn about people's behavior by interacting with them.

The Laboratory-Observation Method In the laboratory-observation method, people engage in the behavior under study in the laboratory setting. When methods of observation influence the behavior under study, that behavior may be distorted.

The Correlational Method

Correlational studies reveal the strength and direction of the relationships between variables. However, they do not show cause and effect.

The Experimental Method

Experiments allow scientists to draw conclusions about cause-and-effect relationships because they directly control or manipulate the variables of interest and observe their effects. Well-designed experiments randomly assign individuals to experimental and control groups.

Ethics in Sex Research

Ethics concerns the ways in which researchers protect participants from harm.

Pain and Stress Ethical standards require that research may be conducted only when the expected benefits of the research outweigh the anticipated risks to participants and when the experimenter attempts to minimize expected risks.

Confidentiality Sex researchers keep the identities and responses of participants confidential to protect them from embarrassment and other potential sources of harm.

Informed Consent The principle of informed consent requires that people agree to participate in research only after being given enough information about the purposes, procedures, risks, and benefits to make informed decisions.

The Use of Deception Some research cannot be conducted without deceiving people as to its purposes and procedures. In such cases the potential harm and benefits of the proposed research are weighed carefully.

Debriefing When people are deceived in research studies, they are debriefed afterward to minimize the risk of harm.

 # CHAPTER 3

Henri Matisse, *The Dance, first version,* 1932. Palais Des Beaux-Arts, Paris.
Bridgeman Art Library, London/Superstock. © 1996 Succession H. Matisse/
Artist Rights Society (ARS), New York.

Female Sexual Anatomy and Physiology

Truth OR Fiction?

__T__ A name for the external female genitals is derived from Latin roots that mean "something to be ashamed of."

__T__ Women, but not men, have a sex organ whose only known function is the experiencing of sexual pleasure.

_____ One may determine whether a woman is a virgin by examining the hymen.

_____ Women with larger breasts produce more milk while nursing.

_____ The incidence of breast cancer is on the rise in the United States.

_____ The ancient Romans believed that menstrual blood soured wine and killed crops.

_____ At menopause, women suffer debilitating hot flashes.

_____ Menopause signals an end to women's sexual appetite.

The French saying *Vive la différence!* ("Long live the difference!") celebrates the differences between men and women. The differences between the genders, at least their anatomic differences, have often been met with prejudice and misunderstanding, however. Men have historically exalted their own genitals. Too often, the less visible genitals of women have been deemed inferior. T he derivation of the word **pudendum,** which refers to the external female genitals, speaks volumes about sexism in the ancient Mediterranean world. *Pudendum* derives from the Latin *pudendus*. It literally means "something to be ashamed of."

Truth **OR** Fiction?
R E V I S I T E D

It is true that a name for the external female genitals is derived from Latin roots that mean "something to be ashamed of." It is the Latin *pudendus*. ■

Pudendum
The external female genitals.

Even today, this cultural heritage may lead women to develop negative attitudes toward their genitals. Girls and boys are both sometimes reared to regard their genitals with a sense of shame or disgust. Both may be reprimanded for expressing normal curiosity about them. They may be reared with a "hands-off" attitude, to keep their "private parts" private, even to themselves. Touching them except for hygienic purposes may be discouraged. One woman recalls:

> When I was six years old I climbed up on the bathroom sink and looked at myself naked in the mirror. All of a sudden I realized I had three different holes. I was very excited about my discovery and ran down to the dinner table and announced it to everyone. "I have three holes!" Silence. "What are they for?" I asked. Silence even heavier than before. I sensed how uncomfortable everyone was and answered for myself. "I guess one is for pee-pee, the other for doo-doo and the third for ca-ca." A sigh of relief; no one had to answer my question. But I got the message—I wasn't supposed to ask "such" questions, though I didn't fully realize what "such" was about at that time.

> (Boston Women's Health Book Collective, *The New Our Bodies, Ourselves,* 1992)

Ova
Egg cells. (Singular: ovum.)

In this chapter we tour the female sex organs. Even generally sophisticated students may fill in some gaps in their knowledge. Most of us know what a vagina is, but how many of us realize that only the female gender has an organ that is exclusively dedicated to pleasure? Or that a woman's passing of urine does not involve the vagina? How many of us know that a newborn girl already has all the **ova** she will ever produce?

As women readers encounter the features of their sexual anatomy in their reading, they may wish to examine their own genitals with a mirror. By following the text and the illustrations, students may discover some new anatomic features. They will see that their genitals can resemble those in the illustrations yet also be unique.

External Sex Organs

Vulva
The external sexual structures of the female.

Taken collectively, the external sexual structures of the female are termed the pudendum or the **vulva.** Pudendum, because of its derivation, may be a less desirable term than *vulva*. Vulva is a Latin word that means "wrapper" or "covering." The vulva consists of the *mons veneris,* the *labia majora* and *minora* (major and minor lips), the *clitoris,* and the vaginal opening (see Figure 3.1). Figure 3.2 shows variations in the appearance of women's genitals.

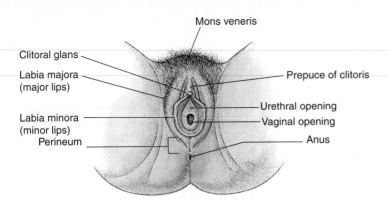

Mons veneris

Clitoral glans

Labia majora
(major lips)

Prepuce of clitoris

Urethral opening

Vaginal opening

Labia minora
(minor lips)

Perineum

Anus

Figure 3.1. Female External Sex Organs. This figure shows the vulva with the labia opened to reveal the urethral and vaginal openings.

The Mons Veneris

Mons veneris

A mound of fatty tissue that covers the joint of the pubic bones in front of the body, below the abdomen and above the clitoris. (The name is a Latin phrase meaning hill or "mount of Venus," the Roman goddess of love. Also known as the *mons pubis*, or simply *mons*.)

The **mons veneris** consists of fatty tissue that covers the joint of the pubic bones in front of the body, below the abdomen and above the clitoris. At puberty the mons becomes covered with pubic hair that is often thick and curly, but varies from person to person in waviness, texture, and color. The pubic hair captures the chemical secretions that exude from the vagina during sexual arousal. Despite the preoccupation in the United States with chemicals that mask odors, these secretions produce a scent that may allure lovers.

The mons cushions a woman's body during sexual intercourse, protecting her and her partner from the pressure against the pubic bone that stems from thrusting motions. There is an ample supply of nerve endings in the mons, so that caresses of the area can produce pleasurable sexual sensations.

The Labia Majora

Labia majora

Large folds of skin that run downward from the mons along the sides of the vulva. (Latin for "large lips" or "major lips.")

The **labia majora** are large folds of skin that run downward from the mons along the sides of the vulva. The labia majora of some women are thick and bulging. In other women, they are thinner, flatter, and less noticeable. When close together, they hide the labia minora and the urethral and vaginal openings.

The outer surfaces of the labia majora, by the thighs, are covered with pubic hair and darker skin than that found on the thighs or labia minora. The inner surfaces of the labia majora are hairless and lighter in color. They are amply supplied with nerve endings that

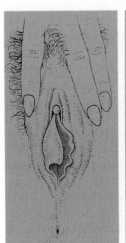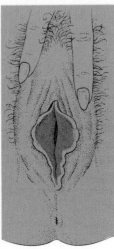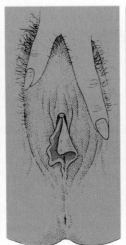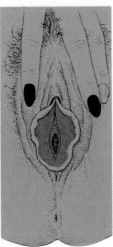

Figure 3.2. Normal Variations in the Vulva. The features of the vulva show a great deal of variation. A woman's attitude toward her genitals is likely to reflect her general self-concept and early childhood messages rather than the appearance of her vulva per se.

respond to stimulation and can produce sensations of sexual pleasure. The labia majora also shield the inner portion of the female genitals.

The Labia Minora

Labia minora
Hairless, light-colored membranes, located between the labia majora. (Latin for "small lips" or "minor lips.")

The **labia minora** are two hairless, light-colored membranes, located between the major lips. They surround the urethral and vaginal openings. The outer surfaces of the labia minora merge with the major lips. At the top they join at the prepuce (hood) of the clitoris.

The labia minora differ markedly in appearance from woman to woman. The labia minora of some women form protruding flower shapes that are valued greatly in some cultures, such as that of the Hottentots of Africa. In fact, Hottentot women purposely elongate their labia minora by tugging at them.

Rich in blood vessels and nerve endings, the labia minora are highly sensitive to sexual stimulation. When stimulated they darken and swell, indicating engorgement with blood.

The Clitoris

What's the matter, papa? Please don't stall.
Don't you know I love it and want it all?
I'm wild about that thing. Just give my bell a ring.
You pressed my button. I'm wild about that thing.

("I'm Wild About That Thing," recorded by Bessie Smith, 1929)

Worldwide, the clitoris is known by many names, from *bijou* (French for "jewel") to *pokhotnik* (Russian for "lust"). The Tuamotuan people of Polynesia have ten words for it, emblematic of their cultivated interest in female sexuality. By any name, however, the clitoris is the only sex organ whose only known function is the experiencing of pleasure.

Clitoris
A female sex organ consisting of a shaft and glans located above the urethral opening. It is extremely sensitive to sexual sensations.

Clitoris (see Figure 3.1) derives from the Greek word *kleitoris,* meaning "hill" or "slope." The clitoris receives its name from the manner in which it slopes upward in the shaft and forms a mound of spongy tissue at the glans. The body of the clitoris, termed the clitoral shaft, is about 1 inch long and ¼-inch wide. The clitoral shaft consists of erectile tissue that contains two spongy masses called **corpora cavernosa** ("cavernous bodies") that fill with blood (become engorged) and become erect in response to sexual stimulation. The stiffening of the clitoris is less apparent than the erection of the penis, because the clitoris does not swing free from the body as the penis does. The **prepuce** (meaning "before a swelling"), or hood, covers the clitoral shaft. It is a sheath of skin formed by the upper part of the labia minora. The clitoral glans is a smooth, round knob or lump of tissue. It resembles a button and is situated above the urethral opening. The clitoral glans may be covered by the clitoral hood but is readily revealed by gently separating the labia minora and retracting the hood. It is highly sensitive to touch because of the rich supply of nerve endings.

Corpora cavernosa
Masses of spongy tissue in the clitoral shaft that become engorged with blood and stiffen in response to sexual stimulation. (Latin for "cavernous bodies.")

The clitoris is the female sex organ that is most sensitive to sexual sensation. The size of the clitoris varies from woman to woman, just as the size of the penis varies among men. There is no known connection between the size of the clitoris and sensitivity to sexual stimulation. The clitoral glans is highly sensitive to touch. Women thus usually prefer to be stroked or stimulated on the mons, or on the clitoral hood, rather than directly on the glans.

Prepuce
The fold of skin covering the glans of the clitoris (or penis). (From Latin roots meaning "before a swelling.")

In some respects, the clitoris is the female counterpart of the penis. Both organs develop from the same embryonic tissue, which makes them similar in structure, or **homologous.** They are not fully similar in function, or **analogous,** however. Both organs receive and transmit sexual sensations, but the penis is directly involved in reproduction and excretion by serving as a conduit for sperm and urine, respectively. The clitoris, however, seems to be a unique sex organ. It serves no known purpose other than sexual pleasure. It is ironic that many cultures—including Victorian culture—have viewed women as unresponsive to sexual stimulation. It is ironic because women, not men, possess a sex organ that is apparently solely devoted to pleasurable sensations. The clitoris is the

Homologous
Similar in structure; developing from the same embryonic tissue.

Analogous
Similar in function.

woman's most erotically charged organ, which is borne out by the fact that women most often masturbate through clitoral stimulation, not vaginal insertion.

T r u t h **OR** *Fiction?*
R E V I S I T E D

It is true that women, but not men, have a sex organ whose only known function is the experiencing of sexual pleasure. That organ is the clitoris. ■

Surgical removal of the clitoral hood, a form of female circumcision, is common among Muslims in the Near East and Africa. As we see in the nearby World of Diversity feature, it aims to control female sexuality.

The Vestibule

The word *vestibule,* which means "entranceway," refers to the area within the labia minora that contains the openings to the vagina and the urethra. The vestibule is richly supplied with nerve endings and is very sensitive to tactile or other sexual stimulation.

The Urethral Opening

Urethral opening
The opening through which urine passes from the female's body.

Urine passes from the female's body through the **urethral opening** (see Figure 3.1), which is connected by a short tube called the urethra to the bladder (see Figure 3.3), where urine collects. The urethral opening lies below the clitoral glans and above the vaginal opening. The urethral opening, urethra, and bladder are unrelated to the reproductive system. Many males (and even some females), however, believe erroneously that for women urination and coitus occur through the same bodily opening. The confusion may arise from the fact that urine and semen both pass through the penis of the male or because the urethral opening lies near the vaginal opening.

The proximity of the urethral opening to the external sex organs may pose some hygienic problems for sexually active women. The urinary tract, which includes the urethra, bladder, and kidneys, may become infected from bacteria that are transmitted from the vagina or rectum. Infectious microscopic organisms may also pass from the male's sex organs to the female's urethral opening during sexual intercourse. Manual stimulation of the vulva with dirty hands may also transmit bacteria through the urethral opening to the bladder. Anal intercourse followed by vaginal intercourse may transfer microscopic organisms from the rectum to the bladder and cause infection. For similar reasons, women should first wipe the vulva, then the anus, when using the bathroom.

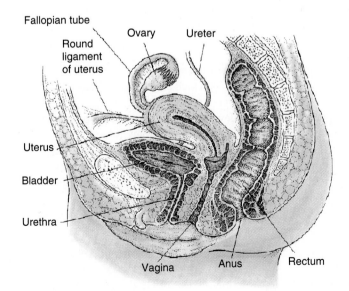

Figure 3.3. The Female Reproductive System. This cross-section locates many of the internal sex organs that compose the female reproductive system. Note that the uterus is normally tipped forward.

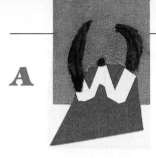

RITUAL GENITAL MUTILATION

Cultures in some parts of Africa and the Middle East ritually mutilate or remove the entire clitoris, not just the clitoral hood. Removal of the clitoris, or **clitoridectomy,** is a rite of initiation into womanhood in many of these predominantly Islamic cultures. It is often performed as a puberty ritual in late childhood or early adolescence (not at birth, like male circumcision).

The clitoris gives rise to feelings of sexual pleasure in women. Its removal or mutilation represents an attempt to ensure the girl's chastity since it is assumed that uncircumcised girls are consumed with sexual desires (Ahmed, 1991). Some groups in rural Egypt and in the northern Sudan, however, perform clitoridectomies primarily because it is a social custom that has been passed down from ancient times (Toubia, 1994). Some perceive it as part of their faith in Islam. However, neither Islam nor any other religion requires it (Ahmed, 1991; Rosenthal, 1993). Ironically, many young women do not grasp that they are victims. They assume that clitoridectomy is part of being female (Rosenthal, 1994).

Clitoridectomies are performed under unsanitary conditions without benefit of anesthesia (Rosenthal, 1993). Medical complications are common, including infections, bleeding, tissue scarring, painful menstruation, and obstructed labor (Toubia, 1994). The procedure is psychologically traumatizing (Toubia, 1994). An even more radical form of clitoridectomy, called *infibulation* or pharaonic circumcision, is practiced widely in the Sudan. Pharaonic circumcision involves complete removal of the clitoris along with the labia minora and the inner layers of the labia majora. After

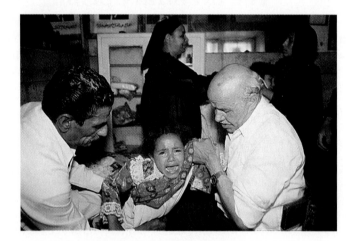

Ritual Genital Mutilation. Some predominantly Islamic cultures in Africa and the Middle East ritually mutilate or remove the clitoris as a rite of initiation into womanhood. Novelist Alice Walker drew attention to the practice in her novel *Possessing the Secret of Joy*. She has called for its abolition in her book and film, *Warrior Marks*.

Clitoridectomy
Surgical removal of the clitoris.

Cystitis
An inflammation of the urinary bladder. (From the Greek *kystis*, meaning "sac.")

Gynecologist
A physician who treats women's diseases, especially of the reproductive tract. (From the Greek *gyne*, meaning "woman.")

Cystitis is a bladder inflammation that may stem from any of these sources. Its primary symptoms are burning and frequent urination (also called *urinary urgency*). Pus or a bloody discharge is common, and there may be an intermittent or persistent ache just above the pubic bone. These symptoms may disappear after several days, but consultation with a **gynecologist** is recommended, because untreated cystitis can lead to serious kidney infections.

So-called honeymoon cystitis is caused by the tugging on the bladder and urethral wall that occurs during vaginal intercourse. It may occur upon beginning coital activity (though not necessarily on one's honeymoon) or upon resuming coital activity after lengthy abstinence. Figure 3.3 shows the close proximity of the urethra and vagina.

A few precautions may help women prevent serious inflammation of the bladder:

- Drinking two quarts of water a day to flush the bladder
- Drinking orange or cranberry juice to maintain an acid environment that discourages growth of infectious organisms
- Decreasing use of alcohol and caffeine (from coffee, tea, or cola drinks) that may irritate the bladder

removal of the skin tissue, the raw edges of the labia majora are sewn together. Only a tiny opening is left to allow passage of urine and menstrual discharge. The sewing together of the vulva may be intended to ensure the girls' chastity until marriage. Medical complications are common, including menstrual and urinary problems, and even death. After marriage, the opening is enlarged to permit intercourse. Enlargement is a gradual process that is often made difficult by scar tissue from the circumcision. Hemorrhaging and tearing of surrounding tissues are common consequences. It may take three months or longer before the opening is large enough to allow penile penetration. Mutilation of the labia is now illegal in the Sudan, although the law continues to allow removal of the clitoris. Some African countries have outlawed clitoridectomies, although such laws are rarely enforced (Rosenthal, 1993).

A shockingly high number of women in Africa and the Middle East—85 to 114 million by some estimates (Kaplan, 1993)—have undergone removal of the clitoris and the labia minora. Clitoridectomies remain common or even universal in nearly 30 countries in Africa, in many countries in the Middle East, and in parts of Malaysia, Yemen, Oman, Indonesia, and the India-Pakistan subcontinent (Rosenthal, 1995). Thousands of African immigrant girls living in European countries are also at risk of having their genitals mutilated by their parents (Tempest, 1993). Even in the United States, some girls have been subjected to ritual mutilation (Rosenthal, 1993).

Do not confuse male circumcision with the maiming inflicted on girls in the name of circumcision. Former Representative Patricia Schroeder of Colorado depicts the male equivalent of female genital mutilation as involving the amputation or cutting off of the penis and its surrounding tissue (Rosenthal, 1993). *The New York Times* columnist A. M. Rosenthal (1995) calls female genital mutilation the most widespread existing violation of human rights in the world. The Pulitzer Prize–winning, African American novelist Alice Walker has drawn attention to the practice of female genital mutilation in her best-selling novel *Possessing the Secret of Joy* (1992). She has called for its abolition in her book and movie *Warrior Marks*. Rosenthal (1995) argues that pressure should be placed on nations that fail to take meaningful action to stop this ritual mutilation of women. He suggests that Western nations could tie economic aid to efforts to eliminate clitoridectomies in developing countries. The United Nations as well could treat clitoridectomies as a permanent priority. Yet calls from Westerners to ban female circumcision in parts of Africa and the Middle East have sparked controversy on grounds of "cultural condescension"—that people in one culture cannot dictate the cultural traditions of another. A leader of an influential women's rights organization in Kenya put the issue thus: "Let indigenous people fight it [female circumcision] according to their own traditions. . . . It will die faster than if others tell us what to do." Yet for Alice Walker, "torture is not culture." As the debate continues, the reality is that 2 million African girls continue to undergo ritual genital mutilations each year.

Want to do something about it? Contact one of the groups who are trying to fight female genital torture:

- Equality Now, 226 West 88th Street, New York, NY 10019
- Women's International Network, 187 Grant Street, Lexington, MA 02173
- FORWARD, 38 King Street, London, England WC2B 8JT

- Washing the hands prior to masturbation or self-examination
- Washing one's partner's and one's own genitals before and after intercourse
- Preventing objects that have touched the anus (fingers, penis, toilet tissue) from subsequently coming into contact with the vulva
- Urinating soon after intercourse to help wash away bacteria

These measures do not guarantee protection against transmission of infectious organisms, but they may help.

The Vaginal Opening

When I was five or six, my mother told me about sex. I remember that I was confused about what my mother said, because somehow I couldn't conceptualize what the female vagina looked like. I was curious to see an actual vagina and not just how it looked diagrammed in a book.

(Morrison et al., 1980, p. 35)

Introtus
The vaginal opening. (From the Latin for "entrance.")

Hymen
A fold of tissue across the vaginal opening that is usually present at birth and remains at least partly intact until a woman engages in coitus. (Greek for "membrane.")

T r u t h **OR** *Fiction?*
R E V I S I T E D

One does not see an entire vagina, but rather the vaginal opening, or **introitus,** when one parts the labia minora, or minor lips. The introitus lies below and is larger than the urethral opening. Its shape resembles that of the **hymen.**

The hymen is a fold of tissue across the vaginal opening that is usually present at birth and may remain at least partly intact until a woman engages in coitus. For this reason the hymen has been called the "maidenhead." Its presence has been taken as proof of virginity, and its absence as evidence of coitus. However, some women are born with incomplete hymens, and other women's hymens are torn accidentally, such as during horse-back riding, strenuous exercise, or gymnastics—or even when bicycle riding. A punctured hymen is therefore poor evidence of coital experience. A flexible hymen may also withstand many coital experiences, so its presence does not guarantee virginity. Some people believe incorrectly that virgins cannot insert tampons or fingers into their vaginas, but most hymens will accommodate these intrusions without great difficulty. Some hymens, however, are torn accidentally when inserting tampons.

Contrary to myth, it is not true that one may determine whether a woman is a virgin by examination of the hymen. Examination of the hymen may yield false information. ■

Figure 3.4 illustrates various vaginal openings. The first three show common shapes of hymens among women who have not had coitus. The fifth drawing shows a *parous* ("passed through") vaginal opening, typical of a woman who has delivered a baby. Now and then the hymen consists of tough fibrous tissue and is closed, or *imperforate,* as in the fourth drawing. An imperforate hymen may not be discovered until after puberty, when menstrual discharges begin to accumulate in the vagina. In these rare cases, a simple surgical incision will perforate the hymen. A woman may also have a physician surgically perforate her hymen if she would rather forgo the tearing and discomfort that may accompany her initial coital experiences. This procedure is unnecessary, however, for the great majority of women. They experience little pain or distress during initial coitus despite old horror stories. A woman may also stretch the vaginal opening in preparation for intercourse by inserting a finger—preferably lubricated with saliva or K-Y jelly—and gently pressing downward toward the anus. After several repetitions, she may insert two fingers and repeat the process, spreading the fingers slightly after insertion. This procedure is sometimes followed over several days or weeks.

The hymen is found only in female horses and humans. It is not present in animal species closest to humans on the evolutionary scale, such as chimps and gorillas. The hymen remains something of a biological mystery, since it serves no apparent biological function.

Defloration
Destruction of the hymen (especially as a cultural ritual).

Defloration   The hymen has been of great cultural significance because of the (erroneous) association between it and virginity. In some societies its destruction, or **defloration,** is ritualized. For example, in some ancient religious rites, young girls were

Figure 3.4. **Appearance of Various Types of Hymens and the Introitus (at right) As It Appears Following Delivery of a Baby.**

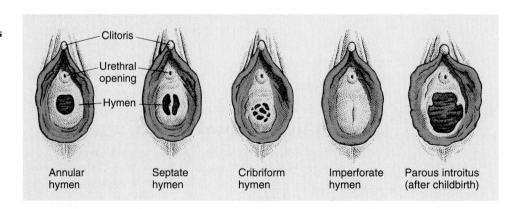

Annular hymen   Septate hymen   Cribriform hymen   Imperforate hymen   Parous introitus (after childbirth)

deflowered by sculpted phalluses in ceremonies conducted on the temple steps. During the Middle Ages, the lord of the manor held the *droit du seigneur* (French for "right of the lord") to deflower (by means of intercourse) a maiden on her wedding night, after which she became her husband's sexual property. Among the Yungar of Australia, older women deflowered maidens prior to marriage. Girls who were found to have ruptured hymens might be tortured or killed. Since some girls are born with minimal hymens, many have probably been unjustly punished for purported sexual indiscretions.

Defloration usually leads to at least minor bleeding, and in cultures as diverse as the traditional Arabian and the European, bloody bed sheets have been paraded around villages on the wedding night. Woe to the virgin who, through no fault of her own, failed to bleed! In rural villages in seventeenth- and eighteenth-century Europe and Latin America, the well-prepared bride would have pigeon or dove blood handy to smear upon her sheets, in case hymenal blood failed to flow.

The Perineum

The **perineum** incorporates the skin and underlying tissue between the vaginal opening and the anus. The perineum is rich in nerve endings. Stimulation of the area may heighten sexual arousal. Many physicians make a routine perineal incision during labor, called an **episiotomy,** to facilitate childbirth.

Structures That Underlie the External Sex Organs

Figure 3.5 shows what lies beneath the skin of the vulva. The vestibular bulbs and Bartholin's glands are active during sexual arousal and are found on both sides (shown on the right in Figure 3.5). Muscular rings (**sphincters**) that constrict bodily openings such as the vaginal and anal openings are also found on both sides.

The clitoral **crura** are wing-shaped, leglike structures that attach the clitoris to the pubic bone beneath. The crura contain corpora cavernosa, which engorge with blood and stiffen during sexual arousal.

The **vestibular bulbs** are attached to the clitoris at the top and extend downward along the sides of the vaginal opening. Blood congests them during sexual arousal, swelling the vulva and lengthening the vagina. This swelling contributes to coital sensations for both partners.

Perineum
The skin and underlying tissue that lies between the vaginal opening and the anus. (From Greek roots meaning "around" and "to empty out.")

Episiotomy
A surgical incision in the perineum that may be made during childbirth to protect the vagina from tearing. (From the Greek roots *epision*, meaning "pubic region," and *tome*, meaning "cutting.")

Sphincters
Ring-shaped muscles that surround body openings and open or close them by expanding or contracting. (From the Greek for "that which draws close.")

Crura
Anatomical structures resembling legs that attach the clitoris to the pubic bone. (Singular: crus. A Latin word meaning "leg" or "shank.")

Vestibular bulbs
Cavernous structures that extend downward along the sides of the introitus and swell during sexual arousal.

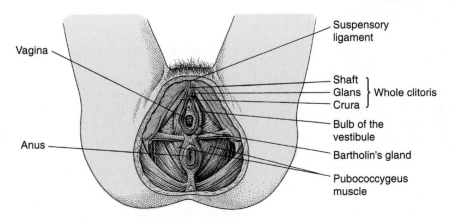

Figure 3.5. **Structures That Underlie the Female External Sex Organs.**
If we could see beneath the vulva, we would find muscle fibers that constrict the various body openings, plus the crura ("legs") of the clitoris, the vestibular bulbs, and Bartholin's glands.

Bartholin's glands
Glands that lie just inside the minor lips and secrete fluid just before orgasm.

Pubococcygeus muscle
The muscle that encircles the entrance to the vagina.

Bartholin's glands lie just inside the minor lips on each side of the vaginal opening. They secrete a couple of drops of lubrication just before orgasm. This lubrication is not essential for coitus. In fact, the fluid produced by the Bartholin's glands has no known purpose. If the glands become infected and clogged, however, a woman may notice swelling and local irritation. It is wise to consult a gynecologist if these symptoms do not fade within a few days.

It was once believed that the source of the vaginal lubrication or "wetness" that women experience during sexual arousal was produced by the Bartholin's glands. It is now known that engorgement of vaginal tissues during sexual excitement results in a form of "sweating" by the lining of the vaginal wall. During sexual arousal the pressure from this engorgement causes moisture from the many small blood vessels that lie in the vaginal wall to be forced out and to pass through the vaginal lining, forming the basis of the lubrication. In less time than it takes to read this sentence (generally within 10 to 30 seconds), beads of vaginal lubrication or "sweat" appear along the interior lining of the vagina in response to sexual stimulation, in much the same way that rising temperatures cause water to pass through the skin as perspiration.

Pelvic floor muscles permit women to constrict the vaginal and anal openings. They contract automatically, or involuntarily, during orgasm, and their tone may contribute to coital sensations. Gynecologist Arnold Kegel (1952) developed a set of exercises to help build pelvic muscle tone in women who had problems controlling urination after childbirth. The stress of childbirth on the pelvic muscles sometimes reduces muscle tone, leading to an involuntary loss of urine when a woman sneezes or coughs. Kegel also observed that women with thin or weak **pubococcygeus (P-C) muscles** reported they had little or no vaginal sensations during coitus or experienced unpleasant vaginal sensations. Some women with weak P-C muscles complained, "I just don't feel anything" (during coitus), or "I don't like the feeling" (Kegel, 1952, p. 522). Kegel found that women who practiced his exercises improved their urinary control along with their genital sensations during coitus. He believed that many women could enhance vaginal sensations during coitus by exercising their P-C muscles through exercises that have since become known as "Kegels."

A L O S E R   L O O K

KEGELS

Kegel exercises are commonly used to help women heighten their awareness of vaginal sensations. They may also have a psychological benefit, because women who perform Kegel exercises assume a more active role in enhancing their genital sensations. Sex therapist Lonnie Barbach (1975) offers instructions for Kegel exercises:

1. Locate the P-C muscle by purposely stopping the flow of urine. The muscle you squeeze to stop the urine flow is the P-C muscle. (The P-C muscle acts as a sphincter for both the urethral and vaginal openings.)
2. In order to learn to focus consciously on contracting the P-C muscle, insert a finger into the vaginal opening, and contract the muscle so that it can be felt to squeeze or contain the finger. (The P-C muscle can contract to contain objects as narrow as a finger. Thus men need not fear that a large penis is required in order to induce stimulating vaginal sensations in a woman.)
3. Remove your finger, squeeze the P-C muscle for three seconds, and then relax. Repeat several times. This part of the exercise may be performed while seated at a classroom or business desk. No one (except the woman herself) will be the wiser. Many women practice a series of Kegel exercises consisting of 10 contractions, 3 times a day.
4. The P-C muscle may also be tensed and relaxed in rapid sequence. Since this exercise may be more fatiguing than the above, women may choose to practice it perhaps 10 to 25 times, once a day.

What are your attitudes toward your own genital organs? Where do you think your attitudes come from?

What are the roles of the female external sex organs in reproduction?

What measures can you take to ensure the health of your own sex organs and those of the people you care about? Are you doing everything you can? If not, why not?

Internal Sex Organs

The internal sex organs of the female include the innermost parts of the vagina, the cervix, the uterus, and two ovaries, each connected to the uterus by a fallopian tube (see Figures 3.3, 3.6). These structures comprise the female reproductive system.

The Vagina

Vagina

The tubular female sex organ that contains the penis during sexual intercourse and through which a baby is born. (Latin for "sheath.")

The **vagina** extends back and upward from the vaginal opening (see Figure 3.3). It is usually 3 to 5 inches long at rest. Menstrual flow and babies pass from the uterus to the outer world through the vagina. During coitus, the penis is contained within the vagina.

The vagina is commonly pictured as a canal or barrel, but when at rest, it is like a collapsed muscular tube. Its walls touch like the fingers of an empty glove. The vagina expands in length and width during sexual arousal. The vagina can also expand to allow insertion of a tampon, as well as the passage of a baby's head and shoulders during childbirth.

The vaginal walls have three layers. The inner lining, or *vaginal mucosa,* is made visible by opening the labia minora. It is a mucous membrane similar to the skin that lines the inside of the mouth. It feels fleshy, soft, and corrugated. It may vary from very dry (especially if the female is anxious about something like examinations) to very wet, in which case fingers slide against it readily. The middle layer of the vaginal wall is muscular. The outer or deeper layer is a fibrous covering that connects the vagina to other pelvic structures.

The vaginal walls are rich with blood vessels but poorly supplied with nerve endings. Unlike the sensitive outer third of the vaginal barrel, the inner two thirds are so insensitive to touch that minor surgery may sometimes be performed on those portions without anesthesia. The entire vaginal barrel is sensitive to pressure, however, which can be experienced as sexually pleasurable.

The vaginal walls secrete substances that help maintain the vagina's normal acidity (pH 4.0 to 5.0). Normally the secretions taste salty. The odor and taste of these secretions may vary during the menstrual cycle. Although the evidence is not clear, the secretions are

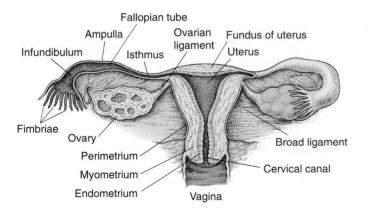

Figure 3.6. Female Internal Reproductive Organs. This drawing highlights the relationship of the uterus to the fallopian tubes and ovaries. Note the layers of the uterus, the ligaments that attach the ovaries to the uterus, and the relationship of the ovaries to the fimbriae of the fallopian tubes.

Douche
Application of a jet of liquid to the vagina as a rinse. (From the Italian *doccia*, meaning "shower bath.")

Vaginitis
Vaginal inflammation.

thought to contain substances that may act as sexual attractants. Women who frequently **douche** or use feminine deodorant sprays may remove or mask substances that may arouse sex partners. Douching or spraying may also alter the natural chemical balance of the vagina, which can increase the risk of vaginal infections. Feminine deodorant sprays can also irritate the vagina and evoke allergic reactions. The normal, healthy vagina cleanses itself through regular chemical secretions that are evidenced by a mild white or yellowish discharge.

Vaginitis refers to any vaginal inflammation, whether it is caused by an infection, an allergic reaction, or chemical irritation. Vaginitis may also stem from use of birth-control pills or antibiotics that alter the natural body chemistry, or from other factors, such as lowered resistance (from fatigue or poor diet). Changes in the natural body chemistry or lowered resistance permit microscopic organisms normally found in the vagina to multiply to infectious levels. Vaginitis may be recognized by abnormal discharge, itching, burning of the vulva, and, sometimes, urinary urgency. The causes and treatments of vaginitis are elaborated in Chapter 16. Women with vaginitis are advised to seek medical attention, but let us note some suggestions that may help prevent vaginitis (Boston Women's Health Book Collective, 1992):

1. Wash your vulva and anus regularly with mild soap. Pat dry (taking care not to touch the vulva after dabbing the anus).
2. Wear cotton panties. Nylon underwear retains heat and moisture that cause harmful bacteria to flourish.
3. Avoid pants that are tight in the crotch.
4. Be certain that sex partners are well-washed. Condoms may also reduce the spread of infections from one's sex partner.
5. Use a sterile, water-soluble jelly such as K-Y jelly if artificial lubrication is needed for intercourse. Do *not* use Vaseline. Birth-control jellies can also be used for lubrication.
6. Avoid intercourse that is painful or abrasive to the vagina.
7. Avoid diets high in sugar and refined carbohydrates since they alter the normal acidity of the vagina.
8. Women who are prone to vaginal infections may find it helpful to douche occasionally with plain water, a solution of 1 or 2 tablespoons of vinegar in a quart of warm water, or a solution of baking soda and water. Douches consisting of unpasteurized, plain (unflavored) yogurt may help replenish the "good" bacteria that are normally found in the vagina and that may be destroyed by use of antibiotics. Be careful when douching, and do not douche when pregnant or when you suspect you may be pregnant. Consult your physician before deciding to douche or to apply any preparations to the vagina.
9. Watch your general health. Eating poorly or getting insufficient rest will reduce your resistance to infection.

The Cervix

When someone first said to me two years ago, "You can feel the end of your own cervix with your finger," I was interested but flustered. I had hardly ever put my finger in my vagina at all, and felt squeamish about touching myself there, in that place "reserved" for lovers and doctors. It took me two months to get up nerve to try it, and then one afternoon, pretty nervously, I squatted down in the bathroom and put my finger in deep, back into my vagina. There it was, feeling slippery and rounded, with an indentation at the center through which, I realized, my menstrual flow came. It was both very exciting and beautifully ordinary at the same time. Last week I bought a plastic speculum so I can look at my cervix. Will it take as long this time?

(Boston Women's Health Book Collective, *The New Our Bodies, Ourselves,* 1992)

Cervix
The lower end of the uterus. (Latin for "neck.")

Os
The opening in middle of the cervix. (Latin for "mouth.")

The **cervix** is the lower end of the uterus. Its walls, like those of the vagina, produce secretions that contribute to the chemical balance of the vagina. The opening in the middle of the cervix, or **os,** is normally about the width of a straw, although it expands to permit passage of a baby from the uterus to the vagina during childbirth. Sperm pass from the vagina to the uterus through the cervical canal.

Cervical cancer is one of the most common forms of cancer in women. An estimated 16,000 new cases of cervical cancer are reported annually (American Cancer Society, 1995). Cervical cancer is more common among women who have had many sex partners, who became sexually active at a relatively early age, who come from lower socioeconomic status, and who smoke. All women are at risk, however.

A **Pap test** examines a sample of cervical cells that are smeared on a slide to screen for cervical cancer and other abnormalities. The American Cancer Society (1995) recommends annual Pap tests along with a pelvic examination for women who are, or have been, sexually active or who have reached age 18. Most cases of cervical cancer can be successfully treated by surgery and **radiotherapy** if they are detected early. The five-year survival rate for women with cervical cancer is 67%. For women diagnosed with localized cancer, the survival rate is 90% (American Cancer Society, 1995). There were approximately 4,800 deaths from cervical cancer in 1995. The mortality rate is more than twice as high for African American women as for White women (American Cancer Society, 1995).

The Uterus

The **uterus,** or womb, (see Figures 3.3, 3.6) is the organ in which a fertilized ovum implants and develops until birth. The uterus usually slants forward (is *antroverted*), although about 10% of women have uteruses that tip backward (are *retroverted*). In most instances a retroverted uterus causes no problems, but some women with retroverted uteruses find coitus in certain positions painful. (They quickly learn more comfortable positions by trial and error.) A retroverted uterus normally tips forward during pregnancy. This condition probably does not interfere with conception, although at one time it was thought that it might do so. The uterus is suspended in the pelvis by flexible ligaments. In a woman who has not given birth, it is about 3 inches long, 3 inches wide, and 1 inch thick near the top. The uterus expands to accommodate a fetus during pregnancy and shrinks after pregnancy, though not to its original size.

The uppermost part of the uterus is called the **fundus** (see Figure 3.6). The uterus is shaped like an inverted pear. If a ceramic model of a uterus were placed on a table, it would balance on the fundus. The central region of the uterus is called the body. The narrow lower region is the cervix, which leads downward to the vagina.

Like the vagina, the uterus has three layers (also shown in Figure 3.6). The innermost layer, or **endometrium,** is richly supplied with blood vessels and glands. Its structure varies according to a woman's age and phase of the menstrual cycle. Endometrial tissue is discharged through the cervix and vagina at menstruation. For reasons not entirely understood, in some women endometrial tissue may also grow in the abdominal cavity or elsewhere in the reproductive system. This condition is called **endometriosis,** and the most common symptom is menstrual pain. If left untreated, endometriosis may lead to infertility.

Cancer of the endometrial lining, called endometrial cancer, occurs more commonly in obese women, women with early menarche or late menopause, women with a history of failure to ovulate, and women who are obtaining estrogen-replacement therapy (American Cancer Society, 1995). Endometrial cancer is symptomized by abnormal uterine staining or bleeding, especially after menopause. The five-year survival rate for endometrial cancer is 83% overall, and 94% if discovered at an early stage (American Cancer Society, 1995).

The second layer of the uterus, the **myometrium,** is well muscled. It endows the uterus with flexibility and strength, and creates the powerful contractions that propel a fetus outward during labor. The third or outermost layer, the **perimetrium,** provides an external cover.

One woman in three in the United States has a **hysterectomy** by the age of 60. Most hysterectomy patients are between the ages of 35 and 45. The hysterectomy is now the second most commonly performed operation on women in this country. (Cesarean sections

Pap test
A test of a sample of cervical cells that screens for cervical cancer and other abnormalities. (Named after the originator of the technique, Dr. Papanicolaou.)

Radiotherapy
Treatment of a disease by X-rays or by emissions from a radioactive substance.

Uterus
The hollow, muscular, pear-shaped organ in which a fertilized ovum implants and develops until birth.

Fundus
The uppermost part of the uterus. (*Fundus* is a Latin word meaning "base.")

Endometrium
The innermost layer of the uterus. (From Latin and Greek roots meaning "within the uterus.")

Endometriosis
A condition caused by the growth of endometrial tissue in the abdominal cavity or elsewhere outside the uterus, and characterized by menstrual pain.

Myometrium
The middle, well-muscled layer of the uterus. (*Myo-* stems from the Greek *mys*, meaning "muscle.")

Perimetrium
The outer layer of the uterus. (From roots meaning "around the uterus.")

Hysterectomy
Surgical removal of the uterus.

Complete hysterectomy
Surgical removal of the ovaries, fallopian tubes, cervix, and uterus.

are the most common.) A hysterectomy may be performed when women develop cancer of the uterus, ovaries, or cervix, or other diseases that cause pain or excessive uterine bleeding. A hysterectomy may be partial or complete. A **complete hysterectomy** involves the surgical removal of the ovaries, fallopian tubes, cervix, and uterus. It is usually performed to reduce the risk of cancer spreading throughout the reproductive system. A partial hysterectomy removes the uterus but spares the ovaries and fallopian tubes. Sparing the ovaries allows the woman to continue to ovulate and produce adequate quantities of female sex hormones.

The hysterectomy has become steeped in controversy. In many cases it is possible that less radical medical interventions might successfully treat the problem. Based on a sample of more than 5,000 hysterectomies performed in seven health maintenance organizations (HMOs) across the country, a panel of experts in gynecology and obstetrics reported that 28% of these operations in younger women, and 16% in women overall, were inappropriate (Bernstein et al., 1993). We advise women whose physicians recommend a hysterectomy to seek a second opinion before proceeding.

The Fallopian Tubes

Fallopian tubes
Tubes that extend from the upper uterus toward the ovaries and conduct ova to the uterus. (After the Italian anatomist Gabriel Fallopio, who is credited with their discovery.)

Two uterine tubes, also called **fallopian tubes,** are about 4 inches in length and extend from the upper end of the uterus toward the ovaries (see Figure 3.6). The part of each tube nearest the uterus is the **isthmus,** which broadens into the **ampulla** as it approaches the ovary. The outer part, or **infundibulum,** has fringelike projections called **fimbriae** that extend toward, but are not attached to, the ovary.

Isthmus
The segment of a fallopian tube closest to the uterus. (A Latin word meaning "narrow passage.")

Ova pass through the fallopian tubes on their way to the uterus. The fallopian tubes are not inert passageways. They help nourish and conduct ova. These tubes are lined with tiny hairlike projections termed cilia ("lashes") that help move ova through the tube. The exact mechanisms by which ova are guided are unknown, however. It is tempting to say that ova move at a snail's pace, but a snail would leave them far behind. They journey toward the uterus at about 1 inch per day. Since ova must be fertilized within a day or two after they are released from the ovaries, fertilization usually occurs in the infundibulum within a couple of inches of the ovaries. The form of sterilization called tubal ligation ties off the fallopian tubes, so that ova cannot pass through them or become fertilized.

Ampulla
The wide segment of a fallopian tube near the ovary. (A Latin word meaning "bottle.")

Infundibulum
The outer, funnel-shaped part of a fallopian tube. (A Latin word meaning "funnel.")

In an **ectopic pregnancy,** the fertilized ovum implants outside the uterus, most often in the fallopian tube where fertilization occurred. Ectopic pregnancies can eventually burst fallopian tubes, causing hemorrhaging and death. Ectopic pregnancies are thus terminated before the tube ruptures. They are not easily recognized, however, because their symptoms—missed menstrual period, abdominal pain, irregular bleeding—suggest many conditions. Experiencing any of these symptoms is an excellent reason for consulting a gynecologist. Women who have had pelvic inflammatory disease (PID), undergone tubal surgery, or used intrauterine devices (IUDs) are at increased risk of developing ectopic pregnancies (Marchbanks, 1988).

Fimbriae
Projections from a fallopian tube that extend toward an ovary. (Singular: fimbria. Latin for "fiber" or "fringe.")

The Ovaries

Ectopic pregnancy
A pregnancy in which the fertilized ovum implants outside the uterus, usually in the fallopian tube. (*Ectopic* derives from Greek roots meaning "out of place.")

The two **ovaries** are almond-shaped organs that are each about 1½ inches long. They lie on either side of the uterus, to which they are attached by ovarian ligaments. The ovaries produce ova (egg cells) and the female sex hormones **estrogen** and **progesterone.**

Estrogen is a generic term for several hormones (such as estradiol, estriol, and estrone) that promote the changes of puberty and regulate the menstrual cycle. Estrogen also helps older women maintain cognitive functioning and feelings of psychological well-being (Sourander, 1994). Progesterone also has multiple functions, including regulating the menstrual cycle and preparing the uterus for pregnancy by stimulating the development of the endometrium (uterine lining). Estrogen and progesterone levels vary with the phases of the menstrual cycle.

The human female is born with all the ova she will ever have (about 2 million), but they are immature in form. Of these, about 400,000 survive into puberty, each of which is

Ovaries
Almond-shaped organs that produce ova and the hormones estrogen and progesterone.

Estrogen
A generic term for female sex hormones (including estradiol, estriol, estrone, and others) or synthetic compounds that promote the development of female sex characteristics and regulate the menstrual cycle. (From the roots meaning "generating" [-*gen*] and "estrus.")

Progesterone
A steroid hormone secreted by the corpus luteum or prepared synthetically that stimulates proliferation of the endometrium and is involved in regulation of the menstrual cycle. (From the root *pro-*, meaning "promoting," and the words *gestation*, *steroid*, and *one*.)

Follicle
A capsule within an ovary that contains an ovum. (From a Latin word meaning "small bag.")

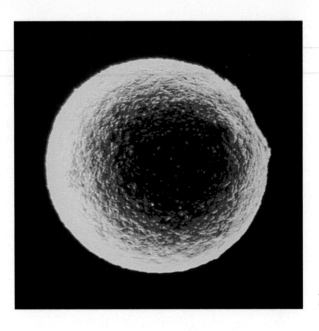

A Magnified Human Ovum (Egg Cell).

contained in the ovary within a thin capsule, or **follicle.** During a woman's reproductive years, from puberty to menopause, only 400 or so ripened ova, typically 1 per month, will be released by their rupturing follicles for possible fertilization. How these ova are selected is among the mysteries of nature.

The American Cancer Society (1995) estimates that each year some 27,000 women in the United States are diagnosed with ovarian cancer, and 14,500 die from it. It most often strikes women between the ages of 40 and 70 and ranks as the fourth leading cancer killer of women, behind lung cancer, breast cancer, and colon cancer. Women most at risk are those with blood relatives who had the disease, especially a first-degree relative (mother, sister, or daughter). Other risk factors are also important, since about 9 women in 10 who develop ovarian cancer do not have a family history of it. Researchers have identified several risk factors that increase the chances of developing the disease: never having given birth, prolonged use of talcum powder between the anus and the vagina, infertility, a history of breast cancer, and a diet rich in meat and animal fats. Questions have been raised as to whether the use of clomiphene, a fertility drug, increases the risk of ovarian cancer (Del Priore et al., 1995; Whittemore, 1994).

Early detection is the key to fighting ovarian cancer. When it is detected before spreading beyond the ovary, 90% of victims survive. However, the overall survival rate is only 42% (American Cancer Society, 1995). Unfortunately, ovarian cancer is often "silent" in the early stages, showing no obvious signs or symptoms. The most common sign is enlargement of the abdomen, which is caused by the accumulation of fluid. Periodic, complete pelvic examinations are important. The Pap test, which is useful in detecting cervical cancer, does not reveal ovarian cancer. The American Cancer Society (1995) advises women over the age of 40 to have a cancer-related checkup every year.

Surgery, radiation therapy, and drug therapy are treatment options. Surgery usually includes the removal of one or both ovaries, the uterus, and the fallopian tubes.

The Pelvic Examination

Women are advised to have an internal (pelvic) examination at least once a year by the time they reach their late teens (or earlier if they become sexually active) and twice yearly if they are over age 35 or use birth-control pills. The physician (usually a gynecologist) first examines the woman externally for irritations, swellings, abnormal vaginal discharges, and clitoral adhesions. The physician normally inserts a speculum to help inspect the cervix

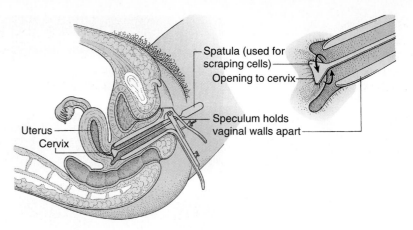

Figure 3.7. Use of the Speculum and Spatula During a Pelvic Examination. The speculum holds the vaginal walls apart while the spatula is used to gently scrape cells from the cervix. The Pap test screens for cervical cancer and other abnormalities.

and vaginal walls for discharges (which can be signs of infection), discoloration, lesions, or growths. This examination is typically followed by a Pap test to detect cervical cancer. A sample of vaginal discharge may also be taken to test for the sexually transmitted disease gonorrhea.

To take a Pap smear, the physician will hold open the vaginal walls with a plastic or (hopefully prewarmed!) metal speculum so that a sample of cells (a "smear") may be scraped from the cervix with a wooden spatula (see Figure 3.7). Women should not douche prior to Pap tests or schedule them during menstruation, since douches and blood confound analysis of the smear.

The speculum exam is normally followed by a bimanual vaginal exam in which the index and middle fingers of one hand are inserted into the vagina while the lower part of the abdomen is palpated (touched) by the other hand from the outside. The physician uses this technique to examine the location, shape, size, and movability of the internal sex organs, searching for abnormal growths and symptoms of other problems. Palpation may be somewhat uncomfortable, but severe pain is a sign that something is wrong. A woman should not try to be "brave" and hide such discomfort from the examiner. She may only be masking a symptom (that is, depriving the physician of useful information). Physical discomfort is usually mild, however, and psychological discomfort may often be relieved by discussing it frankly with the examiner.

Finally, the physician should do a recto-vaginal examination in which one finger is inserted into the rectum while the other is inserted into the vagina. This procedure provides additional information about the ligaments of the uterus, the ovaries, and the fallopian tubes. The procedure also helps the physician evaluate the health of the rectum.

Although it may be somewhat uncomfortable, the pelvic examination is not ordinarily painful. It is normal for a woman who has not had one, or who is visiting a new doctor, to be anxious about the exam. The doctor should be reassuring if the woman expresses concern. If the doctor is not, the woman should feel free to consult another doctor. She should not forgo the pelvic examination itself, however. It is essential for early detection of problems.

~ *Reflections* ~

Are the female internal sex organs more complex than you had believed? If so, how?

What are the risk factors for cancer of the female internal sex organs? What can be done to prevent them or to detect them early?

If you are a woman, would you prefer a female or male physician to conduct a pelvic exam? Why?

The Breasts

The degree of attention which breasts receive, combined with the confusion about what the breast fetishists actually want, makes women unduly anxious about them. They can never be just right; they must always be too small, too big, the wrong shape, too flabby. The characteristics of the mammary stereotype are impossible to emulate because they are falsely simulated, but they must be faked somehow or another. Reality is either gross or scrawny.

(Germaine Greer, *The Female Eunuch*)

Some college women recall:

I was very excited about my breast development. It was a big competition to see who was wearing a bra in elementary school. When I began wearing one, I also liked wearing see-through blouses so everyone would know. . . .

My breasts were very late in developing. This brought me a lot of grief from my male peers. I just dreaded situations like going to the beach or showering in the locker room. . . .

All through junior high and high school I felt unhappy about being "overendowed." I felt just too uncomfortable in sweaters—there was so much to reveal and I was always sure that the only reason boys liked me was because of my bustline. . . .

By the time I was eleven I needed a bra. . . . The girls in my gym class in sixth grade laughed at me because my breasts were pretty big and I still didn't have a bra. I tried to cover myself up when I dressed and undressed. On my eleventh birthday my mom gave me a sailor blouse and inside was my first bra. . . . (It) was the best present I could have received. The bra made me feel a lot better about myself, but I was still unsure of my femininity for a long time. . . .

(Morrison et al., 1980, pp. 66–70)

Secondary sex characteristics
Traits that distinguish women from men but are not directly involved in reproduction.

Mammary glands
Milk-secreting glands. (From the Latin *mamma*, which means both "breast" and "mother.")

In some cultures the breasts are viewed merely as biological instruments for feeding infants. In our culture, however, breasts have taken on such erotic significance that a woman's self-esteem may become linked to her bustline.

The breasts are **secondary sex characteristics.** That is, like the rounding of the hips, they distinguish women from men, but they are not directly involved in reproduction. Each breast contains 15 to 20 clusters of milk-producing **mammary glands** (Figure 3.8). Each gland opens at the nipple through its own duct. The mammary glands are separated by soft, fatty tissue. It is the amount of this fatty tissue, not the amount of glandular tissue, that largely determines the size of the breasts. Women vary little in their amount of glandular tissue, so breast size does not determine the quantity of milk that can be produced.

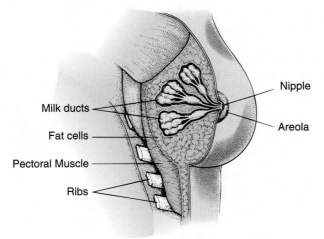

Milk ducts

Fat cells

Pectoral Muscle

Ribs

Nipple

Areola

Figure 3.8. **A Breast of an Adult Woman.** This drawing reveals the structures underlying the breast, including milk ducts and fat cells.

It is not true that women with larger breasts produce more milk while nursing. It is the amount of fatty tissue, not the amount of glandular milk-producing tissue, that largely determines the size of the breasts. ■

Areola
The dark ring on the breast that encircles the nipple.

The nipple, which lies in the center of the **areola,** contains smooth muscle fibers that make the nipple become erect when they contract. The areola, or area surrounding the nipple, darkens during pregnancy and remains darker after delivery. Oil-producing glands in the areola help lubricate the nipples during breast-feeding. Milk ducts conduct milk from the mammary glands through the nipples. Nipples are richly endowed with nerve endings, so that stimulation of the nipples heightens sexual arousal for many women. Male nipples are similar in sensitivity. Gay males often find nipple stimulation pleasurable. Male heterosexuals generally do not. Perhaps heterosexual men have learned to associate breast stimulation with the female sexual role. It is not that their nipples are less sensitive.

Figure 3.9 shows normal variations in the size and shape of the breasts of adult women. The sensitivity of the breasts to sexual stimulation is unrelated to their size. Small breasts may have as many nerve endings as large breasts, but they will be more densely packed.

Women can prompt their partners to provide breast stimulation by informing them that their breasts are sensitive to stimulation. They can also guide a partner's hands in ways that provide the type of stimulation they desire. The breasts vary in sensitivity with the phases of the menstrual cycle, and some women appear less responsive to breast stimulation than others. However, some less sensitive women may learn to enjoy breast stimulation by focusing on breast sensations during lovemaking in a relaxed atmosphere.

Breast Cancer

Breast cancer strikes about 182,000 women and takes some 46,000 lives annually. It is the second leading cause of cancer deaths among women, after lung cancer (American Cancer Society, 1995). (An estimated 240 men also die of breast cancer annually.) The National Cancer Institute estimates that in the United States, 1 woman in 8 will develop breast cancer ("Chance of breast cancer," 1993). The disease takes the lives of nearly 3 of 10 women who develop it. It is not cancer in the breast that causes death, but rather its spread to vital body parts, such as the brain, the bones, the lungs, or the liver.

Mammography
A special type of X-ray test that detects cancerous lumps in the breast.

Despite the popular impression to the contrary, rates of breast cancer in the United States are not on the increase (American Cancer Society, 1995). Rather, more early cases of breast cancer are being detected because of an increased use of **mammography,** a specialized X-ray that detects cancerous lumps in the breast. Advances in early detection and treatment have led to increased rates of recovery. The five-year survival rate for women

Figure 3.9. Normal Variations in the Size and Shape of the Breasts of Adult Women. The size and shape of the breasts have little bearing on ability to produce milk or on sensitivity to sexual stimulation. Breasts have become highly eroticized in our culture.

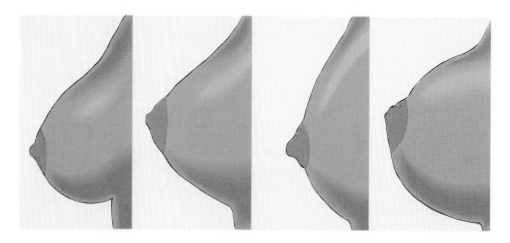

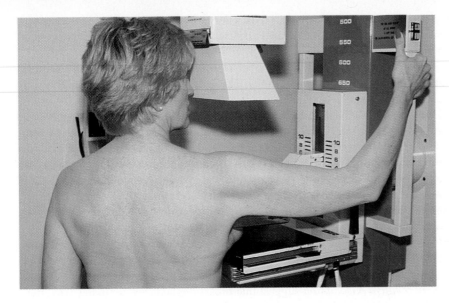

Mammography. Early detection is a key to effective treatment of cancer. Mammography uses specialized X-ray technology to detect cancerous lumps in the breast before they can be felt. The goal is to detect tumors before they have metastasized to other parts of the body.

whose breast cancers have not metastasized—that is, spread beyond the breast—is 91%, up from 78% in the 1940s (American Cancer Society, 1994). The five-year survival rate drops to 69% if the cancer has spread to the surrounding region and to 18% if it has spread to distant sites in the body.

Truth OR Fiction?
R E V I S I T E D

It is not true that the incidence of breast cancer is on the rise in the United States. Instead, breast cancer is being detected earlier through means such as mammography. ■

Breast cancer is rare in women under age 25. The risk increases sharply with age. About four of five cases develop in women over the age of 50 ("Chance of breast cancer," 1993). The National Cancer Institute (NCI) estimates that from birth to age 40, 1 in 217 women will develop breast cancer. From birth to age 50 the risk rises to 1 in 50. By age 60, the risk rises to 1 in 24, and by age 70, to 1 in 14 (Ochs, 1993a).

The risk of breast cancer is higher among women with a family history of the disease (Slattery & Kerber, 1993). A study of more than 100,000 women nurses showed that those with mothers or sisters who had breast cancer had nearly twice the chance of developing the disease themselves (Colditz et al., 1993). Women who had both a mother and a sister with the disease had between two and three times greater risk. Still, about 80% of women with breast cancer have no family history of the disease (Brody, 1995a). Only about 6% of the women with breast cancer in the nurses' study had either a mother or sister with the disease (Johnson & Williams, 1993).

Other risk factors include early onset of menstruation (before age 12), late menopause (after age 50), delayed childbearing (after age 30), never giving birth, hormone-replacement therapy (HRT) in postmenopausal women, and heavy drinking of alcohol (American Cancer Society, 1994; Colditz et al., 1995; Fuchs et al., 1995). The first five factors apparently create greater risk because of prolonged exposure to estrogen. Estrogen stimulates breast development in young women. Earlier onset of menstruation, later menopause, delayed childbearing, and HRT are all connected to longer, uninterrupted exposure to high levels of estrogen. Despite widespread opinion to the contrary, it has *not* been shown that a diet high in fats contributes to breast cancer (Hunter et al., 1996).

Cysts
Saclike structures filled with fluid or diseased material.

Benign
Doing little or no harm.

Fibroadenoma
A benign, fibrous tumor.

Malignant
Lethal; causing or likely to cause death.

Detection   Women with breast cancer have lumps in the breast, *but most lumps in the breasts are not cancerous.* Most are either **cysts** or **benign** tumors called **fibroadenomas.** Breast cancer involves lumps in the breast that are **malignant.**

Lumpectomy

Surgical removal of a lump from the breast.

Mastectomy

Surgical removal of the entire breast.

There is no clear-cut way to prevent breast cancer, but early detection and treatment reduce the risk of mortality. The sooner cancer is detected, the less likely it is to have spread to critical organs.

Breast cancer may be detected in a number of ways, including breast self-examination, medical examination, and mammography. Through mammography, tiny, highly curable cancers can be detected—and treated—before they can be felt by touch (Brody, 1995a). By the time a malignant lump is large enough to be felt by touch, it already contains millions of cells. It may even have metastasized—that is, splintered off to form colonies elsewhere in the body. A mammography can detect tiny tumors before metastasis. One study found that 82% of women whose breast cancers were detected early by mammography survived for at least five years following surgery, as compared to 60% of those whose cancers were discovered later. Early detection may offer another benefit. Smaller cancerous lumps can often be removed by **lumpectomy,** which spares the breast. More advanced cancers are likely to be treated by **mastectomy.**

Many women who have had mastectomies have had surgical breast implants to replace the tissue that has been removed. Other women have breast implants to augment their breast size. Articles published in *The New England Journal of Medicine* and *The Journal of the American Medical Association* suggest that breast implants appear to have no effect on the probability of developing breast cancer (Bryant & Brasher, 1995), rheumatoid arthritis (Kolata, 1996), and a number of other health problems (Sanchez-Guerrero et al., 1995), casting doubt on previous studies that had implicated them in the development of these problems. However, this issue remains quite controversial as this book goes to press. Readers are advised to consult their gynecologists for the latest research information.

The American Cancer Society recommends that women have a breast exam every three years when they are between 20 and 39 years of age, every one or two years between ages 40 and 49, and then annually thereafter ("Breast fears fade," 1993). They also recommend that young women receive a baseline mammogram for comparison with later tests. The mortality rate from breast cancer may be cut by 30% or more if women follow these guidelines (Brody, 1990b). Mammography is not foolproof, however. Thus, the chances of early detection are optimized through a combination of monthly breast self-examinations (see the nearby A Closer Look feature), annual breast examinations by a physician, and regular mammograms.

Questions have been raised about the recommendation that women in their 40s obtain regular mammograms. The results of a controversial 1992 Canadian study showed that women in their 40s who had received mammograms had the same death rates from breast cancer as women who did not (Kolata, 1993a, 1993c). Yet analysis of data from eight major studies, including the Canadian study, suggests that mammography in younger women can reduce their death rate from breast cancer by about 14% (Smart et al., 1995). When the results of the Canadian study are left out, analysis suggests that women of ages 40 to 49 can reduce their death rate from breast cancer by 23% (Smart et al., 1995). Mammograms reduce the death rate from breast cancer in women age 50 and above by 25% to 30% (Kolata, 1993f). Why the difference? It is possible that since younger women have denser breasts, mammograms in younger women are more difficult for doctors to read and so may be less reliable indicators of early cancers.

The decision as to whether a woman should have a mammogram rests with the woman and her doctor. We note, however, that only one study—the 1992 Canadian study—suggests that mammography is not of use in women under age 50. Moreover, the Canadian study has been criticized for relatively small sample size, relatively brief follow-ups of the women in the study, and failure to use the most up-to-date screening technology (Brody, 1995a). We therefore support the recommendations of the American Cancer Society that women of ages 40 to 50 have a mammogram every one to two years, and that women age 50 and above have an annual mammogram.

The number of women who have had mammographies has risen dramatically in recent years. By 1990, three of four women over the age of 40 had at least one mammogram, up from 54% just three years earlier ("Mammograms on rise," 1992). Women who receive regular health care are more likely to also have mammograms (Siegler et al., 1995). A study of 670 Californian African American women found that women with more social ties were

A CLOSER LOOK

BREAST SELF-EXAMINATION

Regular breast self-examination and regular visits to a physician provide the best protection against breast cancer, since they may lead to early detection and treatment. A woman may wish to undertake an initial breast self-examination with a physician in order to determine the degree of "lumpiness" that seems normal for her. Then she should conduct a breast self-examination at least once a month, preferably about a week after her period ends (when the breasts are least influenced by hormones), so that any changes can be reported promptly to a physician (see Figure 3.10).

The following instructions for breast self-examination are based on American Cancer Society guidelines. Additional material on breast self-examination may be obtained from the American Cancer Society by calling this toll-free number: (800) ACS-2345.

1. *In the shower.* Examine your breasts during your bath or shower; hands glide more easily over wet skin. Keep your fingers flat, and move gently over every part of each breast. Use the right hand to examine the left breast and the left hand for the right breast. Check for any lump, hard knot, or thickening.

2. *Before a mirror.* Inspect your breasts with your arms at your sides. Next, raise your arms high overhead. Look for any changes in the contour of each breast, a swelling, dimpling of skin, or changes in the nipple. Then rest your palms on your hips and press down firmly to flex your chest muscles. Your left and right breasts will not exactly match—few women's breasts do. Regular inspection shows what is normal for you and will give you confidence in your examination.

3. *Lying down.* To examine your right breast, put a pillow or folded towel under your right shoulder. Place your right arm behind your head—this distributes breast tissue more evenly on the chest. With your left hand, fingers flat, press gently with the finger pads (the top thirds of the fingers) of the three middle fingers in small circular motions around an imaginary clock face. Begin at the outermost top of your right breast for 12 o'clock, then move to 1 o'clock, and so on around the circle back to 12. A ridge of firm tissue in the lower curve of each breast is normal. Then move in 1 inch, toward the nipple. Keep circling to examine *every part of your breast*, including the nipple. This requires at least three more circles. Now slowly repeat the procedure on your left breast. Place the pillow beneath your left shoulder, your left arm behind your head, and use the finger pads on your right hand.

After you examine your left breast fully, squeeze the nipple of each breast gently between your thumb and index finger. Any discharge, clear or bloody, should be reported to your doctor immediately.

Research shows that many women who know how to do breast self-examinations do not do them regularly. Why? There are many reasons, including fear of what one will find and doubts as to whether self-examination will make a difference. But the most frequently mentioned reasons are being too busy or forgetting (Friedman et al., 1994).

Figure 3.10. **Woman Examining Her Breast for Lumps.**

A CLOSER LOOK

*WOMEN WHO LOSE BREASTS DEFINE THEIR OWN FEMININITY**

Twenty to 30 years ago, women with breast cancer worried that even if they survived the disease, the loss of a breast would somehow diminish their femininity and sexual attractiveness. Many women hid their mastectomies, disguising their single-breasted figures with cumbersome prostheses even around family members.

Today, women are less likely to perceive breast cancer as an attack on their feminine nature. For one thing, more and more women are having surgery that removes the malignancy but spares the breast. When a mastectomy is necessary, many women have reconstructive surgery to implant their own fatty tissue (Figure 3.11). One recent study, in fact, found no differences in self-esteem among women who had had mastectomies and wore external breast prostheses, women who had had mastectomies and had reconstructive surgery, and women who had not had mastectomies (Reaby et al., 1994).

And although breasts are still viewed in many societies and cultures as a symbol of womanhood, nurturing, and sexuality, many men no longer consider the loss of a woman's breast as having lessened her physical attributes or sexual desirability.

"We Are What We Are"

"When it comes to self-image, you can't let cancer dictate who and what you are," said Jean Ettesvold, a 60-year-old retired social worker from Grand Rapids, Michigan, who had a mastectomy. "We are what we are, in spite of the trauma we have suffered."

In a recent study of the effects of breast cancer on sexuality, body image, and intimate relationships, Leslie R. Schover, a staff psychologist at the Center for Sexual Function at the Cleveland Clinic Foundation in

Ohio, concluded, "The majority of women cope well with the stress of cancer surgery and the loss of a breast. The options of breast conservation and reconstruction give women a new sense of control over their treatment and are quite successful in helping women feel comfortable with their bodies again."

In more than a dozen recent interviews, women who had lost a breast to cancer, ranging in age from their 30s to their 60s, said they did not feel less attractive than women with natural breasts. Most chose reconstructive surgery, though some used prostheses.

Some breast cancer survivors reject any kind of camouflage after mastectomy. They say cosmetic remedies undermine efforts to focus attention on thousands of women suffering and dying from the disease.

"When other one-breasted women hide behind the mask of prosthesis or reconstruction, I find little support in the broader female environment for my rejection of what feels like a cosmetic sham," said one women who has chosen not to wear a prosthesis for philosophical and political reasons. "The social and economic discrimination practiced against women who have breast cancer is not diminished by pretending that mastectomies do not exist. . . . I would lie if I did not also speak of loss. Any amputation is a physical and psychic reality that must be integrated into a new sense of self. The absence of my breast is a recurrent sadness, but certainly not one that dominates my life."

Most of the married women said their mastectomies had not harmed their marriages or their sex lives. The single women said their surgery had not impaired their relationships with men or dating. Some said they found men to be even more

supportive after their mastectomies than before. Others said men seemed emotionally moved by their stories, often calling them courageous or survivors.

Other Traumas

Ann Marcou, the founder of Y-Me, a national support network for women with cancer, said: "I think [mastectomy] doesn't have quite the stigma it did. . . . People used to hide in the closet. Individual women still tussle with their body because it's so valued in society. Every woman who goes through this will wonder about her femininity and sexuality. But it comes down to this: 'Your femininity is not determined by whether or not you have breasts.' "

*Adapted from Williams, L. (1991, December 25). Women Who Lose Their Breasts Define Their Own Femininity. *The New York Times*, p. 39.

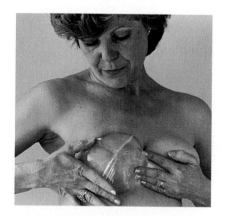

Alternatives Following Mastectomy. After removal of a breast, some women prefer not to camouflage a missing breast. Others use external prostheses. Still others select artificial breast implants or breast reconstruction using tissue from elsewhere in the body.

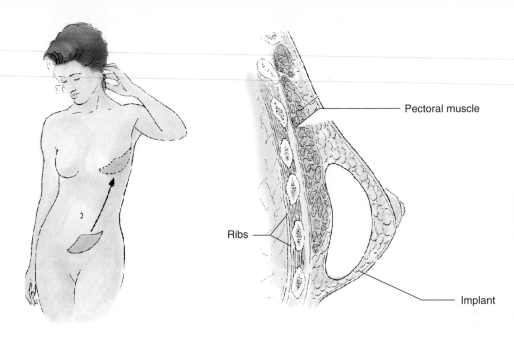

Pectoral muscle

Ribs

Implant

Figure 3.11. Breast Reconstruction. For women who decide on breast reconstruction there are two major surgical approaches. Flap surgery (left), using tissue from elsewhere in the body, can cost $20,000 for two breasts. Silicone implants (right) are less expensive.

more likely to obtain mammograms (Kang et al., 1994). That is, people with concerned families and friends are more likely to take care of themselves.

Nearly half (45%) of the women over age 40 who have not had mammograms explain that their doctors have not recommended it. Some women forgo mammograms because of the cost (Blustein, 1995). Some wonder whether their efforts at self-detection will actually be effective (Aiken et al., 1994). Others fear finding out that something is wrong; they may be encouraged to learn that more than 95% of women who receive a mammogram are given a clean bill of health. Most of the remaining 5%, moreover, show no evidence of cancer on follow-up tests. Even if cancer is present, it is best discovered and treated early.

~ *Reflections* ~

■ How important is the size and shape of your breasts (or your partner's breasts) to you? Why?

■ If you are a woman, what should you be doing at your age to prevent or detect breast cancer early? Are you doing everything you can? If not, why not?

■ How do you believe you would react if you (or your partner) had a mastectomy? Why?

The Menstrual Cycle

Menstruation

The cyclical bleeding that stems from the shedding of the uterine lining (endometrium).

Menstruation is the cyclical bleeding that stems from the shedding of the uterine lining (endometrium.) Menstruation takes place when a reproductive cycle has not led to the fertilization of an ovum. The word *menstruation* derives from the Latin *mensis,* meaning "month." The human menstrual cycle averages about 28 days in length.

The menstrual cycle is regulated by the hormones estrogen and progesterone, and can be divided into four phases. During the first phase of the cycle, the *proliferative phase,* which follows menstruation, estrogen levels increase, causing the ripening of perhaps 10 to 20 ova (egg cells) within their follicles and the proliferation of endometrial tissue in the uterus. During the second phase of the cycle, estrogen reaches peak blood levels, and

Ovulation
The release of an ovum from an ovary.

Corpus luteum
The follicle that has released an ovum and then produces copious amounts of progesterone and estrogen during the luteal phase of a woman's cycle. (From Latin roots meaning "yellow body.")

Endocrine gland
A ductless gland that releases its secretions directly into the bloodstream.

Menarche
The first menstrual period.

Estrous cycle
The female reproductive cycle of most mammals (other than primates), which is under hormonal control and includes a period of heat, followed by ovulation.

Estrus
The periodic sexual excitement in which female mammals (other than primates) are most receptive to the sexual advances of males.

Hypothalamus
A bundle of neural cell bodies near the center of the brain that are involved in regulating body temperature, motivation, and emotion.

Pituitary gland
The gland that secretes growth hormone, prolactin, oxytocin, and others.

ovulation occurs. Normally only 1 ovum reaches maturity and is released by an ovary during ovulation. Then the third phase—the *secretory,* or *luteal,* phase—of the cycle begins. The luteal phase begins right after ovulation and continues through the beginning of the next cycle.

The term *luteal phase* is derived from **corpus luteum,** the name given the follicle that releases an ovum. The corpus luteum functions as an **endocrine gland** and produces copious amounts of progesterone and estrogen. Progesterone causes the endometrium to thicken, so that it will be able to support an embryo if fertilization occurs. If the ovum goes unfertilized, however, estrogen and progesterone levels plummet. These falloffs provide the trigger for the fourth phase, the *menstrual phase,* which leads to the beginning of a new cycle.

Ovulation may not occur in every menstrual cycle. Anovulatory ("without ovulation") cycles are most common in the years just after **menarche.** They may become frequent again in the years prior to menopause, but they may also occur irregularly among women in their 20s and 30s.

Although the menstrual cycle averages about 28 days, variations among women, and in the same woman from month to month, are quite common. Girls' cycles are often irregular for a few years after menarche, but later assume reasonably regular patterns. Variations from cycle to cycle tend to occur during the proliferative phase that precedes ovulation. That is, menstruation tends to reliably follow ovulation by about 14 days. Variations of more than 2 days in the postovulation period are rare.

Although hormones regulate the menstrual cycle, psychological factors can influence the secretion of hormones. Stress can delay or halt menstruation. Anxiety that she may be pregnant and thus miss her period may also cause a woman to be late. Many women in otherwise good health stopped menstruating during imprisonment in Nazi concentration camps during World War II.

Menstruation Versus Estrus

The menstrual cycle is found only in women, female apes, and female monkeys. It differs from an ovarian, or **estrous cycle,** which occurs in "lower" mammals such as rodents, cats, and dogs. **Estrus** is the periodic sexual excitement (otherwise referred to as being "in heat") when the female is most receptive to the advances of the male. Estrus occurs when the animal is ovulating and hence most likely to conceive offspring. Women (and other female primates), however, ovulate about halfway through the cycle and may be interested in sexual activity at any time during their cycles. Estrous cycles, moreover, may be characterized by little bleeding ("spotting") or no bleeding. Menstruation typically involves a heavier flow of blood.

Regulation of the Menstrual Cycle

The menstrual cycle involves finely tuned relationships between structures in the brain—the **hypothalamus** and the **pituitary gland**—and the ovaries and uterus. All these structures are parts of the endocrine system, which means that they secrete chemicals directly into the bloodstream (see Figure 3.12). The ovaries and uterus are also reproductive organs. The chemicals secreted by endocrine glands are called **hormones.** (Other bodily secretions, such as milk, saliva, sweat, and tears, arrive at their destinations by passing through narrow, tubular structures in the body called ducts.)

Behavioral and social scientists are especially interested in hormones because of their behavioral effects. Hormones regulate bodily processes such as the metabolic rate, growth of bones and muscle, production of milk, metabolism of sugar, and storage of fats, among others. Several hormones play important roles in sexual and reproductive functions.

The gonads—the **testes** (or testicles) in the male and the ovaries in the female—secrete sex hormones directly into the bloodstream. The female gonads, the ovaries, produce the sex hormones estrogen and progesterone. The male gonads, the testes, produce the male

Hormone

A substance secreted by an endocrine gland that regulates various body functions. (From the Greek *horman*, meaning "to stimulate" or "to excite.")

Testes

The male gonads.

Testosterone

The male sex hormone that fosters the development of male sex characteristics and is connected with the sex drive.

Prolactin

A pituitary hormone that stimulates production of milk.

Oxytocin

A pituitary hormone that stimulates uterine contractions in labor and the ejection of milk during nursing.

Gonadotropins

Pituitary hormones that stimulate the gonads. (Literally, "that which 'feeds' the gonads.")

Follicle-stimulating hormone (FSH)

A gonadotropin that stimulates development of follicles in the ovaries.

Luteinizing hormone (LH)

A gonadotropin that helps regulate the menstrual cycle by triggering ovulation.

Gonadotropin-releasing hormone (Gn-RH)

A hormone secreted by the hypothalamus that stimulates the pituitary to release gonadotropins.

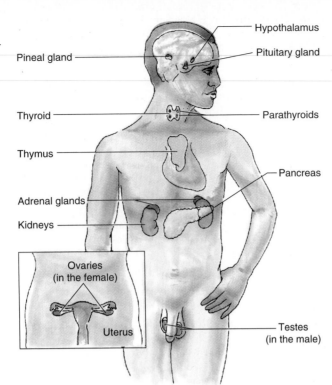

Figure 3.12. Major Glands of the Endocrine System. The endocrine system consists of glands that secrete chemicals called hormones directly into the bloodstream.

sex hormone **testosterone.** Males and females also produce sex hormones of the other gender, but in relatively small amounts.

The hypothalamus is a pea-sized structure in the front part of the brain. It weighs about 4 to 5 grams and lies above the pituitary gland and below (hence the prefix *hypo-,* for "under") the thalamus. Despite its small size, it is involved in regulating many states of motivation, including hunger, thirst, aggression, and sex. For example, when the rear part of a male rat's hypothalamus is stimulated by an electric probe, the rat runs through its courting and mating sequence. It nibbles at a female's ears and at the back of her neck. When she responds, they copulate. Human sexuality is not so stereotyped or mechanical—although in the cases of some people who are highly routinized in their behavior, it may appear so.

The pituitary gland, which is about the size of a pea, lies below the hypothalamus at the base of the brain. Because many pituitary secretions regulate other endocrine glands, the pituitary has also been called the *master gland.* Pituitary hormones regulate bone and muscle growth and urine production. Two pituitary hormones are active during pregnancy and motherhood: **prolactin,** which stimulates production of milk; and **oxytocin,** which stimulates uterine contractions in labor and the ejection of milk during nursing. The pituitary gland also produces **gonadotropins** (literally, "that which 'feeds' the gonads") that stimulate the ovaries: **follicle-stimulating hormone (FSH)** and **luteinizing hormone (LH).** These hormones play central roles in regulating the menstrual cycle.

The hypothalamus receives information about bodily events through the nervous and circulatory systems. It monitors the blood levels of various hormones, including estrogen and progesterone, and releases a hormone called **gonadotropin-releasing hormone (Gn-RH),** which stimulates the pituitary to release gonadotropins. Gonadotropins, in turn, regulate the activity of the gonads. It was once thought that the pituitary gland ran the show, but it is now known that the pituitary gland is regulated by the hypothalamus. Even the "master gland" must serve another.

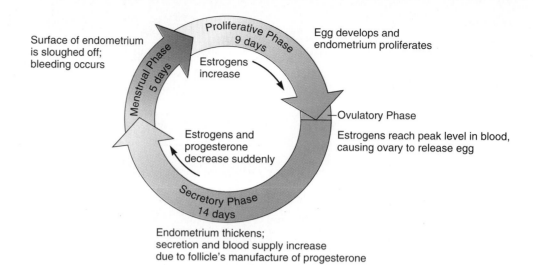

Surface of endometrium
is sloughed off;
bleeding occurs

Egg develops and
endometrium proliferates

Proliferative Phase
9 days

Menstrual Phase
5 days

Estrogens
increase

Ovulatory Phase

Estrogens reach peak level in blood,
causing ovary to release egg

Estrogens and
progesterone
decrease suddenly

Secretory Phase
14 days

Endometrium thickens;
secretion and blood supply increase
due to follicle's manufacture of progesterone

Figure 3.13. **The Four Phases of the Menstrual Cycle.** The menstrual cycle includes proliferative, ovulatory, secretory (luteal), and menstrual phases.

Phases of the Menstrual Cycle

We noted that the menstrual cycle has four stages or phases: proliferative, ovulatory, secretory, and menstrual (see Figure 3.13). It might seem logical that a new cycle begins with the first day of the menstrual flow, since this is the most clearly identifiable event of the cycle. Many women also count the days of the menstrual cycle beginning with the onset of menstruation. Biologically speaking, however, menstruation is really the culmination of the cycle. In fact, the cycle begins with the end of menstruation and the initiation of a series of biological events that lead to the maturation of an immature ovum in preparation for ovulation and possible fertilization.

Proliferative phase

The first phase of the menstrual cycle, which begins with the end of menstruation and lasts about 9 or 10 days. During this phase, the endometrium proliferates.

The Proliferative Phase The first phase, or **proliferative phase,** begins with the end of menstruation and lasts about 9 or 10 days in an average 28-day cycle (see Figures 3.13, 3.14). During this phase the endometrium develops, or "proliferates." This phase is also known as the *preovulatory* or *follicular* phase, because certain ovarian follicles mature and the ovaries prepare for ovulation.

Low levels of estrogen and progesterone are circulating in the blood as menstruation draws to an end. When the hypothalamus senses a low level of estrogen in the blood, it increases its secretion of Gn-RH, which in turn triggers the pituitary gland to release FSH. When FSH reaches the ovaries, it stimulates some follicles (perhaps 10 to 20) to begin to mature. As the follicles ripen, they begin to produce estrogen. Normally, however, only one of them—called the *graafian follicle*—will reach full maturity in the days just preceding ovulation. As the graafian follicle matures, it moves toward the surface of the ovary, where it will eventually rupture and release a mature egg (see Figures 3.14, 3.15).

Estrogen causes the endometrium in the uterus to thicken to about $\frac{1}{8}$ inch. Glands develop that would eventually nourish an embryo. Estrogen also stimulates the appearance of a thin cervical mucus. This mucus is alkaline and provides a hospitable, nutritious medium for sperm. The chances are thus increased that sperm that enter the female reproductive system at the time of ovulation will remain viable.

Ovulatory phase

The second stage of the menstrual cycle, during which a follicle ruptures and releases a mature ovum.

Zygote

A fertilized ovum (egg cell).

The Ovulatory Phase During ovulation, or the **ovulatory phase,** the graafian follicle ruptures and releases a mature ovum *near* a fallopian tube—not actually *into* a fallopian tube (see Figure 3.15 on page 88). The other ripening follicles degenerate and are harmlessly reabsorbed by the body. If two ova mature and are released during ovulation, which happens occasionally, and both are fertilized, fraternal (nonidentical) twins will develop. Identical twins develop when one fertilized ovum divides into two separate **zygotes.**

Ovulation is set into motion when estrogen production reaches a critical level. The high level of estrogen is detected by the hypothalamus, which triggers the pituitary to

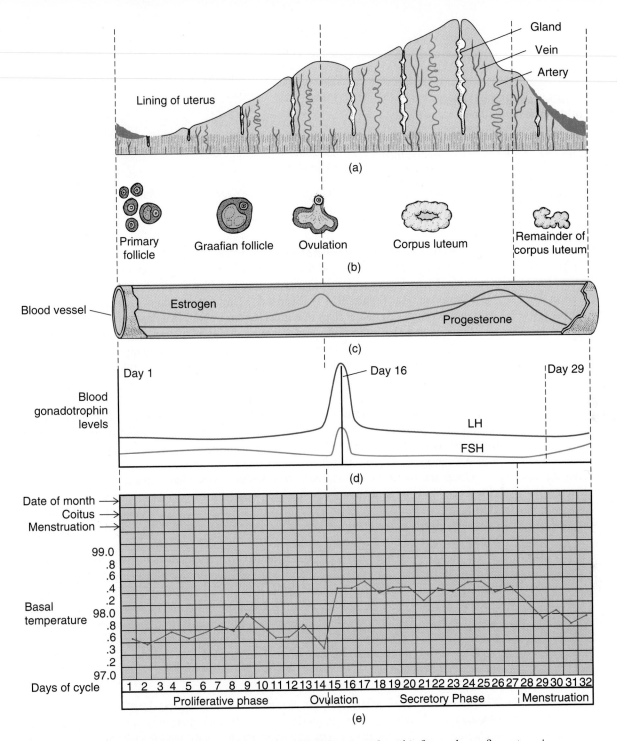

Figure 3.14. **Changes That Occur During the Menstrual Cycle.** This figure shows five categories of biological change: (a) changes in the development of the uterine lining (endometrium), (b) follicular changes, (c) changes in blood levels of ovarian hormones, (d) changes in blood levels of pituitary hormones, and (e) changes in basal temperature. Note the dip in temperature that is connected with ovulation.

Clomiphene
A synthetic hormone that is chemically similar to LH and induces ovulation.

release copious amounts of FSH and LH (see Figure 3.14). The surge of LH triggers ovulation, which usually begins 12 to 24 hours after the level of LH in the body has reached its peak.

The synthetic hormone **clomiphene** is chemically similar to LH and has been used by women who ovulate irregularly to induce reliable ovulation. The induction and accurate prediction of the timing of ovulation increase the chances of conceiving.

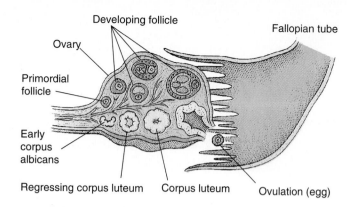

Figure 3.15. Maturation and Eventual Decomposition of an Ovarian Follicle. Many follicles develop and produce estrogen during the proliferative phase of the menstrual cycle. Usually only one, the graafian follicle, ruptures and releases an ovum. The graafian follicle then develops into the corpus luteum, which produces copious quantities of estrogen and progesterone. When fertilization does not occur, the corpus luteum decomposes.

Mittelschmerz
Pain that occurs during ovulation. (German for "middle pain," reflecting the fact that the pain occurs midway between menstrual periods).

A woman's *basal body temperature,* taken by oral or rectal thermometer, dips slightly at ovulation (see Figure 3.14) and rises by about 1 degree Fahrenheit on the day following ovulation. Many women use this information to help them conceive or avoid conceiving. Note, however, that Figure 3.14 is idealized. Many women show greater fluctuations in daily temperature or gradual rises in temperature for about two days after ovulation.

Some women have discomfort or cramping during ovulation, termed **mittelschmerz.** Mittelschmerz is sometimes confused with appendicitis. Mittelschmerz, however, may occur on either side of the abdomen, depending on which ovary is releasing an ovum. A ruptured appendix always causes pain on the right side.

Secretory phase
The third phase of the menstrual cycle, which follows ovulation. Also referred to as the *luteal phase,* after the *corpus luteum,* which begins to secrete large amounts of progesterone and estrogen following ovulation.

The Secretory Phase The phase following ovulation is called the postovulatory or **secretory phase.** Some people refer to it as the *luteal phase,* which reflects the name given the ruptured (graafian) follicle—the *corpus luteum.* Figures 3.14 and 3.15 show the transformation of the graafian follicle into the corpus luteum.

Under the influence of LH, the corpus luteum, which has remained in the ovary, begins to produce large amounts of progesterone and estrogen. Levels of these hormones peak at around the 20th or 21st day of an average cycle (see Figure 3.14). These hormones cause the glands in the endometrium to secrete nutrients to sustain a fertilized ovum that becomes implanted in the uterine wall.

If implantation does not occur, the hypothalamus responds to the peak levels of progesterone in the blood by signaling the pituitary to stop producing LH and FSH. Although certainly more complex, this feedback process is similar to that of a thermostat in a house reacting to rising temperatures by shutting down the furnace. The levels of LH and FSH decline rapidly, leading the corpus luteum to decompose. After its decomposition, levels of estrogen and progesterone fall precipitously. In this sense, the corpus luteum sows the seeds of its own destruction: Its hormones signal the brain to shut down secretion of substances that maintain it.

Menstrual phase
The fourth phase of the menstrual cycle, during which the endometrium is sloughed off in the menstrual flow.

The Menstrual Phase: An End and a Beginning The **menstrual phase** is the sloughing off of the uterine lining (the endometrium) in the menstrual flow. Menstruation occurs when estrogen and progesterone levels decline to the point where they can no longer sustain the uterine lining. The lining then disintegrates and is discharged from the body along with the menstrual flow. Menstruation itself is the passing of the lining through the cervix and vagina.

The low estrogen levels of the menstrual phase signal the hypothalamus to release Gn-RH, which in turn stimulates the pituitary to secrete FSH. FSH, in turn, prompts ovarian secretion of estrogen and the onset of another proliferative phase. Thus a new cycle begins. The menstrual phase is a beginning as well as an end.

Menstrual flow contains blood from the endometrium (uterine lining), endometrial tissue, and cervical and vaginal mucus. Although the flow can appear persistent and last for five days or more, most women lose only a total of 2 or 3 ounces of blood (4 to 6 tablespoonfuls). A typical blood donor, by contrast, donates 16 ounces of blood at a sitting. A woman's blood loss through menstruation is thus usually harmless. Extremely heavy or prolonged (over a week) menstrual bleeding may reflect health problems and should be discussed with a health care provider.

Tampon

A cylindrical plug of cotton that is inserted into the vagina and left in place to absorb menstrual fluid. (A French word, meaning a gun barrel "plug.")

Prior to 1933, women generally used external sanitary napkins or pads to absorb the menstrual flow. In that year, however, **tampons** were introduced and altered the habits of millions of women. Women who use tampons can swim without concern while menstruating, wear more revealing or comfortable apparel, and feel generally less burdened.

Tampons are inserted into the vagina and left in place to absorb menstrual fluid. In recent years, questions have arisen about whether or not tampons cause or exacerbate infections. For example, tampon use has been linked to toxic shock syndrome (TSS), an infection that is sometimes fatal. Signs of TSS include fever, headache, sore throat, vomiting, diarrhea, muscle aches, rash, and dizziness. Peeling skin, disorientation, and a plunge in blood pressure may follow.

TSS is caused by the *Staphylococcus aureus* ("staph") bacterium. In 1980, the peak year for cases of TSS, there were 344 recorded cases of TSS and 28 fatalities. Proctor and Gamble removed its "extra absorbent" tampon Rely from the market when it was discovered that 71% of these TSS victims had used the product. Plugging the vagina with a highly absorbent tampon that remains in place for six hours or more may create an ideal breeding ground for staph. The number of TSS cases has declined dramatically since then.

Some researchers believe that concern over TSS has been exaggerated. Nevertheless, many women now use regular rather than superabsorbent tampons to reduce the chance of creating a breeding ground for staph bacteria. Some women alternate tampons with sanitary napkins during each day of menstruation. Some change their tampons three or four times a day. These alternatives may also present problems, however. If more tampons are used, the increased number of insertions may increase the chances of transferring staph from the fingers or vaginal opening into the vagina. Other women have returned to external sanitary napkins. Still others use natural sponges. Women are encouraged to consult their health care providers about TSS.

Coitus During Menstruation

Many couples continue to engage in coitus during menstruation, but others abstain. One study found that men and women are less likely to initiate sexual activity during menstruation than during any other phase of the woman's cycle (Harvey, 1987). Some people abstain because of religious prohibitions. Others express concern about the "fuss" or the "mess" of the menstrual flow. Despite traditional attitudes that associate menstruation with uncleanliness, there is no evidence that coitus during menstruation is physically harmful to either partner. Ironically, menstrual coitus may be helpful to the woman. The uterine contractions that occur during orgasm may help relieve cramping by dispelling blood congestion. Orgasm achieved through masturbation may have the same effect.

Women may be sexually aroused at any time during the menstrual cycle. The preponderance of the research evidence, however, points to a peak in sexual desire in women around the time of ovulation (Kresin, 1993).

Human coital patterns during the phases of the menstrual cycle apparently reflect personal decisions, not hormone fluctuations. Some couples may decide to increase their frequency of coitus at ovulation in order to optimize the chances of conceiving, or to abstain during menstruation because of religious beliefs or beliefs linking menses with uncleanliness. Some may also increase their coital activity preceding menstruation to compensate for anticipated abstinence during menses, or increase coital activity afterwards to make up for deprivation. In contrast, females of other species that are bound by the estrous cycle respond sexually only during estrus, except in relatively rare cases in which the female submits to sexual advances to fend off attacks from an aggressive male.

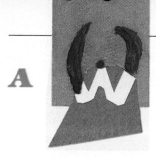

A World of Diversity

HISTORICAL AND CROSS-CULTURAL PERSPECTIVES ON MENSTRUATION

In Peru, they speak of a "visit from Uncle Pepe," whereas in Samoa, menstruation is referred to as "the boogie man." One of the more common epithets given menstruation through the course of history is "the curse." The Fulani of Upper Volta in Africa use a term for it that translates "to see dirt." Nationalism also rises to the call, with some nations blaming "the curse" on their historical enemies. In earlier times the French referred to menstruation as "the English" and to its onset as "the English are coming."

It is a common folk belief that menstruating women are contaminated. Men thus avoid contact with menstruating women for fear of their lives. To prevent their contaminating others, menstruating women in tribal societies may be dispatched to special huts on the fringe of the village. In the traditional Navajo Indian culture, for instance, menstruating women would be consigned to

huts that were set apart from other living quarters. In many Islamic societies, a menstruating woman is considered polluted and is not permitted either to pray or to enter a mosque.

Women in industrialized nations are not consigned to special huts, but throughout the history of Western culture, menstruation has been seen as unclean, contaminating, and even magical. In A.D. 77, the Roman historian Pliny summed up Roman misbeliefs about menstrual blood:

> Contact with it turns new wine sour, crops touched by it become barren, grafts die, seeds in gardens are dried up, the fruit of trees falls off. . . . [The] edge of steel and the gleam of ivory are dulled, hives of bees die, even bronze and iron are at once seized by rust, and a horrible smell fills the air; to taste it drives dogs mad and infects their bites with an incurable poison.

The Old Testament (Leviticus 15:19) warns against any physical contact with a menstruating woman, including, of course, coitus:

> And if a woman have an issue, and her issue in her flesh be blood, she shall be put apart seven days; and whosoever toucheth her shall be unclean.

Orthodox Jews still abstain from coitus during menstruation and the week afterward. Prior to resuming sexual relations, the woman must attend a *mikvah*—a ritual cleansing in which the genitals are washed and

Truth **OR** Fiction?
REVISITED

Yes, the ancient Romans did believe that menstrual blood soured wine and killed crops. Negative views of menstruation and menstrual blood have persisted throughout history. ■

Menopause

Menopause
The cessation of menstruation.

Climacteric
A long-term process, including menopause, that involves the gradual decline in the reproductive capacity of the ovaries.

Menopause, or the "change of life," is the cessation of menstruation. Menopause is a process that most commonly occurs between the ages of 46 and 50 and lasts for about two years. However, it may begin any time between the ages of 35 and 60. There is at least one case of a woman who became pregnant at age 61.

Menopause is a specific event in a long-term process known as the **climacteric** ("critical period"), which refers to the gradual decline in the reproductive capacity of the ovaries. The climacteric generally lasts for about 15 years, from ages 45 to 60 or so. After about the age of 35, the menstrual cycles of many women shorten, from an average of 28 days to 25 days at age 40 and to 23 days by the mid-40s. By the end of her 40s, a woman's cycles often become erratic, with some periods close together and others missed.

In menopause, the pituitary gland continues to pour normal levels of FSH and LH into the bloodstream, but for reasons that are not well understood, the ovaries gradually lose their capacity to respond. The ovaries no longer ripen egg cells or produce the sex hormones estrogen and progesterone.

The deficit in estrogen may lead to a number of unpleasant physical sensations, such as night sweats and hot flashes (suddenly feeling hot) and hot flushes (suddenly looking

all foreign substances are removed. Such practices are grounded in religious tradition, not science. The attitudes of people in ancient and present-day preliterate societies toward menstruation should be understood in terms of their limited understanding of bodily processes. Because they lack knowledge that menstruation is a part of the woman's natural menstrual cycle, they may regard the flow of blood from a woman's loins as a sign of filth or contamination and believe that it is healthier for others to temporarily avoid physical contact with her. Science teaches that there is no medical basis to these fears, and that there are no dangers in menstrual coitus, despite the persistence of superstition.

Fears of contamination by menstruating women are nearly universal across cultures and remain quite current in some circles. As late as the 1950s, women were not allowed in some European breweries for fear that the beer would turn sour. Some Indian castes still teach that a man who touches a woman during menses be-

comes contaminated and must be purified by a priest.

We might laugh off these misconceptions as folly and ignorance, if it were not for their profound effect on women. Women who believe the

myths about menstruation may see themselves as sources of pollution and endure anxiety, depression, and lowered self-esteem. Negative cultural beliefs concerning menstruation may also contribute to menstrual distress.

The Menstrual Hut. Cultural beliefs linking menstruation with impurity and uncleanliness are common in preliterate and advanced societies. This engraving shows a Navajo village in which women were consigned to special huts during menstruation to prevent contamination.

reddened). Hot flashes and flushes may alternate with cold sweats, in which a woman feels suddenly cold and clammy. Anyone who has experienced "cold feet" or hands from anxiety or fear will understand how dramatic the shifting patterns of blood flow can be. Hot flashes and flushes stem largely from "waves" of dilation of blood vessels across the face and upper body. All of these sensations reflect "vasomotor instability." That is, there are disruptions in the body mechanisms that dilate or constrict the blood vessels to maintain an even body temperature. Additional signs of estrogen deficiency include dizziness, headaches, pains in the joints, sensations of tingling in the hands or feet, burning or itchy skin, and heart palpitations. The skin usually becomes drier. There is some loss of breast tissue and decreased vaginal lubrication during sexual arousal. Women may also encounter sleep problems, such as awakening more frequently at night and having difficulty falling back to sleep.

Long-term estrogen deficiency has been linked to brittleness and porosity of the bones (**osteoporosis**). In this condition, bones break more readily, and some women develop so-called dowager's hump. Osteoporosis is potentially severely handicapping, even life threatening. The increased brittleness of the bones increases the risk of serious fractures, especially of the hip, and many elderly women never recover from these fractures.

Osteoporosis
A condition caused by estrogen deficiency and characterized by a decline in bone density, such that bones become porous and brittle. (From the Greek *osteon*, meaning "bone," and the Latin *porus*, meaning "pore.")

MYTHS ABOUT MENOPAUSE

Menopause is certainly a major life change for most women. For many women, menopause symbolizes the many midlife issues they face, including changes in appearance, sexuality, and health (Jones, 1994). Yet exactly what types of changes do we find? Many of us harbor misleading ideas about menopause—ideas that can be harmful to women. Consider the following myths and the realities. To which myths have you fallen prey?

Myth 1. *Menopause is abnormal.* Of course not. Menopause is a normal development in women's lives.

Myth 2. *The medical establishment considers menopause a disease.* No longer. Menopause is described as a "deficiency syndrome" today, referring to the decline in secretion of estrogen and progesterone. Unfortunately, the term *deficiency* also has negative meanings.

Myth 3. *After menopause, women need complete replacement of estrogen.* Not necessarily. Some estrogen continues to be produced by the adrenal glands, fatty tissue, and the brain.

Myth 4. *Menopause is accompanied by depression and anxiety.* Not necessarily. Karen Matthews and her colleagues (1990) followed 541 healthy women through menopause and found that menopause was not significantly connected to depression, anxiety, stress, anger, or job dissatisfaction. (Outcomes may differ for women who have psychological problems prior to menopause.) Another group of researchers reported finding no overall relationship between mental health symptoms and menopausal status in a sample of 522 African American women (Jackson et al., 1991).

Much of a woman's response to menopause reflects its meaning to her, not physical changes (Jones, 1994). Women who adopt the commonly held belief that menopause signals the beginning of the end of life may develop a sense of hopelessness about the future, which in turn can set the stage for depression. Women whose entire lives have centered around childbearing and child rearing are more likely to suffer a strong sense of loss. Moreover, there is a cultural bias to explain depression and other complaints of middle-aged women in terms of menopause, rather than to explore psychosocial factors.

Myth 5. *At menopause, women suffer debilitating hot flashes.* Many women do not have hot flashes at all. Among those who do, the flashes are often relatively mild.

Myth 6. *A woman who has had a hysterectomy will not undergo menopause afterward.* It depends on whether or not the ovaries (the major producers of estrogen) were also removed. If they were not, menopause should proceed normally.

Myth 7. *Menopause signals an end to a woman's sexual appetite.* Not at all. Many women feel liberated by the severing of the ties between sex and reproduction.

Myth 8. *Menopause ends a woman's childbearing years.* Not necessarily! Postmenopausal women do not produce ova. However, ova from donors have been fertilized

---

Hormone-replacement therapy (HRT) Replacement of naturally occurring estrogen or estrogen and progesterone with synthetic equivalents, following menopause.

Estrogen deficiency also has psychological effects. It can impair cognitive functioning and feelings of psychological well-being (Sourander, 1994).

Some women who experience severe physical symptoms have been helped by **hormone-replacement therapy (HRT),** which typically consists of synthetic estrogen and progesterone. These synthetic hormones are used to offset the losses of their naturally occurring counterparts. HRT may help reduce the hot flushes and other symptoms brought about by hormonal deficiencies during menopause. It is especially helpful in protecting the woman against the development of osteoporosis (Davidson, 1995).

HRT is not without controversy. Although HRT has certainly been helpful to many menopausal women, some studies link use of estrogen to an increased risk of breast cancer and uterine cancer (Colditz et al., 1995; Goldman & Tosteson, 1991). On the other hand, estrogen replacement lowers the woman's risk of cardiovascular disorders (heart and artery disease), osteoporosis (Davidson, 1995; Everson et al., 1995), and colon cancer

in laboratory dishes, and the developing embryos have been implanted in the uteruses of postmenopausal women and carried to term (Bohlen, 1995; Sauer et al., 1990).

Myth 9. *A woman's general level of activity is lower after menopause.* Many postmenopausal women become peppier and more assertive.

Myth 10. *Men are not affected by their wives' experience of menopause.* Many men are, of course. Men could become still more understanding if they learned about menopause and if their wives felt freer to talk to them about it.

Menopause and Sexuality Menopause does not mark the end of a woman's sex life. Many women, in fact, feel sexually liberated by the biological severing of the traditional link between sexual activity and reproduction.

(Newcomb & Storer, 1995). HRT may reduce the risk of cardiovascular disease by lowering the levels of cholesterol in the bloodstream. A study of 49,000 postmenopausal nurses found that HRT was connected with 44% fewer heart attacks and a reduced risk of death from heart disease of 39% (Stampfer et al., 1991). Use of progestin along with estrogen does not mitigate the health benefits of estrogen on the heart (Davidson, 1995).

Hormone-replacement therapy is not recommended for women whose medical conditions or family histories make it inadvisable for them (Brody, 1992b). It is usually not recommended, for example, for women with a family history of breast cancer. Women are advised to explore the health benefits and risks of HRT with their gynecologists.

Overall, fewer than one in five postmenopausal women receive hormone-replacement therapy (Brody, 1992b). For those who do not receive replacement hormones, other drugs are available, when they are needed, to help them deal with menopausal complaints, such as hot flashes.

Menstrual Problems

Although menstruation is a natural biological process, the majority of women experience some discomfort prior to or during menstruation. Table 3.1 contains a list of commonly reported symptoms of menstrual problems. The problems we explore in this section include dysmenorrhea; mastalgia; menstrual migraine headaches; amenorrhea; and premenstrual syndrome (PMS).

Dysmenorrhea

Dysmenorrhea
Pain or discomfort during menstruation.

Primary dysmenorrhea
Menstrual pain or discomfort that occurs in the absence of known organic problems.

Secondary dysmenorrhea
Menstrual pain or discomfort that is caused by identified organic problems.

Pain or discomfort during menstruation, or **dysmenorrhea,** is the most common type of menstrual problem. Most women at some time have at least mild menstrual pain or discomfort. Pelvic cramps are the most common manifestation of dysmenorrhea. They may be accompanied by headache, backache, nausea, or bloated feelings. Women who develop severe cases usually do so within a few years of menarche. **Primary dysmenorrhea** refers to menstrual pain or discomfort in the absence of known organic pathology. Women with **secondary dysmenorrhea** have identified organic problems that are believed to cause their menstrual problems. Their pain or discomfort is caused by, or is *secondary to,* these problems. Endometriosis, pelvic inflammatory disease, and ovarian cysts are just a few of the organic disorders that can give rise to secondary dysmenorrhea. Yet evidence is accumulating that supposed primary dysmenorrhea is often *secondary* to hormonal changes, although the precise causes have not been delineated. For example, menstrual cramps sometimes decrease dramatically after childbirth, as a result of the massive hormonal changes that occur with pregnancy.

Painful menstruation was reported by nearly 75% of the participants in a sample of college women (Wildman & White, 1986). The symptoms varied not only from person to person but also according to whether or not the women had been pregnant. Women who had been pregnant reported a lower incidence of menstrual pain but a higher incidence of premenstrual symptoms and menstrual discomfort.

Biological Aspects of Dysmenorrhea   Menstrual cramps appear to result from uterine spasms that may be brought about by copious secretion of hormones called

---

TABLE 3.1   Common symptoms of menstrual problems

Physical Symptoms	Psychological Symptoms
Swelling of the breasts	Depressed mood, sudden tearfulness
Tenderness in the breasts	Loss of interest in usual social or recreational activities
Bloating	
Weight gain	Anxiety, tension (feeling "on edge" or "keyed up")
Food cravings	
Abdominal discomfort	Anger
Cramping	Irritability
Lack of energy	Changes in body image
Sleep disturbance, fatigue	Concern over skipping routine activities, school, or work
Migraine headache	
Pains in muscles and joints	A sense of loss of control
Aggravation of chronic disorders such as asthma and allergies	A sense of loss of ability to cope

---

Prostaglandins

Prostaglandins
Hormones that cause muscle fibers in the uterine wall to contract, as during labor.

Mastalgia
A swelling of the breasts that sometimes causes premenstrual discomfort.

prostaglandins. Prostaglandins apparently cause muscle fibers in the uterine wall to contract, as during labor. Most contractions go unnoticed, but powerful, persistent contractions are discomfiting in themselves and may temporarily deprive the uterus of oxygen, another source of distress. Women with more intense menstrual discomfort apparently produce higher quantities of prostaglandins. Prostaglandin-inhibiting drugs, such as ibuprofen, indomethacin, and aspirin are thus often of help. Menstrual pain may also be secondary to endometriosis.

Pelvic pressure and bloating may be traced to pelvic edema (Greek for "swelling")—the congestion of fluid in the pelvic region. Fluid retention can lead to a gain of several pounds, sensations of heaviness, and **mastalgia**—a swelling of the breasts that sometimes causes premenstrual discomfort. Masters and Johnson (1966) noted that orgasm (through coitus or masturbation) can help relieve menstrual discomfort by reducing the pelvic congestion that spawns bloating and pressure. Orgasm may also increase the menstrual flow and shorten this phase of the cycle.

Headaches frequently accompany menstrual discomfort. Most headaches (in both sexes) stem from simple muscle tension, notably in the shoulders, the back of the neck, and the scalp. Pelvic discomfort may cause muscle contractions, thus contributing to the tension that produces headaches. Women who are tense about their menstrual flow are thus candidates for muscle tension headaches. Migraine headaches may arise from changes in the blood flow in the brain, however. Migraines are typically limited to one side of the head and are often accompanied by visual difficulties.

Amenorrhea

Amenorrhea
The absence of menstruation.

Primary amenorrhea
Lack of menstruation in a woman who has never menstruated.

Secondary amenorrhea
Lack of menstruation in a woman who has previously menstruated.

Anorexia nervosa
A psychological disorder of eating characterized by intense fear of putting on weight and refusal to eat enough to maintain normal body weight.

Premenstrual syndrome (PMS)
A combination of physical and psychological symptoms (e.g., anxiety, depression, irritability, weight gain from fluid retention, and abdominal discomfort) that regularly afflicts many women during the four- to six-day interval that precedes their menses each month.

Amenorrhea is the absence of menstruation and is a primary sign of infertility. **Primary amenorrhea** describes the absence of menstruation in a woman who has not menstruated at all by about the age of 16 or 17. **Secondary amenorrhea** describes delayed or absent menstrual periods in women who have had regular periods in the past. Amenorrhea has various causes, including abnormalities in the structures of the reproductive system, hormonal abnormalities, growths such as cysts and tumors, and psychological problems, such as stress. Amenorrhea is normal during pregnancy and following menopause. Amenorrhea is also a symptom of **anorexia nervosa,** an eating disorder characterized by an intense fear of putting on weight and a refusal to eat enough to maintain a normal body weight, which often results in extreme (and sometimes life-threatening) weight loss. Hormonal changes that accompany emaciation are believed responsible for the cessation of menstruation. Amenorrhea may also occur in women who exercise strenuously, such as competitive long-distance runners. It is unclear whether the cessation of menstruation in female athletes is due to the effects of strenuous exercise itself, to related physical factors such as low body fat, to the stress of intensive training, or to a combination of factors.

Premenstrual Syndrome (PMS)

In late 1980, in a town about 50 miles from London, a 37-year-old woman, Christiana English, rammed her car into her boyfriend and killed him. She was subsequently convicted of manslaughter but released on probation. Her attorney persuaded the court that English was not fully responsible for her violent behavior, because it was induced by **premenstrual syndrome (PMS)** (Parlee, 1982). This case and similar ones received widespread attention in the press and provoked a storm of controversy. The sensationalism that attended the English case has died down, but the belief that premenstrual women are prone to otherwise uncharacteristic emotional turbulence and violence remains widespread. It has even been argued by some that the tumult associated with PMS makes women incapable of assuming positions of responsibility in government and industry.

What is PMS? How are women affected by it? Let us see if we can separate truth from fiction.

The term *PMS* describes the combination of bodily and psychological symptoms that may afflict women during the four- to six-day interval that precedes their menses each month. The constellation of symptoms includes some combination of anxiety, depression, irritability, weight gain from fluid retention, and abdominal discomfort. PMS also appears to be linked with imbalances in serotonin (Steiner et al., 1995), which is a chemical messenger in the nervous system. Serotonin imbalances are also linked to changes in appetite. In one study, women who suffered from PMS and nonsufferers alike showed increased appetite during the luteal phase, but the increases were greater for women with PMS (Both-Orthman et al., 1988). For many women, premenstrual symptoms persist during menstruation.

Nearly three women in four experience some form of PMS (Brody, 1989a). The great majority of cases involve mild to moderate levels of discomfort. About 10% of women report menstrual symptoms severe enough to impair their social, academic, or occupational functioning (Brody, 1989a). However, fewer than 1% of the employed women in a survey by Gruber and Wildman (1987) reported *ever* missing work because of menstrual problems. Fewer still commit violent crimes or wind up in mental wards. Most studies concur that cyclical changes in mood and behavior are generally minor.

PMS is not unique to our culture. Researchers find premenstrual symptoms to be equally prevalent among women studied in the United States, Italy, and in the Islamic nation of Bahrain (Brody, 1992c).

The causes of PMS are unclear, but evidence is accumulating for a biological basis to premenstrual symptoms (Asso & Magos, 1992). Researchers are looking to possible relationships between menstrual problems, including PMS, and chemical imbalances in the body. Researchers have yet to find differences in levels of estrogen or progesterone between women with severe PMS and those with mild symptoms or no symptoms (Rubinow & Schmidt, 1995). Perhaps it is not hormone levels themselves but the sensitivity of brain centers to these hormones that predisposes some women to PMS.

Treatments for PMS range from exercise and dietary control (for example, limiting salt and sugar), to use of vitamin supplements, to hormone treatments (usually progesterone), to drugs that increase the amount of serotonin in the nervous system (Steiner et al., 1995). Check with your physician about the most up-to-date research findings.

How to Handle Menstrual Discomfort

Most women suffer from some degree of menstrual discomfort. Women with persistent menstrual distress may profit from the suggestions listed below. Researchers are exploring the effectiveness of these techniques in controlled studies. For now, you might consider running a personal experiment. Adopt the techniques that sound right for you—all of them, if you wish. Try them out for a few months to see if you reap any benefits. Such personal experiments are uncontrolled, and it is scientifically difficult to pin down the reasons for results. (You may feel better simply because you *expect* to do so or because of overall improvements in health.) Still, the methods may enhance your comfort, your health, and your outlook on menstruation—not bad outcomes at all!

1. Don't blame yourself! Menstrual problems were once erroneously attributed to women's "hysterical" nature. This is nonsense. Menstrual problems appear, in large part, to reflect hormonal variations or chemical fluctuations in the brain during the menstrual cycle. Researchers have not yet fully identified all the causal elements and patterns, but their lack of knowledge does not mean that women who suffer from menstrual complaints are "hysterical."

2. Keep a menstrual calendar, so that you can track your menstrual symptoms systematically and identify patterns.

3. Develop strategies for dealing with days that you experience the greatest distress—strategies that will help enhance your pleasure and minimize the stress affecting you on those days. Activities that distract you from your menstrual discomfort may be helpful. Go see a movie or get into that novel you've been meaning to read.

4. Ask yourself whether you harbor any self-defeating attitudes toward menstruation that might be compounding distress. Do close relatives or friends see menstruation as an illness, a time of "pollution," a "dirty thing"? Have you adopted any of these attitudes—if not verbally, then in ways that affect your behavior, such as by restricting your social activities during your period?

A CLOSER LOOK

TRACKING YOUR PREMENSTRUAL COMPLAINTS WITH A PMS CALENDAR

Do you have PMS? Clinicians often determine whether PMS is present by asking the woman to track her physical and emotional complaints over at least two cycles. PMS is suspected if the same complaints appear during the week preceding menstruation and then disappear within a few days of the start of her period on two successive cycles.

Researchers at the University of California at San Diego have developed a PMS calendar that flags the 22 most common premenstrual complaints (Podolsky, 1991). Using the calendar, the researchers correctly identified 35 of 36 women who had previously been diagnosed with PMS; none of a comparison group of non-PMS sufferers was selected. The calendar is not a substitute for a medical evaluation, but may provide helpful information that the woman can bring to her physician's attention. Using the PMS calendar involves these steps (Podolsky, 1991):

1. Using graph paper, set up a chart like Figure 3.16, numbering the columns across the page to 28 or to the number of days that correspond to the length of your own menstrual cycle. Day 1 corresponds to the first day of your period.
2. For each day, rate the severity of any noticeable symptoms using a three point scale, where 1=noticeable, 2=moderate, and 3=intolerable.
3. Shade the boxes in the row marked "Bleeding" for days of menstrual bleeding. Use an X to mark days in which there is spotting.
4. Start a new calendar for your next cycle.
5. When you have completed a calendar for two successive cycles, add up the scores for each of the cycles for the week preceding your period (Day 1). You should consider seeking a medical consultation if *all of the following criteria are met:*

a. The scores for both weeks are 30 or greater.
b. You marked 5 or more of the first 10 listed symptoms each cycle.
c. The symptoms decline within four days after active bleeding starts.
d. These symptoms do not return for at least a week.
e. You find that your symptoms interfere with either your personal or professional life.

Whatever your score or pattern of symptoms, bring any troubling symptom or complaint to the attention of your physician. Check it out.

PMS Calendar

Jane Doe

CYCLE DAY	1	2	3	4	5		24	25	26	27	28
Bleeding	X				X						
Date March	3	4	5	6	7		26	27	28	29	30
Weight (Before Breakfast)	126	126	126	124	126		128	129	130	130	130

SYMPTOMS

	1	2	3	4	5		24	25	26	27	28
*Depression	2	1	1				2	2	2	1	2
*Anger, violent tendencies							2	2	1	2	3
*Irritability	1							2	2	2	2
*Anxiety, tension, nervousness	1						2	2	2	2	2
*Confusion, difficulty concentrating											
*Desire to be left alone											
*Tender breasts	1						2	2	3	3	3
*General bloated feeling							2	2	2	3	3
*Headaches	2	1					2	2	3	3	3
*Swelling of hands, ankles or breasts	1						2	2	2	3	3
Acne	2	1	1				1	1	1	1	1
Dizziness											
Fatigue	2	2	1	1			2	2	2	2	2
Hot flashes											
Nausea, diarrhea, constipation										1	1
Racing or pounding heart											
Crying easily	2						2	2	1	2	3
Food cravings (sweet, salty)							1	1	1	1	1
Forgetfulness											
Increased appetite									1	1	1
Mood swings	1						1	2	2	2	2
Overly sensitive	1						2	2	2	3	3

a. None											
b.											

MEDICATIONS

a. None											
b.											

*Especially significant PMS symptoms.

Figure 3.16. The PMS Calendar. Keeping a PMS calendar may provide helpful information regarding the pattern of PMS symptoms that women may experience. Symptoms should be tracked for at least two cycles to reveal the pattern of complaints.

Exercise as a Strategy for Coping with Menstrual Discomfort. Some women find that vigorous exercise helps relieve menstrual discomfort.

5. See a doctor about your concerns, especially if you suffer severe symptoms. Severe menstrual symptoms are often secondary to medical disorders such as endometriosis and pelvic inflammatory disease (PID). Check it out.
6. Develop nutritious eating habits—and continue them throughout the entire cycle (that means always). Consider limiting intake of alcohol, caffeine, fats, salt, and sweets, especially during the days preceding menstruation.
7. Some women find that vigorous exercise—jogging, swimming, bicycling, fast walking, dancing, skating, even jumping rope—helps relieve premenstrual and menstrual discomfort. Evidence suggests that exercise helps to relieve and possibly prevent menstrual discomfort (Choi, 1992). By the way, develop regular exercise habits—don't seek to become solely a premenstrual athlete.
8. Check with your doctor about vitamin and mineral supplements (such as calcium and magnesium). Vitamin B6 appears to have helped some women.
9. Ibuprofen (brand names: Medipren, Advil, Motrin, etc.) and other medicines available over the counter may be helpful for cramping. Prescription drugs such as fluoxetine may also be of help. Ask your doctor for a recommendation.
10. Remind yourself that menstrual problems are time-limited. Don't worry about getting through life or a career. Just get through the next couple of days.

∼ *Reflections* ∼

▪ What are the phases of the menstrual cycle?

▪ Are any particular attitudes toward menstruation held by most people from your sociocultural background? What are they? Do you share these attitudes? Why, or why not?

▪ Do you (or your loved ones) experience menstrual problems? Have they been discussed with a health care specialist? If not, why not?

In this chapter we have explored female sexual anatomy and physiology. In the following chapter, we turn our attention to the male.

Summing Up

External Sex Organs

The female external sexual structures are collectively known as the vulva and consist of the mons veneris, labia majora and minora, the clitoris, the vestibule, and the vaginal opening.

The Mons Veneris The mons veneris consists of fatty tissue that covers the joint of the pubic bones in front of the body.

The Labia Majora The labia majora are large folds of skin that run downward from the mons along the sides of the vulva.

The Labia Minora The labia minora are hairless, light-colored membranes that surround the urethral and vaginal openings.

The Clitoris The clitoris is the female sex organ that is most sensitive to sexual sensation, but it is not directly involved in reproduction.

The Vestibule The vestibule contains the openings to the vagina and the urethra.

The Urethral Opening Urine passes from the female's body through the urethral opening.

The Vaginal Opening The vaginal opening, or introitus, lies below the urethral opening.

The Perineum The perineum is the area that lies between the vaginal opening and the anus.

Structures That Underlie the External Sexual Structures These structures include the vestibular bulbs, Bartholin's glands, the sphincters, the clitoral crura, and the pubococcygeus (P-C) muscle.

Internal Sex Organs

The internal female sex organs—or female reproductive system—include the innermost parts of the vagina, the cervix, the uterus, the ovaries, and the fallopian tubes.

The Vagina   Menstrual flow and babies pass from the uterus to the outer world through the vagina. During coitus, the vagina contains the penis.

The Cervix   The cervix is the lower end of the uterus.

The Uterus   The uterus or womb is the pear-shaped organ in which a fertilized ovum implants itself and develops until birth.

The Fallopian Tubes   Two fallopian tubes extend from the upper end of the uterus toward the ovaries. Ova pass through the fallopian tubes on their way to the uterus and are normally fertilized within these tubes.

The Ovaries   The ovaries lie on either side of the uterus and produce ova and the sex hormones estrogen and progesterone.

The Pelvic Examination   Regular pelvic examinations are essential for early detection of problems involving the reproductive track.

The Breasts

In some cultures the breasts are viewed merely as biological instruments for feeding infants. In our culture, however, they have taken on erotic significance. The breasts are secondary sex characteristics that contain mammary glands.

Breast Cancer   Breast cancer is the second leading cancer killer in women, after lung cancer. Women with breast cancer will have lumps in the breast, but most lumps in the breasts are benign. Breast cancer may be detected in a number of ways, including breast self-examination, medical examinations, and mammography. Early detection yields the greatest chance of survival.

The Menstrual Cycle

Menstruation is the cyclical bleeding that stems from the shedding of the endometrium when a reproductive cycle has not led to the fertilization of an ovum. The menstrual cycle is regulated by estrogen and progesterone.

Regulation of the Menstrual Cycle   The menstrual cycle involves finely tuned relationships between the hypothalamus, the pituitary gland, and the ovaries and uterus. Hormones produced by the hypothalamus regulate the pituitary, which in turn secretes hormones that regulate the secretions of the ovaries and uterus.

Phases of the Menstrual Cycle   The menstrual cycle has four stages or phases: proliferative, ovulatory, secretory, and menstrual. During the first phase of the cycle, which follows menstruation, ova ripen within their folli-

cles and endometrial tissue proliferates. During the second phase, ovulation occurs. During the third phase, the corpus luteum produces copious amounts of progesterone and estrogen that cause the endometrium to thicken. If the ovum goes unfertilized, a plunge in estrogen and progesterone levels triggers the fourth, or menstrual, phase, which leads to the beginning of a new cycle.

Coitus During Menstruation   Couples are apparently less likely to initiate sexual activity during menstruation than during any other phase of the woman's cycle.

Menopause   Menopause is the cessation of menstruation, which most commonly occurs between the ages of 46 and 50. Estrogen deficiency in menopause may give rise to night sweats, hot flashes, hot flushes, cold sweats, dry skin, loss of breast tissue, and decreased vaginal lubrication. Long-term estrogen deficiency has been linked to osteoporosis. Hormone-replacement therapy can offset losses of estrogen and progesterone but has been linked to a slightly increased risk of breast and endometrial cancers, though also to a marked reduction in risk of cardiovascular disease and osteoporosis. For most women, menopausal problems are mild. Psychological problems can reflect the meaning of menopause to the individual.

Menstrual Problems

Most women experience some discomfort prior to or during menstruation. Common menstrual problems include dysmenorrhea, amenorrhea, and premenstrual syndrome (PMS).

Dysmenorrhea   Dysmenorrhea is the most common menstrual problem, and pelvic cramps are the most common symptom. Dysmenorrhea can be caused by problems such as endometriosis, pelvic inflammatory disease, and ovarian cysts.

Amenorrhea   Amenorrhea can be caused by problems such as abnormalities in the structures of the reproductive system, hormonal abnormalities, cysts, tumors, and stress.

Premenstrual Syndrome (PMS)   As many as three women in four have some form of PMS. The causes of PMS are unclear, but most researchers look to potential links between menstrual problems and hormone levels. Women have long suffered from the stereotype that they are incapable of managing responsibility because of cyclical hormone fluctuations, but evidence contradicts the stereotype.

How to Handle Menstrual Distress   Women with persistent menstrual problems may benefit from a number of active coping strategies for handling menstrual distress.

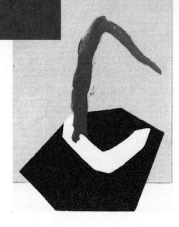

CHAPTER 4

Henri Matisse, *Music,* 1910. Hermitage Museum, St. Petersburg, Russia.
Scala/Art Resource, NY. © 1996 Succession H. Matisse/Artist Rights
Society (ARS), New York.

Male Sexual Anatomy and Physiology

Truth OR Fiction?

_F_ The penis contains bone and muscle.

_F_ Uncircumcised men are more sensitive than circumcised men to sexual stimulation.

_T_ The father determines the baby's gender.

_T_ The sperm of the tiny fruit fly are longer than human sperm.

_F_ Morning erections reflect the need to urinate.

_F_ Men can will themselves to have erections.

_F_ The penis has a mind of its own.

_T_ Many men paralyzed below the waist can attain erection, engage in sexual intercourse, and ejaculate.

_T_ Men can have orgasms without ejaculating.

From the earliest foundations of Western civilization, male-dominated societies elevated men and exalted male genitalia. The ancient Greeks carried oversized images of fish as **phallic symbols** in their Dionysian processions, which celebrated the wilder and more frenzied aspects of human sexuality. In the murky predawn light of Western civilization, humankind engaged in phallic worship. Phallic symbols played roles in religious worship and became glorified in art in the form of ploughs, axes, and swords.

The tradition of phallic worship became raised to higher aesthetic levels. The ancient Greeks adorned themselves with phallic rings and necklaces. In ancient Rome, celebrations were held to honor Venus, the goddess of love. The Romans outfitted a float in the shape of a large phallus and paraded it through the streets. There were no tributes to the female genitals. Even though Venus was being honored, no artisans devoted themselves to creating floats in the likeness of the vulva or the clitoris.

Men held their own genitals in such high esteem that it was common courtroom practice for them to swear to tell the truth with their hands on their genitals—as we swear to tell the truth in the name of God or by placing our hands on the Bible. The words **testes** and **testicles** derive from the same Latin word as "testify." The Latin *testis* means "a witness."

Even today, we see evidence of pride—indeed veneration!—of the male genitalia. Men with large genitals are accorded respect from their male peers and sometimes adoration from female admirers. In *The Sun Also Rises*, Ernest Hemingway describes how matadors stuffed the front of their trousers with fabric. With their "manhood" fully packed, they plunged the sword into the poor animal's head before their adoring public. U.S. slang describes men with large genitals as "well-hung" or "hung like a bull" (or stallion).

Given these cultural attitudes, it is not surprising that young men (and some not-so-young men) belittle themselves if they feel, as many do, that they are little— that is, that their penises do not measure up to some ideal. Boys who mature late may be ridiculed by their peers for their small genitals. Their feelings of inadequacy may persist into adulthood. Adult men, too, may harbor doubts that their penises are large enough to satisfy their lovers. Or they may fear that their partners' earlier lovers had larger genitals.

In this chapter we examine male sexual anatomy and physiology, and we attempt to sort out truth from fiction. We see, for example, that despite his lingering doubts, a man's capabilities as a lover do not depend on the size of his penis (at least within broad limits). For a man to judge his sexual prowess on the basis of locker-room comparisons makes about as much sense as choosing a balloon by measuring it when it is deflated.

In our exploration of male sexual anatomy and physiology, as in our exploration of female sexual physiology and anatomy, we begin with the external genitalia and then move inward. Once inside, we focus on the route of sperm through the male reproductive system.

Phallic symbols
Images of the penis that are usually suggestive of generative power.

Testes
The male sex glands, suspended in the scrotum, that produce sperm cells and male sex hormones. Singular: *testis*.

Testicles
Testes.

External Sex Organs

The male external sex organs include the penis and the scrotum (Figures 4.1, 4.2).

The Penis

The penis mightier than the sword.
(Mark Twain)

Is that a gun in your pocket, or are you just glad to see me?
(Mae West)

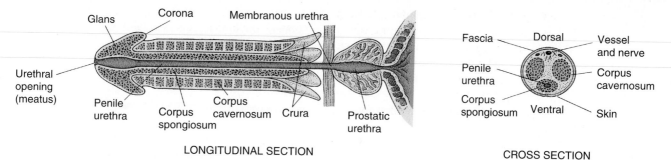

Glans Corona Membranous urethra

Urethral opening (meatus) Penile urethra Corpus spongiosum Corpus cavernosum Crura Prostatic urethra

LONGITUDINAL SECTION

Fascia Dorsal Vessel and nerve

Penile urethra Corpus cavernosum

Corpus spongiosum Ventral Skin

CROSS SECTION

Figure 4.1. **The Penis.** During sexual arousal the corpora cavernosa and corpus spongiosum become congested with blood, causing the penis to enlarge and stiffen.

Penis

The male organ of sexual intercourse. (From the Latin for "tail.")

Cloaca

The cavity in birds, reptiles, and many fish into which the genitourinary and intestinal tracts empty. (From the Latin *cluere*, meaning "to cleanse.")

At first glance the **penis** may seem rather simple and obvious in its structures, particularly when compared to women's organs. This apparent simplicity may have contributed to cultural stereotypes that men are straightforward and aggressive, whereas women tend to be complicated, and perhaps, mysterious. Yet, as Figure 4.1 shows, the apparent simplicity of the penis is misleading. Much goes on below the surface. Gender stereotypes regarding anatomy are as misleading as those regarding personality (see Chapter 6).

The penis, like the vagina, is the sex organ used in sexual intercourse. Unlike the vagina, however, the penis serves as a conduit for urine. Semen and urine pass out of the penis through the urethral opening. The opening is called the urethral *meatus* (pronounced me-ATE-us), meaning "passage."

The penis arrived on the evolutionary scene some 100 million years ago. It was first found in reptiles—the ancestors of present-day crocodiles and lizards, and dinosaurs. Earlier in the evolutionary process, male and female animals each had a genital opening called a **cloaca.** The cloaca functioned as both an excretory and a sex organ. It took some fancy bodywork for couples to align their cloacae so that the male's sperm could find their way into the female's cloacal cavity. The penis is a more efficient shape—a shaft—for funneling sperm into the female. It gives them a head start on their journey toward the ovum.

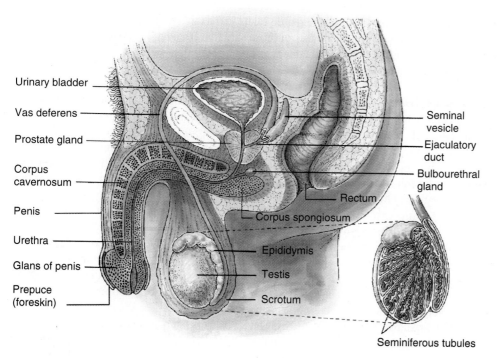

Urinary bladder

Vas deferens

Prostate gland

Corpus cavernosum

Penis

Urethra

Glans of penis

Prepuce (foreskin)

Seminal vesicle

Ejaculatory duct

Bulbourethral gland

Rectum

Corpus spongiosum

Epididymis

Testis

Scrotum

Seminiferous tubules

Figure 4.2. **The Male Reproductive System.** The external male sex organs include the penis and the scrotum.

Many mammals, including dogs, have penile bones that stiffen the penis to facilitate copulation. Despite the slang term "boner," the human penis contains no bones. Nor, despite another slang term, "muscle," does the penis contain muscle tissue. However, muscles at the base of the penis, like the muscles surrounding the vaginal and urethral openings in women, are involved in controlling urination and ejaculation.

Truth **OR** *Fiction?*
R E V I S I T E D

Despite the slang terms, there is no bone or muscle tissue in the penis. ■

Rather than bones or muscles, the penis contains three cylinders of spongy material that run its length. The larger two of these cylinders, the **corpora cavernosa** (see Figure 4.1), lie side by side and function like the cavernous bodies in the clitoris. These cylinders fill up with blood and stiffen during sexual arousal. In addition, a **corpus spongiosum** (spongy body) runs along the bottom, or ventral, surface of the penis. It contains the penile urethra that conducts urine through the penis to the urinary opening (urethral meatus) at the tip. At the tip of the penis, the spongy body enlarges to become the glans, or head, of the penis.

Corpora cavernosa
Cylinders of spongy tissue in the penis that become congested with blood and stiffen during sexual arousal.

All three cylinders consist of spongy tissue that swells (becomes engorged) with blood during sexual arousal, resulting in erection. The urethra is connected to the bladder, which is unrelated to reproduction, and to those parts of the reproductive system that transport semen.

Corpus spongiosum
The spongy body that runs along the bottom of the penis, contains the penile urethra, and enlarges at the tip of the penis to form the glans.

The glans of the penis, like the clitoral glans, is extremely sensitive to sexual stimulation. Direct, prolonged stimulation can become irritating, even painful. Men generally prefer to masturbate by stroking the shaft of the penis rather than the glans, although some prefer the latter. The **corona,** or coronal ridge, separates the glans from the body of the penis. It is also quite sensitive to sexual stimulation. After the glans, the parts of the penis that men tend to find most sensitive are the corona and an area on the underside of the penis called the **frenulum.** The frenulum is a thin strip of tissue that connects the underside of the glans to the shaft. Most men find the top part of the penis to be the least sensitive part.

Corona
The ridge that separates the glans from the body of the penis. (From the Latin for "crown.")

The base of the penis, called the **root,** extends into the pelvis. It is attached to pelvic bones by leglike structures, called crura, that are like those that anchor the female's clitoris. The body of the penis is called the penile **shaft.** The penile shaft, unlike the clitoral shaft, is free-swinging. Thus, when sexual excitement engorges the penis with blood, the result—erection—is obvious. The expression "getting shafted," which means being taken advantage of, presumably refers to the penile shaft. Another phrase, "getting screwed," refers more directly to sexual intercourse.

Frenulum
The sensitive strip of tissue that connects the underside of the penile glans to the shaft. (From the Latin *frenum,* meaning "bridle.")

The skin of the penis is hairless and loose, allowing expansion during erection. It is fixed to the penile shaft just behind the glans. Some of it, however, like the labia minora in the female, folds over to partially cover the glans. This covering is the prepuce, or **foreskin.** It covers part or all of the penile glans just as the clitoral prepuce (hood) covers the clitoral shaft. The prepuce consists of loose skin that freely moves over the glans. However, in the male, as in the female, smegma may accumulate below the prepuce, causing the foreskin to adhere to the glans.

Root
The base of the penis, which extends into the pelvis.

Shaft
The body of the penis, which expands as a result of vasocongestion.

Circumcision   **Circumcision** is the surgical removal of the prepuce. Advocates of circumcision believe that it is hygienic because it eliminates a site where smegma might accumulate and bacteria might grow. Opponents of circumcision believe that it is unnecessary because regular cleaning is sufficient to reduce the risk of these problems.

Foreskin
The loose skin that covers the penile glans. Also referred to as the *prepuce.*

Male circumcision has a long history as a religious rite. Jews traditionally carry out male circumcision shortly after a baby is born. Circumcision is performed as a sign of the covenant between God and the people of Abraham—and for purposes of hygiene (see Figure 4.3). Muslims also have ritual circumcisions for religious reasons. Circumcision is common among Christians for hygienic reasons.

Circumcision
Surgical removal of the foreskin of the penis. (From the Latin *circumcidere,* meaning "to cut around.")

Evidence concerning the health benefits of circumcision seems mixed and inconclusive. For example, Jewish women, whose husbands are universally circumcised, were found in some early research to have a somewhat lower incidence of cervical cancer than Christian women (Weiner et al., 1951). The wives of Lebanese Muslims, however, who also practiced circumcision, were no less prone to cervical cancer than were the wives of Lebanese Christians, who did not (Abou-David, 1967). There is also some evidence that penile cancer, a rare form of cancer, is slightly more common among uncircumcised men

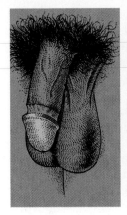
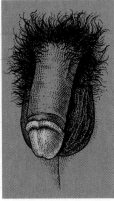

Figure 4.3. Circumcision. Circumcision is the surgical removal of the foreskin, or prepuce, of the penis. Circumcision has a long history as a religious rite among Jews. Many Christians also practice circumcision for hygienic reasons.

Phimosis
An abnormal condition in which the foreskin is so tight that it cannot be withdrawn from the glans. (From the Greek *phimos*, meaning "muzzle.")

Premature ejaculation
A sexual dysfunction in which the male persistently ejaculates too early to afford the couple adequate sexual gratification.

Truth **OR** *Fiction?*
R E V I S I T E D

(Harahap & Siregar, 1988). Physicians continue to debate the health benefits of circumcision. They do agree, however, that circumcision is the treatment of choice for **phimosis,** a condition in which it is difficult to retract the foreskin from the glans.

In 1971 the American Academy of Pediatrics announced that it did not recommend routine circumcision as a means of enhancing health. Their position has not changed. Perhaps as a result, the incidence of circumcision declined in the United States from 90% of newborn males in 1970 to 59% in the 1980s (Lindsey, 1988).

Recent research suggests, however, that urinary tract infections are more common among uncircumcised male infants than among circumcised infants (Herzog, 1989; Wiswell et al., 1987). Still, it has been argued that the risks associated with urinary tract infections in infancy are too low to justify routine circumcision (King, 1988; Lohr, 1989). Emerging evidence also suggests that uncircumcised men may be at greater risk than circumcised men of becoming infected by the AIDS virus. Certain cells in the foreskin may be especially susceptible to it (Touchette, 1991).

Questions have also been raised about the *sexual* effects of circumcision. One argument is that circumcised males may have more difficulty controlling ejaculation since the penile glans is directly exposed to sexual stimulation. As a result, the argument goes, such men would be more likely to suffer from **premature ejaculation.** Common sense—or should we say, common nonsense?—has actually had it both ways: that circumcised men are more *and* less sensitive to sexual stimulation than the uncircumcised. The first belief rests shakily on the assumption that circumcised men are more "exposed," thus *more* sensitive and less capable of controlling ejaculation. The latter argument is based on the fact that circumcised men have lost some sexually sensitive skin. Thus they should be *less* sensitive to erotic stimulation. Perhaps the debate has continued this long because of the virtual absence of well-controlled scientific research comparing the sexual sensitivity of circumcised and uncircumcised men. The only clinical study ever reported found no significant differences in sensitivity to various forms of tactile stimulation between circumcised and uncircumcised men (Masters & Johnson, 1966). Moreover, the foreskin retracts during sexual arousal in uncircumcised men, directly exposing the clitoral glans to stimulation. It is thus unlikely that there are significant differences in coital sensitivity between circumcised and uncircumcised men that might lead to premature ejaculation.

There is actually no reliable empirical evidence that uncircumcised men are more sensitive to sexual stimulation. ∎

Penis Size

IRAS: Am I not an inch of fortune better than she?

CHARMIAN: Well, if you were but an inch of fortune better than I, where would you choose it?

IRAS: Not in my husband's nose.

(William Shakespeare, *Antony and Cleopatra*)

In our culture the size of the penis is sometimes seen as a measure of a man's masculinity and his ability to please his sex partner (see the nearby A Closer Look feature). Shakespeare and other writers inform us that men have looked down at themselves for centuries, sometimes in delight but more often in chagrin. Men who are heralded for their sexual or reproductive feats are presumed to have more prominent "testaments" to their manhood.

It may be of some comfort to note that even the smallest normal human penis is between three and four times the length of the phallus of the burly gorilla. Even so, the human penis does not merit comparison with the phallus of the blue whale. This ocean-dwelling mammal, the largest animal on earth, is about 100 feet from end to end and possesses a penis about 7 feet in length. When not in use, the penis is cached in the male's abdomen, which is a fortunate thing. If it were to trail down permanently, it might act as a rudder and muddle the animal's internal navigational system.

Masters and Johnson (1966) reported that the penises of the 312 male subjects they studied generally ranged in length from 3½ inches to a little more than 4 inches when flaccid (soft). The average erect penis ranges from 5 to 7 inches in length (Reinisch, 1990). Erect penises differ less in size than flaccid penises do (Jamison & Gebhard, 1988). Penises that are small when flaccid tend to gain more size when they become erect. Larger flaccid penises gain relatively less. Size differences in flaccid penises may thus be largely canceled out by erection. Nor is there a relationship between penis size and body weight, height, or build (Money et al., 1984).

Even when flaccid, the same penis can vary in size. Factors such as cold air or water, or emotions of fear or anxiety can cause the penis (along with the scrotum and testicles) to draw closer to the body, reducing its size. The flaccid penis may also grow in size in warm water or when the man is relaxed.

A CLOSER LOOK

ON PENIS SIZE AND SEXUAL PERFORMANCE

Perhaps most men have had concerns about the size of their penises. As sex therapist Bernard Zilbergeld put it in his book *Male Sexuality*, "Women, we are given to believe, crave nothing so much as a penis that might be mistaken for a telephone pole" (1978, p. 27). Think critically about the belief that men with bigger penises make more effective lovers. What assumptions is it based upon? Is there supportive evidence?

The belief that the size of the man's penis determines his sexual prowess is based upon the assumption that men with bigger penises are better equipped to satisfy a woman sexually. Zilbergeld and others point out, however, that women rarely mention

penis size as an important element in their sexual satisfaction. Quite regularly they *do* mention ability to communicate with partners, the emotional atmosphere of the relationship, and sensitivity to employing sexual techniques that enhance the partner's pleasure.

Does your knowledge of female sexual physiology support or challenge the assumption that bigger is necessarily better? From your reading of Chapter 3, what do you know about how the vagina accommodates the penis? What is the role of the P-C muscle? Which part of the vagina is most sensitive to tactile stimulation? What, if any, might be the relationships between the clitoris—the

woman's most erotically sensitive organ—and the size of the penis? Which seems more crucial: sexual technique and the quality of the relationship, or penis size? Why?

The diameter of the penis, rather than its length, may actually have a greater bearing on a partner's sexual sensations, since thicker penises may provide more clitoral stimulation during coital thrusting. Nonetheless, even though the inner vagina is relatively insensitive to touch, some women find the *pressure* of deeper penetration sexually pleasurable. Others, however, find deeper penetration to be uncomfortable or painful, especially if thrusting is too vigorous.

Scrotum

The pouch of loose skin that contains the testes. (From the same linguistic root as the word *shred*, meaning "a long, narrow strip," and probably referring to the long furrows on the scrotal sac.)

Spermatic cord

The cord that suspends a testicle within the scrotum and contains a vas deferens, blood vessels, nerves, and the cremaster muscle.

Vas deferens

A tube that conducts sperm from the testicle to the ejaculatory duct of the penis. (From Latin roots meaning "a vessel" that "carries down.")

Cremaster muscle

The muscle that raises and lowers the testicle in response to temperature changes and sexual stimulation.

Dartos muscle

The muscle in the middle layer of the scrotum that contracts and relaxes in response to temperature changes.

Germ cell

A cell from which a new organism develops. (From the Latin *germen*, meaning "bud" or "sprout.")

Sperm

The male germ cell. (From a Greek root meaning "seed.")

Androgens

Male sex hormones. (From the Greek *andros*, meaning "man" or "males," and *-gene*, meaning "born.")

Testosterone

A male steroid sex hormone.

Interstitial cells

Cells that lie between the seminiferous tubules and secrete testosterone. (*Interstitial* means "set between.")

Leydig's cells

Another term for *interstitial cells.*

The Scrotum

The **scrotum** is a pouch of loose skin that becomes covered lightly with hair at puberty. The scrotum consists of two compartments that hold the testes. Each testicle is held in place by a **spermatic cord,** a structure that contains the **vas deferens,** blood vessels and nerves, and the cremaster muscle. The **cremaster muscle** raises and lowers the testicle within the scrotum in response to temperature changes and sexual stimulation. (The testes are drawn closer to the body during sexual arousal.)

Sperm production is optimal at a temperature that is slightly cooler than the 98.6 degrees Fahrenheit that is desirable for most of the body. Typical scrotal temperature is 5 to 6 degrees lower than body temperature. The scrotum is loose-hanging and flexible. It permits the testes and nearby structures to escape the higher body heat, especially in warm weather. In the middle layer of the scrotum is the **dartos muscle,** which (like the cremaster) contracts and relaxes reflexively in response to temperature changes. In cold weather, or when a man jumps into a body of cold water, it contracts to bring the testes closer to the body. In warm weather, it relaxes, allowing the testes to dangle farther from the body. The dartos muscle also increases or decreases the surface area of the scrotum in response to temperature changes. Smoothing allows greater dissipation of heat in hot weather. Tightening or constricting the skin surface helps retain heat and gives the scrotum a wrinkled appearance in the cold.

The scrotum is developed from the same embryonic tissue that becomes the labia majora of the female. Thus, like the labia majora, it is quite sensitive to sexual stimulation. It is somewhat more sensitive than the top side of the penis but less so than other areas of the penis.

~ *Reflections* ~

Agree or disagree with the following statement, and support your answer: Men with bigger penises make more effective lovers.

Are you or are the men in your family circumcised? If so, why? If not, why not? Are you aware of any effects of circumcision? (Are you sure?)

Were you knowledgeable about the penis and scrotum prior to reading this section? What was new to you? What mistaken ideas had you held?

Internal Sex Organs

The male internal sex organs consist of the testes, the organs that manufacture sperm and the male sex hormone testosterone; the system of tubes and ducts that conduct sperm through the male reproductive system; and the organs that help nourish and activate sperm and neutralize some of the acidity that sperm encounter in the vagina.

The Testes

The testes are the male gonads (*gonad* derives from the Greek *gone,* meaning "seed"). In slang the testes are frequently referred to as "balls" or "nuts." These terms are considered vulgar, but they are reasonably descriptive. They also make it easier for many people to refer to the testes in informal conversation.

The testes serve two functions analogous to those of the ovaries. They secrete sex hormones and produce mature **germ cells.** In the case of the testes, the germ cells are **sperm** and the sex hormones are **androgens.** The most important androgen is **testosterone.**

Testosterone   Testosterone is secreted by **interstitial cells,** which are also referred to as **Leydig's cells.** Interstitial cells lie between the seminiferous tubules and re-

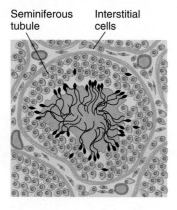

Seminiferous   Interstitial
tubule   cells

Figure 4.4. Interstitial Cells. Testosterone is produced by the interstitial cells, which lie between the seminiferous tubules in each testis. Sperm (seen in the middle of the diagram) are produced within the seminiferous tubules.

Figure 4.5. Hormonal Control of the Testes. Several endocrine glands—the hypothalamus, the pituitary gland, and the testes—keep blood testosterone levels at a more or less constant level. Low testosterone levels signal the hypothalamus to secrete LH-releasing hormone (LH-RH). Like dominoes falling in a line, LH-RH causes the pituitary gland to secrete LH, which in turn stimulates the testes to release testosterone. Follicle-stimulating, hormone-releasing hormone (FSH-RH) from the hypothalamus causes the pituitary to secrete FSH, which in turn causes the testes to produce sperm cells.

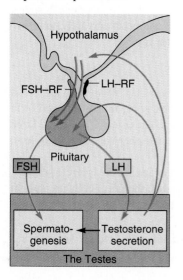

lease testosterone directly into the bloodstream (see Figure 4.4). Testosterone stimulates prenatal differentiation of male sex organs, sperm production, and development of **secondary sex characteristics,** such as the beard, deep voice, and growth of the muscle mass.

In men, several endocrine glands—the hypothalamus, pituitary gland, and testes (see Figure 4.5)—keep blood testosterone levels at a more or less even level. This contrasts with the peaks and valleys in levels of female sex hormones during the phases of the menstrual cycle. Testosterone levels vary slightly with stress, time of day or month, and other factors, but a feedback loop among the endocrine glands keeps them relatively stable.

The same pituitary hormones, FSH and LH, that regulate the activity of the ovaries also regulate the activity of the testes. FSH regulates the production of sperm by the testes. LH stimulates secretion of testosterone by the interstitial cells. Low testosterone levels signal the hypothalamus to secrete a hormone, called LH-releasing hormone (LH-RH). Like dominoes falling in a line, LH-RH causes the pituitary gland to secrete LH, which in turn stimulates the testes to release testosterone into the blood system. LH is also referred to as *interstitial-cell-stimulating hormone,* or ICSH.[1]

When the level of testosterone in the blood system reaches a certain peak, the hypothalamus directs the pituitary gland *not* to secrete LH. This system for circling information around these three endocrine glands is called a *feedback loop.* This feedback loop is *negative.* That is, increases in hormone levels in one part of the system trigger another part to shut down, and vice versa.

The testes usually range between 1 and $1^3/_4$ inches in length. They are about half as wide and deep. The left testicle usually hangs lower, because the left spermatic cord tends to be somewhat longer.

Sperm   Each testicle is divided into many lobes. The lobes are filled with winding **seminiferous tubules** (see Figure 4.2). Although packed into a tiny space, these tubules, placed end to end, would span the length of several football fields. Through a process called **spermatogenesis,** these threadlike structures produce and store hundreds of billions of sperm through the course of a lifetime.

Sperm cells develop through several stages. It takes about 72 days for the testes to manufacture a mature sperm cell (Leary, 1990). In an early stage, sperm cells are called **spermatocytes.** Each one contains 46 chromosomes, including one X and one Y sex chromosome. Each spermatocyte divides into two **spermatids,** each of which has 23 chromosomes. Half the spermatids have X sex chromosomes, and the other half have Y sex chromosomes. Looking something like tadpoles when examined under a microscope, mature sperm cells, called **spermatozoa,** each have a head, a cone-shaped midpiece, and a tail. The head is about 5 microns ($1/_{50,000}$ of an inch) long and contains the cell nucleus that houses the 23 chromosomes. The midpiece contains structures that provide the energy that the tail needs to lash back and forth in a swimming motion. Each sperm cell is about 50 microns ($1/_{5,000}$ of an inch) long, one of the smallest cells in the body (Thompson, 1993).

During fertilization, the 23 chromosomes from the father's sperm cell combine with the 23 chromosomes from the mother's ovum, furnishing the standard ensemble of 46 chromosomes in the offspring. Among the 23 chromosomes borne by sperm cells is one sex chromosome—an X sex chromosome or a Y sex chromosome. Ova contain X sex chromosomes only. The union of an X sex chromosome and a Y sex chromosome leads to the development of male offspring. Two X sex chromosomes combine to yield female offspring. So the presence of an X or Y sex chromosome from the father determines the baby's gender.

[1]We do not throw such terms at you willy-nilly or to complicate matters. In future years, you will be reading and hearing about the biology of sex in the popular media, and since it is unlikely that all commentators will agree on the terminology that is to be used, we want you to be able to recognize the meanings of various terms.

A CLOSER LOOK

IS THERE A MANOPAUSE?

Men cannot undergo menopause; they have never menstruated. Yet one now and then hears of a so-called male menopause, occasionally referred to as "manopause." Some men during their later years are informally referred to as menopausal. Sadly, this description is usually meant to convey the negative, harmful stereotype of the aging person as crotchety and irritable. Such stereotypes of menopause are unfortunate reminders of sexism and ageism, and are not necessarily consistent with the biology or psychology of aging.

The scientific jury is still out on the existence of the male menopause. Women encounter relatively sudden age-related declines in sex hormones and fertility during menopause. Men experience a gradual decline in testosterone levels as they age, but nothing like the sharp plunge in estrogen levels that women experience during menopause. Testosterone levels begin to fall at about age 40 or 50 and may decline to one third or one half of their peak levels by age 80 (Brody, 1995c).

The drop in testosterone levels that occurs as men age may be connected to a variety of age-related symptoms, including reduced muscle mass and strength, accumulation of body fat, reduced energy levels, lowered fertility, and reduced erectile ability. However, despite a decline in testosterone levels, most men remain potent throughout their lives. Little is known about the critical levels of testosterone that are needed to maintain erectile ability. Certain age-related changes, such as reduced muscle mass and strength and increased body fat, may be due to other factors associated with aging rather than to declining testosterone production, such as a gradual loss of *human growth hormone,* a hormone that helps maintain muscle strength and that may prevent fat buildup. Some experts believe that testosterone replacement may help avert erectile problems, bone loss, and frailty, in much the same way that estrogen replacement benefits postmenopausal women (Brody, 1995c). Others worry that excessive use of the hormone may increase the risks of prostate cancer and cardiovascular disease.

Although men do experience a gradual decline in the number and motility of sperm as they age, which reduces their fertility, some viable sperm continue to be produced even into late adulthood. It is not surprising, from a physical standpoint, to find a man in his 70s or older fathering a child.

Men can remain sexually active and father children at advanced ages. For both genders, marital satisfaction and attitudes toward aging can affect sexual behavior as profoundly as physical changes can.

Is There a *Manopause*? The term *menopause* is sometimes used to convey the negative, harmful stereotype of the aging person as crotchety and irritable. The scientific jury is still out on whether there is a "male menopause," but men do experience a gradual decline in testosterone levels as they age. The decline in testosterone is connected with age-related symptoms such as reduced muscle strength, accumulation of fat, reduced energy, lowered fertility, and reduced erectile ability. Nevertheless, most men maintain erectile ability throughout their lives.

Truth OR Fiction? REVISITED It is true that the father determines the baby's gender through the presence of an X or Y sex chromosome from the father. If the fertilizing sperm has an X sex chromosome, the child will be a girl. If it has a Y sex chromosome, the child will be a boy. ∎

The testes are veritable dynamos of manufacturing power, churning out about 1,000 sperm per second or about 30 billion—yes, *billion*—per year (Elmer-Dewitt, 1991). Mathematically speaking, 10 to 20 ejaculations hold enough sperm to populate Earth. (Men are always so taken with themselves, notes the third author.)

Belgian researchers have discovered that sperm cells possess the same kind of receptors that the nose uses to sense odors (Angier, 1992). This discovery suggests that sperm may find their way to an egg cell by detecting its scent. Researchers at the Texas

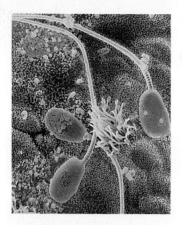

**Human Sperm Cells
Magnified Many Times.**

**Secondary sex
characteristics**
Traits that distinguish the genders but are not directly involved in reproduction.

Seminiferous tubules
Tiny, winding, sperm-producing tubes that are located within the lobes of the testes. (From Latin roots meaning "seed bearing.")

Spermatogenesis
Process by which sperm cells are produced and developed.

Spermatocyte
An early stage in the development of sperm cells, in which each parent cell has 46 chromosomes, including one X and one Y sex chromosome.

Spermatids
Cells formed by the division of spermatocytes. Each spermatid has 23 chromosomes.

Spermatozoa
Mature sperm cells.

Epididymis
A tube that lies against the back wall of each testicle and serves as a storage facility for sperm. (From Greek roots meaning "upon testicles.")

Southwestern Medical Center in Dallas had earlier discovered that the fertile egg cells emit a compound that attracts the interest of sperm cells. These odor receptors may be the mechanism by which sperm recognize these attractants. If this turns out to be the case, it could lead to the development of contraceptives that prevent fertilization by blocking these receptors.

Sperm proceed from the seminiferous tubules through an intricate maze of ducts that converge in a single tube called the **epididymis.** The epididymis lies against the back wall of the testicle and serves as a storage facility for sperm. The epididymis, which is some 2 inches in length, consists of twisted passages that would be 10 to 20 feet in length if stretched end to end. Sperm are inactive when they enter the epididymis. They continue to mature as they slowly make their way through the epididymis for another two to four weeks.

The Vas Deferens

Each epididymis empties into a vas deferens (also called *ductus deferens*). The vas is a thin, cylindrical tube about 16 inches long that serves as a conduit for mature sperm. In the scrotum, the vas deferens lies near the skin surface within the spermatic cord. Therefore, a **vasectomy,** an operation in which the right and left vas deferens are severed, is a convenient means of sterilization. The tube leaves the scrotum and follows a circuitous path up into the abdominal cavity. Then it loops back along the rear surface of the bladder (see Figure 4.6).

The Seminal Vesicles

The two **seminal vesicles** are small glands, each about 2 inches long. They lie behind the bladder and open into the **ejaculatory ducts,** where the fluids they secrete combine with sperm (see Figure 4.6). A vesicle is a small cavity or sac; the seminal vesicles were so named because they were mistakenly believed to be reservoirs for semen, rather than glands.

The fluid produced by the seminal vesicles is rich in fructose, a form of sugar, which nourishes sperm and helps them become active, or motile. Sperm motility is a major factor in male fertility. Before reaching the ejaculatory ducts, sperm are propelled along their journey by contractions of the epididymis and vas deferens and by **cilia** that line the walls of the vas deferens. Once they become motile, they propel themselves by whipping their tails.

At the base of the bladder, each vas deferens joins a seminal vesicle to form a short ejaculatory duct that runs through the middle of the prostate gland (see Figure 4.6). In the prostate the ejaculatory duct opens into the urethra, which leads to the tip of the penis. The urethra carries sperm and urine out through the penis, but normally not at the same time.

Chromosomes. The normal human cell contains 46 chromosomes which are arranged in pairs. When a sperm cell and ovum unite, 23 chromosomes from the father's sperm cell combine with 23 chromosomes from the mother's ovum, to form the normal complement of 46 chromosomes in the offspring. The presence of an X or Y sex chromosome from the father determines the baby's gender.

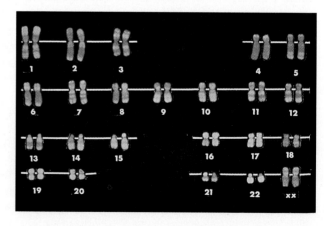

Vasectomy

A sterilization procedure in which the vas deferens is severed, preventing sperm from reaching the ejaculatory duct.

Seminal vesicles

Small glands that lie behind the bladder and secrete fluids that combine with sperm in the ejaculatory ducts.

Ejaculatory duct

A duct formed by the convergence of a vas deferens with a seminal vesicle through which sperm pass through the prostate gland and into the urethra.

Cilia

Hairlike projections from cells that beat rhythmically to produce locomotion or currents.

Prostate gland

The gland that lies beneath the bladder and secretes prostatic fluid, which gives semen its characteristic odor and texture.

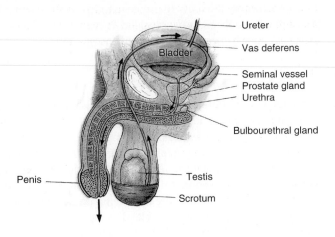

Ureter
Vas deferens
Bladder
Seminal vessel
Prostate gland
Urethra
Bulbourethral gland
Penis
Testis
Scrotum

Figure 4.6. Passage of Spermatozoa. Each testicle is divided into lobes that contain threadlike seminiferous tubules. Through spermatogenesis, the tubules produce and store hundreds of billions of sperm over the course of a lifetime. During ejaculation, sperm cells travel through the vas deferens, up and over the bladder, into the ejaculatory duct, and then through the urethra. Secretions from the seminal vesicles and the bulbourethral glands join with sperm to compose semen.

The Prostate Gland

The **prostate gland** lies beneath the bladder and approximates a chestnut in shape and size (about 3/4 inch in diameter). Note the spelling of the name of the gland—pros*tate,* not pros*trate.* (*Prostrate* means lying with one's face on the ground, as in some forms of prayer.) The prostate gland contains muscle fibers and glandular tissue that secrete prostatic fluid. Prostatic fluid is milky and alkaline. It provides the characteristic texture and odor of the seminal fluid. The alkalinity neutralizes some of the acidity of the vaginal tract, prolonging the life span of sperm as seminal fluid spreads through the female reproductive system. The prostate is continually active in mature males, but sexual arousal further stimulates secretions. Secretions are conveyed into the urethra by a sievelike duct system. There the secretions combine with sperm and fluid from the seminal vesicles.

A C L O S E R L O O K

BIG!

Truth OR Fiction?
REVISITED

It is true that the sperm of the tiny fruit fly are longer than human sperm. In fact, they are longer than the sperm of any mammal.

Don't be fooled by his size. The tiny fruit fly, *Drosophila bifurca,* is only a fraction of an inch long. You can crush it easily with the tip of your finger. But this little insect holds the distinction of being number 1 in the *Guinness Book*

of Records for length of sperm. He produces coiled sperm that stretch out to nearly 2½ inches, or 20 times the length of his own body! How does the fruit fly accomplish this feat? By devoting about 11% of his body weight to his testes.

This fruit fly's sperm are 1,000 times as long as human sperm (Pitnick, 1995). Remember that a human sperm cell is about 1/5,000 of an inch long, and is one of the smallest cells in the body (Thompson, 1993). In order to match the achievement of the fruit fly, a man would have to produce sperm that are 100 to 120 feet long (Leary, 1995).

There may be many more fruit flies than people, but fruit flies are no match for people in terms of numbers of sperm. Men can ejaculate several hundred million sperm at a time, whereas the fruit fly releases only about 50 (Pitnick, 1995). Moreover, human sperm are strong swimmers, whereas the rolled-up fruit fly sperm slowly unwinds in the female and apparently relies on transportation mechanisms within the female to reach its goal.

Why, the third author wishes to ask, must men be so competitive—even with fruit flies?

A vasectomy prevents sperm from reaching the urethra but does not cut off fluids from the seminal vesicles or prostate gland. A man who has had a vasectomy thus emits an ejaculate that appears normal but contains no sperm.

Cowper's Glands

Cowper's glands
Structures that lie below the prostate and empty their secretions into the urethra during sexual arousal.

Bulbourethral glands
Another term for *Cowper's glands.*

The **Cowper's glands** are also known as the **bulbourethral glands,** in recognition of their shape and location. These two structures lie below the prostate and empty their secretions into the urethra. During sexual arousal they secrete a drop or so of clear, slippery fluid that appears at the urethral opening. The functions of this fluid are not entirely understood. It may help buffer the acidity of the male's urethra and lubricate the urethral passageway to ease the passage of seminal fluid. The fluid is not produced in sufficient amounts to play a significant role in lubricating the vagina during intercourse.

Fluid from the Cowper's glands precedes the ejaculate and often contains viable sperm. Thus, coitus may lead to pregnancy even if the penis is withdrawn prior to ejaculation. This is one reason why people who practice the "withdrawal method" of birth control are frequently called "parents."

Semen

Semen
The whitish fluid that constitutes the ejaculate, consisting of sperm and secretions from the seminal vesicles, prostate, and Cowper's glands.

Sperm and the fluids contributed by the seminal vesicles, the prostate gland, and the Cowper's glands make up **semen,** or whitish seminal fluid, which is expelled through the tip of the penis during ejaculation. The seminal vesicles secrete about 70% of the fluid that constitutes the ejaculate. The remaining 30% of seminal fluid consists of sperm and fluids produced by the prostate gland and the Cowper's gland. Sperm themselves account for only about 1% of the volume of semen. This is why men with vasectomies continue to ejaculate about as much semen as before, although their ejaculates are devoid of sperm.

Semen is the medium that carries sperm through much of the male's reproductive system and the reproductive tract of the female. Semen contains water, mucus, sugar (fructose), acids, and bases. It activates and nourishes sperm, and the bases help shield sperm from vaginal acidity. The typical ejaculate contains between 200 and 400 million sperm and ranges between 3 and 5 milliliters in volume. (Five milliliters is equal to about 1 tablespoon.) The quantity of semen decreases with age and frequency of ejaculation.

~ *Reflections* ~

- How are the testes analogous to the ovaries?
- What are the components of semen? Where do they come from?
- What is the evidence for the existence of "manopause"?

Diseases of the Urogenital System

Urologist
A physician who specializes in the diagnosis and treatment of diseases of the urogenital system.

Because the organs that comprise the urinary and reproductive systems are near each other and share some "piping," they are referred to as the urinogenital or urogenital system. A number of diseases affect the urogenital system. The type of physician who specializes in their diagnosis and treatment is a **urologist.**

Urethritis

Urethritis
An inflammation of the bladder or urethra.

Men, like women, are subject to bladder and urethral inflammations, which are generally referred to as **urethritis.** The symptoms include frequent urination (urinary frequency), a strong need to urinate (urinary urgency), burning during urination, and a penile discharge. People with symptoms of urinary frequency and urinary urgency feel the pressing need to urinate repeatedly, even though they may have just done so and may have but another drop or two to expel. The discharge may dry on the urethral opening, in which case it may have to be peeled off or wiped away before it is possible to urinate. The urethra also may become constricted when it is inflamed, slowing or halting urination. It is a frightening sensation for a male to feel the urine rush from his bladder and then suddenly stop at the urethral opening!

Preventive measures for urethritis parallel those suggested for cystitis (bladder infection): drinking more water, drinking cranberry juice (4 ounces, two or three times a day), and lowering intake of alcohol and caffeine. Cranberry juice is highly acidic, and acid tends to eliminate many of the bacteria that can give rise to urethritis.

Cancer of the Testes

Cancer of the testicles remains a relatively rare form of cancer, accounting for about 6,000 new cases annually, or about 1% of all new cancers in men (American Cancer Society, 1991). It is the most common form of solid-tumor cancer to strike men between the ages of 20 and 34, however (Vazi et al., 1989). It accounts for nearly 10% of all deaths from cancer among men in that age group.

Cryptorchidism
A condition in which one or two testicles fail to descend from the abdomen into the scrotum.

There is no evidence that testicular cancer results from sexual overactivity or masturbation. Men who had **cryptorchidism** as children (a condition in which one or both testicles fail to descend from the abdomen into the scrotum) stand about a 40 times greater chance of contracting testicular cancer. Undescended testicles appear to occur more commonly in boys born to mothers who used the hormone diethylstilbestrol (DES) during pregnancy. In the 1940s and 1950s, pregnant women were often prescribed DES to help prevent miscarriages.

Although testicular cancer was generally fatal in earlier years, the prognosis today is quite favorable, especially for cases that are detected early. Treatments include surgical removal of the diseased testis, radiation, and chemotherapy. The survival rate among cases that are detected early, before the cancer has spread beyond the testes, is 96% (American Cancer Society, 1991). Delayed treatment markedly reduces the chances of survival, because survival is connected with the extent to which the cancer has spread.

The surgical removal of a testicle may have profound psychological implications. Some men who have lost a testicle feel less "manly." Fears related to sexual performance can engender sexual dysfunctions. From a physiological standpoint, sexual functioning should remain unimpaired, as adequate quantities of testosterone are produced by the remaining testis.

The early stages of testicular cancer usually produce no symptoms, other than the mass itself. Because early detection is crucial to survival, men are advised to examine themselves monthly, following puberty (Reinisch, 1990) and to have regular medical checkups. Self-examination may also reveal evidence of sexually transmitted diseases and other problems.

Disorders of the Prostate

The prostate gland is tiny at birth and grows rapidly at puberty. It may shrink during adulthood, but usually becomes enlarged past the age of 50. Hormonal changes associated with aging have been implicated in enlargement of the prostate. There may also be other causes, such as inflammation resulting from sexually transmitted diseases.

Enlargement of the Prostate   The prostate surrounds the upper part of the urethra (see Figure 4.2). As the prostate enlarges, it constricts the urethra, causing symptoms such as urinary frequency (including increased frequency of nocturnal urination), urinary urgency, and difficulty starting the flow of urine. Surgical removal of a part of the prostate can help relieve the pressure on the urethra and is considered more or less routine. Many nonsurgical treatments are also under development, including chemotherapy and use of microwave radiation.

A **_CLOSER LOOK_**

SELF-EXAMINATION OF THE TESTES

Self-examination (see Figure 4.7) is best performed shortly after a warm shower or bath, when the skin of the scrotum is most relaxed. The man should exam the scrotum for evidence of pea-sized lumps. Each testicle can be rolled gently between the thumb and the fingers. Lumps are generally found on the side or front of the testicle. The presence of a lump is not necessarily a sign of cancer, but it should be promptly reported to a physician for further evaluation. The American Cancer Society (1990) lists these warning signals:

1. A slight enlargement of one of the testicles.
2. A change in the consistency of a testicle.
3. A dull ache in the lower abdomen or groin.
   (Pain may be absent in cancer of the testes, however).
4. Sensation of dragging and heaviness in a testicle.

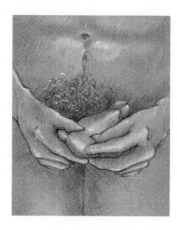

**Figure 4.7.
Testicular Self-
Examination.**

Cancer of the Prostate   A more serious and life-threatening problem is prostate cancer. The American Cancer Society estimates that about one man in eight in the United States will develop prostate cancer (Ochs, 1993b). Prostate cancer is the second most common form of cancer among men, after skin cancer, and the second leading cause of cancer deaths in men, after lung cancer. According to the American Cancer Society (1995), there were 244,000 new cases of prostate cancer in the United States in 1995, and 40,400 men died from the disease.

Prostate cancer involves the growth of malignant prostate tumors that can metastasize to bones and lymph nodes if not detected and treated early. African American men are one-third more likely than White men to develop prostate cancer (American Cancer Society, 1995). African American men may also have less access to routine medical evaluations than White men do, so that disease is diagnosed at a later stage. Researchers have identified intake of animal fat as a potential risk factor. Men whose diets are rich in animal fats,

A Blood Test for Detection of Cancer of the Prostate.
The PSA test assists in the early detection of prostate cancer.

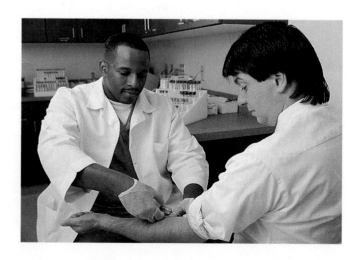

especially fats from red meat, have a substantially higher chance of developing advanced prostate cancer than do men with a low intake of animal fat. The incidence of prostate cancer also increases with age. Over 80% of all prostate cancers are diagnosed in men over the age of 65 (American Cancer Society, 1995). Genetic factors may also be involved (Wilson, 1995).

The early symptoms of cancer of the prostate may mimic those of benign prostate enlargement: urinary frequency and difficulty in urinating. Later symptoms include blood in the urine, pain or burning on urination, and pain in the lower back, pelvis, or upper thighs (American Cancer Society, 1995). Most cases occur without noticeable symptoms in the early stages.

The American Cancer Society (1995) recommends that men receive annual rectal examinations beginning at about age 40. The physician inserts a finger into the rectum and feels for abnormalities in the prostate gland. The procedure may be uncomfortable, but it is brief and not particularly painful. Unfortunately, many men are reluctant to undergo a rectal examination, even though it is only mildly uncomfortable and may save their lives. Some are embarrassed or reluctant to discuss urinary problems with their physicians. Some may even resist the rectal examination because they associate rectal insertion with male–male sex. Still others are fearful that they may have cancer and choose to remain ignorant. Avoidance of, or ignorance of the need for, annual rectal exams among men is a major contributor to the death rate from prostate cancer.

A blood test can detect evidence of prostate cancer even among men whose prostates feel normal upon physical examination. A study of more than 10,000 men found that the blood test was about twice as successful in detecting early prostate cancer than were physical examinations (Catalona et al., 1993). The blood test measures prostate-specific antigen, or PSA, which is a type of protein that seeps out of the prostate gland when it is cancerous or enlarged ("Blood test's value in early prostate cases," 1993). The American Cancer Society (1995) recommends that men of age 50 and above have an annual PSA blood test.

When a cancerous growth is suspected on the basis of a rectal examination or a PSA blood test, the American Cancer Society (1995) recommends further testing with ultrasound. Fifty-eight percent of cases of prostate cancer are discovered while they are still localized. The five-year survival rate is 94% for prostate cancer that has not metastasized (American Cancer Society, 1995). The five-year survival rate drops dramatically if the cancer has metastasized. The overall survival rate has improved in the past 30 years from 50% to 80% (American Cancer Society, 1995).

The most widely used treatment for prostate cancer is surgical removal of the prostate gland. Years ago there was a notable risk of surgical complications from prostate removal, usually because of damage to the surrounding nerves. Problems in controlling the flow of urine or achieving erection or ejaculation often resulted. Surgical techniques that have been introduced in the past 15 years tend to spare the surrounding nerves and reduce, though they do not eliminate, the risk of complications. Other treatments include radiation, hormone treatment, and anticancer drugs. Hormone treatment and anticancer drugs may shrink the size of the tumor and relieve pain for long periods of time.

Prostatitis
Inflammation of the prostate gland.

Prostatitis   Many infectious agents can inflame the prostate, causing **prostatitis.** The chief symptoms are an ache or pain between the scrotum and anal opening and painful ejaculation. Prostatitis is usually treated with antibiotics. Although aspirin and ibuprofen may relieve the pain, men with these symptoms should consult a physician. Painful ejaculation may discourage masturbation or coitus, which is ironic, since regular flushing of the prostate through ejaculation may be helpful in the treatment of prostatitis.

～ *Reflections* ～

■ Why is it important for men to detect cancers of the testes and prostate early? What can men do to detect them early?

■ A question to male readers: What are *you* doing to try to ensure the health of your sex organs?

Male Sexual Functions

The male sexual functions of erection and ejaculation provide the means for sperm to travel from the male's reproductive tract to the female's. There the sperm cell and ovum unite to conceive a new human being. Of course, the natural endowment of reproduction with sensations of pleasure helps ensure that it will take place with or without knowledge of these biological facts.

Erection

Erection
The enlargement and stiffening of the penis as a consequence of engorgement with blood.

Erection is the engorgement of the penis with blood, such that the penis grows in size and stiffens. The erect penis is an efficient conduit, or funnel, for depositing sperm deep within the vagina.

In mechanical terms, erection is a hydraulic event. The spongy, cavernous masses of the penis are equipped to hold blood. Filling them with blood causes them to enlarge, much like a sponge swells as it absorbs water. This simple description belies the fact that erection is a remarkable feat of biological engineering (there they go again, notes the third author) that involves the cooperation of the vascular (blood) system and the nervous system.

In a few moments—as quickly as 10 or 15 seconds—the penis can double in length, become firm, and shift from a funnel for passing urine to one that expels semen. Moreover, the bladder is closed off when the male becomes sexually aroused, decreasing the likelihood that semen and urine will mix.

Yes, the blood that fills the penis during sexual arousal causes erectile tissue to expand. But what accounts for the firmness of an erection? A sponge that fills with water expands but does not grow hard. It turns out that the two corpora cavernosa are surrounded by a tough, fibrous covering called the *tunica albuginea*. As the rubber of a balloon resists the pressure of pumped-in air, this housing resists expansion, causing the penis to rigidify. The corpus spongiosum, which contains the penile urethra, also engorges with blood during erection. It does not become hard, however, since it lacks the fibrous casing. The penile glans, which is formed by the crowning of the spongiosum at the tip of the penis, turns a dark purplish hue as it becomes engorged, but it too does not stiffen.

Despite the advanced state of biological knowledge, some mechanics of erection are not completely understood. It is not entirely clear, for example, whether penile cavities become engorged because the veins that carry blood away from the penis do not keep pace with the rapid flow of blood entering the penis, or whether the returning blood flow is reduced by compression of the veins at the base of the penis (as stepping lightly on a hose slows the movement of water).

Performance anxiety
Feelings of dread and foreboding experienced in connection with sexual activity (or any other activity that might be judged by another person).

We do know that erection is reversed when more blood flows out of the erectile tissue than flows in, restoring the pre-erectile circulatory balance and shrinking the erectile tissue or spongy masses. The erectile tissue thus exerts less pressure against the fibrous covering, resulting in a loss of rigidity. Loss of erection occurs when sexual stimulation ceases, or when the body returns to a (sexual) resting state following orgasm. Loss of erection can also occur in response to anxiety or perceived threats. Loss of erection in response to threat can be abrupt, as when a man in the "throes of passion" suddenly hears a suspicious noise in the adjoining room, suggestive of an intruder. Yet the "threats" that induce loss of erection are more likely to be psychological than physical. In our culture, men often measure their manhood by their sexual performance. A man who fears that he will be unable to perform successfully may experience **performance anxiety** that can prevent him from achieving erection or lead to a loss of erection at penetration.

The male capacity for erection quite literally spans the life cycle. Erections are common in babies, even within minutes after birth. Evidence from ultrasound studies shows that male fetuses may even have erections months prior to birth. Men who are well into their 80s and 90s continue to experience erections and engage in coitus.

Nor are erections limited to the conscious state. Men have nocturnal erections every 90 minutes or so as they sleep. They generally occur during REM (rapid eye movement) sleep. REM sleep is associated with dreaming. It is so named because the sleeper's eyes dart about rapidly under the closed eyelids during this stage. Erections occur during most periods of REM sleep.

The mechanism of nocturnal erection appears to be physiologically based. That is, erections occur along with dreams that may or may not have erotic content. Morning erections are actually nocturnal erections. They occur when the man is awakened during REM sleep, as by an alarm clock. Men sometimes erroneously believe that a morning erection is caused by the need to urinate. When the man awakens with both an erection and the need to urinate, he may mistakenly assume that the erection was caused by the pressure of his bladder.

Truth **OR** Fiction?
R E V I S I T E D

It is not true that morning erections reflect the need to urinate. Morning erections are actually a form of nocturnal erection. ∎

Spinal Reflexes and Sexual Response

Reflex
A simple, unlearned response to a stimulus that is mediated by the spine rather than the brain.

Men may become sexually aroused by a range of stimulation, including tactile stimulation provided by their partners, visual stimulation (such as from scanning photos of nude models in men's magazines), or even mental stimulation from engaging in sexual fantasies. Regardless of the source of stimulation, the man's sexual responses, erection and ejaculation, occur by **reflex.**

Erection and ejaculation are reflexes: automatic, unlearned responses to sexual stimulation. So too are vaginal lubrication and orgasm in women. We do not control sexual reflexes voluntarily, as we might control the lifting of a finger or an arm. We can set the stage for them to occur by ensuring the proper stimulation. Once the stage is set, the reflexes are governed by automatic processes, not by conscious effort. Efforts to control sexual responses consciously by "force of will" can backfire and make it more difficult to become aroused (for example, to attain erection or vaginal lubrication). We need not "try" to become aroused. We need only expose ourselves to effective sexual stimulation and allow our reflexes to do the job for us.

Truth **OR** Fiction?
R E V I S I T E D

It is not true that men can will themselves to have erections. Men can only set the stage for erections by providing physical or cognitive sexual stimulation. ∎

The reflexes governing erection and ejaculation are controlled at the level of the spinal cord. Thus, they are considered spinal reflexes. How does erection occur? Erections may occur in response to different types of stimulation. Some erections occur from direct stimulation of the genitals, as from stroking, licking, or fondling the penis or scrotum. Erectile responses to such direct stimulation involve a simple spinal reflex that does not require the direct participation of the brain.

Erections can also be initiated by the brain, without the genitals being touched or fondled at all. Such erections may occur when a man has sexual fantasies, when he views erotic materials, or when he catches a glimpse of a woman in a bikini on a beach. In the case of the "no-hands" type of erections, stimulation from the brain travels to the spinal cord, where the erectile reflex is triggered. To better understand how this reflex works, we need to first explain the concept of the reflex arc.

The Reflex Arc When you withdraw your hand from a hot stove or blink in response to a puff of air, you do so before you have any time to think about it. These responses, like erection, are reflexes that involve sensory neurons and effector neurons (see Figure 4.8 on page 118). In response to a stimulus like a touch or a change in temperature, sensory neurons or receptors in the skin "fire" and thereby send messages to the spinal cord. The message is then transmitted to effector neurons that begin in the spinal cord and cause muscles to contract or glands to secrete chemical substances. So if you accidentally touched a hot stove, sensory neurons in your fingers or hand would deliver a message to the spinal cord, which would trigger effector neurons to contract muscles that pull your

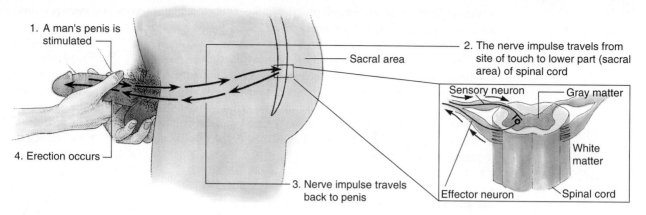

1. A man's penis is stimulated

2. The nerve impulse travels from site of touch to lower part (sacral area) of spinal cord

Sacral area

Sensory neuron — Gray matter

White matter

4. Erection occurs

Effector neuron — Spinal cord

3. Nerve impulse travels back to penis

Figure 4.8. **Reflexes.** Reflexes involve sensory neurons, effector neurons, and, sometimes, interneurons that connect the two in the spinal cord. Reflexes need not involve the brain, although messages to the brain may make us aware when reflexes are occurring. Reflexes are the product of "local government" in the spine. *(Source:* From *Human Sexuality* by S. A. Rathus. Copyright © 1983 by Holt, Rinehart & Winston, Inc. Reprinted by permission of the publisher.)

hand away from the stove. The brain does not control this spinal reflex arc. That is not to say that the brain fails to "get the message" shortly afterwards. Sensory messages usually rise from the spinal cord to the brain to make us aware of stimulation. (Awareness "dwells" within the nerve cells, or gray matter, of the brain.) The experience of pain occurs when a message travels from the site of the injury to the spinal cord and then to receiving stations in the brain that "interpret" the message to produce the sensation of pain. The withdrawal of your hand from a harmful object begins before your brain even gets the message.

Sacrum

The thick, triangular bone located near the bottom of the spinal column.

The Role of the Spinal Cord   Let us look more closely at the spinal reflex that produces erection in response to tactile stimulation (touch). Tactile stimulation of the penis or nearby areas (lower abdomen, scrotum, inner thighs) causes sensory neurons to transmit nerve messages (signals) to an erection center in the lower back, in an area of the spinal cord called the **sacrum.** The sacral erection center controls reflexive erections—that is, erections occurring in response to direct stimulation of the penis and nearby areas (Spark, 1991). When direct penile stimulation occurs, messages in the form of nerve impulses are received by this erection center, which in turn sends impulses to the genitalia via nerves that service the penis. These impulses cause arteries carrying blood to the corpora cavernosa and corpus spongiosum to dilate, so that more blood flows into these tissues; as these tissues expand, the penis becomes erect.

The existence of the sacral erection center makes it possible for men whose spinal cords have been injured or severed above the center to achieve erections (and ejaculate) in response to direct tactile stimulation of the penis. Erection occurs even though their injuries prevent nerve signals from reaching their brains. Because of the lack of communication between the genital organs and the brain, there are no sensations, no physical pleasure. Many spinal-injured men report that sex remains psychologically pleasurable and fulfilling nonetheless. They can observe the responses of their partners, and perhaps the brain fills in some sensations from memory or imagination.

The Role of the Brain   If direct penile stimulation triggers erection at the spinal level, what is the role of the brain? Although it may seem that the penis sometimes has a mind of its own, the brain plays an important role in regulating sexual responses.

Tactile (touch) stimulation of the penis may trigger the erection reflex through a simple reflex arc in the spinal cord. Penile sensations are then normally relayed to the brain, which generally results in sensations of pleasure and perhaps in a decision to focus on erotic stimulation. The sight of one's partner, erotic fantasies, memories, and so forth can result in messages being sent by the brain through the spinal cord to the arteries servicing the penis, helping to maintain the erection.

The brain can also originate messages that trigger the erectile reflex. The "no-hands" type of erection can occur while recalling sexual memories, entertaining sexual fantasies, viewing erotic stimuli, or even while asleep. In such cases the brain plays a more direct role in the erectile response by transmitting nerve impulses to a second and higher erection center located in the upper back in the lumbar region of the spinal cord. This higher spinal erection center serves as a "switchboard" between the brain and the penis, allowing perceptual, cognitive, and emotional responses to make their contributions. When the nerve pathways between the brain and the upper spinal cord are blocked or severed, men cannot achieve "psychogenic erections"—that is, erections in response to mental stimulation alone.

The brain can also stifle sexual response. A man who is highly anxious about his sexual abilities may be unable to achieve an erection even with the most direct, intense penile stimulation. Or a man who believes that sexual pleasure is sinful or dirty may be filled with anxiety and guilt and be unable to achieve erection when he is sexually stimulated by his partner.

In some males, especially adolescents, the erectile reflex is so easily tripped that incidental rubbing of the genitals against his own undergarments, the sight of an attractive passer-by, or a fleeting sexual fantasy produces erection. Spontaneous erections may occur under embarrassing circumstances, such as before classes change in junior or senior high school, or on a public beach. In an effort to distract himself from erotic fantasies and to allow an erection to subside, many a male adolescent in the classroom has desperately renewed his interest in his algebra or foreign language textbook before the bell has rung. (A well-placed towel may serve in a pinch on a public beach.)

As men mature they require more penile stimulation to achieve full erection. Partners of men in their 30s and 40s need not feel that their attractiveness has waned if their lovers no longer have instant "no-hands" erections when they disrobe. It takes men longer to achieve erection as they age, and direct penile stimulation becomes a more critical source of arousal.

The Role of the Autonomic Nervous System

Although stimulation that brings about an erection can originate in the brain, this does not mean that erection is a voluntary response, like raising your arm. Whatever the original or dominant source of stimulation—direct penile stimulation or sexual fantasy—erection remains an unlearned, automatic reflex.

Automatic responses, such as erection, involve the division of the nervous system called the **autonomic nervous system** (ANS). *Autonomic* means "automatic." The ANS controls automatic bodily processes such as heartbeat, pupil dilation, respiration, and digestion. In contrast, voluntary movement (like raising an arm) is under the control of the *somatic* division of the nervous system.

The ANS has two branches, the **sympathetic** and the **parasympathetic.** These branches have largely opposing effects; when they are activated at the same time, their effects become balanced out to some degree. In general, the sympathetic branch is in command during processes that involve a release of bodily energy from stored reserves, such as during running, performing some other athletic task, or being gripped by fear or anxiety. The sympathetic branch also governs the general mobilization of the body, such as by increasing the heart rate and respiration rate in response to threat.

The parasympathetic branch is most active during processes that restore reserves of energy, such as digestion. When we experience fear or anxiety, the sympathetic branch of the ANS quickens the heart rate. When we relax, the parasympathetic branch curbs the heart rate. The parasympathetic branch activates digestive processes, but the sympathetic branch inhibits digestive activity. Since the sympathetic branch is in command when we feel fear or anxiety, such stimuli can inhibit the activity of the parasympathetic system, thereby slowing down digestive process and possibly causing indigestion.

Autonomic nervous system
The division of the nervous system that regulates automatic bodily processes, such as heartbeat, pupil dilation, respiration, and digestion. Abbreviated *ANS*.

Sympathetic
The branch of the ANS most active during emotional responses that spend the body's reserves of energy, such as fear and anxiety. The sympathetic ANS largely controls ejaculation.

Parasympathetic
The branch of the ANS most active during processes that restore the body's reserves of energy, such as digestion. The parasympathetic ANS largely controls erection.

The divisions of the autonomic nervous system play different roles in sexual arousal and response. The nerves that cause penile arteries to dilate during erection belong to the parasympathetic branch of the autonomic nervous system. It is thus the parasympathetic system that largely governs erection. The nerves governing ejaculation belong to the sympathetic branch, however. One implication of this division of neural responsibility is that intense fear or anxiety, which involves sympathetic nervous system activity, may inhibit erection by counteracting the activity of the parasympathetic nervous system. Since sympathetic arousal is involved in triggering the ejaculatory reflex, anxiety or fear may also accelerate ejaculation, causing premature ejaculation. Intense emotions like fear and anxiety can thus lead to problems in achieving or maintaining erection as well as causing hasty ejaculation.

The connection between the emotions, sympathetic activity, and ejaculation can set up a vicious cycle. Anxiety in a sexual encounter may trigger premature ejaculation. During a subsequent sexual encounter, the man might fear a recurrence of premature ejaculation. This fear may engender the reality. He may thus face further sexual encounters with yet greater fear, possibly further hastening ejaculation—and possibly inhibiting erection itself. Methods for helping men with erectile dysfunction and premature ejaculation aim at reducing their levels of anxiety and thereby lessening sympathetic activity.

Because erections seem spontaneous at times, and often occur when the man would rather not have them, it may seem to men that the penis has a mind of its own. Despite this common folk belief, however, the penis possesses no guiding intelligence. It consists of spongy masses of erectile tissue, not the lovely dense gray matter that renders your thought processes so incisive.

Truth OR Fiction?
R E V I S I T E D

It is not true that the penis has a mind of its own. Although it may seem that the penis follows its own mind at times, it is governed by the autonomic (automatic) nervous system. ∎

Peyronie's disease
An abnormal condition characterized by an excessive curvature of the penis that can make erections painful.

Erectile Abnormalities Some men find that their erect penises are slightly curved or bent. Some degree of curvature is perfectly normal, but men with **Peyronie's disease** have excessive curvature that can make erections painful or make it difficult to enjoy coitus. The condition is caused by buildup of fibrous tissue in the penile shaft. Although some cases of Peyronie's disease appear to clear up on their own, most require medical attention.

Some men experience erections that persist for hours or days. This condition is called *priapism*, after Priapus of Greek myth, the son of Dionysus and Aphrodite who personified male procreative power. Priapism is often caused by leukemia, sickle cell anemia, or diseases of the spinal cord, although in some cases the cause remains unknown. Priapism occurs when the mechanisms that drain the blood that make the penis erect are damaged and so cannot return the blood to the circulatory system. The name of the disorder is truly a misnomer, because Priapus had a voracious sexual appetite. Men with priapism instead suffer from a painful condition that should receive medical attention. Priapism may become a medical emergency, since erection prolonged beyond six hours can starve penile tissues of oxygen, leading to tissue deterioration. Immediate medical intervention in the form of drugs or even surgery may be required to reverse the condition and allow blood to drain from the penis (Spark, 1991).

Ejaculation

Orgasm
The climax of sexual excitement.

Paraplegic
A person with sensory and motor paralysis of the lower half of the body.

Ejaculation, like erection, is a spinal reflex. It is triggered when sexual stimulation reaches a critical point or threshold. Ejaculation generally occurs together with **orgasm**, the sudden muscle contractions that occur at the peak of sexual excitement and result in the abrupt release of sexual tension that had built up during sexual arousal. Orgasm is accompanied by subjective sensations that are generally intensely pleasurable. Ejaculation, however, refers only to the expulsion of semen from the tip of the penis. Orgasm and ejaculation are *not* synonymous, however. Nor do they always occur simultaneously. For example, **paraplegics** can ejaculate if the area of the lower spinal cord that controls ejaculation is

120 ~ CHAPTER 4   MALE SEXUAL ANATOMY AND PHYSIOLOGY

intact. They do not experience the subjective aspects of orgasm, however, since the sensations of orgasm do not reach the brain.

T r u t h OR *Fiction?*

R E V I S I T E D

It is true that men who are paralyzed below the waist can attain erection, engage in sexual intercourse, and ejaculate, if the spinal centers controlling erection and ejaculation remain intact. ■

Conversely, prepubertal boys may experience orgasms even though they emit no ejaculate. Orgasms without ejaculate are termed "dry orgasms." Boys do not begin to produce seminal fluid (and sperm) until puberty. Mature men, too, can experience dry orgasms. They can take the form of "little orgasms" preceding a larger orgasm, or they can follow "wet orgasms" when sexual stimulation is continued but seminal fluids have not been replenished. These dry orgasms are perfectly normal. Dry orgasms can also be a result of retrograde ejaculation, however, as we shall see below.

T r u t h OR *Fiction?*

R E V I S I T E D

It is true that men can have orgasms without ejaculating. Such orgasms are termed dry orgasms. ■

Ejaculation occurs in two stages. The first phase, often called the **emission stage,** involves contractions of the prostate, seminal vesicles, and the upper part of the vas deferens (the **ampulla**). The force of these contractions propels seminal fluid into the prostatic part of the urethral tract—a small tube called the **urethral bulb**—which balloons out as muscles close at either end, trapping the semen. It is at this point that the man perceives that orgasm is inevitable. Masters and Johnson term this feeling a sense of "ejaculatory inevitability" (Masters & Johnson, 1966). Men might colloquially describe the feeling as being about to "come." The man feels that a point of no return has been passed, that nothing can prevent ejaculation.

The second stage, which is often referred to as the **expulsion stage,** involves the propulsion of the seminal fluid through the urethra and out of the urethral opening at the tip of the penis. In this stage, muscles at the base of the penis and elsewhere contract rhythmically, forcefully expelling semen. The second stage is generally accompanied by the highly pleasurable sensations of orgasm.

In ejaculation, the seminal fluid is released from the urethral bulb and expelled by forceful contractions of the pelvic muscles that surround the urethral channel and the crura of the penis. The first few contractions are most intense and occur at 0.8-second intervals. Subsequent contractions lessen in intensity. The interval between them gradually increases. Seminal fluid is expelled in spurts during the first few contractions. The contractions are so powerful that seminal fluid may be propelled to distances of 12 to 24 inches, according to observations made by Masters and Johnson. Some men, however, report that semen travels but a few inches or just oozes from the penile opening. The force of the expulsion varies with the condition of the man's prostate, his general health, and his age. There is some correspondence between the force of the expulsion and the pleasure of orgasm. That is, more intense orgasms, psychologically speaking, often accompany more forceful ejaculations.

Like erection, ejaculation is regulated by two centers in the spinal cord, one in the sacral region and one in the higher lumbar region. When sexual arousal rises to a critical level—the point of ejaculatory inevitability—the lumbar ejaculatory center triggers the first stage of ejaculation, seminal emission. The lower, or sacral, ejaculatory center triggers the second stage of orgasm: the rhythmic muscle contractions that expel the ejaculate from the body.

Although ejaculation occurs by reflex, a man can delay ejaculation by maintaining the level of sexual stimulation below the critical threshold, or "point of no return." Men who suffer from premature ejaculation have been successfully treated in programs that train them to learn to recognize their "point of no return" and maintain sexual stimulation below it. (Issues concerning the definition and treatment of premature ejaculation are explored in Chapter 15 on sexual dysfunction.) Recognizing the point of no return and keeping stimulation beneath the critical level can also prolong coitus and enhance sexual pleasure for couples even when the man does not experience premature ejaculation.

Emission stage
The first phase of ejaculation, which involves contractions of the prostate gland, seminal vesicles, and the upper part of the vas deferens.

Ampulla
A sac or dilated part of a tube or canal.

Urethral bulb
The small tube that makes up the prostatic part of the urethral tract, which balloons out as muscles close at either end, trapping semen prior to ejaculation.

Expulsion stage
The second stage of ejaculation, during which muscles at the base of the penis and elsewhere contract rhythmically, forcefully expelling semen and providing pleasurable sensations.

Retrograde ejaculation
Ejaculation in which the ejaculate empties into the bladder. (From the Latin *retrogradi*, meaning "to go backward.")

Retrograde Ejaculation   Some men experience **retrograde ejaculation,** in which the ejaculate empties into the bladder rather than being expelled from the body. During normal ejaculation an external sphincter opens, allowing seminal fluid to pass out of the body. Another sphincter, this one internal, closes off the opening to the bladder, preventing the seminal fluid from backing up into the bladder. In retrograde ejaculation, the actions of these sphincters are reversed. The external sphincter remains closed, preventing the expulsion of the seminal fluid, while the internal sphincter opens, allowing the ejaculate to empty into the bladder. The result is a dry orgasm. No ejaculate is apparent because semen has backed up into the bladder. Retrograde ejaculation condition may be caused by prostate surgery (much less so now than in former years), drugs such as tranquilizers, certain illnesses, and accidents. Retrograde ejaculation is usually harmless in itself, since the seminal fluid is later discharged with urine. Infertility can result, however, and there may be some changes in the sensations associated with orgasm. Persistent dry orgasms should be medically evaluated, since their underlying cause may be a threat to health.

～ *Reflections* ～

- Did you know how erection occurred before taking this course? Do the facts differ from your assumptions?
- Agree or disagree with the following statement, and support your answer: The penis has a mind of its own.
- What roles do the brain and spinal cord play in erection and ejaculation?

Male sexual functions, like female sexual functions, are incredibly complex. They involve the cooperation of the nervous system, the endocrine system, the cardiovascular system, and the musculoskeletal system. In Chapter 5 we learn more about how the female and male sex organs respond to sexual stimulation. In Chapter 6 we examine the similarities and differences between the genders with respect to sexual differentiation, behavior, and personality.

Summing Up

External Sex Organs

The male external sex organs include the penis and the scrotum.

The Penis   Semen and urine pass out of the penis through the urethral opening. The penis contains cylinders that fill with blood and stiffen during sexual arousal. Circumcision—the surgical removal of the prepuce—has been carried out for religious and hygienic reasons. In our culture the size of the penis is sometimes seen as a measure of a man's masculinity and his ability to please his sex partners, although there is little if any connection between the size of the penis and sexual performance.

The Scrotum   The scrotum is the pouch of loose skin that contains the testes. Each testicle is held in place by a spermatic cord, which contains the vas deferens and the cremaster muscle.

Internal Sex Organs

The male internal sex organs consist of the testes, a system of tubes and ducts that conduct sperm, and organs that nourish and activate sperm.

The Testes   The testes serve two functions analogous to those of the ovaries. They secrete male sex hormones (androgens) and produce germ cells (sperm). The hypothalamus, pituitary gland, and testes keep blood testosterone levels at a more or less constant level through a hormonal negative feedback loop. Testosterone is produced by interstitial cells. Sperm are produced by seminiferous tubules. Sperm are stored and mature in the epididymis.

The Vas Deferens   Each epididymis empties into a vas deferens that conducts sperm over the bladder.

The Seminal Vesicles   The seminal vesicles are glands that open into the ejaculatory ducts where the fluids they secrete combine with and nourish sperm.

The Prostate Gland   The prostate gland secretes fluid that provides the characteristic texture and odor of semen.

Cowper's Glands   During sexual arousal, the Cowper's glands secrete a drop or so of clear, slippery fluid that appears at the urethral opening.

Semen   Sperm and the fluids contributed by the seminal vesicles, prostate gland, and Cowper's glands make up semen, the whitish fluid that is expelled through the tip of the penis during ejaculation.

Diseases of the Urogenital System

Urethritis   Men, like women, are subject to bladder and urethral inflammations, which are generally referred to as urethritis.

Cancer of the Testes   This is the most common form of solid-tumor cancer to strike young men between the ages of 20 and 34.

Disorders of the Prostate   The prostate gland generally becomes enlarged in men past the age of 50. Prostate cancer involves the growth of malignant prostate tumors that can metastasize to bones and lymph nodes. The chief symptoms of prostatitis are an ache or pain between the scrotum and anal opening and painful ejaculation.

Male Sexual Functions

Erection   Erection is the process by which the penis becomes engorged with blood, increases in size, and stiffens. Erection occurs in response to sexual stimulation but is also common during REM sleep.

Spinal Reflexes and Sexual Response   Erection and ejaculation occur by reflex. Reflexes involve sensory neurons and effector neurons, which meet in the spinal cord. There are two erection centers in the spinal cord. Although erection is a reflex, penile sensations are relayed to the brain, where they generally result in pleasure. Erection and ejaculation also involve the autonomic nervous system (ANS). The parasympathetic branch of the ANS largely governs erection, whereas the sympathetic branch largely controls ejaculation.

Ejaculation   Ejaculation, like erection, is a reflex. It is triggered when sexual stimulation reaches a critical threshold. Ejaculation usually but not always occurs with orgasm, but the terms are not synonymous. The emission phase of ejaculation involves contractions of the prostate, seminal vesicles, and the upper part of the vas deferens. In the expulsion stage, semen is propelled through the urethra and out of the penis. In this stage, muscles at the base of the penis and elsewhere contract rhythmically, forcefully expelling semen. There are two ejaculation centers in the spinal cord. In retrograde ejaculation, the ejaculate empties into the bladder rather than being expelled from the body.

C H A P T E R   5

Henri Matisse, *The Knife Thrower,* Plate 15 from *Jazz.* The Metropolitan
Museum of Art, Gift of Lila Acheson Wallace, 1983. © 1996 Succession
H. Matisse/Artist Rights Society (ARS), New York. © 1985 by The
Metropolitan Museum of Art.

Sexual Arousal and Response

Outline

Truth OR Fiction?

_____ The menstrual cycles of women who live together tend to become synchronized.

_____ The primary erogenous zone is the brain.

_____ "Spanish fly" will not turn your date on, but it may cure his or her warts.

_____ Electrical stimulation of certain areas in the human brain can yield sensations similar to those of sexual pleasure and gratification.

_____ Normal men produce estrogen, and normal women produce androgens.

_____ Written descriptions of men's and women's experiences during orgasm cannot be differentiated.

_____ Orgasms attained through sexual intercourse are more intense than those attained through masturbation.

What turns you on? What springs your heart into your mouth, tightens your throat, and opens the floodgates into your genitals? The sight of your lover undressing, a photo of Denzel Washington or Cindy Crawford, a sniff of some velvety perfume, a sip of wine?

Many factors contribute to sexual arousal. Some people are aroused by magazines with photographs of nude or seminude models that have been airbrushed to perfection. Some need only to imagine Hollywood's latest sex symbol. Others become aroused by remembrances of past lovers. Others are stimulated by sexual fantasies of flings with strangers.

People vary greatly in the cues that excite them sexually and in the frequency with which they experience sexual thoughts and feelings. Some young people seem perpetually aroused or arousable. Other people rarely or never entertain sexual thoughts or fantasies.

In this chapter we look at factors that contribute to sexual arousal and the processes that relate to sexual response. Since our experience of the world is initiated by our senses, we begin the chapter by focusing on the role of the senses in sexual arousal.

Making Sense of Sex: The Role of the Senses in Sexual Arousal

We come to apprehend the world around us through our senses—vision, hearing, smell, taste, and the skin senses, which include that all-important sense of touch. Each of the senses plays a role in our sexual experience, but some senses play larger roles than others.

Vision: The Better to See You With

It was the face of Helen of Troy, not her scent or her melodic voice, that "launched a thousand ships." Men's and women's magazines are filled with pictures of comely members of the other gender, not with "scratch and sniff" residues of their scents (but wait, a new marketing idea dawns!).

In matters of sexual attraction, people seem to have more in common with birds than with fellow mammals such as dogs and cats. Birds identify prospective mates within their species on the basis of their plumage and other visual markings. People also tend to be visually oriented when it comes to sexual attraction. By contrast, dogs and cats are more attracted to each other on the basis of scents that signal sexual receptivity.

Visual cues can be sexual turn-ons. We may be turned on by the sight of a lover in the nude, disrobing, or dressed in evening wear. Lingerie companies hope to convince customers that they will enhance their sex appeal by wearing strategically concealing and revealing nightwear. Some couples find it arousing to observe themselves making love in an overhead mirror or on videotape. Some people find sexually explicit movies arousing. Others are bored or offended by them. Though both genders can be sexually aroused by visually mediated erotica (a technical term for "porn flicks"), men are more interested in them (see Chapter 20).

Smell: Does the Nose Know Best?

Although the sense of smell plays a lesser role in governing sexual arousal in humans than in lower mammals, odors can be sexual turn-ons or turn-offs. Perfume companies, for example, bottle fragrances purported to be sexually arousing.

Visual Cues Can Be Sexual Turn-Ons or Turn-Offs.
Despite cross-cultural differences in standards of physical attractiveness, a clear complexion has universal appeal.

Aphrodisiac
Any drug or other agent that is sexually arousing or increases sexual desire. (From *Aphrodite*, the Greek goddess of love and beauty.)

Most Westerners prefer their lovers to be clean and fresh-smelling. People in our society learn to remove or mask odors by the use of soaps, deodorants, and so on. The ancient Egyptians invented the practice of scented bathing to rid themselves of offensive odors (Ramirez, 1990). The ancient Romans had such a passion for perfume that they would bathe in fragrances and even dab their horses and household pets (Ackerman, 1990).

Inclinations to find underarm or genital odors offensive may reflect cultural conditioning and not biological predispositions. In some societies, genital secretions are considered **aphrodisiacs.**

Menstrual Synchrony   Research by several investigators suggests that exposure to other women's sweat can modify a woman's menstrual cycle. In one study, women exposed to underarm secretions from other women, which may contain some as yet unidentified pheromones, showed converging shifts in their menstrual cycles (Bartoshuk & Beauchamp, 1994; Preti et al., 1986). Similar synchronization of menstrual cycles has also been observed among women who share dormitory rooms. In another study, 80% of the women who dabbed their upper lips with an extract of perspiration from other women began to menstruate in sync with the cycles of the donors after about three menstrual cycles (Cutler & Preti, 1986). A control group, who dabbed their lips with alcohol, showed no changes in their menstrual cycles. In yet another study from this research group, the length of the cycles of women with unusually short or long cycles began to normalize when they were exposed to an extract of *male* underarm perspiration (Preti et al., 1986).

Truth OR Fiction?
R E V I S I T E D

The menstrual cycles of women who live together do tend to become synchronized, possibly in response to pheromones. ■

The Skin Senses: Sex as a Touching Experience

Our skin senses enable us to sense pain, changes in temperature, and pressure (or touch). Whatever the roles of vision and smell in sexual attraction and arousal, the sense of touch

DO WE HAVE A "SIXTH SENSE" FOR SEX?

Pheromones are chemicals that drive the libido to do the lambada.

(Stephanie Strom, 1993)

For centuries, people have searched for a love potion—a magical formula that could make others fall in love with them or be strongly attracted to them. Some scientists, such as David Berliner (1993), suggest that such potions may indeed exist, in the form of chemical secretions known as **pheromones.**

Pheromones are odorless chemicals that in people would be detected through a "sixth sense"—the *vomeronasal organ.* This organ, located in the nose (hence, *nasal*) would detect these odorless chemicals and communicate information about them to the brain, where they might

affect sexual response (Blakeslee, 1993b).

Pheromones trigger sexual behavior in many organisms, from insects to reptiles to mammals (Cobb & Jallon, 1990; Eggert & Muller, 1989; Mason et al., 1989). Lower animals also use pheromones to organize food gathering, maintain pecking orders, sound alarms, and mark territories (Strom, 1993). Pheromones are commonly contained in vaginal secretions and in urine. In mice, exposure to male urine, which contains male pheromones, can induce estrus in the female (i.e., put her "in heat"). Female dogs deposit drops of urine on the ground that serve as scent markings to signal sexual receptivity.

People may also use pheromones. Infants, for example, may use them to

recognize their mothers. Adults might respond to them in seeking a mate. Only a few years ago, most researchers did not believe that people had a vomeronasal organ. Therefore, it was unlikely that pheromones played a role in human behavior. Today, however, research findings suggest that people may possess such a sensory organ (Bartoshuk & Beauchamp, 1994). David Berliner has jumped ahead of the research enterprise by forming companies that commercialize the use of pheromones with people. As the new millennium rolls in, might people be using perfumes and colognes that have a double impact—one on the sense of smell and another on a "sixth sense for sex"?

Pheromones
Chemical substances secreted externally by certain animals, which convey information to, or produce specific responses in, other members of the same species. (From the Greek *pherien*, meaning "to bear [a message]" and *hormone.*)

Erogenous zones
Parts of the body that are especially sensitive to tactile sexual stimulation. (*Erogenous* is derived from roots meaning "giving birth to erotic sensations.")

Primary erogenous zones
Erogenous zones that are particularly sensitive because they are richly endowed with nerve endings.

Secondary erogenous zones
Parts of the body that become erotically sensitized through experience.

has the most direct effects on sexual arousal and response. Any region of that sensitive layer we refer to as skin can become eroticized. The touch of your lover's hand upon your cheek, or your lover's gentle massage of your shoulders or back, can be sexually stimulating.

Erogenous Zones   **Erogenous zones** are parts of the body that are especially sensitive to tactile sexual stimulation—to strokes and other caresses. **Primary erogenous zones** are erotically sensitive because they are richly endowed with nerve endings. **Secondary erogenous zones** are parts of the body that become erotically sensitized through experience.

Primary erogenous zones include the genitals; the inner thighs, perineum, buttocks, and anus; the breasts (especially the nipples); the ears (particularly the earlobes); the mouth, lips, and tongue; the neck; the navel; and, yes, the armpits. Preferences vary somewhat from person to person, reflecting possible biological, attitudinal, and experiential differences. Areas that are exquisitely sensitive for some people may produce virtually no reaction, or discomfort, in others. Many women, for example, report little sensation when their breasts are stroked or kissed. Many men are uncomfortable when their nipples are caressed. On the other hand (or foot), many people find the areas between their toes sensitive to erotic stimulation and enjoy keeping a toehold on their partners during coitus.

Secondary erogenous zones become eroticized through association with sexual stimulation. For example, a woman might become sexually aroused when her lover gently caresses her shoulders, because such caresses have been incorporated as a regular feature of the couple's lovemaking. A few of the women observed by Masters and Johnson (1966) reached orgasm when the smalls of their backs were rubbed.

A Touching Experience. The sense of touch is intimately connected with sexual experience. The touch of a lover's hand on the cheek, or gentle massage, can be sexually stimulating. Certain parts of the body—called erogenous zones—have special sexual significance because of their response to erotic stimulation.

People are also highly responsive to images and fantasies. This is why the brain is sometimes referred to as the primary sexual organ, or an erogenous zone. Some women report reaching orgasm through fantasy alone (Kinsey et al., 1953). Men regularly experience erection and nocturnal emissions ("wet dreams") without direct stimulation of the genitals.

Ironically, the brain is not an erogenous zone. It is not stimulated directly by touch. (The brain processes tactile information from the skin, but it does not have sensory neurons to directly gather this information itself.) However, the etymology (word origins) of the term *erogenous* clearly applies to the brain. It *can* give birth to erotic sensations through production of fantasy, erotic memories, and other thoughts.

Truth  *Fiction?*
R E V I S I T E D

It is not true that the primary erogenous zone is the brain. The brain is not an erogenous zone in the strict sense of the term. Erogenous zones are directly sensitive to touch. The brain, however, processes information received through erogenous zones and can have such an impact on sexual arousal that it has been dubbed an erogenous zone in recognition of its importance. ■

Taste: On Savory Sex

Taste appears to play a minor role in sexual arousal and response, unless we digress into puns and note that taste in the form of a zesty meal or a delicate wine may contribute to arousal. In any event, some people are sexually aroused by the taste of genital secretions, such as vaginal secretions or seminal fluid. We do not know, however, whether these secretions are laced with chemicals that have biologically arousing effects, or whether arousal reflects the meaning that these secretions have to the individual. That is, we may learn to become aroused by, or to seek out, flavors or odors that have been associated with sexual pleasure. Others are turned off by them.

Hearing: The Better to Hear You With

The sense of hearing also provides an important medium for sexual arousal and response. Like visual and olfactory cues, sounds can be turn-ons or turn-offs. The sounds of one's lover, whether whispers, indications of pleasure, or animated sounds that may attend orgasm, may be arousing during the heat of passion. For some people, key words or vocal intonations may become as arousing as direct stimulation of an erogenous zone. Many people are aroused when their lovers "talk dirty." Spoken vulgarities spur their sexual arousal. Others find vulgar language offensive.

The sultry voices of screen sirens Lauren Bacall and Kathleen Turner have aroused the ardor of many a moviegoer. Teenagers may shriek at the music of groups such as Aerosmith or Pearl Jam, just as their parents (and grandparents) did when they heard the Beatles, Frank Sinatra, Johnny Mathis, or the King himself (Elvis, that is). Of course, the sex appeal of these performers goes beyond the sounds that they produce.

Music itself can contribute to sexual arousal. Music can relax us and put us "in the mood" or have associations ("They're playing our song!"). Many couples find background music "atmospheric"—a vital accoutrement of lovemaking.

Sounds can also be sexual turn-offs. Most of us would find funeral music a damper on sexual arousal. We may also be inhibited by scratchy, unnerving voices. Heavy metal rock might be a sexual turn-off to many (are your authors showing their age?), but it could help set the right tone for others.

~ *Reflections* ~

- Do you find photos of scantily clad or nude people to be sexually arousing? Why, or why not?
- Do you find perfumes or colognes to enhance the attractiveness of other people? Why, or why not?
- What kinds of touches do you find to be erotic? Do you have any secondary erogenous zones?

Aphrodisiacs: Of Spanish Flies and Rhino Horns

The only known aphrodisiac is variety.

(Marc Connolly)

An aphrodisiac is a substance that arouses or increases one's capacity for sexual pleasure or response. You may have heard of "Spanish fly," an alleged aphrodisiac once extracted from a Spanish beetle. (The beetle from which it was taken, *Lytta vesicatoria,* is near extinction.) A few drops in a date's drink was believed to make you irresistible. Spanish fly is but one of many purported aphrodisiacs. It is toxic, however, not sexually arousing. Spanish fly is now synthesized—but not as an aphrodisiac. The active ingredient, *cantharidin,* is a skin irritant that can burn off warts. If it can burn off warts, consider the damage it can do when taken internally. It irritates the urinary tract and can cause severe tissue damage or death. It inflames the urethra, producing a burning sensation in the penis that is sometimes misinterpreted as sexual feelings.

We should also be concerned about an expectancy, or placebo effect, when evaluating the effectiveness of a purported aphrodisiac (Brody, 1993b). The belief that a substance has sexually stimulating effects may itself inspire sexual excitement. If a person tries a supposed aphrodisiac and feels sexually aroused, the person may well attribute the turn-on to the effects of the substance, even if the substance had no direct effect on sex drive.

Truth OR Fiction? REVISITED

It is true that "Spanish fly" will not turn your date on, but may cure his or her warts. Spanish fly contains cantharidin, a skin irritant that can in fact burn off warts. Cantharidin is not an aphrodisiac, but it can inflame the urethra, producing a burning sensation that could be misinterpreted as sexual feelings. ■

Foods that in some way resemble male genitals have now and then been considered aphrodisiacs. They include oysters, clams, bull's testicles ("prairie oysters"), tomatoes, and "phallic" items such as celery stalks, bananas, and even ground-up rhinoceros, reindeer, and elephant horns (which is one derivation of the slang term "horny").

Even potatoes have been held to be aphrodisiacs. Yes, potatoes. Shakespeare echoed this belief when he wrote, "Let the sky rain potatoes . . . ; let a tempest of provocation come." None of these foods or substances has been shown to be sexually stimulating, however—not even deep-fried potato skins with cheddar cheese and bacon. Sadly, myths about the sexually arousing properties of substances drawn from rhinoceroses or elephants may be contributing to the rapidly diminishing numbers of these animals.

Other drugs and psychoactive substances may have certain effects on sexual arousal and response. The drug *yohimbine,* an extract from the African yohimbe tree, does stimulate blood flow to the genitals (Brody, 1993b). Although it appears to increase sexual arousal and performance in male rats, researchers have failed to show similar aphrodisiac effects of the drug on men (Buffum, 1985). Yohimbine also happens to be toxic (Brody, 1993b).

Amyl nitrate (in the form of "snappers" or "poppers") has been used mostly by gay men (and by some heterosexuals) in the belief that it heightens sensations of arousal and orgasm. Poppers dilate blood vessels in the brain and genitals, producing sensations of warmth in the pelvis and possibly facilitating erection and prolonging orgasm. Amyl nitrate does have some legitimate medical uses, such as helping reduce heart pain (angina) among cardiac patients. It is inhaled from ampules that "pop" open for rapid use when heart pain occurs. Poppers can cause dizziness, fainting, and migraine-type headaches, however. They should be taken only under a doctor's care for a legitimate medical need, not to intensify sexual sensations.

Certain drugs appear to have aphrodisiac effects by acting on the brain mechanisms controlling sex drive. For example, drugs that affect brain receptors for the neurotransmitter dopamine, such as the antidepressant drug *bupropion* (trade name: Wellbutrin) and the drug L-dopa used in the treatment of Parkinson's disease, can increase the sex drive (Brody, 1993b).

The most potent chemical aphrodisiac may be a naturally occurring substance in the body, the male sex hormone testosterone. It is the basic fuel of sexual desire in both genders (Brody, 1993b).

The safest and perhaps most effective method for increasing the sex drive may not be a drug or substance, but exercise. Regular exercise not only enhances general health. It also boosts energy and increases the sex drive in both genders (Brody, 1993b). Perhaps the most potent aphrodisiac of all is novelty. Partners can invent new ways of sexually discovering one another. They can make love in novel places, experiment with different techniques, wear provocative clothing, share or enact fantasies, or whatever their imaginations inspire.

Some substances, such as potassium nitrate (saltpeter), have been considered inhibitors of sexual response—anaphrodisiacs. Saltpeter, however, only indirectly dampens sexual arousal. As a diuretic that can increase the need for urination, it may make the thought of sex unappealing. It does not directly dampen sexual response, however.

Other chemicals do dampen sexual arousal and response. Tranquilizers and central nervous system depressants, such as barbiturates, can lessen sexual desire and impair sexual performance. These drugs may paradoxically enhance sexual arousal in some people, however, by lessening sexual inhibitions or fear of possible repercussions from sexual activity. Antihypertensive drugs, which are used in the treatment of high blood pressure, may produce erectile and ejaculatory difficulties in men, and reduction of sexual desire in both genders. Certain antidepressant drugs, such as fluoxetine (brand name: Prozac), amitriptyline (brand: name Elavil), and imipramine (brand name: Tofranil) appear to dampen sex drive (Brody, 1993b; Meston & Gorzalka, 1992). Antidepressants may also impair erectile response and delay ejaculation in men and orgasmic responsiveness in women (Meston & Gorzalka, 1992). (Because they delay ejaculation, some of these drugs are being used to treat premature ejaculation.)

Nicotine, the stimulant in tobacco smoke, constricts the blood vessels. Thus it can impede sexual arousal by reducing the capacity of the genitals to become engorged with blood. Chronic smoking can also reduce the blood levels of testosterone in men, which can in turn lessen sex drive or motivation.

Antiandrogen

A substance that decreases the levels of androgens in the bloodstream.

Antiandrogen drugs may have anaphrodisiac effects (see Chapters 18 and 19). Their effectiveness in modifying deviant behavior patterns such as sexual violence and sexual interest in children is questionable.

Psychoactive Drugs

Psychoactive drugs, such as alcohol and cocaine, are widely believed to have aphrodisiac effects. Yet their effects may reflect our expectations of them, or their effects on sexual inhibitions, rather than direct stimulation of sexual response.

Alcohol: The "Great Provoker of Three Things"
In Shakespeare's *Macbeth,* the following exchange takes place between Macduff and a porter:

PORTER: . . . Drink, sir, is a great provoker of three things.

MACDUFF: What three things does drink especially provoke?

PORTER: Marry,[1] sir, nose-painting,[2] sleep, and urine. Lechery,[3] sir, it provokes, and unprovokes; it provokes the desire, but it takes away the performance.

Small amounts of alcohol are stimulating, but large amounts curb sexual response. This fact should not be surprising because alcohol is a depressant. Alcohol reduces central nervous system activity. Large amounts of alcohol can severely impair sexual performance in both men and women.

People who drink moderate amounts of alcohol may feel more sexually aroused because of their expectations about alcohol, not because of its chemical properties. That is, people who expect alcohol to enhance sexual responsiveness may act the part. Expectations that alcohol serves as an aphrodisiac may lead men with problems achieving erection to turn to alcohol as a cure (Roehrich & Kinder, 1991). The fact is, alcohol is a depressant and can reduce sexual potency rather than restore it.

Alcohol may also lower sexual inhibitions, because it allows us to ascribe our behavior to the effects of the alcohol rather than to ourselves (Crowe & George, 1989; Lang, 1985). Alcohol is connected with a liberated social role and thus provides an excuse for dubious behavior. "It was the alcohol," people can say, "not me." People may express their sexual desires and do things when drinking that they would not do when sober. For example, a person who feels guilty about sex may become sexually active when drinking because he or she can later blame the alcohol.

Consider a survey of 1,100 undergraduates taken at the University of Virginia (Grossman, 1991). Forty-three percent of the respondents were classified as "heavy drinkers." That is, they had had at least five alcoholic beverages in a row on one occasion within the two weeks preceding the survey. *More than half* of the heavy drinkers reported that under the influence of alcohol, they had engaged in sexual activity with someone they would not ordinarily have become involved with. All in all, between 20% and 25% of the total sample had engaged in sexual activity they deemed unwise when under the influence of alcohol!

In laboratory studies, men who were misled into believing that they had drunk alcohol spent more time lingering over pornographic pictures as researchers looked on than did men who thought they had not. Did they believe that they would avert the censure of the onlookers because they could attribute their prurience to the alcohol? If so, perhaps alcohol provides an excuse for socially deviant behavior. The amount of time the men lingered over the pornographic material was unaffected by whether or not they had actually drunk alcohol (Lang et al., 1980; Lansky & Wilson, 1981).

---

[1]Contraction of the expression "By the Virgin Mary"; used by Elizabethans like Shakespeare to speak emphatically yet avoid disrespect to the Virgin Mary.

[2]The reddening of the nose that occurs in many chronic alcoholics as a result of the bursting of small blood vessels.

[3]Excessive indulgence of sexual desire. (Related to the German *lecken,* meaning "to lick.")

Effects of Alcohol on Sexual Behavior—A Complex Picture. Small doses of alcohol can be stimulating and induce feelings of euphoria, both of which would appear to be connected with sexual interest. Alcohol can also reduce fear of consequences of engaging in risky behavior—sexual and otherwise. Drinkers sometimes say, "It was the alcohol, not me." Alcohol is also expected to be sexually liberating, and people often live up to social and cultural expectations. Yet, as a depressant drug, alcohol biochemically dampens sexual response.

Alcohol can also induce feelings of euphoria. Euphoric feelings may enhance sexual arousal and also wash away qualms about expressing sexual desires. Alcohol also appears to impair the ability to weigh information ("information processing") that might otherwise inhibit sexual impulses (Steele & Josephs, 1990). When people drink, they may be less able to foresee the consequences of misconduct and less likely to ponder their standards of conduct.

Hallucinogenics   There is no evidence that marijuana and other hallucinogenic drugs directly stimulate sexual response. However, fairly to strongly intoxicated marijuana users claim to have more empathy with others, to be more aware of bodily sensations, and to experience time as passing more slowly. These sensations could heighten subjective feelings of sexual response. Some marijuana users report that the drug inhibits their sexual responsiveness, however (Wolman, 1985). The effects of the drug on sexual response may depend upon the individual's prior experiences with the drug, attitudes toward the drug, and the amount taken.

Other hallucinogenics, such as LSD and mescaline, have also been reported by some users to enhance sexual response. Again, these effects may reflect dosage level, as well as expectations, user experiences, attitudes toward the drugs, and altered perceptions.

Stimulants   Stimulants such as amphetamines ("speed," "uppers," "bennies," "dexies") have been reputed to heighten arousal and sensations of orgasm. High doses can give rise to irritability, restlessness, hallucinations, paranoid delusions, insomnia, and loss of appetite. These drugs generally activate the central nervous system but are not known to have specific sexual effects. Nevertheless, arousing the nervous system can contribute to sexual arousal (Palace, 1995). The drugs can also elevate the mood, and perhaps sexual pleasure is heightened by general elation.

Cocaine is a natural stimulant that is extracted from the leaves of the coca plant—the plant from which the soft drink Coca-Cola obtained its name. In fact, Coke—Coca-Cola—contained cocaine as part of its original formula. Cocaine was removed from the secret formula in 1906. Cocaine is ingested in various forms, snorted as a powder, smoked in hardened rock form ("crack" cocaine) or in a freebase form, or injected directly into the bloodstream in liquid form. Cocaine produces a euphoric rush, which tends to ebb quickly. Physically, cocaine constricts blood vessels (reducing the oxygen supply to the heart), elevates the blood pressure, and accelerates the heart rate.

Despite the popular belief that cocaine is an aphrodisiac, frequent use can lead to sexual dysfunctions, such as erectile disorder and failure to ejaculate among males, decreased vaginal lubrication in females, and decreased sexual interest in both men and women

(Weiss & Mirin, 1987). Some people do report initial increased sexual pleasure with cocaine use; however, that increase may reflect cocaine's loosening of inhibitions. Over time, though, regular users may become dependent on cocaine for sexual arousal or lose the ability to enjoy sex (Weiss & Mirin, 1987).

～ *Reflections* ～

▪ What are the effects of alcohol on sexual arousal? Do the scientific "facts" contradict any beliefs you had held about alcohol?

▪ Have you done anything under the influence of alcohol or other drugs that you otherwise would not have done? What role did the drug play?

▪ Before reading this section, did you believe that some substances serve as aphrodisiacs? What are they?

Sexual Response and the Brain: Cerebral Sex?

The brain may not be an erogenous zone, but it plays a central role in sexual functioning. Direct genital stimulation may trigger spinal reflexes that produce erection in the male and vaginal lubrication in the female without the direct involvement of the brain. The same reflexes may also be triggered by sexual stimulation that originates in the brain in the form of erotic memories, fantasies, visual images, and thoughts, however. The brain may also inhibit sexual responsiveness, as when we experience guilt or anxiety in a sexual situation, or when we suddenly realize in the midst of a sexual encounter that we have left the car lights turned on. Let us explore the brain mechanisms involved in sexual functioning.

The Geography of the Brain

The brain consists of three major parts, the hindbrain, the midbrain, and the forebrain (see Figure 5.1). The lower part of the brain, called the hindbrain, consists of the **medulla,** the **pons,** and the **cerebellum.** The medulla plays a role in regulating vital functions such as heart rate, respiration, and blood pressure. The pons relays information about body movement and plays a role in states or functions such as attention, sleep, and respiration. The cerebellum is involved in balance and coordination. Rising from the hindbrain into the forebrain is the **reticular activating system,** or RAS, which is involved in attention, arousal, and sleep.

Key areas in the forebrain, or frontal part of the brain, are the **thalamus, hypothalamus, limbic system,** and **cerebrum.** The thalamus, which lies in the center of the brain, plays a role in regulating sleep and attention, and relays sensory information to the cerebral cortex. Sensory information from the eyes, for example, is relayed by the thalamus to the visual areas of the cerebral cortex, where the information is processed. The hypothalamus lies between the thalamus and the pituitary gland and is involved in motivation and emotion; in body functions such as control of body temperature, concentration of fluids, and storage of nutrients; and in regulation of the menstrual cycle.

The limbic system consists of parts of the hypothalamus and contains other structures such as the hippocampus and the septum (see Figure 5.2). The limbic system is involved in memory and in regulation of hunger, aggression, and sexual behavior.

Your cerebrum is your crowning glory. The large mushroom-shaped outer surface of the cerebrum, convoluted with ridges and valleys, is called the **cerebral cortex.** It has two hemispheres and is involved in thinking, language, memory, and fantasy.

Brain Mechanisms in Sexual Functioning

Parts of the brain, in particular the cerebral cortex and the limbic system, play key roles in sexual functioning. Cells in the cerebral cortex fire (transmit messages) when we experience

Medulla
An oblong area of the hindbrain involved in regulation of heartbeat and respiration.

Pons
A structure of the hindbrain that regulates respiration, attention, sleep, and dreaming.

Cerebellum
A part of the hindbrain that governs muscle coordination and balance.

Reticular activating system
A part of the brain active during attention, sleep, and arousal.

Thalamus
An area near the center of the brain involved in the relay of sensory information to the cortex and in the functions of sleep and attention.

Hypothalamus

A brain structure below the thalamus that regulates body temperature, motivation, and emotion.

Limbic system

A group of structures active in memory, motivation, and emotion; the structures that are part of this system form a fringe along the inner edge of the cerebrum.

Cerebrum

The large mass of the forebrain, which consists of two hemispheres.

Cerebral cortex

The wrinkled surface area (gray matter) of the cerebrum.

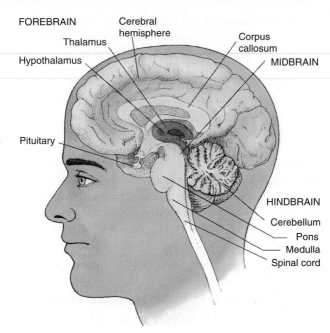

Figure 5.1. The Geography of the Brain. A view of the brain, split from top to bottom.

sexual thoughts, images, wishes, fantasies, and the like. Cells in the cerebral cortex interpret sensory information as sexual turn-ons or turn-offs. The sight of your lover disrobing, the anticipation of a romantic kiss, a passing sexual fantasy, or the viewing of an erotic movie can trigger the firing of cortical cells. These cells, in turn, transmit messages through the spinal cord that send blood rushing to the genitals, causing erection or vaginal lubrication. The cortex also provides the conscious sense of self. The cortex judges sexual behavior to be proper or improper, moral or immoral, relaxing or anxiety- or guilt-provoking.

Areas of the brain below the cortex, especially the limbic system, also play roles in sexual processes (Everitt, 1990; Kimble, 1992). For example, when the rear part of a male rat's hypothalamus is stimulated by an electrical probe, the animal mechanically runs through its courting and mounting routine. It nibbles at the ears and the back of the neck

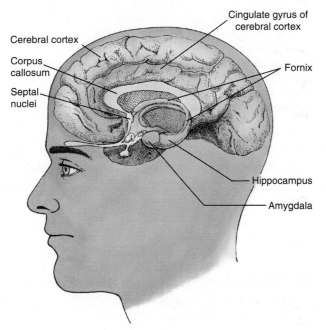

Figure 5.2. The Limbic System. The limbic system lies along the inner edge of the cerebrum.

of a female rat and mounts her when she responds. People, of course, are influenced by learning, fantasy, and values as well as simple brain (or spinal) stimulation.

The importance of the limbic system in the sexual behavior in animals was demonstrated in experiments by Heinrich Klüver and Paul Bucy of the University of Chicago in 1939. Klüver and Bucy reported that destruction of areas of the limbic system triggered persistent sexual behaviors that included masturbation and male–female and male–male mounting attempts. The monkeys even tried to mount the experimenters. For obvious ethical reasons, researchers have not injured or destroyed parts of people's brains to observe the effects on humans.

Electrical stimulation of the hippocampus and septum of the limbic system has also been found to produce erections in laboratory monkeys (MacLean et al., 1976). Electrical stimulation of a pathway in the thalamus, moreover, produced a seminal discharge in these monkeys—without erection. Stimulation of certain areas in the thalamus and hypothalamus may induce ejaculation. Still, the precise relationships among brain structures that regulate erection and ejaculation in animals or humans have not been fully mapped out.

On Pushing the Right Buttons: Are There Pleasure Centers in the Brain?

Research with electrical probes suggests that "pleasure centers" may exist in and near the hypothalamus in other animals and perhaps even in people. When electrodes are implanted in certain parts of the limbic system, investigators find that laboratory animals such as rats (Olds, 1956; Olds & Milner, 1954) will repeatedly press controls to receive bursts of electricity. Of course we cannot know what the rats experience, but men to whom this was done reported that stimulation of these so-called pleasure centers led to feelings of sexual arousal and gratification.

Heath (1972) found that electrical stimulation of the septal region of the limbic system resulted in orgasmlike sensations in two people. Delgado (1969) reported that two female epileptic patients who received limbic stimulation as part of a diagnostic evaluation became sexually aroused by the stimulation:

> [One] reported a pleasant tingling sensation in the left side of her body "from my face down to the bottom of my legs." She started giggling and . . . [stated] that she enjoyed the sensation "very much." Repetition of these stimulations made the patient more communicative and flirtatious, and she ended by openly expressing her desire to marry the therapist. [The other patient reported] a pleasant sensation of relaxation and considerably increased her verbal output, which took on a more intimate character. [She] expressed her fondness for the therapist [whom she had just met], kissed his hands, and talked about her immense gratitude. (p. 145)

Truth OR Fiction? REVISITED

It is true that electrical stimulation of certain areas in the human brain can yield sensations similar to those of sexual pleasure and gratification. Electrical stimulation of certain parts of the limbic system yielded sensations similar to those of sexual gratification—at least in the relatively small number of people who have been studied. ∎

We cannot say whether specific "pleasure centers" in the brain are responsible for sexual pleasure. We might wonder, however, whether we would bother to develop sexual relationships if pleasure centers could be accessed through direct stimulation. Before you run to the store for electrodes, you should note that very few researchers suggest that we may someday replace our lovers with battery-powered kits.

～ Reflections ～

▪ What are the roles of the limbic system and cerebral cortex in sexual behavior?
▪ If you could electrically stimulate a pleasure center in your brain and find as much pleasure as you do in sexual activity with another person, do you think you would bother to form romantic relationships? Why, or why not?

Sex Hormones: Do They "Goad" Us into Sex?

Hormone

A substance secreted by an endocrine gland that regulates various body functions. (From the Greek *horman*, meaning "to stimulate" or "to goad.")

In a TV situation comedy, a male adolescent was described as a "hormone with feet." Ask parents why teenagers act the way they do, and you are likely to hear a one-word answer: hormones! **Hormones** are chemical substances that are secreted by the ductless glands of the endocrine system and discharged directly into the bloodstream. The word *hormone* derives from the Greek *horman*, meaning "to stimulate" or "to goad." And we could say that they very much goad us into sexual activity. Hormones also regulate various bodily functions, including growth and resistance to stress as well as sexual functions.

Both men and women produce small amounts of the sex hormones of the other gender in their bodies. Testosterone, the major form of androgen, or male sex hormone, is secreted in small amounts by the adrenal glands (located above the kidneys) in both genders, but in much larger amounts by the testes. The ovaries produce small amounts of androgens but much larger amounts of the female sex hormones, estrogen and progesterone. The testes similarly produce small amounts of estrogen and progesterone.

Truth **OR** *Fiction?*
R E V I S I T E D

It is true that normal men produce estrogen, and normal women produce androgens. However, men do not produce as much estrogen as women do, and women do not produce as much of the male sex hormones as men do. ■

Secondary sex characteristics

Physical traits that differentiate males from females but are not directly involved in reproduction.

The hypothalamus and pituitary gland regulate gonadal secretion of sex hormones, specifically testosterone in males and estrogen and progesterone in females. At puberty a surge of sex hormones causes the blossoming of reproductive maturation: the sperm-producing ability of the testes in males and the maturation of ova and ovulation in females (see Chapter 13). Sex hormones released at puberty also cause the flowering of **secondary sex characteristics.** In males, these include the lengthening of the vocal cords (and consequent lowering of the voice) and the growth of facial and pubic hair. In females, the breasts and hips become rounded with fatty tissue, and pubic hair grows.

Are Adolescents "Hormones with Feet"? Research shows that levels of androgens are connected with sexual interest in both male and female adolescents. Hormone levels are more likely to predict sexual behavior in adolescent males, however, perhaps because society places greater restraints on female sexuality.

Sex Hormones and Sexual Behavior: Organizing and Activating Influences

Sex hormones have organizing and activating effects on behavior. That is, they exert an influence on the type of behavior that is expressed (an *organizing* effect) and the frequency or intensity of the drive that motivates the behavior and the ability to perform the behavior (*activating* effects). For example, sex hormones predispose lower animals and possibly people toward stereotypical masculine or feminine mating behaviors (an organizing effect). They also facilitate sexual response and influence sexual desire (activating effects).

Though sex hormones clearly determine the sexual "orientations" and drives of many lower animals, their roles in human sexual behavior may be relatively more subtle and are not as well understood. Much of our knowledge of the organizing and activating effects of sex hormones comes from research with other species in which hormone levels were manipulated by castration or injection. Ethical standards prohibit such research with human infants, for obvious reasons.

The activating effects of testosterone can be clearly observed among male rats. For example, males who are castrated in adulthood and thus deprived of testosterone discontinue sexual behavior. If they are given injections of testosterone, however, they resume stereotypical male sexual behaviors, such as attempting to mount receptive females.

In rats, testosterone organizes or differentiates the brain in the masculine direction. As a result, adult male rats display stereotypical masculine behaviors upon activation by testosterone. Male fetuses and newborns normally have sufficient amounts of testosterone in their blood systems to organize their brains in the masculine direction. Female fetuses and newborns normally have lesser amounts of testosterone. Their brains thus become organized in a feminine direction. When female rats are prenatally exposed to large doses of testosterone, their sexual organs became somewhat masculinized, and they are predisposed toward masculine mating behaviors in adulthood (Kimble, 1992).

In rats and other rodents, sexual differentiation of the brain is not complete at birth. Female rodents who are given testosterone injections shortly before or shortly following birth (depending on the species) show typical masculine sexual patterns in adulthood, attempting to mount other females and resisting mounting by males (Ellis & Ames, 1987).

Questions remain about the organizing effects of sex hormones on human sexual behavior. Prenatal sex hormones are known to play a role in the sexual differentiation of the genitalia and of the brain structures in the fetus, such as the hypothalamus (see Chapter 6). Their role in patterning sexual behavior in adulthood remains unknown, however. Researchers have speculated that the brains of **transsexual** individuals may have been prenatally sexually differentiated in one direction, while their genitals were being differentiated in the other (Money, 1994). It has been speculated that prenatal sexual differentiation of the brain may also be connected with sexual orientation (see Chapter 10).

What of the activating effects of sex hormones on human sex drive and behavior? Though the countless attempts to extract or synthesize aphrodisiacs have failed to produce the real thing, men and women normally produce one genuine aphrodisiac—testosterone. Whatever the early organizing effects of sex hormones in humans, testosterone activates the sex drives of both men and women.

Sex Hormones and Male Sexual Behavior

Evidence of the role for hormones in sex drive is found among men who have declines in testosterone levels as the result of castration. Castration (removal of the testes) is sometimes performed as a medical treatment for cancer of the prostate or other diseases of the male reproductive tract, such as genital tuberculosis. In Europe, however, some convicted sex offenders have voluntarily undergone castration as a condition of release.

Regardless of the reason for castration, men who are surgically or chemically castrated usually exhibit a gradual loss of sexual desire. They also gradually tend to lose the capacities to attain erection and to ejaculate—an indication that testosterone is important in maintaining sexual functioning as well as drive, at least in males. Castrated men show great variation in their sexual interest and functioning, however. Some continue to experience sexual desires and are able to function sexually for years, even decades. Learning appears to play a large role in determining continued sexual response following castration. Males who were sexually experienced before castration show a more gradual decline in sexual activity. Those who were sexually inexperienced at the time show relatively little or no interest in sex. Male sexual motivation and functioning thus involve an interplay of hormonal influences and experience.

Further evidence of the relationship between hormonal levels and male sexuality is found in studies of men with **hypogonadism,** a condition marked by abnormally low levels of testosterone production. Hypogonadal men generally suffer loss of sexual desire and a decline in sexual activity (Carani et al., 1990). Here again, hormones do not tell the whole story. Hypogonadal men are capable of erection, at least for a while, even though their sex drives may wane (Bancroft, 1984). The role of testosterone as an activator of sex drives in men is further supported by evidence of the effects of testosterone replacement in hypogonadal men. When such men obtain testosterone injections, their sex drives, fantasies, and activity are often restored to former levels (Cunningham et al., 1989; Goleman, 1988).

Though minimal levels of androgens are critical to male sexuality, there is no one-to-one correspondence between hormone levels and the sex drive or sexual performance in adults. In men who have ample supplies of testosterone, sexual interest and functioning depend more on learning, fantasies, attitudes, memories, and other psychosocial factors than on hormone levels. At puberty, however, hormonal variations may play a more direct role in stimulating sexual interest and activity in males. Udry and his colleagues (Udry et al., 1985; Udry et al., 1986; Udry & Billy, 1987) found, for example, that testosterone levels predicted sexual interest, masturbation rates, and the likelihood of engaging in sexual intercourse among teenage boys. A positive relationship also has been found between testos-

Transsexual
A person with a gender-identity disorder who feels that he or she is really a member of the other gender and trapped in a body of the wrong gender.

Hypogonadism
An abnormal condition marked by abnormally low levels of testosterone production.

terone levels in adult men and frequency of sexual intercourse (Dabbs & Morris, 1990; Knussman et al., 1986). Moreover, drugs that reduce the levels of androgen in the blood system, called *antiandrogens,* lead to reductions in sex drive and related fantasies and urges (Berlin, 1983; Money, 1987b) (see Chapters 18 and 19).

Sex Hormones and Female Sexual Behavior

The female sex hormones estrogen and progesterone play prominent roles in promoting the changes that occur during puberty and in regulating the menstrual cycle. Female sex hormones do not appear to play a direct role in determining sexual motivation or response in human females, however.

In most mammals, females are sexually receptive only during estrus. Estrus is a brief period of fertility that corresponds to time of ovulation, and during estrus, females are said to be "in heat." Estrus occurs once a year in some species; in others, it occurs periodically during the year in so-called sexual or mating seasons. Estrogen peaks at time of ovulation, so there is a close relationship between fertility and sexual receptivity in most female mammals. Women's sexuality is not clearly linked to hormonal fluctuations, however. Unlike females of most other species of mammals, the human female is sexually responsive during all phases of the reproductive (menstrual) cycle—even during menstruation, when ovarian hormone levels are low—and after menopause.

There is some evidence, however, that sexual responsiveness in women is influenced by the presence of circulating androgens, or male sex hormones, in their bodies. The adrenal glands of women produce small amounts of androgens, just as they do in males. The fact that women normally produce smaller amounts of androgens than men does not mean that they necessarily have weaker sex drives. Rather, women appear to be more sensitive to smaller amounts of androgens (Bancroft, 1984). For women, it seems that less is more.

Ovariectomy
Surgical removal of the ovaries.

Women who receive **ovariectomies,** which are sometimes carried out when a hysterectomy is performed, no longer produce female sex hormones. Nevertheless, they continue to experience sex drives and interest as before. Loss of the ovarian hormone estradiol may cause vaginal dryness and make coitus painful, but it does not reduce sexual desire. (The dryness can be alleviated by a lubricating jelly or by estrogen-replacement therapy.) However, women whose adrenal glands *and* ovaries have been removed (so that they no longer produce androgens) gradually lose sexual desire. An active and enjoyable sexual history seems to ward off this loss, however, providing further evidence of the impact of cognitive and experiential factors on human sexual response.

Research provides further evidence on the links between androgens and women's sex drives. Levels of testosterone in the bloodstream have been associated with increased sexual interest in women (Persky et al., 1982; Sherwin et al., 1985). The frequency of masturbation in women appears to be associated with changes in androgen levels (Bancroft et al., 1983)—another indication of the activating role of androgens in female sexuality. In the studies by Udry and his colleagues mentioned earlier, androgen levels were also found to predict sexual interest among teenage girls. In contrast to boys, however, girls' androgen levels were unrelated to the likelihood of coital experience. Androgens apparently affect sexual desire in both genders, but sexual interest may be more likely to be directly translated into sexual activity in men than in women (Bancroft, 1990). This gender difference may be explained by society's placement of greater restraints on adolescent female sexuality.

Other researchers report that women's sexual activity increases at points in the menstrual cycle when levels of androgens in the bloodstream are high (Morris et al., 1987). Another study was conducted with women whose ovaries had been surgically removed ("surgical menopause") as a way of treating disease. The ovaries supply major quantities of estrogen. Following surgery, the women in this study were treated either with estrogen-replacement therapy (ERT), with ERT *plus* androgens, or with a placebo (an inert substance made to resemble an active drug) (Sherwin et al., 1985). This was a double-blind study. Neither the women nor their physicians knew which drug the women were receiving. The results showed that the combination of androgens and ERT heightened sexual desire and sexual fantasies more than ERT alone or the placebo.

Androgens thus play a more prominent role than ovarian hormones in activating and maintaining women's sex drives. As with men, however, women's sexuality is too complex to be explained fully by hormone levels. For example, an active and enjoyable sexual history seems to ward off the loss of sexual interest that generally follows the surgical removal of the adrenal glands and ovaries.

~ *Reflections* ~

- What are the organizing and activating effects of sex hormones?
- Do you know people who have taken testosterone or estrogen for medical or other reasons? What were the reasons for using hormones? What were their effects?

The Sexual Response Cycle

Sexual response cycle
Masters and Johnson's model of sexual response, which consists of four phases.

Vasocongestion
The swelling of the genital tissues with blood, which causes erection of the penis and engorgement of the area surrounding the vaginal opening.

Myotonia
Muscle tension.

Although we may be culturally attuned to focus on gender differences rather than similarities, Masters and Johnson (1966) found that the physiological responses of men and women to sexual stimulation (whether from coitus, masturbation, or other sources) are quite alike. The sequence of changes in the body that takes place as men and women become progressively more aroused is referred to as the **sexual response cycle**. Masters and Johnson divided the cycle into four phases: *excitement, plateau, orgasm,* and *resolution.* Figure 5.3 suggests the levels of sexual arousal associated with each phase.

Both males and females experience **vasocongestion** and **myotonia** early in the response cycle. Vasocongestion is the swelling of the genital tissues with blood, which causes erection of the penis and engorgement of the area surrounding the vaginal opening. The testes, nipples, and even earlobes become engorged as blood vessels in these areas dilate.

Myotonia refers to muscle tension. Myotonia causes voluntary and involuntary muscle contractions, which produce facial grimaces, spasms in the hands and feet, and eventually, the spasms of orgasm. Let us follow these and the other bodily changes that constitute the sexual response cycle.

Figure 5.3. Levels of Sexual Arousal During the Phases of the Sexual Response Cycle.
Masters and Johnson divide the sexual response cycle into four phases: excitement, plateau, orgasm, and resolution. During the resolution phase, the level of sexual arousal returns to the prearoused state. For men there is a refractory period following orgasm. As shown by the broken line, however, men can become rearoused to orgasm once the refractory period is past and their levels of sexual arousal have returned to pre-plateau levels. Pattern A for women shows a typical response cycle, with the broken line suggesting multiple orgasms. Pattern B shows the cycle of a woman who reaches the plateau phase but for whom arousal is "resolved" without reaching the orgasmic phase. Pattern C shows the possibility of orgasm in a highly aroused woman who passes quickly through the plateau phase.

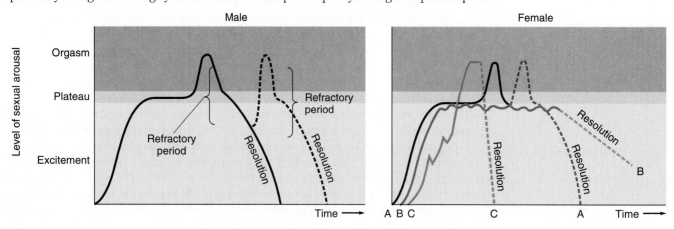

Excitement Phase

Excitement phase
The first phase of the sexual response cycle, which is characterized by erection in the male, vaginal lubrication in the female, and muscle tension and increases in heart rate in both males and females.

In younger men, vasocongestion during the **excitement phase** produces penile erection as early as 3 to 8 seconds after stimulation begins. Erection may occur more slowly in older men, but the responses are essentially the same. Erection may subside and return as stimulation varies. The scrotal skin thickens, losing its baggy appearance. The testes increase in size. The testes and scrotum become elevated.

In the female, vaginal lubrication may start 10 to 30 seconds after stimulation begins. Vasocongestion swells the clitoris, flattens the labia majora and spreads them apart, and increases the size of the labia minora. The inner two thirds of the vagina expand. The vaginal walls thicken, and because of the inflow of blood, turn from their normal pink to a deeper hue. The uterus becomes engorged and elevated. The breasts enlarge, and blood vessels near the surface become more prominent.

Sex flush
A reddish rash that appears on the chest or breasts late in the excitement phase of the sexual response cycle.

The skin may take on a rosy **sex flush** late in this phase. It varies with intensity of arousal and is more pronounced in women. The nipples may become erect in both genders, especially in response to direct stimulation. Men and women show some increase in myotonia, heart rate, and blood pressure.

Plateau Phase

Plateau phase
The second phase of the sexual response cycle, which is characterized by increases in vasocongestion, muscle tension, heart rate, and blood pressure in preparation for orgasm.

A plateau is a level region, and the level of arousal remains somewhat constant during the **plateau phase** of sexual response. Nevertheless, the plateau phase is an advanced state of arousal that precedes orgasm. Men in this phase show a slight increase in the circumference of the coronal ridge of the penis. The penile glans turns a purplish hue, a sign of vasocongestion. The testes are elevated further into position for ejaculation and may reach one and a half times their unaroused size. The Cowper's glands secrete a few droplets of fluid that are found at the tip of the penis (see Figure 5.4).

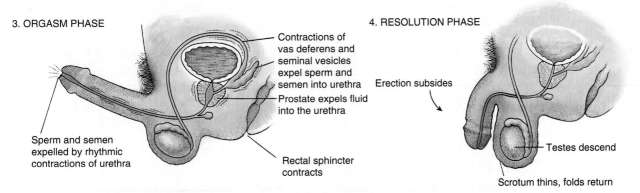

Figure 5.4. The Male Genitals During the Phases of the Sexual Response Cycle.

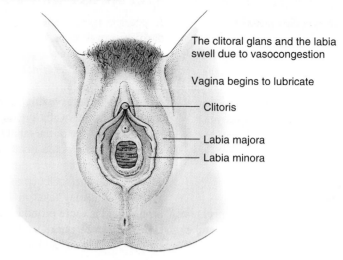

1. EXCITEMENT PHASE

The clitoral glans and the labia swell due to vasocongestion

Vagina begins to lubricate

Clitoris

Labia majora

Labia minora

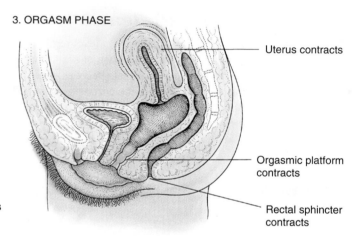

3. ORGASM PHASE

Uterus contracts

Orgasmic platform contracts

Rectal sphincter contracts

Figure 5.5. **The Female Genitals During the Phases of the Sexual Response Cycle.**

Orgasmic platform
The thickening of the walls of the outer third of the vagina, due to vasocongestion, that occurs during the plateau phase of the sexual response cycle.

Sex skin
Reddening of the labia minora that occurs during the plateau phase.

In women, vasocongestion swells the tissues of the outer third of the vagina, contracting the vaginal opening (thus preparing it to "grasp" the penis) and building the **orgasmic platform** (see Figure 5.5). The inner part of the vagina expands fully. The uterus becomes fully elevated. The clitoris withdraws beneath the clitoral hood and shortens. Thus a women (or her partner) may feel that the clitoris has become lost. This may be mistaken as a sign that the woman's sexual arousal is waning, although it is actually increasing.

Coloration of the labia minora appears, which is referred to as the **sex skin.** The labia minora become a deep wine color in women who have borne children and bright red in women who have not. Further engorgement of the areolas of the breasts may make it seem that the nipples have lost part of their erection (see Figure 5.6). The Bartholin's glands secrete a fluid that resembles mucus.

About one man in four, and about three women in four, show a sex flush, which often does not appear until the plateau phase. Myotonia may cause spasmodic contractions in the hands and feet and facial grimaces. Breathing becomes rapid, like panting, and the heart rate may increase to 100 to 160 beats per minute. Blood pressure continues to rise. The increase in heart rate is usually less dramatic with masturbation than during coitus.

Orgasmic Phase

The orgasmic phase in the male consists of two stages of muscular contractions. In the first stage, contractions of the vas deferens, the seminal vesicles, the ejaculatory duct, and the

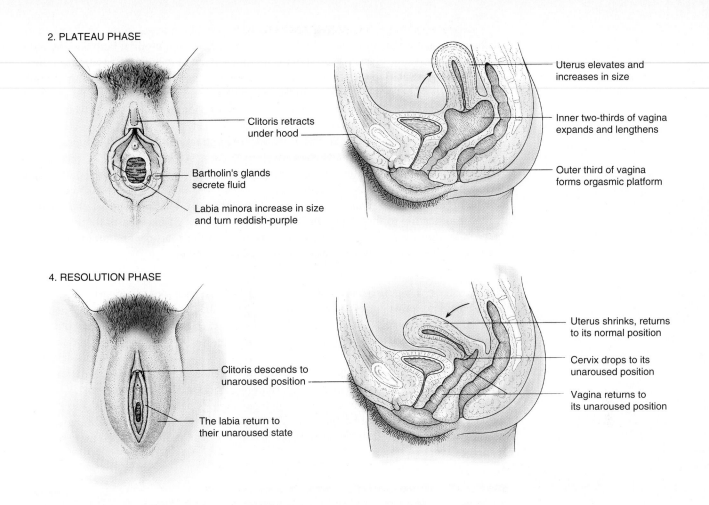

2. PLATEAU PHASE

Clitoris retracts
under hood

Bartholin's glands
secrete fluid

Labia minora increase in size
and turn reddish-purple

Uterus elevates and
increases in size

Inner two-thirds of vagina
expands and lengthens

Outer third of vagina
forms orgasmic platform

4. RESOLUTION PHASE

Clitoris descends to
unaroused position

The labia return to
their unaroused state

Uterus shrinks, returns
to its normal position

Cervix drops to its
unaroused position

Vagina returns to
its unaroused position

prostate gland cause seminal fluid to collect in the urethral bulb at the base of the penis (see Figure 5.4). The bulb expands to accommodate the fluid. The internal sphincter of the urinary bladder contracts, preventing seminal fluid from entering the bladder in a backward, retrograde ejaculation. The normal closing off of the bladder also serves to prevent urine from mixing with semen. The collection of semen in the urethral bulb produces feelings of ejaculatory inevitability—the sensation that nothing will stop the ejaculate from "coming." This sensation lasts for about 2 to 3 seconds.

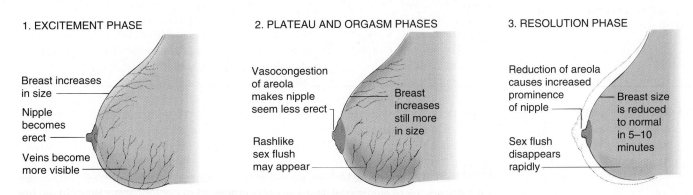

1. EXCITEMENT PHASE

Breast increases
in size

Nipple
becomes
erect

Veins become
more visible

2. PLATEAU AND ORGASM PHASES

Vasocongestion
of areola
makes nipple
seem less erect

Rashlike
sex flush
may appear

Breast
increases
still more
in size

3. RESOLUTION PHASE

Reduction of areola
causes increased
prominence
of nipple

Sex flush
disappears
rapidly

Breast size
is reduced
to normal
in 5–10
minutes

Figure 5.6. **The Breast During the Phases of the Sexual Response Cycle.**

In the second stage, the external sphincter of the bladder relaxes, allowing the passage of semen. Contractions of muscles surrounding the urethra and urethral bulb and the base of the penis propel the ejaculate through the urethra and out of the body. Sensations of pleasure tend to be related to the strength of the contractions and the amount of seminal fluid. The first 3 to 4 contractions are generally most intense and occur at 0.8-second intervals (5 contractions every 4 seconds). Another 2 to 4 contractions occur at a somewhat slower pace. Rates and patterns vary somewhat from man to man.

Orgasm in the female is manifested by 3 to 15 contractions of the pelvic muscles that surround the vaginal barrel. The contractions first occur at 0.8-second intervals, producing, as in the male, a release of sexual tension. Another 3 to 6 weaker and slower contractions follow. The spacing of these contractions is generally more variable in women than in men. The uterus and the anal sphincter also contract rhythmically. Uterine contractions occur in waves from the top to the cervix. In both genders, muscles go into spasm throughout the body. Blood pressure and heart rate reach a peak, with the heart beating up to 180 times per minute. Respiration may increase to 40 breaths per minute.

Subjective Experience of Orgasm   The sensations of orgasm have challenged the descriptive powers of poets. Words like "rush," "warmth," "explosion," and "release" do not adequately capture them. We may assume (rightly or wrongly) that others of our gender experience pretty much what we do, but can we understand the sensations of the other gender?

Several studies suggest that the orgasms of both genders may feel quite similar. In one, 48 men and women provided written descriptions of orgasms. The researchers (Proctor et al., 1974) modified the language (for example, changing "penis" to "genitals") so that the authors' genders would not be apparent. They then asked 70 "experts" (psychologists, gynecologists, etc.) to indicate the gender of each author. The ratings were no more reliable than guesswork.

Truth OR Fiction?
REVISITED

It is true that written descriptions of men's and women's experiences during orgasm cannot be differentiated—at least when they are altered to exclude language that gives away exactly which anatomic features are involved. Thus, this Truth or Fiction item is only qualifiedly "true." (Listen: Life is complex. Be tolerant.) ■

Resolution Phase

Resolution phase

The fourth phase of the sexual response cycle, during which the body gradually returns to its prearoused state.

The period following orgasm, in which the body returns to its prearoused state, is called the **resolution phase.** Following ejaculation, the man loses his erection in two stages. The first occurs in about a minute. Half the volume of the erection is lost as blood from the corpora cavernosa empties into the other parts of the body. The second stage occurs over a period of several minutes: The remaining tumescence subsides as the corpus spongiosum empties. The testes and scrotum return to normal size, and the scrotum regains its wrinkled appearance.

In women orgasm also triggers release of blood from engorged areas. In the absence of continued stimulation, swelling of the areolas decreases; then the nipples return to normal size. The sex flush lightens rapidly. In about 5 to 10 seconds the clitoris descends to its normal position. The clitoris, vaginal barrel, uterus, and labia gradually shrink to their prearoused sizes. The labia minora turn lighter (the "sex skin" disappears) in about 10 to 15 seconds.

Most muscle tension (myotonia) tends to dissipate within 5 minutes after orgasm in both men and women. Blood pressure, heart rate, and respiration may also return to their prearousal levels within a few minutes. About 30% to 40% of men and women find their palms, the soles of their feet, or their entire bodies covered with a sheen of perspiration. Both men and women may feel relaxed and satiated. However, . . .

Refractory period

A period of time following a response (e.g., orgasm) during which an individual is no longer responsive to stimulation (e.g., sexual stimulation).

Although the processes by which the body returns to its prearousal state are similar in men and women, there is an important gender difference during the resolution phase. Unlike women, men enter a **refractory period** during which they are physiologically incapable of experiencing another orgasm or ejaculation (in much the same way that the flash attachment to a camera cannot be set off again immediately after it is used—it has to be recharged). The refractory period of adolescent males may last only minutes, whereas that of men age 50 and above may last from several minutes (yes, "it could happen") to a day. Women do not undergo a refractory period and so can become quickly rearoused to the point of repeated (multiple) orgasm if they desire and receive continued sexual stimulation (see Figure 5.3).

Myotonia and vasocongestion may take an hour or more to dissipate in people who are aroused but who do not reach orgasm. Persistent pelvic vasocongestion may cause "blue balls" in males—the slang term for a throbbing ache. Some men insist that their dates should consent to coitus, since it is unfair to stimulate them to the point where they have this condition. This condition can be relieved through masturbation as well as coitus, however—or allowed to dissipate naturally. Although it may be uncomfortable, it is not dangerous and should not be an excuse to pressure or coerce another person into any sexual activity. "Blue" sensations are not limited to men. Women, too, may experience unpleasant pelvic throbbing if they have become highly aroused and do not find release (Barbach, 1975). Women, too, can relieve pelvic throbbing through masturbation.

Kaplan's Three Stages of Sexual Response: An Alternative Model

Helen Singer Kaplan is a prominent sex therapist and author of several professional books (1974, 1979, 1987) on sex therapy. Whereas Masters and Johnson had proposed a four-stage model of sexual response, Kaplan developed a three-stage model consisting of (1) desire, (2) excitement, and (3) orgasm. Kaplan's model is an outgrowth of her clinical experience in working with people with sexual dysfunctions. She believes that their problems can best be classified according to these three phases. Kaplan's model makes it convenient for clinicians to classify sexual dysfunctions involving desire (low or absent desire), excitement (such as problems with erection in the male or lubrication in the female), and orgasm (such as premature ejaculation in the male or orgasmic dysfunction in the female).

Masters and Johnson focus on physiological changes that occur during sexual stimulation. Kaplan's model includes two phases that are primarily physiological (*excitement,* consisting of initial vasocongestion of the genitals, resulting in erection in the male and vaginal lubrication in the female, and *orgasm,* marked by pelvic muscular contractions) and one that is primarily psychological (desire). Kaplan's stages of excitement and orgasm are clearly differentiated along physiological lines. (Masters and Johnson's excitement and plateau stages are less clearly differentiated in terms of differences in biological processes. Both primarily involve vasocongestion.)

Masters and Johnson view sexual response as composed of *successive* stages; the order is crucial and invariant. Kaplan treats her phases as relatively independent components of sexual response whose sequence is somewhat variable. For example, a person may experience sexual excitement and even orgasm, though sexual desire remains low. Excitement may also precede desire in some situations. For example, people with low sexual desire may find their sexual appetites sparked as their bodies respond to their partners' sexual stimulation. A person who lacks desire may not be motivated to seek sexual stimulation or be able to respond adequately to sexual stimuli, however.

Kaplan's model is noteworthy for designating desire as a separate phase of sexual response. Problems in lack of sexual interest or desire are among the most common brought to the attention of sex therapists (see Chapter 15).

~ *Reflections* ~

How do you know when you are becoming sexually aroused? Do the phases of the sexual response cycle describe your reactions to sexual stimulation?

Were you surprised to learn that the sensations of orgasm are apparently quite similar among women and men? Why, or why not?

Controversies About Orgasm

Are women capable of experiencing multiple orgasms? Are men? Physiologically speaking, is there but one type of orgasm? Or are there different types of orgasm, depending on the site of stimulation? Do women ejaculate during orgasm? If so, what fluid do they emit?

Few other topics in human sexuality have aroused more controversies over the years than orgasm. We do not have all the answers, but some intriguing research findings have shed light on some of these continuing controversies.

Multiple Orgasms: When You're Having More Than One

Multiple orgasms

One or more additional orgasms following the first, which occur within a short period of time and before the body has returned to a pre-plateau level of arousal.

Kinsey's report (Kinsey et al., 1953) that 14% of his female respondents regularly had **multiple orgasms** sent shock waves through the general community and even surprised his fellow scientists. Many people were aghast that women could have more than one orgasm at a time. There were comments (mostly by men, of course!) that the women in the Kinsey surveys must be "nymphomaniacs" who were incapable of being satisfied with the "normal" complement of one orgasm per occasion. However, only 13 years later, Masters and Johnson (1966) reported that most if not all women are capable of multiple orgasms. Though all women may have a biological capability for multiple orgasms, not all women report them. A recent survey of 720 nurses showed that only 43% reported experiencing multiple orgasms (Darling et al., 1991).

It is difficult to offer a precise definition of multiple orgasms. In Masters and Johnson's view, multiple orgasms involves the occurrence of one or more *additional* orgasms following the first, within a short period of time and before the body has returned to a pre-plateau level of arousal. By this definition, a person would not have experienced multiple orgasms if he or she had two or more successive orgasms that were separated by a return to a prearoused state or a pre-plateau (excitement stage) level of arousal. (Note that the pattern shown by the broken line for the male in Figure 5.3 does *not* constitute multiple orgasms, even if it occurs reasonably rapidly after the first orgasm, because he *does* return to a pre-plateau level of sexual arousal between orgasms.) The lines of demarcation between the excitement and plateau stages of arousal are not too obvious, however. Therefore, a person may experience two or more successive orgasms within a short time but not

Reproduced by special permission of Playboy Magazine, © 1984.

"Front desk? Look, I hate to sound like a prude, but the folks in room 614 seem to be having an excessive number of orgasms."

know whether these are, technically speaking, "multiple orgasms." Whether or not the orgasm fits the definition does not diminish the experience, but it does raise the question of whether both men and women are capable of multiple orgasms.

By Masters and Johnson's definition, men are not capable of achieving multiple orgasms, because they enter a refractory period following ejaculation during which they are physiologically incapable of achieving another orgasm or ejaculation for a time. Put more simply, men who want more than one orgasm during one session may have to relax for a while and allow their sexual arousal to subside. Yet women can maintain a high level of arousal between multiple orgasms and have them in rapid succession.

Women do not enter a refractory period. Women can continue to have orgasms if they continue to receive effective stimulation (and, of course, are interested in continuing). Some men thus refrain from reaching orgasm until their partners have had the desired number. The differential capacity for multiple orgasms is one of the major gender differences in sexual response.

Some men have two or more orgasms without ejaculation ("dry orgasms") preceding a final ejaculatory orgasm. These men may not enter a refractory period following their initial dry orgasms and may therefore be able to maintain their level of stimulation at near-peak levels. Some men report multiple orgasms in which dry orgasms follow an ejaculatory orgasm, with little or no loss of erection between orgasms (Dunn & Trost, 1989). Some men report more varied patterns, with ejaculatory orgasms and dry orgasms preceding or following each other in different sequences.

Men who report multiple orgasms indicate that if they are highly aroused following an initial orgasm, and if sexual stimulation continues, they can achieve one or more subsequent orgasms before losing their erections (Dunn & Trost, 1989). Still, the evidence for multiple orgasms in men is largely anecdotal and limited to a relatively few case examples. Nor is it known whether such "multiple" orgasms meet the technical definition given by Masters and Johnson of two or more orgasms in rapid succession without a return to a *pre-plateau* stage of arousal in between. Nor do we know what percentage of men might be multiply orgasmic (Dunn & Trost, 1989).

Masters and Johnson found that some women experienced 20 or more orgasms by masturbating. Still, few women have multiple orgasms during most sexual encounters, and many are satisfied with just one per occasion. Some women who have read or heard about female orgasmic capacity wonder what is "wrong" with them if they are content with just one. Nothing is wrong with them, of course: A biological capacity does not create a behavioral requirement.

How Many Kinds of Orgasms Do Women Have? One, Two, or Three?

Until Masters and Johnson published their laboratory findings, many people believed that there were two types of female orgasm, as proposed by the psychoanalyst Sigmund Freud: the *clitoral orgasm* and the *vaginal orgasm*. Clitoral orgasms were achieved through direct clitoral stimulation, such as by masturbation. Clitoral orgasms were seen by psychoanalysts (mostly male psychoanalysts, naturally) as emblematic of a childhood fixation—a throwback to an erogenous pattern acquired during childhood masturbation.

The term vaginal orgasm referred to an orgasm achieved through deep penile thrusting during coitus and was theorized to be a sign of mature sexuality. Freud argued that women achieve sexual maturity when they forsake clitoral stimulation for vaginal stimulation. This view would be little more than an academic footnote but for the fact that some adult women who continue to require direct clitoral stimulation to reach orgasm, even during coitus, have been led by traditional (generally male) psychoanalysts to believe that they are sexually "fixated" at an immature stage, or are, at least, sexually inadequate.

Despite Freudian theory, Masters and Johnson (1966) were able to find only one kind of orgasm, physiologically speaking, regardless of the source of stimulation (manual–clitoral or penile–vaginal). By monitoring physiological responses to sexual stimulation, they found that the female orgasm involves the same biological events whether it is reached through masturbation, petting, coitus, or just breast stimulation. All orgasms involve spasmodic contractions of the pelvic muscles surrounding the vaginal barrel, leading to a release of sexual tension. The bard wrote, "A rose is a rose is a rose." Biologically speaking, the same principle can be applied to orgasm: "An orgasm is an orgasm is an orgasm." In men, it also matters not how orgasm is achieved—through masturbation, petting, oral sex, coitus, or by fantasizing about a fellow student in chem lab. Orgasm still involves the same physiological processes: Involuntary contractions of the pelvic muscles at the base of the penis expel semen and release sexual tension. A woman or a man might prefer one source of orgasm to another—she or he might prefer achieving orgasm with a lover rather than by masturbation, but the biological events that define orgasm remain the same.

Though orgasms attained through coitus or masturbation may be physiologically alike, there are certainly key psychological or subjective differences. (Were it not so, there would be fewer sexual relationships.) The coital experience, for example, is often accompanied by feelings of attachment, love, and connectedness toward one's partner. Masturbation, by contrast, is more likely to be experienced solely as a sexual release.

Orgasms experienced through different means may also vary in physiological and subjective intensity. Masters and Johnson (1966) found that orgasms experienced during masturbation were generally more physiologically intense than those experienced during intercourse, perhaps because masturbation allows one to focus only on one's own pleasure and on ensuring that one receives effective stimulation to climax. This does not mean that orgasms during masturbation are more enjoyable or gratifying than those experienced through coitus, however. Given the emotional connectedness we may feel toward our lovers, we are unlikely to break off our relationships in favor of masturbation. Thus, "physiological intensity," as measured by laboratory instruments, does not translate directly into subjective pleasure or fulfillment.

T r u t h **OR** *Fiction?*
R E V I S I T E D

Actually, orgasms attained through masturbation appear to be more intense than those attained through coitus—at least in terms of physiological measurements. (That does not mean that they are more enjoyable.) ◼

The purported distinction between clitoral and vaginal orgasms also rests on an assumption that the clitoris is not stimulated during coitus. Masters and Johnson showed this to be a *false* assumption. Penile coital thrusting draws the clitoral hood back and forth against the clitoris. Vaginal pressure also heightens blood flow in the clitoris, further setting the stage for orgasm (Lavoisier et al., 1995).

One might think that Masters and Johnson's research settled the question of whether or not there are different types of female orgasm. Other investigators, however, have proposed that there are distinct forms of female orgasm, yet not those suggested by psychoanalytic theory. For example, Singer and Singer (1972) suggested that there are three types of female orgasm: *vulval, uterine,* and *blended.* According to the Singers, the vulval orgasm represents the type of orgasm described by Masters and Johnson (1966) that involves *vulval* contractions; that is, contractions of the vaginal barrel. Consistent with the findings of Masters and Johnson (1966), they note that the vulval orgasm remains the same regardless of the source of stimulation, clitoral or vaginal.

According to the Singers, the uterine orgasm does not involve vulval contractions. It occurs only in response to deep penile thrusting against the cervix. This thrusting slightly displaces the uterus and stimulates the tissues that cover the abdominal organs. The uterine orgasm is accompanied by a certain pattern of breathing: gasping or gulping of air is followed by an involuntary holding of the breath as orgasm approaches. When orgasm is reached, the breath is explosively exhaled. The uterine orgasm is accompanied by deep feelings of relaxation and sexual satisfaction.

The third type, or blended orgasm, is described as combining features of the vulval and uterine orgasms. It involves both an involuntary breath-holding response and contractions of the pelvic muscles. The Singers note that the type of orgasm a woman experiences—vulval, uterine, or blended—depends on factors such as the parts of the body that are stimulated and the duration of stimulation. Each produces its own kind of satisfaction, and no one type is necessarily better or preferable to any other.

The Singers' hypothesis of three distinct forms of female orgasm remains controversial. Researchers initially scoffed at the idea that orgasms could arise from vaginal stimulation alone. The vagina, after all, especially the inner two thirds of the vaginal cavity, is relatively insensitive to stimulation (erotic or otherwise). Proponents of the Singers' model counter that the type of uterine orgasm described by the Singers is induced more by pressure resulting from deep pelvic thrusting than by touch.

The G-Spot

Grafenberg spot
A part of the anterior wall of the vagina, whose prolonged stimulation is theorized to cause particularly intense orgasms and a female ejaculation. Abbreviated *G-spot*.

A part of the vagina, notably a bean-shaped area within the anterior wall, may have special erotic significance. This area is believed to lie about 1 to 2 inches from the vaginal entrance and to consist of a soft mass of tissue that swells from the size of a dime to a half dollar when stimulated (Davidson et al., 1989). It has been called the **Grafenberg spot**—the "G-spot" for short (see Figure 5.7). The spot can be directly stimulated by the woman's or her partner's fingers or by penile thrusting in the rear entry or the female-superior positions. Some researchers suggest that stimulation of the spot produces intense erotic sensations and that with prolonged stimulation, a distinct form of orgasm occurs. This orgasm is characterized by intense pleasure and, in some cases, by a biological event earlier thought to be exclusively male in nature: ejaculation (Perry & Whipple, 1981; Whipple & Komisaruk, 1988). These claims, as with other claims of distinct forms of female orgasm, have been steeped in controversy.

The G-spot was named after a gynecologist, Ernest Grafenberg, who first suggested the erotic importance of this area. Grafenberg observed that orgasm in women could be induced by stimulating this area. He also claimed that such orgasms may be accompanied by the discharge of a milky fluid or "ejaculate" from the urethra. In a laboratory experiment, Zaviacic and his colleagues (1988a, 1988b) found evidence of an ejaculate in 10 of 27 women studied. Some researchers believe that this fluid is urine that some women release involuntarily during orgasm (Alzate, 1985). Other researchers believe that it differs from urine (Zaviacic et al., 1988; Zaviacic & Whipple, 1993). The nature of this fluid and its source remains a source of controversy, but Zaviacic and Whipple (1993) suggest that it may represent a fluid that is released during sex by a "female prostate," a system of ducts and glands called *Skene's glands,* in much the same way that semen is released by the prostate gland in men. Zaviacic and Whipple suggest that "many women who felt that they may be urinating during sex . . . [may be helped by] the knowledge that the fluid they expel may be different from urine and a normal phenomenon that occurs during sexual response" (1993, p. 149). Some women, however, may expel urine during sex, perhaps because of urinary stress incontinence (Zaviacic & Whipple, 1993). Zaviacic and Whipple also note that stimulation of the G-spot and ejaculation may be related in some women but not in others.

Figure 5.7. The Grafenberg Spot (G-Spot).

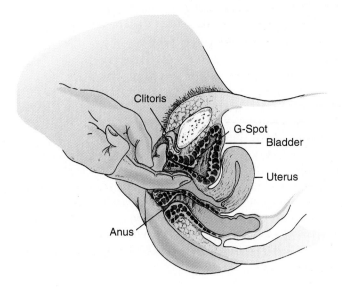

Even proponents of the existence of the G-spot recognize that it is difficult to locate, since it is not apparent to the eye (Ladas et al., 1982). Perry and Whipple (1981) suggest that women may try to locate the spot either by self-exploration or with the assistance of a partner. In either case, two fingers should be used to press deeply but gently into the front, or anterior, wall of the vagina to locate the spot, which may feel like a small lump within the anterior wall (see Figure 5.7). When the spot is stimulated by stroking, the woman may initially experience an urge to urinate, perhaps because the sensitive area lies close to the bladder and urethra. A few minutes of continued stimulation lead to strong sensations of sexual pleasure in some women, which is accompanied by vasocongestion that swells the area. More prolonged stimulation may lead to an intense orgasm; however, fear of loss of urinary control leads some women to avoid such prolonged stimulation (Ladas et al., 1982).

Perry and Whipple (1981) relate the G-spot to the Singers' model of three kinds of orgasm. They suggest that sustained stimulation of the G-spot can produce a uterine orgasm that is characterized by deeper sensations than those that occur during the vulval orgasm that is produced by clitoral stimulation. The connection between the G-spot and the Singers' model is controversial.

The very existence of the G-spot remains debatable. Ladas, Whipple, and Perry (1982) reported locating the G-spot in every one of more than 400 women they examined. Zaviacic and his colleagues (1988) reported finding the spot in each of 27 women they examined. Other researchers have been unable to find an area of heightened sensitivity corresponding to the G-spot, however (Alzate & Londono, 1984; Masters et al., 1989). Some researchers (e.g., Hock, 1983) deny the existence of the G-spot as a distinct anatomical structure. They argue that the entire anterior wall of the vagina, and not any one spot or area, is richly supplied with nerve endings and sensitive to erotic stimulation.

Although the existence of the G-spot continues to be debated among researchers, a recent survey of 1,289 professional women in the health and counseling professions revealed that a majority believe that the G-spot exists and that they have experienced sexual pleasure when it has been stimulated (Davidson et al., 1989). Still, there was considerable confusion among these women as to the precise location of this sensitive area. About three out of four women reported experiencing an orgasm from stimulation of this area, most frequently from manual stimulation.

More research is needed to determine the scientific basis of the claims for different kinds of orgasm in women and whether there are specific sites in the vagina, such as the G-spot, that may be especially sensitive to erotic stimulation.

~ *Reflections* ~

▪ Have you ever felt pressured to have multiple orgasms? If so, why?
▪ Do you believe that you have experienced more than one kind of orgasm? Do your own experiences coincide with any of the descriptions of orgasm in the text?
▪ Do you believe that women have a G-spot? Why, or why not?

Summing Up

Making Sense of Sex: The Role of the Senses in Sexual Arousal

Each sense plays a role in sexual experience, but some play more of a role than others.

Vision: The Better to See You With   Visual information plays a major role in human sexual attraction. Visual cues can be sexual turn-ons or turn-offs.

Smell: Does the Nose Know Best?   Although the sense of smell plays a lesser role in governing sexual arousal in humans than in lower mammals, particular odors can be sexual turn-ons or turn-offs. Many organisms are sexually aroused by naturally produced chemicals called pheromones, but their role in human sexual behavior remains unclear.

The Skin Senses: Sex as a Touching Experience
The sense of touch has the most direct effects on sexual arousal and response. Erogenous zones are especially sensitive to tactile sexual stimulation.

Taste: On Savory Sex   Taste appears to play only a minor role in sexual arousal and response.

Hearing: The Better to Hear You With   Like visual and olfactory cues, sounds can be turn-ons or turn-offs.

Aphrodisiacs: Of Spanish Flies and Rhino Horns

Alleged aphrodisiacs such as Spanish fly and foods that in some way resemble the genitals have not been shown to contribute to sexual arousal or response.

Psychoactive Drugs   The alleged aphrodisiac effects of psychoactive drugs, such as alcohol and cocaine, may reflect our expectations of them or their effects on sexual inhibitions, rather than direct stimulation of sexual response. Alcohol is also connected with a liberated social role and thus provides an external excuse for dubious behavior. Some people report initial increased sexual pleasure with cocaine use, but frequent use can lead to sexual dysfunctions.

Sexual Response and the Brain: Cerebral Sex?

The brain plays a central role in sexual functioning.

The Geography of the Brain   The brain consists of three major parts, the hindbrain, the midbrain, and the forebrain.

Brain Mechanisms in Sexual Functioning   The cerebral cortex interprets sensory information as sexual turn-ons or turn-offs. The cortex transmits messages through the spinal cord that cause vasocongestion. Direct stimulation of parts of the limbic system may cause erection and ejaculation in male animals.

On Pushing the Right Buttons: Are There Pleasure Centers in the Brain?   Electrical stimulation of certain parts of the limbic system apparently yields sensations similar to those of sexual gratification.

Sex Hormones: Do They "Goad" Us into Sex?

Sex hormones have organizing and activating effects on behavior. Men and women normally produce one genuine aphrodisiac: testosterone. Female sex hormones do not appear to play a direct role in determining sexual motiva-

tion or response in human females. Yet levels of testosterone in the bloodstream have been associated with sexual interest in women.

The Sexual Response Cycle

Masters and Johnson found that the physiological responses of men and women to sexual stimulation are quite alike. Both experience vasocongestion and myotonia early in the response cycle.

Excitement Phase   Sexual excitement is characterized by erection in the male and vaginal lubrication in the female.

Plateau Phase   The plateau phase is an advanced state of arousal that precedes orgasm.

Orgasmic Phase   The third phase of the sexual response cycle is characterized by orgasmic contractions of the pelvic musculature. Orgasm in the male occurs in two stages of muscular contractions. Orgasm in the female is manifested by contractions of the pelvic muscles that surround the vaginal barrel.

Resolution Phase   During the resolution phase, the body returns to its prearoused state.

Kaplan's Three Stages of Sexual Response: An Alternative Model   Kaplan developed a three-stage model of sexual response consisting of desire, excitement, and orgasm. Kaplan's model makes it more convenient for clinicians to classify and treat sexual dysfunctions.

Controversies About Orgasm

Multiple Orgasms: When You're Having More Than One   Multiple orgasm is the occurrence of one or more additional orgasms following the first, within a short period of time and before the body has returned to a pre-plateau level of arousal. Most women, but not most men, are capable of multiple orgasms.

How Many Kinds of Orgasms Do Women Have? One, Two, or Three?   Freud theorized the existence of two types of orgasm in women: clitoral and vaginal. Masters and Johnson found only one kind of orgasm among women. Singer and Singer suggested that there are three types of female orgasm: vulval, uterine, and blended.

The G-Spot   The G-spot—an allegedly distinct area of the vagina within the anterior wall—may have special erotic significance. Some researchers suggest that prolonged stimulation of the spot produces an orgasm that is characterized by intense pleasure and, in some women, by a type of ejaculation. The nature of this ejaculate remains in doubt.

CHAPTER 6

Henri Matisse, Sketch for *"The Joy of Living"*, 1905. San Francisco Museum of Modern Art. Bequest of Elise S. Haas. © 1996 Succession H. Matisse/Artist Rights Society (ARS), New York.

Gender Identity and Gender Roles

Outline

Truth OR Fiction?

_____ If male sex hormones were not present during critical stages of prenatal development, we would all develop female sexual organs.

_____ The sex of a baby crocodile is determined by the temperature at which the egg develops.

_____ Thousands of people have changed their genders through gender-reassignment surgery.

_____ Men act more aggressively than women do.

_____ A 2½-year-old child may know that he is a boy but think that he can grow up to be a mommy.

_____ Adolescent girls who show a number of masculine traits are more popular than girls who thoroughly adopt the traditional feminine gender role.

We're halfway there. We've begun to raise our daughters more like sons—so now women are whole people. But fewer of us have the courage to raise our sons more like daughters. Yet until men raise children as much as women do—and are raised to raise children, whether or not they become fathers—they will have a far harder time developing in themselves those human qualities that are wrongly called "feminine," but are really those necessary to raise children: empathy, flexibility, patience, compassion, and the ability to let go.

(Gloria Steinem, graduation speech at Smith College, 1995)

Whatever women do they must do twice as well as men to be thought half as good. Luckily, this is not difficult.

(Charlotte Whitton)

I like men to behave like men—strong and childish.

(French author Françoise Sagan)

These remarks from war correspondents in the battle of the genders signify key issues in the study of gender: gender roles, the actual differences between the genders, and the enduring problem of sexism. This chapter addresses the biological, psychological, and sociological aspects of gender. First we focus on sexual differentiation—the process by which males and females develop distinct reproductive anatomy. We then turn to gender roles—the complex behavior patterns that are deemed "masculine" or "feminine" in a particular culture. The chapter examines empirical findings on actual gender differences, which may challenge some of the preconceptions that many of us hold regarding the differences between men and women. We next consider gender typing—the processes by which boys come to behave in line with what is expected of men (most of the time) and girls with what is expected of women (most of the time). We shall also explore the concept of psychological androgyny, which applies to people who display characteristics associated with both genders.

Prenatal Sexual Differentiation

Sexual differentiation
The process by which males and females develop distinct reproductive anatomy.

Over the years many ideas have been proposed to account for **sexual differentiation,** such as the belief that sperm from the right testicle make females, but sperm from the left testicle make males (Angier, 1990). If this were so, males would indeed be sinister, because *sinister* means "left-hand" or "unlucky side" in Latin.

According to the Bible, Adam was created first, and Eve issued forth from one of his ribs. From the standpoint of modern biological knowledge, however, it would be more accurate to say that "Adams" (that is, males) develop from "Eves" (females). Let us trace the development of sexual differentiation.

Chromosome
One of the rodlike structures, found in the nucleus of every living cell, that carries the genetic code in the form of genes.

When a sperm cell fertilizes an ovum, 23 **chromosomes** from the male parent normally combine with 23 chromosomes from the female parent. The **zygote,** the beginning of a new human being, is only 1/175 of an inch long. Yet, on this tiny stage, one's stamp as a unique individual has already been ensured—whether one will have black or blond hair, grow bald or develop a widow's peak, or become male or female.

Zygote
A fertilized ovum (egg cell).

The chromosomes from each parent combine to form 23 pairs. The 23rd pair are the sex chromosomes. An ovum carries an X sex chromosome, but a sperm carries either an X or a Y sex chromosome. If a sperm with an X sex chromosome fertilizes the ovum, the newly conceived person will normally develop as a female, with an XX sex chromosomal structure. If the sperm carries a Y sex chromosome, the child will normally develop as a male (XY).

Embryo
The stage of prenatal development that begins with implantation of a fertilized ovum in the uterus and concludes with development of the major organ systems at about two months after conception.

After fertilization, the zygote divides repeatedly. After a few short weeks one cell has become billions of cells. At about 3 weeks a primitive heart begins to drive blood through the embryonic bloodstream. At about 5 to 6 weeks, when the **embryo** is only ¼ to ½ inch long, primitive gonads, ducts, and external genitals whose gender cannot be distinguished visually have formed (see Figure 6.1 and Figure 6.2 on page 156). Each embryo possesses

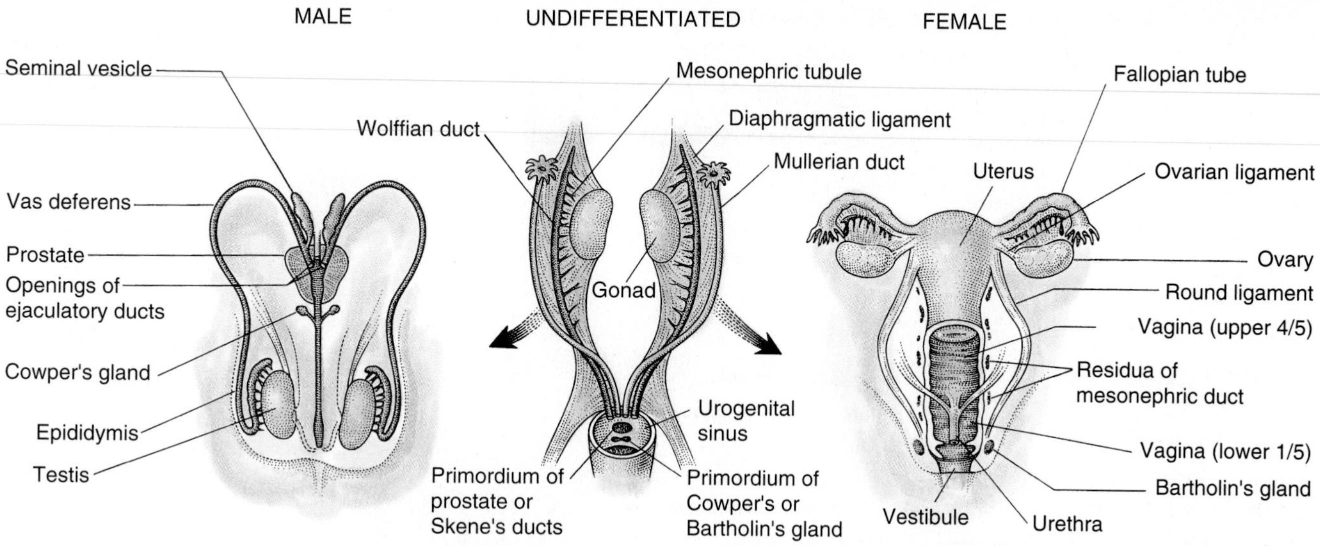

Figure 6.1. Development of the Internal Sexual Organs from an Undifferentiated Stage at About 5 or 6 Weeks Following Conception.

primitive external genitals, a pair of sexually undifferentiated gonads, and two sets of primitive duct structures, the Müllerian (female) ducts and the Wolffian (male) ducts.

During the first 6 weeks or so of prenatal development, embryonic structures of both genders develop along similar lines and resemble primitive female structures. At about the seventh week after conception, the genetic code (XX or XY) begins to assert itself, causing changes in the gonads, genital ducts, and external genitals. The Y sex chromosome causes the testes to begin to differentiate. Ovaries begin to differentiate if the Y chromosome is absent. Some rare individuals who have only one X sex chromosome instead of the typical XY or XX arrangement also become females, since they too lack the Y chromosome (Angier, 1990).

Thus, the basic blueprint of the human embryo is female. The genetic instructions in the Y sex chromosome cause the embryo to deviate from the female developmental course. "Adams" develop from embryos that otherwise would become "Eves."

By about the seventh week of prenatal development, the Y sex chromosome stimulates the production of *H-Y* antigen, a protein that fosters the development of testes. Strands of tissue begin to organize into seminiferous tubules. Female gonads begin to develop somewhat later than male gonads. The forerunners of follicles that will bear ova are not found until the fetal stage of development, about 10 weeks after conception. Ovaries begin to form at 11 or 12 weeks.

The Role of Sex Hormones in Sexual Differentiation

Androgens
Male sex hormones.

Testosterone
The male sex hormone that fosters the development of male sex characteristics and is connected with the sex drive.

Without the influence of male sex hormones, or **androgens,** we would all develop into females (Angier, 1994; Federman, 1994). Once the testes develop in the embryo, they begin to produce androgens. The most important androgen, **testosterone,** spurs differentiation of the male (Wolffian) duct system (see Figure 6.1). Each Wolffian duct develops into an epididymis, vas deferens, and seminal vesicle. The external genitals, including the penis, begin to take shape at about the eighth week of development under the influence of another androgen, *dihydrotestosterone* (DHT). Yet another testicular hormone, one secreted during the fetal stage, prevents the Müllerian ducts from developing into the female duct system. It is appropriately termed the Müllerian inhibiting substance (MIS).

Small amounts of androgens are produced in female fetuses, but they are not normally sufficient to cause male sexual differentiation. In female fetuses, the relative absence of an-

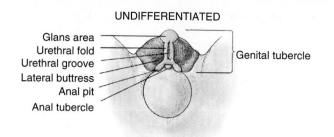

UNDIFFERENTIATED

Glans area
Urethral fold
Urethral groove
Lateral buttress
Anal pit
Anal tubercle

Genital tubercle

45–50 mm

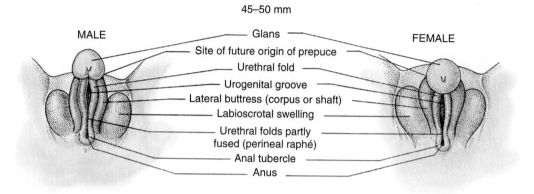

MALE   Glans   FEMALE
Site of future origin of prepuce
Urethral fold
Urogenital groove
Lateral buttress (corpus or shaft)
Labioscrotal swelling
Urethral folds partly
fused (perineal raphé)
Anal tubercle
Anus

FULLY DEVELOPED

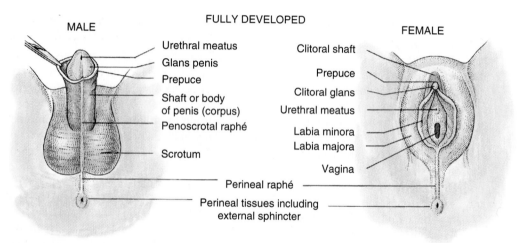

MALE   FEMALE

Urethral meatus   Clitoral shaft
Glans penis   Prepuce
Prepuce   Clitoral glans
Shaft or body   Urethral meatus
of penis (corpus)
Penoscrotal raphé   Labia minora
                                   Labia majora
Scrotum
                                   Vagina
Perineal raphé
Perineal tissues including
external sphincter

Figure 6.2. **Development of the External Sexual Organs from an Undifferentiated Stage at About 5 or 6 Weeks Following Conception.**

drogens causes degeneration of the Wolffian ducts and prompts development of female sexual organs. The Müllerian ducts evolve into fallopian tubes, the uterus, and the upper two thirds of the vagina. These developments occur even in the absence of female sex hormones. Although female sex hormones are crucial in puberty, they are not involved in fetal sexual differentiation. If a fetus with an XY sex chromosomal structure failed to produce testosterone, it would develop female sexual organs.

T r u t h   **OR**   *Fiction?*

R E V I S I T E D

It is true that we would all develop female sexual organs if male sex hormones were not present during critical stages of prenatal development. Embryos develop female sexual organs in the absence of male sex hormones. ■

Descent of the Testes and the Ovaries

The testes and ovaries develop from slender structures high in the abdominal cavity. By about 10 weeks after conception, they have descended so that they are almost even with

Inguinal canal
A fetal canal that connects the scrotum and the testes, allowing their descent. (From the Latin *inguinus*, meaning "near the groin.")

Cryptorchidism
The condition defined by undescended testes. (From roots meaning "hidden testes.")

Klinefelter's syndrome
A sex-chromosomal disorder caused by an extra X sex chromosome.

Turner syndrome
A sex-chromosomal disorder caused by loss of some X chromosome material.

the upper edge of the pelvis. The ovaries remain there for the rest of the prenatal period. Later they rotate and descend farther to their adult position in the pelvis. About four months after conception the testes normally descend into the scrotal sac through the **inguinal canal.** After their descent, this passageway is closed.

In a small percentage of males, one or both testes remain undescended. They remain in the abdomen at birth. The condition is termed **cryptorchidism.** In most cases of cryptorchidism, the testes migrate to the scrotum during infancy. In still other cases the testes descend by puberty. Men with undescended testes are usually treated through surgery or hormonal therapy, since they are at higher risk for cancer of the testes. Sperm production is also impaired because the undescended testes are subjected to a higher-than-optimal body temperature, causing sterility.

Sex Chromosomal Abnormalities

Abnormalities of the sex chromosomes can have profound effects on sexual characteristics, physical health, and psychological development. **Klinefelter syndrome,** a condition that affects about 1 in 500 males, is caused by an extra X sex chromosome, so the man has an XXY rather than an XY pattern. Men with this pattern fail to develop appropriate secondary sex characteristics. They have enlarged breasts, poor muscular development, and, because they fail to produce sperm, they are infertile. They also tend to be mildly retarded.

Turner syndrome, found only in women, occurs in 1 in 2,000–5,000 girls. It is caused by the loss of some X sex chromosome material. These girls develop typical external genital organs, but they are short in stature and their ovaries do not develop or function normally. Girls with Turner syndrome tend to be involved in fewer social activities and to have more academic problems relative to girls without Turner syndrome (Rovet & Ireland, 1994). However, they do not have major social or behavioral problems.

Prenatal Sexual Differentiation of the Brain

The brain, like the genital organs, undergoes prenatal sexual differentiation. Testosterone causes cells in the hypothalamus of male fetuses to become insensitive to the female sex hormone estrogen. In the absence of testosterone, as in female fetuses, the hypothalamus does develop sensitivity to estrogen.

Sensitivity to estrogen is important in the regulation of the menstrual cycle of women after puberty. The hypothalamus detects low levels of estrogen in the blood at the end of each cycle and initiates a new cycle by stimulating the pituitary gland to secrete FSH. FSH, in turn, stimulates estrogen production by the ovaries and the ripening of an immature follicle in an ovary. Sexual differentiation of the hypothalamus most likely occurs during the second trimester of fetal development (Pillard & Weinrich, 1986).

～ *Reflections* ～

What is the relationship between sex chromosomes and anatomic sex? Do you know anyone with one of the chromosomal abnormalities discussed in this section? How did it affect her or him?

What is the role of sex hormones in sexual differentiation?

Gender Identity

Gender identity
The psychological sense of being male or female.

Gender assignment
The labeling of a newborn as a male or female.

For all of us, our awareness of being male or being female—our **gender identity**—is one of the most obvious and important aspects of our self-concepts. Our gender identity is not an automatic extension of our anatomic gender. Gender identity is a psychological construct, a sense of being male or being female. **Gender assignment** reflects the child's anatomic gender and usually occurs at birth. Gender identity is so important to parents that they may want to know "Is it a boy or a girl?" before they begin to count fingers and toes.

Most children first become aware of their anatomic gender by about the age of 18 months. By 36 months, most children have acquired a rather firm sense of gender identity (Etaugh & Rathus, 1995; McConaghy, 1979).

Nature and Nurture in Gender Identity

What determines gender identity? Are our brains biologically programmed along masculine or feminine lines by prenatal sex hormones? Does the environment, in the form of postnatal learning experiences, shape our self-concepts as males or females? Or does gender identity reflect an intermingling of biological and environmental influences?

Gender identity is almost always consistent with chromosomal gender. Such consistency does not certify that gender identity is biologically determined, however. We also tend to be reared as males or females, according to our anatomic genders. How, then, might we sort out the roles of nature and nurture, of biology and the environment?

Pseudohermaphrodites

People who possess the gonads of one gender but external genitalia that are ambiguous or typical of the other gender.

Clues may be found in the experiences of rare individuals, **pseudohermaphrodites,** who possess the gonads of one gender but external genitalia that are ambiguous or typical of the other gender. Pseudohermaphrodites are sometimes reared as members of the other gender (the gender other than their chromosomal gender). Researchers wondered whether the gender identity of these children reflects their chromosomal and gonadal gender or the gender according to which they were reared. Before going further with this, let us distinguish between true hermaphroditism and pseudohermaphroditism.

Hermaphroditism

Hermaphrodites

People who possess both ovarian and testicular tissue. (From the names of the male and female Greek gods *Hermes* and *Aphrodite.*)

Hormonal errors during prenatal development produce various congenital defects. Some individuals are born with both ovarian and testicular tissue. They are called **hermaphrodites,** after the Greek myth of the son of Hermes and Aphrodite, whose body became united with that of a nymph while he was bathing. True hermaphrodites may have one gonad of each gender (a testicle and an ovary), or gonads that combine testicular and ovarian tissue.

Regardless of their genetic gender, hermaphrodites usually assume the gender identity and gender role of the gender assigned at birth. Figure 6.3 shows a genetic female (XX) with a right testicle and left ovary. This person married and became a stepfather with a firm male identity. The roles of biology and environment remain tangled, however, since true hermaphrodites have gonadal tissue of both genders.

Figure 6.3. **A True Hermaphrodite.** This genetic (XX) female has one testicle and one ovary and the gender identity of a male.

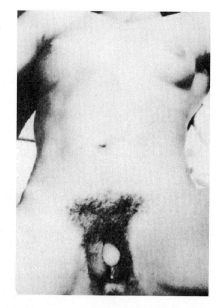

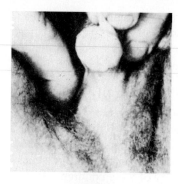

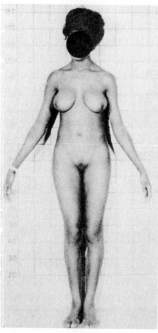

Figure 6.4. Pseudo-hermaphroditism. In androgenital syndrome (top photo), a genetic (XX) female has female internal sexual structures (ovaries) but masculinized external genitals. The bottom photo shows a genetic (XY) male with androgen-insensitivity syndrome. The external genitals are feminized, and the person has always lived as a female.

Androgenital syndrome

A form of pseudohermaphroditism in which a genetic female has internal female sexual structures but masculinized external genitals.

True hermaphroditism is extremely rare. More common is pseudohermaphroditism, which occurs in perhaps 1 infant in 1,000. The occurrence of pseudohermaphroditism has given scientists an opportunity to examine the roles of nature (biology) and nurture (environmental influences) in the shaping of gender identity.

Pseudohermaphroditism *Pseudohermaphrodites* ("false" hermaphrodites) have testes or ovaries, but not both. Unlike true hermaphrodites, their gonads (testes or ovaries) match their chromosomal gender. Because of prenatal hormonal errors, however, their external genitals and sometimes their internal reproductive anatomy are ambiguous or resemble those of the other gender.

The most common form of female pseudohermaphroditism is **androgenital syndrome**, in which a genetic (XX) female has female internal sexual structures (ovaries), but masculinized external genitals (see Figure 6.4). The clitoris is so enlarged that it may resemble a small penis. The syndrome occurs as a result of excessive levels of androgens. In some cases the fetus's own adrenal glands produce excess androgen (the adrenal glands usually produce low levels of androgen). In other cases mothers may have received synthetic androgens during their pregnancies. In the 1950s and 1960s, before these side effects were known, synthetic androgens were sometimes prescribed to help prevent miscarriages in women with histories of spontaneous abortions.

Another type of pseudohermaphroditism, **androgen-insensitivity syndrome**, describes genetic (XY) males who had lower-than-normal prenatal sensitivity to androgens. As a result their genitals did not become normally masculinized. At birth their external genitals are feminized, including a small vagina, and their testes are undescended. Because of insensitivity to androgens, the male duct system (epididymis, vas deferens, seminal vesicles, and ejaculatory ducts) fails to develop. Nevertheless, the fetal testes produce Müllerian inhibiting substance, preventing the development of a uterus or fallopian tubes.

A third type of pseudohermaphroditism is named **Dominican Republic syndrome** because it was first documented in a group of 18 affected boys in two rural villages in that nation (Imperato-McGinley et al., 1974). Dominican Republic syndrome is a genetic enzyme disorder that prevents testosterone from masculinizing the external genitalia. The boys were born with normal testes and internal male reproductive organs, but their external genitals were malformed. Their penises were stunted and resembled clitorises. Their scrotums were incompletely formed and resembled female labia. They also had partially formed vaginas.

Pseudohermaphroditism and Gender Identity The experiences of pseudohermaphrodites have provided insights into the origins of gender identity. The genitals of girls with androgenital syndrome are normally surgically feminized in infancy. The girls also receive hormone treatments to correct excessive adrenal output of androgens. As a result, they usually acquire a feminine gender identity and develop physically as normal females.

What if the syndrome is not identified early in life, however? Consider the cases of two children who were treated at Johns Hopkins University Hospital. The children both suffered from androgenital syndrome, but their treatments and the outcomes were very different. Each child was genetically female (XX). Each had female internal sex organs. Because of prenatal exposure to synthetic male sex hormones, however, each developed masculinized external sex organs (Money & Ehrhardt, 1972).

The problem was identified in one child (let's call her Abby) in infancy. Her masculinized sex organs were removed surgically when she was age 2. Like many other girls, Abby was tomboyish during childhood, but she was always feminine in appearance and had a female gender identity. She began to develop breasts by the age of 12, but did not begin to menstruate until age 20. She dated boys, and her fantasy life centered around marriage to a man.

The other child (let's call him James) was initially mistaken for a genetic male with stunted external sex organs. The error was discovered at the age of 3½. By then he had a firm male gender identity, so surgeons further masculinized his external sex organs rather

Androgen-insensitivity syndrome

A form of pseudohermaphroditism in which a genetic male is prenatally insensitive to androgens. As a result his genitals do not become normally masculinized.

Dominican Republic syndrome

A form of pseudohermaphroditism in which a genetic enzyme disorder prevents testosterone from masculinizing the external genitalia.

than remove them. At puberty, hormone treatments stoked the development of body hair, male musculature, and other male secondary sex characteristics.

As an adolescent, James did poorly in school. Possibly in an effort to compensate for his poor grades, he joined a gang of semidelinquents. He became one of the boys. In contrast to Abby, James was sexually attracted to women.

Both children were pseudohermaphrodites. Both had internal female sexual organs and masculinized external organs, but they were treated and reared differently. In Abby's case, the newborn was designated female, surgically altered to remove the masculinized genitals, and reared as a girl. In James's case, the infant was labeled and reared as a boy. Each child acquired the gender identity of the assigned gender. Environmental influences appeared to play the critical role in shaping the gender identity of these children.

Further evidence for the importance of psychosocial influences on gender identity is found in studies of genetic (XY) males with androgen-insensitivity syndrome. They possess testes but are born with feminine-appearing genitals and are typically reared as girls. They develop a female gender identity and stereotypical feminine interests. They show as much interest in dolls, dresses, and future roles as mothers and housewives as do genetic (XX) girls of the same ages and social class (Brooks-Gunn & Matthews, 1979; Money & Ehrhardt, 1972).

The boys with Dominican Republic syndrome also resembled girls at birth and were reared as females. At puberty, however, their testes swung into normal testosterone production, causing startling changes: their testes descended, their voices deepened, their musculature filled out, and their "clitorises" expanded into penises. Of the 18 boys who were reared as girls, 17 shifted to a male gender identity. Sixteen of the 18 assumed a stereotypical masculine gender role. Of the remaining 2, 1 adopted a male gender identity but continued to maintain a feminine gender role, including wearing dresses. The other maintained a female gender identity and later sought a sex-change operation to "correct" the pubertal masculinization.

The Dominican transformations suggest that gender identity is malleable. What of the roles of nature and nurture in the formation of gender identity, however? If environmental forces (nurture) were predominant, gender identity would be based on the gender in which the person is reared, regardless of biological abnormalities. With the Dominicans, however, pubertal biological changes led to changes in both gender identity and gender roles. Is nature (biology) then the primary determinant of gender identity? Unfortunately, the Dominican study does not allow clear separation of the effects of nature and nurture. One intriguing hypothesis is that the pubertal surges of testosterone may have activated brain structures that were masculinized during prenatal development. Prenatal testosterone levels in these boys were presumably normal and could have affected the sexual differentiation of brain tissue, even though the genetic defect prevented the hormone from masculinizing the external genitalia.

Consider some other possibilities: Did the children, seeing themselves transforming into men, begin to change their self-concepts to be consistent with their anatomic changes? Did the children choose to assume male gender identities because the masculine gender role was positively valued in their culture? Either possibility permits a psychological or cultural explanation of gender identity.

What, then, can we conclude from studies of pseudohermaphrodites? For one thing, gender identity and the assumption of gender roles are strongly influenced by psychosocial factors. Pseudohermaphrodites can acquire the gender identity of the other chromosomal gender when they are reared as members of that gender. The genetic (XX) females—Abby and James—were reared as members of different genders and acquired the gender identity in which they were reared. Yet both were treated with sex hormones appropriate to their assigned gender. Thus, we cannot be certain that sex hormones did not influence their subsequent gender identity. The Dominican study also suggests that gender identity may not be fixed by early learning influences, but may be subject to subsequent biological and/or psychosocial influences.

We should also recognize that the experiences of people affected by these hormonal errors may not generalize to others. Perhaps the brains of these children had not been clearly gender-typed prenatally and were thus capable of an unusual degree of postnatal flexibility in the assumption of gender identity. Perhaps in normal people the brain is more clearly differentiated prenatally, so that gender identity is not so readily influenced by experience.

Most scientists conclude that gender identity is influenced by complex interactions between biological and psychosocial factors. Some place relatively greater emphasis on psychosocial factors (Money, 1987a; Money & Ehrhardt, 1972). Others emphasize the role of biological factors (Collaer & Hines, 1995). The debate over the relative contributions of nature and nurture is likely to continue.

In case you have had enough discussion of the complex issues surrounding the origins of gender in human beings, consider the crocodile. Crocodile eggs do not carry sex chromosomes. The baby's sex is determined, instead, by the temperature at which the eggs develop (Ackerman, 1991). Some (males) like it hot (at least in the mid-90s Fahrenheit), and some (females) like it, not cold perhaps, but under the mid-80s Fahrenheit.

Truth **OR** Fiction?
R E V I S I T E D

It is true that the sex of a baby crocodile is determined by the temperature at which the egg develops. ■

Transsexualism

Transsexuals
People who have a gender-identity disorder in which they feel trapped in the body of the wrong gender.

In 1953 an ex-GI who journeyed to Denmark for a "sex-change operation" made headlines. She became known as Christine (formerly George) Jorgensen. Since then, thousands of **transsexuals** have undergone gender-reassignment surgery. Among the better known is the tennis player Dr. Renée Richards, formerly Dr. Richard Raskin.

Gender-reassignment surgery cannot implant the internal reproductive organs of the other gender. Instead, it generates the likeness of external genitals typical of the other gender. This can be done more precisely with male-to-female than female-to-male transsexuals. After such operations, people can participate in sexual activity and even attain orgasm, but they cannot conceive or bear children.

Renée Richards (née Richard Raskin). Physician Richard Raskin (left) underwent gender reassignment to become Renée Richards (right). Richards played professional tennis on the women's circuit.

It is not true that people have changed their genders through gender-reassignment surgery. Gender-reassignment surgery cannot implant the internal reproductive organs of the other gender. It only generates the appearance of the external genitals typical of the other gender. ■

Gender dysphoria
The subjective experience of incongruity between genital anatomy and gender identity or role.

Transsexuals experience **gender dysphoria.** That is, according to John Money (1994), they have the subjective experience of incongruity between their genital anatomy and their gender identity or role. They have the anatomic sex of one gender but feel that they are members of the other gender. As a result of this discrepancy, they wish to be rid of their own primary sex characteristics (their external genitals and internal sex organs) and to live as members of the other gender. A male transsexual perceives himself to be a female who, through some quirk of fate, was born with the wrong genital equipment. A female transsexual perceives herself as a man trapped in a woman's body. Although the prevalence of transsexualism remains unknown, it is thought to be rare. Pauly (1974) estimated the prevalence at 1 in 100,000 males and 1 in 130,000 females. Experts estimate the number of transsexuals in the United States to be about 25,000. Perhaps 6,000 to 11,000 of them have undergone gender-reassignment surgery (Selvin, 1993).

Patterns of sexual attraction do not appear to be central in importance. Some transsexuals report never having had strong sexual feelings. Others are attracted to members of their own (anatomic) gender. They are unlikely to regard themselves as gay or lesbian, however. From their perspective, their lovers are members of the other gender. Still others are attracted to members of the other anatomic gender. Nonetheless, they all want to be rid of their own sex organs and to live as members of the other gender.

Transsexualism is not to be confused with a gay male or lesbian sexual orientation (Selvin, 1993). Gay males and lesbians are erotically attracted to members of their own gender. A gay man may desire another man as a lover; a lesbian may sexually desire another woman. Gay men and lesbians perceive their gender identities to be consistent with their anatomic gender, however. They would no more want to be rid of their own genitals than would heterosexuals. As one gay man put it, "Just because I'm turned on by other men doesn't make me feel less like a man."

Transsexuals usually show cross-gender preferences in play and dress in early childhood. Many report that they felt they belonged to the other gender for as long as they can remember. Only a few were unaware of their transsexual feelings until adolescence. Male transsexuals generally recall that as children, they preferred playing with dolls, enjoyed wearing frilly dresses, and disliked rough-and-tumble play. They were often perceived by their peers as "sissy boys." Female transsexuals usually report that as children they disliked dresses and acted much like "tomboys." They also preferred playing "boys' games" and doing so with boys. Female transsexuals appear to have an easier time adjusting than male transsexuals (Selvin, 1993). "Tomboys" generally find it easier to be accepted by their peers than "sissy boys." Even in adulthood, it may be easier for a female transsexual to don men's clothes and "pass" as a slightly built man than it is for a brawnier man to pass for a tall woman.

The transition to adolescence is particularly difficult for transsexuals. They find their bodies changing in ways that evoke their disgust. Female transsexuals abhor the onset of menstruation and the development of breasts. They may seek to disguise their budding breasts by binding them or wearing loose clothing. Some have mastectomies at the age of consent to remove the obvious reminder of what they perceive as "nature's mistake."

Theoretical Perspectives   No clear understanding of the nature or causes of transsexualism has emerged (Money, 1994). Views on its origins somewhat parallel those on the origins of a gay male or lesbian sexual orientation, which is surprising, given the fundamental differences that exist between the two.

Identification
In psychoanalytic theory, the process of incorporating within ourselves our perceptions of the behaviors, thoughts, and feelings of others.

Psychoanalytic theorists have focused on early parent–child relationships. Male transsexuals, in this view, may have had "close-binding mothers" (extremely close mother–son relationships) and "detached–hostile fathers" (fathers who were absent or disinterested) (Stoller, 1969). Such family circumstances may have fostered intense **identification** with the mother, to the point of an inversion of typical gender roles and identity. Girls with weak, ineffectual mothers and strong, masculine fathers may identify with their fathers, rejecting their own female identities.

There is some evidence that male transsexuals tend to have had unusually close relationships with their mothers during childhood. Female transsexuals tend to have identified more with their fathers and to have perceived their mothers as cold and rejecting (Pauly, 1974). Yet one problem with the psychoanalytic view is that the roles of cause and effect may be reversed. It could be that in childhood, transsexuals gravitate toward the parent of the other gender and reject the efforts of the parent of the same gender to reach out to them and engage them in gender-typed activities. These views also do not account for the many transsexuals whose family backgrounds fail to match these patterns. Moreover, these views lack predictive power. Most children—in fact, the vast majority!—with such family backgrounds do *not* become transsexuals.

The early onset of transsexual feelings suggests that critical early learning experiences, if they exist, might occur in the preschool years. Transsexuals may also be influenced by prenatal hormonal imbalances. The brain is in some ways "masculinized" or "feminized" by sex hormones during prenatal development. The brain could be influenced in one direction, even as the genitals are being differentiated in the other direction (Money, 1987a).

Gender Reassignment   Gender reassignment for transsexuals has been controversial since its inception. Yet psychotherapy is not considered a reasonable alternative, because it has been generally unsuccessful in helping transsexuals accept their anatomic genders (Roberto, 1983; Tollison & Adams, 1979).

Surgery is one element of gender reassignment. Since the surgery is irreversible, health professionals conduct careful evaluations to determine that people seeking reassignment are competent to make such decisions and have thought through the consequences. They usually require that the transsexual live openly as a member of the other gender for a trial period of at least a year before surgery.

Once the decision is reached, a lifetime of hormone treatments is begun. Male-to-female transsexuals receive estrogen, which fosters the development of female secondary sex characteristics. It causes fatty deposits to develop in the breasts and hips, softens the skin, and inhibits growth of the beard. Female-to-male transsexuals receive androgens, which promote male secondary sex characteristics. The voice deepens, hair becomes distributed according to the male pattern, muscles enlarge, and the fatty deposits in the breasts and hips are lost. The clitoris may also grow more prominent.

Gender-reassignment surgery is largely cosmetic. Medical science cannot construct internal genital organs or gonads. Male-to-female surgery is generally more successful. The penis and testicles are first removed. Tissue from the penis is placed in an artificial vagina so that sensitive nerve endings will provide sexual sensations. A penis-shaped form of plastic or balsa wood is used to keep the vagina distended during healing.

In female-to-male transsexuals, the internal sex organs (ovaries, fallopian tubes, uterus) are removed, along with the remaining fatty tissue in the breasts. The nipples are moved to keep them at the proper height on the torso. The urethra is rerouted through the enlarged clitoris, or an artificial penis and scrotum are constructed from tissue from the abdomen, the labia, and the perineum through a series of operations. In either case, the patient can urinate while standing, which appears to provide psychological gratification. Although the artificial penis does not stiffen and become erect naturally, a variety of methods, including implants, can be used to allow the artificial penis to approximate erection.

Some transsexuals hesitate to undertake surgery because they are repulsed by the prospect of such extreme medical intervention. Others forgo surgery so as not to jeopardize high-status careers or family relationships (Kockott & Fahrner, 1987). Such people continue to think of themselves as members of the other gender, however, even without surgery.

Outcomes of Gender-Reassignment Surgery   Following the introduction of gender-reassignment surgery in the the United States in 1960s, most reports of postoperative adjustment were positive (Pauly, 1986). An influential study in the 1970s conducted at the Gender Identity Clinic at Johns Hopkins University was quite negative, however (Meyer & Reter, 1979). The study included a control group of transsexuals who did not receive gender-reassignment surgery. Psychological adjustment was more positive among transsexuals in the control group than among those who had undergone surgery.

Other reviews report more positive outcomes for gender-reassignment surgery (Kockott & Fahrner, 1987; Lundstrom et al., 1984; Pauly & Edgerton, 1986). One study of 42 postoperative male-to-female transsexuals found that all but one would repeat the surgery. Moreover, the great majority found sexual activity more pleasurable as a "woman" (Bentler, 1976).

Reviewers of the international literature reported in 1984 that about 90% of transsexuals who undergo gender-reassignment surgery experience positive results (Lundstrom et al., 1984). In Canada, a follow-up study of 116 transsexuals (female-to-male and male-to-female) at least one year after surgery found that most of them were content with the results and were reasonably well adjusted (Blanchard et al., 1985). Positive results for surgery were also reported in a study of 141 Dutch transsexuals (Kuiper & Cohen-Kettenis, 1988). Nearly 9 of 10 male-to-female and female-to-male transsexuals in a study of 23 transsexuals reported they were very pleased with the results of their gender-reassignment surgery (Lief & Hubschman, 1993). Still another study (Abramowitz, 1986) reported that about two out of three cases showed at least some postoperative improvement in psychological adjustment. These favorable results do not mean that postoperative transsexuals were ecstatic about their lives. In many cases it meant that they were less unhappy. Most transsexuals are socially maladjusted prior to gender reassignment, and many remain lonely and isolated afterward. Moreover, about half incur postoperative medical complications (Lindermalm et al., 1986).

Male-to-female transsexuals whose surgery permitted them to pass as members of the other gender showed better adjustment than those whose surgery left telltale signs (such as breast scarring and leftover erectile tissue) that they were not "real" women (Ross & Need, 1989). Social and family support also contributed to postsurgical adjustment (Ross & Need, 1989).

Male-to-female transsexuals outnumber female-to-males, but postoperative adjustment is apparently more favorable for female-to-males. Nearly 10% of male-to-female cases, as compared to 4% to 5% of female-to-males, have had disturbing outcomes, such as severe psychological disorders, hospitalization, requests for reversal surgery, and even suicide (Abramowitz, 1986). One reason for the relatively better postoperative adjustment of the female-to-male transsexuals may be society's more accepting attitudes toward women who desire to become men (Abramowitz, 1986). Female-to-male transsexuals tend to be better adjusted socially before surgery as well (Kockott & Fahrner, 1988; Pauly, 1974), so their superior postoperative adjustment may be nothing more than a selection factor.

A growing number of programs across the country have been established to help transsexuals come to terms with themselves and adjust to living in a society in which they rarely feel welcome (Selvin, 1993). One example is the Gender Identity Project in New York City's Greenwich Village, which sponsors meetings where transsexuals get together and share common concerns. Such programs help create a sense of community for a group of people who feel alienated from the larger society.

~ *Reflections* ~

- What is your gender identity? What is the relationship between your anatomic sex and your gender identity?
- Had you heard of transsexualism before taking this course? How do the facts on transsexualism differ from what you had heard?
- What is the difference between transsexualism and a gay male or lesbian sexual orientation?

Gender Roles and Stereotypes

"Why can't a woman be more like a man?" You may recall this lyric from the song that Professor Henry Higgins sings in the musical *My Fair Lady*. In the song the professor laments that women are emotional and fickle, whereas men are logical and dependable.

Stereotype
A fixed, conventional idea about a group of people.

Gender roles
Complex clusters of ways in which males and females are expected to behave.

The "emotional woman" is a **stereotype**—a fixed, oversimplified, and often severely distorted idea about a group of people. The "logical man" is also a stereotype—albeit more generous. Gender roles are stereotypes in that they evoke fixed, conventional expectations of men and women.

Our gender identities—our personal identification of ourselves according to our concepts of masculinity and femininity—do not determine the roles or behaviors that are deemed masculine or feminine in our culture. Cultures have broad expectations of men and women that are termed **gender roles.**

Some might think that people "play" gender roles in the same way that many actors play roles. That is, they sense that they are pretending, and they conform to what the director wants. (The "director" here may be society at large.) John Money, however, writes that gender roles are very much a part of the person:

> In the language of the theater, a gender role is not a script handed to an actor but a role incorporated into the actor, who, [changed] by it, manifests it in person. An actor does not simply learn a role, he or she assimilates and lives it. So also with gender role: a child assimilates and lives it, is inhabited by it, has it as a belonging, and manifests it to others . . . in word and deed. There is no one cause of a gender role. It develops under the influence of multiple factors, sequentially over time, from prenatal life onwards. Nature alone is not responsible, nor is nurture alone. They work together, hand in glove.
>
> (Money, 1994, p. 166)

In our culture the stereotypical female exhibits traits such as gentleness, dependency, kindness, helpfulness, patience, and submissiveness (Cartwright et al., 1983). The masculine gender-role stereotype is one of toughness, gentlemanliness, and protectiveness (Myers & Gonda, 1982). Females are generally seen as warm and emotional; males as independent, assertive, and competitive. The times are a-changing, somewhat. Women, as well as men, now bring home the bacon, but women are still more often expected to fry it in the pan and bear the primary responsibility for child rearing (Deaux & Lewis, 1983). In some cultures, however, women are reared to be the hunters and food gatherers while men stay close to home and tend the children.

～ *Reflections* ～

- Agree or disagree with the following statement, and support your answer: A woman's place is in the home.
- How do most people from your sociocultural background feel about traditional gender roles? Why?

A Woman's Place? Contemporary men and women are entering occupations that had been traditionally associated with the other gender. Women fight fires and pilot aircraft; men pursue careers in nursing and primary education.

MACHISMO/MARIANISMO *STEREOTYPES AND HISPANIC CULTURE**

The term *Hispanic* is generally used to describe Spanish-speaking peoples of Latin America whose cultures were influenced by a mixture of Spanish, African, and Native American (Indian) cultures. Although Hispanic peoples share some common cultural traditions, most notably the Spanish language and devotion to Christianity, each Spanish-speaking nation in Latin America has its own cultural tradition, as well as distinct subcultures. The differences among the peoples of Latin America can be seen in their dress styles, their use of language, and their musical and literary traditions. Argentinians, for example, tend to be more Europeanized in their style of dress and tastes in music. In the Dominican Republic and Puerto Rico, the influence of African and native Carib Indian cultures blossoms forth in the colorful style of dress and in the use of percussion instruments in music.

The *machismo* tradition should be evaluated in this light. *Machismo* is a cultural stereotype that defines masculinity in terms of an idealized view of manliness. To be *macho* is to be

strong, virile, and dominant. Each Hispanic culture puts its own particular cultural stamp on the meaning of *machismo*, however. In the Spanish-speaking cultures of the Caribbean and Central America, the macho code encourages men to restrain their feelings and maintain an emotional distance. In my travels in Argentina and some other Latin American countries, however, I have observed that men who are sensitive and emotionally expressive are not perceived as compromising their macho code.

Marianismo

In counterpoint to the macho ideal among Hispanic peoples is the cultural idealization of femininity embodied in the concept of *marianismo*. The *marianismo* stereotype, which derives its name from the Virgin Mary, refers to the ideal of the virtuous woman as one who "suffers in silence," submerging her needs and desires to serve those of her husband and children. With the marianismo stereotype, the image of a woman's role as a martyr is raised to the level of a cultural ideal. According to this cultural stereotype, a woman is

expected to demonstrate her love for her husband by waiting patiently at home and having dinner prepared for him at any time of day or night he happens to come home, to have his slippers ready for him, and so on. The feminine ideal is one of suffering in silence and being the provider of joy, even in the face of pain. Strongly influenced by the patriarchal Spanish tradition, the *marianismo* stereotype has historically been used to maintain women in a subordinate position in relation to men.

Acculturation: When Traditional Stereotypes Meet the Financial Realities of Life in the United States

Acculturation—the merging of cultures that occurs when immigrant groups become assimilated into the mainstream culture—has challenged this traditional *machismo/marianismo* division of marital roles among Hispanic couples in the United States. I have seen in my own work in treating Hispanic couples in therapy that marriages are under increasing strain from the conflict between traditional and modern expectations about marital roles. Hispanic American women have

Sexism

Sexism

The prejudgment that because of gender, a person will possess negative traits.

We have all encountered the effects of **sexism**—the prejudgment that because of gender, a person will possess certain negative traits. These negative traits are assumed to disqualify the person for certain vocations or prevent him or her from performing adequately in these jobs or in some social situations.

Sexism may even lead us to interpret the same behavior in prejudicial ways when performed by women or by men. We may see the man as "self-assertive," but the woman as "pushy." We may look upon *him* as flexible, but brand *her* fickle and indecisive. *He* may be rational, whereas *she* is cold. *He* is tough when necessary, but *she* is bitchy. When the businesswoman engages in stereotypical masculine behaviors, the sexist reacts negatively by branding her abnormal or unhealthy.

Sexism may make it difficult for men to act in ways that are stereotyped as feminine. A "sensitive" woman is simply sensitive, but a sensitive man may be seen as a "sissy." A woman may be perceived as polite, whereas a man showing the same behavior seems passive or weak. Only recently have men begun to enter occupational domains previously re-

been entering the workforce in increasing numbers, usually in domestic or child-care positions, but they are still expected to assume responsibility for tending their own children, keeping the house, and serving their husbands' needs when they return home. In many cases, a reversal of traditional roles occurs, in which the wife works and supports the family while the husband remains at home because he is unable to find or maintain employment.

It is often the Hispanic American husband who has the greater difficulty accepting a more flexible distribution of roles within the marriage and giving up a rigid set of expectations tied to traditional *machismo/marianismo* gender expectations. Although some couples manage to reshape their expectations and marital roles in the face of changing conditions, many relationships buckle under the strain and are terminated in divorce. While I do not expect either the *machismo* or *marianismo* stereotype to disappear entirely, I would not be surprised to find a greater flexibility in gender-role expectations as a product of continued acculturation.

*This World of Diversity feature was written by Rafael. Javier, Ph.D. Dr. Javier is associate clinical professor of psychology and director of the Center for Psychological Services and Clinical Studies at St. John's University in Jamaica, New York. Dr. Javier was born in the Dominican Republic and educated in philosophy in the Dominican Republic, Puerto Rico, and Venezuela, and in psychology and psychoanalysis at New York University. He is a practicing psychoanalyst and maintains a research interest in psycholinguistics and psychotherapy with ethnic minorities. All rights are reserved by Dr. Javier.

Hispanic-American Women. Many Hispanic Americans adhere to the machismo stereotype of men as restraining their feelings and maintaining an emotional distance. The marianismo stereotype for women idealizes women who suffer in silence, who subordinate their needs to those of their husbands and children.

stricted largely to women, such as secretarial work, nursing, and teaching in the primary grades. Only recently have the floodgates opened for women into traditionally masculine professions such as engineering, law, and medicine.

Although children of both genders have about the same general learning ability, stereotypes limit their horizons. Children tend to show preferences for gender-typed activities and toys by as early as 2 or 3 years of age. If they should stray from them, their peers are sure to remind them of the "errors of their ways." How many little girls are discouraged from considering professions like architecture and engineering because they are handed dolls, not blocks and fire trucks? How many little boys are discouraged from pursuing child-care and nursing professions because of the "funny" looks they get from others when they reach for dolls?

Children not only develop stereotyped attitudes about play activities; they also develop stereotypes about the differences between "man's work" and "woman's work." Women have been historically excluded from "male occupations," and stereotypical expectations concerning "men's work" and "women's work" filter down to the primary grades. For example, according to traditional stereotypes, women are *not expected* to excel in math. Exposure to such negative expectations may discourage women from careers in science and technology.

MOM THE BREADWINNER

Why do women work? To buy the family a second car? To provide vacation money? To send the kids to camp? According to a poll by Louis Harris and Associates (1995), these stereotypes no longer hold water. Women's work is no longer supplemental. Women, like men, work to support the family.

Yes, we are all familiar with the high-powered mothers like Michelle Pfeiffer, Hillary Clinton, and Marcia Clark, who outearn their husbands or support their children on their own. But out of the spotlight, the earning power of the ordinary woman has been growing by leaps and bounds. According to the Harris poll, wives share about equally with their husbands in supporting their families. Nearly half of them—48%—reported that they provided at least half of their family's income, and not just vacation money—half of the mortgage, half of the clothing, half of the medical bills, half of the new pairs of Reeboks and mountain bikes (Lewin, 1995).

Why is it that we still think of women as primarily mothers? Why haven't we paid more attention to their new roles as providers? Perhaps it is because working mothers continue to do what mothers in general have done. That is, 9 of 10 still bear the primary responsibility for the children, cooking, and cleaning (Lewin, 1995). Are they overburdened? Perhaps. The survey reveals that working mothers are pressed for time. They are worried about not having enough time with their families and about balancing the demands of work and a home life. Nevertheless, when they were asked whether they would like to surrender some of their responsibilities, 53% of working women said no. Even more ironic, full-time working mothers reported that they felt more likely to feel valued for their contributions at

home than full-time homemakers were.

Despite their roles as providers, women still don't rank their values in the same way that men do. The poll inquired as to what made working women feel successful at work. Most of the respondents mentioned the quality of the work they did (51%), its meaning (17%), the magnitude of what they produced (16%), and the recognition of supervisors and co-workers (12%). Only 7% of them said money.

Despite their new earning power, working mothers are still primarily concerned about their children. When they were asked what made them feel successful at home, about one man and woman in four mentioned good relationships and spend-

ing time together. The next-largest group of women (22%) reported good, well-adjusted, healthy children. But 20% of men mentioned money, or being able to afford things. Only 8% of the men mentioned well-adjusted kids. Just 5% of the women mentioned money.

And despite the work ethic, working mothers still value a caring and generous nature above other human qualities (49%). They rate honesty second (37%). Being good wives or mothers comes in third (16%), and a strong work ethic comes in only fourth (13%).

So mom is still doing what mom has been expected to do. She is still looking after the house and kids. But now she also pays half the bills.

Why Do Women Work? To support the family. We are familiar with high-profile mothers like Marcia Clark, Michelle Pfeiffer, and Hillary Clinton, who outearn their husbands or support their children on their own. But the earning power of the ordinary woman has been growing such that wives now share about equally with their husbands in supporting their families.

~ *Reflections* ~

▪ Have you encountered sexism? Under what circumstances? What was its effect on you?

▪ Have you been guilty of sexism? (Are you sure?) What are you going to do about it?

Gender Differences: *Vive la Différence* or *Vive la Similarité?*

If the genders were not anatomically different, this book would never have been written. How do the genders differ in cognitive abilities and personality, however?

Differences in Cognitive Abilities

A classic review by Eleanor Maccoby and Carol Nagy Jacklin (1974) found persistent evidence that females are somewhat superior to males in verbal ability. But a more recent review of the accumulated evidence found no overall gender differences in verbal abilities, with the exception that boys are more often slower to develop language skills (Hyde & Linn, 1988). Far more boys than girls have reading problems, ranging from reading below grade level to severe disabilities.

Males generally exceed females in visual–spatial abilities (Voyer et al., 1995). Visual–spatial skills include the ability to follow a map when traveling to an unfamiliar location, to construct a puzzle or assemble a piece of equipment, and to perceive relationships between figures in space (see Figure 6.5).

Differences in math are small and narrowing at all ages (Hyde et al., 1990). Females excel in computational ability in elementary school, however. Males excel in mathematical problem solving in high school and in college (Hyde et al., 1990). Differences in problem solving are reflected on the mathematics test of the Scholastic Aptitude Test (SAT). The mean score is 500, and about two thirds of the test takers receive scores between 400 and 600. Boys outperform girls on SAT math items (Byrnes & Takahira, 1993). Twice as many boys as girls attain scores over 500. According to Byrnes and Takahira (1993), boys' superiority in math does not reflect gender per se. Instead, boys do well because of prior knowledge of math and their strategies for approaching math problems.

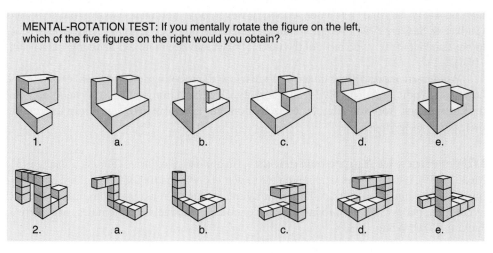

MENTAL-ROTATION TEST: If you mentally rotate the figure on the left, which of the five figures on the right would you obtain?

Figure 6.5. Rotating Geometric Figures in Space. Visual–spatial skills—for example, the ability to rotate geometric figures in space—have been considered part of the male gender-role stereotype. Gender differences in visual–spatial skills are small, however, and can be modified by training. (*Source:* From Rathus, S. A., et al. (1990). *Psychology.* [4th ed.]. Copyright © 1990 by Holt, Rinehart & Winston, Inc. Reprinted by permission of the publishers.)

In our culture, then, girls are somewhat advanced in their development of verbal abilities. Boys apparently show greater math ability, beginning in adolescence. Three factors should caution us not to attach too much importance to these gender differences, however:

1. In most cases, the differences are small (Hyde & Plant, 1995). Differences in verbal, mathematical, and spatial abilities are also getting smaller (Hyde et al., 1990; Maccoby, 1990; Voyer et al., 1995).
2. These gender differences are *group* differences. Variation in ability on tests of verbal or math skills is larger *within,* than between, the genders (Maccoby, 1990). Despite differences between groups of boys and girls, millions of boys exceed the "average" girl in writing and spelling skills. Likewise, millions of girls outperform the "average" boy in problem-solving and spatial tasks. The male gender has produced its Shakespeares and the female gender its Madame Curies.
3. The small differences that may exist may largely reflect environmental influences and cultural expectations (Tobias, 1982). Spatial and math skills are stereotyped in our culture as masculine, whereas reading skills are stereotyped as feminine. In one study, however, female introductory psychology students who were given but three hours of training in performing visual–spatial skills such as rotating geometric figures performed these tasks as well as men (Stericker & LeVesconte, 1982).

Differences in Personality

There are also many gender differences in personality. According to a meta-analysis of the research literature, females exceed males in extraversion, anxiety, trust, and nurturance (Feingold, 1994). Males exceed females in assertiveness, tough-mindedness, and self-esteem. The assertiveness is connected with aggressiveness, as we see below. The tough-mindedness has unfortunate implications for men's health, as we also see. Your third author notes, with some displeasure, two factors that may largely account for the relatively lower self-esteem of females:

- Parents, on the average, prefer to have boys.
- Society has created an unlevel playing field in which females have to perform better than males to be seen as doing equally well.

Differences in Communication Styles: "He's Just an Old Chatterbox"
We have been inundated with cartoons of suburban housewives gossiping across the fence or pouring endless cups of coffee when the "girls" drop by for a chat. Research has shown, however, that in many situations men spend more time talking than women do. Men are also more likely to introduce new topics and interrupt others (Brooks, 1982; Deaux, 1985; Hall, 1984). Girls tend to be more talkative during early childhood than boys. By the time they enter school, however, boys dominate classroom discussions (Sadker & Sadker, 1994). As girls mature, it appears that they learn to "take a back seat" to boys and let the boys do most of the talking when they are in mixed-gender groups (Hall, 1984).

Women are more willing than men to disclose their feelings and personal experiences, however (Dindia & Allen, 1992). The stereotype of the "strong and silent" male may not discourage men from hogging the conversation, but it may inhibit them from expressing their personal feelings.

Differences in Aggressiveness
In almost all cultures (Ford & Beach, 1951; Mead, 1935), it is the males who march off to war and who battle for fame, glory, and shaving-cream-commercial contracts in stadiums and arenas. In most psychological studies on aggression, males have been found to behave more aggressively than females (Maccoby & Jacklin, 1980; White, 1983).

Truth OR Fiction?

REVISITED

It is true that men act more aggressively, on the whole, than women do. The question remains, *why?* ■

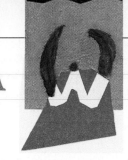

A WORLD OF DIVERSITY

ON THE EDGE OF REBELLION—JAPANESE STYLE

Traditional Japanese women have literally trailed their husbands for centuries. They have scrubbed the men's muddy footprints, made their baths, and, in the olden days, paid for infidelity with their heads. Their servitude was so complete that a sixteenth-century Spanish trader referred to Japanese women as "pious" and "excellent," and to Japanese men as "cruel" (WuDunn, 1995).

In the workplace of today, Japanese women are last to be hired and first to be fired. They are rarely allowed to carry the business cards of their companies. Japanese women are no longer resigned or reticent. Many, in fact, could not be more scathing in their opinions about Japanese men.

"My father almost never steps inside the kitchen," says 23-year-old Chie Suziki, a systems analyst. "If Mom is around, he wouldn't even serve tea—he'd just yell 'Tea!' But of course if my mother isn't around, he has to do it by himself. Would I marry someone like my dad? No way!" (WuDunn, 1995).

Japan's feminist movement is only in the formative stages, but women of all ages are nevertheless quietly rebelling. They call new hot lines; they organize pressure groups; they even file suits for sex discrimination. Today's Japanese women are also placing more emphasis on their careers. As a result, they are getting married later and having fewer children—all of which alarms Japanese men.

Kayo Enomoto is a 23-year-old travel agency worker who spent a year in the United States. She doubts that she will find a tolerable husband in Japan. "I think Japanese men are dreaming," says the independent Enomoto. "They have this ideal figure of a woman that's different from reality. Men like women who will make them three square meals a day and wait patiently for their return home."

A Mini-Experiment
To make her point about Japanese men, Enomoto conducted a mini-

experiment. One evening at a drinking party, she decided to role-play the obedient woman. She attended the men, refilling their beer glasses and wiping the tables clean.

"At the end of the party, I was the most popular girl," she complained. "Half of the guys wanted my phone number. I was so disappointed. I wondered how stupid the guys could be."

On Large Chunks of Garbage and Soggy Leaves
While Japanese women have been traditionally wedded to their marriages, their husbands have been traditionally wedded to their jobs. Many women refer to their husbands as "seven-elevens"—meaning that they are on the job at 7:00 in the morning and do not leave until 11:00 in the evening.

These men often have no hobbies. The lack of outside interests creates special problems when they retire. Some wives who have spent their lives in the home refer to a retired husband as *sodai-gomi*, "a large chunk of garbage," something lying around on the sofa like a worn-out accessory that needs to be tossed out. Some retired

husbands are dubbed *nure-ochiba*. Here the metaphor refers to a soggy fallen leaf, the sort that sticks annoyingly to the body.

The "large chunks of garbage" and "soggy fallen leaves" are sometimes divorced by their wives when they retire. If servitude is difficult for women when men are away on the job, it apparently becomes suffocating when men lie around the house all day.

Raised to Be Spoiled
In Japan, "men are raised to be spoiled," laments Yumiko Hamada, a writer who lived with her husband in the United States for many years. During this period, the couple's gender roles had become somewhat flexible, so that Hamada's husband had begun to help with the dishes and other household chores. Now that they have returned to Japan, the husband still helps with the dishes at home, but not when they visit his parents. "When we go over there, it's constant work for me," says Hamada (WuDunn, 1995). "His parents would still be horrified to see him do 'woman's work,' " she explains.

A Woman's Place—in Japan, That Is. Traditional Japanese women have literally trailed their husbands for centuries. Even in today's workplace, Japanese women are last to be hired and first to be fired. Yet many Japanese women are no longer resigned or reticent. Some are quite scathing about Japanese men who harbor traditional expectations.

Differences in Willingness to Seek Health Care   Men's life expectancies are seven years shorter, on the average, than women's. Part of the difference, according to a survey of 1,500 physicians, is due to women's greater willingness to seek health care ("Doctors tie male mentality," 1995). Men often let symptoms go until a problem that could have been prevented or readily treated becomes serious or life threatening. Women, for example, are much more likely to check themselves for breast cancer than men are to even recognize the symptoms of prostate cancer. Many men, according to the survey, have a "bullet-proof mentality." They are too strong to see the doctor in their 20s, too busy in their 30s, and too frightened later on.

On Becoming a Man or a Woman: Gender Typing

Gender typing
The process by which children acquire behavior that is deemed appropriate to their gender.

We have chronicled the biological process of sexual differentiation, and we have explored some gender differences in cognitive abilities and behavior. In this section we consider various explanations of **gender typing.**

Biological Perspectives

Biological views on gender typing tend to focus on the roles of genetics and prenatal influences in predisposing men and women to gender-linked behavior patterns. Biological perspectives have also focused on the possible role of hormones in sculpting the brain during prenatal development.

Sociobiology: It's Only Natural   To the sociobiologist, the story of the survival of our ancient ancestors is etched in our genes. Sociobiologists propose that those genes that bestow attributes that increase an organism's chances of surviving to produce viable offspring are most likely to be transmitted to future generations. We thus possess the genetic remnants of traits that helped our ancestors survive and reproduce. This heritage, according to sociobiologists, influences our social and sexual behavior as well as our anatomic features.

According to sociobiologists, men's traditional roles as hunters and warriors, and women's roles as caregivers and gatherers of fruits and vegetables, are bequeathed to us in our genes. Men are better suited to war and the hunt because of physical attributes passed along since ancestral times. Upper-body strength, for example, would have enabled them to throw spears and overpower adversaries. Men also possess perceptual–cognitive advantages, such as superior visual–motor skills that favor aggression. Visual–motor skills would have enabled men to aim spears or bows and arrows.

Women, it is argued, are genetically predisposed to be empathic and nurturant because these traits enabled ancestral women to respond to children's needs and enhance the likelihood that their children would flourish and eventually reproduce, thereby transmitting their own genetic legacy to future generations. Prehistoric women thus tended to stay close to home, care for the children, and gather edible plants, whereas men ventured from home to hunt and raid their neighbors' storehouses.

Sociobiology is steeped in controversy. Although scientists do not dispute the importance of evolution in determining physical attributes, many are reluctant to attribute complex social behaviors, such as aggression and gender roles, to heredity. The sociobiological argument implies that stereotypical gender roles—men as breadwinners and women as homemakers, for example—reflect the natural order of things. Critics contend that biology is not destiny, that our behavior is not dictated by our genes.

Prenatal Brain Organization   Researchers have sought the origins of gender-typed behavior in the organization of the brain. Is it possible that the cornerstone of gender-typed behavior is laid in the brain before the first breath is taken?

The hemispheres of the brain are specialized to carry out certain functions (Levy, 1985). In most people, the right hemisphere ("right brain") appears to be specialized to perform visual–spatial tasks. The "left brain" appears to be more essential to verbal functions, such as speech, in most people.

We know that sex hormones are responsible for prenatal sexual differentiation of the genitals and for the gender-related structural differences in the hypothalamus of the developing prenatal brain. Sexual differentiation of the brain may also partly explain men's (slight!) superiority at spatial-relations tasks, such as interpreting road maps and visualizing objects in space. Testosterone in the brains of male fetuses spurs greater growth of the right hemisphere and slows the rate of growth of the left hemisphere. This difference may be connected with the ability to accomplish spatial-relations tasks.

Might boys' inclinations toward aggression and rough-and-tumble play also be prenatally imprinted in the brain? Some theorists argue that prenatal sex hormones may masculinize or feminize the brain by creating predispositions that are consistent with gender-role stereotypes, such as rough-and-tumble play and aggressive behavior in males (Collaer & Hines, 1995). Money (1987a) allows a role for prenatal dispositions but argues that social learning plays a stronger role in gender typing. He claims that social learning is even potent enough to counteract prenatal predispositions.

Cross-Cultural Perspectives

Sociobiology cannot account for differences in gender roles that exist across cultures, especially neighboring cultures. The anthropologist Margaret Mead (1935) lived among several tribes on the South Pacific island of New Guinea and found that gender roles in these tribes differed not only from those of Western culture, but also from one another.

Among the Mundugumor, a tribe of headhunters and cannibals, both men and women were warlike and aggressive. The women disdained bearing and rearing children because it interrupted participation in warring parties against neighboring villages. The men and women of the Arapesh tribe were gentle and peaceful, by contrast. Both genders nurtured the children. The Tchambuli were even more unusual in terms of what we consider stereotypical behavior in our society. The men spent most of their time caring for children, gossiping, bickering, primping and applying makeup, and haggling over prices. Fish was the staple diet of the Tchambuli, and women brought home the daily catch. Women kept their heads shaven, disdained ornaments, and were more highly sexed and aggressive than men.

Whatever the influence of biology on behavior, biological factors alone do not make men aggressive or independent, or women passive or submissive (Havemann & Lehtinen, 1990). Cultural expectations and learning play a large role.

Gender Roles as a Cultural Adaptation   The Mundugumor, Arapesh, and Tchambuli peoples of New Guinea—and members of modern industrialized societies—all share the same biological makeup. Within each gender, the same sex hormones pulse through the arteries of the peoples of New Guinea as through the arteries of stockbrokers on Wall Street. (Yes, even stockbrokers are warm-blooded.) Yet despite this common biological makeup, wide cultural variations exist with respect to gender roles.

Anthropologists believe that cultural differences in gender roles can be explained in terms of the adaptations that cultures make to their social and natural environments (Werner & Cohen, 1990). Consider differences in gender roles between the Sambian people of New Guinea and the !Kung people of Africa. The Sambians have rigidly defined gender roles. Boys are socialized to become warriors, whereas women tend the children and keep a discreet distance from men (Herdt, 1987). Among the !Kung people, however, women play a more active role in tribal affairs and are permitted more autonomy (Drapers, 1975).

How might such differences arise? The Sambians, until recently, were subject to repeated attacks from enemies and could survive only by rearing their sons as warriors (Wender & Cohen, 1990). Sambians' rigid gender roles may be seen as an adaptation to these onslaughts. The !Kung live in small scattered groups and forage for their food. Both genders make substantial contributions to the food supply. In this egalitarian society, gender roles are more flexible. Both men and women enjoy considerable autonomy and influence.

Psychological Perspectives

Children acquire awareness of gender-role stereotypes by the tender ages of 2½ to 3½ (Kuhn et al., 1978). Both boys and girls generally agree, when asked to describe the differences between the genders, that boys build things, play with transportation toys such as cars and fire trucks, enjoy helping their fathers, and hit other children. Both boys and girls also agree that girls enjoy playing with dolls and helping their mothers cook and clean, and are talkative, dependent on others for help, and nonviolent. They perceive the label "cruel" to be a masculine trait, whereas "cries a lot" is perceived as a feminine trait. By the time they are age 3, most children have become aware of the differences in stereotypical ways men and women dress and the types of occupations that are considered appropriate for each gender (Ruble & Ruble, 1982). Psychologists have attempted to explain how children acquire such knowledge and adopt stereotypical behavior patterns in terms of psychodynamic, social-learning, and cognitive–developmental theories.

Psychodynamic Theory   Sigmund Freud explained gender typing in terms of identification. Appropriate gender typing, in Freud's view, requires that boys come to identify with their fathers and girls with their mothers. Identification is completed, in Freud's view, as children resolve the **Oedipus complex** (sometimes called the Electra complex in girls).

According to Freud, the Oedipus complex occurs during the phallic period of psychosexual development, from the ages of 3 to 5. During this period the child develops incestuous wishes for the parent of the other gender and comes to perceive the parent of the same gender as a rival. The complex is resolved by the child's forsaking incestuous wishes for the parent of the other gender and identifying with the parent of the same gender. Through identification with the same-gender parent, the child comes to develop gender-typed behaviors that are typically associated with that gender. Children display stereotypical gender-typed behaviors earlier than Freud would have predicted, however. Even during the first year, boys are more independent than girls. Girls are more quiet and restrained. Girls show preferences for dolls and soft toys, and boys for hard transportation toys, by the ages of 1½ to 3.

Social-Learning Theory   Social-learning theorists explain the development of gender-typed behavior in terms of processes such as observational learning, identification, and socialization. Children can learn what is deemed masculine or feminine by observational learning, as suggested by the results of an experiment by Perry and Bussey (1979). In this study, 8- and 9-year-old boys and girls watched adult role models indicate their preferences for each of 16 pairs of items—pairs such as toy cows versus toy horses and oranges versus apples. What the children didn't know was that the expressed preferences were made arbitrarily. The children then were asked to indicate their own preferences for the items represented in the pairs. The boys' choices agreed with the adult men's an average of 14 out of 16 times. Girls chose the pair item selected by the men, on the average, only 3 out of 16 times.

In social-learning theory, identification is viewed as a continuing and broadly based learning process in which rewards and punishments influence children to imitate adult models of the same gender—especially the parent of the same gender (Storms, 1979). Identification is more than imitation, however. In identification, the child not only imitates the behavior of the model, but tries to become like the model in broad terms.

Socialization also plays a role in gender typing. Almost from the moment a baby comes into the world, it is treated according to its gender. Parents tend to talk more to baby girls, and fathers especially engage in more roughhousing with boys (Jacklin et al., 1984). When children are old enough to speak, parents and other adults—even other children—begin to instruct children as to how they are expected to behave. Parents may reward children for behavior they consider gender-appropriate and punish (or fail to reinforce) them for behavior they consider inappropriate for their gender. Girls are encouraged to practice caretaking behaviors, which are intended to prepare them for traditional feminine adult

---

Oedipus complex

A conflict of the phallic stage in which the boy wishes to possess his mother sexually and perceives his father as a rival in love.

Socialization

The process of guiding people into socially acceptable behavior patterns by means of information, rewards, and punishments.

roles. Boys are handed erector sets or doctor sets to help prepare them for traditional masculine adult roles.

Fathers generally encourage their sons to develop assertive, instrumental behavior (that is, behavior that gets things done or accomplishes something) and their daughters to develop nurturant, cooperative behavior. Fathers are likely to cuddle their daughters gently. They are likely to carry their sons like footballs or toss them into the air. Fathers also tend to use heartier and harsher language with their sons, such as "How're yuh doin', Tiger?" and "Hey you, get your keester over here" (Jacklin et al., 1984). Being a nontraditionalist, your first author made sure to toss his young daughters into the air, which raised immediate objections from the relatives, who chastised him for being too rough. This, of course, led him to modify his behavior. He learned to toss his daughters into the air when the relatives were not around.

Generally speaking, from an early age boys are more likely to receive toy cars and guns and athletic equipment and to be encouraged to compete aggressively. Even relatively sophisticated college students are likely to select traditionally masculine toys as gifts for boys and traditionally feminine toys for girls (Fisher-Thompson, 1990). Girls are spoken to more often, whereas boys are handled more frequently and more roughly. Whatever the biological determinants of gender differences in aggressiveness and verbal skills, early socialization experiences clearly contribute to gender typing.

Parental roles in gender typing are apparently changing. With more mothers working outside the home, daughters today are exposed to more women who represent career-minded role models than was the case in earlier generations. More parents today are encouraging their daughters to become career-minded and to engage in strenuous physical activities, such as organized sports. Many boys today are exposed to fathers who take a larger role than men used to in child care and household responsibilities.

Schools are also important socialization influences. Schools have been slow to adapt to recent changes in gender roles (Sadker & Sadker, 1994). They may be exposing children to masculine and feminine images that are even more rigid and polarized than those currently held in society at large. Teachers often expect girls to perform better than boys in reading and language arts and have higher expectations of boys in math and science. These expectations may be conveyed to children, patterning their choices of careers.

Sexism in America's schools is widespread. Many tests remain biased against girls, which reduces their chances of obtaining scholarships and gaining admission to more competitive colleges (Chira, 1992). Many science teachers and some math teachers tend to ignore girls in favor of boys. Such biases may discourage young women with aptitude in math and science from pursuing careers in these areas. Yet the report highlighted some promising developments. The traditional gender gap in math scores is narrowing; girls have made significant gains in catching up to boys. Moreover, special programs in math and science for girls held after school and in the summer have helped bolster the girls' confidence and interest in these subjects.

The popular media—books, magazines, radio, film, and especially television—also convey gender stereotypes (Remafedi, 1990). The media by and large portray men and women in traditional roles (Signorielli, 1990). Men more often play doctors, attorneys, and police officers. Women more often play nurses, secretaries, paralegals, and teachers. Even when women portray attorneys or police officers, they are more likely than men to handle family disputes. The male police officer is more likely to be shown in action roles; the male attorney holds the court spellbound with a probing cross-examination. Working women are also more likely than men to be portrayed as undergoing role conflict—being pulled in opposite directions by job and family. One study reported that despite current awareness of sexism, "Women are often still depicted on television as half-clad and half-witted, and needing to be rescued by quick-thinking, fully clothed men" (Adelson, 1990). Ageism buttresses sexism in that female characters age 40 and above are only rarely depicted in roles other than mothers and grandmothers.

Social-learning theorists believe that aggression is largely influenced by learning. Boys are permitted, even encouraged, to engage in more aggressive behavior than girls. Nonetheless, females are likely to act aggressively under certain conditions. Ann Frodi and her colleagues (1977) reviewed 72 studies that examined gender differences in aggression. All in all, females acted as aggressively as men when they were given the physical means to do so and believed that aggression was justified. In an influential review article, Maccoby and Jacklin commented on the socialization influences that discourage aggression in girls:

> Aggression in general is less acceptable for girls, and is more actively discouraged in them, by either direct punishment, withdrawal of affection, or simply cognitive training that "that isn't the way girls act." Girls then build up greater anxieties about aggression, and greater inhibitions against displaying it. (1974, p. 234)

Social-learning theorists have made important contributions to our understanding of how rewards, punishments, and modeling influences foster gender-typed behavior patterns. How do children integrate gender-role expectations within their self-concepts? And how do their concepts concerning gender influence their development of gender-typed behavior? Let us consider two cognitive approaches to gender typing that shed light on these matters: cognitive–developmental theory and gender schema theory.

Schema
Concept; way of interpreting experience or processing information.

Cognitive–Developmental Theory Psychologist Lawrence Kohlberg (1966) proposed a cognitive–developmental view of gender typing. From this perspective, gender typing is not the product of environmental influences that mechanically "stamp in" gender-appropriate behavior. Rather, children themselves play an active role. They form concepts, or **schemas,** about gender and then conform their behavior to their gender concepts. These developments occur in stages and are entwined with general cognitive development.

According to Kohlberg, gender typing entails the emergence of three concepts: *gender identity, gender stability,* and *gender constancy.* Gender identity is usually acquired by the age of 3. By the age of 4 or 5, most children develop a concept of **gender stability**—the recognition that people retain their genders for a lifetime. Prior to this age, boys may think that they will become mommies when they grow up, and girls, daddies.

Gender stability
The concept that people retain their genders for a lifetime.

Truth **OR** *Fiction?*
REVISITED

It is true that a 2½-year-old child may know that he is a boy but think that he can grow up to be a mommy. Children at this age have not yet developed gender stability. ■

Gender Typing. According to cognitive theories of gender typing, children are motivated to behave in ways that are consistent with their genders. Children seek information as to what behaviors are deemed appropriate for people of their gender.

Gender constancy
The concept that people's genders do not change, even if they alter their dress or behavior.

The more sophisticated concept of **gender constancy** develops in most children by the age of 7 or 8. They recognize that gender does not change, even if people alter their dress or behavior. So gender remains constant even when appearances change. A woman who wears her hair short (or shaves it off) remains a woman. A man who dons an apron and cooks dinner remains a man.

According to cognitive–developmental theory, children are motivated to behave in gender-appropriate ways once they have established the concepts of gender stability and gender constancy. They then make an active effort to obtain information as to which behavior patterns are considered "masculine" and which "feminine" (Perry & Bussey, 1979). Once they obtain this information, they imitate the "gender-appropriate" pattern. So boys and girls who come to recognize that their genders will remain a fixed part of their identity will show preferences for "masculine" and "feminine" activities, respectively. Researchers find, for instance, that boys who had achieved gender constancy played with an uninteresting gender-typed toy for a longer period of time than did boys who hadn't yet achieved gender constancy (Frey & Ruble, 1992). Both groups of boys played with an interesting gender-typed toy for about an equal length of time.

Cross-cultural studies of the United States, Samoa, Nepal, Belize, and Kenya find that the concepts of gender identity, gender stability, and gender constancy emerge in the order predicted by Kohlberg. However, gender-typed play often emerges at an earlier age than would be predicted by the cognitive–developmental theory. Many children make gender-typed choices of toys by the age of 2. Children as young as 18 months are likely to have developed a sense of gender identity, but gender stability and constancy are some years off. Gender identity alone thus seems sufficient to prompt children to assume gender-typed behavior patterns. Psychologist Sandra Bem (1983) also notes that Kohlberg's theory does not explain why the concept of gender plays such a prominent role in children's classification of people and behavior. Another cognitive view, gender schema theory, attempts to address these concerns.

Gender Schema Theory: An Information-Processing Approach

Gender schema
A cluster of mental representations about male and female physical qualities, behaviors, and personality traits.

Gender schema theory proposes that children develop a **gender schema** as a means of organizing their perceptions of the world (Bem, 1981, 1985; Martin & Halverson, 1981). A gender schema is a cluster of mental representations about male and female physical qualities, behaviors, and personality traits. Gender gains prominence as a schema for organizing experience because of society's emphasis on it. Even young children start to mentally group people of the same gender according to the traits that represent that gender.

Children's gender schemas determine how important gender-typed traits are to them. Consider the dimension of *strength–weakness*. Children may learn that strength is connected with maleness and weakness with femaleness. (Other dimensions, such as *light–dark,* are not gender-typed and thus may fall outside children's gender schemas.) Children also gather that some dimensions, such as strong–weak, are more important to one gender (in this case, male) than the other.

Once children acquire a gender schema, they begin to judge themselves according to traits considered relevant to their genders. In doing so, they blend their developing self-concepts with the prominent gender schema of their culture. The gender schema furnishes standards for comparison. Children with self-concepts that are consistent with the prominent gender schema of their culture are likely to develop higher self-esteem than children whose self-concepts are inconsistent. Jack learns that muscle strength is a characteristic associated with "manliness." He is likely to think more highly of himself if he perceives himself as embodying this attribute than if he does not. Barbara is likely to discover that the dimension of kindness–cruelty is more crucial than strength–weakness to the way in which women are perceived in society.

According to gender schema theory, gender identity itself is sufficient to inspire gender-appropriate behavior. Once children develop a concept of gender identity, they begin to seek information concerning gender-typed traits and strive to live up to them. Jack will retaliate when provoked, because boys are expected to do so. Barbara will be "sugary and sweet" if such is expected of little girls. Thus, gender-typed behavior emerges earlier than would be proposed by cognitive–developmental theory. Jack and Barbara's self-esteem depends in part on how they measure up to the gender schema.

Research suggests that children do process information according to a gender schema (Levy & Carter, 1989; Stangor & Ruble, 1989). Objects and activities pertinent to a child's own gender are better retained in memory. Boys, for example, do a better job of remembering transportation toys they have been shown previously, whereas girls are better at recalling dolls and other "feminine" objects (Bradbard & Endsley, 1983). In another study, Martin and Halverson (1983) showed elementary school children pictures of children involved in "gender-consistent" or "gender-inconsistent" activities. Gender-consistent pictures showed boys doing things like sawing wood and playing with trains. Girls were shown doing things like cooking and cleaning. Gender-inconsistent pictures showed models of the other gender involved in gender-typed endeavors. A week later, the children were asked whether boys or girls had engaged in each activity. Boys and girls both made errors recalling the genders of the models shown engaging in "gender-inconsistent" behavior.

Once established, gender schemas resist change, even when broad social changes occur. For this reason, many parents cannot accept their sons' wearing ("feminine") earrings. A generation earlier, parents had similar difficulty accepting daughters in jeans or sons in long hair.

~ *Reflections* ~

- Summarize gender differences in cognitive functioning and personality. Do research findings on the nature of gender differences fit your own ideas about gender differences? How, or how not?
- What biological and psychological factors contribute to gender differences?
- How would you explain gender differences in aggressive behavior? Do you know some men who are aggressive and some who are not? How would you explain the differences from person to person?

Gender Roles and Sexual Behavior

Gender roles have had a profound influence on dating practices and sexual behavior. Children learn at an early age that men usually make dates and initiate sexual interactions, whereas women usually serve as the "gatekeepers" in romantic relationships. In their traditional role as gatekeepers, women are expected to wait to be asked out and to screen suitors. Men are expected to make the first (sexual) move and women to determine how far advances will proceed. Regrettably, some men refuse to take no for an answer. They feel that they have the right to force their dates into sexual relations.

Men as Sexually Aggressive, Women as Sexually Passive

The cultural expectation that men are initiators and women are gatekeepers is embedded within the larger stereotype that men are sexually aggressive and women are sexually passive. Men not only initiate sexual encounters; they are expected to dictate all the "moves" thereafter, just as they are expected to take the lead on the dance floor. According to the stereotype, women are to let men determine the choice, timing, and sequence of sexual positions and techniques. Unfortunately, the stereotype favors men's sexual preferences, denying women the opportunity to give and receive their preferred kinds of stimulation.

A woman may more easily reach orgasm in the **female-superior position,** but her partner may prefer the **male-superior position.** If the man is calling the shots, she may not have the opportunity to reach orgasm. Even the expression of her preferences may be deemed "unladylike."

Female-superior position
A coital position in which the woman is on top.

Male-superior position
A coital position in which the man is on top.

The stereotypical masculine role also imposes constraints on men. Men are expected to take the lead in bringing their partners to orgasm, but they should not ask their partners what they like because they are expected to be natural experts. ("Real men" not only don't eat quiche; they also need not ask women how to make love.)

Fortunately, more flexible attitudes are emerging. Women are becoming more sexually assertive, and men are becoming more receptive to expressing tenderness and gentleness. Still, the roots of traditional gender roles run deep. A recent survey of students in human sexuality classes in colleges in the New York–New Jersey area showed that males reported more instances of women initiating sex than women reported initiating (Anderson & Aymami, 1993). Who got it right? Are women who initiate sex less willing to admit they do so, perhaps even to themselves, because they hold to the stereotypical expectation that "nice girls don't"? Are men so taken with themselves that they believe that women can't help pursuing them for sexual relations? Perhaps a combination of factors is involved in explaining this discrepancy. What do you think?

Men as Overaroused, Women as Underaroused

According to another stereotype, men become sexually aroused at puberty and remain at the ready throughout adulthood. Women, however, do not share men's natural interests in sex, and a woman discovers her own sexuality only when a man ignites her sexual flame. Men must continue to stoke women's sexual embers, lest they die out. The stereotype denies that "normal" women have spontaneous sexual desires or are readily aroused.

It was widely believed in the Victorian period (even by so-called sex experts!) that women are naturally asexual and "unbothered" by sexual desires. The contemporary residues of this stereotype hold that women do not enjoy sex as much as men and that women who openly express their sexual desires are "whores" or "sluts." The stereotype that women are undersexed also supports the traditional double standard: it is natural for men to sow their wild oats, but women who are sexually active outside of committed relationships are sluts or *nymphomaniacs.*

Despite the stereotype, women are no less arousable than men. Nor do they wait upon the attentions of a man to discover their sexuality. Children of both genders routinely discover that touching their genitals produces pleasurable sensations long before they have intimate relationships.

~ *Reflections* ~

- Are the men you know sexually aggressive? Are the women you know sexually passive? How do you account for differences in sexual aggressiveness and sexual passivity among the people you know?
- Do you notice gender differences in sexual arousability? If so, what are they? How do you account for them?
- Which do you find to be more noticeable among the people you know: gender differences in sexual arousability or individual differences in sexual arousability? Explain.

Psychological Androgyny: The More Traits, the Merrier?

Most people think of masculinity and femininity as opposite ends of one continuum (Storms, 1980). People tend to assume that the more masculine a person is, the less feminine he or she must be, and vice versa. So a man who exhibits stereotypical feminine traits of nurturance, tenderness, and emotionality is often considered less masculine than other

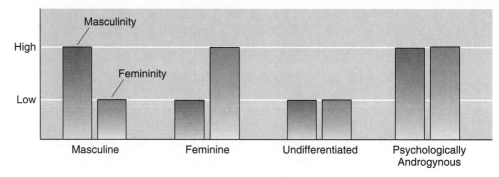

Figure 6.6. **A Model of Psychological Androgyny.** Some behavioral scientists argue that masculinity and femininity are independent personality dimensions. People who exhibit "masculine" assertiveness and instrumental skills along with "feminine" nurturance and cooperation are said to be psychologically androgynous. People high in assertiveness and instrumental skills fit only the masculine stereotype. People high in traits such as nurturance and cooperation fit only the feminine stereotype. People low in the stereotypical masculine and feminine patterns are considered undifferentiated. (*Source:* From Rathus, S. A. and Nevid, J. S. [1989]. *Psychology and the challenges: Adjustment and growth* [4th ed.]. Copyright © 1989 by Holt, Rinehart & Winston, Inc. Reprinted by permission of the publisher.)

men. Women who compete with men in business are perceived not only as more masculine but also as less feminine than other women.

Psychological androgyny
Possession of stereotypical masculine traits, such as assertiveness and instrumental skills, along with stereotypical feminine traits, such as expressiveness, nurturance, and cooperation.

Some behavioral scientists, such as Sandra Bem, argue that masculinity and femininity comprise separate personality dimensions. A person who is highly masculine, whether male or female, may also possess feminine traits—and vice versa. People who exhibit "masculine" assertiveness and instrumental skills (skills in the sciences and business, for example) along with "feminine" nurturance and cooperation fit both the masculine and feminine gender-role stereotypes. They are said to show **psychological androgyny** (see Figure 6.6). People high in assertiveness and instrumental skills fit only the masculine stereotype. People high in traits such as nurturance and cooperation fit only the feminine stereotype. People low in the stereotypical masculine and feminine patterns are considered "undifferentiated" according to gender-role stereotypes.

People who are psychologically androgynous may be capable of summoning a wider range of masculine and feminine traits to meet the demands of various situations and to express their desires and talents. Researchers, for example, have found psychologically androgynous persons of both genders to show "masculine" independence under group pressures to conform and "feminine" nurturance in interactions with a kitten or baby (Bem, 1975; Bem et al., 1976). Androgynous men and women are more apt to share leadership responsibilities in mixed-gender groups (Porter et al., 1985). By contrast, "masculine" men and women tend to dominate such groups, whereas "feminine" men and women are likely to take a back seat.

Many people who oppose the constraints of traditional gender roles may perceive psychological androgyny as a desirable goal. Some feminist writers, however, criticize psychological androgyny on grounds that the concept is defined in terms of, and thereby perpetuates, belief in the existence of masculine and feminine gender roles (Lott, 1985).

Psychological Androgyny, Psychological Well-Being, and Personal Development

Psychologically androgynous people tend to have higher self-esteem and to be generally better adjusted psychologically than people who are feminine or undifferentiated. Yet it appears that these benefits are more strongly related to the presence of masculine traits than to the combination of masculine and feminine traits (Whitley, 1983; Williams & D'Alessandro, 1994). That is, masculine traits such as assertiveness and independence may be related to psychological well-being, whether or not they are combined with feminine traits such as warmth, nurturance, and cooperation.

There is also evidence that feminine traits, such as nurturance and sensitivity, appear to predict success in intimate relationships—in *men* as well as in women. Marital happiness as rated by husbands is positively related to femininity in the wives (Antill, 1983). More interestingly, perhaps, ratings of marital happiness from the wives were also positively correlated with their husbands' femininity. Androgynous men are more likely to express tender feelings of love toward their partners and to be more accepting of their partner's faults than are masculine-typed ("macho") men (Coleman & Ganong, 1985). It seems that both genders appreciate spouses who are sympathetic, able to express warmth and tenderness, and nurturant toward children.

Masculine and androgynous adolescents of both genders tend to be more popular and to have higher self-esteem than other adolescents (Lamke, 1982b). We might not be surprised, given the prevalence of sexism, that adolescent boys fare better if they possess stereotypical masculine traits. What is more surprising is that adolescent girls also fare better when they exhibit stereotypical masculine traits, such as assertiveness and independence. It seems that young women do not risk having others question their femininity if they exhibit masculine traits, providing more evidence that the constellations of traits we call masculinity and femininity are independent clusters.

Truth OR Fiction?
REVISITED

It is true that adolescent girls who show a number of masculine traits are more popular than girls who thoroughly adopt the traditional feminine gender role. Masculine traits such as independence and assertiveness apparently do not compromise their friends' perceptions of their femininity. ■

Psychological Androgyny and Sexual Behavior

Some evidence shows psychologically androgynous men and women to be more comfortable with their sexuality than are masculine men and feminine women (Walfish & Mayerson, 1980). Perhaps they can draw upon a broader repertoire of sexual behaviors. They may be comfortable with cuddling and tender holding, and also with initiating and directing sexual interactions. Researchers also find that androgynous women experience orgasm more frequently (Radlove, 1983) and express greater sexual satisfaction (Kimlicka et al., 1983) than feminine women do.

Who Is Androgynous?

Sandra Bem (1974) reported that about 50% of her college student samples adhered to their own gender-role stereotypes. About 15% were cross-typed (described by traits stereotypical of the other gender), and 35% were androgynous. In more recent research, other researchers found a somewhat lower incidence of androgyny, about 25%, based upon samples of high school students (e.g., Lamke, 1982a).

A sample of African American and White women showed that relatively more African American women could be classified as psychologically androgynous. Relatively more White women were categorized as undifferentiated (Binion, 1990). Although the African American women were more psychologically androgynous in terms of their personality traits, they held predominantly traditional beliefs about the woman's role in the family.

In this chapter we have focused on the biology and psychology of gender. Our gender, both anatomically and psychologically, is a primary aspect of our sexuality. In the next chapter we begin to explore how we express our sexuality through intimate relationships with others.

~ Reflections ~

Would you consider yourself to be a highly masculine man? A highly feminine woman? Why, or why not?

How is your masculinity or femininity related to your sense of who you are and to your self-esteem? Explain.

Would most people from your sociocultural background believe that psychological androgyny is desirable? Why, or why not?

Summing Up

Prenatal Sexual Differentiation

During the first six weeks or so of prenatal development, embryonic structures of both genders develop along similar lines and resemble primitive female structures. At about the seventh week after conception, the genetic code (XX or XY) begins to assert itself, causing changes in the gonads, genital ducts, and external genitals.

The Role of Sex Hormones in Sexual Differentiation Testosterone spurs differentiation of the male (Wolffian) duct system. In the absence of testosterone, the Wolffian ducts degenerate, and female sex organs develop.

Descent of the Testes and the Ovaries The testes and ovaries develop in the abdominal cavity. About four months after conception, the testes descend into the scrotal sac.

Sex Chromosomal Abnormalities Abnormalities of the sex chromosomes can have profound effects on sexual characteristics, physical health, and psychological development. Examples include Klinefelter syndrome and Turner syndrome.

Prenatal Sexual Differentiation of the Brain Gender-specific changes occur in the hypothalamus during prenatal development. Testosterone causes cells in the hypothalamus of male fetuses to become insensitive to estrogen.

Gender Identity

One's gender identity is one's sense of being male or being female.

Nature and Nurture in Gender Identity Gender identity is almost always consistent with anatomic gender.

Hermaphroditism Some individuals—hermaphrodites—are born with both ovarian and testicular tissue. Hermaphrodites usually assume the gender identity and gender role of the gender assigned at birth. Pseudohermaphrodites can acquire the gender identity of the other chromosomal gender when they are reared as members of that gender.

Transsexualism Transsexuals harbor a deep sense of discomfort about their anatomic gender. Hormone treatments and gender-reassignment surgery provide transsexuals with many of the characteristics of the other gender.

Gender Roles and Stereotypes

Cultures have broad expectations of men and women that are termed *gender roles.* In our culture the stereotypical female is seen as gentle, dependent, kind, helpful, patient, and submissive. The stereotypical male is tough, competitive, gentlemanly, and protective.

Sexism

Sexism is the prejudgment that because of gender, a person will possess certain negative traits that disqualify him or her for certain vocations or prevent him or her from performing adequately in these jobs or in some social situations. Women have been historically excluded from "male occupations," and stereotypical expectations concerning "men's work" and "women's work" filter down to the primary grades.

Gender Differences: Vive la Différence or Vive la Similarité?

Differences in Cognitive Abilities Boys have historically been seen as excelling in math and spatial-relations skills, whereas girls have been viewed as excelling in language skills. Gender differences in these areas are small, however, and cultural expectations play a role in them.

Differences in Personality Stereotypical gender preferences for toys and play activities are in evidence at an early age. Males are more aggressive than females, but the question is, *why?*

On Becoming a Man or a Woman: Gender Typing

Biological Perspectives Biological views on gender typing focus on the roles of genetics and prenatal influences in predisposing men and women to gender-linked behavior patterns. Testosterone in the brains of male fetuses spurs greater growth of the right hemisphere, which may be connected with the ability to manage spatial-relations tasks.

Cross-Cultural Perspectives Anthropologists have found that differences in gender roles exist among preliterate cultures and even between neighboring cultures.

Psychological Perspectives Psychologists have attempted to explain gender typing in terms of psychodynamic, social-learning, and cognitive–developmental theories. Freud explained gender typing in terms of identification with the parent of the same gender through resolution of the Oedipus complex.

Social-learning theorists explain the development of gender-typed behavior in terms of processes such as observational learning, identification, and socialization.

According to the cognitive–developmental view, children form concepts about gender and then make their behavior conform to their gender concepts. According to Kohlberg, gender typing entails the emergence of three concepts: gender identity, gender stability, and gender constancy.

Gender schema theory proposes that children develop a gender schema as a means of organizing their perceptions of the world. Once children acquire a gender schema, they begin to judge themselves according to traits considered relevant to their genders. In doing so they blend their developing self-concepts with the prominent gender schema of their culture.

Gender Roles and Sexual Behavior

Stereotypical gender-role expectations affect dating practices and sexual behavior.

Men as Sexually Aggressive, Women as Sexually Passive   According to this stereotype, men are sexual initiators and women are sexual gatekeepers. Men not only initiate sexual encounters; they are expected to initiate all the "moves."

Men as Overaroused, Women as Underaroused   According to another stereotype, women do not share men's interests in sex and discover their own sexuality only when a man ignites their sexual flame.

Psychological Androgyny: The More Traits, the Merrier?

Masculinity and femininity may comprise two independent personality dimensions. People who combine stereotypical masculine and feminine behavior patterns are psychologically androgynous.

Psychological Androgyny, Psychological Well-Being, and Personal Development   Masculine and androgynous people of both genders tend to be better psychologically adjusted than people who are feminine or undifferentiated.

Psychological Androgyny and Sexual Behavior   Psychologically androgynous men and women are more comfortable with their sexuality than masculine men and feminine women.

Who Is Androgynous?   Estimates of psychological androgyny among high school and college samples based on previous research range from 25% to 35%.

CHAPTER 7

Henri Matisse, *The Heart,* Plate 7 from *Jazz.* The Metropolitan Museum
of Art, Gift of Lila Acheson Wallace, 1983. © 1996 Succession H. Matisse/Artist
Rights Society (ARS), New York. © 1985 by The Metropolitan Museum of Art.

Attraction and Love

Truth OR Fiction?

_____ Beauty is in the eye of the beholder.

_____ College men would like women to be thinner than the women want to be.

_____ People are regarded as more attractive when they are smiling.

_____ Women who are randomly assigned names like Kathy and Jennifer are rated as more attractive than women assigned names like Harriet and Gertrude.

_____ Physical appeal is the most important trait we seek in partners for long-term relationships.

_____ "Opposites attract." We are more apt, that is, to be attracted to people who disagree with our views and tastes than to people who share them.

_____ It is possible to be in love with someone who is not also a friend.

Candy and Stretch. A new technique for controlling weight gain? No, these are the names of a couple who have just met at a camera club that doubles as a meeting place for singles.

Candy and Stretch stand above the crowd—literally. She is almost 6 feet tall, an attractive woman in her early 30s. He is more plain looking, but "wholesome." He is in his late 30s and 6 feet 5 inches tall. Stretch has been in the group for some time. Candy is a new member. Let us follow them as they meet during a coffee break. As you will see, there are some differences between what they say and what they think.[1]

THEY SAY	*THEY THINK*
STRETCH: Well, you're certainly a welcome addition to our group.	(Can't I ever say something clever?)
CANDY: Thank you. It certainly is friendly and interesting.	(He's cute.)
STRETCH: My friends call me Stretch. It's left over from my basketball days. Silly, but I'm used to it.	(It's safer than saying my name is David Stein.)
CANDY: My name is Candy.	(At least my nickname is. He doesn't have to hear Hortense O'Brien.)
STRETCH: What kind of camera is that?	(Why couldn't a girl named Candy be Jewish? It's only a nickname, isn't it?)
CANDY: Just this old German one of my uncle's. I borrowed it from the office.	(He could be Irish. And that camera looks expensive.)
STRETCH: May I? (He takes her camera, brushing her hand and then tingling with the touch.) Fine lens. You work for your uncle?	(Now I've done it. Brought up work.)
CANDY: Ever since college.	(Okay, so what if I only went for a year?)
It's more than being just a secretary. I get into sales, too.	(If he asks what I sell, I'll tell him anything except underwear.)
STRETCH: Sales? That's funny. I'm in sales, too, but mainly as an executive. I run our department.	(Is there a nice way to say used cars? I'd better change the subject.)
I started using cameras on trips. Last time I was in the Bahamas, I took—	(Great legs! And the way her hips move—)
CANDY: Oh! Do you go to the Bahamas, too? I love those islands.	(So I went just once, and it was for the brassiere manufacturers' convention. At least we're off the subject of jobs.)
STRETCH:	(She's probably been around. Well, at least we're off the subject of jobs.)
I did a little underwater work there last summer. Fantastic colors. So rich in life.	(And lonelier than hell.)
CANDY:	(Look at that build. He must swim like a fish. I should learn.)
I wish I'd had time when I was there. I love the water.	(Well, I do. At the beach, anyway, where I can wade in and not go too deep.

So begins a relationship. Candy and Stretch have a drink and talk, talk, talk—sharing their likes and dislikes. Amazingly, they seem to agree on everything, from clothing to cars to politics. The attraction they feel is very strong, and neither of them is willing to turn the other off by disagreeing.

They fall in love. Weeks later they still agree on everything, even though there is one topic they avoid scrupulously: religion. Their different backgrounds became apparent once they exchanged last names. That doesn't mean they have to talk about it, however.

[1]Bach and Deutsch (1970).

186 ~ CHAPTER 7 ATTRACTION AND LOVE

They delay introductions to their parents. The O'Briens and the Steins are narrow-minded about religion. If the truth be known, so are Candy and Stretch. Candy errs by telling Stretch, "You're not like other Jews I know." Stretch also voices his feelings now and then. After Candy has nursed him through a cold, he remarks, "You know, you're very Jewish." Candy and Stretch play the games required to maintain the relationship. They tell themselves that their remarks were mistakes, and, after all, anyone can make mistakes. They were meant as compliments, weren't they? Yet each is becoming isolated from family and friends.

One of the topics they ignore is birth control. As a Catholic, Candy does not take oral contraceptives. (Stretch later claimed that he had assumed she did.) Candy becomes pregnant, and they get married. Only through professional help do they learn each other's genuine feelings. And on several occasions, the union comes close to dissolving.

How do we explain the goings-on in this tangled web of deception? Candy and Stretch felt strongly attracted to each other. What determines who is attractive? Why did Candy and Stretch pretend to agree on everything? Why did they put off introductions to their parents?

Two possible consequences of attraction are friendship and love. Candy and Stretch "fell in love." What *is* love? When the first author was a teenager, the answer was, "Five feet of heaven in a ponytail." However, this answer may lack scientific merit. We see that there are different forms of love and that our concepts of love are far from universal.

 **Attraction**

Let us explore some of the factors that determine interpersonal attraction.

Physical Attractiveness: How Important Is Looking Good?

We might like to think of ourselves as so sophisticated that physical attractiveness does not move us. We might like to claim that sensitivity, warmth, and intelligence are more important to us. However, we may never learn about other people's personalities if they do not meet our minimal standards for physical attractiveness. Research shows that physical attractiveness is a major determinant of interpersonal and sexual attraction (Hensley, 1992). In fact, physical appearance is the key factor in consideration of partners for dates, sex, and marriage (Hatfield & Sprecher, 1986).

Is Beauty in the Eye of the Beholder?
What determines physical attractiveness? Are our standards fully subjective, or is there broad agreement on what is attractive? Cross-cultural studies show that people universally want physically appealing partners (Ford & Beach, 1951). However, is that which appeals in one culture repulsive in others?

In certain African tribes, long necks and round, disklike lips are signs of feminine beauty. Women thus stretch their necks and lips to make themselves more appealing. Women of the Nama tribe persistently tug at their labia majora to make them "beautiful"—that is, prominent and elongated (Ford & Beach, 1951).

T r u t h **OR** *Fiction?*
R E V I S I T E D

Beauty may not be completely in the eye of the beholder. Although personal tastes may vary within and across cultures, there are cultural standards for physical attractiveness. ∎

Beauty and Culture. Can you find Mr. or Ms. Right among these people? Are your judgments of physical beauty based on universal standards or on your cultural experiences?

In our culture, taller men are considered to be more attractive by women (Hensley, 1994; Sheppard & Strathman, 1989). Undergraduate women prefer their dates to be about 6 inches taller than they are. Undergraduate men, on the average, prefer women who are about 4½ inches shorter (Gillis & Avis, 1980). Tall women are not viewed so positively. Shortness, though, is perceived to be a liability for both men and women (Jackson & Ervin, 1992).

Some women of Candy's stature find that shorter men are discouraged from asking them out. Some walk with a hunch, as if to minimize their height. A neighbor of the first and third authors refers to herself as 5 feet 13 inches tall.

Anorexia nervosa
A potentially life-threatening eating disorder characterized by refusal to maintain a healthy body weight, intense fear of being overweight, a distorted body image, and, in females, lack of menstruation (amenorrhea).

Female plumpness is valued in many, perhaps most, preliterate societies (Anderson et al., 1992; Frayser, 1985). Wide hips and a broad pelvis are widely recognized as sexually appealing. In our culture, however, slenderness is in style. Some young women suffer from an eating disorder called **anorexia nervosa,** in which they literally starve themselves to conform to the contemporary ideal. Both genders find slenderness (though not anorexic thinness) attractive, especially for females (Fallon & Rozin, 1985; Franzoi & Herzog, 1987; Rozin & Fallon, 1988).

The hourglass figure is popular in the United States. In one study, 87 African American college undergraduates—both male and female—rated women of average weight with a waist-to-hip ratio of 0.7 to 0.8 as most attractive and desirable for long-term relationships

(Singh, 1994a). Neither very thin nor obese women were found to be as attractive, regardless of the waist-to-hip ratio. Findings were similar for a sample of 188 White students (Singh, 1994b).

Do men idealize the *Penthouse* centerfold? What size busts do men prefer? Women's beliefs that men prefer large breasts may be somewhat exaggerated. The belief that men want women to have bursting bustlines leads many women to seek breast implants in the attempt to live up to an ideal that men themselves don't generally hold (Rosenthal, 1992). Researchers in one study showed young men and women (ages 17 to 25 years) a continuum of male and female figures that differed only in the size of the bust for the female figures and of the pectorals for the male figures (Thompson & Tantleff, 1992). The participants were asked to indicate the ideal size for their own gender and the size they believed the average man and woman would prefer.

The results show some support for the "big is better" stereotype—for both men and women. Women's conception of ideal bust size was greater than their actual average size. Men preferred women with still larger busts, but not nearly as large as the busts women *believed* that men prefer. Men believed that their male peers preferred women with much bustier figures than their peers themselves said they preferred. Ample breast or chest sizes may be preferred by the other gender, but people seem to have an exaggerated idea of the sizes the other gender actually prefers.

Both genders find obese people unattractive, but there are gender differences in impressions of the most pleasing body shape. On the average, college men think that their present physiques are close to ideal and appealing to women (Fallon & Rozin, 1985). Col-

Slim Is In. Pressure to conform to an idealized slender image play a key role in the development of eating disorders among young women.

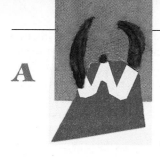 

WIDE-EYED WITH . . . BEAUTY?

Some aspects of beauty seem to be largely cross-cultural. Research suggests that White people, African Americans, Asian Americans, and Hispanic Americans tend to agree on the facial features that they find to be attractive (Cunningham et al., 1995). They all prefer female faces with large eyes; greater distance between the eyes; small noses; narrower faces with smaller chins; high, expressive eyebrows; larger lower lips; and a well-groomed, full head of hair.

Consider the methodology of a study that compares the facial preferences of people in Japan and England. Perrett (1994) created computer composites of the faces of 60 women. Part A of Figure 7.1 is a composite of the 15 women who were rated the most attractive. He then used computer enhancement to exaggerate the differences between the composite of

the 60—that is, the average face—and the composite of the 15 most attractive women. He found that both Japanese and British men deemed women with large eyes, high cheekbones, and narrow jaws to be the most attractive (Perret, 1994). Computer enhancement resulted in the image shown in Part B of Figure 7.1. The enhanced composite has still higher cheekbones and a narrower jaw than Part A. Part B was then rated as the most attractive image. Similar results were found for the image of a Japanese woman.

Cunningham and his colleagues (1995) reported historical anecdotes that suggest that the facial preferences of people as diverse as Europeans, Black Africans, Native Americans, Indians (in India, that is), and Chinese are quite consistent. They quoted from Charles Darwin's 1871 treatise, *The*

Descent of Man, and Selection in Relation to Sex:

> Mr. Winwood Reade . . . who has had ample opportunities for observation [with Black Africans] who have never associated with Europeans is convinced that their ideas of beauty are, on the whole, the same as ours; and Dr. Rohlfs writes to me the same effect with respect to Borneo and the countries inhabited by the Pullo tribes. . . . Capt. Burton believes that a woman whom we consider beautiful is admired throughout the world.

Darwin believed that our physical preferences were largely inborn and related to survival of our species. What do you think? Do you believe that "their ideas of beauty are, on the whole, the same as ours"? Or do you think that research hasn't yet ferreted out significant cultural or ethnic differences that might exist? If there is ethnic consistency in these preferences, how would you explain them? For example, do you believe

- that they are coincidental?
- that there has been more exchange of ideas among cultures than has been believed?
- that there is something instinctive about them?

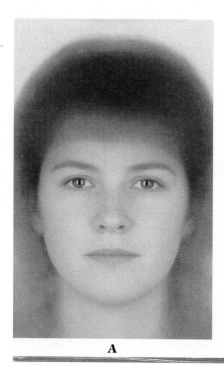

A

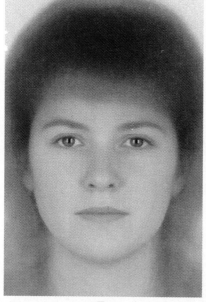

B

Figure 7.1. What Features Contribute to Facial Attractiveness? In both England and Japan, features such as large eyes, high cheekbones, and narrow jaws contribute to perceptions of the attractiveness of women. Part A is a computer composite of the faces of 15 women rated as the most attractive of a group of 60. Part B is a computer composite that exaggerates the features of these 15 women. That is, they are developed further in the direction that separates them from the average of the full group.

lege women generally see themselves as much heavier than the figure that is most alluring to men, and heavier still than the figure they perceive as the ideal feminine form. Both genders are wrong about the preferences of the other gender, however. Men actually prefer women to be somewhat heavier than the women imagine they would. Women prefer their men to be a bit leaner than the men would have expected.

It is not true that college men would like women to be thinner than the women want to be. College men actually prefer women who are heavier, though still slender, than the women expect. On the other hand, college women prefer men who are thinner than the men imagine. ∎

How Traits and Names Affect Perceptions of Physical Attractiveness: On the Importance of *Not* Being Ernest

Both genders rate the attractiveness of faces higher when they are shown smiling in photographs than when they are shown in a nonsmiling pose (Mueser et al., 1984). (Photographers are not ignorant of this fact.) So there is reason to "put on a happy face" when you meet people socially or ask someone out on a date. Context is important, however. It may be more appropriate in a business context to maintain a more serious countenance. The effects of a smile may also be a greater determinant of attractiveness in women than in men (Deutsch et al., 1987).

It is true that people are regarded as more attractive when they are smiling. Thus, it may make sense to "put on a happy face" when meeting people. ∎

Gender-role expectations may affect perceptions of attractiveness. Women who viewed videos of prospective dates found men who acted outgoing and self-expressive more appealing than men who were passive (Riggio & Woll, 1984). Another study found that highly feminine women are more likely to be attracted to dominant "macho" men than less feminine women are (Maybach & Gold, 1994). Yet men who viewed videos in the Riggio and Woll (1984) study were put off by outgoing, self-expressive behavior in women. In yet another study, women rated videos of dominant college men (defined in this study as social control over a troublesome interaction with an instructor) as more appealing than submissive men. Again, male viewers were put off by similarly dominant women (Sadalla et al., 1987). Despite recent changes in traditional gender-role stereotypes, many men in the United States still prefer demure women. This is not to suggest that dominant, self-expressive women should stifle themselves to attract traditional men; the relationships would probably rub them both the wrong way.

Names also may affect perceptions of physical appeal. In one study, women who were randomly assigned names like Kathy, Jennifer, and Christine were rated more attractive than women assigned the names Harriet, Gertrude, and Ethel (Garwood et al., 1980). Seems silly, does it not? After all, our parents name us, and there need be no relationship between our names and our physical appeal. On the other hand, we may choose to keep our names or to use nicknames. So if you are unhappy with your name, why not assume a more popular nickname? Beginning college or a new job is an ideal time for doing so. Men, too, can doff their Sylvesters and Ernests, if they prefer. If you have an unusual name and are content with it, be yourself, however.

It is true that women who are randomly assigned names like Kathy and Jennifer are rated as more attractive than women assigned names like Harriet and Gertrude. Perhaps observers thought that the Harriets and Gertrudes of the world would use more contemporary nicknames if they were "with it." ∎

What Do You Look for in a Long-Term, Meaningful Relationship?

Your second author conducted a survey of college men and women in the early 1980s and found that psychological characteristics such as warmth, fidelity, honesty, and sensitivity were rated higher in importance than physical attractiveness as desirable qualities in a prospective partner for a meaningful, long-term relationship (Nevid, 1984). Physical attractiveness won out when students were asked to consider the qualities that are most important in a partner for a sexual relationship. Overall, however, men placed greater emphasis on the physical characteristics of their partners for both types of relationships than did women. Women placed more value on qualities such as warmth, assertiveness, wit, and ambition. The single most highly desired quality students wanted in long-term partners was honesty. Honestly.

Truth **OR** *Fiction?*
R E V I S I T E D

It is not true that physical appeal is the most important trait we seek in partners for long-term relationships. According to the results of one study, honesty was reported to be more vital in partners for long-term relationships. ∎

Although personal qualities may assume more prominent roles in determining partner preferences in long-term relationships, physical appeal probably plays a "filtering" role. Unless a prospective date meets minimal physical standards, we might not look beneath the surface for "more meaningful" traits.

Nevid's results have been replicated in studies on initial attraction and on choice of mates. Women place relatively greater emphasis than men on traits like vocational status, earning potential, expressiveness, kindness, consideration, dependability, and fondness for children. Men give relatively more consideration to youth, physical attractiveness, cooking ability (can't they switch on the microwave by themselves?), and frugality (Howard et al., 1987; Sprecher et al., 1994). When it comes to mate selection, females in a sample of students from Germany and the Netherlands also emphasized the financial prospects and status of a potential mate, whereas males emphasized the importance of physical attractiveness (de Raad & Doddema-Winsemius, 1992). A study of more than 200 Korean college students found that in mate selection, women placed relatively more emphasis on education, jobs, and family of origin than men did (Brown, 1994). Men placed relatively more emphasis on physical attractiveness and affection. (Yes, men were more "romantic." Women were more pragmatic.)

Susan Sprecher and her colleagues (1994) surveyed a national probability sample of 13,017 English- or Spanish-speaking people, age 19 or above, living in households in the United States. In one section of their questionnaire, they asked respondents how willing they would be to marry someone who was older, younger, of a different religion, not likely to hold a steady job, not good-looking, and so forth. Each item was followed by a 7-point scale in which 1 meant "not at all" and 7 meant "very willing." As shown in Table 7.1, women were more willing than men to marry someone who was not good-looking. On the other hand, women were less willing to marry someone not likely to hold a steady job.

Are Attractiveness Preferences Inherited?   On the surface, gender differences in perceptions of attractiveness seem unbearably sexist—and perhaps they are. Yet some sociobiologists believe that evolutionary forces favor the continuation of gender differences in preferences for mates because certain preferred traits provide reproductive advantages. Some physical features, like cleanliness, good complexion, clear eyes, good teeth, good hair, firm muscle tone, and a steady gait are universally appealing to both genders (Ford & Beach, 1951). Perhaps they are markers of reproductive potential (Symons, 1995). Age and health may be relatively more important to a woman's appeal, since these characteristics tend to be associated with her reproductive capacity: the "biological clock" limits her reproductive potential. Physical characteristics associated with a woman's youthfulness, such as smooth skin, firm muscle tone, and lustrous hair, may thus have become more closely linked to a woman's appeal (Buss, 1994). A man's reproductive value, however, may depend more on how well he can provide for his family than on his age or physical appeal. The value of men as reproducers, therefore, is more intertwined with factors that contribute to a stable environment for child rearing—such as economic status and reliability. Sociobiologists argue that these gender differences in mate preferences may have been passed down through the generations as part of our genetic heritage (Buss, 1994; Symons, 1995).

TABLE 7.1 Gender differences in mate preferences

How willing would you be to marry someone who ...	Men	Women
• was not "good-looking"?	3.41	4.42†
• was older than you by 5 or more years?	4.15	5.29†
• was younger than you by 5 or more years?	4.54	2.80†
• was not likely to hold a steady job?	2.73	1.62†
• would earn much less than you?	4.60	3.76†
• would earn much more than you?	5.19	5.93†
• had more education than you?	5.22	5.82†
• had less education than you?	4.67	4.08†
• had been married before?	3.35	3.44
• already had children?	2.84	3.11*
• was of a different religion?	4.24	4.31
• was of a different race?	3.08	2.84†

Based on a 7 point scale where 1 = not at all, and 7 = very willing.
*Difference statistically significant at the .01 level of confidence.
†Difference statistically significant at the .001 level of confidence.
Source: Based on information in Susan Sprecher, Quintin Sullivan, & Elaine Hatfield (1994). Mate Selection Preferences: Gender Differences Examined in a National Sample. *Journal of Personality and Social Psychology, 66* (6), 1074–1080.

Men's interest in younger women is apparently universal. It occurs in both preliterate and industrialized societies (Buss, 1994; Symons, 1979). Female jealousy of younger women is another thread that spans cultures. Sexual competition, according to Margaret Mead, generally involves

> the struggle between stronger older men and weaker younger men or between more attractive younger women and more entrenched older ones.
>
> (Mead, 1967, p. 198)

Sociobiological views of gender differences in mate preferences are largely speculative and not fully consistent with the evidence. Despite gender differences, both men and women report that they place greater weight on personal characteristics than on physical features in judging prospective mates (Buss, 1994). Many women, like men, still prefer physically appealing partners (Bixler, 1989). Women also tend to marry men similar to themselves in physical attractiveness as well as socioeconomic standing. Note also that older men are more likely than younger men to die from natural causes. From the standpoint of reproductive advantages, women would thus achieve greater success by marrying fit, younger males who are likely to survive during the child-rearing years than by marrying older, higher-status males. Moreover, similar cultural influences, rather than inherited dispositions, may explain commonalities across cultures in gender differences in mate preferences. For example, in societies in which women are economically dependent on men, a man's appeal may depend more on his financial resources than on his physical appeal.

The Matching Hypothesis: Who Is "Right" for You?

Do not despair if you are less than exquisite in appearance, along with most of us mere mortals. You may be saved from permanently blending in with the wallpaper by the effects

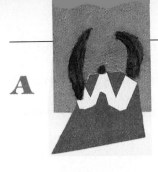

A WORLD OF DIVERSITY

GENDER DIFFERENCES IN PREFERENCES IN MATES ACROSS 37 CULTURES

What do men in Nigeria, Japan, Brazil, Canada, and the United States have in common? For one thing, men in these countries report that they prefer mates who are younger than themselves. Buss (1994) reviewed survey evidence on the preferred age difference between oneself and one's mate in 37 cultures (representing 33 countries) in Europe, Africa, Asia, Australia, New Zealand, and North and South America. In every culture men preferred younger mates (the range was from 0.38 years to 6.45 years). Women, however, preferred older mates (the range was from 1.82 years to 5.1 years).

Gender differences in the preferred age of mates paralleled actual differences in age of men and women at the time of marriage. Men were between two and five years older on the average than their brides at the time of

marriage. The smallest age difference at marriage, 2.1 years, was found in Poland. The largest difference, 4.92 years, was found in Greece. Men in the mainland United States are 2.71 years older than women at the time of marriage. In Canada, men are 2.51 years older than their mates, on the average.

Buss finds that in all 37 cultures, men placed greater value on a prospective partner's "good looks" than did women. On the other hand, women in 36 of 37 cultures placed greater value on "good earning capacity" of prospective mates.

The consistency of Buss' findings lends credence to the notion that there are widespread gender differences in preferences with respect to age, physical characteristics, and financial status of prospective mates. Generally speaking, men across cultures place greater

value on the physical attractiveness and relative youth of prospective mates, whereas women place relatively greater value on the earning capacity of prospective mates. Buss interprets women's preferences for relatively older mates as additional evidence that women appraise future mates on the basis of their ability to provide for a wife and family, since age and income tend to be linked among men.

Despite these gender differences in preferences for mates, Buss finds that both men and women placed greater weight on personal qualities than on looks or income potential of prospective mates. In *all* 37 cultures, the characteristics "kind, understanding" and "intelligent" were rated higher than earning power or physical attractiveness.

Matching hypothesis
The concept that people tend to develop romantic relationships with people who are similar to themselves in attractiveness.

of the **matching hypothesis.** This concept holds that people tend to develop romantic relationships with people who are similar to themselves in physical attractiveness rather than the local Denzel Washington or Cindy Crawford look-alike.

Researchers have found that people who are dating steadily, engaged, or married tend to be matched in physical attractiveness (Kalick, 1988). Young married couples even tend to be matched in weight (Schafer & Keith, 1990). The central motive for seeking "matches" seems to be fear of rejection by more appealing people (Bernstein et al., 1983).

There are exceptions to the matching hypothesis. Now and then we find a beautiful woman married to a plain or ugly man (or vice versa). How do we explain it? What, after all, would *she* see in *him?* According to one study (Bar-Tal & Saxe, 1976), people judging "mismatched" pairs may tend to ascribe wealth, intelligence, or success to the man. We seek an unseen factor that will balance the physical attractiveness of one partner. For some mismatched couples, similarities in attitudes and personalities may balance out differences in physical attractiveness.

More Than Beauty   Matching applies not only to physical appeal. Our sex and marital partners tend to be like us in race and ethnicity, age, level of education, and religion. Consider some findings of the NHSLS study (Michael et al., 1994, pp. 45–47):

- The sex partners of nearly 94% of unmarried White men are White women. About 2% of single White men are partnered with Hispanic American women, 2% with Asian American women, and less than 1% with African American women.
- The sex partners of nearly 82% of African American men are African American women. Nearly 8% of African American men are partnered with White women. Under 5% are partnered with Hispanic American women.

- About 83% of the women and men in the study chose partners within 5 years of their own age and of the same or a similar religion.
- Of all the women in the study, *not one* with a graduate college degree had a partner who had not finished high school.
- Men with a college degree almost never had sexual relationships with women with much more or much less education than they had.

Similarity in Attitudes: Do Opposites Attract?

Why do the great majority of us have partners from our own backgrounds? One reason is that marriages are made in the neighborhood and not in heaven (Michael et al., 1994). That is, we tend to live among people who are similar to us in background, and thus come into contact with them. Another is that we are drawn to people who are similar in their attitudes. People similar in background are more likely to be similar in their attitudes. Similarity in attitudes and tastes is a key contributor to attraction, friendships, and love relationships (Cappella & Palmer, 1990; Griffin & Sparks, 1990; Laumann et al., 1994).

Let us also note a gender difference. Evidence shows that women place greater weight on attitude similarity as a determinant of attraction to a stranger of the other gender than do men, whereas men place more value on physical attractiveness (Feingold, 1991).

We also tend to *assume* that people we find attractive share our attitudes (Dawes, 1989; Marks et al., 1981). The physical attraction between Candy and Stretch motivated them to pretend that their preferences, tastes, and opinions coincided. They entered into a nonspoken agreement not to discuss their religious differences. When sexual attraction is strong, perhaps we want to think that the kinks in the relationship will be small or that we can iron them out. Let us also note that though similarity may be important in determining initial attraction, compatibility appears to be an even stronger determinant of maintaining an enduring intimate relationship (Vinacke et al., 1988).

Truth **OR** Fiction?
R E V I S I T E D

Actually, it is not true that "opposites attract." We are actually *less* apt, that is, to be attracted to people who disagree with our views and tastes than to people who share them. ∎

Reciprocity: If You Like Me, You Must Have Excellent Judgment

Has anyone told you that you are good-looking, brilliant, and emotionally mature to boot? That your taste is elegant? Ah, what superb judgment!

Who Is Right for You? Research shows that people tend to pair off with others who are similar in physical characteristics and personality traits.

Reciprocity
Mutual exchange.

When we feel admired and complimented, we tend to return these feelings and behaviors. This is called **reciprocity.** Reciprocity is a potent determinant of attraction (Condon & Crano, 1988). We tend to be much more warm, helpful, and candid when we are with strangers whom we believe like us (Clark et al., 1989; Curtis & Miller, 1986). We even tend to welcome positive comments from others when we know them to be inaccurate (Swann et al., 1987).

Perhaps the power of reciprocity has enabled many couples to become happy with one another and reasonably well adjusted. By reciprocating positive words and actions, a person can perhaps stoke neutral or mild feelings into robust, affirmative feelings of attraction.

～ *Reflections* ～

▪ How important is physical attractiveness to you in your evaluation of partners for dating, sex, and marriage? (Are you being truthful?)

▪ What personality traits are most important to you in your evaluation of partners for dating, sex, and marriage?

▪ Would you date someone of another race? Another religion? Why, or why not? What would be the response of your parents or other members of your sociocultural group if you did?

Attraction can lead to feelings of love. Let us now turn to that most fascinating topic.

Love

For thousands of years, poets have sought to capture love in words. A seventeenth-century poet wrote that his love was like "a red, red rose." In Sinclair Lewis' novel *Elmer Gantry,* love is "the morning and the evening star." Love is beautiful and elusive. It shines, brilliant and heavenly. Passion and romantic love are also earthy and sexy, brimming with sexual desire.

Romantic love is hardly unique to our culture. Researchers report finding evidence of romantic love in 147 of the 166 different cultures they studied in a recent cross-cultural comparison (Jankowiak & Fischer, 1992). Romantic love occurs even in most preliterate societies. The absence of romantic love in the remaining 19 cultures, the investigators suspect, was most probably due to the limitations of their study methods (Gelman, 1993).

Our culture idealizes the concept of romantic love. Thus we readily identify with the plight of the "star-crossed" lovers in *Romeo and Juliet* and *West Side Story,* who sacrificed for love. We learn that "love makes the world go round" and that "love is everything." Virtually all of the participants in the Janus and Janus nationwide survey (96% of the men and 98% of the women) reported that love is important to them (Janus & Janus, 1993). Like other aspects of sexual and social behavior among humans, the concept of love must be understood within a cultural context. Luckily (or miserably), we have such a context in Western culture. . . .

The Greek Heritage

The concept of love can be traced back at least as far as the classical age of Greece. The Greeks distinguished four concepts related to the modern meanings of love: *storge, agape, philia,* and *eros.*

Storge
(STORE-gay) Loving attachment and nonsexual affection; the type of emotion that binds parents to children.

Storge is loving attachment, deep friendship, or nonsexual affection. It is the emotion that binds friends and parents and children. Some scholars believe that even romantic love is a form of attachment that is similar to the types of attachments infants have to their mothers (Hazan & Shaver, 1987).

Agape
(AH-gah-pay) Selfless love; a kind of loving that is similar to generosity and charity.

Agape is similar to generosity and charity. It implies the wish to share one's bounty, and is epitomized by anonymous donations of money. In relationships, it is characterized by selfless giving (Lee, 1988). Agape, according to Lee's research, is the kind of love least frequently found between adults in committed relationships.

Philia

(FEEL-yuh) Friendship love, which is based on liking and respect rather than sexual desire.

Eros

The kind of love that is closest in meaning to the modern-day concept of passion.

Philia is closest in meaning to friendship. It is based on liking and respect, rather than sexual desire. It involves the desire to do and enjoy things with the other person, and to see him or her when one is lonely or bored.

Eros is closest in meaning to our concept of passion. Eros was a character in Greek mythology (transformed in Roman mythology into Cupido, now called Cupid) who would shoot unsuspecting people with his love arrows, causing them to fall madly in love with the person who was nearest to them at the time. Erotic love embraces sudden passionate desire: "love at first sight" and "falling head over heels in love." Passion can be so gripping that one is convinced that life has been changed forever. This feeling of sudden transformation was captured by the Italian poet Dante Alighieri (1265–1321), who exclaimed upon first beholding his beloved Beatrice, "*Incipit vita nuova,*" which can be translated as "My life begins anew." Romantic love can also be earthy and sexy. In fact, sexual arousal and desire may be the strongest component of passionate or romantic love (Berscheid, 1988). Romantic love begins with a powerful physical attraction or feelings of passion, and is associated with strong physiological arousal (Lee, 1988).

Unlike the Greeks, we tend to use the word *love* to describe everything from feelings of affection toward another to romantic ardor to sexual intercourse ("making love"). Still, different types or styles of love are recognized in our own culture, as we shall see.

Romantic Love in Contemporary Western Culture

The experience of *romantic love,* as opposed to loving attachment or sexual arousal per se, occurs within a cultural context in which the concept is idealized. Western culture has a long tradition of idealizing the concept of romantic love, as represented, for instance, by romantic fairy tales that have been passed down through the generations. In fact, our exposure to the concept of romantic love may begin with hearing the fairy tales of Sleeping Beauty, Cinderella, and Snow White—along with their princes charming. Later perhaps, the concept of romantic love blossoms with exposure to romantic novels, television and film scripts, and the heady tales of friends and relatives.

During adolescence, strong sexual arousal along with an idealized image of the object of our desires leads us to label our feelings as love. We may learn to speak of "love" rather than "lust," because sexual desire in the absence of a committed relationship might be viewed as primitive or animalistic. Being "in love" enables attraction and sexual arousal, not only to society but also to oneself. Unlike lust, love can even be discussed at the dinner table. If others think we are too young to experience "the real thing"—which presumably includes knowledge of and respect for the other person's personality traits—our feelings may be called "puppy love" or a "crush."

Western society maintains much of the double standard toward sexuality. Thus, women are more often expected to justify sexual experiences as involving someone they love. Young men usually need not attribute sexual urges to love. So men are more apt to deem love a "mushy" concept. The vast majority of people in the United States nonetheless believe romantic love is a prerequisite for marriage. Romantic love is rated by young people as the single most important reason for marriage (Roper Organization, 1985). Over 80% of college men and women subscribe to the belief that "being in love" is a precondition for marriage (Berscheid, 1988; Simpson et al., 1986). More than half also believe that falling out of love justifies divorce.

Which is the more romantic gender? Although the question may well incite an argument in mixed company, the Janus and Janus (1993) nationwide survey of adult Americans found that a slightly greater percentage of the single men (82%) perceived themselves as being romantic than did single women (77%). Yet among married people, the figures were reversed, with 79% of the women describing themselves as romantic as compared to 72% of the men. Perhaps there is some truth to the stereotype that men are more romantic during the courtship stage of relationships than the marriage stage. Then again, maybe self-perceptions of being romantic don't quite jibe with the reality. In any event, you can explore self-perceptions of being a romantic or a realist when it comes to love by completing the nearby Love Attitudes Scale.

QUESTIONNAIRE

ARE YOU A ROMANTIC OR A REALIST? THE LOVE ATTITUDES SCALE

David Knox of East Carolina University contrasts romantic love with *realistic love*—the kind of love that is maintained across the years. Partners who share a realistic love have the blinders off. They accept and cherish each other, warts and all.

    Knox (1983) developed the Love Attitudes Scale to evaluate the degree to which people hold a romantic or realistic view of love. How about you? Are you a realist or a romantic when it comes to matters of the heart? To find out, complete the scale, and then turn to the scoring key in the Appendix.

    Directions: Circle the number that best represents your opinion on each item according to the following code. Add up your scores to arrive at a total score.

1 = Strongly agree (SA)
2 = Mildly agree (MA)
3 = Undecided (U)
4 = Mildly disagree (MD)
5 = Strongly disagree (SD)

1. Love doesn't make sense. It just is.
1 2 3 4 5
2. When you fall "head over heels" in love, it's sure to be the real thing.
1 2 3 4 5
3. To be in love with someone you would like to marry but can't is a tragedy.
1 2 3 4 5
4. When love hits, you know it.
1 2 3 4 5
5. Common interests are really unimportant; as long as each of you is truly in love, you will adjust.
1 2 3 4 5
6. It doesn't matter if you marry after you have known your partner for only a short time as long as you know you are in love.
1 2 3 4 5
7. If you are going to love a person, you will "know" after a short time.
1 2 3 4 5
8. As long as two people love each other, the educational differences they have really do not matter.
1 2 3 4 5
9. You can love someone even though you do not like any of that person's friends.
1 2 3 4 5
10. When you are in love, you are usually in a daze.
1 2 3 4 5
11. Love "at first sight" is often the deepest and most enduring type of love.
1 2 3 4 5
12. When you are in love, it really does not matter what your partner does because you will love him or her anyway.
1 2 3 4 5
13. As long as you really love a person, you will be able to solve the problems you have with that person.
1 2 3 4 5
14. Usually you can really love and be happy with only one or two people in the world.
1 2 3 4 5

15. Regardless of other factors, if you truly love another person, that is a good enough reason to marry that person.
1 2 3 4 5
16. It is necessary to be in love with the one you marry to be happy.
1 2 3 4 5
17. Love is more of a feeling than a relationship.
1 2 3 4 5
18. People should not get married unless they are in love.
1 2 3 4 5
19. Most people truly love only once during their lives.
1 2 3 4 5
20. Somewhere there is an ideal mate for most people.
1 2 3 4 5
21. In most cases, you will "know it" when you meet the right partner.
1 2 3 4 5
22. Jealousy usually varies directly with love; that is, the more you are in love, the greater your tendency to become jealous will be.
1 2 3 4 5
23. When you are in love, you are motivated by what you feel rather than by what you think.
1 2 3 4 5
24. Love is best described as an exciting rather than a calm thing.
1 2 3 4 5
25. Most divorces probably result from falling out of love rather than failing to adjust.
1 2 3 4 5
26. When you are in love, your judgment is usually not too clear.
1 2 3 4 5
27. Love often comes only once in a lifetime.
1 2 3 4 5
28. Love is often a violent and uncontrollable emotion.
1 2 3 4 5
29. When selecting a marriage partner, differences in social class and religion are of small importance compared with love.
1 2 3 4 5
30. No matter what anyone says, love cannot be understood.
1 2 3 4 5

Total Score on the Love Attitudes Scale:

Source: From Knox, D. (1983). *The Love Attitudes Inventory* (rev. ed.). Saluda, NC: Family Life Publications. Reprinted with permission.

When reciprocated, romantic love is usually a source of deep fulfillment and ecstasy (Hatfield, 1988). How wonderful when love meets its match. When love is unrequited, however, it can lead to emptiness, anxiety, or despair. Romantic love can thus teeter between states of ecstasy and misery (Hatfield, 1988). Perhaps no other feature of our lives can lift us up as high or plunge us as low as romantic love.

Infatuation Versus "True Love": Will Time Tell?   Perhaps you first noticed each other when your eyes met across a crowded room, like the star-crossed lovers in *West Side Story*. Or perhaps you met when you were both assigned to the same Bunsen burner in chemistry lab—less romantic, but closer to the flame. However it happened, the meeting triggered such an electric charge through your body that you could not get him (or her) out of your mind. Were you truly in love, however, or was it merely a passing fancy? Was it infatuation or the "real thing"—a "true," lasting, and mutual love? How do you tell them apart?

Perhaps you don't, at least not at first. **Infatuation** is a state of intense absorption in or focus on another person. It is usually accompanied by sexual desire, elation, and general physiological arousal or excitement. Some refer to passion as infatuation. Others dub it a "crush." Both monickers suggest that it is a passing fancy. In infatuation, your heart may pound whenever the other person draws near or enters your fantasies.

For the first month or two, infatuation and the more enduring forms of romantic love are essentially indistinguishable (Gordon & Snyder, 1989). At first, both may be characterized by intense focusing or absorption. Infatuated people may become so absorbed that they cannot sleep, work, or carry out routine chores. Logic and reason are swept aside. Infatuated people hold idealized images of their love objects and overlook their faults. Caution may be cast to the winds. In some cases, couples in the throes of infatuation rush to get married, only to find a few weeks or months later that they are not well suited.

As time goes on, signs that distinguish infatuation from a lasting romantic love begin to emerge. The partners begin to view each other more realistically and determine whether or not the relationship should continue.

Infatuation has been likened to a state of passionate love (Sternberg, 1986) that is based on intense feelings of passion but not on the deeper feelings of attachment and caring that typify a more lasting mutual love. Although infatuation may be a passing fancy, it can be supplanted by the deeper feelings of attachment and caring that characterize more lasting love relationships.

Note, too, that infatuation is not a necessary first step on the path to a lasting mutual love. Some couples develop deep feelings of love without ever experiencing the fireworks of infatuation (Sternberg, 1986). Or sometimes one partner is infatuated while the other manages to keep his or her head below the clouds.

Contemporary Models of Love: Dare Science Intrude?

Despite the importance of love, scientists have historically paid little attention to it. Some people believe that love cannot be analyzed scientifically. Love, they maintain, should be left to the poets, philosophers, and theologians. Yet researchers are now applying the scientific method to the study of love. They recognize that love is a complex concept, involving many areas of experience—emotional, cognitive, and motivational (Sternberg & Grajek, 1984). They have reinforced the Greek view that there are different kinds and styles of love. Let us consider some of the views of love that have emerged from modern theorists and researchers.

Love as Appraisal of Arousal   Social psychologists Ellen Berscheid and Elaine Hatfield (Berscheid & Walster, 1978; Walster & Walster, 1978) define **romantic love** in terms of a state of intense physiological arousal and the cognitive appraisal of that arousal as love. The physiological arousal may be experienced as a pounding heart, sweaty palms, and butterflies in the stomach when one is in the presence of or thinking about one's love interest. Cognitive appraisal of the arousal means attributing it to some cause, such as fear or love. The perception that one has fallen in love is thus derived from several simultaneous events: (1) a state of intense physiological arousal that is connected with an appropriate love

Infatuation
A state of intense absorption in or focus on another person, which is usually accompanied by sexual desire, elation, and general physiological arousal or excitement; passion.

Romantic love
A kind of love characterized by feelings of passion and intimacy.

object (that is, a person, not an event like a rock concert), (2) a cultural setting that idealizes romantic love, and (3) the attribution of the arousal to feelings of love toward the person.

Styles of Love   Some psychologists speak in terms of *styles* of love. Clyde and Susan Hendrick (1986) developed a love attitude scale that suggests the existence of six styles of love among college students. The following is a list of the styles. Each one is exemplified by statements similar to those on the original scale. As you can see, the styles owe a debt to the Greeks:

1. *Romantic love (eros):* "My lover fits my ideal." "My lover and I were attracted to one another immediately."
2. *Game-playing love (ludus):* "I keep my lover up in the air about my commitment." "I get over love affairs pretty easily."
3. *Friendship (storge, philia):* "The best love grows out of an enduring friendship."
4. *Logical love (pragma):* "I consider a lover's potential in life before committing myself." "I consider whether my lover will be a good parent."
5. *Possessive, excited love (mania):* "I get so excited about my love that I cannot sleep." "When my lover ignores me, I get sick all over."
6. *Selfless love (agape):* "I would do anything I can to help my lover." "My lover's needs and wishes are more important than my own."

Most people who are "in love" experience a number of these styles, but the Hendricks (1986) found some interesting gender differences in styles of love. College men are significantly more likely to develop game-playing and romantic love styles. College women are more apt to develop friendly, logical, and possessive love styles. (There were no gender differences in selfless love.) The Hendricks and their colleagues (1988) have also found that romantically involved couples tend to experience the same kinds of love styles. They also showed that couples with romantic and selfless styles of love are more likely to remain together. A game-playing love style leads to unhappiness, however, and is one reason that relationships come to an end.

Sternberg's Triangular Theory of Love   Psychologist Robert Sternberg (1986, 1987, 1988) offers a triangular theory of love. In his view there are three distinct components of love:

1. *Intimacy:* the experience of warmth toward another person that arises from feelings of closeness, bondedness, and connectedness to the other. Intimacy also involves the desire to give and receive emotional support and to share one's innermost thoughts with the other.
2. *Passion:* an intense romantic or sexual desire for another person, which is accompanied by physiological arousal.
3. *Decision/commitment:* a component of love that involves both short-term and long-term issues. In the short term there is the issue of deciding that one loves the other person. In the long term there is the issue of one's willingness to make a *commitment* to maintain the relationship through good times and bad. Decision and commitment need not go hand in hand. Although decision generally precedes commitment, some people become committed to a relationship before they even decide whether they love the other person. Others, however, never make a lasting commitment or openly acknowledge loving the other person.

According to Sternberg's model, love can be conceptualized in terms of a triangle in which each vertex represents one of these basic elements of love (see Figure 7.2). The way the components are balanced can be represented by the shape of the triangle. For example, a love in which all three components were equally balanced would be represented by an equilateral triangle, as in Figure 7.2.

Sternberg believes that couples are well matched if they possess corresponding levels of passion, intimacy, and commitment. Compatibility can be represented visually in terms of the congruence of the love triangles. Figure 7.3(A) on page 202 shows a perfect match, in which the triangles are congruent. Figure 7.3(B) depicts a good match; the partners are similar in the three dimensions. Figure 7.3(C) shows a mismatch; major differences exist between the partners on all three components. Relationships may run aground when part-

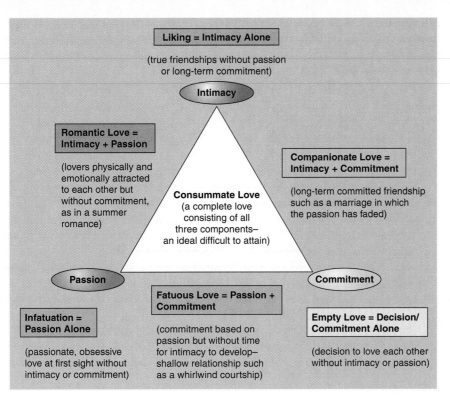

Figure 7.2. The Triangular Model of Love. According to psychologist Robert Sternberg, love consists of three components, as shown by the vertices of this triangle. Various kinds of love consist of different combinations of these components. Romantic love, for example, consists of passion and intimacy. Consummate love—a state devoutly to be desired—consists of all three.

ners are mismatched. A relationship may fizzle, rather than sizzle, when one partner experiences more passion than the other, or when one wants a long-term commitment when the other's idea of commitment is to stay the night.

According to the Sternberg model, various combinations of the three elements of love characterize different types of love relationships (Sternberg, 1986, 1988) (see Figure 7.3 and Table 7.2, both on page 202). For example, *infatuation* (passionate love) is typified by strong sexual desire, but not by intimacy and commitment. The partners may each feel passionate love for the other, or, as in the case of Tom, such feelings may go unrequited:

> Tom sat behind Lisa in physics class. Tom hated physics, but he could not say the same for Lisa. One look at her was enough to change his life. He had fallen madly in love with her. Instead of listening to the teacher or looking at the blackboard, he would gaze at Lisa throughout the class. Lisa was aware of this and was not happy about it. She did not much care for Tom, and when he tried to start a conversation with her, she moved on as quickly as possible. Tom's staring and his awkwardness in talking to her made her feel uncomfortable. Tom, on the other hand, could think of little else besides Lisa, and his grades began to suffer as he spent the time he should have been devoting to his homework thinking about her. He was a man obsessed. The obsession might have gone on for quite some time had not both Tom and Lisa graduated that June and gone to different colleges. Tom never saw Lisa again, and after several unanswered love letters, he finally gave up on her.
> (Sternberg, 1988, p. 123)

Liking is very much like friendship. It consists of feelings of closeness and emotional warmth without passion or decision/commitment. Liking is not felt toward passing acquaintances. It is reserved for people to whom one feels close enough to share one's innermost feelings and thoughts. We sometimes develop these intimate relationships without making the commitment to maintaining a long-term relationship that typifies other types of love, however. Liking may develop into a passionate love, however, or into a more committed form of friendship (called *companionate love* in Sternberg's model).

Should lovers also be friends, or are lovers and friends part of the twain that never meet? Candy and Stretch's relationship lacked the quality most often associated with true friendship: the willingness to share confidences. Despite their physical intimacy, their relationship remained so superficial that they couldn't even share information about their religious backgrounds.

It is indeed possible to be in love with someone who is not also a friend. Being in love can refer to states of passion or infatuation, whereas friendship is usually based on shared interests, liking, and respect. ∎

Candy and Stretch were "in love" although they were far from friends. Friendship and passionate love do not necessarily overlap. There is nothing that prevents people in love from becoming good friends, however—perhaps even the best of friends. Sternberg's model recognizes that the intimacy we find in true friendships and the passion we find in love are blended in two forms of love—romantic love and consummate love. These love types differ along the dimension of decision/commitment, however.

Romantic love has both passion and intimacy but lacks commitment. Romantic love may burn brightly and then flicker out. Or it may develop into a more complete love, called *consummate love,* in which all three components flower. Desire is accompanied by a deeper intimacy and commitment. The flames of passion can be stoked across the years, even if they do not burn quite as brightly as they once did. Consummate love is most special, and certainly an ideal toward which many Westerners strive. In *empty love,* by contrast, there is nought but commitment. Neither the warm emotional embrace of intimacy nor the flame of passion exists. With empty love, one's lover is a person whom one tolerates and remains with because of a sense of duty.

Sometimes a love relationship has both passion and commitment but lacks intimacy. Sternberg calls this *fatuous (foolish) love.* Fatuous love is associated with whirlwind courtships that burn brightly but briefly as the partners come to the realization that they are

Figure 7.3. Compatibility and Incompatibility, According to the Triangular Model of Love. Compatibility in terms of Sternberg's types of love can be represented as triangles. Part A shows a perfect match, in which triangles are congruent. Part B depicts a good match; the partners are similar according to the three dimensions. Part C shows a mismatch. Major differences exist between the partners on all three components.

A

Perfectly matched involvements

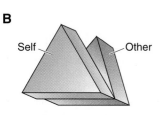

B

Closely matched involvements

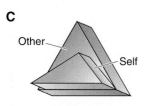

C

Severely mismatched involvements

TABLE 7.2	Types of love according to Sternberg's triangular model	
1. Nonlove	A relationship in which all three components of love are absent. Most of our personal relationships are of this type—casual interactions or acquaintances that do not involve any elements of love.	
2. Liking	A loving experience with another person or friendship in which intimacy is present but passion and commitment are lacking.	
3. Infatuation	A kind of "love at first sight" in which one experiences passionate desires for another person in the absence of both intimacy and decision/commitment components of love.	
4. Empty love	A kind of love characterized by the decision (to love) and the commitment (to maintain the relationship) in the absence of either passion or intimacy. Stagnant relationships that no longer involve the emotional intimacy or physical attraction that once characterized them are of this type.	
5. Romantic love	A loving experience characterized by the combination of passion and intimacy, but without decision/commitment components of love.	
6. Companionate love	A kind of love that derives from the combination of intimacy and decision/commitment components of love. This kind of love often occurs in marriages in which passionate attraction between the partners has died down and has been replaced by a kind of committed friendship.	
7. Fatuous love	The type of love associated with whirlwind romances and "quicky marriages" in which the passion and decision/commitment components of love are present, but intimacy is not.	
8. Consummate love	The full or complete measure of love involving the combination of passion, intimacy, and decision/commitment. Many of us strive to attain this type of complete love in our romantic relationships. Maintaining it is often harder than achieving it.	

Source: Adapted from Sternberg, 1988.

ＱUESTIONNAIRE

STERNBERG'S TRIANGULAR LOVE SCALE

Which are the strongest components of your love relationship? Intimacy? Passion? Decision/commitment?
All three components? Two of them?

    To complete the following scale, fill in the blank spaces with the name of one person you love or
care about deeply. Then rate your agreement with each of the items by using a nine point scale in
which 1 = "not at all," 5 = "moderately," and 9 = "extremely." Use points in between to indicate intermediate levels of agreement between these values. Then consult the scoring key in the Appendix.

Intimacy Component

_____ 1. I am actively supportive of _____'s well-being.

_____ 2. I have a warm relationship with _____.

_____ 3. I am able to count on _____ in times of need.

_____ 4. _____ is able to count on me in times of need.

_____ 5. I am willing to share myself and my possessions with _____.

_____ 6. I receive considerable emotional support from _____.

_____ 7. I give considerable emotional support to _____.

_____ 8. I communicate well with _____.

_____ 9. I value _____ greatly in my life.

_____ 10. I feel close to _____.

_____ 11. I have a comfortable relationship with _____.

_____ 12. I feel that I really understand _____.

_____ 13. I feel that _____ really understands me.

_____ 14. I feel that I can really trust _____.

_____ 15. I share deeply personal information about myself with _____.

Passion Component

_____ 16. Just seeing _____ excites me.

_____ 17. I find myself thinking about _____ frequently during the day.

_____ 18. My relationship with _____ is very romantic.

_____ 19. I find _____ to be very personally attractive.

_____ 20. I idealize _____.

_____ 21. I cannot imagine another person making me as happy as _____ does.

_____ 22. I would rather be with _____ than anyone else.

_____ 23. There is nothing more important to me than my relationship with _____.

_____ 24. I especially like physical contact with _____.

_____ 25. There is something almost "magical" about my relationship with _____.

_____ 26. I adore _____.

_____ 27. I cannot imagine life without _____.

_____ 28. My relationship with _____ is passionate.

_____ 29. When I see romantic movies and read romantic books, I think of _____.

_____ 30. I fantasize about _____.

Decision/Commitment Component

_____ 31. I know that I care about _____.

_____ 32. I am committed to maintaining my relationship with _____.

_____ 33. Because of my commitment to _____, I would not let other people come between us.

_____ 34. I have confidence in the stability of my relationship with _____.

_____ 35. I could not let anything get in the way of my commitment to _____.

_____ 36. I expect my love for _____ to last for the rest of my life.

_____ 37. I will always feel a strong responsibility for _____.

_____ 38. I view my commitment to _____ as a solid one.

_____ 39. I cannot imagine ending my relationship with _____.

_____ 40. I am certain of my love for _____.

_____ 41. I view my relationship with _____ as permanent.

_____ 42. I view my relationship with _____ as a good decision.

_____ 43. I feel a sense of responsibility toward _____.

_____ 44. I plan to continue my relationship with _____.

_____ 45. Even when _____ is hard to deal with, I remain committed to our relationship.

Source: Sternberg, 1988. Reprinted by permission of Basic Books, Inc., Publishers, New York.

not well matched. Intimacy can develop in such relationships, but couples who rush into marriage often find that the realities of marriage give the lie to their expectations:

> They expect a marriage made in heaven, but do not realize what they must do truly to maintain such a marriage. They base the relationship on passion and are disappointed when the passion starts to fade. They feel shortchanged—they have gotten much less than they bargained for. The problem, of course, is that they bargained for too much of one thing [passion] and not enough of another [intimacy].

> (Sternberg, 1988, p. 128)

In *companionate love,* finally, intimacy and commitment are strong, but passion is lacking. This form of love typifies long-term (so-called Platonic) friendships and marriages in which passion has ebbed but a deep and abiding friendship remains. Berscheid and Walster defined companionate love as "the affection we feel for those with whom our lives are deeply entwined" (1978, p. 9).

Although romantic love may become transformed into companionate love, the process by which this transformation takes place remains vague (Shaver et al., 1988). Companionate love need not be sexless or lacking in romance, however. Although passion may have ebbed, the giving and receiving of sexual pleasure can help strengthen bonds. Partners may feel that their sex lives have even become more deeply satisfying as they seek to please each other by practicing what they have learned about each other's sexual needs and wants.

The balance among Sternberg's three aspects of love is likely to shift through the course of a relationship. A healthful dose of all three components—found in consummate love—typifies, for many of us, an ideal marriage. At the outset of marriage, passions may be strong but intimacy weak. Couples may only first be getting to know each other's innermost thoughts and feelings. Time alone does not cause intimacy and commitment to grow, however. Some couples are able to peer into each other's deeper selves and form meaningful commitments at relatively early stages in their relationships. Yet some long-married couples may remain distant or waver in their commitment. Some couples experience only a faint flickering of passion early in the relationship. Then it becomes quickly extinguished. For some the flames of passion burn ever brightly. Yet many married couples find that passion tends to fade while intimacy and commitment grow stronger.

Knowing about these components of love may help couples avoid pitfalls. Couples who recognize that passion exerts a strong pull early in a relationship may be less likely to let passion rush them into marriage. Couples who recognize that it is normal for passions to fade may avoid assuming that their love is at an end when it may, in fact, be changing into a deeper, more intimate and committed form of love. This knowledge may also encourage couples to focus on finding ways of rekindling the embers of romance, rather than looking to escape at the first signs that the embers have cooled.

Researchers have tested some facets of the triangular model. One study reported mixed results. As the model would predict, married adults reported higher levels of commitment to their relationships than did unmarried adults (Acker & Davis, 1992). Yet the expected

Consummate Love. According to Sternberg, romantic love may develop into a more complete love, called consummate love, in which desire is accompanied by deep intimacy and commitment. Consummate love is the special ideal toward which many Westerners strive.

decline in passion over time was found only for women. Critics contend that Sternberg's model does not account for all the nuances and complexities of love (Murstein, 1988). The model tells us little, for example, about the *goals* of love or the *sources* of love. In fairness, Sternberg's model is a major contribution to the scientific study of love, which is only now beginning. Poets, philosophers, and theologians, by comparison, have been writing about love for millennia.

~ *Reflections* ~

■ Have you been in romantic love? How did you know you were in love?
■ Consider the kinds of love discussed in this chapter. What kind of love have you felt for family members? For friends? For people with whom you have had romantic relationships? Has one kind of love ever changed into another?

In this chapter we have discussed interpersonal attraction—the force that initiates social contact. In the next chapter we follow the development of social contacts into intimate relationships.

Summing Up

Attraction

A number of factors determine interpersonal attraction.

Physical Attractiveness: How Important Is Looking Good? Physical attractiveness is a major determinant of sexual attraction. In our culture, slenderness is in style. Both genders consider smiling faces more attractive. Socially dominant men, but not dominant women, are usually found attractive. Women place relatively greater emphasis on traits like vocational status and earning potential, whereas men give relatively more consideration to physical attractiveness. Some sociobiologists believe that evolutionary forces favor the continuation of such gender differences in preferred traits because certain preferred traits provide reproductive advantages.

The Matching Hypothesis: Who Is "Right" for You? According to the matching hypothesis, people tend to develop romantic relationships with people who are similar to themselves in attractiveness.

Similarity in Attitudes: Do Opposites Attract? Similarity in attitudes and tastes is a strong contributor to attraction, friendships, and love relationships.

Reciprocity: If You Like Me, You Must Have Excellent Judgment Through the reciprocation of positive words and actions, neutral or mild feelings may be stoked into feelings of attraction.

Love

In our culture we are brought up to idealize the concept of romantic love.

The Greek Heritage The Greeks had four concepts related to the modern meanings of love: storge, agape, philia, and eros.

Romantic Love in Contemporary Western Culture Western culture has a long tradition of idealizing the concept of romantic love. Most people in the United States see romantic love as prerequisite to marriage. At first, infatuation and more enduring forms of romantic love may be indistinguishable.

Contemporary Models of Love: Dare Science Intrude? Researchers are now applying the scientific method to the study of love.

Berscheid and Hatfield define romantic love in terms of intense physiological arousal and cognitive appraisal of that arousal as love.

Hendrick and Hendrick suggest that there are six styles of love among college students: romantic love, game-playing love, friendship, logical love, possessive love, and selfless love.

Sternberg suggests that there are three distinct components of love: intimacy, passion, and commitment. Various combinations of these components typify different kinds of love. Romantic love is characterized by the combination of passion and intimacy.

CHAPTER 8

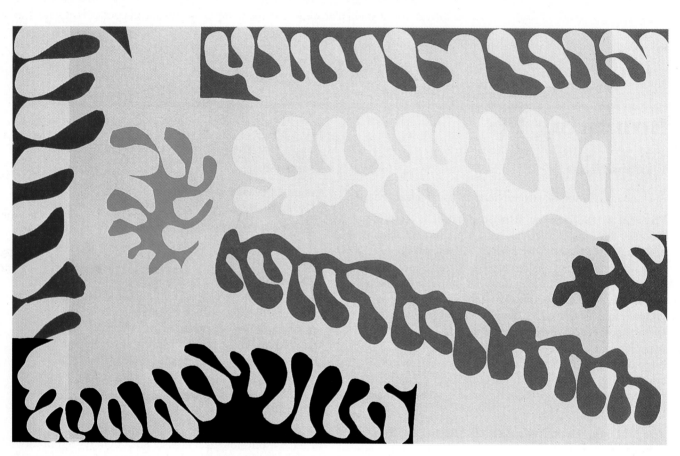

Henri Matisse, *Lagoon,* Plate 17 from *Jazz.* The Metropolitan Museum
of Art, Gift of Lila Acheson Wallace, 1983. © 1996 Succession H. Matisse/Artist
Rights Society (ARS), New York. © 1985 by The Metropolitan Museum of Art.

Relationships, Intimacy, and Communication

Outline

Truth OR Fiction?

_____ Small talk is an insincere method of initiating a relationship.

_____ Only phonies practice opening lines.

_____ Swift self-disclosure of intimate information is the best way to deepen a new relationship.

_____ Many people remain lonely because they fear being rejected by others.

_____ People can have intimate relationships without being sexually intimate.

_____ "Love is all you need." That is, when partners truly love one another, they instinctively know how to satisfy each other sexually.

_____ If you are criticized, the best course is to retaliate.

_____ Relationships come to an end when the partners cannot resolve their differences.

_____ Disagreement is destructive to a relationship.

ill you, won't you, will you, won't you, will you join the dance?

(Lewis Carroll, *Alice in Wonderland*)

No man is an island, entire of itself.

(John Donne)

"One, two. One, two." A great opening line? In the film *Play It Again, Sam*, Woody Allen plays the role of Allan Felix, a social klutz who has just been divorced. Diane Keaton plays his platonic friend Linda. At a bar one evening with Linda and her husband, Allan Felix spots a young woman on the dance floor who is so attractive that he wishes *he* could have *her* children.

The thing to do, Linda prompts him, is to begin dancing, then dance over to her and "say something." With a bit more prodding, Linda convinces Allan to dance. It's so simple, she tells him. He need only keep time—"One, two, one, two."

"One, two," repeats Allan. Linda shoves him off to his dream woman.

Hesitantly, Allan dances up to her. Working up courage, he says, "One, two. One, two, one, two." He is ignored and finds his way back to Linda.

"Allan, try something more meaningful," Linda implores.

Once more, Allan dances nervously back toward the woman of his dreams. He stammers, "Three, four, three, four."

"*Speak* to her, Allan," Linda insists.

He dances up to her again and tries, "You interested in dancing at all?"

"Get lost, creep," she replies.

Allan dances rapidly back toward Linda. "What'd she say?" Linda asks.

"She'd rather not," he shrugs.

So much for "One, two, one, two," and, for that matter, for "Three, four, three, four." Striking up a relationship requires some social skills, and the first few conversational steps can be big ones.

In this chapter we first define the stages that lead to intimacy in relationships. We define intimacy and see that not all relationships achieve this level of interrelatedness, even some supposedly deep and permanent relationships such as marriage. Moreover, we do not all have partners with whom we can develop intimate relationships; some of us remain alone, and, perhaps, lonely. There are steps we can take to overcome loneliness, however, as we illustrate in the pages ahead. Finally, we discuss the ways that communication contributes to relationships and sexual satisfaction, and we enumerate ways of enhancing communication skills.

Social-exchange theory
The view that the development of a relationship reflects the unfolding of social exchanges—that is, the rewards and costs of maintaining the relationship as opposed to ending it.

ABCDE model
Levinger's view, which approaches romantic relationships in terms of five stages: attraction, building, continuation, deterioration, and ending.

The ABC(DE)s of Romantic Relationships

Romantic relationships, like people, undergo stages of development. According to **social-exchange theory,** the development reflects the unfolding of social exchanges, which involve the rewards and costs of maintaining the relationship as opposed to dissolving it. During each stage, positive factors sway partners toward maintaining and enhancing their relationship. Negative factors incline them toward letting it deteriorate and end (Karney & Bradbury, 1995).

George Levinger (1980) proposes an **ABCDE model** to describe the stages of romantic relationships: (1) *Attraction,* (2) *Building,* (3) *Continuation,* (4) *Deterioration,* and (5) *Ending.*

The A's—Attraction

Attraction occurs when two people become aware of each other and find one another appealing or enticing. We may find ourselves attracted to an enchanting person "across a crowded room," in a nearby office, or in a new class. We may meet others through blind dates, introductions by mutual friends, computer match-ups, or by "accident." Initial feelings of attraction are largely based on visual impressions, though we may also form initial impressions by overhearing people speak or hearing others talk about them.

According to the NHSLS study (Michael et al., 1994), married people are most likely to have met their spouses through mutual friends (35%) or by self-introductions (32%) (see Figure 8.1). Other sources of introductions are family members (15%) and coworkers, classmates, or neighbors (13%). Mutual friends and self-introductions are also the most common ways of meeting for unmarried couples (Michael et al., 1994).

The B's—Building

Building a relationship follows initial attraction. Factors that motivate us to try to build relationships include similarity in the level of physical attractiveness, similarity in attitudes, and mutual liking and positive evaluations. Factors that may deter us from trying to build relationships include lack of physical appeal, dissimilarity in attitudes, and negative mutual evaluations.

Not-So-Small Talk: An Audition for Building a Relationship
In the early stages of building a relationship, we tend to probe each other with **surface contact:** We typically look for common ground in the form of overlapping attitudes and interests, and we check out our feelings of attraction. At this point the determination of whether to strive to develop the relationship is often made, at least in part, on the basis of **small talk.** Small talk allows an exchange of information but stresses breadth of topic coverage rather than in-depth discussion. Engaging in small talk may seem "phony," but premature self-disclosure of intimate information may repel the other person, as we shall see.

Small talk is a trial balloon for friendship. Successful small talk encourages a couple to venture beneath the surface. At a cocktail party, people may flit about from person to person, exchanging small talk, but now and then a couple finds common ground and pairs off.

Truth OR Fiction?
R E V I S I T E D

It is not true that small talk is an insincere method of initiating a relationship. Actually, small talk is a realistic way to begin a relationship. It allows couples to search for common ground and test feelings of attraction. ■

The "Opening Line": How Do You Get Things Started?
One kind of small talk is the greeting, or opening line. We usually precede verbal greetings with eye contact and decide to begin talking if eye contact is reciprocated. Avoidance of eye contact may mean that the person is shy, but it could also signify lack of interest. If you would

Surface contact
A probing phase of building a relationship in which people seek common ground and check out feelings of attraction.

Small talk
A superficial kind of conversation that allows exchange of information but stresses breadth of topic coverage rather than in-depth discussion.

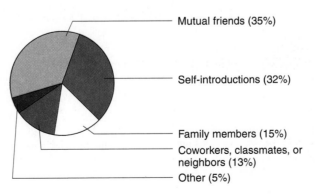

Figure 8.1. How Married People Meet Their Partners.

- Mutual friends (35%)
- Self-introductions (32%)
- Family members (15%)
- Coworkers, classmates, or neighbors (13%)
- Other (5%)

like to progress from initial attraction to surface contact, try a smile and direct eye contact. If the eye contact is reciprocated, choose an opening line, or greeting. Since your opening line can be important, you may prefer to say something more meaningful than "One, two, one, two."

Consider some greetings, or opening lines:

Verbal salutes, such as "Good morning."
Personal inquiries, such as "How are you doing?"
Compliments, such as "I like your outfit."
References to your mutual surroundings, such as "What do you think of that painting?" or "This is a nice apartment house, isn't it?"
References to people or events outside the immediate setting, such as "How do you like this weather we've been having?"
References to the other person's behavior, such as "I couldn't help noticing you were sitting alone," or "I see you out on this track every Saturday morning."
References to your own behavior, or to yourself, such as "Hi, my name is Allan Felix" (feel free to use your own name, if you prefer).

The simple "Hi" or "Hello" is very useful. A friendly glance followed by a cheerful hello ought to give you some idea of whether the attraction is reciprocated. If the hello is returned with a friendly smile and inviting eye contact, follow it up with another greeting, such as a reference to your surroundings, the other person's behavior, or your name.

Truth **OR** Fiction?
R E V I S I T E D

Actually, it can be helpful for everyone to practice opening lines. People are social beings, and opening lines help us initiate social relationships—with new friends as well as dates. ■

Exchanging "Name, Rank, and Serial Number"   Early exchanges are likely to include name, occupation, marital status, and hometown. This has been likened to exchanging "name, rank, and serial number" with the other person. Each person seeks a sociological profile of the other to discover common ground that may provide a basis for pursuing the conversation. An unspoken rule seems to be at work: "If I provide you with some information about myself, you will reciprocate by giving me an equal amount of information about yourself. Or . . . 'I'll tell you my hometown if you tell me yours' " (Knapp, 1978, p. 114). If the other person is unresponsive, she or he may not be attracted to you, and you may wish to try someone else. But you may also be awkward in your approach or perhaps turn the other person off by disclosing too much about yourself at once. The nearby 'What Do You Say Now?' feature suggests ways of improving date-seeking skills.

Self-disclosure
The revelation of personal, perhaps intimate, information.

Self-Disclosure: You Tell Me and I'll Tell You . . . Carefully
Opening up, or **self-disclosure,** is central to building intimate relationships. But just what sort of information is safe to disclose upon first meeting someone? If you refuse to go beyond name, rank, and serial number, you may look uninterested or as if you are trying to keep things under wraps. If, on the other hand, you spill out the fact that you have a terrible rash on your thigh, it's likely that you have disclosed too much too soon.

By permission of Johnny Hart and Creators Syndicate Inc.

HOW TO IMPROVE DATE-SEEKING SKILLS

All right, now you know that Mr. or Ms. Right exists. So what do you do? How do you go about making a date?

Psychologists have learned that we can enhance our social skills, including our date-seeking skills, through the technique of *successive approximations.* (The third author interjects: "See here, you two psychologists, if you *mean* building skills step by step, why not just *say* 'step by step'?") That means that we can practice a series of tasks that are *graded in difficulty.* (The third author surrenders!) We can hone our social skills and gain self-confidence at each step. We can try out some of our skills on friends. Friends can role-play the prospective date and give honest feedback about our behavior.

Here is an example of a series of graduated (*step-by-step*)* tasks that may help you sharpen your own date-seeking skills:

Easy Practice Level

Select a person with whom you are friendly, but one whom you have no desire to date. Practice making small talk about the weather, new films, TV shows, concerts, museum shows, political events, and personal hobbies.

Select a person you might have some interest in dating. Smile when you pass this person at work, school, or elsewhere, and say "Hi." Engage in this activity with other people of both genders to increase your skills at greeting others.

Speak into your mirror, using behavior rehearsal and role playing. Pretend you are in the process of sitting next to the person you would like to date, say, at lunch or in the laundry room. Say "Hello" with a broad smile, and introduce yourself. Work on the smile until it looks inviting and genuine. Make some comment about the food or the setting—the cafeteria, the office, whatever. Use a family member or confidant to obtain feedback about the effectiveness of the smile, your tone of voice, posture, and choice of words.

Medium Practice Level

Sit down next to the person you want to date, and engage in small talk. If you are in a classroom, talk about a homework assignment, the seating arrangement, or the instructor (be kind). If you are at work, talk about the building or some recent interesting event in the neighborhood. Ask your intended date how he or she feels about the situation. If you are at a group meeting, such as Parents Without Partners, tell the other person that you are there for the first time and ask for advice on how to relate to the group.

Engage in small talk about the weather and local events. Channel the conversation into an exchange of personal information. Give your "name, rank, and serial number"—who you are, your major field or your occupation, where you're from, why or how you came to the school or company. The other person is likely to reciprocate and provide equivalent information. Ask how he or she feels about the class, place of business, city, hometown, and so on.

Rehearse asking the person out before your mirror, a family member, or a confidant. You may wish to ask the person out for a cup of coffee or to a film. It is somewhat less threatening to ask someone out to a gathering at which "some of us will be getting together." Or you may rehearse asking the person to accompany you to a cultural event, such as an exhibition at a museum or a concert—it's "sort of" a date, but also less anxiety inducing.

Target Behavior Level

Ask the person out on a date in a manner consistent with your behavior rehearsal. If the person says he or she has a previous engagement or can't make it, you may wish to say something like, "That's too bad," or "I'm sorry you can't make it," and add something like, "Perhaps another time." You should be able to get a feeling for whether the person you asked out was just seeking an excuse or has a genuine interest in you and, as claimed, could not in fact accept the specific invitation.

Before asking the date out again, pay attention to his or her apparent comfort level when you return to small talk on a couple of occasions. If there is still a chance, the person should smile and return your eye contact. The other person may also offer you an invitation. In any event, if you are turned down twice, do not ask a third time. And don't make a catastrophe out of the refusal. Look up. Note that the roof hasn't fallen in. The birds are still chirping in the trees. You are still paying taxes. Then give someone else a chance to appreciate your fine qualities.

*Happy now?

If the surface contact provided by small talk and initial self-disclosure has been mutually rewarding, partners in a relationship tend to develop deeper feelings of liking for each other (Collins & Miller, 1994). Self-disclosure may continue to build gradually through the course of a relationship as partners come to trust each other enough to share confidences and more intimate feelings.

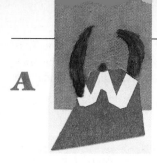 

SELF-DISCLOSURE: EAST MAY BE EAST AND WEST MAY BE WEST, BUT HERE, PERHAPS, THE TWAIN DO (ALMOST) MEET

Research suggests that we should refrain from disclosing certain types of information too rapidly if we want to make a good impression. In one study, confederates of the experimenters (Wortman et al., 1976) engaged in 10-minute conversations with study participants. Some confederates were "early disclosers," who shared intimate information early. Others, "late disclosers," shared intimate information toward the end of the conversation only. In either case, the information was identical. Study participants then rated the disclosers. Early disclosers were rated less mature, secure, well adjusted, and genuine than the late disclosers. Study participants also preferred to continue relationships with the late disclosers. We may say we value "openness" and "honesty" in our relationships, but it may be a social mistake to open up too soon.

T r u t h OR F i c t i o n ?
R E V I S I T E D

It is not true that swift self-disclosure of intimate information is the best way to deepen a new relationship. Actually, swift or premature self-disclosure can make one seem distraught or awkward and turn people off. ∎

A Japanese study showed similar results. Japanese college students rated actors in a mock conversation more favorably when they disclosed less about themselves (Nakanishi, 1986). Chinese people also responded negatively to others who are prone to early self-disclosure.

Despite such cross-cultural similarities, self-disclosure in general may be viewed less favorably in

Eastern cultures. In Japanese society, for example, self-disclosure is often seen as inappropriate in social relationships (Nakanishi, 1986). Not surprisingly, researchers find that people in the United States tend to disclose much more about themselves in social interactions than do the Japanese (Gudykunst & Nishida, 1984).

Do You Dare Let It All Hang Out? Despite the common belief that one should be honest and open, research suggests that people who self-disclose too much too soon are seen as socially inept. Researchers find that people in Japan tend to disclose less personal information in social interactions than people in the United States do.

Gender Differences in Self-Disclosure   A woman complains to a friend: "He never opens up to me. It's like living with a stone wall." Women commonly declare that men are loath to express their feelings (Tannen, 1990). Researchers find that men tend to be less willing to disclose their feelings, perhaps in adherence to the traditional "strong and silent" male stereotype (see Chapter 6).

Yet gender differences in self-disclosure tend to be small. Overall, researchers find that women are only slightly more revealing about themselves than men (Dindia & Allen, 1992). We should thus be careful not to rush to the conclusion that men are always more "tight-lipped." The belief that there are large gender differences in self-disclosure appears to be something of a myth.

Stereotypes are also a-changing—somewhat. We now see depictions in the media of the "new" man as someone who is able to express feelings without compromising his masculinity. We shall have to wait to see whether this "new" sensitive image replaces the rugged, reticent stereotype, or is a passing fancy.

Mutuality: When the "We," Not the "I's," Have It   When feelings of attraction and the establishment of common ground lead a couple to regard themselves as "we"—not just two "I's" who happen to be in the same place at the same time—they have

A CLOSER LOOK

WHO ARE THE IDEAL MEN FOR THE 1990S?

We thank readers for assuming that the first and second authors are referring to themselves in the title of this piece. (The third author is considering abandoning this project.) However, the title refers to a recent poll by *Psychology Today* magazine (Keen & Zur, 1989). *Psychology Today* readers are wealthier and better educated (66% had earned at least a baccalaureate degree) than the public at large, but they are reasonably similar to readers of this textbook in their educational and socioeconomic backgrounds.

The study found that hard-driving businessmen and John Wayne types are "on the outs" for the 1990s. The compassionate, communicative man is definitely "in." Table 8.1 shows the percentages of women respondents who endorsed certain traits ascribed to the masculine ideal. Social receptivity, a powerful presence, and health were viewed as desirable. Macho, urbane, and Type A men needn't apply.

It appears that many men are living up to the new ideal, at least in the opinion of women who know them well. The *Psychology Today* article reported that 37% of the women respondents rated the men to whom they felt closest (fathers, brothers, friends, lovers, or husbands) as "ideal." Another 52% considered the man to whom they were closest as "good." That may be good enough. The categories "ideal" and "good" add up to 89%.

Perhaps male readers need to unstiffen their upper lips and start listening and sharing their feelings—if they want to approximate the ideal for the 1990s (Tannen, 1990).

TABLE 8.1   Qualities ascribed to the ideal man by *Psychology Today* readers

Trait	Percentage Who Endorse Trait
Is receptive, responsive to the initiatives of others	89%
Has strong intellectual, moral, or physical presence	87
Attends to diet, exercise, health	87
Expresses feelings of sadness	86
Stops often to wonder, to appreciate, perchance to dream	82
Follows inner authority	77
Is even-tempered, moderate	77
Is easy to be with	75
Is nonjudgmental	74
Accepts help willingly	70
Takes charge, is a doer	68
. . .	
Is urbane, suave	22
Has Type A personality	20
Is always found where the action is	20
Is introverted	16
Is critical	14
Has mood swings	10
Never shows pain	6
Basically ignores his body	2

Source: Reprinted with permission from *Psychology Today* magazine. Copyright © 1989 (Sussex Publishers, Inc.).

Mutuality

A phase in building a relationship in which members of a couple come to regard themselves as "we," no longer two "I's" who happen to be in the same place at the same time.

attained what Levinger terms a state of **mutuality.** The development of mutuality favors the continuation and further deepening of the relationship.

The C's—Continuation

Once a relationship has been established, the couple embarks upon the stage of continuation. Factors that encourage continuation include seeking ways to introduce variety and maintain interest (such as trying out new sexual practices and social activities), showing evidence of caring and positive evaluation (such as sending birthday or Valentine's Day cards), showing lack of jealousy, perceiving fairness in the relationship, and experiencing mutual feelings of general satisfaction.

Factors in this stage that can throw the relationship into a downward spiral include boredom (e.g., falling into a rut in leisure activities, sexual practices, etc.), displaying evidence of negative evaluation (such as bickering, and forgetting anniversaries and other important dates or pretending that they do not exist), perceiving a lack of fairness in the relationship (such as one partner's always deciding how the couple will spend their free time), or experiencing feelings of jealousy and general dissatisfaction.

Jealousy

> O! beware, my lord, of jealousy;
> It is the green-ey'd monster . . .
>
> (William Shakespeare, *Othello*)

Thus was Othello, the Moor of Venice, warned of jealousy in the Shakespearean play that bears his name. Yet Othello could not control his feelings and slew his beloved Desdemona. The English poet John Dryden labeled jealousy a "tyrant of the mind." Anthropologists find evidence of jealousy in all cultures, although it may vary in amount and intensity across and within cultures. It appears to be more common and intense among cultures with a stronger *machismo* tradition, in which men are expected to display their virility.

Sexual jealousy is aroused when we suspect that an intimate relationship is threatened by a rival. Lovers can become jealous when others show sexual interest in their partners or when their partners show an interest (even a casual or nonsexual interest) in another. Jealousy can impair a relationship and produce feelings of mistrust of one's partner or toward potential rivals.

Sexual jealousy may be associated with a range of negative emotions, including fear of losing the loved one and anger toward the rival, the loved one, or both. Feelings of possessiveness, which are related to jealousy, can also stress a relationship. In extreme cases jealousy can cause depression or give rise to spouse abuse, suicide, or, as with Othello, murder. But milder forms of jealousy are not necessarily destructive to a relationship. They may even serve the positive function of revealing how much one cares for one's partner.

How common is sexual jealousy? Common. In a survey of 103 women at various stages of involvement in an intimate relationship, 3 out of 4 reported feelings of jealousy (Pines & Aronson, 1983). Fifty-four percent described themselves as jealous. Women who were in nonmonogamous relationships or were dissatisfied with their relationships were more likely to describe themselves as jealous. A typical situation that prompted jealousy was a party at which the woman's partner spent time talking to, or dancing or flirting with, other women.

What causes jealousy? In some cases, people become mistrustful of their current partners because their former partners had cheated. Jealousy may also derive from low self-esteem or a lack of self-confidence. People with low self-esteem may experience sexual jealousy because they become overly dependent on their partners. They may also fear that they will not be able to find another partner if their present lover leaves.

White (1981) has concluded from his research on jealousy that feelings of inadequacy lead to jealousy in women. In men, the reverse seems to be the case. For men, that is, feelings of jealousy tend to give rise to feelings of inadequacy. It is as if jealousy leads them to question whether they are worthy of their partners' affections. For both men and women, however, feelings of jealousy can lead to perceiving anyone as a rival, which can make them continually mistrustful.

Unfortunately many lovers—including many college students—play jealousy games. They let their partners know that they are attracted to other people. They flirt openly and even manufacture tales to make their partners pay more attention to them, to test the relationship, to inflict pain, or to take revenge for a partner's disloyalty.

The D's—Deterioration

Deterioration is the fourth stage of a relationship. It is not necessarily a stage that we seek, and certainly not an inevitability. Positive factors that can deter or slow deterioration include putting time and energy into the relationship, striving to cultivate the relationship, and showing patience—for example, giving the relationship a reasonable opportunity to improve. Negative factors that foster deterioration include failure to invest time and energy in the relationship, deciding to put an end to it, or simply permitting deterioration to proceed unchecked.

A relationship begins to deteriorate when one or both partners deem the relationship to be less enticing or rewarding than it had been. Couples who work toward maintaining and enhancing their relationships may find that they become stronger and more meaningful.

Active and Passive Responses to Deterioration   When a couple perceives their relationship to be deteriorating, they can respond in active or passive ways. Active means of response include doing something that may enhance the relationship (such as working on improving communication skills, negotiating differences, or seeking professional help) or making a decision to end the relationship. Passive methods of responding are basically characterized by waiting for something to happen, by just doing nothing. People can sit back passively and wait for the relationship to improve on its own (once in a great while, it does) or for the relationship to deteriorate to the point where it ends. ("Don't look at me; these things happen.")

It is irrational (and damaging to a relationship) to assume that suitable relationships require no investment of time and effort. No two of us—with the possible exceptions of your first and third authors—are matched perfectly. Unless one member of a couple does double duty as a doormat, inevitable frictions will surface. When problems arise, it is better to work to resolve them than to act as if they don't exist and hope that they will disappear of their own accord.

The E's—Ending

Ending is the fifth and final stage of a relationship. Although it may be the ultimate stage of development, like deterioration, it need not be inevitable or desirable. Various factors can prevent a deteriorating relationship from ending. For example, people who continue to find some sources of satisfaction, who are committed to maintaining the relationship, or who believe that they will eventually be able to overcome their problems are more likely to invest what they must to prevent the collapse.

According to social-exchange theory, relationships draw to a close when negative forces are in sway—when the partners find little satisfaction in the affiliation, when the barriers to leaving the relationship are low (that is, the social, religious, and financial constraints are manageable), and especially when alternative partners are available (Karney & Bradbury, 1995).

The swan song of a relationship is not always a bad thing. When people are definitely incompatible, and when genuine attempts to preserve the relationship have faltered, ending the relationship can offer each partner a chance for happiness with someone else.

~ *Reflections* ~

- What opening lines, if any, have you used to begin relationships? Do you find it difficult to make small talk? Why, or why not?
- Have you ever had trouble deciding how much intimate information to disclose to a dating partner? What are the dangers in disclosing too much too soon to a partner? Are there some things that you feel that you should never share with a partner?
- Have you ever experienced feelings of jealousy? How did they affect your relationship? Your self-esteem? Did you handle the feelings well? Why, or why not?

Loneliness: "All the Lonely People, Where Do They All Come From?"

Many people start relationships because of loneliness. Loneliness and being alone are not synonymous. Loneliness is a state of painful isolation, of feeling cut off from others. Being alone, a state of solitude, can be quite desirable since it allows us to work, study, or reflect on the world around us. Solitude is usually a matter of choice; loneliness is not.

Lonely people tend to spend a lot of time by themselves, eat dinner alone, spend weekends alone, and participate in few social activities. They are unlikely to date. Some lonely people report having many friends, but a closer look suggests that these "friendships" are shallow. Lonely people are unlikely to share confidences. Loneliness tends to peak during adolescence. This is when most young people begin to supplant family ties with peer relationships. Loneliness is often connected with feelings of depression and with feelings of being "sick at heart."

Loneliness is even reported among some married people. In one study (Sadava & Matejcic, 1987), lonely wives tended to feel less liking and love for their partners and expressed less marital satisfaction. Lonely husbands reported less liking for their wives and less intimacy in their relationships.

Causes of Loneliness

The causes of loneliness are many and complex. Lonely people tend to have several of the following characteristics:

1. *Lack of social skills.* Lonely people often lack the interpersonal skills needed to make friends or to cope with disagreements.
2. *Lack of interest in other people.*
3. *Lack of empathy.*
4. *Fear of rejection.* This fear is often connected with self-criticism of social skills and expectations of failure in relating to others (Schultz & Moore, 1984).
5. *Failure to disclose personal information to potential friends* (Solano et al., 1982).
6. *Cynicism about human nature* (e.g., seeing people as only out for themselves).
7. *Demanding too much too soon.* They perceive other people as cold and unfriendly in the early stages of a relationship.
8. *General pessimism.* When we expect the worst, we often get . . . you guessed it.
9. *An external locus of control.* That is, they do not see themselves as capable of taking their lives into their own hands and achieving their goals.

 **Truth OR Fiction? REVISITED** It is true that many people remain lonely because they fear being rejected by others. ■

Coping with Loneliness

Psychologists have helped people cope with loneliness by fostering more adaptive ways of thinking and behaving. Lonely people often have distorted views of other people. They may have had one or two unfortunate experiences and jump to the conclusion that people are generally selfish and not worth the effort of getting involved. Let's face it: Some people *are* basically out for themselves, but the expectation that everyone is can perpetuate loneliness by motivating avoidance of social activities.

What can you do to deal with loneliness in your own life? We are all different, and the methods that might help one person may not aid another. But here is a list of suggestions compiled by Rathus and Fichner-Rathus (1994):

1. *Challenge your feelings of pessimism.* Adopt the attitude that things happen when you make them happen.
2. *Challenge your cynicism about human nature.* Yes, lots of people are selfish and not worth knowing, but if you assume that all people are like that, you can doom yourself to a lifetime of loneliness. Your task is to find people who possess the qualities that you value.
3. *Challenge the idea that failure in social relationships is awful and is thus a valid reason for giving up on them.* Sure, social rejection can be painful, but unless you happen to be Harrison Ford or Julia Roberts, you may not appeal to everyone. We must all learn to live with some rejection. But keep looking for the people who possess the qualities you value and who will find things of equal value in you.
4. *Follow the suggestions for improving your date-seeking skills spelled out in the What Do You Say Now? feature.* Sit down at a table with people in the cafeteria, not off in a corner by yourself. Smile and say hi to people who interest you. Practice opening lines for different occasions—and a few follow-up lines. Try them out in the mirror.
5. *Make numerous social contacts.* Join committees for student activities. Try intramural sports. Join social-action groups, such as environmental groups and community betterment groups. Join clubs, such as the photography club or the ski club. Get on the school yearbook or newspaper staff.
6. *Be assertive.* Express your genuine opinions.
7. *Become a good listener.* Ask people how they're doing. Ask them for their opinions about classes, politics, the campus events of the day. Then actually *listen* to what they have to say. Tolerate diverse opinions; remember that no two of us are identical in our outlooks (not even your "perfectly" matched first and third authors). Maintain eye contact. Keep your face friendly. (No, you don't have to remain neutral and friendly if someone becomes insulting toward a religious or ethnic group.)
8. *Give people the chance to know you.* Exchange opinions, and talk about your interests. Yes, you'll turn some people off—who doesn't?—but how else will you learn whether you and another person share common ground?
9. *Fight fair.* Friends will inevitably disappoint you, and you'll want to tell them about it. Do so, but fairly. You can start by asking if it's okay to be open about something. Then say, "I feel upset because you . . . " You can ask your friend if he or she realized that his or her behavior upset you. Try to work together to find a way to avoid recurrences. Finish by thanking your friend for helping you resolve the problem.
10. *Remember that you're worthy of friends.* It's true—warts and all. None of us is perfect. We're all unique, but you may connect with more people than you imagine. Give people a chance.
11. *Use your college counseling center.* Many thousands of students are lonely but don't know what to do about it. Others just cannot find the courage to approach others. College counseling centers are very familiar with the problem of loneliness, and you should consider them a valuable resource. You might even ask if there's a group at the center for students seeking to improve their dating or social skills.

~ *Reflections* ~

What is the difference between loneliness and solitude?
Have you ever been lonely? What were the reasons for it?
Did you do anything to overcome your loneliness? What? Would you now do anything differently?

Intimacy

Intimacy
Feelings of closeness and connectedness that are marked by sharing of inmost thoughts and feelings.

Intimacy involves feelings of emotional closeness and connectedness with another person and the desire to share each other's inmost thoughts and feelings. Intimate relationships are also characterized by attitudes of mutual trust, caring, and acceptance.

Sternberg's (1986) triangular theory of love (see Chapter 7) regards intimacy as a basic component of romantic love. But people can be intimate and not in love, at least not in romantic love. Close friends and family members become emotionally intimate when they care deeply for each other and share their private feelings and experiences. It is not necessary for people to be *sexually* intimate to have an emotionally intimate relationship. Nor does sexual intimacy automatically produce emotional intimacy. People who are sexually involved may still fail to touch each other's lives in emotionally intimate ways. Even couples who fall in love may not be able to forge an intimate relationship because of unwillingness or inability to exchange inmost thoughts and feelings. Sometimes husbands or wives share greater emotional intimacy with friends than with their spouses.

Truth  Fiction?
R E V I S I T E D

It is true that people can have intimate relationships without being sexually intimate. Close friends and relatives can have nonsexual but intimate relationships. ∎

Let us now consider some of the factors that are involved in building and maintaining intimate relationships.

Knowing and Liking Yourself

Some social scientists suggest that an initial step toward intimacy with others is getting to know and like yourself. By coming to know and value yourself, you identify your inmost feelings and needs and develop the security to share them.

Trusting and Caring

Two of the most important ingredients of an intimate relationship are trust and caring. When trust exists in a relationship, partners feel secure that disclosing intimate feelings will not lead to ridicule, rejection, or other kinds of harm. Trust usually builds gradually, as partners learn whether or not it is safe to share confidences. Caring is an emotional bond that allows intimacy to develop. In caring relationships, partners seek to gratify each other's needs and interests.

Building Intimacy. Intimate couples share each other's inmost thoughts and feelings. Intimacy also involves mutual trust, caring, and acceptance.

Try a Little Tenderness? Tenderness is expressed physically and verbally—by kissing, hugging, cuddling, or holding hands, and by words of caring and appreciation.

Tenderness is expressed by putting one's arm around a partner's shoulder to offer support, or by verbalizations of love, caring, and appreciation. In romantic relationships, tenderness also takes the form of kissing, hugging, cuddling, and holding hands.

Being Honest

Since intimacy involves the sharing of one's inmost thoughts and feelings, honesty is a core feature of intimacy. Without honesty, partners see only each other's facades. A person need not be an "open book" to develop and maintain intimacy, however. Some aspects of experience are kept even from one's most intimate partners, for they may be too embarrassing or threatening to reveal (Kammeyer et al., 1990). For example, we would not expect partners to disclose every passing sexual fantasy.

Intimate relationships thus usually involve balances in which some things are revealed and others are not. Total honesty could devastate a relationship. It would not be reasonable, for example, to expect intimate partners to divulge the details of past sexual experiences. The recipient may wonder: "Why is Kimball telling me this? Am I as good a lover as _____? Is Kimball still in love with _____? What else did Kimball do with _____?" Discretion thus also buttresses intimate relationships. As Gordon and Snyder (1989) put it, "Honesty means *saying what you mean,* not revealing every detail" (p. 24). Nor is intimacy established by frank but brutal criticism, even if it is honest.

Making a Commitment

Have you ever noticed that people may open up to strangers on airplanes or trains, yet find it hard to talk openly with people to whom they are closest? An intimate relationship involves more than the isolated act of baring one's soul to a stranger. Truly intimate relationships are marked by commitment or resolve to maintain the relationship through thick and thin. When we open up to strangers on a plane, we know it is unlikely that we will have to face them again.

This does not mean that intimate relationships require indefinite or lifelong commitments. A commitment, however, carries an obligation that the couple will work to overcome problems in the relationship rather than run for the exit at the first sign of trouble.

Maintaining Individuality When the *I* Becomes *We*

In committed relationships, a delicate balance exists between individuality and mutuality. In healthy unions, a strong sense of togetherness does not eradicate individuality. Partners in such relationships remain free to be themselves. Neither seeks to dominate or submerge himself or herself into the personality of the other. Each partner maintains individual interests, likes and dislikes, needs and goals.

Communicating

Good communication is another hallmark of an intimate relationship. Partners are able to share their most personal thoughts and feelings clearly and honestly. Communication is a two-way street. It embraces sending and receiving messages. The good communicator is thus a skilled listener as well as a clear speaker (Tannen, 1990). We generally associate communication with *talk,* which involves the use of verbal messages to convey a thought or a feeling. Through talk, the speaker *encodes* a thought or a feeling into words. The listener *decodes* the words to extract the meaning of the message. Problems in verbal communication can arise at several levels:

1. *The speaker may use words differently than the listener, leading to misunderstandings or miscommunication.* For example, the speaker might say, "You look really cute tonight." The listener might object, saying, "You think I look *cute?* What's wrong with the way I look?" The speaker protests, "No, I didn't mean it that way. I meant you look good. Yes, good."
2. *The speaker's words may not match his or her tone of voice, facial expression, or body gestures.* For example, the speaker says, "Darling, I really *don't mind* if we visit your mother this weekend." But the speaker did not say, "I really *want* to visit your mother," so the words "don't mind" come across as a kind of snarl. In such cases, the listener is likely to place greater weight on *how* something is said rather than on *what* is said.
3. *The speaker may not be able to put into words what he or she truly means or feels.* Sometimes we grasp for words to express our feelings, but they do not come, or those that do come miss the mark.

Nonverbal Communication: The Body Speaks   Though the spoken word is a primary form of communication, we often express our feelings through nonverbal channels as well, such as by tone of voice, gestures, body posture, and facial expressions (Tannen, 1990). People may place more weight on how words are said than on their denotative meaning. People also accentuate the meaning of their words through gestures, raising or lowering their voices, or using a sterner or softer tone of voice.

The Body Speaks. Nonverbal cues such as posture, eye contact, and physical distance convey information about a person's underlying feelings toward another. What might you infer about the couple's attitudes on the basis of their body language?

Nonverbal communication is used not only to accentuate the spoken word, but also to directly express feelings. We sometimes are better able to convey our feelings through body language than by the use of words. A touch or a gaze into someone's eyes may express more about our feelings than words can. Parents express feelings of tenderness and caring toward infants by hugging, holding, and caressing them, and by speaking in a gentle and soothing tone of voice, even though the meanings of the words cannot yet be grasped.

Let us examine some aspects of nonverbal communication:

On "Being Uptight" and "Hanging Loose" The ways that people carry themselves offer cues about their feelings and potential actions. People who are emotionally "uptight" often stand or sit rigidly and straight-backed. People who feel more relaxed literally "hang loose."

People who face us and lean toward us are in effect saying that they like us or care about what we are saying. If we overhear a conversation between a couple and see that the woman is leaning toward the man, but he is leaning back and playing with his hair, we tend to infer that he is not accepting what she is saying or has lost interest.

Touching Touching is a powerful form of communication. Women are more apt than men to touch the people with whom they interact. When touching suggests too much intimacy, however, it can be annoying. Touching may also establish "property rights" over one's partner. People may touch their partners in public or hold their hands, not as a sign of affection, but as a signal to others that their partners are taken and that others should keep a respectful distance. Similarly, the wearing of an engagement or wedding ring signals unavailability.

Gazing and Staring: The Look of Love? We gather information about the motives, feelings, and attitudes of others through eye contact. In Western culture, looking other people "squarely in the eye"—at least among men—is positively valued. People who do so appear self-assertive, direct, and candid. When people look away, they may be perceived as shy, deceitful, or depressed. In some Asian cultures, however, looking other people directly in the eye may seem an aggressive invasion.

Unaggressive gazing into another person's eyes—especially the eyes of a person whom one considers attractive—can create deep feelings of intimacy in our culture. In a laboratory study, couples who had just met were instructed to gaze into each other's eyes for two minutes. Afterwards, many reported experiencing feelings of passion (Kellerman et al., 1989). Is this what is meant by "the look of love"?

All in all, there are many ways in which we communicate with others through verbal and nonverbal channels. Let us now look at ways in which partners can learn to communicate better with each other, especially about sex. Many couples, even couples who are able to share deepest thoughts and feelings, may flounder at communicating their sexual needs and preferences. Couples who have lived together for decades may know each other's tastes in food, music, and movies about as well as they know their own but still be hesitant to share their sexual likes and dislikes (Havemann & Lehtinen, 1990). They may also be reluctant, for fear of opening wounds in the relationship, to exchange their feelings about other aspects of their relationship, including each other's habits, appearance, and gender-stereotypical attitudes.

∼ *Reflections* ∼

▪ What are the various meanings of *intimacy?* Are you or have you been involved in an intimate relationship?

▪ Do you touch people when you are communicating with them? How do you touch them? What does the touching mean?

▪ Have you ever stared at anyone you disliked? What was the message of your eye contact? Have you ever gazed into the eyes of someone who appealed to you? What was the message of this eye contact?

Communication Skills for Enhancing Relationships and Sexual Relations

Marital counselors and sex therapists might be as busy as the proverbial Maytag repair-person ("A bow in the direction of political correctness?" asks the third author) if more couples communicated with each other about their sexual feelings. Unfortunately, when it comes to sex, *talk* may be the most overlooked four-letter word.

Many couples suffer for years because one or both partners are unwilling to speak up. Or problems arise when one partner misinterprets the other. One partner might interpret the other's groans or grimaces of pleasure as signs of pain and pull back during sex, leaving the other frustrated. Improved communication may be no panacea, but it helps. Clear communication can take the guesswork out of relationships, avert misunderstandings, relieve resentments and frustrations, and increase both sexual and general satisfaction with the relationship.

Common Difficulties in Sexual Communication

Why is it so difficult for couples to communicate about sex? Here are some possibilities:

On "Making Whoopie"—Is Sex Talk Vulgar? Vulgarity, like beauty, is to some degree in the eye of the beholder. One couple's vulgarity may be another couple's love talk. Some people may maintain a Victorian belief that any talk about sex is not fit for mixed company, even between intimate partners. Sex, that is, is something you may do, but not something to be talked about. Other couples may be willing in principle to talk about sex, but find the reality difficult because of the lack of an agreeable, common language.

How, for example, are they to refer to their genitals or to sexual activities? One partner may prefer to use coarse four-letter (or five-letter) words to refer to them. The other might prefer more clinical terms. A partner who prefers slang for the sexual organs might be regarded by the other as vulgar or demeaning. (But as the forbidden fruit is often the sweetest, some people feel sexually aroused when they or their partners "talk dirty.") One who uses clinical terms, such as fellatio or coitus, might be regarded as, well, clinical. Some couples try to find a common verbal ground, one that is not vulgar at one extreme, or clinical at the other. They might speak, for example, of "doing it" rather than "engaging in sexual intercourse." (The title of the Eddie Cantor musical of the 1930s suggests that some people once spoke of "making whoopie.") Or they might speak of "kissing me down there" rather than practicing fellatio or cunnilingus.

In some cases of gross mismatch in partners' choices for the language of love, the differences run much deeper than choice of words.

On Irrational Beliefs Many couples also harbor irrational beliefs about relationships and sex, such as the notion that people should somehow *know* what their partners want, without having to ask. The common misconception that people should know what pleases their partners undercuts communication. Men, in particular, seem burdened with the stereotype that they should have a natural expertise at sex. Women may feel it is "unladylike" to talk openly about their sexual needs and feelings. Both partners may hold the idealized romantic notion that "love is all you need" to achieve sexual happiness. But such knowledge does not arise from instinct nor love. It is learned—or it remains unknown.

A related irrational belief is that "my partner will read my mind." We may erroneously assume that if our partners truly loved us, they would somehow "read our minds" and know what types of sexual stimulation we desire. Unfortunately, or fortunately, others cannot read our minds. We must assume the responsibility for communicating our preferences.

It is not true that "Love is all you need." Even when partners truly love each other, they do not instinctively know how to satisfy each other sexually. Communication is required. ■

Some people communicate more effectively than others, perhaps because they are more sensitive to others' needs or because their parents served as good models as communicators. But communication skills can be acquired at any time. Learning takes time and work, but the following guidelines should prove helpful if you want to enhance your communication skills. The skills discussed can also be used to improve communication in areas of intimate relationships other than the sexual.

Getting Started

How do you broach tough topics? Here are some ideas.

Talking About Talking
You can start by talking about talking. You can inform your partner that it is difficult for you to talk about problems and conflicts: "You know, I've always found it awkward to find a way of bringing things up," or, "You know, I think other people have an easier time than I do when it comes to talking about some things." You can allude to troublesome things that happened in the past when you attempted to resolve conflicts. This approach encourages your partner to invite you to proceed.

Broaching the topic of sex is perhaps the most difficult step in communicating with your partner. Couples who gab endlessly about their finances, their children, their work, and so on, suddenly clam up when sex comes up. So it may be helpful for you and your partner to first agree to talk about talking about sex. You can begin by admitting that it is hard or embarrassing for you to talk about sex. You can say that your sexual relationship is important to you and that you want to do everything you can to enhance it. Gently probe your partner's willingness to set aside time to talk about sex, preferably when you can dim the lights and not be interrupted.

The "right time" may be when you are both relaxed, rested, and unpressed for time. The "right place" can be any place where you can enjoy privacy and go undisturbed. Sex talk need not be limited to the bedroom. Couples may feel more comfortable talking about sex over dinner, when cuddling on the sofa, or when just relaxing together.

Requesting Permission to Bring Up a Topic
Another possibility is to request permission to raise an issue. You can say something like this: "There's something on my mind. Do you have a few minutes? Is now a good time to tell you about it?" Or you can say, "There's something that we need to talk about, but I'm not sure how to bring it up. Can you help me with it?"

Giving Your Partner Permission to Say Something That Might Be Upsetting to You
You can tell your partner that it is okay to point out ways in which you can become a more effective lover. For example, you can say, "I know that you don't want to hurt my feelings, but I wonder if I'm doing anything that you'd rather I didn't do?"

Listening to the Other Side

Skilled listening involves skills such as active listening, paraphrasing, the use of reinforcement, and valuing your partner even when the two of you disagree.

Active Listening. Effective communication requires listening to the other person's side. We can listen actively rather than passively by maintaining eye contact and showing that we understand the other person's feelings and ideas.

Listening Actively   To listen actively rather than passively, first adopt the attitude that you may actually learn something—or perceive things from another vantage point—by listening. Second, recognize that even though the other person is doing the talking, you need not sit back passively. In other words, it is not helpful to stare off into space while your partner is talking, or to offer a begrudging "mm-hmm" now and then to be "polite." Instead, you can listen actively by maintaining eye contact and modifying your facial expression to show that you understand his or her feelings and ideas. For example, nod your head when appropriate.

Listening actively also involves asking helpful questions, such as "Would you please give me an example?" or "Was that good for you?"

An active listener does not simply hear what the other person is saying, but also focuses attentively on the speaker's words and gestures to grasp meaning. Nonverbal cues may reveal more about the speaker's inner feelings than the spoken word. Good listeners do not interrupt, change the topic, or walk away when their partners are speaking.

Paraphrasing   Paraphrasing shows that you understand what your partner is trying to say. In paraphrasing, you recast or restate the speaker's words to confirm your comprehension. For example, suppose your partner says, "You hardly ever say anything when we're making love. I don't want you to scream or make obligatory grunts, or do something silly, but sometimes I wonder if I'm trying to make love to a brick wall." You can paraphrase it by saying something like this: "So it's sort of hard to know if I'm really enjoying it."

Reinforcing the Other Person for Communicating   Even when you disagree with what your partner is saying, you can maintain good relations and keep channels of communication open by saying something like "I really appreciate your taking the time to try to work this out with me" or "I hope you'll think it's okay if I don't see things entirely in the same way, but I'm glad that we had a chance to talk about it."

Showing That You Value Your Partner, Even When the Two of You Disagree   When you disagree with your partner, do so in a way that shows that you still value your partner as a person. In other words, say something like "I love you very much, but it annoys me when you . . . " rather than "You're really contemptible for doing . . . " By so doing, you encourage your partner to disclose sensitive material without fear of personal attack or the risk of losing your love or support.

Learning About Your Partner's Needs

Listening is basic to learning about another person's needs, but sometimes it helps to go a few steps further.

Asking Questions to Draw the Other Person Out   You can ask open-ended questions that allow for a broader exploration of issues, such as these:

"What do you like best about the way we make love?"
"Do you think that I do things to bug you?"
"Does it bother you that I go to bed later than you do?"
"Does anything disappoint you about our relationship?"
"Do you think that I do things that are inconsiderate when you're studying for a test?"

Closed-ended questions that call for a limited range of responses would be most useful when you're looking for a simple yes-or-no type of response, such as "Would you rather make love with the stereo off?"

Using Self-Disclosure   Self-disclosure is essential to developing intimacy. You can also use self-disclosure to learn more about your partner's needs, because communicating your own feelings and ideas invites reciprocation. For example, you might say,

"There are times when I feel that I disappoint you when we make love. Should I be doing something differently?"

Granting Permission for the Other Person to Say Something That Might Upset You
You can ask your partner to level with you about an irksome issue. You can say that you recognize that it might be awkward to discuss it, but that you will try your best to listen conscientiously and not get too disturbed. You can also limit communication to one such difficult issue per conversation. If the entire emotional dam were to burst, the job of mopping up could be overwhelming.

Providing Information

There are many skillful ways of communicating information, including "accentuating the positive" and using verbal and nonverbal cues. When you want to get something across, remember that it is irrational to expect that your partner can read your mind. He or she can tell when you're wearing a grumpy face, but your expression does not provide much information about your specific feelings. When your partner asks, "What would you like me to do?" responding with "Well, I think you can figure out what I want" or "Just do whatever you think is best" is not very helpful. Only you know what pleases you. Your partner is not a mind-reader.

Accentuating the Positive
Let your partner know when he or she is doing something right! Speak up or find another way to express your appreciation. Accentuating the positive is rewarding and also informs your partner about what pleases you. In other words, don't just wait around until your partner does something wrong and then seize the opportunity to complain!

Using Verbal Cues
Sexual activity provides an excellent opportunity for direct communication. You can say something like "Oh, that's great" or "Don't stop." Or you can ask for feedback, as in "How does that feel . . . ?"

Feedback provides direct guidance about what is pleasing. Partners can also make specific requests and suggestions.

Using Nonverbal Cues
Sexual communication also occurs without words. Couples learn to interpret each other's facial expressions as signs of pleasure, boredom, even disgust. Our body language also communicates our likes and dislikes. Our partners may lean toward us or away from us when we touch them, or relax or tense up; in any case, they speak volumes in silence.

The following exercises may help couples use nonverbal cues to communicate their sexual likes and dislikes. Similar exercises are used by sex therapists to help couples with sexual dysfunctions.

1. *Taking turns petting.* Taking turns petting can help partners learn what turns one another on. Each partner takes turns caressing the other, stopping frequently enough to receive feedback by asking questions like "How does that feel?" The recipient is responsible for giving feedback, which can be expressed either verbally ("Yes, that's it—yes, just like that" or "No, a little lighter than that") or nonverbally, as by making certain appreciative or disapproving sounds. Verbal feedback is usually more direct and less prone to misinterpretation. The knowledge gained through this exercise can be incorporated into the couple's regular pattern of lovemaking.

2. *Directing your partner's hand.* Gently guiding your partner's hand—to show your partner where and how you like to be touched—is a most direct way of communicating sexual likes. While taking turns petting, and during other acts of lovemaking, one partner can gently guide the other's fingers and hands through the most satisfying strokes and caresses. Women might show partners how to caress the breasts or clitoral shaft in this manner. Men might cup their partners' hands to show them how to stroke the penile shaft or caress the testes.

3. *Signaling.* Couples can use agreed-upon nonverbal cues to signal sexual pleasure. For example, one partner may rub the other in a certain way, or tap the other, to signal that something is being done right. The recipient of the signal takes mental notes and incorporates the pleasurable stimulation into the couple's lovemaking. This is a sort of "hit or miss" technique, but even near misses can be rewarding.

Making Requests

A basic part of improving relationships or lovemaking is asking partners to change their behavior—to do something differently or to stop doing something that hurts or is ungratifying. The skill of making requests now comes to the fore.

Being Specific   Be specific in requesting changes. Telling your partner something like "I'd like you to be nicer to me" may accomplish little. Your partner may not know that his or her behavior is *not* nice and may not understand how to be "nicer." It is better to say something like "I would appreciate it if you would get coffee for yourself, or at least ask me in a more pleasant way." Or, "I really have a hard time with the way you talk to me in front of your friends. It's as if you're trying to show them that you have control over me or something." Similarly, it may be less effective to say "I'd like you to be more loving" than to say, "When we make love, I'd like you to kiss me more and tell me how you care about me."

Of course, you can precede your specific requests with openers such as "There's something on my mind. Is this a good time for me to bring it up with you?"

Using "*I*-Talk"   Using the word *I* is an excellent way of expressing your feelings. Psychologists who help people become more assertive often encourage them to use the words *I, me,* and *my* in their speech, not just to express their feelings, but to buttress their sense of self-worth.

You are more likely to achieve desired results by framing requests in *I*-talk than by heaping criticisms on your partner. For example, "I would like it if we spent some time cuddling after sex" is superior to "You don't seem to care enough about me to want to hold me after we make love." Saying "I find it very painful when you use a harsh voice with me" is probably more effective than "Sometimes people's feelings get hurt when their boyfriends [girlfriends] speak to them harshly in front of their friends or families."

You may find it helpful to try out *I*-talk in front of a mirror or with a confidant before using it with your partner. In this way, you can see whether your facial expression and tone

Cathy © 1968, Cathy Guisewhite. Reprinted with permission of Universal Press Syndicate. All rights reserved.

of voice are consistent with what you are saying. Friends may also provide pointers on the content of what you are saying.

Delivering Criticism

Delivering criticism effectively is a skill. It requires focusing partners' attention on the problem without inducing resentment or defensiveness, or reducing them to trembling masses of guilt or fear.

Evaluating Your Motives   First, weigh your goals forthrightly. Is your primary intention to punish your partner, or are you more interested in gaining cooperation? If your goal is punishment, you may as well be coarse and disparaging, but expect to invite reprisals. If your goal is to improve the relationship, however, a tactful approach may be in order.

Picking the Right Time and Place   Deliver criticism privately—not in front of friends or family members. Your partner has a right to be upset when you make criticism public. Making private matters public induces indignation and cuts off communication.

Being Specific   Being specific may be even more important when delivering criticism than when making requests. By being specific about the *behavior* that disturbs you, you bypass the trap of disparaging your partner's personality or motives. For example, you may be more effective by saying "I could lose this job because you didn't write down the message" than by saying "You're completely irresponsible" or "You're a flake." Similarly, you may achieve better results by saying "The bathroom looks and smells dirty when you throw your underwear on the floor" rather than "You're a filthy pig." It is more to the point (and less intimidating) to complain about specific, modifiable behavior than to try to overhaul another person's personality.

Expressing Displeasure in Terms of Your Own Feelings   Your partner is likely to feel less threatened if you express displeasure in terms of your own feelings than by directly attacking his or her personality. Attacks often arouse defensive behavior, and sometimes retaliation, rather than enhance relationships. When confronting your partner for failing to be sensitive to your sexual needs when making love, it may be more effective to say "You know, it really *upsets* me that you don't seem to care about my feelings when we make love" than "You're so wrapped up in yourself that you never think about anyone else."

Keeping Criticism and Complaints to the Present   How many times have you been in an argument and heard things like "You never appreciated me!" or "Last summer you did the same thing!" Bringing up the past during conflicts muddles current issues and heightens resentments. When your partner forgets to jot down the details of the telephone message, it is more useful to note that "This was a vital phone call" than "Three weeks ago you didn't tell me about the phone call from Chris and as a result I missed out on seeing *Home Alone: The College Years.*" It's better to leave who did what to whom last year (or even last week) alone. Focus on the present.

Expressing Criticism Constructively   Be sensitive to your partner's needs by avoiding blunt criticisms or personal attacks and by suggesting constructive alternatives. Avoid saying things like "You're really a lousy lover." Say instead, "Can I take your hand and show you what I'd like?" As a rule of thumb, unless you can criticize your partner constructively, it may be best not to criticize at all.

Expressing Criticism Positively   Whenever possible, express criticism positively, and combine it with a concrete request. When commenting upon the lack of affection your partner displays during lovemaking, say, "I love it when you kiss me. Please kiss me more" rather than "You never kiss me when we're in bed and I'm sick of it."

Receiving Criticism

Honest criticism is hard to take, particularly from a relative, a friend, an acquaintance, or a stranger.

(Franklin P. Jones)

Delivering criticism can be tricky, especially when you want to inspire cooperation. Receiving criticism can be even trickier. Nevertheless, the following suggestions offer some help.

Clarifying Your Goals   When you hear "It's time you did something about . . . ," it would be understandable if the hair on the backs of your arms did a headstand. After all, it's a blunt challenge. When we are confronted harshly, we are likely to become defensive and think of retaliating. But if your objective is to enhance the relationship, take a few moments to stop and think. To resolve conflicts, we need to learn about the other person's concerns, keep lines of communication open, and find ways of changing problem behavior.

So when your partner says, "It's about time you did something about the bathroom," stop and think before you summon up your most menacing voice and say, "Just what the hell is that supposed to mean?" Ask yourself what you want to find out.

Asking Clarifying Questions   Just as it's important to be specific when delivering criticism, it helps if you encourage the other person to be specific when you are on the receiving end of criticism. In the example of the complaint about the bathroom, you can help your partner be specific and, perhaps, avert the worst by asking clarifying questions, such as "Can you tell me exactly what you mean?" or "The bathroom?"

Consider a situation in which a lover says something like "You know, you're one of the most irritating people I know." Rather than retaliate and perhaps hurt the relationship further, you can say something like "How about forgoing the character assassination and telling me what I did that's bothering you?" This response assertively asks an end to insults and requests that your partner be specific.

Acknowledging the Criticism   Even when you disagree with a criticism, you can keep lines of communication open and show some respect for your partner's feelings by acknowledging and paraphrasing the criticism.

On the other hand, if you are at fault, you can acknowledge that forthrightly. For example, you can say, "You're right. It was my day to clean the bathroom and it totally slipped my mind" or "I was so busy, I just couldn't get to it." Now the two of you should look for a way to work out the problem. When you acknowledge criticism, you cue your partner to back off a bit and look for ways to improve the situation. But what if your partner then becomes abusive and says something like "So you admit you blew it?" You might then try a little education in conflict resolution. You could say, "I admitted that I was at fault. If you're willing to work with me to find a way to handle it, great; but I'm not going to let you pound me into the ground over it."

Rejecting the Criticism   Now, if you think that you were not at fault, express your feelings. Use *I*-talk, and be specific. Don't seize the opportunity to angrily point out your partner's shortcomings. By doing so, you may shut down lines of communication.

Negotiating Differences   Negotiate your differences if you feel that there is merit on both sides of the argument. You may want to say something like "Would it help if I . . . ?" And if there's something about your obligation to clean the bathroom that seems totally out of place, perhaps you and your partner can work out an exchange—that is, you get relieved of cleaning the bathroom in exchange for tackling a chore that your partner finds equally odious.

If none of these approaches helps resolve the conflict, consider the possibility that your partner is using the comment about the bathroom as a way of expressing anger over other issues. You may find out by saying something like "I've been trying to find a way to resolve this thing, but nothing I say seems to be helping. Is this really about the bathroom, or are there other things on your mind?"

And notice that we haven't suggested that you seize the opportunity to strike back by saying "Who're you to complain about the bathroom? What about your breath and that pig sty you call your closet?" Retaliation is tempting and may make you feel good in the short run, but it can do a relationship more harm than good in the long run.

It is not true that retaliation is the best course of action if you are criticized. Retaliation is an inferior way to handle criticism—that is, if your goal is to resolve conflict. ∎

When Communication Is Not Enough: Handling Impasses

Communication helps build and maintain relationships, but sometimes partners have profound, substantial disagreements. In fact, it is normal to have disagreements from time to time. Even when their communication skills are superbly tuned, partners now and then reach an impasse.

Opening the lines of communication may also elicit hidden frustrations. These frustrations can lead partners to seriously question the value of continuing the relationship or to agree to consult a helping professional. Though some people feel it is best to "let sleeping dogs lie," the *skillful* airing of underlying dissatisfactions can be healthful for a relationship. Couples who reach an impasse can follow several courses of action that may be helpful:

Looking at the Situation from the Other Person's Perspective
Some of the conflict may be resolved by (honestly!) saying something like "I still disagree with you, but I can understand why you take your position." In this way, you recognize your partner's goodwill and, perhaps, lessen tensions.

Seeking Validating Information
On the other hand, if you do not follow your partner's logic, you can say something like "Please believe me: I'm trying very hard to look at this from your point of view, but I can't follow your reasoning. Would you try to help me understand your point of view?"

Taking a Break
Sometimes when you reach a stalemate, it helps to allow the problem to "incubate" for a while. If you and your partner put the issue aside for a while, perhaps a resolution will dawn on one of you later on. If you wish, schedule a follow-up discussion so that the issue won't be swept under the rug.

Tolerating Differentness
Although we tend to form relationships with people who share similar attitudes, there is never a perfect overlap. A partner who pretends to be your clone will most likely become a bore. Assuming that your relationship is generally rewarding and pleasurable, you may find it possible to tolerate certain differences between yourself and your partner. Respecting other people in part means allowing them to be who they are. When we have a solid sense of who we are as individuals and what we stand for, we are more apt to tolerate differentness in our partners.

Many relationships do come to an end when the partners cannot resolve their differences. However, it is possible for relationships to continue and improve even when we reach impasses. We need to be able to tolerate differentness in other people if relationships are to improve. ∎

Agreeing to Disagree
When all else fails, you can agree to disagree on various issues. You can remain a solid, respected individual, and your partner can remain a worthwhile, effective person even if the two of you disagree from time to time.

Disagreement is not necessarily destructive to a relationship—unless you are convinced that it must be. Two people cannot see everything in the same way. Failure to ever disagree will have to leave at least one partner feeling frustrated now and then.

Truth OR Fiction?
R E V I S I T E D

It is not true that disagreement is destructive to a relationship. Everyone disagrees with her or his partner now and then (whether or not disagreements are expressed). The important thing is to try to resolve disagreements and, when they cannot be resolved, to handle the impasse productively. ■

You can handle an impasse by focusing on the things that you and your partner have in common. Presumably there will be a number of them—some of them with little feet.

~ *Reflections* ~

- Have you had arguments with dates or lovers? Was part of the problem difficulty in communicating? What methods of communication discussed in this chapter might have been of help to you?
- Do you have difficulty criticizing another person or accepting criticism? Why? How can you become better at delivering or receiving criticism?
- Have you ever arrived at an impasse in a disagreement with a partner? What did you do about it? How did it work out?

Summing Up

The ABC(DE)S of Romantic Relationships

Levinger proposes an ABCDE model of romantic relationships, which refers to five stages: attraction, building, continuation, deterioration, and ending.

The A's—Attraction The major promoter of attraction is propinquity.

The B's—Building Similarity in the level of physical attractiveness, similarity in attitudes, and liking motivate us to build relationships.

The C's—Continuation Factors such as variety, caring, positive evaluations, lack of jealousy, perceived fairness in the relationship, and mutual feelings of satisfaction encourage us to continue relationships.

The D's—Deterioration Factors that foster deterioration include failure to invest time and energy in the relationship, deciding to put an end to it, or simply permitting deterioration to proceed unchecked.

The E's—Ending Relationships tend to end when the partners find little satisfaction in the affiliation, when alternative partners are available, when couples are not committed to preserving them, and when they expect them to falter.

Loneliness: "All the Lonely People, Where Do They All Come From?"

Loneliness is a state of painful isolation, of feeling cut off from others.

Causes of Loneliness The causes of loneliness include lack of social skills, lack of interest in other people, lack of empathy, fear of rejection, lack of self-disclosure, cynicism about human nature, demanding too much too soon, general pessimism, and an external locus of control.

Coping with Loneliness People are helped to overcome loneliness by challenging self-defeating attitudes and acquiring social-skills training.

Intimacy

Intimacy involves feelings of emotional closeness with another person and the desire to share each other's inmost thoughts and feelings.

Knowing and Liking Yourself An initial step toward intimacy with others is getting to know and like yourself so that you can identify your inmost feelings and develop the security to share them.

Trusting and Caring   Intimate relationships require trust, caring, and tenderness.

Being Honest   Honesty is a core feature of intimacy.

Making a Commitment   Truly intimate relationships are marked by commitment, a resolve to maintain the relationship through thick and thin.

Maintaining Individuality When the *I* Becomes *We*   In healthy unions, a strong sense of togetherness does not eradicate individuality.

Communicating   Communication is a two-way street. It embraces sending and receiving messages. We often express feelings through nonverbal channels such as tone of voice, gestures, body posture, and facial expressions.

Communication Skills for Enhancing Relationships and Sexual Relations

Common Difficulties in Sexual Communication   Couples may find it difficult to talk about sex because of the lack of an agreeable common language. Many couples also harbor irrational beliefs about relationships and sex.

Getting Started   Ways of getting started in communicating include talking about talking, requesting permission to raise an issue, and granting one's partner permission to say things that might be upsetting.

Listening to the Other Side   Skilled listening involves elements such as active listening, paraphrasing, the use of reinforcement, and valuing your partner even when the two of you disagree.

Learning About Your Partner's Needs   You can learn about your partner's needs by asking questions, using self-disclosure, and asking your partner to level with you about an irksome issue.

Providing Information   You can provide information by "accentuating the positive" and using verbal and nonverbal cues.

Making Requests   In making requests, it is helpful to take responsibility for what happens, to be specific, to be assertive, and to use "*I*-talk."

Delivering Criticism   In delivering criticism, it is helpful to evaluate your motives, pick a good time and place, be specific, express displeasure in terms of your own feelings, keep complaints to the present, and express criticism constructively and positively.

Receiving Criticism   To receive criticism effectively, it is helpful to clarify goals, ask clarifying questions, acknowledge the criticism, reject inappropriate criticisms, and negotiate differences.

When Communication Is Not Enough: Handling Impasses   Partners can help manage impasses by trying to see things from the partner's perspective, seeking validating information, taking a break, tolerating differentness, and, when necessary, agreeing to disagree.

CHAPTER 9

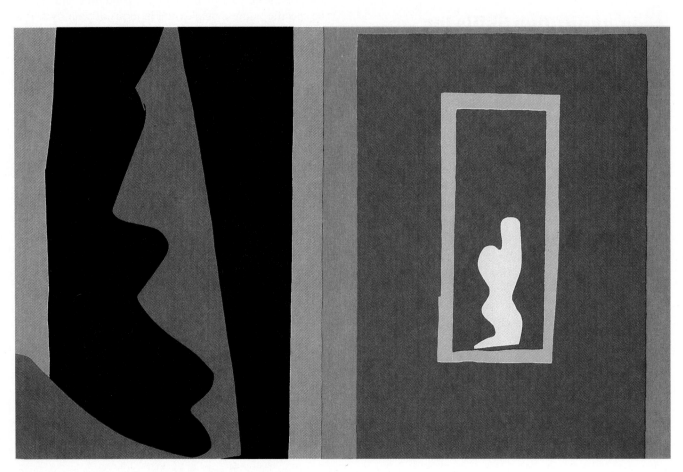

Henri Matisse, *Destiny,* Plate 16 from *Jazz.* The Metropolitan Museum
of Art, Gift of Lila Acheson Wallace, 1983. © 1996 Succession H. Matisse/Artist
Rights Society (ARS), New York. © 1984 by The Metropolitan Museum of Art.

Sexual Techniques and Behavior Patterns

Truth OR Fiction?

_____ Married people rarely if ever masturbate.

_____ White men are more likely to masturbate than African-American men are.

_____ Women who masturbate during adolescence are less likely to find gratification in marital coitus than women who do not.

_____ Women are more likely to reach orgasm through sexual intercourse than masturbation.

_____ Most women masturbate by inserting a finger or other object into the vagina.

_____ Heterosexual people do not fantasize about sexual activity with people of their own gender.

_____ Statistically speaking, oral sex is the norm for today's young married couples.

_____ African-Americans are more likely than white Americans to engage in oral sex.

_____ When lovers fantasize about other people, the relationship is in trouble.

_____ Anal sex is more common among less well educated people.

This is the chapter that describes sexual techniques and statistical breakdowns of "who does what with whom." There is great variety in human sexual expression. Some of us practice few, if any, of the techniques in the chapter. Some of us practice most or all of them. Some of us practice some of them some of the time. Our knowledge of the prevalences of these techniques comes from sex surveys that began with Kinsey and have continued with the work of Hunt, the University of Chicago group, and others. Of course surveys are plagued by problems such as nonrepresentative sampling, social desirability, and volunteer bias. Therefore, we must be cautious in generalizing their results. Surveys provide our best "guestimates" of the prevalences of sexual behaviors. They do not provide precise figures.

Readers of this textbook are as varied in their sexual values, preferences, and attitudes as is society in general. Some of the techniques discussed may thus strike some readers as indecent. Our aim is to provide information about the diversity of sexual expression. We are not seeking common ground as to what is acceptable. Nor do we pass judgments or encourage readers to expand their sexual repertoires.

The human body is sensitive to many forms of sexual stimulation. Yet we reiterate the theme that biology is not destiny: A biological capacity does not impose a behavioral requirement. Cultural expectations, personal values, and individual experience—not only our biological capacities—determine our sexual behavior. What is right for you is right for you—not necessarily for your neighbor.

We begin by reviewing the techniques that people practice by themselves to derive sexual pleasure—masturbation and sexual fantasy. We then consider techniques that involve a partner.

Solitary Sexual Behavior

Various forms of sexual expression do not require a partner or are not generally practiced in the presence of a partner. Masturbation is one of the principal forms of one-person sexual expression. Masturbation involves direct stimulation of the genitals. Other forms of individual sexual experience, such as sexual fantasy, may or may not be accompanied by genital stimulation.

Masturbation

In solitude he pollutes himself, and with his own hand blights all his prospects for both this world and the next. Even after being solemnly warned, he will often continue this worse than beastly practice, deliberately forfeiting his right to health and happiness for a moment's mad sensuality.

(J. H. Kellogg, M.D., *Plain Facts for Old and Young,* 1888)

Masturbation
Sexual self-stimulation.

Dildo
A penis-shaped object used in sexual activity.

The word *masturbation* derives from the Latin *masturbari,* from the roots for "hand" and "to defile." The derivation provides clues to historical cultural attitudes toward the practice. Masturbation may be practiced by manual stimulation of the genitals, perhaps with the aid of artificial stimulation, such as a vibrator. It may employ an object, such as a pillow or a **dildo,** that touches the genitals. Even before we conceive of sexual experiences with others, we may learn early in childhood that touching our genitals can produce pleasure.

Pleasure is not the only reason that people masturbate. Table 9.1 lists reasons for masturbation, according to the findings of the NHSLS study.

Within the Judeo-Christian tradition, masturbation—"onanism"—has been strongly condemned as sinful. Early Judeo-Christian attitudes toward masturbation reflected the censure that was applied toward nonprocreative sexual acts. In the Judeo-Christian tradi-

TABLE 9.1 Reasons for masturbation by respondents to NHSLS study

Reasons for Masturbation	Men (%)	Women (%)
To relax	26	32
To relieve sexual tension	73	63
Partners are unavailable	32	32
Partner does not want to engage in sexual activity	16	6
Boredom	11	5
To obtain physical pleasure	40	42
To help get to sleep	16	12
Fear of AIDS and other STDs	7	5
Other reasons	5	5

Source: Adapted from Laumann, E. O., Gagnon, J. H., Michael, R. T., & Michaels, S. (1994). *The Social Organization of Sexuality: Sexual Practices in the United States.* Chicago: University of Chicago Press, Table 3.3, p. 86.

tion, masturbation has been referred to as "onanism," a name that is derived from the biblical story of Onan. According to the Book of Genesis (38:9–11), Onan was the second-born son of Judah. Judah's first son, Er, had died without an heir. Biblical law required that if a man died without leaving a male heir, his brother must take the widow as a wife (a union called a levirate marriage) and rear their first son as his brother's heir. Judah thus directed Onan to "Go in unto thy brother's wife, and perform the duty of a husband's brother unto her, and raise up seed to thy brother." But Onan "spilled [his seed] upon the ground" during relations with his deceased brother's wife and was struck down by God for his deed.

Though "onanism" has come to be associated with Judeo-Christian condemnation of masturbation, Onan's act was one of **coitus interruptus,** not masturbation. Both acts, however, involve nonprocreative sex—spilling the seed. Moreover, Onan's punishment seems to have more to do with his failure to fulfill his lawful obligations than for spilling his seed. Whatever its biblical origins, masturbation is prohibited under Jewish law. Historians suspect that Jews and Christians in ancient times condemned sexual practices that did not lead to pregnancy because of the need for an increase in their numbers. The need for progeny is also linked to the widespread view that coitus in marriage is the only morally acceptable avenue of sexual expression.

The history of cultural attitudes toward masturbation in Western society has been, until very recently, one of almost continual condemnation of the practice on moral and religious grounds—even on medical grounds.

Coitus interruptus
The practice of withdrawing the penis prior to ejaculation during sexual intercourse.

Historical Medical Views of Masturbation   Until recent years masturbation was thought to be physically and mentally harmful, as well as degrading. The eighteenth-century physicians S. A. D. Tissot and Benjamin Rush (a signer of the Declaration of Independence) believed that masturbation caused tuberculosis, "nervous diseases," poor eyesight, memory loss, and epilepsy.

Many clergy and medical authorities of the nineteenth century were persuaded that certain foods had a stimulating effect on the sex organs. So one form of advice to parents focused on modifying their children's diets to eliminate foods that were believed to excite the sexual organs, notably meat, coffee, tea, and chocolate, and to substitute "unstimulating" foods in their place, most notably grain products. In the 1830s the Reverend Sylvester Graham developed a cracker, since called the graham cracker, to help people control their sexual impulses.

Yet another household name belongs to a man who made his mark by introducing a bland diet that was also intended to help people, especially youngsters, control their sexual impulses. In the nineteenth-century United States, medical advice was largely disseminated to the general public through pamphlets and guides written by leading medical authorities. One of the more influential writers was the superintendent of the Battle Creek Sanatorium in Michigan, Dr. J. H. Kellogg (1852–1943), better known to you as the creator of the modern breakfast cereal. Kellogg identified 39 signs of masturbation, including acne, paleness, heart palpitations, rounded shoulders, weak backs, and convulsions. Kellogg, like Graham, believed that sexual desires could be controlled by a diet of simple foods, especially grains, including the corn flakes that have since borne his name. (We wonder how Kellogg would react to the energizing, sugar-coated cereals that now bear his name.)

Many nineteenth-century physicians also advised parents to take measures to prevent their children from masturbating. Kellogg suggested that parents bandage or cage their children's genitals, or tie their hands. Some of the contraptions devised to prevent masturbation were barbarous (see Figure 9.1).

Several nineteenth-century scholars of sexuality joined the crusade against masturbation. Richard von Krafft-Ebing (in *Psychopathia Sexualis,* 1886) and Havelock Ellis (in *Studies in the Psychology of Sex,* 1900) condemned masturbation as psychologically dangerous. Krafft-Ebing linked masturbation to sexual orientation. Male masturbation, or so it was mistakenly believed, arrested the development of normal erotic instincts and led to **impotence** with women. Thus, it encouraged male–male sexual activity.

Masturbation Today   Despite this history, there is no scientific evidence that masturbation is harmful. Masturbation does not cause insanity, grow hair on the hands, or cause warts or any of the other psychological and physical ills once ascribed to it. Masturbation is physically harmless, save for rare injuries to the genitals due to rough stimulation. Nor is masturbation in itself psychologically harmful, although it may be a sign of an adjustment problem if people use masturbation as an exclusive sexual outlet when opportunities for sexual relationships are available. Sex therapists have even found therapeutic benefits for masturbation. It has emerged as a treatment for women who have difficulty reaching orgasm (Kay, 1992) (see Chapter 15).

Of course, people who consider masturbation wrong, harmful, or sinful may experience anxiety or guilt if they masturbate or wish to masturbate. These negative emotions are linked to their attitudes toward masturbation, not to masturbation per se (Michael et al., 1994).

Despite the widespread condemnation of masturbation in our society, surveys indicate that most people masturbate at some time. The incidence of masturbation is generally greater among men than women. However, there are women who masturbate frequently and men who rarely if ever do so (Michael et al., 1994).

Nearly all of the adult men and about two thirds of the adult women in Kinsey's samples (Kinsey et al., 1948, 1953) reported that they had masturbated at some time. In a study of students in an urban university, 85% of the women and 95% of the men reported that they had masturbated (Person et al., 1989). Seventy-one percent of the women and 83% of the men reported masturbating during the previous three months.

Not all researchers find that the gender gap has narrowed to such an extent. A survey of students in a New England college found nearly twice as many men (81%) as women (45%) reporting some experience with masturbation (Leitenberg et al., 1993). About three

Figure 9.1. Devices Designed to Curb Masturbation. Because of widespread beliefs that masturbation was harmful, various contraptions were introduced in the nineteenth century to prevent the practice in children. Some of the devices were barbarous.

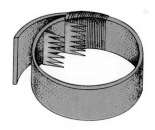

TABLE 9.2 Sociocultural factors and frequency of masturbation during past 12 months, as found in the NHSLS study

Sociocultural Characteristics	Frequency of Masturbation (%)			
	Not at All		At Least Once a Week	
	Men	Women	Men	Women
Total population	36.7	58.3	26.7	7.6
Age 18–24	41.2	64.4	29.2	9.4
25–29	28.9	58.3	32.7	9.9
30–34	27.6	51.1	34.6	8.6
35–39	38.5	52.3	20.8	6.6
40–44	34.5	49.8	28.7	8.7
45–49	35.2	55.6	27.2	8.6
50–54	52.5	71.8	13.9	2.3
55–59	51.7	77.6	10.3	2.4
Marital Status Never married (not cohabiting)	31.8	51.8	41.3	12.3
Married	42.6	62.9	16.5	4.7
Formerly married (not cohabiting)	30.2	52.7	34.9	9.6
Education Less than high school	54.8	75.1	19.2	7.6
High school graduate	45.1	68.4	20.0	5.6
Some college	33.2	51.3	30.8	6.9
College graduate	24.2	47.7	33.2	10.2
Advanced degree	18.6	41.2	33.6	13.7
Religion None	32.6	41.4	37.6	13.8
Liberal, moderate Protestant	28.9	55.1	28.2	7.4
Conservative Protestant	48.4	67.3	19.5	5.8
Catholic	34.0	57.3	24.9	6.6
Race/Ethnicity White (non-Hispanic)	33.4	55.7	28.3	7.3
African American	60.3	67.8	16.9	10.7
Hispanic American	33.1	65.5	24.4	4.7
Asian American	38.7	—*	31.3	—*
Native American	—*	—*	—*	—*

*Sample sizes too small to report findings.

Source: Adapted from Laumann, E. O., Gagnon, J. H., Michael, R. T., & Michaels, S. (1994). *The Social Organization of Sexuality: Sexual Practices in the United States.* Chicago: University of Chicago Press, Table 3.1, p. 82.

in four men, as compared to only one in three women, reported masturbating during the previous year.

The NHSLS study also found a notable gender gap in reported frequencies of masturbation (Laumann et al., 1994). Table 9.2 shows how the sample group reported the frequency of masturbation during the past 12 months, broken down according to gender, age, marital status, level of education, religion, and race/ethnicity. Overall, 37% of the men and

58% of the women sampled reported that they had *not* masturbated during the past 12 months. Within every social category, men reported masturbating more frequently than women did. Despite the sexual revolution, women may still find masturbation less pleasurable or acceptable than men do (Leitenberg et al., 1993). Women may still be subject to traditional socialization pressures that teach that sexual activity for pleasure's sake is more of a taboo for women than for men. Then, too, women are more likely to pursue sexual activity within the context of a relationship.

Married people are less likely to have masturbated during the past 12 months than never married and formerly married people. Nevertheless, only 43% of the married men and 63% of the married women sampled said that they did not masturbate at all during the past year.

Truth  Fiction?
R E V I S I T E D

It is not true that married people rarely if ever masturbate. The majority of married men and a sizable minority of married women in the United States report masturbating at least occasionally. ■

Education would appear to be a clear liberating influence on masturbation. For both genders, people with more education reported more frequent masturbation. Perhaps better-educated people are less likely to believe the old horror stories about masturbation or to be subject to traditional social restrictions. Conservative religious beliefs appear to constrain masturbation. Conservative Protestants are apparently less likely to masturbate than liberal and moderate Protestants are. African Americans are notably less likely to report masturbating over a 12-month period than are other ethnic groups.

Truth OR Fiction?
R E V I S I T E D

It is true that white men are more likely to masturbate than African-American men are. Perhaps African-American men are relatively more likely to adhere to traditional views concerning masturbation. ■

There appears to be a link between attitudes toward masturbation and orgasmic potential. A study of women revealed more negative attitudes toward masturbation among a group of 21- to 40-year-olds who had never achieved orgasm than among a comparison group of women who had (Kelly et al., 1990). Kinsey and his colleagues had reported links between prior masturbation and sexual satisfaction in marriage. Women who had masturbated during adolescence were more likely to find gratification in marital coitus than women who did not (Kinsey et al., 1953).

This evidence does not suggest that adolescents should be encouraged to masturbate to enhance the likelihood of sexual fulfillment as adults. A selection factor probably explains the link (see Figure 9.2). That is, people who masturbate early are probably generally more open to exploring their sexuality and learning about the types of stimulation that arouse them. These attitudes would carry over into marriage and increase the likelihood that women would

Figure 9.2. **What Are the Connections Between Masturbation During Adolescence and Sexual Satisfaction in Marriage?** There is a positive correlation between masturbation during adolescence and sexual satisfaction in marriage. What hypotheses can we make about the causal connections? Does experience with masturbation teach people about their sexual needs so that they are more likely to obtain adequate sexual stimulation in marriage? Are people who masturbate early generally more open to exploring their sexuality and learning about the types of stimulation that arouse them? Such attitudes might also increase the likelihood that people would seek the coital stimulation they need to achieve sexual gratification in marriage.

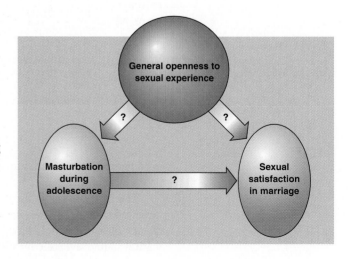

seek the coital stimulation they need to achieve sexual gratification. Nevertheless, adolescent masturbation probably does also set the stage for marital sexual satisfaction by yielding information about the types of stimulation people need to obtain sexual gratification.

 Actually, women who masturbate during adolescence are *more* likely to find gratification in marital coitus than women who do not. ■

Other researchers find that women achieve orgasm more reliably through masturbation than through coitus. Based on her magazine survey, Hite (1977) reported that 92% of her sample could reliably achieve orgasm through masturbation. Only 30% regularly did so through coitus. Masters and Johnson (1966) also found that masturbation was a more reliable means for women to achieve orgasm than coitus, at least for women who accept masturbation as a sexual outlet.

 Women are actually *more* likely to reach orgasm through masturbation than through coitus. ■

In our efforts to correct misinformation about masturbation, we do not wish to leave the impression that there is anything wrong with people who choose *not* to masturbate. Nor do we wish to imply that people should masturbate. Although we may all be able to experience pleasure from self-stimulation, let us say once more that biology is not destiny. It is illogical to transform a biological capacity into a behavioral requirement.

Techniques of Male Masturbation

Sex is like bridge—if you don't have a good partner, you'd better have a good hand.

(Contemporary bathroom graffiti)

Although masturbation techniques vary widely, most men report that they masturbate by manual manipulation of the penis (see Figure 9.3). Typically they take one or two minutes to reach orgasm (Hite, 1981; Kinsey et al., 1948). Men tend to grip the penile shaft with one hand, jerking it up and down in a milking motion. Some men move the whole hand up and down the penis, while others use just two fingers, generally the thumb and index finger. Men usually shift from a gentler rubbing action during the flaccid or semi-erect state of arousal

Figure 9.3. Male Masturbation. Masturbation techniques vary widely, but most men report that they masturbate by manual manipulation of the penis. They tend to grip the penile shaft with one hand and jerk it up and down in a milking motion.

to a more vigorous milking motion once full erection takes place. Men are also likely to stroke the glans and frenulum lightly at the outset, but their grip tightens and their motions speed up as orgasm nears. At orgasm, the penile shaft may be gripped tightly, but the glans has become sensitive, and contact with it is usually avoided. (Likewise, women usually avoid stimulating the clitoris directly during orgasm because of increased sensitivity.)

Some men use soapsuds (which may become irritating) as a lubricant for masturbation during baths or showers. Other lubricants, such as petroleum jelly or K-Y jelly, may also be used to reduce friction and to simulate the moist conditions of coitus.

A few men prefer to masturbate by rubbing the penis and testicles against clothing or bedding (Kinsey et al., 1948). A very few men rub their genitals against inflatable dolls sold in sex shops. These dolls may come with artificial mouths or vaginas that can be filled with warm water to mimic the sensations of coitus. Artificial vaginas are also for sale.

Some men strap vibrators to the backs of their hands. Electrical vibrators save labor but do not simulate the type of up-and-down motions of the penis that men favor. Hence, they are not used very often. Most men rely heavily on fantasy or erotic photos or videos, but do not use sex-shop devices.

Techniques of Female Masturbation   Techniques of female masturbation also vary widely. In fact, Masters and Johnson reported never observing two women masturbate in precisely the same way. Even when the general technique was similar, women varied in the tempo and style of their self-caresses. But some general trends have been noted. Most women masturbate by massaging the mons, labia minora, and clitoral region with circular or back-and-forth motions (Hite, 1976; Kinsey et al., 1953). They may also straddle the clitoris with their fingers, stroking the shaft rather than the glans (see Figure 9.4). The glans may be lightly touched early during arousal, but because of its ex-

Figure 9.4. Female Masturbation. Techniques of female masturbation vary so widely that Masters and Johnson reported never observing two women masturbating in precisely the same way. However, most women masturbate by massaging the mons, labia minora, and clitoral region, either with circular or back-and-forth motions.

quisite sensitivity, it is rarely stroked for any length of time during masturbation. Women typically achieve clitoral stimulation by rubbing or stroking the clitoral shaft or pulling or tugging on the vaginal lips. Some women also massage other sensitive areas, such as their breasts or nipples, with the free hand. Many women, like men, fantasize during masturbation (Leitenberg & Henning, 1995).

In contrast to the male myth (Kinsey and his colleagues [1953] describe it as a "male conceit") that women usually masturbate by simulating penile thrusting through the insertion of fingers or phallic objects into their vaginas, relatively few women actually do (Hite, 1976; Kinsey et al., 1953). Hite reported that only 1.5% of her respondents exclusively relied on vaginal insertion as a means of masturbation. Kinsey and his colleagues found that only one in five women had sometimes used vaginal insertions of objects during masturbation. Some women first experimented with the technique of vaginal insertions but then gave it up as they became more familiar with their sexual anatomy and capabilities. Others practiced the technique because their male partners found it sexually stimulating to watch them engage in this type of activity. Still, some women reported experiencing erotic pleasures from deep vaginal penetration.

It is not true that most women masturbate by inserting a finger or other object into the vagina. Most women rely on clitoral stimulation. ■

Even when women do use insertion, they usually precede or combine it with clitoral stimulation. Sex shops sell dildos, which women can use to rub their vulvas or to insert them vaginally. Penis-shaped vibrators may be used in a similar fashion. Many women masturbate during baths, some by spraying their genitals with water-massage shower heads.

Handheld electrical vibrators (see Figure 9.5) provide a constant massaging action against the genitals that can be erotic. Some women find this type of stimulation too intense, however, and favor vibrators that strap to the back of the hand and cause the fingers to vibrate during manual stimulation of the genitals. This type of vibration may numb the hand that is attached to the vibrator, however. Women who use vibrators often experiment with different models to find one with the shape and intensity of vibration that suits them.

Sexual Fantasy

Sexual fantasies are sexual experiences that can occur without a partner, but many people also fantasize during lovemaking (Leitenberg & Henning, 1995). Some couples find it sex-

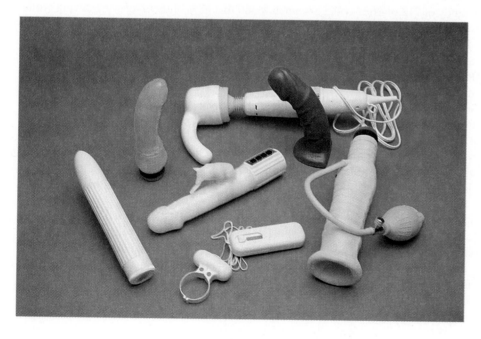

Figure 9.5. **Electric Vibrators.**

Sexual Fantasy. Sexual fantasies can be a powerful source of sexual stimulation, when people are masturbating or making love.

ually arousing to share their fantasies or to enact them with their partners. Strictly speaking, however, a fantasy is a private mental experience involving thoughts or images that are sexually arousing to the individual. Sexual fantasies may be experienced without sexual behavior, as in erotic dreams or daydreams. Sexual fantasies can also be used to heighten sexual response during masturbation or sexual activity with another person. Masturbators often require some form of cognitive stimulation, such as fantasy or reading or viewing erotica, to increase their arousal to the point of orgasm.

How common are sexual fantasies? It is a popular belief that only people with deficient sex lives engage in sexual fantasies. However, evidence shows that the majority of men and women engage in sexual fantasies from time to time, especially during masturbation (Reinisch, 1990). Men fantasize more often than women do (Hsu et al., 1994). In their national survey, Laumann and his colleagues (1994) found that 54% of men and 19% of women said they thought about sex at least one time a day.

A study of 212 married college women found that 88% of them reported having erotic fantasies. Most of them fantasized both during masturbation and coitus (Davidson & Hoffman, 1986). Another study showed that sexual daydreaming or fantasy in women was associated with a greater sex drive, more sexual activity, and a more positive attitude toward sex (Purifoy et al., 1992). We would hardly expect to find such a pattern among people with deficient sex lives.

Sexual fantasies may be reasonably realistic, such as imagining sexual activity with an attractive classmate. They may involve flights of fancy, such as making love to a movie star. The most common fantasy theme reported among women involves someone they are or have been involved with (Leitenberg & Henning, 1995). In contrast to men's fantasies, women are more likely to focus on the partner's feelings, touching, their own responses to what is happening, and the general feeling tone of the sexual encounter (Leitenberg & Henning, 1995).

The most common masturbation fantasy reported by both genders in the *Playboy* sample was "having intercourse with a loved one" (Hunt, 1974). But note some interesting gender differences: Men are more likely to assume aggressive, dominant roles. Women are more apt to enact passive, submissive roles (Leitenberg & Henning, 1995; Person et al., 1989). Women are more likely to connect sexual activity to relationships and emotional involvement than men are (Barbach, 1995; Leitenberg & Henning, 1995).

Fantasy themes apparently parallel traditional gender stereotypes but may also reflect deeper currents. Sociobiologists might conjecture that women are relatively more likely to fantasize about the images of familiar lovers because female reproductive success in ancestral times was more likely to depend on a close, protective relationship with a stable partner (Symons, 1995). Women can bear and rear relatively few offspring. Thus, they would have had (and might still have) a relatively greater genetic investment in each reproductive opportunity.

Whether or not the wellsprings of sexual fantasy themes lie in our genetic heritages, we should not confuse sexual fantasies with behavior. Fantasies are imaginary. Most people do not intend to act out their fantasies. They use them as a means of inducing or enhancing sexual pleasure (Reinisch, 1990). As one woman noted,

> My fantasies are so personal, and the pleasure I get from them derives so much, I think, from the fact that they are private and locked away in my imagination, that I wouldn't dream of trying to make them come true.... But act my fantasies out? Make them come true? No, absolutely not. My real life's not what they're about; I don't want those things to really happen to me, I simply want to imagine what it would be like. So that's where they'll stay.

(Friday, 1973, p. 288)

What Friday says here of women's fantasies also applies to men:

> For many women, fantasy is a way of exploring, safely, all the ideas and actions which might frighten them in reality. In fantasy they can expand their reality, play out certain sexual variables and images in much the same way that children enter into fantasy as a form of play, of trying out desires, releasing energies for which they have no outlet in reality. Thinking about it, even getting excited over the image doesn't mean you want it as your reality ... or else we all, night dreamers that we are, would be suppressed robbers, bisexuals, murderers, or even inanimate objects. (p. 41)

Fantasizing about forcing someone into sexual activity, or about being victimized, does not mean that one wants these events to occur (Leitenberg & Henning, 1995; Reinisch, 1990). Women who imagine themselves being sexually coerced remain in control of their fantasies. Real assault victims are not. Nor is it unusual for heterosexual people to have episodic fantasies about sexual activity with people of their own gender, or for gay males or lesbians to fantasize about sexual activity with people of the other gender. In neither case does the person necessarily intend to carry out the fantasy.

Truth OR Fiction?
REVISITED

Heterosexual people may in fact fantasize about sexual activity with people of their own gender. People do not necessarily express their fantasies in their behavior. ■

Why do people fantasize when they masturbate? Masturbation fantasies serve several functions. For one, they increase or facilitate sexual arousal. Sex therapists encourage clients to use sexual fantasies to enhance sexual arousal (e.g., Heiman & LoPiccolo, 1987). Sexual fantasies are highly arousing, in part because fantasizers can command the imagined sexual encounter. They may imagine that people who will not give them the time of day find them irresistible and are willing to fulfill their sexual desires. Or fantasizers may picture improbable or impossible arousing situations, such as sexual activity on a commercial airliner or while skydiving. Some masturbation fantasies may be arousing because they permit us to deviate from traditional gender roles. Women might fantasize about taking an aggressive role or forcing someone into sexual activity. Men, by contrast, may imagine being overtaken by a horde of sexually aggressive women. Other fantasies involve sexual transgressions or "forbidden" behaviors, such as exposing oneself, doing a striptease before strangers, engaging in sexual activity with strangers, or sadomasochistic sex (S&M).

Masturbation fantasies can also allow people to rehearse sexual encounters. We may envision the unfolding of an intended sexual encounter, from greeting a date at the door, through dinner and a movie, and finally to the bedroom. We can mentally rehearse what we would say and do as a way of preparing for the date. Finally, masturbation fantasies may fill in the missing love object when we are alone or our partners are away.

MY SECRET GARDEN

In her book *My Secret Garden*, Nancy Friday (1973) compiled an anthology of erotic fantasies that women reported having during masturbation, daydreaming, and coitus. Here are some examples:

Sometimes during sex, or just during the day, I think of what it would be like to trade husbands, that is, for me and my husband to have sex with a couple with whom we are good friends . . . me with the guy and my husband with the other wife. (p. 47)

I save my fantasizing for when I'm alone. I wait till evening, take a couple of drinks, and curl up in bed with a sexy book. Then when the drinks take hold I can imagine my hands are those of my lover.

Other fantasies are just day-dreams, which I have constantly. My favorite daydream is of me cooking or washing dishes, my lover comes in, puts his arms around me, and as we kiss and press against one another and our passion builds, I just reach behind me and turn off the stove, the dishes are forgotten, everything left wonderfully unfinished in this very interrupted state, as we go off to the bedroom to make love. (p. 68)

~ *Reflections* ~

- What are the beliefs of most people from your sociocultural group about masturbation? Do you share these beliefs? Why, or why not?
- What misinformation, if any, did you receive about masturbation as you were growing up? What was the source of the misinformation?
- Do you have sexual fantasies? What do you fantasize about? Do you—or did you—wonder whether your fantasies are "normal"? If so, why?

Sex with Others

Partners' feelings for one another, and the quality of their relationships, may be stronger determinants of their sexual arousal and response than the techniques that they employ. Partners are most likely to experience mutually enjoyable sexual interactions when they are sensitive to each other's sexual needs and incorporate techniques with which they are both comfortable. As with other aspects of sharing relationships, communication is the most important "sexual" technique.

Foreplay

Foreplay
Physical interactions that are sexually stimulating and set the stage for intercourse.

Various forms of noncoital sex, such as cuddling, kissing, petting, and oral–genital contact, are used as **foreplay.** The pattern and duration of foreplay vary widely within and across cultures. Broude and Greene (1976) found that prolonged foreplay was the norm in about half of the societies in their cross-cultural sample. Foreplay was minimal in one in ten societies and virtually absent in about one third of them.

Within the United States, there is a gender difference in the amount of foreplay desired. A survey of college students revealed that women wanted longer periods of foreplay (and "afterplay") than men did (Denny et al., 1984). Since women usually require a longer period of stimulation during sex with a partner to reach orgasm, increasing the duration of foreplay may increase female coital responsiveness.

Foreplay is not limited to the human species. Virtually all species of mammals, from horses and sheep to dogs and chimpanzees, engage in some kind of foreplay. Depending on the particular species, mating pairs may rub, playfully nip, lick, or nuzzle each other's genitals for minutes or hours preceding coitus (Geer et al., 1984).

Kissing, genital touching, and oral–genital contact may also be experienced as ends in themselves, not as preludes to coitus. Yet some people object to petting for petting's sake, equating it with masturbation as a form of sexual activity without a "product." Many people behave as though all sexual contact must lead to coitus, perhaps because of the importance that our culture places on it.

Kissing

Kissing is almost universal in our culture, but it occurs less often among the world's cultures than manual or oral stimulation of the genitals (Frayser, 1985). Kissing is unknown in some cultures, such as among the Thonga of Africa and the Siriono of Bolivia. Variations in styles of kissing also exist across cultures (Ford & Beach, 1951). Kissing is now becoming practiced in Japan because of the influence of Western culture but was previously unknown there. Instead of kissing, the Balinese of the South Pacific bring their faces close enough to each other to smell each other's perfume and feel the warmth of each other's skin. This practice has been wrongly dubbed "rubbing noses" by Europeans. Among some preliterate societies, kissing consists of sucking the partner's lips and tongue and allowing saliva to pass from one mouth to the other.

Couples may kiss for its own enjoyment or as a prelude to intercourse, in which case it is a part of foreplay. In *simple kissing,* the partners keep their mouths closed. Simple kissing may develop into caresses of the lips with the tongue, or into nibbling of the lower lip. In what Kinsey called *deep kissing,* which is also called French or soul kissing, the partners part their lips and insert their tongues into each other's mouths. Some prefer the lips parted slightly. Others open their mouths widely.

Kissing may also be an affectionate gesture without erotic significance, as in kissing someone good-night. Some people are accustomed to kissing relatives and close friends affectionately on the lips. Others limit kissing relatives to the cheek. Sustained kissing on the lips and deep kissing are almost always erotic gestures.

Kissing is not limited to the partner's mouth. Kinsey found that more than nine husbands in ten kissed their wives' breasts. Women usually prefer several minutes of body contact and gentle caresses before desiring to have their partner kiss their breasts, or suck or lick their nipples. Women also usually do not prefer a hard sucking action unless they are highly aroused. Many women are reluctant to tell their partners that sucking hurts because they do not want to interfere with their partner's pleasure.

Other parts of the body are also often kissed, including the hands and feet, the neck and earlobes, the insides of the thighs, and the genitals themselves.

Touching

Touching or caressing erogenous zones with the hands or other parts of the body can be highly arousing. Even simple hand-holding can be sexually stimulating for couples who are sexually attracted to one another. The hands are very rich in nerve endings.

Touching is a common form of foreplay. Both men and women generally prefer manual or oral stimulation of the genitals as a prelude to intercourse. Women generally prefer that direct caressing of the genitals be focused around the clitoris but not directly on the extremely sensitive clitoral glans. Men sometimes assume (often mistakenly) that their partners want them to insert their finger or fingers into the vagina as a form of foreplay. But not all women enjoy this form of stimulation. Some women go along with it because it's what their partners want or something they think their partners want. Ironicallly, men may do it because they assume that their partners want it. When in doubt, it would not hurt to *ask*. If you are not sure what to say, you can always blame us: "Listen, I read this thing in my human sexuality text, and I was wondering . . . "

Masters and Johnson (1979) noted gender differences with respect to preferences in foreplay. Men typically prefer direct stroking of their genitals by their partner early in lovemaking. Women, however, tend to prefer that their partners caress their genitals after a period of general body contact that includes holding, hugging, and nongenital massage. This is not a hard and fast (or slow) rule, but it concurs with other observations that men tend to be more genitally oriented than women. Women are more likely to view sex within a broader framework of affection and love.

Techniques of Manual Stimulation of the Genitals   Here again, variability in technique is the rule, so partners need to communicate their preferences. The man's partner may use two hands to stimulate his genitals. One may be used to fondle the scrotum, by gently squeezing the skin between the fingers (taking care not to apply pressure to the testes themselves). The other hand may circle the coronal ridge and engage in gentle stroking of the penis, followed by more vigorous up and down movements as the man becomes more aroused.

The penis may also be gently rolled back and forth between the palms as if one were making a ball of clay into a sausage—increasing pressure as arousal progresses. Note that men who are highly aroused or who have just had an orgasm may find direct stimulation of the penile glans uncomfortable.

The woman may prefer that her partner approach genital stimulation gradually, following stimulation of other body parts. Genital stimulation may begin with light, stroking motions of the inner thighs and move on to the vaginal lips (labia) and the clitoral area. Women may enjoy pressure against the mons pubis from the heel of the hand, or tactile stimulation of the labia, which are sensitive to stroking motions. Clitoral stimulation can focus on the clitoral shaft or the region surrounding the shaft, rather than the clitoris itself, because of the extreme sensitivity of the clitoral glans to touch.

Moreover, the clitoris should not be stroked if it is dry, lest it become irritated. Since it produces no lubrication of its own, a finger may enter the outer portion of the vagina to apply some vaginal lubrication to the clitoral region.

Some, but not all, women enjoy having a finger inserted into the vagina, which can stroke the vaginal walls or simulate thrusting of the penis. Vaginal insertion is usually not preferred, if at all, until the woman has become highly aroused. Many women desire that their partners discontinue stroking motions while they are experiencing orgasm, but others wish stimulation to continue. Men and women woman may physically guide their partners' hands or otherwise express their preferences as to the types of strokes they find most pleasurable.

If a finger is to be inserted into the vagina, it should be clean. Fingernails should be well trimmed. Inserting fingers that have been in the anus into the vagina is dangerous. The fingers may transfer microbes from the woman's digestive tract, where they do no harm, to the woman's reproductive tract, where they can cause serious infections.

Breast Stimulation

Men are more likely to stimulate women's breasts than to have their own breasts fondled, even though the breasts (and especially the nipples) are erotically sensitive in both genders. Most, but not all, women enjoy breast stimulation. Masters and Johnson report that some women are capable of achieving orgasm from breast stimulation alone.

The hands and the mouth can be used to stimulate the breasts and the nipples. Since the desired type and intensity of breast stimulation varies from person to person, partners need to communicate their preferences.

Masters and Johnson (1979) find that gay men frequently stroke their partners' nipples before stimulating the penis itself. Although some heterosexual men enjoy having their breasts and nipples stimulated by their partners, many, if not most, do not. Many men are simply unaware that their breasts are erotically sensitive. Cultural conditioning may also play a major part in men's reluctance to having their breasts stimulated: Men may feel uncomfortable receiving a form of stimulation that they have learned to associate with the stereotypical feminine sexual role.

Fellatio
Oral stimulation of the male genitals.

Cunnilingus
Oral stimulation of the female genitals.

Oral–Genital Stimulation

Oral stimulation of the male genitals is called **fellatio.** Fellatio is referred to by slang terms such as "blow job," "sucking," "sucking off," or "giving head." Oral stimulation of the female genitals is called **cunnilingus,** which is referred to by slang expressions such as "eating" (a woman) or "going down" on her.

The popularity of oral–genital stimulation has increased dramatically since Kinsey's day, especially among young married couples. Kinsey and his colleagues (1948, 1953) found that at least 60% of married, *college-educated* couples had experienced oral–genital contact. Such experiences were reported by only about 20% of couples who only had a high school education and 10% who only had a grade school education.

The incidence of oral sex may have peaked during the sexual revolution. The *Playboy* survey in the early 1970s found that more than 90% of the married couples under 25 years of age—*across all educational levels*—reported they had engaged in oral–genital sex (Hunt, 1974). But remember that 80% of the people approached by Hunt refused to participate in the survey. Therefore, there is likely to be a volunteer bias in his statistics. (The researchers who conducted the NHSLS study are less kind in discussion of the representativeness of Hunt's sample.)

According to the NHSLS study, the incidence of oral sex is somewhat lower in the 1990s (Laumann et al., 1994). About three of four men (77%) and two of three women (68%) report playing the active role in oral sex during their lifetimes. Nearly four men in five (79%) and three of four women (73%) report having been the recipients of oral–genital sex during their lifetimes. Among married couples, 80% of the men and 71% of the women have performed oral sex. Eighty percent of the men and 74% of the women have received oral sex. These are dramatic increases since Kinsey's day. Among young White women (ages 18 to 36) in Kinsey's sample, 48% reported ever engaging in fellatio. Fifty-one percent of their partners had engaged in cunnilingus.

Truth OR Fiction?
R E V I S I T E D

It is true that oral sex is the norm for today's young married couples, statistically speaking. A majority of them report participating in this form of sexual expression. ■

As with touching, oral–genital stimulation can be used as a prelude to intercourse or as a sexual end in itself. If orgasm is reached through oral–genital stimulation, a woman may be concerned about tasting or swallowing a man's ejaculate. There is a lack of scientific evidence that swallowing semen is harmful to one's health, unless the man is infected with a sexually transmitted disease, in which case semen can act as a conduit of infections (Reinisch, 1990). Note that oral–genital contact with the genitals of an infected partner, even without contact with semen, may transmit harmful organisms. Couples are thus advised to practice "safer sex" techniques (see Chapters 16 and 17) unless they know that they and their partners are free of sexually transmitted diseases (Reinisch, 1990).

Techniques of Fellatio   Although the word *fellatio* is derived from a Latin root meaning "to suck," a sucking action is generally not highly arousing. The up-and-down movements of the penis in the partner's mouth, or the licking of the penis, are generally the most stimulating. Gentle licking of the scrotum may also be highly arousing.

The mouth is stimulating to the penis because it contains warm, moist mucous membranes, as does the vagina. Muscles of the mouth and jaw can create varied pressure and movements. Erection may be stimulated by gently pulling the penis with the mouth (being careful never to touch the penis with the teeth) and simultaneously providing manual stimulation, as described earlier.

Higher levels of sexual arousal or orgasm can be promoted by moving the penis in and out of the mouth, simulating the motion of the penis in the vagina during intercourse. The speed of the motions can be varied, and manual stimulation near the base of the penis (firmly encircling the lower portion of the penis or providing pressure behind the scrotum) can also be stimulating.

Some people may gag during fellatio, a reflex that is triggered by pressure of the penis against the back of the tongue or against the throat. Gagging may be avoided if the man's partner grasps the shaft of the penis with one hand and controls the depth of penetration. Gagging is less likely to occur if the partner performing fellatio is on the top, rather than below, or if there is verbal communication about how deep the man may comfortably penetrate. Gagging may also be overcome by allowing gradually deeper penetrations of the penis over successive occasions while keeping the throat muscles relaxed.

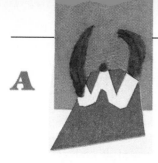

SOCIOCULTURAL FACTORS AND ORAL SEX

Table 9.3 shows the incidence of oral sex among men and women with various levels of education and from different racial/ethnic backgrounds in the NHSLS survey. As with masturbation, the incidence of oral sex correlates with level of education. That is, more highly educated individuals are more likely to have practiced oral sex. Why? Perhaps education encourages experimentation. Perhaps education dispels myths that nontraditional behavior patterns are necessarily harmful. Note also that African American men and women are less likely to

TABLE 9.3 NHSLS study respondents who report experience with oral sex

		Performed Oral Sex (%)		Received Oral Sex (%)	
		Men	Women	Men	Women
Education	Less than high school	59.2	42.1	60.7	49.6
	High school graduate	75.3	59.6	76.6	67.1
	Some college	80.0	78.2	84.0	81.6
	College graduate	83.7	78.9	84.6	83.1
	Advanced college degree	80.5	79.0	81.4	81.9
Race/Ethnicity	White	81.4	75.3	81.4	78.9
	African American	50.5	34.4	66.3	48.9
	Hispanic American	70.7	59.7	73.2	63.7
	Asian American	63.6	—*	72.7	—*

*There were not enough Asian-American women in the sample to allow for the reporting of meaningful findings.

Source: Adapted from Laumann, E. O., Gagnon, J. H., Michael, R. T., & Michaels, S. (1994). *The Social Organization of Sexuality: Sexual Practices in the United States.* Chicago: University of Chicago Press, Table 3.6, p. 98.

Techniques of Cunnilingus   Women can be highly aroused by their partner's tongue because it is soft, warm, and well lubricated. In contrast to a finger, the tongue can almost never be used too harshly. A woman may thus be more receptive to direct clitoral contact by a tongue. Cunnilingus provides such intense stimulation that many women find it to be the best means for achieving orgasm. Some women cannot reach orgasm in any other way (Hite, 1976).

In performing cunnilingus, the partner may begin by kissing and licking the woman's abdomen and inner thighs, gradually nearing the vulva. Gentle tugging at or sucking of the labia minora can be stimulating, but the partner should take care not to bite. Many women enjoy licking of the clitoral region, and others desire sucking of the clitoris itself. The tongue may also be inserted into the vagina where it may imitate the thrusts of intercourse.

"69"   The term *sixty-nine*, or *soixante-neuf* in French (pronounced swah-sahnt nuff), describes simultaneous oral–genital stimulation (see Figure 9.6 on page 250). The numerals *6* and *9* are used because they resemble two partners who are upside-down and facing each other.

The "69" position has the psychologically positive feature of allowing couples to experience simultaneous stimulation, but it can be an awkward position if two people are not sim-

have engaged in oral sex than people from other racial/ethnic backgrounds. African-American men and women were also less likely than other ethnic groups to report masturbating during the past 12 months. African Americans may adhere more strictly to traditional ideas as to what kinds of sexual behavior are and are not proper.

Findings from a national survey of more than 3,000 sexually active men between the ages of 20 and 39 conducted by the Battelle Human Affairs Research Center in Seattle are consistent with the NHSLS findings. Seventy-five percent of the men reported performing oral sex. Seventy-nine percent reported receiving oral sex (Billy et al., 1993). Mirroring the racial differences observed by Laumann and his colleagues (1994), African-American men in the Battelle survey were also much less likely than their white counterparts to have performed or received oral sex.

The results of a 1980s survey of college students are also consistent with the NHSLS data. Eighty-one percent of white females reported they had engaged in fellatio, as compared to 47% of African-American females (Belcastro, 1985). Seventy-two percent of white males had performed cunnilingus, compared to 50% of African-American males. Although the prevalence of oral–genital sex since Kinsey's time has increased for both African Americans and white Americans, African Americans remain relatively less likely than white Americans to engage in oral sexual activity.

Truth OR Fiction?
REVISITED

It is not true that African Americans are more likely than white Americans to engage in oral sex. A review of the available survey evidence shows that white Americans are more likely than African Americans to engage in oral–genital sexual activity ■

Ethnicity and Oral Sex. According to the NHSLS study and others, African Americans report that they are less likely than people from other racial/ethnic backgrounds to engage in oral sex. Why do you think that this is so?

ilar in size. Some couples avoid 69 because it deprives each partner of the opportunity to focus fully on receiving or providing sexual pleasure. A person may find it distracting when receiving stimulation to have to focus on providing effective stimulation to someone else.

The 69 technique may be practiced side by side or with one partner on top of the other. But here again there are no strict rules, and couples often alternate positions.

Abstaining from Oral Sex Despite the popularity of oral sex among couples today, those who desire to abstain from it have no reason to consider themselves abnormal.

People offer various reasons for abstaining from oral sex. Although natural body odors may be arousing to some people, others are disturbed by the genital odors to which they are exposed. Some people object on grounds of cleanliness. They view the genitals as "dirty" because of their proximity to the urinary and anal openings. Concerns about offensive odors or cleanliness may be relieved by thoroughly washing the genitals beforehand.

Some women prefer not to taste or swallow semen because they find it to be "dirty," sinful, or repulsive. Others are put off by the taste or texture. Semen has a salty taste and a texture similar to the white of an egg. If couples are to engage in unprotected oral sex, open discussion of feelings can enhance pleasure and diminish anxiety. For example, the

Figure 9.6. **Simultaneous Oral–Genital Contact.** The "69" position allows partners to engage in simultaneous oral–genital stimulation.

man can be encouraged to warn his partner or remove his penis from her mouth when he is nearing ejaculation.

Let us dispel a couple of myths about semen. For one thing, it is impossible to become pregnant by swallowing semen. For another, semen is not fattening. Reinisch (1990) notes that the average amount of semen expelled in the ejaculate contains only about 5 calories. On the other hand, it is not our intention to encourage swallowing of semen. The aesthetics of swallowing semen have little or nothing to do with concerns about pregnancy or weight. They involve the preferences of the individual.

Some of the objections expressed by people who are reluctant to engage in oral sex may be overcome. Others, such as beliefs that oral–genital contact is offensive or repulsive, are more deeply rooted. Shyness and embarrassment may also deter oral sex. A survey of college students found that shyness and embarrassment were the two most frequent reasons given for not engaging in oral sex (Gagnon & Simon, 1987). In one respect, oral sex is one of the most intimate types of lovemaking. After all, it provides a direct view of parts of the body we have been reared to keep private.

People may also object to oral sex because it is condemned by Judeo-Christian moral codes. In the Judeo-Christian tradition, any sexual contact that does not lead to procreation has been considered sinful. Couples may also be deterred from oral sex because it is illegal in many states, even for married couples. Some people object to oral sex on grounds that it is unnatural, even though many other species practice some form of oral–genital contact (Ford & Beach, 1951).

Sexual Intercourse: Positions and Techniques

Sexual intercourse, or *coitus* (from the Latin *coire,* meaning "to go together"), is sexual activity in which the penis is inserted into the vagina. Intercourse may take place in many different positions. Each position, however, must allow the genitals to be aligned so that the penis is contained by the vagina. In addition to varying positions, couples also vary the depth and rate of thrusting (in-and-out motions) and sources of additional sexual stimulation.

Though the number of possible coital positions is virtually endless, we will focus on four of the most commonly used positions: the male-superior (man-on-top) position, the female-superior (woman-on-top) position, the lateral-entry (side-entry) position, and the rear-entry position. Although not properly fitting the definition of sexual intercourse, we shall discuss anal intercourse as well, a sexual technique used by both male–female and male–male couples.

Missionary position
The coital position in which the man is on top. Also termed the *male-superior position*.

The Male-Superior (Man-on-Top) Position   The male-superior position ("superiority" is used purely in relation to body position, but has sometimes been taken as a symbol of male domination) has also been called the **missionary position.** In this position the partners face one another. The man lies above the woman, perhaps supporting himself on his hands and knees rather than applying his full weight against his partner (see Figure 9.7). Still, movement is easier for the man than for the woman, which suggests that he is responsible for directing their activity.

Many students of human sexuality suggest that it is preferable for the woman to guide the penis into the vagina, rather than having the man do so. The idea is that the woman can feel the location of the vaginal opening and determine the proper angle of entry. To accomplish this, the woman must feel comfortable "taking charge" of the couple's lovemaking. With the breaking down of the traditional stereotype of the female as passive, women are feeling more comfortable taking this role. On the other hand, if the couple prefers that the man guide his penis into his partner's vagina, the slight loss of efficiency need not trouble them, as long as he moves prudently to avoid hurting his partner.

Figure 9.7. The Male-Superior Coital Position. In this position the couple face one another. The man lies above the woman, perhaps supporting himself on his hands and knees rather than allowing his full weight to press against his partner. The position is also referred to as the *missionary position.*

The male-superior position has the advantage of permitting the couple to face one another so that kissing is easier. The woman may run her hands along her partner's body, stroking his buttocks and perhaps cupping a hand beneath his scrotum to increase stimulation as he reaches orgasm.

But the male-superior position makes it difficult for the man to caress his partner while simultaneously supporting himself with his hands. So the position may not be favored by women who enjoy having their partners provide manual clitoral stimulation during coitus. This position can be highly stimulating to the man, which can make it difficult for him to delay ejaculation. The position also limits the opportunity for the woman to control the angle, rate, and depth of penetration. It may thus be more difficult for her to attain the type of stimulation she may need to achieve orgasm, especially if she favors combining penile thrusting with manual clitoral stimulation. Finally, this position is not advisable during the late stages of pregnancy. At that time the woman's distended abdomen would force the man to arch severely above her, lest he place undue pressure against the woman's abdomen.

The Female-Superior (Woman-on-Top) Position

In the female-superior position the couple face one another with the woman on top. The woman straddles the male from above, controlling the angle of penile entry and the depth of thrusting (see Figure 9.8). Some women maintain a sitting position; others lie on top of their partners. Many women vary their position.

In the female-superior position the woman is psychologically, and to some degree physically, in charge. She can move as rapidly or as slowly as she wishes with little effort, adjusting her body so as to vary the angle and depth of penetration. She can reach behind her to stroke her partner's scrotum, or lean down to kiss him.

As in the male-superior position, kissing is relatively easy. This position has additional advantages. The man may readily reach the woman's buttocks or clitoris in order to provide manual stimulation. Assuming that the woman is shorter than he is, it is rather easy for him to stimulate her breasts orally (a pillow tucked behind his head may help). The woman can, in effect, guarantee that she receives adequate clitoral stimulation, either by the penis or manually by his hand or her own. This position thus facilitates orgasm in the woman. As it tends to be less stimulating for the male, it may help him to control ejaculation. For these reasons this position is commonly used by couples who are learning to overcome sexual difficulties.

The Lateral-Entry (Side-Entry) Position

In the lateral-entry position, the man and woman lie side by side, facing one another (see Figure 9.9 on page 254). This position has the advantages of allowing each partner relatively free movement and easy access to the other. The man and woman may kiss freely, and they can stroke each other's bodies with a free arm. The position is not physically taxing, because both partners are resting easily on the bedding. Thus it is an excellent position for prolonged coitus or for coitus when couples are somewhat fatigued.

Let us note some disadvantages to this position. First, inserting the penis into the vagina while lying side by side may be awkward. Many couples thus begin coitus in another position and then change into the lateral-entry position—often because they wish to prolong coitus. Second, one or both partners may have an arm lying beneath the other that will "fall asleep" or become numb because of the constricted blood supply. Third, women may not receive adequate clitoral stimulation from the penis in this position. Of course, such stimulation may be provided manually (by hand) or by switching to another position after a while. Fourth, it may be difficult to achieve deeper penetration of the penis. The lateral position is useful during pregnancy (at least until the final stages, when the distension of the woman's abdomen may make lateral entry difficult).

The Rear-Entry Position

In the rear-entry position, the man faces the woman's rear. In one variation (see Figure 9.10 on page 255), the woman supports herself on her hands and knees while the man supports himself on his knees, entering her from behind. In another, the couple lie alongside one another and the woman lifts one leg, draping it backward over her partner's thigh. The latter position is particularly useful during the later stages of pregnancy.

The rear-entry position may be highly stimulating for both partners. Men may enjoy viewing and pressing their abdomens against their partner's buttocks. The man can reach

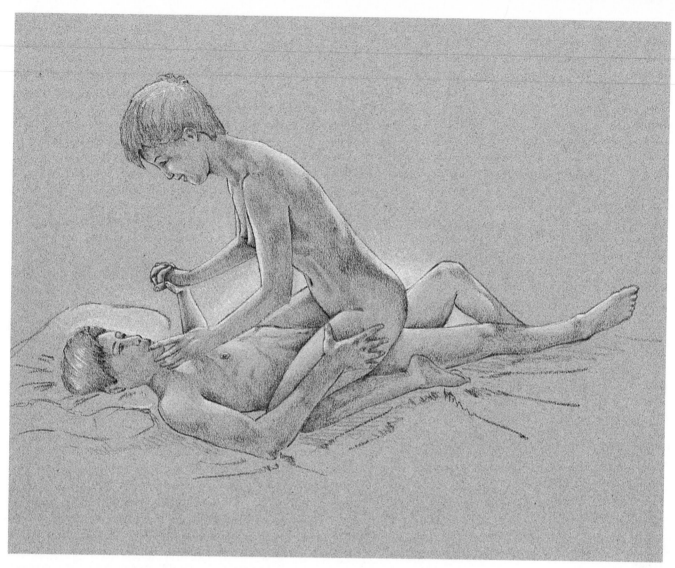

Figure 9.8. **The Female-Superior Coital Position.** The woman straddles the male from above, controlling the angle of penile entry and the depth of thrusting. The female-superior position puts the woman psychologically and physically in charge. The woman can ensure that she receives adequate clitoral stimulation from the penis or the hand. The position also tends to be less stimulating for the male and may thus help him to control ejaculation.

around or underneath to provide additional clitoral or breast stimulation, and she may reach behind (if she is on her hands and knees) to stroke or grasp her partner's testicles.

Potential disadvantages to this position include the following: First, this position is the mating position used by most other mammals, which is why it is sometimes referred to as *doggy style.* Some couples may feel uncomfortable about using the position because of its association with animal mating patterns. The position is also impersonal in the sense that the partners do not face one another, which may create a sense of emotional distance. Since the man is at the woman's back, the couple may feel that he is very much in charge—he can see her, but she cannot readily see him. Physically, the penis does not provide adequate stimulation to the clitoris. The penis also tends to pop out of the vagina from time to time. Finally, air tends to enter the vagina during rear-entry coitus. When it is expelled, it can sound as though the woman has passed air through the anus—a possibly embarrassing though harmless occurrence.

Use of Fantasy During Coitus   As with masturbation, mental excursions into fantasy during coitus may be used to enhance sexual arousal and response (Davidson &

Figure 9.9. The Lateral-Entry Coital Position. In this position the couple face each other side by side. Each partner has relatively free movement and easy access to the other. Because both partners rest easily on the bedding, it is an excellent position for prolonged coitus or for coitus when couples are fatigued.

Hoffman, 1986). In a sense, coital fantasies allow couples to inject sexual variety and even offbeat sexual escapades into their sexual activity, without being unfaithful. Fantasies were historically viewed as evil. People believed that fantasies, like dreams, were placed in the mind by agents of the Devil. Despite this tradition, researchers find that most married people have engaged in coital fantasies (Davidson & Hoffman, 1986). In one study, 71% of the men and 72% of the women reported engaging in coital fantasies to enhance their sexual arousal (Zimmer et al., 1983). A more recent survey of a sample of 178 students, faculty, and staff members at a college in Vermont found that 84% reported fantasizing at least occasionally during intercourse (Cado & Leitenberg, 1990). Nor does there appear to be any connection between sexual dissatisfaction with one's relationship and the use of coital fantasies (Davidson & Hoffman, 1986). Thus coital fantasies are not a form of compensation for an unrewarding sexual relationship.

Lest you think that coital fantasies arise only out of sexual monotony in marriage, many, if not most, unmarried people also fantasize during sexual relations. In one study of sexually experienced, single undergraduates, Sue (1979) found that virtually the same percentages of men (58.6%) and women (59.4%) reported "sometimes" or "almost always" fantasizing during coitus.

Coital fantasies, like masturbation fantasies, run a gamut of themes. They include making love to another partner, group sex, orgies, images of past lovers or special erotic experiences, and making love in fantastic and wonderful places, among others.

Table 9.5 on page 258 shows the coital fantasies reported to Hariton and Singer (1974) by a sample of married women from an affluent New York City suburb. The women included PTA members and regular churchgoers. Yet 65%—a strong majority—used coital fantasies. The use of fantasies was not a sign of marital difficulty. In fact, women who fantasized reported *better* sexual relations with their partners than did those who did not. The content of these fantasies suggests that they serve to introduce novelty or variety into their sexual relationships.

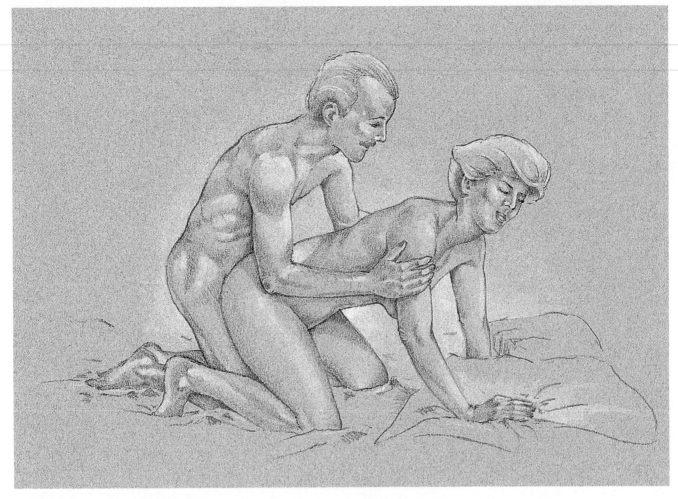

Figure 9.10. **The Rear-Entry Coital Position.** The rear-entry position is highly erotic for men who enjoy viewing and pressing their abdomens against their partners' buttocks. Some couples feel uncomfortable about the position because of its association with animal mating patterns. The position is also impersonal in that the partners do not face one another. Moreover, some couples dislike the feeling that the man is psychologically in charge because he can see his partner but she cannot readily see him.

Relationship Issues and Coital Fantasies   Studies of coital fantasies by Hariton and Singer (1974) and Sue (1979), among others, find that sexual fantasies during intercourse are common among couples with close relationships and are a means of facilitating sexual arousal. By facilitating sexual arousal, coital fantasies may help strengthen the intimate bond between the partners. Evidence does not show coital fantasies to be a sign of a troubled relationship.

T r u t h   **OR**   *Fiction?*
R E V I S I T E D

Evidence fails to show that coital fantasies are a sign of a troubled relationship. ■

Partners are often reluctant to share their coital fantasies, or even to admit to them. This is especially true when the fantasy is about someone other than the partner. The fantasizer might fear being accused of harboring extramarital desires. Or the fantasizer might fear that the partner will interpret fantasies as a sign of rejection: "What's the matter, don't I turn you on anymore?" The advisability of self-disclosure is best weighed against one's partner's potential reactions to coital fantasies.

Anal Intercourse   Anal intercourse can be practiced by male–female couples and male–male couples. It involves insertion of the penis into the rectum. The rectum is richly endowed with nerve endings and is thus highly sensitive to sexual stimulation. Anal inter-

ARE AFRICAN AMERICANS SEXUALLY PERMISSIVE? CULTURAL MYTHOLOGY VERSUS SOME FACTS

African Americans have long been stereotyped as more sexually permissive than white Americans (Wyatt, 1989). The perpetuation of this stereotype is based more on cultural biases than on scientific evidence. Evidence from Kinsey's time through the 1980s has shown that African-American teenagers begin intercourse at earlier ages, on the average, than white teenagers (Wyatt, 1989). Such research has largely failed to account for socioeconomic (social class) differences between the groups, however.

Researchers have begun to critically examine existing stereotypes of African-American sexuality. The 1988 National Survey of Family Growth, which surveyed nearly 8,500 American women ages 15 to 44, found that white women were more likely to have had 10 or more sex partners than either African-American or Hispanic women (Lewin, 1992b). In another research effort, Philip Belcastro (1985) administered an anonymous sex survey to a racially mixed sample of more than 1,000 never-married, undergraduate students at a midwestern university. Belcastro found that the similarities in the sexual behaviors of African-American and white students outweighed the differences. African-American and white students did not differ with respect to incidence of premarital coitus, coitus with a stranger, abortion, coital frequency, number of coital partners, use of condoms or diaphragms, and number of pregnancies (see Table 9.4). Some differences did emerge, however. African-American males had their first coital experiences at an earlier age than white males and had younger first partners. White females had relatively more coital partners with whom they had long-term (six months or longer) relationships. White males reported more masturbatory experience than African-American males. White females were more likely than African-American females to perform fellatio, manually stimulate their partners, and use birth-control pills and coitus interruptus. Belcastro's survey did not control for socioeconomic differences between the African-American and white American samples, however. In addition, college students—African American and white American—are likely to be more affluent and better educated than their counterparts in the general population.

Gail Wyatt (1989) used Kinsey-style interviews to examine various aspects of sexual behavior among 126 African-American and 122 white American women, ages 18 to 36, from Los Angeles County. Wyatt's study is noteworthy for balancing White and African-American samples with respect to sociodemographic factors such as income level, education, and marital status. Wyatt reported no significant differences in age of first intercourse between the African-American and white American women in her sample. The average age at first intercourse was 16.6 years for the total sample—16.5 years for African-American women and 16.7 years for white women, respectively—an insignificant difference. (These data are also remarkably similar to those obtained by Belcastro—see Table 9.4.) Factors that predicted age of first intercourse were similar across groups. For both groups, perceptions that one's parents were more influential than one's friends during adolescence and the eventual attainment of higher educational levels were associated with a delay in the age of first intercourse.

All in all, results of the Belcastro and Wyatt surveys fail to support the stereotype of African-American sexual permissiveness. The similarities between the races overshadowed their differences. We should caution, however, that neither sample was a national probability sample. The results may thus not generalize to all African Americans or white Americans.

Determining whether or not a group is sexually permissive depends on the criteria that one uses to define permissiveness. If age of coital initiation were the criterion of permissiveness, African-American males would be considered more permissive than white American males, according to Belcastro's findings. If masturbating, performing fellatio, or masturbating one's partner were the criteria of permissiveness, white Americans would be deemed more permissive than African Americans.

course is also referred to as "Greek culture," or lovemaking in the "Greek style" because of bisexuality in ancient Greece among males. It is also the major act that comes under the legal definition of sodomy. Both women and men may reach orgasm through receiving the penis in the rectum and thrusting.

In anal intercourse, the penetrating male usually situates himself behind his partner. (He can also lie above or below his partner in a face-to-face position.) The receiving partner can supplement anal stimulation with manual stimulation of the clitoral region or penis to reach orgasm.

Although more interracial research would be of interest, an even richer understanding of sexual behavior patterns might be gained by examining variability within racial groups according to factors such as socioeconomic status and family background.

TABLE 9.4 Sexual behaviors of African-American and white American college students

Behavior	Males % (Means)		Females % (Means)	
	African Americans	White Americans	African Americans	White Americans
Your age at first intercourse (years)	13.6	16.3*	16.2	16.8
Age of your first coital partner	14.8	16.9*	18.6	19.2
Your age when you first masturbated (years)	13.3	13.1	12.6	14.3
Number of times you masturbate per month	4.7	6.5	2.2	3.4
Number of times you have intercourse per month	7.5	8.9	8.5	9.7
Number of coital partners you have dated for 6 months or longer	2.9	2.2	1.5	2.0*
Number of partners with whom you have cohabited	2.4	1.9	2.0	1.2
Number of times you or your partner have become pregnant	1.5	1.0	1.2	1.1
Number of different coital partners in your lifetime	7.4	7.6	4.8	6.6

*Denotes statistically significant results comparing African Americans and white Americans within the same gender.
Source: Adapted from Belcastro, 1985, p. 65.

Women often report wanting their partner's fingers in the anus at the height of passion or at the moment of orgasm. A finger in the rectum at time of orgasm can heighten sexual sensation because the anal sphincters contract during orgasm. Although some men also want a finger in the anus, many resist because they associate anal penetration with the female role or with male–male sexual activity. However, the desire to be entered by one's partner is not necessarily connected with sexual orientation. A gay male or lesbian sexual orientation refers to the eroticization of members of one's own gender, not the desire to penetrate or be penetrated.

TABLE 9.5 Coital fantasies of married women

Fantasy	Women Reporting Fantasy (%)
Thoughts of an imaginary romantic lover enter my mind.	56
I relive a previous sexual experience.	52
I enjoy pretending that I am doing something forbidden.	50
I imagine that I am being overpowered or forced to surrender.	49
I am in a different place, like a car, motel, beach, woods, etc.	47
I imagine myself delighting many men.	43
I pretend that I struggle and resist before being aroused to surrender.	40
I imagine that I am observing myself or others having sex.	38
I pretend that I am another irresistibly sexy female.	38
I daydream that I am being made love to by more than one man at a time.	36
My thoughts center around feelings of weakness or helplessness.	33
I see myself as a striptease dancer, harem girl, or other performer.	28
I pretend that I am a whore or a prostitute.	25
I imagine that I am being forced to expose my body to a seducer.	19
My thoughts center around urination or defecation.	2

Source: Hariton & Singer, 1974.

Many couples are repulsed by the idea of anal intercourse. They view it as unnatural, immoral, or risky. Yet others find anal sex to be an enjoyable sexual variation, though perhaps not a regular feature of their sexual diet.

The NHSLS survey found that 1 man in 4 (26%) and 1 woman in 5 (20%) reported having engaged in anal sex at some time during their lives (Laumann et al., 1994). Yet only about 1 person in 10 (10% of the men and 9% of the women) had engaged in anal sex during the past year. As with oral sex, there was a higher incidence of anal sex among more highly educated people in the NHSLS survey. For example, about 30% of the male college graduates had engaged in anal sex, as compared with 23% of male high school graduates. About 29% of the women with advanced college degrees had engaged in anal sex, as compared with about 17% of the women who had graduated only from high school (Laumann et al., 1994). Education appears to be a liberating experience in sexual experimentation. About 1 in 5 men in the Battelle sample reported having engaged in anal intercourse (Billy et al., 1993). As in the NHSLS survey, anal intercourse was more commonly reported among better-educated men.

Truth OR Fiction?
REVISITED

Anal sex actually turns out to be *less* common among less well educated people. Perhaps education is a liberating influence on sexual experimentation. ■

Religion appears to be a restraining influence on anal sex. About 34% of the men and 36% of the women in the NHSLS survey who said they had no religion reported engaging in anal sex during their lifetimes. Percentage figures for male Christians ranged from the lower to upper 20s, and for female Christians, from the midteens to the lower 20s (Laumann et al., 1944, p. 99). There were too few Jews in the sample to report meaningful figures for Jewish men and women.

Many couples kiss or lick the anus in their foreplay. This practice is called **anilingus.** Oral–anal sex carries a serious health risk, however, because microorganisms causing in-

Anilingus
Oral stimulation of the anus.

testinal diseases and various sexually transmitted diseases can be spread through oral–anal contact.

Many couples today hesitate to engage in anal intercourse because of the fear of AIDS and other sexually transmitted diseases (STDs). The AIDS virus and other microorganisms causing STDs such as gonorrhea, syphilis, and hepatitis can be spread by anal intercourse, because small tears in the rectal tissues may allow the microbes to enter the recipient's blood system. Women also incur a greater risk of contracting HIV, the virus that causes AIDS, from anal intercourse than from vaginal intercourse—just as receptive anal intercourse in gay men carries a high risk of infection (Voeller, 1991). However, partners who are both infection-free are at no risk of contracting HIV or other STD-causing organisms through anal or vaginal intercourse, or any other sexual act.

～ *Reflections* ～

▪ How do our attitudes and values influence the kinds of foreplay and sexual techniques we will enjoy?

▪ What is the connection between level of education and sexual practices such as oral sex? Do you believe that your college experience will have any effects on your own sexual behavior? Explain.

▪ Do the "missionary," female-superior, or rear-entry positions for intercourse seem to you to express any political attitudes concerning male–female relationships? Explain.

In this chapter, we have observed many of the variations in human sexual expression. No other species shows such diversity in sexual behavior. People show diversity not only in sexual behavior, but also in sexual orientation—which is the focus of the following chapter.

Summing Up

Solitary Sexual Behavior

Masturbation   Masturbation may be practiced by means of manual stimulation of the genitals, perhaps with the aid of an electric vibrator or object that provides tactile stimulation. Within the Judeo-Christian tradition, masturbation has been condemned as sinful. Until recent years, masturbation was thought to be physically and mentally harmful, yet contemporary scholars see masturbation as harmless. Surveys indicate that most people have masturbated at some point in their lives.

Sexual Fantasy   Sexual fantasies are often incorporated with masturbation or with sex with another person to heighten sexual response. Sexual fantasies range from the realistic to flights of fancy. Many people fantasize about sexual activities that they would not actually engage in.

Sex with Others

Foreplay   The pattern and duration of foreplay varies widely within and across cultures. Women usually desire longer periods of foreplay than men do.

Kissing   Couples kiss for its own enjoyment or as a prelude to intercourse.

Touching   Touching or caressing erogenous zones with the hands or other parts of the body can be highly arousing. Men typically prefer direct stroking of their genitals by their partner early in lovemaking. Women, however, tend to prefer that their partners caress their genitals after a period of general body contact.

Breast Stimulation   Most, but not all, women enjoy breast stimulation. The hands and the mouth can be used to stimulate the breasts.

Oral–Genital Stimulation   The popularity of oral–genital stimulation has increased dramatically since Kinsey's day, but survey researchers find persistent differences in the frequency of these activities between African and White Americans.

Sexual Intercourse: Positions and Techniques   Couples today use a greater variety of coital positions than in Kinsey's time. Four of the most commonly used coital positions are the male-superior position, the female-superior position, the lateral-entry position, and the rear-entry position.

CHAPTER 10

Henri Matisse, *Two Odalisques*. Moderna Museet, SKM, Stockholm. © 1996
Succession H. Matisse/Artist Rights Society (ARS), New York.

Sexual Orientation

Outline

Truth ◆OR◆ Fiction?

_____ Gay males and lesbians would prefer to be members of the other gender.

_____ Gay males and lesbians suffer from hormonal imbalances.

_____ Gay males unconsciously fear women's genitals because they associate them with castration.

_____ The American Psychiatric Association considers homosexuality to be a mental disorder.

_____ Many gay couples have lifestyles similar to those of married heterosexual couples and are as well adjusted.

ohn, a nurse, was awarded custody of his 7-year-old son, Jacob, after a divorce. John's companion, Don, often picks Jacob up after school. "Who is that?" a teacher unfamiliar with the situation asked Jacob one day.

"That's my father's husband," Jacob replied matter-of-factly.

Alyson Publications, a Boston publisher, added two titles to its children's list: *Heather Has Two Mommies* and *Daddy's Roommate.*

As suggested by these slices of contemporary life reported by Gross (1991), many children are reared openly by gay male or lesbian couples. In most states, a gay male or lesbian sexual orientation is no longer grounds for parents to lose custody of their children (Dunlap, 1995). States have become more accepting of this living arrangement because of a lack of evidence that children reared by gay male and lesbian parents are less well adjusted than other children (Baggett, 1992; Patterson, 1995). Nor does being reared by a parent with a gay male or lesbian sexual orientation cause children to develop such sexual orientations or gender identity confusion (Patterson, 1995).

In this chapter we discuss **sexual orientation.** Sexual orientation concerns the *direction* of one's romantic interests and erotic attractions—toward members of the same gender, the other gender, or both. We will see that gay people, like heterosexual people, struggle to incorporate their sexuality within their personal identity, to find lovers, and to establish satisfying lifestyles. Unlike heterosexual people, however, gay people in our culture must come to terms with their sexuality against a backdrop of societal intolerance.

Sexual orientation
The directionality of one's sexual interests—toward members of the same gender, the other gender, or both genders.

Heterosexual orientation
Erotic attraction to, and preference for, developing romantic relationships with members of the other gender.

Homosexual orientation
Erotic attraction to, and preference for, developing romantic relationships with members of one's own gender. (From the Greek *homos*, meaning "same," not the Latin *homo*, which means "man").

Gay males
Males who are erotically attracted to and desire to form romantic relationships with other males.

Lesbians
Females who are erotically attracted to and desire to form romantic relationships with other females. (After *Lesbos,* the Greek island on which, legend has it, female–female sexual activity was idealized.)

Sexual Orientation

Sexual orientation refers to one's erotic attractions toward, and interests in developing romantic relationships with, members of one's own or the other gender. A **heterosexual orientation** refers to an erotic attraction to, and preference for developing romantic relationships with, members of the other gender. (Many gay people refer to heterosexual people as being *straight,* or as *straights.*) Notice that we say *other gender,* not *opposite gender.* Social critics note that many of the problems that arise between men and women are based on the notion that men and women are polar opposites (Bem, 1993). Research and common sense both support the view that men and women are more alike in personality and behavior than they are different, however.

A **homosexual orientation** refers to an erotic attraction to, and interest in forming romantic relationships with, members of one's own gender. The term *homosexuality* denotes sexual interest in members of one's own gender and applies to both men and women. Homosexual men are often referred to as **gay males.** Homosexual women are also called **lesbians** or *gay women.* Gay males and lesbians are also referred to collectively as "gays" or "gay people." The term **bisexuality** refers to an orientation in which one is sexually attracted to, and interested in forming romantic relationships with, both males and females.

Coming to Terms with Terms

Now that we have defined the term *homosexuality,* let us note that we will use it only sparingly. Many gay people object to the term *homosexual* because they feel that it draws too much attention to sexual behavior. Moreover, the term bears a social stigma. Many gays would prefer terms such as *gay male* or *lesbian sexual orientation,* or a term such as *homophile,* if a term must be used to set them apart. The Greek root *philia* suggests love and friendship rather than sexual behavior. Thus, a homophile is a person who develops romantic love and emotional commitment to members of her or his own gender. Sexual activity is secondary.

A Slice of Contemporary Life. Some gay couples consider themselves to be married, although their unions are not legally recognized in nearly all jurisdictions.

Bisexuality
Erotic attraction to, and interest in developing romantic relationships with, both males and females.

We therefore use the terms *gay male* and *lesbian* instead of *homosexual* when we refer to sexual orientation. As noted by the American Psychological Association's Committee on Lesbian and Gay Concerns (1991), the word *homosexual* has also been historically associated with concepts of deviance and mental illness. It perpetuates negative stereotypes of gay people. Also, the term is often used to refer to men only. It thus renders lesbians invisible.

Then, too, the word *homosexual* is ambiguous in meaning—that is, does it refer to sexual behavior or sexual orientation (Suppe, 1994)? In this book, your authors speak of male–female sexual behavior (not *heterosexual* behavior), male–male sexual behavior, and female–female sexual behavior.

Sexual Orientation and Gender Identity

Since gay people are attracted to members of their own gender, some people assume that they would prefer to be members of the other gender. Like heterosexual people, however, gay people have a gender identity that is consistent with their anatomic gender. Unlike transsexuals, gay people do not see themselves as being trapped in the body of the other gender.

T r u t h **OR** *Fiction?*
R E V I S I T E D

It is not true that gay males and lesbians would prefer to be members of the other gender. Their gender identity is consistent with their anatomic gender. ■

Heterosexuals tend to focus almost exclusively on sexual aspects of male–male and female–female relationships. But the love relationships of gay people, like those of heterosexual people, involve more than sex. Gay people, like heterosexual people, spend only a small proportion of their time in sexual activity. More basic to a gay male or lesbian sexual orientation is the formation of romantic attachments with members of one's own gender. These attachments, like male–female attachments, provide a framework for love and intimacy. Although sex and love are common features of relationships, neither is a *necessary* prerequisite for a relationship. Sexual orientations are not defined by sexual activity per se, but rather by the *direction* of one's romantic interests and erotic attractions.

Classification of Sexual Orientation

Determining a person's sexual orientation might seem to be a clear-cut task. Some people are exclusively gay and limit their sexual activities to partners of their own gender. Others are strictly heterosexual and limit their sexual activities to partners of the other gender. Many people fall somewhere in between, however. Where might we draw the line between a gay male and lesbian sexual orientation, on the one hand, and a heterosexual orientation, on the other? Where do we draw the line between these orientations and bisexuality?

It is possible, indeed not unusual, for heterosexual people to have had some sexual experiences with people of their own gender. Consider a survey of more than 7,000 male readers of *Playboy* magazine. Among those reporting sexual experiences with both men and women in adulthood, more than 2 out of 3 perceived themselves to be heterosexual rather than bisexual (Lever et al., 1992). For many of these men, sexual experiences with other men were limited to a brief period of their lives and did not alter their sexual orientations. Lacking heterosexual outlets, prison inmates may have sexual experiences with people of their own gender while they maintain their heterosexual identities. Inmates would form sexual relationships with people of the other gender if they were available, and they return to male–female sexual behavior upon release from prison. Physical affection also helps some prisoners, male and female, cope with loneliness and isolation. Males who engage in prostitution with male clients may separate their sexual orientation from their "trade." Many fantasize about a female when permitting a client to fellate them. The behavior is male–male. The person's sexual *orientation* may be heterosexual.

Gay males and lesbians, too, may engage in male–female sexual activity while maintaining a gay sexual orientation. Some gay males and lesbians marry members of the other gender but continue to harbor unfulfilled desires for members of their own gender. Then, too, some people are bisexual but may not have acted upon their attraction to members of their own gender.

Sexual orientation is not necessarily expressed in sexual behavior. Many people come to perceive themselves as gay or heterosexual long before they ever engage in sex with members of their own gender. Some people, gay and heterosexual alike, adopt a celibate lifestyle for religious or ascetic reasons and abstain from sexual relationships. Some remain celibate not by choice but because of lack of partners.

People's erotic interests and fantasies may also shift over time. Gay males and lesbians may experience sporadic **heteroerotic** interests. Heterosexual people may have occasional **homoerotic** interests. Many heterosexual people report fantasies about sexual activity with people of their own gender. Many gay people have fantasies about sex with people of the other gender (Masters & Johnson, 1979). About 50% of one sample of lesbians reported that they are sometimes attracted to men (Bell & Weinberg, 1978).

Attraction to people of the other gender and people of one's own gender may thus not be mutually exclusive. People may have various degrees of sexual interest in, and sexual experience with, people of either gender. Kinsey and his colleagues recognized that the boundaries between gay male and lesbian sexual orientations, on the one hand, and a heterosexual orientation, on the other, are sometimes blurry. They thus proposed a continuum of sexual orientation rather than two poles.

The Kinsey Continuum   Before Kinsey, scientists generally viewed gay and heterosexual orientations as separate categories. People were viewed as either gay or heterosexual in their psychological makeup and erotic interests. Kinsey and his colleagues (1948, 1953) found evidence of degrees of gay and heterosexual orientations among people he surveyed, however, with bisexuality representing a midpoint between the two. As Kinsey and his colleagues noted,

> The world is not to be divided into sheep and goats. . . . Only the human mind invents categories and tries to force facts into separated pigeonholes. The living world is a continuum in each and every one of its aspects. (1948, p. 639)

Kinsey and his colleagues (1948, 1953) conceived a 7-point "heterosexual–homosexual continuum" (see Figure 10.1). People are located on the continuum according to their patterns of sexual attraction and behavior. People in category 0 are considered exclusively heterosexual. People in category 6 are considered exclusively gay.

Picking Criteria   What percentage of the population, then, is gay? The percentages depend on the criteria one uses. Kinsey and his colleagues reported that about 4% of men and 1% to 3% of women in their samples were exclusively gay (6 on their scale). A

Heteroerotic

Of an erotic nature and involving members of the other gender.

Homoerotic

Of an erotic nature and involving members of one's own gender.

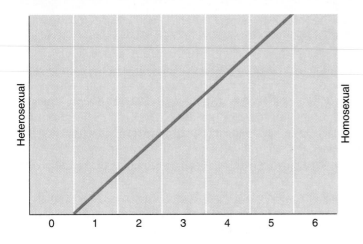

Figure 10.1. **The Kinsey Continuum.** Kinsey and his colleagues conceived a 7-point heterosexual–homosexual continuum that classifies people according to their homosexual behavior and the magnitude of their attraction to members of their own gender. People in category 0, who accounted for most of Kinsey's study participants, were considered exclusively heterosexual. People in category 6 were considered exclusively homosexual.

larger percentage of people were considered predominantly gay (scale points 4 or 5) or predominantly heterosexual (1 or 2 on their scale). Some were classified as equally gay and heterosexual in orientation and could be labeled bisexual (scale point 3). Most people were classified as exclusively heterosexual (scale point 0). Table 10.1 indicates the percentage of people who were classified according to the seven categories in Figure 10.1. Percentages varied according to marital status, age, level of education, and other factors. This particular table is based on people ages 20 to 35.

TABLE 10.1 Percentages of respondents ages 20 to 35 at each level of the Kinsey Continuum of Sexual Orientation

Rating Category		Females (%)	Males (%)
0:	*Entirely heterosexual experience*		
	Single	61–72	53–78
	Married	89–90	90–92
	Previously married	75–80	
1–6:	*At least some sexual experience with people of one's own gender*	11–20	18–42
2–6:	*More than incidental sexual experience with people of one's own gender*	6–14	13–38
3–6:	*Homosexual as much or more than heterosexual*	4–11	9–32
4–6:	*Mostly homosexual*	3–8	7–26
5–6:	*Almost exclusively homosexual*	2–6	5–22
6:	*Exclusively homosexual*	1–3	3–16

Adapted from Kinsey, A. C., et al. (1953). *Sexual Behavior in the Human Female.* Philadelphia: W. B. Saunders, p. 488. Reprinted by permission of the Kinsey Institute for Research in Sex, Gender, and Reproduction, Inc.

Married people were more likely than single people to be classified as exclusively heterosexual. During Kinsey's day, single young people had fewer heterosexual outlets, which may have encouraged them to seek partners of their own gender. A gay male or lesbian sexual orientation may have influenced some to delay marriage, however. Men, overall, were more likely than women to report sexual experiences with people of their own gender.

Between the poles of the continuum lie people with various degrees of sexual interest in, and sexual experience with, people of their own gender. Thirty-seven percent of men and 13% of the women told interviewers they had reached orgasm through sexual activity with someone of their own gender at some time after puberty. Fifty percent of men who remained single until age 35 reported they had reached orgasm through sexual activity with other males.

Many people in Kinsey's day were startled by these figures. They meant that sexual activity with people of one's own gender, especially among males, was more widespread than had been believed. But Kinsey's figures for male–male sexual activity may have been exaggerated. For instance, his finding that 37% of males had reached orgasm through sexual activity with other males was based on a sample that included a high proportion of former prisoners. Findings may also have been distorted by the researchers' efforts to recruit known gay people into their samples. Once these sources of possible bias are corrected, the incidence of male–male sexual activity drops from 37% to about 25%. (Even this percentage is much higher than people suspected at the time.) Because Kinsey's sample was not drawn at random, however, we cannot say whether it represented the general population.

A 1970 nationwide survey conducted by the Kinsey Institute obtained results (published in 1989) that were strikingly similar to Kinsey's early (adjusted) estimates. At least 20% of the randomly selected adult men in the United States had reached orgasm through male–male sexual activity at some point in their lives (Fay et al., 1989). Between 1% and 2% of men in the United States reported male–male sexual experiences within the past year. A 1993 Louis Harris poll found that 4.4% of men and 3.6% of women reported sexual activity with a member of their own gender within the past 5 years (Barringer, 1993b). Kinsey Institute director June Reinisch (1990) examined the available evidence and estimated that more than 25% of men in the United States have had a male–male sexual experience in their teens or adult years.

Statistics concerning *past* sexual activity with a member of one's own gender can be misleading. They may represent a single episode or a brief period of adolescent experimentation. Half of the men who reported male–male sexual activity in Kinsey's sample had limited their experiences to the ages of 12 to 14. Another third had male–male sexual experience by the age of 18, but not again.

Kinsey's research also showed that sexual behavior patterns could shift during a person's lifetime, sometimes dramatically so (Sanders et al., 1990). Sexual experiences or feelings involving people of one's own gender are common, especially in adolescence, and do not mean that one will engage in sexual activity exclusively with people of one's own gender in adulthood (Bullough, 1990).

What did Kinsey find with respect to more enduring patterns of male–male and female–female sexual activity? Estimates based on an analysis of Kinsey's data (Gebhard, 1977) suggest that 13% of the men and 7% of the women, or 10% for both genders combined, were either predominantly or exclusively interested in, and sexually active with, people of their own gender for at least three years between the ages of 16 and 55.

Lately there has been considerable controversy concerning the percentages of people believed to be gay. Current estimates generally find lower percentages of gay people in the population than Kinsey did. Considering data drawn from studies conducted in the United States, Asia, and Pacific island countries, Milton Diamond (1993) estimates that only about 5% of men and 2% to 3% of women across different cultures have engaged in sexual activity with someone of their own gender on at least one occasion since adolescence. No cross-cultural studies show rates of sexual activity with people of the same gender to reach Kinsey's often-cited figure of 10% of predominant or exclusive sexual behavior with partners of one's own gender. Diamond also finds fewer people to have a bisexual orientation than a gay male or lesbian sexual orientation.

Research in the United States, Britain, France, and Denmark finds that about 3% of men surveyed *identify* themselves as gay (Hamer et al., 1993; Laumann et al., 1994). About 2% of the U.S. women surveyed *identify* themselves as having a lesbian sexual orientation (Janus & Janus, 1993; Laumann and others, 1994). Surveys in the United States, Britain, and France find that larger numbers of men (5% to 11%) and women (2% to 4%) report *engaging in sexual behavior* with members of their own gender within the past five years (Sell et al., 1995). Surveys show that still larger numbers of men (8% to 9%) and women (8% to 12%) report some *sexual attraction* to members of their own gender, but no sexual interaction since the age of 15 (Sell et al., 1995).

Sex surveys reveal the percentages only of people *willing to admit* to certain behaviors or sexual orientations (Cronin, 1993; Isay, 1993). "We can't count people who simply don't want to be counted" (Cronin, 1993). Surveys may omit gay people who hesitate to proclaim their sexual orientation because of social stigma or repression of their sexual feelings.

Keep in mind that the following factors affect survey results:

- The ways in which the questions are phrased (for example, do they look into sexual identity, sexual behavior, or sexual attraction—and over what period of time?)
- The social desirability of the professed behavior
- The gender of the interviewer
- The manner in which the survey was conducted, such as by means of personal interviews, phone calls, or written surveys
- The biases of respondents, such as volunteer bias

Challenges to the Kinsey Continuum   Although the Kinsey continuum has been widely adopted by sex researchers, it is not universally accepted. Kinsey believed that exclusive heterosexual and gay sexual orientations lay at opposite poles of one continuum. Therefore, the more heterosexual a person is, the less gay that person is, and vice versa (Sanders et al., 1990).

Viewing gay and heterosexual orientations as opposite poles of one continuum is akin to the traditional view of masculinity and femininity as opposite poles of one continuum, such that the more masculine one is, the less feminine, and vice versa. Viewing men and women as opposites has led to misunderstandings, even hostility, between the genders (Bem, 1993). As noted in Chapter 6, however, we may also regard masculinity and femininity as independent personality dimensions. Similarly, the view of gay people and heterosexuals as opposites has also led to misunderstandings and hostility (Katz, 1995). Yet these sexual orientations may also be separate dimensions, rather than polar opposites.

Psychologist Michael Storms (1980) suggests that gay and heterosexual orientations are independent dimensions. Thus, one can be high or low on both dimensions simultaneously. Storms (1980) suggests that there are separate dimensions of responsiveness to male–female stimulation (heteroeroticism) and sexual stimulation that involves someone of the same gender (homoeroticism), as shown in Figure 10.2 on page 268. According to this model, bisexuals are high in both dimensions, whereas people who are low in both are essentially asexual. According to Kinsey, bisexual individuals would be *less* responsive to stimulation by people of the other gender than heterosexual people are, but *more* responsive to stimulation by people of their own gender. According to the two-dimensional model, however, bisexual people may be as responsive to stimulation by people of the other gender as heterosexual people are, and as responsive to stimulation by people of their own gender as gay people are.

Fantasy as the Measure   Kinsey had argued that the content of erotic fantasies was an excellent gauge of sexual orientation. To test this formulation, Storms (1980) investigated the erotic fantasies of heterosexual, gay, and bisexual people. Kinsey might have predicted that bisexual individuals would have *fewer* heteroerotic fantasies than heterosexual people, and *more* homoerotic fantasies than heterosexual people. But Storms predicted that "bisexuals will report *as much* heteroerotic fantasy as heterosexual people and *as much* homoerotic fantasy as homosexuals" (p. 786).

Storms found that heterosexual students reported significantly more fantasies about the other gender than their own gender. Gay students reported more frequent fantasies

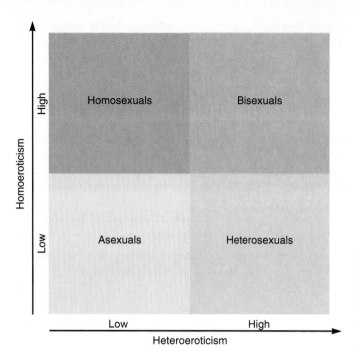

Figure 10.2. Heterosexuality and Homosexuality as Separate Dimensions. According to this model, homosexuality and heterosexuality are independent dimensions. One can thus be high or low on both dimensions at the same time. Most people are high in one dimension. Bisexuals are high in both dimensions. People who are low in both are considered *asexual*.

about their own gender. Bisexuals, as predicted, reported a high level of both kinds of fantasies. Gay students were also more likely to have fantasies about the other gender than heterosexual students were to have fantasies about their own gender. Given the stigma attached to homosexuality, it may be that heterosexual people are less likely to admit to fantasies about their own gender (even to themselves). It may also be that gay males and lesbians are influenced by the media and the culture at large, which, of course, continually portray socially desirable male–female interactions.

Whatever the reasons, Storms did find that many bisexual people show a high level of sexual interest, as measured by erotic fantasies, in both men and women. Thus, it may be that sexual interest in the other gender and in one's own gender are independent dimensions rather than opposite poles of one continuum. Yet most sex researchers continue to use the Kinsey scale, or some derivative of it, for classifying sexual orientation (Sanders et al., 1990).

Bisexuality

To me, I never felt like I had a stronger attraction to men or women. I didn't have a problem identifying myself as gay, but I knew that wasn't the whole picture.

(A 29-year-old social worker from North Carolina who fell in love with a woman and then had a sexual relationship with his male roommate)

I don't limit myself to a guy or a girl. Whoever comes into my life, if we hit it off, great. That's happened with a lot of people I know. They'll say, "Guess what happened last night." It's very accepted.

(A 22-year-old political science major)

She finally came out of the closet and said, "Mom, there's this girl and she's the most gorgeous girl you've ever seen." I said, "You're only for girls?" She said: "No, it's not just the girls. I can see a really good-looking guy, too."

(The mother of a 19-year-old woman who uses a computer bulletin board to meet other bisexuals)

(Adapted from Gabriel, 1995b)

Bisexual people are sexually attracted to both males and females. Many bisexual people have somewhat stronger attraction to one gender than the other, yet they remain bisexual (Weinberg et al., 1994). Kinsey and his colleagues considered people rated as 3s to be bisexual (see Figure 10.1).

Depending on how one defines bisexuality, perhaps 1% to 4% of the population is bisexual. About 1% of the people (0.8% of the men and 0.9% of the women) surveyed in the NHSLS study (Laumann et al., 1994) reported having a bisexual *identity.* However, about 4% (3.9% of the men and 4.1% of the women) reported that they were sexually attracted to both women and men.

Bisexual people are sometimes said to "swing both ways," or to be "A/C-D/C" (as in "alternating current" and "direct current"). Some gay people (and some heterosexual people) believe that claims to bisexuality are a "cop-out" that people use to deny being gay. Perhaps they fear leaving their spouses or "coming out" (declaring their gay male or lesbian sexual orientation publicly). Others view bisexuality as a form of sexual experimentation with people of one's own gender by people who are predominantly heterosexual. But many avowed bisexual people disagree. They report that they can maintain erotic interests in, and romantic relationships with, members of both genders. Some authors (e.g., Garber, 1995; Weinberg et al., 1994) insist that bisexuality is an authentic sexual orientation and not simply a "cover" for a gay male or lesbian sexual orientation.

Some bisexual people follow lifestyles that permit them to satisfy their dual inclinations. Others feel pressured by heterosexual and gay people alike to commit themselves one way or the other (Garber, 1995; Weinberg et al., 1994). Some gay people also mask their sexual orientation by adopting a bisexual lifestyle. That is, they get married but also enter into clandestine sexual liaisons with members of their own gender.

~ *Reflections* ~

- Agree or disagree with the following statement, and support your answer: Gay males and lesbians should be permitted to adopt children.
- We prefer to use the terms *gay males* and *lesbians* rather than *homosexuals.* Do you endorse the use of our terminology? Why, or why not?
- Does it make sense to you to distinguish between one's sexual orientation and one's sexual behavior? For example, do you believe that males may engage in sexual activity with other males and maintain a heterosexual orientation? Why, or why not?

Perspectives on Gay Male and Lesbian Sexual Orientations

Gay male and lesbian sexual orientations have existed throughout history. Attitudes toward them have varied widely. They have been tolerated in some societies, openly encouraged in others, but condemned in most (Bullough, 1990). In this section we review historical and other perspectives on gay male and lesbian sexual orientations.

Historical Perspectives

In Western culture, few sexual practices have met with such widespread censure as sexual activities with members of one's own gender. Throughout much of history, male–male and female–female sexual behavior were deemed sinful and criminal—an outrage against God and humanity. Within the Judeo-Christian tradition, male–male sexual activity was regarded as a sin so vile that no one dared speak its name. Our legal system, grounded in this religious tradition, maintains criminal penalties for sexual practices commonly associated with male–male and female–female sex, such as anal and oral sex. Much of the criminalization of male–male and female–female sex has been directed against men (Bullough, 1990; Katz, 1995).

Jews and Christians have traditionally referred to male–male sexual activity as the sin of Sodom. Hence the origins of the term *sodomy,* which generally alludes to anal intercourse (and sometimes to oral–genital contact). According to the Book of Genesis, the city of Sodom was destroyed by God. Yet it is unclear what behavior incurred God's wrath.

Pope Gregory III was not ambiguous, however, in his eighth-century account of the city's obliteration as a punishment for sexual activity with members of one's own gender.

The Book of Leviticus was also clear in its condemnation:

> If a man lies with a man as with a woman, both of them have committed an abomination; they shall be put to death, their blood is upon them.

(Leviticus 20:13)

Sexual activity with members of one's own gender was not the only sexual act considered sinful by the early Christians. Any nonprocreative sexual act was considered sinful, even within marriage. With the fall of the Roman Empire, the influence of Christianity spread across western Europe. Christian beliefs were eventually encoded into secular law. By the late Middle Ages, most civil statutes throughout Western Europe contained penalties for nonprocreative sexual acts involving the discharge of semen, including oral or anal sex, masturbation, male–male sexual behavior, and bestiality (Boswell, 1990). Male–male and female–female sexual practices continue to be condemned by most Christian and Jewish denominations, and by Islam.

The Roman Catholic Church draws a distinction between a gay male or lesbian sexual orientation on the one hand, and male–male or female–female sexual behavior on the other, however (Donoghue, 1995; Sullivan, 1995). The behavior is the sin, not the orientation. The church sees sin as a temporary state from which a sinner, including a gay male or lesbian sinner, can be freed by behavioral change, contrition, and repentance.

Cross-Cultural Perspectives

Male–male sexual behavior has been practiced in many preliterate societies. In their review of the literature on 76 preliterate societies, Ford and Beach (1951) found that in 49 societies (64%), male–male sexual interactions were viewed as normal and deemed socially acceptable for some members of the group. The other 27 societies (36%) had sanctions against male–male sexual behavior. Nevertheless, male–male sexual activity persisted. In another cross-cultural analysis, Broude and Greene (1976) found that male–male sexual behavior was present but uncommon in 41% of a sample of 70 of the world's non-European societies. It was rare or absent in 59% of these societies. Broude and Greene also found evidence of societal disapproval and punishment of male–male sexual activity in 41% of a sample of 42 societies for which information was available.

Sexual behavior between adult males appears to be more common in societies that highly value female virginity before marriage and segregate young men and women (Davenport, 1977). Such factors may increase juvenile male–male sexual experimentation, which may then persist into adulthood.

Some societies permit or require some forms of male–male sexual activity. In some societies, sexual activities are acceptable between older and younger males or between adolescents, but not between adult men. At the turn of the century, the Swans of North Africa expected all juvenile males to engage in sexual relations with older men. Fathers arranged for unmarried sons to be given to older men. Almost all men were reported to have had such sexual relationships as boys. Later, between the ages of 16 and 20, they all married women.

Sexual activities between males are sometimes limited to rites that mark the young male's initiation into manhood. In some preliterate societies, semen is believed to boost strength and virility. Older males thus transmit semen to younger males through oral or anal sexual activities. Among the Sambian people of New Guinea, a tribe of warlike headhunters, 9- to 12-year-old males leave their parents' households and live in a "clubhouse" with other prepubertal and adolescent males. There they undergo sexual rites of passage. To acquire the fierce manhood of the headhunter, they perform fellatio on older males and drink "men's milk" (semen) (Herdt, 1981; Money, 1990; Stoller & Herdt, 1985). The initiate is enjoined to ingest as much semen as he can, "as if it were breast milk or food" (Herdt, 1981, p. 235). Ingestion of semen is believed to give rise to puberty. Following puberty, adolescents are fellated by younger males (Baldwin & Baldwin, 1989). By the age of 19, however, young men are expected to take brides and enter exclusively male–female sexual relationships.

These practices of Sambian culture might seem to suggest that the sexual orientations of males are fluid and malleable. The practices involve *behavior,* however, and not *sexual orientation.* Male–male sexual behavior among Sambians takes place within a cultural context that bears little resemblance to consensual male–male sexual activity in Western society. The prepubertal Sambian male does not *seek* sexual liaisons with other males. He is removed from his home, by force if necessary, and thrust into male–male sexual encounters by older males (Baldwin & Baldwin, 1989).

Little is known about female–female sexual activity in non-Western cultures. Evidence of female–female sexual behavior was found by Ford and Beach in only 17 of the 76 societies they studied. Perhaps it was more difficult to acquire data about female sexuality. Perhaps female sexual behavior in general, not just sexual activity with other females, was more likely to be repressed. Of course, it is also possible that women are less likely than men to develop sexual interests in, or romantic relationships with, members of their own genders. Whatever the reasons, this cross-cultural evidence is consistent with data from our own culture. Here, too, males are more likely than females to develop sexual interests in, or romantic relationships with, members of their own genders (Katz, 1995; Laumann et al., 1994).

Cross-Species Perspectives

Many of us have observed pets and other animals engaging in sexual behaviors that resemble male–male or female–female contacts among humans, such as attempting to mount others of their own sex. We should be careful, though, about drawing comparisons between the behavior of people and lower animals. Superficially similar behaviors may not have the same function in other species.

A male baboon may present his rear and allow himself to be mounted by another male. This behavior may resemble anal intercourse among gay men. Is the behavior sexually motivated, however? Mounting behavior among male baboons may represent a type of dominance ritual in which lower-ranking males adopt a submissive (feminine) posture to ward off attack from dominant males (Nadler, 1990). (Some male–male acts among people also involve themes of dominance, as in the case of a dominant male prisoner forcing a less dominant one to submit to anal intercourse.) In other cases, male baboons may be seeking favors or protection from more dominant males (Nadler, 1990). Among juvenile animals, male–male behaviors may also be a form of play. Females may also attempt to mount other females, but here too, the motivations may not be the same as those of humans.

Sexual motivation appears to play a role in some, but not all, male–male and female–female sexual interactions among animals. Fellatio and anal intercourse to ejaculation among juvenile male orangutans may be a case in point, as may be thrusting by one adult female gorilla against another. Some male–male encounters among rhesus monkeys also appear to be sexually motivated. However, researchers have not found evidence among nonhuman primates of the prolonged, exclusive male–male sexual activity found among humans that occurs when male–female opportunities are available.

Attitudes Toward Sexual Orientation in Contemporary Society

Toni, a 20-year-old lesbian college student, was incredulous that her parents believed she had *chosen* her sexual orientation. They saw her lesbianism as linked to the general rebelliousness that had been stirred by attending a school known for its "radical" image. Toni was infuriated that they believed that she would "get over" her lesbian sexual orientation once she decided to accept adult responsibilities.

(The Authors' Files)

Negative attitudes toward gay people pervade our society (Katz, 1995). A national survey of men of ages 15 to 19 showed that 9 of 10 felt that sex between men was "disgusting." Three of five could not even see themselves being friends with a gay man (Marsiglio, 1993b).

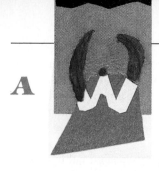

A WORLD OF DIVERSITY

ETHNICITY AND SEXUAL ORIENTATION: A MATTER OF BELONGING

Lesbians and gay men frequently suffer the slings and arrows of an outraged society. Because of societal prejudices, it is difficult for many young people to come to terms with an emerging lesbian or gay male sexual orientation. You might assume that people who have been subjected to prejudice and discrimination—members of ethnic minority groups in the United States—would be more tolerant of a lesbian or gay male sexual orientation. However, according to psychologist Beverly Greene (1994) of St. John's University, such an assumption might not be warranted.

In an article that addresses the experiences of lesbians and gay men from ethnic minority groups, Greene (1994) notes that it is difficult to generalize about ethnic groups in the United States. For example, African Americans may find their cultural origins in the tribes of West Africa, but they have also been influenced by Christianity and the local subcultures of their North American towns and cities. Native Americans represent hundreds of tribal groups, languages, and cultures. By and large, however, a lesbian or gay male sexual orientation is rejected by ethnic minority groups in the United States. Lesbians and gay males are pressured to keep their sexual orientations a secret or to move to communities where they can live openly without sanction.

Within traditional Hispanic-American culture, the family is the primary social unit. Men are expected to support and defend the family, and women are expected to be submissive, respectable, and deferential to men (Morales, 1992). Because women are expected to remain virgins until marriage, men sometimes engage in male–male sexual behavior without considering themselves gay (Greene, 1994). Hispanic-American culture frequently denies the sexuality of women. Thus, women who label themselves lesbians are doubly condemned—because they are lesbians and because they are confronting others with their sexuality. Because lesbians are independent of men, most Hispanic-American heterosexual people view Hispanic-American lesbians as threats to the tradition of male dominance (Trujillo, 1991).

Asian-American cultures emphasize respect for one's elders, obedience to parents, and sharp distinctions in masculine and feminine gender roles (Chan, 1992). The topic of sex is generally taboo within the family. Asian Americans, like Hispanic Americans, tend to assume that sex is unimportant to women. Women are also considered to be less important than men. Open admission of a lesbian or gay male sexual orientation is seen as a rejection of one's traditional cultural roles and a threat to the continuity of the family line (Chan, 1992; Garnets & Kimmel, 1991).

Because many African-American men have had difficulty finding jobs, gender roles among African Americans have been more flexible than those found among white Americans

Seventy-five percent of respondents to a 1987 survey felt that sexual relations between members of the same gender are "always wrong" (Davis & Smith, 1987). Forty percent would bar gay people from teaching in a college or university. A 1992 national Gallup poll found that the great majority (78%) of Americans favor equal employment opportunities for gay people ("Job rights," 1992). Two out of three Americans favor health insurance and inheritance rights for gay spouses. Yet fewer than one in three favors legally sanctioned gay marriages. Only about a third supported the right of gay couples to adopt children. Americans were about equally split on the issues of whether gay people should be permitted to teach in elementary schools or become members of the clergy.

Some of those who would bar gay people from teaching and other activities believe that gay people, given the chance, will seduce and recruit children into a gay lifestyle. Such beliefs have been used to prevent gay couples from becoming adoptive or foster parents and to deny them custody or visitation rights to their own children, following divorce. Some people who would bar gay people from interactions with children fear that the children will be molested. Yet more than 90% of cases of child molestation involve heterosexual male assailants (Gelles & Cornell, 1985; Gordon & Snyder, 1989). Nor are children who are reared or taught by gay men or lesbians more likely to become gay themselves. One study found that 36 of 37 children who were reared by lesbian or transsexual couples developed a heterosexual orientation (Green, 1978). Nor has it been shown that children reared by gay parents are more likely to encounter gender identity conflicts (Patterson, 1995).

and most other ethnic minority groups (Greene, 1994). Nevertheless, the African-American community appears to strongly reject gay men and lesbians, pressuring them to remain secretive about their sexual orientations (Gomez & Smith, 1990; Poussaint, 1990). Greene (1994) hypothesizes a number of factors that influence African Americans to be hostile toward lesbians and gay men. One is strong allegiance to Christian beliefs and biblical scripture. Another is internalization of the dominant culture's stereotyping of African Americans as highly sexual beings. That is, many African Americans may feel a need to assert their sexual "normalcy" or even a sense of sexual superiority.

Prior to the European conquest, sex may not have been discussed openly by Native Americans, but sex was generally seen as a natural part of life. Individuals who incorporated both traditional feminine and masculine styles were generally accepted and even admired. The influence of the religions of colonists led to greater rejection of lesbians and gay men, and

pressure to move off the reservation to the big city (Greene, 1994). Native-American lesbians and gay men, like Asian-American lesbians and gay men, thus often feel doubly removed from their families.

If any generalization is possible, it may be that lesbians and gay men find more of a sense of belonging in the gay community than in their ethnic communities.

A Matter of Belonging. Gay couples who are members of ethnic minority groups often report that they feel more a part of the gay community than of their ethnic group.

Homophobia
A cluster of negative attitudes and feelings toward gay people, including intolerance, hatred, and fear. (From Greek roots meaning "fear" [of members of the] "same" [gender].)

Gay bashing
Violence against homosexuals.

Homophobia **Homophobia** takes many forms, including
- use of derogatory names (such as *queer, faggot,* and *dyke*).
- telling disparaging "queer jokes."
- barring gay people from housing, employment, or social opportunities.
- taunting (verbal abuse).
- **gay bashing** (physical abuse).

Homophobia derives from root words meaning "fear of homosexuals." Although homophobia is more common among heterosexual people, gay people themselves can be homophobic. Homophobia among gay people is called *internalized homophobia*. It is believed to stem from the internalization of negative societal attitudes toward gay people (Gonsiorck, 1988).

Although some psychologists link homophobia to fears of a gay male or lesbian sexual orientation within oneself, homophobic attitudes may also be embedded within a cluster of stereotypical gender-role attitudes toward family life (Kerns & Fine, 1994). These attitudes support male dominance and the belief that it is natural and appropriate for women to sacrifice for their husbands and children (Katz, 1995; Marsiglio, 1993b). People who have a strong stake in maintaining stereotypical gender roles may feel more readily threatened by the existence of the gay male or lesbian sexual orientation, since gay people appear to confuse or reverse these roles.

Homophobic attitudes are more common among males who identify with a traditional male gender role and those who hold a fundamentalist religious orientation (Kerns & Fine, 1994; Marsiglio, 1993b). Similarly, researchers find that college students who hold a conservative political orientation tend to be more accepting of negative attitudes toward gay people than are liberal students (Lottes & Kuriloff, 1992). Another university sample found male students to be more homophobic than women in their attitudes (Kunkel & Temple, 1992).

Generally speaking, heterosexual men are relatively less tolerant of gay people than are heterosexual women (Kerns & Fine, 1994; Seltzer, 1992; Whitley & Kite, 1995). Perhaps some heterosexual men are threatened by the possibility of discovering male–male sexual impulses within themselves (Freiberg, 1995). Consistent with this view, heterosexual males tend to hold more negative attitudes toward gay men than toward lesbians (Kite, 1992).

In a study conducted by your second author (Nevid, 1983), college men and women were shown explicit films of either male–male, female–female, or male–female sexual activity. Their emotional responses and their attitudes toward gay people were measured. The male–male and female–female films elicited more negative emotional states—more anger, anxiety, and depression—in both genders than did the male–female films. However, negative *attitudes* toward gay people were exacerbated by exposure to the films only in men, and only in those men who viewed films of male–male sexual activity. Nevid surmised that men are more sensitive to cues of the threat of a gay male sexual orientation. Men are more likely than women to respond negatively to displays of sexual interactions between members of their own gender. Such displays harden their attitudes toward gay people.

Gay Bashing and the AIDS Epidemic   Although strides toward social acceptance of gay people have been made since Kinsey's day, the advent of AIDS has added fuel to the fire of hatred and prejudice. When AIDS first appeared, it primarily struck the gay male community. Some people in the larger society believed that the epidemic was a God-sent plague intended to punish gay people for sinful behavior.

The advent of the epidemic has been accompanied by a dramatic rise in the incidence of gay bashing (Freiberg, 1995). Perhaps the epidemic has served as a pretext for some people to attack gay males, whom they blame for spreading the disease (Katz, 1995). Violent incidents against gay people rose by an average of 42% in 1990 over the previous year in Boston, Chicago, Los Angeles, Minneapolis/St. Paul, New York City, and San Francisco (Brozan, 1991). Anti-gay incidents in these cities included harassment, physical assault, robbery, arson, extortion, vandalism, bomb threats, and homicide.

Gay bashing also occurs on college campuses. A large percentage (77%) of 121 lesbian and gay male undergraduate students in one survey at Pennsylvania State University reported they had been verbally insulted. Nearly 1 in 3 (31%) reported being chased or followed (D'Augelli, 1992a). Nearly 20% said they had been physically assaulted. Most of the victimizers were fellow students. Few of these incidents were reported to the authorities.

Students, too, tend to hold gay men more responsible for behaviors that put themselves at risk of contracting AIDS. One study found that students assigned a greater amount of blame to a hypothetical person who had contracted AIDS when the person was identified as a gay male than when the person was identified as a heterosexual male (Anderson, 1992).

Ironically, the percentage of gay men who account for new cases of AIDS has been steadily declining (see Chapter 17). By contrast, the percentages of persons who contract AIDS by sharing contaminated hypodermic syringes while injecting drugs, and by male–female sexual intercourse, have been on the upswing.

Sexual Orientation and the Law   During the past generation, gay people have organized effective political groups to fight discrimination and to overturn the sodomy laws that have traditionally targeted them. Despite their success, sodomy laws are still on the books in about half of our states. Sodomy laws prohibit "unnatural" sexual acts, even between consenting adults. A gay male or lesbian sexual orientation is not illegal in itself. However, certain sexual acts which many gay people (and heterosexual people) practice, such as anal intercourse and oral–genital contact, fall under the legal definition of sodomy in many states. Sodomy laws also typically prohibit sexual contacts with animals. Although sodomy laws are usually intended to apply equally to all adults, married or unmarried, heterosexual or gay, the vast majority of prosecutions have been directed against gay people.

A 1986 Supreme Court decision (*Hardwick v. Bowers*) let stand a Georgia sodomy law that makes oral–genital and anal–genital sexual contact crimes punishable by up to 20 years in prison. Whether the acts occur between consenting adults is irrelevant. The decision was a blow to gay rights organizations, which had looked to the Supreme Court to overturn sodomy laws nationwide. Instead, the court held that states retain the right to enact sodomy laws and impose criminal penalties.

Many other countries, including Mexico, Holland, Italy, Spain, England, France, and the Scandinavian countries have decriminalized male–male and female–female sexual activity (Carrera, 1981). In Canada, a consensual sexual act is prosecutable under sodomy laws only if one of the participants is under 21 years of age or the act is performed in public.

Gay Activism   Nowhere in the United States have gay people been more politically effective than in San Francisco. They are well represented on the city police force and in other public agencies. The coming out of many gay people, and their flocking to more tolerant urban centers, have rendered them formidable political forces in these locales.

The Mattachine Society, named after gay medieval court jesters, was the first powerful gay rights organization. At first, membership was kept secret to protect members' social standing in the community. Today, however, members' names are published, and many heterosexual supporters are listed in their ranks. Founded in Los Angeles in 1950, the Mattachine Society now has chapters in most metropolitan areas. The society publishes the *Mattachine Newsletter* and *Homosexual Citizen.* Another newsletter, the *Advocate,* has become the nation's best-known gay newsletter.

The largest lesbian organization is the Daughters of Bilitis, named after the Greek courtesan who was loved by the lesbian poet Sappho. Founded in 1956, the group provides a forum for sharing social experiences and pursuing equal rights. The organization's newsletter is the *Ladder.*

The AIDS epidemic has had a profound effect on the political agenda of gay rights organizations. These organizations have mounted a vigorous effort to combat the AIDS epidemic on several fronts:

1. To lobby for increased funding for AIDS research and treatment
2. To educate the gay and wider communities of the dangers associated with high-risk sexual behavior
3. To encourage gay men and others to adopt safer sex practices, including the use of latex condoms (see Chapter 17)
4. To protect the civil rights of people with AIDS and carriers of the virus that causes AIDS (the *human immunodeficiency virus [HIV]*) with respect to employment, housing, medical and dental treatment, and medical insurance
5. To provide counseling and support services for people with AIDS and those infected with HIV

Outing
The revelation of the identities of gay people by other gay people. The method is intended to combat discrimination against gay people by forcing individuals out of the closet and into the fray.

Some gay rights organizations work within the mainstream political process. Others, such as the militant *Act-Up* organization, have taken a more strident and confrontational stance to secure more funding for AIDS research and treatment.

Some militant gay groups have resorted to the method of **outing** to combat discrimination. In this method, gay people unmask other gay people without their consent, forcing them "out of the closet." Many gay people have responded vehemently to this practice. They term it a "gay witch hunt."

Stereotypes and Sexual Behavior   Among heterosexual people, sexual aggressiveness is linked to the masculine gender role. Sexual passivity is linked to the feminine role. Some heterosexual people assume (often erroneously) that in gay male and lesbian relationships, one partner consistently assumes the masculine role in sexual relations, and the other, the feminine.

Gay Rights. Gay men, lesbians, and those who care about them have participated in demonstrations demanding equal access to housing, jobs, and other opportunities.

Butch
A lesbian who assumes a traditional masculine gender role.

Femme
A lesbian who assumes a traditional feminine gender role.

Many gay couples vary the active and passive roles, however. Among gay male couples, for example, roles in anal intercourse (*inserter* versus *insertee*) and in fellatio are often reversed. Contrary to popular assumptions, sexual behavior between lesbians seldom reflects distinct **butch–femme** gender roles. Most lesbians report providing and receiving oral–genital stimulation. Typically, partners alternate roles or simultaneously perform and receive oral stimulation. Many gay people claim that the labels of *masculine* and *feminine* only represent the "straight community's" efforts to pigeonhole them in terms "straights" can understand.

Biological Perspectives

Is sexual orientation an *inborn* trait that is transmitted genetically, like eye color or height? Does it reflect hormonal influences? Biological perspectives focus on the role of genetics and hormonal influences in shaping sexual orientation.

Monozygotic (MZ) twins
Twins who develop from the same fertilized ovum; identical twins.

Dizygotic (DZ) twins
Twins who develop from different fertilized ova; fraternal twins.

Concordance
Agreement.

Genetics and Sexual Orientation   Considerable evidence exists that gay male and lesbian sexual orientations run in families (Bailey et al., 1993; Pillard, 1990). In one study, for example, 22% of the brothers of a sample of 51 predominantly gay men were either gay or bisexual themselves. This is nearly four times the proportion expected in the general population (Pillard & Weinrich, 1986). Although such evidence is consistent with a genetic explanation, families also share a common environment.

Twin studies also shed light on the possible role of heredity (Rose, 1995). **Monozygotic (MZ) twins,** or identical twins, develop from a single fertilized ovum and share 100% of their heredity. **Dizygotic (DZ) twins,** or fraternal twins, develop from two fertilized ova. Like other brothers and sisters, DZ twins share only 50% of their heredity. Thus if a gay male or lesbian sexual orientation were transmitted genetically, it should be found about twice as often among identical twins of gay people as among fraternal twins. Since MZ and DZ twins who are reared together share similar environmental influences, differences in the degree of **concordance** for a given trait between the types of twin pairs are further indicative of genetic origins.

Several studies have identified gay men who had either identical (MZ) or fraternal (DZ) twin brothers in order to examine the prevalences of a gay male sexual orientation in their twin brothers (Rose, 1995). In an early study, Kallmann (1952) found 100% concordance for a gay male sexual orientation among the identical twin brothers of gay men, as compared to 12% concordance for fraternal twin pairs in which one of the brothers was identified as gay. This seemed strong evidence indeed of genetic factors in sexual orientation. However, later studies have found much lower concordance rates among MZ twins (Bailey & Pillard, 1991; Eckert et al., 1986; McConaghy & Blaszczynski, 1980). These studies found many instances of MZ twins in which one identical twin member was gay and the other in the pair was not. Still, MZ twins do appear to have a higher concordance rate for a gay male sexual orientation than DZ twins. Bailey and Pillard (1991) reported a 52% concordance rate among MZ twin pairs versus a 22% rate among DZ twin pairs in their sample. In another study, researchers reported a concordance rate for a gay sexual orientation of 66% in MZ twins, as compared to 30% among DZ twins (Whitam et al., 1993).

Bear in mind that MZ twins are more likely to be dressed alike and treated alike than DZ twins. Thus, their greater concordance for a gay sexual orientation may at least in part reflect environmental factors. The greater concordance between MZ twins may only signify that MZ twins are likely to react more similarly than DZ twins to the same *environmental* influences (Bancroft, 1990).

Researchers at the National Cancer Institute have found evidence linking a region on the X sex chromosome to a gay male sexual orientation (Hamer et al., 1993). The researchers found that gay males in a sample of 114 gay men were more likely to have gay male relatives on their mothers' side of the family than would be expected, based on the prevalence of a gay male sexual orientation in the general population. Yet they did not have a greater than expected number of gay male relatives on their paternal side of the family. This pattern of inheritance is consistent with genetic traits, like hemophilia, that are linked to the X sex chromosome, which men receive from their mothers.

The researchers then went on to examine the X sex chromosome in 40 pairs of gay male, non-twin brothers. In 33 of the pairs, the brothers had identical DNA markers on the end tip of the X chromosome. For brothers overall in the general population, about half would be expected to have inherited this chromosomal structure. It is suspected, therefore, that this chromosomal region may hold a gene that predisposes men to a gay male sexual orientation.

The researchers cautioned that they had not found a particular gene linked to sexual orientation, just a general location of where the gene may be found. Nor do scientists know how such a gene, or combination of genes, might account for sexual orientation. Perhaps a particular gene or genes govern the development of proteins that sculpt parts of the brain in ways that favor the development of a gay male sexual orientation. On the other hand, a number of the gay brothers, 7 of the 40 pairs, did *not* share the chromosomal marker.

Sexologist John Money (1994) agrees that genetic factors may play a role in the development of sexual orientation. However, genetic factors do not fully govern sexual orientation. Most researchers believe that sexual orientation is affected by a complex interplay of biological and psychosocial influences (Barlow & Durand, 1995).

Hormonal Influences and Sexual Orientation

Sex hormones strongly influence the mating behavior of other species (Crews, 1994). Researchers have thus looked into possible hormonal factors in determining sexual orientation in humans.

Activating effects
Those effects of sex hormones that influence the level of the sex drive but not sexual orientation.

Testosterone is essential to male sexual differentiation. Thus, the levels of testosterone and its by-products in the blood and urine have been suspected as a possible influence of sexual orientation, at least in males. Research has failed to connect sexual orientation in either gender with differences in the levels of either male or female sex hormones in adulthood (Friedman & Downey, 1994). In adulthood, testosterone appears to have **activating effects.** That is, it affects the intensity of sexual desire, but not the preference for partners of the same or the other gender (Whalen et al., 1990).

What of the possible *prenatal* effects of sex hormones? Experiments have been performed in which pregnant rats were given antiandrogen drugs that block the effects of testosterone. When the drugs were given during critical periods in which the fetuses' brains were becoming sexually differentiated, male offspring were likely to show feminine mating patterns as adults (Ellis & Ames, 1987). The adult males became receptive to mounting attempts by other males and failed to mount females.

Do prenatal sex hormones play a similar role in determining sexual orientation in people? There is suggestive evidence. For example, Meyer-Bahlburg and his colleagues (1995) interviewed groups of women exposed prenatally to DES—a synthetic estrogen. They found that these women were more likely to be rated as lesbian or bisexual than women who were not exposed to DES. We do know that the genitals of gay people differentiate prenatally in accord with their chromosomal gender (Whalen et al., 1990). It remains possible that imbalances in prenatal sex hormones may cause brain tissue to be sexually differentiated in one direction even though the genitals are differentiated in the other (Collaer & Hines, 1995).

Truth OR Fiction?
REVISITED

It is not true that gay males and lesbians suffer from hormonal imbalances. Gay males and lesbians do not show imbalances of sex hormones in adulthood. However, the role of prenatal hormonal factors in the development of sexual orientation remains an open question. ■

The Structure of the Brain   Evidence suggests that there may be structural differences between the brains of heterosexual and gay men. In 1991, Simon LeVay, a neurobiologist at the Salk Institute in La Jolla, California, carried out autopsies on the brains of 35 AIDS victims—19 gay men and 16 (presumably) heterosexual men. He found that a segment of the hypothalamus—specifically, a cell group called the third interstitial nucleus of the anterior hypothalamus—in the brains of the gay men was less than half the size of the same segment in the heterosexual men. The same brain segment was larger in the brain tissues of heterosexual men than in brain tissues obtained from a comparison group of 6 presumably heterosexual women. No significant differences in size were found between the brain tissues of the gay men and the women, however.

LeVay's findings are intriguing, but they are preliminary. We do not know, for example, whether the structural differences found by LeVay are innate. Nor should LeVay's findings be taken to mean that biology is destiny. As Richard Nakamura, a scientist with the National Institute of Mental Health, commented, "This [LeVay's findings] shouldn't be taken to mean that you're automatically [gay] if you have a structure of one size versus a structure of another size" (Angier, 1991).

The belief that sexual orientation is innate or inborn has many adherents—both in the scientific and general communities. Support for the possible influences of prenatal hormonal factors in "sculpting" the brain in a masculine or feminine direction is based largely on animal studies, however. Direct evidence with people is lacking. We must also be careful in generalizing results from other species to our own.

Psychological Perspectives

Do family relationships play a role in the origins of sexual orientation? What are the effects of childhood sexual experiences? Psychoanalytic theory and learning theory provide two of the major psychological approaches to understanding the origins of sexual orientation.

Polymorphously perverse
In psychoanalytic theory, being receptive to all forms of sexual stimulation.

Displacement
In psychoanalytic theory, a defense mechanism that allows one to transfer unacceptable wishes or desires onto more appropriate or less threatening objects.

Castration anxiety
In psychoanalytic theory, a man's fear that his genitals will be removed. Castration anxiety is an element of the Oedipus complex and is implicated in the directionality of erotic interests.

Psychoanalytic Views   Sigmund Freud, the originator of psychoanalytic theory, believed that children enter the world **polymorphously perverse.** That is, prior to internalizing social inhibitions, children are open to all forms of sexual stimulation. However, through proper resolution of the Oedipus complex, a boy will forsake his incestuous desires for his mother and come to identify with his father. As a result, his erotic attraction to his mother will eventually be transferred, or **displaced,** onto more appropriate *female* partners. A girl, through proper resolution of her Electra complex, will identify with her mother and seek erotic stimulation from men when she becomes sexually mature.

In Freud's view, a gay male or lesbian sexual orientation results from failure to successfully resolve the Oedipus complex by identifying with the parent of the same gender. In men, faulty resolution of the Oedipus complex is most likely to result from the so-called classic pattern of an emotionally "close-binding" mother and a "detached–hostile" father. A boy reared in such a family may come to identify with his mother and even to "transform himself into her" (Freud, 1922/1959, p. 40). He may thus become effeminate and develop sexual interests in men.

Freud believed that the mechanism of unresolved **castration anxiety** plays a role in a gay male sexual orientation. By the time the Oedipus complex takes effect, the boy will have learned from self-stimulation that he can obtain sexual pleasure from his penis. In his youthful fantasies, he associates this pleasure with mental images of his mother. He is also likely to have learned that females do not possess a penis. Somewhere along the line the psychoanalyst theorizes that the boy may also have been warned that his penis will be removed if he plays with himself. From all this, the boy may surmise that females—including his mother—once had penises, but that they were removed.

During the throes of the Oedipus complex, the boy unconsciously comes to fear that his father, his rival in love for the mother, will retaliate by removing the organ that the boy has come to associate with sexual pleasure. His fear causes him to repress his sexual desire for his mother and to identify with the potential aggressor—his father. The boy thus overcomes his castration anxiety and is headed along the path of adult heterosexuality.

If the Oedipus complex is not successfully resolved, castration anxiety may persist. When sexually mature, the man will not be able to tolerate sex with women. Their lack of a penis will arouse unconscious castration anxiety within himself. According to psychoanalytic theory, the boy may unconsciously associate the vagina with teeth, or other sharp instruments, and be unable to perform sexually with a woman.

The Electra complex in little girls follows a somewhat different course. Freud believed that little girls become envious of boys' penises, since they lack their own. This concept of **penis envy** was one of Freud's most controversial beliefs. In Freud's view, jealousy leads little girls to resent their mothers, whom they blame for their anatomic "deficiency," and to turn from their mothers to their fathers as sexual objects. They now desire to possess the father, because the father's penis provides what they lack. But incestuous desires bring the girl into competition with her mother. Motivated by fear that her mother will withdraw her love if the desires persist, the girl normally represses them and identifies with her mother. She then develops traditional feminine interests and eventually seeks erotic stimulation from men. She supplants her childhood desire for a penis with a desire to marry a man and bear children. The baby, emitted from between her legs, serves as the ultimate penis substitute.

A girl who does not resolve her penis envy in childhood may "manifest homosexuality, . . . exhibit markedly masculine traits in the conduct of her later life, choose a masculine vocation, and so on" (Freud, 1922/1959, p. 50). The residue of this unresolved complex is continued penis envy, the striving to become a man by acting like a man and seeking sexual satisfaction with women: lesbianism.

In Freud's view, a gay male or lesbian sexual orientation is one result of assuming the gender role normally taken up by the other gender. The gay male is expected to be effeminate; the lesbian, masculine. But, as noted in research into gender-typed behavior and sexual orientation, this stereotypical view of gay people is far from universal. Nor do the behaviors stereotypical of the other gender found in some adult gay men or women necessarily derive from Oedipal problems. Biological and other psychosocial factors may be involved.

A nagging problem of Freudian theory is that many of its concepts, such as castration anxiety and penis envy, are believed to operate at an unconscious level. As such, they lie beyond the scope of scientific observation and measurement. We cannot learn whether boys experience castration anxiety by asking them, since the theory claims that **repression** will keep such anxieties out of awareness. Nor can we directly learn about penis envy by interviewing girls.

Penis envy
In psychoanalytic theory, the girl's wish to have a penis.

Repression
In psychoanalytic theory, the most basic defense mechanism through which threatening ideas and impulses are ejected from conscious awareness.

Truth OR Fiction?
REVISITED

Actually, the idea that "castration anxiety" in gay males is aroused by heterosexual intercourse has not been scientifically demonstrated and remains speculative. ▪

Research on Psychoanalytic Theories of Sexual Orientation
Psychoanalysts—psychotherapists trained in the Freudian tradition—have researched sexual orientation largely through case studies. These studies have been carried out almost exclusively with gay males who were in therapy at the time.

In 1962, psychoanalyst Irving Bieber reported the results of questionnaires filled out by 77 psychiatrists on 106 gay male clients. In 1976, he reported the results of similar surveys of gay men in therapy.

Bieber claimed to find the "classic pattern" among gay males—their orientation was determined by having a dominant, "smothering" mother and a passive, detached father. As the clients described them, the mothers were overprotective, seductive, and jealous of their sons. The fathers were aloof, unaffectionate, and hostile toward them. The father, being detached, may have failed to buffer the close mother–son relationship. The mother's relationship with the father was typically disturbed, and the mother may have substituted a

Father–Son Relationship. Does the quality of the father-son relationship play a role, as some theorists suspect, in the development of homosexuality in men? According to a recent study, gay men perceived themselves as having been more distant from their fathers during childhood than did heterosexual men. The question is, why?

"close-binding" relationship with her son. This classic pattern was believed to result in the boy's developing a fear of sexual contacts with women. Though he would be unconscious of this dynamic, for him, any female partner would represent his mother. Desire for her would stir unconscious fears of retaliation by the father—that is, castration anxiety.

Bieber's findings may be criticized on several grounds:

1. The study participants were all in analysis, and many wanted to become heterosexual. Thus we cannot generalize the results to well-adjusted gay men.
2. The analysts may have chosen cases that confirmed their theoretical perspectives. Or perhaps over the course of analysis, clients were subtly encouraged to provide "evidence" that was consistent with psychoanalytic theory.
3. No clear evidence exists that gay males either fear or are repulsed by female genitalia. To the contrary, many gay males have successfully, and often repeatedly, engaged in coitus with women. They may simply not be sexually attracted to women or may find relationships with men more satisfying.
4. Many *heterosexual* men have family backgrounds that fit the classic pattern, and the families of many gay men do *not* fit the pattern. Researchers from the Kinsey Institute found that heterosexual males identified with their mothers as often as gay males did. A seductive mother–son relationship had little if any bearing on sexual orientation (Bell et al., 1981). Parent–child relations were only weakly linked to lesbianism as well.
5. Retrospective accounts of childhood relationships with parents are subject to gaps in memory and distortions.

More recent evidence has brought the issue of familial closeness between gay men and their parents into closer perspective. Richard Pillard and his colleagues (Pillard & Weinrich, 1986; Pillard, 1990) found that gay males described themselves as more distant from their fathers during childhood than did either heterosexual controls or the gay men's own heterosexual brothers. The gay men in their sample also reported greater closeness to their mothers. Still, the father's psychological distance from the son may have reflected the *son's* alienation from him, not the reverse. That is, the son may have been so attached to his mother, or so uninterested in traditional masculine activities, that he rebuffed paternal attempts to engage him in conventional father–son activities.

In sum, family characteristics may play a role in the development of sexual orientation. However, there is great variation among the families of gay males and lesbians. No single pattern applies in all cases (Isay, 1990). Family dynamics may be one of many factors that shape sexual orientation.

Learning Theories   Learning theorists agree with Freud that early experiences play an important role in the development of sexual orientation. They focus on the role of reinforcement of early patterns of sexual behavior, however, rather than on the resolution of unconscious conflicts. People generally repeat pleasurable activities and discontinue painful ones. Thus, people may learn to engage in sexual activity with people of their own gender if childhood sexual experimentation with them is connected with sexual pleasure.

If sexual motivation is high, as it tends to be during adolescence, and the only outlets are with others of one's own gender, adolescents may experiment sexually with them. If these encounters are pleasurable, and heterosexual experiences are unpleasant, a firmer gay male or lesbian sexual orientation may develop (Gagnon & Simon, 1973). Conversely, pain, anxiety, or social disapproval may be connected with early contacts with people of one's own gender. In such cases, the child may learn to inhibit feelings of attraction to people of his or her own gender and develop a firmer heterosexual orientation.

Although learning may play a role in the development of a gay male or lesbian sexual orientation, learning theorists have not identified specific learning experiences that would lead to these orientations. Moreover, most adolescent encounters with people of the same gender, even if pleasurable, do not lead to an adult gay male or lesbian sexual orientation. Many heterosexual people have had adolescent encounters with members of their own gender without being swayed in their adult orientations. This is true even of people whose early sexual interactions with the other gender were fumbling and frustrating. Moreover, the overwhelming majority of gay males and lesbians were aware of sexual interest in people of their own gender *before* they had sexual encounters with them, pleasurable or otherwise (Bell et al., 1981).

Gender Nonconformity

Stereotypes of the effeminate gay male and the masculine lesbian are exaggerated. Nevertheless, research finds that gay males and lesbians are more likely than heterosexuals to report childhood behavior stereotypical of the other gender (Bailey & Zucker, 1995; Friedman & Downey, 1994). Many gay males and lesbians have childhood recollections of acting and feeling "different" from their peers from a young age. Some gay males can recall feeling different as early as age 3 or 4 (Isay, 1990). Feelings of differentness were often related to behavior that is stereotypical of the other gender.

It would appear that the majority of gay males perceive themselves to have been effeminate during childhood (Bailey & Zucker, 1995). Gay males from various groups, such as prisoners, psychiatric patients, and members of gay rights organizations more often reported that they avoided participating in competitive sports as children, were more fearful of physical injury, and were more likely to avoid getting into fights, than did heterosexual males (McConaghy, 1987).

Gay males are also more likely to recall feeling more sensitive than their peers during childhood (Isay, 1990). They cried more easily. Their feelings were more readily hurt. They had more artistic interests. They had fewer male buddies but more female playmates. Gay males were also more likely than their heterosexual counterparts to have preferred "girls' toys." They preferred playing with girls to playing with trucks or guns, or engaging in rough-and-tumble play. Their preferences often led to their being called "sissies" (Bell et al., 1981; Green, 1987). Gay men also recall more cross-dressing during childhood. They preferred the company of older women to older men and engaged in childhood sex play with other boys rather than with girls (Whitam, 1977).

There is also evidence of masculine-typed behavior among lesbians as children (Bailey & Zucker, 1995). Lesbians were more likely than heterosexual women to perceive themselves as having been "tomboys" as children. They were more likely to have preferred rough-and-tumble games to playing with dolls and to have enjoyed wearing boy's clothing rather than "cutesy" dresses.

How might extreme childhood effeminacy lead to a gay male sexual orientation? Green (1987) speculates that the social detachment of these boys from male peers and role models (especially fathers) creates strong, unfulfilled cravings for male affection. This craving then leads them to seek males as partners in sex and love relationships in adolescence and adulthood.

Alan Bell of the Kinsey Institute offers a different explanation. He believes that self-perceptions of differentness and social distance from other males during childhood lead these boys to develop erotic attractions that are also different from the other boys'. These are erotic attractions toward members of their own gender.

Bear in mind that not all of these highly effeminate boys turned out to be gay. Note, too, that these studies followed only boys who were stereotypically effeminate in childhood. Thus it failed to address the development of gay males who do *not* show behavior stereotypical of the other gender as children. Some gay men report engaging in few if any gender-conforming behaviors in childhood. Others report as many typically masculine behaviors and as few feminine behaviors in childhood as heterosexual men. Moreover, perhaps 5% of heterosexual males cross-dressed as children (Carrier, 1986). Still, there appears to be a general connection between excessive behavior stereotypical of the other gender and the development of a gay male sexual orientation in some cases (McConaghy, 1987). It remains unclear whether early effeminacy reflects genetic factors, prenatal influences (such as hormonal imbalances), early experiences, or some combination of these.

All in all, the origins of a gay male or lesbian sexual orientation remain mysterious and complex, just as mysterious as the origins of heterosexuality. In reviewing theories and research, we are left with the impression that sexual orientation is unlikely to have a single cause. Sexual orientation appears to spring from multiple origins, including biological and psychosocial factors (Strickland, 1995). Genetic and biochemical factors (such as hormone levels) may affect the prenatal organization of the brain (Money, 1994). These factors may predispose people to a certain sexual orientation. But it may be that early socialization experiences are also required to give rise to a gay male, lesbian, heterosexual, or bisexual sexual orientation. The precise influences and interactions of these factors have so far eluded researchers.

～ *Reflections* ～

What are the attitudes of people from your sociocultural group toward gay males and lesbians? Do you share these attitudes? Why, or why not?

Why do you believe men tend to be more homophobic than women?

Evaluate the evidence for biological and psychological theories of sexual orientation.

Adjustment of Gay Males and Lesbians

Despite the widespread belief that there is something wrong with gay men and lesbians, evidence has failed to show that they are more emotionally unstable or more subject to psychological disorders (such as anxiety and depression) than other people (Reiss, 1980). Nor have researchers been able to distinguish between gay and heterosexual people on the basis of psychological tests (Reiss, 1980). A gay male or lesbian sexual orientation is no longer itself considered a form of mental illness. In 1973 the American Psychiatric Association voted to drop a gay male or lesbian sexual orientation from its list of mental disorders, although a diagnostic category remains for people with persistent and marked distress about their sexual orientation (American Psychiatric Association, 1994, p. 538).

Truth OR Fiction?
R E V I S I T E D

It is not true that the American Psychiatric Association considers homosexuality a mental disorder. The American Psychiatric Association has not considered a gay male or lesbian sexual orientation to be a mental disorder since 1973. ∎

Gay men, lesbians, and bisexuals occupy all socioeconomic and vocational levels and follow a variety of lifestyles. Researchers find gay men and lesbians overall to be more

Sexual Orientation and Adjustment. Researchers find that gay men and lesbians are about as well adjusted as heterosexuals. Gay couples who are closely committed to one another are also as well adjusted as committed heterosexual couples.

highly educated than most Americans (Cronin, 1993). Bell and Weinberg (1978) found variations in adjustment in the gay community that seem to mirror the variations in the heterosexual community. Gay people who lived with partners in stable, intimate relationships—so-called close couples—were about as well adjusted as married people. Older gay people who lived alone and had few sexual contacts were more poorly adjusted. So, too, are many heterosexual people who have similar lifestyles. All in all, differences in adjustment seem more likely to reflect the lifestyle than the sexual orientation.

Most gay males and lesbians who share close relationships with their partners are satisfied with the quality of their relationships. Researchers find that heterosexual and gay couples report similar levels of satisfaction with their relationships (Kurdek & Schmitt, 1986a; Peplau & Cochran, 1990). Gay males and lesbians in enduring relationships generally report high levels of love, attachment, closeness, caring, and intimacy (Peplau & Cochran, 1980).

As is the case with heterosexual people, not all of the relationships of gay people are satisfying. Among both groups, satisfaction is higher when both partners feel that the benefits they receive from the relationship outweigh the costs (Duffy & Rusbult, 1985/1986). Like heterosexual people, gay men and lesbians are happier in relationships in which they share power and make joint decisions (Kurdek & Schmitt, 1986b). In sum, researchers have not found that gay men and lesbians suffer from more psychological distress than heterosexual people.

Treatment of Gay Male and Lesbian Sexual Orientations

Despite the judgment of the American Psychiatric Association, some people still view a gay male or a lesbian sexual orientation as an illness. If it is an illness, then it is something to be "cured," perhaps by medical or psychological means. However, the great majority of gay men and lesbians do not seek professional assistance to change their sexual orientations. Most see their sexual orientations as integral parts of their personal identities. Bell and Weinberg (1978) found only a few gay people who were interested in changing their sexual orientation—even if a "magic pill" were available to bring about the change (see Table 10.2). Only a minority of Bell and Weinberg's sample had *ever* considered discontinuing male–male or female–female sexual activity.

A few gay men and women do express an interest in changing their orientations, however. Helping professionals have tried to help them do so in a variety of ways. At one time, when it was commonly believed that hormonal imbalances influenced one's sexual orientation, hormone treatments were in vogue. There is no evidence that they were effective.

TABLE 10.2 Percentages of gay people who wish they had received a "magic heterosexuality pill" at birth or could receive one today

	White Males (%)	African-American Males (%)	White Females (%)	African-American Females (%)
Desire magic pill at birth?	28	23	16	11
Desire magic pill today?	14	13	5	6

Source: Reprinted by permission of Simon & Schuster from Bell, A. P., & Weinberg, M. S. (1978). *Homosexualities: A Study of Diversity Among Men and Women.* New York: Simon & Schuster, p. 339.

A few psychotherapists have reported changing the sexual orientations of some individuals. For example, Bieber (1976) claimed that about one in four clients changed his or her sexual orientation through psychoanalytic psychotherapy. But critics charge that these clients were highly motivated to change. Moreover, some of them began therapy as bisexuals. Their change in lifestyle may be attributable to their initial motivation to change and not to the therapy itself.

Masters and Johnson (1979) employed methods used to treat sexual dysfunctions (see Chapter 15) to "reverse" patients' gay male or lesbian sexual orientations. For example, they involved gay males in a graded series of pleasurable activities with women, such as massage and genital stimulation. Masters and Johnson reported a failure rate of 20% for the gay men and 23% for the lesbians they treated in their therapy program. At a five-year follow-up, more than 70% of the clients continued to engage in male–female sexual activity (Schwartz & Masters, 1984). For many reasons, however, these patients do not seem to represent the general gay population:

- Most of them were bisexuals. Only about one in five engaged exclusively in male–male or female–female sexual activities.
- More than half were married.
- They all were motivated to switch their sexual orientations.

Regardless of these people's changes in sexual behavior, remember that sexual behavior is not the equivalent of sexual orientation. (It was thus inaccurate for Masters and Johnson to claim that they had reversed an individual's sexual *orientation.*) That is, many gay people engage in sexual activities with people of the other gender. Nevertheless, they still prefer to have such relationships with people of their own gender.

Isay (1990), a psychoanalyst, argues that gay men and women often enter therapy because of conflicts that arise from social pressure and prejudice. Such pressures can create problems in the acceptance of one's gay male or lesbian sexual orientation. The role of the therapist, he argues, should be to help unburden the client of conflict and promote a more gratifying life as a gay person.

～ *Reflections* ～

▪ Agree or disagree with the following statement, and support your answer: Gay males and lesbians are maladjusted.
▪ Agree or disagree with the following statement, and support your answer: We should help gay males and lesbians change their sexual orientation whenever possible.

Coming Out: Coming to Terms with Being Gay

You must worship rugby and beer. And if you don't, God help you.

(A Roman Catholic priest in New Zealand, cited in Shenon, 1995)

Because of the backdrop of social condemnation and discrimination, gay males and lesbians in our culture often struggle to come to terms with their sexual orientation. Gay men and lesbians usually speak of the process of accepting their sexual orientation as "coming out" or as "coming out of the closet." Coming out is a two-pronged process: coming out to oneself (recognizing one's gay male or lesbian sexual orientation) and coming out to others (declaring one's orientation to the world). Coming out can create a sense of pride in one's sexual orientation and foster the ability to form emotionally and sexually satisfying relationships with gay male or lesbian partners.

Coming Out to Oneself

Many gay people have a difficult time coming to recognize, let alone accept, their sexual orientation. Some have even considered or attempted suicide because of problems in self-acceptance:

> It (suicidal thinking) was because of my homosexuality. I was completely depressed that my homosexuality was leading me nowhere. My life seemed to be going around in a circle. I was still fighting against recognition of my homosexuality. I knew what I was but I didn't want to be.
>
> [I had] the feeling that homosexuality was a hopeless existence. I felt there was no future in it, that I was doomed to be alone. And from my Catholic background, I felt that homosexuality was very evil.
>
> (Bell & Weinberg, 1978, p. 202)

Consider the experience of a New Zealand gay adolescent who was subjected to merciless taunting until his parents pulled him out of school. "He threw a ball like a girl does," said a hot-line worker (cited in Shenon, 1995), "and the hassling just wouldn't stop. He was hassled nonstop from the day he got to that school until the day he left."

"You're judged constantly on your maleness," adds a Roman Catholic priest in New Zealand (cited in Shenon, 1995). "It can be a very intolerant country. You must worship rugby and beer. And if you don't, God help you. I think we've just been dreadful about this macho-ness."

For some people, coming to recognize and accept a gay male or lesbian sexual orientation involves gradually stripping away layers of denial. For others it may be a sudden awakening. Long-standing sexual interests in members of one's own gender may rush into focus on a particular person, as happened with a graduate student named David:

> In college [David's] closest friend was gay. Although this friend had wanted to have sex with David and the attraction was mutual, David still could not associate this attraction with a sexuality that was not acceptable to him. In his first year of graduate school, when he was about 23, he fell in love and then suddenly and with a great sense of relief recognized and acknowledged to himself that he was homosexual. He then had sex for the first time and has subsequently been . . . open about his sexuality.
>
> (Isay, 1990, p. 295)

Recognition of a gay sexual orientation may be only the first step in a lifelong process of sexual identity formation. Acceptance of being gay becomes part of one's self-definition (Isay, 1990). The term *gay,* or *homosexual, identity* refers to the subjective or psychological sense of being gay.

Some gay men and lesbians who have not yet come to recognize or accept their gay sexual orientation get married. For some, marriage is a means of testing feelings toward people of the other gender. For others, marriage represents an attempt to conceal or overcome their sexual orientation (Buxton, 1994; Gabriel, 1995a). Perhaps 20% of gay males and a higher percentage of lesbians get married at least once (Bell & Weinberg, 1978). But such marriages tend to be unhappy and short-lived. They may be strained by one partner's concealing her or his gay sexual orientation. Alternatively, they may buckle from the open acknowledgment of being gay. Virtually all such marriages in Bell and Weinberg's study eventually ended in separation or divorce.

In the 1990s, many American couples have a gay or lesbian spouse. Thousands of gay men and lesbians who had conformed to social pressures by getting married are now coming out of the closet and sometimes leaving home (Buxton, 1994; Gabriel, 1995a).

Coming Out to Others

There are different patterns of coming out to others. Coming out occasionally means an open declaration to the world. More often a person may inform only one or a few select people. The person might tell friends but not family members.

Many gay men and lesbians remain reluctant to declare their sexual orientation, even to friends and family. Disclosure is fraught with the risk of loss of jobs, friendships, and social standing (Padesky, 1988). A social worker who counsels lesbians described some fears of coming out to others expressed by her clients:

> Will I lose my job, will I lose my house, will I lose my children, will I be attacked? I've seen people lose a job. Even if you don't lose it, you become marginal, excluded either actively or through uncomfortable vibes.

(Cited in Barrett, 1990, p. 470)

Gay men and lesbians often anticipate negative reactions from informing family members, including denial, anger, and rejection. Family members and loved ones may refuse to hear or be unwilling to accept reality, as Martha Barron Barrett notes in her book *Invisible Lives,* which chronicles the lives of a sample of lesbians in the United States:

> Parents, children, neighbors, and friends of lesbians deny, or compartmentalize, or struggle with their knowledge in the same way the women themselves do. "My parents know I've lived with my partner for six years. She goes home with me. We sleep in the same bed there. The word *lesbian* has never been mentioned." "I told my mother and she said, 'Well, now that's over with. We don't need to mention it again.' She never has, and that was ten years ago. I don't know if she ever told my father." A husband may dismiss it as "just a phase," a boyfriend may interpret it as a sexual tease, a straight woman may believe "she's just saying that because she couldn't get a man."
>
> The strong message is, "Keep it quiet." Many lesbians do that by becoming invisible. . . . They (lesbians) leave their lesbian persona at home when they go to work on Monday morning. On Friday they don it again. That weekend at home, the flip side of the double life, is what most of heterosexual society never sees.

(Barrett, 1990, p. 52)

Some families are more accepting. They may in fact have had suspicions and prepared themselves for such news. Then, too, many families are initially rejecting but often eventually come to at least grudging acceptance that their child is gay.

A CLOSER LOOK

OUT INTO THE "GAY GLOBAL VILLAGE" OF CYBERSPACE

The gay community has been active on-line for quite some time. An *Out* magazine survey shows that gay men and lesbians are more likely than the general population to use personal computers, modems, and on-line services at home. In an average month in 1995, 40,000 gay people spent more than 100,000 hours on-line with America Online's Gay and Lesbian Community Forum. Planet Out, the electronic media company, debuted on the Microsoft Network in 1995. It seeks to become the "gay global village" of cyberspace. Planet Out is also extending its reach to America Online, the Internet's World Wide Web, and other international networks.

Planet Out received the endorsement of virtually all leading gay organizations. The following agreed to provide information on the new service: the Human Rights Campaign Fund, the National Gay and Lesbian Task Force, Parents and Friends of Lesbians and Gays, the Gay and Lesbian Victory Fund, Digital Queers, and the Gay and Lesbian Alliance Against Defamation.

Planet Out is a meeting place for millions of gay men, lesbians, bisexuals, and others who may be reluctant to associate publicly. Its services include news, arts and entertainment, "chat rooms" with personal ads, human rights action alerts, surveys, celebrity interviews, health forums, and travel tips.

Hugh Dubberly, 37, creative director of Netscape Communications and former head of design at Apple Computer, said chatting electronically with gay men and lesbians on America Online had given him the courage to openly discuss his gay male sexual orientation. "It's something that would have been unthinkable for me even a year or two ago," he said. "If I had relied on more traditional ways of meeting people, like going to bars, or going to meetings of various organizations, or picking up gay publications, it never would have happened" (Lewis, 1995).

Do you know any gay males or lesbians? Have they shared with you their experiences in coming out? What did they go through? Why?

Are you a gay male or lesbian? If so, have you come out? If so, what was the experience like? If not, why not?

Patterns of Sexual Activity Among Gay Males and Lesbians

Heterosexual people are often confused about the sexual practices of gay couples. They may wonder, "Just what do they do?" Generally speaking, gay couples express themselves sexually through as wide a range of activities as heterosexual couples, with the exception of vaginal intercourse. But there are shades of difference between gay and heterosexual couples in sexual techniques.

Sexual Techniques

Gay male couples tend to engage in sexual activities such as kissing, hugging, petting, mutual masturbation, fellatio, and anal intercourse. Laboratory observations of sexual relations between gay males by Masters and Johnson (1979) showed that gay males spent a good deal of time caressing their partners' bodies before approaching the genitals. After hugging and kissing, 31 of 42 gay male couples observed by Masters and Johnson used oral or manual nipple stimulation.

Not all gay males enjoy or practice anal intercourse. Of those who do, most alternate between being the inserter and the insertee. The frequency of anal intercourse among gay males is apparently declining in the face of the AIDS epidemic (Catania et al., 1991; Centers for Disease Control, 1990a; Sonenstein et al., 1989).

Risks of infection and of injury to the rectum or anus are associated with another sexual practice called "fisting." Fisting is the insertion of the fist or hand into the rectum, usually after the bowels have been evacuated with an enema.

Facing the Crisis. The gay male community has responded to the AIDS crisis through the development of telephone hot-lines, support services, and safer sex programs, among other initiatives and programs.

Sexual techniques practiced by lesbians vary. Lesbian couples report kissing, manual and oral breast stimulation, and manual and oral stimulation of the genitals (Kinsey et al., 1953). Manual genital stimulation is the most common and frequent sexual activity among lesbian couples (Bell & Weinberg, 1978). Most lesbian couples also engage in genital apposition. That is, they position themselves so as to rub their genitals together rhythmically (Kinsey et al., 1953). Like gay males, lesbians spend a good deal of time holding, kissing, and caressing each other's bodies before they approach the breasts and genitals. By contrast, heterosexual males tend to move quickly to stimulate their partners' breasts or start directly with genital stimulation (Masters & Johnson, 1979).

Like heterosexual women, lesbians are less genitally oriented and less fixated on orgasm than men. Lesbians generally begin stimulating their partners with more general genital stimulation rather than direct clitoral stimulation, whereas heterosexual males often begin by stimulating the clitoris (Masters & Johnson, 1979). Nor do lesbian couples generally engage in deep penetration of the vagina with fingers. Rather, they may use more shallow vaginal penetration, focusing stimulation on the vaginal lips and entrance. Images of lesbians strapping on dildos for vaginal penetration exist more in the imagination of uninformed heterosexual people than in the sexual repertoire of lesbian couples (Masters & Johnson, 1979). The emotional components of lovemaking—gentle touching, cuddling, and hugging—are important elements of sexual sharing in lesbian relationships.

~ *Reflections* ~

Agree or disagree with the following statement, and support your answer: The sexual practices of gay males and lesbians are more similar to, than different from, the sexual practices of heterosexuals.

Gay Lifestyles

One of the mistakes that lay people (and some researchers) make is to treat gay people as if they were all the same. According to Bell and Weinberg (1978), gay people do not adopt a single, stereotypical lifestyle. That is why the authors termed their report *Homosexualities: A Study of Diversity Among Men and Women*. Variations in sexual expression exist within and across sexual orientations. Descriptions of gay and heterosexual lifestyles must consider individual differences.

Gay men and lesbians in larger U.S. urban centers can usually look to gay communal structures to provide services and support. These include gay rights organizations and gay-oriented newspapers, magazines, bookstores, housing cooperatives, medical services, and other support services (Gagnon, 1990). The gay community provides a sense of acceptance and belonging that gay people do not typically find in society at large. Gay people still encounter discrimination in the workplace, in housing, and in the military.

Restrictions on gay males participating in the armed services has been a continuing controversy. In 1993, President Bill Clinton encountered stiff opposition when he sought to follow through on his campaign pledge to permit openly gay men and women to serve in the military. As a compromise measure, he instituted a "don't ask, don't tell" policy. It permits gay males and lesbians to serve so long as they do not publicly express or reveal their sexual orientation. Moreover, military officials are prohibited from inquiring about the sexual orientation of recruits or initiating investigations in the absence of a public display or disclosure of a gay male or lesbian sexual orientation ("Defense dept. suspends," 1993). The constitutionality of this policy has been challenged since it may restrict free speech.

Gay rights organizations fight for rights for gay people to participate fully in society—to teach in public schools, to adopt children, to live together in sanctioned relationships, and to serve openly and proudly in the military. Cafés and social clubs provide places where gay men and lesbians can socialize and be open about their sexual orientations. Many such establishments also serve as meeting places for casual sexual "pickups," although the advent of AIDS may have curtailed such activity. Organizations such as New York's Gay Men's Health Crisis (GMHC) provide medical, social, and psychological assistance to gay males who have been afflicted by AIDS.

Not all gay people feel that they are a part of the "gay community" or participate in gay rights organizations, however. For many, their sexual orientation is a part of their identity, but not a dominant theme that governs their social and political activities.

Lifestyle Differences Between Gay Males and Lesbians

Much of our knowledge of lifestyle patterns among gay males and lesbians comes from research that predates the AIDS epidemic. Researchers in the 1970s found that gay males were more likely than lesbians to engage in casual sex with many partners. Lesbians more often confined their sexual activity to a committed, affectionate relationship (Bell & Weinberg, 1978). Bell and Weinberg reported that 84% of gay males, as compared to about 7% of lesbian women, reported having more than 50 partners in their lifetimes. Seventy-nine percent of gay males in their study, as compared to only 6% of lesbians, reported that more than half of their partners had been strangers.

Even in this age of AIDS, a recent survey found that only about half of gay men (40% to 60%), but about three in four lesbians, are currently involved in a steady relationship (Peplau & Cochran, 1990). Even gay males within committed relationships have more permissive attitudes toward extracurricular sexual activity than lesbians do (Blumstein & Schwartz, 1990; Peplau & Cochran, 1990).

Traditionally, the gay bar was an arena for making sexual contacts (Bell & Weinberg, 1978). **Cruising** is the name gay people give to searching for a sex partner, principally for casual sex. One can "cruise," and one can "be cruised." Gay males were more likely than lesbians to cruise in public places like gay bars. Lesbians were more likely to find partners among friends, at work, and at informal social gatherings.

Today, with the threat of AIDS hanging over every casual sexual encounter, cruising has lost popularity. Many gay baths, long a setting for casual sexual contacts, have closed down—or been closed down by authorities—because of AIDS. The closing of many gay bathhouses is but one sign of changes in gay communities that have occurred since the advent of AIDS. Many gay males have changed their behavior to prevent contracting or spreading AIDS. Evidence shows that, as a group, gay males have become more likely to limit or avoid anal and oral sex, especially with new partners. They are now more likely to use latex condoms when they do practice these techniques, to limit their sexual contacts to partners they know, and to rely more on masturbation as a sexual outlet (Centers for Disease Control, 1990a, 1990b; Siegel et al., 1988). Despite the advent of AIDS, some gay men, like some heterosexual people, continue high-risk behavior. For example, they engage in unprotected anal intercourse and sexual activity with multiple partners.

Research also shows that extracurricular sexual activity continues to be commonplace among gay male couples. One study surveyed 943 gay males and 1,510 married heterosexual males who had been living with a partner for 2 to 10 years. Four of five (79%) of the gay males reported sex with another partner during the preceding year, as compared to only 11% of the heterosexual males (Blumstein & Schwartz, 1990). Among couples who had been together for longer than 10 years, 94% of gay men reported extracurricular activity at some time during their primary relationships.

Variations in Gay Lifestyles

Bell and Weinberg (1978) found that about 3 out of 4 gay couples they studied could be classified according to 1 of 5 lifestyles: *close couples, open couples, functionals, dysfunctionals,* and *asexuals*. **Close couples** strongly resembled married couples. They evidenced deep emotional commitment and few outside sexual relationships. Almost three times as many lesbians (28%) as gay males (10%) lived in such committed, intimate relationships. Gay people living in close relationships showed fewer social and psychological problems than those with any other lifestyle.

Cruising
The name homosexuals give to searching for a sex partner.

Close couples
Bell and Weinberg's term for gay couples whose relationships resemble marriage in their depth of commitment and exclusiveness.

It is true that many gay couples have lifestyles similar to those of married heterosexual couples and are as well adjusted. They are referred to as *close couples* by Bell and Weinberg. ■

Open couples

Bell and Weinberg's term for gay couples who live together but engage in secret affairs.

Functionals

Bell and Weinberg's term for gay people who live alone, have adapted well to a swinging lifestyle, and are sociable and well adjusted.

Dysfunctionals

Bell and Weinberg's term for gay people who live alone and have sexual, social, or psychological problems.

Asexuals

Bell and Weinberg's term for gay people who live alone and have few sexual contacts.

Partners in **open couples** lived together but engaged in clandestine affairs. Gay people in open couples were not as well adjusted as those in close couples. Nevertheless, their overall adjustment was similar to that of heterosexual people. Still other gay people lived alone and had sexual contacts with numerous partners—a kind of "swinging singles" gay lifestyle. Some of those who lived alone, **functionals,** appeared to have adapted well to their swinging lifestyle and were sociable and well adjusted. Others, called **dysfunctionals,** had sexual, social, or psychological problems. Dysfunctionals were often anxious, unhappy, and found it difficult to form intimate relationships. **Asexuals** also lived alone but were distinguished by having few sexual contacts. Asexuals tended to be older than gay people in the other groups. Although they did not have the adjustment problems of dysfunctionals, they too did not form intimate relationships. Despite being largely asexual in terms of their behavior, their sexual orientation was clearly gay.

The Bell and Weinberg study described diversity of lifestyles in the gay community in the 1970s, before the AIDS epidemic struck. Although such lifestyles continue today to a certain extent, the AIDS epidemic has inhibited promiscuous sex within the gay community. The specter of AIDS has had a more profound effect on the lifestyles and sexual practices of gay males than on any other group in society.

~ *Reflections* ~

■ Agree or disagree with the following statement, and support your answer: Gay males and lesbians lead a wild, swinging sexual lifestyle. (Hint: Critical thinkers avoid overgeneralizations.)

■ What did you learn about gay males and lesbians from this chapter? What misinformation has been corrected? What is completely new to you?

■ Do you believe that the information in this chapter has been presented in a straightforward or a biased manner? Explain.

Summing Up

Sexual Orientation

Coming to Terms with Terms   Sexual orientation describes the directionality of one's sexual and romantic interests—toward members of the same gender, the other gender, or both. Gay male and lesbian sexual orientations denote sexual and romantic interest in members of one's own gender.

Sexual Orientation and Gender Identity   Gay males and lesbians have a gender identity that is consistent with their chromosomal and anatomic sex.

Classification of Sexual Orientation   Kinsey and his colleagues found evidence of degrees of homosexuality and heterosexuality, with bisexuality representing a midpoint between the two. Heterosexuality and homosexuality may be separate dimensions rather than polar opposites, however.

Perspectives on Gay Male and Lesbian Sexual Orientations

Historical Perspectives   Throughout much of Western history, gay people have been deemed sinful and criminal.

Cross-Cultural Perspectives   Male–male sexual behavior is practiced by at least some members of many preliterate societies.

Cross-Species Perspectives   Many animals engage in behaviors that resemble male–male contacts among humans, but we must be cautious in ascribing motives to animals.

Attitudes Toward Sexual Orientation in Contemporary Society   The majority of people in our society view gay people negatively. During the past generation, gay males and lesbians have organized effective political groups to fight discrimination and overturn antisodomy laws that have traditionally targeted them.

Biological Perspectives Evidence of a genetic contribution to sexual orientation is accumulating. Research has failed to connect sexual orientation with differences in current (adult) levels of sex hormones. Prenatal sex hormones may play a role in determining sexual orientation in humans, however.

Psychological Perspectives Psychoanalytic theory connects sexual orientation with unconscious castration anxiety and improper resolution of the Oedipus complex. Learning theorists focus on the role of reinforcement of early patterns of sexual behavior.

Gender Nonconformity Although only a few gay people fit the stereotypes of swishy men and butch women, research finds that homosexuals report a greater incidence of behavior stereotypical of the other gender as children than do heterosexual reference groups.

Adjustment of Gay Males and Lesbians

Evidence has failed to show that gay males, lesbians, and bisexuals are more emotionally unstable or more subject to psychiatric disorders than heterosexual people are.

Coming Out: Coming to Terms with Being Gay

Gay people in our culture struggle to come to terms with their sexual orientation against a backdrop of social condemnation and antagonism. Coming out is a two-pronged process: coming out to oneself and coming out to others. Coming to recognize and accept one's gay sexual orientation may occur as a gradual process or a sudden awakening.

Patterns of Sexual Activity Among Gay Males and Lesbians

Gay people generally express themselves sexually through as wide a range of activities as heterosexual people do, with the exception of vaginal intercourse.

Gay Lifestyles

Gay people do not adopt a single, stereotypical lifestyle.

Lifestyle Differences Between Gay Males and Lesbians Gay males are more likely than lesbians to engage in casual sex with many partners. Lesbians more often confine sexual activity to a committed, affectionate relationship. Many gay males have changed their sexual behavior to prevent contracting or spreading AIDS.

Variations in Gay Lifestyles The majority of gay people studied by Bell and Weinberg could be classified according to one of five lifestyles: close couples, open couples, functionals, dysfunctionals, and asexuals.

C HAPTER 11

Henri Matisse, *The Yellow Curtain,*
Bridgeman Art Library/Superstock.
© 1996 Succession H. Matisse/Artist
Rights Society (ARS), New York.

Conception, Pregnancy, and Childbirth

Outline

Truth OR Fiction?

_____ There is an all-female species of lizard that lays unfertilized eggs that develop into identical females generation after generation.

_____ Prolonged athletic activity may decrease fertility in the male.

_____ A "test-tube baby" is grown in a large laboratory dish throughout the nine-month gestation period.

_____ For the first week following conception, a fertilized egg cell is not attached to its mother's body.

_____ Pregnant women can have one or two alcoholic beverages a day without harming their babies.

_____ A baby signals its mother when it is ready to be born.

_____ One U.S. birth in four is by caesarean section.

_____ Couples should abstain from sexual activity for at least six weeks following childbirth.

O n a balmy day in October, Elaine and her husband Dennis rush to catch the train to their jobs in the city. Elaine's workday is outwardly much the same as any other. Within her body, however, a drama is unfolding. Yesterday, hormones had caused a follicle in her ovary to rupture, releasing its egg cell, or ovum. Like all women, Elaine possessed at birth all the ova she would ever have, each encased in a sac, or follicle. How this particular follicle was selected to mature this month and release its ovum remains a mystery. For the next day or so, however, Elaine will be capable of conceiving.

When Elaine used her ovulation-timing kit the previous morning, it showed that she was about to ovulate. So later that night, Elaine and Dennis had made love, hoping that Elaine would conceive. When Dennis ejaculated, hundreds of millions of sperm were deposited within Elaine's vagina. Only a few thousand survived the journey through the cervix and uterus to the fallopian tube that contained the ovum, released just hours earlier. Of these, a few hundred remained to bombard the ovum. Only one succeeded in penetrating the ovum's covering, resulting in conception. From a single cell formed by the union of sperm and ovum, a new life begins to form. The **zygote** is but 1/175 of an inch across—a tiny beginning. But Elaine must wait a few weeks before a pregnancy test will reveal that she is pregnant.

Elaine is 37. Four months into her pregnancy, Elaine obtains **amniocentesis** in order to check for the presence of chromosomal abnormalities, such as **Down syndrome.** (Down syndrome is more common among children born to women in their late 30s and older.) Amniocentesis also indicates the gender of the fetus. Although many parents prefer to know the gender of their baby before it is born, Elaine and Dennis ask their doctor not to inform them. "Why ruin the surprise?" Dennis explains to his friends. Elaine and Dennis are left to debate boys' names and girls' names for the next few months.

Conception: Against All Odds

Zygote
A fertilized ovum.

Amniocentesis
A procedure for drawing off and examining fetal cells in the amniotic fluid to determine the presence of various disorders in the fetus.

Down syndrome
A chromosomal abnormality that leads to mental retardation, caused by an extra chromosome on the 21st pair.

Spontaneous abortion
The sudden, involuntary expulsion of the embryo or fetus from the uterus before it is capable of independent life.

Conception is the union of a sperm cell and an ovum. On one hand, conception is the beginning of a new human life. Conception is also the end of a fantastic voyage, however, in which a viable ovum, one of only several hundred that will mature and ripen during a woman's lifetime, unites with one of several hundred *million* sperm produced by the man in the average ejaculate.

Ova carry X sex chromosomes. Sperm carry either X or Y sex chromosomes. Girls are conceived from the union of an ovum and an X-bearing sperm, boys from the union of an ovum and a Y-bearing sperm. Sperm that bear Y sex chromosomes appear to be faster swimmers than those bearing X sex chromosomes. This is one of the reasons that between 120 and 150 boys are conceived for every 100 girls. What seem to be natural balancing factors favor the survival of female fetuses, however. Male fetuses are more likely to be lost in a **spontaneous abortion,** which often occurs during the first month of pregnancy. In many cases of early spontaneous abortion, the woman never realizes that she had been pregnant. Despite spontaneous abortions, boys still outnumber girls at birth. Boys suffer from a higher incidence of infant mortality, however. Thus the numbers of boys and girls in the population are further equalized by the time they mature to the point of pairing off.

The 200 to 400 million sperm in an average ejaculate may seem excessive, since only 1 can fertilize an egg. Only 1 in 1,000 will ever arrive in the vicinity of an ovum, however. Millions deposited in the vagina simply flow out of the woman's body because of gravity, unless she remains prone for quite some time. Normal vaginal acidity kills many more. Many surviving sperm swim against the current of fluid coming from the cervix, through the os and into the uterus. Surviving sperm may reach the fallopian tubes 60 to

Figure 11.1. **Human Sperm Swarming Around an Ovum in a Fallopian Tube.** Fertilization normally occurs in a fallopian tube, not in the uterus.

Zona pellucida

A gelatinous layer that surrounds an ovum. (From roots meaning "zone that light can shine through.")

Hyaluronidase

An enzyme that briefly thins the zona pellucida, enabling one sperm to penetrate. (From roots meaning "substance that breaks down a glasslike fluid.")

90 minutes after ejaculation. About half the sperm end up in the wrong tube—that is, the one not containing the egg. Perhaps some 2,000 sperm find their way into the right tube. Fewer still manage to swim the final 2 inches against the currents generated by the cilia that line the tube.

The journey of sperm may not be random or blind. Fertile ova secrete a compound that appears to attract sperm cells (Angier, 1992, p. A19). Sperm cells contain odor receptors that were once thought to be found only in the nasal cavity. It is thus conceivable (pardon the pun) that sperm cells are attracted to ova through a variation of the sense of smell.

Fertilization normally occurs in a fallopian tube. (Figure 11.1 shows sperm swarming around an egg in a fallopian tube.) Ova contain chromosomes, proteins, fats, and nutritious fluid and are surrounded by a gelatinous layer called the **zona pellucida.** This layer must be penetrated if fertilization is to occur. Sperm that have completed their journey secrete the enzyme **hyaluronidase,** which briefly thins the zona pellucida, enabling one sperm to penetrate. Once a sperm has entered, the zona pellucida thickens, locking other sperm out. The corresponding chromosomes in the sperm and ovum line up opposite each other. Conception occurs as the chromosomes from the sperm and ovum combine to form 23 new pairs, which carry a unique set of genetic instructions.

Optimizing the Chances of Conception

Some couples may wish to optimize their chances of conceiving during a particular month so that birth occurs at a desired time. Others may have difficulty conceiving and wish to maximize their chances for a few months before consulting a fertility specialist. Some fairly simple procedures can dramatically increase the chances of conceiving for couples without serious fertility problems.

The ovum can be fertilized for about 4 to 20 hours after ovulation. Sperm are most active within 48 hours after ejaculation. So one way of optimizing the chances of conception is to engage in coitus within a few hours of ovulation. There are a number of ways to predict ovulation.

Using the Basal Body Temperature Chart   Few women have perfectly regular cycles, so they can only guess when they are ovulating. A basal body temperature (BBT) chart (see Figure 11.2) may help provide a more reliable estimate.

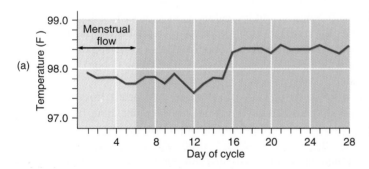

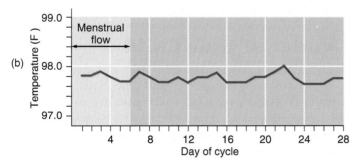

Figure 11.2. **A Basal Body Temperature (BBT) Chart.** Body temperature dips slightly just prior to ovulation, rises about 0.4 to 0.8 of a degree following ovulation, and remains elevated through the course of the cycle. Part (a) represents a cycle in which a sustained elevation in temperature occurred following ovulation on day 15. Part (b) shows no sustained temperature rise, which is indicative of an absence of ovulation in this cycle. *Source:* Adapted from Kolodny, R. C., Masters, W. H., and Johnson, V. E. (1979). *Textbook of sexual medicine.*

As shown in the figure, body temperature is fairly even before ovulation, and early morning body temperature is generally below 98.6 degrees Fahrenheit. But just prior to ovulation, basal temperature dips slightly. Then, on the day following ovulation, temperature tends to rise by about 0.4 to 0.8 degrees and to remain higher until menstruation. In using the BBT method, a women attempts to detect these temperature changes by tracking her temperature just after awakening each morning but before rising from bed. Thermometers that provide finely graded readings, such as electronic digital thermometers, are best suited for determining these minor changes. The couple record the woman's temperature and the day of the cycle (as well as the day of the month) and indicate whether they have engaged in coitus. With regular charting for six months, the woman may learn to predict the day of ovulation more accurately—assuming that her cycles are fairly regular.

Opinion is divided as to whether it is better for couples to have coitus every 24 hours or every 36 to 48 hours for the several-day period during which ovulation is expected. More frequent coitus around the time of ovulation may increase the chances of conception. Relatively less frequent (that is, every 36 to 48 hours) coitus leads to a higher sperm count during each ejaculation. Most fertility specialists recommend that couples seeking to conceive a baby have intercourse once every day or two during the week in which the woman expects to ovulate. Men with lower than normal sperm counts may be advised to wait 48 hours between ejaculations, however (Speroff et al., 1985).

Analyzing Urine for Luteinizing Hormone   Over-the-counter kits are more accurate than the BBT method and predict ovulation by analyzing the woman's urine for the surge in luteinizing hormone (LH) that precedes ovulation by about 12 to 24 hours. The kits are expensive, however, and careful testing of the woman's urine each morning is required.

Tracking Vaginal Mucus   Women can track the thickness of their vaginal mucus during the phases of the menstrual cycle by rolling it between their fingers and noting changes in texture. The mucus is thick, white, and cloudy during most phases of the cycle. It becomes thin, slippery, and clear for a few days preceding ovulation. A day or so after ovulation the mucus again thickens and becomes opaque.

Additional Considerations   Coitus in the male-superior position allows sperm to be deposited deeper in the vagina and minimizes leakage of sperm out of the vagina due to gravity. Women may improve their chances of conceiving by lying on their backs and drawing their knees close to their breasts following ejaculation. This position, perhaps aided by the use of a pillow beneath the buttocks, may prevent sperm from dripping out quickly and elevates the pool of semen in relation to the cervix. It thus makes gravity work for, rather than against, conception. Women may also avoid standing and may lie as still as possible for about 30 to 60 minutes following ejaculation to help sperm move toward the cervical opening.

Women with severely retroverted or "tipped" uteruses may profit from supporting themselves on their elbows and knees and having their partners enter them from behind. Again, this position helps prevent semen from dripping out of the vagina.

The man should penetrate the woman as deeply as possible just prior to ejaculation, hold still during ejaculation, then withdraw slowly in a straight line to avoid dispersing the pool of semen.

Selecting the Gender of Your Child

Folklore is replete with methods for preselecting the gender of one's children. Some cultures have advised coitus under the full moon to conceive boys. The Greek philosopher Aristotle suggested that making love during a north wind would beget sons. A south wind would produce daughters. Sour foods were once suggested for parents desirous of having boys. Those who wanted girls were advised to consume sweets. Husbands who yearned to have boys might be advised to wear their boots to bed. The thesis that the right testicle was responsible for seeding boys was popular at one time. Eighteenth-century Frenchnoble-men were advised to have their left testicles removed if they wanted to sire sons. It should go without saying that none of these methods worked. More recent methods sound more reasonable, if less colorful. However, serious questions remain about their reliability.

Shettles's Approach   Sperm bearing the Y sex chromosome are smaller than those bearing the X sex chromosome and are faster swimmers. But sperm with the X sex chromosome are more durable. From these assumptions, Shettles (1982) and other re-searchers derive a number of strategies for choosing the gender of one's children.

These techniques may increase the chances of having a boy:

1. The man should not ejaculate for several days preceding his partner's expected time of ovulation.
2. The couple should engage in coitus on the day of ovulation.
3. The man should be penetrating deeply at the moment of ejaculation.
4. The woman can lower the acidity of the vagina and make it more hospitable to sperm bearing Y sex chromosomes by douching with 2 tablespoons of baking soda to a quart of warm water before coitus.

These techniques may increase the chances of having a girl:

1. The couple should engage in coitus two days (or slightly more) before ovulation.
2. The woman should raise the acidity of the vagina by douching with 2 tablespoons of vinegar per quart of warm water before coitus.
3. The woman should avoid orgasm following her partner's ejaculation on the (debat-able) assumption that orgasm facilitates the journey of sperm.
4. The man should ejaculate at a shallow depth of penetration.

A combination of these methods has been asserted to result in the conception of a child of the desired gender in about 80% of cases, but many observers regard these figures as exaggerated (Carson, 1988). Other researchers report that timing intercourse to coincide with ovulation leads to the conception of more girls than boys (Zarutskie et al., 1989) or has no effect on the gender of the baby (Wilcox et al., 1995).

Sperm-Separation Procedures   Several sperm-separation procedures are in use. One is based on the relative swimming rates of Y- and X-bearing sperm. Another re-lies on the differences in electrical charges of the two types of sperm to separate them. Sperm-separation approaches reportedly have success rates of about 80% (Carson, 1988).

～ Reflections ～

▢ Where does conception normally take place? Did you know this?
▢ Agree or disagree with the following statement, which is based on the remarks of a social critic: Gender selection technology is sexist.

Infertility and Alternative Ways of Becoming Parents

Infertility
Inability to conceive a child.

For couples who want children, few problems are more frustrating than inability to con-ceive. Physicians often recommend that couples try to conceive on their own for six months before seeking medical assistance. The term **infertility** is usually not applied until the fail-ure to conceive has persisted for more than a year.

Infertility concerns millions of Americans. Because the incidence of infertility in-creases with age, it is partially the result of a rise in couples who postpone childbearing until

A CLOSER LOOK

SEX AND THE SINGLE LIZARD

Some years back, a scandalous book emerged on the scene—*Sex and the Single Woman*. A somewhat different scandal has now emerged in the animal world. It could be dubbed "Sex and the Single Lizard."

National Geographic reports the discovery of a most unusual all-female species of lizard found in South America and the West Indies. At time for reproduction, no males need apply. With no male contact, the lizards lay unfertilized eggs. The hatchlings develop into identical fe-

males generation after generation (Cole, 1995). Why? They derive all of their hereditary material from their mothers. The scientific name of the species is *Gymnophthalmus under-woodi*. (We include the scientific name so that you will think that there is some value to this A Closer Look feature.)

The lizards are hybrids of two species of lizard, each of which reproduces normally—that is, by having male lizards fertilize the females' eggs.

The third author notes that she has three perfect daughters and no sons. The first author does not wish to discuss the matter further.

Truth **OR** Fiction?
R E V I S I T E D

It is true that there is an all-female species of lizard that lays unfertilized eggs that develop into identical females generation after generation. ■

---

their 30s and 40s (Sheehy, 1995). All in all, about 15% of American couples have fertility problems (Howards, 1995). However, about half of them eventually succeed in conceiving a child (Jones & Toner, 1993). Many treatment options are available, ranging from drugs to stimulate ovulation to newer reproductive technologies, such as in vitro fertilization.

Male Fertility Problems

Although most concerns about fertility have traditionally centered on women, the problem lies with the man in about 30% of cases (Howards, 1995). In about 20% of cases, problems are found in both partners (Hatcher et al., 1990; Howards, 1995).

Fertility problems in the male reflect abnormalities such as these:

1. Low sperm count
2. Irregularly shaped sperm—for example, malformed heads or tails
3. Low sperm **motility**
4. Chronic diseases such as diabetes, as well as infectious diseases such as sexually transmitted diseases
5. Injury to the testes
6. An **auto-immune response,** in which antibodies produced by the man deactivate his own sperm
7. A pituitary imbalance and/or thyroid disease

Problems in producing normal, abundant sperm may be caused by genetic factors, advanced age, hormonal problems, diabetes, injuries to the testes, varicose veins in the scrotum, drugs (alcohol, narcotics, marijuana, tobacco), antihypertensive medications, environmental toxins, excess heat, and emotional stress.

Sperm production gradually declines with age, but normal aging does not produce infertility. Men in late adulthood father children, even though conception may require more attempts.

Low sperm count (or the absence of sperm) is the most common problem. Sperm counts of 40 million to 150 million sperm per milliliter of semen are considered normal. A count of fewer than 20 million is generally regarded as low. Sperm production may be

Motility

Self-propulsion. A measure of the viability of sperm cells.

Auto-immune response

The production of antibodies that attack naturally occurring substances that are (incorrectly) recognized as being foreign or harmful.

low among men with undescended testes that were not surgically corrected prior to puberty. Frequent ejaculation can reduce sperm counts. Sperm production may also be impaired in men whose testicles are consistently 1 or 2 degrees above the typical scrotal temperature of 94 to 95 degrees Fahrenheit (Leary, 1990). Frequent hot baths and tight-fitting underwear can also reduce sperm production, at least temporarily. Some men may encounter fertility problems from prolonged athletic activity, use of electric blankets, or even long, hot baths. In such cases the problem can be readily corrected. Male runners with fertility problems are often counseled to take time off to increase their sperm counts.

Sometimes the sperm count is adequate, but prostate, hormonal, or other factors deprive sperm of motility or deform them. Motility can also be hampered by scar tissue from infections. Scarring may prevent sperm from passing through parts of the male reproductive system, such as the vas deferens. To be considered normal, sperm must be able to swim for at least two hours following coitus, and most (60% or more) must be normal in shape.

Truth **OR** *Fiction?* REVISITED

It is true that prolonged athletic activity may decrease fertility in the male. Such activity can raise the temperature of the scrotum, providing a less-than-optimal environment for sperm. ■

Sperm counts have been increased by surgical repair of the varicose veins in the scrotum. Microsurgery can open blocked passageways that prevent the outflow of sperm (Howards, 1995). Researchers are also investigating the effects on sperm production of special cooling undergarments. One device, a kind of athletic supporter that is kept slightly damp with distilled water, has been approved by the Federal Drug Administration. Seventy percent of the men whose infertility is due to higher-than-normal scrotal temperatures show increased sperm count and quality with the wearing of cooling undergarments (Leary, 1990; Silber, 1991).

Artificial insemination
The introduction of sperm in the reproductive tract through means other than sexual intercourse.

Artificial Insemination   The sperm of men with low sperm counts can be collected and quick-frozen. The sperm from multiple ejaculations can then be injected into a woman's uterus at the time of ovulation. This is one kind of **artificial insemination.** The sperm of men with low sperm motility can also be injected into their partners' uteruses, so that the sperm begin their journey closer to the fallopian tubes. Sperm from a donor can be used to artificially inseminate a woman whose partner is completely infertile or has an extremely low sperm count. The child then bears the genes of one of the parents, the mother. A donor can be chosen who resembles the man in physical traits and ethnic background.

A variation of artificial insemination has been used with some men with very low (or zero!) sperm counts in the semen, immature sperm, or immotile sperm. Immature sperm can be removed from a testicle by a thin needle and then directly injected into an egg in a laboratory dish (Brody, 1995b). The method has even been successful with a few men who only have tailless spermatids in the testes.

Female Fertility Problems

Major causes of infertility in women include the following:

1. Irregular ovulation, including failure to ovulate
2. Obstructions or malfunctions of the reproductive tract, which are often caused by infections or diseases involving the reproductive tract
3. Endometriosis
4. Declining hormone levels of estrogen and progesterone that occur with aging and may prevent the ovum from becoming fertilized or remaining implanted in the uterus

Ten percent to 15% of female infertility problems stem from failure to ovulate (Frisch, 1988). Many factors can play a role in failure to ovulate, including hormonal irregularities, malnutrition, genetic factors, stress, and chronic disease. Failure to ovulate may occur in response to extreme dieting, as in the case of the eating disorder *anorexia nervosa*. But even women who are only 10% to 15% below their normal body weights may fail to ovulate (Frisch, 1988).

Ovulation may often be induced by the use of fertility drugs such as *clomiphene* (Clomid). Clomiphene stimulates the pituitary gland to secrete FSH and LH, which in turn stimulate maturation of ova. Clomiphene leads to conception in the majority of cases of infertility that are due *solely* to irregular or absent ovulation (Reinisch, 1990). But since infertility can have multiple causes, only about 50% of women who use clomiphene become pregnant. Another infertility drug, Pergonal, contains a high concentration of FSH, which directly stimulates maturation of ovarian follicles. Like clomiphene, Pergonal has high success rates with women whose infertility is due to lack of ovulation. Clomiphene and Pergonal have been linked to multiple births, including quadruplets and even quintuplets. However, fewer than 10% of such pregnancies result in multiple births.

Local infections that scar the fallopian tubes and other organs impede the passage of sperm or ova. Such infections include pelvic inflammatory disease—an inflammation of the woman's internal reproductive tract that can be caused by various infectious agents, such as the bacteria responsible for gonorrhea and chlamydia (see Chapter 16).

In **endometriosis,** cells break away from the uterine lining (the endometrium) and become implanted and grow elsewhere. When they develop on the surface of the ovaries or fallopian tubes, they may block the passage of ova or impair conception. About one case in six of female sterility is believed to be due to endometriosis. Hormone treatments and surgery sometimes reduce the blockage to the point that women can conceive. A physician may suspect endometriosis during a pelvic exam, but it is diagnosed with certainty by **laparoscopy.** A long, narrow tube is inserted through an incision in the navel, permitting the physician to inspect the organs in the pelvic cavity visually. The incision is practically undetectable.

Suspected blockage of the fallopian tubes may also be checked by a **Rubin test** or a **hysterosalpingogram.** In a Rubin test, carbon dioxide gas is blown through the cervix. Its pressure is then monitored to determine whether it flows freely through the fallopian tubes into the abdomen or is trapped in the uterus. In the more common hysterosalpingogram, the movement of an injected dye is monitored by X-rays. This procedure may be uncomfortable.

Several new methods help many couples with problems, such as blocked fallopian tubes, bear children.

In Vitro Fertilization

When Louise Brown was born in England in 1978 after being conceived by the method of **in vitro fertilization** (IVF), the event made headlines around the world. Louise was dubbed the world's first "test-tube baby." However, conception took place in a laboratory dish (not a test tube), and the fetus was implanted in the mother's uterus, where it developed to term. Prior to in vitro fertilization, fertility drugs stimulate ripening of ova. Ripe ova are then surgically removed from an ovary and placed in a laboratory dish along with the father's sperm. Fertilized ova are then injected into the mother's uterus to become implanted in the uterine wall.

It is not true that a "test-tube baby" is grown in a large laboratory dish throughout the nine-month gestation period. A test-tube baby is actually conceived in a laboratory dish (which is similar to a test tube, perhaps), but the fertilized egg is then placed in the mother's uterus where it must become implanted if it is to develop to term. ■

GIFT

In **gamete intrafallopian transfer,** or GIFT, sperm and ova are inserted together into a fallopian tube for fertilization. Unlike in vitro fertilization, conception occurs in a fallopian tube rather than a laboratory dish.

ZIFT

ZIFT (**zygote intrafallopian transfer**) involves a combination of IVF and GIFT. Sperm and ova are combined in a laboratory dish. Following fertilization, the zygote is placed in the mother's fallopian tube to begin its journey to the uterus for implantation. ZIFT has an advantage over GIFT in that the fertility specialists can ascertain that fertilization has occurred before insertion is performed.

Donor IVF

Donor IVF is a variation of the IVF procedure in which the ovum is taken from another woman, fertilized, and then injected into the uterus or fallopian tube of the intended mother. The procedure is used in cases in which the intended mother does not produce ova.

Endometriosis
An abnormal condition in which endometrial tissue is sloughed off into the abdominal cavity rather than out of the body during menstruation. The condition is characterized by abdominal pain and may cause infertility.

Laparoscopy
A medical procedure in which a long, narrow tube (laparoscope) is inserted through an incision in the navel, permitting the visual inspection of organs in the pelvic cavity. (From the Greek *lapara*, meaning "flank.")

T r u t h **OR** *Fiction?*
R E V I S I T E D

Rubin test
A test in which carbon dioxide gas is blown through the cervix and its progress through the reproductive tract is tracked to determine whether or not the fallopian tubes are blocked.

Hysterosalpingogram

A test in which a dye is injected into the reproductive tract and its progress is tracked by X-rays to determine whether or not the fallopian tubes are blocked. (From roots meaning "record of," "uterus," and "fallopian tubes.")

In vitro fertilization

A method of conception in which mature ova are surgically removed from an ovary and placed in a laboratory dish along with sperm.

Gamete intrafallopian transfer (GIFT)

A method of conception in which sperm and ova are inserted into a fallopian tube to encourage conception.

Zygote intrafallopian transfer (ZIFT)

A method of conception in which an ovum is fertilized in a laboratory dish and then placed in a fallopian tube.

Donor IVF

A variation of in vitro fertilization in which the ovum is taken from one woman, fertilized, and then injected into the uterus or fallopian tube of another woman.

Embryonic transfer

A method of conception in which a woman volunteer is artificially inseminated by the male partner of the intended mother, after which the embryo is removed from the volunteer and inserted within the uterus of the intended mother.

Intracytoplasmic injection

A method of conception in which sperm is injected directly into an ovum.

Surrogate mother

A woman who is impregnated through artificial insemination, with the sperm of a prospective father, carries the embryo and fetus to term, and then gives the child to the prospective parents.

Embryonic Transfer   A similar method for women who do not produce ova of their own is **embryonic transfer.** In this method a woman volunteer is artificially inseminated by the male partner of the infertile woman. Five days later the embryo is removed from the volunteer and inserted within the uterus of the mother-to-be, where it is hoped that it will become implanted.

In vitro and transfer methods are costly. Success with in vitro fertilization drops from nearly 30% in women in their mid-20s to 10% to 15% in women in their late 30s (Toner et al., 1991). As success remains elusive in many cases, frustration and lack of hope often lead couples to consider dropping out of infertility treatment programs (Blenner, 1992). Moreover, coping with infertility often stresses the marriage (Ulbrich et al., 1990).

Intracytoplasmic Injection   **Intracytoplasmic injection** has been used when the man has too few sperm for IVF, or when IVF fails (Howards, 1995). In this method, sperm is injected directly into an ovum. To date, the method has resulted in pregnancy in about 35% of cases (Van Steirteghem et al., 1993).

Surrogate Motherhood   A **surrogate mother** is artificially inseminated by the husband of the infertile woman and carries the baby to term. The surrogate signs a contract to turn the baby over to the infertile couple. Such contracts have been invalidated in some states, however, so that surrogate mothers in these states cannot be compelled to hand over the babies.

Adoption   Adoption is yet another way for people to obtain children. Despite the occasional conflicts in which adoptive parents are pitted against biological parents who change their minds about giving their children up for adoption, most adoptions result in the formation of loving new families. Many people in the United States find it easier to adopt infants from other countries, infants with special needs, or older children.

∼ Reflections ∼

▪ Do you know of any couples who have had difficulty conceiving a child? Did they consult a health professional about the problem? What was recommended? How did it work out? What did the couple experience during the process?

▪ Today's reproductive technologies make it possible for women to have babies after menopause (by receiving donor eggs) or to become grandmothers to their own children (by using eggs donated by their daughters). It may even become possible for a woman to receive a transplanted ovary from an aborted fetus and later give birth to a child whose biological mother is the aborted fetus. These reproductive technologies have leapfrogged ahead of society's efforts to grapple with their ethical, moral, and legal implications. Where should the line be drawn in determining how far medical science should go in providing reproductive alternatives to infertile people?

Pregnancy

People react to becoming pregnant in different ways. For those who are psychologically and economically prepared, pregnancy may be greeted with joyous celebration. Some women feel that pregnancy helps fulfill their sense of womanhood:

Being pregnant meant I was a woman. I was enthralled with my belly growing. I went out right away and got maternity clothes.

It gave me a sense that I was actually a woman. I had never felt sexy before. . . . I felt very voluptuous.

(Boston Women's Health Book Collective, *The New Our Bodies, Ourselves,* 1992)

QUESTIONNAIRE

SHOULD YOU HAVE A CHILD?

Whether or not to have children is one of the most significant life decisions you will face. Children have a way of needing a generation (or a lifetime) of love and support. We have no simplistic answers to this question, no standardized questionnaire that yields a score for a "Go."

Instead, we offer the following questionnaire to help you consider some of the reasons to have or not to have children. This listing of reasons may offer you some insight into your own motives. You can check the blank spaces to see how many pros you come up with and how many cons. The items are not intended to be equal in weight. Nor should your total score govern your decision. You be the judge. It's your life and your choice.

Reasons to Have Children

Couples offer reasons such as the following for having children. Check those that seem to apply to you:

_____ 1. *Personal experience.* Having children is a unique experience. To many people, no other experience compares with having the opportunity to love children, experience their love, help shape their lives, and watch them develop.

_____ 2. *Personal pleasure.* There is fun and pleasure in playing with children, taking them to the zoo and the circus, and viewing the world through their fresh, innocent eyes.

_____ 3. *Personal extension.* Children carry on our family heritage and some of our own wishes and dreams beyond the confines of our own mortality. We name them after ourselves or others in our families and see them as extensions of ourselves. We identify with their successes.

_____ 4. *Loving relationship.* Parents have the opportunity to establish extremely close and cherished bonds with other human beings.

_____ 5. *Personal status.* Within our culture, parents are afforded respect *just because* they are parents. Consider the commandment "Honor thy father and thy mother."

_____ 6. *Personal competence.* Parenthood is a challenge. Competence in the social roles of mother or father is a potential source of gratification to many people.

_____ 7. *Personal responsibility.* Parents have the opportunity to be responsible for the welfare and education of their children.

_____ 8. *Companionship for the later years.* Many people expect their children will provide them with comfort, companionship, and perhaps crucial aid in their later years.

On the other hand, an unwanted pregnancy may evoke feelings of fear and hopelessness, as occurs with many teenagers.

In this section we examine biological and psychological aspects of pregnancy: signs of pregnancy, prenatal development, complications, effects of drugs and sex, and the psychological experiences of pregnant women and fathers. The nearby questionnaire invites you to consider whether you should have a child.

Early Signs of Pregnancy

For many women the first sign of pregnancy is missing a period. But some women have irregular menstrual cycles or miss a period because of stress. Missing a period is thus not a fully reliable indicator. Some women also experience cyclic bleeding or spotting during pregnancy, although the blood flow is usually lighter than normal. If a woman's basal body temperature remains high for about three weeks after ovulation, there is reason to suspect pregnancy even if she spots two weeks after ovulation.

_____ 9. *Moral worth.* Some people feel that having children provides the opportunity for a moral, selfless act in which they place the needs of others—their children—ahead of their own.

_____ 10. *Religious beliefs.* The biblical injunction to "bear fruit and multiply" is followed by many people across a range of religious affiliations.

Reasons Not to Have Children

Many couples who decide not to have children cite reasons such as the following. Check those that you endorse:

_____ 1. *Strain on Earth's resources.* Because the world is overpopulated, it is wrong to place additional strain on limited resources. More children will only geometrically increase the problem of overpopulation.

_____ 2. *Time together.* Child-free couples may be able to spend more time together as a couple and develop a more intimate relationship.

_____ 3. *Freedom.* Children have a way of erasing leisure time. They may also make it more difficult to pursue educational and vocational advancement. Child-free couples may be more able to live spontaneously, to go where they please and do as they please.

_____ 4. *Dual careers.* Both members of child-free couples may pursue careers without distraction.

_____ 5. *Financial drain.* Children are a financial burden, especially considering the costs of child care and education.

_____ 6. *Difficulty.* Parenthood is demanding. It requires sacrifice of time, money, and energy, and not everyone makes a good parent.

_____ 7. *Irrevocable decision.* Once you have children, the decision cannot be changed.

_____ 8. *Failure.* Some people fear that they will not be good parents. People with poor relationships with their own parents may fear that they will repeat the same mistakes their parents made with them.

_____ 9. *Other children.* People can enjoy children other than their own, such as nieces and nephews, or become "Big Brothers" or "Big Sisters," without assuming the full burden of parental responsibility.

_____ 10. *Sense of danger.* The world is perceived to be a dangerous place, with the threats, for example, of crime, environmental destruction, and nuclear war. It is better not to bring children into such a world.

Pregnancy Tests

Human chorionic gonadotropin
A hormone produced by women shortly after conception, which stimulates the corpus luteum to continue to produce progesterone. The presence of HCG in a woman's urine indicates that she is pregnant.

You may have heard your parents say that they learned your mother was pregnant by means of the "rabbit test," in which a sample of the woman's urine was injected into a laboratory animal. This procedure, which was once commonly used to confirm pregnancy, relied on the fact that women produce **human chorionic gonadotropin** (HCG) shortly after conception. HCG causes rabbits, mice, or rats to ovulate.

Today, pregnancy can be confirmed in minutes by tests that directly detect HCG in the urine as early as the third week of pregnancy. A blood test—the *beta subunit HCG radioimmunoassay* (RIA)—can detect HCG in the woman's blood as early as the eighth day of pregnancy, about five days preceding her expected period.

Over-the-counter home pregnancy tests are also available. They too test the woman's urine for HCG and are intended to be used as early as one day after a missed period. Laboratory-based tests are considered 98% or 99% accurate. Home-based tests performed by lay people are somewhat less accurate. Women are advised to consult their physicians if they suspect that they are pregnant or wish to confirm a home pregnancy test result.

Hegar's sign
Softness of a section of the uterus between the uterine body and the cervix, which indicates that a woman is pregnant.

About a month after a woman misses her period, a health professional may be able to confirm pregnancy by pelvic exam. Women who are pregnant usually show **Hegar's sign.** Hegar's sign is softness of a section of the uterus between the uterine body and the cervix, which may be palpated (felt) by the woman's physician by placing a hand on the abdomen and two fingers in the vagina.

Early Effects of Pregnancy

Just a few days after conception, a woman may note tenderness of the breasts. Hormonal stimulation of the mammary glands may make the breasts more sensitive and cause sensations of tingling and fullness.

Morning sickness
Symptoms of pregnancy, including nausea, aversions to specific foods, and vomiting.

Morning sickness, which may actually occur throughout the day, refers to the nausea, food aversions, and vomiting experienced during pregnancy. About half of all pregnant women experience morning sickness during the first few months of pregnancy (Thompson, 1993). In some cases, morning sickness is so severe that the woman cannot eat regularly and must be hospitalized to ensure that she and the fetus receive adequate nutrition. Morning sickness usually subsides by about the twelfth week of pregnancy. Pregnant women may also experience greater-than-normal fatigue during the early weeks, so that they sleep longer and fall asleep more readily than usual. Frequent urination, which may also be experienced, is caused by pressure from the swelling uterus on the bladder.

Miscarriage (Spontaneous Abortion)

Miscarriage
A spontaneous abortion.

Miscarriages have many causes, including chromosomal defects in the fetus and abnormalities of the placenta and uterus. About three in four miscarriages occur in the first 16 weeks of pregnancy, and the great majority of these occur in the first 7 weeks. Some miscarriages occur so early that the woman is not aware that she was pregnant.

Following a miscarriage, a couple may feel a deep sense of loss and undergo a period of mourning. Emotional support from friends and family often helps the couple cope with the loss. In most cases women who miscarry can carry subsequent pregnancies to term.

Sex During Pregnancy

Most health professionals concur that coitus is safe throughout the course of pregnancy until the start of labor, provided that the pregnancy is developing normally and the woman has no history of miscarriages. Women who experience bleeding or cramps during pregnancy may be advised by their obstetricians not to engage in coitus (Samuels & Samuels, 1986).

Masters and Johnson (1966) reported an initial decline in sexual interest among pregnant women during the first trimester. There is increased interest during the second trimester and another decline in interest during the third. Many women show declines in sexual interest and activity during the first trimester because of fatigue, nausea, or misguided concerns that coitus will harm the embryo or fetus. Also during the first trimester, vasocongestion may cause tenderness of the breasts, discouraging fondling and sucking. Researchers in Israel reported a gradual decline in sexual interest and frequency of intercourse and orgasm during pregnancy among a sample of 219 women. The greatest decline occurred during the third trimester (Hart et al., 1991). Pain during intercourse is also commonly reported, especially in the third trimester (Ulbrich et al., 1990).

As the woman's abdominal region swells, the popular male-superior position becomes unwieldy. The female-superior, lateral-entry, and rear-entry positions are common alternatives. Of course, manual and oral sex can continue as usual. Although oral sex is generally considered safe during pregnancy, blowing air into the pregnant woman's vagina is to be avoided, since it can introduce life-threatening air bubbles into the mother's bloodstream (Samuels & Samuels, 1986).

Some women are concerned that the uterine contractions of orgasm may dislodge an embryo. Such concerns are usually unfounded, unless the woman has a history of miscarriage or is presently at risk of miscarriage. Women may also be concerned that orgasmic contractions during the final month may induce labor. Evidence on the issue is mixed, however. Women and their partners are advised to consult their obstetricians. (Few obstetricians in the 1990s will make parents feel guilty that they retain their interest in sex during pregnancy.)

Psychological Changes During Pregnancy

A woman's psychological response to pregnancy reflects her desire to be pregnant, her physical changes, and her attitudes toward these changes. Women with the financial, social, and psychological resources to meet the needs of pregnancy and child rearing may welcome pregnancy. Some describe it as the most wondrous experience of their lives. Other women may question their ability to handle their pregnancies and childbirth. Or they may fear that pregnancy will interfere with their careers or their mates' feelings about them. In general, women who want to have a baby and choose to become pregnant are better adjusted during their pregnancies.

The first trimester may be difficult for women who are ambivalent about pregnancy. At that stage symptoms like morning sickness are most pronounced, and women must come to terms with being pregnant. The second trimester is generally less tempestuous. Morning sickness and other symptoms have largely vanished. It is not yet difficult to move about, and the woman need not yet face the delivery. Women first note fetal movement during the second trimester, and for many the experience is stirring:

> I was lying on my stomach and felt—something, like someone lightly touching my deep insides. Then I just sat very still and . . . felt the hugeness of having something living growing in me. Then I said, No, it's not possible, it's too early yet, and then I started to cry. . . . That one moment was my first body awareness of another living thing inside me.
>
> (*The New Our Bodies, Ourselves,* 1992)

During the third trimester it is normal, especially for first-time mothers, to worry about the mechanics of delivery and whether the child will be normal. The woman becomes increasingly heavy and literally "bent out of shape." It may become difficult to get up from a chair or out of bed. She must sit farther from the steering wheel when driving. Muscle tension from supporting the extra weight in her abdomen may cause backaches. She may feel impatient in the days and weeks just prior to delivery.

Men, like women, respond to pregnancy according to the degree to which they want the child. Many men are proud and look forward to the child with great anticipation. In such cases, pregnancy may bring parents closer together. But fathers who are financially or emotionally unprepared may consider the pregnancy a "trap." Now and then an expectant father experiences some signs of pregnancy, including morning sickness and vomiting. This reaction is termed a **sympathetic pregnancy.**

Looking Forward to Parenthood. A couple's reactions to pregnancy reflect the degree to which they want and are prepared for the child.

Sympathetic pregnancy The experiencing of a number of signs of pregnancy by the father.

～ *Reflections* ～

How did people in your life react on learning that they were pregnant? Why?

Has anyone you know had a miscarriage? How did she react?

Do you believe that it is appropriate to engage in sexual activity during pregnancy? Why, or why not?

Prenatal Development

We can date pregnancy from the onset of the last menstrual cycle before conception, which makes the normal gestation period 280 days. We can also date pregnancy from the date at which fertilization was assumed to have taken place, which normally corresponds to two weeks after the beginning of the woman's last menstrual cycle. In this case, the normal gestation period is 266 days.

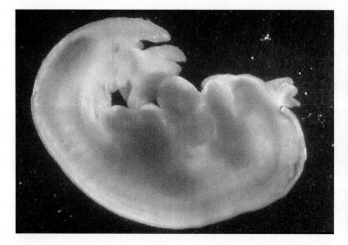

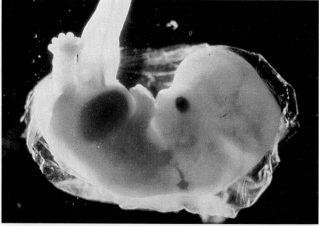

Prenatal Development. The rates of human growth and development are most dramatic prior to birth. Within a few months, a human fetus advances from weighing a fraction of an ounce to several pounds, and from one cell to billions of cells.

Once pregnancy has been confirmed, the delivery date may be calculated by *Nagele's rule:*

- Jot down the date of the first day of the last menstrual period.
- Add seven days.
- Subtract three months.
- Add one year.

For example, if the last period began on November 12, 1998, adding seven days yields November 19, 1998. Then subtracting three months yields August 19, 1998. Adding one year gives a "due date" of August 19, 1999. Few babies are born exactly when they are due,[1] but the great majority are delivered during a ten-day period that spans the date.

Shortly following conception, the single cell that results from the union of sperm and egg begins to multiply—becoming two cells, then four, then eight, and so on. During the weeks and months that follow, tissues, structures, and organs begin to form, and the fetus gradually takes on the shape of a human being. By the time the fetus is born, it consists of hundreds of billions of cells—more cells than there are stars in the Milky Way galaxy. Prenatal development can be divided into three periods: the *germinal stage,* which corresponds to about the first two weeks, the *embryonic stage,* which coincides with the first

---

[1]The first and third authors wish to boast, however, that their daughters Allyn and Jordan were born precisely on their due dates. At least one of them has been just as compulsive ever since. The second author adds that he and his wife Judy had their son Michael within one day of the due date. (Close but no cigar, notes the first author.)

T r u t h **OR** *Fiction?*
R E V I S I T E D

two months, and the *fetal stage.* We also commonly speak of prenatal development in terms of three trimesters of three months each.

The Germinal Stage

Within 36 hours after conception, the zygote divides into 2 cells. It then divides repeatedly, becoming 32 cells within another 36 hours as it continues its journey to the uterus. It takes the zygote perhaps three or four days to reach the uterus. This mass of dividing cells then wanders about the uterus for perhaps another three or four days before it begins to become implanted in the uterine wall. The process of implantation takes about another week. This period from conception to implantation is termed the **germinal stage,** or the **period of the ovum** (see Figure 11.3).

It is true that for the first week following conception, a fertilized egg cell is not attached to its mother's body. Later it becomes implanted in the uterine wall. ■

Several days into the germinal stage, the cell mass takes the form of a fluid-filled ball of cells, which is called a **blastocyst.** Already some cell differentiation has begun. Cells begin to separate into groups that will eventually become different structures. Within a thickened mass of cells that is called the **embryonic disk,** two distinct inner layers of cells are beginning to form. These cells will become the embryo and eventually the fetus. The outer part of the blastocyst, called the **trophoblast,** consists of several membranes from which the amniotic sac, placenta, and umbilical cord eventually develop.

Implantation may be accompanied by some bleeding, which results from the usual rupturing of some small blood vessels that line the uterus. Bleeding can also be a sign of

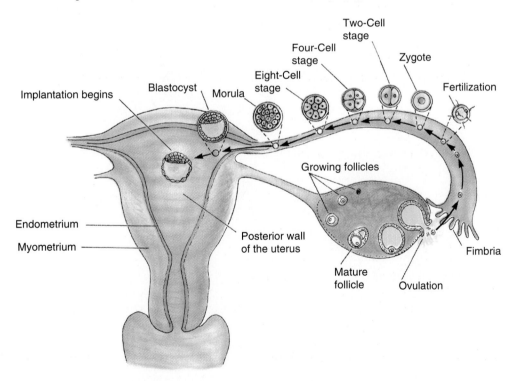

Figure 11.3. The Ovarian Cycle, Conception, and the Early Days of the Germinal Stage. The zygote first divides about 36 hours after conception. Continuing division creates the hollow sphere of cells termed the blastocyst. The blastocyst normally becomes implanted in the wall of the uterus.

a miscarriage—though most women who experience implantation bleeding do not miscarry but go on to have normal pregnancies and deliver healthy babies.

The Embryonic Stage

Embryonic stage

The stage of prenatal development that lasts from implantation through the eighth week and is characterized by the differentiation of the major organ systems.

Cephalocaudal

From the head downward. (From Latin roots meaning "head" and "tail.")

Proximodistal

From the central axis of the body outward. (From Latin roots meaning "near" and "far.")

The period from implantation to about the eighth week of development is called the **embryonic stage.** The major organ systems of the body begin to differentiate during this stage.

Development of the embryo follows two trends—**cephalocaudal** and **proximodistal.** The apparently oversized heads depicted in Figure 11.4 represent embryos and fetuses at various stages of prenatal development. Growth of the head (the cephalic region) takes precedence over the growth of the lower parts of the body. You can also think of the body as containing a central axis that coincides with the spinal cord. The growth of the organ

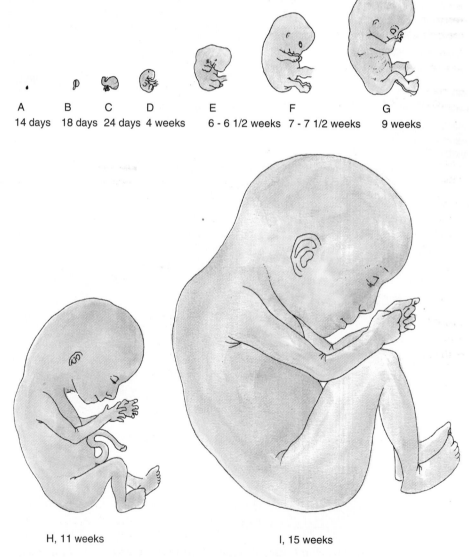

A	B	C	D	E	F	G
14 days	18 days	24 days	4 weeks	6 - 6 1/2 weeks	7 - 7 1/2 weeks	9 weeks

H, 11 weeks   I, 15 weeks

Figure 11.4. Human Embryos and Fetuses. Development is cephalocaudal and proximodistal. Growth of the head takes precedence over the growth of the lower parts of the body.

systems that lie close to this axis (that is, *proximal* to the axis) takes precedence over the growth of those that lie farther away toward the extremities (that is, *distal* to the axis). Relatively early maturation of the brain and organ systems that lie near the central axis allows these organs to facilitate further development of the embryo and fetus.

As the embryonic stage unfolds, the nervous system, sensory organs, hair, nails, teeth, and the outer layer of skin begin to develop from the outer layer of cells, or **ectoderm,** of the embryonic disk. By about three weeks after conception, two ridges appear in the embryo. The ridges fold together to form the **neural tube.** This tube develops into the nervous system. The inner layer of the embryonic disk is called the **endoderm.** From this layer develop the respiratory and digestive systems, and organs such as the liver and the pancreas. A short time later in the embryonic stage, the middle layer of cells, or **mesoderm,** differentiates and develops into the reproductive, excretory, and circulatory systems, as well as the skeleton, muscles, and the inner layer of the skin.

During the third week of development, the head and blood vessels begin to form. By the fourth week, a primitive heart begins to beat and pump blood in an embryo that measures but a fifth of an inch in length. The heart will normally continue to beat without rest for every minute of every day for the better part of a century. By the end of the first month of development we can see the beginnings of the arms and legs—"arm buds" and "leg buds." The mouth, eyes, ears, and nose begin to take shape. The brain and other parts of the nervous system begin to develop.

The arms and legs develop in accordance with the proximodistal principle. First the upper arms and legs develop. Then the forearms and lower legs. Then the hands and feet form, followed by webbed fingers and toes by about six to eight weeks into development. The webbing is gone by the end of the second month. By this time the head has become rounded, and the limbs have elongated and separated. Facial features are visible. All this has occurred in an embryo that is about 1 inch long and weighs 1/30 of an ounce. During the second month, nervous impulses also begin to travel through the developing nervous system.

The Amniotic Sac

The embryo—and later on, the fetus—develops within a protective environment in the mother's uterus called the **amniotic sac,** which is surrounded by a clear membrane. The embryo and fetus are suspended within the sac in **amniotic fluid.** The amniotic fluid acts like a shock absorber. It cushions the embryo from damage that might result from the mother's movements. The fluid also helps maintain a steady temperature.

The Placenta

Nutrients and waste products are exchanged between mother and embryo (or fetus) through a mass of tissue called the **placenta.** The placenta is unique in origin. It develops from material supplied by both mother and embryo. Toward the end of the first trimester, it becomes a flattish, round organ about 7 inches in diameter and 1 inch thick—larger than the fetus itself. The fetus is connected to the placenta by the **umbilical cord.** The mother is connected to the placenta by the system of blood vessels in the uterine wall. The umbilical cord develops about five weeks after conception and reaches 20 inches in length. It contains two arteries through which maternal nutrients reach the embryo. A vein transports waste products back to the mother.

The circulatory systems of mother and embryo do not mix. A membrane in the placenta permits only certain substances to pass through, such as oxygen (from the mother to the fetus); carbon dioxide and other wastes (from the embryo or fetus to the mother, to be eliminated by the mother's lungs and kidneys); nutrients; some microscopic disease-causing organisms; and some drugs, including aspirin, narcotics, alcohol, and tranquilizers.

The placenta is also an endocrine gland. It secretes hormones that preserve the pregnancy, stimulate the uterine contractions that induce childbirth, and help prepare the breasts for breast-feeding. Some of these hormones may also cause the signs of pregnancy. HCG (human chorionic gonadotropin) stimulates the corpus luteum to continue to produce progesterone. The placenta itself secretes increasing amounts of estrogen and progesterone. Ultimately, the placenta passes from the woman's body after delivery. For this reason it is also called the "afterbirth."

Ectoderm
The outermost cell layer of the newly formed embryo, from which the skin and nervous system develop.

Neural tube
A hollow area in the blastocyst from which the nervous system will develop.

Endoderm
The inner layer of the newly formed embryo, from which the lungs and digestive system develop.

Mesoderm
The central layer of the embryo, from which the bones and muscles develop.

Amniotic sac
The sac containing the fetus.

Amniotic fluid
Fluid within the amniotic sac that suspends and protects the fetus.

Placenta
An organ connected to the fetus by the umbilical cord. The placenta serves as a relay station between mother and fetus, allowing the exchange of nutrients and wastes.

Umbilical cord
A tube that connects the fetus to the placenta.

The Fetal Stage

The fetal stage begins by the ninth week and continues until birth. By about the ninth or tenth week, the fetus begins to respond to the outside world by turning in the direction of external stimulation. By the end of the first trimester, the major organ systems, the fingers and toes, and the external genitals have been formed. The gender of the fetus can be determined visually. The eyes have become clearly distinguishable.

During the second trimester the fetus increases dramatically in size, and its organ systems continue to mature. The brain now contributes to the regulation of basic body functions. The fetus increases in weight from 1 *ounce* to 2 *pounds* and grows from about 4 to 14 inches in length. Soft, downy hair grows above the eyes and on the scalp. The skin turns ruddy because of blood vessels that show through the surface. (During the third trimester, layers of fat beneath the skin will give the red a pinkish hue.)

Fetal Movements   Usually by the middle of the fourth month the mother can feel the first fetal movements. By the end of the second trimester, the fetus moves its limbs so vigorously that the mother may complain of being kicked—often at 4:00 A.M. It opens and shuts its eyes, sucks its thumb, alternates between periods of wakefulness and sleep, and perceives lights and sounds. The fetus also does somersaults, which the mother will definitely feel. Fortunately, the umbilical cord will not break or strangle the fetus, no matter what acrobatic feats the fetus performs.

Near the end of the second trimester the fetus approaches the **age of viability.** Still, only a minority of babies born at the end of the second trimester who weigh under 2 pounds will survive—even with intense medical efforts.

During the third trimester, the organ systems continue to mature and enlarge. The heart and lungs become increasingly capable of maintaining independent life. Typically, during the seventh month the fetus turns upside down in the uterus so that it will be headfirst, or in a **cephalic presentation,** for delivery. But some fetuses do not turn during this month. If such a fetus is born prematurely it can have either a **breech presentation** (bottom first) or a shoulder-first presentation, which can complicate problems of prematurity. The closer to term (the full nine months) the baby is born, the more likely it is that the presentation will be cephalic. If birth occurs at the end of the eighth month, the odds are overwhelmingly in favor of survival.

During the final months of pregnancy, the mother may become concerned that the fetus seems to be less active than before. Most of the time the change in activity level is normal. The fetus has grown so large that it is cramped, and its movements are restricted.

Environmental Influences on Prenatal Development

Advances in scientific knowledge have made us more aware of the changes that take place during prenatal development. They have also heightened our awareness of the problems that can occur and what might be done to prevent them. We focus in this next section on the environmental factors that affect prenatal development. These include the mother's diet, maternal diseases and disorders, and the mother's use of drugs.

The Mother's Diet   It is a common misconception that the fetus will take what it needs from its mother. Actually, malnutrition in the mother can adversely affect fetal development. Maternal malnutrition during the third trimester, when the fetus normally makes sharp gains in weight, is linked to low birthweight and increased infant mortality. Pregnant women who are well nourished are more likely to deliver babies of average or above average size. Their infants are also less likely to develop colds and serious respiratory disorders.

A woman can expect to gain at least 20 pounds during pregnancy because of the growth of the placenta, amniotic fluid, and the fetus itself. Most women will gain about 25 pounds or so (Thompson, 1993). Overweight women may gain less. Slender women may

Age of viability
The age at which a fetus can sustain independent life.

Cephalic presentation
Emergence of the baby headfirst from the womb.

Breech presentation
Emergence of the baby feet first from the womb.

gain 30 pounds. Regular weight gains are most desirable, about ½ pound a week during the first half of pregnancy and about 1 pound a week during the second half.

Teratogens
Environmental influences or agents that can damage an embryo or fetus. (From the Greek *teras*, meaning "monster.")

Maternal Diseases and Disorders Environmental influences or agents that can harm the embryo or fetus are called **teratogens.** These include drugs taken by the mother, such as alcohol and even aspirin, as well as substances produced by the mother's body, such as Rh-positive antibodies. Other teratogens include the metals lead and mercury, radiation, and disease-causing organisms such as viruses and bacteria. Although many disease-causing organisms cannot pass through the placenta to infect the embryo or fetus, some extremely small organisms, such as those causing syphilis, measles, mumps, and chicken pox, can. Some disorders such as toxemia are not transmitted to the embryo or fetus but can adversely affect the environment in which it develops.

Critical period of vulnerability
A period of time during which an embryo or fetus is vulnerable to the effects of a teratogen.

Critical Periods of Vulnerability The times at which exposure to particular teratogens can cause the greatest harm are termed **critical periods of vulnerability.** Critical periods correspond to the times at which the structures most affected by the teratogens are developing (see Figure 11.5). The heart, for example, develops rapidly from the third to the fifth week following conception. It may be most vulnerable to certain teratogens at this time. The arms and legs, which develop later, are most vulnerable from the fourth through the eighth week of development. Since the major organ systems differentiate during the embryonic stage, the embryo is most vulnerable to the effects of teratogens during this stage.

Let us now consider some of the most damaging effects of specific maternal diseases and disorders.

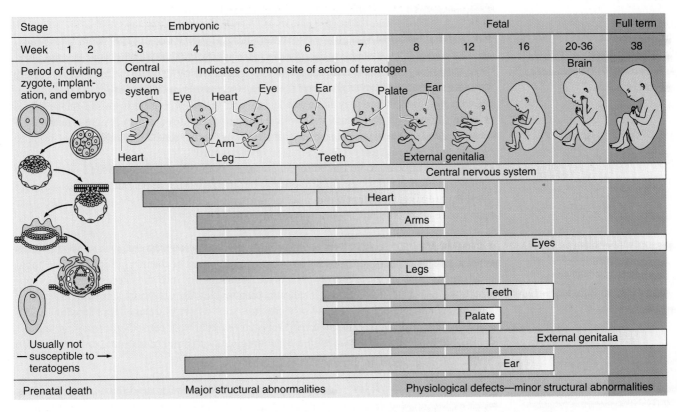

Figure 11.5. Critical Periods in Prenatal Development. The developing embryo is most vulnerable to teratogens when the organ systems are taking shape. The periods of greatest vulnerability of organ systems are shown in blue. Periods of lesser vulnerability are shown in yellow. *Source:* Rathus, S. A. (1988). *Understanding Child Development.* Copyright © 1988 by Holt, Rinehart, & Winston, Inc. Reprinted with permission.

Rubella
A viral infection that can cause mental retardation and heart disease in an embryo. Also called *German measles*.

Rubella (German Measles) **Rubella** is a viral infection. Women who contract rubella during the first month or two of pregnancy, when rapid differentiation of major organ systems is taking place, may bear children who are deaf or who develop mental retardation, heart disease, or cataracts. Risk of these defects declines as pregnancy progresses.

Nearly 85% of women in the United States had rubella as children and so acquired immunity. Women who do not know whether they have had rubella may be tested; if they are not immune, they can be vaccinated *prior to pregnancy*. Inoculation during pregnancy is considered risky because the vaccine causes a mild case of the disease in the mother, which can affect the embryo or fetus. Increased awareness of the dangers of rubella during pregnancy, and of the preventative effects of inoculation, has led to a dramatic decline in the number of children born in the United States with defects caused by rubella.

Syphilis
A sexually transmitted disease caused by a bacterial infection.

Stillbirth
The birth of a dead fetus.

Syphilis Maternal **syphilis** may cause miscarriage or **stillbirth,** or be passed along to the child in the form of congenital syphilis. Congenital syphilis can impair the vision and hearing, damage the liver, or deform the bones and teeth.

Routine blood tests early in pregnancy can diagnose syphilis and other problems. Because the bacteria that cause syphilis do not readily cross the placental membrane during the first months of pregnancy, the fetus will probably not contract syphilis if an infected mother is treated successfully with antibiotics before the fourth month of pregnancy.

Acquired immunodeficiency syndrome (AIDS)
A sexually transmitted disease that destroys white blood cells in the immune system, leaving the body vulnerable to various "opportunistic" diseases.

Acquired Immunodeficiency Syndrome (AIDS) **Acquired immunodeficiency syndrome (AIDS)** is caused by the *human immunodeficiency virus* (HIV). HIV is blood-borne and is sometimes transmitted through the placenta to infect the fetus. The rupturing of blood vessels in mother and baby during childbirth provides another opportunity for transmission of HIV (Peckham & Gibb, 1995). *However, the majority of babies born to mothers who are infected with HIV do not become infected themselves.* As we will see in Chapter 17, measures can be taken to minimize the probability of transmission. HIV can also be transmitted to children by breast-feeding.

Toxemia
A life-threatening condition that is characterized by high blood pressure.

Toxemia **Toxemia** is a life-threatening condition characterized by high blood pressure that may afflict women late in the second or early in the third trimester of pregnancy. The first stage is termed *preeclampsia*. It is diagnosed by protein in the urine, swelling from fluid retention, and high blood pressure, and may be relatively mild. As preeclampsia worsens, the mother may have headaches and visual problems from the raised blood pressure, along with abdominal pain. If left untreated, the disease may progress to the final stage, termed *eclampsia*. Eclampsia can lead to maternal or fetal death. Babies born to women with toxemia are often undersized or premature.

Toxemia appears to be linked to malnutrition. Ironically, undernourished women may gain weight rapidly through fluid retention, but their swollen appearance may discourage them from eating. Pregnant women who gain weight rapidly but have not increased their food intake should consult their obstetricians.

Ectopic pregnancy
A pregnancy in which the fertilized ovum becomes implanted someplace other than the uterus.

Ectopic Pregnancy In an **ectopic pregnancy,** the fertilized ovum implants itself someplace other than the uterus. Most ectopic pregnancies occur in a fallopian tube ("tubal pregnancies") when the ovum is prevented from moving into the uterus because of obstructions caused by infections. If ectopic pregnancies do not abort spontaneously, they must be removed by surgery or use of medicines such as methotrexate (Hausknecht, 1995), since the fetus cannot develop to term. Delay in removal may cause hemorrhaging and the death of the mother. A woman with a tubal pregnancy will not menstruate, but may notice spotty bleeding and abdominal pain.

Rh incompatibility
A condition in which antibodies produced by a pregnant woman are transmitted to the fetus and may cause brain damage or death.

Rh Incompatibility In **Rh incompatibility,** antibodies produced by the mother are transmitted to a fetus or newborn infant. *Rh* is a blood protein found in some people's red blood cells. Rh incompatibility occurs when a woman who does not have this blood factor, and is thus *Rh negative,* is carrying an *Rh-positive* fetus, which can happen if the father is Rh-positive. The negative–positive combination is found in about 10% of U.S. marriages. However, it becomes a problem only in a minority of the resulting pregnancies. In such cases the mother's antibodies attack the red blood cells of the fetus, which can cause brain damage or death. Rh incompatibility does not usually adversely affect a first child because women will usually not yet have formed antibodies to the Rh factor.

Since mother and fetus have separate circulatory systems, it is unlikely that Rh-positive fetal red blood cells will enter the Rh-negative mother's body. The probability of an exchange of blood increases during childbirth, however, especially when the placenta becomes detached from the uterine wall. If an exchange of blood occurs, the mother will then produce antibodies to the baby's Rh-positive blood. The mother's antibodies may enter the fetal bloodstream and cause a condition called *fetal erythroblastosis,* which can result in anemia, mental deficiency, or even the death of the fetus or newborn infant.

Fortunately, blood-typing of pregnant women significantly decreases the threat of uncontrolled erythroblastosis. If an Rh-negative mother is injected with the vaccine Rhogan within 72 hours after delivery of an Rh-positive baby, she will not develop the dangerous antibodies and thus will not pass them on to the fetus in a subsequent pregnancy. A fetus or newborn child at risk for erythroblastosis may also receive a preventive blood transfusion, in order to remove the mother's Rh-positive antibodies from its blood.

Drugs Taken by the Mother (and the Father)   Some widely used drugs, including nonprescription drugs like aspirin, are linked with birth abnormalities. In the 1960s the drug thalidomide was marketed to pregnant women as a presumably safe treatment for nausea and insomnia. However, the drug caused birth deformities, including stunted or missing limbs. Maternal use of illegal drugs such as cocaine and marijuana may also place the fetus at risk.

Paternal use of certain drugs also may endanger the fetus. One question is whether drugs alter the genetic material in the father's sperm. The use of certain substances by those who come into contact with a pregnant woman can harm the fetus. For example, the mother's inhalation of second-hand tobacco or marijuana smoke can hurt the fetus.

Several antibiotics may harm a fetus, especially if they are taken during certain periods of fetal development. Tetracycline may yellow the teeth and deform the bones. Other antibiotics have been implicated in deafness and jaundice.

Acne drugs can cause physical and mental handicaps in the children of women who use them during pregnancy (Mills, 1995). Antihistamines, used commonly for allergies, may deform the fetus.

If you are pregnant, or suspect that you are, it is advisable to consult your obstetrician before taking any and all drugs, not just prescription drugs. Your obstetrician can usually direct you to a safe and effective substitute for a drug that could harm a fetus.

Hormones   The hormones progestin and DES have sometimes been used to help women at risk of miscarriage maintain their pregnancies. When taken at about the time that sex organs differentiate, progestin—which is similar in composition to male sex hormones—can masculinize the external sex organs of embryos with female (XX) sex chromosomal structures. Progestin taken during the first trimester has also been linked to increased levels of aggressive behavior during childhood.

DES (short for *diethylstilbestrol*), a powerful estrogen, was given to many women at risk for miscarriage from the 1940s through the 1960s to help maintain their pregnancies. DES is suspected of causing cervical and testicular cancer in some of the children whose mothers used it when pregnant. Other problems have been reported as well. Daughters whose mothers used DES during their pregnancies have a higher-than-expected rate of miscarriages and premature deliveries. It was once suspected that men who were exposed prenatally to DES had higher than expected rates of infertility. However, research reveals no connection between in utero exposure to DES and male infertility (Wilcox et al., 1995). DES users themselves appear to be at high risk of some serious medical problems, such as breast cancer (Greenberg et al., 1984).

DES
Diethylstilbestrol: an estrogen that was once given to women at risk for miscarriage to help maintain pregnancy.

Vitamins   Many pregnant women are prescribed daily doses of multivitamins to maintain their own health and to promote the development of a healthy pregnancy. "Too much of a good thing" may be hazardous, however. High doses of vitamins such as A, B$_6$, D, and K have been linked to birth defects. Vitamin A excesses have been linked with cleft palate and eye damage, whereas excesses of vitamin D are linked to mental retardation.

Narcotics   Narcotics such as heroin and methadone can readily pass from mother to fetus through the placental membrane. Narcotics are addictive. Fetuses of mothers who use them regularly during their pregnancies can become addicted in utero. At birth, such babies may undergo withdrawal and show muscle tension and agitation. Women who use narcotics are advised to notify their obstetricians so that measures can be taken to aid the infants prior to and following delivery.

Tranquilizers and Sedatives   The tranquilizers Librium and Valium cross the placental membrane and may cause birth defects such as harelip. Sedatives, such as the barbiturate *phenobarbital,* are suspected of decreasing testosterone production and causing reproductive problems in the sons of women who use them during pregnancy.

Hallucinogenics   Use of hallucinogenic drugs such as marijuana and LSD during pregnancy has been linked to chromosomal damage in fetuses (National Academy of Sciences, 1982). The active ingredient in marijuana, THC, readily crosses the placenta, as does LSD. Use of marijuana can lead to decreased androgen production in male fetuses, which can interfere with the process of sexual differentiation. Research provides evidence that preschoolers whose mothers used marijuana during their pregnancies suffered more neurological and visual problems than did children of nonusers (Fried, 1986).

Fetal alcohol syndrome
A cluster of symptoms caused by maternal drinking, in which the child shows developmental lags and characteristic facial features such as an underdeveloped upper jaw, flattened nose, and widely spaced eyes.

Alcohol   Mothers who drink heavily during pregnancy expose the fetus to greater risk of birth defects, infant mortality, sensory and motor problems, and mental retardation (Barr et al., 1990; Coles, 1994). Nearly 40% of children whose mothers drank heavily during pregnancy develop **fetal alcohol syndrome** (FAS). FAS is a cluster of symptoms typified by developmental lags and characteristic facial features, such as an underdeveloped upper jaw, flattened nose, and widely spaced eyes. Infants with FAS are often smaller than average and have smaller than average brains. They may be mentally retarded, lack coordination, and have deformed limbs and heart problems.

Although research suggests that light drinking is unlikely to harm the fetus in most cases (Jacobson & Jacobson, 1994), FAS has been found even among the children of mothers who drank only two ounces of alcohol a day during the first trimester (Astley et al., 1992). Moreover, individual sensitivities to alcohol may vary widely (Jacobson & Jacobson, 1994). The critical period for the development of the facial features associated with FAS seems to be the first two months of prenatal development, when the head is taking shape (Coles, 1994).

T r u t h   OR   *Fiction?*
R E V I S I T E D

It is not true that pregnant women can have one or two alcoholic beverages a day without harming their babies. No safe minimal amount of drinking for pregnant women has been established. Therefore, pregnant women are advised to abstain from alcohol, period.   ■

Cigarette Smoking   At least 1 in 4 pregnant women in 1990 smoked (USDHHS, 1991; Floyd et al., 1993). Cigarette smoke contains chemicals such as carbon monoxide and the stimulant nicotine that are transmitted to the fetus. Maternal smoking increases the risk of spontaneous abortion and complications during pregnancy such as premature rupturing of the amniotic sac, stillbirth, premature birth, low birthweight, and early infant mortality (English & Eskenazi, 1992; Floyd et al., 1993; USDHHS, 1992a). Women who smoke less than a pack a day stand a higher risk of pregnancy and birth complications than do nonsmokers (Floyd et al., 1993; Mayer et al., 1990). The health risks generally increase with the amount smoked.

Low birthweight is the most common risk factor for infant disease and mortality (USDHHS, 1992a). Maternal smoking during pregnancy more than doubles the risk of low birthweight (Mayer et al., 1990). The combination of smoking and drinking alcohol places the child at greater risk of low birthweight than either practice alone (Day & Richardson, 1994). As many as 1 in 4 cases of low birthweight could be prevented if mothers-to-be quit smoking during pregnancy (USDHHS, 1990). The earlier the pregnant smoker quits, the better for the baby (and herself!). Simply cutting down on smoking during pregnancy may not offer much protection in preventing low birthweight, however (USDHHS, 1990a).

Maternal smoking also has important acute effects on fetal heart rate (Graca et al., 1991) and increases the risk of sudden infant death syndrome (SIDS) (Feng, 1993; Haglund & Cnattingius, 1990; Malloy et al., 1992; Schoendorf & Kiely, 1992; Zhang & Fried, 1992). Maternal smoking has also been linked to reduced lung function in newborns (Hanrahan et al., 1992) and asthma in childhood (Martinez et al., 1992). Evidence also points to reduced attentions spans, hyperactivity, and lower IQs and achievement test scores in children exposed to maternal smoking during and following pregnancy (Barr et al., 1990).

Smoking by the father (or other household members) may be dangerous to a fetus because secondary smoke (smoke exhaled by the smoker or emitted from the tip of a lit cigarette) may be absorbed by the mother and passed along to the fetus. Passive exposure to second-hand smoke during infancy is also linked to increased risk of SIDS (Schoendorf & Kiely, 1992).

The majority of women in the United States of reproductive age drink alcohol, at least occasionally. More than one in four smoke cigarettes. Many of them do not suspend drug use until they learn that they are pregnant. Unfortunately, this knowledge may not be obtained until a woman is weeks into the pregnancy. Damage to the fetus may thus have already occurred. Many women are unwilling or unable to change their drug use habits even after learning they are pregnant. Among women who smoke, only one in five quits smoking when she becomes pregnant (Floyd et al., 1993).

Our clinical experience suggests that it may be easier for women to quit if they conceptualize their quitting as limited in time to the terms of their pregnancies rather than as permanent. Then, of course, if they should remain abstinent after delivery, perhaps they will not be disappointed.

Other Agents   X-rays increase the risk of malformed organs in the fetus, especially within a month and a half following conception. (Ultrasound has *not* been shown to harm the embryo or fetus.)

Chromosomal and Genetic Abnormalities

Not all of us have the normal complement of chromosomes. Some of us have genes that threaten our health or our existence (see Table 11.1 on page 316).

Down Syndrome   Children with Down syndrome have characteristic round faces; wide, flat noses; and protruding tongues. They often suffer from respiratory problems and heart malformations, problems that tend to claim their lives by middle age—the "prime of life" when most of us are reaching our vocational heights. People with Down syndrome are also moderately mentally retarded, but they usually can learn to read and write. With a little help from family and social agencies, they may hold jobs and lead largely independent lives.

The risk of a child's having Down syndrome increases with the mother's age (see Table 11.2 on page 317). Down syndrome is usually caused by an extra chromosome on the 21st pair. In about 95% of cases, Down syndrome is transmitted by the mother (Antonarakas et al., 1991). The inner corners of the eyes of people with the syndrome have a downward-sloping crease of skin that gives them a superficial likeness to Asians. This is why the syndrome was once dubbed *mongolism,* a moniker that has since been rejected because of its racist overtones.

Sickle Cell Anemia and Tay-Sachs Disease   Sickle cell anemia and Tay-Sachs disease are genetic disorders that are most likely to afflict certain racial and ethnic groups. Sickle cell anemia is most prevalent in the United States among African Americans. One of every 375 African Americans is affected by the disease, and 8% are carriers of the

TABLE 11.1 Some chromosomal and genetic abnormalities

Cystic fibrosis	A genetic disease in which the pancreas and lungs become clogged with mucus, which impairs the processes of respiration and digestion.
Down syndrome	A condition characterized by a 3rd chromosome on the 21st pair. The child with Down syndrome has a characteristic fold of skin over the eye and mental retardation. The risk of a child's exhibiting the syndrome increases as parents increase in age.
Hemophilia	A sex-linked disorder in which the blood fails to clot properly.
Huntington's chorea	A fatal neurological disorder whose onset occurs in middle adulthood.
Neural-tube defects	Disorders of the brain or spine, such as *anencephaly,* in which part of the brain is missing, and *spina bifida,* in which part of the spine is exposed or missing. Anencephaly is fatal shortly after birth, but some spina bifida victims survive for a number of years, albeit with severe handicaps.
Phenylketonuria	A disorder in which children cannot metabolize phenylalanine, which builds up in the form of phenylpyruvic acid and causes mental retardation. The disorder can be diagnosed at birth and controlled by diet.
Retina blastoma	A form of blindness caused by a dominant gene.
Sickle cell anemia	A blood disorder that mostly afflicts African Americans, in which deformed blood cells obstruct small blood vessels, decreasing their capacity to carry oxygen and heightening the risk of occasionally fatal infections.
Tay Sachs disease	A fatal neurological disorder that primarily afflicts Jews of European origin.

Source: Etaugh & Rathus (1995).

sickle cell trait (Leary, 1993). In sickle cell anemia, the red blood cells assume a sickle shape—hence the name—and they form clumps that obstruct narrow blood vessels and diminish the supply of oxygen. As a result, victims can suffer problems ranging from swollen, painful joints to potentially lethal problems such as pneumonia and heart and kidney failure. Infections are a leading cause of death among those with the disease (Leary, 1993a).

Tay Sachs disease is a fatal neurological disease of young children. Only 1 in 100,000 people in the United States is affected, but among Jews of Eastern European background the figure rises steeply to 1 in 3,600 (Hubbard & Wald, 1993). The disease is characterized by degeneration of the central nervous system and gives rise to retardation, loss of muscle control and paralysis, blindness, and deafness. Victims seldom live beyond the age of 5.

Recessive trait

A trait that is not expressed when the gene or genes involved have been paired with dominant genes. Recessive traits are transmitted to future generations, however, and are expressed if they are paired with other recessive genes.

Sex-Linked Genetic Abnormalities
Some genetic defects, such as hemophilia, are sex linked, in that they are carried only on the X sex chromosome. They are transmitted from generation to generation as **recessive traits.** Females, each of whom has two X sex chromosomes, are less likely than males to be afflicted by sex-linked disorders, because the genes that carry the disorder would have to be present on both of their sex chromosomes for the disorder to be expressed. Sex-linked disorders are more likely to afflict sons of female carriers because they have only one X sex chromosome, which they inherit from their mothers. England's Queen Victoria was a hemophilia carrier and transmitted the condition to many of her children, who in turn carried it into several ruling houses of Europe. For this reason hemophilia has been dubbed the "royal disease."

Methods of Averting Chromosomal and Genetic Abnormalities
Based upon information about a couple's medical background and family history of genetic defects, genetic counselors help couples appraise the risks of passing along genetic

TABLE 11.2 Risk of giving birth to an infant with Down syndrome, according to age of the mother

Age of Mother	Probability of Down Syndrome
30	1/885
31	1/826
32	1/725
33	1/592
34	1/465
35*	1/365
36	1/287
37	1/225
38	1/176
39	1/139
40	1/109
41	1/85
42	1/67
43	1/53
44	1/41
45	1/32
46	1/25
47	1/20
48	1/16
49	1/11

*Age at which testing for Down syndrome is usually first recommended.
Source: Adapted from Samuels & Samuels, 1986, p. 240. Reprinted with permission.

defects to their children. Some couples facing a high risk of passing along genetic defects to their children decide to adopt. Other couples decide to have an abortion if the fetus is determined to have certain abnormalities.

Various medical procedures are used to detect the presence of these disorders in the fetus. *Amniocentesis* is usually performed about four months into pregnancy but is sometimes done earlier. Fluid is drawn from the amniotic sac (or "bag of waters") with a syringe. Fetal cells in the fluid are grown in a culture and examined under a microscope for the presence of biochemical and chromosomal abnormalities. *Chorionic villus sampling (CVS)* is performed

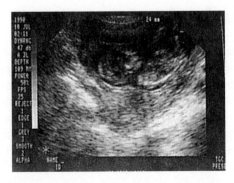

An Ultrasound Image. An ultrasound image of the second author's son, Michael, at 12 weeks following conception. The head and upper torso (facing upwards) can be seen in the upper middle section of the picture. He was handsome even then, his perfectly objective father points out.

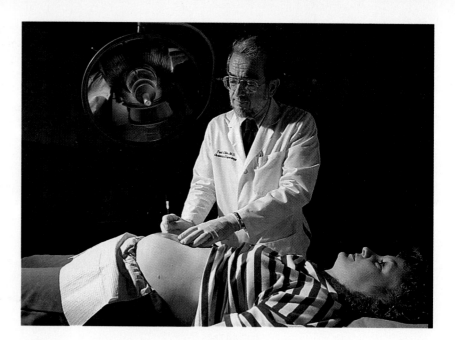

Amniocentesis. In this form of prenatal testing, cells sloughed off by the fetus into amniotic fluid are withdrawn by a syringe and examined for genetic and chromosomal abnormalities.

several weeks earlier. A narrow tube is used to snip off material from the chorion, which is a membrane that contains the amniotic sac and fetus. The material is analyzed. CVS is somewhat riskier than amniocentesis, so most obstetricians prefer to use the latter. The tests detect Down syndrome, sickle cell anemia, Tay-Sachs disease, spina bifida, muscular dystrophy, Rh incompatibility, and other conditions. The tests also identify the gender of the fetus.

In ultrasound, high-pitched sound waves are bounced off the fetus, like radar, revealing a picture of the fetus on a TV monitor and allowing the obstetrician to detect certain abnormalities. Obstetricians also use ultrasound to locate the fetus during amniocentesis in order to lower the probability of injuring it with the syringe.

Parental blood tests can suggest the presence of problems such as sickle cell anemia, Tay-Sachs disease, and neural-tube defects. Still other tests examine fetal DNA and can indicate the presence of Huntington's chorea, cystic fibrosis, and other disorders.

~ *Reflections* ~

- Have you been with anyone during a pregnancy? (Don't exclude yourself!) How did she react when she first detected fetal movements?
- Do you know anyone who drank alcohol or smoked during pregnancy? Would she talk about her drinking or smoking? What did she say?
- Do you know of anyone who has been tested to learn whether her or his child is likely to have a genetic or chromosomal abnormality? Which test was used? Why?

Childbirth

Early in the ninth month of pregnancy, the fetus's head settles in the pelvis. This shift is called "dropping" or "lightening." The woman may actually feel lighter because of lessened pressure on the diaphragm. About a day or so before the beginning of labor, the woman may notice blood in her vaginal secretions because fetal pressure on the pelvis may rupture superficial blood vessels in the birth canal. Tissue that had plugged the cervix, possibly preventing entry of infectious agents from the vagina, becomes dislodged. There is a resultant discharge of bloody mucus. At about this time one woman in ten also has a rush of warm "water" from the vagina. The "water" is amniotic fluid, and it means that the amniotic sac has burst. Labor usually begins within a day after rupture of the amniotic sac. For most women the amniotic sac does not burst until the end of the first stage of childbirth. Other signs of impending labor include indigestion, diarrhea, abdominal cramps, and an ache in the small of the back. Labor begins with the onset of regular uterine contractions.

The first uterine contractions are relatively painless and are called **Braxton-Hicks contractions,** or "false" labor contractions. They are false because they do not widen the cervix or advance the baby through the birth canal. They tend to increase in frequency but are less regular than labor contractions. "Real" contractions, by contrast, become more intense when the woman moves around or walks.

The initiation of labor may involve the secretion of hormones by the fetal adrenal and pituitary glands that stimulate the placenta and mother's uterus to secrete **prostaglandins.** Prostaglandins stimulate the uterine musculature to contract. It would make sense for the fetus to have a mechanism for signaling the mother that it is mature enough to sustain independent life. The mechanisms that initiate and maintain labor are not fully understood, however. Later in labor the pituitary gland releases **oxytocin,** a hormone that stimulates contractions strong enough to expel the baby.

Braxton-Hicks contractions
So-called false labor contractions that are relatively painless.

Prostaglandins
Uterine hormones that stimulate uterine contractions.

Oxytocin
A pituitary hormone that stimulates uterine contractions.

Truth **OR** Fiction?
REVISITED

It is probably true that a baby signals its mother (chemically) when it is ready to be born (that is, to sustain independent life). ■

The Stages of Childbirth

Childbirth begins with the onset of labor and progresses through three stages.

Efface
To become thin.

Dilate
To open or widen.

The First Stage   In the first stage uterine contractions **efface** and **dilate** the cervix to about 4 inches (10 cm) in diameter, so that the baby may pass. Stretching of the cervix causes most of the pain of childbirth. A woman may experience little or no pain if her

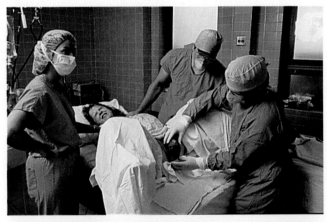

Coming into the World. Childbirth progresses through three stages. In the first stage, uterine contractions efface and dilate the cervix so that the baby may pass. The second stage lasts from a few minutes to a few hours and ends with the birth of the baby. During the third stage the placenta is expelled.

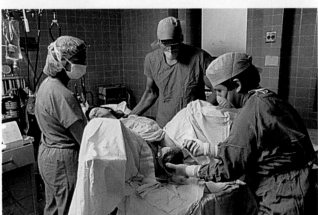

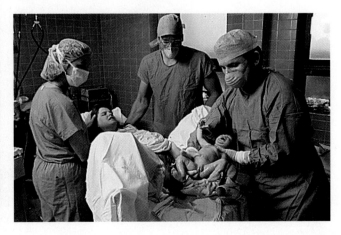

cervix dilates easily and quickly. The first stage may last from a couple of hours to more than a day. Twelve to 24 hours of labor is considered about average for a first pregnancy. In later pregnancies labor takes about half this time.

The initial contractions are usually mild and spaced widely, at intervals of 10 to 20 minutes. They may last 20 to 40 seconds. As time passes, contractions become more frequent, long, strong, and regular.

Transition is the process that occurs when the cervix becomes nearly fully dilated and the baby's head begins to move into the vagina, or birth canal. Contractions usually come quickly during transition. Transition usually lasts about 30 minutes or less and is often accompanied by feelings of nausea, chills, and intense pain.

Transition

The process during which the cervix becomes nearly fully dilated and the head of the fetus begins to move into the birth canal.

The Second Stage   The second stage of childbirth follows transition and begins when the cervix has become fully dilated and the baby begins to move into the vagina and first appears at the opening of the birth canal (see Figure 11.6). The woman may be taken

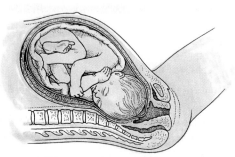

1. The second stage of labor begins

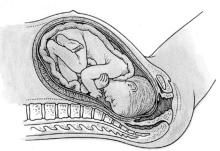

2. Further descent and rotation

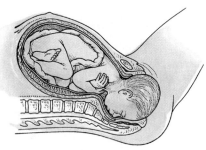

3. The crowning of the head

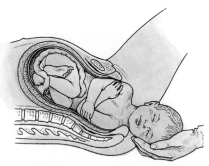

4. Anterior shoulder delivered

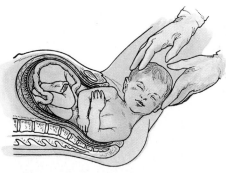

5. Posterior shoulder delivered

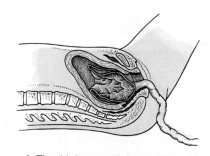

6. The third stage of labor begins with separation of the placenta from the uterine wall

Figure 11.6.   The Stages of Childbirth. In the first stage, uterine contractions efface and dilate the cervix to about 4 inches so that the baby may pass. The second stage begins with movement of the baby into the birth canal and ends with birth of the baby. During the third stage the placenta separates from the uterine wall and is expelled through the birth canal.

to a delivery room for the second stage of childbirth. The second stage is shorter than the first stage. It lasts from a few minutes to a few hours and ends with the birth of the baby.

Each contraction of the second stage propels the baby farther along the birth canal (vagina). When the baby's head becomes visible at the vaginal opening, it is said to have *crowned*. The baby typically emerges fully a few minutes after crowning.

Episiotomy

A surgical incision in the perineum that widens the birth canal, preventing random tearing during childbirth.

Perineum

The area between the vulva and the anus.

An **episiotomy** may be performed on the mother when the baby's head has crowned. Episiotomies are controversial, however. The incision can be painful in itself and cause discomfort and itching as it heals. In some cases the discomfort interferes with coitus for months. Many obstetricians no longer perform episiotomies routinely. However, most health professionals concur that an episiotomy is preferable to the random tearing that can occur if the tissues of the **perineum** become extremely effaced.

With or without an episiotomy, the baby's passageway to the external world is a tight fit at best. As a result, the baby's facial features and the shape of its head may be temporarily distended. The baby may look as if it has been through a prizefight. Its head may be elongated, its nose flattened, and its ears bent. Although parents may be concerned about whether the baby's features will assume a more typical shape, they almost always do.

The Third Stage   The third, or placental, stage of childbirth may last from a few minutes to an hour or more. During this stage, the placenta is expelled. Detachment of the placenta from the uterine wall may cause some bleeding. The uterus begins the process of contracting to a smaller size. The attending physician sews up the episiotomy or any tears in the perineum.

In the New World   As the baby's head emerges, mucus is cleared from its mouth by means of suction aspiration to prevent the breathing passageway from being obstructed. Aspiration is often repeated once the baby is fully delivered. (Newly delivered babies are no longer routinely held upside down to help expel mucus. Nor is the baby slapped on the buttocks to stimulate breathing, as in old films.)

Once the baby is breathing adequately, the umbilical cord is clamped and severed about 3 inches from the baby's body. (After the birth of your first and third authors' third child, your first author was invited by the obstetrician to cut the umbilical cord—but the third author seized the scissors and cut the umbilical cord herself, squirting blood on the glasses of the obstetrician. "Who gave the obstetrician the right to determine who would cut the umbilical cord!" she wanted to know.) The stump of the umbilical cord dries and falls off in its own time, usually in seven to ten days.

While the mother is in the third stage of labor, the nurse may perform procedures on the baby, such as placing drops of silver nitrate or an antibiotic ointment into the eyes. This procedure is required by most states to prevent bacterial infections in the newborn's eyes. Typically the baby is also footprinted and (if the birth has taken place in a hospital) given an identification bracelet. Since neonates do not manufacture vitamin K on their own, the baby may also receive an injection of the vitamin to ensure that her or his blood will clot normally in case of bleeding.

Methods of Childbirth

Until this century childbirth was usually an event that happened at home and involved the mother, a midwife, family, and friends. These days women in the United States and Canada typically give birth in hospitals, attended by obstetricians who use surgical instruments and anesthetics to protect mothers and children from infection, complications, and pain. Medical procedures save lives but also make childbearing more impersonal. Social critics argue that these procedures have "medicalized" a natural process. They have usurped control over women's bodies and, through the use of drugs, denied many women the experience of giving birth.

Anesthetized Childbirth

In sorrow thou shalt bring forth children.

(Genesis 3:16)

The Bible suggests that the ancients saw suffering as a woman's lot. But during the past two centuries, science and medicine have led to the expectation that women should experience minimal discomfort during childbirth. Today some anesthesia is used to minimize or eliminate pain in most U.S. deliveries.

General anesthesia first became popular when Queen Victoria of England delivered her eighth child under chloroform in 1853. General anesthesia, like the chloroform of old, induces unconsciousness. The drug sodium pentothal, a barbiturate, induces general anesthesia when it is injected into a vein. Barbiturates may also be taken orally to reduce anxiety while the woman remains awake. Women may also receive tranquilizers like Valium or narcotics like Demerol to help them relax and to blunt pain without inducing sleep.

Anesthetic drugs, as well as tranquilizers and narcotics, decrease the strength of uterine contractions during delivery. They may thus delay the process of cervical dilation and prolong labor. They also weaken the woman's ability to push the baby through the birth canal. Because they cross the placental membrane, they also lower the newborn's overall responsiveness.

Regional or **local anesthetics** block pain in parts of the body without generally depressing the mother's alertness or putting her to sleep. In a *pudendal block,* the external genitals are numbed by local injection. In an *epidural block* and a *spinal block,* an anesthetic is injected into the spinal canal, which temporarily numbs the mother's body below the waist. To prevent injury, the needles used for these injections do not come into contact with the spinal cord itself. Although local anesthesia decreases the responsiveness of the newborn baby, there is little evidence that medicated childbirth has serious, long-term consequences on children (Ganitsch, 1992).

Natural Childbirth   Partly as a reaction against the use of anesthetics, English obstetrician Grantly Dick-Read endorsed **natural childbirth** in his 1944 book *Childbirth Without Fear.* Dick-Read argued that women's labor pains were heightened by their fear of the unknown and resultant muscle tensions. Many of Dick-Read's contributions came to be regarded as accepted practice in modern childbirth procedures, such as the emphasis on informing women about the biological aspects of reproduction and childbirth, the encouragement of physical fitness, and the teaching of relaxation and breathing exercises.

Prepared Childbirth: The Lamaze Method   The French obstetrician Fernand Lamaze visited the Soviet Union in 1951 and found that many Russian women bore babies without anesthetics and without reporting a great deal of pain. Lamaze returned to western Europe with some of the techniques the women used, and they are now usually termed the **Lamaze method,** or *prepared childbirth.* Lamaze (1981) argued that women can learn to conserve energy during childbirth and reduce the pain of uterine contractions by associating the contractions with other responses, such as thinking of pleasant mental images such as beach scenes, or engaging in breathing and relaxation exercises.

A pregnant woman typically attends Lamaze classes with a "coach"—usually the father—who will aid her in the delivery room by timing contractions, offering emotional support, and coaching her in the breathing and relaxation exercises. The woman and her partner also receive more general information about childbirth. The father is integrated into the process, and many couples report that their marriages are strengthened as a result.

The Lamaze method is flexible concerning the use of anesthetics. Many women report some pain during delivery and obtain anesthetics. However, the Lamaze method appears to enhance women's self-esteem by helping them gain a greater sense of control over the delivery process.

Cesarean Section   In a **cesarean section,** the baby is delivered through surgery rather than naturally through the vagina. The term is derived from the Latin for "to cut." Julius Caesar is said to have been delivered in this way, but health professionals believe this unlikely (Brody, 1989b). In a cesarean section (C-section for short) the woman is anesthetized, and incisions are made in the abdomen and uterus so that the surgeon can remove the baby. The incisions are then sewn up and the mother can begin walking, often on the same day, although generally with some discomfort for a while.

General anesthesia
The use of drugs to put people to sleep and eliminate pain, as during childbirth.

Local anesthesia
Anesthesia that eliminates pain in a specific area of the body, as during childbirth.

Natural childbirth
A method of childbirth in which women use no anesthesia but are given other strategies for coping with discomfort and are educated about childbirth.

Lamaze method
A childbirth method in which women learn about childbirth, learn to relax and to breathe in patterns that conserve energy and lessen pain, and have a coach (usually the father) present at childbirth. Also termed *prepared childbirth.*

Cesarean section
A method of childbirth in which the fetus is delivered through a surgical incision in the abdomen.

Transverse position
A crosswise birth position.

C-sections are most likely to be advised when normal delivery is difficult or threatening to the health of the mother or child. Vaginal deliveries can become difficult if the baby is large or the mother's pelvis is small or misshapen, or if the mother is overly tired or weakened. Herpes and HIV infections in the birth canal can be bypassed by C-section. C-sections are also likely to be performed if the baby presents for delivery in the breech position (feet downward) or the **transverse position** (lying crosswise), or if the baby is in distress.

Use of the C-section has mushroomed. In the 1990s, nearly 1 million births each year are by cesarean section, which works out to nearly 1 of every 4 births. Compare this figure to about 1 in 10 births in 1975. The increased rate of C-sections in part reflects advances in medical technology, such as use of fetal monitors that allow doctors to detect fetal distress ("Fetal heart," 1995). Critics claim that many C-sections are unnecessary and reflect overly aggressive medical practices. Even the Centers for Disease Control and Prevention (CDC) believes that as many as one in three C-sections are unnecessary ("U.S. says," 1993). The CDC hopes to lower the rate of cesareans in the United States to 15 per 100 births by the year 2000, a level the agency considers to be medically appropriate.

Truth **OR** *Fiction?*
R E V I S I T E D

It is true that one U.S. birth in four is by cesarean section. The use of cesarean section has mushroomed to nearly 25% of deliveries in the 1990s. Critics of this trend have raised concerns as to how many of them are medically necessary. ∎

Medical opinion once held that after a woman had a C-section, subsequent deliveries also had to be performed by C-section. Otherwise, uterine scars might rupture during labor. Evidence has shown that rupture is rare, however (Samuels & Samuels, 1986). Today, many obstetricians encourage women with prior C-sections who fall into certain low-risk groups to attempt subsequent vaginal deliveries. The number of women who are delivering vaginally after an earlier C-section section has thus been increasing.

Alternatives to the Hospital: Where Should a Child Be Born?

In the United States, most births occur in hospitals. Medical equipment and personnel are thus available to handle complications. But hospital deliveries have their disadvantages. Hospitals are often impersonal and very expensive, although the costs may be offset by medical insurance. Giving birth in a hospital tends to instill the perception that pregnancy is an illness, rather than a healthy, natural process. In addition, the hospital environment tends to encourage mothers to assume a passive role and surrender responsibility for their care to the doctor. For various reasons, then, many pregnant women and their partners have sought alternative places to deliver their children.

Birth Centers   Birth centers seek to provide the atmosphere associated with home delivery. Birth centers typically have some medical equipment available and are frequently located within or adjacent to medical centers to permit immediate access to medical facilities (e.g., if an emergency C-section is needed). Such centers are intended for women who are deemed to be at low risk for birth complications.

The birthing room itself is typically decorated and furnished cheerfully, like a bedroom. Family members, friends, and siblings of the baby may be present to share the experience. Women in labor can move about the room freely and eat, drink, rest, or chat with friends and family as they wish. Following the birth the family generally remains together in the room, sharing what for most is a loving and joyous experience. These days even maternity wards in U.S. hospitals seem to be assuming much of the comforting ambience of birthing centers.

Home Births   Home birth provides familiar surroundings and the psychological sense that the woman and her family are more in control. Some advocates of home childbirth argue that it is safe enough for women who have been medically screened for potential complications and who have a history of normal births. Critics charge that it is not possible to screen women for every possible complication, however, and that home delivery exposes the mother and child to unnecessary risks, especially if unexpected complications occur. Many physicians refuse to deliver babies in the home.

～ *Reflections* ～

■ Do you know anyone who has used the Lamaze method? What does she (or he) say about it?
■ Do you know anyone who had a cesarean section? What was the reason for it? What are the mother's feelings about it? Did the C-section affect subsequent deliveries?
■ Where were you born? Who was present during delivery? Why?

Birth Problems

Most deliveries are uncomplicated, or "unremarkable" in the medical sense—although childbirth is the most remarkable experience of many parents' lives. Problems can and do occur, however. Some of the most common birth problems are anoxia and the birth of preterm and low-birthweight babies.

Anoxia

Anoxia
Oxygen deprivation.

Prenatal **anoxia** can cause various problems in the neonate and affect later development. It leads to complications such as brain damage and mental retardation. Prolonged anoxia during delivery can also result in cerebral palsy and possibly death.

The baby is supplied with oxygen through the umbilical cord. Passage through the birth canal squeezes the umbilical cord. Temporary squeezing, like holding one's breath for a moment, is unlikely to cause problems. (In fact, slight oxygen deprivation at birth is not unusual because the transition from receiving oxygen through the umbilical cord to breathing on its own may not happen immediately after the baby emerges.) Anoxia can result if constriction of the cord is prolonged, however. Prolonged constriction is more likely to occur with a breech presentation, because the baby's head presses the umbilical cord against the birth canal during delivery. Fetal monitoring can help detect anoxia early, however, before damage occurs. A C-section can be performed if the fetus appears to be in distress.

Preterm and Low-Birthweight Children

Preterm
Born prior to 37 weeks of gestation.

A neonate is considered to be premature, or **preterm,** if it is born before 37 weeks of gestation. The normal period of gestation is 40 weeks. Prematurity is generally linked with low birthweight, since the fetus normally makes dramatic gains in weight during the last weeks of pregnancy. Regardless of the length of its gestation period, a newborn baby is considered to have a low birthweight if it weighs less than 5 pounds (about 2,500 grams).

Preterm or low-birthweight babies face a heightened risk of infant mortality (Singh & Yu, 1995). A birthweight of 3¼ pounds (1,500 grams) is considered to be the cutoff with respect to the likelihood of mortality.

Surfactants
Substances that prevent the walls of the airways from sticking together.

Respiratory distress syndrome
A cluster of breathing problems, including weak and irregular breathing, to which preterm babies are especially vulnerable.

Preterm babies are relatively thin because they have not yet formed the layer of fat that accounts for the round, robust appearance of most full-term babies. Their muscles are immature, which weakens their sucking and breathing reflexes. Also, in the last weeks of pregnancy fetuses secrete **surfactants** that prevent the walls of their airways from sticking together. Muscle weakness and incomplete lining of the airways with surfactants can cause a cluster of problems known as **respiratory distress syndrome,** which is responsible for many neonatal deaths. Preterm babies may also suffer from underdeveloped immune systems, which leave them more vulnerable to infections.

Preterm infants usually remain in the hospital for a time. There they can be monitored and placed in incubators that provide a temperature-controlled environment and offer some protection from disease. If necessary, they may also receive oxygen.

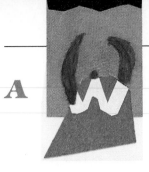 
ETHNICITY AND INFANT MORTALITY

Back in 1950, there were more than 25 infant deaths per 1,000 live births in the United States. Because the United States now has some of the world's most sophisticated medical technology, that number has been dropping sharply, to 8.5 in 1992 and 7.9 in 1994. Yet within the United States, there are also dramatic ethnic differences in rates of infant mortality. Infant mortality rates are lowest for Chinese Americans and Japanese Americans (Singh & Yu, 1995). Hispanic Americans of Cuban, Mexican, or Central or South American descent have the next lowest infant mortality rates. Non-Hispanic White Americans follow, and then come African Americans. The infant mortality rate for African Americans is about twice that for non-Hispanic White Americans (Singh & Yu, 1995). In the year 1992, African Americans made up about 12% of the U.S. population. However, they accounted for about 17% of the live births and one third of the infant deaths in the nation (Singh & Yu, 1995).

Much of the ethnic difference in infant mortality can apparently be attributed to differences in prenatal health care. Table 11.3 shows 1990 infant health statistics obtained from public records in New York City. Residents of the affluent White Kips Bay–Yorkville area have healthier newborns than residents of East Harlem (a low-income neighborhood made up mostly of African Americans) or of middle-income and mainly White Astoria–Long Island City. East Harlem mothers, like other low-income mothers (McLaughlin et al., 1992), were more likely than their middle- and upper-income counterparts to have babies with low birthweights and babies who died during infancy. Maternal malnutrition and use of chemical substances such as alcohol and tobacco during pregnancy have all been

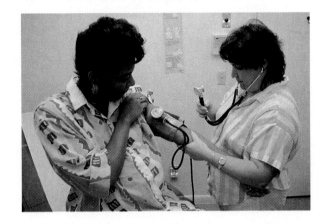

Prenatal Care. The incidence of low-birth-weight babies is clearly connected to the quality of prenatal care. Many women in the United States—especially women from minority groups—do not receive adequate prenatal care. Some receive no prenatal care at all.

linked to low birthweights and increased mortality during the first year of life (Barr et al., 1990; McLaughlin et al., 1992).

The differences in infant health shown in the table are also connected with the incidence of prenatal care received by the mothers in the three neighborhoods. According to 1990

New York City Department of Health records, nearly 36% of East Harlem mothers received either late prenatal care or none, as compared with about 6% in Kips Bay–Yorkville and about 10% in Astoria–Long Island City. Research has shown that comprehensive prenatal care is connected with higher birthweights (McLaughlin et al., 1992).

TABLE 11.3 Infant health statistics for three New York City neighborhoods

Infant Health Statistics	East Harlem	Astoria–Long Island City	Kips Bay–Yorkville
Infant deaths per 1,000 live births	23.4	14.9	7.3
Low birthweight babies per 100 live births (less than 5.5 pounds)	18.5	6.1	6.0
Very low birthweight babies per 100 live births (less than 3.3 pounds)	3.8	0.98	0.87
Live births per 100 in which mothers received late or no prenatal care	35.8	10.4	6.1

This table shows infant health statistics for three New York City neighborhoods. East Harlem is a heavily studied inner-city area characterized by poverty, a high proportion of minority residents, and many teenage pregnancies. The Astoria–Long Island City area is populated by middle-income residents. Kips Bay–Yorkville is a high-income area.
Source: Department of Health, City of New York, 1990.

■ Do you know of anyone who experienced birth problems such as anoxia or low birthweight? What was the outcome?

The Postpartum Period

Postpartum
Following birth.

The weeks following delivery are called the **postpartum** period. The first few days postpartum are frequently happy ones. The long wait is over, as are the discomforts of childbirth. A sizable number of women experience feelings of depression, however, in the days and sometimes weeks and months following childbirth.

Maternal Depression

Mood changes following childbirth are experienced by many new mothers. During the days or weeks following the delivery of their babies, anywhere from 50% to 80% of new mothers (Harding, 1989) experience periods of sadness, tearfulness, and irritability that are commonly called the "postpartum blues," the "maternity blues," or the "baby blues." This downswing in mood typically occurs around the third day after delivery (Samuels & Samuels, 1986). The baby blues usually last about 48 hours and are generally believed to be a normal response to hormonal and psychological changes that attend childbirth (Harding, 1989; Samuels & Samuels, 1986).

Postpartum depression
Persistent and severe mood changes during the postpartum period, involving feelings of despair and apathy and characterized by changes in appetite and sleep, low self-esteem, and difficulty in concentrating.

Some mothers experience more persistent and severe mood changes, called **postpartum depression** (PPD) (Whiffen, 1992). PPD may last a year or even longer. PPD can involve extreme sadness or despair, apathy, changes in appetite and sleep patterns, low self-esteem, and difficulty concentrating. A study of 1,033 married, middle-class, first-time mothers from the Pittsburgh area who had full-term, healthy infants found that 9.3% of them had experienced PPD (Campbell & Cohn, 1991). Some researchers (e.g., Gitlin & Pasnau, 1989) estimate that PPD affects up to 15% of new mothers.

Like the "maternity blues," PPD may reflect a combination of physiological and psychological factors. Hormonal changes may play a role in PPD, but women with PPD are more likely than those with the maternity blues to have been susceptible to depression before and during their pregnancies (O'Hara et al., 1984). Psychosocial factors such as stress, a troubled marriage, or the need to adjust to an unwanted or sick baby may all increase a woman's susceptibility to PPD (Gitlin & Pasnau, 1989; O'Hara et al., 1984, 1991). Adjusting to a new baby imposes inevitable changes on parents, and change is usually stressful in itself. Depression is likely to be prolonged in women who feel helpless in meeting the demands they face (Cutrona, 1983). First-time mothers, single mothers, and mothers who lack social support from their partners or family members face the greatest risk of PPD (Gitlin & Pasnau, 1989).

New fathers may also have bouts of depression. New mothers are not the only ones who must adjust to the responsibilities of parenthood. Fathers too may feel overwhelmed or unable to cope. Perhaps more fathers might experience the "paternity blues" but for the fact that mothers generally shoulder the lion's share of child-rearing chores.

Breast-Feeding Versus Bottle-Feeding

Only a minority of U.S. women breast-feed their children. One reason is that many women return to the workforce shortly following childbirth. Some choose to share feeding chores with the father, who is equally equipped to prepare and hold a bottle, but not to breast-feed. Other women find breast-feeding inconvenient or unpleasant. Long-term comparisons of breast-fed and bottle-fed children show few, if any, significant differences. Breast-feeding does reduce the general risk of infections to the baby, however, by transmitting the mother's antibodies to the baby. Breast-feeding also reduces the incidence of allergies in babies, particularly in allergy-prone infants (Wardlaw & Insel, 1990).

The hormones prolactin and oxytocin are involved in breast-feeding. **Prolactin** stimulates production of milk, or **lactation,** two to three days after delivery. Oxytocin causes the breasts to eject milk and is secreted in response to suckling. When an infant is weaned, secretion of prolactin and oxytocin is discontinued, and lactation comes to an end.

Uterine contractions that occur during breast-feeding help return the uterus to its typical size. Breast-feeding also delays resumption of normal menstrual cycles. Breast-feeding is not a perfectly reliable birth-control method, however. (But nursing women are advised not to use birth-control pills, since the hormone content of the pills is passed to the infant through the milk.)

Should a woman breast-feed her baby? Although breast-feeding has benefits for both mother and infant, each woman must weigh these benefits against the difficulties breast-feeding may pose for her. These include assuming the sole responsibility for nighttime feedings, the physical demands of producing and expelling milk, tendency for soreness in the breasts, and the inconvenience of being continually available to meet the infant's feeding needs. Women should breast-feed because they want to, not because they feel they must.

Resumption of Ovulation and Menstruation

For close to a month after delivery, women experience a reddish vaginal discharge called **lochia.** A nonnursing mother does not resume actual menstrual periods until two to three months postpartum. The first few cycles are likely to be irregular. Many women incorrectly assume that they will resume menstruating following childbirth by first having a menstrual period and then ovulating two weeks later. In most cases the opposite is true. Ovulation precedes the first menstrual period after childbirth. Thus, a woman may become pregnant before the menstrual phase of her first postpartum cycle. Some women, but not all, who suffered premenstrual syndrome before their pregnancies are often delighted to find that their periods give them less discomfort after the birth of their children.

Resumption of Sexual Activity

The resumption of coitus depends on a couple's level of sexual interest, the healing of episiotomies or other injuries, fatigue, the recommendations of obstetricians, and, of course, tradition. Obstetricians usually advise a six-week waiting period for safety and comfort.

It is true that couples should abstain from coitus for at least six weeks following childbirth. However, many other kinds of sexual activities are safe and do not cause discomfort. (Check with your obstetrician.) ■

Women will typically prefer to delay coitus until it becomes physically comfortable, generally when the episiotomy or other lacerations have healed and the lochia has ended. This may take several weeks. Women who breast-feed may also find they have less vaginal lubrication, which can cause some discomfort during coitus. K-Y jelly or other lubricants may help in such cases.

The return of sexual interest and resumption of sexual activity may take longer for some couples than for others. Sexual interest depends more on psychological than on physical factors. Many couples encounter declining sexual interest and activity in the first year following childbirth, generally because child care can sap energy and limit free time. Generally speaking, couples whose sexual relationships were satisfying before the baby arrived tend to show greater sexual interest and to resume sexual activity earlier than those who had less satisfying relationships beforehand. (No surprise.)

Prolactin
A pituitary hormone that stimulates production of milk. (From roots meaning "for milk.")

Lactation
Production of milk by the mammary glands.

Lochia
A reddish vaginal discharge that may persist for a month after delivery. (From the Greek *lochios,* meaning "of childbirth.")

■ Do you know of anyone who was depressed after delivering a baby? How serious was the depression? Do you have any idea what caused it? Was it treated? If so, how? How long did the depression last?
■ Would you prefer that your children be breast-fed or bottle-fed? (Or, were your children breast-fed or bottle-fed?) Why?
■ Do you have any opinion as to how long following delivery a woman should wait to resume sexual activity? Explain.

Summing Up

Conception: Against All Odds

Conception is the union of a sperm cell and an ovum. Fertilization normally occurs in a fallopian tube.

Optimizing the Chances of Conception   Optimizing the chances of conception means engaging in coitus at the time of ovulation. Ovulation can be predicted by calculating the woman's basal body temperature, analyzing the woman's urine for luteinizing hormone, or tracking the thickness of vaginal mucus.

Selecting the Gender of Your Child   Strategies for gender preselection have been derived from the fact that sperm bearing the Y sex chromosome are faster swimmers but less durable than those bearing the X sex chromosome. Sperm-separation procedures are also used. None of these methods is perfectly reliable, however.

Infertility and Alternative Ways of Becoming Parents

Male Fertility Problems   Fertility problems in the male include low sperm count, irregularly shaped sperm, low sperm motility, certain chronic or infectious diseases, trauma to the testes, an auto-immune response to sperm, and pituitary imbalances and/or thyroid disease.

Female Fertility Problems   The major causes of infertility in women include irregular ovulation, obstructions or malfunctions of the reproductive tract, and endometriosis. Failure to ovulate may often be overcome by fertility drugs. Methods for overcoming other female fertility problems include in vitro fertilization, GIFT, ZIFT, donor IVF, embryonic transfer, and surrogate motherhood.

Pregnancy

Early Signs of Pregnancy   Early signs include a missed period, presence of HCG in the blood or urine, and Hegar's sign.

Pregnancy Tests   Pregnancy tests detect the presence of HCG—human chorionic gonadotropin—in the woman's urine or blood.

Early Effects of Pregnancy   Early effects include tenderness in the breasts and morning sickness.

Miscarriage (Spontaneous Abortion)   Miscarriages have many causes, including chromosomal defects in the fetus and abnormalities of the placenta and uterus.

Sex During Pregnancy   Most health professionals concur that in most cases coitus is safe until the start of labor.

Psychological Changes During Pregnancy   A woman's psychological response to pregnancy reflects her desire to be pregnant, her physical changes, and her attitudes toward these changes. Men, like women, respond to pregnancy according to the degree to which they want the child.

Prenatal Development

The Germinal Stage   The germinal stage is the period from conception to implantation.

The Embryonic Stage   The embryonic stage begins with implantation and extends to about the eighth week of development and is characterized by differentiation of the major organ systems.

The Fetal Stage   The fetal stage begins by the ninth week and continues until the birth of the baby. The fetal stage is characterized by continued maturation of the fetus's organ systems and dramatic increases in size.

Environmental Influences on Prenatal Development   Environmental factors that affect prenatal development include the mother's diet, maternal diseases and disorders, and drugs. Maternal malnutrition has been linked to low birthweight and infant mortality. Exposure to particular teratogens causes the greatest harm during critical periods of vulnerability.

Chromosomal and Genetic Abnormalities Chromosomal and genetic abnormalities can lead to cystic fibrosis, Down syndrome, hemophilia, Huntington's chorea, neural-tube defects, phenylketonuria, retina blastoma, sickle cell anemia, and Tay-Sachs disease. Parental blood tests, amniocentesis, and ultrasound allow parents to learn whether their children have or are at risk for many such disorders.

Childbirth

The Stages of Childbirth In the first stage uterine contractions efface and dilate the cervix so that the baby may pass. The first stage may last from a couple of hours to more than a day. The second stage lasts from a few minutes to a few hours and ends with the birth of the baby. During the third stage the placenta is expelled.

Methods of Childbirth Contemporary methods for facilitating childbirth include anesthetized childbirth, natural childbirth, the Lamaze method, and cesarean section.

Alternatives to the Hospital: Where Should a Child Be Born? In the United States most births occur in hospitals. Some parents seeking more intimate arrangements, however, opt for a birth center or home delivery.

Birth Problems

Anoxia Prenatal anoxia can cause brain damage and mental retardation in the child.

Preterm and Low-Birthweight Children Preterm and low-birthweight babies have a heightened risk of infant mortality.

The Postpartum Period

Maternal Depression Transient mood changes following childbirth are experienced by many new mothers. Women with postpartum depression experience lingering depressions following childbirth.

Breast-Feeding Versus Bottle-Feeding Breast-feeding is connected with fewer infections and allergic reactions in the baby than bottle-feeding. Long-term studies show few differences between children whose parents used one or the other feeding method, however.

Resumption of Ovulation and Menstruation The first few menstrual cycles following childbirth are likely to be irregular.

Resumption of Sexual Activity Obstetricians usually advise a 6-week waiting period following childbirth before resuming coitus, but couples need not wait this long to enjoy other forms of sexual activity.

CHAPTER 12

Henri Matisse, *The Trapeze Artists,* Plate 11 from *Jazz.* The Metropolitan
Museum of Art, Gift of Lila Acheson Wallace, 1983. © 1996 Succession
H. Matisse/Artist Rights Society (ARS), New York. © 1985 by The Metropolitan
Museum of Art.

Contraception and Abortion

Outline

Truth OR Fiction?

_____ Ancient Egyptians used crocodile dung as a contraceptive substance.

_____ Contraceptives not only prevent conception; they also prevent sexually transmitted diseases (STDs).

_____ There is an oral contraceptive that can be taken the morning after intercourse.

_____ Sterilization operations can be surgically reversed.

_____ Testosterone can be used as a male *contraceptive* device.

_____ Abortions were legal in the United States prior to the Civil War.

_____ The D&C is the most widely used abortion method in the United States.

It was a stifling day in July 1912. Margaret Sanger (1883–1966), a nurse practitioner, was summoned to the house of a woman near death from a botched self-induced abortion. Her husband had called a doctor, and the doctor sent for Sanger. Together, doctor and nurse worked feverishly through the days and nights that followed to stem an infection that had taken hold in the woman. Sanger later commented,

> Never had I worked so fast, never so concentratedly. The sultry days and nights were melted into a torpid inferno. It did not seem possible there could be such heat, and every bit of food, ice, and drugs had to be carried up three flights of stairs. . . .

After two interminable weeks, the woman began to recover. Her neighbors, who had feared the worst, came to express their joy. But the woman, who smiled wanly at those who came to see her, appeared more depressed and anxious than would be expected of someone who was recovering from a grave illness. By the end of the third week, when Sanger prepared to leave her patient, the woman, Mrs. Sachs, voiced the fear that was haunting her. Her face registered deep despair as she explained to Sanger that she dreaded becoming pregnant again and facing a choice between attempting another abortion, which she feared might kill her, and bearing a baby whose care it was beyond her means to support. She pleaded for information about contraception but Sanger could offer none. In 1912 it was a crime even for health professionals like Margaret Sanger to dispense information about contraceptives. Abortions, too, were illegal. Sanger tried to comfort her and promised to return to talk again.

Three months later she received another urgent call. It was Mr. Sachs. His wife was sick again—from the same cause. As Sanger recalled,

> For a wild moment I thought of sending someone else, but actually, of course, I hurried into my uniform, caught up my bag, and started out. All the way I longed for a subway wreck, an explosion, anything to keep me from having to enter that home again. But nothing happened, even to delay me. I turned into the dingy doorway and climbed the familiar stairs once more. The children were there, young little things.
>
> Mrs. Sachs was in a coma and died within ten minutes. I folded her still hands across her breast, remembering how they had pleaded with me, begging so humbly for the knowledge which was her right. I drew a sheet over her pallid face. Jake was sobbing, running his hands through his hair and pulling it out like an insane person. Over and over again he wailed, "My God! My God! My God!"
>
> (Sanger, 1938)

Today, partly because of the work of Margaret Sanger, who went on to become a key advocate for birth control, information about contraceptives is disseminated freely throughout the United States.

Methods of birth control include contraception and abortion. Contraception refers to techniques that prevent conception. Abortion refers to the termination of a pregnancy before the embryo or fetus is capable of surviving outside the womb.

Contraception

Coitus interruptus
A method of contraception in which the penis is withdrawan from the vagina prior to ejaculation. Also referred to as the *withdrawal method.*

People have been devising means of contraception since they became aware of the relationship between coitus and conception. Ironically, the safest and most effective method of contraception is also the least popular: abstinence. The Bible contains many references to contraceptive techniques, including vaginal sponges and contraceptive concoctions. It also refers to **coitus interruptus,** or withdrawal. The story of Onan, for example, implies knowledge of the withdrawal method.

Margaret Sanger. Sanger was a key advocate for birth control in the United States. She established the National Birth Control League and a birth-control clinic in Brooklyn, New York. She was instrumental in the dismantling of the Comstock law, which prevented physicians from disseminating information about birth control and prevention of sexually transmitted diseases.

Ancient Egyptian methods of birth control included douching with wine and garlic after coitus, and soaking crocodile dung in sour milk and stuffing the mixture deep within the vagina.

T r u t h OR *Fiction?*
R E V I S I T E D

It is true that ancient Egyptians used crocodile dung as a contraceptive substance. ■

The dung blocked the passage of many—if not all—sperm through the cervix and also soaked up sperm. The dung may also have done its job through a social mechanism. It may have discouraged all but the most ardent suitors.

Greek and Roman women placed absorbent materials within the vagina to absorb semen. The use of sheaths or coverings for the penis has a long history. Sheaths worn over the penis as decorative covers can be traced to ancient Egypt (1350 B.C.). Sheaths of linen were first described in European writings in 1564 by the Italian anatomist Fallopius (from whom the name of the fallopian tube is derived). Linen sheaths were used, without success, as a barrier against syphilis. The term **condom** was not used to describe penile sheaths until the eighteenth century. At that time, sheaths made of animal intestines became popular as a means of preventing sexually transmitted diseases and unwanted pregnancies. Among the early advocates of condoms as a method of contraception was the Italian adventurer and writer Giovanni Casanova (1725–1798). We now associate his name with men who are known for their amorous adventures. James Boswell (1740–1795), the biographer of Samuel Johnson, described his use of "armor," or condoms, in his graphic *London Journal.* On one occasion, however, he was so enamored with a street prostitute that he neglected to use his armor and contracted gonorrhea. Condoms made of rubber (hence the slang "rubbers") were introduced shortly after Charles Goodyear invented vulcanization of rubber in 1843. Many other forms of contraception were also used widely in the nineteenth century, including withdrawal, vaginal sponges, and douching.

Condom
A sheath made of animal membrane or latex that covers the penis during coitus and serves as a barrier to sperm following ejaculation.

Contraception in the United States: The Legal Battle

As methods of contraception grew more popular in the nineteenth century, opponents waged a battle to make contraception illegal. One powerful opponent of contraception was Anthony Comstock, who served for a time as the secretary of the New York Society for the Suppression of Vice. Comstock lobbied successfully for passage of a federal law in 1873—the Comstock law—that prohibited the dissemination of birth-control information through the mail on the grounds that it was "obscene and indecent." Many states passed even more restrictive laws. They outlawed passage of information from one person to another, even from physician to patient.

Consider the resistance that Margaret Sanger met when she challenged the laws restricting information about contraception. In 1914 she established the National Birth Control League, which published the magazine *The Woman Rebel*. *Rebel* did not publish birth-control information but challenged the view that it was obscene. Nevertheless, charges were brought against Sanger, and she fled to Europe before her trial. During her self-imposed exile, she visited birth-control clinics in the Netherlands. When the charges against her in the United States were dropped in 1916, Sanger returned and established a birth-control clinic in Brooklyn, New York. The clinic was closed by the police, and Sanger was arrested. Released on bail, she reopened the clinic and was thereupon sentenced to 30 days in jail. She successfully appealed the sentence. In 1918 the courts ruled that physicians must be allowed to disseminate information that might aid in the cure and prevention of disease. Dismantling of the Comstock law had begun. With the financial support of a wealthy friend, Katherine Dexter McCormack, Sanger spurred research into the use of hormones as one approach to contraception. In 1960, only six years before Sanger's death, oral contraception—"the pill"—was finally marketed in the United States. In 1965 the Supreme Court struck down the last impediment to free use of contraception: a law preventing the sale of contraceptives in Connecticut (*Griswold v. Connecticut,* 1965). In 1973 abortion was in effect legalized by the Supreme Court in the case of *Roe v. Wade,* permitting women to terminate unwanted pregnancies.

Today, contraceptives are advertised in popular magazines and sold through vending machines in college dormitories. U.S. history is not a one-way road to unrestricted use of birth control, however. Recent Supreme Court decisions have set aside bits and pieces of *Roe v. Wade,* giving the states more discretion over the regulation of abortion and restricting access to abortions for minors. Use of **artificial contraception** continues to be opposed by many groups, including the Roman Catholic Church. Yet many individual Catholics, including many priests, hold liberal attitudes toward contraception.

Artificial contraception
A method of contraception that applies a human-made device.

Selecting a Method of Contraception

If you believe that you and your partner should use a method of contraception, how will you determine which one is right for you? There is no simple answer. What is right for your friends may be wrong for you. You and your partner will make your own selections, but there are some issues you may want to consider:

1. *Convenience.* Is the method convenient? The convenience of a method depends on a number of factors: Does it require a device that must be purchased in advance? If so, can it be purchased over the counter as needed, or are a consultation with a doctor and a prescription required? Will the method work at a moment's notice, or, as with the birth-control pill, will it require time to reach maximum effectiveness? Some couples feel that few things dampen ardor and spontaneity more quickly than the need to pay attention to a contraceptive device in the heat of passion. Use of contraceptives like the condom and the diaphragm need not interrupt sexual activity, however. Both partners can share in applying the device. Some couples find that this becomes an erotic aspect of their lovemaking.

2. *Moral acceptability.* A method that is morally acceptable to one person may be objectionable to another. For example, some oral contraceptives prevent fertilization;

TALKING TO YOUR PARTNER ABOUT CONTRACEPTION

When is the right time to discuss contraception? On a first date? When you are invited to meet your partner's family? When you are lost in amorous embraces? Broaching the topic can be awkward. *Not* broaching the issue can be disastrous. Often a man responds to news that his partner is pregnant by saying something like this: "But I thought you were using *something!*"

Technically speaking, the right time to discuss birth control is *anytime* that allows your contraceptive to become effective before you engage in coitus. That can mean weeks or months before, if you decide to use a prescription contraceptive such as the birth-control pill, the IUD, the diaphragm, or the cervical cap. Or it can mean a few moments before coitus, if you decide to use a condom and have one ready. Despite the obvious advantage to deciding upon contraception before coitus, the issue is often broached, if it is broached at all, only after the partners become sexually intimate.

Practically speaking, it is awkward—and perhaps presumptuous!—to discuss contraception when you meet or are on a first date. But at the very least, it is advisable to prepare oneself for the possibility of coitus. The man or woman may bring along a condom. The woman may already be on the pill, have an IUD in place, or a diaphragm.

Talking about contraception helps many couples make the transition from a casual relationship to an intimate one. Talking enables partners to share responsibility for their behavior. As a result, the woman is less likely to be resentful that the responsibility rests entirely on her.

Yes, it can be awkward or difficult to raise the topic. Couples may not feel that their relationship is secure enough. They may take the view, "We'll cross that bridge when we come to it." Not planning ahead, however, prevents the effective use of contraceptives that require advance planning.

Couples who choose to discuss contraception before engaging in coitus may benefit from these communication guidelines:

1. *Pick a strategic time and place.* Choose a time when the two of you are alone and are free of distractions. Pick a place that is comfortable and private.
2. *Couch your discussion in terms of your feelings about your partner and your relationship.* Talk about your general feelings toward your partner and your general relationship before you narrow in on contraception.
3. *Don't apologize for raising the topic.* You may feel embarrassed talking about sensitive topics like birth control. But you need not apologize for bringing up the subject. Apologizing suggests that you think you are doing something wrong.
4. *Raise the subject in a way that encourages candid discussion.* Use open-ended questions to explore your partner's attitudes. Say something like "I think our relationship has reached the point where we need to talk about contraception. I know we're not sleeping together yet, but some forms of contraception require advanced planning. Have you been thinking about it?"
5. *Explore options.* Don't make demands of your partner. Don't say "Since we may start sleeping together, I think you should go on the pill." Rather, say something like "I know that many different types of contraceptives are available. Why don't we discuss which method might be best for us if we become intimate?" Use the opportunity to explore each other's views about birth control in general and specific techniques in particular.

others allow fertilization to occur but then prevent implantation of the fertilized ovum in the uterus. In the second case, the method of contraception may be considered to produce a form of early abortion, which is likely to concern people who object to abortion no matter how soon after conception it occurs. Yet the same people may have no moral objection to preventing fertilization.

3. *Cost.* Methods vary in cost. Some more costly methods involve devices (such as the diaphragm, the cervical cap, and the IUD) or hormones (pills or Norplant) that require medical visits in addition to the cost of the devices themselves. Other methods, such as rhythm methods, are essentially free.
4. *Sharing responsibility.* Most forms of birth control place the burden of responsibility largely, if not entirely, on the woman. The woman must consult with her doctor to obtain birth-control pills or other prescription devices such as diaphragms, cervical caps,

Norplant, and IUDs. The woman must take birth-control pills reliably or check to see that her IUD remains in place. Some couples prefer methods that allow for greater sharing of responsibility, such as alternating use of the condom and diaphragm. A man can also share the responsibility for the birth-control pill by accompanying his partner on her medical visits, sharing the expense, and helping her remember to take her pill.

5. *Safety.* How safe is the method? What are the side effects? What health risks are associated with its use? Can your partner's health or comfort be affected by its use?

6. *Reversibility.* Reversibility refers to the effects of a birth-control technique or device. In most cases the effects of birth-control methods can be fully reversed by discontinuing their use. In other cases reversibility may not occur immediately, as with oral contraceptives. One form of contraception, sterilization, should be considered irreversible, although many attempts at reversal have been successful.

7. *Protection against STDs.* Birth-control methods vary in the degree of protection they afford against STDs such as gonorrhea, chlamydia, and AIDS. This is especially important to people who are sexually active with one or more partners who are *not known* to be free of infectious diseases.

Some contraceptives prevent sexually transmitted diseases as well as conception. Most methods, however, offer no protection against STDs. Therefore, this Truth or Fiction item is too broad to be true. ■

8. *Effectiveness.* Techniques and devices vary widely in their effectiveness in actual use. Despite the widespread availability of contraceptives, about two of three pregnancies in the United States are unplanned, and of these, about half result from contraceptive failures (Angier, 1993a). The failure rate for a particular method refers to the percentage of women who become pregnant when using the method for a given period of time, such as during the first year of use. Most contraceptive methods are not used correctly all or even much of the time. Thus it is instructive to compare the failure rate among people who use a particular method or device *perfectly* (consistently and correctly) with the failure rate among *typical* users. Failure rates among typical users are often considerably higher because of incorrect, unreliable, or inconsistent use. Table 12.1 on page 338 shows the failure rates, continuation rates, reversibility, and degree of protection against STDs associated with various contraceptive methods.

～ *Reflections* ～

▪ What is your personal reaction to the true story told by Margaret Sanger? Why?
▪ What problems would you anticipate in trying to discuss contraception with a partner? Why?
▪ Which of the factors in selecting a method of contraception would seem to be most important to you? Explain.

Methods of Contraception

There are many methods of contraception, including oral contraceptives (the pill), Norplant, intrauterine devices (IUDs), diaphragms, cervical caps, spermicides, condoms, douching, withdrawal (coitus interruptus), timing of ovulation (rhythm), and some devices under development.

Oral contraceptive
A contraceptive, consisting of sex hormones, which is taken by mouth.

Oral Contraceptives ("the Pill")

An **oral contraceptive** is commonly referred to as a birth-control pill, or simply "the pill." However, there are many kinds of birth-control pills that vary in the type and dosages of

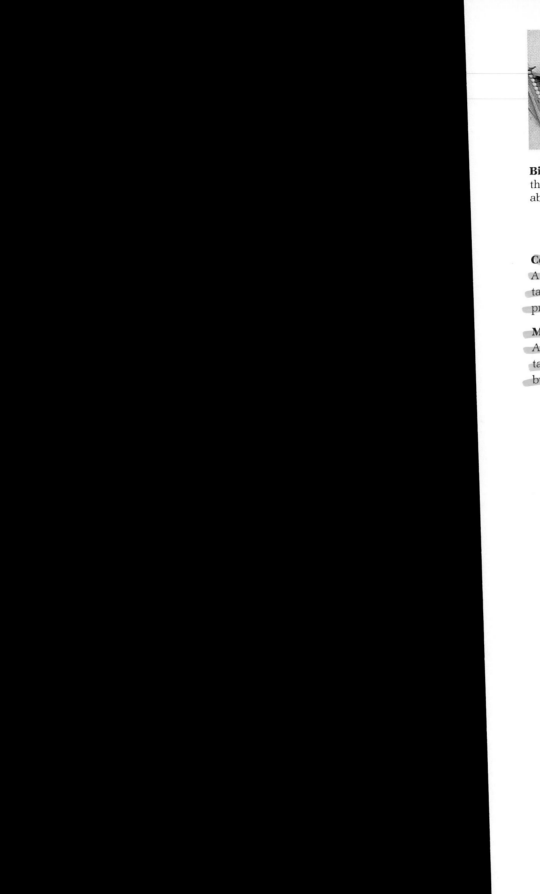

Birth-Control Pills. Some of the oral contraceptives available today.

Combination pill
A birth-control pill that contains synthetic estrogen and progesterone.

Minipill
A birth-control pill that contains synthetic progesterone but no estrogen.

hormones they contain. Birth-control pills fall into two major categories: combination pills and minipills.

Combination pills (such as Ortho-Novum, Ovcon, and Loestrin) contain a combination of synthetic forms of the hormones estrogen and progesterone (progestin). Most combination pills provide a steady dose of synthetic estrogen and progesterone. Other combination pills, called *multiphasic* pills, vary the dosage of these hormones across the menstrual cycle to reduce the overall dosages to which the woman is exposed and possible side effects. The **minipill** contains synthetic progesterone (progestin) only.

Available only by prescription, oral contraceptives are used by 28% of women in the United States who use reversible (nonsterilization) forms of contraception, or some 19 million women (Angier, 1993a). Use of the pill has been on the increase in recent years, especially among married women (Forrest & Fordyce, 1993). Birth-control pills are the most popular forms of contraception among single women of reproductive age.

How They Work   Women cannot conceive when they are already pregnant because their bodies suppress maturation of egg follicles and ovulation. The combination pill fools the brain into acting as though the woman is already pregnant, so that no additional ova mature or are released. If ovulation does not take place, a woman cannot become pregnant.

In a normal menstrual cycle, low levels of estrogen during and just after the menstrual phase stimulate the pituitary gland to secrete FSH, which in turn stimulates the maturation of ovarian follicles. The estrogen in the combination pill inhibits FSH production, so follicles do not mature. The progesterone (progestin) inhibits the pituitary's secretion of LH, which would otherwise lead to ovulation. The woman continues to have menstrual periods, but there is no unfertilized ovum to be sloughed off in the menstrual flow.

The combination pill is taken for 21 days of the typical 28-day cycle. Then, for 7 days, the woman either takes no pill at all or an inert placebo pill to maintain the habit of taking a pill a day. The sudden drop in hormone levels causes the endometrium to disintegrate and menstruation to follow 3 or 4 days after the last pill has been taken. Then the cycle is repeated.

The progestin in the combination pill also increases the thickness and acidity of the cervical mucus. The mucus thus becomes a more resistant barrier to sperm and inhibits development of the endometrium. Therefore, even if an egg were somehow to mature and become fertilized in a fallopian tube, sperm would not be likely to survive the passage through the cervix. Even if sperm were somehow to succeed in fertilizing an egg, the failure of the endometrium to develop would mean that the fertilized ovum could not become implanted in the uterus. Progestin may also impede the progress of ova through the fallopian tubes and make it more difficult for sperm to penetrate ova.

The minipill contains progestin but no estrogen. Minipills are taken daily through the menstrual cycle, even during menstruation. They act in two ways. They thicken the cervical mucus to impede the passage of sperm through the cervix, and they render the inner lining of the uterus less receptive to a fertilized egg. Thus, even if the woman does conceive, the fertilized egg will pass from the body rather than becoming implanted in the uterine wall. Since it contains no estrogen, the minipill does not usually prevent ovulation. The combination pill, by contrast, works directly to prevent ovulation. Since ovulation and fertilization may occur in women who use the minipill, some people see use of the minipill as an early abortion method. Others, however, reserve the term "abortion" for methods of terminating pregnancy following successful implantation.

Effectiveness of Birth-Control Pills   The failure rate of the birth-control pill associated with perfect use is very low—0.5% or less depending on the type of pill (see Table 12.1). The failure rate increases to 3% in typical use. Failures can occur when women forget to take the pill for two days or more, when they do not use backup methods when they first go on the pill, and when they switch from one brand to another. But forgetting to take the pill even for one day may alter the woman's hormonal balance, allowing ovulation—and fertilization—to occur.

TABLE 12.1 Approximate failure rates of various methods of birth control, their reversibility, and protection against STDs

| Method | Women Experiencing an Accidental Pregnancy within the First Year of Use (%) | | Women Continuing Use at One Year[3] (%) | Reversibility | Protection Against Sexually Transmitted Diseases (STDs) |
	Typical Use[1]	Perfect Use[2]			
Chance[4]	85	85		Yes (unless fertility has been impaired by exposure to STDs)	No
Spermicides[5]	21	6	43	Yes	Some
Periodic Abstinence	20		67	Yes	No
Calendar		9			
Ovulation Method		3			
Sympto-Thermal[6]		2			
Postovulation		1			
Withdrawal	19	4		Yes	No
Cervical Cap[7]					
Parous Women*	36	26	45	Yes	Some[8]
Nulliparous† Women	18	9	58	Yes	Some[8]
Diaphragm[7]	18	6	58	Yes	Some[8]
Condom Alone					
Female (Reality)	21	5	56	Yes	Yes[8]
Male	12	3	63	Yes	Yes[8]
Pill	3		72	Yes	No, but may reduce the risk of PID[9]
Progestin Only		0.5			
Combined		0.1			
IUD					
Progestasert T	2.0	1.5	81	Yes, except if fertility is impaired	No, and may increase the risk of PID
Copper T 380A	0.8	0.6	78		
LNg 20	0.1	0.1	81		

Reversibility   Use of oral contraceptives may temporarily reduce fertility after they are discontinued but is not associated with permanent infertility (Mishell, 1989). Nine of ten women begin ovulating regularly within three months of suspending use (Reinisch, 1990). Users of the pill who frequently start and stop usage may later incur fertility problems, however (Reinisch, 1990). When a woman appears not to be ovulating after going off the pill, a drug like clomiphene is often used to induce ovulation.

Advantages and Disadvantages   The great advantage of oral contraception is that when used properly it is nearly 100% effective. Unlike many other forms of contraception, such as the condom or diaphragm, its use does not interfere with sexual spontaneity or diminish sexual sensations. The sex act need not be interrupted, as it would be by use of a condom.

Method	Women Experiencing an Accidental Pregnancy within the First Year of Use (%)		Women Continuing Use at One Year[3] (%)	Reversibility	Protection Against Sexually Transmitted Diseases (STDs)
	Typical Use[1]	Perfect Use[2]			
Depo-Provera	0.3	0.3	70	Yes	No
Norplant (6 capsules)	0.09	0.09	85	Yes	No
Female Sterilization	0.4	0.4	100	Not usually	No
Male Sterilization	0.15	0.10	100	Not usually	No

[1]Among typical couples who initiate use of a method (not necessarily for the first time), the percentage who experience an accidental pregnancy during the first year if they do not stop use for any other reason.

[2]Among couples who initiate use of a method (not necessarily for the first time) and who use it perfectly (both consistently and correctly), the percentage who experience an accidental pregnancy during the first year if they do not stop use for any other reason.

[3]Among couples attempting to avoid pregnancy, the percentage who continue to use a method for one year.

[4]The percentages failing in columns 2 and 3 are based on data from populations in which contraception is not used and from women who cease using contraception in order to become pregnant. Among such populations, about 89% become pregnant within one year. This estimate was lowered slightly (to 85%) to represent the percentage who would become pregnant within one year among women now relying on reversible methods of contraception if they abandoned contraception altogether.

[5]Foams, creams, gels, vaginal suppositories, and vaginal film.

[6]Cervical mucus (ovulation) method supplemented by calendar in the preovulatory and basal body temperature in the postovulatory.

[7]With spermicidal cream or jelly.

[8]These methods provide better protection against STDs if a spermicide such as nonoxynol-9 is used simultaneously.

[9]Pelvic inflammatory disease.

*Women who have borne children.

†Women who have not borne children.

Sources: For failure rates and percentages of women discontinuing use, adapted from Hatcher et al. (1994). For reversibility and protection against sexually transmitted diseases, adapted from Reinisch (1990).

Copyright © 1990 by The Kinsey Institute for Research in Sex, Gender, and Reproduction. From THE KINSEY INSTITUTE NEW REPORT ON SEX. Reprinted with permission from St. Martin's Press, New York, NY.

Birth-control pills may also have some *healthful* side effects. They appear to reduce the risk of rheumatoid arthritis, ovarian cysts, pelvic inflammatory disease (PID), and fibrocystic (benign) breast growths. The use of the pill regularizes menstrual cycles and reduces menstrual cramping and premenstrual discomfort. The pill may also be helpful in the treatment of iron-deficiency anemia and facial acne. Considerable scientific evidence shows that the use of the combination pill reduces the risks of ovarian and endometrial cancer, even for a number of years after the woman has stopped taking the pill (Hatcher et al., 1994; Mishell, 1989). Moreover, the pill's protective effects against invasive ovarian cancer increases steadily with the length of use (Whittemore et al., 1992).

The pill does have some disadvantages. It confers no protection against STDs. Moreover, it may reduce the effectiveness of antibiotics used to treat STDs. Going on the pill requires medical consultation, so a woman must plan to begin using the pill at least several weeks before becoming sexually active or before discontinuing the use of other contraceptives and must incur the expense of medical visits.

The main drawbacks of birth-control pills are potential side effects and possible health risks. The estrogen in combination pills may produce side effects such as nausea and vomiting, fluid retention (feeling "bloated"), weight gain, increased vaginal discharge, headaches, tenderness in the breasts, and dizziness. Many of these side effects are temporary, but when they persist, women may be switched from one pill to another, perhaps to one with lower doses of hormones. Pregnant women produce high estrogen levels in the corpus luteum and placenta. The combination pill artificially raises levels of estrogen, so it is not surprising that women who use it may have side effects that mimic the early signs of pregnancy, such as weight gain or nausea ("morning sickness"). Weight gain can result from estrogen (through fluid retention) or progestin (through increased appetite and development of muscle). Oral contraceptives may also increase blood pressure in some women, but clinically significant elevations are rare in women using the low-dose pills that are available today (Hatcher et al., 1994). Still, it is wise for women who use the pill to have their blood pressure checked regularly (Mishell, 1989). Women who encounter problems with high blood pressure from taking the pill are usually switched to another form of contraception.

Many women have avoided using the pill because of the risk of blood clots. The lower dosages of estrogen found in most types of birth-control pills today are associated with much lower risk of blood clots than was the case in the 1960s and 1970s when higher dosages were typically used (Wharton & Blackburn, 1988). Still, women who are at increased risk for blood clotting problems, such as those with a history of circulatory problems or stroke, are typically advised not to use the pill.

Women who are considering using the pill need to weigh the benefits and risks in terms of their own health profile in consultation with their gynecologists or health care providers. For the great majority of young, healthy women in their 20s and early 30s, there is very little chance of developing blood clots or other cardiovascular problems from using the pill (Hatcher et al., 1994). Moreover, women who use the pill are no more likely than nonusers to develop cardiovascular problems later in life—even women who have used the pill for more than ten years (Stampfer et al., 1988).

Some women, however, should simply not be on the pill (Calderone & Johnson, 1989; Hatcher et al., 1994; Reinisch, 1990). These include women with a history of circulatory problems or blood clots, and those who have suffered a heart attack or stroke or have a history of coronary disease, breast or uterine cancer, undiagnosed genital bleeding, liver tumors, or sickle cell anemia (because of associated blood-clotting problems). Because of their increased risk of cardiovascular problems, caution should be exercised when the combination pill is used by women over 35 years of age who are heavy smokers (15 or more cigarettes daily) (Hatcher et al., 1994). Nursing mothers should also avoid using the pill, as the hormones may be passed to the baby in the mother's milk.

Since the risks of cardiovascular complications generally increase with age, many women over the age of 35 have been encouraged by their gynecologists to use other forms of birth control. As a result, the pill is used by only 1 women in 50 between the ages of 35 and 44, as compared to 1 women in 6 in the 25 to 34 age category and one woman in four in the 15-to-24 age group (U.S Bureau of the Census, 1990b). Recent studies, however, show no increased risk of serious cardiovascular disease among healthy, nonsmoking women up to the age of 45 who use oral contraceptives containing lower dosages of estrogen (Mishell, 1989). Many health professionals, including the American College of Obstetricians and Gynecologists, believe that healthy nonsmokers age 35 to 44 can continue to use oral contraceptives safely (Mishell, 1989).

The pill may also have psychological effects. Some users report depression or irritability. Switching brands or altering doses may help. Evidence is lacking concerning the effects of lower-estrogen pills on sexual desire.

Progestin fosters male secondary sex characteristics, so women who take the minipill may develop acne, facial hair, thinning of scalp hair, reduction in breast size, vaginal dryness, and missed or shorter periods. Irregular or so-called breakthrough bleeding between menstrual periods is a common side effect of the minipill (Reinisch, 1990). Irregular bleeding should be brought to the attention of a health professional. Because they can produce vaginal dryness, minipills can hinder vaginal lubrication during intercourse, decreasing sexual sensations and rendering sex painful.

Researchers have also examined suspected links between the use of the pill and certain forms of cancer, especially breast cancer, since breast cancer is sensitive to hormonal changes. Results from several large-scale studies show no overall increase in the rates of breast cancer among pill users, but it remains possible that some subgroups of women who use the pill may be at increased risk (Hatcher et al., 1994). The evidence linking use of the pill with increased risk of cervical cancer is mixed, with some studies showing such a link and others showing none (Hatcher et al., 1994).

Women considering the pill are advised to have a thorough medical evaluation to rule out contraindications (reasons for *not* using the pill). The evaluation should include a detailed medical and family history, and a physical exam including a Pap smear, assessment of blood pressure, screening for STDs, urinalysis, breast and pelvic exam, and possibly an EKG (electrocardiogram). Women who begin to use the pill, regardless of their age or risk status, should pay attention to changes in their physical condition, have regular checkups, and promptly report any physical complaints or unusual symptoms to their physicians.

"Morning-After" Pills   The so-called morning-after pill, or postcoital contraceptive, actually refers to several types of pills that have high doses of estrogen and progestin. Since they are not taken regularly, they do not prevent ovulation from occurring. Instead, they stop fertilization from taking place or prevent the fertilized egg from implanting itself in the uterus (Hoffman, 1993). In that respect, then, some people consider them an early abortion technique. Morning-after pills are most effective when taken within 72 hours after ovulation. Women who wait to see whether they have missed a period are no longer candidates for the morning-after pill. Depending on the brand, four, six, or eight pills are prescribed.

Truth **OR** *Fiction?*

R E V I S I T E D

It is true that there are effective oral contraceptives that can be taken the morning after unprotected intercourse. They are termed "morning-after" pills.

Morning-after pills have a higher hormone content than most birth-control pills. For this reason, nausea is a common side effect, occurring in perhaps 70% of users. Nausea is usually mild and passes within a day or two after treatment, but it can be treated with antinausea medication (Hatcher et al., 1994). Vomiting should be brought to the attention of a physician, since the woman may need to take additional pills to make up for ones possibly lost in vomiting (Hatcher et al., 1994).

Because of the strength of the dosage, the morning-after pill is not recommended as a regular form of birth control. We also know little about possible long-term health complications. Morning-after pills are *one-time* forms of "emergency" protection (Hatcher et al., 1994), which may be most appropriate to use following rape or when regular contraceptive devices fail (for example, if a condom breaks or a diaphragm becomes dislodged). The morning-after pill is generally effective in preventing implantation of a fertilized ovum, but health professionals caution that when it fails, the fetus may be damaged by exposure to the hormones it contains.

Norplant

The contraceptive implant *Norplant* consists of six matchstick-sized silicone tubes that contain progestin and are surgically embedded in a woman's upper arm. About 1 million women in the United States have received Norplant since FDA approval in 1990 (Kolata, 1995).

How It Works   Norplant, like the pill, relies on female sex hormones to suppress fertility. But rather than taking a pill once a day, tubes implanted in the woman's body

release a small, steady dose of progestin into her bloodstream, providing continuous contraceptive protection for as long as five years (Hatcher et al., 1994). The progestin in the Norplant system suppresses ovulation and thickens the cervical mucus so that sperm cannot pass. The contraceptive effect occurs within 24 hours of insertion. After five years the spent tubes are replaced. An alternative implant, Norplant-2, consists of two hormone-releasing tubes that provide at least three years of protection.

Norplant. Norplant consists of silicone rods that are surgically implanted in the woman's arm. They gradually dispense progestin, the same female sex hormone found in the minipill. Their effectiveness lasts about five years.

How It Is Used   Implantation takes a few minutes in a doctor's office and is carried out under local anesthesia.

Effectiveness   Norplant is reported to have an extremely low failure rate of less than 1% per year across five years (see Table 12.1). The failure rate approximates that of surgical sterilization.

Reversibility   Although the failure rate of Norplant approximates that of sterilization, Norplant is fully reversible. Removal restores a normal likelihood of pregnancy.

Advantages and Disadvantages   The key advantage of Norplant is its convenience. The hormone is dispensed automatically. The woman need not remember to take a pill each day, insert a device before coitus, or check that an IUD is in place. The most commonly reported side effect is abnormal menstrual bleeding (Hatcher et al., 1994; Mishell, 1989).

Many health professionals concerned about finding ways to reduce teenage pregnancy rates are enthusiastic about Norplant. School-based programs have been initiated to make Norplant available to young women, which has fueled the debate concerning whether schools should be involved in distributing contraceptives to minors (see Chapter 13).

The nearby A Closer Look recounts another use of Norplant.

Intrauterine Devices (IUDs)

Camel drivers setting out on long desert journeys placed round stones in the uteruses of female camels to prevent them from becoming pregnant and lost to service. The stones may

A   C L O S E R   L O O K

HOLD THAT BEAVER!

The quality of mercy was seriously strained in a Denver suburb recently, when the town of Wheat Ridge had to bite the bullet and press the pause button it its nonviolent plan for curbing beaver proliferation. (Beavers, you see, have the horrendous habits of burrowing beneath walking paths [*flop!*] and of turning trees into taste treats.)

According to Nick Fisher (1992) of the town's Animal and Park Enforcement Department, Wheat Ridge

chewed over the situation and decided to defang its gnawing wildlife problem by biting into the mammals' reproductive patterns with Norplant. TV cameras were about to record the first implanting of the birth-control device on an anesthetized beaver when a veterinarian declared, at the last moment, "It's a male." Beavers, it happens, are "darn hard to sex," explained Dr. Robinson, because their sex organs are deep inside their bod-

ies. (Is it possible that the good doctor meant to say "*dam* hard to sex" but was too genteel?) The program will have to await the identification of a toothsome tootsie.

Apparently Wheat Ridge had bitten off more than it could chew. By the time the town finds and identifies a female, we may all be long in the tooth. Frankly, dear readers, we wonder whether the beavers give a dam about all this.

Intrauterine device

A small object that is inserted into the uterus and left in place to prevent conception. Abbreviated *IUD*.

have acted as primitive **intrauterine devices** (IUDs). IUDs are small objects of various shapes that are inserted into the uterus. IUDs have been used by humans since Greek times. Today, they are inserted into the uterus by a physician or nurse practitioner and usually left in place for a year or more. Fine plastic threads or strings hang down from the IUD into the vagina, so that the woman can check to see that it remains in place.

IUDs are used by about 1.5 million women in the United States and more than 80 million women around the world (Altman, 1991). Nearly 60 million IUD users are in China, where nearly one in three married women uses an IUD during her childbearing years. By contrast, IUDs are used by only about 3% of married women of childbearing age in the United States. Married women in the United States are more than twice as likely as single women to use an IUD (U.S. Bureau of the Census, 1990b).

IUDs achieved their greatest popularity in the United States in the 1960s and 1970s. Then there was a sharp drop off in their use during the 1980s after use of a popular model, the Dalkon Shield, was linked to a high incidence of pelvic infections and tubal infertility (Darling et al., 1992).

Figure 12.1 shows two IUDs: the Progestasert T, which releases small quantities of progesterone (progestin) daily, and the Copper T 380A (ParaGard), a T-shaped, copper-based device. Because the Progestasert T must be replaced annually, and any insertion carries some risk of infection, health authorities recommend the use of the ParaGard device, which can be used for upwards of eight years, unless the woman is allergic to copper (Hatcher et al., 1994).

How It Works   We do not know exactly how IUDs work. A foreign body, such as the IUD, apparently irritates the uterine lining. This irritation gives rise to mild inflammation and the production of antibodies that may be toxic to sperm or to fertilized ova and/or may prevent fertilized eggs from becoming implanted. Inflammation may also impair proliferation of the endometrium—another impediment to implantation. Progestin released by the Progestasert T also has effects like the progestin-only minipill: It lessens the likelihood of fertilization and implantation. Action on fertilized ova may be considered to constitute an early abortion. Since IUDs may not prevent fertilization, people who oppose abortion, regardless of how soon it occurs after conception, also oppose the IUD.

Effectiveness   The failure rate associated with typical use of the Progestasert T is about 2% (see Table 12.1). Most failures occur within three months of insertion, often be-

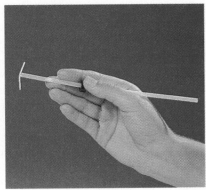

Figure 12.1. Two IUDs: The Progestasert T and the Copper T 380A (ParaGard). The Progestasert T releases small quantities of progesterone (progestin) daily. The Copper T 380A is a T-shaped, copper-based device.

cause the device shifts position or is expelled. ParaGard is the most effective IUD. The first-year failure rate in typical use is 0.8%.

The IUD may irritate the muscular layer of the uterine wall, causing contractions that expel it through the vagina. The device is most likely to be expelled during menstruation, so users are advised to check their sanitary napkins or tampons before discarding them. Women who use IUDs are advised to check the string several times a month to ensure that the IUD is in place. Spontaneous expulsions occur in 2% to 10% of users within the first year of use (Hatcher et al., 1994). Women who have not borne children have a higher expulsion rate (about 7%) than women who have (3%) (Reinisch, 1990). Some family-planning clinics advise women to supplement their use of IUDs with other devices for the first three months, when the risks of a shift in position or expulsion are greatest.

Anti-inflammatory drugs, such as aspirin, and antibiotics may also decrease IUD effectiveness. Since many physicians recommend an aspirin every other day as a way of helping prevent certain kinds of cancer (Marcus, 1995), women are advised to discuss these issues with their gynecologists.

Reversibility IUDs may be removed readily by professionals. Nine out of ten former IUD users who wish to do so become pregnant within a year (Reinisch, 1990).

Advantages and Disadvantages The IUD has three major advantages: (1) it is highly effective; (2) it does not diminish sexual spontaneity or sexual sensations; and (3) once in place, the woman need not "do anything" more to prevent pregnancy (other than check that it remains in place). The small risk of failure is reduced in effect to zero if the couple also use an additional form of birth control, such as the diaphragm or condom.

The IUD also does not interfere with the woman's normal hormonal production. Users continue to produce pituitary hormones that stimulate ovarian follicles to mature and rupture, thereby releasing mature ova and producing female sex hormones.

If IUDs are so effective and relatively "maintenance free," why are they not more popular? One reason is that insertion can be painful. Another reason is side effects. The most common side effects are excessive menstrual cramping, irregular bleeding (spotting) between periods, and heavier than usual menstrual bleeding (Reinisch, 1990). These usually occur shortly following insertion and are among the primary reasons women ask to have the device removed. A more serious concern is the possible risk of pelvic inflammatory disease (PID), a serious disease that can become life threatening if left untreated (Hatcher et al., 1994). A recent review of the scientific evidence suggests that women who use the IUD may have a small increased risk of PID (Cates & Stone, 1992b). It appears that the risk of infection is associated more with the insertion of the device (bacteria may enter the woman's reproductive tract during insertion) than with use of the device itself (Cates & Stone, 1992b).

PID can produce scar tissue that blocks the fallopian tubes, causing infertility. Women with pelvic infections should not use an IUD (Hatcher et al., 1994). Women who have risk factors for PID may also wish to consider the advisability of an IUD. Risk factors include a recent episode of gonorrhea or chlamydia, recurrent episodes of these STDs, sexual contact with multiple partners, or sexual contact with a partner who has multiple sexual partners. All in all, the IUD may be best suited to women who have completed their families and are advised not to use oral contraceptives (Mishell, 1989).

Another risk in using an IUD is that the device may perforate (tear) the uterine or cervical walls, which can cause bleeding, pain, and adhesions and become life threatening. Perforations are usually caused by improper insertion and occur in perhaps 1 case in 1,000 (Reinisch, 1990). IUD users are also at greater risk for ectopic pregnancies, both during and after usage, and for miscarriage. Ectopic pregnancies occur in about 5% of women who become pregnant while using an IUD (Cole, 1989). IUD use is not recommended for women with a history of ectopic pregnancy (Cole, 1989). Women who become pregnant while using the IUD stand about a 50–50 chance of miscarriage (Hatcher et al., 1994).

Despite the fact that the IUD irritates uterine tissues, there is no evidence that IUD users run a greater risk of cancer. Long-term data on the health effects of IUD use are limited, however.

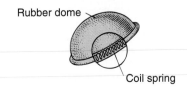

Rubber dome

Coil spring

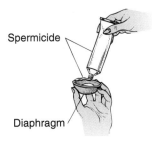

Spermicide

Diaphragm

Figure 12.2. A Diaphragm. The diaphragm is a shallow cup or dome made of latex. Diaphragms must be fitted to the contour of the vagina by a health professional. The diaphragm forms a barrier to sperm but should be used in conjunction with a spermicidal cream or jelly.

Diaphragm

A shallow rubber cup or dome, fitted to the contour of a woman's vagina, that is coated with a spermicide and inserted prior to coitus to prevent conception.

Another drawback to the IUD is its cost. The typical cost of an IUD insertion in a family-planning clinic ranges from $200 to $300 (Hatcher et al., 1994). Potential expulsion of the IUD presents yet another disadvantage. Moreover, the IUD, like the pill, offers no protection against STDs. Finally, like the pill, IUDs place the burden of contraception entirely on the woman.

The Diaphragm

Diaphragms were once used by about one third of United States couples who practiced birth control. When invented in 1882, they were a breakthrough. Their popularity declined only in the 1960s with the advent of the pill and the IUD. Today, only 1 married White woman in 20 and 1 married African American woman in 50 under the age of 44 regularly use the diaphragm (U.S. Bureau of the Census, 1990b). Overall, 3% of U.S. women using reversible forms of contraception use the diaphragm (Angier, 1993b).

The diaphragm is a shallow cup or dome made of thin latex rubber (see Figure 12.2). The rim is a flexible metal ring covered with rubber. Diaphragms come in different sizes, to allow a precise fit.

Diaphragms are available by prescription and must be fitted to the contour of the vagina by a health professional. Several sizes and types of diaphragms may be tried during a fitting. Women practice insertion in a health professional's office so they can be guided as needed.

How It Works The diaphragm is inserted and removed by the woman, much like a tampon. It is akin to a condom in that it forms a barrier against sperm when placed snugly over the cervical opening. Yet it is unreliable as a barrier alone. Thus, the diaphragm should be used in conjunction with a spermicidal cream or jelly. The diaphragm's main function is to keep the spermicide in place.

How It Is Used The diaphragm should be inserted no more than two hours before coitus, since the spermicides that are used may begin to lose effectiveness beyond this time. Some health professionals, however, suggest that the diaphragm may be inserted up to six hours preceding intercourse. (It seems reasonable to err on the side of caution and assume that there is a two-hour time limit.) The woman or her partner places a tablespoonful of spermicidal cream or jelly on the inside of the cup and spreads it inside the rim. (Cream spread outside the rim might cause the diaphragm to slip.) The woman opens the inner lips of the vagina with one hand and folds the diaphragm with the other by squeezing the ring. She inserts the diaphragm against the cervix, with the inner side facing upward (see Figure 12.3 on page 346). Her partner can help insert the diaphragm, but the woman is advised to check its placement. Some women prefer a plastic insertion device, but most find it easier to insert the diaphragm without it. The diaphragm should be left in place *at least six hours* to allow the spermicide to kill any remaining sperm in the vagina (Hatcher et al., 1994). It should not be left in place for longer than 24 hours, to guard against toxic shock syndrome (TSS).

After use, the diaphragm should be washed with mild soap and warm water and stored in a dry, cool place. When cared for properly, a diaphragm can last about two years. Women may need to be refitted after pregnancy or a change in weight of about ten pounds or more.

Effectiveness If used consistently and correctly, the failure rate of the diaphragm is estimated to be 6% during the first year of use (see Table 12.1). In typical use, however, the failure rate is believed to be three times as high—18%. Some women become pregnant because they do not use the diaphragm during every coital experience. Others may insert it too early or not leave it in long enough. The diaphragm may not fit well, or it may slip—especially if the couple is acrobatic. A diaphragm may develop tiny holes or cracks. Women are advised to inspect the diaphragm for signs of wear and consult their health professionals when in doubt. Effectiveness also is seriously compromised when the diaphragm is not used along with a correctly applied spermicide (Trussell et al., 1993).

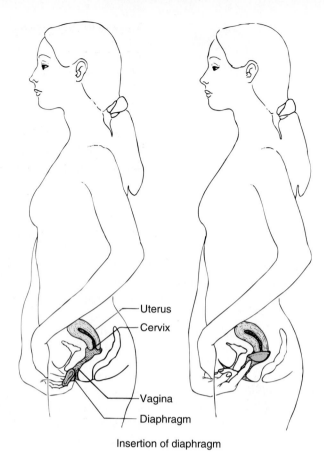

Figure 12.3. Insertion and Checking of the Diaphragm.
Women are instructed in insertion of the diaphragm by a health
professional. In practice, a woman and her partner may find
joint insertion an erotic experience.

Uterus
Cervix

Vagina
Diaphragm

Insertion of diaphragm

Reversibility The effects of the diaphragm are fully reversible. In order to become
pregnant, the woman simply stops using it. The diaphragm has not been shown to influence subsequent fertility.

Advantages and Disadvantages The major advantage of the diaphragm is
that when used correctly it is a safe and effective means of birth control and does not alter
the woman's hormone production or reproductive cycle. The diaphragm can be used as
needed, whereas the pill must be used daily and the IUD remains in place whether or not
the woman engages in coitus. Another advantage is the virtual absence of side effects. The
few women who are allergic to the rubber in the diaphragm can switch to a plastic model.
Another advantage is that spermicides that contain nonoxynol-9 may provide some, but not
total, protection against STDs, including AIDS, genital herpes, trichomoniasis ("trich"),
syphilis, and perhaps chlamydia (Reinisch, 1990).

The major disadvantage is the high pregnancy rate associated with typical use. Nearly
1 in 5 typical users (18%) of the diaphragm combined with spermicidal cream or jelly becomes pregnant during the first year of use (Hatcher et al., 1994). Another disadvantage is
the need to insert the diaphragm prior to intercourse, which the couple may find disrup-
tive. Another disadvantage is that the woman's partner may find the taste of the spermicides used in conjunction with the diaphragm to be unpleasant during oral sex. The
pressure exerted by the diaphragm against the vaginal and cervical walls may also irritate
the urinary tract and cause urinary or even vaginal infections. Switching to a different size
diaphragm or one with a different type of rim may help alleviate this problem. About 1
woman or man in 20 may develop allergies to the particular spermicide that is used, which
can lead to irritation of the genitals. This problem may also be alleviated by switching to
another brand.

Spermicides

Spermicides are chemical agents that kill sperm. They come in different forms, including jellies and creams, suppositories, aerosol foam, and a contraceptive film. Spermicides should be left in place in the vagina (no douching) for *at least 6–8 hours* after coitus (Hatcher et al., 1994).

How They Are Used Spermicidal jellies, creams, foam, and suppositories should be used no more than 60 minutes preceding coitus to provide for maximum effectiveness (Hatcher et al., 1994). Spermicidal jellies and creams come in tubes with plastic applicators that introduce the spermicide into the vagina (see Figure 12.4). Spermicidal foam is a fluffy white cream with the consistency of shaving cream. It is contained in a pressurized can and is introduced with a plastic applicator in much the same way as spermicidal jellies and creams.

Vaginal suppositories are inserted into the upper vagina, near the cervix, where they release spermicide as they dissolve. Unlike spermicidal jellies, creams, and foam, which become effective immediately when applied, suppositories must be inserted no less than 10 to 15 minutes before coitus so that they have sufficient time to dissolve (Hatcher et al., 1994).

Spermicidal film consists of thin, 2-inch-square sheets that are saturated with spermicide. When placed in the vagina, they dissolve into a gel and release the spermicide. The spermicidal film should be inserted at least five minutes before intercourse to allow it time to melt and for the spermicide to be dispersed (Hatcher et al., 1994). It remains effective for upwards of one hour (Hatcher et al., 1994). One disadvantage of the film that some users have noted is a tendency for it to adhere to the fingertips, which makes it difficult to insert correctly.

How They Work Spermicides coat the cervical opening, blocking the passage of sperm and killing sperm by chemical action.

Effectiveness In typical use, the first-year failure rate of spermicides used alone is 21 pregnancies per year per 100 users (Hatcher et al., 1994; Reinisch, 1990). When used correctly and consistently, the failure rate is estimated to drop to about 6 pregnancies per 100 users in the first year. All forms of spermicide are more effective when they are combined with other forms of contraception, such as the condom.

Reversibility Spermicides have not been linked with any changes in reproductive potential. Couples who wish to become pregnant simply stop using them.

Advantages and Disadvantages The major advantages of spermicides are that they do not alter the woman's natural biological processes and are applied only as

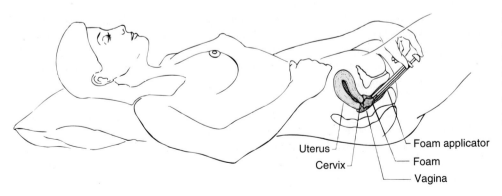

Figure 12.4. The Application of Spermicides. Spermicidal jellies and creams come in tubes with plastic applicators. Spermicidal foam comes in a pressurized can and is applied with a plastic applicator in much the same way as spermicidal jellies and creams.

Uterus
Cervix
Foam applicator
Foam
Vagina

needed. Unlike a diaphragm, they do not require a doctor's prescription or a fitting. They can be bought in virtually any drugstore, and the average cost per use of the foam variety is modest—about 50 cents. Spermicides that contain nonoxynol-9 may also provide some protection against organisms that give rise to STDs.

The major disadvantage is the high failure rate among typical users. Foam often fails when the can is not shaken enough, when too little is used, when it is not applied deeply enough within the vagina near the cervix, or when it is used after coitus has begun.

Spermicides are generally free of side effects but occasionally cause vaginal or penile irritation. Irritation is sometimes alleviated by changing brands. Some partners find the taste of spermicides unpleasant. (Couples can engage in oral sex before applying spermicides.) Spermicides may pose a danger to an embryo, so women who suspect they are pregnant are advised to suspend use until they find out for certain.

The Cervical Cap

The cervical cap, like the diaphragm, is a dome-shaped rubber cup. It comes in different sizes and must be fitted by a health professional. It is smaller than the diaphragm, however—about the size of a thimble—and is meant to fit snugly over the cervical opening.

How It Is Used   Like the diaphragm, the cap is intended to be used with a spermicide applied inside it (Hatcher et al., 1994). When inserting it, the woman (or her partner) fills the cap about a third full of spermicide. Then, squeezing the edges together, the woman inserts the cap high in the vagina, so that it presses firmly against the cervix. The woman can test the fit by running a finger around the cap to ensure that the cervical opening is covered. It should be left in place for at least 8 hours after intercourse. The cap provides continuous protection for upwards of 48 hours without the need for additional spermicide. To reduce the risk of toxic shock syndrome, the cap should not be left in place longer than 48 hours. Like the diaphragm, the cap should be cleaned after use and checked for wear and tear. When cared for properly, the cap should last for upwards of three years.

How It Works   Like the diaphragm, the cervical cap forms a barrier and also holds spermicide in place against the cervix. It prevents sperm from passing into the uterus and fallopian tubes and kills sperm by chemical action.

Effectiveness   The failure rate in typical use is estimated to be high, ranging from 18% in women who have not borne children to 36% in women who have (Hatcher et al., 1994). Failures may be attributed, at least in part, to the cap's becoming dislodged and to changes in the cervix during the menstrual cycle, which can cause the cap to fit less snugly over the cervix.

Reversibility   There is no evidence that the cervical cap affects fertility.

Advantages and Disadvantages   Like the diaphragm, the cap is a mechanical device that does not affect the woman's hormonal production or reproductive cycle. The cap may be especially suited to women who cannot support a diaphragm because of lack of vaginal muscle tone. Because of concern that the cap may irritate cervical tissue, however, Mishell (1989) recommends that repeat Pap tests be performed with users.

Some women find the cap uncomfortable. The cap can also become dislodged during sexual activity or lose its fit as the cervix changes over the menstrual cycle. Reported side effects include urinary tract infections and allergic reactions or sensitivities to the rubber or spermicide. Other potential disadvantages include the expense and inconvenience of being fitted by a health professional. Moreover, some women are shaped so that the cap does not remain in place. For these reasons, and because they may be hard to obtain, cervical caps are not very popular in the United States (Reinisch, 1990).

The effectiveness of the cervical cap is considerably greater among women who have not given birth (Trussell et al., 1993). Women who have given birth may wish to consult their gynecologists concerning the suitability of the cap.

Condoms

Prophylactic

An agent that protects against disease.

Condoms are also called "rubbers," "safes," **prophylactics** (because latex condoms protect against STDs), and "skins" (referring to those that are made from lamb intestines). Condoms lost popularity with the advent of the pill and the IUD. They are less effective than the pill or IUD, may disrupt sexual spontaneity, and can decrease coital sensations because they prevent the penis from actually touching the vaginal wall.

Condoms have been making a comeback, however, because those made of latex rubber can help prevent the spread of the AIDS virus (the *human immunodeficiency virus* [HIV]) and other STDs and, to a lesser extent, because of concerns about side effects of the pill and the IUD. Largely because of concerns about AIDS and other STDs, use of condoms among unmarried women jumped from 18% in 1987 to 33% in 1992 (Forrest & Fordyce, 1993). Unmarried women are more likely to report using condoms than are married women (33% vs. 19%). Overall, 17% of U.S. women who use reversible forms of contraception use condoms (Angier, 1993b).

Condom advertisements have appeared in mainstream media, including magazines such as *People* and *Cosmopolitan,* and on major TV networks. In a TV commercial, a man and a woman are shown hurriedly undressing. The man tells the woman that he forgot to bring a condom with him. She then tells him that he'd best forget it (making love, that is). Whether the media campaign will increase condom usage remains to be seen.

The renewed popularity of condoms has also been spurred by the increased assertiveness of contemporary women. They make the point (which should be obvious, but all too often is not) that contraception is as much the man's responsibility as the woman's. Condoms alter the psychology of sexual relations. By using a condom the man assumes much of the responsibility for contraception. Condoms are the only contraceptive device worn by men, and the only readily reversible method of contraception that is available to men. Condoms are inexpensive and can be obtained without prescription from pharmacies, family-planning clinics, rest rooms, and even from vending machines in some college dormitories.

Some condoms are made of latex rubber. Thinner, more expensive condoms ("skins") are made from the intestinal membranes of lambs. The latter allow greater sexual sensation but do not protect as well against STDs. Only latex condoms are effective against the tiny AIDS virus. Condoms made of animal intestines have pores large enough to permit the AIDS virus and other viruses, such as the one that causes hepatitis B, to slip through (Consumer's Union, 1995). A few condoms are made from other materials, such as plastic (polyurethane). Questions remain about the effectiveness of polyurethane condoms (Consumer's Union, 1995). Some condoms have plain ends. Others have nipples or reservoirs (see Figure 12.5) that catch semen and may help prevent the condom from bursting during ejaculation.

How It Works   A condom is a cylindrical sheath that serves as a barrier, preventing the passage of sperm and disease-carrying microorganisms from the man to his partner. It

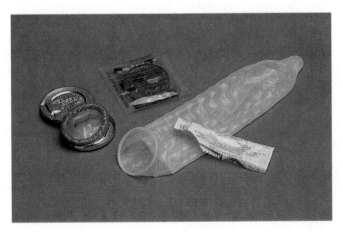

Figure 12.5. Condoms. Some condoms are plain-tipped, whereas others have nipples or reservoirs that catch semen and may help prevent the condom from bursting during ejaculation. Latex condoms form effective barriers to the tiny AIDS virus.

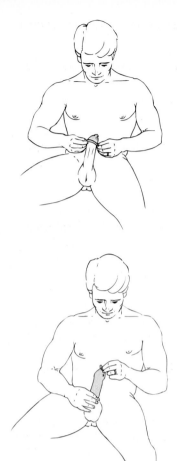

Figure 12.6. **Applying a Condom.** First the rolled-up condom is placed on the head of the penis, and then it is rolled down the shaft of the penis. If a condom without a reservoir tip is used, a ½-inch space should be left at the tip for the ejaculate to accumulate.

also helps prevent infected vaginal fluids (and microorganisms) from entering the man's urethral opening or from penetrating through small cracks in the skin of the penis.

How It Is Used   The condom is rolled onto the penis once erection is achieved and before contact between the penis and the vagina (see Figure 12.6). If the condom is *not* used until moments before the point of ejaculation, sperm-carrying fluid from the Cowper's glands or from preorgasmic spasms may already have passed into the vagina. Nor does the condom afford protection against STDs if it is fitted after penetration.

Condoms sometimes fall off or break. Between 1% and 2% of condoms break or fall off during intercourse or when withdrawing the penis afterward (Cates & Stone, 1992a; Trussell et al., 1992). Condoms also sometimes slip down the shaft of the penis without falling off. To use a condom most effectively and to help prevent it from either breaking or falling off, a couple should observe the following guidelines:[1]

- Use a condom each and every time you have intercourse. Inexperienced users should also practice putting on a condom before they have the occasion to use one with a partner.
- Handle the condom carefully, making sure not to damage it with your fingernail, teeth, or sharp objects.
- Place the condom on the erect penis before it touches the vulva.
- Uncircumcised men should pull back the foreskin before putting on the condom.
- If you use a spermicide, place some inside the tip of the condom before placing the condom on the penis. You may also wish to use additional spermicide applied by an applicator inside the vagina to provide extra protection, especially in the event of breakage of the condom.
- Do not pull the condom tightly against the tip of the penis.
- For a condom without a reservoir tip, leave a small empty space—about a half-inch—at the end of the condom to hold semen, yet do not allow any air to be trapped at the tip. Some condoms come equipped with a reservoir (nipple) tip that will hold semen.
- Unroll the condom all the way to the bottom of the penis.
- Ensure that adequate vaginal lubrication during intercourse is present, possibly using lubricants if necessary. But use only water-based lubricants such as contraceptive jelly or K-Y jelly. Never use an oil-based lubricant that can weaken the latex material, such as petroleum jelly (Vaseline), cold cream, baby oil or lotion, mineral oil, massage oil, vegetable oil, Crisco, hand or body lotions, and most skin creams. Do not use saliva as a lubricant because it may contain infectious organisms, such as viruses.
- If the condom breaks during intercourse, withdraw the penis immediately, put on a new condom, and use more spermicide.
- After ejaculation, carefully withdraw the penis while it is still erect.
- Hold the rim of the condom firmly against the base of the penis as the penis is withdrawn, to prevent the condom from slipping off.
- Remove the condom carefully from the penis, making sure that semen doesn't leak out.
- Check the removed condom for tears or cracks. If any are found, immediately apply a spermicide containing nonoxynol-9 directly to the penis and within the vagina. Wrap the used condom in a tissue, and discard it in the garbage. Do not flush it down the toilet, as condoms may cause problems in the sewers. Wash your hands thoroughly with soap and water.

Since condoms can be eroded by exposure to body heat or other sources of heat, they should not be kept for any length of time in a pocket or the glove compartment of a car.

---

[1]Adapted from the Centers for Disease Control pamphlet *Condoms and Sexually Transmitted Diseases . . . Especially AIDS* (HHS Publication FDA 90–4329) and other sources.

Nor should a condom be used more than once. Here are some other things you should *never* do with a condom:

- Never use teeth, scissors, or sharp fingernails to open a package of condoms. Open the condom package carefully to avoid tearing or puncturing the condom.
- Never test a condom by inflating it or stretching it.
- Never use a condom after its expiration date.
- Never use damaged condoms. Condoms that are sticky, gummy, discolored, brittle, or appear otherwise damaged, or that show signs of deterioration should be considered damaged.
- Never use a condom if the sealed packet containing the condom is damaged, cracked, or brittle, as the condom itself may be damaged or defective.
- Do not open the sealed packet until you are ready to use the condom. A condom contained in a packet that has been opened can become dry and brittle within a few hours, causing it to tear more easily. The box that contains the condom packets, however, may be opened at any time.
- Never use the same condom twice. Use a new condom if you switch the site of intercourse, such as from the vagina to the anus, or from the anus to the mouth, during a single sexual act.
- If you want to carry a condom with you, place it in a loose jacket pocket or purse, not in your pant's pocket or in a wallet held in your pant's pocket, where it might be exposed to body heat.
- Never buy condoms from vending machines that are exposed to extreme heat or placed in direct sunlight.

Effectiveness   In typical use, the failure rate of the male condom is estimated at 12% (see Table 12.1). That is, 12 out of 100 women whose partners rely on condoms alone for contraception can expect to become pregnant during the first year of use. This rate can be reduced to perhaps 2% or 3% if the condom is used correctly and combined with the use of a spermicide (Hatcher et al., 1994; Reinisch, 1990). The effectiveness of a condom and spermicide combined rivals that of the birth-control pill when used correctly and consistently.

Reversibility   The condom is simply a mechanical barrier to sperm and does not compromise fertility. Therefore, a couple who wish to conceive a child simply discontinue its use.

Advantages and Disadvantages   Condoms have the advantage of being readily available. They can be purchased without prescription. They require no fitting and can remain in sealed packages until needed. They are readily discarded after use. The combination of condoms and spermicides containing the ingredient nonoxynol-9 increases contraceptive effectiveness and protection against various STD-causing organisms, including HIV. Some condoms contain this spermicidal agent as a lubricant. When in doubt, ask the pharmacist.

Condoms do not affect production of hormones, ova, or sperm. Women whose partners use condoms ovulate normally. Men who use them produce sperm and ejaculate normally. With all these advantages, why are condoms not more popular?

One disadvantage of the condom is that it may render sex less spontaneous. The couple must interrupt lovemaking to apply the condom. Condoms may also lessen sexual sensations, especially for the man. Latex condoms do so more than animal membrane sheaths. Condoms also sometimes slip off or tear, allowing sperm to leak through.

On the other hand, condoms are almost entirely free of side effects (an advantage reported by 70% of female respondents to a *Consumer Reports* survey). They offer protection against STDs that is unparalleled among contraceptive devices. They can also be used without prior medical consultation. Both partners can share putting on the condom, which makes it an erotic part of their lovemaking, not an intrusion. The use of textured or ultrathin condoms may increase sensitivity, especially for the male. Thus many couples find that advantages outweigh disadvantages. Sex in the age of AIDS has given condoms a new respectability, even a certain trendiness. Notice, for example, the new "designer colors" and styles on display at your local pharmacy. Advertisers now also target women in their ads, suggesting that women, like men, can come prepared with condoms.

It is tempting to claim that the condom has a perfect safety record and no side effects. Let us settle for "close to perfect." Some people may have allergic reactions to the spermicides with which some lubricated condoms are coated or that the woman may apply. In such cases the couple may need to use a condom without a spermicidal lubricant or stop using supplemental spermicides. Some people are allergic to latex.

Women have an absolute right to insist that their male sex partners wear latex condoms, assuming that their partners are not latex-sensitive. STDs such as gonorrhea and chlamydia (see Chapter 16) do far more damage to a woman's reproductive tract than to a man's. Condoms can help protect women from vaginitis, pelvic inflammatory disease (PID), infections that can harm a fetus or cause infertility, and most important, AIDS.

Douching

Douche

To rinse or wash the vaginal canal by inserting a liquid and allowing it to drain out.

Many couples believe that if a woman **douches** shortly after coitus, she will not become pregnant. Women who douche for contraceptive purposes often use syringes to flush the vagina with water or a spermicidal agent. The water is intended to wash sperm out; the spermicides, to kill them. Douching is ineffective, however, because large numbers of sperm move beyond the range of the douche seconds after ejaculation. In addition, squirting a liquid into the vagina may even propel sperm *toward* the uterus. Douching, at best, has a failure rate among typical users of 40% (Reinisch, 1990), too high to be considered reliable.

Regular douching may also alter the natural chemistry of the vagina, increasing the risk of vaginal infection. In short, douching is a "nonmethod" of contraception.

Withdrawal (Coitus Interruptus)

Withdrawal means that the man removes his penis from the vagina before ejaculating. Withdrawal has a first-year failure rate among typical users ranging from 19 to 23% (Hatcher et al., 1994; Reinisch, 1990). There are several reasons for these failures. The man may not withdraw in time. Even if the penis is withdrawn just before ejaculation, some ejaculate may still fall on the vaginal lips, and sperm may find their way to the fallopian tubes. Active sperm may also be present in the *pre*-ejaculatory secretions of fluid from the Cowper's glands, a discharge of which the man is usually unaware and cannot control. These sperm are capable of fertilizing an ovum even if the man withdraws before orgasm. Because of its unreliability and high failure rate, withdrawal, like douching, is also a nonmethod of contraception.

Fertility Awareness Methods (Rhythm Methods)

Fertility awareness, or *rhythm*, methods rely on awareness of the fertile segments of the woman's menstrual cycle. Terms such as *natural birth control* or *natural family planning* also refer to these methods. The essence of such methods is that coitus is avoided on days when conception is most likely. Fertility awareness methods are used by about 3% of married women ages 15 to 44, but by less than 1% of single women (U.S. Bureau of the Census, 1990b). Women of ages 25 to 44 are more than twice as likely as 15- to 24-year-olds to use rhythm methods. Since the rhythm method does not employ artificial devices, it is acceptable to the Roman Catholic Church.

How They Work   A number of rhythm methods are used to predict the likelihood of conception. They are the mirror images of the methods that couples use to increase their chances of conceiving (see Chapter 11). Methods for enhancing the chances of conception seek to predict time of ovulation so the couple can arrange to have sperm present in the woman's reproductive tract at about that time. As methods of *birth control,* rhythm methods seek to predict ovulation so that the couple can *abstain* from coitus when the woman is fertile.

The Calendar Method

Calendar method
A fertility awareness (rhythm) method of contraception that relies on prediction of ovulation by tracking menstrual cycles, typically for a 10- to 12-month period, and assuming that ovulation occurs 14 days prior to menstruation.

The Calendar Method   The **calendar method** assumes that ovulation occurs 14 days prior to menstruation. The couple abstains from intercourse during the period that begins 3 days prior to day 13 (because sperm are unlikely to survive for more than 72 hours in the female reproductive tract) and ends 2 days after day 15 (because an unfertilized ovum is unlikely to remain receptive to fertilization for longer than 48 hours). The period of abstention thus covers days 10 to 17 of the woman's cycle.

When a woman has regular 28-day cycles, predicting the period of abstention is relatively straightforward. Women with irregular cycles are generally advised to chart their cycles for 10 months to a year to determine their shortest and longest cycles. The first day of menstruation counts as day 1 of the cycle. The last day of the cycle is the day preceding the onset of menstruation.

Consider a woman whose cycles vary from 23 to 33 days. In theory she will ovulate 14 days before menstruation begins. (To be safe she should assume that ovulation will take place anywhere from 13 to 15 days before her period.) Applying the rule of "three days before" and "two days after," she should avoid coitus from day 5 of her cycle, which corresponds to 3 days before her earliest expected ovulation (computed by subtracting 15 days from the 23 days of her shortest cycle and then subtracting 3 days), through day 22, which corresponds to 2 days after her latest expected ovulation (computed by subtracting 13 days from the 33 days of her longest cycle and then adding 2 days). Another way of determining this period of abstention would be to subtract 18 days from the woman's shortest cycle to determine the start of the "unsafe" period and 11 days from her longest cycle to determine the last "unsafe" day. The woman in the example has irregular cycles. She thus faces an 18-day abstention period each month—quite a burden for a sexually active couple.

Most women who follow the calendar method need to abstain from coitus for at least 10 days during the middle of each cycle (Reinisch, 1990). Moreover, the calendar method cannot ensure that the woman's longest or shortest menstrual cycles will occur during the 10- to 12-month period of baseline tracking. Some women, too, have such irregular cycles that the range of "unsafe" days cannot be predicted reliably even if baseline tracking is extended.

The Basal Body Temperature (BBT) Method

Basal body temperature (BBT) method
A fertility awareness method of contraception that relies on prediction of ovulation by tracking the woman's temperature during the course of the menstrual cycle.

The Basal Body Temperature (BBT) Method   In the **basal body temperature (BBT) method,** the woman tracks her body temperature upon awakening each morning to detect the small changes that occur directly before and after ovulation. A woman's basal body temperature sometimes dips slightly just before ovulation and then tends to rise between 0.4 and 0.8 degrees Fahrenheit just before, during, and after ovulation. It remains elevated until the onset of menstruation. (The rise in temperature is caused by the increased production of progesterone by the corpus luteum during the luteal phase of the cycle.) Thermometers that provide finely graded readings, such as electronic thermometers, are best suited for determining minor changes. A major problem with the BBT method is that it does not indicate the several *unsafe* preovulatory days during which sperm deposited in the vagina may remain viable. Rather, the BBT method indicates when a woman *has* ovulated. Thus, many women use the calendar method to predict the number of "safe" days prior to ovulation and the BBT method to determine the number of "unsafe" days after. A woman would avoid coitus during the "unsafe" preovulatory period (as determined by the calendar method) and then for three days when her temperature rises and remains elevated. A drawback of the BBT method is that changes in body temperature may also result from factors unrelated to ovulation, such as infections, sleeplessness, or stress. So some women triple-check themselves by also tracking their cervical mucus.

The Cervical Mucus (Ovulation) Method

Ovulation method
A fertility awareness method of contraception that relies on prediction of ovulation by tracking the viscosity of the cervical mucus.

Viscosity
Stickiness, consistency.

The Cervical Mucus (Ovulation) Method   The **ovulation method** tracks changes in the **viscosity** of the cervical mucus. Following menstruation, the vagina feels

Peak days
The days during the menstrual cycle during which a woman is most likely to be fertile.

rather dry. There is also little or no discharge from the cervix. These dry days are relatively safe. Then a mucous discharge appears in the vagina that is first thick and sticky, and white or cloudy in color. Coitus (or unprotected coitus) should be avoided at the first sign of any mucous. As the cycle progresses, the mucus discharge thins and clears, becoming slippery or stringy, like raw egg white. These are the **peak days.** This mucus discharge, called the *ovulatory mucus,* may be accompanied by a feeling of vaginal lubrication or wetness. Ovulation takes place about a day after the last peak day (about four days after this ovulatory mucus first appears). Then the mucus becomes cloudy and tacky once more. Intercourse may resume four days following the last peak day.

One problem with the mucus method is that some women have difficulty detecting changes in the mucus discharge. Such changes may also result from infections, certain medications, or contraceptive creams, jellies, or foam. Sexual arousal may also induce changes in viscosity.

Ovulation-Prediction Kits   Predicting ovulation is more accurate with an ovulation-prediction kit. Kits allow women to test their urine daily for the presence of luteinizing hormone (LH). LH levels surge about 12 to 24 hours prior to ovulation. Ovulation-prediction kits are more accurate than the BBT method. Some couples use the kits to enhance their chances of conceiving a child by engaging in coitus when ovulation appears imminent. Others use them as a means of birth control to find out when to avoid coitus. When used correctly, ovulation-predicting kits are between 95% to 100% accurate (Reinisch, 1990).

Ovulation kits are expensive and require that the woman's urine be tested each morning. Nor do they reveal the full range of the unsafe *pre*ovulatory period during which sperm may remain viable in the vagina. A couple might thus choose to use the kits to determine the unsafe period following ovulation, and the calendar method to determine the unsafe period preceding ovulation.

Effectiveness   The estimated first-year failure rate in typical use is 20%, which is high but no higher than the use of contraceptive devices such as the cervical cap or the female condom (see Table 12.1). Still, perhaps one in five typical users will become pregnant during the first year of use. (You may have heard the joke "What do you call people who use the rhythm method? Parents!") Fewer failures occur when these methods are applied conscientiously, when a combination of rhythm methods is used, and when the woman's cycles are quite regular. Restricting coitus to the postovulatory period can reduce the pregnancy rate to 1% (Hatcher et al., 1994). The trick is to be able to reliably determine when ovulation occurs. The pregnancy rate can be reduced to practically zero if rhythm methods are used with other forms of birth control, such as the condom or diaphragm.

Advantages and Disadvantages   Because they are a natural form of birth control, rhythm methods appeal to many people who, for religious or other reasons, prefer not to use artificial means. Since no devices or chemicals are used, there are no side effects. Nor do they cause any loss of sensation, as condoms do. Nor is there disruption of lovemaking, as with condoms, diaphragms, or foam, although lovemaking could be said to be quite "disrupted" during the period of abstention. Rhythm methods are inexpensive, except for ovulation-prediction kits. Both partners may share the responsibility for rhythm methods. The man, for example, can take his partner's temperature or assist with the charting. All rhythm methods are fully reversible.

A disadvantage is the fact that the reliability of rhythm methods is low. Rhythm methods may be unsuitable for women with irregular cycles. Women with irregular cycles who ovulate as early as a week after their menstrual flows can become pregnant even if they engage in unprotected intercourse only when they are menstruating, since some sperm remaining in a woman's reproductive tract may survive for up to eight days and fertilize an ovum that is released at that time (Reinisch, 1990). Moreover, the rhythm method requires abstaining from coitus for several days, or perhaps weeks, each month. Rhythm methods also require that records of the menstrual cycle be kept for many months prior to implementation. Unlike diaphragms, condoms, or spermicides, rhythm methods cannot be used at a moment's notice. Finally, rhythm methods do not offer any protection against STDs.

Sterilization

Sterilization

Surgical procedures that render people incapable of reproduction without affecting sexual activity.

Many people decide to be sterilized when they plan to have no children or no more children. With the exception of abstinence, sterilization is the most effective form of contraception. Yet the prospect of **sterilization** arouses strong feelings because a person is transformed all at once, and presumably permanently, from someone who might be capable of bearing children to someone who cannot. This transformation often involves a profound change in self-concept. These feelings are especially strong in men and women who link fertility to their sense of masculinity or femininity.

Still, more than a million sterilizations are performed in the United States each year. It is the most widely used form of birth control among married couples age 30 and above (Reinisch, 1990). Nineteen percent of the respondents in a 1992 national sample of nearly 7,000 women ages 15 to 50 reported being sterilized; 12% reported having partners who had undergone a vasectomy. Married women were far more likely to rely on a permanent method of contraception (tubal sterilization or vasectomy) than were single women (48% vs. 11%).

Vasectomy

The surgical method of male sterilization in which sperm are prevented from reaching the urethra by cutting each vas deferens and tying it back or cauterizing it.

Male Sterilization The male sterilization procedure used today is the **vasectomy.** About 500,000 vasectomies are performed each year in the United States (Altman, 1993b). More than 15% of men in the United States have had vasectomies.

A vasectomy is usually carried out in a doctor's office, under local anesthesia, in 15 to 20 minutes. Small incisions are made in the scrotum. Each vas is cut, a small segment is removed, and the ends are tied off or cauterized (to prevent them from growing back together) (see Figure 12.7). Now sperm can no longer reach the urethra. Instead, they are harmlessly reabsorbed by the body.

Figure 12.7. Vasectomy. The male sterilization procedure is usually carried out in a doctor's office, using local anesthesia. Small incisions are made in the scrotum. Each vas deferens is cut, and the ends are tied off or cauterized to prevent sperm from reaching the urethra. Sperm are harmlessly reabsorbed by the body after the operation.

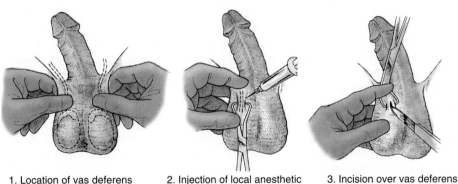

1. Location of vas deferens

2. Injection of local anesthetic

3. Incision over vas deferens

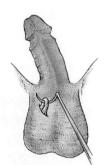

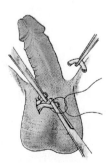

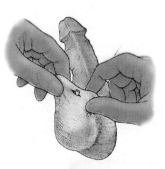

4. Isolation of vas from surrounding tissue

5. Removal of segment of vas; tying of ends

6. Return of vas to position; incision is closed and process is repeated on the other side

The man can usually resume sexual relations within a few days. Since some sperm may be present in his reproductive tract for a few weeks, however, he is best advised to use an additional contraceptive method until his ejaculate shows a zero sperm count. Some health professionals recommend that the man have a follow-up sperm count a year after his vasectomy, to ensure that the cut ends of the vas deferens have not grown together—a complication that occurs in about 1% of cases (Reinisch, 1990).

Vasectomy does not diminish sex drive or result in any change in sexual arousal, erectile or ejaculatory ability, or sensations of ejaculation. Male sex hormones and sperm are still produced by the testes. Without a passageway to the urethra, however, sperm are no longer expelled with the ejaculate. Since sperm account for only about 1% of the ejaculate, the volume of the ejaculate is not noticeably different.

Though there are no confirmed long-term health risks of vasectomy (Reinisch, 1990), two recent studies of more than 73,000 men who had undergone vasectomies raise concerns that the procedure may not be as risk-free as people generally believe. The studies showed that men who had had vasectomies more than 20 years earlier faced a slightly increased risk of prostate cancer (Altman, 1993a; Giovannucci et al., 1993a, 1993b). The studies found a correlation between vasectomies and the risk of prostate cancer, but did not establish a causal connection. It is possible that other factors than the vasectomy itself may explain the greater risk faced by vasectomized men. The results also conflict with earlier studies showing either no link between vasectomies and the risk of prostate cancer or even a *lower* risk among vasectomized men. More research is needed to clarify the relationship between vasectomy and prostate cancer. In the meantime, medical experts recommend that men who have had vasectomies get annual checkups for signs of prostate cancer (Altman, 1993a).

The vasectomy is nearly 100% effective. Fewer than 2 pregnancies occur during the first year among 1,000 couples in which the man has undergone a vasectomy (see Table 12.1). The few failures stem from sperm remaining in the male's genital tract shortly after the operation, or the growing together of the segments of a vas deferens.

Reversibility is simple in concept but not in practice. Thus, vasectomies should be considered permanent. In an operation to reverse a vasectomy, called a **vasovasotomy,** the ends of the vas deferens are sewn together, and in a few days they grow together. Estimates of success at reversal, as measured by subsequent pregnancies, range from 16% to 79% (Hatcher et al., 1994). Some vasectomized men develop antibodies that attack their own sperm. The production of antibodies does not appear to endanger the man's health (Hatcher et al., 1994), but it may contribute to infertility following reconnection (Reinisch, 1990).

Major studies conducted over a 15-year period revealed no deaths due to vasectomy in the United States (Reinisch, 1990). Few documented complications of vasectomies have been reported in the medical literature. Minor complications are reported in 4% or 5% of cases, however. They typically involve temporary local inflammation or swelling after the operation. Ice packs and anti-inflammatory drugs, such as aspirin, may help reduce swelling and discomfort. More serious but rarer medical complications include infection of the epididymis (Reinisch, 1990).

Female Sterilization Nearly four in ten (39%) married women under the age of 45 have been surgically sterilized (U.S. Bureau of the Census, 1990b). **Tubal sterilization,** also called *tubal ligation,* is the most common method of female sterilization. Tubal sterilization prevents ova and sperm from passing through the fallopian tubes. About 650,000 tubal sterilizations are performed each year in the United States (Altman, 1993c).

The two main surgical procedures for tubal sterilization are *minilaparotomy* and *laparoscopy*. In a **minilaparotomy,** a small incision is made in the abdomen, just above the pubic hairline, to provide access to the fallopian tubes. Each tube is cut and either tied back or clamped with a clip. In a **laparoscopy** (see Figure 12.8), sometimes called "belly button surgery," the fallopian tubes are approached through a small incision in the abdomen just below the navel. The surgeon uses a narrow, lighted viewing instrument called a *laparoscope* to locate the tubes. A small section of each of the tubes is cauterized, cut, or clamped. The woman usually returns to her daily routine in a few days and can resume

Vasovasotomy

The surgical method of reversing vasectomy in which the cut or cauterized ends of the vas deferens are sewn together.

Tubal sterilization

The most common method of female sterilization, in which the fallopian tubes are surgically blocked to prevent the meeting of sperm and ova. Also called *tubal ligation.*

Minilaparotomy

A kind of tubal sterilization in which a small incision is made in the abdomen to provide access to the fallopian tubes.

Laparoscopy

Tubal sterilization by means of a *laparoscope,* which is inserted through a small incision just below the navel and used to cauterize, cut, or clamp the fallopian tubes. Sometimes referred to as "belly button surgery."

Depo-Provera   *Depo-Provera* (medroxyprogesterone acetate) is a long-acting, synthetic form of progesterone that works as a contraceptive by inhibiting ovulation. The progesterone signals the pituitary gland in the brain to stop producing hormones that would lead to the release of mature ova by the ovaries. Administered by injection once every three months, Depo-Provera is an effective form of contraception, with reported failure rates of less than 1 pregnancy per 100 women during the first year of use (Hatcher et al., 1994). Depo-Provera has been used by more than 30 million women in more than 90 countries worldwide since it was first marketed in 1969. However, approval in the United States was held up because of concerns over side effects, including the risk of breast cancer. A review by the Food and Drug Administration (FDA) finally found the cancer risk to be minimal and approved Depo-Provera as a contraceptive in 1992. A World Health Organization study of 12,000 women found no links between the drug and the risk of ovarian or cervical cancer (Walt, 1993). Yet the drug may produce side effects such as weight gain, menstrual irregularity, and spotting between periods (Hatcher et al., 1994). Use of Depo-Provera has also been linked to *osteoporosis,* a condition involving bone loss that can cause bones to become brittle and fracture easily.

Devices Under Development   Other methods of contraception are in experimental stages, including sterilization techniques that promise greater reversibility. Also in the experimental stage is a so-called male pill, an oral contraceptive for men. The male sex hormone testosterone has shown promise in reducing sperm production ("Male birth control," 1995). The pituitary gland normally stimulates the testes to produce sperm. Testosterone suppresses the pituitary, in turn suppressing sperm production. Men who have received testosterone injections have shown declines in sperm production. Potential complications include an increased risk of prostate cancer. Testosterone also appears to increase cholesterol levels in the bloodstream, which may heighten the risk of cardiovascular disease.

T r u t h   **OR**   *Fiction?*   It is true that testosterone can be used as a male contraceptive. However, side effects and other

R E V I S I T E D   questions have prevented testosterone from being marketed for such usage. ■

In any event, a survey of college men found that only one in five expressed willingness to take a male pill (Laird, 1994). The men believed that taking a male pill would be more of a bother than having one's partner take a female pill and more "contrary to nature"!

Another approach was suggested when investigators in China found extremely low birth rates in communities in which cottonseed oil was used in cooking. They extracted a drug from the cotton plant, *gossypol,* which shows promise as a male contraceptive. Chinese studies reveal the drug to be nearly 100% effective in preventing pregnancies. The drug appears to nullify sperm production without affecting hormone levels or the sex drive. However, toxic effects of gossypol have limited its acceptability as a male contraceptive.

Some men are infertile because they produce antibodies that destroy their own sperm. It is also speculated that vasectomy causes some men's bodies to react to their own sperm as foreign substances and produce antibodies. This is an immunological response to sperm. Some researchers have suggested that it may be possible to develop ways to induce the body to produce such antibodies. Ideally this procedure would be reversible.

Applying ultrasound waves to the testes has been shown to produce reversible sterility in laboratory rats, dogs, and monkeys. No one is quite certain how ultrasound works in inducing temporary sterilization. Moreover, its safety has not been demonstrated.

～ *Reflections* ～

▪ Have you discussed methods of contraception with your peers? If so, what factors account for your peers' choices?

▪ Are some or all of the methods of contraception morally and ethically unacceptable to you? Explain.

▪ Do you believe that your views on contraception are consistent with those of most people from your sociocultural background? Explain.

Abortion

Induced abortion

The purposeful termination of a pregnancy before the embryo or fetus is capable of sustaining independent life. (From the Latin *abortio*, meaning "that which is miscarried.")

An **induced abortion** (in contrast to a spontaneous abortion, or miscarriage) is the purposeful termination of a pregnancy. Perhaps more than any other contemporary social issue, induced abortion (hereafter referred to simply as abortion) has divided neighbors and family members into opposing camps.

Thirty-seven million abortions worldwide, including more than 1.5 million in the United States, are performed each year (Smolowe, 1993; U.S. Bureau of the Census, 1990b). The great majority of abortions in the United States—nearly 90%—occur during the first trimester. This is when they are safest to the woman and least costly (Centers for Disease Control, 1992a). Nearly four women in five who have abortions are unmarried.

Women of color in the United States have proportionally more abortions than White women (Centers for Disease Control, 1992a). There are about 55 abortions per 1,000 women of color reported each year, as compared to 23 for White women. These statistics may underestimate the rates of abortion, especially for higher-income women who have greater access to private health care providers. Many abortions performed in private settings are reported under a medical classification other than abortion.

Abortion is practiced widely in Canada, Japan, Russia, and many European nations. It is less common in developing nations, largely because of sparse medical facilities. Abortion is rarely used as a primary means of birth control. It usually comes into play when other methods have failed.

More than half (55%) of the women having abortions are in their 20s. Women ages 15 to 19 account for about one in four (25%) abortions. The remainder of women having abortions are either under the age of 15 (1%), between 30 and 39 years of age (18%), or are 40 or older (1%) (Henshaw & Silverman, 1988). Nearly half of women seeking abortions are mothers who bear substantial family responsibilities (Russo et al., 1992).

There are many reasons why women have abortions, including psychological factors as well as external circumstances. Abortion is often motivated by a desire to reduce the risk of physical, economic, psychological, and social disadvantages that the woman perceives for herself and her present and future children should she take the pregnancy to term (Russo et al., 1992).

The national debate over abortion has been played out in recent years against a backdrop of demonstrations, marches, and occasional acts of violence, such as firebombings of abortion clinics and even murder. (See the nearby A Closer Look feature.) The right-to-life (pro-life) movement asserts that human life begins at conception and thus views abortion as the murder of an unborn child (Sagan & Dryan, 1990). Some in the pro-life movement brook no exception to their opposition to abortion. Others would permit abortion to save the mother's life or when a pregnancy results from rape or incest.

The pro-choice movement contends that abortion is a matter of personal choice and that the government has no right to interfere with a woman's right to terminate a pregnancy. Pro-choice advocates argue that women are free to control what happens within their bodies, including pregnancies.

When Does Human Life Begin?

Moral concerns about abortion often turn on the question of when human life begins. For some Christians, the matter revolves around when they believe the fetus obtains a soul.

In his thesis on *ensoulment,* the thirteenth-century Christian theologian Saint Thomas Aquinas wrote that a male fetus does not acquire a human soul until 40 days after conception. A female fetus does not acquire a soul until after 80 days. Scientists, too, have attempted to define when human life can be said to begin. Astronomer Carl Sagan, for example, writes that fetal brain activity can be considered a secular or scientific marker of human life (Sagan & Dryan, 1990). Brain activity is needed for thought, the quality that is considered most "human" by many. Brain wave patterns typical of children do not begin

A CLOSER LOOK

FROM THOUGHT TO DEED: IN THE MIND OF A KILLER WHO SAYS HE SERVED GOD[2]

Sandy-haired and bespectacled with a well-muscled, 6-foot frame, Paul Jennings Hill has an appearance that might be described as Computer Programmer All-American. The 41-year-old former Presbyterian minister presents such an air of cordiality and evenness that he hardly seems a homicidal religious fanatic at all.

Yet Mr. Hill is an unapologetic killer, condemned to die in Florida's electric chair for the shotgun slayings of a doctor, John Bayard Britton, and a security escort, James H. Barrett, outside a Pensacola abortion clinic (in July 1994). To talk to him is to encounter a calm zealot's eerily disarming, internally consistent logic—an impermeable personal conviction of the sort that often fatefully haunts society. (In a September 1995 prison interview), Mr. Hill spoke not of remorse but of relief for having killed.

"I would feel more stress if I were in your shoes, with my core beliefs," he said to a visitor across the table who had commented on how oddly relaxed he looked, even clad in handcuffs and the prison-issue orange of the condemned. "Y'know, there was the *burden* of, what am I going to do for these thousands and thousands of children being killed, and here I am watching them go by and being killed every week?

"Of course, I still have struggles every day to walk with the Lord, but I feel like I'm much more at peace now than prior to shooting the abortionist," he said. "I honestly feel better now about myself, about life and about everything than I ever have because I know I did the right thing."

Mr. Hill occupies a singular place in this country's multifaceted debate over whether it can be morally justified to snuff out life, for he is the only one of several recent anti-abortion killers to be sentenced to death. As it

happens, Mr. Hill says he believes in the death penalty—"I couldn't have shot that abortionist if I didn't"—but says it is unjustified in his case because he was "effectually defending" unborn human lives in immediate mortal peril.

This argument of "justifiable homicide" is one he intends to press in [the] appeals process. A judge denied him that defense at his trial (in the fall of 1994). If he is again thwarted, he said, he is prepared to abandon appeals and die for his cause, if that is the best way to bring what he calls the "holocaust" of abortion to the world's attention. . . .

In his extreme fervor he parts company with the anti-abortion movement's more moderate majority, whose leaders have condemned his actions and for whom he reserves some of his most caustic comments (he likens them to acquiescent church leaders in Hitler's Germany). Mr. Hill's logic is simple: If you believe that abortion is murder, you are morally obligated under God not only to try to legislate and instruct against it but also to act forcefully to defend the innocent unborn. That means killing. . . .

Dr. Britton, clad in his bulletproof vest, arrived [at the clinic] shortly be-

fore 7:30 A.M. in the covered blue pickup truck of his two unarmed volunteer escorts: Mr. Barrett, 74, a retired Air Force officer, and Mr. Barrett's wife, June, 68, in the jumpseat in back. . . .

Dead in the front seat with [shotgun] wounds to the head were Mr. Barrett (closest to [Hill] as he approached the vehicle on the driver's side) and Dr. Britton. Cowering in the shattered glass on the pickup's floor was June Barrett, with a shotgun wound in her left arm.

Asked why he had killed Mr. Barrett—who was not his target—Mr. Hill said matter-of-factly: "Because he was directly between the abortionist and me. I was actually aiming at the abortionist, but he was directly between us, so for me to shoot the abortionist and to aim and shoot at him was one and the same thing."

To his interviewer's expression of amazement, Mr. Hill added: "Y'know, it happens all the time. Police kill people to prevent other people from being killed. . . . "

[2]Interview by Tom Kuntz, adapted from Kuntz, T. (1995, September 24). From Thought to Deed: In the Mind of a Killer Who Says He Served God. *The New York Times*, p. E7.

Paul Hill on Death Row. Hill, accompanied by two policemen, is sentenced to death in Florida's electric chair for the shotgun slaying of medical doctor John Bayard Britton and his security escort, James H. Barrett. Hill killed both men outside a Pensacola (FL) abortion clinic.

QUESTIONNAIRE

PRO-CHOICE OR PRO-LIFE? WHERE DO YOU STAND?

What does it mean to be "pro-life" on the abortion issue? What does it mean to be "pro-choice"? Which position is closer to your own views on abortion?

    The *Reasoning About Abortion Questionnaire (RAQ)* (Parsons et al., 1990) assesses agreement with pro-life or pro-choice lines of reasoning about abortion. To find out which position is closer to your own, indicate your level of agreement or disagreement with each of the following items by circling the number that most closely represents your feelings. Then refer to the key in the appendix to interpret your score.

        1 = Strongly Agree 2 = Agree 3 = Mixed Feelings
        4 = Disagree 5 = Strongly Disagree

1. Abortion is a matter of personal choice.
   1 2 3 ④ 5
2. Abortion is a threat to our society.
   ① 2 3 4 5
3. A woman should have control over what is happening to her own body by having the option to choose abortion.
   1 2 3 ④ 5
4. Only God, not people, can decide if a fetus should live.
   1 2 ③ 4 5
5. Even if one believes that there may be some exceptions, abortion is still basically wrong.
   ① 2 3 4 5
6. Abortion violates an unborn person's fundamental right to life.
   ① 2 3 4 5
7. A woman should be able to exercise her rights to self-determination by choosing to have an abortion.
   1 2 ③ 4 5
8. Outlawing abortion could take away a woman's sense of self and personal autonomy.
   1 2 ③ 4 5
9. Outlawing abortion violates a woman's civil rights.
   1 2 3 ④ 5
10. Abortion is morally unacceptable and unjustified.
    ① 2 3 4 5

11. In my reasoning, the notion that an unborn fetus may be a human life is not a deciding issue in considering abortion.
    1 2 ③ 4 5
12. Abortion can be described as taking a life unjustly.
    ① 2 3 4 5
13. A woman should have the right to decide to have an abortion based on her own life circumstances.
    1 2 3 ④ 5
14. If a woman feels that having a child might ruin her life, she should consider an abortion.
    1 2 3 4 ⑤
15. Abortion could destroy the sanctity of motherhood.
    1 ② 3 4 5
16. An unborn fetus is a viable human being with rights.
    1 ② 3 4 5
17. If a woman feels she can't care for a baby, she should be able to have an abortion.
    1 2 3 ④ 5
18. Abortion is the destruction of one life for the convenience of another.
    ① 2 3 4 5
19. Abortion is the same as murder.
    ① 2 3 4 5
20. Even if one believes that there are times when abortion is immoral, it is still basically the woman's own choice.
    1 2 3 ④ 5   �50⌐

---

until about the 30th week of pregnancy. Before then, the human fetus lacks the brain architecture to begin thinking (Sagan & Dryan, 1990). Of course, this line of thinking raises the question of whether fetal brain wave activity can be equated with thought. (What would a fetus "think" about?) Moreover, some argue that a newly fertilized ovum carries the *potential* for human thought in the same way that the embryonic or fetal brain does. It could even be argued that sperm cells and ova are living things in that they carry out the biological processes characteristic of cellular life. All in all, the question of when *human* life begins is a matter of definition that is apparently unanswerable by science.

Historical and Legal Perspectives on Abortion

Societal attitudes toward abortion have varied across cultures and times in history. Abortion was permitted in ancient Greece and Rome, but women in ancient Assyria were impaled on stakes for attempting abortion. The Bible does not specifically prohibit abortion (Sagan & Dryan, 1990). For much of its history, the Roman Catholic Church held to Thomas Aquinas's belief that ensoulment of the fetus did not occur for at least 40 days after conception. In 1869, Pope Pius IX declared that human life begins at conception. Thus an abortion at any stage of pregnancy became murder in the eyes of the church and grounds for excommunication. The Roman Catholic Church has since opposed abortion during any stage of pregnancy.

In colonial times and through the mid-nineteenth century, women in the United States were permitted to terminate a pregnancy until such time as the "quickening" (the point at which the woman was first able to feel the fetus stirring within her) (Sagan & Dryan, 1990). Few women were prosecuted for abortion, because quickening was determined by the woman's self-report (Sagan & Dryan, 1990). More restrictive abortion laws emerged after the American Civil War, spurred by the need to increase the population and by concerns voiced by physicians about protecting women from botched abortions. By 1900 virtually all states in the union had enacted legislation banning abortion *at any point* during pregnancy, except when necessary to save the woman's life.

T r u t h  *Fiction?*
R E V I S I T E D

It is true that abortions were legal in the United States prior to the Civil War—until the point in the pregnancy when the woman sensed fetal movements. ∎

Abortion laws remained essentially unchanged until the late 1960s, when some states liberalized their abortion laws under mounting public pressure. Then, in 1973, the U.S. Supreme Court in effect legalized abortion nationwide in the landmark *Roe v. Wade* decision.

Roe v. Wade held that a woman's right to an abortion was protected under the right to privacy guaranteed by the Constitution. The decision legalized abortions for any reason during the first trimester, leaving the decision to have an abortion entirely in the hands of the woman. In its ruling, the Court also noted that a fetus is not considered a person and is thus not entitled to constitutional protection. The Court ruled that states may regulate a woman's right to have an abortion during the second trimester to protect her health, such

Polarization. Abortion is an issue that continues to deeply polarize the United States. Pro-choice groups assert that women have the right to control what happens within their bodies. Pro-life groups argue that abortion is the taking of a human life.

as by requiring her to obtain an abortion in a hospital rather than a doctor's office. The Court also held that when a fetus becomes viable, its rights override the mother's right to privacy. Because the fetus may become viable early in the third trimester, states may prohibit third-trimester abortions, except in cases in which an abortion is necessary to protect a woman's health or life.

In 1977, Congress enacted the Hyde amendment, which denies Medicaid funding for abortions except in cases in which the woman's life is endangered. In *Harris v. McRae* (1980), the U.S. Supreme Court essentially upheld the Hyde amendment (and similar state legislation) by ruling that federal and state governments are not required to pay for abortions for poor women who are receiving public assistance.

Since *Roe v. Wade,* 33 states have also enacted laws requiring parental consent or notification before a minor may have an abortion (Carlson, 1990). Sixty-nine percent of adults in the United States believe that parental permission should be required before teenage girls can have abortions (Carlson, 1990). Many pregnant teenage girls, however, especially those living in families with alcoholic or abusive parents, fear telling their parents that they are pregnant. In 1990 rulings involving state laws in Ohio and Minnesota, the U.S. Supreme Court upheld the rights of states to require that a minor seeking an abortion notify at least one parent and wait 48 hours before an abortion can be performed. The Court provided an "escape clause," however: The minor girl may go before a judge instead. Carlson (1990) notes that many pregnant teenagers who are reluctant to reveal pregnancies to their parents may also hesitate to reveal them to authority figures such as judges. A 1993 U.S. Supreme Court ruling let stand a Mississippi law requiring minors to obtain approval either from both parents or from a judge.

Parental consent laws have widespread popular support. Three of four adults support such provisions, including many abortion rights supporters (Lewin, 1992b). Yet, with or without the rules, the majority of girls seeking abortions do consult their parents before going through with their plans. One of the arguments favoring parental approval is the belief that parents know what is best for their children. However, opponents say that parental consent laws only serve to delay girls from getting safer early abortions, and force them to postpone abortions until the second trimester, when the risks are greater. Even in states that allow minors seeking abortions to obtain consent from a third party, most usually a judge, the delays involved can heighten the risks the girl faces (Pliner & Yates, 1992).

In 1989 a decision by the U.S. Supreme Court in a Missouri case, *Webster v. Reproductive Health Services,* considerably narrowed abortion rights granted previously under *Roe v. Wade.* By a 5–4 split decision, the Supreme Court upheld Missouri state laws (1) restricting public employees from performing or assisting in abortions, except in cases in which an abortion was needed to save a woman's life; (2) prohibiting the use of public facilities for performing abortions; and (3) requiring doctors to perform medical tests to determine the viability of a fetus before granting a woman's request for an abortion if she is believed to be at least 20 weeks pregnant. Although the *Webster* decision did not ban abortions, it made it more difficult (and expensive) for women to obtain late second-trimester abortions by allowing states to require medical testing for viability at 20 weeks. (The 20-week stipulation is unlikely to have a major impact, however, because 91% of abortions occur within the first 12 weeks of pregnancy) (McKinney, 1989). States would also be permitted to ban abortions performed in public facilities or by public employees, which would make it more difficult for poor women to obtain abortions.

Attitudes Toward Legalized Abortion National public opinion polls taken since *Roe v. Wade* have consistently shown that a majority of people in the United States support the decision legalizing abortion (Gordon & Snyder, 1989). There is little difference in support for abortion between Catholics, Jews, and Protestants (Gordon & Snyder, 1989). On the other hand, African Americans are less likely than White Americans to support abortion. Researchers find that higher levels of education are associated with pro-choice attitudes. Reduced support for legal abortion is associated with religious commitment, conservative attitudes on premarital sex, and belief in having large families

(Lynxwiler & Gay, 1994). Public support for abortion increased during the 1960s and 1970s but decreased slightly between 1980 and 1985 (Gillespie et al., 1988).

Most people in the United States favor legalized abortion but not under all circumstances. A 1993 ABC News/*Washington Post* poll found that a woman's right to have an abortion was approved by a margin of 2 to 1, 65% versus 33%. Yet, according to a 1989 Gallup poll, only 27% of Americans believe that a woman should have a right to an abortion for any reason. A large majority believe that women should be permitted to have an abortion if the pregnancy results from rape or incest, if the woman's life or health is threatened, or if the child is likely to be born seriously deformed. A majority feel that abortion should be illegal, however, for a woman who does not want or cannot afford a child. Even a great majority of American Catholics and Protestants endorse abortion under certain conditions, such as when the woman's health is endangered, when there is chance of birth defects, or when a woman becomes pregnant as the result of rape. Support for abortion under other conditions is lower, however, with fewer than half endorsing abortions in the case of a single woman who doesn't want to marry (38% of Catholics and 44% of Protestants approving) or of a married woman who doesn't want more children (37% of Catholics and 43% of Protestants approving).

Although some consider abortion a "women's issue," men are as likely—if not more likely—to be pro-choice (Scott & Schuman, 1980). Among people who support abortion rights, however, women as a group feel more strongly about the issue than men do, are more likely to consider a congressional candidate's stance on abortion to be a litmus test for support, and are more likely to take social action.

The controversy over abortion has led to a decline in the numbers of abortion providers (Boodman, 1993; Lacayo, 1993; National Abortion Rights Action League Fact Sheet, 1993). Nationwide, 83% of counties have no abortion provider. Many women who seek abortions at abortion clinics must navigate past pro-life picketers to gain entrance.

Many people in the pro-choice movement argue that if abortions were to be made illegal again, thousands of women, especially poor women, would die or suffer serious physical consequences from botched or nonsterile abortions. People in the pro-life movement counter that alternatives to abortion such as adoption are available to pregnant women and that no one is forced to have an abortion. Pro-choice advocates argue that the debate about abortion should be framed not only by notions of the mother's right to privacy but also by the issue of the quality of life of an unwanted child. They argue that minority and physically or mentally disabled children are often hard to place for adoption. These children often spend their childhoods being shuffled from one foster home to another. Pro-life advocates counter that killing a fetus eliminates any potential that it might have, despite hardships, of living a fruitful and meaningful life. The debate about abortion continues, with no consensus in the offing.

Methods of Abortion

Regardless of the moral, legal, and political issues that surround abortion, many abortion methods are in use today.

Vacuum aspiration
Removal of the uterine contents by suction. An abortion method used early in pregnancy. (From the Latin *aspirare*, meaning "to breathe upon.")

Vacuum Aspiration
Vacuum aspiration, or suction curettage, is the safest and most common method of abortion. It accounts for more than 90% of abortions in the United States. It is relatively painless and inexpensive. It can be done with little or no anesthesia in a medical office or clinic, but only during the first trimester. Later, thinning of the uterine walls increases the risks of perforation and bleeding.

In the procedure the cervix is usually dilated first by insertion of progressively larger curved metal rods, or "dilators," or by insertion, hours earlier, of a stick of seaweed called *Laminaria digitata. Laminaria* expands as it absorbs cervical moisture, providing a gentler means of opening the os. Then an angled tube connected to an aspirator (suction machine) is inserted through the cervix into the uterus. The uterine contents are then evacuated (emptied) by suction (see Figure 12.9 on page 366). Possible complications include perforation of the uterus, infection, cervical lacerations, and hemorrhaging, but these are rare.

ABORTION ~ **365**

Figure 12.9. Vacuum Aspiration. This is the safest and most common method of abortion, but it can be performed only during the first trimester. An angled tube is inserted through the cervix into the uterus, and the uterine contents are then evacuated (emptied) by suction.

1. Vacurette is inserted through cervical canal

2. Suction is turned on; material flows through tubing

3. Empty uterus collapses

Collection hose
Vacuum tube to bottles
Collection bottles
Pump compartment

T r u t h **OR** *Fiction?*
R E V I S I T E D

It is not true that the D&C is the most widely used type of abortion method in the United States today. Vacuum aspiration is the most widely used abortion method. ■

Dilation and Curettage (D&C)

The **D&C** was once the customary method of performing abortions. It now accounts for only a small number of abortions in the United States. It is usually performed 8 to 20 weeks following the last menstrual period (LMP). Once the cervix has been dilated, the uterine contents are scraped from the uterine lining with a blunt scraping tool.

D&C's are carried out in a hospital, usually under general anesthesia. The scraping increases the chances of hemorrhaging, infection, and perforation. Because of these risks, D&C's have largely been replaced by the vacuum aspiration method. D&C's are still used to treat various gynecological problems, however, such as abnormally heavy menstrual bleeding.

Dilation and Evacuation (D&E)

The **D&E** is used most commonly during the second trimester, when vacuum aspiration alone would be too risky. The D&E combines suction and the D&C. First the cervix is dilated. The cervix must also be dilated more fully than with vacuum aspiration to allow for passage of the larger fetus. Then a suction tube is inserted to remove some of the contents of the uterus. But suction alone cannot safely remove all uterine contents. So the remaining contents are removed with forceps. A blunt scraper may also be used to scrape the uterine wall to make sure that the lining has been removed fully. Like the D&C, the D&E is usually performed in the hospital under general anesthesia. Most women recover quickly and relatively painlessly. In rare instances, however, complications can arise. These include excessive bleeding, infection, and perforation of the uterine lining (Thompson, 1993).

Inducing Labor by Intra-amniotic Infusion

Second-trimester abortions are sometimes performed by chemically inducing premature labor and delivery. The procedure, which must be performed in a hospital, is called instillation, or **intra-amniotic infusion.** It is usually performed when fetal development has progressed beyond the point at which other methods are deemed safe. A saline (salt) solution or a solution of prostaglandins (hormones that stimulate uterine contractions during labor) is injected into the amniotic sac. Prostaglandins may also be administered by vaginal suppository. Uterine contractions (labor) begin within a few hours after infusion. The fetus and placenta are expelled from the uterus within the next 24 or 48 hours.

D&C
Abbreviation for *dilation and curettage,* an operation in which the cervix is dilated and uterine contents are then gently scraped away.

D&E
Abbreviation for *dilation and evacuation,* an abortion method in which the cervix is dilated prior to vacuum aspiration.

Intra-amniotic infusion
An abortion method in which a substance is injected into the amniotic sac to induce premature labor. Also called *instillation.*

Intra-amniotic infusion accounts for only a small number of abortions. Medical complications, risks, and costs are greater with this procedure than with other methods of abortion. Overly rapid labor can tear the cervix, but previous dilation of the cervix with *Laminaria* lessens the risk. Perforation, infection, and hemorrhaging are rare if prostaglandins are used, but about half the recipients experience nausea and vomiting, diarrhea, or headaches. Saline infusion can cause shock and even death if the solution is carelessly introduced into the bloodstream.

Hysterotomy

An abortion method in which the fetus is removed by cesarean section.

Hysterotomy   The **hysterotomy** is, in effect, a cesarean section. Incisions are made in the abdomen and uterus, and the fetus and uterine contents are removed. Hysterotomy may be performed during the late second trimester, between the 16th and 24th weeks LMP. It is performed very rarely, usually only when intra-amniotic infusion is not advised. A hysterotomy is major surgery that must be carried out under general anesthesia in a hospital. Hysterotomy involves risks of complications from the anesthesia and the surgery itself.

A C L O S E R L O O K

ABORTION DRUGS

Most early abortions are accomplished by vacuum aspiration, which is a surgical technique. Although vacuum aspiration is safe enough for the woman, 60% to 70% of women in the United States would prefer a drug-induced abortion if it were available (Population Council, 1995).

RU-486
One drug-induced abortion method is available in France and many other parts of the world. RU-486 is an abortion pill. It contains *mifepristone*, a chemical that induces early abortion by blocking the effects of progesterone. Progesterone is the hormone that stimulates proliferation of the endometrium, allowing implantation of the fertilized ovum and, subsequently, development of the placenta. Today, nearly half of French women seeking abortion prefer RU-486 to surgical methods, including vacuum aspiration.

Supporters of RU-486 argue that it offers a safe, noninvasive substitute for more costly and unpleasant abortion procedures (Segal, 1990). Moreover, use of RU-486 means that a woman need not run a gauntlet of

demonstrators to visit an abortion clinic or hospital. Supporters also note that RU-486 may reduce the numbers of women who die each year from complications from self-induced abortions. Such women are usually too poor to avail themselves of legally sanctioned abortion facilities. Or else they live in Third World countries that lack adequate medical services.

RU-486 may make abortion physically easier, but not necessarily psychologically easier. The developer of the RU-486, Dr. Étienne-Émile Baulieu, remarks "It's insulting to women to say that abortion now will be as easy as taking aspirins. . . . It is always difficult, psychologically and physically, sometimes tragic" (Smolowe, 1993, p. 51). Moreover, questions remain about the safety of the procedure (Carper, 1993). Commonly reported side effects include heavy menstrual bleeding, lasting about ten days on the average, and menstrual cramping.

RU-486 has not yet been introduced in the United States, largely because of opposition by pro-life groups (Hausknecht, 1995; Segal, 1990). Opponents argue that RU-486 makes

abortions more accessible and difficult to regulate (Smolowe, 1993). Pro-life groups consider abortion murder, whether induced by surgery or a pill.

Other Methods
As the abortion debate continues, so does research into the use of other drugs. A combination of the cancer drug *methotrexate* and the ulcer drug *misoprostol*, for example, can be used to terminate early pregnancy. Methotrexate is toxic to the trophoblastic tissue of the embryo, and misoprostol causes uterine contractions. Hausknecht (1995) reported a pilot study in which an injection of methotrexate followed by a vaginal suppository with misoprostol led to successful abortions in 171 of 178 women. (The remaining 7 subsequently underwent aspiration.) Moreover, it would appear that the combination of methotrexate and misoprostol has fewer side effects than RU-486.

It seems likely that additional methods of chemical induction of abortion will become available as the years go on. None of them is likely to defuse the abortion debate, however.

A WORLD OF DIVERSITY

JAPAN'S ABORTION AGONY: IN A COUNTRY THAT PROHIBITS THE PILL, REALITY COLLIDES WITH RELIGION

Yuka Sugimoto winds her way among thousands of miniature stone statues in a hillside Buddhist temple (WuDunn, 1996). She finds the one she is seeking—the proper *mizuko jizo*—and lingers to ponder the clandestine act that resulted in this.

Buddhists come to the temples to pray for health, wealth, or a wife or husband. Not Ms. Sugimoto. She comes to this ancient temple once a month as a way of making amends with the fetus she aborted 2 years earlier, when she was an unmarried student.

Japan may be the richest, most technologically advanced nation in the world, but it depends on an antiquated system of birth control that forces women to rely heavily on abortion in a society that at the same time disapproves of it.

Japan's abortion rate is one of the highest among the world's industrialized nations. One reason for this is the lack of birth-control alternatives. The government bans the use of the birth-control pill as a contraceptive, and doctors do not encourage the

Offerings Made at a Buddhist Temple in Japan by Women Who Have Had Abortions. Japan prohibits women from using the birth-control pill, thereby increasing the incidence of abortion.

use of sterilization, IUDs, or diaphragms. Nearly 75% of Japanese continue to use condoms and rhythm methods despite their high failure rate.

Over the years Japanese officials defended the ban against the pill by arguing that oral contraceptives are unsafe and would promote promiscuity ("Still no pill for Japan," 1992). In

Psychological Consequences of Abortion

The woman who faces an unwanted pregnancy may experience a range of negative emotions, including

> fear ("What will I do now?"), self-anger ("How could I let this happen?"), guilt ("What would my parents think if they knew I was pregnant?"), ambivalence ("Will I be sorry if I have an abortion? Will I be sorry if I don't?"), and sometimes desperation ("Is suicide a way out?").
>
> (Knox, 1988, p. 455)

Whether to have an abortion is typically a painful decision—perhaps the most difficult decision a woman will ever make. Even women who apparently make the decision without hesitation may later have feelings of guilt, remorse, anger, and sadness. Although the woman's partner is often overlooked in the research on abortion, he may encounter similar feelings.

1992, a review by the Health and Welfare Ministry found birth-control pills to be safe, but decided to uphold the ban because of concerns about AIDS. Though Japan has had relatively few AIDS cases by international standards (fewer than 500 by mid-1991), the health ministry feared that lifting the ban on the pill might discourage condom use and lead to an epidemic of AIDS. Some women in Japan are able to skirt the ban by consulting sympathetic physicians who are willing to prescribe them presumably to treat gynecological complaints.

In part because of limited contraceptive options, the Japanese use condoms more than any other people in the world. They are widely available in drugstores, supermarkets, and vending machines; embarrassed housewives can buy them from door-to-door saleswomen. Abortion is the widely used backup for failed contraception. And yet, although abortions have now been legal and easily accessible in Japan for over 40 years, women who have them feel stigmatized because abortion is regarded by many Japanese, even those who accept it, as "killing a baby."

The majority of Japanese draw little distinction between a fetus and an infant. According to Samuel Coleman, the author of *Family Planning in Japanese Society*, the reasons lie at least partially in Shinto and Buddhism, Japan's two major religions. Although neither religion promotes active opposition to abortion, Buddhism is based on the ideal of overcoming one's sense of ego. In this context, a woman who aborts wrongly puts her ego before her fetus. Shinto, an ancient religion based on ancestor and nature worship, holds that an aborted fetus can place a curse on the woman who aborts.

Offerings at the Temple

Hiroshi Hihara is a gynecologist in Tokyo. He makes his living on infertility work and abortions, many of them for married women whose method of contraception has failed. Although Hihara is a member of a Buddhist temple, he does not consider himself religious. But he says he is not comfortable with abortion. "Abortion is legal and approved of by the government, and if a patient wants it, I can't turn her down," he says. "She's entitled to it. But I am not happy to do it."

And yet, he performs some 200 abortions a year and quietly admits, when asked, that his fees from abortion represent "a large portion of my income."

Caught in this moral and economic trap, he resolves his feelings in a uniquely Japanese way. First, he tells each abortion patient to make an offering after the operation at any of the Buddhist temples selling miniature stone statues, or *mizuko jizo*, which women can buy in memory of an aborted fetus. Thousands of such statues stand on display at temples these days, and although some are for miscarriages and stillborn children, the vast majority are for abortions. Many of the statues are decorated with crocheted hats, plastic bibs, and little pinwheels, all put there by women to keep the soul of the aborted fetus warm and amused.

Debate is going on over whether to legalize the pill and promote other forms of birth control such as the diaphragm. Whether Japanese women will use the pill if legalized is an open question. In a June 1990 survey released by one of Japan's largest newspapers, results showed that fewer than 10% of Japanese women would use it even if it were available.

Women's reactions depend on various factors, including the support they receive from others (or the lack thereof) and the strength of their relationships with their partners. Women with greater support from their male partners or parents tend to show a more positive emotional reaction following an abortion (Armsworth, 1991). Generally speaking, the sooner the abortion occurs, the less stressful it is. Women who have a difficult time reaching an abortion decision, who blame the pregnancy on their character, who have lower coping ability, and who have less social support experience more distress following abortion (Major & Cozzarelli, 1992).

Many men are very concerned and supportive of their partners. Others seek to detach themselves from the situation. And of course there are some cases in which the identity of the father is unknown. Some men consider pregnancy the woman's responsibility: "She's the one who let herself get pregnant." Some men reproach the woman for failing to take precautions. No wonder feminists insist that men share full responsibility for pregnancies.

Women's negative feelings tend to be more severe before the abortion than afterward. Afterward, feelings may alternate between a sense of relief and regrets. Women interviewed after an abortion generally show positive psychological adjustment (Adler, 1990; Stotland, 1992). Recollection of the abortion may evoke passing feelings of sadness for years afterward, however. Women who have had abortions in their youth may have regrets if they have difficulty becoming pregnant later on.

The nearby World of Diversity feature provides some perspective on the ways in which some citizens of the wealthiest nation on the Pacific Rim cope with their feelings about abortion.

~ *Reflections* ~

▪ Do you know anyone who has had an abortion? What motivated the abortion? How did she react to the abortion? How did you feel at the time?

▪ One of the issues concerning abortion is whether it is the taking of a human life. How do *you* define *human life*? When do *you* believe human life begins? At conception? When the embryo becomes implanted in the uterus? When the fetus begins to assume a human shape or develops human facial features? When the fetus is capable of sustaining independent life? Explain.

▪ What are your own views on abortion? Are some abortion methods more acceptable to you than others? Why or why not?

Summing Up

Birth control methods include contraception and induced abortion.

Contraception

Contraception in the United States: The Legal Battle
In the United States, Anthony Comstock lobbied successfully for passage of a federal law in 1873 that prohibited the dissemination of birth-control information through the mail on the grounds that it was obscene and indecent. In 1918 the courts ruled that physicians must be allowed to disseminate information that might aid in the cure and prevention of disease, and dismantling of the Comstock law had begun.

Selecting a Method of Contraception   Issues surrounding the choice of a method of contraception involve their convenience, moral acceptability, cost, sharing of responsibility between the partners, safety, reversibility, the protection they afford from STDs, and effectiveness.

Methods of Contraception

Oral Contraceptives ("the Pill")   Birth-control pills include combination pills and minipills. Combination pills contain estrogen and progestin and fool the brain into acting as though the woman is already pregnant, so that no additional ova mature or are released. Minipills contain progestin, thicken the cervical mucus to impede the passage of sperm through the cervix, and render the inner lining of the uterus less receptive to a fertilized egg. Oral contraception is nearly 100% effective. The main drawbacks are side effects and potential health risks.

"Morning-after" pills prevent implantation of a fertilized ovum in the uterus.

Norplant   Norplant consists of tubes containing progestin that are surgically embedded under the skin of the woman's upper arm. Norplant provides continuous contraceptive protection for as long as five years.

Intrauterine Devices (IUDs)   The IUD apparently irritates the uterine lining, causing inflammation and the production of antibodies that may be toxic to sperm or fertilized ova and/or may prevent fertilized eggs from becoming implanted. The IUD is highly effective, but there are possible troublesome side effects and the potential for serious health complications.

The Diaphragm   The diaphragm covers the cervix and should be used with a spermicidal cream or jelly. It must be fitted by a health professional.

Spermicides   Spermicides block the passage of sperm and kill sperm. Their failure rate is high, but spermicides that contain nonoxynol-9 may also provide some protection against organisms that give rise to STDs.

The Cervical Cap   Like the diaphragm, the cap covers the cervix and is most effective when used with a spermicide.

Condoms   Latex condoms afford protection against STDs. Condoms are the only contraceptive device worn by men and the only readily reversible method of contraception that is available to men.

Douching   Douching is ineffective as a contraceptive because large numbers of sperm may pass beyond the range of the douche within seconds after ejaculation.

Withdrawal (Coitus Interruptus)   Withdrawal requires no special equipment but has a high failure rate.

Fertility Awareness Methods (Rhythm Methods)
Rhythm methods rely on awareness of the fertile segments of the woman's menstrual cycle. Rhythm methods include the calendar method, the basal body temperature method, and the cervical mucus method. Their failure rate is high in typical use.

Sterilization   Sterilization methods should be considered permanent, although they may be reversed in many cases. The vasectomy is usually carried out under local anesthesia in 15 to 20 minutes. Female sterilization methods prevent ova and sperm from passing through the fallopian tubes.

Other Devices   The female condom is fitted over the vaginal opening and provides a shield that blocks sperm but allows the penis to move freely.

The vaginal ring can be worn in the vagina for three months and delivers a continuous dose of hormones that relieves a woman of having to remember to take a pill.

Depo-Provera is injected and supplies a continuous dosage of long-acting progesterone, which acts to inhibit ovulation.

Abortion

Historical and Legal Perspectives on Abortion   In colonial times and through the mid-nineteenth century, women in the United States were permitted to terminate a pregnancy until "quickening" occurred. More restrictive abortion laws came into being after the Civil War. In 1973, the U.S. Supreme Court in effect legalized abortion nationwide in the landmark *Roe v. Wade* decision.

Methods of Abortion   Abortion methods in use today include vacuum aspiration, D&C, D&E, induction of labor by intra-amniotic infusion, and hysterotomy.

Psychological Consequences of Abortion   Although choosing to have an abortion is typically a painful decision, women interviewed about a year after an abortion generally show good psychological adjustment.

CHAPTER 13

Henri Matisse, *The Swimmer in the Aquarium,* Plate 12 from *Jazz.* The Metropolitan Museum of Art, Gift of Lila Acheson Wallace, 1983. © 1996 Succession H. Matisse/Artist Rights Society (ARS), New York. © 1985 by The Metropolitan Museum of Art.

Sexuality in Childhood and Adolescence

Outline

Infancy (0 to 2 Years): The Search for the Origins of Human Sexuality
The Infant's Capacity for Sexual Response
Masturbation
Genital Play

Early Childhood (3 to 8 Years)
Masturbation
Male–Female Sexual Behavior
Male–Male and Female–Female Sexual Behavior

Preadolescence (9 to 13 Years)
Masturbation
Male–Female Sexual Behavior
Male–Male and Female–Female Sexual Behavior
Sex Education and Miseducation

Adolescence
Puberty
Masturbation
Male–Female Sexual Behavior
Male–Male and Female–Female Sexual Behavior

Teenage Pregnancy
Contraceptive Use Among Sexually Active Teens

Summing Up

A World of Diversity / Cross-Cultural Perspectives on Childhood Sexuality; Menarche in Cross-Cultural Perspective; Ethnic Differences in Premarital Intercourse, Adolescent Use of Contraception, and Resolution of Unwanted Pregnancies; Rates of Teenage Pregnancy at Home and Abroad

What Do You Say Now? / How Should a Parent React to Childhood Masturbation?; Talking to Your Children About Sex

A Closer Look / The First Time; Should Public Schools Provide Students with Contraceptives?

Truth OR Fiction?

___ T Many boys are born with erections.

___ T Infants often engage in pelvic thrusting at 8 to 10 months of age.

___ F Most children learn the facts of life from parents or from school sex-education programs.

___ F Sex education encourages sexual activity among children and adolescents.

___ T Nocturnal emissions in boys accompany erotic dreams.

___ T Petting is practically universal among adolescents in the United States.

___ T Nearly 1 million adolescent girls in the United States become pregnant each year.

___ T In some school districts, condoms are distributed to adolescents without parental consent.

M y heart leaps up when I behold
A rainbow in the sky:
So was it when my life began,
So is it now I am a man,
So be it when I shall grow old
Or let me die!
The Child is father of the Man:
And I could wish my days to be
Bound each to each by natural piety.

(William Wordsworth, "My Heart Leaps Up")

What a life it would be, indeed, were our hearts to swell with the wonders of the world throughout our lives. In this chapter we begin our chronicle of sexual behavior across the life span, and we see the ways in which the child is father of the man. Within children's personal and social experiences lie the seeds of later sexual competence and self-esteem—or the seeds of incompetence, guilt, and shame. In the next chapter we shall see that our sexuality remains an integral part of our lives throughout our lives—one that has the potential to help our hearts leap up for all our days.

Infancy (0 to 2 Years): The Search for the Origins of Human Sexuality

Fetuses not only have erections. They also suck their fingers. The sucking reflex allows babies to gain nourishment, which is necessary for survival. But as Sigmund Freud hypothesized, infants also seem to reap sensual pleasure from sucking fingers, pacifiers, nipples, or whatever else fits into the mouth. This is not surprising, given the sensitivity of the mouth's mucosal lining.

Stimulation of the genitals in infancy may also produce sensations of pleasure. Parents who touch their infants' genitals while changing or washing them may discover the infants smiling or becoming excited. Infants discover the pleasure of self-stimulation (masturbation) for themselves when they gain the capacity to manipulate their genitals with their hands.

The Infant's Capacity for Sexual Response

Boys are often born with erections. Most have erections during the first few weeks.

It is true that many boys are born with erections. Ultrasound has revealed erections even in fetuses. ■

Signs of sexual arousal in infant girls, such as vaginal lubrication, are less readily detected. Yet evidence of lubrication and genital swelling has been reported (Martinson, 1976).

Do not interpret children's responses according to adult concepts of sexuality, however. Lubrication and erection are reflexes, not necessarily signals of "interest" in sex. Infants have the biological capacity for these reflexes, but we cannot say what, if anything, the reflexes "mean" to them.

Parent-Child Bonding. Parents who form warm and affectionate relationships with their children may help them develop the ability to form loving attachments later in life.

Pelvic Thrusting Pelvic thrusting is observed in infant monkeys, apes, and humans. These observations led ethologist John Bowlby (1969) to suggest that infantile sexual behavior may be the rule in mammals, not the exception. Thrusting has been observed in humans at 8 to 10 months of age and may be an expression of affection. Typically, the infant clings to the parent, nuzzles, and thrusts and rotates the pelvis for several seconds.

T r u t h **OR** *Fiction?*
R E V I S I T E D

It is true that infants often engage in pelvic thrusting at 8 to 10 months of age. However, there is no reason to believe that thrusting means the same thing to infants that it does to adults. ∎

Orgasm At least some infants seem capable of sexual responses that closely resemble orgasm. Kinsey and his colleagues (1953) noted that baby boys show behaviors that resemble adult orgasm by as early as 5 months; baby girls, as early as 4 months. Orgasmic responses in boys are similar to those in men—but without ejaculation. Ejaculation occurs only after puberty.

Masturbation

Masturbation is typical for infants and young children and tends to start between 6 and 12 months. At early ages children usually masturbate by rubbing the genitals against a soft object, such as a towel, bedding, or a doll. As the child matures and becomes capable of more coordinated hand movements, direct manual stimulation of the genitals often becomes preferred.

Masturbation to orgasm is rare until the second year, however (Reinisch, 1990). Some children begin masturbating to orgasm later. Some never do. All in all, however, an orgasmic response from masturbation is common among children, as it is among adults (Reinisch, 1990).

Genital Play

Children in the United States typically do not engage in genital play with others until about the age of 2. Then, as an expression of their curiosity about their environment and other people, they may investigate other children's genitals, or hug, cuddle, kiss, or climb on top

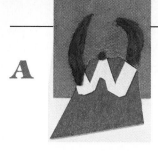
CROSS-CULTURAL PERSPECTIVES ON CHILDHOOD SEXUALITY

Though we are born with the capacity for sexual response, our expression of sexuality largely reflects the culture in which we are reared. Every culture encourages people to conform to socially acceptable behavior. Most people in a given culture develop similar behavior patterns and attitudes.

Cultures vary in their attitudes and practices concerning human sexuality—in particular, childhood and adolescent sexuality. Some may be characterized as sexually permissive, others as sexually restrictive. Broude and Greene (1976) analyzed attitudes toward, and frequency of, premarital sex among 114 of the world's societies. Most societies (55%) either disapproved of or disallowed premarital sex among females. About one in four societies (24%) permitted girls to engage in premarital sex. Another 21% tolerated discreet premarital sex for females. Despite societal prohibitions, premarital sex among females was common or universal in two thirds of the societies sampled. Female premarital sex was uncommon or absent in the other third. Premarital sex among males was even more common. Among 107 societies in their cross-cultural sample, male premarital sex was universal or typical in 78%. It was atypical in the other 22%.

Sexually Permissive Societies

Ford and Beach (1951) noted that when masturbation was permitted in a society, children progressed from occasional genital touching to more purposeful masturbation by about 6 to 8 years of age. Sexually permissive cultures also permit sexual expression among peers. Among the Seniang people of Oceania, boys and girls publicly simulated coitus without fear of reproach by adults (Ford & Beach, 1951). The Lesu of Oceania believed that it is normal for children to imitate coital positions. The Chewu people of Africa believed that childhood sexual experimentation is necessary for adult fertility.

The Lecha people of the Himalayas believed that girls do not attain physical maturity unless they engage in early sexual intercourse. During early childhood, Lecha children engaged in mutual masturbation and attempted copulation. Girls began to engage in regular sexual intercourse by age 11 or 12. Among the Trobrianders of the South Pacific, girls were usually initiated into sexual intercourse by 6 or 8 years of age, boys by age 10 or 12. Among the Muria Gond of India, boys and girls as young as 10 lived together in dormitories and spent their evenings dancing, singing, and pairing off for sex.

Societies that permit sex play among children also tend to encourage open discussion of sex and to allow children to observe sexual behavior among adults. Among the Trukese of the South Pacific, children learned about sex by observing and asking adults. Lesu children, too, would observe adults, but there was at least one taboo: they were not to watch their own mothers.

Sexually Restrictive Societies

Ford and Beach (1951) found that only a minority of preliterate societies were sexually restrictive. The Apinaye people of South America warned their children not to masturbate and thrashed them if they were suspected of doing so. The Kwoma of New Guinea warned boys never to touch their genitals, even when urinating. They risked having their penises beaten with a stick if they touched them.

Sexually restrictive societies discourage masturbation and sex play among children. Children who disobey are punished. Such societies also tend to be closed-lipped about sex. Parents try to keep their children ignorant about reproduction. Premarital sex and watching adults engage in sex are also restricted.

Many societies hold to a sexual double standard by which boys are allowed greater sexual freedom than girls.

of them. None of this need cause concern. Spiro (1965) describes 2-year-olds at play in an Israeli kibbutz:

> Ofer [a boy] and Pnina [a girl] sit side by side on chamber pots. . . . Ofer puts his foot on Pnina's foot, she then does the same—this happens several times. . . . Finally, Pnina shifts her pot away, then moves back, then away . . . they laugh. . . . Pnina stands up, lies on the table on her stomach, . . . Ofer pats her buttocks. . . . Ofer kicks Pnina gently, and they laugh . . . Pnina touches and caresses Ofer's leg with her foot . . . says "more more" . . . Ofer stands, then Pnina stands, both bounce up and down . . . both children are excited, bounce, laugh together . . . Pnina grabs Ofer's penis, and he pushes her away . . . she repeats, he pushes her away, and turns around . . . Pnina touches his buttocks. (p. 225)

There is no reason to infer that Ofer and Pnina were seeking sexual gratification. Rough-and-tumble play, including touching the genitals, is common among children.

～ Reflections ～

- How did you feel when you saw that we were covering sexuality during infancy? Did it seem to you that we ought not be discussing sexuality during infancy (or childhood)? Why, or why not?
- Was any of the information about infant sexuality surprising to you? If so, what?
- Would you characterize your own sociocultural background as sexually permissive or restrictive? Why?

Early Childhood (3 to 8 Years)

SUSAN: Once my younger sister and I were over at a girl friend's house playing in her bedroom. For some reason she pulled her pants down and exposed her rear to us. We were amazed to see she had an extra opening down there we didn't know about. My sister reciprocated by pulling her pants down so we could see if she had the same extra opening. We were amazed at our discovery, our mothers not having mentioned to us that we had a vagina!

CHRISTOPHER: Nancy was a willing playmate, and we spent many hours together examining each other's bodies as doctor and nurse. We even once figured out a pact that we would continue these examinations and watch each other develop. That was before we had started school.

(Morrison et al., 1980, p. 19)

These recollections of early childhood show children's curiosity about sexual anatomy. Children often show each other their bodies. The unwritten rule seems to be, "I'll show you mine if you'll show me yours."

Masturbation

KIM: I began to masturbate when I was 3 years old. My parents . . . tried long and hard to discourage me. They told me it wasn't nice for a young lady to have her hand between her legs.

When I was five I remember my mother discovering that I masturbated with a rag doll I slept with. She was upset, but she didn't make a big deal about it. She just told me in a matter-of-fact way, "Do you know that what you're doing is called masturbating?" That didn't make much sense to me, except I got the impression she didn't want me to do it.

(Morrison et al., 1980, pp. 4, 5)

Because of the difficulties in conducting such research, statistics concerning the incidence of masturbation in children is largely speculative. Parents may not wish to respond to questions concerning the sexual conduct of their children. Or if they do, they may have a tendency to present their children as little "gentlemen" and "ladies" and perhaps underreport their sexual activity. Their biases may also lead them not to perceive their children's genital touching as masturbation. Many parents will not even permit adolescents to be interviewed about their sexual behavior (Fisher & Hall, 1988), let alone younger children. When we are asked to look back as adults, our memories may be less than accurate.

We can only conclude that some children masturbate whereas others do not. Prevalences are highly speculative. But it does appear that children masturbate more frequently by the age of 4 or 5 (Reinisch, 1990).

HOW SHOULD A PARENT REACT TO CHILDHOOD MASTURBATION?

Few parents today believe that childhood masturbation sets the stage for physical and mental maladies. Still, they may react with concern, disgust, or shock when their children masturbate.

Parents who are unaware that masturbation is commonplace among children may erroneously assume that children who masturbate are oversexed or aberrant. The parent may pull a child's hands away and scold her or him. Some may even slap the child's hand. Once the child is capable of understanding speech, the parent may say things like "Don't touch down there! That's a bad thing to do. Stop doing that." Threats and punishments may be used. Or parents may fail to acknowledge the behavior openly, but move the hands away from the genitals or pick up the child whenever he or she is discovered masturbating.

Sex educators Mary Calderone and Eric Johnson (1989) argue that punishment will not stop children from masturbating. It may cause them to become secretive and guilty about it, however. Sex guilt tends to persist and may impede sexual pleasure in marriage. June Reinisch (1990), director of the Kinsey Institute, notes that

> parents who scowl, scold, or punish in response to a child's exploring his or her genitals may be teaching the child that this kind of pleasure is wrong

and that the *child* is "bad" for engaging in this kind of behavior. This message may hinder the ability to give and receive erotic pleasures as an adult and ultimately interfere with the ability to establish a loving and intimate relationship. (p. 248)

Calderone, Johnson, and Reinisch concur that children need to learn that masturbation in public is not acceptable in our culture, however. Calderone and Johnson suggest that the child who masturbates in front of others can be told something like this:

> I'm glad you've found your body feels good, but when you want to touch your body that way, it's more private to be in your room by yourself. (p. 138)

Reinisch adds that parents are important shapers of their children's sexuality, and more broadly, of their self-esteem. Acknowledging the child's sexuality, rather than rejecting and discouraging it, can strengthen children's self-esteem, build a positive body image, and encourage competence and assertiveness.

Not all authorities, and certainly not all parents, endorse such views. Some object to masturbation on religious or moral grounds. Others feel uncomfortable or conflicted about masturbation themselves. Parents must decide for themselves how best to react when they discover their children masturbating.

Childhood Sexuality? Children are naturally inquisitive about sexual behavior and anatomy.

Male–Female Sexual Behavior

ALICIA: On my birthday when I was in the second grade, I remember a classmate, Tim, walked home with a friend and me. He kept chasing me to give me kisses all over my face, and I acted like I didn't want him to do it, yet I knew I liked it a lot; when he would stop, I thought he didn't like me anymore.

(Morrison et al., 1980, pp. 21, 29)

Three- and 4-year-olds commonly express affection through kissing. Curiosity about the genitals may also occur by this stage. Sex games like "show" and "playing doctor" may begin earlier but become common between the ages of 6 and 10 (Reinisch, 1990). Much of this sexual activity takes place in same-gender groups, although mixed-gender sex games are not uncommon. Children may exhibit their genitals to each other, touch each other's genitals, or even masturbate together.

Male–Male and Female–Female Sexual Behavior

> ARNOLD: When I was about 5, my cousin and I . . . went into the basement and dropped our pants. We touched each other's penises, and that was it. I guess I didn't realize the total significance of the secrecy in which we carried out this act. For later . . . my parents questioned me . . . and I told them exactly what we had done. They were horrified and told me that that was definitely forbidden.
>
> (Morrison et al., 1980, p. 24)

Despite Arnold's parents' "horror," same-gender sexual play in childhood does not presage adult sexual orientation (Reinisch, 1990). It may, in fact, be more common than heterosexual play. It typically involves handling the other child's genitals, although it may include oral or anal contact. It may also include an outdoor variation of the game of "show" in which boys urinate together and see who can reach farthest or attain the highest trajectory.

～ Reflections ～

■ Have you ever discussed masturbation with your friends? At what age did your friends or you begin to masturbate? Did you know what you were doing (that is, that you were masturbating)? How did you feel about it? Why?

■ Did you ever play "show" or "doctor" as a child? What were your feelings about it?

■ Did your parents or other adults find you masturbating or playing "doctor"? What was their response? Has their response contributed to your own attitudes? If so, how?

Preadolescence (9 to 13 Years)

During preadolescence children typically form relationships with a close "best friend" that enable them to share secrets and confidences. The friends are usually peers of the same gender. Preadolescents also tend to socialize with larger networks of friends in gender-segregated groups. At this stage boys are likely to think that girls are "dorks." To girls at this stage, "dork" is too good a word to apply to most boys.

Preadolescents grow increasingly preoccupied with and self-conscious about their bodies. Their peers pressure preadolescents to conform to dress codes, standards of "correct" slang, and to group standards concerning sex and drugs. Peer disapproval can be an intense punishment.

Sexual urges are experienced by many preadolescents, but they may not emerge until adolescence. Sigmund Freud had theorized that sexual impulses are hidden, or latent, during preadolescence, but many preadolescents are quite active sexually during the so-called latency period.

Masturbation

> PAUL: When I was about 10, stories about masturbation got me worried. A friend and I went to a friend's older brother whom we respected and asked, "Is it really bad?" His reply stuck in my mind for years. "Well, it's like a bottle of olives—every time you take one out, there is one less in there." We were very worried because we thought we'd run out before we got to girls.
>
> (Morrison et al., 1980, pp. 6–8)

Kinsey and his colleagues (1948, 1953) reported that masturbation is the primary means of achieving orgasm during preadolescence for both genders. They found that 45% of males and 15% of females masturbated by age 13.

Male–Female Sexual Behavior

Preadolescent sex play often involves mutual display of the genitals, with or without touching. Such sexual experiences are quite common and do not appear to impair future sexual adjustment (Leitenberg et al., 1989).

Although preadolescents tend to socialize in same-gender groups, interest in the other gender among heterosexuals tends to gradually increase as they approach puberty. Group dating and mixed-gender parties often provide preadolescents with their first exposure to heterosexual activities. Couples may not begin to pair off until early or midadolescence.

Male–Male and Female–Female Sexual Behavior

Much preadolescent sexual behavior among members of the same gender is simply exploration. Some incidents reflect lack of availability of partners of the opposite gender. As with younger children, experiences with children of the same gender during preadolescence may be more common than heterosexual experiences (Leitenberg et al., 1989). These activities are usually limited to touching of each other's genitals or mutual masturbation. Since preadolescents generally socialize within their genders, it is not surprising that their sexual explorations may also be within their genders. Most same-gender sexual experiences involve single episodes or short-lived relationships and are not signs of a budding gay orientation.

Sex Education and Miseducation

How do people learn about sex? Studies have consistently shown that in the United States, peers are the main source of sexual information for both genders. According to an ABC News *Nightline* poll (1995), 53% of American adults had learned about sex from their friends. Thirty percent had learned from their parents. Ten percent had learned from school sex-education programs. When asked where teenagers today learn about sex, five of six (83%) said from friends.

Truth **OR** *Fiction?*
R E V I S I T E D

It is not true that most children learn the facts of life from parents or from school sex-education programs. Most children learn about sex from peers. Is the lamp on the street corner the key guiding light for U.S. youth? ■

School-based sex-education programs were relatively rare as late as the early 1970s, despite the fact that an overwhelming majority of parents supported sex education in the schools (Norman & Harris, 1981). Sex-education programs became more common in the 1970s and 1980s. By the late 1980s, about six in ten teenagers received some form of sex education in the schools (Kenney et al., 1989).

The ABC News *Nightline* poll (1995) found that most American adults believe that sex-education programs should teach students to use contraceptives if they are going to engage in premarital sexual activity (91%), that condoms can prevent AIDS (85%), and that early sex is a bad idea (80%). On the other hand, there is great disagreement as to whether school sex-education programs should discuss masturbation, abortion, and sexual orientation.

Today, nearly all states mandate or recommend sex-education programs. The content and length of sex-education programs vary widely. Most programs emphasize the biological aspects of puberty and reproduction (Haffner, 1993). In keeping with parents' preferences, few focus on abortion, masturbation, and sexual orientation. Sexual pleasure is rarely mentioned.

Sex education in the schools, especially about value-laden topics, remains a source of controversy. Some people argue that sex education ought to be left to parents and religious authorities. But the data suggest that the real alternatives to the schools are peers and the corner newsstand, which sells more copies of "adult" magazines than of textbooks. Many parents are also concerned that teaching subjects such as sexual techniques and contraception encourages sexual experimentation. Yet research has failed to demonstrate that sex education increases early sexual experimentation (Eisen & Zellman, 1987; Hayes, 1987).

Truth OR Fiction?
REVISITED

There is actually no evidence that sex education encourages sexual activity among children and adolescents. ■

Many school programs that offer information about contraception and other sensitive topics are limited to high school juniors and seniors. Sexual experimentation often begins earlier, however. Most sexually active teens in Coles and Stokes's (1985) sample began engaging in intercourse by age 15. Fifty percent of the sexually active teenage boys and 18% of the sexually active teenage girls began by age 13.

Accurate information in preadolescence might prevent various sexual mishaps (Coles & Stokes, 1985). Many teens, for example, erroneously believe that a female cannot get pregnant from her first coital experience. Others believe that douching protects them from sexually transmitted diseases (STDs) or unwanted pregnancies.

~ Reflections ~

■ How old were you when you learned "the facts of life"? What was your reaction?
■ How did you learn about reproduction and sexuality? What inaccuracies were there in your early sources of information?
■ Do you support sex education in the schools? If so, what topics should be covered? Which should not? Why?

Adolescence

Adolescence is bounded by the advent of puberty at the lower end and the capacity to take on adult responsibilities at the upper end. In our society adolescents are "neither fish nor fowl," as the saying goes—neither children nor adults. Adolescents may be able to reproduce and be taller than their parents, but they may not be allowed to get driver's licenses or attend R-rated films. They are prevented from working long hours and must usually stay in school until age 16. They cannot marry until they reach the "age of consent." The message is clear: Adults see adolescents as impulsive, and they must be restricted for "their own good." Given these restrictions, a sex drive heightened by surges of sex hormones, and media inundation with sexual themes, it is not surprising that many adolescents are in conflict with their families about "going around" with certain friends, sex, and using the family car.

Puberty

Puberty begins with the appearance of **secondary sex characteristics** and ends when the long bones make no further gains in length (see Table 13.1 on page 384). The appearance of strands of pubic hair are often the first visible signs of puberty. Pubic hair tends to be light colored, sparse, and straight at first. Then it spreads and grows darker, thicker, and coarser. Puberty also involves changes in **primary sex characteristics.** Once puberty begins, most major changes occur within three years in girls and within four years in boys (Etaugh & Rathus, 1995).

Toward the end of puberty, reproduction becomes possible. The two principal markers of reproductive potential are **menarche** in the girl and the first ejaculation in the boy. But these events do not generally herald immediate fertility.

Girls typically experience menarche between the ages of 10 and 18. In the mid-1800s, European girls typically achieved menarche by about age 17 (see Figure 13.1). The age of menarche has declined sharply since then among girls in Western nations, most likely be-

Puberty
The stage of development during which reproduction first becomes possible. Puberty begins with the appearance of *secondary sex characteristics* and ends when the long bones make no further gains in length. (From the Latin *puber*, meaning "of ripe age.")

Secondary sex characteristics
Physical characteristics that differentiate males and females and that usually appear at puberty but are not directly involved in reproduction, such as the bodily distribution of hair and fat, development of the muscle mass, and deepening of the voice.

Primary sex characteristics
Physical characteristics that differentiate males and females and are directly involved in reproduction, such as the sex organs.

Menarche
The onset of menstruation; first menstruation. (From Greek roots meaning "month" [*men*] and "beginning" [*arche*].)

TALKING TO YOUR CHILDREN ABOUT SEX

"Daddy, where do babies come from?"

"What are you asking me for? Go ask your mother."

Most children do not find it easy to talk to their parents about sex (Coles & Stokes, 1985). The parents may not find it any easier. Nearly half (47%) of the teens polled in a national survey said they would ask their friends, siblings, or sex partners if they desired information about sex. Only about a third (36%) would turn to their parents (Coles & Stokes, 1985). Three out of four say that it is hard to talk about sex with their fathers. More than half (57%) find it difficult to approach their mothers. Regrettably, information received from peers is likely to be strewn with inaccuracies. Misinformed teenagers run a higher risk of unwanted pregnancies and STDs.

Yet most young children are curious about where babies come from, about what makes little girls different from little boys, and so on. Parents who avoid answering such questions convey their own uneasiness about sex and may teach children

that sex is something to be ashamed of, not something they should discuss openly.

Some parents resist talking about sex with their children because they are insecure in their own knowledge. Reinisch (1990) argues that parents need not be sex experts to talk to their children about sex, however. Parents can turn to books in the local bookstore to fill in gaps in knowledge, or to books that are intended for parents to read to their children. They can also admit that they do not know the answer to a particular question. Reinisch suggests that children will respect parents who display such honesty.

In answering children's questions, parents need to be sensitive to what their children can understand. The 4-year-old who wants to know where babies come from is probably not interested in detailed biological information. It may be sufficient to say "from Mommy's uterus" and then point to the mother's abdominal region. Why say "tummy"? "Tummy" is wrong and confusing.

In their *Family Book About Sexuality*, Calderone and Johnson (1989) offer parents some pointers:

1. *Be willing to answer your child's questions about sex.* Parents who respond to their children's questions about sex by saying, "Why do you want to know that?" squelch further questioning. The child is likely to interpret the parent's response as meaning "You shouldn't be interested in that."

2. *Use appropriate language.* As children develop awareness of their sexuality, they need to learn the names of their sex organs. They also need to learn that the "dirty words" that others use to refer to the sexual parts of the body are not acceptable in most situations, since they carry emotional connotations that can arouse negative feelings.

Nor should parents use "silly words" to describe sexual organs. As June Reinisch (1990) notes,

> Another way parents send out negative messages about sexuality is by using silly words (or no words at all) to describe sexual anatomy. Whether they call genitals "pee-pee" or "privates" or

cause of improved nutrition and health care. In the United States, the average age of menarche by the 1960s and 1970s had dropped to between 12½ and 13 (Etaugh & Rathus, 1995).

One view is that a critical body weight (perhaps 103 to 109 pounds) triggers pubertal changes such as menarche, and children today do tend to achieve larger body sizes sooner. Menarche may also be triggered by the accumulation of a certain percentage of body fat. This theory is supported by the finding that menarche comes later to girls who have a lower percentage of body fat, such as athletes (Frisch, 1983). Whatever the exact triggering mechanism, the average age at which girls experience menarche has leveled off in recent years.

Pubertal Changes in the Female   First menstruation, or menarche, is the most obvious sign of puberty in girls. Yet other, less obvious changes have already taken place that have set the stage for menstruation. Between 8 and 14 years of age, release of FSH by the pituitary gland causes the ovaries to begin to secrete estrogen. Estrogen has several major effects on pubertal development. For one, it stimulates the growth of breast

nothing at all, parents are telling children that these body parts are significantly different, embarrassing, mysterious, or taboo compared to such other body parts as the eyes, nose, and knees, which have names openly used in conversation. (p. 248)

3. *Give advice in the form of information that the child can use to make sound decisions, not as an imperial edict.* State your own convictions, but label your beliefs as your own rather than as something you are trying to impose on your child. Parents are not as likely to be effective by "laying down the law" as by relating convictions in firm but loving ways—by providing information and encouraging discussion. Reinisch (1990) suggests combining information about sex with expressions of the parents' values and beliefs.

    Parents of teenage children often react to sexual experimentation with threats or punishments, which may cause adolescents to rebel or tune them out. Or the adolescent may learn to associate sex with fear and anger, which may persist even in adult relationships. Parents may find it more constructive to convey concern about the consequences of children's actions in a loving and nonthreatening way that invites an open response. Say, for example, "I'm worried about the way you are experimenting, and I'd like to give you some information that you may not have. Can we talk about it?" (Calderone & Johnson, 1989, p. 141).

4. *Share information in small doses.* Pick a time and place that feels natural for such discussions, such as when the child is preparing for bed or when you are riding in the car.

5. *Encourage the child to talk about sex.* Children may feel embarrassed about talking about sex, especially with family members. Make the child aware that you are always available to answer questions. Be "askable." But let the child postpone talking about a sensitive topic until the two of you are alone or the child feels comfortable. Books about sexuality may help a child open up. They can be left lying around or given to the child with a suggestion such as "This is a good book about sex, or at least I thought so. If you read it, then maybe we can talk about it" (Calderone & Johnson, 1989, p. 136).

6. *Respect privacy rights.* Most of us, parents and children alike, value our privacy at certain times. A parent who feels uncomfortable sharing a bathroom with a child can simply tell the child that Daddy (or Mommy) likes to be alone when using the bathroom. Or the parent might explain, "I like my privacy, so please knock and I'll tell you if it's okay to come in. I'll do the same for you" (Calderone & Johnson, 1989, p. 137). This can be said without a scolding or harsh tone. Privacy rights in the bedroom can be established by saying in a clear and unthreatening way, "Please knock when the door's closed and wait to be invited in" (Calderone & Johnson, 1989, p. 138). But it is just as important for the parent to respect the same rights to privacy that the parent expects from the child. The child is likely to feel grateful for the respect and to show respect in return.

tissue ("breast buds"), perhaps as early as age 8 or 9. The breasts usually begin to enlarge during the tenth year.

Estrogen also promotes the growth of the uterus and the thickening of the vaginal lining. It also stimulates growth of fatty and supporting tissue in the hips and buttocks. This tissue and the widening of the pelvis cause the hips to become rounded and permit childbearing. But growth of fatty deposits and connective tissue varies considerably. Some women may have pronounced breasts; others may have relatively large hips.

Small amounts of androgens produced by the female's adrenal glands, along with estrogen, stimulate development of pubic and underarm hair, beginning at about age 11. Excessive androgen production can darken or thicken facial hair.

Estrogen causes the labia to grow during puberty, but androgens cause the clitoris to develop. Estrogen stimulates growth of the vagina and uterus. Estrogen typically brakes the female growth spurt some years before that of the male. Girls deficient in estrogen during their late teens may grow quite tall, but most tall girls reach their heights because of normal genetically determined variations, not estrogen deficiency.

TABLE 13.1 Stages of pubertal development

IN FEMALES

Beginning sometime between ages 8 and 11	Pituitary hormones stimulate ovaries to increase production of estrogen. Internal reproductive organs begin to grow.
Beginning sometime between ages 9 and 15	First the areola (the darker area around the nipple) and then the breasts increase in size and become more rounded. Pubic hair becomes darker and coarser. Growth in height continues. Body fat continues to round body contours. A normal vaginal discharge becomes noticeable. Sweat and oil glands increase in activity, and acne may appear. Internal and external reproductive organs and genitals grow, which makes the vagina longer and the labia more pronounced.
Beginning sometime between ages 10 and 16	Areola and nipples grow, often forming a second mound sticking out from the rounded breast mound. Pubic hair begins to grow in a triangular shape and to cover the center of the mons. Underarm hair appears. Menarche occurs. Internal reproductive organs continue to develop. Ovaries may begin to release mature eggs capable of being fertilized. Growth in height slows.
Beginning sometime between ages 12 and 19	Breasts near adult size and shape. Pubic hair fully covers the mons and spreads to the top of the thighs. The voice may deepen slightly (but not as much as in males). Menstrual cycles gradually become more regular. Some further changes in body shape may occur into the young woman's early 20s.

*This table is a general guideline. Changes may normally appear sooner or later than shown, and not always in the indicated sequence.

Anovulatory
Without ovulation.

Estrogen production becomes cyclical in puberty and regulates the menstrual cycle. Following menarche, a girl's early menstrual cycles are typically **anovulatory.** Girls cannot become pregnant until ovulation occurs, which may lag behind menarche by as much as two years. At first ovulation may not be reliable, so a girl may be relatively infertile. Some teenagers are highly fertile soon after menarche, however (Reinisch, 1990).

Pubertal Changes in the Male   At puberty the hypothalamus signals the pituitary to increase production of FSH and LH. These releasing hormones stimulate the testes to increase their output of testosterone. Testosterone prompts growth of the male genitals: the testes, scrotum, and penis. It fosters differentiation of male secondary sex characteristics: the growth of facial, body, and pubic hair, and the deepening of the voice. Testicle growth, in turn, accelerates testosterone production and pubertal changes. The testes continue to grow, and the scrotal sac becomes larger and hangs loosely from the body. The penis widens and lengthens, and pubic hair appears.

By age 13 or 14, erections become frequent. Indeed, many junior high school boys dread that they may be caught between classes with erections, or asked to stand before the

IN MALES

Beginning sometime between ages 9 and 15	Testicles begin to grow. Skin of the scrotum becomes redder and coarser. A few straight pubic hairs appear at the base of the penis. Muscle mass develops, and the boy begins to grow taller. The areola grows larger and darker.
Beginning sometime between ages 11 and 16	The penis begins to grow longer. The testicles and scrotum continue to grow. Pubic hair becomes coarser, more curled, and spreads to cover the area between the legs. The body gains in height. The shoulders broaden. The hips narrow. The larynx enlarges, resulting in a deepening of the voice. Sparse facial and underarm hair appears.
Beginning sometime between ages 11 and 17	The penis begins to increase in circumference as well as in length (though more slowly). The testicles continue to increase in size. The texture of the pubic hair is more like an adult's. Growth of facial and underarm hair increases. Shaving may begin. First ejaculation occurs. In nearly half of all boys, gynecomastia (breast enlargement) occurs, which then decreases in a year or two. Increased skin oils may produce acne.
Beginning sometime between ages 14 and 18	The body nears final adult height, and the genitals achieve adult shape and size, with pubic hair spreading to the thighs and slightly upward toward the belly. Chest hair appears. Facial hair reaches full growth. Shaving becomes more frequent. For some young men, further increases in height, body hair, and muscle growth and strength continue into their early 20s.

Source: Copyright © 1990 by the Kinsey Institute for Research in Sex, Gender, and Reproduction. From THE KINSEY INSTITUTE NEW REPORT ON SEX. Reprinted with permission from St. Martin's Press, New York, NY.

Nocturnal emission
Involuntary ejaculation of seminal fluid while asleep. Also referred to as a "wet dream," although the individual need not be dreaming about sex, or dreaming at all, at the time.

Truth **OR** Fiction?
R E V I S I T E D

class. Under the influence of testosterone, the prostate and seminal vesicles—the organs that produce semen—increase in size, and semen production begins. Boys typically experience their first ejaculation by age 13 or 14, most often through masturbation. There is much variation, however. First ejaculations may occur as early as age 8 or not until the early 20s (Reinisch, 1990). Mature sperm are not usually found in the ejaculate until about a year after the first ejaculation, at age 14 on the average (Kulin et al., 1989). But sperm may be present in the first ejaculate (Reinisch, 1990), so pubertal boys should not assume that they have an infertile "grace period" following first ejaculation. About a year after first ejaculation, boys may also begin **nocturnal emissions,** which are also called "wet dreams" because of the belief that nocturnal emissions accompany erotic dreams—which need not be so.

Despite the term "wet dreams," nocturnal emissions in boys need not accompany erotic dreams. ■

Underarm hair appears at about age 15. Facial hair is at first a fuzz on the upper lip. A beard does not appear for another two or three years. Only half of U.S. boys shave (of

Figure 13.1. Age at Menarche. The age at menarche has been declining since the mid-1800s among girls in Western nations apparently because of improved nutrition and health care. Menarche may be triggered by the accumulation of a critical percentage of body fat. *Source:* Etaugh, C., and Rathus, S. A. [1995]. The World of Children. Fort Worth: Harcourt Brace.

Larynx

A structure of muscle and cartilage at the upper end of the trachea that contains the vocal cords; the voice box.

Gynecomastia

Overdevelopment of a male's breasts. (From Greek roots meaning "woman" [*gyne*] and "breast" [*mastos*].)

necessity) by age 17. The beard and chest hair continue to develop past the age of 20. At age 14 or 15 the voice deepens because of the growth of the **larynx** and the lengthening of the vocal cords. Development is gradual, and the voices of adolescent boys sometimes crack embarrassingly.

Boys and girls undergo general growth spurts during puberty. Girls usually shoot up before boys. Individuals differ, however, and some boys spurt sooner than some girls.

Increases in muscle mass produce increases in weight. The shoulders and the circumference of the chest widen. At the age of 18 or so, men stop growing taller because estrogen prevents the long bones from making further gains in length (Smith et al., 1994). Males normally produce some estrogen in the adrenal glands and testes. Nearly one in two boys experiences temporary enlargement of the breasts, or **gynecomastia,** during puberty, which is also caused by estrogen.

Masturbation

Masturbation is a major sexual outlet during adolescence. About half of the adolescent boys (46%) in Coles and Stokes's (1985) national survey of 1,067 teenagers and about a

Puberty. Puberty is the beginning of adolescence. Toward the end of puberty, reproduction becomes possible. Reproductive maturity, however, does not necessarily go hand-in-hand with responsible sexual decision-making.

A WORLD OF DIVERSITY

MENARCHE IN CROSS-CULTURAL PERSPECTIVE

I'll never forget seventh grade when it seemed all my friends were menstruating but me. At first I was thinking of coming to school one day and telling them I had gotten my first period but I was afraid that they'd know I was lying so I didn't. Pretty soon no one talked about it much so by the time I did get my first period no one really cared—except my mother who told me I was now a woman.

I began menstruating when I was twelve. I remember feeling great ambivalence about it. I was a little frightened by the blood, and resented having to wear a "diaper." I was sure everyone would be able to tell I had a belt and pad on! On the other hand, I was excited to know that I could become pregnant—that I had become a woman.

My mother showed me how to roll up and wrap a used sanitary napkin in Kleenex. I really did it perfectly my first try and went out to show my mother, who had company in the living room. They giggled; though I got no negative messages about it, I felt embarrassed.

(Morrison et al., 1980, *Growing Up Sexual*, pp. 70–73)

These recollections of college women reflect common attitudes toward menstruation. Some pubescent girls see it as a sign of "becoming a woman." They anxiously await menarche. They compete with friends to see who will be first to arrive on the doorstep of adulthood. The second quotation shows that many people mistakenly believe that menstruation signals reproductive capacity. Yet such capacity may lag behind menarche by more than a year.

Girls tend to be more likely to share news of first menstruation with friends than boys are to tell other boys of their first ejaculation (Brooks-Gunn et al., 1986; Gaddis & Brooks-Gunn, 1985). Menstruation is perceived as a biological event that signals a passage to womanhood. Ejaculation is perceived as a sexual event, however. Boys may also feel embarrassed to disclose the experience to friends because it typically occurs during masturbation.

In different times, in different places, menarche has had different meanings. The Thais view menarche as transforming a girl into a complete woman (Gardiner & Gardiner, 1991). The Kurtatchi, who live on an island off the green coast of New Guinea, greet menarche with an elaborate ceremony (Matlin, 1993). The girl's mother announces the event to friends and relatives, who go into seclusion with the girl. They paint their bodies in preparation for public ceremonies. The girl and her entourage emerge from seclusion, perform a dance, and blow on a conch shell. The girl parades among the rejoicing villagers. Then there is a feast.

Among Hindu families in India, the onset of menstruation signifies the loss of the girl's purity (Kumar, 1991). During menstruation, she is expected to abstain from cooking food for the family or participating in religious ceremonies. A menstruating girl may be expected to cease daily activities and spend time alone in her room, a practice of isolation that may continue even into her marriage.

---

quarter of the girls (24%) reported masturbating. The average age at which teenagers in the Coles and Stokes survey reported they started to masturbate was 11 years 8 months.

A southern California survey of 641 teenagers showed that boys who masturbate do so two to three times a week, on the average, as compared to about once a month for girls (Hass, 1979). Researchers find no links between adolescent masturbation and early sexual activity (for example, frequency of intercourse, number of different partners, or age upon first intercourse) and sexual adjustment during young adulthood (Leitenberg et al., 1993).

Many teens still think of masturbation as shameful (Coles & Stokes, 1985). Only about one in three (31%) of the teens surveyed by Coles and Stokes reported feeling completely free of guilt over masturbation. One in five felt a "large amount" or "a great deal" of guilt. The others felt a "small" or "medium" amount of guilt.

Male–Female Sexual Behavior

Young people today start dating and "going steady" earlier than in past generations. These changes have implications for teenage pregnancy. Teens who date earlier (by age 14) are more likely to engage in coitus during high school (Miller et al., 1986). Teens who initiate sexual intercourse earlier are also less likely to use contraception and more likely to incur

ADOLESCENCE ~ **387**

an unwanted pregnancy. If the young woman decides to keep her baby, she is also more likely to have to leave school and scuttle educational and vocational plans. Early dating does not always lead to early coitus, however. Nor does early coitus always lead to unwanted pregnancies. Still, some young women find their options in adulthood restricted by a chain of events that began in early adolescence.

Petting   Many adolescents use petting to express affection, satisfy their curiosities, heighten their sexual arousal, and reach orgasm while avoiding pregnancy and maintaining virginity.

An overwhelming majority (97%) of teenagers sampled in the Coles and Stokes (1985) survey had engaged in kissing (a form of light petting) by the age of 15 (Coles & Stokes, 1985). Girls tended to engage in kissing earlier than boys, perhaps because girls tend to mature faster. By age 13, 73% of the girls and 66% of the boys had engaged in kissing.

Truth OR Fiction?
REVISITED

It is true that petting is practically universal among adolescents in the United States. ▪

Oral Sex   The incidence of premarital oral sex has increased two- or threefold since Kinsey's time. About four in ten (41%) of the 17- and 18-year-old girls in the Coles and Stokes (1985) survey of the 1980s reported that they had performed fellatio. About a third of the boys reported performing cunnilingus. Many girls reported they had engaged in fellatio for the partner's pleasure, not their own.

A 1982 survey of 16-year-old high school students revealed even higher rates of oral sex (Newcomer & Udry, 1985). Fifty-three percent of the 256 boys sampled and 42% of the 289 girls reported engaging in oral sex. More students had engaged in oral sex than in coitus. Some couples maintain *technical virginity* by substituting oral sex for intercourse (Gagnon & Simon, 1987). This seems to represent a reversal of the traditional sexual script in which couples do not engage in oral sex, if at all, until after they have begun to engage in coitus.

Some adolescent couples use oral sex as a means of birth control. As one 17-year-old New York girl put it, "That's what we used to do before we could start having sex, because we didn't have protection and stuff" (Coles & Stokes, 1985, p. 60).

Premarital Intercourse   In the 1990s, more than half of our teenagers engage in coitus (Haffner, 1993). Many young people feel as if they are caught betwixt and between. On the one hand, adults tell them to wait until they're older, to "just say no." On the other hand, the movies and television programs they see, and the stories they hear from their peers, reinforce the belief that everybody's "doing it."

The incidence of premarital intercourse, especially for females, has increased dramatically since Kinsey's day. In Kinsey's time, the sexual double standard held firm. Women were expected to remain virgins until marriage, but society looked the other way for men. Not surprisingly, Kinsey and his colleagues found a much greater incidence of premarital coitus among men. By the age of 20, 77% of the single men but only 20% of the single women reported that they had engaged in premarital coitus. Of those still single by age 25, the figures rose to 83% for men but only 33% for women. The discrepancy between the genders is partly explained by the fact that men were often sexually initiated by prostitutes (Hunt, 1974). Rates of premarital coitus among young women should not be confused with sexual promiscuity. Kinsey found that 53% of the females who had engaged in premarital coitus had done so with one partner only (Kinsey et al., 1953).

Sexual activity among adolescents in the United States has increased since the 1970s. Surveys in the early 1970s found that about half (46% to 57% across studies) of the women sampled had engaged in premarital sex by the age of 19 (Kantner & Zelnik, 1972; Sorensen, 1973). This figure compares to fewer than 20% in Kinsey's day. By 1979, 65%—nearly two out of three—young, never-married women 19 years of age who lived in metropolitan areas of the United States had engaged in sexual intercourse (Zeman, 1990) (see Table 13.2). By 1988, among 19-year-old, never-married adolescents living in metropoli-

TABLE 13.2 Percentages of adolescent boys and girls in metropolitan areas of the United States who engaged in sexual intercourse, 1979 vs. 1988

Age	BOYS (%)		GIRLS (%)	
	1979	1988	1979	1988
15	n/a	33	22	27
16	n/a	50	27	34
17	56	66	47	52
18	66	72	54	70
19	78	86	65	78

Source: Newsweek, 1990. Reprinted with permission. Source of data for girls: National Survey of Family Growth; for boys: Urban Institute.

tan areas of the United States, 78% of the girls and 86% of boys had initiated sexual intercourse (Zeman, 1990).

The Janus and Janus nationwide sample taken during the late 1980s and early 1990s found that even among adults today who identify themselves as very religious, seven in ten reported having had premarital sexual experiences (Janus & Janus, 1993). Young people today are also initiating sexual intercourse at younger ages. Kinsey found that 7% of White females had engaged in intercourse by the age of 16. By 1979, 22% of 15-year-old girls in U.S. metropolitan areas had engaged in coitus, with the figure rising to 27% by 1988 (Zeman, 1990). By 1988, about one in three 15-year-old boys also reported coital experiences (Zeman, 1990). Today, the average age of first intercourse among girls in the United States is 16; for boys, 15.5 (USDHHS, 1990b).

Although teenage sexual activity has increased nationwide, sexual activity appears to have declined in the 1980s among college women on some campuses, perhaps in response to mounting fears of AIDS and increased conservatism. For example, 37% of college women at one university who were surveyed during the early 1980s reported they were sexually active, as compared to about 50% of the women surveyed five years earlier (Gerrard, 1987). Moreover, sexual activity among teenagers tends to be episodic. Only half of the sexually experienced adolescents in one survey reported engaging in sexual intercourse during the month before the interview (Leigh et al., 1994).

In sum, the incidence of premarital sex has increased since Kinsey's day, dramatically so among females. Rates of premarital sex among young men have traditionally been higher, but the gender gap has narrowed considerably.

Motives for Intercourse Premarital intercourse is motivated by a number of factors. Sex hormones, especially testosterone, activate sexual arousal. Thus the pubertal surge of hormones directly activates sexual arousal, at least among boys (Brooks-Gunn & Furstenberg, 1989). Hormonal changes may also have indirect effects on sexual experimentation (Brooks-Gunn & Furstenberg, 1989). About half of the men (51%) and one quarter of the women (24%) in the NHSLS study report that their primary reason for the first coital experience was curiosity, or "readiness for sex" (Michael et al., 1994, p. 93).

Hormonal changes stoke the development of secondary sex characteristics. Adolescents whose secondary sex characteristics develop early may begin dating earlier, which may increase the likelihood of progressing toward sexual intercourse at an earlier age. Some early maturers may be pressured into dating or sex—psychologically ready or not.

For some adolescents, sexual intercourse is perceived as the natural outgrowth of love (Thompson, 1995). The NHSLS study found that affection for her partner was the primary reason for first intercourse among nearly half (48%) of the women and one quarter (25%) of the men sampled (Michael et al., 1994). Betsy believed that she was in love:

> I was seventeen when I had my first sexual experience. I had been going out with my boyfriend for about five months, during which time he had been continually pressuring me to have sex. He made it seem as though I had to comply or he would end the relationship. Because I was deeply in love with him (or so I thought), I allowed it to happen.
>
> (Copyright © 1991 by McIntyre, Formichella, Osterhout, and Gresh by arrangement with AVON BOOKS, p. 64)

Adolescents may consider intercourse a sign of maturity, a way for girls to reward a boyfriend for remaining loyal, or a means of punishing parents (Thompson, 1995). Some adolescents engage in coitus in response to peer pressure, especially from close friends. Adolescents whose friends have engaged in sexual intercourse are more likely to engage in intercourse themselves. Coles and Stokes (1985) found that for 78% of the virgins in their national sample, few if any of their friends had engaged in intercourse. This was true of only 28% of the nonvirgins.

Sometimes the pressure comes from dating partners. About one quarter (24%) of the women sampled in the NHSLS study said that they went along with intercourse only for the sake of their partners (Michael et al., 1994):

> MEGAN (18, California): I have felt pressure before. My first boyfriend pressured me because he knew I loved him and that he could take advantage of my feelings. I was blinded by my feelings and I had sex with him. I hated it.
>
> AMY (18, Washington, D.C.): I was sexually pressured by my second boyfriend. He didn't love me, but he did want to have sex. I helped him sneak into my room in the middle of the night. Just before we were about to have sex, I realized that it wasn't something I wanted to do. I wanted my first time to be with someone I loved and who loved me. I stopped him, although he tried everything to get me to say yes. The next day we broke up, and I couldn't have been happier.
>
> (Copyright © 1991 by McIntyre, Formichella, Osterhout, and Gresh by arrangement with AVON BOOKS, pp. 4–6)

About 8% of the men in the NHSLS study say they went along with intercourse for the sake of their partners (Michael et al., 1994). As one young man describes it:

> MATT (18, New York): My girlfriend pressured me and I didn't handle it very well. I submitted so she wouldn't be mad or disappointed.
>
> (Copyright © 1991 by McIntyre, Formichella, Osterhout, and Gresh by arrangement with AVON BOOKS, p. 65)

Factors in Premarital Intercourse   Many young people abstain from premarital coitus for religious or moral reasons (Coles & Stokes, 1985; Miller & Bingham, 1989). Family influences and religious values are important determinants of adolescent sexual experience (White & DeBlassie, 1992). Other reasons include fear of being caught, fear of pregnancy, or fear of disease.

A study of 142 low-income, African American adolescent females (ages 13–18) at an inner-city health clinic in Dallas found that girls who were not sexually active tended to be younger and more career oriented, to have a father at home, to hold more conservative values about sexuality, and to be more influenced by family values, than sexually active girls (Keith et al., 1991).

Teens who have higher educational goals and do better in school are less likely to engage in coitus than less academically oriented teens (Brooks-Gunn & Furstenberg, 1989; Hofferth & Hayes, 1987). The causal connection between school performance and premarital sex is difficult to discern, because adolescents who do well in school are also more likely to come from better-functioning families.

Not surprisingly, older teens are more likely than younger ones to engage in premarital intercourse (Miller & Bingham, 1989). The likelihood of premarital intercourse is also

linked to early dating, especially early steady dating (Brooks-Gunn & Furstenberg, 1989; Miller et al., 1986). Adolescents who begin dating earlier may be more likely to progress through stages of petting to coitus.

Teenagers' Values and the Sexual Double Standard   Do young people today subscribe to the traditional double standard that allows greater sexual freedom for men than for women? It may be premature to drive the nails into the coffin of the sexual double standard, but a common standard for judging acceptability of premarital sex may be emerging. A study of 666 undergraduate students in a midwestern university showed no evidence of the double standard; students were not differently disposed toward the acceptability of premarital sex for one gender or the other (Sprecher, 1989). According to the Coles and Stokes (1985) national survey, teenagers express only slightly more approval of casual sex for boys than for girls.

Male–Male and Female–Female Sexual Behavior

About 5% of the adolescents in the Coles and Stokes (1985) national survey reported sexual experiences with people of their own gender. More than nine out of ten experiences among adolescents of the same gender are between peers (Sorensen, 1973). Seduction of adolescents by gay male and lesbian adults is relatively rare. Most adolescent sexual encounters with people of the same gender are transitory. They most often include mutual masturbation, fondling, and genital display.

Many gay males and lesbians, of course, develop a firm sense of being gay during adolescence. Coming to terms with adolescence is often a difficult struggle, but it is often more intense for gay people (Baker, 1990) (see Chapter 10). Adolescents can be particularly cruel in their stigmatization, referring to gay peers as "homos," "queers," "faggots," and so on. Many adolescent gays thus feel isolated and lonely and decide to cloak their sexual orientation. Many do not express their sexual orientation at all until after their high school years.

Adding to the strain of developing a gay identity in a largely hostile society is the threat of AIDS, which is all the more pressing a threat to young gay males because of the toll that AIDS has inflicted on the gay male community (Baker, 1990).

Teenage Pregnancy

About 10% of American girls of ages 15 to 19 become pregnant each year ("Rate of births," 1995). This amounts to one in five sexually active girls and nearly 1 million pregnancies a year. About 40% of teenage pregnancies, or nearly 400,000 annually, end in abortion. Although some of the remainder of these pregnancies result in miscarriages, nearly 500,000 produce live births (Kantrowitz, 1990a).

Truth *OR* Fiction?
R E V I S I T E D

It is true that there are more than 1 million adolescent pregnancies in the United States each year. Nearly 40% of them end in abortion. ■

Although these figures are cause for concern, the rate of births for teenagers was actually dropping modestly during the mid-1990s ("Rate of births," 1995). The proportion of out-of-wedlock births among teenagers shot up during the 1970s and 1980s. Among young women 15 to 17 years of age in the period 1985–1989, 81% of births occurred out of wedlock, as compared to 41% in 1965–1969 and 59% in 1975–1979 (Pear, 1991). Two of three teenage mothers in the 1990s are unmarried, as compared to 15% in 1960. Among African American teenage mothers, 92% are unmarried (National Research Council, 1993).

Some pregnant teenagers plan their pregnancies, but the great majority do not. Nine in ten pregnancies among unmarried teenagers are unplanned (Alan Guttmacher Institute, 1991).

ETHNIC DIFFERENCES IN PREMARITAL INTERCOURSE, ADOLESCENT USE OF CONTRACEPTION, AND RESOLUTION OF UNWANTED PREGNANCIES

African American teenagers become sexually active two years earlier, on the average, than White teenagers. They are more likely in dating relationships to progress directly from light petting to intercourse (Brooks-Gunn & Furstenberg, 1989). Earlier initiation to coitus and more rapid progression from petting to intercourse may place African American females at greater risk of unwanted pregnancies (Brooks-Gunn & Furstenberg, 1989; Smith & Udry, 1985).

A review of the available research on ethnicity and sexual behavior in college students shows Asian American and Hispanic American students to be somewhat more conservative sexually than their African American or (non-Hispanic) White American counterparts (Baldwin et al., 1992; Padilla & O'Grady, 1987). A survey of 114 Chinese American students attending the University of California at Berkeley showed that more than 60% approved of premarital intercourse for couples who are in love or engaged to be married (Huang & Uba, 1992). Four in ten reported engaging in premarital intercourse themselves. By contrast, a much lower proportion (fewer than one in ten) of the respondents in a survey of Chinese students in Hong Kong reported having premarital intercourse (Chan, 1990). The experience of living in a sexually permissive culture like the United States seems to liberalize the sexual behavior and attitudes of young Chinese Americans. Lending support to this interpretation is the finding from the Berkeley survey that the level of acculturation to the United States was associated with both greater sexual experience and more permissive attitudes. Still, the prevalence of premarital sex among Asian American students, including the Chinese American students

Ethnic Differences in Use of Contraception. Researchers find ethnic differences in contraceptive use among sexually active adolescents. How do sociocultural factors affect use of contraceptives?

in the Berkeley sample, is low by comparison with the general U.S. college population.

There are also informative ethnic group differences in the use of contraception. Hispanic American adolescents, for example, are less likely than non-Hispanics to use contraception (Darabi et al., 1986). Horowitz (1983) attributes the low rate of use of contraceptives by Hispanic American teens not to lack of knowledge about birth control, but to conflict between sexual activity and the conservative sexual values with which they are reared. The use of contraception may be a nagging reminder that one's sexual behavior is inconsistent with one's sexual values. A survey of Mexican American and Anglo undergraduates at a southern California state university with a large Mexican American enrollment found that Mexican American students were more conservative and traditional in their sexual attitudes and reported *less* sexual experience than their Anglo counterparts (Padilla & O'Grady, 1987). Another researcher reports that Mexican American women tend to delay first intercourse in comparison to non-Hispanic White women (Slonim-Nevo, 1992).

Yet other research shows that the more often Hispanic American adolescent females engage in intercourse, the more likely they are to use effective contraception (DuRant et al., 1990). Perhaps it becomes more difficult to maintain a veneer of denial of sexual activity as the young woman becomes more sexually active.

The survey by Padilla and O'Grady (1987) also revealed that Mexican American students held more conservative attitudes than Anglo students concerning masturbation, abortion, and premarital and extramarital relationships. Mexican American students less frequently engaged in sexual intercourse, had fewer coital partners, and reported masturbating less often than their Anglo counterparts. They also identified more strongly than Anglo students with a traditional Judeo-Christian value system. The Padilla and O'Grady survey was based on one college sample of 165 Mexican American students (86 male, 79 female) and 99 Anglo students (47 male, 52 female). They may not represent the Mexican American community at large.

A longitudinal study in Houston, Texas, sheds light on some ethnic dif-

TABLE 13.3 Resolution of adolescent pregnancies by racial/ethnic group

	Of those whose partners experienced pregnancy			
	Percentage whose partners experienced pregnancy by age 21	Percentage whose partners had abortions	Percentage whose partners had the child; couple did not marry or cohabit	Percentage whose partners had the child; couple married or cohabited
African American *(N=627)*	24	16	56	28
White *(N=1,666)*	12	58	8	34
Hispanic American *(N=240)*	16	29	16	55
Total *(N=2,533)*	15	38	28	34

Source: Adapted from Buchanan, M., & Robbins, C. (1990). Early Adult Psychological Consequences for Males of Adolescent Pregnancy and Its Resolution. *Journal of Youth and Adolescence, 19,* 413–424. Reprinted with permission.

ferences in the resolution of teenage pregnancies (Buchanan & Robbins, 1990). The data shown in Table 13.3 are based on a sample of more than 2,000 males from the Houston school district who were first evaluated in seventh grade and then ten years later. By age 21, rates of adolescent pregnancies among the sexual partners of these young men were greater among African Americans (24%) than White (12%) or Hispanic Americans (16%).

Abortions were more often used as a means for resolving adolescent pregnancies among White teenagers in this sample than among African Americans or Hispanic Americans. Among African Americans and Hispanic Americans, adolescent pregnancies were more often carried to term, with a greater percentage of adolescent fathers among the Hispanics either marrying or living with the mothers.

The problem of teen pregnancy cuts across all ethnic, religious, and socioeconomic groupings and has be-

come a major social problem in our society. Although most everyone agrees with the need to prevent teens from becoming pregnant, how to accomplish this goal has become the subject of a major national debate, as we will see later in the chapter.

Other researchers focus on relationships between family factors and premarital intercourse. Children whose parents are separated or divorced are more likely than those from intact homes to engage in premarital intercourse (Coles & Stokes, 1985). Perhaps parents who have "failed" in their marital relationships lack credibility in advising their adolescent children (Coles & Stokes, 1985). Perhaps divorced mothers communicate more permissive attitudes than married mothers (Thornton & Camburn, 1987). Single parents, because of time constraints, may also be less capable of supervising their children (Newcomer & Udry, 1987). So teenagers from single-parent homes may have greater op-

portunities for privacy, especially when the parent is employed outside the home (Coles & Stokes, 1985). Moreover, a teenager may interpret a single parent's becoming sexually active with dates as tacit approval of premarital sex.

The quality of the relationship between teens and their parents may also be important (Brooks-Gunn & Furstenberg, 1989). Teens who feel that they can talk to their parents are less likely to engage in coitus than those who describe communication with their parents as poor.

Adolescents whose parents are very permissive and impose very few rules and restrictions are also more likely to engage in premarital intercourse (Hogan & Kitigawa, 1985; Miller et al., 1986). Parents who show an interest in their children's behavior and communicate their concerns and expectations with understanding and respect may best influence their children to show sexual restraint.

THE FIRST TIME

MARK: As we had no place to go, we went out into the woods with several blankets and made love. It was like something out of a Woody Allen movie. I couldn't get my pants off because I was shaking from nerves and from the cold. The nerves and cold made it all but impossible for me to get an erection and then after I had and we made love I couldn't find the car keys.

AMY: My first sexual experience occurred after the Junior Prom in high school in a car at the drive-in. We were both virgins, very uncertain, but very much in love. We had been going together since eighth grade. The experience was somewhat painful. I remember wondering if I would look different to my mother the next day. I guess I didn't because nothing was said.

(Morrison et al., 1980, p. 608)

For those who do not remain celibate, there must be a first time. Given the inexperience and awkwardness of at least one member of the couple, and frequent feelings of guilt and fear, it is not surprising that most people, like Mark and Amy, don't get it quite right the first time. Adoles-cent boys and girls often report different concerns about first intercourse. The girl is more likely to be concerned about whether she is doing the right thing. The boy is more likely to be concerned about whether he is doing the thing right. Women are more likely than men to be physically and psychologically disappointed with the experience and to feel guilty afterwards (Darling et al., 1992; Sprecher et al., 1995). One study of 300 sexually experienced college students found that only 28% of the women considered their first encounter physically or psychologically satisfying. Yet 81% of college men were physically satisfied, and 67% were psychologically satisfied (Darling & Davidson, 1986).

Negative attitudes among women toward their first coital experience may have cultural roots. A comparison between American and Swedish women showed that American women reported more negative emotional experiences to their first premarital coitus (Schwartz, 1993). In general, the Swedish have more permissive attitudes about sex than do people in the United States. Negative emotional consequences of first intercourse reflect cultural norms or standards as well as the act itself. Of course, Swedish men may also be more responsive to their partners' needs.

Coles and Stokes (1985) found that most adolescent boys (60%) reported feeling "glad" after their first intercourse (see Table 13.4). Most adolescent girls (61%) expressed ambivalence. One in ten girls (11%) reported feeling "sorry," as compared to only 1% of boys. Some females feel guilty about ending their virginity. Others find first intercourse painful or uncomfortable, in part because of the tearing of the hymen, in part because penetration may have been rushed or forced. The pain was more than one 15-year-old New York girl had anticipated:

[I] wasn't expecting it to hurt that much. It was like total pain. Even after the first minutes of pain, it's still like you're too sore to enjoy anything. I didn't expect that at all.

(Coles & Stokes, 1985, p. 74)

The consequences of unplanned teenage pregnancies can devastate young mothers, their children, and society at large. Even young people themselves perceive teenage parenthood to be disastrous (Moore & Stief, 1992). Teenage mothers are more likely to live in poverty and to receive welfare than their peers (Grogger & Bronars, 1993). Poverty, joblessness, and lack of hope for the future are recurrent themes in adolescent pregnancy (Desmond, 1994). Half of teenage mothers quit school and go on public assistance (Kantrowitz, 1990a). Few receive consistent emotional or financial help from the fathers, who generally cannot support themselves, much less a family. Working teenage mothers earn just half as much as those who give birth in their 20s (National Research Council, 1993). Barely able to cope with one baby, many young mothers who give birth at age 15 or 16 have at least one more baby by the time they are 20. Among teenage girls who become pregnant, nearly one in five will become pregnant again within a year. More than 31% will have a repeat pregnancy within two years (Alan Guttmacher Institute, 1991). Undereducated, unskilled, and overburdened, these young mothers face a constant uphill struggle.

Medical complications associated with teenage childbearing are highest of any group of fertile women except for those in their late 40s (Hess et al., 1993). In addition to high rates of miscarriage and stillbirths, children born to teenagers are at greater risk of prema-

Yet for some, the quality of the relationship tempered pain:

> We were both so excited. We hadn't been able to sleep the night before. I can't remember that much leading up to it, but we had sex a few times—I guess about three times—that night. He really enjoyed it; I found it emotionally nice, but painful. It was like a *good* hurt, but still it hurt; it was uncomfortable. But it was something we both felt really good about.
>
> (Coles & Stokes, 1985, p. 74)

Young women are more likely to find their first coital experience satisfying when their partners are loving, gentle, and considerate (Weiss, 1983).

First intercourse is often awkward, even fumbling. The partners are still learning about their own sexual responses and how to please each other:

> KAREN (23, New York): I had sexual intercourse for the first time at age 18. My boyfriend and I had been going out for a year. For several months before we had intercourse we engaged in a lot of petting but not much genital contact. I was the more aggressive partner and I was the one who suggested we have intercourse. It was very awkward; the first time we tried, he couldn't get in.
>
> (Copyright © 1991 by McIntyre, Formichella, Osterhout, and Gresh by arrangement with AVON BOOKS, pp. 50–51)

Let us note some gender differences in choice of first partners. For first-time intercourse, survey evidence shows that females are more likely than males to report having been in a committed relationship with their partners (Darling et al., 1992; Sprecher et al., 1995). In the study of some 1,600 college students by Susan Sprecher and her colleagues (1995), 60% of the women reported that their first partner was someone they were dating seriously, as opposed to 36% of the men. Men were more likely than women (23% versus 8%) to engage in first intercourse with someone they were seeing for less than a week. Men experienced more pleasure, largely because they were more likely to reach orgasm. Women experienced more guilt. These gender differences are consistent with the traditional double standard that accords greater sexual freedom to men. Men are expected to "sow their wild oats" with casual partners. Women are expected to save themselves for a man with whom they share strong emotional ties and an enduring relationship.

TABLE 13.4 Feelings about first intercourse

	Sorry (%)	Ambivalent (%)	Glad (%)	No Feelings (%)
Males	1	34	60	5
Females	11	61	23	4

Source: From SEX AND THE AMERICAN TEENAGER by R. Coles and G. Stokes. Copyright © 1985 by Rolling Stone Press. Reprinted by permission of HarperCollins Publishers.

turity, birth complications, and infant mortality (Fraser et al., 1995; Goldenberg & Klerman, 1995). These problems are often the result of inadequate prenatal care. However, even when prenatal care is taken into consideration, the children of teenagers are at greater risk than those of women in their 20s (Fraser et al., 1995; Goldenberg & Klerman, 1995).

Children of teenage mothers are at greater risk of physical, emotional, and intellectual problems in their preschool years, due to poor nutrition and health care, family instability, and inadequate parenting (Furstenberg et al., 1989; Hechtman, 1989). They are more aggressive and impulsive as preschoolers than are children of older mothers (Furstenberg et al., 1989). They do more poorly in school. They are also more likely to suffer maternal abuse or neglect (Felsman et al., 1987; Kinard & Reinherz, 1987).

A number of factors have contributed to the increase in teenage pregnancy, including a loosening of traditional taboos on adolescent sexuality (Hechtman, 1989). Impaired family relationships, problems in school, emotional problems, misunderstandings about reproduction or contraception, and lack of contraception also play roles (Hechtman, 1989). Some adolescent girls believe that a baby will elicit a commitment from their partners or fill an emotional void. Some become pregnant as a way of rebelling against parents. Some poor teenagers view early childbearing as the best of the severely limited options they perceive for their futures. But the largest number become pregnant because

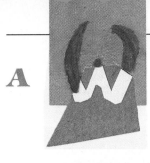 
RATES OF TEENAGE PREGNANCY AT HOME AND ABROAD

There are ethnic and social class differences in rates of teenage pregnancy. Rates of teenage pregnancy are higher among women of color, women from lower socioeconomic classes, and urbanites (Hechtman, 1989). Poverty is an especially strong predictor of teenage pregnancy (Jencks & Mayer, 1990). African American and Hispanic American teenagers, many of whom are poor, are twice as likely as White teenagers to become pregnant (Alan Guttmacher Institute, 1991). African American girls have the highest birth rate overall. The majority of residents of District of Columbia (DC) are African American, and DC had the highest rate of teenage pregnancy in the mid-1990s: 208 per 1,000 female teenagers ("Rate of births," 1995). Among the states, the rate varied from 54 per 1,000 in largely White Wyoming to 107 per 1,000 in Georgia ("Rate of births," 1995). Yet the Hispanic teenage pregnancy rate has been growing faster than those of all other ethnic and racial groups (Shapiro, 1992).

The rate of teenage pregnancy in the United States is more than double the rates in Canada, France, Great Britain, and Sweden, and more than five times greater than the rates in the Netherlands (Jones, 1985). Adolescent females in the United States, however, are no more likely to engage in sexual intercourse than adolescents in these other countries. What, then, might account for the two- to fivefold greater number of teenage pregnancies in the United States?

Several factors appear to account for these international differences

(Jones, 1985; Wallace & Vienonen, 1989). First, fewer U.S. teenagers have access to family-planning services that provide contraceptives at low or no cost. Second, U.S. teenagers who use contraception are much less likely to use birth-control pills, one of the most effective forms of contraception. Third, the other countries, except for

Canada, provide more extensive community- and school-based sex-education programs. Other factors, too, may be involved. For example, young men in these other countries tend to accept somewhat more responsibility for birth control than American males do (Hess et al., 1993).

Teenage Pregnancy. Nearly 1 million teenage girls in the United States become pregnant each year. Rates of teenage pregnancy are more prevalent among girls from minority groups, lower socioeconomic classes, and urban areas.

of misunderstandings about reproduction and contraception or miscalculations about the odds of conception. Even many who are relatively well informed about contraception fail to use it consistently (Hechtman, 1989).

More attention has been focused on teenage mothers, but young fathers bear an equal responsibility for teenage pregnancies. A survey based on a nationally representative sample of 1,880 young men ages 15 through 19 showed that socioeconomically disadvantaged young men in particular appeared to view paternity as a source of self-esteem and were consequently more likely than more affluent young men to say that fathering a child would make them feel like a real man and that they would be pleased, or at least not as upset, with an unplanned pregnancy (Marsiglio, 1993a). Consistent with these attitudes, young men living in poorer conditions were less likely to have used an effective contraceptive method during their most recent sexual experience.

Teenage fathers are more likely to have problems in school—both behavioral and academic—and to hold more pessimistic attitudes toward the future than their peers (Hanson et al., 1989). Steady dating also increased the risk of teenage fatherhood.

Contraceptive Use Among Sexually Active Teens

Sexually active teenagers use contraception inconsistently, if at all. Contraception is most likely to be used by teens in stable, monogamous relationships (Baker et al., 1988). Even teens in monogamous relationships tend to use ineffective methods of contraception or to use effective methods inconsistently, however (Polit-O'Hara & Kahn, 1985). About one in five sexually active teens in the Coles and Stokes (1985) national sample relied on withdrawal or the rhythm method the first and the most recent times they engaged in intercourse (see Table 13.5).

Various factors determine use of contraceptives (Beck & Davies, 1987). Teenage girls who engage in more frequent intercourse are more likely to use contraception and to use more effective methods (DuRant & Sanders, 1989). Teens whose peers use contraceptives are more likely to use them themselves (Jorgensen et al., 1980). Older teenagers are more likely than younger ones to use contraception (Mosher & Bachrach, 1987). Younger teens who are sexually active may be less likely to use contraception because they lack information about contraception and because they do not always perceive the repercussions of their actions (Handler, 1990). Younger teens may also have less access to contraceptives.

Teenage boys are more likely than teenage girls to know how to obtain and use condoms correctly, according to the results of a California survey of more than 1,000 high school students (Leland & Barth, 1992). Boys are also more likely to have used birth control during their first or most recent sexual experience. It appears that girls are more uncomfortable than boys in obtaining or using contraception, especially condoms (Leland & Barth, 1992).

Poor family relationships and poor communication with parents are associated with inconsistent contraceptive use (Brooks-Gunn & Furstenberg, 1989). Poor performance in school and low educational ambitions predict irregular contraceptive use, as they also predict early sexual initiation.

TABLE 13.5 Type of birth control used by sexually active teenagers

	First Time (%)	Most Recent Time (%)
Rhythm	3	4
Withdrawal	18	17
Condom	62	54
The pill	11	45
Diaphragm	3	4
Spermicidal foam	1	4
IUD	0	2

Source: From SEX AND THE AMERICAN TEENAGER by R. Coles and G. Stokes. Copyright © 1985 by Rolling Stone Press. Reprinted by permission of HarperCollins Publishers.

SHOULD PUBLIC SCHOOLS PROVIDE STUDENTS WITH CONTRACEPTIVES?

Alarmed by the threat of AIDS and the epidemic of teenage pregnancy, some school districts now distribute contraceptives, such as condoms, to students. Most school districts require parental consent. Others, such as the New York City school system, do not. Clinics that protect the confidentiality of their teenage clients often make active attempts to involve the parents in some way, usually by providing opportunities for family counseling, parent advisory groups, and parent–child communication training (Beck & Davies, 1987).

T r u t h OR *Fiction?*
R E V I S I T E D

It is true that condoms are distributed to adolescents without parental consent in some school districts. They are not distributed without controversy, however. ∎

Today only a few contraceptive counseling programs specifically reach out to males. Those that do so are typically stymied by poor participation rates (e.g., Gordon & DeMarco, 1984). There is a discrepancy between the attitudes of teenage males and their behavior (Beck & Davies, 1987). Young men generally voice strong opinions that birth control is the responsibility of both partners, but few use family-planning services even when they are available.

Adults voice hope that sex education will prevent teenage pregnancies. According to the ABC News (1995) poll, nine Americans in ten say that sex-education classes should teach pupils to practice birth control if they engage in sexual activity. However, 80% favor teaching that sex at an early age is a bad idea. A small majority (59%) say that school health clinics should provide students with condoms and other forms of contraceptives. However, about the same number (58%) say that students who use this

service should be required to get parental permission. Many parents oppose programs that do not require parental consent for fear that they compromise family cohesiveness and parental authority.

Of course, many parents believe that they, not the schools, should dispense information to their children about contraception and that they should be the ones who decide whether their children are given contraceptives. Many oppose giving adolescents contraceptives on moral and religious grounds. They argue that the emphasis should be on abstinence rather than on contraception. Some opponents believe that distributing contraceptives to teens encourages premarital sex.

Advocates of these programs argue that requiring parental consent would discourage participation by large numbers of sexually active teens. They note that many teens become sexually active despite educators' encouragement to abstain. Given this re-

When asked to explain why they don't use contraceptives, sexually active teens often cite factors such as sexual infrequency ("don't have intercourse often enough to use it") and disruption of sexual spontaneity ("interferes with sex") (Coles & Stokes, 1985). Some teenagers get "carried away" and do not wish to disrupt sex by applying birth-control devices. For others, coitus is an unplanned, "spur of the moment" experience.

Myths also decrease likelihood of using birth control. Some adolescents believe that they are too young to become pregnant. Others believe that pregnancy results only from repeated coitus or will not occur if they are standing up. Still other adolescents simply do not admit to themselves that they are engaging in coitus. Concerns about side effects are also given as reasons for failure to use contraception (Washington et al., 1983).

Teenagers who focus on the long-term consequences of their actions are more likely to use contraceptives. The quality of the relationship is also a factor. Satisfaction with the relationship is associated with more frequent intercourse *and* more consistent use of contraception (Jorgensen et al., 1980). More consistent contraceptive use is found in relationships in which the young woman takes the initiative in making decisions and resolving conflicts.

ality, they argue, society has a responsibility to help protect sexually active teens from unwanted pregnancies and AIDS.

Handing out condoms is not likely to reduce teenage pregnancy or the spread of sexually transmitted diseases unless the "handouts" are accompanied by counseling that focuses on their proper use. Sexually active teenagers also need to learn how to communicate the need for contraception with their partners. More comprehensive reproductive health care clinics have been established in some schools, which combine condom distribution with counseling about sex. But are they effective in lowering the rates of teenage pregnancy? Thus far, these programs have failed to dent schoolwide pregnancy rates (Kirby et al., 1992, 1993).

Enter Norplant

The introduction of the contraceptive device Norplant has added a new wrinkle to the debate over distributing contraceptives in the schools. The advantage of Norplant is that once implanted, it offers around-the-clock protection against unwanted pregnancies for several years. Baltimore, which is beset with one of the highest teen pregnancy rates in the United States, became the first city in the nation to offer Norplant to teenage girls in a school-based clinic in the attempt to combat teenage pregnancies (Kantrowitz, 1992; Lewin, 1992b). In Baltimore, 1 in 10 girls of ages 15 to 17 have babies ("For high school girls," 1993). Most live in poverty. Until the experimental program, Norplant was too expensive for most teens. The Norplant program is located in a school in an impoverished, inner-city community, where the problem of teenage pregnancy is most acute. Here, a 16-year-old teenage mother in Baltimore expresses her hopes that Norplant will enable her to finish high school and pursue a college education without becoming pregnant again:

> I don't know what I would do if I had another baby. . . . I share a crowded bedroom with two younger sisters, and it's so small and cluttered with bunk beds and cribs. I've tried to find a job, but there aren't any, and my stepfather is out of work. I want to go to art school, and I always dreamed of having fun on a college campus. . . . I wanted Norplant to help me finish school.

(*Source: The New York Times*, March 7, 1993, p. 28)

The Baltimore Norplant program has sparked considerable controversy. Although some proponents hail Norplant as a "silver bullet" against teen pregnancies, others believe that it will encourage teenage promiscuity. As one local clergyman put it, "Norplant sends a message that it is O. K. to have sex as long as you don't get pregnant" ("Plan for wider use of Norplant," 1993). Norplant also does not offer protection against sexually transmitted diseases. Some opponents consider the use of Norplant in inner-city schools to be a racist tool. Some worry about potential side effects or medical risks, especially in a population of inner-city teens who may not see a physician regularly. Proponents argue that Norplant is needed because teens fail to use other forms of contraception consistently or at all, even if they are made available to them.

Let us note that many adolescents today who use condoms do so more because of fear of AIDS than to protect themselves against unwanted pregnancies (Lewin, 1991). A reduction in teenage pregnancies may be a side effect of this trend.

Combating Teenage Pregnancy: A Role for the Schools?   Various means have been recommended to combat the problem of teenage pregnancy, including universal sex education, free contraceptive services for teenagers, open discussion of sex between parents and children, and dissemination of information about responsible sex practices and contraception through the media. Given the effects of sex education in other industrialized countries, many helping professionals believe that the rate of teenage pregnancy and the spread of sexually transmitted diseases in the United States could be curtailed through sex education about contraception and provision of contraceptives.

Pregnancy prevention programs in the schools range from encouraging teens to delay sex ("saying no to early sex") to providing information about contraception to distributing condoms or referring students to contraceptive clinics (Furstenberg et al., 1989; Hayes,

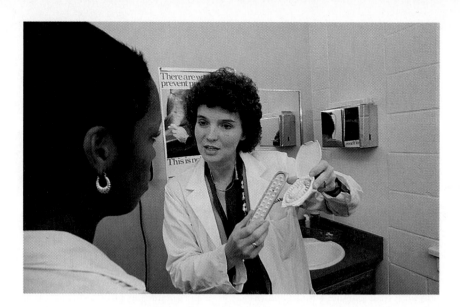

Contraception Clinic. A teenager is counseled about use of birth-control pills. Should schools provide contraceptives to students? Should parents have a say in whether their children receive them?

1987). The vast majority of sex educators (86%) recommend abstinence to their students as the best way to prevent pregnancy and AIDS (Kantrowitz, 1990b). Fewer than half inform their students about how to obtain contraceptives. Three out of four large school districts in the United States provide some instruction about the methods of contraception and the use of condoms to prevent the spread of AIDS and other sexually transmitted diseases. About four in ten provide information about clinics or doctors whom students can contact to receive contraceptives (Kenney et al., 1989).

Evidence supports the effectiveness of programs that counsel abstinence, at least among younger teens. A school-based sex-education program focused on the development of skills needed to resist social and peer pressure to initiate sexual activity encouraged younger (junior high school) teens to postpone sexual involvement (Howard & McCabe, 1990). Program participants also had fewer pregnancies than students who did not participate in the program. However, programs that rely on the "just say no" model to encourage abstinence are less effective in persuading high school students to abstain from sexual activity (Wilson & Sanderson, 1988).

Because many teenagers are or will become sexually active, our society faces the question of whether the public schools should make contraceptive services or contraceptives themselves available to sexually active teens. This issue is the focus of heated debate among parents, educators, health officials, and other public officials in various communities in the United States and Canada. We explore this question further in the nearby A Closer Look feature.

～ *Reflections* ～

◾ At what ages did you experience the changes of puberty? Were you early or late compared with your friends? Did it matter? If so, how?

◾ At what ages did you or your friends become sexually active? What were your or their motives for becoming sexually active? Were your or their early sexual experiences as exciting or pleasurable as expected?

◾ What are the attitudes of most people from your sociocultural background toward premarital sexuality? Do you share their attitudes? Why or why not?

In this chapter we have chronicled sexuality in childhood and adolescence. In the next chapter we continue our journey through the life span.

Summing Up

Infancy (0 to 2 Years): The Search for the Origins of Human Sexuality

The Infant's Capacity for Sexual Response   Fetuses have been found to have erections and suck their fingers. Stimulation of the genitals in infancy may produce sensations of pleasure. Pelvic thrusting has been observed in humans as early as 8 months of age. Masturbation may begin as early as 6 to 12 months. Some infants seem capable of sexual responses that closely resemble orgasm.

Masturbation   Self-stimulation for pleasure (masturbation) typically occurs among children as young as 6 to 12 months of age.

Genital Play   U.S. children typically do not engage in genital play with others until about the age of 2.

Early Childhood (3 to 8 Years)

Masturbation   Statistics concerning the incidence of masturbation at ages 3 to 8 are speculative.

Male–Female Sexual Behavior   In early childhood, children show curiosity about the genitals and may play "doctor."

Male–Male and Female–Female Sexual Behavior   Same-gender sexual activity play may be more common than heterosexual play and does not presage adult sexual orientation.

Preadolescence (9 to 13 Years)

Preadolescents tend to socialize with best friends and with large groups, and to become self-conscious about their bodies.

Masturbation   Masturbation is apparently the primary means of achieving orgasm during preadolescence for both genders.

Male–Female Sexual Behavior   Preadolescent sex play often involves mutual display of the genitals, with or without touching. Group dating and mixed-gender parties often provide preadolescents with their first exposure to heterosexual activities.

Male–Male and Female–Female Sexual Behavior   Much preadolescent same-gender sexual behavior involves sexual exploration and is short-lived.

Sex Education and Miseducation   Despite the increased availability of sex-education programs, peers apparently remain the major source of sexual information.

Adolescence

Adolescence is bounded by the advent of puberty at the lower end and the capacity to take on adult responsibilities at the upper end. The conflicts and distress experienced by many adolescents apparently reflect the cultural expectations to which they are exposed.

Puberty   Pubertal changes are ushered in by sex hormones. Puberty begins with the appearance of secondary sex characteristics and ends when the long bones make no further gains in length. Once puberty begins, most major changes in primary sex characteristics occur within three years in girls and within four years in boys.

Masturbation   Masturbation is a major sexual outlet during adolescence.

Male–Female Sexual Behavior   Adolescents today date and "go steady" earlier than in past generations, a change that has apparently increased the incidence of teenage pregnancy. Many adolescents use petting as a way of achieving sexual gratification without becoming pregnant or ending one's virginity. The incidence of premarital intercourse, especially for females, has increased dramatically since Kinsey's day.

Male–Male and Female–Female Sexual Behavior   Most adolescent same-gender sexual encounters are transitory. Coming to terms with adolescence is often more intense for gay males and lesbians, largely because gay male and lesbian sexual orientations are stigmatized in our society.

Teenage Pregnancy

Nearly 1 million adolescents in the United States become pregnant each year. Rates of teenage pregnancy are connected with socioeconomic status.

Contraceptive Use Among Sexually Active Teenagers   Sexually active teenagers use contraception inconsistently, if at all. Thus, more than 1 million teenage girls in the United States become pregnant each year.

CHAPTER 14

Henri Matisse, *The Dance,* 1910. Hermitage Museum, St. Petersburg, Russia.
Scala/Art Resource, NY. © 1996 Succession H. Matisse/Artist Rights
Society (ARS), New York.

Sexuality in Adulthood

Outline

Singlehood

Cohabitation: Darling, Would You Be My POSSLQ?
Who Are the Cohabitors? * Reasons for Cohabitation *
Cohabitation and Later Marriage: Benefit or Risk?

Marriage
Historical Perspectives * Why Do People Marry? *
Types of Marriage * Whom Do We Marry: Are Marriages
Made in Heaven or in the Neighborhood?

Marital Sexuality
The Sexual Revolution Hits Home * Sexual Satisfaction

Extramarital Sex
Patterns of Extramarital Sex *
Attitudes Toward Extramarital Sex *
Effects of Extramarital Sex * Swinging

Divorce
The Cost of Divorce

Alternative Forms of Marriage
Open Marriage * Group Marriage

Sex in the Later Years
Physical Changes * Patterns of Sexual Activity

Sex and Disability
Physical Disabilities * Psychological Disabilities

Summing Up

A World of Diversity / Snug in Their Beds for Christmas
Eve—In Japan, December 24 Has Become the Hottest Night
of the Year; Ethnicity, Babies, and Marriage—Not Exactly
Like the Horse and Carriage

A Closer Look / A Kind of Sexual Revolution:
At Some Nursing Homes, Intimacy Is a Matter of Policy

Truth OR Fiction?

_____ "Singlehood" (forgive the word) has become a more
common U.S. lifestyle over the past few decades.

_____ Cohabitation is most common among college students.

_____ In the ancient Hebrew and Greek civilizations, wives
were viewed as their husbands' property.

_____ Men are more romantic than women.

_____ Most of today's sophisticated young people see nothing wrong with an occasional extramarital fling.

_____ Few women can reach orgasm after the age of 70.

_____ People who are paralyzed due to spinal-cord injuries
cannot become sexually aroused or engage in coitus.

People entering adulthood today face a wider range of sexual choices and lifestyles than those of earlier generations. The sexual revolution loosened traditional constraints on sexual choices, especially for women. Couples experiment with lifestyles that would have been unthinkable in earlier generations. An increasing number of young people choose to remain single as a way of life, not merely as a way station preceding the arrival of Mr. or Ms. Right.

In this chapter, we discuss diverse forms of adult sexuality in the United States today, including singlehood, marriage, and alternative lifestyles such as cohabitation, open marriage, and group marriage. Let us begin as people begin—with singlehood.

Singlehood

Recent years have seen a sharp increase in the numbers of single young people in our society. "Singlehood," not marriage, is now the most common lifestyle among people in their early 20s. Though marriages may be made in heaven, many Americans are saying heaven can wait. By the early 1990s, one in four people in the United States 18 years of age and older had never married, as compared to about one in six in 1970 and one in five in 1980 (Barringer, 1992a, 1992b). The rate of marriages had also fallen off. The proportion of people tying the knot reached a 25-year low (Barringer, 1992b). Nearly 80% of single men in the 20-to-24 age range were unmarried, up from 55% in 1970 (U.S. Bureau of the Census, 1990a). The percentage of single women in this age group grew from 36% in 1970 to 61%. About one in four U.S. households consisted of a single adult. This represented a threefold increase since 1960.

Although most people do get married by their late 20s, never-married singles still account for some 43% of the men and 30% of the women in the 25-to-29 age group (U.S. Bureau of the Census, 1990a). In fact, the proportion of people who remain single into their late 20s and early 30s has more than doubled since 1970 (U.S. Bureau of the Census, 1990a).

Truth **OR** Fiction?
R E V I S I T E D

It is true that "singlehood" has become a more common U.S. lifestyle over the past few decades. More people are remaining single into their 20s and 30s than was the case a generation or two ago. ■

Several factors contribute to the increased proportion of singles. For one thing, more people are postponing marriage to pursue educational and career goals (Barringer, 1991). Many young people are deciding to "live together" (cohabit), at least for a while, rather than get married. Also, people are getting married at later ages (Kornblum, 1994). The increased prevalence of divorce also swells the ranks of single adults.

Less social stigma is attached to remaining single today. Though single people are less likely today to be perceived as socially inadequate or as failures, some unmarried people still encounter stereotypes. Men who have never married may be suspected of being gay. Single women may feel that men perceive them as "loose."

Many single people do not choose to be single. Some remain single because they have not yet found Mr. or Ms. Right. Yet many young people see singlehood as an alternative, open-ended way of life, however—not just a temporary stage that precedes marriage. As career options for women have expanded, they are not as financially dependent on men as were their mothers and grandmothers. A number of career women, like young career-oriented men, choose to remain single (at least for a time) to focus their energies on their careers.

Singlehood is not without its problems. Some singles express concerns about a lack of a steady, meaningful social relationship. Others, usually women, worry about their physical safety. Some people living alone may find it difficult to satisfy their needs for intimacy, companionship, sex, and emotional support. Despite these concerns, most singles are well

Singles. There is no one "singles scene" today. While some singles meet in singles' bars, many singles meet in more casual settings, such as the neighborhood laundromat. Some singles advertise in newspapers and magazines, or online.

adjusted and content. Singles who have a greater number of friends and a supportive social network tend to be more satisfied with their lifestyles.

There is no single "singles scene." Single people differ in their sexual interests and lifestyles. Many achieve emotional and psychological security through a network of intimate relationships with friends. Most are sexually active, and many practice **serial monogamy.** Other singles have a primary sexual relationship with one steady partner but occasional flings with others. A few, even in this age of AIDS, are "swinging singles." That is, they pursue casual sexual encounters, or "one-night stands."

Some singles remain celibate, either by choice or for lack of opportunity. People choose **celibacy** for a number of reasons. Nuns and priests do so for religious reasons. Others believe that celibacy allows them to focus their energies and attention on work or to commit themselves to an important cause. They see celibacy as a temporary accommodation to other pursuits. Others remain celibate because they view sex outside of marriage as immoral. Still others remain celibate because they find the prospects of sexual activity aversive or unalluring, or because of fears of STDs.

Serial monogamy
A pattern of involvement in one exclusive relationship after another, as opposed to engaging in multiple sexual relationships at the same time.

Celibacy
Complete sexual abstinence. (Sometimes used to describe the state of being unmarried, especially in the case of people who take vows to remain single.)

~ *Reflections* ~

- At what age do most of your peers plan to get married? (Or at what age *did* most of your peers get married?) Why?
- Is remaining single an option for you? Why, or why not?

Cohabitation: Darling, Would You Be My POSSLQ?

There is nothing I would not do
If you would be my POSSLQ.

(Charles Osgood)

Cohabitation
Living together as though married but without legal sanction.

POSSLQ? This unromantic abbreviation was introduced by the U.S. Bureau of the Census to refer to **cohabitation.** It stands for People of Opposite Sex Sharing Living Quarters and applies to unmarried couples who live together.

SNUG IN THEIR BEDS FOR CHRISTMAS EVE—IN JAPAN, DECEMBER 24 HAS BECOME THE HOTTEST NIGHT OF THE YEAR*

For young people all over the Christian world, Christmas Eve is a night of magic and wonder. In Japan as well, Christmas Eve has become immensely important—but for rather different reasons.

It has become the sexiest night of the year.

Japanese popular culture has made Christmas Eve a night, similar to our New Year's Eve, when unmarried people are expected to have a date. It has now come to be expected that the date include an overnight stay. For weeks prior to this night, TV shows, magazines, and *manga* (adult comic books) are full of reports and advice on which hotels are best for young couples to stay in on Christmas Eve, what each partner should wear, and where the pair should have breakfast the following morning.

"Christmas Eve is now important as a night for making love," complains poet and social critic Hazuki Kajiwara.

This is such a widely accepted aspect of the day here known as *eebu*, the Japanese pronunciation of "eve," that December 24 is frequently referred to as "H-day." The letter *H*, taken from the English word "hormone," is a common symbol here for sex.

The *eebu* phenomenon is carried out in an intensely materialistic, free-spending atmosphere, reflecting the commercial nature of the Christmas season in Japan. In a country less than 1% Christian, December 25 is just another working day. Yet stores and restaurants here have more Christmas trees, wreaths, and reindeer on display than most places in the United States.

For a couple's Christmas Eve fling, the man is expected to bear all costs. Many "salary men" save all year for this one date. The news magazine *Asahi Journal* printed a breakdown of a fairly standard "Eve course": When the man arrives to pick up his date, he should present her with a $215 silver

heart pendant from Tiffany's and then take her out for an evening at Tokyo Disneyland, where admission and extras will cost $100 or so. Then it's on to dinner for two at a French or American restaurant ($385) and a room for the night overlooking Tokyo Bay at the Hilton or the Sheraton Grande ($300, or $650 for a suite). Breakfast in the hotel coffee shop should cost only $35, but a rental limousine to take the couple to their homes so they can quickly change and go to work will cost another $150.

But *eebu* is hardly a free ride for Japanese women. They must pay the emotional cost.

Women between college age and their mid-30s have more money and more independence today than ever before in Japanese history. But they are losing their connection to family and peer groups, and are struggling to survive on their own.

Some social scientists believe that cohabitation has become accepted within the social mainstream (Bumpass, 1995). Whether or not this is so, society in general has become more tolerant of it. We seldom hear cohabitation referred to as "living in sin" or "shacking up" as we once did. People today are more likely to refer to cohabitation with value-free expressions such as "living together."

Perhaps the current tolerance reflects societal adjustment to the increase in the numbers of cohabiting couples. Or perhaps the numbers of cohabiting couples have increased as a consequence of tolerance. The numbers of households consisting of unmarried adults of the other gender living together in the United States doubled between 1980 and the early 1990s (Steinhauer, 1995). They grew from 1.6 million couples in 1980 to 2.9 million couples in 1990 and 3.3 million in 1992.

Who Are the Cohabitors?

Much of the attention on cohabitation has been focused on college students living together, but cohabitation is more prevalent among the less well educated and less affluent classes (Willis & Michael, 1994). The cohabitation rate is about twice as high among African American couples as White couples. Fifty-five percent of male cohabitors and 41% of female cohabitors have never been married (U.S. Bureau of the Census, 1990a). Children live with about one cohabiting couple in three (Saluter, 1992).

"Behind the traditional Japanese groupism is a fear of being alone," says Hikaru Hayashi, senior research director at the Hakuhodo Institute, a sociological think tank. For single women, "Christmas Eve enhances the fear that they are not rooted in society."

With virtually everyone making elaborate plans for *eebu*, it has become something of a social necessity for single men and women to have a date that night. The tribulations of those who don't have one become the subject of enormous media attention.

A travel agency has been advertising excursion trips for singles under the headline "Find a Boyfriend by Christmas!" The Tokyo Broadcasting System ran a miniseries called "Christmas Eve." The story concerned a young "office lady" who listened to her friends chattering about the fancy restaurants and hotels they were going to for *eebu* but was ashamed to admit she had no date. In the final episode, a young man called her at the last minute. The two walked off happily

Eebu. Japanese popular culture has made Christmas Eve into a night similar to our New Year's Eve. Unmarried people are expected to have a date, and that date is usually expected to include an overnight stay.

into the night, presumably in search of a hotel with a vacant room.

The idea that it might be shameful for a single woman to spend the night with her date is less commonly expressed, but it does occur. Sampei Sato, the editorial cartoonist for the newspaper *Asahi Shimbun*, devoted his space one day to an appeal to young unmarried women to sleep at home rather than in a hotel on Christmas Eve.

The new view of *eebu* has increased the Japanese people's belief that they are unique. "In all the world," said the lead-in to a TV talk show, "only Japan has turned the day before Christmas into a day for sex."

*Adapted from Reid, T. R. (1990, December 24). Snug in Their Beds for Christmas Eve: In Japan, Dec. 24 Has Become the Hottest Night of the Year. *The Washington Post.*

About one cohabitor in three is divorced. Divorced people are more likely than people who never married to enter cohabiting relationships. Apparently, the experience of divorce makes some people more willing to share their lives than their bank accounts—the second or third time around (Steinhauer, 1995).

Willingness to cohabit is related to more liberal attitudes toward sexual behavior, less traditional views of marriage, and less traditional views of gender roles (Huffman et al., 1994). Cohabitors are less likely than noncohabitors to attend church regularly (Laumann et al., 1994). Six out of ten male cohabitors and nearly seven out of ten female cohabitors are under 35 years of age (U.S. Bureau of the Census, 1990a). Yet the greatest increase since 1980 in the numbers of people cohabiting has not been among young romantics, but among people age 35 and above (Bumpass, 1995).

Truth **OR** Fiction?

R E V I S I T E D

It is not true that cohabitation is most common among college students. Cohabitation is actually more prevalent among the less well educated and the less affluent. ■

Reasons for Cohabitation

Why do people cohabit? Cohabitation, like marriage, is an alternative to the loneliness that can accompany living alone. Romantic partners may have deep feelings for each other but not be ready to get married. Some couples prefer cohabitation because it provides a

Source: Reprinted with special permission of King Features Syndicate.

consistent relationship without the legal and economic entanglements of marriage (Steinhauer, 1995).

Many cohabitors feel less commitment toward their relationships than married people do (Nock, 1995). Ruth, an 84-year-old woman, has been living with her partner, age 85, for four years. "I'm a free spirit," she says. "I need my space. Sometimes we think of marriage, but then I think that I don't want to be tied down" (cited in Steinhauer, 1995, p. C7).

Ruth's comments are of interest because they counter stereotypes of women and older people. However, it is more often the man who is unwilling to make a marital commitment (Yorburg, 1995), as in the case of Mark. Mark, a 44-year-old computer consultant, lives with Nancy and their 7-year-old daughter, Janet. Mark says, "We feel we are not primarily a couple but rather primarily individuals who happen to be in a couple. It allows me to be a little more at arm's length. Men don't like committing, so maybe this is just some sort of excuse" (cited in Steinhauer, 1995, p. C7).

Economic factors come into play as well. Emotionally committed couples may decide to cohabit because of the economic advantages of sharing household expenses. Cohabiting individuals who receive public assistance (social security or welfare checks) risk losing support if they get married (Steinhauer, 1995). Some older people live together rather than marry because of resistance from adult children (Yorburg, 1995). Some children fear that a parent will be victimized by a needy senior citizen. Others may not want their inheritances to come into question or may not want to decide where to bury the remaining parent. Younger couples may cohabit secretly to maintain parental support that they might lose if they were to get married or to openly reveal their living arrangements.

Cohabitation and Later Marriage: Benefit or Risk?

Cohabiting couples may believe that cohabitation will strengthen eventual marriage by helping them iron out the kinks in their relationship. Yet cohabitors who later marry may run a greater—not lesser—risk of divorce than noncohabitors. Statistics from a national survey of households reveal that the likelihood of divorce within ten years of marriage is nearly twice as great among married couples who cohabited before marriage (Riche, 1988). A Swedish study found that the likelihood of marital dissolution was 80% greater among women who had cohabited before a first marriage than among women who had not (Bennett et al., 1988).

We must be cautious about drawing causal conclusions from correlational data, however. None of the couples in these studies were *randomly assigned* to cohabitation or noncohabitation. Therefore, *selection factors*—the factors that lead some couples to cohabit and others not to cohabit—may explain the results (see Figure 14.1). Cohabitors tend to be more committed to personal independence (Bumpass, 1995). They also tend to be less traditional and less religious than noncohabitors. All in all, people who cohabit prior to marriage tend to be less committed to the values and interests traditionally associated with the institution of marriage. The attitudes of cohabitors, and not cohabitation itself, may thus account for their higher rates of marital dissolution.

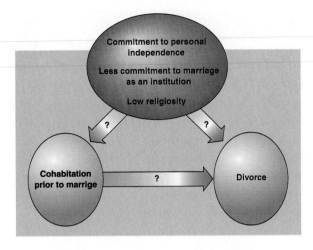

Figure 14.1. Does Cohabitation Prior to Marriage Increase the Risk of Eventual Divorce? There is a correlational relationship between cohabitation prior to marriage and the risk of divorce later on. Does cohabitation increase the risk of divorce, or do other factors—such as a commitment to personal independence—contribute to both the likelihood of cohabitation and eventual divorce?

About 40% of cohabiting couples eventually marry (Laumann et al., 1994). The majority of couples break up within three years. Termination of the relationship, not marriage, is the more likely outcome of cohabitation (Willis & Michael, 1994).

~ *Reflections* ~

Do you know people who are living together without being married? What is their motivation for doing so? How do most people from their sociocultural background feel about cohabitation? Why?

Agree or disagree with the following statement, and support your answer: Cohabitation helps couples determine whether they are compatible before they get married.

Agree or disagree with the following statement, and support your answer: Cohabitation is a normal variation in lifestyle.

Marriage

Marriage is found in all human societies. Most people in every known society, sometimes nearly all, get married at least once (Ember & Ember, 1990; Kammeyer, 1990).

Marriage is our most common lifestyle. In some cultures, such as among the Hindu of India, marriage is virtually universal, with more than 99% of the females eventually marrying. In the United States, most people still get married, but today one in four people of age 18 and above has never married (Steinhauer, 1995). In 1970, the number of never-married adults was only one in six (Steinhauer, 1995). However, cohabitation is becoming widespread in the United States as well. University of Wisconsin researcher Larry Bumpass has been following 10,000 people since the late 1980s. In 1995, he reported that 49% of people ages 35 to 39 were cohabiting, as compared to 34% in the late 1980s. Bumpass estimates that nationwide, half of the adult population under age 40 is cohabiting. In 1995, he estimated that in ten years, half of the adult population under the age of 50 will be cohabiting.

In the United States, about 65% of the adult men and 60% of the adult women are married and living with their spouses (U.S. Bureau of the Census, 1990a). With more people delaying marriage in favor of pursuing educational and career goals, the average (median) age of first marriage has been rising steadily over the past few decades and is now 26.5 years for men and 24.4 years for women (Saluter, 1992). This represents an increase of three years for both men and women since 1975.

Wedding Daze. The social institution of marriage is found in all human societies. Why has marriage retained its popularity, even in these relatively liberated times?

Historical Perspectives

Marriage in Western culture has a long and varied history. Among the ancient Hebrews, men dominated most aspects of life. This system was known as **patriarchy.** The man of the house had the right to choose wives for his sons and could himself take concubines or additional wives. He alone could institute divorce—a practice still found among Orthodox Jews. Although he could dally, his wife had to be scrupulous in the maintenance of her virtue. Failure to bear children was grounds for divorce. The wife was clearly considered to be part of the property of the man of the house: a **chattel.**

In classical Greece, women were also viewed as the property of men. Their central purposes were to care for the household and to bear children. Rarely were they viewed as suitable companions for men. During the golden age of Greece, men would turn to high-class prostitutes for sensual sex and sophisticated conversation—not to their wives.

It is true that in the ancient Hebrew and Greek civilizations, wives were viewed as their husbands' property—as chattels. The women's movement has fought to throw off the weight of millennia of such oppressive practices. ■

The Romans also had a powerful patriarchy. The oldest man directed family life and could, if he wished, sell his children into slavery and arrange their marriages and divorces. Marriages were typically arranged for financial or political gain. Women were in effect given by their fathers to their husbands.

The Christian tradition also has a strong patriarchal foundation. Male dominance was legitimized by biblical scripture, as we can see in this passage from the New Testament: "Wives, submit to your own husbands, as unto the Lord. For the husband is the head of the wife, as Christ is the head of the church" (Ephesians 5:23–24).

Patriarchal traditions in Western culture gradually weakened with time, and women came to be viewed as loving companions rather than mere chattels. They gradually gained more household responsibilities and were recognized as being capable of profiting from education. The notion that a married woman might rightfully seek personal fulfillment through a career unrelated to her husband's needs is a relatively recent development, however. The perception that married women have a right to sexual fulfillment is also new. As late as the nineteenth century, sex in marriage was largely seen as a means for bearing children and satisfying the husband's sexual needs. Although there were some caring and sen-

Patriarchy

A form of social organization in which the father or eldest male runs the group or family; government, rule, or domination by men. (From the Greek *pater*, meaning "father," and *archein*, meaning "to rule.")

T r u t h **OR** *Fiction?*
R E V I S I T E D

Chattel

A movable piece of personal property, such as furniture or livestock. (From the Old French word meaning "cattle.")

sitive husbands, typical nineteenth-century sexual relations between husbands and wives were brief and brutal. Women derived little pleasure from them. Sex was viewed, even among educated classes, as a husband's right and a wife's duty. Marriage manuals of the time held that a woman's role was to submit to her husband's advances in order to please him. Women were assumed to be motivated sexually only by the desire for children.

Marital roles in modern society have changed and are changing still. Some couples still adhere to traditional gender roles that ascribe breadwinning responsibilities to the husband and child care and homemaking roles to the wife. U.S. couples today are more likely to share or even reverse marital roles, however. Table 14.1 lists some of the discriminating features of traditional and so-called modern marriages.

Why Do People Marry?

Marriage meets personal and cultural needs. It legitimizes sexual relations and provides a legal sanction for deeply committed relationships. It permits the maintenance of a home life and provides an institution in which children can be supported and socialized into adopting the norms of the family and the culture at large. Marriage restricts sexual relations so that a man can be assured—or at least could assume—that his wife's children are his. Marriage also permits the orderly transmission of wealth from one family to another and from one generation to another. As late as the seventeenth and eighteenth centuries, most European marriages were arranged by the parents of the bride and groom, generally on the basis of how the marriage would benefit the families.

Notions like romantic love, equality, and the very radical concept that men as well as women would do well to aspire to the ideal of faithfulness are recent additions to the structure of marriage in Western society. Not until the nineteenth century did the notion of love

---

TABLE 14.1 A comparison of traditional and modern marriages

Traditional Marriage	Modern Marriage
The emphasis is on ritual and traditional roles.	The emphasis is on companionship.
Couples do not live together before marriage.	Couples may live together before marriage.
The wife takes the husband's last name.	The wife may choose to keep her maiden name.
The husband is dominant; the wife is submissive.	Neither spouse is dominant or submissive.
The roles for the husband and the wife are specific and rigid.	Both spouses have flexible roles.
There is one income (the husband's).	There may be two incomes; that is, the couple may share the breadwinning role. In many cases, the woman is the breadwinner.
The husband initiates sexual activity; the wife complies.	Either spouse may initiate (or refuse) sex.
The wife cares for the children.	The parents share child-rearing chores.
Education is considered important for the husband, not for the wife.	Education is considered equally important for both spouses.
The husband's career decides the location of the family residence.	The career of either spouse may determine the location of the family residence.

Source: Adapted by permission from CHOICES IN RELATIONSHIPS by D. Knox; Copyright © 1988 by West Publishing Company. All rights reserved.

A WORLD OF DIVERSITY

ETHNICITY, BABIES, AND MARRIAGE—NOT EXACTLY LIKE THE HORSE AND CARRIAGE

Once upon a time, it is said, babies and marriage went together like the proverbial horse and carriage. Today, however, the connection is no longer so solid. The percentage of single-parent families has been heading upward, more than doubling from 12% to 26% between 1970 and 1990 (Barringer, 1992b). More than half of the children born to 18- and 19-year-olds in the United States are born out of wedlock (O'Connell, 1991). Nearly one in four (24%) never-married women become mothers, up from 15% in 1982 (DeParle, 1993; "More single mothers," 1993). The sharpest increases are found among White women (more than doubling, from 6.7% to 14.6%), among women who have graduated from college (also more than doubling, from 3.0% to 6.4%), and among women in professional and managerial jobs (nearly tripling, from 3.1% to 8.3%). The numbers of unmarried African American and Hispanic American women becoming mothers have also risen, but not as sharply as among White women (DeParle, 1993) (see Figure 14.2).

Demographers and sociologists suggest a number of reasons for the upturn in out-of-wedlock births. For one thing, less stigma is now attached to bearing children out of wedlock

(Bachu, 1991). Unmarried women who become pregnant are thus less likely to seek the sanction of marriage. Another reason is that more people are postponing marriage to pursue educational or career goals, or because they haven't met someone that meets their marital expectations (Barringer, 1992b). The state of the economy may also play an important role. Troubled economic conditions may discourage people from making a commitment during times they don't feel economically secure (Barringer, 1992b). Whatever the reason, women who delay marriage spend a longer period of

time as singles during which they can become accidentally pregnant (Bumpass, 1991). Day care has also become more available, making it easier for single women to rear children (Rindfuss, 1991).

Why the sharp increase in out-of-wedlock births among better-educated, professionally employed women? It appears that the social acceptability of single parenthood within the middle class has risen while women's increased earning power provides them with the economic means to raise a child alone (Seligmann, 1993). Although women's earn-

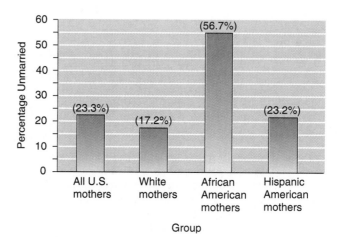

Figure 14.2
Percentage of U.S. Women Who Gave Birth Out of Wedlock.
Source: U.S. Bureau of the Census, 1991.

as a basis for marriage become widespread in Western culture. In some preliterate societies, the very idea of being in love is considered a laughable concept—hardly a basis for marriage.

Today, because more people believe that premarital sex is acceptable between two people who feel affectionate toward each other, the desire to engage in sexual intercourse is less likely to motivate marriage. Marriage provides a sense of emotional and psychological security, however, and opportunities to share feelings, experiences, and ideas with someone with whom one forms a special attachment. Desires for companionship and intimacy are thus central goals in contemporary marriages. Even in these more liberated times, young people (ages 17 to 23) today strongly endorse the traditional ideal that marriage is a lifetime commitment (Moore & Stief, 1992).

ings, on the average, still fall below those of men, the earning power of well-educated professional women has risen to the point that they are no longer economically dependent on men. DeParle (1993) observes that the "feminist revolution has left many women with a new sense of independence. Witnessing the high divorce rates around them, many women no longer trust the institution of marriage." Moreover, many single, well-educated women today who face the relentless ticking of their biological clocks with no prospective partner in the offing are opting for motherhood anyway (Lawson, 1993). As one 39-year-old single mother, whose son is now nearly 4 years old, commented,

> Ideally, [my son] . . . would have a father who adored me and adored him . . . but we don't have that. . . . I always wanted to have a child, . . . I knew so many women who were waiting for that Alan Alda type to come along, and wanting a committed relationship. And they were waiting and waiting.
>
> (Seligmann, 1993, p. 53.)

A national organization, Single Mothers by Choice, which was formed to help single mothers cope with raising children alone, now has some 2,000 members in 20 chapters nationwide (Lawson, 1993).

Most single mothers, however, are neither well educated nor professionally employed. Most are women with little education who are either unemployed or underemployed. The challenges they face are not those of balancing the responsibilities of career and motherhood but of coping with the daily struggles of survival. The U.S. Census Bureau reports that nearly 50% of unwed mothers failed to finish high school and only 6% had bachelor's degrees (Lawson, 1993). A record number of unmarried mothers now depend on welfare payments to survive (DeParle, 1993). Children from single-parent households, overall, have more educational, financial, and emotional problems than those from dual-parent households.

Out-of-wedlock births have shot up since the 1960s, especially among African Americans (Chideya, 1993). Two of three first births to African American women under the age of 35 are now out of wedlock (Chideya, 1993). A majority of African American children (58%) now live in single-parent households, as compared to 20% of White children (Barringer, 1992b; Chideya, 1993). (About 25% of these new parents of children born out of wedlock are, however, living together, or cohabiting [Bumpass, 1991]. Children born within these relationships will thus be reared in two-parent families.)

The greater prevalence of out-of-wedlock births among African Americans is found at both the low and high ends of the income spectrum. It's not that the institution of marriage has lost favor. A *Newsweek* poll of single African American adults showed that 88% wanted to get married (Chideya, 1993). But the dream of marriage has been hammered in the last 25 years. Chideya (1993) attributes the discrepancy between the dream and the reality to the economic dislocation that began in the 1970s and 1980s, when the nation shifted from an industrial to a service base. The change was particularly devastating to African American men, who had migrated north in vast numbers to take well-paying manufacturing jobs that have now become scarce.

The connection between marriage and bearing children varies widely among industrialized nations. In Japan, for example, only 1% of children are born out of wedlock (O'Connell, 1991). In Sweden, however, cohabitation is so common that about 50% of children are born out of wedlock (O'Connell, 1991). Sharp increases in the numbers of unmarried mothers have occurred in recent years in industrialized democracies other than Japan, as they have in the United States (DeParle, 1993).

Types of Marriage

There are two major types of marriage: **monogamy** and **polygamy.** In monogamy, a husband and wife are wed only to each other. But let us not confuse monogamy, which is a form of matrimony, with sexual exclusivity. People who are monogamously wedded often do have extramarital affairs, as we shall see, but they are considered to be married to only one person at a time. In polygamy, a person has more than one spouse and is permitted sexual access to each of them.

Polygyny is by far the most prevalent form of polygamy among the world's preliterate societies (Ford & Beach, 1951; Frayser, 1985). **Polyandry** is practiced only rarely (see Chapter 1). In polygynous societies, men are permitted to have multiple wives if they can

Monogamy
Marriage to one person.

Polygamy
Simultaneous marriage to more than one person.

Polygyny
A form of marriage in which a man is married to more than one woman at the same time.

Polyandry

A form of marriage in which a woman is married to more than one man at the same time.

support them; more rarely, a man will have one wife and one or more concubines. The man's first wife typically has higher status than the others. Economic factors and the availability of prospective mates usually limit the opportunities for men to wed more than one woman at a time, however. In many cases, only wealthy men can afford to support multiple wives and the children of these unions. In addition, few if any societies have enough women to allow most men to have two or more wives (Ember & Ember, 1990). For these reasons, even in societies that prefer polygyny, fewer than half of the men at any given time actually have multiple mates (Ford & Beach, 1951).

Whom Do We Marry: Are Marriages Made in Heaven or in the Neighborhood?

Most preliterate societies regulate the selection of spouses in some way. The universal incest taboo proscribes matings between close relatives. Societal rules and customs also determine which persons are desirable mates and which are not.

In Western cultures, mate selection is presumably free. Parents today seldom arrange marriages, although they may still encourage their child to date that wonderful son or daughter of the solid churchgoing couple who live down the street. Nevertheless, factors such as race, social class, and religion often determine the categories of persons within which we may seek mates (Laumann et al., 1994). People in our culture tend to marry others from the same geographical area and social class. Since neighborhoods are often made up of people from a similar social class, storybook marriages like Cinderella's are the exception to the rule.

Because we make choices, we tend to marry people who attract us. These people are usually similar to us in physical attractiveness and attitudes, even in minute details. We are more often than not similar to our mates in characteristics such as height, weight, personality traits, and intelligence (Buss, 1994; Lesnik-Oberstein & Cohen, 1984; Schafer & Keith, 1990). Those we marry also seem likely to meet our material, sexual, and psychological needs.

Homogamy

The practice of marrying people who are similar in social background and standing. (From Greek roots meaning "same" [*homos*] and "marriage" [*gamos*].)

The concept of "like marrying like" is termed **homogamy.** We usually marry people of the same racial/ethnic background, educational level, and religion. Interracial marriages account for fewer than 1 in every 200 marriages (U.S. Bureau of the Census, 1991). Moreover, more than 9 of 10 marriages are between people of the same religion. Marriages between individuals who are alike may stand a better chance of survival, since the partners are more likely to share their values and attitudes (Michael et al., 1994). Dissimilar couples, however, can work to overcome the barriers that divide them by developing shared interests and mutual respect for their differences.

We also tend to follow *age homogamy* (Michael et al., 1994). Age homogamy—the selection of a partner who falls in one's own age range—may reflect the tendency to marry early in adulthood. Persons who marry late or who remarry tend not to select partners so close in age. Bridegrooms tend to be two to five years older than their wives, on the average, in European, North American, and South American countries (Buss, 1994).

Mating gradient

The tendency for women to "marry up" (in social or economic status) and for men to "marry down."

Some marriages also show a **mating gradient.** The stereotype has been that an economically established older man would take an attractive, younger woman as his wife. But by and large, with boring predictability, we are attracted to and marry the boy or girl (almost) next door. Most marriages seem to be made not in heaven, but in the neighborhood.

Who Has His Head in the Clouds? (Hint: The Question Is *Not* Phrased in Sexist Language)
When it comes to picking a mate, men tend to be the romantics; women, the pragmatists. Men are more likely to believe that each person has one true love whom they are destined to find (Peplau & Gordon, 1985). Men are more likely to believe in love at first sight. Women, on the other hand, are more likely to value financial security as much as passion. Women are more likely to believe that they could form a loving relationship with many individuals. Women are also less likely to believe that love conquers all—especially economic problems.

It is true that men are more romantic than women—when we define being romantic as believing in love at first sight or that there is one person who is right for oneself. (Who is more "romantic" if we define romantic to mean that one wishes to confine sexual activity to a romantic relationship?) ■

~ *Reflections* ~

■ Agree or disagree with the following statement, and support your answer: There is a right person for everyone, and they are destined to meet.

■ Agree or disagree with the following statement, and support your answer: Marriage is an old-fashioned, outdated lifestyle that has become irrelevant for today's sophisticated young people.

■ Agree or disagree with the following statement, and support your answer: Children are best reared by married parents.

Marital Sexuality

Patterns of marital sexuality vary across cultures, yet anthropologists have noted some common threads (Ember & Ember, 1990). Privacy for sexual relations is valued in almost all cultures. Most cultures also place restrictions on coitus during menstruation, during at least some stages of pregnancy, and for a time after childbirth.

Until the sexual revolution of the 1960s and 1970s, Western culture could be characterized as sexually restrictive, even toward marital sex. Hunt noted that "Western civilization has long had the rare distinction of contaminating and restricting the sexual pleasure of married couples more severely than almost any other" (1974, p. 175).

The Sexual Revolution Hits Home

We usually think of the sexual revolution in terms of the changes in sexual behaviors and attitudes that occurred among young, unmarried people. It also ushered in profound changes in marital sexuality, however. Compared to Kinsey's "prerevolution" samples from the late 1930s and 1940s, married couples today engage in coitus more frequently, with greater variety, and for longer durations of time. They report higher levels of sexual satisfaction.

The sexual revolution also helped dislodge traditional male dominance in sexual behavior. In essence, male dominance is the view that sexual pleasure is meant for men but not women and that it is the duty of women to satisfy their husbands' sexual needs and serve as passive "receptacles." Assumptions of male dominance are found even in the writing of the (for his time) liberated Kinsey. Nowhere are they more evident than in his (and his colleagues') comment that men, who have the biological capacity to ejaculate a few moments after entry, need not feel bound to "wait" for women to reach orgasm (Kinsey et al., 1948, p. 580).

People caught up in social revolutions may not perceive themselves as revolutionaries. They may not even be aware that a "revolution" is taking place. The sexual revolution was not heralded by parades or massive demonstrations. There was no "storming of the Bastille" to proclaim sexual freedom. Organizations promoting "free love" did not attract large followings. Even the most famous slogan of the sexual revolution—"Make love, not war"— was more an indictment of the Vietnam War than a call for free love. Moreover, social movements are begun by a few but are spread by the perception that they define popular trends. Married people, as well as singles, thus made sexual decisions not only on the basis of their religious teachings and personal values, but also on their perceptions of the norm.

Liberalizing trends were communicated through popular media. Hundreds if not thousands of books and magazines with sexual content crammed bookstore shelves and supermarket display cases. During Kinsey's day, books like Henry Miller's *Tropic of Cancer* and

D. H. Lawrence's *Lady Chatterley's Lover* were censored in the United States. Now they are readily available but so tame when compared to today's explicit books and magazines that they barely raise an eyebrow. Similarly, since the late 1960s pornographic films have been shown in adult theaters across the nation. In many places the audiences include middle-class couples and college students, not just "dirty old men." The VCR has brought sexually explicit films into middle-class suburban homes.

Scientific findings were also liberalizing influences. Kinsey's and Masters and Johnson's findings that normal women were capable not only of orgasm but also of multiple orgasms punctured traditional beliefs that sexual gratification was the birthright of men alone. TV shows, films, and radio talk shows began to portray women as sexual initiators who enjoy sex. All of these influences have encouraged U.S. women to forgo the traditional passive approach to sexuality.

The affluence of the post–World War II years also encouraged more young people to pursue a college education and live away from home. College liberates not only through exposure to great books and scientific knowledge, but also through challenging students' attitudes by bright, knowledgeable peers from different backgrounds. Prejudice and myth are often analyzed and discarded.

Americans have also become more mobile. Jobs carry young people thousands of miles from home. Their sexual attitudes are influenced by new acquaintances from many parts of the country and from people from other nations, not just by a few people from "the neighborhood."

The development of effective contraceptives also separated sex from reproduction. Motives for sexual pleasure became more open. The term *recreational sex* came into play. All these liberalizing forces have led to changes in the frequency of marital sex and in techniques of foreplay and coitus since Kinsey's day.

Changes in Duration and Techniques of Foreplay   Married women in Kinsey's sample reported an average (median) length of foreplay of about 12 minutes. This figure rose to nearly 15 minutes among the wives in the *Playboy* survey (Hunt, 1974). Kinsey found that men at lower educational levels engaged in briefer periods of foreplay, generally lasting but a minute or two before penetration. The length of foreplay rose to 5-to-15 minutes among college-educated men. In a dramatic shift in sophistication since Kinsey's day, Hunt found that the typical duration of foreplay in the 1970s was 15 minutes for college-educated and noncollege males alike. Foreplay was relatively longer in duration among younger married couples than their elders, however.

Marital foreplay has also become more varied since Kinsey's day. Couples in more recent surveys report using a wider variety of foreplay techniques, including oral stimulation of the breasts and oral–genital contact (Blumstein & Schwartz, 1983; Hunt, 1974).

Changes in Frequency of Marital Coitus   How frequently do married couples engage in coitus? A comparison of the reports from Kinsey's couples and the *Playboy* survey couples (see Table 14.2) shows increases in coital frequency at every age level. However, keep in mind that 80% of those contacted by the *Playboy* survey refused to participate. Thus the figures in the table may represent a strong volunteer bias. Because volunteers tend to be more open about their sexuality than people who refuse to divulge information about sex, this bias would tend to inflate the statistical results (Laumann et al., 1994).

The data reported by the NHSLS study do not allow a direct comparison with the Kinsey and *Playboy* figures. As shown in Table 14.3, however, the overwhelming majority of married men and women in the United States now report engaging in sexual relations either a few times per month or two to three times a week (Laumann et al., 1994). The average is seven times a month (Michael et al., 1994, p. 136). These figures are somewhat more in keeping with Kinsey's than with the *Playboy* survey's, which may cast doubt on the *Playboy* survey's statistics.

Kinsey and the University of Chicago group (who conducted the NHSLS study) did not find strong links between coital frequency and educational level. The NHSLS study,

TABLE 14.2 Median weekly frequency of marital coitus, male and female estimates combined (Kinsey and *Playboy* surveys)

KINSEY (1948, 1953)		PLAYBOY (1974)	
Age	Frequency	Age	Frequency
16–25	2.45	18–24	3.25
26–35	1.95	25–34	2.55
36–45	1.40	35–44	2.00
46–55	0.85	45–54	1.00
55–60	0.50	55 and over	1.00

Source: Hunt, M. (1974). *Sexual Behavior in the 1970's.* New York: Dell Books, p. 191.

like the Kinsey surveys, found that the frequency of sexual relations declined with age, but not as dramatically. At the ages of 50–59, for example, people reported an average of four to five times per month. Regardless of a couple's age, sexual frequency also appears to decline with years of marriage (Blumstein & Schwartz, 1990).

Changes in Techniques and Duration of Coitus

In coitus, as in foreplay, the marital bed since Kinsey's day has become a stage on which the players act more varied roles. Today's couples use greater variety in coital positions.

Kinsey's study participants mainly limited coitus to the male-superior position. As many as 70% of Kinsey's males used the male-superior position exclusively (Kinsey et al., 1948). Perhaps three couples in ten used the female-superior position frequently. One in four or five used the lateral-entry position frequently, and about one in ten, the rear-entry position. Younger and more highly educated men showed greater variety, however. Hunt (1974), by comparison, found that three quarters of the married couples in the *Playboy* survey used the female-superior position at least occasionally. More than half had used the lateral-entry position, and about four in ten had used the rear-entry position.

TABLE 14.3 Frequency of marital sexual relations during the past year, according to NHSLS study

Frequency of Sexual Relations	Men (%)	Women (%)
Not at all	1.3	3.0
A few times per year	12.8	11.9
A few times per month	42.5	46.5
Two to three times a week	36.1	31.9
Four or more times a week	7.3	6.6

Source: Adapted from Laumann, E. O., Gagnon, J. H., Michael, R. T., & Michaels, S. (1994). *The Social Organization of Sexuality: Sexual Practices in the United States.* Chicago: University of Chicago Press, Table 3.4, pp. 88–89.

An often overlooked but important difference between Kinsey's and current samples involves the length of intercourse. In Kinsey's time it was widely believed that the "virile" man ejaculated rapidly during intercourse. Kinsey estimated that most men reached orgasm within 2 minutes after penetration, many within 10 or 20 seconds. Kinsey recognized that women usually took longer to reach orgasm through coitus, and that some clinicians were already asserting that a man's ejaculation was "premature" unless he delayed it until "the female (was) ready to reach orgasm" (1948, p. 580)

Even today's less-educated couples appear to be more sophisticated than Kinsey's in their recognition of the need for sexual variety and their focus on exchanging sexual pleasure rather than rapidly reaching orgasm (Michael et al., 1994). According to the NHSLS study, the "duration of the last sexual event" of three out of four married couples was 15 minutes to an hour. Eight percent to 9% of couples exceeded an hour (Michael et al., 1994). (About one unmarried, noncohabiting couple in three made love for an hour or more, suggesting that novelty and youth have their motivational aspects.)

Sexual Satisfaction

One index by which researchers measure sexual satisfaction is orgasmic consistency. Men tend to reach orgasm more consistently than women do. After 15 years of marriage, 45% of the wives in Kinsey's study reported reaching orgasm 90% to 100% of the time. After 15 years of marriage, 12% of the wives in Kinsey's study had not experienced orgasm.

Orgasmic consistency now seems higher than in Kinsey's day. The NHSLS study found that more than 90% of the men and about 70% of women reported reaching orgasm "always" or "usually" with their primary partner during the 12 months prior to the survey (Laumann et al., 1994; Michael et al., 1994) (see Table 14.4). Three of four men (75%) and nearly three women in ten (28.6%) reported reaching orgasm on every occasion (not shown in Table 14.4). Only 2% of the married women reported never reaching orgasm with their husbands during the past year (not shown).

Women in their 40s were somewhat more likely to reach orgasm consistently than younger and older women. Perhaps women in their 40s have had more time to get in touch with their sexuality and may be more secure in their relationships as compared with younger women. The falloff for women and men in their 50s may be biologically related. The nature of the relationship is a factor for women. Married women were most likely to reach orgasm consistently, followed by cohabiting, and then noncohabiting women. Security in the relationship apparently promotes orgasmic consistency. There do not seem to be notable racial or ethnic differences.

Orgasm is not the only criterion for measuring pleasure or satisfaction in marital sex. The NHSLS study asked participants whether they had been extremely physically satisfied

Sexual Satisfaction. Marital closeness is linked to sexual satisfaction. Perhaps sexual pleasure contributes to marital closeness, or perhaps closeness helps couples achieve greater sexual satisfaction.

TABLE 14.4 Sociocultural factors and sexual satisfaction in primary relationship during past year

Sociocultural Characteristics	Always or Usually Had an Orgasm with Partner		Has Been Extremely Physically Satisfied with Partner		Has Been Extremely Emotionally Satisfied with Partner	
	Men (%)	Women (%)	Men (%)	Women (%)	Men (%)	Women (%)
Age						
18–24	92	61	44	44	41	39
25–29	94	71	50	39	46	40
30–39	97	70	45	41	39	38
40–49	97	78	44	42	38	42
50–59	91	73	53	32	52	32
Marital Status						
Noncohabiting	94	62	39	40	32	31
Cohabiting	95	68	44	46	35	44
Married	95	75	52	41	49	42
*Race/Ethnicity**						
White (non-Hispanic)	96	70	47	40	43	38
African American	90	72	43	44	43	38
Hispanic American	96	68	51	39	43	39

*The numbers of Asian Americans and Native Americans were too small to report reliable statistics.

Source: Combined from Laumann, E. O., Gagnon, J. H., Michael, R. T., & Michaels, S. (1994). *The Social Organization of Sexuality: Sexual Practices in the United States.* Chicago: University of Chicago Press, Table 3.7, pp. 116–117, and Michael, R. T., Gagnon, J. H., Laumann, E. O., & Kolata, G. (1994). *Sex in America: A Definitive Survey.* Boston: Little, Brown, Table 9, pp. 128–129.

with their primary partners during the past year. It is apparent, from Table 14.4, that men's and women's general physical satisfaction is comparable—about 47% and 41%, respectively. Orgasm, then, is not a guarantee of satisfaction. And lack of orgasm is not necessarily a sign of dissatisfaction.

The emotional satisfaction in a marital relationship is also linked to sexual satisfaction. Table 14.4 shows that about 40% of men and women report being extremely emotionally satisfied with their primary partners. Closer relationships are connected with more consistent orgasm.

Other researchers have found that wives who talk openly to their husbands about their sexual feelings and needs report higher levels of sexual satisfaction (Banmen & Vogel, 1985; Tavris & Sadd, 1977). Women respondents to the *Redbook* survey who took an active role during sex were more satisfied with their sex lives than those who assumed the traditional passive female role (Tavris & Sadd, 1977).

~ *Reflections* ~

Agree or disagree with the following statement, and support your answer: Sexual pleasure is meant for men but not women, and it is the duty of women to satisfy their husbands' sexual needs.

- What has been the role of contraceptives as a liberating force in the expression of human sexuality?
- Agree or disagree with the following statement, and support your answer: Marital sex tends to become routine, repetitious, and unexciting.

Extramarital Sex

Extramarital sex (or "affairs") is usually conducted without the spouse's knowledge or approval. Such clandestine affairs are referred to as **conventional adultery,** infidelity, or simply "cheating." Some extramarital affairs are "one-night stands." Others persist for years.

In **consensual adultery,** extramarital relationships are conducted openly with the knowledge and consent of the partner and sometimes even with the partner's participation, as in **swinging.**

Some people engage in extramarital sex for variety. Some have affairs to break the routine of a confining marriage. Others enter affairs for reasons similar to the nonsexual reasons adolescents often have for coitus: as a way of expressing hostility toward a spouse or retaliating for injustice. Husbands and wives who engage in affairs often report that they are not satisfied with, or fulfilled by, their marital relationships.

Sometimes the sexual motive is less pressing than the desire for emotional closeness. In one study, some women who reported affairs said they had been seeking someone whom they could "talk" to or "communicate" with (Atwater, 1982). Curiosity and desire for personal growth were more prominent motives for affairs than marital dissatisfaction among Atwater's (1982) respondents. Middle-aged people may have affairs to boost their self-esteem or prove that they are still attractive.

Men (whether single, married, or cohabiting) are generally more approving of extramarital affairs than are women (Glass & Wright, 1992). Men who have had affairs are more likely to cite a need for sexual excitement as a justification than women are—75% versus 55% (Glass & Wright, 1992). Women are less accepting of sex without emotional involvement (Townsend, 1995). Women are more likely to cite "falling in love" as a justification for their affairs than do men: 77% versus 43%. These data support the widely held view that "men separate sex and love; women appear to believe that love and sex go together and that falling in love justifies sexual involvement" (Glass & Wright, 1992, p. 361).

Patterns of Extramarital Sex

How many people "cheat" on their spouses? Viewers of TV talk shows may get the impression that everyone cheats, but surveys paint a different picture. In a study conducted between 1988 and 1992 by the respected National Opinion Research Center, 21% of the husbands and 12% of the wives acknowledged marital infidelity ("Cheating," 1993). More than 90% of the married women and 75% of the married men in the NHSLS study reported remaining loyal to their spouses (Laumann et al., 1994). The vast majority of those who were cohabiting also reported that they were loyal to their partners while they were living together (Laumann et al., 1994).

Having presented the percentages of reported extramarital sex, let us note one compelling limitation to these data. These reports cannot be verified. People may be reluctant to reveal they have "cheated" on their spouses even when they are assured of anonymity. There is likely to be an overall tendency to underreport the incidence of extramarital sex.

Attitudes Toward Extramarital Sex

The sexual revolution does not seem to have changed attitudes toward extramarital sex. Most people in the United States disapprove of it. Eighty percent to 98% of the *Playboy* sample reported that they would object to their mates' engaging in affairs (Hunt, 1974). Moreover, only 20% of those in the sample who reported having had affairs said that their

Extramarital sex
Sexual relations between a married person and someone other than his or her spouse.

Conventional adultery
Extramarital sex that is kept clandestine (hidden) from one's spouse.

Consensual adultery
Extramarital sex that is engaged in openly with the knowledge and consent of one's spouse.

Swinging
A form of consensual adultery in which both spouses share extramarital sexual experiences. Also referred to as *mate-swapping.*

mates were aware of them. Most married couples espouse the value of monogamy as the cornerstone of their marital relationship (Blumstein & Schwartz, 1990).

Truth **OR** Fiction?

REVISITED

It is not true that most of today's sophisticated young people see nothing wrong with an occasional extramarital fling. The sexual revolution never extended itself to extramarital affairs—at least among the majority of married people. ■

Cross-Cultural Perspectives on Extramarital Sex   Most preliterate societies prohibit extramarital relationships for one or both spouses (Frayser, 1985). In cultures in which extramarital sex is permitted, husbands are typically allowed greater sexual freedom than wives. Frayser could find no societies that allowed extramarital sex for wives but not husbands.

Slightly more than half (54%) of the preliterate societies around the world permit men to have extramarital partners (Ember & Ember, 1990). Only 11% allow women the same opportunity. In some societies extramarital affairs are formalized within rules of social conduct. Among the Aleut people of Alaska's Aleutian Islands, for example, men may offer visitors the opportunity to sleep with their wives as a gesture of hospitality. Among the Chukchee of Siberia, who often travel long distances from their homes, a married man is allowed to engage in sexual activity with his host's wife. The understanding is that he would reciprocate when the host visited him (Ford & Beach, 1951).

Kinship ties often determine sexual access to extramarital partners (Frayser, 1985). Among the people of the Marshall Islands in the Pacific, a woman is allowed to have a sexual relationship with her sister's husband. Among the Native American Comanches, a man is permitted to have intercourse with his brother's wife, if his brother consents. Customs sometimes limit extramarital intercourse to ceremonial occasions. The Fijians of Oceania, for example, engage in extramarital relationships only following the return of their men from warfare. In Western society, Mardi Gras and some out-of-town conventions represent ceremonial occasions for extramarital liaisons that might not be tolerated otherwise.

Effects of Extramarital Sex

The discovery of infidelity can evoke a range of emotional responses. The spouse may be filled with anger, jealousy, even shame. Feelings of inadequacy and doubts about one's attractiveness and desirability may surface. Infidelity may be seen by the betrayed spouse as a serious breach of trust and intimacy. Marriages that are not terminated in the wake of the disclosure may survive in a damaged condition (Charny & Parnass, 1995).

The harm an affair does to a marriage may reflect the meaning of the affair to the individual and his or her spouse. If a person has an affair because the marriage is deeply troubled, the affair may be one more factor that speeds its dissolution. The effects on the marriage may depend on the nature of the affair. It may be easier to understand that a spouse has fallen prey to an isolated, unplanned encounter than to accept an extended affair (Charny & Parnass, 1995). In some cases the discovery of infidelity stimulates the couple to work to improve their relationship. If the extramarital activity continues, however, it may undermine the couple's efforts to restore their relationship.

Swinging

Comarital sex
Swinging; mate-swapping.

Swinging—also called "mate-swapping" or **comarital sex**—is a form of consensual adultery in which both partners openly share sexual experiences with other people. Some swingers argue that swinging can help improve a marriage by reducing sexual boredom and increasing togetherness. This view draws support from studies that show that swinging leads to increased rates of coitus *between* the spouses and is associated with higher levels of marital satisfaction (Gilmartin, 1975; Wheeler & Kilmann, 1983). But these studies were limited to swinging couples who had made an adjustment to swinging. We do not know about the much larger numbers of couples who dropped out from swinging. Another study of 56 swinging couples showed no consistent relationship between swinging and marital satisfaction. Swinging was as likely to disrupt a marital relationship as to improve it (Levitt, 1988).

Most swingers seek to avoid emotional entanglements with their swinging partners, but they may fail to separate their emotions from their sexual activity. Emotional intimacy between swinging partners can be even more threatening to the swingers' primary relationships than sexual intimacy. For various reasons, most swinging couples drop out after a short period of experimentation.

Swingers tend to be White, fairly affluent, well-educated, and to have but nominal religious affiliations (Jenks, 1985). Solid statistics on the prevalence of swinging are lacking, however. Observers of sexual trends suggest that swinging, like other nontraditional forms of matrimony, seems to have largely vanished from the social scene (Havemann & Lehtinen, 1990). Concern over AIDS, coupled with the more conservative social climate of recent years, seems to have restricted swinging to a few devotees. Even during the heyday of the sexual revolution, only 2% of married males and fewer than 2% of married females in the *Playboy* survey had "swung," and many of these individuals had tried it just once (Hunt, 1974).

~ *Reflections* ~

▪ Why do you think that even the majority of "sexually liberated" people draw the line at extramarital sex?

▪ Agree or disagree with the following statement, and support your answer: Extramarital sex is more exciting and satisfying than marital sex.

▪ How would you account for gender differences in the incidence of extramarital sex?

Divorce

Nearly half of the marriages in the United States end in divorce (Davies & Cummings, 1994; Laumann et al., 1994). The divorce rate in the United States rose steadily through much of the twentieth century (see Figure 14.3) before leveling off in the 1980s. About one quarter (26%) of children below the age of 18 live in single-parent households (Barringer, 1991). Divorced women outnumber divorced men, in part because men are more likely to remarry following divorce (Saluter, 1992).

The relaxation of legal restrictions on divorce, especially the introduction of the so-called no-fault divorce, has made divorces easier to obtain. Until the mid-1960s, adultery

Figure 14.3. Divorce Rates in the United States. The divorce rate in the United States rose steadily through much of the twentieth century before leveling off in the 1980s.

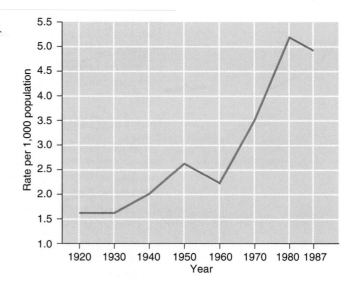

was the only legal grounds for divorce in New York State. Other states were equally strict. But now no-fault divorce laws have been enacted in nearly every state, allowing a divorce to be granted without a finding of marital misconduct. The increased economic independence of women has also contributed to the rising divorce rate. More women today have the economic means of breaking away from a troubled marriage. Today, more people consider marriage an alterable condition than in prior generations. People today hold higher expectations of marriage than did their parents or grandparents. They expect marriage to be personally fulfilling as well as meet the traditional expectation of marriage as an institution for rearing children. Many demand the right to be happy in marriage. The most common reasons given for a divorce today are problems in communication and a lack of understanding. Years ago it was more likely to be lack of financial support.

The Cost of Divorce

Divorce is often associated with financial and emotional problems. When a household splits, the resources often cannot maintain the earlier standard of living for each partner. A woman who has not pursued a career may struggle to compete with younger, more experienced workers. Divorced mothers often face the combined stress of the sole responsibility for rearing their children (women receive custody in the majority of divorce cases) and the need to increase their incomes to make ends meet. Not surprisingly, single mothers (including divorced and never-married mothers) are more likely to report depression and less satisfaction with life than either single fathers or married parents (Burden, 1986). Divorced fathers may also find it difficult to pay alimony and child support while attempting to establish a new lifestyle.

Divorce may also prompt feelings of failure as a spouse and parent, loneliness and uncertainty about the future, and depression. Married people appear to be better able to cope with the stresses and strains of life, perhaps because they can rely on each other for emotional support. Divorced and separated people have the highest rates of physical and men-

Who Pays for Divorce? Divorce often compounds financial and emotional problems. In the majority of cases, divorced mothers who received custody of their children often face the combined stress of the sole responsibility for rearing the children and the need to increase their incomes to make ends meet.

tal illness in the population (Bloom et al., 1978; Nevid et al., 1997). Divorced people also have higher rates of suicide than married people (Trovato, 1986). On the other hand, divorce may be a time of personal growth and renewal. It can provide an opportunity for people to take stock of themselves and establish a new, more rewarding life for themselves.

Children also suffer in a divorce. On the other hand, marital conflict or fighting is connected with the same kinds of problems (Amato & Keith, 1991; Davies & Cummings, 1994). Marital relations spill over into parent–child relations and affect children's behavior (Erel & Burman, 1995). Boys tend to show greater problems in adjusting to conflict or divorce, such as conduct problems at school and increased anxiety and dependence (Grych & Fincham, 1993; Holden & Ritchie, 1991).

Wallerstein and Blakeslee (1989) reported that about four out of ten children in their case studies showed problems such as anxiety, academic underachievement, decreased self-worth, and anger ten years after the divorce. A "sleeper effect" was also described. Apparently well-adjusted children of divorce developed problems in early adulthood, especially difficulties trusting that their partners in intimate relationships would make lasting commitments. Researchers attribute children's problems following divorce not only to the divorce itself but also to a subsequent decline in the quality of parenting. Children's adjustment is enhanced when parents maintain their parenting responsibilities and set aside their differences long enough to agree upon child-rearing practices (Wallerstein & Blakeslee, 1989). Children of divorce also benefit when divorced parents encourage each other to continue to play important roles in their children's lives and avoid saying negative things about each other in their children's presence.

Despite the difficulties in adjusting to a divorce, most divorced people eventually bounce back. The majority remarry. Among older people, divorced men are more likely than divorced women to remarry—in part because men usually die earlier than women (and so fewer prospective husbands are available), in part because older men tend to remarry younger women. The proportion of divorced women who remarry appears to be declining. Census data suggest that only about three of ten women over the age of 40 who got divorced in the 1980s will eventually remarry (Bumpass et al., 1988). (A similar situation exists among people who are widowed. Only about one in four widows, as compared to about one in two widowers, eventually remarry [Lown & Dolan, 1988].)

Remarriages are even more likely than first marriages to end in divorce (Lown & Dolan, 1988). One reason is the selection factor. That is, divorced people are a subgroup of people who get married who are relatively less inclined than others to persist in a troubled marriage. Many divorced people who remarry are also encumbered with alimony and child-support payments that strain their new marriages. Many bring children from their earlier marriages to their new ones.

By the beginning of the next century, the stepfamily may be the most common family unit in the United States (CBS News, 1991). Six of ten stepfamilies eventually disband, often under the weight of the financial and emotional pressures of coping with the demands of a reconstituted family (CBS News, 1991). However, among remarriages that survive, the level of personal happiness in spouses is as high as among spouses in first marriages and much higher than the level among divorced people (Weingarten, 1985).

What of the long-term consequences of divorce? In one study, only one person in five reported that divorce had been a mistake five years after the fact (Wallerstein & Kelly, 1980). Most felt that the divorce had enhanced their lives. Most, however, also reported that they had underestimated the emotional pain they would encounter.

～ *Reflections* ～

■ Agree or disagree with the following statement, and support your answer: Falling out of love is sufficient reason for a divorce.

■ Do you think that parents should remain together "for the sake of the children," regardless of the nature of the marital relationship? Explain.

■ Do most people from your sociocultural background approve or disapprove of divorce as a remedy for an unhappy marriage? Do you agree with their beliefs? Why, or why not?

Alternative Forms of Marriage

Marriages are generally based on the expectation of sexual exclusivity. Alternative or non-traditional marital styles, however, such as open marriages and group marriages, permit intimate relationships with people outside the marriage. Such alternative lifestyles attracted a flurry of attention during the heyday of the sexual revolution in the 1970s, but were even then more often talked about than practiced (Havemann & Lehtinen, 1990). Today, they find still fewer adherents.

Open Marriage

Open marriage
A marriage that is characterized by the personal privacy of the spouses and the agreed-upon liberty of each spouse to form intimate relationships, which may include sexually intimate relationships, with people other than the spouse.

Open marriage is based on the view that people's needs for intimacy are unlikely to be gratified through one relationship. Proponents argue that the core marriage can be enhanced if the partners have the opportunity to develop emotionally intimate relationships with others (O'Neill & O'Neill, 1972).

The prevalence of open marriages, like that of swinging, remains unknown. Nor is there much data upon which to base conclusions about the success of open marriages. Rubin found no meaningful differences in marital adjustment between 130 couples with sexually open marriages and 130 couples who maintained sexual exclusivity. Still another study found no differences in the longevity of sexually open and sexually exclusive marriages over a five-year period (Rubin & Adams, 1986).

Group Marriage

Group marriage
A social arrangement in which three or more people share an intimate relationship. Group marriages are illegal in the United States.

Group marriage also attracted some adherents during the sexual revolution of the 1960s and 1970s. In a group marriage, three or more people share an intimate relationship, although they are not legally married. Each member feels committed or married to at least two others. The major motive for group marriage is extension of intimacy beyond one spouse in order to increase personal fulfillment (Constantine & Constantine, 1973). Members of eight out of nine group marriages surveyed by the Constantines also admitted interest in a variety of sexual partners, however.

Group marriages differ from swinging in that participants share inmost thoughts and feelings and expect their bonds to be permanent. Group marriages, therefore, are not perceived merely as vehicles for legitimizing mate-swapping. Adherents expect children to profit by observing several adult role models and by escaping the "smothering" possessiveness of exclusive parent–child relationships.

Although they provide sexual variety, group marriages require adjustment to at least two other people—not just one. Moreover, legal and social problems can arise with respect to issues such as paternity and inheritance. Managing money may also be stressful, with arguments arising over joint accounts and who can spend how much for what. Sexual jealousies often arise as well. Given these problems, it is not surprising that group marriages are rare and have a high failure rate.

Group marriages are not unique to our culture. Although rare, other cultures have developed analogous marital customs (Werner & Cohen, 1990). Among the Chukchee people of Siberia, for example, group marriages sometimes involved as many as 10 couples. The men in such marriages, who considered themselves "companions-in-wives," had sexual rights to each wife.

All in all, the ideal of the traditional marriage remains strong in our culture. In a survey of 500 college students, only 13% of the males and a mere 3% of the females acknowledged willingness to participate in swinging (Billingham & Sack, 1986). Fewer still—5% of the males and 1% of the females—were willing to enter into group marriage. Men are somewhat more likely than women to participate or express an interest in lifestyles that permit greater sexual freedom and, perhaps, less personal responsibility (Knox, 1988). (Why is the third author not surprised?) But even most of those who have tried alternative lifestyles such as cohabitation, open marriage, or group marriage enter into traditional marriages at some time.

All in all, most adults in the United States still seem to feel about marriage the way Winston Churchill felt about democracy: It's flawed, laden with problems, and frustrating—but preferable to the alternatives.

~ *Reflections* ~

Can you imagine yourself in an open marriage or a group marriage? Why, or why not?

Sex in the Later Years

Which is the fastest growing segment of the U.S. population? People age 65 and above. More than 30 million people in the United States are senior citizens, and their number is growing fast. This "graying" of the United States may have a profound effect on the views we hold of older people, especially concerning their sexuality. Many people in our culture see sexual activity as appropriate only for the young (Reiss, 1988). This belief falls within a constellation of unfounded cultural myths about sexuality among older people, which includes the notions that older people are sexless, older people with sexual urges are abnormal, and older men with sexual interests are "dirty old men."

Researchers find that sexual daydreaming, sex drive, and sexual activity tend to decline with age, whereas negative sexual attitudes tend to increase (Purifoy et al., 1992). However, research does not support the belief that people lose their sexuality as they age. Nearly all (95%) of the older people in one sample reported that they liked sex, and 75% reported that orgasm was essential to their sexual fulfillment (Starr & Weiner, 1981). People who are exposed to cultural views that sex among older people is deviant may renounce sex as they age, however. Those who remain sexually active may be bothered by guilt (Reiss, 1988).

Sexual activity among older people, as among other groups, is influenced not only by physical structures and changes, but by psychological well-being, feelings of intimacy (Shaw, 1994), and cultural expectations.

Physical Changes

Although many older people retain the capacity to respond sexually, physical changes do occur as the years pass (see Table 14.5). If we are aware of them, we will not view them as abnormal or find ourselves unprepared to cope with them. Many potential problems can be averted by changing our expectations or making some changes to accommodate the aging process.

Changes in the Female   Many of the physical changes in women stem from decline in the production of estrogen around the time of menopause. The vaginal walls lose much elasticity and the thick, corrugated texture of the childbearing years. They grow paler and thinner. Thus, coitus may become irritating. The thinning of the walls may also place greater pressure against the bladder and urethra during coitus, leading in some cases to symptoms of urinary urgency and burning urination. The condition, similar to honeymoon cystitis, may persist for days.

The vagina also shrinks in size. The labia majora lose much of their fatty deposits and become thin. The introitus becomes relatively constricted, and penile entry may become somewhat difficult. This "problem" has a positive aspect: increased friction between the penis and vaginal walls may heighten sexual sensations. The body of the uterus decreases in size after menopause and no longer becomes so congested during sexual arousal. Following menopause, women also produce less vaginal lubrication, and the lubrication that

TABLE 14.5 Changes in sexual arousal often associated with aging

Changes in the Female	Changes in the Male
Reduced myotonia (muscle tension)	Longer time to erection and orgasm
Reduced vaginal lubrication	Need for more direct stimulation for erection and orgasm
Reduced elasticity of the vaginal walls	Less semen emitted during ejaculation
Smaller increases in breast size during sexual arousal	Erections may be less firm
Reduced intensity of muscle spasms at orgasm	Testicles may not elevate as high into scrotum
	Less intense orgasmic contractions
	Lessened feeling of a need to ejaculate during sex
	Longer refractory period

Source: Copyright © 1990 by The Kinsey Institute for Research in Sex, Gender, and Reproduction. From THE KINSEY INSTITUTE NEW REPORT ON SEX. Reprinted with permission from St. Martin's Press, New York, NY.

is produced may take minutes, not seconds, to appear. Lack of adequate lubrication is also a major reason for painful coitus.

Many of these changes may be slowed or reversed through estrogen-replacement therapy (see Chapter 3). Natural lubrication may also be increased through more elaborate foreplay. The need for more foreplay may encourage the man to become a more considerate lover. (He too will likely need more time to become aroused.) An artificial lubricant may also ease problems posed by difficult entry or painful thrusting.

Women's breasts show smaller increases in size with sexual arousal as they age, but the nipples still become erect. Because the muscle tone of the urethra and anal sphincters

Sexuality and Aging. Despite stereotypes that stigmatize older people who are sexually active as abnormal or deviant, it is normal for older people to have sexual urges and maintain an active sex life.

decreases, the spasms of orgasm become less powerful and fewer in number. Thus orgasms may feel less intense. The uterine contractions that occur during orgasm may become discouragingly painful for some postmenopausal women. Despite these changes, women can retain their ability to achieve orgasm well into their advanced years. The subjective experience of orgasm also remains highly satisfying, despite the lessened intensity of muscular contractions.

T r u t h OR *Fiction?*

R E V I S I T E D

It is not true that only a few women can reach orgasm after the age of 70. Actually, healthy women can retain the capacity for orgasm well into their advanced years. ■

Changes in the Male   Age-related changes tend to occur more gradually in men than in women and are not clearly connected with any one biological event, as they are with menopause in the woman. Male adolescents may achieve erection in a matter of seconds through sexual fantasy alone. After about age 50, men take progressively longer to achieve erection. Erections become less firm, perhaps because of lowered testosterone production. Older men may require minutes of direct stimulation of the penis to achieve an erection. Couples can adjust to these changes by extending the length and variety of foreplay.

Most men remain capable of erection throughout their lives. Erectile dysfunction is not inevitable with aging. Men generally require more time to reach orgasm as they age, however, which may also reflect lowered testosterone production. In the eyes of their sex partners, however, delayed ejaculation may make them better lovers.

The testes may decrease slightly in size and produce less testosterone with age. Testosterone production usually declines gradually from about age 40 to age 60 and then begins to level off. However, the decline is not inevitable and may be related to the man's general health. Sperm production tends to decline as the seminiferous tubules degenerate, but viable sperm may be produced quite late in life. Men in their 70s, 80s, and even 90s have fathered children.

Nocturnal erections tend to diminish in intensity, duration, and frequency as men age, but they do not normally disappear in healthy men (Reinisch, 1990; Schiavi et al., 1990). The refractory period tends to lengthen with age. An adolescent may require only a few minutes to regain erection and ejaculate again after a first orgasm, whereas a man in his 30s may require half an hour. Past age 50, the refractory period may increase to several hours.

Older men produce less ejaculate, and it may seep rather than shoot out. Though the contractions of orgasm still begin at 0.8-second intervals, they become weaker and fewer. Still, the number and strength of spasms do not translate precisely into subjective pleasure. An older male may enjoy orgasm as thoroughly as he did at a younger age. Attitudes and expectations can be as important as the contractions themselves.

An 82-year-old man commented on his changing sexual abilities:

> I come maybe once in every three sexual encounters these days with my wife. My erection comes and goes, and it's not a big concern to us. I get as much pleasure from touching and thrusting as I do from an ejaculation. When I was younger it was inconceivable to me that I might enjoy sex without an orgasm, but I can see now that in those days I missed out on some pleasure by making orgasm such a focus.
>
> (Gordon & Snyder, 1989, p. 153)

Following orgasm, erection subsides more rapidly than it does in a younger man. A study of 65 healthy men ages 45 to 74 showed an age-related decline in sexual desire, arousal, and activity. Yet there were no differences between younger and older men in level of sexual satisfaction or enjoyment (Schiavi et al., 1990).

In sum, most physical changes do not bring a man's or a woman's sex life to a grinding halt. People's attitudes, sexual histories, and partners are usually more important factors in sexual behavior and enjoyment.

Patterns of Sexual Activity

Despite the decline in certain physical functions, older people can continue to lead a vibrant, fulfilling sex life. In fact, years of sexual experience may more than compensate for any diminution of physical responsiveness (Hodson & Skeen, 1994). In one survey of 800 people in the United States, ages 60 through 91, nearly three out of four who had remained sexually active reported that lovemaking had become more rewarding over the years (Starr & Weiner, 1981). Unfortunately, people who overreact to expected changes in sexual response may conclude that their sex lives are over and give up on sexual activity or even on expressing any physical affection (Reinisch, 1990).

Ninety-four percent of the men and 84% of the women in Kinsey's samples remained sexually active at the age of 60. Half of the 60- to 91-year-olds surveyed by Starr and Weiner (1981) reported sexual relations on a regular basis; and half of these, at least once a week. A study of 200 healthy 80- to 102-year olds reported that 30% of the women and 62% of the men still engaged in intercourse (Bretschneider & McCoy, 1988). A study of 100 older men in England found that the key factor in whether they continued to engage in sexual activity was the availability of a partner—not physical condition (Jones et al., 1994). Sex therapist Helen Singer Kaplan (1990) concludes:

> The loss of sexuality is not an inevitable aspect of aging. . . . The results of these studies are remarkable in their consensus: Without exception, each investigator found that, providing they are in good health, the great majority of people remain sexually functional and active on a regular basis until virtually the end of life. Or, to put it more succinctly, 70% of healthy 70-year-olds remain sexually active, and are having sex at least once a week, and typically more often than that. . . .
>
> Although it is widely believed that sex no longer matters after middle age, the opposite is true, and sex often becomes *more* and not *less* important as a person grows older. Because sex is among the last pleasure-giving biological processes to deteriorate, it is potentially an enduring source of gratification at a time when these are becoming fewer and fewer, and a link to the joys of youth. These are important ingredients in the [older] person's emotional well-being. (pp. 185, 204)

Coital frequency tends to decline with age (Laumann et al., 1994). One study of people married for more than 50 years showed that nearly half (47%) had discontinued intercourse, and 92% reported a decline over the years (Ade-Ridder, 1985). Several factors played a role in declining activity, including physical problems, boredom, and cultural attitudes toward sex among the aging. Despite general trends, sexuality among older people is variable (Knox, 1988). Many older people engage in intercourse, oral sex, and masturbation at least as often as when younger; some become disgusted by sex; others simply lose interest. A six-year longitudinal study of older married couples found that one in five actually increased their coital frequency over time (Palmore, 1981).

Coital frequency, however, is not synonymous with sexual satisfaction. In a Canadian study of 215 married people who were middle-aged and older (51 to 81 years of age), those age 65 or above showed lower coital frequency than younger respondents (Libman, 1989). No sizable differences emerged in the level of sexual satisfaction between older and younger groups, however.

Masturbation also generally declines with age for both men and women, although an increase may occur following a marital separation, divorce, or death of a spouse (Hegeler & Mortensen, 1977). Still, continued masturbation was reported by nearly half (46%) among a sample of people ages 60 to 91 (Starr & Weiner, 1981). This is a high level of acceptance among people who were reared during a time when masturbation was generally viewed as harmful (Kammeyer, 1990).

Couples may accommodate to the physical changes of aging by broadening their sexual repertoire to include more diverse forms of stimulation. Many respondents to a *Consumer Reports* survey reported using oral–genital stimulation, sexual fantasy, sexually explicit materials, anal stimulation, vibrators, and other sexual techniques to offset problems in achieving lubrication or erection (Brecher, 1984). Sexual satisfaction may be derived from manual or oral stimulation, cuddling, caressing, and tenderness, as well as from intercourse to orgasm.

The availability of a sexually interested and supportive partner may be the most important determinant of continued sexual activity. Many women discontinue sexual activity because of the death of their husbands. Women's life expectancy exceeds men's by an average of seven years (71.3 years for men versus 78.3 years for women). This is one reason that one older woman in two lives without a spouse, as compared to one man in five. About 50% of all women over the age of 65 have been widowed, as compared to only 13% of

A C L O S E R L O O K

*A KIND OF SEXUAL REVOLUTION: AT SOME NURSING HOMES, INTIMACY IS A MATTER OF POLICY**

They met last New Year's Eve. He was tall with an easy manner. She was petite with a girlish smile. He asked her to dance and held her close. "I didn't push him away," she said. "I've been around awhile. I've pushed a lot of men away."

It was a modern romance, at once pure and complicated. First, there was his wife. He was still married, although separated. Then, there was his walker.

Fritzie Heilbron's prince came to her not astride a white horse, but in black orthopedic shoes, shuffling along with the help of a walker. He is 76, impaired by Parkinson's disease, and with enough fear of his wife to want his name kept private. But Mrs. Heilbron is smitten. She's 85 and has waited 45 years since her husband died to fall in love again.

This is not a case of geriatrics going clubbing. It is a scene from a nursing home, where those who care for the elderly and infirm report a kind of sexual revolution. The revolution is not among the elderly, who experts say have always demonstrated an enduring urge for intimacy, but in the attitude of those who provide care. They are beginning to recognize that sexual activity is normal and beneficial for patients—even for those with Alzheimer's disease.

"It's not just a matter of dirty old men and disgusting old women," said Robert N. Butler, the director of the International Longevity Center at Mount Sinai Hospital. "The impor-

tance of tenderness, touching, being together in bed is an expression that remains vital to the end of life."

At the Hebrew Home for the Aged, a 1,200-bed nursing home and Alzheimer's research center in the Riverdale section of the Bronx where Mrs. Heilbron and her companion found each other, a new policy gives patients the right to privacy so they can carry on intimate relationships. In confronting the issue directly, the Hebrew Home is in the vanguard of the shift away from seeing sex in nursing homes as a behavior problem.

The policy states that "residents have the right to seek out and engage in sexual expression" and the right to obtain "materials with sexually explicit content," including books, magazines, and videos. The home is training its staff to recognize and respect intimate relationships, and officials there say they will try to assist budding romances by moving one member of a couple to a single room to provide privacy. (None have asked to live together.) In the case of Alzheimer's patients or other cognitively impaired residents, the nursing home officials consult with social workers, nurses, and families to determine if both residents are willing participants and decide whether the relations should continue.

"A couple of years ago, when there were people who were sexually involved, we thought we had to separate them," said Robin Bouru, a social worker at the Hebrew Home.

Because most nursing home residents share rooms, some homes around the country have set aside rooms that couples can use for privacy, and others have formalized policies for addressing sexual activity, like the one at the Hebrew Home. But Meredith Wallace, a geriatric nurse at the Hospital of Saint Raphael in New Haven who has written about sexuality of the aged, said many homes are moving slowly, if at all, to break down "the old stereotypes."

The Conjunction of Two Taboos
Antonette Zeiss, a clinical psychologist at the Veterans Administration Health Care System in Palo Alto, California, who has instructed nursing home administrators in California on sexual relations among patients, said the subject is difficult to confront because "it's the conjunction of two taboos about sex."

"The first," she said, "is that sex is for the young. The second is that sex is for the cognitively intact."

She said that in her experience most people who run nursing homes agree that residents have a right to sexual expression, but it is difficult for staff members to support "because they feel uncomfortable with it."

Others have raised more straightforward objections, from the danger of patients physically hurting themselves to the violation of moral laws at homes that are run by religious organizations.

men over age 65 (U.S. Bureau of the Census, 1987). Not surprisingly, loneliness was the problem most frequently reported (55%) among a sample of 36 widows (Haas-Hawkings et al., 1985).

Perhaps nowhere is sexuality among older people subject to greater distortions than in nursing homes and "old-age" homes (Pratt & Schmall, 1989). Staff members of these facilities tend to treat the residents as sexless beings and may be stunned to discover them involved in sexual activity. In many cases sexual activities among residents are actively discouraged (see the nearby A Closer Look feature).

"You Don't Think of Your Grandparents Having Sex"

Janet Lowe, a nurse's aide at the Hebrew Home, said that the first time she realized two unwed residents were having a relationship, "I was shocked. You don't think of your grandparents having sex."

Ms. Lowe said other members of the staff had stronger objections. "Some people thought it should be stopped because they weren't married."

Jacob Reingold, the vice chairman of the Hebrew Home, which is run according to Orthodox Jewish law, acknowledges that the home would face a quandary if two unwed patients wanted to live together as a couple.

But Reingold, who directed the sexual expression policy at the home, said he was intent on fighting the tendency in the nursing home industry "to sweep this issue under the cover."

For many at the Hebrew Home, romance is a welcome relief from the unbroken landscape of aches and pains and dwindling days. "I think it's beautiful, seeing a man and a woman walking together holding hands," said Ethel Hoberman, who is 81, healthy, spry, and available. "It sort of gives the place the feeling of being alive, rather than waiting to die."

Some staff members and residents find the sexual relationships between unwed, elderly people immoral or distasteful, or both. "There are some women who say: 'Yuck, that's disgusting. They're going to give them rooms so they can do things there?' " said Grace Meltzer, a resident of the Hebrew Home.

Sonya Kantor, who is 86 and president of the resident's council at the home, discreetly said, "I have a gentleman friend here" and explained the negative comments this way: "The disapproval of some of the women may come from the fact that they don't have male friends."

Officials at the Hebrew Home said intimate relationships return some dignity to residents who give up privacy and freedom in exchange for assistance and security. "Can't we allow them to have some vestige of normalcy in this critical area?" said Douglas Holmes, a psychologist who heads the home's research division. "I'm totally pro-sex as long as no one is victimized."

The thorniest issue of sexual conduct at nursing homes involves relations between patients with dementia. Psychologists and doctors say aberrant behavior like public masturbation and unwanted kissing and touching of others is common with Alzheimer's patients, who often lose the ability to make social judgments. But, said Dr. Philip D. Sloane, a professor at the University of North Carolina medical school who advises the Manor Health Care chain of 170 nursing homes on Alzheimer's care, "a lot of the time, the activity we think of as sexually deviant behavior is just reaching out for intimacy."

But determining what sexual behavior is appropriate for patients with dementia is difficult for nursing home administrators, who not only have to worry about what is best for their patients, but also what is acceptable to patients' families and what will keep them out of court.

Like the Hebrew Home, the Manor Health Care homes have a protocol for evaluating instances in which patients with dementia exhibit a strong attraction. He said it is not unusual for the staff, in conjunction with a resident's family, to allow casual intimacy—holding hands, hugging—but that sex is rarely if ever allowed, out of concern for the patients' safety and the difficulty of determining whether they consent.

"It's pretty hard to feel comfortable that there's consent when you have two people who don't know what they're doing," Sloane said.

At the Hebrew Home, Mrs. Meltzer, who lives on a different floor than her husband because he suffers from dementia, said even in his confused state his need for closeness emerges. "I think intimate sex is the farthest thing from his mind," she said. "He reaches for my hand and kisses me. And he says why don't you just get undressed and get into bed. I think he just wants intimacy."

Mrs. Meltzer said the need for companionship doesn't fade with age. She said that when she first moved to the home, she was told about a man who was found naked and dead in the bed of a woman who lives there. Mrs. Meltzer said she still remembered her reaction: "I said, 'Well, anyway, he died happy.' "

*Reprinted from Purdy, M. (1995, November 6). A Kind of Sexual Revolution: At Some Nursing Homes, Intimacy Is a Matter of Policy. *The New York Times*, pp. B1, B6. Copyright © 1995 by The New York Times Company. Reprinted by permission.

- Did any of the information presented about sexuality among older people surprise you? What was it? Why was it a surprise?
- What stereotypes of older people do you hold? Do you believe that sexual activity is proper for people in their 60s or older? Why, or why not?

Sex and Disability

Like older people, people with disabilities (especially those whose physical disabilities render them dependent on others) are often seen as sexless and childlike (Nosek et al., 1994). Such views are based on misconceptions about the sexual functioning of people with disabilities. Some of these myths and stereotypes may be eroding, however, in part due to the success of the civil and social rights movements of the disabled in the 1970s and the attention focused on the sexuality of people with disabilities in films such as *Coming Home, Born on the Fourth of July,* and *My Left Foot.*

A person may have been born with or acquire a bodily impairment, or suffer a loss of function or a disfiguring change in appearance. Although the disability may require the person to make adjustments in order to perform sexually, most people with disabilities have the same sexual needs, feelings, and desires as people without disabilities. Their ability to express their sexual feelings and needs depends on the physical limitations imposed by their disabilities, their adjustment to their disabilities, and the availability of partners. The establishment of mature sexual relationships generally demands some distance from one's parents. Therefore, persons with disabilities who are physically dependent on their parents may find it especially difficult to develop sexual relationships (Knight, 1989). Parents who acknowledge their children's sexual development can be helpful by facilitating dating. Far too often, parents become overprotective:

> Adolescent disabled girls have the same ideas, hopes, and dreams about sexuality as able-bodied girls. They will have learned the gender role expectations set for them by the media and others and may experience difficulty if they lack more substantive educational information about sexuality and sex function. In addition their expectations may come in conflict with the family which may have consistently protected or overindulged the child and not permitted her to "grow up." . . . In many cases the families are intensely concerned about the sexual and emotional vulnerability of the daughter and hope that "nothing bad" will happen to her. They may, therefore, encourage her to wear youthful clothing and to stay a safe little girl. The families can mistakenly assume there may be no sexual life ahead of her and protect her from this perceived bitter reality with youthful clothing and little-girlish ways. The result can be, of course, that the young emerging woman may become societally handicapped in learning how to conduct herself as a sexual woman. She will be infantilized.
>
> (Cole, 1988, pp. 282–283)

In such families young people with disabilities get the message that sex is not for them. As they mature they may need counseling to help them recognize the normalcy of their sexual feelings and to help them make responsible choices for exploring their sexuality.

Physical Disabilities

According to Margaret Nosek and her colleagues (1994), sexual wellness, even among the disabled, involves five factors:

- Positive sexual self-concept; seeing oneself as valuable sexually and as a person
- Knowledge about sexuality
- Positive, productive relationships

Sex and Disabled People. Most people with disabilities have the same sexual needs, feelings, and desires as people without disabilities. They are capable of expressing their sexuality in ways that can be pleasurable for themselves and their partners.

- Coping with barriers to sexuality (social, environmental, physical, and emotional)
- Maintaining the best possible general and sexual health, given one's limitations

This model applies to all of us, of course. Let us now consider aspects of specific physical disabilities and human sexuality.

Cerebral palsy

A muscular disorder that is caused by damage to the central nervous system (usually prior to or during birth) and characterized by spastic paralysis.

Cerebral Palsy   Cerebral palsy does not generally impair sexual interest, capacity for orgasm, or fertility (Reinisch, 1990). Depending on the nature and degree of muscle spasticity or lack of voluntary muscle control, however, afflicted people may be limited to certain types of sexual activities and coital positions.

The importance of sex education for disabled people is highlighted by a case of a man with cerebral palsy:

> A 40-year-old man with moderate cerebral palsy came to see me for sexual counseling. When asked why he came for counseling, he said, "I think I'm old enough to learn about sex." He was college educated, fully employed, and had been living by himself, away from his parents, for three years. In questioning him further, I found that the extent of his sexual knowledge was he knew he had a penis but knew nothing about the human sexual response or about female anatomy. When I asked him if any "white, sticky stuff" ever came out of his penis, he replied, "Yes, and doesn't that have something to do with my cerebral palsy?"
>
> (Knight, 1989, p. 186)

People with disabilities such as cerebral palsy often suffer social rejection during adolescence and perceive themselves as unfit or unworthy of intimate sexual relationships, especially with people who are not disabled. They are often socialized into an asexual role. Sensitive counseling can help them understand and accept their sexuality, promote a more positive body image, and provide the social skills to establish intimate relationships (Edmonson, 1988).

Spinal-Cord Injuries   Persons who suffer physical disabilities as the result of traumatic injuries or physical illness must not only learn to cope with their physical limitations but also adjust to a world designed for nondisabled people (Trieschmann, 1989). Spinal-cord injuries affect about 6,000 to 10,000 people annually in the United States (Seftel et al., 1991). The majority of persons who suffer disabling spinal-cord injuries are young, active males. Automobile or pedestrian accidents account for about half of these cases. Other common causes include stabbing or bullet wounds, sports injuries, and falls. Depending on the location of the injury to the spinal cord, a loss of voluntary control (paralysis) can occur in either the legs (*paraplegia*) or all four limbs (*quadriplegia*). A loss of sensation may also occur in parts of the body that lie beneath the site of injury. Most people who suffer such injuries have relatively normal life spans, but the quality of their lives is profoundly affected.

The effect of spinal-cord injuries on sexual response depends on the site and severity of the injury. Men have two erection centers in the spinal cord: a higher center in the lumbar region that controls psychogenic erections and a lower one in the sacral region that controls reflexive erections. When damage occurs at or above the level of the lumbar center, the man loses the capacity for psychogenic erections, the kinds of erections that occur in response to mental stimulation alone, such as when viewing erotic films or fantasizing. They may still be able to achieve reflexive erections from direct stimulation of the penis, as these erections are controlled by the sacral erection center located in a lower portion of the spinal cord. However, they cannot feel any genital sensations because the nerve connections to the brain are severed. Men with damage to the sacral erection center lose the capacity for reflexive erections but can still achieve psychogenic erections so long as their upper spinal cords remains intact (Spark, 1991). Overall, researchers find that about three of four men with spinal-cord injuries are able to achieve erections but only about one in ten continue to ejaculate naturally (Geiger, 1981; Spark, 1991). Others can be helped to ejaculate with the aid of a vibrator (Szasz & Carpenter, 1989). Their brains may help to fill in some of the missing sensations associated with coitus and even orgasm. When direct stimulation does not cause erection, the woman can stuff the limp penis into the vagina and gently thrust her hips, taking care not to dislodge the penis.

Although the frequency of sexual activity among spinal-cord-injured men tends to decline following the injury (Alexander et al., 1993), a study of almost 1,300 men with these injuries found that about one out of three (35%) continued to engage in sexual intercourse (Spark, 1991). Only about one in five of the men received any kind of sexual counseling to help them adjust sexually to their disability. The men typically reported increased interest in alternative sexual activities, especially those involving areas above the level of the spinal injury, such as those involving the mouth, lips, neck, and ears.

Retention of sexual response depends on the site and severity of the injury (Seftel et al., 1991). Women may lose the ability to experience genital sensations or to lubricate normally during sexual stimulation. However, breast sensations may remain intact, making this area even more erotogenic. Most women with spinal-cord injuries can engage in coitus, become impregnated, and deliver vaginally. A survey of 27 spinal-cord-injured women showed that about half were able to experience orgasm (Kettl et al., 1991). Some also report "phantom orgasms" that provide intense psychological pleasure and that are accompanied by nongenital physical sensations that are similar to those experienced by nondisabled women (Perduta-Fulginiti, 1992). Spinal-cord-injured women can heighten their sexual pleasure by learning to use fantasized orgasm, orgasmic imagery, and amplification of their physical sensations (Perduta-Fulginiti, 1992).

Truth OR Fiction?
R E V I S I T E D

Actually, people who are paralyzed due to spinal-cord injuries usually *can* become sexually aroused and engage in coitus. Most spinal-cord-injured women can become impregnated and bear healthy children. ■

Couples facing the challenge of spinal-cord injury may expand their sexual repertoire to focus less on genital stimulation (except to attain the reflexes of erection and lubrication) and more on the parts of the body that retain sensation. Stimulation of some areas of the body, such as the ears, the neck, and the breasts (in both men and women) can yield pleasurable erotic sensations (Knight, 1989; Seftel et al., 1991).

Sensory Disabilities   Sensory disabilities, such as blindness or deafness, do not directly affect genital responsiveness. Still, sexuality may be affected in many ways. A person who has been blind since birth or early childhood may have difficulty understanding a partner's anatomy. Sex-education curricula have been designed specifically to enable visually impaired people to learn about sexual anatomy via models. Anatomically correct dolls may be used to simulate positions of intercourse.

Deaf persons, too, often lack knowledge about sex. Their ability to comprehend the social cues involved in forming and maintaining intimate relationships may also be impaired. Sex-education programs based on sign language are helping many hearing-impaired people become more socially perceptive as well as knowledgeable about the physical aspects of sex. Persons with visual and hearing impairments often lack self-esteem and self-confidence, which makes it difficult for them to establish intimate relationships. Sexual counseling may help them become more aware of their sexuality and develop social skills.

Arthritis
A progressive disease that is characterized by inflammation or pain in the joints.

Other Physical Disabilities and Impairments   Specific disabilities pose particular challenges to, and limitations on, sexual functioning. **Arthritis** may make it difficult or painful for sufferers to bend their arms, knees, and hips during sexual activity (Ehrlich, 1988). Coital positions that minimize discomfort and the application of moist heat to the joints before sexual relations may be helpful.

A male amputee may find that he is better balanced in the lateral or female-superior position than in the male-superior position (Knight, 1989). A woman with limited hand function may find it difficult or impossible to insert a diaphragm and may need to request assistance from her partner or switch to another contraceptive (Cole, 1988). Sensitivity to each other's needs is as vital to couples in which one member has a disability as it is to nondisabled couples.

Psychological Disabilities

Persons with psychological disabilities, such as mental retardation, are often stereotyped as incapable of understanding their sexual impulses. Retarded people are sometimes assumed to maintain childlike innocence through their lives, or to be devoid of sexuality. Some stereotype retarded people in the opposite direction: as having stronger-than-normal sex drives and being incapable of controlling them (Reinisch, 1990). Some mentally retarded people do act inappropriately—by masturbating publicly, for example. The stereotypes are exaggerated, however, and even many of those who act inappropriately can be trained to follow social rules (Reinisch, 1990).

Parents and caretakers often discourage retarded people from learning about their sexuality or teach them to deny or suppress their sexual feelings. Although the physical changes of puberty may be delayed in mentally retarded people, most develop normal sexual needs (Edmonson, 1988). Most are capable of learning about their sexuality and can be guided into rewarding and responsible intimate relationships.

One of the greatest impediments to sexual fulfillment among people with disabilities is finding a loving and supportive partner. Some people engage in sexual relations with people with disabilities out of sympathy. By and large, however, the partners are other people with disabilities or nondisabled people who have overcome stereotypes that portray disabled people as undesirable. Many partners have had some prior positive relationship with a person with a disability, usually during childhood (Knight, 1989). Experience facilitates acceptance of the idea that a disabled person can be desirable. Depending on the nature of the disability, the nondisabled partner may need to be open to assuming a more active sexual role to compensate for the limitations of the partner with the disability. Two partners with disabilities need to be sensitive to each other's needs and physical limitations. People with disabilities and their partners may also need to expand their sexual repertoires to incorporate ways of pleasuring each other that are not as fixated on genital stimulation.

The message is simple: Sexuality may enrich the lives of nearly all adults at virtually any age.

~ Reflections ~

Do you know anyone with one of the disabilities discussed in the chapter? What do you know of the role of sexuality in that individual's life? What are your thoughts on the subject? Why?

Why do you think that people with disabilities tend to be stereotyped as asexual?

Why do you think parents and caretakers discourage retarded people from learning about their sexuality or teach them to suppress their sexual feelings?

Summing Up

Singlehood

Recent years have seen a sharp increase in the numbers of single young people in our society. Reasons include increased permissiveness toward premarital sex and, particularly for women, the desire to become established in a career. No one lifestyle characterizes single people.

Cohabitation: Darling, Would You Be My POSSLQ?

Who Are the Cohabitors? Cohabitation is more prevalent among less well educated and less affluent people.

Reasons for Cohabitation Some couples prefer cohabitation because it provides a consistent intimate relationship without the legal and economic entanglements of marriage. Some emotionally committed couples cohabit because of the economic advantages of sharing household expenses.

Cohabitation and Later Marriage: Benefit or Risk? Cohabitors who later marry may run a greater risk of divorce than noncohabitors, perhaps because cohabitors are a more liberal group.

Marriage

Marriage is found in all human societies and is our most common lifestyle.

Historical Perspectives In historical patriarchies, the man of the house had the right to choose wives for his sons and could himself take concubines or additional wives.

Why Do People Marry? Throughout Western history, marriages have legitimized sexual relations, sanctioned the permanence of a deeply committed relationship, and provided for the orderly transmission of wealth and a setting for child rearing. In Western society today, romantic love is seen as an essential aspect of marriage.

Types of Marriage The major types of marriage are monogamy and polygamy. Polygamy includes polygyny and polyandry.

Whom Do We Marry: Are Marriages Made in Heaven or in the Neighborhood? People in the United States tend to marry within their geographical area and social class. They tend to marry people similar in physical attractiveness, who share similar attitudes, and who seem likely to meet their material, sexual, and psychological needs.

Marital Sexuality

Until the sexual revolution, Western culture could be characterized as sexually restrictive, even in its attitudes toward marital sex.

The Sexual Revolution Hits Home Married couples today engage in coitus more frequently and for longer durations of time than in Kinsey's day. They report higher levels of sexual satisfaction and engage in a greater variety of sexual activities.

Sexual Satisfaction U.S. women are more likely to reach orgasm through marital sex than in Kinsey's day. Wives take more active sexual roles than in Kinsey's day.

Extramarital Sex

In most cases extramarital relationships are conducted without the spouse's knowledge or approval. People may have affairs for sexual variety, to punish their spouses, to achieve emotional closeness, or to prove that they are attractive.

Patterns of Extramarital Sex Precise figures on the prevalence of extramarital sex are lacking.

Attitudes Toward Extramarital Sex Extramarital sex continues to be viewed negatively by the majority of married people in our society.

Effects of Extramarital Sex The discovery of infidelity can evoke anger, jealousy, even shame. Affairs often, but not always, damage marriages.

Swinging Only a small minority of married couples engage in swinging.

Divorce

About half the marriages in the United States end in divorce. Reasons include relaxed restrictions on divorce, greater financial independence among women, and the idea that marriages should be happy.

The Cost of Divorce Divorce is often associated with financial and emotional problems, however. Divorce can give rise to feelings of failure and depression, and make it difficult to rear children.

Alternative Forms of Marriage

Alternative marital styles such as open marriages and group marriages permit intimate relationships with people outside the marriage.

Open Marriage Open marriages allow each partner open companionship and personal privacy, which may allow sexual intimacy with others.

Group Marriage In a group marriage, three or more people share an intimate relationship, although they are not legally married.

Sex in the Later Years

There are a number of unfounded cultural myths about sexuality among older people, including the stereotypes that older people are sexless and that older people with sexual urges are abnormal.

Physical Changes Physical changes as the years pass can impair sexual activity. Many potential problems can be averted by changing our expectations and making changes to accommodate the aging process.

Patterns of Sexual Activity Sexual activity tends to decline with age, but continued sexual activity can boost self-esteem and be an important source of gratification.

Sex and Disability

People with disabilities may suffer from prejudice that depicts them as sexless or as lacking the means to express their sexual needs or feelings.

Physical Disabilities Cerebral palsy does not usually impair sexual interest, capacity for orgasm, or fertility, but afflicted people may be limited to certain types of sexual activities and coital positions. People with spinal-cord injuries may be paralyzed and lose sensation below the waist. They often respond reflexively to direct genital stimulation. Sensory disabilities do not directly affect sexual response but may impair sexual knowledge and social skills.

Psychological Disabilities Most mentally retarded people can learn the basics of their own sexuality and develop responsible intimate relationships.

# CHAPTER 15

Henri Matisse, French, 1869–1954, *Bathers by a River*, oil on canvas, 1909,
1913, and 1916, 259.7 x 389.9 cm, Charles H. and Mary F. S. Worcester Collection, 1953.158. Photograph © 1995, The Art Institute of Chicago. All Rights
Reserved. © 1996 Succession H. Matisse/Artist Rights Society (ARS), New York.

Sexual Dysfunctions

Outline

Truth OR Fiction?

_____ Sexual dysfunctions are rare occurrences.

_____ Only men can reach climax too early.

_____ The most common cause of painful intercourse in women is vaginal infection.

_____ During the 1980s, 2,000 people fell prey to the belief that their genitals were shrinking and retracting into their bodies.

_____ In sex therapy a man with erectile disorder is taught how to will an erection.

_____ Many sex therapists recommend masturbation as the treatment for women who have never been able to reach orgasm.

_____ A man can be prevented from ejaculating by squeezing his penis when he feels that he is about to do so.

_____ Drugs are available to treat premature ejaculation and erectile disorder.

Derek Jones, 39, and his wife Pam, 37, had not attempted coitus for five years. Their sexual relations had been limited to fondling and caressing each other and to occasional oral–genital contact. They had given up at coitus because of Derek's persistent difficulty in attaining and sustaining erections. But recently they had begun trying again. Some nights Derek would have an erection enabling him to penetrate, only to find that he ejaculated too rapidly. Many nights he was unable to perform at all. Each failure was yet another blow to Derek's self-esteem. Pam kept secret her belief that he could not perform because he was no longer sexually attracted to her.

Terry, 24, has decided she is built differently from friends and women she reads about. They all reach orgasm, it seems, at the drop of a hat. But she has never managed "one of those things." Her husband David, also 24, is considerate, but Terry knows that he, too, is frustrated and feels guilty with every ejaculation. Why should he enjoy sex if Terry cannot? Sex has become a chore rather than a source of pleasure, and David has been having some difficulty attaining erection. Terry wonders whether she should try to fake orgasm to hold on to him. But she is too embarrassed to ask a friend how to act.

(The Authors' Files)

Derek and Terry have **sexual dysfunctions.** That is, they have difficulties in becoming sexually aroused or reaching orgasm. Many of us are troubled by sexual problems from time to time. Men occasionally have difficulty achieving an erection or ejaculate more rapidly than they would like. Most women occasionally have difficulty achieving orgasm or becoming sufficiently lubricated. People are not considered to have a sexual dysfunction unless the problem is persistent and causes distress, however.

Although there are different types of sexual dysfunctions, they share some features. People with sexual dysfunctions may avoid sexual opportunities for fear of failure. They may anticipate that sex will result in frustration or physical pain rather than pleasure and gratification. Because of the emphasis placed upon sexual competence, people with sexual dysfunctions may feel inadequate or incompetent, feelings that diminish their self-esteem. They may experience feelings such as guilt, shame, frustration, depression, and anxiety.

Many people with sexual dysfunctions find it difficult to talk about them, even with their spouses or helping professionals. A woman who cannot reach orgasm with her husband may fake orgasms rather than "make a fuss." A man may find it difficult to admit erectile problems to his physician during a physical. Many physicians are also uncomfortable talking about sexual matters. They may never inquire about sexual problems.

Because many people are reluctant to admit to sexual problems, we do not have precise figures on their frequencies. The best current information we have may be based on the National Health and Social Life Survey (Laumann et al., 1994) (see Table 15.1). The NHSLS group asked respondents for a yes or no answer to the question "During the last 12 months has there ever been a period of several months or more when you lacked interest in having sex; were unable to come to a climax; came to a climax too quickly; experienced physical pain during intercourse; did not find sex pleasurable; felt anxious about your ability to perform sexually; or (for men) had trouble achieving or maintaining an erection or (for women) had trouble lubricating?" Overall, women reported more problems than men in the areas of painful sex, lack of pleasure, inability to reach orgasm, and lack of interest in sex. Men were more likely than women to report reaching climax too early and being anxious about their performance. Difficulty keeping an erection (erectile disorder) increases with age from about 6% in the 18- to 24-year-old age group to about 20% in the 55- to 59-year-old age group. The NHSLS figures represent persistent current problems. The incidences of occasional problems and of lifetime problems would be higher.

Sexual dysfunctions
Persistent or recurrent difficulties in becoming sexually aroused or reaching orgasm.

It is not true that sexual dysfunctions are rare. To the contrary, they are quite common. It also turns out that women, as well as men, report reaching climax too early. Women, however, generally complain that they have reached climax too early to experience a fully enjoyable orgasm. The issue as to whether men reach climax prematurely tends to focus on the fact that they usually lose their erections and thus cannot continue to engage in sexual intercourse.

TABLE 15.1 Current sexual dysfunctions according to the NHSLS study (respondents reporting the problem within the past year)

	Men (%)	Women (%)
Pain during sex	3.0	14.4
Sex not pleasurable	8.1	21.2
Unable to reach orgasm	8.3	24.1
Lack of interest in sex	15.8	33.4
*Anxiety about performance**	17.0	11.5
Reaching climax too early	28.5	10.3
Unable to keep an erection	10.4	—
Having trouble lubricating	—	18.8

*Anxiety about performance is not itself a sexual dysfunction. However, it figures prominently in sexual dysfunctions.

Source: Adapted from Tables 10.8A and 10.8B, pp. 370–371, in Laumann, E. O., Gagnon, J. H., Michael, R. T., & Michaels, S. (1994). *The Social Organization of Sexuality: Sexual Practices in the United States.* Chicago: University of Chicago Press.

Sexual desire disorders
Sexual dysfunctions in which people have persistent or recurrent lack of sexual desire or aversion to sexual contact.

Sexual arousal disorders
Sexual dysfunctions in which people persistently or recurrently fail to become adequately sexually aroused to engage in or sustain sexual intercourse.

Orgasmic disorders
Sexual dysfunctions in which people persistently or recurrently have difficulty reaching orgasm or reach orgasm more rapidly than they would like, despite attaining a level of sexual stimulation of sufficient intensity to normally result in orgasm.

Sexual pain disorders
Sexual dysfunctions in which people persistently or recurrently experience pain during coitus.

Dyspareunia
A sexual dysfunction characterized by persistent or recurrent pain during sexual intercourse. (From roots meaning "badly paired.")

Vaginismus
A sexual dysfunction characterized by involuntary contraction of the muscles surrounding the vaginal barrel, preventing penile penetration or rendering penetration painful.

Types of Sexual Dysfunctions

The most widely used system of classification of sexual dysfunctions is based upon the American Psychiatric Association's *Diagnostic and Statistical Manual of Mental Disorders* (the DSM of 1994). The DSM, which is now in its fourth edition, groups sexual dysfunctions into four categories:

1. **Sexual desire disorders.** These involve dysfunctions in sexual desire, interest, or drive, in which the person experiences a lack of sexual desire or an aversion to genital sexual contact.
2. **Sexual arousal disorders.** Sexual arousal is principally characterized by erection in the male and vaginal lubrication and swelling of the external genitalia in the female. In men, sexual arousal disorders involve recurrent difficulty in achieving or sustaining erections sufficient to successfully engage in sexual intercourse. In women, they typically involve failure to become sufficiently lubricated.
3. **Orgasmic disorders.** Men or women may encounter difficulties achieving orgasm or may reach orgasm more rapidly than they would like. Women are more likely to encounter difficulties reaching orgasm; men are more likely to experience overly rapid orgasm (premature ejaculation). But some men inhibit orgasm during coitus, and a few women complain of overly rapid orgasms.
4. **Sexual pain disorders.** Both men and women may suffer from **dyspareunia** (painful intercourse). Women may experience **vaginismus,** which prevents penetration by the penis or renders penetration painful.

Sexual dysfunctions may also be classified as either lifelong or acquired. *Lifelong* dysfunctions have existed throughout the person's lifetime. *Acquired* dysfunctions develop following a period of normal functioning. They also may be classified as generalized or situational. *Generalized* dysfunctions affect a person's general sexual functioning. *Situational* dysfunctions affect sexual functioning only in some sexual situations (such as during coitus but not during masturbation) or occur with some partners but not with others. Consider, for example, a man who has never been able to achieve or maintain an erection during sexual relations with a partner but can do so during masturbation. His dysfunction would be classified as lifelong *and* situational.

Sexual Desire Disorders

Sexual desire disorders involve lack of sexual desire or interest and/or aversion to genital sexual activity. Although the prevalence of these disorders in the general population is not known, sex therapists report an increase in their frequency over the past generation (Schmidt, 1994).

Lack of Sexual Desire   People with little or no sexual interest or desire are said to have *hypoactive sexual desire disorder.* They also often report an absence of sexual fantasies. According to the NHSLS Study (Laumann et al., 1994), the problem is more common among women than men. Nevertheless, the belief that men are always eager and willing to engage in sexual activity is no more than a myth.

Lack of sexual desire does not imply that a person is unable to achieve erection, lubricate adequately, or reach orgasm. Some people with low sexual desire do have such problems. Others can become sexually aroused and reach orgasm when stimulated adequately. Many enjoy sexual activity, even if they are unlikely to initiate it. Many appreciate the affection and closeness of physical intimacy, but have no interest in genital stimulation.

Hypoactive sexual desire is one of the most commonly diagnosed sexual dysfunctions (Letourneau & O'Donohue, 1993). Yet there is no clear consensus among clinicians and researchers concerning the definition of low sexual desire. How much sexual interest or desire is "normal"? There is no standard level of sexual desire—no 98.6 degree reading on the "sexual thermometer." Lack of desire is usually considered a problem when couples recognize that their level of sexual interest has gotten so low that little remains. Sometimes the lack of desire is limited to one partner. When one member of a couple is more interested in sex than the other, sex therapists often recommend that couples try to reach a compromise. They also try to uncover and resolve problems in the relationship that may dampen the sexual ardor of one or both partners.

Biological and psychosocial factors—hormonal deficiencies, depression, marital dissatisfaction, and so on—contribute to lack of desire. Among the medical conditions that diminish sexual desire are testosterone deficiencies, thyroid overactivity or underactivity, and temporal lobe epilepsy (Kresin, 1993). Sexual desire is stoked by testosterone, which

Parents as Models. Parental examples are important modeling influences in shaping a child's development. Parents who are warm and affectionate toward each other model loving interactions which can help children develop positive attitudes toward intimate relationships.

Hypogonadism
An endocrine disorder that reduces the output of testosterone.

is produced by men in the testes and by both genders in the adrenal glands. Women may experience less sexual desire when their adrenal glands are surgically removed. Low sexual interest, along with erectile difficulties, are also common among men with **hypogonadism.** (Hypogonadism is treated with testosterone [Brody, 1995c; Carani et al., 1990].) However, women with inhibited sexual desire usually have normal levels of the hormones testosterone, estrogen, and progesterone (Schreiner-Engle et al., 1989; Stuart et al., 1987). The role of hormones in lack of desire among physically healthy men and women remains unclear.

Researchers find men with hypoactive sexual desire disorder to be older than women with the disorder (Segraves & Segraves, 1991a). A gradual decline in sexual desire, at least among men, may be explained in part by the reduction in testosterone levels that occurs in middle and later life (Brody, 1995c). Abrupt changes in sexual desire, however, are more often explained by psychological and interpersonal factors such as depression, emotional stress, and problems in the relationship (Leiblum & Rosen, 1988; Schreiner-Engle & Schaivi, 1986).

Psychological problems can contribute to low sexual desire (Letourneau & O'Donohue, 1993). Anxiety is the most commonly reported factor. Various types of anxiety may be involved in dampening sexual desire, including performance anxiety (anxiety over being evaluated negatively), anxiety involving fears of pleasure or loss of control, and deeper sources of anxiety relating to fears of castration or injury. Depression is also a common cause of inhibited desire. A history of sexual assault has also been linked to low sexual desire.

Some medications, including those used to control anxiety or hypertension, may also reduce desire. Changing medications or dosage levels may return the person's previous level of desire.

Sexual Aversion Disorder   People with low sexual desire may have little or no interest in sex, but they are not repelled by genital contact. Some people, however, find sex disgusting or aversive and avoid genital contact.

Sexual aversions are less common than lack of desire and remain poorly understood (Spark, 1991). Some researchers consider sexual aversion to be a *sexual phobia* or *sexual panic state* with intense, irrational fears of sexual contact and a pressing desire to avoid sexual situations (Kaplan, 1987). A history of erectile problems can cause sexual aversion in men (Spark, 1991). Men with such histories may be anxious in sexual situations because they trigger feelings of failure and shame. Their partners may also develop an aversion to sexual contact because of this anxiety and because of their own frustration. A history of sexual trauma, such as rape or childhood sexual abuse or incest, often figures prominently in cases of sexual aversion, especially in women.

Sexual Arousal Disorders

Vasocongestion
Engorgement of blood vessels with blood, which swells the genitals and breasts during sexual arousal.

When we are sexually stimulated, our bodies normally respond with **vasocongestion,** which produces erection in the male and vaginal lubrication in the female. People with sexual arousal disorders, however, fail to achieve or sustain the lubrication or erection necessary to facilitate sexual activity. Or they lack the subjective feelings of sexual pleasure or excitement that normally accompany sexual arousal (American Psychiatric Association, 1994).

Problems of sexual arousal have sometimes been labeled *impotence* in the male and *frigidity* in the female. But these terms are pejorative, so many professionals prefer to use less threatening, more descriptive, labels.

Male erectile disorder
Persistent difficulty achieving or maintaining an erection sufficient to allow the man to engage in or complete sexual intercourse. Also termed *erectile dysfunction.*

Male Erectile Disorder   Sexual arousal disorder in the male is called **male erectile disorder** or *erectile dysfunction.* It is characterized by persistent difficulty in achieving or maintaining an erection sufficient to allow the completion of sexual activity. In most cases the failure is limited to sexual activity with partners, or with some partners and not others. It can thus be classified as *situational.* In rare cases the dysfunction is found during any sexual activity, including masturbation. In such cases, it is considered *generalized.* Some men with erectile disorder are unable to attain an erection with their partners. Others can achieve erection but not sustain it (or recover it) long enough for penetration and ejaculation.

Perhaps 10 to 15 million men in the United States suffer from erectile disorder (Leary, 1992). Another 10 million may suffer from partial dysfunction. The incidence of erectile disorder increases with age and is believed to affect one in three men over the age of 60. Men with *lifelong* erectile disorder (formerly called *primary* erectile dysfunction) never had adequate erectile functioning. Erectile disorder far more commonly develops after a period of normal functioning and is classified as *acquired erectile disorder* (formerly called *secondary* erectile dysfunction). Many such men engaged in years of successful coitus prior to the problem.

Performance anxiety
Anxiety concerning one's ability to perform behaviors, especially behaviors that may be evaluated by other people.

Occasional problems in achieving or maintaining erection are quite common. Fatigue, alcohol, anxiety over impressing a new partner, and other factors may account for a transient episode. Even an isolated occurrence can lead to a persistent problem if the man fears recurrence, however. The more anxious and concerned the man becomes about his sexual ability, the more likely he is to suffer **performance anxiety.** This anxiety can contribute to repeated failure, and a vicious cycle of anxiety and failure may develop.

A man with erectile difficulties may try to "will" an erection, which can compound the problem. Each failure may further demoralize and defeat him. He may ruminate about his sexual inadequacy, setting the stage for yet more anxiety. His partner may try to comfort and support him by saying things like "It can happen to anyone," "Don't worry about it," or "It will get better in time." But attempts at reassurance may be to no avail. As one client put it,

> I always felt inferior, like I was on probation, having to prove myself. I felt like I was up against the wall. You can't imagine how embarrassing this (erectile failure) was. It's like you walk out in front of an audience that you think is a nudist convention and it turns out to be a tuxedo convention.
>
> (The Authors' Files)

The vicious cycle of anxiety and erectile failure may be interrupted if the man recognizes that occasional problems are normal and does not overreact. The emphasis in our culture on men's sexual prowess may spur them to view occasional failures as catastrophes rather than

A CLOSER LOOK

FROM THE AUTHORS' FILES: "THE CASE OF THE SINGER IN THE BAND"

Cliff, 29, was a singer in a rock band, playing local clubs and private parties. His hair was styled in the contemporary fashion of a rock star, but very little else about him fit the stereotype. He didn't drink, smoke, take drugs, or party to all hours of the night. Perhaps most surprisingly, Cliff was still a virgin. He did not expose this "secret," as he put it, to anyone but his therapist. The members of the band had wondered about his sexual orientation, since Cliff would reject the advances of female admirers. He dated infrequently and hardly ever beyond a first date. His hesitation to engage in coitus

did not reflect a personal commitment to celibacy, a gay male sexual orientation, or lack of sexual interest. He was immobilized by an overwhelming fear of failure to perform sexually. Cliff reported that he always felt best when he was singing—like he was on top of the world. "It was funny," he would say, "people would think I had everything going for me." They would not know that Cliff felt inadequate and inferior to other men because he couldn't perform "like a man."

Cliff had first attempted intercourse at 17 with a girl from the neighborhood. She had aggressively

pursued him, even giving him written sexual invitations. He described their first encounter as a disaster. He lost his erection at the point of penetration and tried desperately but unsuccessfully to penetrate with a flaccid penis. There were several other such frustrating experiences in the next few years, always with the same disappointing outcome. Eventually, he gave up trying, finding excuses with his dating partners for his fear of pursuing sexual activity, breaking off relationships that had become too intimate.

transient disappointments, however. Viewing occasional problems as an inconvenience, rather than a tragedy, may help avert the development of persistent erectile difficulties.

Performance anxiety is a prominent cause of erectile disorder. So are other psychological factors such as depression, lack of self-esteem, and problems in the relationship (Leary, 1992). Physiological factors can also play a causative role, as we shall see.

Female Sexual Arousal Disorder   Women may encounter persistent difficulties becoming sexually excited or sufficiently lubricated in response to sexual stimulation. In some cases these difficulties are lifelong. In others they develop after a period of normal functioning. In some cases difficulties are pervasive and occur during both masturbation and sex with a partner. More often they occur in certain situations. For example, they occur with some partners and not with others, or during coitus but not during oral–genital sex or masturbation.

Female sexual arousal disorder often accompanies other sexual disorders such as hypoactive sexual desire disorder and orgasmic disorders (Segraves & Segraves, 1991b). Despite problems in becoming sexually aroused, women with sexual arousal disorders can often engage in coitus. Vaginal dryness may produce discomfort, however.

Female sexual arousal disorder, like its male counterpart, may have physical causes (Graber, 1993). A thorough evaluation by a medical specialist (a urologist in the case of a male; a gynecologist in the case of a female) is recommended. Any neurological, vascular, or hormonal problem that interferes with the lubrication or swelling response of the vagina to sexual stimulation may contribute to female sexual arousal disorder. For example, diabetes mellitus may lead to diminished sexual excitement in women because of the degeneration of the nerves servicing the clitoris and the blood vessel (vascular) damage it causes. Reduced estrogen production can also result in vaginal dryness.

Female sexual arousal disorder more commonly has psychological causes, however. In some cases, women harbor deep-seated anger and resentment toward their partners. They thus find it difficult to turn off these feelings when they go to bed. In other cases, sexual trauma is implicated. Survivors of sexual abuse often find it difficult to respond sexually to their partners. Childhood sexual abuse is especially prevalent in cases of female sexual arousal disorder (Morokoff, 1993). Feelings of helplessness, anger, or guilt, or even flashbacks of the abuse, may surface when the woman begins sexual activity, dampening her ability to become aroused. Other psychosocial causes include anxiety or guilt about sex and ineffective stimulation by the partner (Morokoff, 1993).

Orgasmic Disorders

Three disorders concern the orgasm phase of the sexual response cycle: (1) female orgasmic disorder, (2) male orgasmic disorder, and (3) premature ejaculation.

In female or male orgasmic disorder, the woman or man is persistently delayed in reaching orgasm or does not reach orgasm at all, despite achieving sexual stimulation of sufficient intensity to normally result in orgasm. The problem is more common among women than men. In some cases a person can reach orgasm without difficulty while engaging in sexual relations with one partner, but not with another.

Male Orgasmic Disorder   Male orgasmic disorder has also been termed *delayed ejaculation, retarded ejaculation,* or *ejaculatory incompetence.*[1] The problem may be lifelong or acquired, generalized or situational. There are very few cases of men who have never ejaculated. In most cases the disorder is limited to coitus. The man may be capable of ejaculating during masturbation or oral sex, but find it difficult, if not impossible—despite high levels of sexual excitement—to ejaculate during intercourse. There is a myth that men with male orgasmic disorder and their female partners enjoy his condition, because it enables him to "go on forever" (Dekker, 1993). Actually, the experience is frustrating for both partners.

---

[1]Just as we find terms like *impotence* and *frigidity* unnecessarily pejorative, we prefer to use the more clinical-sounding but less offensive *male orgasmic disorder* or *delayed ejaculation* rather than "retarded" ejaculation or ejaculatory "incompetence."

Male orgasmic disorder is relatively infrequent in the general population and in clinical practice, where it is among the least frequently diagnosed disorders (Dekker, 1993). Research on the problem has been scarce (Dekker, 1993), and only a few individual or multiple case reports have appeared in the literature (e.g., Masters & Johnson, 1970; Rathus, 1978).

Male orgasmic disorder may be caused by physical problems such as multiple sclerosis (Kedia, 1983) or neurological damage that interferes with neural control of ejaculation. It may also be a side effect of certain drugs. Various psychological factors may also play a role, including performance anxiety, sexual guilt, and hostility toward the partner. Helen Singer Kaplan (1974) suggests that some men with male orgasmic disorder may be unconsciously "holding back" their ejaculate from their partners because of underlying hostility or resentment. Masters and Johnson (1970) found that men with this problem frequently have strict religious backgrounds that may leave a residue of unresolved guilt about sex, which inhibits ejaculation. Emotional factors such as fears of pregnancy and anger toward one's partner can also play a role.

As with other sexual dysfunctions, men with male orgasmic disorder and their partners may "try harder." But trying harder often compounds rather than alleviates sexual problems. Sexual relations become a job to get done, a chore rather than an opportunity for pleasure and gratification.

Anorgasmic
Never having reached orgasm. (Literally, "without orgasm.")

Spectator role
A role, usually taken on because of performance anxiety, in which people observe rather than fully participate in their sexual encounters.

Female Orgasmic Disorder
Women with female orgasmic disorder are unable to reach orgasm or have difficulty reaching orgasm following what would usually be an adequate amount of sexual stimulation. Women who have never achieved orgasm through any means are sometimes labeled **anorgasmic** or *preorgasmic*.

A woman who reaches orgasm through masturbation or oral sex may not necessarily reach orgasm dependably during coitus with her partner (Stock, 1993). Penile thrusting during coitus may not provide sufficient clitoral stimulation to facilitate orgasm. An orgasmic disorder may be diagnosed, however, if orgasm during coitus was impaired by factors such as sexual guilt or performance anxiety. Women who try to force an orgasm may also find themselves unable to do so. They may assume a **spectator role** and observe rather than fully participate in their sexual encounters. "Spectatoring" may further decrease the likelihood of orgasm.

Premature ejaculation
A sexual dysfunction in which ejaculation occurs with minimal sexual stimulation and before the man desires it.

Premature Ejaculation
A second type of male orgasmic disorder, premature ejaculation, was the most common male sexual dysfunction reported in the NHSLS study (see Table 15.1). Men with **premature ejaculation** ejaculate too rapidly to permit their partners or themselves to fully enjoy sexual relations. The degree of prematurity varies. Some men ejaculate during foreplay, even at the sight of their partner disrobing. But most ejaculate either just prior to or immediately upon penetration, or following a few coital thrusts (Kaplan, 1974).

Just what constitutes *prematurity*? Some definitions focus on a particular time period during which a man should be able to control ejaculation. Is ejaculation within 30 seconds of intromission premature? Within one minute? Ten minutes? There is no clear cutoff. Some scholars argue that the focus should be on whether the couple is satisfied with the duration of coitus rather than on a specific time period.

Helen Singer Kaplan (1974) suggested that the label "premature" should be applied to cases in which men persistently or recurrently lack voluntary control over their ejaculations. This may sound like a contradiction in terms since ejaculation is a reflex, and reflexes need not involve thought or conscious control. Kaplan means, however, that a man may control his ejaculation by learning to regulate the amount of sexual stimulation he experiences so that it remains below the threshold at which the ejaculation reflex is triggered.

Rapid Female Orgasm: Can Women Reach Orgasm Too Quickly?
The female counterpart to premature ejaculation, *rapid orgasm*, is so rarely recognized as a problem that it is generally ignored by clinicians and is not classified as a sexual dysfunction in the DSM system. Still, some women experience orgasm rapidly and show little interest in continuing sexual activity so that their partners can achieve gratification. Many women who reach orgasm rapidly are open to continued sexual stimulation and capable of experiencing successive orgasms, however.

Sexual Pain Disorders

For most of us, coitus is a source of pleasure. For some of us, however, coitus gives rise to pain and discomfort.

Dyspareunia   Dyspareunia, or painful coitus, can afflict men or women. Dyspareunia is one of the most common sexual dysfunctions and is also a common complaint of women seeking gynecological services (Quevillon, 1993).

Pain is a sign that something is wrong—physically or psychologically. Dyspareunia may result from physical causes, emotional factors, or an interaction of the two (Meana & Binik, 1994). The most common cause of coital pain in women is inadequate lubrication. In such a case, additional foreplay or artificial lubrication may help. Vaginal infections or sexually transmitted diseases (STDs) may also produce coital pain, however. Allergic reactions to spermicides, even the latex material in condoms, can give rise to coital pain or irritation. Pain during deep thrusting may be caused by endometriosis or pelvic inflammatory disease (PID), from other diseases or structural disorders of the reproductive organs (Reid & Lininger, 1993), or by penile contact with the cervix.

T r u t h   **OR**   *Fiction?*   R E V I S I T E D

The most common cause of painful intercourse in women is not vaginal infection. Lack of adequate lubrication is the most common cause of coital pain in women. ■

Psychological factors such as unresolved guilt or anxiety about sex or the lingering effects of sexual trauma may also be involved. These factors may inhibit lubrication and cause involuntary contractions of the vaginal musculature, making penetration painful or uncomfortable.

Painful intercourse is less common in men and is generally associated with genital infections that cause burning or painful ejaculation. Smegma under the penile foreskin of uncircumcised men may also irritate the penile glans during sexual contact.

Vaginismus   Vaginismus involves an involuntary contraction of the pelvic muscles that surround the outer third of the vaginal barrel. Vaginismus occurs reflexively during attempts at vaginal penetration, making entry by the penis painful or impossible. These reflexive contractions are accompanied by a deep-seated fear of penetration (Beck, 1993). Some women with vaginismus are unable to tolerate penetration by any object, including a finger, tampon, or a physician's speculum. The prevalence of vaginismus is unknown.

The woman with vaginismus usually is not aware that she is contracting her vaginal muscles. In some cases, husbands of women with vaginismus develop erectile disorder after repeated failures at penetration (Masters & Johnson, 1970; Speckens et al., 1995).

Vaginismus is caused by a psychological fear of penetration, rather than by a physical injury or defect (LoPiccolo & Stock, 1986). Women with vaginismus often have histories of sexual trauma, rape, or botched abortions that resulted in vaginal injuries. They may desire sexual relations. They may be capable of becoming sexually aroused and achieving orgasm. However, fear of penetration triggers an involuntary spasm of the vaginal musculature at the point of penile insertion. Vaginismus can also be a cause or an effect of dyspareunia. Women who experience painful coitus may develop a fear of penetration. Fear then leads to the development of involuntary vaginal contractions. Women with vaginismus may also experience pain during coital attempts if the couple tries to force penetration. Vaginismus and dyspareunia may also give rise to, or result from, erectile disorder in men (Speckens et al., 1995). Feelings of failure and anxiety come to overwhelm both partners.

Table 15.2 on page 448 shows differences between white Americans and African Americans in the incidences of current sexual dysfunctions and other problems, according to the NHSLS study (Laumann et al., 1994). The African American men report a higher incidence than White men of each of the sexual dysfunctions surveyed. African American women report a higher incidence of most sexual dysfunctions, with the exceptions of painful sex and trouble lubricating.

TABLE 15.2 White and African American differences in the incidence of current sexual problems (respondents reporting the problem within the past year)

	White Men (%)	African American Men (%)	White Women (%)	African American Women (%)
Pain during sex	3.0	3.3	14.7	12.5
Sex not pleasurable	7.0	15.2	19.7	30.0
Unable to reach orgasm	7.4	9.9	23.2	29.2
Lack of interest in sex	14.7	20.0	30.9	44.5
Anxiety about performance	16.8	23.7	10.5	14.5
Reaching climax too early	27.7	33.8	7.5	20.4
Unable to keep an erection	9.9	14.5	—	—
Having trouble lubricating	—	—	20.7	13.0

Source: Adapted from Tables 10.8A and 10.8B, pp. 370–371, in Laumann, E. O., Gagnon, J. H., Michael, R. T., & Michaels, S. (1994). *The Social Organization of Sexuality: Sexual Practices in the United States.* Chicago: University of Chicago Press.

~ *Reflections* ~

Why do you believe that so many people have difficulty talking about sexual problems or sexual dysfunctions? Why do you think that men have more difficulty talking about them than women do?

The text notes that there is no consensus among clinicians and researchers concerning the definition of low sexual desire. How much sexual interest or desire would seem to be normal to you? Why?

How would *you* define "premature" ejaculation? Explain.

Origins of Sexual Dysfunctions

Since sexual dysfunctions involve the sex organs, it was once assumed that they stemmed largely from organic or physical causes. Today the pendulum has swung. It is now widely believed that many or most cases reflect psychosocial factors such as sexual anxieties, lack of sexual knowledge, or marital dissatisfaction. Many cases involve the interaction of organic and psychological factors (Meisler & Carey, 1990; Mohr & Beutler, 1990).

Organic Causes

Physical factors, such as fatigue and lowered testosterone levels, can dampen sexual desire and reduce responsiveness. Fatigue may lead to male erectile disorder and male orgasmic disorder, and to female orgasmic disorder and inadequate lubrication in women. But these will be isolated incidents unless the person attaches too much meaning to them and becomes concerned about future performances. Painful coitus, however, often reflects organic factors such as underlying infections. Various medical conditions can affect orgasmic functioning in both men and women, including diabetes mellitus, multiple sclerosis, spinal-cord injuries, complications from certain surgical procedures (such as removal of the prostate in men), endocrinological problems, and use of some pharmacological agents, such as drugs used to treat hypertension and psychiatric disorders (Segraves & Segraves, 1993).

It was once believed that 95% of cases of erectile disorder resulted from psychological causes (Masters & Johnson, 1970). It is now thought that organic factors are also widely involved (Rajfer et al., 1992). Psychological factors such as anxiety or depression may serve to perpetuate or exacerbate the problem even when there are underlying organic causes.

Organic causes of erectile disorder affect the flow of blood to and through the penis or damage to nerves involved in erection (Appell, 1986; Spark, 1991). Erectile problems can arise when clogged or narrow arteries leading to the penis deprive the penis of oxygen (Blakeslee, 1993a). Erectile disorder occurs in as many as 35% of 20- to 60-year-old men with diabetes mellitus, a disease that can damage blood vessels and nerves. Nerve damage resulting from prostate surgery may also impair erectile response. Erectile disorder may also result from multiple sclerosis (MS), a disease in which nerve cells lose the protective coatings that facilitate transmission of neural messages. As many as 50% of adult men with MS may have erectile disorder. MS has also been implicated in male orgasmic disorder (Kedia, 1983).

Syphilis, a sexually transmitted disease, can result in erectile failure if the bacteria that cause the disease invade the spinal cord and affect the cells that control erection (Spark, 1991). Chronic kidney disease, hypertension, cancer, emphysema, and heart disease can all impair erectile response. So too can endocrine disorders that impair testosterone production.

Rajfer and his colleagues (1992) believe that most cases of erectile disorder involve failure of the body to produce sufficient quantities of the substance nitric oxide. When nitric oxide comes into contact with the muscles encircling blood vessels in the penis, the muscles relax, allowing vasocongestion to occur and causing the penis to swell. A lack of nitric oxide allows blood to leak out of the penis and be reabsorbed by the body, thereby preventing the degree of engorgement necessary for the attainment and maintenance of erection. One approach to erectile disorder is to inject the penis with a chemical that raises nitric oxide levels and thus relaxes the penile muscles to permit blood to flow more freely. (Unfortunately, no pill with a similar effect is in the offing [Kessler, 1992].)

Women may also encounter vascular or nerve disorders that impair genital blood flow, reducing lubrication and sexual excitement, rendering intercourse painful, and reducing their ability to reach orgasm.

Tumescence
Swelling; erection. (From the Latin *tumere*, meaning "to swell." *Tumor* has the same root.)

People with sexual dysfunctions are generally advised to undergo a physical examination to determine whether their problems are biologically based. Men with erectile disorder may be evaluated in a sleep center to determine whether they attain erections while asleep. Healthy men usually have erections during rapid-eye-movement (REM) sleep, which occurs every 90 to 100 minutes. Men with organically based erectile disorder often do not have nocturnal erections. However, this technique, called nocturnal penile **tumescence** (NPT), may lead to misleading results in perhaps 20% of cases (Meisler & Carey, 1990). NPT may thus be helpful but not definitive in suggesting whether erectile disorder is organically based (Mohr & Beutler, 1990).

Prescription drugs and illicit drugs are believed to account for one in four cases of erectile disorder (Leary, 1992b). Antidepressant medication and antipsychotic drugs may impair erectile functioning and cause orgasmic disorders (Segraves, 1988b; Spark, 1991). Tranquilizers like Valium and Xanax may cause orgasmic disorder in either gender (Segraves, 1988b). Antihypertensive drugs can lead to erectile failure (Segraves, 1988b). Switching to hypertensive drugs that do not impair sexual response or adjusting dosage levels may help (Spark, 1991).

Central nervous system depressants such as alcohol, heroin, and morphine can reduce sexual desire and impair sexual arousal (Segraves, 1988a). Regular marijuana use has also been associated with reduced sexual desire and performance (Nelson, 1988). Heavy drinking can damage the nerves that control erection and ejaculation (Spark, 1991). Narcotics also depress testosterone production, which can further reduce sexual desire and lead to erectile failure (Spark, 1991).

It is commonly believed that cocaine is an aphrodisiac. However, regular use can cause erectile disorder or male orgasmic disorder and can reduce sexual desire in both genders (Weiss & Mirin, 1987). Some people report increased sexual pleasure from the initial use of cocaine, but repeated use can lead to dependency on the drug for sexual arousal. Long-term use may compromise the ability to experience sexual pleasure (Weiss & Mirin, 1987).

A WORLD OF DIVERSITY

INIS BEAG AND MANGAIA—WORLDS APART

Let us invite you on a journey to two islands that are a world apart—sexually as well as geographically. The sexual attitudes and practices within these societies will shed some light on the role of cultural values in determining what is sexually normal and what is sexually dysfunctional.

Our first stop is the island of Inis Beag, which lies off the misty coast of Ireland. From the air Inis Beag is a green jewel, fertile and inviting. At ground level things do not appear quite so warm, however.

The residents of this Irish folk community do not believe that it is normal for women to experience orgasm. Anthropologist John Messenger (1971), who visited Inis Beag in the 1950s and 1960s, reported that any woman who finds pleasure in sex—especially the intense waves of pleasure that can accompany orgasm—is viewed as deviant. *Should women on Inis Beag, then, be diagnosed as orgasmically impaired?*

Premarital sex is all but unknown on Inis Beag. Prior to marriage, men and women socialize apart. Marriage comes relatively late—usually in the middle 30s for men and the middle 20s for women. Mothers teach their daughters that they will have to submit to their husbands' animal cravings in order to obey God's injunction to "be fruitful and multiply." *After this indoctrination, women show little interest in sex. Should they be diagnosed as having hypoactive sexual desire disorder?*

Polynesia. Cultural expectations affect our judgments as to what kinds of sexual behavior are functional and dysfunctional. Some Polynesian cultures are sexually permissive. They encourage children to explore their sexuality. Men may be expected to bring their partners to orgasm several times before ejaculating. In such cultures, should men who ejaculate before their partners have multiple orgasms be diagnosed with premature ejaculation?

Occasional use of alcohol and other drugs can also lead to sexual difficulties when people misattribute their sexually dampening effects to causes within themselves. If you are unable to perform sexually when you have had a few drinks and do not recognize that alcohol can depress your performance, you may believe that something else is wrong with you. This belief can create anxiety at your next sexual opportunity, which can prevent normal functioning. A second failure may set off a vicious cycle in which self-doubts prompt more anxiety, and anxiety results in repeated failure and heightened anxiety.

Psychosocial Causes

Psychosocial factors are connected with sexual dysfunctions. These include—but are not necessarily limited to—cultural influences, psychosexual trauma, a gay sexual orientation, marital dissatisfaction, psychological conflict, lack of sexual skills, irrational beliefs, and performance anxiety.

The women of Inis Beag need not be overly concerned about frequent sexual intercourse, however, since the men of the island believe, erroneously, that sexual activity will drain their strength. Consequently, men avoid sex on the eve of sporting activity or strenuous work. Because of taboos against nudity, married couples engage in intercourse with their underclothes on. Intercourse takes place in the dark—literally as well as figuratively.

During intercourse the man takes the male-superior position. The male is always the initiator. Foreplay is brief, rarely involving manual stimulation of the breasts and never including oral stimulation of the genitals. *Should people who have difficulty becoming sexually aroused under these circumstances be diagnosed as having sexual arousal disorders?* The man ejaculates as rapidly as he can, in the belief that he is the only partner with sexual needs and to spare his wife as best he can. Then he turns over and rapidly falls asleep. Once more the couple have done their duty. *Since the man ejaculates rapidly, should he be diagnosed as having premature ejaculation?*

Our next stop is Mangaia. Mangaia is a Polynesian pearl of an island. It lifts languidly out of the blue waters of the Pacific. It lies on the other side of the world from Inis Beag—in more ways than one.

From an early age, Mangaian boys and girls are encouraged to get in touch with their own sexuality through sexual play and masturbation (Marshall, 1971). At about the age of 13, Mangaian boys are initiated into manhood by adults who instruct them in sexual techniques. Mangaian males are taught the merit of bringing their female partners to multiple orgasms before ejaculating. *Are Mangaian males who ejaculate before their partners have multiple orgasms suffering from premature ejaculation?*

Boys practice their new techniques with girlfriends on secluded beaches or beneath the listing fronds of palms. They may visit girlfriends in the evening in the huts where they sleep with their families. Parents often listen for their daughters to laugh and gasp so that they will know that their daughters have reached orgasm with a visiting young man, called a "sleep-crawler." Usually they pretend to be asleep so as not to interfere with

courtship and impede their daughters' chances of finding a suitable mate. Daughters may receive a nightly succession of sleepcrawlers.

Girls, too, learn techniques of coitus from their elders. Typically they are initiated by an experienced male relative. Mangaians look on virginity with disdain, because virgins do not know how to provide sexual pleasure. Thus, the older relative makes his contribution to the family by initiating the girl.

Mangaians, by the way, expressed concern when they learned that many European and U.S. women do not regularly experience orgasm during coitus. Orgasm is apparently universal among Mangaian women. Therefore, Mangaians could only assume that Western women suffered from some abnormality of the sex organs. *Do they?*

All in all, the sharp contrasts between Inis Beag and Mangaia illustrate how concepts of normality are embedded within a cultural context. Behavior that is judged to be normal in one culture may be regarded as abnormal in another. How might our own cultural expectations influence our judgments about sexual dysfunction?

Cultural Influences   Children reared in sexually repressive cultural or home environments may learn to respond to sex with feelings of anxiety and shame, rather than sexual arousal and pleasure. People whose parents instilled in them a sense of guilt over touching their genitals may find it difficult to accept their sex organs as sources of pleasure.

In Western cultures, sexual pleasure has traditionally been a male preserve. Young women may be reared to believe that sex is a duty to be performed for their husbands, not a source of personal pleasure. Although the traditional double standard may have diminished in the United States in recent years, girls may still be exposed to relatively more repressive attitudes. Women are more likely than men in our culture to be taught to repress their sexual desires and even to fear their sexuality (Nichols, 1990a). Self-control and vigilance—not sexual awareness and acceptance—become identified as feminine virtues. Women reared with such attitudes may be less likely to learn about their sexual potentials or express their erotic preferences to their partners. Compared to women who readily reach orgasm, sexually active but anorgasmic women report more negative attitudes toward

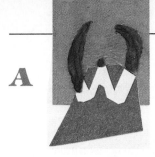

AN ODD COUPLE: KORO AND DHAT SYNDROMES

Many men in the United States are concerned that their penises are too small. However, they are not usually concerned that their genitals will retract into their bodies. It is also still believed by some people in the United States that men should avoid sex on the eve of an athletic event, because sex saps the body of strength. This belief has a counterpart in the country of India.

Let us consider two Far Eastern sexual disorders: Koro and Dhat syndromes.

Koro Syndrome

Koro syndrome is found primarily in China and some other Far Eastern countries. People with Koro syndrome fear that their genitals are shrinking and retracting into the body, a problem that they believe will be fatal. Koro syndrome has been identified mainly in young men, although some cases have also been reported in women. People with Koro syndrome show signs of acute anxiety, including profuse sweating, breathlessness, and heart palpitations. Men with the disorder have been known to use mechanical devices, such as chopsticks, to try to prevent the penis from retracting into the body.

Koro syndrome has been traced as far back as 3000 B.C. Epidemics involving hundreds or thousands of people have been reported in parts of Asia such as China, Singapore, Thailand, and India (Tseng et al., 1992). In Guangdong Province in China, an epidemic involving more than 2,000 persons occurred during the 1980s. Guangdong residents who did not fall victim to Koro were less superstitious and more intelligent than those who fell victim to the epidemic (Tseng et al., 1992).

Reassurance by a health professional that fears that the genitals will retract into the body are unfounded often put an end to Koro episodes. In any event, Koro episodes tend to pass with time.

Truth **OR** Fiction? REVISITED

It is true that 2,000 people fell prey to the belief that their genitals were shrinking and retracting into their bodies in the 1980s. The syndrome is known as Koro and is found in the Far East. ∎

Dhat Syndrome

Dhat syndrome is found among young Asian Indian males and involves excessive fears over the loss of seminal fluid during nocturnal emissions (Akhtar, 1988). Some men with Dhat syndrome also believe (incorrectly) that semen mixes with urine and is excreted by urinating.

There is a widespread belief within Indian culture (and other Near and Far Eastern cultures) that the loss of semen is harmful because it depletes the body of physical and mental energy (Chadda & Ahuja, 1990). Therefore, men with Dhat syndrome may visit physician after physician to find help in preventing nocturnal emissions or the imagined loss of semen mixed with urine. Dhat syndrome can best be understood within its cultural context:

> In India, attitudes toward semen and its loss constitute an organized, deep-seated belief system that can be traced back to the scriptures of the land. . . . [even as far back as the classic Indian sex manual, the *Kama Sutra*, which was believed to be written by the sage Vatsayana between the third and fifth centuries A.D.] . . . Semen is considered to be the elixir of life, in both a physical and mystical sense. Its preservation is supposed to guarantee health and longevity.
>
> (Akhtar, 1988, p. 71)

It is a commonly held Hindu belief that it takes "40 meals to form one drop of blood; 40 drops of blood to fuse and form one drop of bone marrow; and 40 drops of this produce one drop of semen" (Akhtar, 1988, p. 71). Some Indian males thus experience great anxiety over the involuntary loss of the fluid through nocturnal emissions (Akhtar, 1988). Dhat syndrome has also been associated with difficulty in achieving or maintaining erection, apparently due to excessive concern about loss of seminal fluid through ejaculation.

---

masturbation, greater sexual guilt, and greater discomfort talking with their partners about sexual activities that involve direct clitoral contact (cunnilingus and manual stimulation) (Kelly et al., 1990).

Many women who are exposed to negative attitudes about sex during childhood and adolescence find it difficult to suddenly view sex as a source of pleasure and satisfaction once they are married. The result of a lifetime of learning to turn themselves off sexually may lead to difficulties experiencing the full expression of sexual arousal and enjoyment when an acceptable opportunity arises (Morokoff, 1993).

Psychosexual Trauma   Learning theorists focus on the role of conditioned anxiety in explaining sexual dysfunctions. Sexual stimuli come to elicit anxiety when they have been paired with physically or psychologically painful experiences, such as rape, incest, or sexual molestation. Strong conditioned anxiety can stifle sexual arousal. Unresolved anger and misplaced guilt can also make it difficult for victims of rape and other sexual traumas to respond sexually, even years afterward. Persons who have been sexually victimized may harbor feelings of disgust and revulsion toward sex, or deep-seated fears of sex that make it difficult for them to respond sexually, even with loving partners.

Sexual Orientation   Some gay males and lesbians test their sexual orientation by developing heterosexual relationships, even marrying and rearing children with partners of the other gender. Others may wish to maintain the appearance of heterosexuality to avoid the social stigma that society attaches to a gay sexual identity. In such cases, problems in arousal or performance with heterosexual partners can be due to a lack of heteroerotic interests. A lack of heterosexual response is not a problem for people who are committed to a gay lifestyle, however. Sexual dysfunctions may also occur in gay relationships, as they do in heterosexual relationships.

Ineffective Sexual Techniques   In some marriages couples practice a narrow range of sexual techniques because they have fallen into a certain routine or because one partner controls the timing and sequence of sexual techniques. A woman who remains unknowledgeable about the erotic importance of her clitoris may be unlikely to seek direct clitoral stimulation. The man who responds to a temporary erectile failure by trying to force an erection may be unintentionally setting himself up for repeated failure. The couple who fail to communicate their sexual preferences or to experiment with altering their sexual techniques may find themselves losing interest. Brevity of foreplay and coitus may contribute to female orgasmic disorder.

Emotional Factors   Orgasm involves a sudden loss of voluntary control. Fear of losing control or "letting go" may block sexual arousal. Other emotional factors, especially depression, are often implicated in sexual dysfunctions (Beck, 1988). Women with hypoactive sexual desire are more likely to report a history of depressive episodes (Schreiner-Engle & Schiavi, 1986). People who are depressed frequently report lessened sexual interest and may find it difficult to respond sexually. People who are exposed to a high level of emotional stress may also experience an ebbing of sexual interest and response.

Problems in the Relationship   Problems in the relationship are important and often pivotal factors in sexual dysfunctions (Catalan et al., 1990; Fish et al., 1994; Leiblum & Rosen, 1991). Problems in a relationship are not so easily left at the bedroom door. Couples usually find that their sexual relationships are no better than the other facets of their relationships. Couples who harbor resentments toward one another may make sex their arena of combat. They may fail to become aroused by their partners or "withhold" orgasm to make their partners feel guilty or inadequate.

Problems in communication may also play a role. Troubled relationships are usually characterized by poor communication. Partners who have difficulty communicating about other matters may be unlikely to communicate their sexual desires to each other.

The following case highlights how sexual dysfunctions can develop against the backdrop of a troubled relationship:

> After living together for six months, Paul and Petula are contemplating marriage. But a problem has brought them to a sex therapy clinic. As Petula puts it, "For the last two months he hasn't been able to keep his erection after he enters me." Paul is 26, a lawyer; Petula, 24, is a buyer for a large department store. They both grew up in middle-class, suburban families, were introduced through mutual friends and began having intercourse,

A Failure to Communicate. Problems in communication cause or exacerbate sexual problems. It is irrational to believe that one's partner would know what to do if she or he "really loved me." Sex therapy enhances communication skills.

without difficulty, a few months into their relationship. At Petula's urging, Paul moved into her apartment, although he wasn't sure he was ready for such a step. A week later he began to have difficulty maintaining his erection during intercourse, although he felt strong desires for his partner. When his erection waned, he would try again, but would lose his desire and be unable to achieve another erection. After a few times like this, Petula would become so angry that she began striking Paul in the chest and screaming at him. Paul, who at 200 pounds weighed more than twice as much as Petula, would just walk away, which angered Petula even more.

It became clear that sex was not the only trouble spot in their relationship. Petula complained that he preferred to be with his friends and go to baseball games than to spend time with her. When they were together at home, he would become absorbed in watching sports events on television, and showed no interest in activities she enjoyed—attending the theater, visiting museums, etc. Since there was no evidence that the sexual difficulty was due to either organic problems or depression, a diagnosis of male erectile disorder was given. Neither Paul or Petula were willing to discuss their nonsexual problems with a therapist. While the sexual problem was treated successfully with a form of sex therapy modeled after techniques developed by Masters and Johnson [see discussion later in the chapter] and the couple later married, Paul's ambivalence continued well into their marriage, and there were future recurrences of sexual problems as well.

(Adapted from Spitzer et al., 1989, pp. 149–150)

Though couples with strongly committed and supportive relationships can generally develop effective coping strategies for overcoming even the most severe sexual problems, couples in relationships with unresolved conflicts may derive little if any benefit from even the most advanced psychological, medical, or surgical treatments of sexual dysfunctions (Leiblum & Rosen, 1991).

Psychological Conflicts   Within Freud's psychoanalytic theory, sexual dysfunctions are rooted in the failure to successfully resolve the Oedipus or Electra complexes of early childhood. Sexual encounters in adulthood arouse unconscious anxieties and hostilities that are believed to reflect unresolved conflicts, thereby inhibiting sexual response.

A modern psychoanalytic theorist, Helen Singer Kaplan (1974), believes that sexual dysfunctions represent an interaction of *immediate* causes (such as poor techniques, marital conflict, performance anxiety, and lack of effective communication) and deep-seated or *remote* causes (such as unresolved childhood conflicts that predispose people to encounter sexual anxiety and hostility in adulthood). Kaplan believes there is value in combining direct behavioral techniques, which deal with the immediate causes of sexual dysfunctions, with psychoanalytic (insight-oriented) techniques that deal with the remote causes.

Lack of Sexual Skills   Sexual competency involves the acquisition of sexual knowledge and skills and is based largely on learning. We generally learn what makes us and others feel good through trial and error and by talking and reading about sex. Some people may not develop sexual competency because of a lack of opportunity to acquire knowledge and experience—even within marriage. People with sexual dysfunctions may have been reared in families in which discussions of sexuality were off limits and early sexual experimentation was harshly punished. Such early influences may have squelched the young person's sexual learning and experimentation or led her or him to associate anxiety or guilt with sex.

Helen Singer Kaplan (1974) notes that premature ejaculators may have failed to learn to recognize the level of sexual arousal that directly precedes their ejaculatory threshold— the level of stimulation that triggers the ejaculatory reflex. As a result they may be less able to employ self-control strategies to delay ejaculation such as temporarily halting genital stimulation when they approach their "point of no return." Men with limited sexual experience are particularly unlikely to recognize their ejaculatory threshold and to regulate sexual stimulation so that it remains below this triggering point. Some men may try to delay ejaculation by keeping their minds blank or diverting their attention from sex (as by thinking about their forthcoming calculus exam). In so doing, they ignore their own sexual stimulation and do not learn "when to say when."

Although some men with premature ejaculation may have difficulty gauging their level of sexual arousal, research fails to show that premature ejaculators in general are less accurate than other men in making such judgments (Kinder & Curtiss, 1988; Strassberg et al., 1990). It may be that premature ejaculators are more physiologically sensitive to sexual stimulation, not that they are less capable of assessing their sexual arousal (Strassberg et al., 1990). Perhaps premature ejaculators simply require less stimulation to achieve orgasm. Though this may be the case, it does not account for the factors explaining these differences in sensitivity levels (O'Donohue et al., 1993).

Irrational Beliefs   Psychologist Albert Ellis (1962, 1977) points out that irrational beliefs and attitudes may contribute to sexual dysfunctions. Negative feelings like anxiety and fear, Ellis submits, do not stem directly from the events we experience, but rather from our interpretations of these events. If a person encounters a certain event, like an erectile or orgasmic disorder on a given day, and then *believes* that the event is awful or catastrophic, he or she will exaggerate feelings of disappointment and set the stage for future problems.

Performance Anxiety   Anxiety—especially performance anxiety—plays important roles in the development of sexual dysfunctions. Performance anxiety occurs when a person becomes overly concerned with how well he or she performs a certain act or task. Performance anxiety may place a dysfunctional individual in a spectator rather than a performer role. Rather than focusing on erotic sensations and allowing involuntary responses like erection, lubrication, and orgasm to occur naturally, he or she focuses on self-doubts and fears, and thinks, "Will I be able to do it this time? Will this be another failure?"

Performance anxiety can set the stage for a vicious cycle in which a sexual failure increases anxiety. Anxiety then leads to repeated failure, and so on. Sex therapists emphasize the need to break this vicious cycle by removing the need to perform.

In men, performance anxiety can inhibit erection while also triggering a premature ejaculation. (Erection, mediated by the parasympathetic nervous system, can be blocked by activation of the sympathetic nervous system in the form of anxiety. Since ejaculation, like anxiety, is mediated by the sympathetic nervous system, arousal of this system in the form of anxiety can increase the level of stimulation and thereby heighten the potential for premature ejaculation.)

In women, performance anxiety can reduce vaginal lubrication and contribute to orgasmic disorder. Women with performance anxieties may try to force an orgasm, only to find that the harder they try, the more elusive it becomes.

~ *Reflections* ~

Do you know of anyone who has sexual problems or dysfunctions that are apparently related to traumatic sexual experiences as a child or an adult? Explain.

■ Are there any sexual attitudes common to people of your sociocultural background that can give rise to sexual problems or dysfunctions? What are the attitudes? Do you share these attitudes? Why, or why not?

■ What kinds of vicious cycles characterize sexual problems and feelings of anxiety? Have you known anyone with similar concerns about taking tests in college? How does anxiety interact with test performance for them?

Treatment of Sexual Dysfunctions

When Kinsey conducted his surveys in the 1930s and 1940s, there was no effective treatment for sexual dysfunctions. At the time the predominant model of therapy for sexual dysfunctions was long-term psychoanalysis. Psychoanalysts believed that the sexual problem would abate only if the presumed unconscious conflicts that lay at the root of the problem were resolved through long-term therapy. Evidence of the effectiveness of psychoanalysis in treating sexual dysfunctions is still lacking, however.

Sex therapy
A collective term for short-term behavioral models for treatment of sexual dysfunctions.

Since that time behavioral models of short-term treatment, collectively called **sex therapy**, have emerged. These models aim to modify the dysfunctional behavior as directly as possible. Sex therapists also recognize the roles of childhood conflicts, self-defeating attitudes, and the quality of the partners' relationship. Therefore, they draw upon various forms of therapy, as needed (LoPiccolo, 1994; Rosen et al., 1994).

Although the particular approaches vary, sex therapies aim to:

1. Change self-defeating beliefs and attitudes
2. Teach sexual skills
3. Enhance sexual knowledge
4. Improve sexual communication
5. Reduce performance anxiety

Sex therapy usually involves both partners, although individual therapy is preferred in some cases. Therapists find that granting people "permission" to sexually experiment or discuss negative attitudes about sex helps many people overcome sexual problems without the need for more intensive therapy.

Let us begin with the groundbreaking work of Masters and Johnson.

The Masters-and-Johnson Approach

Masters and Johnson pioneered the use of direct behavioral approaches to treating sexual dysfunctions (Masters & Johnson, 1970). A female–male therapy team focuses on the couple as the unit of treatment during a two-week residential program. Masters and Johnson consider the couple, not the individual, dysfunctional. A couple may describe the husband's erectile disorder as the problem, but this problem is likely to have led to problems in the couple by the time they seek therapy. Similarly, a man whose wife has an orgasmic disorder is likely to be anxious about his ability to provide effective sexual stimulation.

Sensate focus exercises
Exercises in which sex partners take turns giving and receiving pleasurable stimulation in non-genital areas of the body.

The dual-therapist team permits each partner to discuss problems with a member of his or her own gender. It reduces the chance of therapist bias in favor of the female or male partner. It allows each partner to hear concerns expressed by another member of the other gender. Anxieties and resentments are aired, but the focus of treatment is behavioral change. Couples perform daily sexual homework assignments, such as **sensate focus exercises**, in the privacy of their own rooms.

Sensate focus sessions are carried out in the nude. Partners take turns giving and receiving stimulation in nongenital areas of the body. Without touching the breasts or genitals, the giver massages or fondles the receiving partner in order to provide pleasure under relaxing and nondemanding conditions. Since genital activity is restricted, there is no pressure to "perform." The giving partner is "freed" to engage in trial-and-error learning about the receiving partner's sensate preferences. The receiving partner is also "freed" to enjoy the experience without feeling rushed to reciprocate or obliged to perform by becoming sexually aroused. The receiving partner's only responsibility is to direct the giving partner as needed. In addition to these general sensate focus exercises, Masters and Johnson used specific assignments designed to help couples overcome particular sexual dysfunctions.

Masters and Johnson were pioneers in the development of sex therapy. Yet many sex therapists have departed from the Masters-and-Johnson format. Many do not treat clients in an intensive residential program. Many question the necessity of female–male therapist teams. Researchers find that one therapist is about as effective as two, regardless of her or his gender (Libman et al., 1985). Nor does the therapeutic benefit seem to depend to any great extent on whether the sessions are conducted within a short period of time, as in the Masters-and-Johnson approach, or spaced over time (Libman et al., 1985). Some success has also been reported in minimal contact programs in which participants are given written instructions rather than live therapy sessions (Mohr & Beutler, 1990). Therapists have also departed from the Masters-and-Johnson approach by working individually with preorgasmic women rather than the couple. Group treatment programs have also been used successfully in treating female orgasmic disorder (Killmann et al., 1987).

The Helen Singer Kaplan Approach

Kaplan (1974) calls her approach *psychosexual therapy*. Psychosexual therapy combines behavioral and psychoanalytic methods. Kaplan, as noted, believes that sexual dysfunctions have both *immediate* causes and *remote* causes (underlying intrapsychic conflicts that date to childhood). Kaplan begins therapy with the behavioral approach. She focuses on improving the couple's communication, eliminating performance anxiety, and fostering sexual skills and knowledge. She uses a brief form of insight-oriented therapy when it appears that remote causes impede response to the behavioral program. In so doing, she hopes to bring to awareness unconscious conflicts that are believed to have stifled the person's sexual desires or responsiveness. Although Kaplan reports a number of successful case studies, there are no controlled studies demonstrating that the combination of behavioral and insight-oriented, or psychoanalytic, techniques is more effective than the behavioral techniques alone.

Let us now consider some of the specific techniques that sex therapists have introduced in treating several of the major types of sexual dysfunction.

Sexual Desire Disorders

Some sex therapists help kindle the sexual appetites of people with hypoactive sexual desire by prescribing self-stimulation exercises combined with erotic fantasies (LoPiccolo & Friedman, 1988). Sex therapists may also assist dysfunctional couples by prescribing sensate focus exercises, enhancing communication, and expanding the couple's repertoire of sexual skills. Sex therapists recognize that hypoactive sexual desire is often a complex problem that requires more intensive treatment than do problems of the arousal or orgasm phases (Leiblum & Rosen, 1988). Helen Singer Kaplan (1987) argues that insight-oriented approaches are especially helpful in the treatment of hypoactive sexual desire and sexual aversion to uncover and resolve deep-seated psychological conflicts.

When lack of desire is connected with depression, sexual interests may rebound when the depression lifts. Treatment in such cases may involve psychotherapy or chemotherapy, not sex therapy per se. Some cases of hypoactive sexual desire involve hormonal deficiencies, especially deficiencies in testosterone. But testosterone-replacement therapy is believed to be successful only in the relatively few cases of bona fide testosterone deficiencies (Spark, 1991). When problems in the relationship are involved, marital or couples therapy may be indicated to improve the relationship. Once interpersonal problems are ironed out, sexual interest may return.

Treatment of sexual aversion disorder may involve a multifaceted approach, including biological treatments such as the use of medications to reduce anxiety, and psychological treatments designed to help the individual overcome the underlying sexual phobia. Couples therapy may be used in cases in which sexual aversions arise from problems in relationships (Gold & Gold, 1993). Sensate focus exercises may be used to lessen generalized anxiety about sexual contact. But fears of specific aspects of the sexual act may need to be overcome through behavioral exercises in which the client learns to manage the stimuli that evoke fears of sexual contact:

> Bridget, 26, and Bryan, 30, were married for four years but had never consummated their relationship because Bridget would panic whenever Bryan attempted coitus with her. While she enjoyed foreplay and was capable of achieving orgasm with clitoral stimulation, her fears of sexual contact were triggered by Bryan's attempts at vaginal penetration. The therapist employed a program of gradual exposure to the feared stimuli to allow Bridget the opportunity to overcome her fears in small, graduated steps. First she was instructed to view her genitals in a mirror when she was alone—this in order to violate her long-standing prohibition against looking at and enjoying her body. While this exercise initially made her feel anxious, with repeated exposure she became comfortable performing it and then progressed to touching her genitals directly. When she became comfortable with this step, and reported experiencing pleasurable erotic sensations, she was instructed to insert a finger into the vagina. She encountered intense anxiety at this step and required daily practice for two weeks before she could tolerate inserting her finger into her vagina without discomfort. Her husband was then brought into the treatment process. The couple was instructed to have Bridget insert her own finger in her vagina while Bryan watched. When she was comfortable with this exercise, she then guided his finger into her vagina. Later he placed one and then two fingers into her vagina, while she controlled the depth, speed and duration of penetration. When she felt ready, they proceeded to attempt penile penetration in the female superior position, which allowed her to maintain control over penetration. Over time, Bridget became more comfortable with penetration to the point that the couple developed a normal sexual relationship.

> (Adapted from Kaplan, 1987, pp. 102–103)

Sexual Arousal Disorders

Men with chronic erectile disorder may believe that they have "forgotten" how to have an erection. They may ask their therapists to "teach" them or "show them" how. Some of our clients have asked us to tell them what they should think or picture in their minds to achieve an erection, or how they should touch their partners or be touched. Erection is an involuntary reflex, however, not a skill. A man need not learn how to have an erection any more than he need learn how to breathe.

In sex therapy, women who have trouble becoming lubricated and men with erectile problems learn that they need not "do" anything to become sexually aroused. As long as their problems are psychologically and not organically based, they need only receive sexual stimulation under relaxed circumstances so that anxiety does not inhibit their natural reflexes.

Truth OR Fiction? REVISITED

It is not true that sex therapy teaches a man with erectile disorder how to will an erection. Men with erectile disorder are actually taught that it is not possible to will an erection. One can only set the stage for erection (or vaginal lubrication) to occur and then allow it to happen reflexively. ■

In order to reduce performance anxiety, the partners engage in nondemanding sexual contacts: contacts that do not demand lubrication or erection. They may start with nongenital sensate focus exercises in the style of Masters and Johnson. After a couple of sessions, sensate focus extends to the genitals. The position shown in Figure 15.1 allows the woman easy access to her partner's genitals. She repeatedly "teases" him to erection and allows the erection to subside. Thus she avoids creating performance anxiety that could lead to loss of erection. By repeatedly regaining his erection, the man loses the fear that loss of erection means it will not return. He learns also to focus on erotic sensations for their own sake. He experiences no demand to perform, as the couple is instructed to refrain from coitus.

When the dysfunctional partner can reliably achieve sexual excitement (denoted by erection in the male and lubrication in the female), the couple does not immediately attempt coitus, since this might rekindle performance anxiety. Rather, the couple engages in a series of nondemanding, pleasurable sexual activities, eventually culminating in coitus.

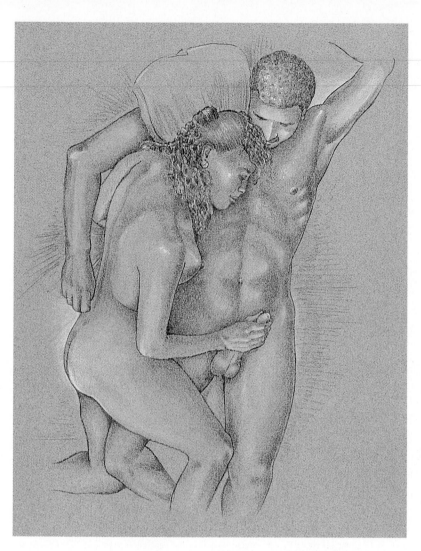

Figure 15.1. **The Training Position Recommended by Masters and Johnson for Treatment of Erectile Disorder and Premature Ejaculation.** By lying in front of her partner who has his legs spread, the woman has ready access to his genitals. In one part of a program designed to overcome erectile disorder, she repeatedly "teases" him to erection and allows the erection to subside. Thus she avoids creating performance anxiety that could lead to loss of erection. Through repeated regaining of erection, the man loses the fear that loss of erection means it will not return.

In Masters and Johnson's approach, the couple begin coitus after about 10 days of treatment. The woman teases the man to erection while she is sitting above him, straddling his thighs. When he is erect, *she* inserts the penis—to avoid fumbling attempts at entry—and moves slowly back and forth in a *nondemanding way*. Neither attempts to reach orgasm. If erection is lost, teasing and coitus are repeated. Once the couple become confident that erection can be retained—or reinstated if lost—they may increase coital thrusting gradually to reach orgasm.

Orgasmic Disorders

Women who have never experienced orgasm often harbor negative sexual attitudes that cause anxiety and inhibit sexual response. Treatment in such cases may first address these attitudes.

Masters and Johnson use a couples-oriented approach in treating anorgasmic women. They begin with sensate focus exercises. Then, during genital massage and later during coitus, the woman guides her partner in the caresses and movements that she finds sexually exciting. Taking charge helps free the woman, psychologically speaking, from the traditional stereotype of the passive, subordinate female role.

Masters and Johnson recommend a training position (see Figure 15.2 on page 460) that gives the man access to his partner's breasts and genitals. She can guide his hands to show him the types of stimulation she enjoys. The genital play is *nondemanding*. The goals are to learn to provide and enjoy effective sexual stimulation, not to reach orgasm. The

Figure 15.2. **The Training Position for Nondemanding Stimulation of the Female Genitals.**
This position gives the man access to his partner's breasts and genitals. She can guide his hands to show
him the types of stimulation she enjoys.

clitoris is not stimulated early, since doing so may produce a high level of stimulation before the woman is prepared.

After a number of occasions of genital play, the couple undertake coitus in the female-superior position (see Figure 15.3). This position allows the woman freedom of movement and control over her genital sensations. She is told to regard the penis as her "toy." The couple engages in several sessions of deliberately slow thrusting to sensitize the woman to sensations produced by the penis and break the common counterproductive pattern of desperate, rapid thrusting.

Orgasm cannot be willed or forced. When a woman receives effective stimulation, feels free to focus on erotic sensations, and feels that nothing is being demanded of her, she will generally reach orgasm. Once the woman is able to attain orgasm in the female-superior position, the couple may extend their sexual repertoire to other positions.

Masters and Johnson prefer working with the couple in cases of anorgasmia, but other sex therapists prefer to begin working with the woman individually through masturbation (Barbach, 1975; Heiman & LoPiccolo, 1987). This approach assumes that the woman accepts masturbation as a therapy tool. Masturbation provides women with opportunities to

Figure 15.3. Coitus in the Female-Superior Position. In treatment of female orgasmic disorder, the couple undertake coitus in the female-superior position after a number of occasions of genital play. This position allows the woman freedom of movement and control over her genital sensations. She is told to regard the penis as her "toy." The couple engages in several sessions of deliberately slow thrusting to sensitize the woman to sensations produced by the penis and to break the common counterproductive pattern of desperate, rapid thrusting.

learn about their own bodies at their own pace. It frees them of the need to rely on partners or to please partners. The sexual pleasure they experience helps counter lingering sexual anxieties. Although there is some variation among therapists, the following elements are commonly found in directed masturbation programs:

1. *Education.* The woman and her sex partner (if she has one) are educated about female sexuality.
2. *Self-exploration.* Self-exploration is encouraged as a way of increasing the woman's sense of body awareness. She may hold a mirror between her legs to locate her sexual anatomic features. Kegel exercises may be prescribed to help tone and strengthen the pubococcygeus (PC) muscle that surrounds the vagina and increase her awareness of genital sensations and sense of control.
3. *Self-massage.* Once the woman feels comfortable about exploring her body, she creates a relaxing setting for self-massage. She chooses a time and place where she is free from external distractions. She begins to explore the sensitivity of her body to touch, discovering and then repeating the caresses that she finds pleasurable. At first self-massage is not concentrated on the genitals. It encompasses other sensitive parts of the body. She may incorporate stimulation of the nipples and breasts and then direct genital stimulation, focusing on the clitoral area and experimenting with hand movements. Nonalcohol-based oils and lotions may be used to enhance the sensuous quality of the massage and to provide lubrication for the external genitalia. Kegel exercises may also be performed during self-stimulation to increase awareness of vaginal sensations and increase muscle tension. Some women use their dominant hand to stimulate their breasts while the other hand massages the genitals. No two women approach masturbation in quite the same way. During the first few occasions the woman does not attempt to reach orgasm, so as to prevent performance anxiety.
4. *Giving oneself permission.* The woman may be advised to practice assertive thoughts to dispel lingering guilt and anxiety about masturbation. For example, she might repeat to herself, "This is my body. I have a right to learn about my body and receive pleasure from it."
5. *Use of fantasy.* Arousal is heightened through the use of sexual images, fantasies, and fantasy aids, such as erotic written or visual materials.

6. *Allowing, not forcing, orgasm.* It may take weeks of masturbation to reach orgasm, especially for women who have never achieved orgasm. By focusing on her erotic sensations and fantasies, but not demanding orgasm, the woman lowers performance anxiety and creates the stimulating conditions needed to reach orgasm.

7. *Use of a vibrator.* A vibrator may be recommended to provide more intense stimulation, especially for women who find that manual stimulation is insufficient.

8. *Involvement of the partner.* Once the woman is capable of regularly achieving orgasm through masturbation, the focus may shift to the woman's sexual relationship with her partner. Nondemanding sensate focus exercises may be followed by nondemanding coitus. The female-superior position is often used. It enables the woman to control the depth, angle, and rate of thrusting. She thus ensures that she receives the kinds of stimulation needed to reach orgasm.

Truth OR Fiction?
REVISITED

It is true that many sex therapists recommend masturbation as the treatment for women who have never been able to reach orgasm. Masturbation allows women (and men) to get in touch with their own sexual responses without relying on a partner. ■

Kaplan (1974) suggests a bridge maneuver to assist couples who are interested in making the transition from a combination of manual and coital stimulation to coital stimulation alone as a means for reaching orgasm. Manual stimulation during coitus is used until the woman senses that she is about to reach orgasm. Manual stimulation is then stopped and the woman thrusts with her pelvis to provide the stimulation necessary to reach orgasm. Over time the manual clitoral stimulation is discontinued earlier and earlier. Although some couples may prefer this "hands-off" approach to inducing orgasm, Kaplan points out that there is nothing wrong with combining manual stimulation and penile thrusting. There is no evidence that reliance on clitoral stimulation means that women are sexually immature. (Evidence has not borne out the theoretical psychoanalytic distinction between clitoral and vaginal orgasms.)

Our focus has been on sexual techniques, but it is worth noting that a combination of approaches that focus on sexual techniques and underlying interpersonal problems may be more effective than focusing on sexual techniques alone, at least for couples whose relationships are troubled (Killmann et al., 1987; LoPiccolo & Stock, 1986).

Male Orgasmic Disorder   Treatment of male orgasmic disorder generally focuses on increasing sexual stimulation and reducing performance anxiety (LoPiccolo & Stock, 1986). Masters and Johnson instruct the couple to practice sensate focus exercises for several days, during which the man makes no attempt to ejaculate. The couple is then instructed to bring the man to orgasm in any way they can, usually by the woman's stroking his penis. Once the husband can ejaculate in the woman's presence, she brings him to the point at which he is about to ejaculate. Then, in the female-superior position, she inserts the penis and thrusts vigorously to bring him to orgasm. If he loses the feeling he is about to ejaculate, the process is repeated. Even if ejaculation occurs at the point of penetration, it often helps break the pattern of inability to ejaculate within the vagina.

Squeeze technique
A method for treating premature ejaculation whereby the tip of the penis is squeezed temporarily to prevent ejaculation.

Premature Ejaculation   In the Masters-and-Johnson approach, sensate focus exercises are followed by practice in the training position shown in Figure 15.1. The woman teases her partner to erection and uses the **squeeze technique** when he indicates that he is about to ejaculate. She squeezes the tip of the penis, which temporarily prevents ejaculation. This process is repeated three or four times in a 15- to 20-minute session before the man purposely ejaculates.

In using the squeeze technique (which should be used only following personal instruction from a sex therapist), the woman holds the penis between the thumb and first two fingers of the same hand. The thumb presses against the frenulum. The fingers straddle the coronal ridge on the other side of the penis. Squeezing the thumb and forefingers together fairly hard for about 20 seconds (or until the man's urge to ejaculate passes) prevents ejaculation. The erect penis can withstand fairly strong pressure without discomfort, but erection may be partially lost.

After two or three days of these sessions, Masters and Johnson have the couple begin coitus in the female-superior position because it creates less pressure to ejaculate. The woman inserts the penis. At first she contains it without thrusting, allowing the man to get used to intravaginal sensations. If he signals that he is about to ejaculate, she lifts off and squeezes the penis. After some repetitions, she begins slowly to move backward and forward, lifting off and squeezing as needed. The man learns gradually to tolerate higher levels of sexual stimulation without ejaculating.

The alternate "stop-start" method for treating premature ejaculation was introduced by urologist James Semans (1956). The method can be applied to manual stimulation or coitus. For example, the woman can manually stimulate her partner until he is about to ejaculate. He then signals her to suspend sexual stimulation and allows his arousal to subside before stimulation is resumed. This process enables the man to recognize the cues that precede his point of ejaculatory inevitability or "point of no return," and to tolerate longer periods of sexual stimulation. When the stop-start technique is applied to coitus, the couple begin with simple vaginal containment with no pelvic thrusting, preferably in the female-superior position. The man withdraws if he feels he is about to ejaculate. As the man's sense of control increases, thrusting can begin, along with variations in coital positions. The couple again stop when the man signals that he is approaching ejaculatory inevitability.

Sexual Pain Disorders

Dyspareunia   Dyspareunia, or painful intercourse, generally calls for medical intervention to ascertain and treat any underlying physical problems, such as genital infections, that might give rise to pain. When dyspareunia is caused by vaginismus, treatment of vaginismus through a behavioral approach, described below, may eliminate pain.

Vaginismus   Vaginismus is generally treated with behavioral exercises in which plastic vaginal dilators of increasing size are inserted to help relax the vaginal musculature. A gynecologist may first demonstrate insertion of the narrowest dilator. Later the woman herself practices insertion of wider dilators at home. The woman increases the size of the dilator as she becomes capable of tolerating insertion and containment (for 10 or 15 minutes) without discomfort or pain. The woman herself—not her partner or therapist—controls the pace of treatment (LoPiccolo & Stock, 1986). The woman's or her partner's fingers (first the littlest finger, then two fingers and so on) may be used in place of the plastic dilators, with the woman controlling the speed and depth of penetration. When the woman is able to tolerate dilators (or fingers) equivalent in thickness to the penis, the couple may attempt coitus. Still, the woman should control insertion. Circumstances should be relaxed and nondemanding. The idea is to avoid resensitizing her to fears of penetration. Since vaginismus often occurs among women with a history of sexual trauma, such as rape or incest, treatment for the psychological effects of these experiences may also be in order (LoPiccolo & Stock, 1986).

Evaluation of Sex Therapy

Masters and Johnson (1970) reported an overall success rate of about 80% in treating sexual dysfunctions in their two-week intensive program. Some dysfunctions proved more difficult to treat than others. An analysis of treatment results from 1950 to 1977 showed success rates ranging from 67% for primary erectile disorder to 99% for vaginismus (Kolodny, 1981) (see Table 15.3 on page 464). A follow-up of 226 initial successes after a five-year period showed that 16 people, or 7%, experienced a "treatment reversal."

Masters and Johnson's critics note that they followed up on a disappointingly small percentage (29%) of their sample over a five-year period. Thus, they may have seriously underestimated the actual number of treatment reversals (Adams, 1980; Zilbergeld &

TABLE 15.3 Outcomes of sex therapy at the Masters & Johnson Institute (1959–1977)

Variables	N	Failures	Successes	Success Rate (%)
Primary (lifelong) erectile disorder	51	17	34	67
Secondary (acquired) erectile disorder	501	108	393	78
Premature ejaculation	432	17	415	96
Male orgasmic disorder	75	18	57	76
Male Totals	1,059	160	899	85
Primary female orgasmic disorder	399	84	315	79
Secondary female orgasmic disorder	331	96	235	71
Vaginismus	83	1	82	99
Female Totals	813	181	632	78
Combined Totals	1,872	341	1,531	82

Source: Adapted from Kolodny, R. C. (1981). Evaluating Sex Therapy: Process and Outcome at the Masters & Johnson Institute. *Journal of Sex Research, 17*,301–318. Reprinted from *The Journal of Sex Research,* a publication of The Society for the Scientific Study of Sex; Mount Vernon, Iowa 42315 USA.

Evans, 1980). Zilbergeld and Evans (1980) also challenged their outcome measures. They argued that Masters and Johnson used a global measure of success or failure that was not tied to specific criteria.

Masters and Johnson's sample may also have been biased in at least two ways. It consisted only of people who were willing and could afford to spend two weeks at their institute for full-time therapy. These people were better educated and more affluent than the general population. Masters and Johnson also denied treatment to a number of people whom they considered not "really interested" in changing. Thus, their final sample may have been limited to people who were highly motivated. So some of the success of treatment may have been due to the clients' high level of motivation rather than to the treatment they received. Finally, the absence of a control group prevents us from knowing whether factors extraneous to the treatment itself may have been responsible for the apparent success.

Other researchers have reported more modest levels of success in treating erectile disorder than those reported at the Masters and Johnson Institute (Barlow, 1986). Nevertheless, long-term follow-up evaluations support the general effectiveness of sex therapy for erectile disorder (Everaerd, 1993). Yet problems do recur in some cases and are not always easily overcome (Everaerd, 1993). Some couples cope with recurring problems by using the techniques they learned during treatment, such as sensate focus exercises. The addition of biological treatments to the arsenal of treatments for erectile disorder has improved success rates to the point that virtually all erection problems can be successfully treated in one way or another (Reinisch, 1990).

We lack controlled studies of treatments of male orgasmic disorder (Dekker, 1993). Other than the original Masters and Johnson studies, results have been generally disappointing, with most people showing only modest if any improvement (Dekker, 1993). New techniques in treating low sexual desire are also needed because the available techniques are often inadequate (Hawton, 1991).

Sex therapy approaches to treating vaginismus and premature ejaculation have produced more consistent levels of success (Beck, 1993; O'Donohue et al., 1993). Reported success in treating vaginismus has ranged as high as 80% (Hawton & Catalan, 1990) to 100% in Masters and Johnson's (1970) original research. Treatment of premature ejaculation has resulted in success rates above 90% using the squeeze or stop-start techniques

(Killmann & Auerbach, 1979). But there are few data on the long-term results of treatment for premature ejaculation (LoPiccolo & Stock, 1986). Nor do we know why these techniques are effective (Kinder & Curtiss, 1988). Because the squeeze technique carries with it some risk of discomfort, many therapists prefer using the stop-start method.

LoPiccolo and Stock (1986) found that 95% of a sample of 150 previously anorgasmic women were able to achieve orgasm through a directed masturbation program. About 85% of these women were able to reach orgasm through manual stimulation by their partners. Only about 40% were able to achieve orgasm during coitus, however. Christensen (1995) argues that prescribing masturbation in sex therapy can have the side effect of damaging the trust and openness couples need for sexually rewarding relationships.

Generally speaking, couples-oriented treatment helps facilitate orgasm during coitus but is no guarantee that women will become orgasmic during coitus (Heiman & LoPiccolo, 1987; LoPiccolo & Stock, 1986). Nevertheless, the goal of achieving orgasm through some form of genital stimulation with a cooperative partner, as through oral sex or by direct manual clitoral stimulation, is realistic for most women (LoPiccolo & Stock, 1986). Many couples who believe it is important for the woman to reach orgasm during coitus are able to accomplish this end by combining direct clitoral stimulation with coital stimulation (LoPiccolo & Stock, 1986).

Researchers have come to understand some of the factors that predict success in sex therapy. Couples are generally more likely to benefit from sex therapy if they have good relationships and are highly motivated (Killmann et al., 1987; McCabe & Delaney, 1992). It should come as little surprise that the success of treatment often depends on the quality of the relationship. Nor is it surprising that people are generally more successful when they are more motivated to take full advantage of the treatments they receive. It also appears that partners who acquire coping skills from therapy that they can use later, such as learning to respond to problems that arise by discussing them openly and by reinstating techniques learned in therapy, are generally better able to overcome recurrences of the problem. Sex therapy techniques may not be appropriate for people in whom profound personal problems or problems in the relationship underlie sexual dysfunctions (Pryde, 1989).

Biological Treatments of Premature Ejaculation and Erectile Disorder

Sex therapy is by definition psychological or behavioral. However, biological treatments are also being used, especially in the cases of premature ejaculation and male erectile disorder.

Premature Ejaculation Pilot studies have recently appeared in which drugs usually used for psychological problems have been helpful in treating premature ejaculation. One, clomipramine, is normally used to treat people with obsessive–compulsive disorder or schizophrenia. However, in a pilot study with 15 couples, low doses of clomipramine helped men engage in coitus five times longer than usual without ejaculating (Althof, 1994). So-called antidepressant drugs have also been helpful in treatment of premature ejaculation (Forster & King, 1994; Waldinger et al., 1994; Wise, 1994).

Neurotransmitter
A chemical that transmits messages from one brain cell to another.

Why do drugs used to treat psychological problems help with premature ejaculation? The psychological problems are frequently connected with imbalances in body chemistry, such as **neurotransmitters**—the chemicals that transmit messages among brain cells. Neurotransmitters are also involved in other bodily functions, including ejaculation. The antidepressant drugs (fluoxetine, paroxetine, and sertraline) all work by increasing the action of the neurotransmitter serotonin. Serotonin, in turn, may inhibit the ejaculatory reflex (Assalian, 1994). It remains to be seen whether medications continue to show positive effects and to compare their effectiveness with psychological sex therapy techniques.

Erectile Disorder Biological or biomedical approaches may also be helpful in treating erectile disorder, especially in cases in which organic factors are involved. Treatments include penile implants, hormone treatments, vascular surgery, and self-injections of drugs that induce erections.

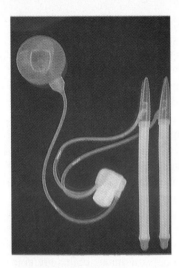

Penile Implants. This implant consists of cylinders which are implanted in the penis. A fluid reservoir (top left) is placed near the bladder. A pump (lower middle) is typically inserted in the scrotum. Squeezing the pump forces fluid into the cylinders, inflating the penis. A release valve returns the fluid to the reservoir, deflating the penis.

Implants A *penile implant* is a prosthetic device that is surgically implanted. About 20,000 men receive penile implants annually in the United States (Blakeslee, 1993a). The costs for the surgery and the prosthesis are as high as $10,000 to $12,000. Most medical insurance plans cover only those cases in which organic causes of erectile disorder are documented (Spark, 1991).

Two general types of implants are currently used, the semirigid and inflatable types (DATTA, 1988). The semirigid implant is made of two rods of silicone rubber that remain in a *permanent* semirigid position. It is rigid enough for intercourse and also permits the penis to hang reasonably close to the body at other times. The inflatable type requires more extensive surgery. Cylinders are implanted in the penis, a fluid reservoir is placed near the bladder, and a tiny pump is inserted in the scrotum. To attain erection, the man squeezes the pump, releasing fluid into the cylinders. When the erection is no longer needed, a release valve returns the fluid to the reservoir, deflating the penis (DATTA, 1988).

Inflatable implants tend to be preferred by men and their partners over the noninflatable, semirigid type (Beutler et al., 1986; DATTA, 1988). The inflatable type more closely duplicates the normal processes of tumescence and detumescence. Couples also find the inflatable type more aesthetically pleasing and sexually satisfying (DATTA, 1988). Some adverse side effects of penile implants have also been reported, including infection, pain, and erosion or perforation of the device (DATTA, 1988). The penile implant also damages the spongy tissues of the penis, impairing the man's ability to have normal erections. Penile implants do not in themselves affect sex drive, sexual sensations, or ejaculation (DATTA, 1988).

Men who receive penile implants, and their partners, are generally pleased with them (Anderson & Wold, 1986; Beutler et al., 1984; Collins & Kinder, 1984). Long-term follow-ups of sexual adjustment place the rate of satisfaction for men and their partners from 60% to 75% (LoPiccolo & Stock, 1986; Spark, 1991). Men with psychologically based erectile disorder tend to show less long-term benefit than men with organically caused dysfunctions (Spark, 1991).

Given the irreversible nature of the surgery, it is important for men and their partners to receive counseling beforehand to correct unrealistic expectations (Shaw, 1989). An expert panel convened by the National Institutes of Health in 1992 called for men and their doctors to consider the alternative treatments that are available. The experts recommended that surgical solutions, such as the use of penile implants or vascular surgery, be employed only if less invasive techniques, such as sex therapy and the use of injections to stimulate erections, prove unsuccessful. Penile implants have been falling out of favor lately, for several reasons, including complications from surgery and mechanical malfunctions (Blakeslee, 1993a).

Vascular Surgery *Vascular surgery* may be helpful in the few cases of specific blockages in the blood vessels that supply the penis, or in which structural defects in the penis restrict blood flow (LoPiccolo & Stock, 1986). An arterial bypass operation may reroute the blood vessels serving the penis around the area of blockage. Such operations have helped increase erections and restore sexual functioning in four out of five cases of men with vascular problems (Carmignani et al., 1987; Goldstein, 1987; Mohr & Beutler, 1990).

Hormone Treatments *Hormone (testosterone) treatments* may help restore sex drive and erectile ability in men with abnormally low levels of testosterone (Bagatell & Bremner, 1996; Carani et al., 1990; Spark, 1991). There is no evidence for its effectiveness in men with normal hormone levels. Testosterone has not been shown to help women who complain of lack of desire (Dow & Gallagher, 1989), unless their problem follows a surgically induced menopause in which the testosterone-producing adrenal glands were removed along with the ovaries (Bagatell & Bremner, 1996).

Penile Injection The muscle relaxants *papaverine* and *alprostadil* work after injection into the corpus cavernosum of the penis. Papaverine-induced erections last 35 to 40 minutes in the absence of ejaculation, or about 15 minutes in case of ejaculation (Levitt &

Mulcahy, 1995). A physician teaches the man how to inject himself. Alprostadil (brand name *Caverject*) was approved by the FDA for treatment of impotence in 1995.

Papaverine and alprostadil induce erection by relaxing the muscles that surround the small blood vessels in the penis. The vessels dilate and allow blood to flow into the penis more freely. Papaverine may also be combined with the drug phentolamine. The latter overcomes nerve signals that would otherwise keep the penis soft (Spark, 1991).

The majority of men with erectile failure achieve an erection sufficient for coitus through injection (Altman, 1995c; Spark, 1991). Injections are most effective for men with problems in the transmission of nerve signals that regulate erection (Altman, 1995c). They are less effective for men with vascular problems that restrict the flow of blood into the penis (Spark, 1991). Injections are also helpful with most men whose erectile problems are psychologically based (Kiely et al., 1987). A long-term study of self-injections with papaverine and phentolamine in 42 men showed significant improvements in sexual satisfaction, frequency of intercourse, and orgasm during coitus as judged by the men and their partners (Althof et al., 1991).

Penile injections may have side effects, including local bruises; prolonged, painful erections (*priapism*); fibrosis and nodules in the penis; difficulty reaching orgasm or ejaculating; abnormal liver functioning; infections; dependency on the injections to induce erections; and diminished quality of erections over time (Altman, 1995c; Mohr & Beutler, 1990; Spark, 1991). Many men find the idea of penile injections distasteful and reject them out of hand or drop out after a trial (Gilbert & Gingell, 1991).[2] Researchers are investigating alternatives to injections, such as creams that can be rubbed on the penis (Blakeslee, 1993a).

T r u t h **OR** *Fiction?*
R E V I S I T E D

It is true that drugs are available to treat premature ejaculation and erectile disorder. Questions remain about the effectiveness of drug therapy as compared to sex therapy. Moreover, drugs may have side effects. In fact, many men with erectile disorder refuse to inject themselves in the penis to attain erection. ■

Vacuum Constriction Device Sounding like something from the "what will they think of next" category, a recently introduced, noninvasive *vacuum constriction device (VCD)* helps men achieve erections through vacuum pressure. The device (brand name: ErecAid) consists of a cylinder that is connected to a hand-operated vacuum pump. It creates a vacuum when it is held over the limp penis to create an airtight seal (Mohr & Beutler, 1990; Spark, 1991). The vacuum increases the flow of blood into the penis, inducing an erection. Rubber bands placed around the base of the penis can maintain the erection for as long as 30 minutes. About 30,000 men were reported to be using the vacuum device by the early 1990s (Blakeslee, 1993a).

The device has been used successfully by men with both organically and psychologically based erectile failure. However, side effects such as pain and black-and-blue marks are common (Spark, 1991). The rubber bands can also injure penile tissue. The rubber bands also prevent normal ejaculation, so semen remains trapped in the urethra until the bands are released (Spark, 1991). The quality of the erections produced by the device is also considered inferior to spontaneous erections (Spark, 1991). The effectiveness of the device in routine use as well as its effects on the couple's sexual relations remain undetermined, however (Mohr & Beutler, 1990; Spark, 1991).

How Do You Find a Qualified Sex Therapist?

How would you find a sex therapist if you had a sexual dysfunction? You might find advertisements for "sex therapists" in the Yellow Pages. But beware. Most states do not restrict usage of the term "sex therapist" to recognized professionals. In these states, anyone who wants to use the label may do so, including quacks and prostitutes.

---

[2]Some women are also disconcerted by the procedure. But not all. One woman who approved the technique said, "When I'm in the mood I simply leave a syringe on the pillow and he gets the message" (Spark, 1991, p. 159).

Thus, it is essential to determine that a sex therapist is a member of a recognized profession (such as psychology, social work, medicine, or marriage and family counseling) with training and supervision in sex therapy. Professionals are usually licensed or certified by their states. All states require licensing of psychologists and physicians, but some states do not license social workers or marriage counselors. If you have questions about the license laws in your state, contact your state's professional licensing board. The ethical standards of these professions prohibit practitioners from claiming expertise in sex therapy without suitable training.

If you are uncertain as to how to locate a qualified sex therapist in your area, you may obtain names of local practitioners from various sources, such as your university or college psychology department, health department, or counseling center; a local medical or psychological association; a family physician; or your instructor. You may also seek services from a sex therapy clinic affiliated with a local medical center or medical school in your area, many of which charge for services on a sliding scale, depending on your income level. You may also contact the American Association of Sex Educators, Counselors, and Therapists (AASECT), a professional organization that certifies sex therapists. They can provide you with the names of certified sex therapists in your area. They are located at 11 Dupont Circle, N. W., Washington, DC.

Ethical professionals are not annoyed or embarrassed if you ask them (1) what their profession is, (2) where they earned their advanced degree, (3) whether they are licensed or certified by the state, (4) their fees, (5) their plans for treatment, and (6) the nature of their training in human sexuality and sex therapy. If the therapist hems and haws, asks why you are asking such questions, or fails to provide a direct answer, beware.

Professionals are also restricted by the ethical principles of their professions from engaging in unethical practices, such as sexual relations with their clients. The nature of therapy creates an unequal power relationship between the therapist and the client. The therapist is perceived as an expert whose suggestions are likely to carry great authority. Clients may thus be vulnerable to exploitation by therapists who misuse their therapeutic authority. Let's be absolutely clear here: There is no therapeutic justification for a therapist to engage in sexual activity with a client. Any therapist who makes a sexual overture toward a client, or tries to persuade a client to engage in sexual relations, is acting unethically.

~ *Reflections* ~

- How do sex therapy programs help people deal with pressure to perform? How can you adapt this knowledge to enhance your own sexual pleasure?
- If you had a sexual dysfunction, do you think that you would be willing to participate in sex therapy? Why, or why not? Do some techniques seem more acceptable to you than others? Explain.
- How would you go about finding a qualified sex therapist if you needed one?

Summing Up

Types of Sexual Dysfunctions

Sexual dysfunctions are difficulties in becoming sexually aroused or reaching orgasm.

Sexual Desire Disorders   These disorders involve dysfunctions in sexual desire, interest, or drive, in which the person experiences a lack of sexual desire or an aversion to genital sexual contact.

Sexual Arousal Disorders   In men, sexual arousal disorders involve recurrent difficulty in achieving or sustaining erections sufficient to successfully engage in sexual intercourse. In women, they typically involve failure to become sufficiently lubricated.

Orgasmic Disorders   Women are more likely to encounter difficulties reaching orgasm. Men are more likely to have premature ejaculation.

Sexual Pain Disorders   These disorders include dyspareunia and vaginismus.

Origins of Sexual Dysfunctions

Many sexual dysfunctions involve the interaction of organic and psychological factors.

Organic Causes   Fatigue may lead to erectile disorder in men and to orgasmic disorder and dyspareunia in women. Dyspareunia often reflects vaginal infections and STDs. Organic factors are believed to be involved in more than 50% of cases of erectile disorder. Medications and other drugs may also impair sexual functioning.

Psychosocial Causes   Psychosocial factors that are connected with sexual dysfunctions include cultural influences, psychosexual trauma, inclinations to a gay sexual orientation, marital dissatisfaction, psychological conflict, lack of sexual skills, irrational beliefs, and performance anxiety. Children reared in sexually repressive cultural or home environments may learn to respond to sex with feelings of anxiety and shame, rather than sexual arousal and pleasure. Many people do not acquire sexual competencies because of a lack of opportunity to acquire knowledge and experience, even within marriage. Irrational beliefs and attitudes such as excessive needs for approval and perfectionism may also contribute to sexual problems. Performance anxiety may place a dysfunctional individual in a spectator rather than performer role.

Treatment of Sexual Dysfunctions

Sex therapy aims to directly modify dysfunctional behavior by changing self-defeating beliefs and attitudes, fostering sexual skills and knowledge, enhancing sexual communication, and suggesting behavioral exercises to enhance sexual stimulation while reducing performance anxiety.

The Masters-and-Johnson Approach   Masters and Johnson pioneered the direct, behavioral approach to treating sexual dysfunctions. They employ a male-and-female therapy team during an in-residence program, which focuses on the couple as the unit of treatment. Sensate focus exercises are used to enable the partners to give each other pleasure in a nondemanding situation.

The Helen Singer Kaplan Approach   Kaplan's *psychosexual therapy* combines behavioral and psychoanalytic methods.

Sexual Desire Disorders   Some sex therapists help kindle the sexual appetites of people with inhibited sexual desire through prescribing self-stimulation exercises combined with erotic fantasies.

Sexual Arousal Disorders   Men and women with impaired sexual arousal receive sexual stimulation from their partners under relaxed circumstances, so that anxiety does not inhibit their natural reflexes.

Orgasmic Disorders   Masters and Johnson use a couples-oriented approach in treating anorgasmic women. Other sex therapists prefer a program of directed masturbation to enable women to learn about their own bodies at their own pace and free them of the need to rely on partners or please partners. Premature ejaculation is usually treated with the squeeze technique or the stop-start method.

Sexual Pain Disorders   Dyspareunia or painful intercourse is generally treated with medical intervention. Vaginismus is generally treated with plastic vaginal dilators of increasing size.

Evaluation of Sex Therapy   The success of sex therapy has varied with the type of sexual dysfunction treated.

Biological Treatments of Premature Ejaculation and Erectile Disorder   Biological approaches may be helpful in treating premature ejaculation and erectile disorder. Treatments include oral drug therapy for premature ejaculation, and penile implants, hormone treatments, vascular surgery, and injections of drugs for erectile disorder.

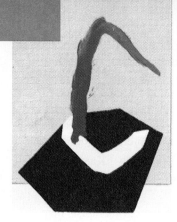

CHAPTER 16

Henri Matisse, *The Clown,*
Plate 1 from *Jazz.* The Metropolitan Museum of Art,
Gift of Lila Acheson Wal-
lace, 1983. © 1996 Succession H. Matisse/Artist Rights
Society (ARS), New York.
© 1985 by The Metropolitan
Museum of Art.

Sexually Transmitted Diseases

Outline

An Epidemic

Bacterial Diseases
Gonorrhea
Syphilis
Chlamydia
Other Bacterial Diseases

Vaginal Infections
Bacterial Vaginosis
Candidiasis
Trichomoniasis

Viral Diseases
Herpes
Viral Hepatitis
Genital Warts
Molluscum Contagiosum

Ectoparasitic Infestations
Pediculosis
Scabies

Prevention of STDs: It's More Than Safer Sex
Prevention Strategies

Summing Up

What Do You Say Now? / Talking to Your Parents About STDs

A Closer Look / What to Do If You Suspect You Have Contracted an STD; Sources of Help

Questionnaire / STD Attitude Scale

Truth OR Fiction?

_____ About 80% of the women who contract gonorrhea do not develop symptoms.

_____ Christopher Columbus brought more than beads, blankets, and tobacco back to Europe from the New World: He also brought syphilis.

_____ Gonorrhea and syphilis may be contracted from toilet seats in public rest rooms.

_____ If a syphilitic chancre (sore) goes away by itself, the infection does not require medical treatment.

_____ Men too can develop vaginal infections.

_____ Vaginitis is often caused by an overgrowth of infectious organisms that normally reside in the vagina.

_____ Many men whose partners have "trich" are also infected themselves, often unknowingly.

_____ Genital herpes can be transmitted only during flare-ups of the disease.

_____ Most people with genital warts have them on visible parts of the body.

_____ Pubic lice are of the same family of animals as crabs.

HAROLD and CARIN, both 20, have been dating for several months. They feel strong sexual attraction toward each other but have hesitated to become sexually intimate because of fears about AIDS. Harold believes that using condoms is no guarantee against infection and wants the two of them to be tested for HIV, the virus that causes AIDS. Carin has resisted undergoing an HIV test, partly because she feels insulted that Harold fears that she may be infected, and frankly, partly in fear of the test results. She has heard that symptoms may not develop for years after infection. She wonders whether she might have been infected by one of the men with whom she slept in the past.

KEISHA has genital herpes. A 19-year-old pre-law student, she has had no recurrences since the initial outbreak two years earlier. But she knows that herpes is a lifelong infection and may recur periodically from time to time. She also knows that she may inadvertently pass the herpes virus along to her sex partners, even to the man she eventually marries. She has begun thinking seriously about Steve, a man she has been dating for the past month. She would like to tell him that she has herpes before they become sexually intimate. Yet she fears that telling him might scare him off.

JOSÉ, 21, a math and computer science major, is planning a career in computer operations, hoping one day to run the computer systems for a large corporation. He lives off-campus with several of his buddies in a run-down house they've dubbed the "Nuclear Dumpsite." He has been dating Maria, a theater major, for several months. They have begun having sexual relations and have practiced "safer sex"—at least most of the time. During the past week he noticed a burning sensation while urinating. It seems to have passed now, so he figures that it was probably nothing to worry about. But he's not sure and wonders whether he should see a doctor.

Harold, Carin, Keisha, and José express some of the fears and concerns of a generation of young people who are becoming sexually active at a time when the threat of AIDS and other STDs (**sexually transmitted diseases**) hangs over every sexual decision.

> **Sexually transmitted diseases**
> Diseases that are communicated through sexual contact. Abbreviated STDs.

AIDS is indeed a scary thing, a very scary thing. But AIDS is only one of many STDs, although certainly the most deadly and frightening. Nearly every time you pick up a newspaper or turn on the radio or TV, you hear about AIDS, yet other STDs pose much wider threats. In a study of more than 16,000 students on 19 U.S. college campuses, HIV (the virus that causes AIDS) was found in 30 blood samples (Gayle et al., 1990), or 0.2% of the students in the sample. *Chlamydia trachomatous* (the bacterium that causes chlamydia) and *human papilloma virus* (HPV) (the organism that causes genital warts) were each found in 1 sample in 10, or 10% of the college population! Chlamydia, virtually unheard of a generation ago, is now the most common bacterial STD in the United States. It has outpaced the old bacterial nemeses, gonorrhea and syphilis (USDHHS, 1992b).

The same study found that college students were reasonably well versed about AIDS. However, many are unaware that chlamydia can go undetected for years. Moreover, if it is left untreated, it can cause pelvic inflammation and infertility. Many, perhaps most, students were completely ignorant of HPV, a virus that causes genital warts and is linked to cervical cancer. Yet the Federal Centers for Disease Control and Prevention (CDC) estimates that as many as 1 million new cases of HPV infection occur each year in the United States—more than syphilis, genital herpes, and AIDS combined (Penn, 1993). Whereas 1 to 1.5 million Americans are thought to be infected with HIV, about 56 million are infected with other STD-causing viruses, such as those causing genital warts, herpes, and hepatitis (Barringer, 1993a). *None of this is intended to downplay the threat of AIDS. AIDS is lethal, and one case is one case too many.*

There are also links between HIV/AIDS and other STDs (USDHHS, 1992b). For one thing, if people with another STD that causes genital lesions or inflammation are exposed to HIV, they are more likely to be infected with it (WHO, 1995). For another, the use of latex (rubber) condoms not only helps prevent the spread of HIV but also many other STD-causing organisms, such as those causing gonorrhea, chlamydia, and genital herpes (Consumer's Union, 1995).

Sexually transmitted diseases (STDs) are transmitted through sexual means, such as vaginal or anal intercourse or oral sex. They were formerly called *venereal diseases* (VD)—after Venus, the Roman goddess of love.

Some STDs can be spread (and often are) through nonsexual contact as well. For example, AIDS and viral hepatitis may be spread by sharing contaminated needles. And yes, a few STDs (like "crabs") may be picked up from bedding or other objects, such as moist towels, that harbor the infectious organisms that cause these STDs.

An Epidemic

STDs are rampant. The World Health Organization (WHO) estimates that at least 333 million people around the world are stricken with curable STDs each year (WHO, 1995). More than 13 million people in the United States, including 2.5 million adolescents (about one in six), contract an STD each year. At least one in four Americans is likely to contract an STD at some point in life (Barringer, 1993a). Two cases in three occur in people under the age of 25. One in four afflicts teenagers. Yet many young people remain largely uninformed about the dangers of STDs.

Some readers have STDs and do not realize it. Ignorance is not bliss, however. Some STDs may not produce noticeable symptoms, but they can be harmful if left untreated. STDs can also be painful and, in the cases of AIDS and advanced syphilis, lethal. Women suffer disproportionately from the effects of STDs. Women are more likely to develop infertility as the result of an STD's spreading through the reproductive system (Barringer, 1993a; Rosenberg & Gollub, 1992). An estimated 100,000 to 150,000 women become infertile each year because of STDs (Barringer, 1993a). Overall, STDs are believed to account for 15% to 30% of cases of infertility among women. In addition to their biological effects, STDs exact an emotional toll and strain relationships to the breaking point.

Why the surge in the incidence of STDs? One is the increased numbers of young people who engage in coitus. Many of them fail to use latex condoms consistently, if at all. Some people do not use condoms because the woman is on the pill. Although birth-control pills are reliable methods of contraception, they do not prevent the spread of STDs. Another reason is that some infections, like chlamydia, often have no symptoms. Therefore, some infected individuals unwittingly pass them along to others. Other risk factors include early sexual

One in Ten. Researchers estimate that chlamydial infections and genital warts afflict one college student in ten. Most students may be aware of the dangers of AIDS, but how many know about the risks posed by these more common STDs?

W H A T   D O   O U   S A Y   N O W ?

TALKING TO YOUR PARTNER ABOUT STDS

Many people find it hard to talk about STDs with their partners. As one young woman explained:

> It's one thing to talk about "being responsible about STD" and a much harder thing to do it at the very moment. It's just plain hard to say to someone I am feeling very erotic with, "Oh, yes, before we go any further, can we have a conversation about STD?" It's hard to imagine murmuring into someone's ear at a time of passion, "Would you mind slipping on this condom or using this cream just in case one of us has STD?" Yet it seems awkward to bring it up any sooner if it's not clear between us that we want to make love.
>
> (Boston Women's Health Book Collective, *The New Our Bodies, Ourselves*, 1992)

Because talking about STDs with sex partners can be awkward, many people wing it. They assume that their partners are free of STDs and hope for the best. Some people act as if not talking about AIDS and other STDs will cause them to go away. But the microbes causing AIDS, herpes, chlamydia, genital warts, and other STDs will not simply go away by not talking about them.

Imagine yourself in this situation: You've gone out with Chris a few times and you're keenly attracted. Chris is attractive, bright, witty, shares some of your attitudes, and, all in all, is a powerful turn-on. Now the evening is winding down. You've been cuddling, and you think you know where things are heading.

Something clicks in your mind! You realize that as wonderful as Chris is, you don't know every place Chris has "been." As healthy as Chris looks and acts, you don't know what's swimming around in Chris's bloodstream. Chris may not know either. In a moment of pent-up desire, Chris may also (how should we put this delicately?) *lie* about not being infected or about past sexual experiences.

What do you say now? How do you protect yourself without turning Chris off? Write some possible responses in the spaces provided, and then keep reading for more ideas.

1. _____
_____
2. _____
_____
3. _____
_____

Ah, the clumsiness! If you ask about condoms or STDs, it is sort of making a verbal commitment to have sexual relations, and perhaps you're not exactly sure that's what your partner intends. And even if it's clear that's where you're heading, will you seem too straightforward? Will you kill the romance? The spontaneity of the moment? Sure you might—life has its risks. But which is riskier: an awkward moment or being infected with a fatal illness? Let's put it another way: Are you *really* willing to die for sex? Given that few verbal responses are perfect, here are some things you can try:

1. You might say something like this: "I've brought something and I'd like to use it. . . . " (referring to a condom).
2. Or you can say, "I know this is a bit clumsy" (you are assertively expressing a feeling and asking permission to pursue a clumsy topic; Chris is likely to respond with "That's okay," or "Don't worry—what is it?") "but the world isn't as safe as it used to be, and I think we should talk about what we're going to do."

The point is that your partner hasn't been living in a cave. Your partner is also aware of the dangers of STDs, especially of AIDS, and ought to be working with you to make things safe and unpressured. If your partner is pressing for unsafe sex and is inconsiderate of your feelings and concerns, you need to reassess whether you want to be with this person. We think you can do better.

---

involvement and sex with multiple partners. Drug use is also associated with an increased risk of STDs. People who abuse drugs are more likely than others to engage in risky sexual practices (Lowry et al., 1994; Rotheram-Borus et al., 1994a). Moreover, certain forms of drug use, such as needle sharing, can directly transmit infectious organisms like HIV.

Education is critical to curtailing the STD epidemic among young people (Yarber & Parillo, 1992). STD instruction is intended to promote responsible sexual decision making and to alter risky behavior patterns. However, education may not be enough. Young people must also want to practice prevention and risk-reduction strategies if education is to have a meaningful effect on their behavior (Yarber & Parillo, 1992).

In this chapter we discuss STDs that are caused by agents as diverse as bacteria, viruses, protozoa, and parasites. In the next chapter we discuss HIV infection and AIDS.

QUESTIONNAIRE

STD ATTITUDE SCALE

Do your attitudes toward sexually transmitted diseases lead you to take risks that increase the chances of contracting one? The STD Attitude Scale (Yarber et al., 1989) was constructed to measure the attitudes of young adults toward STDs and provide insight into these questions.

To complete the questionnaire, read each statement carefully. Record your reactions by circling the letters according to this code:

SA = Strongly Agree
A = Agree
U = Undecided
D = Disagree
SD = Strongly Disagree

Interpret your responses by referring to the scoring key in the Appendix.

1. How one uses her or his sexuality has nothing to do with STD.
SA A U D SD

2. It is easy to use the prevention methods that reduce one's chances of getting an STD.
SA A U D SD

3. Responsible sex is one of the best ways of reducing the risk of STD.
SA A U D SD

4. Getting early medical care is the main key to preventing harmful effects of STD.
SA A U D SD

5. Choosing the right sex partner is important in reducing the risk of getting an STD.
SA A U D SD

6. A high rate of STD should be a concern for all people.
SA A U D SD

7. People with an STD have a duty to get their sex partners to medical care.
SA A U D SD

8. The best way to get a sex partner to STD treatment is to take him or her to the doctor with you.
SA A U D SD

9. Changing one's sex habits is necessary once the presence of an STD is known.
SA A U D SD

10. I would dislike having to follow the medical steps for treating an STD.
SA A U D SD

11. If I were sexually active, I would feel uneasy doing things before and after sex to prevent getting an STD.
SA A U D SD

12. If I were sexually active, it would be insulting if a sex partner suggested we use a condom to avoid STD.
SA A U D SD

13. I dislike talking about STD with my peers.
SA A U D SD

14. I would be uncertain about going to the doctor unless I was sure I really had an STD.
SA A U D SD

15. I would feel that I should take my sex partner with me to a clinic if I thought I had an STD.
SA A U D SD

16. It would be embarrassing to discuss STD with one's partner if one were sexually active.
SA A U D SD

17. If I were to have sex, the chance of getting an STD makes me uneasy about having sex with more than one person.
SA A U D SD

18. I like the idea of sexual abstinence (not having sex) as the best way of avoiding STD.
SA A U D SD

19. If I had an STD, I would cooperate with public health persons to find the sources of STD.
SA A U D SD

20. If I had an STD, I would avoid exposing others while I was being treated.
SA A U D SD

21. I would have regular STD checkups if I were having sex with more than one partner.
SA A U D SD

22. I intend to look for STD signs before deciding to have sex with anyone.
SA A U D SD

23. I will limit my sex activity to just one partner because of the chances I might get an STD.
SA A U D SD

24. I will avoid sexual contact any time I think there is even a slight chance of getting an STD.
SA A U D SD

25. The chance of getting an STD would not stop me from having sex.
SA A U D SD

26. If I had a chance, I would support community efforts toward controlling STD.
SA A U D SD

27. I would be willing to work with others to make people aware of STD problems in my town.
SA A U D SD

Source: Yarber, W. L., Torabi, M. R., & Veenker, C. H. (1989). Development of a Three-Component Sexually Transmitted Diseases Attitude Scale. *Journal of Sex Education & Therapy, 15*, 36–49. Reprinted with permission.

■ Does concern about STDs play a role in your life? If not, why not? (Are you fooling yourself?) If so, how?

■ What problems would you anticipate in discussing concern over STDs with a dating partner? Would these concerns prevent you from talking about STDs? Why, or why not?

■ Would you be insulted if a partner asked you whether you were infected with any STDs? Why, or why not?

Bacterial Diseases

Without the one-celled microorganisms we call **bacteria,** there would be no wine. Bacteria are essential to fermentation. They also play vital roles in our bodies' digestive systems. Unfortunately, bacteria also cause many diseases such as pneumonia, tuberculosis, and meningitis—along with the common STDs gonorrhea, syphilis, and chlamydia.

Gonorrhea

Gonorrhea—also known as "the clap" or "the drip"—was once the most widespread STD in the United States, but the rate of infection declined substantially during the 1980s (Centers for Disease Control [CDC], 1990a). Nearly a million cases of gonorrhea are reported each year. Many cases go unreported, however, so the actual incidence may be much higher. Most new cases of gonorrhea are contracted by people between the ages of 20 and 24.

Gonorrhea is caused by the *gonococcus* bacterium (see Table 16.1). A penile discharge that was probably gonorrhea is described in ancient Egyptian and Chinese writings and is mentioned in the Old Testament (Leviticus 15). Ancient Jews and Greeks assumed that the discharge was an involuntary loss of seminal fluid. In about 400 B.C. the Greek physician Hippocrates suggested that the loss stemmed from excessive sex or "worship" of Aphrodite (whom the Romans would later rename *Venus*). The term *gonorrhea* is credited to the Greek physician Galen, who lived in the second century A.D. Albert L. S. Neisser identified the gonococcus bacterium in 1879. For this reason, the microorganism bears his name: *Neisseria gonorrhoeae.*

Transmission   Gonococcal bacteria require a warm, moist environment, like that found along the mucous membranes of the urinary tract in both genders or the cervix in women. Outside the body, they die in about a minute. There is no evidence that gonorrhea can be picked up from public toilet seats or by touching dry objects. In rare cases, gonorrhea is contracted by contact with a moist, warm towel or sheet used immediately beforehand by an infected person (Calderone & Johnson, 1989). Gonorrhea is almost always transmitted by unprotected vaginal, oral, or anal sexual activity, or from mother to newborn during delivery (Reinisch, 1990).

A person who performs fellatio on an infected man may develop **pharyngeal gonorrhea,** which produces a throat infection. Mouth-to-mouth kissing and cunnilingus are less likely to spread gonorrhea. The eyes provide a good environment for the bacterium. Thus, a person whose hands come into contact with infected genitals and who inadvertently touches his or her eyes afterward may infect them. Babies have contracted gonorrhea of the eyes **(ophthalmia neonatorum)** when passing through the birth canals of infected mothers. This disorder may cause blindness but has become rare because the eyes of newborns are treated routinely with silver nitrate or penicillin ointment, which are toxic to gonococcal bacteria.

A gonorrheal infection may be spread from the penis to the partner's rectum during anal intercourse. A cervical gonorrheal infection can be spread to the rectum if an infected woman and her partner follow vaginal intercourse with anal intercourse. Gonorrhea is less likely to be spread by vaginal than penile discharges.

Bacteria
Plural of *bacterium,* a class of one-celled microorganisms that have no chlorophyll and can give rise to many illnesses. (From the Greek *baktron,* meaning "stick," referring to the fact that many bacteria are rod-shaped.)

Gonorrhea
An STD caused by the *Neisseria gonorrhoeae* bacterium and characterized by a discharge and burning urination. Left untreated, gonorrhea can give rise to pelvic inflammatory disease (PID) and infertility. (From the Greek *gonos,* meaning "seed," and *rheein,* meaning "to flow," referring to the fact that in ancient times the penile discharge characteristic of the illness was erroneously interpreted as a loss of seminal fluid.)

Pharyngeal gonorrhea
A gonorrheal infection of the pharynx (the cavity leading from the mouth and nasal passages to the larynx and esophagus) that is characterized by a sore throat.

Ophthalmia neonatorum
A gonorrheal infection of the eyes of newborn children who contract the disease by passing through an infected birth canal. (From the Greek *ophthalmos,* meaning "eye.")

TABLE 16.1 Causes, modes of transmission, symptoms, diagnosis, and treatment of major sexually transmitted diseases (STDs)

STD and Pathogen	Modes of Transmission	Symptoms	Diagnosis	Treatment
Bacterial Diseases				
Gonorrhea ("clap," "drip"): gonococcus bacterium (*Neisseria gonorrhoeae*).	Transmitted by vaginal, oral, or anal sexual activity, or from mother to newborn during delivery.	In men, yellowish, thick penile discharge; burning urination. In women, increased vaginal discharge, burning urination, irregular menstrual bleeding (most women show no early symptoms).	Clinical inspection, culture of sample discharge.	Antibiotics: ceftriaxone, spectinomycin, penicillin.
Syphilis: *Treponema pallidum.*	Transmitted by vaginal, oral, or anal sexual activity, or by touching an infectious chancre.	In primary stage, a hard, round painless chancre or sore appears at site of infection within 2 to 4 weeks. May progress through secondary, latent, and tertiary stages, if left untreated.	Primary-stage syphilis is diagnosed by clinical examination and by examination of fluid from a chancre. Secondary-stage syphilis is diagnosed by blood test (the VDRL).	Penicillin; or doxycycline, tetracycline, or erythromycin for nonpregnant, penicillin-allergic patients.
Chlamydia and non-gonococcal urethritis (NGU): *Chlamydia trachomatous* bacterium; NGU in men may also be caused by *Ureaplasma urealycticum* bacterium and other pathogens.	Transmitted by vaginal, oral, or anal sexual activity; to the eye by touching one's eyes after touching the genitals of an infected partner, or to newborns passing through the birth canal of an infected mother.	In women, frequent and painful urination, lower abdominal pain and inflammation, and vaginal discharge (but most women are symptom-free). In men, symptoms are similar to but milder than those of gonorrhea—burning or painful urination, slight penile discharge (most men are also asymptomatic). Sore throat may indicate infection from oral–genital contact.	The Abbott Testpack analyzes a cervical smear in women; in men, an extract of fluid from the penis is analyzed.	Antibiotics: doxycycline, tetracycline , or erythromycin.
Vaginitis				
Bacterial vaginosis: *Gardnerella vaginalis* bacterium and others.	Can arise by overgrowth of organisms in vagina, allergic reactions, etc.; also transmitted by sexual contact.	In women, thin, foul-smelling vaginal discharge. Irritation of genitals and mild pain during urination. In men, inflammation of penile foreskin and glans, urethritis, and cystitis. May be asymptomatic in both genders.	Culture and examination of bacterium.	Oral treatment with metronidazole (brand name: Flagyl).

(continued)

TABLE 16.1 Causes, modes of transmission, symptoms, diagnosis, and treatment of major sexually transmitted diseases (STDs) *(continued)*

STD and Pathogen	Modes of Transmission	Symptoms	Diagnosis	Treatment
Candidiasis (moniliasis, thrush, "yeast infection"): *Candida albicans*—a yeastlike fungus.	Can arise by overgrowth of fungus in vagina; may also be transmitted by sexual contact or by sharing a washcloth with an infected person.	In women, vulval itching; white, cheesy, foul-smelling discharge; soreness or swelling of vaginal and vulval tissues. In men, itching and burning on urination, or a reddening of the penis.	Diagnosis usually made on basis of symptoms.	Vaginal suppositories, creams, or tablets containing miconazole, clotrimazole , or terconazole; modification of use of other medicines and chemical agents; keeping infected area dry.
Trichomoniasis ("trich"): *Trichomonas vaginalis*—a protozoan (one-celled animal).	Almost always transmitted sexually.	In women, foamy, yellowish, odorous vaginal discharge; itching or burning sensation in vulva. Many women are asymptomatic. In men, usually asymptomatic, but mild urethritis is possible.	Microscopic examination of a smear of vaginal secretions, or of culture of the sample (latter method preferred).	Metronidazole (Flagyl).
Viral Diseases				
Oral herpes: *Herpes simplex* virus-type 1 (HSV-1).	Touching, kissing, sexual contact with sores or blisters; sharing cups, towels, toilet seats.	Cold sores or fever blisters on the lips, mouth, or throat; herpetic sores on the genitals	Usually clinical inspection.	Over-the-counter lip balms, cold-sore medications; check with your physician, however.
Genital herpes: *Herpes simplex virus-type 2 (HSV-2)*.	Almost always by means of vaginal, oral, or anal sexual activity; most contagious during active outbreaks of the disease.	Painful, reddish bumps around the genitals, thighs, or buttocks; in women, may also be in the vagina or on the cervix. Bumps become blisters or sores that fill with pus and break, shedding viral particles. Other possible symptoms: burning urination, fever, aches and pains, swollen glands; in women, vaginal discharge.	Clinical inspection of sores; culture and examination of fluid drawn from the base of a genital sore.	The antiviral drug acyclovir (brand name: Zovirax) may provide relief and prompt healing, but is not a cure; people with herpes often profit from counseling and group support as well.
Viral hepatitis: hepatitis A, B, C, and D type viruses.	Sexual contact, especially involving the anus (especially for hepatitis A); contact with infected fecal matter; transfusion of contaminated blood (especially for hepatitis B and C).	Ranges from being asymptomatic to mild flulike symptoms and more severe symptoms including fever, abdominal pain, vomiting, and "jaundiced" (yellowish) skin and eyes.	Examination of blood for hepatitis antibodies; liver biopsy.	Treatment usually involves bed rest, intake of fluids, and, sometimes, antibiotics to ward off bacterial infections that might take hold because of lowered resistance. Alpha interferon is sometimes used in treating hepatitis C.

STD and Pathogen	Modes of Transmission	Symptoms	Diagnosis	Treatment
Acquired immunodeficiency syndrome (AIDS): *human immunodeficiency virus (HIV).*	HIV is transmitted by sexual contact; by infusion with contaminated blood; from mother to fetus during pregnancy, or through childbirth or breast-feeding.	Infected people may initially be asymptomatic or develop mild flulike symptoms, which may then disappear for many years prior to the development of "full-blown" AIDS. Full-blown AIDS is symptomized by fever, weight loss, fatigue, diarrhea, and opportunistic infections such as rare forms of cancer (Kaposi's sarcoma) and pneumonia (PCP).	A blood or saliva test detects HIV antibodies in the bloodstream. The Western blot blood test may be used to confirm the results when HIV antibodies are present. The diagnosis of AIDS is usually made on the basis of antibodies, a low count of CD4 cells, and/or presence of indicator diseases.	There is no cure for AIDS. Antiviral drugs like AZT may delay the progress of HIV disease. People with AIDS may profit from good nutrition, exercise, counseling, and stress-management techniques.
Genital warts (venereal warts): *human papilloma virus (HPV).*	Transmission is by sexual and other forms of contact, such as with infected towels or clothing.	Appearance of painless warts, often resembling cauliflowers, on the penis, foreskin, scrotum, or internal urethra in men; on the vulva, labia, wall of the vagina, or cervix in women. May occur around the anus and in the rectum of both genders.	Clinical inspection.	Methods include cryotherapy (freezing), podophyllin, burning, surgical removal.
Ectoparasitic Infestations				
Pediculosis ("crabs"): *Pthirus pubis* (pubic lice).	Transmission is by sexual contact, or by contact with an infested towel, sheet, or toilet seat.	Intense itching in pubic area and other hairy regions to which lice can attach.	Clinical examination.	Lindane (brand name: Kwell)—a prescription shampoo; nonprescription medications containing pyrethrins or piperonal butoxide (brand names: RID, Triple X).
Scabies: *Sarcoptes scabiei.*	Transmission is by sexual contact, or by contact with infested clothing, bed linen, towels, and other fabrics.	Intense itching; reddish lines on skin where mites have burrowed in; welts and pus-filled blisters in affected areas.	Clinical inspection.	Lindane (Kwell).

Source: Adapted from Rathus, S. A. (1996). *Psychology,* 6th ed. Fort Worth: Harcourt Brace College Publishers.

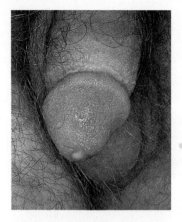

Gonorrheal Discharge.
Gonorrhea in the male often causes a thick, yellowish, pus-like discharge from the penis.

Cervicitis
Inflammation of the cervix.

Asymptomatic
Without symptoms.

T r u t h **OR** *Fiction?*
R E V I S I T E D

Epididymitis
Inflammation of the epididymis.

Pelvic inflammatory disease
Inflammation of the pelvic region—possibly including the cervix, uterus, fallopian tubes, abdominal cavity, and ovaries—that can be caused by organisms such as *Neisseria gonorrhoeae*. Its symptoms are abdominal pain, tenderness, nausea, fever, and irregular menstrual cycles. The condition may lead to infertility. Abbreviated *PID*.

Gonorrhea is highly contagious. Women may stand a slightly greater than 50% chance of contracting gonorrhea after just one exposure. Men have a 20% to 25% risk of infection (Handsfield et al., 1984; Platt et al., 1983). The risks to women are apparently greater because women retain infected semen in the vagina. The risk of infection increases with repeated exposure.

Symptoms   Most men experience symptoms within two to five days after infection. Symptoms include a penile discharge that is clear at first. Within a day it turns yellow to yellow-green, thickens, and becomes puslike. The urethra becomes inflamed, and urination is accompanied by a burning sensation. Thirty percent to 40% of males have swelling and tenderness in the lymph glands of the groin. Inflammation and other symptoms may become chronic if left untreated.

The initial symptoms of gonorrhea usually abate within a few weeks without treatment, leading people to think of gonorrhea as being no worse than a bad cold. However, the gonococcus bacterium will usually continue to damage the body even though the early symptoms fade.

In women the primary site of the infection is the cervix, where it causes **cervicitis.** Cervicitis may cause a yellowish to yellow-green puslike discharge that irritates the vulva. If the infection spreads to the urethra, women may also note burning urination. *About 80% of the women who contract gonorrhea are* **asymptomatic** *during the early stages of the disease, however.* Unfortunately, therefore, many infected women do not seek treatment until more serious symptoms develop. They may also innocently infect another sex partner.

It is true that about 80% of the women who contract gonorrhea do not develop symptoms. However, they may develop quite serious symptoms later on. ∎

When gonorrhea is not treated early, it may spread through the urogenital systems in both genders and strike the internal reproductive organs. In men, it can lead to **epididymitis,** which can cause fertility problems. Swelling and feelings of tenderness or pain in the scrotum are the principal symptoms of epididymitis. Fever may also be present. Occasionally the kidneys are affected.

In women, the bacterium can spread through the cervix to the uterus, fallopian tubes, ovaries, and other parts of the abdominal cavity, causing **pelvic inflammatory disease** (PID). Symptoms of PID include cramps, abdominal pain and tenderness, cervical tenderness and discharge, irregular menstrual cycles, coital pain, fever, nausea, and vomiting. PID may also be asymptomatic. Whether or not women experience symptoms, PID can cause scarring that blocks the fallopian tubes, leading to infertility. PID is a serious illness that requires aggressive treatment with antibiotics. Surgery may be needed to remove infected tissue. Unfortunately, many women become aware of a gonococcal infection only when they develop PID.

These consequences are all the more unfortunate because gonorrhea, when diagnosed and treated early, clears up rapidly in over 90% of cases.

Diagnosis and Treatment   Diagnosis of gonorrhea involves clinical inspection of the genitals by a physician (e.g., a family practitioner, urologist, or gynecologist) and the culturing and examination of a sample of genital discharge (Ison, 1990; Judson, 1990).

Antibiotics are the standard treatment for gonorrhea. Penicillin was once the favored antibiotic, but the rise of penicillin-resistant strains of *Neisseria gonorrhoeae* has required that alternative antibiotics be used (Goldstein & Clark, 1990). An injection of the antibiotic *ceftriaxone* is often recommended. An alternative antibiotic such as *spectinomycin* may be used with people who cannot tolerate ceftriaxone. Since gonorrhea and chlamydia often occur together, persons infected with gonorrhea are usually also treated for chlamydia through the use of another antibiotic. Sex partners of people with gonorrhea should also be examined.

Syphilis

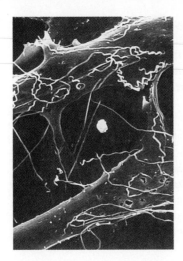

Figure 16.1. Treponema Pallidum. *Treponema pallidum* is the bacterium that causes syphilis. Because of its spiral shape, *T. pallidum* is also called a *spirochete.*

Truth **OR** *Fiction?*

R E V I S I T E D

No society wanted to be associated with the origins of **syphilis.** In Naples they called it "the French disease." In France it was "the Neapolitan disease." Many Italians called it "the Spanish disease," but in Spain they called it "the disease of Española" (modern Haiti).

In 1530 the Italian physician Girolamo Fracastoro wrote a poem about Syphilus, a shepherd boy. Syphilus was afflicted with the disease as retribution for insulting the sun god Apollo. In 1905 the German scientist Fritz Schaudinn isolated the bacterium that causes syphilis (see Figure 16.1). It is *Treponema pallidum* (T. pallidum, for short). The name contains Greek and Latin roots meaning a "faintly colored (pallid) turning thread"— a good description of the corkscrewlike shape of the microscopic organism. Because of the spiral shape, *T. pallidum* is also called a *spirochete,* from Greek roots meaning "spiral" and "hair."

The Origins of Syphilis   The origins of syphilis are controversial. The Columbian theory holds that Christopher Columbus returned to Spain from his first voyage to the West Indies (1492–1493) with more than beads, blankets, and tobacco. Then, from Spain, Spanish mercenaries may have carried the disease to Naples when they were hired to protect that city from French invaders. Then the French army may have contracted syphilis from prostitutes, who also practiced their profession with the Spaniards and Neapolitans. Sailors may have eventually spread syphilis to the East.

It is generally accepted that Columbus exhibited symptoms of advanced syphilis when he died in 1506. However, evidence reported in 1992 shows that syphilis existed in Europe prior to the voyage of Columbus ("Disease discovered Europe first?" 1992; Wilford, 1992).

It is not true that Christopher Columbus brought syphilis back to Europe from the New World. Evidence unearthed in the 1990s refutes this theory. ■

The incidence of syphilis decreased in the United States with the introduction of penicillin (Zenker & Rolfs, 1990). But despite the availability of penicillin and the recent emphasis on safer sex, there has been a resurgence of syphilis (Melvin, 1990; Spark, 1991). The incidence of reported cases of syphilis rose by one third during the 1980s (Rolfs & Nakashima, 1990) (see Figure 16.2). About 45,000 cases of syphilis are reported each year (CDC, 1989a). Many other cases go unreported. By 1988, the rates of syphilis in the United States had reached their highest levels in 40 years.

Researchers believe that the increase in syphilis is linked to increased use of cocaine (Minkoff et al., 1990; Rolfs et al., 1990). Cocaine users risk contracting syphilis through

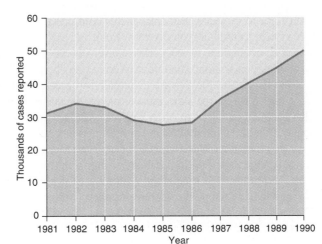

Figure 16.2. Reported Cases of Syphilis in the United States, 1981–1990. The reported incidence of syphilis increased markedly from the middle-to-late 1980s. (The data indicate cases of primary and secondary stage syphilis.) *Source:* Centers for Disease Control.

Syphilis

An STD that is caused by the *Treponema pallidum* bacterium, which may progress through several stages of development—often from a chancre to a skin rash to damage to the cardiovascular or central nervous systems. (From the Greek *siphlos*, meaning "maimed" or "crippled.")

Chancre

A sore or ulcer.

T r u t h **OR** *Fiction?*
R E V I S I T E D

Congenital syphilis

A syphilis infection that is present at birth.

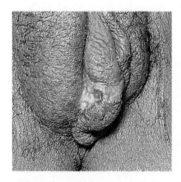

Syphilis Chancre. The first, or primary, stage of a syphilis infection is marked by the appearance of a painless sore or chancre at the site of infection.

Neurosyphilis

Syphilitic infection of the central nervous system, which can cause brain damage and death.

General paresis

A progressive form of mental illness caused by neurosyphilis and characterized by gross confusion.

sex with multiple partners or with prostitutes, not through cocaine use per se (Rolfs et al., 1990). Syphilis and other STDs are often spread among drug users, prostitutes (many of whom abuse drugs themselves), and their sex partners (Farley et al., 1990).

Syphilis is not as widespread as gonorrhea. However, its effects can be more harmful. They can include heart disease, blindness, gross confusion, and death. Syphilis killed the painter Paul Gauguin.

Transmission   Syphilis, like gonorrhea, is most often transmitted by vaginal or anal intercourse, or oral–genital or oral–anal contact with an infected person. The spirochete is usually transmitted when open lesions on an infected person come into contact with the mucous membranes or skin abrasions of the partner's body during sexual activity. The chance of contracting syphilis from one sexual contact with an infected partner is estimated at one in three (Reinisch, 1990). Syphilis may also be contracted by touching an infectious **chancre,** but not from using the same toilet seat as an infected person.

It is not true that gonorrhea and syphilis may be contracted from toilet seats in public rest rooms. Pubic lice can be contracted in this manner, however, as we will see later. ■

Pregnant women may transmit syphilis to their fetuses, because the spirochete can cross the placental membrane. Miscarriage, stillbirth, or **congenital syphilis** may result. Congenital syphilis may impair vision and hearing or deform bones and teeth. Blood tests are administered routinely during pregnancy to diagnose syphilis in the mother so that congenital problems in the baby may be averted. The fetus will probably not be harmed if an infected mother is treated before the fourth month of pregnancy.

Symptoms and Course of Illness   Syphilis develops through several stages. In the first or *primary stage* of syphilis, a painless chancre (a hard, round, ulcerlike lesion with raised edges) appears at the site of infection two to four weeks after contact. When women are infected, the chancre usually forms on the vaginal walls or the cervix. It may also form on the external genitalia, most often on the labia. When men are infected, the chancre usually forms on the penile glans. It may also form on the scrotum or penile shaft. If the mode of transmission is oral sex, the chancre may appear on the lips or tongue. If the infection is spread by anal sex, the rectum may serve as the site of the chancre. The chancre disappears within a few weeks, but if the infection remains untreated, syphilis will continue to work within the body.

The *secondary stage* begins a few weeks to a few months later. A skin rash develops, consisting of painless, reddish, raised bumps that darken after a while and burst, oozing a discharge. Other symptoms include sores in the mouth, painful swelling of joints, a sore throat, headaches, and fever. A person with syphilis may thus wrongly assume that he or she has the flu.

These symptoms also disappear. Syphilis then enters the *latent stage* and may lie dormant for 1 to 40 years. But spirochetes continue to multiply and burrow into the circulatory system, central nervous system (brain and spinal cord), and bones. The person may no longer be contagious to sex partners after several years in the latent stage, but a pregnant woman may pass along the infection to her newborn at any time (Wooldridge, 1991).

In many cases the disease eventually progresses to the late or *tertiary stage.* A large ulcer may form on the skin, muscle tissue, digestive organs, lungs, liver, or other organs. This destructive ulcer can often be successfully treated, but still more serious damage can occur as the infection attacks the central nervous system or the cardiovascular system (the heart and the major blood vessels). Either outcome can be fatal. **Neurosyphilis** can cause brain damage, resulting in paralysis or the mental illness called **general paresis.**

The primary and secondary symptoms of syphilis inevitably disappear. Infected people may thus be tempted to believe that they are no longer at risk and fail to see a doctor. This is indeed unfortunate, because failure to eradicate the infection through proper treatment may eventually lead to dire consequences.

Truth OR Fiction?
R E V I S I T E D

It is not true that if a syphilitic chancre (sore) goes away by itself, the infection does not require medical treatment. The belief that medical treatment is unnecessary if the symptoms of an STD disappear by themselves is unfounded. Gonorrhea and syphilis, for example, both can damage the body even when their early symptoms have abated. ■

VDRL
The test named after the Venereal Disease Research Laboratory of the U.S. Public Health Service that tests for the presence of antibodies to *Treponema pallidum* in the blood.

Antibodies
Specialized proteins produced by the white blood cells of the immune system in response to disease organisms and other toxic substances. Antibodies recognize and attack the invading organisms or substances.

Diagnosis and Treatment   Primary-stage syphilis is diagnosed by clinical examination. If a chancre is found, fluid drawn from it can be examined under a microscope. The spirochetes are usually quite visible. Blood tests are not definitive until the secondary stage begins. The most frequently used blood test is the **VDRL.** The VDRL tests for the presence of **antibodies** to *Treponema pallidum* in the blood.

Penicillin is the treatment of choice for syphilis, although other antibiotics are sometimes used. Successful treatment does not confer immunity to reinfection. Sex partners of persons infected with syphilis should also be evaluated by a physician.

Chlamydia

Although you may be more familiar with gonorrhea and syphilis, chlamydia, another bacterial STD, is actually more common in the United States (CDC, 1993a). Chlamydial infections are caused by the *Chlamydia trachomatis* bacterium, a unique parasitic organism that can survive only within cells (Martin, 1990). This bacterium can cause several different types of infection, including *nongonococcal urethritis (NGU)* in men and women, *epididymitis* (infection of the epididymis) in men, and *cervicitis* (infection of the cervix), *endometritis* (infection of the endometrium), and PID in women (Martin, 1990; Westrom, 1990; Yarber & Parillo, 1992).

The precise prevalences of chlamydial infections are unknown, since there is no national reporting system for chlamydia as there is for gonorrhea and syphilis (CDC, 1993a). As many as 4 million cases may occur annually (Toomey & Barnes, 1990). The incidence of chlamydial infections is especially high among teenagers and college students (Shafer et al., 1993). Researchers estimate that between 8% and 40% of teenage women become infected (Yarber & Parillo, 1992).

Transmission   *Chlamydia trachomatis* is usually transmitted through sexual intercourse—vaginal or anal. *Chlamydia trachomatis* may also cause an eye infection if a person touches his or her eyes after handling the genitals of an infected partner. Oral sex with an infected partner can infect the throat. Newborns can acquire potentially serious chlamydial eye infections as they pass through the cervix of an infected mother during birth. Even newborns delivered by cesarean section may be infected if the amniotic sac breaks before delivery (Reinisch, 1990). Evidence from several studies suggests that between 2% and 26% of pregnant women in the United States carry the *Chlamydia trachomatis* bacterium in the cervix (Reinisch, 1990). Each year more than 100,000 infants are infected with the bacterium during birth (Graham & Blanco, 1990). Of these, about 75,000 develop eye infections and 30,000 develop pneumonia.

Symptoms   Chlamydial infections usually produce symptoms that are similar to, but milder than, those of gonorrhea. In men, *Chlamydia trachomatis* can lead to nongonococcal urethritis (NGU). *Urethritis* is an inflammation of the urethra. NGU refers to forms of urethritis that are not caused by the gonococcal bacterium. (NGU is generally diagnosed only in men. In women, an inflammation of the urethra caused by *Chlamydia trachomatis* is called a chlamydial infection or simply chlamydia.) NGU was formerly called nonspecific urethritis or NSU. Many organisms can cause NGU. *Chlamydia trachomatis* accounts for about half of the cases among men (CDC, 1985).

NGU in men may give rise to a thin, whitish discharge from the penis and some burning or other pain during urination. These contrast with the yellow-green discharge and more intense pain produced by gonorrhea. There may be soreness in the scrotum and feelings of heaviness in the testes. NGU is about two to three times as prevalent among

American men as gonorrhea (CDC, 1989a; Reinisch, 1990). Men in the 20-to-24-year age range are most at risk of contracting gonorrhea and NGU, presumably because of their high levels of sexual activity (Bowie, 1990).

In women, chlamydial infections usually give rise to infections of the urethra or cervix. Women, like men, may experience burning when they urinate, genital irritation, and a mild (vaginal) discharge. Women are also likely to encounter pelvic pain and irregular menstrual cycles. The cervix may look swollen and inflamed.

Yet, as many as 25% of men and 70% of women infected with chlamydia are asymptomatic (Cates & Wasserheit, 1991). For this reason, chlamydia has been dubbed the "silent disease." People without symptoms may go untreated and unknowingly pass along their infections to their partners. In women, an untreated chlamydial infection can spread throughout the reproductive system, leading to PID and to scarring of the fallopian tubes, resulting in infertility (Garland et al., 1990; Hodgson et al., 1990). About half of the more than 1 million annual cases of PID are attributed to chlamydia (Schachter, 1989). Women with a history of exposure to *Chlamydia trachomatis* also stand twice the normal chance of incurring an ectopic (tubal) pregnancy (Sherman et al., 1990).

Untreated chlamydial infections can also damage the internal reproductive organs of men. About 50% of cases of epididymitis are caused by chlamydial infections (Crum & Ellner, 1985). Yet only about 1% or 2% of men with untreated NGU caused by *Chlamydia trachomatis* go on to develop epididymitis (Bowie, 1990). The long-term effects of untreated chlamydial infections in men remain undetermined.

Chlamydial infections also frequently occur together with other STDs, most often gonorrhea. As many as 45% of cases of gonorrhea involve coexisting chlamydial infections (CDC, 1985b; CDC, 1989a).

False positive

An erroneous positive test result or clinical finding.

Diagnosis and Treatment   The Abbott Testpack permits physicians to verify a diagnosis of chlamydia in women in about half an hour (Reichart et al., 1990; Reinisch, 1990). The test analyzes a cervical smear (like a Pap smear) and identifies 75% to 80% of infected cases. There are relatively few **false positives** (incorrect positive findings). In men, a swab is inserted through the penile opening, and the extracted fluid is analyzed to detect the presence of *Chlamydia trachomatis*.

Antibiotics other than penicillin are highly effective in eradicating chlamydial infections (CDC, 1989b; Toomey & Barnes, 1990). (Penicillin, effective in treating gonorrhea, is ineffective against *Chlamydia trachomatis*.) Treatment of sex partners is considered critical regardless of whether the partner shows symptoms, so as to prevent the infection from bouncing back and forth (Martin, 1990). Moreover, a woman whose sex partner develops NGU should be examined for a chlamydial infection herself. At least 30% of these women will test positive for chlamydia even though they (and their partners) may be free of symptoms (Stamm & Holmes, 1990). Likewise, men whose sex partners develop urethral or cervical infections should be medically evaluated, whether or not they notice any symptoms. With chlamydia, both partners may be unaware that they are infected and be oblivious to the internal damage the infection is causing. Because of the risks posed by untreated chlamydial infections, especially to women, and the high rate of asymptomatic infections, many physicians perform diagnostic tests on young women to detect chlamydia during regular checkups.

Other Bacterial Diseases

Several other types of bacterial STDs occur less commonly in the United States and Canada. These include chancroid, shigellosis, granuloma inguinale, and lymphogranuloma venereum.

Chancroid

An STD caused by the *Hemophilus ducreyi* bacterium. Also called *soft chancre*.

Chancroid   Chancroid, or "soft chancre," is caused by the bacterium *Hemophilus ducreyi*. It is more commonly found in the tropics and Eastern nations than in Western countries. The chancroid sore consists of a cluster of small bumps or pimples on the genitals, perineum (the area of skin that lies between the genitals and the anus), or the anus itself. These lesions usually appear within seven days of infection. Within a few days the lesion ruptures, producing an open sore or ulcer. Several ulcers may merge with other ulcers, forming giant ulcers (Ronald & Albritton, 1990). There is usually an accompanying swelling of a nearby lymph node. In contrast to the syphilis chancre, the chancroid ulcer has a soft rim (hence the name) and is painful in men. Women frequently do not experience any pain and may be unaware of being infected (Ronald & Albritton, 1990). The bacterium is typically transmitted through sexual or bodily contact with the lesion or its discharge. Diagnosis is usually confirmed by culturing the bacterium, which is found in pus from the sore, and examining it under a microscope. Antibiotics (erythromycin or ceftriaxone) are usually effective in treating the disease.

Shigellosis
An STD caused by the *Shigella* bacterium.

Shigellosis   Shigellosis is caused by the *Shigella* bacterium and is characterized by fever and severe abdominal symptoms, including diarrhea and inflammation of the large intestine. About 25,000 cases of shigellosis are reported annually (CDC, 1989a). It is often contracted by oral contact with infected fecal material, which may occur as the result of oral–anal sex. It can be treated with antibiotics, such as tetracycline or *ampicillin.*

Granuloma inguinale
A tropical STD caused by the *Calymmatobacterium granulomatous* bacterium.

Elephantiasis
A disease characterized by enlargement of parts of the body, especially the legs and genitals, and by hardening and ulceration of the surrounding skin. (From the Greek *elephas,* meaning "elephant," referring to the resemblance of the affected skin areas to elephant hide.)

Lymphogranuloma venereum
A tropical STD caused by the *Chlamydia trachomatis* bacterium.

Granuloma Inguinale   Rare in the United States, **granuloma inguinale,** like chancroid, is more common in tropical regions. It is caused by the bacterium *Calymmatobacterium granulomatous* and is not as contagious as many other STDs. Primary symptoms are painless red bumps or sores in the groin area that ulcerate and spread. Like chancroid, it is usually spread by intimate bodily or sexual contact with a lesion or its discharge. Diagnosis is confirmed by microscopic examination of tissue of the rim of the sore. The antibiotics tetracycline and streptomycin are effective in treating this disorder. If left untreated, however, the disease may lead to the development of fistulas (holes) in the rectum or bladder, destruction of the tissues or organs that underlie the infection, or scarring of skin tissue that results in a condition called **elephantiasis,** a condition that afflicted the so-called Elephant Man in the nineteenth century.

Lymphogranuloma Venereum (LGV)   Lymphogranuloma venereum (LGV) is another tropical STD that occurs only rarely in the United States and Canada. Some U.S. soldiers returned home from Vietnam with cases of LGV. It is caused by several strains of the *Chlamydia trachomatis* bacterium. LGV usually enters the body through the penis, vulva, or cervix, where a small, painless sore may form. The sore may go unnoticed, but a nearby lymph gland in the groin swells and grows tender. Other symptoms mimic those of flu: chills, fever, and headache. Other symptoms that may occur include backache (especially in women) and arthritic complaints (painful joints). If LGV is untreated, complications such as growths and fistulas in the genitals and elephantiasis of the legs and genitals may occur. Diagnosis is made by skin tests and blood tests. The antibiotic doxycycline is the usual treatment.

~ *Reflections* ~

▨ If you have no symptoms of any STD, do you think it would be wise to have your physician check out your status anyway? Why, or why not?

▨ Agree or disagree with the following statement, and support your answer: Gonorrhea is no worse than a bad cold.

▨ Does it seem that this textbook's presentation of information about STDs is straightforward, or do you think it uses some "scare tactics"? Explain.

◤Vaginal Infections

Vaginitis
Any type of vaginal infection or inflammation.

Vaginitis refers to any kind of vaginal infection or inflammation. Women with vaginitis may encounter genital irritation or itching and burning during urination, but the most common symptom is an odious discharge.

Most cases of vaginitis are caused by organisms that reside in the vagina or by sexually transmitted organisms. Organisms that reside in the vagina may overgrow and cause symptoms when the environmental balance of the vagina is upset by factors such as birth-control pills, antibiotics, dietary changes, excessive douching, or nylon underwear or pantyhose. (See Chapter 3 for suggestions to help reduce the risk of vaginitis.) Still other cases are caused by sensitivities or allergic reactions to various chemicals.

As many as 90% of vaginal infections (Friedrich, 1985; Sobel, 1990) involve bacterial vaginosis (BV), candidiasis (commonly called a "yeast" infection), or trichomoniasis ("trich"). Bacterial vaginosis is the most common form of vaginitis, followed by candidiasis, then by trichomoniasis (Reinisch, 1990), but some cases involve combinations of the three.

The microbes causing vaginal infections in women can also infect the man's urethral tract. In some cases, a "vaginal infection" can be passed back and forth between sex partners.

It is not literally true that men can develop vaginal infections. Only women can have vaginal infections, because only women have vaginas. However, the microbes that cause these infections in women may also cause problems for men. ■

Bacterial Vaginosis

Bacterial vaginosis
A form of vaginitis usually caused by the *Gardnerella vaginalis* bacterium.

Bacterial vaginosis (BV—formerly called *nonspecific vaginitis*) is most often caused by the bacterium *Gardnerella vaginalis* (Briselden & Hillier, 1990; Platz-Christensen et al., 1989). The bacterium is primarily transmitted through sexual contact. The most characteristic symptom in women is a thin, foul-smelling vaginal discharge, but infected women are often asymptomatic. Accurate diagnosis requires culturing the bacterium in the laboratory (Reinisch, 1990). Besides causing troublesome symptoms in some cases, BV may increase the risk of various gynecological problems, including infections of the reproductive tract (Hillier & Holmes, 1990). Oral treatment with *metronidazole* (brand name: Flagyl) for seven days is recommended (CDC, 1989b) and is effective in about 90% of cases (Reinisch, 1990). Recurrences are common, however.

Questions remain about whether the male partner should also be treated. The bacterium can usually be found in the male urethra but does not generally cause symptoms (Reinisch, 1990). Lacking symptoms, the male partner may unknowingly transmit the bacterium to others. There is no evidence that treating the male with metronidazole benefits either him or the female patient, however (CDC, 1989b; Moi et al., 1989).

Candidiasis

Candidiasis
A form of vaginitis caused by a yeastlike fungus, *Candida albicans*.

Also known as *moniliasis, thrush,* or, most commonly, a yeast infection, **candidiasis** is caused by a yeastlike fungus, *Candida albicans*. Candidiasis commonly produces soreness, inflammation, and intense (sometimes maddening!) itching around the vulva that is accompanied by a white, thick, curdlike vaginal discharge. Yeast generally produces no symptoms when the vaginal environment is normal (Reinisch, 1990). Yeast infections can also occur in the mouth in both men and women and in the penis in men.

It is true that vaginitis is often caused by an overgrowth of infectious organisms that normally reside in the vagina. Some cases result from organisms that normally are found in the vagina but become infectious when changes in the vaginal environment allow them to multiply and overgrow. ■

Infections most often arise from changes in the vaginal environment that allow the fungus to overgrow. Factors such as the use of antibiotics or birth-control pills, pregnancy, and diabetes may alter the vaginal balance, allowing the fungus that causes yeast infections to grow to infectious levels. Wearing nylon underwear and tight, restrictive, poorly ventilated clothing may also set the stage for a yeast infection.

Diet may play a role in recurrent yeast infections. Reducing one's intake of substances that produce excessive excretion of urinary sugars (such as dairy products, sugar, and artificial sweeteners) apparently reduces the frequency of recurrent yeast infections (Friedrich, 1985). Recently, researchers reported that the daily ingestion of one pint of yogurt containing active bacterial (*Lactobacillus acidophilus*) cultures actually helped reduce the rate of recurrent infections (Hilton et al., 1992).

Candidiasis can be passed back and forth between sex partners through vaginal intercourse. It may also be passed back and forth between the mouth and the genitals through oral–genital contact and infect the anus through anal intercourse. However, most infections in women are believed to be caused by an overgrowth of "yeast" normally found in the vagina, not by sexual transmission. Still, it is advisable to evaluate both partners simultaneously. Whereas most men with *Candida* are asymptomatic (Hillier & Holmes, 1990), some may develop NGU or a genital thrush that is accompanied by sensations of itching and burning during urination, or a reddening of the penis (Hillier & Holmes, 1990). Candidiasis may also be transmitted by nonsexual means, as between women who share a washcloth.

About 75% of women will experience an episode of candidiasis at some point during their reproductive years (Reinisch, 1990). About half of these women will have recurrent infections. Three days of treatment with vaginal suppositories, creams, or tablets containing miconazole (brand name: Monistat), clotrimazole (brand names: Lotrimin and Mycelex), or terconazole (brand name: Terazol) is usually recommended (CDC, 1989b). Some of these medications are now available without a prescription. Even so, women with vaginal complaints should consult their physicians before taking any medication, to ensure that they receive the proper diagnosis and treatment.

Trichomoniasis

Trichomoniasis
A form of vaginitis caused by the protozoan *Trichomonas vaginalis*.

Trichomoniasis ("trich") is caused by *Trichomonas vaginalis*. *Trichomonas vaginalis* is a parasitic animal that consists of only one cell (technically, a protozoan). Trichomoniasis is the most common parasitic STD (Levine, 1991). It accounts for some 8 million cases a year among women in the United States (Martens & Faro, 1989). Symptoms in women include burning or itching in the vulva, mild pain during urination or coitus, and an odorous, foamy whitish to yellowish green discharge. Lower abdominal pain is reported by 5% to 12% of infected women (Rein & Muller, 1990). Many women notice symptoms appearing or worsening during, or just following, their menstrual periods. Trichomoniasis is also linked to the development of tubal adhesions that can result in infertility (Grodstein et al., 1993). As with many other STDs, about half of infected women are asymptomatic (Reinisch, 1990).

Candidiasis most often reflects an overgrowth of organisms normally found in the vagina. However, trichomoniasis is almost always sexually transmitted (CDC, 1989b). Because the parasite may survive for several hours on moist surfaces outside the body, trich can be communicated from contact with infected semen or vaginal discharges on towels, washcloths, and bedclothes. This parasite is one of the few disease agents that can be picked up from a toilet seat, but it would have to directly touch the penis or vulva (Reinisch, 1990).

Trichomonas vaginalis can cause NGU in the male, which can be asymptomatic or cause a slight penile discharge that is usually noticeable only upon awakening before one first urinates in the morning. There may be tingling, itching, and other irritating sensations in the urethral tract. Yet most infected men are symptom-free (Rein & Muller, 1990). Therefore, they may unwittingly transfer the organism to their sex partners. Perhaps three or four in ten male partners of infected women are found to harbor *Trichomonas vaginalis* themselves (Reinisch, 1990). Diagnosis is frequently made by microscopic examination of a smear of a woman's vaginal fluids in a physician's office (Levine, 1991). Diagnosis based on examination of cultures grown from the vaginal smear is considered more reliable, however (Thomason & Gelbart, 1989).

Truth OR Fiction? It is true that many men whose partners have "trich" are also infected themselves, often un-

REVISITED

knowingly. Perhaps three of four men whose partners have "trich" are infected themselves, and many do not know it. ∎

Except during the first three months of pregnancy, trichomoniasis is treated in both genders with metronidazole (brand name: Flagyl). Both partners are treated, whether or not they report symptoms. When both partners are treated simultaneously, the success rate approaches 100% (Thomason & Gelbart, 1989).

~ *Reflections* ~

▪ What can women do to prevent vaginal infections?
▪ If a woman suspects that she has a vaginal infection, should she attempt a cure with an over-the-counter medicine or see her physician? Explain.
▪ How would you feel if you had been infected with an STD by a partner? What precautions would you expect the partner to have taken? (Would you take such precautions yourself?)

A L O S E R L O O K

WHAT TO DO IF YOU SUSPECT YOU HAVE CONTRACTED AN STD

First, contact your physician right away or call your local health department to see if there is a low-cost clinic available in your community that offers STD treatment. This book may make you better aware of the signs and symptoms of various STDs, but it does not qualify you to diagnose yourself. Second, follow your physician's directions or seek a second medical opinion if you have questions about the recommended treatment.

If You Are Being Treated for an STD...

1. *Take all medication as directed.* Do not skip doses or combine doses. If you should inadvertently skip a dose, call your physician for instructions. Discuss any side effects with your physician. Although the medication may relieve symptoms in a day or two, it may be necessary to continue to take the medication for a week or more to ensure that the infection is completely eliminated.
2. *Understand how to use medication correctly.* Some medication

calls for you to abstain from alcohol or to avoid certain foods, such as dairy products. Some medications should be taken only before or after meals. Check with your physician or pharmacist.

3. *Abstain from sexual contact during an active infection.* Although using a latex condom combined with a spermicidal agent containing the ingredient nonoxynol-9 (which kills many STD-causing organisms) may provide some protection against disease transmission, it is best to abstain from sexual activity until the infection clears. Consult your physician regarding the recommended duration of abstinence.
4. *Contact sex partners who may have infected you or whom you may have infected.* Suggest that they seek a medical evaluation to see if they too are infected. It is possible that they are infected and are unaware of the problem because of a lack of symptoms.
5. *Return for follow-up visits if your physician instructs you to do so.*

Although the symptoms of the infection may be relieved after a few days, return for requested follow-up visits to ensure that you are free of the infection. Your physician may also request that your partner be evaluated so that the two of you do not bounce the STD back and forth.

6. *If you have a continuing STD, such as herpes or HIV, share the information with your partner or partners.* Don't keep it a secret. Your sex partners have a right to know. Make sure that both you and they understand the risks and the necessary precautions that may need to be taken. If you have any doubts about the safety of engaging in sexual relations, consult your physician.

Source: From A Student's Guide to AIDS and Other Sexually Transmitted Diseases by J. S. Nevid. Copyright © 1993 by Allyn & Bacon. Reprinted by permission.

Viral Diseases

Viruses are tiny particles of DNA surrounded by a protein coating. They are incapable of reproducing on their own. When they invade a body cell, however, they can direct the cell's own reproductive machinery to spin off new viral particles that spread to other cells, causing infection. In this chapter we discuss several viral STDs: herpes, viral hepatitis, genital warts, and molluscum contagiosum. AIDS is also caused by a virus and is the topic of the following chapter.

Herpes

The hysteria that surrounded the rapid spread of genital herpes in the 1970s and 1980s has died down since the advent of AIDS. Nevertheless, 500,000 new cases of genital herpes occur each year (Brody, 1993a).

Once you get herpes, it's yours for life. After the initial attack, it remains an unwelcome guest in your body. It finds a cozy place to lie low until it stirs up trouble again. It causes recurrent outbreaks that often happen at the worst times, such as around final exams. This is not just bad luck. Stress can depress the functioning of the immune system and heighten the likelihood of outbreaks.

Not only are you stuck with the virus. You can also pass it along to sex partners for the rest of your life. Flare-ups may continue to recur, sometimes with annoying frequency. On the other hand, some people have no recurrences. Still others have mild, brief recurrences that become less frequent over time.

In the wake of the AIDS epidemic, the threat of genital herpes has not received much attention. Yet the viruses that cause herpes are alive and well. There are actually different types of herpes that are caused by variants of the *Herpes simplex* virus. The most common type, ***Herpes simplex* virus type 1** (HSV-1 virus), causes oral herpes. Oral herpes is denoted by cold sores or fever blisters on the lips or mouth. It can also be transferred to the genitals by the hands or by oral–genital contact (Mertz et al., 1992). **Genital herpes** is caused by a related but distinct virus, the ***Herpes simplex* virus type 2** (HSV-2). This virus produces painful shallow sores and blisters on the genitals. HSV-2 can also be transferred to the mouth through oral–genital contact. Both types of herpes can be transmitted sexually.

Physicians are not required to report cases of herpes to public health officials, so there are no precise statistics on its prevalence. It is estimated that more than 100 million people in the United States are infected with oral herpes and perhaps 30 million with genital herpes (Brody, 1993a).

Transmission   Herpes can be transmitted through oral, anal, or vaginal sexual activity with an infected person (Mertz et al., 1992; Wald et al., 1995). The herpes viruses can also survive for several hours on toilet seats or other objects, where they can be picked up by direct contact. Oral herpes is easily contracted by drinking from the same cup as an infected person, by kissing, even by sharing towels. But genital herpes is generally spread by coitus or by oral or anal sex.

One problem is that many people do not realize that they are infected. They can thus unknowingly transmit the virus through sexual contact. And many of the people who know they are infected don't realize that they can pass along the virus even when they have no noticeable outbreak (Mertz et al., 1992; Wald et al., 1995). Though genital herpes is most contagious during active flare-ups, it may also be transmitted when an infected partner has no symptoms (genital sores or feelings of burning or itching in the genitals). Any intimate contact with an infected person carries some risk of transmission of the virus, even if the infected person never has another outbreak. People may also be infected with the virus and have no outbreaks, yet pass the virus along to others.

Truth OR Fiction?
R E V I S I T E D

It is not true that genital herpes can be transmitted only during flare-ups of the disease. Genital herpes may actually be transmitted between flare-ups, although people are most contagious during outbreaks of the disease. ■

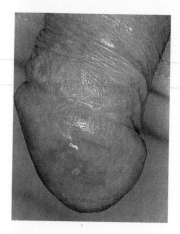

Herpes Lesion on the Male Genitals. Herpes lesions or sores can appear on the genitals in women or men and be associated with flu-like symptoms.

***Herpes simplex* virus type 1**
The virus that causes oral herpes, which is characterized by cold sores or fever blisters on the lips or mouth. Abbreviated *HSV-1*.

Genital herpes
An STD caused by the *Herpes simplex* virus type 2 and characterized by painful shallow sores and blisters on the genitals.

***Herpes simplex* virus type 2**
The virus that causes genital herpes. Abbreviated *HSV-2*.

Ocular herpes

A herpes infection of the eye, usually caused by touching an infected area of the body and then touching the eye.

Prodromal symptoms

Warning symptoms that signal the onset or flare-up of a disease. (From the Greek *prodromos*, meaning "forerunner.")

Herpes may also be spread from one part of the body to another by touching the infected area and then touching another body part. One potentially serious result is a herpes infection of the eye: **ocular herpes.** Thorough washing with soap and water after touching an infected area may reduce the risk of spreading the infection to other parts of the body. Still, it is better to avoid touching the infected area altogether, especially if there are active sores.

Women with genital herpes are more likely than the general population to have miscarriages. Passage through the birth canal of an infected mother can infect babies with genital herpes, damaging or killing them (Whitley et al., 1991). Obstetricians thus often perform cesarean sections if the mother has active lesions or **prodromal symptoms** at the time of delivery (Osborne & Adelson, 1990). Herpes also appears to place women at greater risk of genital cancers, such as cervical cancer (Graham et al., 1982). (All women, not just women with herpes, are advised to have regular pelvic examinations, including Pap tests for early detection of cervical cancer.)

Symptoms   Genital lesions or sores appear about six to eight days after infection with genital herpes. At first they appear as reddish, painful bumps, or papules, along the penis or the vulva. They may also appear on the thighs or buttocks, in the vagina, or on the cervix. These papules turn into groups of small blisters that are filled with fluid containing infectious viral particles. The blisters are attacked by the body's immune system (white blood cells). They fill with pus, burst, and become extremely painful, shallow sores or ulcers that are surrounded by a red ring. People are especially infectious during such outbreaks, as the ulcers shed millions of viral particles. Other symptoms may include headaches and muscle aches, swollen lymph glands, fever, burning urination, and a vaginal discharge. The blisters crust over and heal within one to three weeks. Internal sores in the vagina or on the cervix may take ten days longer than external (labial) sores to heal completely. Physicians thus advise infected women to avoid unprotected intercourse for at least ten days following the healing of external sores.

Although the symptoms disappear, the disease does not. The virus remains in the body permanently, burrowing into nerve cells in the base of the spine, where it may lie dormant for years or a lifetime. The infected person is least contagious during this dormant stage. For reasons that remain unclear, the virus becomes reactivated and gives rise to recurrences in most cases.

Recurrences may be related to factors such as infections (as in a cold), stress, fatigue, depression, exposure to the sun, and hormonal changes, such as those that occur during pregnancy or menstruation. Recurrences tend to occur within 3 to 12 months of the initial episode and to affect the same part of the body.

About 50% of people with recurrent herpes experience prodromal symptoms before an active outbreak (Reinisch, 1990). These warning signs may include feelings of burning, itching, pain, tingling, or tenderness in the affected area. These symptoms may be accompanied by sharp pains in the lower extremities, groin, or buttocks. People with herpes may be more infectious when prodromal symptoms appear. They are advised to avoid unprotected sex until the flare-up subsides.

Symptoms of oral herpes include sores or blisters on the lips, the inside of the mouth, the tongue, or the throat. Fever and feelings of sickness may occur. The gums may swell and redden. The sores heal over in about two weeks, and the virus retreats into nerve cells at the base of the neck, where it lies dormant between flare-ups. About 90% of people with oral herpes experience recurrences. About half of them have five or more recurrences during the first two years after the initial outbreak (Reinisch, 1990).

Diagnosis and Treatment   Genital herpes is first diagnosed by clinical inspection of herpetic sores or ulcers in the mouth or on the genitals. A sample of fluid may be taken from the base of a genital sore and cultured in the laboratory to detect the growth of the virus.

There is no cure or safe, effective vaccine for herpes. Viruses, unlike the bacteria that cause gonorrhea or syphilis, do not respond to antibiotics. The antiviral drug *acyclovir* (brand name: Zovirax) is applied directly to sores in ointment form. It can relieve pain, speed healing, and reduce the duration of viral shedding. Acyclovir must be administered orally, in pill form, to be effective against internal lesions in the vagina or on the cervix. Oral administration of acyclovir may reduce the severity of the initial episode and, if taken regularly, the frequency and duration of recurrent outbreaks (CDC, 1989b; Goldberg et al., 1993). In a study of 389 people who had suffered 12 or more recurrences annually, researchers found that daily doses of acyclovir reduced the number of recurrences, on the average, to 1.7 in the first year, and to less than 1 (0.8) by the fifth year, with few adverse reactions (Brody, 1993a; Goldberg et al., 1993).

Warm baths, loose fitting clothing, aspirin, and cold, wet compresses may relieve pain during flare-ups. People with herpes are advised to maintain regular sleeping habits and to learn to manage stress.

Coping with Genital Herpes　　The psychological problems connected with herpes can be more distressing than the physical effects of the illness. The prospects of a lifetime of recurrences and concerns about infecting one's sex partners exacerbate the emotional impact of herpes. A "herpes syndrome" has been described, which involves feelings of anger, depression, isolation, and shame—even self-perceptions of being tainted, ugly, or dangerous (Mirotznik et al., 1987).

An anonymous survey of Brooklyn College students suggests the emotional toll being exacted by the herpes epidemic. Fifty-five percent of people with herpes reported strong emotional responses to it. Twenty-eight percent reported moderate reactions. Only 17% reported mild reactions (Mirotznik et al., 1987). The majority reported feelings of fear and anger. Half indicated feeling "damaged." Most also felt that herpes had affected their sexual behavior. Seventy-five percent said that they had avoided sex for "a long time" because of herpes. Although most had resumed sexual activity, many sought partners who were also infected so that they would not have to explain the disease, or risk transmitting it, to uninfected people. Given the consequences of herpes, you might think that students would be concerned about contracting the disease. Another survey at Brooklyn College revealed that most sexually active, uninfected students perceived herpes as having serious consequences. However, about three of four were not fearful of contracting the disease, and nearly half had not changed their dating behavior because of it (Mirotznik, 1991).

People with herpes often feel angry, especially toward those who transmitted the disease to them. They may feel anxious about making a long-term commitment or bearing children:

> After the first big episode of herpes, I felt distant from my body. When we began lovemaking again, I had a hard time having orgasms or trusting the rhythm of my responses. I shed some tears over that. I felt my body had been invaded. My body feels riddled with it; I'm somehow contaminated. And there is always that lingering anxiety: is my baby okay? It's unjust that the birth of my child may be affected.

> (*The New Our Bodies, Ourselves,* 1992)

Most people with herpes learn to cope. Some are helped by support groups that share ways of living with the disease. A caring and trusting partner is important. Joanne, a 26-year-old securities analyst, kept her herpes a secret from Jonathan during the first month they were dating. But when they approached the point of becoming sexually intimate, she felt obligated to tell him that she carried the virus:

> "I feared that telling him would scare him off. After all, who wants to have a relationship with someone who can give them herpes? After the first few dates I felt that this was the person I could spend the rest of my life with. I knew he also felt the same way. I had to tell him before things became too intense between us. Believe me, it wasn't easy blurting it out. He wasn't shocked or anything, although he did ask me all kinds of questions about it. I remember telling him that I got recurrences about once a year or so for about a week at a time. I told him that there was always the potential that I could infect him but that we would play it safe and avoid having sex whenever I had an outbreak. I also told him that even at other times I couldn't guarantee that it would be perfectly safe. He said at first that he needed some time to think about it. But later, that very night in fact, he called to tell me that he didn't want this to come between us and that we should try to make our relationship work."

Joanne and Jonathan were married about six months later. A year after that their daughter Andrea was born. Jonathan remains uninfected. Joanne's occasional outbreaks are treated with acyclovir ointment and pass within a week or so.

(The Authors' Files)

The attitudes of people with herpes also play a role in adjusting. People who view herpes as a manageable illness or problem, and not as a medical disaster or character deficit, seem to find it easier to cope.

Viral Hepatitis

Hepatitis
An inflammation of the liver. (From the Greek *hepar*, meaning "liver.")

Jaundice
A yellowish discoloration of the skin and the whites of the eyes. (From the French *jaune*, meaning "yellow.")

Hepatitis is an inflammation of the liver that may be caused by factors such as chronic alcoholism and exposure to toxic materials. Viral hepatitis refers to several different types of hepatitis caused by related, but distinct, viruses. The major types are *hepatitis A* (formerly called infectious hepatitis), *hepatitis B* (formerly called serum hepatitis), *hepatitis C* (formerly called hepatitis non-A, non-B), and *hepatitis D*.

Most people with acute hepatitis have no symptoms. When symptoms do appear, they often include **jaundice,** feelings of weakness and nausea, loss of appetite, abdominal discomfort, whitish bowel movements, and brownish or tea-colored urine. The symptoms of hepatitis B tend to be more severe and long-lasting than those of hepatitis A or C. In about 10% of cases, hepatitis B can lead to chronic liver disease. Hepatitis C tends to have milder symptoms but often leads to chronic liver disease such as cirrhosis or cancer of the liver. Hepatitis D—also called *delta hepatitis* or type D hepatitis—occurs only in the presence of hepatitis B. Hepatitis D, which has symptoms similar to those of hepatitis B, can produce severe liver damage and often leads to death.

The hepatitis A virus is transmitted through contact with infected fecal matter found in contaminated food or water, and by oral contact with fecal matter, as through oral–anal sexual activity (licking or mouthing the partner's anus). (It is largely because of the risk of hepatitis A that restaurant employees are required to wash their hands after using the toilet.) Ingesting uncooked, infested shellfish is also a frequent means of transmission of hepatitis A (Lemon & Newbold, 1990).

Hepatitis B can be transmitted sexually through anal, vaginal, or oral intercourse with an infected partner; through transfusion with contaminated blood supplies; by the sharing of contaminated needles or syringes; and by contact with contaminated saliva, menstrual blood, nasal mucus, or semen (Lemon & Newbold, 1990). Sharing razors, toothbrushes, or other personal articles with an infected person may also transmit hepatitis B. Hepatitis C and hepatitis D may also be transmitted sexually or through contact with contaminated blood. A person can transmit the viruses that cause hepatitis even if he or she is unaware of having any symptoms of the disease.

Hepatitis is usually diagnosed by testing blood samples for the presence of hepatitis antigens and antibodies. There is no cure for viral hepatitis. Bed rest and fluids are usually recommended until the acute stage of the infection subsides, generally in a few weeks. Full recovery may take months. A vaccine provides protection against hepatitis B and also against hepatitis D, since hepatitis D can occur only if hepatitis B is present. In 1992, the federal government and the American Academy of Pediatrics recommended that all adolescents and young adults be immunized against hepatitis B. No vaccine is yet available for hepatitis C or A (Lemon & Newbold, 1990).

Genital Warts. Genital warts are caused by the *human papilloma virus* (HPV) and often have a cauliflower appearance.

Genital Warts

The *human papilloma virus* (HPV) causes **genital warts** (formerly termed *venereal warts*). HPV is extremely widespread, possibly infecting as many as 20% to 30% of sexually active people in the United States (Blakeslee, 1992). Though the warts may appear in visible areas of the skin, in perhaps 7 of 10 cases they appear in areas that cannot be seen, such as on the cervix in women or in the urethra in men (Reinisch, 1990). They occur most commonly among people in the 20- to 24-year-old age range (Reinisch, 1990). Within a few

Genital warts
An STD that is caused by the human papilloma virus and takes the form of warts that appear around the genitals and anus.

T r u t h **OR** *Fiction?*
R E V I S I T E D

months following infection, the warts are usually found in the genital and anal regions. Women are more susceptible to HPV infection because cells in the cervix divide swiftly, facilitating the multiplication of HPV (Blakeslee, 1992). Women who initiate coitus prior to the age of 18 and who have many sex partners are particularly susceptible to infection (Blakeslee, 1992). A study of University of California at Berkeley women revealed that nearly half—46%!—had contracted HPV (Blakeslee, 1992). Similarly, it is estimated that nearly half of the sexually active teenage women in some U.S. cities are infected with HPV (Blakeslee, 1992).

It is not true that most people with genital warts have them on visible parts of the body. Most people with genital warts actually have them on areas that cannot be seen, such as on the cervix in women or in the urethra in men. ■

Genital warts are similar to common plantar warts—itchy bumps that vary in size and shape. Genital warts are hard and yellow-gray when they form on dry skin. They take on pink, soft, cauliflower shapes in moist areas such as the lower vagina. In men they appear on the penis, foreskin, and scrotum, and within the urethra. They appear on the vulva, along the vaginal wall, and on the cervix in women. They can occur outside the genital area in either gender—for example, in the mouth; on the lips, eyelids, or nipples; around the anus; or in the rectum.

Genital warts may not cause any symptoms, but those that form on the urethra can cause bleeding or painful discharges. HPV itself is believed to be harmless in most cases (Penn, 1993), but it has been implicated in cancers of the genital organs, particularly cervical cancer and penile cancer (Koutsky et al., 1992). Cervical cancer is linked to HPV in perhaps as many as 85% to 98% of cases (Blakeslee, 1992; Ochs, 1994). Researchers in one study found that women with a history of HPV infection were 11 times more likely than other women to develop cervical cancer during the two-year study period (Koutsky et al., 1992). However, the odds of HPV's leading to cervical cancer appear rather slim. Only 13,500 new cases of cervical cancer are reported annually in the United States, compared to nearly 1 million new cases of HPV (Penn, 1993). (Penile cancers in men are even rarer.) Even so, it would be wise for women to safeguard themselves from HPV-related cervical cancer by limiting their number of sex partners (to reduce their risk of exposure to HPV) and by having regular Pap smears (Blakeslee, 1992).

HPV can be transmitted sexually through skin-to-skin contact during vaginal, anal, or oral sex (Penn, 1993). It can also be transmitted by other forms of contact, such as touching infected towels or clothing. The incubation period may vary from a few weeks to a couple of years.

Freezing the wart (*cryotherapy*) with liquid nitrogen is the preferred treatment (CDC, 1989b). One alternative treatment involves painting the warts over a period of several days with an alcohol-based podophyllin solution, which causes them to dry up and fall off. Unfortunately, though the warts themselves may be removed, treatment does not rid the body of the virus (CDC, 1989b). There may thus be recurrences. Podophyllin is not recommended for use with pregnant women or for treatment of warts that form on the cervix (CDC, 1989b). If necessary, the warts may also be treated (by a doctor!) with electrodes (burning) or surgery (by laser or surgical removal).

Unfortunately, no vaccine against HPV exists or appears to be in the offing. Latex condoms help reduce the risk of contracting HPV. They do not eliminate the risk entirely because the virus may be transmitted from areas of the skin not protected by condoms, such as the scrotum (Ochs, 1994). People with active warts should probably avoid sexual contact until the warts are removed and the area heals completely.

Molluscum contagiosum
An STD caused by a pox virus that causes painless raised lesions to appear on the genitals, buttocks, thighs, or lower abdomen.

Molluscum Contagiosum

Molluscum contagiosum is caused by a pox virus that may be spread sexually. The virus causes painless raised lesions to appear on the genitals, buttocks, thighs, or lower abdomen. Pinkish in appearance with a waxy or pearly top, they usually appear within two or three months of infection. Most infected people have between 10 and 20 lesions, although the number of lesions may range from 1 to perhaps 100 or more (Douglas, 1990). The lesions are generally not associated with serious complications and often disappear on their own within six months. Or they can be treated by squeezing them (like "popping" a blackhead) to exude the whitish center plug. Freezing with liquid nitrogen may also be used to remove the lesions. However, do not try to treat any lesions on your own. See your doctor.

~ *Reflections* ~

■ Many people with genital herpes feel "damaged" and avoid sex. How do you believe that you would feel if you had genital herpes? Why?
■ How might you discuss an infection of herpes with a prospective lover or mate?
■ Agree or disagree with the following statement, and support your answer: STDs are tougher on women than on men.

Ectoparasitic Infestations

Ectoparasites, as opposed to *endoparasites,* live on the outer surfaces of animals (*ecto* means "outer"). *Trichomonas vaginalis,* which causes trichomoniasis, is an endoparasite (*endo* means "inner"). Ectoparasites are larger than the agents that cause other STDs. In this section we consider two types of STDs caused by ectoparasites: pediculosis and scabies.

Pediculosis

Pediculosis is the name given to an infestation of a parasite whose proper Latin name, *Pthirus pubis* (pubic lice), sounds rather too dignified for these bothersome (dare we say ugly?) creatures that are better known as "crabs." Pubic lice are commonly called "crabs" because under the microscope they are somewhat similar in appearance to crabs (see Figure 16.3). They belong to a family of insects called biting lice. Another member of the family, the human head louse, is an annoying insect that clings to hair on the scalp and often spreads among school children.

It is not true that pubic lice are of the same family of animals as crabs. Viewed under a microscope, however, they appear somewhat similar to crabs. ■

In the adult stage, pubic lice are large enough to be seen with the naked eye. They are spread sexually but may also be transmitted by contact with an infested towel, sheet, or—yes—toilet seat. They can survive for only about 24 hours without a human host, but they may deposit eggs that can take up to seven days to hatch in bedding or towels (Reinisch, 1990). Therefore, all bedding, towels, and clothes that have been used by an infested person must be washed in hot water and dried on the hot cycle, or dry-cleaned to ensure that they are safe. Fingers may also transmit the lice from the genitals to other hair-covered parts of the body, including the scalp and armpits. Sexual contact should be avoided until the infestation is eradicated.

Itching, ranging from the mildly irritating to the intolerable, is the most prominent symptom of a pubic lice infestation. The itching is caused by the "crabs" attaching themselves to the pubic hair and piercing the skin to feed on the blood of their hosts. (Yecch!) The life span of these insects is only about one month, but they are prolific egg-layers and may spawn several generations before they die. An infestation can be treated effectively with a prescription medication, a 1% solution of lindane (brand name: Kwell), which is available as a cream, lotion, or shampoo. Nonprescription medications containing pyrethrins or piperonyl butoxide (brand names: RID, Triple X, and others) will also do the job (Reinisch, 1990). Kwell is not recommended for use by pregnant or lactating women

Ectoparasites
Parasites that live on the outside of the host's body—as opposed to *endo*parasites, which live within the body. (From the Greek *ektos,* meaning "outside.")

Pediculosis
A parasitic infestation by pubic lice (*Pthirus pubis*) that causes itching.

T r u t h **OR** *Fiction?*

R E V I S I T E D

Figure 16.3. Pubic Lice. Pediculosis is an infestation by pubic lice (*Pthirus pubis*). Pubic lice are commonly called "crabs" because of their appearance under a microscope.

(CDC, 1989b). A careful reexamination of the body is necessary after four to seven days of treatment to ensure that all lice and eggs were killed (Reinisch, 1990).

Scabies

Scabies
A parasitic infestation caused by a tiny mite (*Sarcoptes scabiei*) that causes itching.

Scabies (short for *Sarcoptes scabiei*) is a parasitic infestation caused by a tiny mite that may be transmitted through sexual contact or contact with infested clothing, bed linen, towels, and other fabrics. The mites attach themselves to the base of pubic hair and burrow into the skin, where they lay eggs and subsist for the duration of their 30-day life span. Like pubic lice, scabies are often found in the genital region and cause itching and discomfort. They are also responsible for reddish lines (created by burrowing) and sores, welts, or blisters on the skin. Unlike lice, they are too tiny to be seen by the naked eye. Diagnosis is made by detecting the mite or its by-products on microscopic examination of scrapings from suspicious-looking areas of skin (Levine, 1991). Scabies are most often found on the hands and wrists, but they may also appear on the genitals, buttocks, armpits, and feet (Reinisch, 1990). But they do not appear above the neck—thankfully!

Scabies, like pubic lice, may be treated effectively with 1% lindane (Kwell). The entire body from the neck down must be coated with a thin layer of the medication, which should not be washed off for eight hours (CDC, 1989b). But lindane should not be used by women who are pregnant or lactating. To avoid reinfection, sex partners and others in close bodily contact with infected persons should also be treated. Clothing and bed linen used by the infected person must be washed and dried on the hot cycle or dry-cleaned. As with "crabs," sexual contact should be avoided until the infestation is eliminated.

∼ *Reflections* ∼

Had you ever heard of "crabs"? What had you imagined the word meant? Were you correct?

Prevention of STDs: It's More Than Safer Sex

Prevention is the best way to control the spread of STDs, especially those for which there is no cure or vaccine. Prevention of even one case of an STD may prevent its spread to others—perhaps eventually to you.

Prevention Strategies

There are many things that you can do to lower the risk of contracting STDs. As you will see, safer sex is only one aspect of prevention.

Abstinence or Monogamy

> I don't even masturbate anymore. I'm so afraid I'll give myself something. I just want to be friends with myself.
>
> (Richard Lewis)

The only fully effective strategies to prevent the sexual transmission of STDs are abstinence or maintaining a monogamous sexual relationship with an uninfected partner. Thus, if you are celibate, or if you and your sex partner are not infected and neither of you engages in sexual activity with anyone else, you have little to be concerned about. Many people are sexually active and have not committed themselves to a monogamous relationship, however. Even for those who seek monogamous relationships, there must always be that "first time."

Be Knowledgeable About the Risks   Be aware of the risks of STDs. Many of us try to put the dangers of STDs out of our minds—especially in moments of passion. So make a pact with yourself to refuse to play the dangerous game of pretending that the dangers of STDs do not exist or that you are somehow immune.

Remain Sober   Alcohol and other drugs increase the likelihood of engaging in risky sexual behavior.

Inspect Yourself and Your Partner   Inspect yourself for a discharge, bumps, rashes, warts, blisters, chancres, sores, lice, or foul odors. Check out any unusual feature with a physician before you engage in sexual activity.

You may be able to work an inspection of your partner into foreplay—a reason for making love the first time with the lights on. In particular, a woman may hold her partner's penis firmly, pulling the loose skin up and down, as if "milking" it. Then she can check for a discharge at the penile opening. The man may use his fingers to detect any sign of a vaginal discharge. Other visible features of STDs include herpes blisters, genital warts, syphilitic chancres or rashes, and pubic lice.

If you find anything that doesn't look, feel, or smell right, bring it to your partner's attention. Treat any unpleasant odor as a warning sign. Your partner may not be aware of the symptom and may be carrying an infection. If you notice any suspicious signs, refrain from further sexual contact until your partner has the chance to seek a medical evaluation. It is advisable to be informed about the common signs and symptoms of STDs, but you need not become a medical expert. Even if your concerns prove groundless, you can resume sexual relations without the uncertainty that you would have had if you had ignored them.

Of course, your partner may become defensive or hostile if you express a concern that he or she may be carrying an STD. Try to be empathetic. The social stigma attached to people with STDs makes it difficult to accept the possibility of infection. It may be appropriate to point out that STDs are quite common (among college students, bank officers, military personnel, or . . . fill in the blanks) and that many people are unaware that they carry them.

But for your sake as well as your partner's, if you are not sure that sex is safe, stop. Think carefully about the risks, and seek expert advice.

Use Latex Condoms   Latex condoms are effective in blocking nearly all sexually transmissible organisms (Liskin et al., 1990). Latex condoms may be even more effective in preventing STDs when used along with spermicides containing the ingredient nonoxynol-9, which kills STD-causing microorganisms including the viruses that cause AIDS and genital herpes (Heiman & LoPiccolo, 1987; Koop, 1988).

Researchers estimate that in regular use, condoms reduce the rate of STD infections by about 50%, on the average (Rosenberg et al., 1991). Improper use or inconsistent use is a common reason for failures in using condoms to prevent STD transmission (Rosenberg & Gollub, 1992). Yet even when used properly, condoms may be of limited or no value against disease-causing organisms that are transmitted externally, such as those causing herpes, genital warts, and ectoparasitic infestations.

Avoid High-Risk Sexual Behaviors   Anal penetration by a penis or a partner's hand ("fisting") carries a heightened risk of infection because tears in the anal lining can provide microorganisms with a convenient port of entry into the bloodstream. Unless you are absolutely sure that you and your partner are free of STDs, such activities are to be avoided. If you do engage in anal–genital sex and are uncertain as to whether you or your partner is infected, use a latex condom and spermicide. Oral–anal sex, or anilingus (sometimes called *rimming*), should be avoided because of the potential of transmitting microbes between the mouth and the anus.

Also avoid sexual contact with people with STDs, people who practice high-risk sexual behaviors, people who inject drugs, and prostitutes or people who frequent prostitutes.

Wash the Genitals Before and After Sex   Washing the genitals before and after sex removes a quantity of potentially harmful agents. Washing together may be incorporated into erotic foreplay. Right after intercourse, a thorough washing with soap and water may help reduce the risk of infection. Do not, however, deceive yourself into believing that washing your genitals is an effective substitute for safer sex. Most STDs are transmitted internally. Washing is of no avail against them.

There may be some limited benefits to women from douching right after coitus. But frequent douching should be avoided since it may change the vaginal flora and encourage the growth of infectious organisms. Nor is immediate douching possible for women who use a diaphragm and spermicide that must remain in the vagina for at least six to eight hours after intercourse. But such women may profit from washing the external genitals immediately after coitus.

Have Regular Medical Checkups   A sexually active person should have health examinations regularly, at least once a year. Many community clinics and family-planning centers scale their charges to the patient's ability to pay. Checkups are a small enough investment to make in one's own health. Many people are symptomless carriers of STDs, especially of chlamydial infections. Medical checkups enable them to learn about and receive treatment for disorders that might otherwise go unnoticed. Many physicians advise routine testing of asymptomatic young women for chlamydial infections to prevent the hidden damage that may occur if the infection goes untreated (Buhaug et al., 1990).

Discuss Whether You and Your Partner Should Undergo Testing Before Initiating Sexual Relations   Some couples reach a mutual agreement to be tested for HIV and other STDs before they initiate sexual relations. (Some people simply insist that their prospective partners be tested before they initiate sexual relations.) But many people resist testing or feel insulted when their partners raise the issue. People usually assume that they are free of STDs if they are symptom-free and have been reasonably selective in their choice of partners. But STDs happen to the "nicest people," and the absence of symptoms is no guarantee of freedom from infection. Unless you have been celibate or involved in a monogamous relationship with an uninfected partner, you should consider yourself at risk of carrying or contracting an infectious STD.

Consult Your Physician If You Suspect That You Have Been Exposed to an STD   Early intervention may prevent the damage of an STD's spreading to vital body organs. Be sensitive to any physical changes that may be symptomatic of STDs. Consult a physician when in doubt.

Get to Know Your Partner Before Initiating Sexual Relations   Be selective in your choice of sex partners. Having sex with multiple partners—especially "one-night stands"—increases your risk of sexual contact with an infected person. It also lessens the opportunity to get to know your partner well enough to know whether he or she has participated in high-risk sexual practices or has had sex partners in the past who practiced high-risk behaviors.

Avoid Other High-Risk Behaviors   Avoid contact with bodily substances (blood, semen, vaginal secretions, fecal matter) from other people. Do not share hypodermic needles, razors, cuticle scissors, or other implements that may contain another person's blood. Be careful when handling wet towels, bed linen, or other material that may contain bodily substances.

～ *Reflections* ～

▨   Which methods of preventing STDs seem workable to you? Why? Which seem unworkable? Explain.

▨   Will reading this chapter lead to any changes in your behavior? Why, or why not?

▨   Agree or disagree with the following statement, and support your answer: My partner and I should undergo testing before initiating sexual relations.

SOURCES OF HELP

Do you have questions about the signs and symptoms of STDs? Do you need assistance in coping with an STD? A number of organizations have established telephone hotlines that provide anonymous callers with information. Some organizations publish newsletters and other material to help people with particular diseases cope more effectively.

National Toll-Free Hotlines for Information About AIDS and Other STDs
These hotlines provide information about AIDS and other STDs, as well as referral sources. You needn't give your name or identify yourself to obtain information.

National AIDS Hotline, Centers for Disease Control AIDS Hotline: (800) 342-AIDS (information and referral resources nationwide, 24 hours a day)

National STD Hotline: (800) 227-8922 (in California, (800) 982-5883) (a hotline sponsored by the American Social Health Association that dispenses information about STD symptoms and refers callers to local STD clinics that provide confidential, minimum- or no-cost treatment)

Spanish AIDS/SIDA Hotline: (800) 344-7432

AIDS Hotline for Teens: (800) 234-TEEN

AIDS Hotline for the Hearing Impaired: (800) 243-7889

Canadian Toll-Free Hotline (toll-free in Canada): AIDS Committee of Toronto: (800) 267-6600

Where to Obtain Help or Information About Herpes

National Herpes Hotline: (919) 361-8488

The Helper is a newsletter published by HELP (Herpetics Engaged in Living Productively), an organization that helps people with herpes cope with the disease. For copies of the newsletter, and for the address of the HELP chapter closest to you, either call the National STD Hotline listed above or write to HELP, Herpes Resource Center, P. O. Box 13827, Research Triangle Park, NC 27709.

Herpes Resource Center
Box 100
Palo Alto, CA 94302

Summing Up

An Epidemic

More than 13 million people in the United States contract a sexually transmitted disease (STD) each year. Although public attention has been riveted on AIDS for a decade, other STDs such as chlamydia and genital warts pose wider threats.

Bacterial Diseases

Bacteria are one-celled microorganisms that cause many illnesses.

Gonorrhea   Gonorrhea is caused by the *gonococcus bacterium.* For men, symptoms include a penile discharge and burning urination. Most women are asymptomatic. If left untreated, gonorrhea can attack the internal reproductive organs and lead to PID in women. Gonorrhea is treated with antibiotics.

Syphilis   Syphilis is caused by the *Treponema pallidum* bacterium. Syphilis undergoes several stages of development. Although it may lie dormant for many years, it may also be lethal. Syphilis is treated with antibiotics.

Chlamydia   Chlamydia or chlamydial infections are caused by the *Chlamydia trachomatous* bacterium. The symptoms of chlamydial infections resemble those of gonorrhea but tend to be milder. Chlamydial infections also respond to antibiotics.

Vaginal Infections

Vaginitis is usually known by a foul-smelling discharge, genital irritation, and burning during urination. Most cases involve bacterial vaginosis, candidiasis, or trichomoniasis.

Bacterial Vaginosis   Bacterial vaginosis is usually caused by the *Gardnerella vaginalis* bacterium. Oral treatment with metronidazole is recommended.

Candidiasis   Candidiasis is caused by a yeastlike fungus, *Candida albicans.* Infections usually arise from changes in the vaginal environment that allow the fungus to overgrow. Treatment with miconazole, clotrimazole, or terconazole is usually recommended.

Trichomoniasis   "Trich" is caused by a protozoan called *Trichomonas vaginalis.* Trichomoniasis is treated with metronidazole.

Viral Diseases

Viruses are particles of DNA that reproduce by invading a body cell and directing the cell's own reproductive machinery to spin off new viral particles.

Herpes   Oral herpes is caused by the *Herpes simplex* virus type 1 (HSV-1). Genital herpes is caused by the *Herpes simplex* virus type 2 (HSV-2), which produces painful shallow sores and blisters on the genitals. There is no cure or vaccine for herpes, but the antiviral drug acyclovir can relieve pain and speed healing during flare-ups.

Viral Hepatitis   There are several types of hepatitis, and they are caused by different hepatitis viruses. Most cases of hepatitis are transmitted sexually or by contact with contaminated blood or fecal matter.

Genital Warts   Genital warts are caused by the *human papilloma virus (HPV).* HPV has been linked to cancers of the genital tract. Freezing the wart is the preferred treatment for removal of the wart, but the virus remains in the body afterwards.

Molluscum Contagiosum   The viral STD, caused by a pox virus, brings about an outbreak of painless raised lesions on the genitals, buttocks, thighs, or lower abdomen. The lesions usually disappear on their own without serious complications within six months.

Ectoparasitic Infestations

Pediculosis   Pediculosis ("crabs") is caused by pubic lice (*Pthirus pubis*). Pubic lice attach themselves to pubic hair and feed on the blood of their hosts, which often causes itching. Infestations can be treated with a prescription medication, lindane, or with nonprescription medications containing pyrethrins or piperonal butoxide.

Scabies   Scabies (*Sarcoptes scabiei*) is a parasitic infestation caused by a tiny mite that causes itching. Scabies, like pubic lice, is treated with lindane.

Prevention of STDs: It's More Than Safer Sex

Strategies for preventing STDs include abstinence, monogamy, inspecting oneself and one's partner, using latex condoms, avoiding high-risk sex, washing the genitals before and after sex, having regular medical checkups, and getting to know one's partner before engaging in sexual activity.

CHAPTER 17

Henri Matisse, *French
Window at Collioure,*
1914. Museé National
D'Art Moderne, Paris.
© 1996 Succession
H. Matisse/Artist Rights
Society (ARS),
New York.

Acquired Immunodeficiency Syndrome (AIDS)

Outline

Truth OR Fiction?

_____ By the year 2000, 40 million people around the world are likely to be infected by HIV (the virus that causes AIDS).

_____ Only people in high-risk groups are at serious risk for contracting AIDS.

_____ As you are reading this page, you are engaged in search-and-destroy missions against foreign agents within your body.

_____ AIDS does not kill directly; rather, it kills by disabling the body's ability to fend off other life-threatening diseases.

_____ People can pass along HIV to others even if they have no symptoms of the infection themselves.

_____ Most people who are infected by HIV remain symptom-free and appear healthy for years.

_____ You can be infected with HIV by donating blood.

_____ Only a small proportion of AIDS patients are women.

_____ HIV infection is diagnosed by examination of the virus in the bloodstream.

_____ Awareness of the risks of HIV infection and AIDS leads people to engage in "safer sex."

Suddenly it was upon us. As had the sexual revolution, it changed the face of human sexuality. Innocence and spontaneity became things of the past. For millions, the advent of the pill had divorced the free spirit of sex from consequences. Most other repercussions were annoyances—or at least they were not lethal. Now we all had to think again. AIDS had arrived.

The first cases of a mysterious new disease began to appear in medical journals in 1981. Physicians reported treating a number of male patients who were suffering from pneumocystis carinii pneumonia (PCP). PCP is a rare form of pneumonia that had typically been found among cancer patients whose immune systems were suppressed as a side effect of chemotherapy. Some people with PCP showed other disorders associated with suppressed immune systems—high fevers, weight loss, and candidiasis of the mouth. Although people with such conditions normally recover, these people did not. They all died (Gottlieb, 1991). AIDS had arrived.

At first we did not know what had hit us. Then we learned. AIDS had arrived.

AIDS is the acronym for **acquired immunodeficiency syndrome.** AIDS is a fatal disease that is caused by the **human immunodeficiency virus** (HIV). HIV attacks and disables the immune system, the body's natural line of defense, stripping it of its ability to fend off disease-causing organisms. No one knows where HIV originated, but some investigators suspect that it may be a variant of viruses found in monkeys and chimpanzees.

Also in the early 1980s, physicians also began to see cases in young men of a rare form of cancer—Kaposi's sarcoma—that leaves purple spots on the body. This illness usually struck only aging Jewish and Italian men. Though aging men usually live with the disease and die later of other causes, the young men quickly deteriorated and died. Some also had PCP.

When this atypical assortment of symptoms and maladies was first reported in the medical journals, the only clear connection among the afflicted patients was that all of them were gay. The syndrome that struck them became known disparagingly as the "gay cancer" or the "gay plague." Some people viewed the epidemic as an expression of God's wrath against gay men. According to journalist Randy Shilts (1987), the government was slow to respond to the epidemic because of prejudice against gay people. Not until celebrities such as film star Rock Hudson, choreographer Michael Bennett, and fashion designer Perry Ellis died from AIDS did the nation take much note of it. Shilts himself died of AIDS in 1994.

Not until 1982 would the syndrome that first struck gay people be given the name of AIDS. Not until 1983 were cases of AIDS discovered among heterosexuals. Not until 1985 was a test for HIV infection licensed. When AIDS moved into the heterosexual population, it mainly struck people who injected drugs.[1] They spread the virus by sharing contaminated needles and through sexual activity. Other common targets included children who were born after their mothers had been infected, and hemophiliacs and others who had received transfusions of blood that were contaminated with HIV. It became clear that HIV paid no attention to boundaries related to sexual orientation, race, socioeconomic status, or age.

The announcement by basketball great Earvin "Magic" Johnson in 1991 that he was infected with HIV was a watershed event in the history of the AIDS epidemic. Johnson had led the Lakers to five professional basketball championships. Johnson said that he had been infected through male–female sex. Johnson's disclosure that he is HIV-infected (or HIV-positive, which is represented by the expression HIV+) provided graphic evidence that young, vigorous heterosexuals are not invulnerable to HIV infection. If someone as healthy and physically fit as Johnson could be infected by HIV, any of us are potentially at risk. The publicity surrounding Johnson's announcement may have prompted some people to reduce unsafe sexual practices (Centers for Disease Control [CDC], 1993c; "Publicity about Magic," 1993).

Acquired immunodeficiency syndrome (AIDS)
A condition caused by the human immunodeficiency virus (HIV) and characterized by destruction of the immune system so that the body is stripped of its ability to fend off life-threatening diseases.

Human immunodeficiency virus (HIV)
A sexually transmitted virus that destroys white blood cells in the immune system, leaving the body vulnerable to life-threatening diseases.

---

[1]Referred to as *injecting drug users* (IDUs) by the Centers for Disease Control.

Prevalence of HIV Infection and AIDS

Fewer than 100 Americans had died of AIDS in 1981 when the syndrome was first described in the medical journals (Gottlieb, 1991). By July 1995, more than 475,000 Americans would be diagnosed as having AIDS. More than 295,000 would have died from it (CDC, 1996). In 1994 alone there were some 80,000 new cases of AIDS in the United States (CDC, 1996). AIDS had become the leading killer of Americans of ages 25 to 44. The prevalence of AIDS was growing at about 3% a year. AIDS is increasing most rapidly among women, people of color, people who share needles when they inject drugs, and people who engage in unprotected, male–female sex (MMWR, 1995).

Figure 17.1 on page 504 shows the geographical distribution of AIDS cases within the United States. As many as 1.5 million people in the United States are infected with HIV (Fisher et al., 1995). Nearly all of them will eventually develop AIDS. The World Health Organization (WHO) estimated that 20 million people around the world were infected with HIV in 1995. Nearly 4.5 million of them had developed AIDS (WHO, 1995). WHO estimates that the number of persons infected with HIV may soar to 30 to 40 million by the year 2000.

According to a leading official with the World Health Organization, some 30 to 40 million people around the world are likely to be infected by HIV by the year 2000 if present patterns of behavior and infection continue. ■

In the United States, AIDS predominantly affects men who engage in sexual activity with other men or share needles when injecting drugs (CDC, 1995). In 1994, 44% of people with AIDS were infected by male–male sexual contact. Another 27% were infected by sharing contaminated needles for injecting drugs (see Figure 17.2A on page 505). The rate of new cases of AIDS in gay men has been declining—in part due to more widespread use of safer sex practices in the gay male community, including increased use of condoms and reduced numbers of sex partners. Experts remain concerned, however, about the resumption of unsafe sexual practices among older gay men and about younger gay men who may not follow safer sex guidelines (Ehrhardt, 1992).

Male–female sexual contact is the fasting-growing exposure category. Among women, however, male–female sexual contact now accounts for about 38% of cases (see Figure 17.2B). Bear in mind that it is a person's behavior and not the groups to which she or he belongs that determines her or his relative risk of infection. Thus, we speak in terms of high-risk *behaviors* (such as unprotected intercourse) rather than high-risk *groups*.

It is *not* true that only people in high-risk groups are at serious risk for contracting AIDS. One's behavior, not one's group membership, places one at risk for AIDS. ■

Disproportionately high numbers of African Americans and Hispanic Americans have contracted AIDS (Amaro, 1995). Forty-six percent of the men and three quarters of the women with AIDS in the United States are African American or Hispanic American (CDC, 1995). Yet these groups comprise only 21% of the population (see Figure 17.3 on page 505). The number of AIDS cases among African Americans and Hispanic Americans has been increasing, while the number of cases among White people has been modestly declining (Woodard, 1993). Death rates due to AIDS are more than twice as great among African Americans and Hispanic Americans (especially Hispanic people of Puerto Rican origin) than among White Americans (CDC, 1991; 1993f).

Ethnic differences in rates of transmission of HIV appear linked to injecting drugs. People who share needles when they inject drugs can become infected by contaminated needles. They can then transmit the virus to their sex partners through unprotected sex. People who share needles now account for more than one in four AIDS cases (see Figure 17.3). African Americans constitute about 50% of the people who apparently became infected with HIV by injecting drugs (CDC, 1995). Hispanic Americans account for another 29% of cases

Alabama:	13.8%	Louisiana:	28.7	Oklahoma:	8.3
Alaska:	9.7	Maine:	9.4	Oregon:	19.6
Arizona:	15.0	Maryland:	54.4	Pennsylvania:	21.0
Arkansas:	11.6	Massachusetts:	23.2	Rhode Island:	27.7
California:	38.6	Michigan:	10.9	South Carolina:	31.6
Colorado:	22.3	Minnesota:	9.2	South Dakota:	2.6
Connecticut:	27.8	Mississippi:	16.2	Tennessee:	14.8
Delaware:	38.4	Missouri:	13.5	Texas:	32.0
DC:	245.4	Montana:	3.5	Utah:	8.0
Florida:	61.8	Nebraska:	5.5	Vermont:	6.5
Georgia:	31.8	Nevada:	26.6	Virginia:	17.7
Hawaii:	18.3	New Hampshire:	8.1	Washington:	17.4
Idaho:	5.4	New Jersey:	63.2	West Virginia:	5.3
Illinois:	26.4	New Mexico:	12.8	Wisconsin:	7.5
Indiana:	10.8	New York:	82.2	Wyoming:	3.8
Iowa:	4.6	North Carolina:	16.8	Puerto Rico:	64.8
Kansas:	9.6	North Dakota:	3.1		
Kentucky:	8.4	Ohio:	10.7		

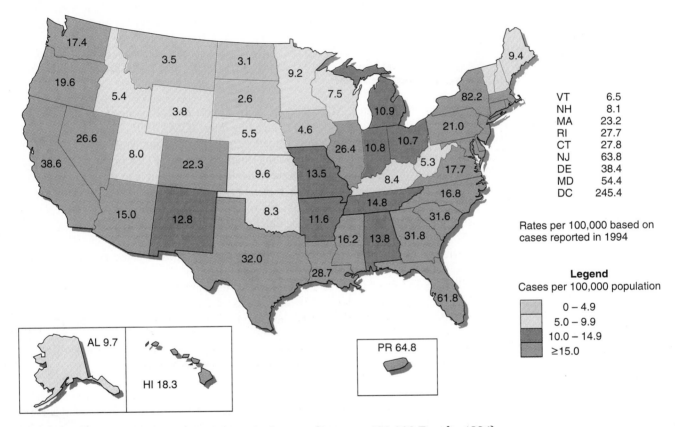

VT	6.5
NH	8.1
MA	23.2
RI	27.7
CT	27.8
NJ	63.8
DE	38.4
MD	54.4
DC	245.4

Rates per 100,000 based on cases reported in 1994

Legend
Cases per 100,000 population

- 0 – 4.9
- 5.0 – 9.9
- 10.0 – 14.9
- ≥15.0

Figure 17.1. AIDS Cases Within the United States (Rate per 100,000 People, 1994).
Source: Table 1, Centers for Disease Control and Prevention (1995). *HIV/AIDS Surveillance Report*, Year-end Edition (U.S. HIV and AIDS cases reported through December 1994), Vol. 6, No. 2.

(CDC, 1995). Drug abuse and the related problem of prostitution occur disproportionately in poor, urban communities with large populations of people of color. Thus, it is not surprising that HIV infection and AIDS have affected these groups disproportionately.

AIDS has ravaged the creative arts, claiming many of its leading talents. The dance world lost the famed ballet star Rudolph Nureyev and the choreographer Michael Bennett, who gave us *A Chorus Line* and *Dreamgirls*. The performing arts lost Liberace, Peter Allen, and Freddie Mercury; the world of fashion, Halston and Perry Ellis; the movie industry, Rock Hudson, Tony Perkins, and Robert Reed; the art world, Robert Mapplethorpe and Keith Haring. In recounting the roster of creative spirits who have been obliterated by

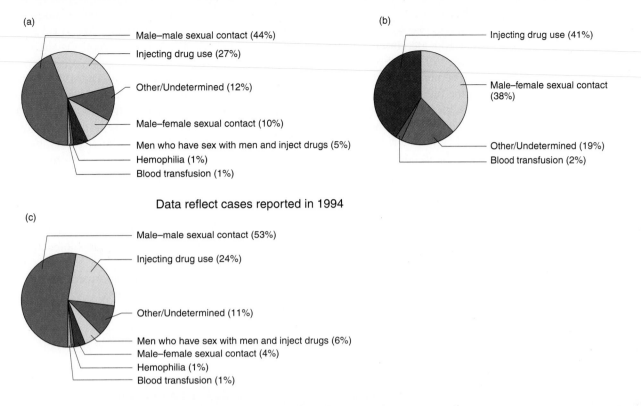

Data reflect cases reported in 1994

Figure 17.2. **AIDS Cases by Exposure Category (1994).** Part A shows men and women combined; Part B, women; and Part C, men. Overall, 10% of cases of AIDS in 1994 were believed to have been transmitted by male–female sexual contact (Part A). Among women, however, more than one in three cases (38%) of AIDS were attributed to male–female sexual contact (Part B). By contrast, only 4% of cases of AIDS among men were attributed to male–female sexual contact (Part C). *Source:* Table 3, Centers for Disease Control and Prevention (1995). *HIV/AIDS Surveillance Report*, Year-end Edition (U.S. HIV and AIDS cases reported through December 1994), Vol. 6, No. 2.

AIDS, Ansen and colleagues (1993) noted that though "all lives are irreplaceable, . . . an artist's death echoes beyond a circle of loved ones" (p. 17).

More than 5,000 HIV-infected children have developed AIDS. The great majority of these children are poor African Americans or Hispanic Americans. HIV-infected children usually develop AIDS-related symptoms by six months of age and full-blown cases of AIDS by their second birthdays (Fletcher et al., 1991). Some, however, do not develop AIDS until the ages of 9 through 11. Some survive into their teens. Most succumb by the age of 10.

Questions remain as to why some children, about one in three, contract the disease from infected mothers, whereas others do not. It appears that the amount of HIV in the mother's bloodstream plays a role (Peckham & Gibb, 1995). Nor is it clear why some die

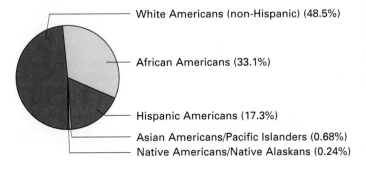

Figure 17.3. **AIDS Cases by Race.** The figure reflects cumulative totals for men and women combined, through December 1994. *Source:* Table 9, Centers for Disease Control and Prevention (1995). *HIV/AIDS Surveillance Report*, Year-end Edition (U.S. HIV and AIDS cases reported through December 1994), Vol. 6, No. 2.

by the ages of 2 through 5, whereas others survive into adolescence. Of course, thousands of children are losing their parents to AIDS. Researchers estimate that AIDS will leave about 100,000 children in the United States motherless by the year 2000 (Michaels & Levine, 1992; Navarro, 1993).

The numbers of cases of AIDS and the death toll are on the rise (CDC, 1995). What will the future bring? Will we still be in the throes of the AIDS epidemic as we enter the new millennium? Have we thus far seen but the tip of the iceberg? Or will our efforts to find a vaccine or a cure succeed? Will people engage in effective means of prevention? Or will they put their lives on the line with every sexual encounter? The answers may be largely up to you.

~ *Reflections* ~

▪ Where were you and what were you doing when you learned that Magic Johnson was infected with HIV? What effect, if any, did knowledge of Johnson's infection have on you? Why?
▪ Why do you think that disproportionately high numbers of African Americans and Hispanic Americans have contracted AIDS within the United States?
▪ Do you think that AIDS is something for you to be concerned about or something that affects "other people"? Explain.

The Immune System and AIDS

Immune system
A term for the body's complex of mechanisms for protecting itself from disease-causing agents such as pathogens.

AIDS is caused by a virus that attacks the body's **immune system**—the body's natural line of defense against disease-causing organisms. Given the intricacies of the human body and the rapid advance of scientific knowledge, we tend to consider ourselves dependent on highly trained specialists to contend with illness. Actually we cope with most diseases by ourselves, through our immune systems.

The immune system combats disease in a number of ways. It produces white blood cells that envelop and kill **pathogens** such as bacteria, viruses, and funguses; worn-out body cells; and cancer cells. White blood cells are referred to as **leukocytes.** Leukocytes engage in microscopic warfare. They undertake search-and-destroy missions. They identify and eradicate foreign agents and debilitated cells.

It is true that as you read this page, you are engaged in search-and-destroy missions against foreign agents within your body. The white blood cells in your immune system continuously seek and destroy foreign pathogens within your body. ▪

Pathogen
An agent, especially a microorganism, that can cause a disease. (From the Greek *pathos*, meaning "suffering" or "disease," and *genic*, meaning "forming" or "coming into being.")

Leukocytes recognize foreign agents by their surface fragments. The surface fragments are termed **antigens** because the body reacts to their presence by developing specialized proteins, or **antibodies.** Antibodies attach themselves to the foreign bodies, inactivate them, and mark them for destruction. (Infection by HIV may be determined by examining the blood or saliva for the presence of antibodies to the virus. Unfortunately, these antibodies are unable to eradicate the infection.)

Rather than mark pathogens for destruction or war against them, special "memory lymphocytes" are held in reserve. Memory lymphocytes can remain in the bloodstream for years, and they form the basis for a quick immune response to an invader the second time around.[2]

Another function of the immune system is to promote **inflammation.** When you suffer an injury, blood vessels in the region initially contract to check bleeding. Then they dilate. Dilation expands blood flow to the injured region, causing the redness and warmth that identify inflammation. The elevated blood supply also brings in an army of leukocytes

Leukocytes
White blood cells that are essential to the body's defenses against infection. (From the Greek *leukos*, meaning "white," and *kytos*, meaning "a hollow," and used in combination with other word forms to mean *cell*.)

[2]Vaccination is the placement of a weakened form of an antigen in the body, which activates the creation of antibodies and memory lymphocytes. Smallpox has been annihilated by vaccination, and researchers are trying to develop a vaccine against the virus that causes AIDS.

to combat invading microscopic life forms, like bacteria, that might otherwise use the local injury to establish a beachhead into the body.

Effects of HIV on the Immune System

Like other viruses, HIV uses the cells it invades to spin off copies of itself. Scientists have identified a key enzyme, *reverse transcriptase* (RT), that HIV uses to cause the genes in the cells it attacks to make proteins that the virus needs in order to reproduce. This discovery may one day lead to the development of drugs that attack HIV by blocking the function of RT without affecting other proteins needed by the body.

Scientists have discovered several types of HIV that cause AIDS. These include *human immunodeficiency virus type 1 (HIV-1),* the most prevalent form, and *human immunodeficiency virus type 2 (HIV-2)*. HIV-1 appears to be the more virulent of the two.

HIV directly attacks the immune system by invading and destroying a type of lymphocyte called the CD4 cell (or helper T-cell).[3] The CD4 cell is the "quarterback" of the immune system. CD4 cells "recognize" invading pathogens and signal B-lymphocytes or B-cells—another kind of white blood cell—to produce antibodies that inactivate pathogens and mark them for annihilation. CD4 cells also signal another class of T-cells, called killer T-cells, to destroy infected cells. By attacking and destroying helper T-cells, HIV disables the very cells that the body relies on to fight off this and other diseases. As HIV cripples the body's defenses, the individual is exposed to serious infections that would not otherwise take hold. Cancerous cells may also proliferate. Although the CD4 cells appear to be its main target, HIV also attacks other types of white blood cells.

The blood normally contains about 1,000 CD4 cells per cubic millimeter. The numbers of CD4 cells may remain at about this level for years following HIV infection. Many people show no symptoms and appear healthy while CD4 cells remain at this level. Then, for reasons that are not clearly understood, the levels of CD4 cells begin to drop off, although symptoms may not appear for a decade or more. As the numbers of CD4 cells decline, symptoms generally increase, and people fall prey to diseases that their weakened immune systems are unable to fight off. People become most vulnerable to opportunistic infections when the level of CD4 cells falls below 200 per cubic millimeter.

Truth **OR** *Fiction?*
REVISITED

It is true that AIDS does not kill directly. HIV kills by disabling the immune system and rendering the body vulnerable to life-threatening diseases that it normally would be capable of fending off. ■

~ *Reflections* ~

▪ What did you learn about the immune system? Had you known that the immune system marks pathogens for destruction? That it routinely sweeps away cancerous cells?

▪ What does HIV do to the immune system? How do the effects of HIV affect the functioning of the immune system?

Progression of HIV Infection and AIDS

HIV follows a complex course once it enters the body. Shortly following infection, the person may experience mild flu-like symptoms—fatigue, fever, headaches and muscle pain, lack of appetite, nausea, swollen glands, and possibly a rash. Such symptoms usually disappear within a few weeks. People may thus dismiss these symptoms as a passing case of flu. People who enter this asymptomatic or carrier state may look and act well and not realize that they are infectious. Thus, they can unwittingly pass along the virus to others.

---

[3]CD4 cells are also known as T_4 cells. The terms are synonymous and completely interchangeable.

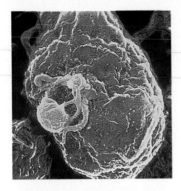

AIDS Virus (HIV) attacking a White Blood Cell.

Antigen
A protein, toxin, or other substance to which the body reacts by producing antibodies. (Combined word formed from *antibody generator*.)

Antibodies
Specialized proteins that attach themselves to foreign substances in the body, inactivating them and marking them for destruction.

Inflammation
Redness and warmth that develop at the site of an injury, reflecting dilation of blood vessels that permits the expanded flow of leukocytes to the region.

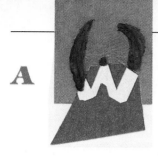
HIV INFECTION AND AIDS: A WORLD EPIDEMIC

HIV disease—HIV infection and AIDS—is a worldwide epidemic that shows no signs of ebbing. AIDS respects no boundaries. It is a merciless killer of men, women, children, and people of all nationalities and races. The rate of HIV infection is increasing faster in areas of the former Soviet Union and many developing countries in Asia, Latin America, and Africa than it is in the United States and other industrialized nations (WHO, 1995). Unless the world community takes effective action in stemming the epidemic, future prospects are indeed harrowing. Consider some facts concerning the spread of HIV and AIDS:

• Sub-Saharan Africa has been most severely hit by the AIDS epi-

demic. This region accounts for nearly 70% of the cases of HIV infection and AIDS cases around the world (see Figure 17.4). Most cases are spread by male–female sexual activity, and most of the infected people are women (Bogert et al., 1995; Lorch, 1993a). The economic and social costs of AIDS have been staggering, especially to some of the developing nations in Africa (Garrett, 1993a). One quarter to one third of adults in urban areas of some countries are believed to be infected with HIV (Shenon, 1992). In Kenya, 12% of young adults in the capital, Nairobi, are believed to be infected (Lorch, 1993b). By the year 2000, 2 mil-

lion Kenyans are expected to be infected, or about one tenth of the total population. In Uganda, deaths from AIDS have touched virtually every family. AIDS has decimated young adults and family breadwinners and left other family members to care for the children.

• The numbers of cases of HIV infection in Asia are skyrocketing (Taylor, 1993a). Asia now ranks as the continent with the second greatest number of cases of HIV infection, after Africa. As in Africa, most cases are spread by male–female sexual activity (Taylor, 1993c). Prostitution is a major route of transmission in Asia, es-

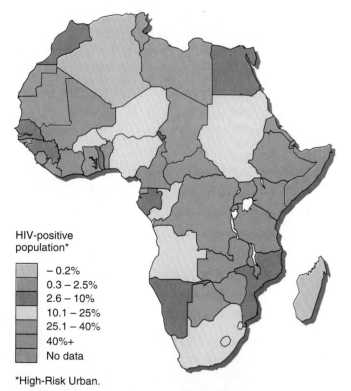

Figure 17.4   Percentage of Population with HIV Infection in Africa.   *Source:* Bogert, C., Chubbuck, K., & Hammer, J. (1995, September 25). Making Men Listen. Africa: Women Bear the Brunt of the AIDS Crisis. *Newsweek*, p. 52. Data source: U.S. Bureau of the Census.

HIV-positive population*

- 0.2%
0.3 – 2.5%
2.6 – 10%
10.1 – 25%
25.1 – 40%
40%+
No data

*High-Risk Urban.

AIDS in Africa. Africa has been harder hit by AIDS than any other continent. Sub-Saharan Africa accounts for nearly 70% of the cases of HIV infection and AIDS in the world. Most cases are spread by male–female sexual activity, and most infected people are women.

pecially in large cities, such as Bombay and Madras in India and Bangkok in Thailand. About one third of the prostitutes in these cities are believed to be infected. The World Health Organization estimates that about 2 million adults in South and Southeast Asia are infected with HIV. Other experts put the figure much higher, at 3.6 million cases, including 2 million in India alone—about twice as many cases as in the United States (Taylor, 1993a). By the end of the decade, the number of cases in Asia may rival or surpass the number in Africa (Taylor, 1993a). The crisis is most severe in India and Thailand (Shenon, 1992).

Asian governments, like those in the West, have been slow to act to stem the epidemic (Shenon, 1992). In India, for example, the government has only recently begun to address the problem by beginning to screen blood sup-

plies for HIV and launching a national HIV education and prevention campaign (Taylor, 1993a).

- The AIDS epidemic in Latin America is well on its way toward surpassing that of the United States (Brooke, 1993). HIV is spreading rapidly through Latin America through male–female sexual activity. Brazil has about as many people infected with HIV as does the United States. However, Brazil's population is only about 60% of that of the United States. In Mexico, government officials believe that between 225,000 and 5 million people are infected, in a population numbering about one third that of the United States. Haiti has the highest rate of HIV infection in Latin America. Infection rates in the largest cities are believed to range between 8% and 10% of the population.

Governments in Latin America are now fighting the epidemic. In

Brazil, AIDS education has become part of the national curriculum. Yet Brazilian men, like many men elsewhere, are reluctant to use condoms. Reluctance partly reflects condoms' dampening of sexual sensations, but also relatively high cost and poor quality.

Cuba has made a dramatic attempt to contain the epidemic. In Cuba, people infected with HIV are quarantined, and testing for infection for most people is mandatory. The stiff measures, despite the cost to individual liberties, are credited with having reduced the spread of the AIDS epidemic. A Cuban official estimated that fewer than 1,000 people in the early 1990s were infected with HIV, out of a population of 10 million.

- Although minuscule by comparison with the United States and some other Asian countries, Japan too is experiencing a rapid rise in the number of AIDS cases (Sterngold, 1992). In the early 1990s, the majority of people in Japan to die from AIDS were foreigners. HIV was predominantly spread via male–female sexual activity with prostitutes. Once the government recognized that HIV and AIDS were affecting its own citizens and not just foreigners, it mounted an AIDS prevention program focused on condom use and encouraging understanding of people infected with the virus. The government also upheld a ban against oral contraceptives by arguing that approving the pill would discourage condom use and lead to an AIDS epidemic.

Truth OR Fiction?
R E V I S I T E D

It is true that people can transmit HIV to others even if they have no symptoms of the infection themselves. ■

Most people who are infected with HIV remain asymptomatic for years. Some enter a symptomatic state (previously labeled *AIDS-related complex,* or ARC) that is typically denoted by symptoms such as chronically swollen lymph nodes and intermittent weight loss, fever, fatigue, and diarrhea. The severity of symptomatic HIV infection depends on various factors, such as the person's general health. This symptomatic state does not constitute full-blown AIDS, but shows that HIV is undermining the integrity of the person's immune system. Like asymptomatic carriers, they may unknowingly pass along the virus to others through sexual contact or needle sharing.

Truth OR Fiction?
R E V I S I T E D

It is true that most people who are infected by HIV remain symptom-free and appear healthy for years. ■

Even during the years when HIV appears to be lying dormant in the body, billions of viral particles are actually being spun off. In a seesaw battle, the great majority of them are wiped out by the immune system. As of this writing, however, cases in which people completely clear HIV from their bodies are extremely rare (Bryson et al., 1995; Groden, 1995).

Eventually, in almost all cases, the balance tips in favor of HIV. Then the virus's numbers swell. Perhaps a decade or more after the person is infected with HIV, and for reasons that remain unclear, the virus begins to overtake the immune system. It obliterates the cells that house it and spreads to other immune-system cells, eventually destroying or disabling the body's ability to defend itself from disease. About half of the people with HIV develop diagnosable AIDS within ten years of initial infection. For this reason, people who know that they are infected with HIV may feel as though they are carrying time bombs within them. AIDS is classified as a *syndrome* because it is characterized by a variety of different symptoms. The beginnings of full-blown cases of AIDS are often marked by symptoms such as swollen lymph nodes, fatigue, fever, "night sweats," diarrhea, and weight loss that cannot be attributed to dieting or exercise.

Opportunistic diseases
Diseases that take hold only when the immune system is weakened and unable to fend them off. Kaposi's sarcoma and pneumocystis carinii pneumonia (PCP) are examples of opportunistic diseases found in AIDS patients.

The diagnosis of AIDS is based on the appearance of indicator diseases, such as PCP; Kaposi's sarcoma; toxoplasmosis of the brain, which is an infection of parasites; or *Herpes simplex* with chronic ulcers. These diseases are termed **opportunistic diseases** because they are not likely to emerge unless a disabled immune system provides the opportunity.

About 10% of people with AIDS have a wasting syndrome (CDC, 1995). Wasting is the unintentional loss of more than 10% of a person's body weight and is connected with AIDS, some other infections, and cancer (Grunfeld, 1995). It appears that people with AIDS who waste away do so because they take in less energy, not because they burn more calories (Macallan et al., 1995). Some people with AIDS eat less because of lack of energy. Eating more often causes people with wasting syndrome to put on fat rather than lean muscle mass, which does not contribute to their overall health.

As AIDS progresses, the individual grows thinner and more fatigued. He or she becomes unable to perform ordinary life functions and falls prey to opportunistic infections. AIDS almost always results in death within a few years.

In 1993, the federal Centers for Disease Control expanded the diagnostic criteria for AIDS. Three additional diseases were added to the list of 23 other AIDS indicators: invasive cancer of the cervix, tuberculosis of the lungs, and recurrent pneumonia. The new criteria provide for an AIDS diagnosis when the CD4 cell count in persons infected with HIV falls to fewer than 200 cells per cubic millimeter, about one fifth the normal amount, irrespective of the presence of indicator diseases. The more inclusive definition has made more people eligible for AIDS benefits. It better accommodates women infected with HIV. Women may develop gynecological conditions, such as persistent and recurrent vaginal yeast infections, that are not seen in men. It also better accommodates people who share needles when they inject drugs, infected children, and unusual cases in which traditional indicator diseases are not present. The expanded definition of AIDS led to an expected surge in the number of diagnosed cases reported in the first few months of 1993.

One of the most baffling puzzles is why some people with HIV remain well for years, whereas others succumb in a relatively short time (Ezzell, 1993). Some people have had HIV for a dozen or more years without developing AIDS (Garrett, 1993b). What distinguishes a long-term survivor of HIV from a short-term survivor remains a mystery (Pfeiffer, 1992). Further study of the immune systems of long-term survivors may shed light on possible protective immunological mechanisms that could help others who are not so fortunate.

~ Reflections ~

- What is meant when we say that HIV and white blood cells fight a "seesaw battle" that can last for a decade or more?
- What is meant by the term *opportunistic diseases?*
- Why do you think some people with HIV remain well for a dozen years or more, whereas others succumb relatively soon?

Transmission

HIV can be transmitted by certain contaminated bodily fluids—blood, semen, vaginal secretions, or breast milk. The first three of these may enter the body through vaginal, anal, or oral–genital intercourse with an infected partner. Other avenues of infection include sharing a hypodermic needle with an infected person (as do many people who inject drugs), transfusion with contaminated blood, transplants of organs and tissues that have been infected with HIV, artificial insemination with infected semen, or being stuck by a needle used previously on an infected person. HIV may enter the body through tiny cuts or sores in the mucosal lining of the vagina, rectum, and even the mouth. These cuts or sores may be so tiny that you may not be aware of them.

Transmission of HIV through kissing, even prolonged kissing or "French" kissing, is considered unlikely (CDC, 1992). We have yet to find any confirmed cases of HIV transmission through kissing.

When a person injects drugs, a small amount of his or her blood remains inside the needle and syringe. If the person is HIV-infected, the virus may be found in the blood remaining in the needle or syringe. When others use the same needle, they inject the infected blood into their bloodstreams. HIV may also be spread by sharing needles used for other purposes, such as injecting steroids, ear piercing, or tattooing. If you are interested in having your ears pierced or getting a tattoo, insist upon seeing a qualified person who uses new or sterilized equipment. Ask questions about the safety measures that are followed before undergoing any such procedure.

Sexual activities may become a means of transmission of HIV only if one of the partners is infected with the virus. *You cannot contract or transmit HIV via sexual activity if neither you nor your partner is infected, no matter what sexual activities you practice.* This is not to say that these activities are entirely free of risk. They may serve as a mode of entry for other STD-causing microorganisms, such as those that cause syphilis, gonorrhea, genital warts, or chlamydia. Anal intercourse may cause injury to sensitive rectal tissue if it is performed too forcefully or without sufficient lubrication.

HIV may also be transmitted from mother to fetus during pregnancy or from mother to child through childbirth or breast-feeding (Peckham & Gibb, 1995). Transmission is most likely to occur during the birth process.

Male-to-female transmission through vaginal intercourse is about twice as likely as female-to-male transmission (Allen & Setlow, 1991), partly because more of the virus is found in the ejaculate than in vaginal secretions. A man's ejaculate may also remain for many days in the vagina, providing greater opportunity for infection to occur. Male–female or male–male anal intercourse is especially risky, particularly to the recipient, since it often tears or abrades rectal tissue, facilitating entry of the virus into the bloodstream (Caceres & van-Griensven, 1994).

Male–female transmission via sexual intercourse is the primary route of HIV infection in Africa, Latin America, and Asia (Altman, 1993c; Quinn, 1990). Worldwide, male–female

Arthur Ashe. Tennis great Arthur Ashe, shown here with his wife at the press conference announcing he had AIDS, is one of thousands who have died of AIDS in the United States. Ashe was infected with HIV from a blood transfusion he received before the blood supply was routinely screened for HIV.

sexual intercourse accounts for 75% of cases of HIV infection (Novello, 1991). In the United States, male–female transmission of HIV accounts for about 10% of AIDS cases and has become the fastest-growing exposure category (CDC, 1995). The numbers of new cases of AIDS in men and women attributable to male–female sexual contact more than doubled between 1989 and 1992 (Haverkos, 1993). Many cases of male–female transmission occur within the community of people who inject drugs and their sex partners. However, one or two cases of male–female transmission in 1993 occurred among people whose partners had risk factors that were either unreported or unknown ("Heterosexual AIDS," 1994). This raises the concern that HIV infection may be spreading more rapidly into the population at large than is generally believed.

In the early years of the AIDS epidemic, HIV spread rapidly among hemophiliacs who had unknowingly been transfused with contaminated blood. Over half of the hemophiliacs in the United States were unknowingly infected with HIV in the early 1980s (Fogle, 1991a). In 1985, the test to detect HIV antibodies (revealing the presence of HIV infection) became available, and blood banks began universal screening of donor blood. Tennis great Arthur Ashe, who died of complications from AIDS in 1993, believed that he had contracted HIV during a blood transfusion he received before the blood supply was routinely screened for HIV (Altman, 1992a). No hemophiliac in the United States is known to have contracted HIV from a blood transfusion since 1987 (Fogle, 1991a). Blood screening is not yet foolproof, however. Though transmission of HIV in the general population from blood transfusions has become quite rare since routine screening of blood supplies began, a remote possibility of infection continues to exist, with estimates indicating a 1 in 75,000 chance of contracting the infection during a single transfusion (Altman, 1992a).

HIV may also be spread by donor semen, such as that used in artificial insemination. Many sperm banks do not test donors for STDs (Meyer, 1994). Cases have been reported of women who have become infected with hepatitis B, gonorrhea, trichomoniasis ("trich"), chlamydia, and even HIV via insemination with donor semen (Meyer, 1994).

Factors Affecting the Risk of Sexual Transmission

Some people are apparently more vulnerable to infection by HIV than others. As a general rule, the probability of sexual transmission rises with the number of coital contacts with an infected partner. Yet there is no predictable connection between the number of episodes of unprotected sex with an infected person and the probability of transmission. Some people seem more likely to communicate the virus, and others seem to be especially vulnerable to contracting it. Why, for instance, are some people infected by one sexual contact with an infected partner, whereas others are not infected during months or years of unprotected coitus?

Some clues have begun to emerge, based on studies in the United States, Europe, and Africa. For one thing, a history of STDs heightens the risk of infection by HIV (WHO, 1995). STDs such as genital warts, gonorrhea, trichomoniasis, and chlamydia inflame the genital region, which may heighten the risk of sexual transmission of other STDs. STDs that produce genital ulcers, such as syphilis and genital herpes, may heighten vulnerability to HIV infection by allowing the virus to enter the circulatory system through the ulcers.

The probability of transmission is also affected by the type of sexual activity, the amount of HIV in the semen, and circumcision. Anal intercourse, for example, is a sexual activity that provides a convenient port of entry for HIV because it often leads to tearing or abrading of the rectal lining. The amount of virus in semen also varies through the course of HIV disease, reaching peaks shortly after initial infection and when full-blown AIDS develops. Circumcised men may have a lower risk of infection because they are less likely to have genital ulcers. Moreover, HIV cannot accumulate under the folds of the foreskin in men who have been circumcised. Cells in the foreskin may be particularly vulnerable to HIV infection as well (Touchette, 1991). Still, more research is necessary to confirm links between circumcision and HIV infection.

Researchers report that alcohol consumption either before, during, or shortly after exposure to HIV can increase the risk of infection (AIDS Update, 1993; Basgara et al., 1993). Alcohol consumption can also make people more likely to engage in risky sexual practices than if they were sober (Lowry et al., 1994; Mulry et al., 1994; Perry et al., 1994). Researchers also suspect that regular consumption of alcohol may impair the immune system and thus hasten the development of AIDS among people who are infected with HIV (Basgara et al., 1993).

A European study of 563 couples in which one member of a couple was infected with HIV found two factors that increased the risk of transmission from the woman to the man: unprotected sexual contact during menses and an advanced stage of HIV infection in the woman (deVincenzi et al., 1992). Among couples in which both of these risk factors were present, 57% of the men became infected, as opposed to 1% of couples who possessed neither of these risk factors. Three factors increased the likelihood that men infected with HIV would transmit the virus to women: anal intercourse, an advanced stage of HIV infection in the man, and female partners who were older than age 45. Among couples with at least two of these risk factors, 54% of the women became infected, as compared with 10% of the women in couples in which none were present.

People in an advanced stage of HIV infection may be more likely to transmit it because there are more viral particles in their genital secretions. Older women may be at increased risk of contracting HIV because the genital mucosa becomes more fragile as the woman ages. Thus the vaginal wall is more likely to become abraded. Sex during menses may increase the likelihood of infection because of a greater concentration of viral particles in the vagina during menstruation. Whatever the particular risk factors, no cases of transmission were reported among partners who regularly used condoms.

How HIV Is *Not* Transmitted

There is much misinformation about the transmission of HIV. Let us consider some of the ways in which HIV is *not* transmitted:

1. *HIV is not transmitted from donating blood.* AIDS cannot be contracted by donating blood because needles are discarded after a single use. Unfortunately, many people have avoided donating blood because of unfounded fears of HIV transmission.

Truth OR Fiction?
REVISITED

It is true that you cannot in fact be infected with HIV by donating blood. The reason is that the needles are used only once. ■

2. *HIV is not transmitted through casual, everyday contact.* There is no evidence of transmission of HIV through hugging someone, shaking hands, bumping into strangers on

buses and trains; handling money, doorknobs, or other objects that have been touched by infected people; sharing drinking fountains, public telephones, public toilets, or swimming pools; or by trying on clothing that has been worn by an infected person (Hatcher et al., 1990). Nor is HIV known to be transmitted by contact with urine, feces, sputum, sweat, tears, or nasal secretions, unless blood is clearly visible in these fluids (Hatcher et al., 1990). (Still, should you need to clean urine, feces, nasal secretions, and especially blood, it would be wise to use rubber gloves and wash your hands thoroughly immediately afterwards.)

3. *HIV is not transmitted by insect bites.* HIV is not transmitted by mosquito bites or from bites by other insects such as bedbugs, lice, or flies (CDC, 1992). Nor can you get HIV from contact with animals.

4. *HIV is not transmitted by airborne germs or contact with contaminated food.* People do not contract HIV from contact with airborne germs, as by sneezing or coughing, or by contact with contaminated food or eating food prepared by a person infected with HIV (CDC, 1992). (However, other disease-causing organisms, such as the virus that causes hepatitis A, may be transmitted by contact with contaminated food.)

5. *HIV is not transmitted through sharing work or home environments.* HIV has not been shown to be transmitted from infected people to family members or others they live with through any form of casual contact, such as hugging or touching, or through sharing bathrooms, food, or eating utensils, so long as there is no exchange of blood or genital secretions (CDC, 1992; Hatcher et al., 1990). There are some isolated reports of nonsexual transmission of HIV between children living together in the same household. Investigators suspect that the route of transmission in these cases involved blood contact, such as the sharing of razor blades in one of the two reported cases and the sharing of a toothbrush in the other (the infected child in this case had bleeding gums) ("AIDS without needles or sex," 1993). No cases of HIV transmission have been documented based on nonsexual contact in schools or in the workplace.

HIV is not transmitted by casual contact, yet many people keep a distance from people with HIV or AIDS. They avoid parties at which people with AIDS are present. They avoid courses taught by a professor with AIDS. They also establish a greater physical distance between themselves and someone believed to have AIDS in a research laboratory (Mooney et al., 1992). Even some physicians and other health care providers are unwilling to have contact with people with HIV and AIDS (Trinkaus & Chow, 1990) or to work on an AIDS unit (Dworkin et al., 1991). A Canadian study showed that people with more accurate knowledge of AIDS and those who are more tolerant of gay people are generally more willing to accept a worker who has AIDS (Summers, 1991).

Transmission via Medical or Dental Treatment

It is theoretically possible for blood to be transferred from health care providers to patients. Yet there is only one known case in which a health care worker transmitted HIV to a patient or patients during treatment (Taylor, 1993b). The case involved an HIV-infected dentist in Florida who apparently infected six of his patients during dental treatment. One was a young women, Kimberly Bergalis, whose poignant testimony before Congress before her death in 1991 came to symbolize the debate as to whether or not health care providers should be tested for HIV.

Infection can work in the opposite direction as well. For example, health care providers risk infection from accidental needle sticks from syringes used on infected patients. The CDC (1995) reports that 42 people nationwide had become infected with HIV by the end of 1994 on the basis of on-the-job accidents. Another 91 were possibly infected on the job. Most of these cases involved lab technicians and nurses who accidentally pricked themselves with a needle or were cut by a scalpel that was used previously on an HIV-infected people. Clearly, health care providers need to exercise caution to avoid contact with infected blood.

Kimberly Bergalis. Bergalis's testimony before Congress prompted public debate over the testing of health-care providers for HIV infection.

Women and AIDS

Lily was not supposed to get AIDS. She was heiress to a cosmetics fortune. She had received her bachelor's degree from Wellesley and had been enrolled in a graduate program in art history when she came down with intractable flu-like symptoms and was eventually diagnosed as having AIDS.

"No one believed it," she said. "I was never a gay male in San Francisco. I never shot up crack in the alleys of The Bronx. My boyfriends didn't shoot up either. There was just Matthew . . ." Now Lily was 24. At 17, in her senior year in high school, she had had a brief affair with Matthew. Later she learned that Matthew was bisexual. Five years ago, Matthew died from AIDS.

"I haven't exactly been a whore," Lily said ironically. "You can count my boyfriends on the fingers of one hand. None of them caught it from me; I guess I was just lucky." Her face twisted in anger. "You may think this is awful," she said, "but there are times when I wish Jerry and Russ had gotten it from me. Why should they get off?"

Lily's family was fully supportive, emotionally and, of course, financially. Lily had been to fine clinics. Physicians from Europe had been brought in. She was on a regimen of three medicines: two antiviral drugs, which singly and in combination had shown some ability to slow the progress of AIDS, and an antibiotic intended to prevent bacterial infections from taking hold. She took some vitamins—but not megavitamin therapy. She exercised almost daily when she felt up to it, and she was doing reasonably well. In fact, there were times when she thought she might get over her illness.

"Sometimes I find myself thinking about children or grandchildren. Or sometimes I find myself looking at all these old pictures [of grandparents and other relatives] and thinking that I'll have silver in my hair, too. Sometimes I really think this is the day the doctors will call me about the new wonder drug that's been discovered in France or Germany."

"I want to tell you about Russ," she said once. "After we found out about me, he went for testing, and he was clear [of antibodies indicative of infection by the AIDS virus]. He stayed with me, you know. When I wanted to do it, we used condoms. A couple of months later, he went for a second test and he was still clear. Then maybe he had second thoughts, because he became impotent—with me. We'd try, but he couldn't do anything. Still he stayed with me, but I felt us drifting apart. After a while, he was just doing the right thing by staying with me, and I'll be damned if anyone is going to be with me because he's doing the right thing."

Lily looked [the interviewer] directly in the eye. "What sane man wants to play Russian roulette with AIDS for the sake of looking like a caring person? And I'll tell you why I eventually sent him away," she added, tears welling. "The one thing I've learned is that you die alone. I don't even feel that close to my parents anymore. Everyone loves you and wishes they could trade places with you, but they can't. You're suddenly older than everyone around you and you're going to go alone. I can't tell you how many times I thought about killing myself, just so that I could be the one who determines exactly where and when I die—how I would be dressed and how I would feel on the final day."

(Adapted from Rathus & Nevid, 1995, pp. 410–411)

Figure 17.5. AIDS Cases by Gender. The figure reflects separate totals for men and women through December 1994. Women now account for about one in seven AIDS cases in the United States. *Source:* Table 9, Centers for Disease Control and Prevention (1995). *HIV/AIDS Surveillance Report,* Year-end Edition (U.S. HIV and AIDS cases reported through December 1994), Vol. 6, No. 2.

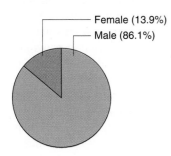

Female (13.9%)
Male (86.1%)

Not so long ago, there were a number of erroneous assumptions about HIV and AIDS—assumptions that have had a disproportionately negative impact on women. They included the notions that women were at low risk of HIV infection and that it was difficult to be infected via male–female sexual intercourse. It was also assumed that HIV infection and AIDS would follow the same course in men and women—a belief that may have delayed diagnosis and intervention with women.

Are Women at Risk of AIDS?   Although AIDS was once considered a syndrome that afflicted only gay men, AIDS cases are rising faster among women than among men. In the mid-1990s, the number of women with AIDS in the United States was doubling every year (Nyamathi et al., 1995). Women now account for 14% of AIDS cases in the United States (see Figure 17.5). The numbers of reported AIDS cases among women may represent the tip of iceberg, because symptoms may not develop for years after infection with HIV. A leading researcher on AIDS, Alexandra Levine of the University of Southern California Medical Center, notes that

> we have not begun to see what's going to happen with women. We are now with women at the same situation we were for gay men in 1983 or 1984. It can happen to you or to me or to any of us. This is a sexually transmitted disease. Period. You must think of yourself as potentially at risk. It's the only way we're going to get on top of this epidemic.
>
> (Cited in Parsons, 1991, A14)

The great majority of cases in women—85%—occur among women of childbearing age. Approximately one in four women with AIDS is 20 to 29 years of age. Therefore, many of them were infected as teenagers (St. Lawrence et al., 1995). The number of deaths from AIDS is also rising rapidly among women. By 1993, AIDS had become the fourth leading killer of women in the 25-to-44 age range.

Women presently account for about one in three cases of AIDS worldwide. If present trends continue, most new cases of HIV worldwide by the year 2000 will be among women (Altman, 1992b). In some countries, women are already surpassing men in the proportions of new cases. In Uganda, for example, the rate of HIV infection among young women is six times greater than it is among young men (Lorch, 1993b).

Truth OR Fiction?
R E V I S I T E D

It is not true that only a small proportion of AIDS patients are women. Women now account for nearly one third of AIDS cases worldwide, and the proportion of women among AIDS cases in the United States, now at 14%, is on the rise. ■

Among women in our society, the risks of HIV infection and deaths from AIDS fall most heavily on poor women, mostly African American or Hispanic American, who live in urban areas (Amaro, 1995). Overall, African American and Hispanic American women account for nearly three of four cases of women with AIDS in the United States, although they make up only 21% of the female population (Amaro, 1995; Nyamathi et al., 1995). Still, as the case of Lily indicates, HIV infection and AIDS cut across all racial, social, and economic boundaries.

Though AIDS prevention programs have focused on increasing condom use among sexually active people, many women cannot compel their partners to use condoms (Amaro, 1995; Weinstock et al., 1993). Moreover, the one barrier method available to women, the female condom, does not seem to be catching on. Sexual counseling programs stress that men need to take more responsibility for wearing condoms and that both partners should learn how to talk about HIV prevention.

Is It Difficult To Be Infected with HIV via Male–Female Sexual Intercourse?   It was once thought unlikely that HIV could be transmitted through male–female sexual intercourse. We now know that male–female sexual intercourse accounts for the majority, about 75%, of cases of HIV transmission worldwide. Moreover, the odds of male-to-female transmission of HIV are about 12 times greater than those of female-to-male transmission (Padian et al., 1991).

In the early years of the epidemic, most women in the United States with AIDS had contracted the disease by sharing contaminated needles when injecting drugs. But male–female sexual activity accounted for about half of the new cases of AIDS reported in American women in 1994 (CDC, 1995). Most women who contract HIV live in large metropolitan areas (73%), often in impoverished inner cities where there is widespread drug use. Like syphilis, HIV infection appears higher among women who use cocaine, perhaps because they often engage in high-risk sexual behaviors, such as prostitution or unprotected intercourse with people who inject drugs (Edlin et al., 1994; Minkoff et al., 1990; Nyamathi et al., 1995).

Do HIV Infection and AIDS Follow the Same Course in Men and Women?   Many questions remain about how HIV infection and AIDS affect women. Much of our knowledge about the course of the illness derives from studies of HIV infection and AIDS in gay men. It is not known whether they follow the same course in women.

Diagnosis and intervention may be delayed in women because of symptoms that go unrecognized or are misdiagnosed (Kent, 1991; Stephens, 1991). Moreover, most of the drug trials have been conducted on men, not on women or children, so questions remain about the effectiveness of AIDS drugs on women and children.

Women die faster from AIDS than men do (Cohen, 1990). Researchers suspect that delayed intervention and treatment of women with AIDS may play a role in this gender difference (Kent, 1991). The fact that AIDS afflicts poor women disproportionately may also in part explain delays in receiving appropriate medical care, since disadvantaged women generally have poorer access to medical care (Stephens, 1991).

~ *Reflections* ~

- What precautions do your dentist and dental hygienist take to avoid being infected with HIV while they work with patients?
- Why is transmission of HIV from mother to child most likely to occur during the birth process? What precautions do health care professionals take to try to prevent such transmission?
- What did you learn about transmission of HIV? Which methods of transmission had you known the least about? Had you thought that HIV could be transmitted through casual contact (as in hugging) or kissing? What does the research show?

Diagnosis of HIV Infection and AIDS

Seropositive

Having a pathogen or antibodies to that pathogen in the bloodstream.

Seronegative

Lacking a pathogen or antibodies to that pathogen in the bloodstream.

Truth **OR** *Fiction?*

R E V I S I T E D

The most widely used test for HIV infection is the enzyme-linked immunosorbent assay (ELISA, for short). ELISA does not directly detect HIV in the circulatory system. Instead, it reveals HIV antibodies. People may show an antibody response to HIV long before they develop symptoms of infection. A positive (**seropositive**) test result means that antibodies were found and usually[4] indicates that the person has HIV in the bloodstream. A negative (**seronegative**) outcome means that antibodies to HIV were not detected (Reinisch, 1990).

Actually, HIV infection is generally diagnosed by examination of HIV *antibodies* in the bloodstream. ■

A saliva test named OraSure was approved by the U.S. Food and Drug Administration (FDA) in 1994. The test is not quite as accurate as a blood test, but it is less expensive and might encourage people who avoid blood tests to be tested. HIV itself is not found in measurable quantities in saliva—which is the reason that kissing is not considered an avenue of transmission of HIV. Saliva is absorbed by a cotton pad on a stick that is placed between the lower gum and the cheek. The saliva in the cotton, like blood, undergoes ELISA in a laboratory.

When people receive positive results on the enzyme-linked immunosorbent assay, the Western blot test can be performed to confirm the findings. The Western blot test detects a particular pattern of protein bands that are linked to the virus. It may take many months for people who have been exposed to HIV to develop antibodies. For this reason, repeated tests over a six-month or even longer period of time from the date of possible exposure may be in order. A seropositive test result means that HIV antibodies have been found, but does not indicate when, or even if, an individual will develop a full-blown case of AIDS.

---

[4]But not always! Fetuses, for example, may receive antibodies from infected mothers, but not the virus itself. Some fetuses, however, do become infected with the virus.

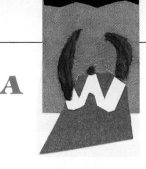

A WORLD OF DIVERSITY

WOMEN WITH AIDS: AGONIZING CHOICES ABOUT MOTHERHOOD

Women infected with HIV face some hard choices about motherhood (Lee, 1995). Studies show that 15% to 30% of the infants born to infected mothers are infected themselves. (However, nearly all babies of infected mothers *test* positive for HIV antibodies because the antibodies are transmitted to them in the uterus, even when the virus itself is not.) Many questions remain unanswered as to why some infants of infected mothers contract the infection whereas most do not.

In addition to concerns over the risks of infection to their babies, infected women confront haunting questions about their own mortality and ability to care for their children: "What will happen to my child if I should fall ill or die? Will I be able to cope with a baby that becomes sick or dies?" Women also have concerns about whether the stress of pregnancy will further strain their physical health, making them more vulnerable to serious opportunistic diseases.

Some infected women who become pregnant opt for abortion, as in the case of Dina M.:

> Dina M. had always envisioned a family of her own. But shortly after learning that she was going to have a baby, the 19-year-old nursing student from Hackensack, N.J., was also told that she had the AIDS virus.

Ten days ago, she had an abortion. The teenager was 4½ months pregnant and had spent most of that time struggling to make a decision.

Torn and scared, she waited until her health began faltering "to go ahead and do it."*

Others decide to continue their pregnancies to term (Lee, 1995). Consider the case of Diane G.:

> Diane G., a 32-year-old Bensonhurst [Brooklyn] resident, chose to continue her pregnancy despite her infection, telling herself that God must have wanted her to keep the baby since she conceived it while practicing birth control.
>
> She said she was infected by her husband of seven years, an intravenous drug user, and that she does not know whether she already had the virus when she had her first two sons, now 5 and 4 and healthy.
>
> After she tested HIV-positive two months into her third pregnancy, she spent weeks calling prenatal clinics, university research centers, and AIDS hot lines, seeking the latest information on the risks to herself and the fetus.
>
> She decided she was healthy enough and found the chances of having a healthy baby acceptable.
>
> The boy, now 2½, has repeatedly tested negative for the virus.*

Some infected women have confronted the agonizing choice of motherhood and decided they have no option but to avoid conception. Consider the case of Heather D., a 30-year-old interior designer who contracted HIV from her husband, who has since died of AIDS:

> "I can't imagine taking that chance, as much as I want a child," she said. "Being sick is physically painful . . . and I wouldn't want to give that to anyone. . . . "
>
> "You know what this is? It's just another loss," she said, of her decision not to conceive. . . . "For me to see a happy couple with a child still brings tears to my eyes."*

Physicians, religious leaders, and lay people are debating the ethics of childbearing by women with HIV. Some note that abortion is not routinely recommended for women who stand a similar risk of transmitting genetic disorders to their offspring. Why, therefore, should women with HIV be singled out? Others question the ethical responsibility of bringing children into the world whose mothers are likely to die during their early childhood. The debate is bound to intensify as the number of women with HIV increases.

*Navarro (1991). Copyright © 1991 by The New York Times Company. Reprinted by permission.

Issues Concerning Testing for HIV Infection

It may come as a surprise that although testing for HIV infection is widely available, those at high risk, or those who suspect that they might "test positive," do not necessarily seek information that will confirm or deny their concerns. Why would someone consciously avoid information that might ultimately assist in prolonging life? Clearly, AIDS testing is not a cut-and-dried matter, as suggested by the following comments:

> PHIL, 20: The only change I've made as a result of the AIDS threat is to use condoms as protection. But when I find a girlfriend who is really special, I plan to be tested for AIDS. Hopefully this would alleviate any fears she might have, and it would show her how much I really care.

MELANIE, 18: How to bring up AIDS with someone you'd like to sleep with confuses me. I mean, what do you say? "Gee, honey, I love you and want to have sex with you, but can you please take an AIDS test today and then lock yourself up for six months so I'm sure you won't sleep with anyone else and then take the test again? Then maybe I'll sleep with you."

DON, 25: I "came out" just as AIDS hit the media in metro-Boston as the Gay Plague. During the first year or so I did very little to practice safe sex. Now, I will not do anything that is against the safe-sex guidelines. I often fear the days I did not follow these guidelines. I often think of being tested, although I am scared. I would not be able to have sexual relations or even date should I test positive, because I am too moral to pretend that nothing is wrong, and too uncomfortable coming forward with this information to my partners. Sometimes I think it is best not to know and to always behave responsibly; other times I think I should know so that I can make plans for my life and if I test negative, seek a long-term relationship "armed" with this information.

(Copyright © 1991 by McIntyre, Formichella, Osterhout, and Gresh by arrangement with AVON Books, pp. 145–147)

Concerns and motivations regarding HIV testing can be complex and contradictory. Although all too many of us engage in sexual practices without regard for potential risk, even in the age of AIDS, some people have become more cautious about their sexual intimacies. This vigilance is evident in a broad spectrum of response. People may feel that they need to know more about each other before they proceed with a sexual relationship. Some, however, will not even consider such a relationship in the absence of testing that finds the prospective partner to be clear of HIV infection. Others might even take the initiative to have themselves tested as a way of assuring a partner that they themselves are safe, or, conversely, to alert their partners that they are indeed infected with HIV. As logical as these measures may seem when weighed against the potential risks, concerned partners may foresee emotional ramifications to such a direct approach. How can one broach such a subject at all? How can a personal relationship get off the ground with concerns and suspicions at its very start? How do you suggest to someone with whom you would like a sexual relationship that he or she be tested for HIV?

And what about obligation? Many believe that people at risk of HIV infection who have not taken steps to determine their HIV status before entering sexual relationships have acted immorally, irresponsibly, and even criminally. A prospective partner has the right, it is argued, to have such information. Its disclosure can lead to appropriate precautions including safer sex practices or the avoidance of needle sharing.

Once again, however, the issues become muddied. Some who are opposed to widespread testing argue that testing is unnecessary and alarmist for people who do not belong to a group that has been hard hit by the epidemic. Such opponents further point out that a person who has been found to be HIV-positive is, in effect, "branded," and can soon fall victim to harsh discrimination regarding employment, as represented in the film *Philadelphia,* as well as in housing or in obtaining medical and life insurance. Moreover, they argue that safer sex guidelines should be practiced as a matter of course in this age of AIDS, regardless of HIV status. Finally, they voice the concern of many that knowledge that one carries HIV antibodies, or has AIDS, can be emotionally devastating and that people may be ill prepared to deal with the enormous stress experienced in the wake of this realization. On the other hand, what they don't know may hurt them, because early detection and intervention may prolong health in infected people.

Disclosure of the Identities of HIV-Infected Health Care Providers

In the wake of the Kimberly Bergalis case, pressure mounted to require mandatory testing of all health care workers. Although Bergalis's death was tragic, health officials believe that the Florida case was an anomaly. No other cases of health care providers' transmitting the virus to their patients through medical or dental treatment have been uncovered among more than 20,000 patients who were treated by infected health care providers (CDC, 1993e; Rogers et al., 1993; von Reyn et al., 1993).

Controversy swirls around the issue of whether health care workers infected with HIV should be prohibited from performing certain procedures, such as surgery. Those favoring restrictions fear that patients might become infected if droplets of blood from tiny cuts in the infected health care worker's skin should enter the patient's bloodstream. Opponents argue that procedures normally followed by health care workers to prevent the spread of infection, such as the wearing of gloves and masks, provide sufficient protection for patients. The issue continues to be debated at the state and national levels.

Many health officials argue that regulations requiring massive testings of health care workers are unnecessary and may unfairly affect the careers of workers infected with the virus, as well as waste millions of dollars that might otherwise be spent on combating or preventing AIDS. Still, a *Newsweek* poll found that more than 90% of people in the United States believe that health care workers who are infected by HIV should be required to inform their patients of the infection (Adler et al., 1991).

Should People Test Themselves for HIV Infection at Home?   As of this writing, the FDA is deciding whether to license diagnostic test kits for sale over the counter (Bayer et al., 1995). Such licensing would make it possible for people to test themselves for HIV infection in the privacy of their own homes.

The main appeal of home testing is that people who have not yet been tested for HIV infection might decide to see whether they have been infected. About 29% of the respondents to the National Health Interview Survey said they would use home testing if it were available (Phillips et al., 1995). As it now stands, many people do not learn that they have been infected until they develop AIDS or shortly before. As a result, they lose out on treatment that might delay the onset of AIDS. Moreover, women with HIV infections who are treated during pregnancy and labor are less likely to transmit the infection to their children (Lee, 1995).

The main impediment to home testing has been the belief that people who are infected with HIV need counseling prior to and after testing. People who test positive for HIV infection are often stunned. They occasionally attempt suicide. Here again, none of the options concerning HIV infection and AIDS presents a rosy picture.

~ *Reflections* ~

▪ Would you be comfortable taking a test to learn whether you were infected with HIV? Why, or why not?

▪ Do you believe that some groups of people, such as health care providers, should have to be tested for HIV infection? Why, or why not?

▪ Agree or disagree with the following statement, and support your answer: Everybody should be tested for HIV infection, and the names of those who are infected should be disclosed to the public.

Treatment of HIV Infection and AIDS

There is neither a cure for HIV infection or AIDS, nor a safe, effective vaccine. The prospects for a cure at this time are grim. On the other hand, a number of experimental AIDS vaccines are being tested on people and animals. Several vaccines have proved somewhat effective in animal trials (e.g., Hu, 1992). Yet the development of an ideal vaccine against AIDS—one that would be safe, inexpensive, and render lifetime protection against all strains of the disease with a single dose—may be decades away.

The mutability of HIV has thus far stymied efforts to find a cure or an effective vaccine. HIV can mutate into forms that are resistant to particular antiviral drugs or vaccines (Ho, 1995). The genes making up HIV mutate a million times more rapidly than human genes, leading scientists on wild goose chases as they try to eradicate a killer that keeps changing its form. A vaccine that might protect against one strain, or a drug that could render a death blow, may hold no value against another. Thus, it may be that no single vaccine will provide a full range of protection against the virus (Cohen, 1993). Moreover, whenever the body's own immune system or a drug may be initially successful in attacking a particular HIV variant, a mutated form capable of resisting the attack arises and takes its place (Ho, 1995). Thus, drugs like zidovudine (AZT), the most widely used HIV/AIDS drug, may delay progression of the disease but may eventually lose effectiveness. AZT appears to have a limited benefit for a limited time (Bartlett, 1993). The symptom complex that defines AIDS eventually develops as more resistant forms of the virus begin to flourish (Hirsch & D'Aquila, 1993).

A sense of gloom was cast over the fight against AIDS when results were reported of a large-scale European study, called the Concorde study, involving the use of AZT in the early asymptomatic stage of HIV infection. Like the airplane of the same name, it represented a cooperative Anglo-French effort. The study compared AZT with a placebo over three years in 1,749 people infected with HIV but symptom-free (Concorde Coordinating Committee, 1994). AZT did not affect either the rates of progression to AIDS or the three-year survival rate. However, other studies suggest that AZT can delay the progression of infection from the asymptomatic to the symptomatic state (Cooper et al., 1993) and increase the blood count of CD4 cells (Kinloch-de Loes et al., 1995). As of this writing, *The New England Journal of Medicine* recommends hitting HIV infection "early and hard" with AZT (Ho, 1995).

AZT has side effects, such as suppression of bone marrow function, which leads to anemia. It also lowers the white blood cell count, further reducing the body's ability to combat infections. Other side effects that are connected with administration of AZT to HIV-infected people who have not developed AIDS include nausea, vomiting, diarrhea, skin rash, and lowering of the number of leukocytes in the bloodstream (Hamilton et al., 1992). Lower-dose formulas of the drug reduce the side effects, however (Fischl et al., 1990).

A new generation of drugs that block the replication of HIV, called *protease inhibitors,* has shown some promise in experimental work but needs to be evaluated further in clinical trials. A naturally occurring protease inhibitor apparently prevents HIV from infecting white blood cells in the saliva (Altman, 1995b). This is why mouth-to-mouth kissing is not considered an avenue for transmission of HIV. One promising approach involves a combination of drugs such as AZT and the protease inhibitor 3TC (*lamivudine*). Preliminary studies suggest that variants of HIV that resist AZT succumb to 3TC, and vice versa (Altman, 1995a).

Research is also underway on the effectiveness of combining AZT with other antiviral drugs, such as didanosine (ddI) and zalcitabine (ddC). In one study, 1,400 people infected with HIV were given the drugs alone or in combination and then were tracked for

Caring for People with AIDS. People with AIDS need love and support, but are often rejected by others, even family members, who fear contracting the disease by touching or hugging them. However, HIV is not transmitted by hugging or touching an infected person, or by being in the same room.

147 weeks. The combination of AZT and ddI led to a 40% lower death rate (6% versus 10%) than AZT alone ("AIDS study," 1995).

Promising results are reported in treating some of the opportunistic infections, such as PCP (Bozzette et al., 1995) and fungal infections (Powderly et al., 1995), that take hold in people with weakened immune systems (Clumeck, 1995). Symptom-free carriers of HIV may also prolong health by taking good care of themselves, getting enough sleep, avoiding unnecessary stress, and eating a balanced diet (Antoni et al., 1990, 1991).

With few if any victories to report in the war against AIDS, one genuine breakthrough occurred when researchers found that AZT administered to HIV-infected pregnant women reduced the rate of HIV infection in their newborns by two thirds (Connor et al., 1994). Scientists had suspected that AZT might help prevent AIDS in children of infected mothers by reducing the amount of the virus in the mother's bloodstream. The research focused on 477 pregnant women, all of whom were infected with HIV but were still healthy, in the United States and France. Half took AZT during pregnancy and through labor and delivery. The other half were given a placebo (a chemically inert pill). After birth, the babies were continued on the treatment the mothers had received for a six-week period. Only 8% of the babies born to the AZT-treated women became infected with HIV, as compared to 25% of the babies born to women in the placebo group. Mild anemia was the only apparent side effect in the children. These striking results offer the best hope yet that many if not most cases of AIDS in children can be prevented by the use of already available drugs.

A complex approach may be needed to combat HIV. It may be necessary to tailor treatment to the strain of the virus, the patient's genetic type, and the ways in which the particular immune system responds to the infection (Garrett, 1993b). Such an approach may yield better results than one in which virtually all patients are treated with the same drug or combination of drugs. For now, however, prevention remains the only known way of stemming the epidemic.

Psychological Adjustment of Persons with HIV Infections and AIDS

The difficulty of living with HIV and AIDS, their symptoms and suffering, is often compounded by psychological problems. Feelings of uncertainty and thoughts of death are common reactions to being told that one is infected with HIV (McCann, 1992). Feelings of hopelessness and anger, guilt about life choices or reckless acts that led to the disease, and even suicidal thoughts and feelings like those experienced by Lily (page 515) are not uncommon. The stress experienced by people with HIV can be overwhelming and may affect the course of the disease by further suppressing the immune system (Goodkin et al., 1992). Not surprisingly, depression in gay men with HIV is higher among those experiencing a greater number of HIV-related symptoms and lower among those expressing greater satisfaction with the social support they received from others (Hays et al., 1992).

Depression and feelings of futility, anger, and frustration stem from the perception of infected persons that they can do little or nothing to help their situation, and that those who might make a difference—the medical profession or the political powers that hold the purse strings of medical research funding—have done and intend to do little or nothing. A cure for AIDS has not been found. A vaccine does not exist. And to complicate the general frustration, many persons with AIDS experience discrimination, social rejection, or open hostility. Though many have reached out to persons with AIDS, others have made it difficult or impossible for them to proceed with a normal life. Adults and children can be ostracized or undergo more subtle social rejection—lack of social invitations, the refusal of other parents to set up play dates, and so on.

Asymptomatic carriers of HIV frequently develop serious adjustment problems. There may be an initial tendency upon learning that one is HIV-positive to deny the harsh reality of the disease. This denial can turn to nagging fears that stem from the uncertainty as to whether or when the virus will lead to AIDS. This state of "suspended animation" can

AIDS Support Group. AIDS support groups provide people with AIDS emotional support and practical assistance.

cause feelings of anxiety, depression and hopelessness, fear of death, guilt, and alienation (Catania et al., 1992b). The stress that this knowledge can impose, or the stress of having lost a lover or close personal friend to the disease, can further compromise the immune system and hasten the progress of the disease.

Prevention

What can we do to curb the spread of AIDS? Given that there is no vaccine or cure, prevention is our best hope. Our discussion of prevention will focus on sexual transmission, but other efforts have been made to prevent transmission of HIV from mother to child, through injection of drugs, and through blood transfusions. For example, HIV-infected women are advised to avoid breast-feeding. AZT and other measures, such as cesarean section, decrease the probability of transmission through childbirth. The screening of blood supplies and potential donors has reduced the probability of infection through blood transfusions to about 1 in 75,000 (Altman, 1992a). We have been less successful in reducing the risk of infection through unsafe sexual contact.

Most prevention efforts focus on education. Sexually active people have been advised to alter their sexual behavior either by practicing abstinence, by limiting their sexual experiences to a lifelong monogamous relationship, or by practicing "safe sex"—which, as we shall see, could be more accurately dubbed "safer sex."

Prevention programs are apparently raising public awareness of AIDS. A 1993 *New York Times*/CBS News national poll showed that knowledge about AIDS is increasing. Seventy-nine percent of respondents correctly recognized that one cannot be infected with HIV by sharing a drinking glass with a person with AIDS, up from 34% in 1985. Eighty-nine percent recognized that you cannot be infected by a toilet seat, up from 49% in 1985. Nearly everyone knew that HIV can be transmitted by male–female sex (96%) and blood transfusions (98%). More people today are also personally acquainted with a person with AIDS. One third of those polled know someone who has died of AIDS or has either HIV infection or AIDS.

Gaps in knowledge about preventing AIDS remain, however. Another survey found that only one in five Americans knew that latex condoms are more effective in preventing the transmission of HIV than natural membrane condoms ("Americans generally well-informed," 1993).

Is Knowing the Same as Doing?

Nor does knowledge about HIV transmission necessarily translate into behavioral change, such as increased use of latex condoms (which can block the transmission of HIV) and other safer sex practices. In fact, knowledge about transmission of HIV and other STDs is not clearly related to condom use (Geringer et al., 1993; Klepinger et al., 1993; Rotheram-Borus & Koopman, 1991a, 1991b). Despite widespread efforts to educate the public about the dangers of unprotected sex, negative attitudes toward using condoms persist, especially among males (Fisher et al., 1995). Consider the litany of complaints we come across: "They reduce sexual pleasure. . . . They're a nuisance to put on. . . . They cost too much. . . . They interrupt sex," and so on.

Yes, concerns about AIDS have led to some changes. About half of the unmarried respondents of ages 18 to 44 to a national telephone poll reported that they had changed their sexual behavior because of fear of AIDS (Kagay, 1991). The most frequently cited changes were increased use of condoms and reductions in the numbers of sex partners. Rising sales of condoms in recent years are consistent with survey evidence. However, condom use in the United States remains relatively low. By the late 1980s, only about one in five sexually active American women used condoms with her partner (Lewin, 1992b). Consider the results of the National AIDS Behavioral Survey, a large probability sample of the U.S. population based on interviews with 10,630 people. Fewer than one in five people (17%) with multiple sex partners, and only 12.6% of those with high-risk sex partners, reported using condoms during *every* sexual encounter (Catania et al., 1992a; Coates, 1993).

The Battelle survey of more than 3,000 sexually active men found a high incidence of unsafe sexual practices (Billy et al., 1993; Tanfer et al., 1993). About 1 in 4 (23%) reported having vaginal intercourse with 20 or more partners in their lifetimes. About 1 in 5 of the single men had 4 or more partners during the preceding 18-month period. Of these men, only half reported using condoms. Overall, only about 1 in 4 sexually active men had used a condom during the four-week period preceding the survey. African American men were more likely than White men to report using condoms (38% vs. 25%). Men younger than age 30 were more likely to do so than older men (36% vs. 19%).

AIDS prevention programs have not succeeded in getting their message across to large numbers of at-risk heterosexuals about the dangers of unprotected sex and sex with multiple partners. Yet concerns and fears of HIV infection are widespread. Four in ten of the men in the Battelle survey believe that there is a chance that they may be infected with HIV. Nearly one in four worries often about AIDS (Klepinger et al., 1993). Many—more than 40%—report having had an HIV blood test. About half of this group had the test specifically to find out if they were infected.

Changes in the Gay Community

Many gay males have adopted safer sexual practices, such as limiting their numbers of sex partners, using latex condoms and spermicides, and decreasing the incidence of anal intercourse (Catania et al., 1991; CDC, 1990e). Researchers find that condoms are used by gay men for anal sex more than 75% of the time (USDHHS, 1992a). These changes have reduced the incidence of new HIV infections (Coates, 1993). However, many gay and bisexual males, both HIV+ and HIV−, continue to engage in unsafe sexual practices (McKirnan et al., 1995; Meyer-Bahlburg et al., 1993). In one sample of 219 gay men, more than 40% reported having had unprotected sex with 3 or more men during the preceding year (Gold & Skinner, 1992). Researchers in Seattle find that although unprotected anal intercourse has decreased in their samples of gay and bisexual men, unprotected oral sex has increased (Seattle-King County Department of Public Health, 1991). Moreover, a sizable number of gay and bisexual men who had adopted safer sexual practices have returned to risky behavior (Schnell & O'Reilly, 1991). A Chicago study found that 31% of bisexual men had engaged in unprotected anal intercourse with another man during the past six months (McKirnan et al., 1995).

High-risk sexual practices are reported to be especially common among gay youth (Rotheram-Borus & Koopman, 1991a). A university investigator found only a few men among 61 gay male students who reported making major changes (such as reducing the number of partners and being more selective when choosing partners) in their sexual behavior because of concerns about HIV (D'Augelli, 1992b). Danish researchers find that a large percentage (43.5%) of the 16- to 19-year-old gay males in their sample had engaged in unsafe sex during the past 12 months (Schmidt et al., 1992).

Researchers in the United States find that frequenting gay bars is associated with greater sexual risk-taking among gay men (Ruefli et al., 1992). Alcohol and drug use preceding or during sex is also associated with riskier behavior in gay males (McCusker et al., 1992), as it is among heterosexuals. Risky sexual behavior among gay males may be more prevalent in the cities outside the epicenter of the epidemic (San Francisco, New York City, Los Angeles) where the gay community has been better organized in marshaling its efforts to combat HIV/AIDS (Ruefli et al., 1992). This evidence underscores the need for increasing AIDS prevention efforts in the gay male population, especially among younger gay males. Sexual practices of bisexual men are also of special concern because they may be a conduit for male–female sexual transmission of HIV (Boulton et al., 1992).

Truth OR Fiction?
REVISITED

It is not true that awareness of the risks of HIV infection and AIDS always leads people to engage in "safer sex." Education about HIV infection and AIDS is an indispensable step, however. ■

Sexual contact between people who inject drugs and their sex partners remains the greatest source of male–female transmission of HIV in North America and Europe. AIDS prevention programs have led to decreases in needle sharing and, on occasion, cessation of injection of drugs. They have had a lesser impact on changing risky sexual behavior among people who inject drugs. Two thirds of a sample of 221 White Americans and 236 heterosexual African Americans who inject drugs in California reported that they never use condoms (Lewis & Watters, 1991). Still, some progress toward safer sex has been reported. Researchers in New York City found a sharp increase from 14% in 1984 to 60% in 1990 of people who inject drugs who report using condoms "at least some of the time" (Kouzi et al., 1992).

A major population group in our society targeted for AIDS prevention efforts is young people. Let us consider the effects that the AIDS epidemic has had on the sexual behavior of young people today.

Coming of Age in the Age of AIDS

Today, for the first time, a generation of young people is becoming sexually active with the threat of a lethal disease hanging over every sexual encounter. How has the threat of AIDS affected the sex lives of young people today? Note these comments:

> ERICA, 18: I am terrified of AIDS. When my boyfriend cheated on me while drunk, I was scared. I now use condoms with him every time.

> A 23-YEAR-OLD MAN: AIDS is a scary thing that always seems to be nagging away at the back of my mind. I've never been promiscuous, and I've never had casual sex. The frightening thing is that you can't be absolutely sure about your partner. With such a long incubation period, one mistake a long time ago can have fatal results.

> RACHEL, 18: AIDS is a definite problem in college because you just don't know. At home, everyone knew who[m] everyone slept with, but here you don't know who[m] they've slept with and they don't know who[m] you've slept with.

> (Copyright © 1991 by McIntyre, Formichella, Osterhout, and Gresh by arrangement with AVON Books, pp. 137–139)

Though the number of AIDS cases among teenagers has remained low (Lewin, 1991), about one in five people with AIDS is in his or her 20s. Most of them were probably infected in their teens (Lewin, 1991). The impact of HIV and AIDS among young people is disproportionate across ethnic groups. Researchers estimate that African American and Hispanic American adolescents are four to five times more likely to be diagnosed with AIDS than White adolescents (DiClemente, 1991). Homeless youth are at special risk of

HIV infection because of the prevalence of unsafe sexual practices and shared drug use in this population group (Goulart & Madover, 1991).

More than three out of four school districts nationwide require some form of AIDS education for grades 6 to 8 (Holtzman et al., 1992). But only about half of the districts require AIDS education at the high school level. Still, evidence shows that AIDS education is having an impact. A survey of 197 predominantly African American students attending an urban high school in the Cleveland area showed that more than half had changed their behavior because of AIDS. For example, they reduced their number of sex partners or the frequency of sexual activity, or they increased their use of condoms (Zimet et al., 1992). A national survey of teenage boys found that exposure to AIDS education was associated with reductions in recent sexual activity (fewer sex partners and less frequent intercourse) and greater use of condoms (Ku et al., 1992). Instruction in skills needed to resist intercourse had a stronger influence on decreasing sexual activity than did instruction about AIDS. Others report that AIDS education programs in the high schools have increased students' knowledge about AIDS (e.g., Ashworth et al., 1992; *Journal of the American Medical Association,* 1993a; Walter & Vaughan, 1993). They have also modestly reduced high-risk sexual behavior (Walter & Vaughan, 1993).

The evidence is not all consistent, however. Researchers in Massachusetts find that only one third of sexually active teens reported always using condoms (Hingson et al., 1990). Nationwide, researchers find that one in five high school students reported engaging in sexual activity with four or more partners, a pattern that puts them at high risk for contracting HIV ("Teen-agers and AIDS," 1992). Nearly one in three high school seniors (29%) reported having had four or more sex partners. The percentages were higher among boys than girls, 27% versus 12%, and among African American males as compared to White males, 60% versus 21%. Fewer than half of the students who reported this level of sexual activity sought to protect themselves or their partners against HIV and other infectious agents. "It's like playing Russian roulette and not knowing how many bullets are in the chambers" said an AIDS expert from the CDC. Moreover, at least half the teenagers sampled in national surveys report that they do not use condoms reliably (CDC, 1993b).

Evidence also shows that many college students continue to engage in high levels of unsafe sexual behavior (Fisher & Misovich, 1991; Miller et al., 1990). Many sexually active college students fail to use condoms consistently, if at all. Many continue to engage in sexual activity with multiple partners. A student survey in an upstate New York college showed that only one in five reported always using condoms (Oswalt & Matsen, 1993). Students in a high-risk category—those with the highest number of partners—used condoms the least often. A survey at a southern California university found that the average student used a condom in fewer than one in three occasions of vaginal intercourse in the previous three-month period (Baldwin et al., 1992). Condoms were used even less frequently (18.5% of the time) during anal intercourse among the 15% of the students who engaged in anal sexual activity.

In another college survey, 70% of University of Massachusetts students polled reported that they had *not* changed their sexual practices despite the threat of AIDS (Johnson, 1990). Another survey found that only 35% of sexually active students at two southeastern state universities used condoms reliably (Hernandez & Smith, 1990). A survey of some 5,500 Canadian first-year students at 51 colleges found them to be well aware of HIV and the ways in which it is transmitted. Nevertheless, only 1 man in 4 (24.8%) and 1 woman in 6 (15.6%) used condoms regularly (MacDonald et al., 1990). One man in 5 and 1 woman in 11 claimed to have had 10 or more sex partners. In this subgroup, only about 20% of the men and 10% of the women used condoms reliably.

Risky Sex: Why So Prevalent in Young People?　Virtually all young people are aware of the sexual transmission of HIV (Wulfert & Wan, 1993). Why, then, do so many of them continue to engage in risky sexual behavior? It is clear that informing young people about how HIV is transmitted is not sufficient to induce more healthful behaviors (Ting & Carter, 1990).

For one thing, teenagers do not perceive risky behavior to be as dangerous as adults do. This generalization extends to drinking, smoking, failure to use seat belts, and drag racing, as well as sexual behavior (Cohn et al., 1995). Young people also profit from being taught specific skills to protect themselves from engaging in risky behaviors, such as communication skills for discussing safer sex options with their partners, assertiveness skills for ensuring that their needs and interests are respected by their partners, social skills to resist peer pressures, and correct use of condoms (St. Lawrence et al., 1995). Greater efforts are needed to reverse peer norms that discourage condom use. For example, it may be advisable for adolescents themselves to support and teach condom use to their peers (Hodges et al., 1992).

Researchers have identified several factors underlying risky sexual behavior among young people:

1. *Perceived low risk of infection.* One of the major stumbling blocks in promoting safer sex practices is that many young heterosexuals perceive a low risk of contracting HIV (Nadeau et al., 1993; Oswalt & Matsen, 1993). People who perceive themselves at low risk are less likely to alter their behavior.

   Given the current low rate of known infections among heterosexuals who do not inject drugs, many heterosexuals may perceive risky sexual practices to be a reasonable gamble (Pinkerton & Abramson, 1992). Heterosexuals who have never had a friend or relative with HIV or AIDS may dismiss HIV infection and AIDS as problems that affect other types of people. Even gay men may operate under the "I'm not the type" fallacy and underestimate their personal risks. According to Pinkerton & Abramson (1992),

   the frightening picture that emerges is one in which it is only the *other guy* (or gal) who gets AIDS: to the heterosexual who does not inject drugs, it's just gays and "druggies" that get AIDS; to the "average" gay man, it's those gay men who are overly promiscuous; and to the bath house participant, it's those who aren't "careful." (pp. 564–565)

2. *Negative attitudes toward condom use.* Many factors discourage condom use. Some people feel embarrassed to buy them. For others, the risk of being infected with HIV seems to fly out of their minds whenever the opportunity for sex arises. Some claim that a condom dampens romantic ardor in moments of passion by requiring an interruption of the sexual act to apply one. Some people just regard them as too much of a fuss. Many men say that condoms deprive them of sexual pleasure. Unless such obstacles to using condoms are overcome, efforts to stem the tide of HIV infection may be thwarted.

3. *Implicit personality theories.* Heterosexuals who engage in sexual relations with casual partners are more likely to use condoms than those with steady partners (Champman et al., 1990; Moore & Rosenthal, 1991). Unsafe sexual encounters (vaginal or anal intercourse without use of a latex condom) are more likely to occur in the context of an established intimate relationship.

Implicit personality theories
Our assumptions about the personalities of other people, which we use to predict their behavior.

   People tend to construct their own personal theories about other people, called **implicit personality theories,** that they use as a basis for predicting which potential partners are risky and which are not. As one student put it, "When you get to know the person . . . as soon as you begin trusting the person . . . you don't really have to use a condom" (Williams et al., 1992, p. 926). Some (mistakenly) believe that knowing something about the sexual history of their partners frees them of the need to take precautions:

   DONNA, 19: I am very selective with my partners. I know all of their sexual histories. I have never taken any other precautions against AIDS or other STDs.

   GINA, 23: I've discussed AIDS with my partner before deciding to have sex. We tried using a condom the first time and hated it. We felt we knew each other well and trusted each other's judgment about who[m] we had been with in the past.

   (Copyright © 1991 by McIntyre, Formichella, Osterhout, and Gresh by arrangement with AVON Books, pp. 137–139)

A person's implicit personality theory may serve to justify the decision not to use condoms, even though such knowledge of the other person may be based on characteristics that in fact are unrelated to HIV status:

[Students] tend to assume that risky people are those who dress provocatively, whom one met in bars, who were older than most college students, who are from large cities, or who are overly anxious for sex.

[Students will use a condom only] with partners they feel they do not know well and whom they perceive might be risky. A typical response was, "If you just met them, you use a condom. . . . If it's long-term, you aren't going to worry."

(Williams et al., 1992, pp. 926–927)

Knowing your partner is not a sufficient basis to evaluate his or her HIV status. You can't know whether your partners are infected with HIV by looking at them, inspecting their genitals, or meeting their folks. The AIDS virus is out there in the general population. You may have a lesser risk of infection than a drug addict in an inner-city neighborhood or a sexually active gay male. You may be at less risk if you have only one or a few sex partners, don't engage in needle sharing, and don't engage in sexual activity with partners who themselves have engaged in dangerous sexual or injection practices or have had other partners who did. But how can you be certain that your partners are telling the truth about their own past sexual practices, let alone vouch for the sexual practices of their previous sex partners? The answer is that you can't. Simply knowing your partner and being monogamous does not constitute safer sex (Williams et al., 1992).

4. *Myth of personal invulnerability.* Another factor underlying risky sexual behaviors is that some people subscribe to a myth of personal invulnerability and believe that they are somehow immune to AIDS and other diseases. Even students who are generally well informed about STDs may perceive themselves as personally immune. One junior at the University of Miami (Ohio) explained to an interviewer why she did not insist that her partners use a condom: "I have an attitude—it may be wrong—that any guy I would sleep with would not have AIDS" (Johnson, 1990, p. A18). The adventurous spirit that we often associate with youth may confer a dangerous sense of immortality and a greater willingness to take risks (Johnson, 1990). Perceptions of personal invulnerability help to explain why AIDS education may not translate into behavioral change (Rosenthal et al., 1992).

Even people who do not believe themselves to be immune may underestimate their risk of being infected with HIV (van der Velde et al., 1994). This finding holds true for impoverished inner-city residents (Hobfoll et al., 1993) as well as college students (Goldman & Harlow, 1993). People tend to view themselves as luckier than the norm. (After all, don't you believe that you alone hold the winning lottery ticket?) Moreover, since the transmission of HIV infection through casual male–female sexual encounters is an infrequent event, people who regularly engage in risky sexual practices and so far have remained uninfected may be lulled into a false sense of security.

Many young people are deeply concerned about the threat of AIDS, however, and have changed their sexual behavior to reduce their risk of exposure:

PATRICK, 21: With AIDS here to stay, I would say safe sex is it. The condom can now be a lifesaver. Being alone now poses the problem that if you're down in the dumps, you can no longer look for quick love and warmth in a bar.

JILL, 26: AIDS has made casual sex out of the question. I take no chances. Sex is not worth dying for. I would only have sex now using a condom and with someone I'm seriously interested in. I would tell others simply that it's life or death. Take precautions or take the consequences.

(Copyright © 1991 by McIntyre, Formichella, Osterhout, and Gresh by arrangement with AVON Books, pp. 137–139)

Even among those who take precautions, feelings of uncertainty may remain:

CONNIE, 23: Unless your partner has never had sex before, you don't know if you can be totally safe, even if you use rubbers.

(Copyright © 1991 by McIntyre, Formichella, Osterhout, and Gresh by arrangement with AVON Books, pp. 137–139)

Many college programs have been introduced to educate students about AIDS and what they can do to prevent it. AIDS prevention programs debunk myths about personal invulnerability and expose the implicit personality theories that people use to (under)estimate their partners' riskiness (Williams et al., 1992).

Information about AIDS often does not produce meaningful behavioral changes. Some AIDS prevention programs and school districts distribute free condoms in the belief that easier access to condoms will encourage their use and thus reduce the risk of HIV transmission.

Targeting Special Populations

Some AIDS experts believe that AIDS prevention programs should be targeted toward the communities that have been hardest hit (St. Lawrence et al., 1995). It is possible, these experts believe, that the epidemic can be all but wiped out if prevention efforts were focused on the communities, especially poor communities, that have been ravaged by the epidemic (Kolata, 1993b; "Research panel," 1993). A 1993 report issued by the prestigious National Research Council lends support to the targeted approach. The council found that AIDS was devastating a handful of communities while leaving much of the nation virtually untouched. As one of the members of the council committee that drafted the report framed the issue, "If we want to really deal with the epidemic, we have to go where the epidemic is" (p. 26). Proponents of this approach point to the city of Tacoma, Washington, which concentrated its prevention efforts on promoting safer injection and sexual practices in people who inject drugs and managed to keep its infection rates in these groups at under 5%, as compared to the skyrocketing rates found in other cities like New York City, where infection rates in people who inject drugs now range between 50% and 80%. But the belief that AIDS prevention efforts should be narrowly but intensively focused on hard-hit communities is not universally supported by AIDS experts. Some believe that since the virus has spread into the more general population, a broader prevention effort is needed. Health officials also fear that AIDS may become largely ignored by the general public if it becomes perceived as a problem that is endemic to socially disadvantaged groups in our society rather than to the society at large.

Some AIDS researchers argue that people who inject drugs should be given sterile needles as well as easier access to drug treatment programs. In 1995, some 75 needle-exchange programs were operating in 55 U.S. cities. A study by the National Academy of Sciences (1995) concluded that these programs slow the spread of HIV without increasing drug abuse. Many political and religious leaders oppose government distribution of condoms or clean-needle programs on moral grounds, however. Meanwhile, many drug treatment programs have long waiting lists. As a result, some infected addicts spread the virus through needle sharing and sexual contact while awaiting entry.

The lack of Spanish-language AIDS education materials and bilingual treatment providers has handicapped efforts to stem the spread of AIDS in the Hispanic community (Fuentes, 1993). Recognizing that drug use is often implicated in the transmission of HIV among Hispanic Americans, the National Latino Coalition on AIDS has called for expanding the availability of drug treatment programs and expanding AIDS prevention efforts in the Hispanic community.

Reducing the Risk of HIV Infection

Two assured ways to avert the sexual transmission of AIDS are celibacy and a lifelong monogamous relationship with a person who is free of HIV. These two sexual lifestyles confer safety but are not followed by most people in the United States or Canada. Still, there are many ways in which sexually active people may reduce the risk of transmitting or contracting the AIDS virus. None of these suggestions is guaranteed to make sexual contact perfectly safe, however. Despite the commonly heard buzz words "safe sex," we can speak only of saf*er* sex—not of absolutely safe sex.

A CLOSER LOOK

SOURCES OF INFORMATION ABOUT HIV INFECTION AND AIDS

We brought you the latest information available on HIV and AIDS when this book went to press. Information about HIV and AIDS, however, changes daily. For the very latest information on HIV infection and AIDS—and for advice on what to do if you are wondering whether or not you have been infected by HIV—contact one or more of the following sources. Many of them, such as the Centers for Disease Control (CDC) AIDS hotline, are toll-free and respect the anonymity of the caller. The CDC, for example, will not ask for your name or attempt to trace the call, even if you inform the listener that you have been involved in illegal drug use. If you or someone to whom you are close is infected by HIV, one of the following groups may be able to lend support. When in doubt, call or write.

Centers for Disease Control AIDS Hotline: (800) 342-AIDS (Information and referral resources nationwide, 24 hours a day)

Canadian Toll-Free Hotline (toll-free in Canada): AIDS Committee of Toronto: (800) 267-6600

If you prefer requesting and receiving your information in Spanish, call: Spanish AIDS/SIDA Hotline: (800) 344-7432

AIDS Hotline for the Hearing Impaired: (800) 243-7889

AIDS Hotline for Teens: (800) 234-TEEN

National Gay and Lesbian Crisis Line—AIDS 800: (800) 221-7044

National AIDS Information Clearinghouse: (800) 458-5231 Education Database Distribution 1600 Research Blvd. Rockville, MD 20850

American Red Cross: (202) 737-8300 AIDS Education Office 1750 K St. NW Washington, DC 20006

National Initiative for AIDS and HIV Prevention Among Adolescents 1025 Vermont Avenue, NW Suite 210 Washington, DC 20005

Teens Teaching AIDS Prevention 3030 Walnut Street Kansas City, MO 64108

National Association of People with AIDS P.O. Box 34056 Washington, DC 20043

The Henry Nichols Foundation P.O. Box 621 Cooperstown, NY 13326

National Council of Churches AIDS Task Force: (212) 870-2421 475 Riverside Drive, Room 572 New York, NY 10115

Sex Information and Education Council of the United States (SIECUS): (212) 819-9770 130 West 42nd St., Suite 2500 New York, NY 10036

American Association of Physicians for Human Rights: (415) 255-4547 273 Church St. San Francisco, CA 94114

1. *Avoid high-risk sexual behaviors, unless you are absolutely certain that your partner is not infected* (Reinisch, 1990). Avoid "unprotected" vaginal intercourse (intercourse without the use of a latex condom and a spermicide containing nonoxynol-9—see the following). Unprotected anal intercourse is one of the riskiest practices. Other high-risk behaviors include unprotected oral–genital activity, oral–anal activity, insertion of a hand or fist into someone's rectum or vagina, or any activity in which you or your partner would come into contact with the other's blood, semen, or vaginal secretions.

2. *Be careful in your choice of partners.* Choose partners carefully. Avoid sexual contact with someone who is seropositive or has engaged in high-risk sexual or drug-use practices and is not known to be seronegative. Uninfected people cannot transmit HIV, but you probably won't know whether prospective partners are free of HIV infection. It is not enough to ask your partner about past sexual behavior and drug use. You need to know the person well enough to judge the truthfulness of his or her answers. Even then, you cannot be sure that the person is truthful or can completely recall all past sexual experiences, let alone verify the sexual histories of all previous partners. To be safe, it is best to abstain or to practice safer sex techniques with any partner who is not known to be free of HIV.

You may reduce the risk of HIV transmission by verifying that you and your partner are seronegative for HIV antibodies before engaging in intimate sexual relations involving the exchange of bodily fluids. Since blood tests for HIV antibodies are not foolproof, however, and a person may be infected with the virus for months or perhaps even a year or longer before antibodies can be detected, it may make sense to use condoms until repeated test results are negative.

3. *Limit your number of sex partners.* The more sexual contacts you have, the greater your risk of exposing yourself to a partner with HIV (or another pathogen). Also avoid sex with a partner who has had multiple partners.

    The NHSLS study was conceived, in part, to study behavior patterns (such as having multiple sex partners) that contribute to becoming infected with HIV. The study found that women had a median number of two sex partners since the age of 18, and men had a median number of six. Young, single (never married and formerly married) women and men (ages 18 to 44) were most likely to have had two or more partners in the past 12 months (Laumann et al., 1994, p. 189). As examples, some 30% of the never-married women and 45% of the never-married men of ages 18–29 reported two or more sex partners in the past 12 months. These people would therefore appear to be at greatest risk.

4. *Inspect your partner's sex organs.* Do not expect to find telltale signs of an HIV infection, but infected people often have other STDs. You may be able to discreetly inspect your partner's sex organs for lice, discharges, rashes, chancres, warts, and blisters during foreplay. Consider any disagreeable odor a warning sign.

5. *Engage in noncoital activities.* Other forms of sexual expression, such as hugging, massage, caressing, mutual masturbation, or rubbing bodies together without vaginal, anal, or oral contact, are low-risk ways of finding sexual pleasure, so long as semen or vaginal fluids do not come into contact with mucous membranes or breaks in the skin. Many sexologists refer to such activities as **outercourse** to distinguish them from sexual intercourse. Sharing sexual fantasies can be very titillating, as can taking a bath or shower together. Vibrators, dildos, and other "sex toys" may also be erotically stimulating and carry a low risk of infection, if they are washed thoroughly with soap and water before use and between uses by two people. If used for penetration, they should be used gently and with plenty of lubricant to avoid irritating or breaking vaginal or rectal tissues (Reinisch, 1990).

6. *Use a latex condom with a spermicide containing nonoxynol-9 before engaging in vaginal intercourse.* Latex condoms are an effective barrier against HIV and many other STD-causing organisms and offer highly effective protection against HIV infection and other STDs when used correctly and consistently (CDC, 1993d). (See Chapter 12 for

Outercourse

Forms of sexual expression, such as massage, hugging, caressing, mutual masturbation, and rubbing bodies together, that do not involve the exchange of body fluids. (Contrast with *intercourse*.)

Encouraging Safer Sex. AIDS prevention programs encourage sexually active people to engage in safer sex. However, many young people, including college students, continue to engage in risky sex.

guidelines for using condoms correctly.) Spermicides containing nonoxynol-9 are toxic to the AIDS virus and other STD-causing organisms, as well as to sperm, and may offer an added level of protection. Yet no evidence exists showing use of nonoxynol-9 alone without a condom to be effective in preventing HIV transmission (CDC, 1993d).

Condoms made from animal membranes ("skins") are less effective as barriers against STD-causing organisms (they contain pores that allow tiny microbes, including HIV, to penetrate). Even latex condoms are not 100% effective in preventing the transmission of the AIDS virus. Condoms (and the people who use them) are fallible. They can break or slip off.

New to the market, the female condom (discussed in Chapter 12) has not been shown to be effective against HIV transmission. To date, latex condoms for men are the only form of contraception proven to provide protection against HIV and other STDs (AIDS Update, 1993).

HIV has been found in the pre-ejaculatory fluid that is emitted before orgasm occurs ("H.I.V. clue supports early use of condom," 1992). This underscores the need for condoms to be used *before* any penile–vaginal contact occurs, not just moments prior to ejaculation.

7. *Use barrier devices when practicing oral sex (fellatio or cunnilingus).* If you decide to practice oral sex, use a condom before practicing fellatio and a dental dam (a square piece of latex rubber used by dentists during oral surgery) to cover the vagina before engaging in cunnilingus (Reinisch, 1990).

8. *Avoid sexual activity when in doubt.* None of the previous practices guarantees protection. Avoid any sexual activity about which you are in doubt.

Reducing the risk of HIV transmission also involves avoiding contact with blood that may be contaminated. Unsafe injection practices ("sharing needles") are the most risky. But do not share cuticle scissors, razor blades, or other implements that might transmit blood from one person to another.

The advent of AIDS presents the medical, mental health, and educational communities with an unparalleled challenge in developing programs to contain the spread of AIDS and for compassionate treatment of people with HIV and AIDS. As frightening as AIDS may be, it is preventable.

∼ *Reflections* ∼

◻ Why do you think that knowledge about the deadliness of AIDS and modes of transmission of HIV does not translate into people's ceasing risky behavior?

◻ Do you favor distribution of condoms in the public schools as a means of attempting to prevent transmission of HIV? Do you support the distribution of free hypodermic needles to people who inject drugs? Why, or why not?

◻ Did you learn anything in this chapter? How has this chapter affected your attitudes toward AIDS and your behavior?

Summing Up

Prevalence of HIV Infection and AIDS

AIDS has claimed hundreds of thousands of lives in the United States. More than 1 million Americans are likely to be infected with HIV. Estimates from health authorities indicate that more than 14 million people worldwide are infected with HIV. The number of people infected with HIV may reach 40 million by the year 2000, according to the World Health Organization.

It is a person's behavior, not the groups to which a person belongs, that determines her or his relative risk of infection.

The Immune System and AIDS

The immune system produces white blood cells (leuko-cytes) that identify, envelop, and kill disease-causing agents (pathogens) such as bacteria and viruses.

Effects of HIV on the Immune System   AIDS is caused by the human immunodeficiency virus (HIV), which attacks the body's immune system. As HIV disables the body's natural defenses, the person becomes vulnerable to opportunistic diseases—such as serious infections and cancers—that are normally held in check.

Progression of HIV Infection and AIDS

Shortly following infection, people may experience mild flu-like symptoms, which usually disappear within a few weeks. They may then remain symptom-free for years. The beginnings of full-blown cases of AIDS are often marked by symptoms such as fatigue, night sweats, persistent fever, swollen lymph nodes, diarrhea, and weight loss.

Transmission

HIV is a blood-borne virus that is also found in semen, vaginal secretions, and breast milk. Common avenues of transmission include sexual intercourse, transfusion with contaminated blood, sharing a hypodermic needle with an infected person, childbirth, and breast-feeding.

Women and AIDS   The number of women who are infected with HIV has been growing rapidly. Many women (and men) contract HIV through male–female sexual intercourse. HIV infection may progress differently in women and men.

Diagnosis of HIV Infection and AIDS

HIV infection can be diagnosed by blood and saliva tests that detect HIV antibodies. Until 1993, the diagnosis of AIDS required the appearance of certain so-called indicator diseases, such as Kaposi's sarcoma or PCP, in a person who was seropositive for HIV. In 1993, the CDC revised the definition of AIDS to include other indicator diseases and to include HIV+ people whose CD4 cell counts had fallen below 200 per cubic millimeter of blood.

Issues Concerning Testing for HIV Infection   Testing for HIV infection raises important emotional, medical, ethical, moral, and lifestyle concerns. Controversy swirls around whether the identities of HIV-infected health care workers should be disclosed, and whether they should be prohibited from performing procedures that might infect patients.

Treatment of HIV Infection and AIDS

There is neither a cure for AIDS nor an effective, safe vaccine. The drug AZT appears to have limited benefits for a limited period of time.

Psychological Adjustment of Persons with HIV Infections and AIDS   People with AIDS often suffer psychological problems, most notably anxiety, depression, guilt about sexual behavior or drug abuse, anger, and suicidal feelings.

Prevention

Coming of Age in the Age of AIDS   For the first time, a generation of Americans is becoming sexually active when the threat of a lethal disease hangs over every sexual encounter. Yet only a minority of young people have made significant preventive changes in their sexual behavior.

Reducing the Risk of HIV Infection   Methods of prevention include celibacy (or abstinence), maintaining a lifelong monogamous relationship with an uninfected partner, and practicing safe(r) sex.

CHAPTER 18

Henri Matisse, *Zulma,* 1950. Statens Museum for Kunst, Copenhagen. J. Rump Collection. © 1996 Succession H. Matisse/Artist Rights Society (ARS), New York.

Atypical Sexual Variations

Outline

Truth OR Fiction?

_____ King Henry III of France insisted on being considered a woman and addressed as "Her Majesty."

_____ Nude sunbathers are exhibitionists.

_____ People who enjoy watching their mates undress are voyeurs.

_____ Exhibitionists and voyeurs are never violent.

_____ Some people cannot become sexually aroused unless they are bound, flogged, or humiliated by their sex partners.

_____ It is considered normal to enjoy some mild forms of pain during sexual activity.

_____ There is a subculture in the United States in which sexual sadists and sexual masochists form liaisons to inflict and receive pain and humiliation during sexual activity.

The following incident took place in New York City. It could have happened anywhere that windows of residences face one other across yards, alleyways, and narrow streets.

A newly married couple were in their apartment, and the wife walked over to the window, which looked into the window of another apartment, and as she put it when recalling the story, "I just couldn't believe my eyes." The couple across the way, who had not pulled down a shade, and who had no curtain on the window, were relaxing on the bed. At least it seemed as if they were relaxing, but soon they became active and energetic, going through all the motions of discovery and exploration, no doubt precoital. There stood the watcher at the window, safe in a perch where she could remain undetected. "Disgusting," she murmured under her breath, but the spectacle held her in fascination. . . . She could not move herself from the window. She did, however, become fearful that the couple might look up and see her, so she stepped inside, and continued to watch by peering out from behind the wall. Still they continued, still she watched. Finally, she called her husband. He too watched, his eyes glued on what had become by then the primal scene. Then he walked away, went to the bedroom, and returned, a pair of opera glasses in his hand.

"No, you will not look with those glasses," the wife indignantly said. "What are you, anyway, a voyeur?"

"But you've been standing over here, watching, all this time, and you called me over," he protested.

"Yes, I called you to see what's going on, but not to get your glasses. I have a right to look out of my own window, and it's their problem if they don't have the decency to pull down a shade. But when you get a telescope, well, that's going too far!" And she insisted at this point that she and her husband, the peepers, pull down the shades.

(Sagarin, 1973, p. 5)

The incident raises questions about our labels for sexual behavior—particularly about the boundaries of what is normal. One couple clearly created conditions under which their sexual activity might become public. Another couple became spellbound by that activity. The exposed couple were in their own home, but could they be considered *exhibitionists?* And were the observers *voyeurs?* The observing wife became indignant when her husband brought out opera glasses. Perhaps she could justify her own "peeping" by thinking that she had stumbled across the other couple. Using opera glasses would transform her accidental discovery into a purposeful act, however. Then, perhaps, she could no longer regard watching as "normal."

What is normal, and what is abnormal or deviant sexual behavior? In this chapter we explore a number of sexual behaviors that deviate from the norm in one sense or another.

Normal Versus Deviant Sexual Behavior

One common approach to defining normality is based on a statistical norm. From this perspective, rare or unusual sexual behaviors are considered abnormal or deviant. The statistical approach may seem value-free, since the yardstick of normality is based on the frequency of behavior, not on judgment of its social acceptability. Engaging in coitus while standing, or more than seven times a week, might be considered deviant by this yardstick. The choice of behaviors we subject to statistical comparison is not divorced from our underlying values, however. Sexual practices such as humming tunes from Rodgers and Hammerstein musicals while making love may be statistically infrequent (at least for people born after 1960) but would not be considered aberrant. Statistical infrequency, then, is not a sufficient criterion for classifying behavior as abnormal or deviant. We must also consider whether the sexual practice deviates from a social norm.

What is considered normal in one culture or at a particular time may be considered abnormal in other cultures and at other times. A gay male or lesbian sexual orientation was considered abnormal and labeled a mental disorder by the American Psychiatric Association throughout most of the century. But in 1973 a gay male or lesbian sexual orientation was dropped as a mental disorder from the association's official diagnostic manual. What is "normal" behavior for the female adolescent Trobriand islander (see Chapter 1) might be considered deviant—even *nymphomaniacal*—by the standards of Western culture.

In our own culture, sexual practices such as oral sex and masturbation were once considered to be deviant or abnormal. Today, however, they are practiced so widely in our society that few people would label them as deviant practices. Concepts of "normalcy" and "deviance," then, reflect the mores and customs of a particular culture at a given time.

Another basis for determining sexual deviance is to classify sexual practices as deviant when they involve the persistent preference for nongenital sexual outlets. If a man prefers fondling a woman's panties to engaging in sexual relations with her, or prefers to masturbate against her foot rather than engage in coitus, his behavior is likely to be labeled deviant.

Because of the confusing array of meanings of the terms *deviant* and *abnormal,* we prefer to speak about unusual patterns of sexual arousal or behavior as "atypical variations" in sexual behavior rather than as "sexual deviations." Atypical patterns of sexual arousal or behavior that become problematic in the eyes of the individual or society are labeled *paraphilias* by the American Psychiatric Association (1994). Clinicians consider paraphilias to be mental disorders. But milder forms of these behaviors may be practiced by many people and fall within the normal spectrum of human sexuality (Brody, 1990a).

The Paraphilias

Paraphilia

A diagnostic category used by the American Psychiatric Association to describe atypical patterns of sexual arousal or behavior that become problematic in the eyes of the individual or society, such as fetishism or exhibitionism. The urges are recurrent and are either acted on or are distressing to the individual. (From Greek roots meaning "to the side of" [*para-*] and "loving" [*philos*].)

Paraphilias involve sexual arousal in response to unusual stimuli such as children or other nonconsenting persons (such as unsuspecting people whom one watches or to whom one exposes one's genitals), nonhuman objects (such as shoes, leather, rubber, or undergarments), or pain or humiliation. The psychiatric diagnosis of paraphilia requires that the person has acted on the urges or is distinctly distressed by them.

People with paraphilias often feel that their urges have an insistent, demanding, or compulsory quality (Money, 1988). They may describe themselves as periodically overcome by them (Brody, 1990a). People with paraphilias tend to experience their urges as beyond their control, much as drug addicts or compulsive gamblers might regard themselves as helpless to avert irresistible urges to gamble or use drugs. For these reasons theorists have speculated that paraphilias may represent a type of sexual compulsion or addiction.

Paraphilias vary in severity. In some cases the person can function sexually in the absence of paraphilic stimuli and seldom if ever acts upon paraphilic urges. In other cases the person resorts to paraphilic behavior only in times of stress. In more extreme forms the person repeatedly engages in paraphilic behavior and may become preoccupied with thoughts and fantasies about these experiences. In such cases the person may not be able to become sexually aroused without either fantasizing about the paraphilic stimulus or having it present. For some people paraphilic behavior is the only means of attaining sexual gratification.

The person with a paraphilia typically replays the paraphilic act in sexual fantasies to stimulate arousal during masturbation or sexual relations. It is as if he or she is mentally replaying a videotape of the paraphilic scene. The scene grows stale after a while, however. According to sex researcher John Money, "the tape wears out and he has to perform another paraphilic act, in effect, to create a new movie" (quoted in Brody, 1990a, p. C12).

Some paraphilias are generally harmless and victimless, such as *fetishism* and cross-dressing to achieve sexual arousal (*transvestic fetishism*). Even being humiliated by one's partner may be relatively harmless if the partner consents. Other paraphilic behaviors, such as exposing oneself in public or enticing children into sexual relations, do have victims and may cause harm, sometimes severe physical or psychological harm. They are also against the law. Sexual sadism, in which sexual arousal is connected to hurting or humiliating another person, can be a most harmful paraphilia when it is forced upon a nonconsenting person. Some brutal rapes involve sexual sadism.

Except in the case of sexual masochism, paraphilias are believed to occur almost exclusively among men (Money & Wiedeking, 1980). The prevalence of paraphilias in the general population remains unknown, because people are generally unwilling to talk about them. Much of what we have learned about paraphilias derives from the reported experiences of people who have been apprehended for performing illegal acts (such as exposing themselves in public) and the few who have voluntarily sought help. The characteristics of others who have not been identified or studied remain virtually unknown.

We discuss the major types of paraphilia in this chapter, with the exception of *pedophilia.* In pedophilia, children become the objects of sexual arousal. Pedophilia often takes the form of sexual coercion of children, as in incest or sexual molestation. It is discussed in Chapter 19, along with other forms of coerced sexuality.

Fetishism

Fetishism

A paraphilia in which an inanimate object, such as an article of clothing or items made of rubber, leather, or silk, elicits sexual arousal.

Partialism

A paraphilia related to fetishism, in which sexual arousal is exaggeratedly associated with a particular body part, such as feet, breasts, or buttocks.

The roots of the word *fetish* come from the French *fétiche,* which is thought to derive from the Portuguese *feitico,* meaning "magic charm." The "magic" in this case lies in an object's ability to arouse a person sexually. In **fetishism,** an inanimate object elicits sexual arousal. Articles of clothing (for example, women's panties, bras, lingerie, stockings, gloves, shoes, or boots) and materials made of rubber, leather, silk, or fur are among the more common fetishistic objects. Leather boots and high-heeled shoes are popular ones.

The fetishist may act on the urges to engage in fetishistic behavior, such as by masturbating by stroking an object or while fantasizing about it, or he may be distressed about such urges or fantasies but not act upon them. In a related paraphilia, **partialism,** people are excessively aroused by a particular body part, such as the feet, breasts, or buttocks.

Most fetishes and partialisms are harmless. Fetishistic practices are almost always private and involve masturbation or are incorporated into coitus with a willing partner. Only rarely have fetishists coerced others into paraphilic activities. Yet some partialists have touched parts of women's bodies in public. And some fetishists have committed burglaries to acquire the fetishistic objects (Sargent, 1988).

Fetishism. In fetishism, inanimate objects such as leather shoes or boots elicit sexual arousal. Fetishists may derive sexual gratification by fondling, manipulating, or fantasizing about the object during masturbation. They may want the object to be present during sexual activity with, or to be worn by, their partners.

Transvestism

Transvestism

A paraphilia in which a person repeatedly cross-dresses to achieve sexual arousal or gratification, or is troubled by persistent, recurring urges to cross-dress. (From the Latin roots *trans-*, meaning "cross," and *vestis*, meaning "garment.") Also known as *transvestic fetishism*.

Transvestism may be viewed as a type of fetish. Whereas other fetishists become sexually aroused by handling the fetishistic object while they masturbate, transvestites become excited by wearing articles of clothing—the fetishistic objects—of the other gender. A fetishist may find the object, or sex involving the object, to be erotically stimulating. For the transvestite, the object is sexually alluring only when it is worn. Transvestites are almost always males. True transvestism has been described only among heterosexual males, although such men may occasionally engage in male–male sexual activity. Most are married and otherwise masculine in behavior and style of dress.

Transvestism is often confused with transsexualism, but there are important differences between them. Transvestites cross-dress because they find it sexually arousing. Most transvestites have masculine gender identities and do not seek to change their anatomic sex. (Some male transvestites show some aspects of a feminine gender identity, however [Doorn et al., 1994].) Transsexuals, by contrast, cross-dress because they are uncomfortable with the attire associated with their anatomic sex.

Like fetishism in general, the origins of transvestism remain obscure. There is no evidence of biological abnormalities in transvestism (Buhrich et al., 1979). Family relationships appear to play a role, however. Transvestites are more likely than other people to be oldest children or only children (Schott, 1995). They also report closer relationships with their mothers than their fathers (Schott, 1995). Some transvestites report a history of "petticoat punishment" during childhood. That is, they were humiliated by being dressed in girl's attire. Some authorities have speculated that the adult transvestite might be attempting psychologically to convert humiliation into mastery by achieving an erection and engaging in sexual activity despite being attired in female clothing (Geer et al., 1984). Transvestism can also be looked at as an attempt by males to escape the narrow confines of the masculine role (Bullough, 1991).

Cross-dressing is common in other cultures and has been reported in historical accounts of figures such as King Henry III of France. This sixteenth-century monarch wanted to be considered a woman and to be addressed as "Her Majesty" (Geer et al., 1984). But cross-dressing may occur in other cultures for reasons other than sexual arousal. In the case of Henry III, it appears that transsexualism, and not transvestism, was involved.

Transvestism. Transvestites cross-dress for the purpose of sexual gratification. Some transvestites sport feminine attire in public. Others cross-dress only in the privacy of their own homes.

It is true that King Henry III of France insisted on being considered a woman and addressed as "Her Majesty." However, the king appears to have been a transsexual rather than a transvestite. ■

Some men cross-dress for reasons other than sexual arousal and so are not "true transvestites." Some men make a living by impersonating women like Marilyn Monroe and Madonna on stage and are not motivated by sexual arousal. Among some segments of the gay male community, it is fashionable to masquerade as women. Gay men do not usually cross-dress to become sexually stimulated, however.

Transvestism behaviors may range from wearing a single female garment when alone to sporting dresses, wigs, makeup, and feminine mannerisms at a transvestite club. Some transvestites become sexually aroused by masquerading as women and attracting the interest of unsuspecting males. They sometimes entice these men or string them along until they find some excuse to back out before their anatomic sex is revealed. The great majority of transvestites do not engage in antisocial or illegal behavior. Most practice their sexual predilection in private and would be horrified or embarrassed to be discovered by associates while dressed in female attire.

Although some transvestites persuade their female partners to permit them to wear feminine attire during their sexual activities, most keep their transvestic urges and activi-

A L O S E R L O O K

A CASE OF TRANSVESTISM

Most transvestites are married and engage in sexual activity with their wives. Yet they seek additional sexual gratification through dressing as women, as in the case of Archie.

Archie was a 55-year-old plumber who had been cross-dressing for many years. There was a time when he would go out in public as a woman, but as his prominence in the community grew, he became more afraid of being discovered in public. His wife Myrna knew of his "peccadillo," especially since he borrowed many of her clothes. She urged him to stay at home, offering to help him with his "weirdness." For many years his paraphilia had been restricted to the home.

The couple came to the clinic at the urging of the wife. Myrna described how Archie had imposed his will on her for 20 years. Archie would wear her undergarments and masturbate while she told him how disgusting he was. (The couple also regularly engaged in "normal" sexual inter-

course, which Myrna enjoyed.) The cross-dressing had come to a head because a teenage daughter had almost walked into the couple's bedroom while they were acting out Archie's fantasies.

With Myrna out of the consulting room, Archie explained how he grew up in a family with several older sisters. He described how underwear had been perpetually hanging to dry in the one bathroom. As an adolescent Archie experimented with rubbing against articles of underwear, then with trying them on. On one occasion a sister walked in while he was modeling panties before the mirror. She told him he was a "dredge to society," and he straightaway experienced unparalleled sexual excitement. He masturbated when she left the room, and his orgasm was the strongest of his young life.

Archie did not think that there was anything wrong with wearing women's undergarments and masturbating. He was not about to give it

up, even if it destroyed his marriage. Myrna's main concern was finally separating herself from Archie's "sickness." She didn't care what he did any more, so long as he did it by himself. "Enough is enough," she said.

That was the compromise the couple worked out. Archie would engage in his fantasies by himself. He would choose times when Myrna was not at home, and she would not be informed of his activities. He would also be very, very careful to choose times when the children would not be around.

Six months later the couple were together and content. Archie had replaced Myrna's input into his fantasies with transvestic–sadomasochistic magazines. Myrna said, "I see no evil, hear no evil, smell no evil." They continued to have sexual intercourse. After a while, Myrna forgot to check to see which underwear had been used.

ties to themselves. A survey of 504 transvestite men showed that most had kept their transvestism a secret from their wives-to-be, hoping that they would not be bothered by their urge to cross-dress once they were married (Weinberg & Bullough, 1986, 1988). The urges continued into their marriages, and the wives eventually discovered their husbands' secrets, however. Seventy of the wives were interviewed (Bullough & Weinberg, 1989). The wives tended to react with confusion, surprise, or shock to discovering their husbands' cross-dressing. Most tried to be understanding at first. Some even assisted their husbands in their cross-dressing, such as by helping them apply makeup. Yet the longer the women were married, the more negative their attitudes tended to become toward their husbands' cross-dressing. Over time, wives generally learned to be tolerant, though not supportive, of their husbands' cross-dressing.

Exhibitionism

Exhibitionism

A paraphilia characterized by persistent, powerful urges and sexual fantasies involving exposing one's genitals to unsuspecting strangers to achieve sexual arousal or gratification.

Exhibitionism ("flashing") involves persistent, powerful urges and sexual fantasies involving exposing one's genitals to unsuspecting strangers for the purpose of achieving sexual arousal or gratification. The urges are either acted upon or are disturbing to the individual. Exhibitionists are almost always males.

What we know of exhibitionists, as with most other people with paraphilias, is almost entirely derived from studies of men who have been apprehended or treated by mental health professionals. Such knowledge may yield a biased picture of exhibitionists. Although about one in three arrests for sexual offenses involves exhibitionism, relatively few reported incidents result in apprehension and conviction (Cox, 1988). Studies in England, Guatemala, the United States, and Hong Kong show that fewer than 20% of occurrences are reported to the police (Cox, 1988). The characteristics of most perpetrators may thus differ from those of people who have been available for study.

The prevalence of exhibitionism in the general population is unknown, but a survey of 846 college women at nine randomly selected U.S. universities found exposure to exhibitionism to be widespread. A third of the women reported that they had run into a "flasher" (Cox, 1988). A majority of the women had been approached for the first time (some had been approached more than once) by 16 years of age. Only 15 of the women had reported these incidents to the police. The clinical definition of exhibitionism involves exposure to a *stranger,* but about a third (36%) of the incidents among the college women were committed by acquaintances, relatives, or "good friends."

The archetypal exhibitionist is young, unhappily married, and sexually repressed. An exhibitionist may claim that marital coitus is reasonably satisfactory, but that he also experiences the compulsion to expose himself to strangers. Many exhibitionists are single, however. They typically have difficulties relating to women and have been unable to establish meaningful heterosexual relationships.

Exhibitionism usually begins before age 18 (American Psychiatric Association, 1994). The urge to exhibit oneself, if not the actual act, usually begins in early adolescence, generally between the ages of 13 and 16 (Freund et al., 1988). The frequency of exhibitionism declines markedly after the age of 40 (American Psychiatric Association, 1994). The typical exhibitionist does not attempt further sexual contact with the victim. Thus, he does not usually pose a physical threat (American Psychiatric Association, 1994).

The police may sometimes trivialize exhibitionism as a "nuisance crime," but the psychological consequences among victims, especially young children, indicate that exhibitionism is not victimless. Victims may feel violated and be bothered by recurrent images or nightmares. They may harbor misplaced guilt that they had unwittingly enticed the exhibitionist. They may blame themselves for reacting excessively or for failing to apprehend the perpetrator. They may also develop fears of venturing out on their own.

Geer and his colleagues (1984) see exhibitionism as an indirect means of expressing hostility toward women. Exposure may be an attempt by the exhibitionist to strike back at women because of a belief that women have wronged him or damaged his self-esteem by failing to notice him or take him seriously. The direct expression of anger may be perceived as too risky, so the exhibitionist vents his rage by humiliating a defenseless stranger. The urge to expose oneself almost always follows a situation in which the exhibitionist feels that his masculinity has been insulted. Some evidence suggests that exhibitionists may be attempting to assert their masculinity by evoking a response from their victims. A number of exhibitionists have reported that they hoped that the women would enjoy the experience and be impressed with the size of their penises (Langevin et al., 1979).

Other studies show exhibitionists to be shy, dependent, passive, lacking in sexual and social skills, even inhibited (Dwyer, 1988). They tend to be self-critical, to have doubts about their masculinity, and to suffer from feelings of inadequacy and inferiority (Blair & Lanyon, 1981; Dwyer, 1988). Many have had poor relationships with their fathers and have overprotective mothers (Dwyer, 1988). Exhibitionists who are socially shy or inadequate may be using exhibitionism as a substitute for the intimate relationships they cannot develop.

The preferred victims are typically girls or young women (Freund & Blanchard, 1986). The typical exhibitionist drives up to, or walks in front of, a stranger and exposes his penis. In one sample of 130 exhibitionists, about 50% reported that they always or nearly always had erections when they exposed themselves (Langevin et al., 1979). After his victim has registered fear, disgust, confusion, or surprise, an exhibitionist will typically cover himself and flee. He usually masturbates, either while exposing himself or shortly afterwards, while thinking about the act and the victim's response (American Psychiatric Association, 1994; Blair & Lanyon, 1981). Some exhibitionists ejaculate during the act. Most of the 238 exhibitionists in a Canadian study reported masturbating to orgasm while exposing themselves or afterwards while fantasizing about it (Freund et al., 1988).

Exhibitionists may also need to risk being caught to experience a heightened erotic response (Stoller, 1977). The exhibitionist may even situate himself to increase the risk. For example, he may repeatedly expose himself in the same location or while sitting in his own easily identifiable car.

Courts nowadays tend to be hard on exhibitionists, partly because of evidence that shows that some exhibitionists progress to more serious crimes of sexual aggression. In one sample, about 10% of rapists and child molesters had begun their "sexual careers" by exposing themselves to strangers (Abel et al., 1984). This does not mean that exhibitionists inevitably become rapists and child molesters. Most do not.

Definitions of exhibitionism also bring into focus the boundaries between normal and abnormal behavior. Are exotic dancers (stripteasers) or nude sunbathers exhibitionists? After all, aren't they also exposing themselves to strangers? But exotic dancers—male or female—usually remove their clothes to sexually excite or entertain an expectant audience, not themselves. Their motive is to earn a living or (arguably) to express themselves in dance. Sunbathers in their "birthday suits" may also seek to sexually arouse others, not themselves. Of course, they may also be seeking an all-over tan or trying to avoid feeling encumbered by clothing. In any case, stripteasers and sunbathers do not expose themselves to unsuspecting others. Thus these behaviors are not regarded as exhibitionistic.

Truth OR Fiction?
R E V I S I T E D

It is not true that nude sunbathers are exhibitionists—at least not in terms of the clinical definition of the disorder. Exhibitionists seek to become sexually aroused by exposing themselves to unsuspecting victims, not to show off their physical attractiveness. ■

It is also normal to become sexually excited while stripping before one's sex partner. Such stripping is done to elicit a positive response from one's partner, not to surprise or shock a stranger.

Obscene Telephone Calling

Telephone scatologia

A paraphilia characterized by the making of obscene telephone calls. (From the Greek *skatos*, meaning "excrement.")

Like exhibitionists, obscene phone callers (almost all of whom are male) seek to become sexually aroused by shocking their victims. Whereas an exhibitionist exposes his genitals to produce the desired response, the obscene phone caller exposes himself verbally by uttering obscenities and sexual provocations to a nonconsenting person. Because of such similarities, obscene telephone calling is sometimes considered a subtype of exhibitionism. The American Psychiatric Association (1994) labels this type of paraphilia **telephone scatologia** (lewdness).

HOW TO RESPOND TO AN EXHIBITIONIST

It is understandable that an unsuspecting woman who is exposed to an exhibitionist may react with shock, surprise, or fear. Unfortunately, her display of shock or fear may reinforce the flasher's tendencies to expose himself. She may fear that the flasher, who has already broken at least one social code, is likely to assault her physically as well. Fortunately, most exhibitionists do not seek actual sexual contact with their victims and run away before they can be apprehended by the police or passersby.

Some women may respond with anger, insults, even arguments that the offender should feel ashamed. A display of anger may reinforce exhibitionism. We do not recommend that the victim insult the flasher, lest it provoke a violent response. Although most exhibitionists are nonviolent, about one in ten has considered or attempted rape (Gebhard et al., 1965).

When possible, showing no reaction or simply continuing on one's way may be the best response. If women do desire to respond to the flasher, they might calmly say something like "You really need professional help. You should see a professional to help you with this problem." They should promptly report the incident to police, so that authorities can apprehend the offender.

Relatively few obscene callers are women (Matek, 1988). Women who are charged with such offenses are generally motivated by rage for some actual or fantasized rejection rather than the desire for sexual arousal. They use the phone to hurl sexual invectives against men whom they feel have wronged them. By contrast, male obscene phone callers are generally motivated by a desire for sexual excitement and usually choose their victims randomly from the phone book or by chance dialing. They typically masturbate during the phone call or shortly afterwards. Despite the offensiveness of their actions, most obscene phone callers are not dangerous. Nor do most make repeat calls to the same person (Reinisch, 1990).

There are many patterns of obscene phone calling (Matek, 1988). Some callers limit themselves to obscenities. Others make sexual overtures. Some just breathe heavily into the receiver. Others describe their masturbatory activity to their victims. Some profess to have previously met the victim at a social gathering or through a mutual acquaintance. Some even present themselves as "taking a sex survey" and ask a series of personally revealing questions.

The typical obscene phone caller is a socially inadequate heterosexual male who has had difficulty forming intimate relationships with women. The relative safety and anonymity of the telephone may shield him from the risk of rejection. A reaction of shock or fright from his victims may fill him with feelings of power and control that are lacking in his life, especially in his relationships with women. The obscenities may vent the rage that he holds against women who have rejected him.

Obscene phone calls are illegal, but it has been difficult to track down perpetrators (Matek, 1988). Call tracing can help police track obscene or offending phone callers. Call tracing works in different ways in different locales. *Caller ID,* which shows the caller's telephone number on a display panel on the receiving party's telephone, is available in many locales. Though this service may deter some obscene callers, others may use public phones instead of their home phones. Callers may also be able to electronically block the display of their telephone numbers. Check with your local telephone company if you are interested in these services.

What should a woman do if she receives an obscene phone call? Advice generally parallels that given to women who are victimized by exhibitionists. Above all, women are advised to remain calm and not reveal shock or fright, since such reactions tend to reinforce the caller and increase the probability of repeat calls. Women may be best advised to say nothing at all and gently hang up the receiver. A woman might alternatively offer a brief response that alludes to the caller's problems before hanging up. She might say in a calm but strong voice, "It's unfortunate you have this problem. I think you should seek professional help." If she should receive repeated calls, the woman might request an unlisted number or contact the police about tracing the calls. Many women list themselves only by their initials in the phone directory so as to disguise their gender. But since this practice is so widespread, obscene callers may surmise that people listed by initials are women living alone.

Voyeurism

Voyeurism involves strong, repetitive urges to observe unsuspecting strangers who are naked, disrobing, or engaged in sexual relations (American Psychiatric Association, 1994). The voyeur becomes sexually aroused by the act of watching and typically does not seek sexual relations with the observed person. Like fetishism and exhibitionism, voyeurism is found almost exclusively among males. It usually begins before the age of 15 (American Psychiatric Association, 1994).

The voyeur may masturbate while "peeping" or afterward while "replaying" the incident in his imagination or engaging in voyeuristic fantasies. The voyeur may fantasize about making love to the observed person but have no intention of actually doing so.

Are people voyeurs who become sexually aroused by the sight of their lovers undressing? What about people who enjoy watching pornographic films or stripteasers? No, no, and no. The people being observed are not unsuspecting strangers. The lover knows that his or her partner is watching. Porn actors and strippers know that others will be viewing them. They would not be "performing" if they did not expect or have an audience.

It is perfectly normal for men and women to be sexually stimulated by the sight of other people who are nude, undressing, or engaged in sexual relations. Voyeurism is characterized by urges to "peep" on *unsuspecting* strangers.

Voyeurism. Voyeurs, or peeping Toms, seek sexual gratification by peering at unsuspecting strangers. Legend has it that Tom was the only townsperson unable to grant Lady Godiva's request to refrain from looking at her while she rode horseback nude to protest a heavy tax on the town.

T r u t h OR *Fiction?*
R E V I S I T E D

Voyeurism
A paraphilia characterized by strong, repetitive urges and related sexual fantasies of observing unsuspecting strangers who are naked, disrobing, or engaged in sexual relations. (From the French verb *voir*, meaning "to see.")

It is not true that people who enjoy watching their mates undress are voyeurs. In such cases the undresser is knowingly and willingly being observed, and the watcher's enjoyment is completely normal. Voyeurs target unsuspecting victims. ■

Voyeurs are also known as "peepers," or *peeping Toms*. Why "peeping Toms"? According to an old English legend, Lady Godiva asked the townspeople not to look upon her while she rode horseback in the nude to protest the oppressive tax that her husband, a landowner, had imposed on them. A tailor named Tom of Coventry was the only townsperson not to grant her request.

Voyeurs often put themselves in risky situations in which they face the prospect of being discovered or apprehended. They may risk physical injury by perching themselves in trees or otherwise assuming precarious positions to catch a preferred view of their target. They will occupy rooftops and fire escapes in brutal winter weather. Peepers can be exceedingly patient in their outings. They may wait hour after hour, night after night, for a furtive glimpse of an unsuspecting person. One 25-year-old recently married man secreted himself in his mother-in-law's closet, waiting for her to disrobe. Part of the sexual excitement seems to stem from the risks voyeurs run. The need for elements of risk in their voyeurism may explain why voyeurs are not known to frequent nude beaches or nudist camps where it is acceptable to look (though not to stare) at others.

Although most voyeurs are nonviolent, some commit violent crimes like assault and rape (Langevin et al., 1985). Voyeurs who break into and enter homes or buildings, or who tap at windows to gain the attention of victims, are among the more dangerous.

T r u t h OR *Fiction?*
R E V I S I T E D

It is incorrect to say that exhibitionists and voyeurs are *never* violent. Exhibitionistic and voyeuristic activities per se do not involve outright violence, but some exhibitionists and voyeurs have been known to be violent, and they may, if provoked or angered, react violently. ■

Compared to other types of sex offenders, voyeurs tend to be less sexually experienced and are less likely to be married (Gebhard et al., 1965). Like exhibitionists, voyeurs tend to harbor feelings of inadequacy and to lack social and sexual skills (Dwyer, 1988). They may thus have difficulty forming romantic relationships with women. For this shy and socially inadequate type of voyeur, "peeping" affords sexual gratification without risk of rejection. Yet not all voyeurs are socially awkward and inept with women.

Sexual Masochism

Sexual masochism

A paraphilia characterized by the desire or need for pain or humiliation to enhance sexual arousal so that gratification may be attained. (From the name of the author Leopold von Sacher-Masoch.)

T r u t h OR *Fiction?*
R E V I S I T E D

Although pleasure and pain may seem like polar opposites, some people experience sexual pleasure through having pain or humiliation inflicted on them by their sex partners. People who associate the receipt of pain or humiliation with sexual arousal are called **sexual masochists.** A sexual masochist either acts upon or is distressed by persistent urges and sexual fantasies involving the desire to be bound, flogged, humiliated, or made to suffer in some way by a sexual partner so as to achieve sexual excitement. In extreme cases the person is incapable of becoming sexually aroused unless pain or humiliation is incorporated into the sexual act.

It is true that some sexual masochists cannot become sexually aroused unless they are bound, flogged, or humiliated by their sex partners. ■

Sexual masochism is the only paraphilia that is found among women with some frequency (American Psychiatric Association, 1994). Even sexual masochism is much more prevalent among men than women, however. Male masochists may outnumber females by a margin of 20 to 1 (American Psychiatric Association, 1994).

The word *masochism* is derived from the name of the Austrian storyteller Leopold von Sacher-Masoch (1835–1895). He wrote tales of men who derived sexual satisfaction from having a female partner inflict pain on them, typically by flagellation (beating or whipping).

Bondage

Ritual restraint, as by shackles, as practiced by many sexual masochists.

Sexual masochists may derive pleasure from various types of punishing experiences, including being restrained (a practice known as **bondage**), blindfolded (*sensory* bondage), spanked, whipped, or made to perform humiliating acts, such as walking around on all fours and licking the boots or shoes of the sex partner, or being subjected to vulgar insults. Some masochists have their partners humiliate them by urinating or defecating on them. Some masochists prefer a particular source of pain. Others seek an assortment. But we should not think that sexual masochists enjoy other types of pain that are not connected with their sexual practices. Sexual masochists are no more likely than anyone else to derive pleasure from the pain they experience when they accidentally stub their toes or touch a hot appliance. Pain has erotic value only within a sexual context. It must be part of an elaborate sexual ritual.

Sexual sadists

People who become sexually aroused by inflicting pain or humiliation on others.

Sexual masochists and **sexual sadists** often form sexual relationships to meet each other's needs. Some sexual masochists enlist the services of prostitutes or obtain the cooperation of their regular sexual partners to enact their masochistic fantasies.

It may seem contradictory for pain to become connected with sexual pleasure. The association of sexual arousal with mildly painful stimuli is actually quite common, however. Kinsey and his colleagues (1953) reported that perhaps as many as one person in four has experienced erotic sensations from being bitten during lovemaking. The eroticization of mild forms of pain (love bites, hair pulls, minor scratches) may fall within the normal range of sexual variation. Pain from these sources increases overall bodily arousal, which may enhance sexual excitement. Some of us become sexually excited when our partners "talk dirty" to us or call us vulgar names. When the urge for pain for purposes of sexual arousal becomes so persistent or strong that it overshadows other sources of sexual stimulation, or when the masochistic experience causes physical or psychological harm, we may say that the boundary between normality and abnormality has been breached.

T r u t h OR *Fiction?*
R E V I S I T E D

It is in fact considered normal to enjoy some mild forms of pain during sexual activity. Love bites, hair pulls, and minor scratches are examples of sources of pain that are considered to fall within normal limits. ■

Baumeister (1988a) proposes that independent and responsible selfhood becomes burdensome or stressful at times. Sexual masochism provides a temporary reprieve from the responsibilities of independent selfhood. It is a blunting of one's ordinary level of self-awareness that is achieved by "focusing on immediate sensations (both painful and pleasant) and on being a sexual object" (Baumeister, 1988a, p. 54).

Sexual masochism can range from relatively benign to potentially lethal practices, like **hypoxyphilia.** People who practice hypoxyphilia may place plastic bags over their heads or nooses around their necks during sexual acts to enhance their sexual arousal by being temporarily deprived of oxygen. Or they may apply pressure to their chests. Oxygen deprivation is usually accompanied by sexual fantasies of being strangled by a lover. People usually discontinue oxygen deprivation before they lose consciousness, but some miscalculations result in death by suffocation (Blanchard & Hucker, 1991; Cosgray et al., 1991).

Sexual Sadism

Sadism is named after the infamous Marquis de Sade (1774–1814), a Frenchman who wrote tales of becoming sexually aroused by inflicting pain or humiliation on others. The virtuous Justine, the heroine of his best-known novel of the same name, endures terrible suffering at the hands of fiendish men. She is at one time bound and spread-eagled so that bloodhounds can savage her. She then seeks refuge with a surgeon who tries to dismember her. Later she falls into the clutches of a saber-wielding mass murderer, but Nature saves her with a timely thunderbolt.

Sexual sadism is characterized by persistent, powerful urges and sexual fantasies involving the inflicting of pain and suffering on others to achieve sexual excitement or gratification. The urges are acted on or are disturbing enough to cause personal distress. Some sexual sadists cannot become sexually aroused unless they make their sex partners suffer. Others can become sexually excited without such acts.

Some sadists hurt or humiliate willing partners, such as prostitutes or sexual masochists. Others—clearly a small minority—stalk and attack nonconsenting victims.

Sadomasochism Sadomasochism (or *S&M*) involves *mutually gratifying sexual interactions* between *consenting partners.* Occasional S&M is quite common among the general population. Couples may incorporate mild or light forms of S&M in their love-making now and then, such as mild dominance and submission games or gentle physical restraint. It is also not uncommon for lovers to scratch or bite their partners to heighten their mutual arousal during coitus. They generally do not inflict severe pain or damage, however.

Twenty-two percent of the men and 12% of the women surveyed by Kinsey and his colleagues (1953) reported at least some sexual response to sadomasochistic stories. Although some milder forms of sadomasochism may fall within the boundaries of normal sexual variation, sadomasochism becomes pathological when such fantasies are acted upon

---

Hypoxyphilia
A practice in which a person seeks to enhance sexual arousal, usually during masturbation, by becoming deprived of oxygen. (From the Greek root meaning "under" [*hypo-*].)

Sadism
A paraphilia characterized by the desire or need to inflict pain or humiliation on others to enhance sexual arousal so that gratification is attained. (From the name of the author Marquis de Sade.)

Sadomasochism
A mutually gratifying sexual interaction between consenting sex partners in which sexual arousal is associated with the infliction and receipt of pain or humiliation. Commonly known as *S&M.*

S&M Paraphernalia. People who participate in S&M often incorporate handcuffs and other paraphernalia into their sadomasochistic encounters.

in ways that become destructive, dangerous, or distressing to oneself or others, as we find in the following case example:

> A 25-year-old female graduate student described a range of masochistic experiences. She reported feelings of sexual excitement during arguments with her husband when he would scream at her or hit her in a rage. She would sometimes taunt him to make love to her in a brutal fashion, as though she were being raped. She found the brutality and sense of being punished to be sexually stimulating. She had also begun having sex with strange men and enjoyed being physically punished by them during sex more than any other type of sexual stimulus. Being beaten or whipped produced the most intense sexual experiences she had ever had. Although she recognized the dangers posed by her sexual behavior, and felt somewhat ashamed about it, she was not sure that she wanted treatment for "it" because of the pleasure that it provided her.
>
> (Adapted from Spitzer et al., 1989, pp. 87–88)

In one subculture, sadomasochism is the preferred or even the exclusive form of sexual gratification. People in this subculture seek one another out through mutual contacts, S&M social organizations, or personal ads in S&M magazines. The S&M subculture has spawned magazines and clubs catering to people who describe themselves as "into S&M," as well as sex shops that sell sadomasochistic paraphernalia. These include leather restraints and leather face masks that resemble the ancient masks of executioners.

Truth **OR** *Fiction?*
R E V I S I T E D

It is true that there is a subculture in the United States in which sexual sadists and sexual masochists form liaisons to inflict and receive pain and humiliation during sexual activity. It is called the *S&M* subculture and is catered to by sex shops and magazines. ■

Participants in sadomasochism often engage in highly elaborate rituals involving dominance and submission. Rituals are staged, as if they were scenes in a play (Weinberg et al., 1984). In the "master and slave" game, the sadist leads the masochist around by a leash. The masochist performs degrading or menial acts. In "bondage and discipline" (B&D), the dominant partner restrains the submissive partner and flagellates (spanks or whips) or sexually stimulates the submissive partner. The erotic appeal of bondage seems connected with controlling or being controlled.

Various types of stimulation may be used to administer pain during S&M encounters, but pain is not always employed. When it is, it is usually mild or moderate. Psychological pain, or humiliation, may be as common as physical pain. Pain may also be used symbolically, as in the case of a sadist who uses a harmless, soft rubber paddle to spank the masochist. So the erotic appeal of pain for some S&M participants may derive from the ritual of control rather than from the pain itself (Weinberg, 1987).

Extreme forms of pain, such as torture or severe beatings, are rarely reported by sadomasochists (Breslow et al., 1985). Masochists may seek pain, but they usually avoid serious injury and dangerous partners (Baumeister, 1988b).

S&M participants may be heterosexual, gay, or bisexual (Breslow et al., 1986). They may assume either the masochistic or the sadistic role, or may alternate roles depending on the sexual script. Persons who seek sexual excitement by enacting both sadistic and masochistic roles are known as *sadomasochists*. In heterosexual relationships the partners may reverse traditional gender roles. The man may assume the submissive or masochistic role, and the woman may take the dominant or sadistic role (Reinisch, 1990).

A survey of S&M participants drawn from ads in S&M magazines found that about three out of four were male and about one in four female (Breslow et al., 1985). Most were married. Women respondents engaged in S&M more frequently and had a greater number of different partners than men. (Apparently a greater number of men than women seek partners for S&M.)

The causes of sexual masochism and sadism, as of other paraphilias, are unclear. Ford and Beach (1951) speculated that humans may possess a physiological capacity to experience heightened sexual arousal from the receipt or infliction of pain (which may explain the prevalence of love bites). Mild pain may heighten physiological arousal both in the aggressor and victim, adding to the effects of sexual stimulation. Yet intense pain is likely to decrease rather than increase sexual arousal.

Pain may also have more direct biological links to pleasure. Natural chemicals called *endorphins,* similar to opiates, are released in the brain in response to pain and produce feelings of euphoria and general well-being. Perhaps, then, pleasure is derived from pain due to the release or augmentation of endorphins (Weinberg, 1987). This theory fails to explain the erotic appeal of sadomasochistic encounters that involve minimal or symbolic pain, however. Nor does it explain the erotic appeal to the sadist of inflicting pain.

Whatever their causes, the roots of sexual masochism and sadism apparently date to childhood. Sadomasochistic behavior commonly begins in early adulthood, but sadomasochistic fantasies are likely to have been present during childhood (American Psychiatric Association, 1994; Breslow et al., 1986).

Frotteurism

Frotteurism
A paraphilia characterized by recurrent, powerful sexual urges and related fantasies involving rubbing against or touching a nonconsenting person. (From the French *frotter,* meaning "to rub.")

Toucherism
A practice related to frotteurism and characterized by the persistent urge to fondle nonconsenting strangers.

Frotteurism (also known as "mashing") is rubbing against or touching a nonconsenting person. As with other paraphilias, a diagnosis of frotteurism requires either acting upon these urges or being distressed by them. Mashing has been reported exclusively among males (Spitzer et al., 1989).

Most mashing takes place in crowded places, such as buses, subway cars, or elevators. The man finds the rubbing or the touching, not the coercive nature of the act, to be sexually stimulating. While rubbing against a woman, he may fantasize a consensual, affectionate sexual relationship with her. Typically the man incorporates images of his mashing within his masturbation fantasies. Mashing also incorporates a related practice, **toucherism:** fondling nonconsenting strangers.

Mashing may be so fleeting and furtive that the woman may not realize what has happened (Spitzer et al., 1989). Mashers thus stand little chance of being caught. Consider the case of a man who victimized a thousand or so women within a decade but was arrested only twice:

> Charles, 45, was seen by a psychiatrist following his second arrest for rubbing against a woman in the subway. He would select as his target a woman in her 20s as she entered the subway station. He would then position himself behind her on the platform and wait for the train to arrive. He would then follow her into the subway car and when the doors closed would begin bumping his penis against her buttocks, while fantasizing that they were enjoying having intercourse in a loving and consensual manner. About half of the time he would ejaculate into a plastic bag that he had wrapped around his penis to prevent staining his pants. He would then continue on his way to work. Sometimes when he hadn't ejaculated he would change trains and seek another victim. While he felt guilty for a time after each episode, he would soon become preoccupied with thoughts about his next encounter. He never gave any thought to the feelings his victims might have about what he had done to them. While he was married to the same woman for 25 years, he appears to be rather socially inept and unassertive, especially with women.
>
> (Adapted from Spitzer et al., 1989, pp. 106–107)

Although this masher was married, many have difficulties forming relationships with women and are handicapped by fears of rejection. Mashing provides sexual contact in a relatively nonthreatening context.

Other Paraphilias

Let us consider some other less common paraphilias.

Zoophilia
A paraphilia involving persistent or repeated sexual urges and related fantasies involving sexual contact with animals.

Zoophilia   A person with **zoophilia** experiences repeated, intense urges and related fantasies involving sexual contact with animals. As with other paraphilias, the urges may be acted upon or cause personal distress. A child or adolescent who shows some sexual response to an occasional episode of rough-and-tumble play with the family pet is thus not displaying zoophilia.

The term *bestiality* applies to actual sexual contact with an animal. Human sexual contact with animals, mythical and real, has a long history. Michelangelo's painting *Leda and the Swan* depicts the Greek god Zeus taking the form of a swan to mate with a woman,

Leda. Zeus was also portrayed as taking the form of a bull or serpent to mate with humans. In the Old Testament, God is said to have put to death people who had relations with animals. The Greek historian Herodotus notes that goats at the Egyptian temple at Mendes were trained to copulate with people.

Although the prevalence of zoophilia in the general population is unknown, Kinsey and his colleagues (1948, 1953) found that about 8% of the men and 3% to 4% of the women interviewed admitted to sexual contacts with animals. Men more often had sexual contact with farm animals, such as calves and sheep. Women more often reported sexual contacts with household pets. Men were more likely to masturbate or copulate with the animals. Women more often reported general body contact. People of both genders reported encouraging the animals to lick their genitals. A few women reported that they had trained a dog to engage in coitus with them. Urban–rural differences also emerged. Rates of bestiality were higher among boys reared on farms. Compared to only a few city boys, 17% of farm boys had reached orgasm at some time through sexual contact with dogs, cows, and goats. These contacts were generally restricted to adolescence, when human outlets were not available. Still, adults sometimes engage in sexual contacts with animals, generally because of curiosity, novelty, or for a sexual release when human partners are unavailable. Whether or not such contacts constitute zoophilia depends upon their frequency and intensity or whether they cause the person distress. In most cases true zoophilia is associated with deep-seated psychological problems and difficulties developing intimate relationships with people.

Necrophilia

A paraphilia characterized by desire for sexual activity with corpses. (From the Greek *nekros*, meaning "dead body.")

Necrophilia

In **necrophilia,** a rare paraphilia, a person desires sex with corpses. Three types of necrophilia have been identified (Rosman & Resnick, 1989). In *regular necrophilia,* the person has sex with a deceased person. In *necrophilic homicide,* the person commits murder to obtain a corpse for sexual purposes. In *necrophilic fantasy,* the person fantasizes about sex with a corpse but does not actually carry out necrophilic acts. Necrophiles often obtain jobs that provide them with access to corpses, such as working in cemeteries, morgues, or funeral homes. The primary motivation for necrophilia appears to be the desire to sexually possess a completely nonresistant and nonrejecting partner (Rosman & Resnick, 1989). Many necrophiles are clearly mentally disturbed.

Klismaphilia

A paraphilia in which sexual arousal is derived from use of enemas.

Coprophilia

A paraphilia in which sexual arousal is attained in connection with feces. (From the Greek *copros*, meaning "dung.")

Urophilia

A paraphilia in which sexual arousal is associated with urine.

Less Common Paraphilias

In **klismaphilia,** sexual arousal is derived from use of enemas. Klismaphiles generally prefer the receiving role to the giving role. Klismaphiles may have derived sexual pleasure in infancy or childhood from the anal stimulation provided by parents giving them enemas.

In **coprophilia,** sexual arousal is connected with feces. The person may desire to be defecated on or to defecate on a sex partner. The association of feces with sexual arousal may also be a throwback to childhood. Many children appear to obtain anal sexual pleasure by holding in and then purposefully expelling feces. It may also be that the incidental connection between erections or sexual arousal and soiled diapers during infancy eroticizes feces.

In **urophilia,** sexual arousal is associated with urine. As with coprophilia, the person may desire to be urinated upon or to urinate upon a sexual partner. Also like coprophilia, urophilia may have childhood origins. Stimulation of the urethral canal during urination may become associated with sexual pleasure. Or urine may have become eroticized by experiences in which erections occurred while the infant was clothed in a wet diaper.

~ Reflections ~

- Are the women on your campus who enjoy dressing in men's-style clothing to be considered transvestites? Why, or why not?
- Are lovers who are excited when their partners see their bodies to be considered exhibitionists? Why, or why not?
- Are lovers who become excited by seeing their partners undressing or in the nude to be considered voyeurs? Why, or why not?

A CLOSER LOOK

PARAPHILIAS AS SEXUAL ADDICTIONS

In his book *The Sexual Addiction* (1983), Patrick Carnes suggests that some people with paraphilias suffer from a sexual addiction, a nonchemical form of addiction. Sexual addicts ("sexaholics") may feel unable to resist their sexual urges and may act upon them indiscriminately, remaining oblivious to resultant harm or damage they cause. Carnes argues that sexual addicts use sex in much the same way that drug addicts and alcoholics use drugs or alcohol: to alter their moods and temporarily relieve psychological states of discomfort, such as depression or anxiety. In the end, however, the destructive nature of the paraphilia reinforces feelings of shame and worthlessness.

Carnes identifies a four-step cycle through which sexual addictions progress and gather strength. Let us apply this model to exhibitionism:

1. *Preoccupation.* The person enters a trancelike state characterized by a preoccupation with thoughts about exposing himself, leading to a strong craving to commit the act.
2. *Ritualization.* The person begins to act upon the exhibitionistic urge. He engages in rituals that precede the act in order to increase his level of sexual arousal, such as driving a route through a park frequented by women walking alone.
3. *Compulsive sexual behavior.* The person exposes himself, while feeling that he cannot control or prevent the act.
4. *Despair.* Whereas most people feel pleasure and a release from sexual tension following sex, the exhibitionist sinks into feelings of hopelessness and despair over his inability to control his exhibitionistic urges. Such feelings may be temporarily offset by recurrent preoccupation with the paraphilia, leading to the completion of a new cycle. But the completion of each cycle provides further confirmation of personal unworthiness.

The concept of sexual addiction may not apply to all paraphilias or all people with paraphilias. Fetishists and transvestites, for example, may feel in control of their sexual urges, not controlled by them. They may not become preoccupied with paraphilic thoughts and fantasies or experience irresistible cravings to perform paraphilic acts.

The view of paraphilias as addictions has met with controversy within the scientific community. Some authorities believe that paraphilias are forms of sexual compulsion, which are more akin to compulsive behaviors such as compulsive hand-washing or compulsive gambling than to chemical addictions (Coleman, 1986; Goldberg, 1987). Other treatment for paraphilias has been modeled after approaches to chemical addictions and alcoholism, such as Alcoholics Anonymous (AA), in which people are encouraged to confront their addictions and learn to cope with their urges. Groups such as Sexaholics Anonymous (SA) and Sex and Love Addicts Anonymous (SLAA), have been formed.

Theoretical Perspectives

The paraphilias are among the most fascinating and perplexing variations in sexual behavior. We may find it difficult to understand how people can become sexually excited by fondling an article of clothing or by cross-dressing. It may also be difficult to identify with people who feel compelled to exhibit their genitals or to rub their genitals against unsuspecting victims in crowded places. Perhaps we can recognize some voyeuristic tendencies in ourselves, but we cannot imagine peeping through binoculars while perched in a nearby tree or, for that matter, risking the social and legal consequences of being discovered in the act. Nor might we understand how people can become sexually turned on by inflicting or receiving pain.

Let us consider explanations that have been advanced from the major theoretical perspectives.

Biological Perspectives

Little is known about whether there are biological factors in paraphilic behavior. Efforts to date to find concrete evidence of brain damage or abnormalities among people with para-

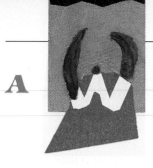

NYMPHOMANIA, SATYRIASIS, AND THE SEXUAL DOUBLE STANDARD

Sarah R., a never-married, 39-year-old artist became sexually active in her junior year in high school and has rarely been without at least one or two lovers ever since. Whenever she has not had an opportunity for sexual intercourse for several weeks or longer, for one reason or another, she has felt quite uncomfortable, or as she put it, "horny and hard-up." She has had two unwanted pregnancies, both of which resulted in abortions, and has contracted gonorrhea on three separate occasions and has suffered several times from infestations of pubic lice. She continues to be troubled with recurrent episodes of genital herpes. She generally limits her sexual relationships to one or two partners, but has on occasion maintained sexual relationships at the same time with three or four men. She engages in sexual intercourse two or three times a week, on the average, and engages in masturbation to relieve her sexual urges when intercourse is not possible.

Both her family practitioner and gynecologist, who have treated her for years, consider her to be a nymphomaniac. Her gynecologist says of her, "Of course she has herpes. What can you expect with the kind of sexual excesses she indulges in? She's a real nympho."

(Goldberg, 1987, p. 204)

Would you have reached the same conclusion as Sarah's physicians did? Why, or why not? What criteria would you use to define **nymphomania**? Perhaps most readers have heard of nymphomania, but only a few are likely to be acquainted with the term describing the same condition in men, **satyriasis. Don Juanism** is another term for the condition.

The fact that nymphomania is more commonly used in our society than the male counterpart underscores the traditional double standard in Western society (Groneman, 1994).

What Is Hypersexuality? Can one really be "oversexed"? Where are the boundaries between a "healthy sexual appetite" and hypersexuality? Why are people usually more familiar with the term *nymphomania* than its male counterpart, *satyriasis*? How do cultural stereotypes affect our perceptions of these behavior patterns?

Greater sexual liberties are accorded to men than women. A man who has a number of flings is likely to be labeled a "playboy," a "Casanova," or even a "stud." A woman who does so is likely to be branded with labels that carry negative connotations, such as "nympho," "slut," or "whore."

Clinicians prefer to use the term **hypersexuality** to refer to nymphomania in women and satyriasis in men, thereby avoiding disparaging connotations. No absolute criteria exist for determining hypersexuality or establishing the boundary between normal sexuality and hypersexuality, however. Some people might consider a person who requires a sexual release through masturbation or coitus more than once daily to be hypersexual. Others draw the line at two, three, or perhaps six or ten or more times daily. Among some couples, the partner desiring less frequent sexual activity may label the other as "oversexed." But what defines "oversexed" in one rela-tionship may be considered normal, or subnormal, in another.

Clinicians may weigh the compulsive or self-defeating nature of the behavior in determining the boundaries of hypersexuality, not the sheer frequency of sexual activity. Hypersexual people may use sex as a means of buttressing a flagging sense of self-esteem. They may feel driven to a series of sexual conquests or brief encounters to reassure themselves that they are desirable, or masculine or feminine enough. Because they lack true intimacy, however, the encounters leave them feeling empty and sexually unfulfilled. Such relationships provide only a temporary salve for feelings of self-doubt or unworthiness. The person quickly loses sexual interest in the new partner once the conquest or brief encounter has occurred and begins searching for another. Partners are treated like objects to be used and discarded.

Return to Sarah. Do the facts of her case suggest hypersexuality? Did Sarah feel a lack of control over her sexual urges? Did she feel compelled to engage in sexual behaviors that put herself at risk of incurring unwanted pregnancies or sexually transmitted diseases?

Goldberg (1987) argues that Sarah's physicians labeled her as a nymphomaniac because her behavior did not meet social expectations of female sexuality. Goldberg (1987) comments, "In all likelihood, a 39-year-old man living the sort of life that Sarah is living would not be regarded as suffering from satyriasis or, indeed, as being sexually abnormal in any way" (p. 204). Does the label of nymphomania represent a sexist tendency to judge women and men by different sets of social standards?

Nymphomania

An excessive, insatiable sexual appetite or drive in women. (From the Greek roots *nymphe*, meaning "a bride," and *mania*, which means "madness.")

Satyriasis

An excessive, insatiable sexual appetite or drive in men. (After *satyr*, a sexually insatiable, goat-legged creature with pointed ears and short horns in Greek mythology. Satyrs were part man, part beast.)

Don Juanism

An excessive, insatiable sexual appetite or drive in men. (After the fictional Spanish nobleman who was unable to obtain true sexual gratification despite numerous affairs.)

Hypersexuality

An excessive or apparently insatiable sex drive that disrupts the person's ability to concentrate on other needs or leads to self-defeating behavior, such as indiscriminate sexual contacts.

philias have failed (Langevin et al., 1989). Because testosterone is linked to sex drive, researchers have also focused on differences in testosterone levels between people with paraphilias and people without them. A recent study found evidence of some hormonal differences between a group of 16 male exhibitionists and controls (Lang et al., 1989). Although no differences in overall levels of testosterone were found, researchers reported that the exhibitionists evidenced significantly elevated levels of the measure of testosterone believed to be most closely linked to sex drive. This difference suggests that exhibitionists may have biologically elevated sex drives. The significance of the finding is limited by the fact that hormone levels among many of the people with paraphilias studied fell within the normal range.

Psychoanalytic Perspectives

Classical psychoanalytic theory suggests that paraphilias are psychological defenses, usually against unresolved castration anxiety dating back to the Oedipus complex (Fenichel, 1945). To the transvestic man, the sight of a woman's vagina threatens to arouse castration anxiety. It reminds him that women do not have penises and that he might suffer the same fate. Sequestering his penis beneath women's clothing symbolically asserts that women do have penises, which provides unconscious reassurance against his own fears of castration.

By exposing his genitals, the exhibitionist unconsciously seeks reassurance that his penis is secure. It is as if he were asserting, "Look! I have a penis!" Shock or surprise on the victim's face acknowledges that his penis still exists, temporarily relieving unconscious castration anxiety.

Masturbation with a fetishistic object (a shoe, for example) allows the fetishist to gratify his sexual desires while keeping a safe distance from the fantasized dangers that he unconsciously associates with sexual contact with women. Or the fetishistic object itself—the shoe—may unconsciously symbolize the penis. Stroking a woman's shoe during sexual relations, or fantasizing about one, may unconsciously provide reassurance that the man's own penis, symbolically represented by the fetishistic object, is secure.

In one psychoanalytic view of voyeurism, the man is unconsciously denying castration by searching for a penis among women victims. Other psychoanalytic views suggest that the voyeur is identifying with the man in the observed couple as he had identified with his own father during childhood observations of the parental coitus—the so-called *primal scene*. Perhaps he is trying to "master" the primal scene by compulsively reliving it.

Psychoanalytic explanations of sadism suggest that sadists are attempting to defend themselves against unconscious feelings of impotence and powerlessness by inflicting pain on others. The recipients' shouts of pain or confessions of unworthiness make sadists feel masculine and powerful.

Psychoanalytic theory suggests that masochism in the male may be the turning inward of aggressive impulses originally aimed toward the powerful, threatening father. The flagellation or bondage may also be unconsciously preferred to castration as a form of punishment for having unacceptable sexual feelings. Like the child who experiences relief when punishment is over, the sexual masochist willingly accepts immediate punishment in the form of flagellation or bondage in place of the future punishment of castration. Or a woman who witnessed her parents having coitus at an early age may have misperceived the father to be assaulting the mother. Her masochism then represents her unconscious reliving of her mother's (imagined) role with her father. Sexual masochists of either gender may also have such high levels of sex guilt that they can permit themselves to experience sexual pleasure only if they are adequately punished for it during sex.

The paraphilias have provided a fertile ground for psychoanalytic theories. There is a lack of evidence to support the role of such unconscious processes as unresolved castration anxiety, however. The basic shortcoming of psychoanalytic theory is that many of its key concepts involve unconscious mechanisms that cannot be directly observed or measured. So psychoanalytic theories remain interesting but speculative hypotheses about the origins of these unusual sexual behavior patterns.

Learning Perspectives

Learning theorists believe that fetishes and other paraphilias are learned behaviors that are acquired through experience. An object may acquire sexually arousing properties through association with sexual arousal or orgasm. Early proponents of the learning theory viewpoint were Alfred Kinsey and his colleagues, who wrote in *Sexual Behavior in the Human Female* (1953):

> Even some of the most extremely variant types of human sexual behavior may need no more explanation than is provided by our understanding of the processes of learning and conditioning. Behavior which may appear bizarre, perverse, or unthinkably unacceptable to some persons, and even to most persons, may have significance for other individuals because of the way in which they have been conditioned. (pp. 645–646)

Like Pavlov's dogs, who learned to salivate to the ringing of a bell that had been repeatedly paired with food, "an animal may become conditioned to respond not only to particular stimuli, but to objects and other phenomena which were associated with the original experience. . . . In the laboratory, male animals may respond to particular dishes, to particular boards, or to particular pieces of furniture with which some female has had contact" (Kinsey et al., 1953, p. 647).

According to the conditioning model, a boy who catches a glimpse of his mother's stockings hanging on the towel rack while he is masturbating may go on to develop a fetish for stockings (Breslow, 1989). Orgasm in the presence of the object would reinforce the erotic connection, especially if the experience occurs repeatedly.

In an early experimental test of the conditioning model, Rachman (1966) showed normal (nonfetishistic) males slides of nude women interspersed with slides of women's boots. After numerous repetitions, the men showed a sexual response to the boots alone. This "fetish" was weak and short-lived, however. It could still be argued that more persistent fetishes might be learned if pairings of such stimuli were to occur repeatedly during childhood. If fetishes were mechanically acquired by association, however, we might expect fetishists to be more attracted to objects that are inadvertently (and often repeatedly) associated with sexual activity, such as pillows, bedsheets, and even ceilings (Breslow, 1989). Yet we do not find this to be the case. The *meaning* of the object also seems to play a role.

Along these lines, Breslow (1989) proposed a learning theory explanation that describes the development of paraphilias in terms of the gradual acquisition of sexual arousal to an unusual object or activity through its incorporation in masturbatory fantasies. A transvestite, for example, may have achieved an erection while trying on his mother's panties in childhood. The paraphilic object or activity is then incorporated within masturbatory fantasies and is reinforced by orgasm. The paraphilic object or activity is then repeatedly used as a masturbatory aid, further strengthening the erotic bond.

We can also consider a role for parental approval as a reinforcing agent in the early development of transvestism. Parents who really wanted to have a girl have been known to occasionally dress their little boys in girls' clothing. The reinforcement of parental approval for cross-dressing may lead the boy to experiment with cross-dressing himself, which may then become eroticized if it is combined with masturbation or sexual fantasies and reinforced by sexual arousal or orgasm.

Fetishistic interests can often be traced to early childhood. Some rubber fetishists, for example, recall erotic interests in rubber objects since early childhood. Reinisch (1990) speculates that for some rubber fetishists, the earliest awareness of sexual arousal or response (such as erection) may have been associated with the presence of rubber pants, diapers, and so forth, such that a connection was formed between the two. Or perhaps the sexual attraction to objects associated with infancy may derive from their association with feelings of being completely loved and cared for. The fetishistic act may represent an attempt to recapture sexual or loving feelings from early childhood.

McGuire and his colleagues (1965) report a case that provides some support for the role of learning in the development of exhibitionism. Two young males were surprised by an attractive woman while urinating. Although embarrassed at the time, their memories of the incident were sexually stimulating, and they masturbated repeatedly while fantasizing about it. The fantasies persisted, possibly reinforced by frequent orgasms. After a while, the young men purposely began to expose themselves to rekindle the high level of sexual excitement. Still, we should caution that only a very small percentage of men who have accidentally been discovered exposed have become exhibitionists.

Friedrich & Gerber (1994) studied five adolescent boys who practiced hypoxyphilia and found extensive early histories of choking in combination with physical or sexual abuse. The combination seems to have encouraged each of the boys to associate choking with sexual arousal.

Blair and Lanyon (1981) suggest that modeling plays a role in some cases. Parents may inadvertently model exhibitionistic behavior to young sons, which can lead the sons to eroticize the act of exposing themselves.

Learning explanations of sexual masochism focus on the pairing of sexual excitement with punishment. For example, a child may be punished when discovered masturbating. Or a boy may reflexively experience an erection if his penis accidentally rubs against the parent's body as he is being spanked. With repeated encounters like these, pain and pleasure may become linked in the person's sexual arousal system. Another learning explanation focuses on the association of pain with parental affection (Breslow, 1989; Sue et al., 1981). A child with cold and indifferent parents may be hugged only following a spanking. The pain or humiliation associated with the spanking becomes associated with the affection of the hug, which leads in later life to pain becoming a prerequisite for sexual pleasure. Yet these learning approaches fail to account for how sexual masochism develops within a larger and more complex sadomasochistic lifestyle (Breslow, 1989).

Learning theories of the origins of paraphilias also fail to consider the predisposing factors that may explain why some people who are exposed to early conditioning experiences develop paraphilic interests and others do not. Such factors may include poor self-esteem and difficulties forming intimate relationships. Many exhibitionists, voyeurs, frotteurs, and other people with paraphilias have few interpersonal skills in relating to women. They may avoid customary social interactions with women for fear of rejection. Their furtive, paraphilic behaviors may provide a sexual release with minimal risks of rejection or apprehension and be maintained because they represent the only available source of sexual gratification or reinforcement. Some paraphilias, such as voyeurism, exhibitionism, and frotteurism, may also be conceptualized as *courtship disorders,* involving an exaggeration or distortion of the steps normally taken during courtship in identifying, approaching, and becoming more intimate with new sexual partners (Freund & Blanchard, 1986).

Sociological Perspectives

Most people indulge paraphilias privately. Sexual masochists and sadists require a partner, however, save for the few masochists who practice only autoerotic forms of masochism and the few sadists who stalk nonconsenting partners. Most sadomasochists also relate in one way or another to the sadomasochistic subculture. It is within the S&M subculture—the loosely connected network of S&M clubs, specialty shops, organizations, magazines, and so on—that S&M rituals are learned, sexual contacts are made, sadomasochistic identities are confirmed, and sexual paraphernalia is acquired. But the S&M subculture exists in the context of the larger society, and the rituals it invents mirror the social and gender roles that exist in the larger society.

Martin Weinberg (1987) proposes a sociological model that focuses on the social context of sadomasochism. Weinberg notes that S&M rituals generally involve some form of dominance and submission and attributes their erotic appeal to the opportunity to reverse the customary power relationships that exist between the genders and social classes in society at large. Within the confines of the carefully scripted S&M encounter, the meek can be powerful and the powerful meek (Geer et al., 1984). People from lower social classes or in menial jobs may be drawn to S&M by the opportunities it affords to enact a dominant role. They may have the opportunity to bark orders and commands that are followed unquestioningly. Those who customarily hold high-status positions that require them to be in control and responsible may be attracted by the opportunity to surrender control to another person. Dominance and submission games also allow opportunities to accentuate or reverse the gender stereotypes that identify masculinity with dominance and femininity with submissiveness.

Individual sadomasochistic interests may become institutionalized as an S&M subculture in societies (like ours) that have certain social characteristics: (1) dominance–submission relationships are embedded within the culture, and aggression is socially valued; (2) there is an unequal distribution of power between people from different gender or social class categories; (3) there are enough affluent people to enable them to participate in such leisure-time activities; and (4) imagination and creativity, important elements in the development of S&M scripts and fantasies, are socially valued and encouraged (Weinberg, 1987).

An Integrated Perspective: The "Lovemap"

Like other sexual patterns, the paraphilias may have multiple biological, psychological, and sociocultural origins (Money, 1994). Our understanding of them may thus be best approached from a theoretical framework that incorporates multiple perspectives, as found in the work of John Money and his colleagues.

Money and Lamacz (1989) trace the origins of paraphilias to childhood. They believe that childhood experiences etch a pattern in the brain, called a **lovemap,** that determines the types of stimuli and activities that become sexually arousing to the individual. In the case of paraphilias, these lovemaps become distorted or "vandalized" by early traumatic experiences, such as incest, overbearing antisexual upbringings, and physical abuse or neglect.

Research suggests that voyeurs and exhibitionists often were the victims of childhood sexual abuse (Dwyer, 1988). Not all children exposed to such influences develop paraphilic compulsions, however. For reasons that remain unknown, some children exposed to such influences appear to be more vulnerable to developing distorted lovemaps than are others. A genetic predisposition, hormonal factors, brain abnormalities, or a combination of these and other factors may play a role in determining one's vulnerability to vandalized lovemaps (Brody, 1990a).

Lovemap
A representation in the mind and in the brain of the idealized lover and the idealized erotic activity with the lover.

～ *Reflections* ～

- Psychoanalytic theories of paraphilias have been quite popular over the years. How would you account for their popularity?
- Agree or disagree with the following statement, and support your answer: Paraphilias are caused by early learning experiences.
- Agree or disagree with the following statement, and support your answer: Despite the amount of theorizing and research that has gone into the paraphilias, we know very little about their origins.

Treatment of the Paraphilias

The treatment of these atypical patterns of sexual behavior raises a number of issues. First, people with paraphilias usually do not want or seek treatment, at least not voluntarily. They often deny that they are offenders, even after they are apprehended and convicted. They are generally seen by mental health workers only when they come into conflict with the law or at the urging of their family members or sexual partners who have discovered them performing the paraphilic behavior or found evidence of their paraphilic interests.

Paraphilic behavior is a source of pleasure, so many people are not motivated to give it up. The individual typically perceives his problems as stemming from society's intolerance, not from feelings of guilt or shame.

Second, helping professionals may encounter ethical problems when they are asked to contribute to a judicial process by trying to persuade a sex offender that he (virtually all are male) *ought* to change his behavior. Helping professionals traditionally help clients clarify or meet their own goals; it is not their role to impose societal goals on the individ-

Psychotherapy and the Paraphilias. Favorable case results have been reported but there is still a great deal of experimental research that needs to be done to evaluate this kind of treatment for paraphilias.

ual. Many helping professionals believe that the criminal justice system, and not they, ought to enforce social standards.

The third issue is a treatment problem. Therapists realize that they are generally less successful with resistant or recalcitrant clients. Unless the motivation to change is present, therapeutic efforts may be wasted.

The fourth problem is the issue of perceived responsibility. Sex offenders almost invariably claim that they are unable to control their urges and impulses. Such claims of uncontrollability are often self-serving and may lead others to treat offenders with greater sympathy and understanding. Most therapies, however, are based on the belief that whatever causes may have led to the problem behavior, and however difficult it may be to resist these unusual sexual urges, accepting personal responsibility for one's actions is a prelude to change. Thus, if therapy is to be constructive, it is necessary to break through the client's personal mythology that he is powerless to control his behavior.

Despite these issues, many offenders are referred for treatment by the courts. A few seek therapy themselves because they have come to see how their behavior harms themselves or others. Let us consider some of the ways in which therapists treat people with these atypical sexual behavior patterns.

Psychotherapy

Psychoanalysis focuses on resolving the unconscious conflicts that are believed to originate in childhood and to give rise in adulthood to pathological problems such as paraphilias. The aim of therapy is to help bring unconscious conflicts, principally Oedipal conflicts, into conscious awareness so that they might be worked through in the light of the individual's adult personality.

Although some favorable case results have been reported (e.g., Rosen, 1967), psychoanalytic therapy of the paraphilias has not been subjected to experimental analysis. We thus do not know whether successes are due to the psychoanalytic treatment itself or to other factors, such as spontaneous improvement or a client's willingness to change.

Behavior Therapy

Behavior therapy

The systematic application of the principles of learning to help people modify problem behavior.

Whereas traditional psychoanalysis tends to entail a lengthy process of exploration of the childhood origins of problem behaviors, **behavior therapy** is relatively briefer and focuses directly on changing behavior. Behavior therapy has spawned a number of techniques to help eliminate paraphilic behaviors and strengthen appropriate sexual behaviors. These techniques include systematic desensitization, aversion therapy, social skills training, covert sensitization, and orgasmic reconditioning, to name a few.

Systematic desensitization

A method for terminating the connection between a stimulus (such as a fetishistic object) and an inappropriate response (such as sexual arousal to the paraphilic stimulus). Muscle relaxation is practiced in connection with each stimulus in a series of increasingly arousing stimuli, so that the person learns to remain relaxed (and not sexually aroused) in their presence.

Systematic desensitization attempts to break the link between the sexual stimulus (such as a fetishistic stimulus) and the inappropriate response (sexual arousal). The client is first taught to relax selected muscle groups in the body. Muscle relaxation is then paired repeatedly with each of a series of progressively more arousing paraphilic images or fantasies. Relaxation comes to replace sexual arousal in response to each of these stimuli, even the most provocative. In one case study, a fetishistic transvestite who had become attracted to his mother's lingerie at age 13 was taught to relax when presented with audiotaped scenes representing transvestite or fetishistic themes (Fensterheim & Kantor, 1980). He played such tapes daily while remaining relaxed. He later reported a complete absence of transvestite thoughts or activities.

In **aversion therapy**, the undesirable sexual behavior (for example, masturbation to fetishistic fantasies) is paired repeatedly with an aversive stimulus (such as a harmless but painful electric shock or a nausea-inducing chemical) in the hope that the client will develop a conditioned aversion toward the paraphilic behavior.

Covert sensitization is a variation of aversion therapy in which paraphilic fantasies are paired with an aversive stimulus in imagination. In a broad-scale application, 38 **pedophiles** and 62 exhibitionists, more than half of whom were court referred, were treated

Aversion therapy
A method for terminating undesirable sexual behavior in which the behavior is repeatedly paired with an aversive stimulus, such as electric shock, so that a conditioned aversion develops.

Covert sensitization
A form of aversion therapy in which thoughts of engaging in undesirable behavior are paired repeatedly with imagined aversive stimuli.

Pedophiles
Persons with pedophilia, a paraphilia involving sexual interest in children.

Social skills training
Behavior therapy methods for building social skills that rely on a therapist's coaching and practice.

Orgasmic reconditioning
A method for strengthening the connection between sexual arousal and appropriate sexual stimuli (such as fantasies about an adult of the other gender) by repeatedly pairing the desired stimuli with orgasm.

by pairing imagined aversive odors with fantasies of the problem behavior (Maletzky, 1980). Clients were instructed to fantasize pedophiliac or exhibitionistic scenes. Then,

> at a point . . . when sexual pleasure is aroused, aversive images are presented. . . . Examples might include a pedophiliac fellating a child, but discovering a festering sore on the boy's penis; an exhibitionist exposing to a woman but suddenly being discovered by his wife or the police; or a pedophiliac laying a young boy down in a field, only to lie next to him in a pile of dog feces.
>
> (Maletzky, 1980, p. 308)

Maletzky used this treatment weekly for six months, then followed it with "booster sessions" every three months over a three-year period. The procedure resulted in at least a 75% reduction of the deviant activities and fantasies for over 80% of the study participants at follow-up periods of up to 36 months.

Social skills training focuses on helping the individual improve his ability to relate to the other gender. The therapist might first model a desired behavior, such as how to ask a woman out on a date or how to handle a rejection. The client might then role play the behavior, with the therapist playing the part of the woman. Following the role-play enactment, the therapist would provide feedback and additional guidance and modeling to help the client improve his skills. This process would be repeated until the client mastered the skill.

Orgasmic reconditioning aims to increase sexual arousal to socially appropriate sexual stimuli by pairing culturally appropriate imagery with orgasmic pleasure. The person is instructed to become sexually aroused by masturbating to paraphilic images or fantasies. But as he approaches the point of orgasm, he switches to appropriate imagery and focuses on it during orgasm. In a case example, Davison (1977) reports reduction of sadistic fantasies in a 21-year-old college man. The client was instructed to attain an erection in any way he could, even through the use of the sadistic fantasies he wished to eliminate. But once erection was achieved, he was to masturbate while looking at photos of *Playboy* models. Orgasm was thus paired with nonsadistic images. These images and fantasies eventually acquire the capacity to elicit sexual arousal. Orgasmic reconditioning is often combined with other techniques, such as social skills training, so that more desirable social behaviors can be strengthened as well (Adams et al., 1981).

Although behavior therapy techniques tend to have higher reported success rates than most other methods, they too are limited by reliance on uncontrolled case studies. Without appropriate controls we cannot isolate the effective elements of therapy or determine that the results were not due merely to the passage of time or other factors unrelated to the treatment. It is possible that clients who are highly motivated to change may succeed in doing so with any systematic approach.

Biochemical Approaches

There is no biological "cure" for the paraphilias. No drug or surgical technique eliminates paraphilic urges and behavior. Yet some progress has recently been reported in using a popular antidepressant, Prozac (fluoxetine hydrochloride), in treating exhibitionism, voyeurism, and fetishism (Emmanuel et al., 1992; Lorefice, 1991; Miller, 1995). Why Prozac? In addition to treating depression, Prozac has been helpful in treating obsessive–compulsive disorder, a type of emotional disorder involving recurrent obsessions (intrusive ideas) and/or compulsions (urges to repeat a certain behavior or thought). Researchers speculate that paraphilias may be linked to obsessive–compulsive disorder (Kruesi et al., 1992). People with paraphilias often experience intrusive, repetitive thoughts or images of the paraphilic object or stimulus, such as mental images of young children. Many also report feeling compelled to repeatedly carry out the paraphilic acts. Paraphilias may belong to what researchers have dubbed an obsessive–compulsive spectrum of behaviors (Kruesi et al., 1992).

People who experience such intense urges that they are at risk of committing sexual offenses may be helped by **antiandrogen drugs,** which reduce the level of testosterone in

Antiandrogen drug
A chemical substance that reduces the sex drive by lowering the level of testosterone in the bloodstream.

the bloodstream (Marshall et al., 1991). Testosterone is closely linked to sex drive and interest. *Medroxyprogesterone acetate* (MPA) (trade name: Depo-Provera), which is administered in weekly injections, is the antiandrogen that has been used most extensively in the treatment of sex offenders. In men, antiandrogens reduce testosterone to a level that is typical of a prepubertal boy (Money, 1987b). They consequently reduce sexual desire and the frequencies of erections and ejaculations (Cooper, 1986; Money, 1987b).

Depo-Provera suppresses the sexual appetite in men. It can lower the intensity of sex drive and erotic fantasies and urges so that the man may feel less compelled to act upon them (Berlin, 1989). Antiandrogens do not, however, eliminate paraphilic urges or behavior. As an analogy, consider the relationship between the accelerator pedal and the steering wheel of a car. The accelerator pedal controls the car's speed but not its direction. In much the same way, releasing pressure on the accelerator pedal slows the car, the use of antiandrogens reduces the intensity of sex drives and desires. The types of stimuli that have erotic value are not affected by antiandrogens, however, any more than easing up on the accelerator alters the direction of a car.

The use of antiandrogens is sometimes incorrectly referred to as *chemical castration.* Surgical castration, the surgical removal of the testes, has sometimes been performed on convicted rapists and violent sex offenders (see Chapter 19). Actual castration eliminates testicular sources of testosterone. Antiandrogens suppress, but do not eliminate, testicular production of testosterone. Also, unlike surgical castration, the effects of antiandrogens can be reversed when the treatment is terminated.

Evidence suggests that antiandrogens may be helpful to some people when they are used in conjunction with psychological treatment (Marshall et al., 1991; Murray, 1988). The value of antiandrogens has been limited by high refusal and dropout rates, however (Marshall et al., 1991). Questions also remain concerning side effects (Money, 1987b).

～ *Reflections* ～

▪ What problems do therapists come across when they seek to "treat" people with paraphilias?
▪ What are the limitations in using antiandrogen drugs to treat people with paraphilias?
▪ Do you have any thoughts on why nearly all people with paraphilias are males?

Although we have amassed a great deal of research on atypical variations in sexual behavior, our understanding of them and our treatment approaches to them remain largely in their infancy.

Summing Up

Normal Versus Deviant Sexual Behavior

What is considered normal in one culture or at a particular time may be considered abnormal in other cultures and at other times. Atypical patterns of sexual arousal or behavior that become problematic in the eyes of the individual or society are labeled *paraphilias.*

The Paraphilias

Paraphilias involve sexual arousal in response to unusual stimuli such as children or other nonconsenting persons, certain objects, or pain or humiliation. The psychiatric diagnosis of paraphilia requires that the person has acted on these persistent urges or is distinctly distressed by them. Except in the case of sexual masochism, paraphilias are believed to occur almost exclusively among men.

Fetishism   In fetishism, an inanimate object comes to elicit sexual arousal. In partialism, people are inordinately aroused by a particular body part, such as the feet.

Transvestism   Whereas other fetishists become sexually aroused by handling the fetishistic object while they masturbate, transvestites become excited by wearing articles of clothing—the fetishistic objects—of the other gender.

Exhibitionism An exhibitionist experiences the compulsion to expose himself to strangers. The typical exhibitionist does not attempt further sexual contact with the victim and so does not usually pose a physical threat.

Obscene Telephone Calling The obscene phone caller is motivated to become sexually aroused by shocking his victim. Such callers typically masturbate during the phone call or shortly afterwards.

Voyeurism Voyeurs become sexually aroused by watching and do not seek sexual relations with the target. The voyeur may masturbate while "peeping" or afterward, while engaging in voyeuristic fantasies. Like exhibitionists, voyeurs tend to harbor feelings of inadequacy and poor self-esteem and to lack social and sexual skills.

Sexual Masochism Sexual masochists associate the receipt of pain or humiliation with sexual arousal. Sexual masochists and sexual sadists may form liaisons to meet each other's needs.

Sexual Sadism Sexual sadism is characterized by persistent, powerful urges and sexual fantasies involving the inflicting of pain and suffering on others to achieve sexual excitement or gratification. Sadomasochists enjoy playing both sadistic and masochistic roles.

Frotteurism Most frotteuristic acts—rubbing against nonconsenting persons—take place in crowded places, such as buses, subway cars, or elevators.

Other Paraphilias Zoophiles desire to have sexual contact with animals. Necrophiles desire to have sexual contact with dead bodies.

Theoretical Perspectives

Biological Perspectives The links between paraphilias and biological factors have yet to be fully explored in research.

Psychoanalytic Perspectives Classical psychoanalytic theory suggests that paraphilias in males are psychological defenses against castration anxiety.

Learning Perspectives Some learning theorists have argued that unusual stimuli may acquire sexually arousing properties through association with sexual arousal or orgasm. Another possibility is that unusual stimuli gradually acquire sexually arousing properties through incorporation in masturbatory fantasies.

Sociological Perspectives According to Weinberg's sociological model, the erotic appeal of S&M rituals may result from the opportunity to reverse the customary power relationships that exist between different gender and social class categories in society at large.

An Integrated Perspective: The "Lovemap" Money and Lamacz suggest that childhood experiences etch a pattern in the brain—a lovemap—that determines the types of stimuli and activities that become sexually arousing. In the case of paraphilias, these lovemaps become distorted by early traumatic experiences.

Treatment of the Paraphilias

People with paraphilias may be motivated to seek help because of fears of exposure, criminal prosecution, or humiliation, but they seldom desire to surrender their sexual preferences.

Psychotherapy Psychoanalysis aims to bring unconscious Oedipal conflicts into awareness so that they can be worked through in adulthood.

Behavior Therapy Behavior therapy attempts to eliminate paraphilic behaviors through techniques such as systematic desensitization, aversion therapy, social skills training, covert sensitization, and orgasmic reconditioning.

Biochemical Approaches The antidepressant Prozac has shown some promise in treating paraphilias. By reducing sex drives, antiandrogen drugs may help people who have difficulty combating paraphilic urges. They may be most helpful when used in conjunction with psychological treatment.

CHAPTER 19

Henri Matisse, *Cowboy,* Plate 14 from *Jazz.* The Metropolitan Museum of Art,
Gift of Lila Acheson Wallace, 1983. © 1996 Succession H. Matisse/Artist Rights
Society (ARS), New York. © 1985 by The Metropolitan Museum of Art.

Sexual Coercion

Outline

Truth OR Fiction?

_____ A woman is raped every five minutes in the United States.

_____ The prevalence of rape is 20 times greater in the United States than in Japan.

_____ The majority of rapes are committed by strangers in deserted neighborhoods or darkened alleyways.

_____ Men who rape other men are gay.

_____ A healthy woman can resist a rapist if she really wants to.

_____ Most rapists are mentally ill.

_____ Women who encounter a rapist should attempt to fight him off.

_____ Father–daughter incest is the most common type of incest.

n recent years the airwaves have been flooded with allegations of sexual assault and sexual harassment involving celebrities, highly placed politicians, and members of the armed services. In late 1991 and early 1992, media sharks went on a feeding frenzy in covering the rape trials of William Kennedy Smith and Mike Tyson, and the Senate confirmation hearings of Supreme Court nominee Clarence Thomas, who faced charges of sexual harassment leveled by a former assistant, law professor Anita Hill.

The Senate hearings failed to determine the truthfulness of the allegations against Clarence Thomas. William Kennedy Smith, a nephew of Senator Edward Kennedy, was acquitted of the rape charges brought against him, but former heavyweight boxing champion Mike Tyson was found guilty and sentenced to prison. (Tyson was released in 1995 and earned $25 million in his first postrelease prizefight.) Some observers of the media frenzy surrounding these cases claimed that *all* men, not just these three, were being judged. Other critics charged that rapes or claims of sexual harassment rarely receive much media coverage unless the accused party is a celebrity, a highly placed official, or a member of a prominent family.

Other high-profile cases include the Tailhook incident and the charges of sexual harassment by more than a dozen women against U.S. Senator, Robert Packwood of Oregon. The Tailhook Association, an organization representing U.S. Navy aviators, held its annual convention in 1991 at a hotel in Las Vegas. It was alleged that during the convention, scores of male aviators sexually harassed and assaulted a number of women, including several fellow aviators. Some women were literally forced to run a gauntlet of drunken male officers along a hotel corridor, where they were fondled, molested, and subjected to sexual insults by many of the men ("Deepening shame," 1992). An internal report commissioned by the Navy secretary was highly critical of the way the higher echelons of the Navy had handled the charges brought against the male officers reportedly involved in the incident, who have yet to be brought to trial. The Senate Ethics Committee voted unanimously to expel Packwood from the Senate in September 1995. Packwood resigned.

A team of professional writers could not have tickled the public's fancy more, but the plots and the characters in these media series were very real. Many observers winced as they saw aspects of themselves—either as aggressors or victims—being laid bare before the nation.

This chapter is about sexual coercion, which includes rape but also encompasses other forms of sexual pressure, including the use of lies and deceit to seduce one's partner and, of course, sexual harassment. Sexual coercion also includes *any* sexual activity between an adult and a child. Even when children cooperate, sexual relations with children are by definition a form of sexual coercion because children are legally below the age of consent. Although sexual coercion is most often perpetrated by men, some offenders are women.

Rape

I wanted to knock the woman off her pedestal, and I felt rape was the worst thing I could do to her.

She wanted it, she was asking for it. She just said "no" so I wouldn't think she was easy. The only reason she yelled rape was she got home late and her husband knew she hadn't been out with her girlfriend.

I found myself having sexual fantasies that would put women in precarious positions. I was thinking about this more and more, like devising a rack, perhaps, that would spread her

Getting the Message. For years, women had complained that U.S. Senator Bob Packwood just didn't "get it." That is, he didn't understand what sexual harassment is, and that it is unacceptable and illegal. Packwood finally got the message when the Senate Ethics Committee voted unanimously to expel him in 1995. He subsequently resigned from the Senate.

legs as wide open as they could possibly be spread—something of this nature. I acted tough with them. The first one and the last pleaded for their virginity. I told them to do what they were told and they wouldn't get hurt. I said that if they didn't do what they were told, they would be sorry. I don't know if I actually threatened to kill them or not, but I very strongly feel that I never would have. The only thing is, perhaps if I continued on and hadn't been caught this time, seeing what happened from the first three times to the second three times—I just wonder—maybe in the next set of three somebody would have gotten hurt, you know, somebody would have really gotten hurt.

(Groth & Birnbaum, *Men Who Rape,* 1979)

Rape
Sexual intercourse that takes place as a result of force or threats of force rather than consent. (The legal definition of rape varies from state to state.) See also *forcible rape* and *statutory rape.*

Forcible rape
Sexual intercourse with a non-consenting person obtained by the use of force or the threat of force.

Statutory rape
Sexual intercourse with a person who is below the age of consent. Sexual intercourse under such conditions is considered statutory rape even though the person attacked may cooperate.

Sexual assault
Any sexual activity that involves the use of force or the threat of force.

These statements made by rapists express the theme that **rape** is the subjugation of women by men by force or threat of force. Many social scientists view rape as an act of violence that is associated with domination, anger, power, and sadism, not with passion or sexual desire (Tedeschi & Felson, 1994). Although sexual motivation plays a role in rape, the use of sex to express domination, anger, and so on is more central to our understanding of rape.

For the first few thousand years of recorded history, the only rapes that were punished were those that defiled virgins, and those were classified as crimes against property (virgins being the property of their fathers)—not as crimes against persons. In ancient Babylonia, rape laws applied to married women as well, but the law required the woman who was raped and her assailant to be bound and thrown into a river. As the injured party (after all, *his* property had been damaged), the husband could choose to let his wife drown or draw her from the water alive. The historical record bears witness to the age-old tradition, carried regrettably to the present day, that stigmatizes rape survivors and ascribes some degree of guilt to them. The ancient Hebrews stoned to death a married women who was raped and her assailant. In both the ancient Babylonian and Hebrew cultures, the wife was seen as guilty of adultery. Virgins who were raped within the protection of the city gates would also be stoned by the Hebrews. It was believed that they could have maintained their purity simply by crying out.

Today the definition of rape varies from state to state. **Forcible rape** is usually defined, however, as sexual intercourse with a nonconsenting person by the use of force or the threat of force. **Statutory rape** refers to sexual intercourse with a person who is below the age of consent, even though the person may cooperate.

Traditionally, a man could not be convicted for raping his wife, though he might have forced her to submit to sexual activity by physical power or threats. This marital exclusion was derived from the English common law that held that a woman "gives herself over" to her husband when she becomes his wife and cannot then retract her consent (Dixon, 1991). Today, however, most states have rape statutes that permit the prosecution of husbands who rape their wives. Many states have also broadened the scope of rape laws to include forced sexual acts other than coitus, such as anal intercourse and oral–genital relations, and to apply rape laws to men who rape other men and to women who coerce men into sexual activity or assist men in raping other women. Forcible rape is a form of **sexual assault.** Even

Forcible Rape. Forcible rape is the use of force or threats of force to compel a person into sexual intercourse. A rapist's motives typically have more to do with the desire to control, abuse, or punish the victim than to attain sexual gratification.

when a sexual attack does not meet the legal definition of rape, as in the case of forced penetration of the anus by an object such as a bottle or a broom handle, it can be classified and prosecuted as a sexual assault (Powell, 1991).

Incidence of Rape

The government's National Crime Victimization Survey (1995) estimates that 500,000 women are sexually assaulted each year. This figure includes 170,000 rapes and 140,000 attempted rapes. This means that a woman was reported to be raped about every three minutes on the average. Moreover, the number of rapes has been swelling faster than the population (FBI, 1991; U.S. Senate Committee on the Judiciary, 1991).

Historical studies have seriously underreported the incidence of rape (Schafran, 1995). They have largely relied on crime statistics. However, the majority of rapes are not reported to the police or prosecuted (Gibbs, 1991). Many women choose not to report assaults because of concern that they will be humiliated by the criminal justice system. Others fear reprisal from their families or the rapist. Some simply assume that the offender will not be apprehended or prosecuted.

It is true that in the United States a woman is raped at least every five minutes. Every three minutes is actually closer to the truth. ■

According to Schafran (1995), there are two reasons that even the National Crime Victimization Survey underestimates the incidence of rape in the United States. First, many women mistakenly believe that coercive sex is rape only when the rapist is a stranger. Second, many women mistakenly assume that only forced vaginal penetration is defined as rape. But many states define rape much more broadly.

Other surveys report the following prevalences of rape or sexual assaults:

- Twenty-one percent of a sample of more than 5,000 female members of a health maintenance plan reported being sexually assaulted (Koss, 1988).
- Eighteen and one-half percent of a sample of women clients of 257 psychotherapists in North Carolina reported being sexually assaulted (Dye & Roth, 1990).
- Fifteen percent of the 3,187 women sampled in a national survey of college students reported that they had been raped. An additional 12% reported that they had been victims of an attempted rape (Koss et al., 1987).
- Nearly 22% of the women in the NHSLS study reported being forced to do something sexual by a man (Laumann et al., 1994).

The weight of the evidence suggests that between 14% and 25% of women in the United States are raped at some point during their lifetimes (Calhoun & Atkeson, 1991; Koss, 1993). The prevalence of reported rapes in the United States is 13 times greater than that in Great Britain and more than 20 times greater than that in Japan (*Newsweek*, 1990). Later we shall consider some of the cultural influences that make our society such a breeding ground for rape.

T r u t h OR *Fiction?*
R E V I S I T E D

It is true that the prevalence of rape is 20 times greater in the United States than in Japan. (That is, the prevalence of *reported* rape is more than 20 times greater in the United States.) ■

Women of all ages, races, and social classes are raped. Young women, however, are at greater risk than older women. Women of ages 16 to 24 are two to three times more likely to be raped than are women in general (National Crime Victimization Survey, 1995).

Types of Rapes

One of the central myths about rape in our culture is that most rapes are perpetrated by strangers lurking in dark alleyways or by intruders who climb through open windows in the middle of the night. Most women are raped by men they know, however—often by men they have come to trust. Figure 19.1 shows that only 4% of the women in the NHSLS study were "forced to do something sexual that they did not want to do" by a stranger. According to the National Crime Victimization Survey, 80% of rapes were committed by acquaintances of the victim (Schafran, 1995).

The types of rape include stranger rape, acquaintance rape, marital rape, male rape, and rape by females.

T r u t h OR *Fiction?*
R E V I S I T E D

It is not true that the majority of rapes are committed by strangers in deserted neighborhoods or darkened alleyways. Most women are raped by men they know, not by strangers. ■

Stranger rape
Rape that is committed by an assailant previously unknown to the person who is assaulted.

Stranger Rape   **Stranger rape** refers to a rape that is committed by an assailant (or assailants) who is not previously known to the person attacked. The stranger rapist often selects targets who seem vulnerable—women who live alone, who are older or retarded, who are walking down deserted streets, or who are asleep or intoxicated. After choosing a target, the rapist may search for a safe time and place to commit the crime—a deserted, run-down part of town, a darkened street, a second-floor apartment without window bars or locks.

Acquaintance rape
Rape by an acquaintance of the person who is assaulted.

Acquaintance Rape   Women are more likely to be raped by men they know, such as classmates, fellow office workers, and even their brothers' friends, than by strangers (Schafran, 1995). **Acquaintance rapes** are much less likely than stranger rapes to be reported to the police (Schafran, 1995). One reason is that rape survivors may not perceive sexual assaults by acquaintances as rapes. Only 27% of the women in the national college survey who had been sexually assaulted saw themselves as rape victims (Koss et al., 1987). Despite the increased public awareness of acquaintance rape, the belief is still common that

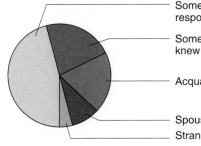

Someone with whom the respondent was in love (46%)

Someone that the respondent knew well (22%)

Acquaintance (19%)

Spouse (9%)

Stranger (4%)

Figure 19.1.   Women's Relationships with Men Who Forced Them to Do Something Sexual That They Did Not Want to Do.   Only 4% of the sexual assaults reported in the NHSLS study were perpetrated by strangers.   *Source:* Adapted from Laumann, E. O., Gagnon, J. H., Michael, R. T., & Michaels, S. (1994). *The Social Organization of Sexuality: Sexual Practices in the United States.* Chicago: University of Chicago Press, Figure 9.3, p. 338.

rapists are strangers lurking in shadows and that a woman should be able to resist a sexual advance unless the man uses a weapon (Calhoun & Atkeson, 1991). Acquaintance rapists tend to believe in myths that serve to legitimize their behavior to themselves, such as the traditional view that men are expected to assume a sexually aggressive role in dating relationships and the belief that rapists are strangers. Even when acquaintance rapes are reported to police, they are often treated as "misunderstandings" or lovers' quarrels rather than as violent crimes.

Date Rape   Date rape is a form of acquaintance rape. Studies of college women show a consistent trend: 10% to 20% of women report being forced into sexual intercourse by dates (Tang et al., 1995). These figures hold at the Chinese University of Hong Kong as well as in the United States (Tang et al., 1995). In one U.S. study, most reported date rapes were committed by men whom the women had known for nearly a year on the average (Muehlenhard & Linton, 1987). Rapes were more likely to occur when the couple had too much to drink and then parked in the man's car or went back to his residence. The man tended to perceive his partner's willingness to return home with him as a signal of sexual interest, even if she resisted his advances. Most of the men ignored women's protests and overcame their resistance by force. None used a weapon. Only a few used threats of violence.

Men who commit date rape may believe that acceptance of a date indicates willingness to engage in coitus. They may think that women should reciprocate with coitus if they are taken to dinner. Other men assume that women who frequent settings such as singles bars are expressing tacit agreement to engage in coitus with men who show interest in them. Some date rapists believe that a woman who resists advances is merely "protesting too much" so that she will not look "easy." They interpret resistance as coyness. It is a ploy in the cat-and-mouse game that typifies the "battle of the sexes" to them. They may believe that when a woman says no, she means maybe. When she says maybe, she means yes. They may thus not see themselves as committing rape. But they are.

The issue of consent lies at the heart of determining whether a sexual act is rape. Unlike cases of stranger rape, date rape occurs within a context in which sexual relations could occur voluntarily. Thus, the issue of consent can become murky. Juries and judges are often faced with a woman complainant who alleges that the male defendant, who may appear neatly dressed and looking like the boy next door, forced her into sexual relations against her will. As in the William Kennedy Smith and Mike Tyson trials, the defendant may concede that sexual intercourse took place but claim that it was consensual. Judges and juries

Combatting Rape on Campus. Many colleges and universities have instituted rape awareness programs to combat the problem of rape on campus. What is the prevalence of rape on your campus? What are you going to do about it?

ANATOMY OF A DATE RAPE: ANN AND JIM

Date rape is a pressing concern on college campuses, where thousands of women have been raped by men they knew or had dated, and where there is much controversy as to what exactly constitutes date rape (Gibbs, 1991). Consider the case of Ann (Trenton State College, 1991):

> I first met him at a party. He was really good looking and he had a great smile. I wanted to meet him but I wasn't sure how. I didn't want to appear too forward. Then he came over and introduced himself. We talked and found we had a lot in common. I really liked him. When he asked me over to his place for a drink, I thought it would be OK. He was such a good listener, and I wanted him to ask me out again.
>
> When we got to his room, the only place to sit was on the bed. I didn't want him to get the wrong idea, but what else could I do? We talked for a while and then he made his move. I was so startled. He started by kissing. I really liked him so the kissing was nice. But then he pushed me down on the bed. I tried to get up and I told him to stop. He was so much bigger and stronger. I got scared and I started to cry. I froze and he raped me.
>
> It took only a couple of minutes and it was terrible, he was so rough. When it was over he kept asking me what was wrong, like he didn't know. He had just forced himself on me and he thought that was OK. He drove me home and said he wanted to see me again. I'm so afraid to see him. I never thought it would happen to me.

College men on dates frequently perceive their dates' protests as part of an adversarial sex game. One male undergraduate said "Hell, no" when asked whether a date had consented to sex. He added, " . . . but she didn't say no, so she must have wanted it, too. . . . It's the way it works" (Celis, 1991). Consider the comments of Jim, the man who raped Ann (Trenton State College, 1991):

> I first met her at a party. She looked really hot, wearing a sexy dress that showed off her great body. We started talking right away. I knew that she liked me by the way she kept smiling and touching my arm while she was speaking. She seemed pretty relaxed so I asked her back to my place for a drink. . . . When she said yes, I knew that I was going to be lucky!
>
> When we got to my place, we sat on the bed kissing. At first, everything was great. Then, when I started to lay her down on the bed, she started twisting and saying she didn't want to. Most women don't like to appear too easy, so I knew that she was just going through the motions. When she stopped struggling, I knew that she would have to throw in some tears before we did it.
>
> She was still very upset afterwards, and I just don't understand it! If she didn't want to have sex, why did she come back to the room with me? You could tell by the way she dressed and acted that she was no virgin, so why she had to put up such a big struggle I don't know.

Accepting a date is not the equivalent of consenting to coitus. Accompanying a man to his room or apartment is not the equivalent of consenting to coitus. Nor are kissing and petting the equivalent of consenting to coitus. Let us reiterate a point worth restating: When the woman says no, the man is obligated to take no for an answer.

---

face the task of discerning subtle shadings in meaning regarding the issue of consent. Attorneys on both sides vie to persuade them to see things their way.

Charges of date rape often come down to a case of his word against hers. Her word often becomes less persuasive in the eyes of the jury if it was clear that she had consented to a series of consensual acts beforehand, such as sharing dinner, attending the movies together, accompanying him to his home, sharing a drink alone, and perhaps kissing or petting. Let us state in no uncertain terms, however, that it does not matter whether the woman wore a "sexy" outfit, was "on the pill," or shared a passionate kiss or embrace with the man. If the encounter ended with the woman's being forcibly violated, then it is rape. When a woman says no, a man must take no for an answer.

The problem of date rape has been brought within closer public scrutiny in recent years. "Take Back the Night" marches have become a common form of student protest on college campuses against the sexual misconduct of men (Gross, 1993). Many colleges have mandated date rape seminars and workshops. Antioch College, a small, traditionally liberal college in Ohio, has gone even further by instituting a sexual offense policy that requires that "willing and verbal consent" be given for every sexual act, from petting to coitus. If you want to hold your partner's hand, you need to ask first. To kiss your partner on the lips, you first have to ask. And so on. . . . This policy was developed by the students themselves. Sanctions for violating the policy can be severe, including expulsion. Supporters claim that the policy is a way of improving communication and ensuring that sexual activity is consensual. Critics claim that it makes sexual relations mechanical and lacking in spontaneity.

The Gang Rape   Groth and Birnbaum (1979) relate the story of Kurt, a 23-year-old White married father of three who was involved in a number of rapes with a friend, Pete:

> I always looked up to Pete and felt second-class to him. I felt I owed him and couldn't chicken out on the rapes. I worshiped him. He was the best fighter, lover, water-skier, motorcyclist I knew. Taking part in the sexual assaults made me feel equal to him. . . . I didn't have any friends and felt like a nobody. . . . He brought me into his bike club. He made me a somebody.

> I'd go to a shopping center and find a victim. I'd approach her with a knife or a gun and then bring her to him. He'd rape her first and then I would. . . . We raped about eight girls together over a four-month period. (p. 113)

By participating in a gang rape, the follower, like Kurt, is attempting to conform to the stereotype of the tough, competent, "masculine" he-man. Followers, however, appear to fortify the courage of the instigator of the act. One of Groth and Birnbaum's planners of such an assault remarks: "Having a partner is like having something to drink. I felt braver. I felt stronger. This gave me the courage to do something I might not have done on my own" (1979, p. 112).

Exercise of power appears to be the major motive behind gang rapes, although some attackers may also be expressing anger against women. Gang members often believe that once women engage in coitus they are "whores." Thus, each offending gang member may become more aggressive as he takes his turn.

The Koss college survey (Koss et al., 1987) showed that sexual assaults involving a group of assailants tend to be more vicious than individual assaults (Gidycz & Koss, 1990). Relatively few survivors of gang rape reported the attack to police or sought support from a crisis center.

Male Rape   The prevalence of male rape is unknown because most assaults are never reported. Some estimates suggest that perhaps 1 in 10 rape survivors is a man, however (Gibbs, 1991). Most men who rape other men are heterosexual. Their motives tend to include domination and control, revenge and retaliation, sadism and degradation, and (when the rape is carried out by a gang member) status and affiliation (Groth & Birnbaum, 1979). Sexual motives are generally absent.

It is not true that men who rape other men are gay. Most men who rape other men are heterosexual. ■

Most male rapes occur in prison settings, but some occur outside prison walls. Male rape survivors tend to suffer greater physical injury than female survivors (Kaufman et al., 1980). Males are more often attacked by multiple assailants, are held captive longer, and are more often reluctant to report the assault (Gerrol & Resick, 1988; Groth & Burgess, 1980; Myers, 1989). After all, victimization does not fit the male stereotype of capacity for self-defense. Men are expected to be not only strong but silent. Male rape survivors may suffer traumatic effects similar to those suffered by female rape survivors, however (Calhoun & Atkeson, 1991).

Marital Rape

The typical marital rapist is a man who still believes that husbands are supposed to "rule" their wives. This extends, he feels, to sexual matters. When he wants her, she should be glad, or at least willing. If she isn't, he has the right to force her. But in forcing her he gains far more than a few minutes of sexual pleasure; he humbles her and reasserts, in the most powerfully emotional way possible, that he is the ruler and she is the subject.

(Hunt, 1979, p. 38)

When Hunt wrote these words, most states would not prosecute husbands for even the most violent of rapes. A number of recent legal changes have made it possible for sexually assaultive husbands to be convicted on rape charges, however. Nearly half the states have completely removed preferential treatment for assaultive husbands. In many other states husbands still receive the benefit of the doubt unless there is evidence of gross brutality (Gibbs, 1991).

Marital rapes are probably more common than date rapes because a sexual relationship has already been established. A husband may believe that he is entitled to sexual access to his wife any time he desires it. He may be less willing to accept a rebuff. He may believe it is his wife's duty to satisfy his sexual needs even when she is uninterested. Although there are no precise statistics on marital rape, a committee of the U.S. Congress estimated that one wife in seven is likely to be raped by her husband (Gibbs, 1991). Marital rape goes largely unreported and unrecognized by survivors as rape (Russell, 1982). Women may fail to report marital rape because of fear that no one will believe them.

Motives for marital rape vary. Some men use sex to dominate their wives. Others degrade their wives through sex, especially after arguments. Sexual coercion often occurs within a context of a pattern of marital violence, battering, and physical intimidation (Finkelhor & Yllo, 1982; Russell, 1982). In some cases, though, violence is limited to the sexual relationship (Finkelhor & Yllo, 1982). Some men see sex as the solution to all marital disputes. They think that if they can force their wives into coitus, "everything will be OK."

Survivors of marital rape may be as fearful as survivors of stranger rape of serious injury or death (Kilpatrick et al., 1987). The long-term effects of marital rape on survivors are also similar to those experienced by survivors of stranger rape (Calhoun & Atkeson, 1991), including fear, depression, and sexual dysfunctions (Kilpatrick et al., 1987). Moreover, the woman who is raped by her husband usually continues to live with her assailant and may fear repeated attacks.

Rape by Women   Rape by women is rare. When it does occur, it often involves aiding or abetting men who are attacking another woman. Rape by women may occur in gang rape in which women follow male leaders to gain their approval. In such cases, a woman may be used to lure another woman to a reasonably safe place for the rape. Or the woman may hold the other woman down while she is assaulted.

But men have actually been raped by women (Sarrel & Masters, 1982; Struckman-Johnson, 1988). Sarrel and Masters reported 11 cases of men who were sexually assaulted by women, including one case of a 37-year-old man who was coerced into sexual intercourse by two women who accosted him at gunpoint. In another case, a 27-year-old man fell asleep in his hotel room with a woman he had just met in a bar and then awakened to find that he was bound to his bed, gagged, and blindfolded. He was then forced into sexual intercourse with four different, who threatened him with castration if he did not perform satisfactorily. Rape of a man may not be recognized as rape in states that adhere to a legal definition that requires forced vaginal penetration of a woman by a man. In such cases, the assailant or assailants may be charged under other statutes governing physical or sexual assaults.

Social Attitudes and Myths That Encourage Rape

Many people believe a number of myths about rape, such as "only bad girls get raped," "any healthy woman can resist a rapist if she really wants to," and "women 'cry rape' only when they've been jilted or have something to cover up" (Burt, 1980, p. 217). Another myth is that rapists are not responsible for their actions but were driven to rape by uncontrollable sexual urges that were aroused by sexually provocative women. Yet another myth is that deep down inside, women want to be raped. Although many women report experiencing rape fantasies, this does not mean that they wish to have the fantasy enacted in real life. The belief that women desire to be overpowered and forced by men into sexual relations is a rationalization for violence (Gordon & Snyder, 1989).

It is not true that a healthy woman can resist a rapist if she really wants to. The belief that a healthy woman can (successfully) resist a rapist—if she "really" wants to—is a cultural myth that has the effect of encouraging rape. ■

Rape myths create a social climate that legitimizes rape. Though both men and women are susceptible to rape myths, researchers find that college men show greater acceptance of rape myths than do college women (Brady et al., 1991; Margolin et al., 1989). Men also cling more stubbornly to myths about date rape than do women, even following date rape education classes designed to challenges these views (Lenihan et al., 1992). College men who endorse rape myths are more likely to see themselves as likely to commit rape (Malamuth, 1981). Such myths do not occur in a social vacuum. They are related to other social attitudes, including gender-role stereotyping, the perception of sex as adversarial, and the acceptance of violence in interpersonal relationships (Burt, 1980).

Sociocultural Factors in Rape

Many observers contend that our society breeds rapists by socializing males into socially and sexually dominant roles (Burt, 1980; Lisak, 1991). Men are often reinforced from early childhood for stereotypical aggressive and competitive behavior (Lisak, 1991). Gender typing may also lead men to reject or repress traits that might restrain sexual aggression but are associated with the feminine gender role, such as tenderness and empathy (Lisak, 1991).

Research with college students supports the connection between stereotypical masculine identification and tendencies to rape or condone rape. One study compared college men who adhered strictly to stereotypical gender-role beliefs with men holding less rigid attitudes. The stereotypical men expressed a greater likelihood of committing rape, were more accepting of violence against women, were more likely to blame rape survivors, and were more aroused by depictions of rape (Check & Malamuth, 1983). Other researchers found that college men who more closely identified with the traditional masculine gender role more often reported having engaged in verbal sexual coercion and forcible rape (Muehlenhard & Falcon, 1990).

Women may be socialized into assuming the helpless role. The stereotypical feminine gender role includes characteristics such as submissiveness, passivity, cooperativeness, even obedience to male authority. Such qualities may make it difficult for a woman to resist when faced with the possibility of rape. A woman may lack skills in aggressiveness and believe that physical resistance is inappropriate or that she is incapable of resisting. Women are also taught that is important to be sexually attractive to men. Women may thus unfairly blame themselves for the assault, believing that they somehow enticed the assailant.

Social influences may reinforce cultural themes that underlie rape, such as the belief that a truly masculine man is expected to be sexually aggressive and overcome a woman's resistance until she "melts" in his arms (Stock, 1991). The popular belief that women fantasize about being overpowered sanctions coercive tactics to "awaken" a woman's sexual desires. Images from popular books and movies reinforce these themes, such as that of Rhett Butler in *Gone with the Wind,* carrying a protesting Scarlett O'Hara up the stairs to her bedroom. Violent pornography, which fuses violence and erotic arousal, may also serve to legitimize rape (Stock, 1991).

Young men may come to view dates not as chances to get to know their partners but as opportunities for sexual conquest, in which the object is to overcome their partners' resistance. In one study, male college students expressed support for a man's right to kiss his female partner even if she resists (Margolin et al., 1989). Malamuth (1981) found that 35% of the college men in his sample said they would force a woman into sexual relations if they knew they could get away with it.

The social philosopher Myriam Miedzian suggests that lessons learned in competitive sports may also predispose young Americans to sexual violence (Levy, 1991). Boys are often exposed to coaches who emphasize winning at all costs. They are taught to be dominant and to vanquish their opponents, even if winning means injuring or "taking out" the opposition. This philosophy, Miedzian argues, may be carried from the playing field into relationships with women. Some athletes distinguish between sports and dating relationships. Others do not. Evidence shows that student athletes commit a disproportionate number of sexual assaults (Eskenazi, 1990). Many of these are gang rapes committed by groups of student athletes who live together and "bond" so strongly that they even share sexual experiences.

Sexual behavior and sports in our culture are linked through common idioms. A young man may be taunted by his friends after a date with a woman with such questions as "Did you score?" or more bluntly, "Did you get in?" Consider, for example, the aggressive competitiveness with which this male college student views dating relationships between men and women:

> A man is supposed to view a date with a woman as a premeditated scheme for getting the most sex out of her. Everything he does, he judges in terms of one criterion—"getting laid." He's supposed to constantly pressure her to see how far he can get. She is his adversary, his opponent in a battle, and he begins to view her as a prize, an object, not a person. While she's dreaming about love, he's thinking about how to conquer her.

(Powell, 1991, p. 55)

Psychological Characteristics of Rapists

Although sexual aggressiveness may be embedded within our social fabric, not all men are equally vulnerable to such cultural influences (Burkhart & Fromuth, 1991). Not all men become rapists. Personal factors are thus also involved. What are they? Are rapists mentally disturbed? Retarded? Driven by insatiable sexual urges?

Much of our knowledge of the psychological characteristics of rapists derives from studies of samples of incarcerated rapists (Harney & Muehlenhard, 1991). One conclusion that emerges is that there is no single type of rapist. Rapists vary in their psychological characteristics, family backgrounds, mental health, and criminal histories (Prentky & Knight, 1991). As a group, rapists are no less intelligent or more likely to be mentally ill than comparison groups (Renzetti & Curran, 1989). Many rapists show no evidence of psychological disturbance (Dean & de Bruyn-Kops, 1982). This does not mean that their behavior is "normal." It means that the great majority of rapists are in control of their behavior, and they know that it is illegal.

Truth OR Fiction?
R E V I S I T E D

It is not true that most rapists are mentally ill, even though their crimes might strike observers as being "sick." ■

Some rapists feel socially inadequate and report that they cannot find willing partners. Some lack social skills and avoid social interactions with women (Overholser & Beck, 1986). Others are no less skillful socially than nonrapists in the same socioeconomic group, however (Segal & Marshall, 1985). Some rapists are basically antisocial and have long histories of violent behavior (Knight et al., 1991). They tend to act upon their impulses regardless of the cost to the person they attack. Some were sexually victimized or physically assaulted as children (Groth, 1978; Sack & Mason, 1980). As adults, they may be identifying with the aggressor role in interpersonal relationships. The use of alcohol may also dampen self-restraint and spur sexual aggressiveness.

For some rapists, violence and sexual arousal become enmeshed. Thus, they seek to combine sex and violence to enhance their sexual arousal (Quinsey et al., 1984). Some rapists are more sexually aroused (as measured by the size of erections) by verbal descriptions, films, or audiotapes that portray themes of rape than are other people (Barbaree & Marshall, 1991). Other researchers, however, have failed to find deviant patterns of arousal in rapists (e.g., Baxter et al., 1986; Hall, 1989). These researchers find that, as a

Rapists. Most incarcerated rapists and other sex offenders will eventually be released, yet few receive little, if any, treatment for rape in prison. Here teenage sex offenders at a state school engage in a role-playing exercise. Should communities be informed when sex offenders are released into their midst? Why or why not?

Anger rape
A vicious, unplanned rape that is triggered by feelings of intense anger and resentment toward women.

Power rape
Rape that is motivated by the desire to control and dominate the person assaulted.

Sadistic rape
A highly ritualized, savage rape in which the person who is attacked is subjected to painful and humiliating experiences and threats.

group, rapists, like most other people, are more aroused by stimuli depicting mutually consenting sexual activity than by rape stimuli.

Studies of incarcerated rapists may be criticized on grounds that the samples may not represent the total population of rapists. It is estimated that fewer than 4% of rapists are caught and eventually imprisoned (Gibbs, 1991). Most rapes are committed by acquaintances. Acquaintance rapists are even less likely than stranger rapists to be arrested, convicted, and incarcerated.

To offset this methodological concern, researchers have turned to the survey method to study men who anonymously report that they have engaged in sexually coercive behaviors, including rape, but have not been identified by the criminal justice system.

Koss and her colleagues (1987) found that about 1 man in 13 (7.7%) in their national college sample of nearly 3,000 college men admitted to committing or attempting rape. Harney and Muehlenhard (1991) summarized research findings on self-identified sexually aggressive men. They are more likely than other men to:

* Condone rape and violence against women
* Hold traditional gender-role attitudes
* Be sexually experienced
* Be hostile toward women
* Engage in sexual activity in order to express social dominance
* Be sexually aroused by depictions of rape
* Be irresponsible and lack a social conscience
* Have peer groups, such as fraternities, that pressure them into sexual activity

The Motives of Rapists: The Search for Types   Although sexual arousal is an obvious and important element in rape (Barbaree & Marshall, 1991), some researchers argue that sexual desire is not the basic motivation for rape (Gebhard et al., 1965; Groth & Birnbaum, 1979). Other researchers believe that sexual motivation plays a key role in at least some rapes (Hall & Hirschman, 1991). Based on their clinical work with more than 1,000 rapists, Groth and Birnbaum believe that there are three basic kinds of rape—anger rape, power rape, and sadistic rape:

1. *Anger rape.* The **anger rape** is a vicious, unplanned attack that is triggered by anger and resentment toward women. The anger rapist usually employs more force than is needed to obtain compliance. The person they rape is often coerced into performing degrading and humiliating acts, fellatio, or anal intercourse. Typically, the anger rapist reports that he had suffered humiliations at the hands of women and used the rape as a means of revenge.
2. *Power rape.* The man who commits a **power rape** is motivated by the desire to control and dominate the woman he rapes. Sexual gratification is secondary. The power rapist uses rape as an attempt "to resolve disturbing doubts about [his] masculine identity and worth, [or] to combat deep-seated feelings of insecurity and vulnerability" (Groth & Hobson, 1983, p. 165). Only enough force to subdue the woman is used.
3. *Sadistic rape.* The **sadistic rape** is a ritualized, savage attack. Sadistic rapists often carefully plan their assaults and use a "con" or pretext to approach their targets, such as asking for directions or offering or requesting assistance (Dietz et al., 1990). Some sadists bind their victims and subject them to humiliating and degrading experiences and threats. Some torture or murder their victims (Dietz et al., 1990). Mutilation of the victim is unfortunately common. Groth and Birnbaum (1979) suggest that sadistic rapists are often preoccupied with violent pornography but have little or no interest in nonviolent (consensual) pornography. Groth (1979) estimated that about 40% of rapes are anger rapes; 55%, power rapes; and 5%, sadistic rapes.

Adjustment of Rape Survivors

Many women who are raped fear for their lives during the attack (Calhoun & Atkeson, 1991). Whether or not weapons or threats are used, the experience of being dominated by

A WORLD OF DIVERSITY

RAPE-PRONE AND RAPE-FREE SOCIETIES: WHITHER THE UNITED STATES?

Cross-cultural studies suggest that sexual violence is not unique to our culture. It may in fact be culturally sanctioned in some societies. Rape is more common in violent cultures, especially in the minority of cultures in which violence toward women is legitimized (Ember & Ember, 1990; Powell, 1991). Among the Yanomamö people of the Amazon jungle, a tribe known to be among the fiercest and most aggressive people in the world, men often raid neighboring villages and literally carry away the women to keep as their wives (Ember & Ember, 1990). Wives are often savagely beaten, stabbed with sticks, or burned with glowing firewood by husbands as punishment for misbehavior. Wives come to accept punishment as part of their marital role. They may also come to regard the scars as signs that their husbands must care deeply for them to have beaten them so badly.

Sanday (1981) characterized 18% of the 156 cultures she studied as *rape-prone*. These rape-prone societies or "cultures of violence" tended to treat women as property. By contrast, Sanday found 45 "rape-free" cultures in which rape was absent or rare. Rape-free societies were characterized by sexual equality in which both genders shared power and were deemed to make important contributions, albeit in different ways, to the welfare of the society. In such societies, women did not economically depend on men and were able to control their own resources. Such societies also rear their children to be nurturant and to shun interpersonal violence. It thus appears that sexual violence occurs within the cultural context of interpersonal violence and male dominance (Stock, 1991).

Such cultural factors may help to explain the high rate of rape in the United States (Renzetti & Curran, 1989). The United States has both a high level of violent behavior, including the highest homicide rate among industrialized nations, and unequal gender relations.

Crisis
A highly stressful situation that can involve shock, loss of self-esteem, and lessened capacity for making decisions.

an unpredictable and threatening assailant is terrifying. The woman does not know whether she will survive and may feel helpless to do anything about it. Afterwards, many survivors enter a state of **crisis.**

Many survivors are extremely distraught in the days and weeks following the rape (Calhoun & Atkeson, 1991; Koss, 1993). They have trouble sleeping and cry frequently. They tend to report eating problems, cystitis, headaches, irritability, mood changes, anxiety and depression, and menstrual irregularity. They may become withdrawn, sullen, and mistrustful (McArthur, 1990). People in the United States tend to believe that women who are raped are at least partly to blame for the assault (Bell et al., 1994). Therefore, some survivors experience feelings of guilt and shame (McArthur, 1990). Some, however, show few negative effects in the aftermath of the assault (Calhoun & Atkeson, 1991). Emotional distress tends to peak in severity by about three weeks following the assault and generally remains high for about a month before beginning to abate about a month or two later (Koss, 1993). About one survivor in four encounters emotional problems that linger beyond a year (Calhoun & Atkeson, 1991; Hanson, 1990).

According to a community survey of sexual assault survivors (both women and men) from Los Angeles, the most frequent emotional reactions to sexual assault were anger (59%), sadness (43%), and anxiety (40%) (see Table 19.1 on page 574). A total of 447 persons from the sample of more than 3,000 adults reported that they had suffered a sexual assault, which included a range of coercive acts from fondling of the breasts or sex organs to sexual intercourse (Siegel et al., 1990). As shown in Table 19.1, women were significantly more likely to report 12 of 14 listed reactions. Survivors who were physically threatened by their assailants reported greater fear and anxiety, depression, and sexual distress (reduced interest and pleasure, fear of sex). Attacks that resulted in forced intercourse were more distressing than those that did not.

TABLE 19.1 Prevalence of emotional and behavioral reactions to sexual assault in a Los Angeles community sample

Reaction	Women (%)	Men (%)	Total (%)
Fearful	45.5	15.9*	35.1
Stopped doing things	31.8	15.2*	25.9
Fearful of sex	21.6	7.9*	16.8
Less sexual interest	32.5	6.9*	23.5
Less sexual pleasure	27.1	8.0*	20.4
Felt dishonored or spoiled	33.9	20.0*	29.1
Guilt	35.0	25.9*	31.8
Sad, blue, or depressed	50.6	28.8*	43.0
Anger	72.0	34.8*	59.0
Tense, nervous, or anxious	49.9	22.9*	40.4
Insomnia	25.2	11.6*	20.4
Loss/increase in appetite	15.8	8.4	13.2
Alcohol/drug use	5.1	5.9	5.4
Fearful of being alone	23.0	2.2*	15.7

*Indicates that the differences between men and women were statistically significant at the .05 level of significance; that is, that there is less than a 5% chance that the differences between men and women were due to chance fluctuations.

Source: Siegel, J. M., et al. (1990). Reactions to Sexual Assault: A Community Study. *Journal of Interpersonal Violence, 5,* 229–246. Reprinted by permission of Sage Publications, Inc.

Rape survivors may also suffer physical injuries and sexually transmitted diseases, even AIDS, as a result of a sexual assault. In one study, concerns about contracting AIDS were reported by about 1 in 4 survivors (Baker et al., 1990).

Rape survivors may also be at risk for long-term health complications. In one study, survivors reported more current physical complaints, including gynecological problems, when they were assessed *two or more years* following the attack than did a reference group matched on demographic variables such as race and age (Waigandt et al., 1990).

Survivors may also encounter problems at work, such as problems relating to coworkers or bosses or difficulties in concentrating. Work adjustment, however, usually returns to normal levels within a year (Calhoun & Atkeson, 1991). Relationships with spouses or partners may also be impaired. Disturbances in sexual functioning are common and may last for years or a lifetime. Survivors often report a lack of sexual desire, fears of sex, and difficulty becoming sexually aroused (Becker et al., 1986). Some women simply do not experience the level of sexual enjoyment they found before the assault (Calhoun & Atkeson, 1991).

Survivors' Reactions to the Assault: Whom to Tell? About two thirds (65%) of the 447 sexual assault survivors in the Los Angeles survey reported they had told someone about the assault (Golding et al., 1989). The person was usually a friend or a relative. Only 1 in 10 reported the assault to the police. Only 1 in 6 consulted a mental health professional. Survivors were more likely to inform police or physicians of attacks by strangers than by acquaintances. Most of the survivors (74%) who disclosed the assault were able to find at least one person who was helpful.

Most women do not report sexual assaults to police. Why? Reasons include fears of retaliation, the social stigma attached to the survivors of rape, doubts that others will believe them, feelings that it would be hopeless to try to bring charges against the perpetrator, concerns about negative publicity, and fears about the emotional distress to which they would be subjected if the case were to go to trial.

Rape Trauma and Psychological Disorders   Rape survivors are at higher-than-average risk of developing psychological disorders such as depression, alcohol and substance abuse, and anxiety (Koss, 1993). Investigators in the United States (Moscarello, 1990) and Norway (Dahl, 1989) report that rape survivors often develop or show signs of **posttraumatic stress disorder** (PTSD). The American Psychiatric Association (1994) describes PTSD as an anxiety disorder that is brought on by exposure to a traumatic event and is also often seen in soldiers who were in combat. Features of PTSD include flashbacks to the traumatic experience in disturbing dreams or intrusive recollections, emotional numbing, and nervousness. PTSD may persist for years. The person may also develop fears of situations connected with the traumatic event. For example, a woman who was raped on an elevator may develop a fear of riding elevators by herself. Researchers also report that women who blame themselves for the rape tend to suffer more severe depression and adjustment problems, including sexual problems (Frazier, 1990; Wyatt et al., 1990).

Rape Trauma Syndrome   Ann Burgess and Lynda Holmstrom (1974) identified some common response patterns in survivors of rape, which they labeled the **rape trauma syndrome.** Through emergency room interviews with 92 women at Boston City Hospital, and telephone or in-person follow-up interviews, Burgess and Holmstrom found two phases in rape trauma syndrome:

The Acute Phase: Disorganization   The acute phase typically lasts for several weeks following the attack. Many survivors are disorganized during this time and may benefit from rape trauma counseling. The woman may cry uncontrollably and experience feelings of anger, shame, fear, and nervousness.

Some women present a calm, composed face to the world, but inwardly have not yet come to terms with the traumatic experience. Calmness often gives way to venting of feelings later on.

The Long-Term Process: Reorganization   The long-term reorganization phase may last for years. The woman gradually comes to deal with her feelings and to reorganize her life (Sales et al., 1984). Lingering fears may lead rape survivors to move to safer surroundings. Women who informed the police may fear retaliation by the rapist. They may change their phone numbers, often to unlisted numbers. Some take out-of-state trips, often visiting parents, although they do not necessarily tell them of the rape. Many survivors continue to be bothered by frightening dreams.

Burgess and Holmstrom noted two variations of the rape trauma syndrome, the compounded reaction and the silent rape reaction.

Compounded Reaction   Survivors with histories of psychological or medical problems sometimes became more severely depressed than other survivors, or became suicidal or psychotic. They required attention for these problems as well as for the rape trauma.

Silent Rape Reaction   Survivors who do not disclose their attacks to anyone may have a silent rape reaction. Unfortunately, concealing the rape may prevent them from receiving social support. If survivors are children or adolescents when assaulted, their feelings may go unresolved for years. They may avoid men or develop sudden panic reactions—like fear of being alone or of going out. They may have frightening dreams and lose self-confidence.

When these survivors seek assistance for other problems, they may show anxiety when the discussion comes around to sexuality. They may even stutter or be silent for long periods. Under these circumstances an empathic interviewer may suspect a silent reaction to a trauma.

Posttraumatic stress disorder
A type of stress reaction brought on by a traumatic event and characterized by flashbacks of the experience in the form of disturbing dreams or intrusive recollections, a sense of emotional numbing or restricted range of feelings, and heightened body arousal. Abbreviated *PTSD*.

Rape trauma syndrome
A two-phase reaction to rape that is characterized by disruption of the survivor's lifestyle (the acute phase) and reorganization of the survivor's life (the long-term phase).

Not all survivors, however, suffer a lengthy or predictable struggle of readjustment (Gordon & Snyder, 1989). For reasons that are not clear, some are able to put the rape behind them with little disruption of their regular lives. Each survivor is an individual, however, and copes with crisis in her own way (Gordon & Snyder, 1989).

Elizabeth Powell (1991, p. 239) offers the following suggestions if you should be raped:

1. Don't change anything about your body—don't wash or even comb your hair. Leave your clothes as they are. Otherwise you could destroy evidence.
2. Strongly consider reporting the incident to police. You may prevent another woman from being assaulted, and you will be taking charge, starting on the path from victim to survivor.
3. Ask a relative or friend to take you to a hospital, if you can't get an ambulance or a police car. If you call the hospital, tell them why you're requesting an ambulance, in case they are able to send someone trained to deal with rape cases.
4. Seek help in an assertive way. Seek medical help. Injuries you are unaware of may be detected. Insist that a written or photographic record be made to document your condition. If you decide to file charges, the prosecutor may need this evidence to obtain a conviction.
5. Question health professionals. Ask about your biological risks. Ask what treatments are available. Ask for whatever will help make you comfortable. Call the shots. Demand confidentiality if that's what you want. Refuse what you don't want.

You may also wish to call a rape hotline or rape crisis center for advice, if one is available in your area. A rape crisis volunteer may be available to accompany you to the hospital and help see you through the medical evaluation and police investigation if you report the attack. It is not unusual for rape survivors to try to erase the details of the rape from their minds. However, trying to remember details clearly will permit you to provide an accurate description of the rapist to the police, including his clothing, type of car, and so on. This information may help police apprehend the rapist and assist in the prosecution.

Treatment of Rape Survivors

Treatment of rape survivors typically involves a two-stage process of helping the woman (the vast majority are female) through the crisis following the attack and then helping to foster long-term adjustment. Crisis intervention typically provides the survivor with support and information to help her express her feelings and develop strategies for coping with the trauma (Resick & Schnicke, 1990). Psychotherapy, involving group or individual approaches, can help the survivor cope with the emotional consequences of rape, avoid self-blame, improve self-esteem, validate the welter of feelings surrounding the experience, and help her establish or maintain loving relationships. Therapists also recognize the importance of helping the rape survivor identify supportive social networks (Ledray, 1990). Family, friends, religious leaders, and health care specialists are all potential sources of help. In major cities and many towns, concerned men and women have formed rape crisis centers and hotlines, peer counseling groups, and referral agencies geared to assessing and treating survivors' needs after the assault. Some counselors are specially trained to mediate between survivors of rape and their loved ones—husbands, lovers, and so forth. These counselors help people to discuss and work through the often complex emotional legacy of rape. Phone numbers for these services can be obtained from feminist groups (for example, your local office of the National Organization for Women [NOW]), the police department, or the telephone directory.

Rape Prevention

The elimination of rape would probably require massive changes in cultural attitudes and socialization processes. Educational intervention on a smaller scale may reduce its incidence, however. A study of 276 undergraduates at Pitzer College in California showed that

Rape Crisis Center. Rape crisis centers provide rape victims with emotional support to help them cope with the traumatic effects of rape. They also help victims obtain medical, legal, and psychological services.

college men who were more knowledgeable about the trauma caused by rape were less likely to report that they might commit a rape (Hamilton & Yee, 1990). Many colleges and universities offer educational programs about date rape. The University of Washington, for example, offers students lectures and seminars on date rape (and also provides women with escorts to their homes or dorms after dark). Brown University requires all first-year students to attend orientation sessions on rape (Celis, 1991). The point of such programs is for men to learn that *no* means *no,* despite the widespread belief that some women like to be "talked into" sex.

Until the basic cultural attitudes that support rape change, however, "rape prevention" will require that women take a number of precautions. Why, a reader may wonder, should women be advised to take measures to avoid rape? Is not the very listing of such measures a subtle way of blaming the woman if she should fall prey to an attacker? No, providing the information does not blame the person who is attacked. The rapist is *always* responsible for the assault. Women can take precautions, as discussed in the nearby A Closer Look feature, that might lower their risk of being assaulted.

Confronting a Rapist: Should you Fight, Flee, or Plead?

What if you are accosted by a rapist? Should you try to fight him off, flee, or try to plead with him to stop? Some women have thwarted attacks by pleading or crying. Yet research has shown that less forceful forms of resistance, such as pleading, begging, or reasoning, can be dangerous strategies. They may not fend off the attack and may heighten the risk of injury (Bart & O'Brien, 1985). Screaming may ward off some attacks (Byers & Lewis, 1988). Running away is sometimes an effective strategy for avoiding a rape (Bart & O'Brien, 1985), for example, but running may not be effective if the woman is outnumbered by a group of assailants (Gidycz & Koss, 1990). No suggestion is likely to be helpful in all rape cases, however.

Self-defense training may help women become better prepared to fend off an assailant. Yet law enforcement officials caution that physical resistance may spur some rapists to become more aggressive (Powell, 1991). Federal statistics show that women who resist increase their chances of preventing the completion of a rape by 80%. However, resistance increases the odds of being physically injured by as much as threefold (Brody, 1992c). A

RAPE PREVENTION

The New Our Bodies, Ourselves (Boston Women's Health Book Collective, 1992) lists several suggestions that may help prevent rape:

- Establish a set of signals with other women in the building or neighborhood.
- List yourself in the phone directory and on the mailbox by your first initials only.
- Use dead-bolt locks.
- Lock windows, and install iron grids on first-floor windows.
- Keep doorways and entries well lit.
- Keep your keys handy when approaching the car or the front door.
- Do not walk by yourself after dark.
- Avoid deserted areas.
- Do not allow strange men into your house or apartment without first checking their credentials.
- Keep your car doors locked and the windows up.
- Check out the back seat of your car before entering.
- Don't live in a risky building. (We realize that this suggestion may be of little use to poor women who have relatively little choice as to where they live.)
- Don't give rides to hitchhikers (including women hitchhikers).

- Don't converse with strange men on the street.
- Shout "Fire!" not "Rape!" People are likely to flock to fires but to avoid scenes of violence.

Powell (1991) adds the following suggestions for avoiding date rape:

- Communicate your sexual limits to your date. Tell your partner how far you would like to go so that he will know what the limits are. For example, if your partner starts fondling you in ways that make you uncomfortable, you might say, "I'd prefer if you didn't touch me there. I really like you, but I prefer not getting so intimate at this point in our relationship."
- Meet new dates in public places, and avoid driving with a stranger or a group of people you've met. When meeting a new date, drive in your own car and meet your date at a public place. Don't drive with strangers or offer rides to strangers or groups of people. In some cases of date rape, the group disappears just prior to the assault.
- State your refusal definitively. Be firm in refusing a sexual overture. Look your partner straight in the eye. The more definite you are,

the less likely your partner will misinterpret your wishes.
- Become aware of your fears. Take notice of any fears of displeasing your partner that might stifle your assertiveness. If your partner is truly respectful of you, you need not fear an angry or demeaning response. But if your partner is not respectful, it is best to become aware of it and end the relationship right there.
- Pay attention to your "vibes." Trust your gut-level feelings. Many victims of acquaintance rape said afterward that they had had a strange feeling about the man but failed to pay attention to it.
- Be especially cautious if you are in a new environment, such as college or a foreign country. You may be especially vulnerable to exploitation when you are becoming acquainted with a new environment, different people, and different customs.
- If you have broken off a relationship with someone you don't really like or feel good about, don't let him into your place. Many so-called date rapes are committed by ex-lovers and ex-boyfriends.

study of 116 rapes showed that women were more likely to physically resist if the attacker was a friend or relative, if the attacker made verbal threats, and if the attacker physically restrained her or injured her (Atkeson et al., 1989).

It is difficult, if not impossible, for people to think through their options clearly and calmly when they are suddenly attacked. Rape experts recommend that women rehearse alternative responses to a rape attack. The Boston Police Department recommends that whatever form of self-defense a woman intends to use, she should carefully think through how it is used and practice using it (Brody, 1992c). Thompson (1991) suggests that effective self-defense is built upon the use of multiple strategies, ranging from attempts to avoid potential rape situations (such as by installing home security systems or by walking only in well-lit areas), to acquiescence when active resistance would seem too risky, to the use of more active verbal or physical forms of resistance in some low-risk situations.

Self-Defense Against Rape. Many women take self-defense classes to help them become better prepared to fend off an assailant. Yet no one strategy is likely to be effective in all situations.

T r u t h **OR** *Fiction?*
R E V I S I T E D

It is questionable whether women who encounter a rapist should attempt to fight off the assailant. Women must make their own decisions about whether to physically resist a rapist, based on their assessment of the rapist, the situation, and their own ability to resist. ■

~ *Reflections* ~

Agree or disagree with the following statement, and support your answer: A woman who walks in a dangerous neighborhood or talks to a stranger deserves what she gets.

Agree or disagree with the following statement, and support your answer: Our society breeds rapists by socializing males into socially and sexually dominant roles.

What can you do to decrease the incidence of rape in our society? Will you do it?

Verbal Sexual Coercion

Verbal sexual coercion is persistent verbal pressure or the use of seduction "lines" to manipulate a person into sexual activity. A study of 194 male undergraduates in a southeastern university showed that 42% admitted to verbally coercing a woman into sex (Craig et al., 1989). In a survey of 325 college undergraduates from a northwestern state university, about 1 in 5 of the men reported having said things to women they didn't mean in order to engage in sexual intercourse (Lane & Gwartney-Gibbs, 1985). Women were more likely than men to have been pressured into sexual relations. One in 4 of the women respondents reported that they engaged in sexual intercourse with someone they would otherwise have rejected because they had "felt pressured by his continual arguments" (p. 56). About 1 in 15 of the *men* reported engaging in sexual intercourse unwillingly as a result of sexual pressure.

The use of verbal pressure and seduction "lines" is so common in dating relationships that they are seldom recognized as coercion. Consider the man who deceives his partner into believing that he really loves her in order to persuade her to engage in sexual activities with him. His use of lies or deception can be considered a form of sexual coercion because it employs devious means to exploit his partner's emotional needs in order to curry sexual favors. Note, however, that the use of the statement "I love you" is not a coercive tactic, sexual pressure, or a seduction line if it is honest (Powell, 1991).

W H A T D O O U S A Y N O W ?

HANDLING SEXUAL PRESSURE LINES

Rape is an extreme form of sexual pressure that involves the use of threats or force to coerce an unwilling person into a sexual act. But sexual pressure may take a more subtle form, such as persistent verbal pressure or the use of seduction "lines" that aim to manipulate, by deception or trickery, another person into having sexual relations.

Following are sexual pressure lines noted by Powell (1991) that men usually use with women. What would you say in response to each of them? Responses as suggested by Powell (1991) are shown in parentheses.

Kind of Pressure Line	The Line	Your Response
Lines that reassure you about the negative consequences	"Don't worry, I'm sterile."	_____ _____ (I know you want to make me feel safer, but . . . well, I'm just not comfortable about sex without a condom. I've known a few people who were more fertile than they thought.)
	"You can't get pregnant the first time."	_____ _____ (Hey, where did you get your sex education? People can get pregnant any time they have intercourse, even if it's just for one second.)
	"Don't worry I'll pull out."	_____ _____ (I know you want to reassure me, but people can get pregnant that way, even without ejaculating.)
Lines that threaten you with rejection	"If you don't have sex, I'll find someone who will."	_____ _____ (I can't believe you are making a threat like this. I'm furious that you would treat lovemaking like some kind of job, as if anyone will do.)
Lines that attempt to put down the refuser	"You're such a bitch."	_____ _____ (I can't believe you want to make love to me and think calling me names will put me in the mood. Good-bye.)

580 ~ CHAPTER 19 SEXUAL COERCION

Kind of Pressure Line	The Line	Your Response
	"Are you frigid?"	_____ _____ _____ (I resent being called names just because I tell you what I want to do with my body.)
Lines that stress the beautiful experience being missed	"Our relationship will grow stronger."	_____ _____ _____ (I know you really would like to get more involved right now. But I need to wait. And lots of people have had their relationship grow stronger without intercourse.)
Lines that might settle for less	"I don't want to do anything. I just want to lie next to you."	_____ _____ _____ (The way we're attracted to each other, I don't think that would be a good idea. As much as I care about you, I'd better not spend the night.)
Lines to make you prove yourself	"If you loved me, you would."	_____ _____ _____ (You know I care a lot about you. But I feel very pressured when you try to get me to do something I'm not ready for. It's not fair to me. Please consider my feelings.)
Lines that attempt to be logical, but aren't	"You're my girlfriend— it's your obligation."	_____ _____ _____ (If you think sex is an obligation, we need to think about this relationship right now.) [*Watch out* for any such talk—it is very common in abusers and rapists. At best, it's an irrational comment by an immature person.]
Lines that are totally transparent	"I'll say I love you after we do it."	_____ _____ _____ (Bye, now.) [There is no way to deal with a person who would say such a thing.]

Although these sample responses can help you resist specific pressure lines, do not think that saying no to sexual pressure is a privilege that you earn by winning an argument. As Powell recognizes, "You don't *have* to explain." Your body is not debatable. You don't have to say anything except " I don't want to."

To what forms of sexual verbal coercion have you been exposed? What forms of verbal coercion have you used?

Have you ever lied to convince someone to engage in sexual activity? Have you lied to avoid sexual activity? Are you happy with the way you handled the situation? Why, or why not?

Sexual Abuse of Children

Many view child sexual abuse as among the most heinous of crimes. Children who are sexually assaulted often suffer social and emotional problems that impair their development and persist into adulthood, affecting their self-esteem and their ability to form intimate relationships.

No one knows how many children are sexually abused. Although most sexually abused children are girls (Knudsen, 1991), one quarter to one third are boys (Finkelhor, 1990). A randomized national telephone survey of more than 2,600 adults showed that 9.5% of the men and 14.6% of the women reported having been sexually abused (a completed or attempted act of sexual intercourse) prior to age 19 (Finkelhor et al., 1990). These estimates may underrepresent the actual prevalences, as people may fail to report such incidents due to faulty memories or because of shame or embarrassment. In addition, about one in four people refused to participate in the survey, casting doubt on the sample's representativeness. Other researchers estimate that the prevalence of sexual abuse among boys ranges from 4% to 16% (Genuis et al., 1991; Janus & Janus, 1993; Kohn, 1987) and among girls exceeds 20% (Janus & Janus, 1993; Kohn, 1987). Whatever the actual prevalences, sexual abuse of children cuts across all racial, ethnic, and economic boundaries (Alter-Reid et al., 1986).

What Is Child Sexual Abuse?

Sexual abuse of children may range from exhibitionism, kissing, fondling, and sexual touching to oral sex and anal intercourse and, in the case of girls, vaginal intercourse (Knudsen, 1991). Any form of sexual contact between an adult and a child is abusive, even if the child is willing, since children are deemed incapable of voluntarily consenting to sexual activity. Although the age of consent varies among the states, sexual relations between adults and children under the age of consent are criminal offenses in every state.

Voluntary sexual activity between children of similar ages is not sexual abuse. Children often engage in consensual sex play with peers or siblings, as in "playing doctor" or in mutual masturbation. Although such experiences may be recalled in adulthood with feelings of shame or guilt, they are not typically as harmful as experiences with adults. When the experience involves coercion, however, or when the other child is significantly older or in a position of power over the younger child, the sexual contact may be considered sexual abuse.

Patterns of Abuse

Children from stable, middle-class families appear to be generally at lower risk of encountering sexual abuse than children from poorer, less cohesive families (Finkelhor, 1984). In most cases, children who are sexually abused are not accosted by the proverbial stranger lurking in the school yard. In perhaps 75% to 80% of cases, instead, the molesters are people who are close to them: relatives, steprelatives, family friends, and neighbors (Waterman & Lusk, 1986). Estimates of the percentage of sexually molested children who are abused by family members have ranged from 10% to 50% of cases (Waterman &

So there really was a monster in her bedroom.

For many kids, there's a real reason to be afraid of the dark.

Last year in Indiana, there were 6,912 substantiated cases of sexual abuse. The trauma can be devastating for the child and for the family. So listen closely to the children around you.

If you hear something you don't want to believe, perhaps you should. For helpful information on child abuse prevention, contact the LaPorte County Child Abuse Prevention Council, 7451 Johnson Road, Michigan City, IN 46360. (219) 874-0007

LaPorte County Child Abuse Prevention Council

The Monster in the Bedroom. Not all monsters are make-believe. Some, like perpetrators of incest, are members of the family.

Lusk, 1986). In a random survey of 521 Boston parents, 55% of the respondents who said they had been sexually abused as children reported that the perpetrator was a family member or acquaintance (Finkelhor, 1984).

Parents who discover that their child has been abused by a family member are often reluctant to notify authorities. Some may feel that such problems are "family matters" that are best kept private. Others may be reluctant to notify authorities for fear that it may shame the family or that they may be held accountable for failing to protect the child. The decision to report the abuse to the police depends largely on the relationship between the abuser and the person who discovers the abuse (Finkelhor, 1984). In the Boston community survey, none of the parents whose children were sexually abused by family members notified the authorities. By contrast, 23% of the parents whose children had been abused by acquaintances notified the authorities; 73% of the parents whose children were abused by strangers did so (Finkelhor, 1984).

Typically, the child initially trusts the abuser. Physical force is seldom needed to gain compliance, largely because of the child's helplessness, gullibility, and submission to adult authority. Whereas most sexually abused children are abused only once, those who are abused by family members are more likely to suffer repeated acts of abuse (Briere & Runtz, 1987; Dube & Hebert, 1988).

Genital fondling is the most common type of abuse (Knudsen, 1991). In one sample of women who had been molested in childhood, most of the contacts involved genital fondling (38% of cases) or exhibitionism (20% of cases). Intercourse occurred in only 4% of cases (Knudsen, 1991). Repeated abuse by a family member, however, commonly follows a pattern that begins with affectionate fondling during the preschool years, progresses to oral sex or mutual masturbation during the early school years, and then to sexual penetration (vaginal or anal intercourse) during preadolescence or adolescence (Waterman & Lusk, 1986).

Abused children rarely report the abuse, often because of fear of retaliation from the abuser or because they believe they will be blamed for it. Adults may suspect abuse if a child shows sudden personality changes or develops fears, problems in school, or eating or sleeping problems. A pediatrician may discover physical signs of abuse during a medical exam.

The average age at which most children are first sexually abused ranges from 6 to 12 years for girls and 7 to 10 years for boys (Knudsen, 1991). Boys are relatively more likely to be abused in public places and by strangers and non–family members (Faller, 1989a; Knudsen, 1991). Boys are also more likely to be threatened and physically injured.

Types of Abusers   Researchers find that the overwhelming majority of perpetrators of child sexual abuse of both boys and girls are males (Thomlison et al., 1991). Although most sexual abusers are adults, some are adolescents. Researchers are only now beginning to focus on this subgroup of offenders. One finding is that male adolescent sexual offenders are more likely than nonoffenders to have been molested themselves as young boys (Becker et al., 1989; Muster, 1992). Some adolescent sexual offenders may be imitating their own victimization. Adolescent child molesters also tend to feel socially inadequate and to be fearful of social interactions with age-mates of the other gender (Katz, 1990).

Although the great majority of sexual abusers are male, the number of female sexual abusers may be greater than has been generally believed (Banning, 1989). Many female sexual abusers may go undetected because society accords women a much freer range of physical contact with children than it does men. A woman who fondles a child might be seen as affectionate, or at worst seductive, whereas a man would be more likely to be perceived as a child molester (Banning, 1989).

What motivates a woman to sexually abuse children, even her own children? Little research has been done to explore this question, but some factors have begun to emerge (Matthews et al., 1990). Some female abusers have histories of becoming dependent on, or rejected by, abusive males. Some appear to have been manipulated into engaging in sexual abuse by their husbands. Others appear to have unmet emotional needs and low self-esteem and may have been seeking acceptance, closeness, and attention through sexual acts with children. Some, motivated by unresolved feelings of anger, revenge, powerlessness, or jealousy, may view their own and others' children as safe targets for venting these feelings. Some view their crimes as expressions of love.

Males account for a disproportionate number of child molesters. Why? Banning (1989), arguing from a sociocultural framework, suggests that males in our culture are socialized into seeking partners who are younger and weaker, whom they can easily dominate. This pattern of socialization may take the extreme form of development of sexual interest in children and adolescent girls, who because of their age are more easily dominated than adult women. Yet sexual interest in children may also be motivated by unusual patterns of sexual arousal in which children become the objects of sexual desire, sometimes to the exclusion of more appropriate (adult) stimuli. This brings us to pedophilia.

Pedophilia

Pedophilia

A type of paraphilia that is defined by sexual attraction to unusual stimuli: children. (From the Greek *paidos*, meaning "child," not the Latin *pedis*, meaning "foot.")

The prevalence of **pedophilia** in the general population is unknown (Ames & Houston, 1990). Some pedophiles are so distressed by their urges that they never act on them. Many, however, molest young children and adolescents, often repeatedly. Some pedophiles are responsible for large numbers of sexual assaults on children. One study of 232 convicted pedophiles showed that they had each molested an average of 76 children (Abel et al., 1989). Incarcerated pedophiles have usually committed many more offenses than those for which they were convicted (Ames & Houston, 1990).

Although pedophiles are sometimes called child molesters, not all child molesters are pedophiles. Pedophilia involves persistent or recurrent sexual attraction to children. Some molesters, however, may seek sexual contacts only with children when they are under unusual stress or lack other sexual outlets. Thus, they do not meet the clinical definition of pedophilia.

Pedophiles are almost exclusively male, although some isolated cases of female pedophiles have been reported (Cooper et al., 1990). Some pedophiles are sexually attracted only to children. Others are sexually attracted to adults as well. Some pedophiles limit their sexual interest in children to incestuous relationships with family members. Others abuse children to whom they are unrelated. Some pedophiles limit their sexual interest in children to looking at them or undressing them. Others fondle them or masturbate in their presence. Some manipulate or coerce children into oral, anal, or vaginal intercourse.

Children tend not to be worldly-wise. They can often be "taken in" by pedophiles who tell them that they would like to "show them something," "teach them something," or do something with them that they would "like." Some pedophiles seek to gain the child's af-

Fired. Former Phillips Academy prep school teacher David Cobb was convicted in 1996 of trying to pay a 12-year-old boy to perform sexual acts on him. He was also convicted for possessing and exhibiting child pornography.

fection and discourage the child from disclosing the sexual activity by showering the child with attention and gifts. Others threaten the child or the child's family to prevent disclosure.

There is no consistent personality profile of the pedophile (Okami & Goldberg, 1992). Most pedophiles do not fit the common stereotype of the "dirty old man" in the trench coat who hangs around school yards. Most are otherwise law-abiding, well-respected citizens, generally in their 30s and 40s. Many are married or divorced, with children of their own.

Research suggests that sexual attraction to children may be more common than is generally believed. Researchers in one study administered an anonymous survey to a sample of 193 college men (Briere & Runtz, 1989). A surprisingly high percentage of the students—21%—admitted to having been sexually attracted to small children. Nine percent reported sexual fantasies involving young children. Five percent reported masturbating to such fantasies. Seven percent reported that there was some likelihood that they would have sex with a young child if they knew they could avoid detection and punishment. Fortunately, most people with such erotic interests never act upon them.

Pedophilia may have complex and varied origins. Some pedophiles who are lacking in social skills may turn to children after failing to establish gratifying relationships with adult women (Overholser & Beck, 1986; Tollison & Adams, 1979). Research generally supports the stereotype of the pedophile as weak, passive, and shy—a socially inept, isolated man who feels threatened by mature relationships (Ames & Houston, 1990; Wilson & Cox, 1983).

Pedophiles who engage in incestuous relationships with their own children tend to present a somewhat different picture. They tend to fall on one or the other end of the dominance spectrum. Some are very dominant; others, very passive. Few are found between these extremes (Ames & Houston, 1990).

Some pedophiles were sexually abused as children and may be attempting to establish feelings of mastery by reversing the situation (De Young, 1982). Cycles of abuse may be perpetuated from generation to generation if children who are sexually abused become victimizers or partners of victimizers as adults.

Incest

Incest

Marriage or sexual relations between people who are so closely related (by "blood") that sexual relations are prohibited and punishable by law. (From the Latin *in-*, meaning "not," and *castus*, meaning "chaste.")

Incest applies to people who are related by blood, or *consanguineous*. The law may also proscribe coitus between, say, a stepfather and stepdaughter, however. Although a few societies have permitted incestuous pairings among royalty, all known cultures have some form of an incest taboo.

Perspectives on the Incest Taboo   Speculations about the origin of incest taboos abound. One explanation holds that the incest taboo developed because it was adaptive for ancient humans to prevent the harmful effects of inbreeding that may result when genetic defects or diseases are carried within family bloodlines (Leavitt, 1990). Our ancient ancestors lacked knowledge of the mechanisms of genetics, but they may have observed that certain diseases or defects tended to run in families. Evidence does show that marriage between close relations is associated with an increased rate of genetic diseases, mental retardation, and other physical abnormalities (Ames & Houston, 1990). Inbreeding may also be counterproductive to survival because it reduces the amount of genetic variation in the gene pool. Therefore, it can reduce the ability of the population to adapt to changes in the environment.

Other theorists explain the incest taboo in terms of the role that it may play in maintaining stability in the family and establishing kinship ties within the larger social grouping (Ember & Ember, 1990). The anthropologist Bronislaw Malinowski (1927), for example, argued that the incest taboo serves to reduce sexual competition within the family. If left uncontrolled, competition would create rivalry and hostility such that the family might be unable to function as a social unit. Since the family unit fosters survival of a society, the incest taboo may have developed as a means of keeping the family intact.

Cooperation theory emphasizes the importance to the survival of the society of cooperative ties between family groups (Ember & Ember, 1990). Society is complex. Its survival requires the cooperation of large numbers of people. Marriage establishes kinship ties that lessen suspiciousness and hostility between family groups and foster cooperation. According to cooperation theory, the incest taboo was established to help ensure that people would marry outside their own families and thus create cohesive communities. Such theories are fascinating but remain speculative.

Types of Incest   Most of our knowledge of incestuous relationships concerns father–daughter incest. Why? Most identified cases involve fathers who were eventually incarcerated.

About 1% of a sample of women in five American cities reported a sexual encounter with a father or stepfather (Cameron et al., 1986). Brother–sister incest, not parent–child incest, is the most common type of incest, however (Waterman & Lusk, 1986). Brother–sister incest is also believed to be greatly underreported, possibly because it tends to be transient and is apparently less harmful than parent–child incest. Finkelhor (1990) found that 21% of the college men in his sample, and 39% of the college women, reported incestuous relationships with a sibling of the other gender. Only 4% reported an incestuous relationship with their fathers. Incest between siblings of the same gender is rare (Waterman & Lusk, 1986). Mother–daughter incest is the rarest form of incest (Waterman & Lusk, 1986).

T r u t h   **OR**   *Fiction?*
R E V I S I T E D

It is not true that father–daughter incest is the most common type of incest. Father–daughter incest may be the most highly publicized variety of incest, but brother–sister incest is actually more common. ■

Let us further consider the two most common incest patterns, father–daughter incest and brother–sister incest.

Father–Daughter Incest   Father–daughter incest often begins with affectionate cuddling or embraces and then progresses to teasing sexual play, lengthy caresses, hugs, kisses, and genital contact, even penetration. In some cases genital contact occurs more abruptly, usually when the father has been drinking, or arguing with his wife. Force is not typically used to gain compliance, but daughters are sometimes physically overcome and injured by their fathers.

Brother–Sister Incest   In sibling incest, the brother usually initiates sexual activity and assumes the dominant role (Meiselman, 1978). Some brothers and sisters may view their sexual activity as natural and not know that it is taboo (Knox, 1988).

Evidence on the effects of incest between brothers and sisters is mixed. In a study of college undergraduates, those who reported childhood incest with siblings did not reveal greater evidence of sexual adjustment problems than other undergraduates (Greenwald & Leitenberg, 1989). Sibling incest may be harmful for some children, however (Sorrenti-Little et al., 1984). Sibling incest is most likely to be harmful when it is recurrent or forced or when parental response is harsh (Knox, 1988; Laviola, 1989).

Family Factors in Incest   Incest frequently occurs within the context of general family disruption, as in families in which there is spouse abuse, a dysfunctional marriage, or alcoholic or physically abusive parents (Alter-Reid et al., 1986; Sirles & Franke, 1989; Waterman, 1986a). Stressful events in the father's life, such as the loss of a job or problems at work, often precede the initiation of incest (Waterman, 1986a).

Fathers who abuse older daughters tend to be domineering and authoritarian with their families (Waterman, 1986a). Fathers who abuse younger, preschool daughters are more likely to be passive, dependent, and low in self-esteem. As Waterman (1986a) notes:

[The fathers] may need soothing and comforting, and may feel especially safe with preschool children: "I felt safe with her. . . . I didn't have to perform. She was so little that I knew she wouldn't and couldn't hurt me." (p. 215)

Marriages in incestuous families tend to be characterized by an uneven power relationship between the spouses. The abusive father is usually dominant. Another thread that frequently runs through incestuous families is a troubled sexual relationship between the spouses. The wife often rejects the husband sexually (Waterman, 1986a).

Gebhard and his colleagues (1965) found that many fathers who committed incest with their daughters were religiously devout, fundamentalist, and moralistic. Perhaps such men, when sexually frustrated, are less likely to seek extramarital and extrafamilial sexual outlets or to turn to masturbation as a sexual release. In many cases the father is under stress but does not find adequate emotional and sexual support from his wife (Gagnon, 1977). He turns to a daughter as a wife surrogate, often when he has been drinking alcohol (Gebhard et al., 1965). The daughter may become, in her father's fantasies, the "woman of the house." This fantasy may become his justification for continuing the incestuous relationship. In some incestuous families, a role reversal occurs. The abused daughter assumes many of the mother's responsibilities for managing the household and caring for the younger children (Waterman, 1986a).

Incestuous abuse is often repeated from generation to generation. One study found that in 154 cases of children who were sexually abused within the family, more than a third of the male offenders and about half of the mothers had either been abused themselves or were exposed to abuse as children (Faller, 1989b).

Sociocultural factors, such as poverty, overcrowded living conditions, and social or geographical isolation, may contribute to incest in some families (Waterman, 1986a). Sibling incest may be encouraged by the crowded living conditions and open sexuality that occur among some economically disadvantaged families (Waterman, 1986a).

Effects of Child Sexual Abuse

Child sexual abuse often inflicts great psychological harm on the child, whether the abuse is perpetrated by a family member, acquaintance, or stranger. Children who are sexually abused may suffer from a litany of short- and long-term psychological complaints, including anger, depression, anxiety, eating disorders, inappropriate sexual behavior, aggressive behavior, self-destructive behavior, sexual promiscuity, drug abuse, suicide attempts, posttraumatic stress disorder, low self-esteem, sexual dysfunction, mistrust of others, and feelings of detachment, (Beitchman, et al., 1992; Finkelhor, 1990; Goodwin et al., 1990; McLaren & Brown, 1989). Child sexual abuse may also have physical effects such as genital injuries and cause psychosomatic problems such as stomachaches and headaches.

Abused children commonly "act out." Younger children have tantrums or display aggressive or antisocial behavior. Older children turn to substance abuse (Finkelhor, 1990; Lusk & Waterman, 1986). Some abused children become withdrawn and retreat into fantasy or refuse to leave the house. Regressive behaviors, such as thumb sucking, fear of the dark, and fear of strangers, are also common among sexually abused children. On the heels of the assault and in the ensuing years, many survivors of childhood sexual abuse—like many rape survivors—show signs of posttraumatic stress disorder. They have flashbacks, nightmares, numbing of emotions, and feelings of estrangement from others (Finkelhor, 1990).

Sexual development of abused children may also become shaped in dysfunctional ways. For example, the survivor may become prematurely sexually active or promiscuous in adolescence and adulthood (Finkelhor, 1988; Lusk & Waterman, 1986; Tharinger, 1990). Researchers find that adolescent girls who are sexually abused tend to engage in consensual coitus at earlier ages than nonabused peers (Wyatt, 1988).

Researchers generally find more similarities than differences between the genders with respect to the effects of sexual abuse in childhood (Finkelhor, 1990). For example, both boys and girls tend to suffer fears and sleep disturbance. There are some gender differences, however. The most consistent gender difference appears to be that boys more often "externalize" their problems, perhaps by becoming more physically aggressive. Girls more often "internalize" their difficulties, as by becoming depressed (Finkelhor, 1990; Gomez-Schwartz et al., 1990).

There has been comparatively little research comparing survivors of child sexual abuse from different ethnic groups. In one of the few reported studies, researchers compared Asian American children who had been sexually abused with random samples of African,

Anatomically Correct Dolls. Therapists and police often use anatomically correct dolls to help sexually abused children describe experiences they cannot put into words. Yet a review of the research by Gerald Koocher and his colleagues in the September 1995 issue of *Psychological Bulletin* suggests that information received in this manner is not always reliable.

White, and Hispanic American sexually abused children drawn from the same child sex-abuse clinic (Rao et al., 1992). As compared to the other groups, Asian American children were more likely to become suicidal. Asian Americans were also less likely to exhibit anger and sexual acting out.

The long-term consequences of sexual abuse in childhood tend to be greater for children who were abused by their fathers or stepfathers, who experienced penetration, who were forced, and who suffered more prolonged and severe abuse (Beitchman et al., 1992; Waterman & Lusk, 1986; Wyatt & Newcomb, 1990). Children who suffer incest often feel a deep sense of betrayal by the offender and, perhaps, by other family members—especially their mothers, whom they perceive as failing to protect them (Finkelhor, 1988). Incest survivors may feel powerless to control their bodies or their lives.

Late adolescence and early adulthood seem to pose especially difficult periods for survivors of childhood sexual abuse. Studies of women in these age groups reveal more psychological and social problems in abused women than are found among nonabused reference groups (Jackson et al., 1990; Roland et al., 1989).

Effects of childhood sexual abuse are often long-lasting. In one study, researchers found evidence of greater psychological distress in a group of 54 adult women, ranging from 23 to 61 years of age, who had been sexually abused as children than in a matched group of nonabused women (Greenwald et al., 1990). Women who blame themselves for the abuse apparently have relatively lower self-esteem and more depression than those who do not (Hoagwood, 1990).

Prevention of Child Sexual Abuse

Many of us were taught by our parents never to accept a ride or an offer of candy from a stranger. However, many instances of child sexual abuse are perpetrated by familiar adults, often a family member or friend. Prevention programs help children understand what sexual abuse is and how they can avoid it. A national survey showed that two of three children in the United States have participated in school-based sex-abuse prevention programs (Goleman, 1993). In addition to learning to avoid strangers, children need to recognize the differences between acceptable touching, as in an affectionate embrace or pat on the head, and unacceptable or "bad" touching. Even elementary-school-age children can learn the distinction between "good touching and bad touching" (Tutty, 1992). Good school-based programs are generally helpful in preparing children to handle an actual encounter with a potential molester (Goleman, 1993). Children who receive comprehensive training are more likely to use strategies such as running away, yelling, or saying no when they are threatened by an abuser. They are also more likely to report incidents to adults.

Researchers recognize that children can easily be intimidated or overpowered by adults or older children. Children may be unable to say no in a sexually abusive situation, even though they want to and know it is the right thing to do (Waterman et al., 1986a). Although children may not always be able to prevent abuse, they can be encouraged to tell someone about it. Most prevention programs emphasize teaching children messages such as "It's not your fault," "Never keep a bad or scary secret," and "Always tell your parents about this, especially if someone says you shouldn't tell them" (Waterman et al., 1986a).

Children also need to be alerted to the types of threats they might receive for disclosing the abuse. They are more likely to resist threats if they are reassured that they will be believed if they disclose the abuse, that their parents will continue to love them, and that they and their families will be protected from the molester.

School-based prevention programs focus on protecting the child. In most states, teachers and helping professionals are required to report suspected abuse to authorities. Tighter controls and better screening are needed to monitor the hiring of day care employees. Administrators and teachers in preschool and day care facilities also need to be educated to recognize the signs of sexual abuse and to report suspected cases (Waterman et al., 1986). Treatment programs to help people who are sexually attracted to children *before* they commit abusive acts would also be of use.

Treatment of Survivors of Child Sexual Abuse

At least 75% of cases of child sexual abuse go unreported. Psychotherapy in adulthood often becomes the first opportunity for survivors to confront leftover feelings of pain, anger, and misplaced guilt (Alter-Reid et al., 1986; Ratican, 1992). Group or individual therapy can help improve survivors' self-esteem and ability to develop intimate relationships. Confronting the trauma within a supportive therapeutic relationship may also help prevent the cycle of abuse from perpetuating itself from one generation to another (Alter-Reid et al., 1986).

Special programs have begun to appear that provide therapeutic services to abused children and adolescents. Most therapists recommend a multicomponent treatment approach, which may involve individual therapy for the child, mother, and father; group therapy for the adolescent or even preadolescent survivor; art therapy or play therapy for the younger child (e.g., using drawings or puppets to express feelings); marital counseling for the parents; and family therapy for the entire family (de Luca et al., 1992; Waterman, 1986b).

∼ *Reflections* ∼

▨ Agree or disagree with the following statement, and support your answer: Any form of sexual contact between an adult and a child is abusive.

▨ Do you know of anyone who was exposed to childhood sexual abuse? What was the experience like at the time? What were its lingering effects? Was the perpetrator reported to authorities? Why, or why not?

▨ Why do you think that males account for a disproportionate number of child molesters?

Treatment of Rapists and Child Molesters

What does *treatment* mean? When a helping professional treats someone, the goal is usually to help that individual. When we speak of treating a sex offender, the goal is as likely, or more likely, to help society by eliminating the problem behavior.

Rapists and child molesters are criminals, not patients. Most convicted rapists and child molesters are incarcerated as a form of punishment, not treatment. They may receive psychological treatment or rehabilitation in prison to help prepare them for release and reentry into society, however. The most common form of treatment is group therapy, which is based on the belief that though offenders may fool counselors, they do not easily fool one another (Kaplan, 1993). Yet the great majority of incarcerated sex offenders receive little or no treatment in prison (Goleman, 1992). In California, for example, which has 15,000 incarcerated sex offenders, treatment has been provided in but one experimental program for only 46 rapists and child molesters (Goleman, 1992).

The results of prison-based treatment programs are mixed at best. Consider a Canadian study of 54 rapists who participated in a treatment program. Following release from prison, 28% were later convicted of a sexual offense, and 43% were convicted of a violent offense (Rice et al., 1990). Treatment also failed to curb recidivism among a sample of 136 child molesters (Rice et al., 1991).

More promising findings resulted from innovative programs in prison facilities in California and Vermont (Goleman, 1992). In the Vermont program, the average rate of conviction for additional sex crimes following release was reduced by at least half in a group of sex offenders who received the treatment program, as compared to a control group who did not. These innovative programs used a variety of techniques. Empathy training was used to increase the offender's sensitivity to his victims. One empathy exercise had offenders write about their crimes from the perspective of the victim. The technique of covert sensitization was used to help offenders resist deviant sex fantasies, which often lead to deviant behavior. The offender would pair, in his imagination, scenes involving rape and molestation with aversive consequences. An exhibitionist, for example, might be asked to practice imagining that he is about to expose himself and is discovered in the act by his parents. A child molester might fantasize about sexually approaching a child, only to find himself confronted by police officers.

Another approach uses medical interventions to reduce testosterone levels and, consequently, offenders' sex drives. In a few European countries, some offenders who claimed they were unable to control their sex drives have been castrated to reduce testosterone levels (Wille & Beier, 1989). The effects of castration are mixed. Many castrated rapists report markedly lowered sex drives, as might be expected from the reductions in testosterone production that result from the removal of the testes. They may retain sexual interest and remain capable of erection, however. And some do repeat their crimes. Other researchers report lower recidivism rates among castrated offenders than among noncastrated offenders. In any event, the use of castration with sex offenders appears to be declining (Wille & Beier, 1989).

Surgical castration is an extreme measure. It raises ethical concerns because of its invasive character and irreversibility. Antiandrogen drugs such as Depo-Provera chemically lessen testicular production of testosterone (Hucker et al., 1988; Ingersoll & Patton, 1991). Unlike surgical castration, the effects of antiandrogen drugs are reversible. Compliance in taking the drugs is a major obstacle to their use, however (Hucker et al., 1988). Nor do drugs help rapists resolve their hostility toward women or their needs for dominance and power.

~ *Reflections* ~

◼ Agree or disagree with the following statement, and support your answer: We should punish sex offenders and not worry about "treating" them.

◼ Agree or disagree with the following statement and support your answer: It is futile to attempt to provide treatment for a sex offender.

Sexual Harassment

Many Americans were spellbound by the Michael Douglas–Demi Moore film, *Disclosure.* In the film, Demi Moore plays Michael Douglas's supervisor. She uses her power over him to attempt to harass him into sexual activity.

Disclosure. The film *Disclosure* revolved around a case in which a female supervisor (Demi Moore) sexually harassed a male employee (Michael Douglas). The film was of interest not only because of the "star power," but also because of the role reversals. That is, the great majority of sexual harassers are men.

Sexual harassment
Deliberate or repeated unsolicited verbal comments, gestures, or physical contact of a sexual nature that is considered to be unwelcome by the recipient.

What *is* **sexual harassment?** Definitions of sexual harassment vary, but its definition in the workplace as the "deliberate or repeated unsolicited verbal comments, gestures, or physical contact of a sexual nature that is considered to be unwelcome by the recipient" has been widely adopted (U.S. Merit Systems Protection Board, 1981, p. 2). Sexual harassment can range from unwelcome sexual jokes, overtures, suggestive comments, and sexual innuendos to outright sexual assault, and may include behaviors such as the following (Powell 1991, p. 110):

- Verbal harassment or abuse
- Subtle pressure for sexual activity
- Remarks about a person's clothing, body, or sexual activities
- Leering at or ogling a person's body
- Unwelcome touching, patting, or pinching
- Brushing against a person's body
- Demands for sexual favors accompanied by implied or overt threats concerning one's job or student status
- Physical assault

Men or women can both commit, and be subjected to, sexual harassment. However, despite the plot of the film *Disclosure,* the great majority of harassers are men.

Charges of sexual harassment are often ignored or trivialized by coworkers and employers. The victim may hear, "Why make a big deal out of it? It's not like you were attacked in the street." Evidence shows, however, that persons subjected to sexual harassment do suffer from it. In one study, 75% of people who were sexually harassed reported reactions such as anxiety, irritability, lowered self-esteem, and anger (Gruber & Bjorn, 1986; Loy & Stewart, 1984). Some find harassment on the job so unbearable that they resign. College women have dropped courses, switched majors, or changed graduate programs or even colleges because they were unable to stop professors from sexually harassing them (Dziech & Weiner, 1984; Fitzgerald, 1993a, 1993b).

One reason that sexual harassment is so stressful is that, as with so many other forms of sexual exploitation or coercion, the blame tends to fall on the victim (Powell, 1991). Some harassers seem to believe that charges of harassment were exaggerated or that the victim "overreacted" or "took me too seriously." In our society, women are expected to be "nice"—to be passive and not "make a scene." The woman who assertively protects her rights may be seen as "strange" and disturbing, or a "troublemaker." "Women are damned if they assert themselves and victimized if they don't" (Powell, 1991, p. 114).

Sexual harassment may have more to do with the abuse of power than with sexual desire (Goleman, 1991; Tedeschi & Felson, 1994). Relatively few cases of sexual harassment involve outright requests for sexual favors. Most involve the expression of power as a tactic to control or frighten someone, usually a woman. The harasser is usually in a dominant position and abuses that position by exploiting the victim's vulnerability. Sexual harassment may be used as a tactic of social control, a means of keeping women "in their place." This is especially so in work settings that are traditional male preserves, such as the firehouse, the construction site, or the military academy. Sexual harassment expresses resentment and hostility toward women who venture beyond the boundaries of the traditional feminine role (Fitzgerald, 1993b).

Sexual harassment is not confined to the workplace or the university. It may also occur between patients and doctors and between therapists and clients. Therapists may use their power and influence to pressure clients into sexual relations. The harassment may be disguised, expressed in terms of the "therapeutic benefits" of sexual activity.

Two of the most common settings in which sexual harassment occurs are the workplace and the university.

Sexual Harassment in the Workplace

Harassers in the workplace can be employers, supervisors, coworkers, or clients of a company. In some cases clients make unwelcome sexual advances to employees that are ignored or approved of by the boss. If a worker asks a coworker for a date and is refused, it is not sexual harassment. If the coworker persists with unwelcome advances and does not take no for an answer, however, the behavior crosses the line and becomes harassment.

Perhaps the most severe form of sexual harassment, short of an outright assault, involves an employer or supervisor who demands sexual favors as a condition of employment or advancement. In 1980, the Equal Employment Opportunity Commission drafted a set of guidelines that expanded the definition of sexual harassment in the workplace to include any behavior of a sexual nature that interferes with an individual's work performance or creates a hostile, intimidating, or offensive work environment.

In 1986, the U.S. Supreme Court recognized sexual harassment as a form of sex discrimination under Title VII of the Civil Rights Act of 1964. It held that employers could be held accountable if such behavior was deemed to create a hostile or abusive work environment or to interfere with an employee's work performance. A 1993 Supreme Court ruling held that a person need not suffer psychological damage to sue an employer on grounds of sexual harassment ("Court, 9–0," 1993). Moreover, employers can be held responsible not only for their own actions, but also for sexual harassment by their employees when they either knew *or should have known* that harassment was taking place and failed to eliminate it promptly (McKinney & Maroules, 1991). To protect themselves, many companies and universities have developed antiharassment programs to educate workers about sexual harassment, established mechanisms for dealing with complaints, and imposed sanctions against harassers.

Under the law, persons subjected to sexual harassment can obtain a court order to have the harassment stopped, have their jobs reinstated (when they have lost them by resisting sexual advances), receive back pay and lost benefits, and obtain monetary awards for the emotional strain imposed by the harassment. However, proving charges of sexual harassment is generally difficult because there are usually no corroborating witnesses or evidence. As a result, relatively few persons who encounter sexual harassment in the workplace file formal complaints or seek legal remedies.

One survey found that most people who were sexually harassed handled the situation by ignoring the harasser (32%) or by saying something directly to the harasser (39%) (Loy & Stewart, 1984). Seventeen percent sought job transfers or quit their jobs. Relatively few, 2%, sought legal help. Only about 3% of women who have been sexually harassed file a formal complaint (Goleman, 1991). Like people subjected to other forms of sexual coercion, persons experiencing sexual harassment often do not report the offense for fear that they will not be believed or will be subjected to retaliation. Some fear that they will be branded as "troublemakers" or that they will lose their jobs (Goleman, 1991).

Sexual Harassment. Where do we draw the line between a sexual invitation and sexual harassment? According to the U.S. government, sexual harassment in the workplace is the "deliberate or repeated unsolicited verbal comments, gestures, or physical contact of a sexual nature that is considered to be unwelcome by the recipient." Sexual harassment can range from unwelcome sexual jokes, overtures, suggestive comments, and sexual innuendos to outright sexual assault.

How common is sexual harassment in the workplace? Although two thirds of the men interviewed by the *Harvard Business Review* said that reports of sexual harassment in the workplace were exaggerated (Castro, 1992), a survey by *Working Woman* magazine showed that more than 90% of the Fortune 500 companies had received complaints of sexual harassment from their employees. More than one third of the companies had been sued on charges of sexual harassment (Sandross, 1988). A survey of federal employees by the U.S. Merit System Protection Board found that 42% of females and 14% of males reported instances of sexual harassment (DeWitt, 1991). A 1991 *The New York Times*/CBS News poll found that 38% of the women sampled reported that they had been the object of sexual advances or remarks from supervisors or other men in positions of power (Kolbert, 1991). Overall, it may be that as many as 1 in 2 women encounters some form of sexual harassment on the job or in college. Sexual harassment would thus be the most common form of sexual victimization (Fitzgerald, 1993b). Research overseas finds that about 70% of the women who work in Japan and 50% of those who work in Europe have encountered sexual harassment (Castro, 1992). Sexual harassment against women is more common in workplaces in which women have traditionally been underrepresented (Fitzgerald, 1993b), such as the construction site or the shipyard.

Sexual Harassment on Campus

Estimates of the frequency of sexual harassment of undergraduate and graduate students vary widely across studies, from 7% to 27% of men and from 12% to 65% of women (McKinney & Maroules, 1991). Overall, 25% to 30% of students report at least one incident of sexual harassment in college. The federal law prohibiting sex discrimination in academic institutions permits students to sue their schools for monetary damages for sexual harassment (Greenhouse, 1992).

Sexual harassment on campus usually involves the less severe forms of harassment, such as sexist comments and sexual remarks, as well as come-ons, suggestive looks, propositions, and light touching (McKinney & Maroules, 1991). Relatively few acts involve the use of direct pressure for sexual intercourse. Harassers are typically (but not always) male. Most students who encounter sexual harassment do not report the incident. If they do, it is usually to a confidant and not a person in authority.

Most forms of harassment involve unequal power relationships between the harasser and the person harassed. *Peer harassment* involves cases between people who are equal in power, as in the cases of repeated sexual taunts from fellow employees, students, or colleagues. In some cases, the harasser may even have less formal power than the person harassed. For example, women professors have been sexually harassed by students (Grauerholz, 1989). Here, of course, the traditional social dominance of the male may override the academic position of the woman—at least in the mind of the offender.

The most common form of harassment by students, reported by nearly one third of the female professors polled in a recent survey, involved sexist remarks. Other common forms of harassment include obscene phone calls, undue attention, and sexual remarks. Outright sexual advances were reported by a few professors (Grauerholz, 1989).

Male faculty and staff members may also be subject to harassment. Six percent of 235 male faculty members polled at one university reported being sexually harassed by a student. Nearly double that percentage (11%) reported that they had attempted to stroke, caress, or touch a student, however (Fitzgerald et al., 1988).

Sexual Harassment in the Schools

Playful sexual antics have long been associated with adolescence. However, unwelcome sexual advances and lewd comments go beyond customary playfulness and have become a troubling concern to many of America's teens. A 1993 nationwide survey of high school and junior high school students found that many boys and girls had encountered harassment in the form of others grabbing or groping them or subjecting them to sexually explicit putdowns when walking through school hallways (Henneberger, 1993).

The picture that emerges from a 1993 Louis Harris nationwide poll of teenagers in grades 8 through 11 indicates that sexual taunts and advances have become part of an unwelcome ritual for many students, especially girls, in trying to make their way through the hallways and stairwells of high schools (Barringer, 1993c; Henneberger, 1993). More than two of three of the girls, and more than four out of ten of the boys, reported being touched, grabbed, or pinched at school. Two of three boys and about one in two girls reported harassing other students. Many of the harassers (41% of the boys and 31% of the girls) viewed their actions as "just part of school life" and "no big deal." Unwelcome sexual comments and advances had negative impact on both boys and girls, but especially on girls. One in three girls who experienced sexual harassment at school reported that it made them feel that they didn't want to go to school. Twenty-eight percent said that it made it more difficult to pay attention in class, and 20% said that it lowered their grades.

One problem is that teachers tend to tolerate sexually harassing behavior by male students against female classmates (Chira, 1992). Most of the harassment (about 80%) reported in the Harris survey was committed by other students, but some students reported being harassed by teachers, coaches, custodians, and other adults.

How to Resist Sexual Harassment

What would you do if you were sexually harassed by an employer or a professor? How would you handle it? Would you try to ignore it and hope that it would stop? What actions might you take? We offer some suggestions, adapted from Powell (1991), that may be helpful. Recognize, however, that responsibility for sexual harassment always lies with the perpetrator and the organization that permits sexual harassment to take place, not with the person subjected to the harassment.

1. *Convey a professional attitude.* Harassment may be stopped cold by responding to the harasser with a businesslike, professional attitude.
2. *Discourage harassing behavior, and encourage appropriate behavior.* Harassment may also be stopped cold by shaping the harasser's behavior. Your reactions to the harasser may encourage businesslike behavior and discourage flirtatious or suggestive behavior. If a harassing professor suggests that you come back after school to review your term paper so that the two of you will be undisturbed, set limits assertively. Tell the professor that you'd feel more comfortable discussing the paper during regular of-

fice hours. Remain task-oriented. Stick to business. The harasser should quickly get the message that you wish to maintain a strictly professional relationship. If the harasser persists, do not blame yourself. You are responsible only for your own actions. When the harasser persists, a more direct response may be appropriate: "Professor Jones, I'd like to keep our relationship on a purely professional basis, okay?"

3. *Avoid being alone with the harasser.* If you are being harassed by your professor but need some advice about preparing your term paper, approach him or her after class when other students are milling about, not privately during office hours. Or bring a friend to wait outside the office while you consult the professor.

4. *Maintain a record.* Keep a record of all incidents of harassment as documentation in the event you decide to lodge an official complaint. The record should include the following: (1) where the incident took place; (2) the date and time; (3) what happened, including the exact words that were used, if you can recall them; (4) how you felt; and (5) the names of witnesses. Some people who have been subjected to sexual harassment have carried a hidden tape recorder during contacts with the harasser. Such recordings may not be admissible in a court of law, but they are persuasive in organizational grievance procedures. A hidden tape recorder may be illegal in your state, however. It is thus advisable to check the law.

5. *Talk with the harasser.* It may be uncomfortable to address the issue directly with a harasser, but doing so puts the offender on notice that you are aware of the harassment and want it to stop. It may be helpful to frame your approach in terms of a description of the specific offending actions (e.g., "When we were alone in the office, you repeatedly attempted to touch me or brush up against me"), your feelings about the offending behavior ("It made me feel like my privacy was being violated. I'm very upset about this and haven't been sleeping well"), and what you would like the offender to do ("So I'd like you to agree never to attempt to touch me again, okay?"). Having a talk with the harasser may stop the harassment. If the harasser denies the accusations, it may be necessary to take further action.

6. *Write a letter to the harasser.* Set down on paper a record of the offending behavior, and put the harasser on notice that the harassment must stop. Your letter might (1) describe what happened ("Several times you have made sexist comments about my body"), (2) describe how you feel ("It made me feel like a sexual object when you talked to me that way"), and (3) describe what you would like the harasser to do ("I want you to stop making sexist comments to me").

7. *Seek support.* Support from people you trust can help you through the often trying process of resisting sexual harassment. Talking with others allows you to express your feelings and receive emotional support, encouragement, and advice. In addition, it may strengthen your case if you have the opportunity to identify and talk with other people who have been harassed by the offender.

8. *File a complaint.* Companies and organizations are required by law to respond reasonably to complaints of sexual harassment. In large organizations, a designated official (sometimes an ombudsman, affirmative action officer, or sexual harassment adviser) is usually charged to handle such complaints. Set up an appointment with this official to discuss your experiences. Ask about the grievance procedures in the organization and your right to confidentiality. Have available a record of the dates of the incidents, what happened, how you felt about it, and so on.

   The two major government agencies that handle charges of sexual harassment are the Equal Employment Opportunity Commission (look under the government section of your phone book for the telephone number of the nearest office) and your state's Human Rights Commission (listed in your phone book under state or municipal government). These agencies may offer advice on how you can protect your legal rights and proceed with a formal complaint.

9. *Seek legal remedies.* Sexual harassment is illegal and actionable. If you are considering legal action, consult an attorney familiar with this area of law. You may be entitled to back pay (if you were fired for reasons arising from the sexual harassment), job reinstatement, and punitive damages.

In closing, we ask not what persons who suffer rape, incest, and sexual harassment will do to redress the harm that has been done to them. We ask what all of us will do to re-shape our society so that sex is no longer used as an instrument of power, coercion, and violence.

~ Reflections ~

- Agree or disagree with the following statement, and support your answer: Because of all the publicity, people who are intolerant of normal sexual advances, or who want to punish their supervisors, are now crying sexual harassment.
- Have you or a friend been exposed to sexual harassment? How did you or the friend handle the situation? Are you happy with the way the situation was handled? Why, or why not?
- Imagine that you are sexually harassed and want to report it, but a friend advises, "Why make such a fuss? Is it really worth it? After all, complaining could backfire." How would you respond?

Summing Up

Rape

Although sexual motivation plays a role in many rapes, the use of sex to express aggression, anger, and power is more central to our understanding of rape. The definition of rape varies from state to state but usually refers to obtaining sexual intercourse with a nonconsenting person by the use of force or the threat of force.

Incidence of Rape Surveys suggest that there are about 310,000 rapes and sexual assaults each year in the United States. Many rapes go unreported.

Types of Rapes Types of rapes include stranger rape, acquaintance rape, marital rape, gang rape, male rape, and rape by females. Women are more likely to be raped by men they know than by strangers. Most male rapes occur in prison settings. Husbands who rape their wives can now be prosecuted under the rape laws in many states.

Social Attitudes and Myths That Encourage Rape
Social attitudes such as gender-role stereotyping, seeing sex as adversarial, and acceptance of violence in interpersonal relationships all help create a climate that encourages rape.

Sociocultural Factors in Rape Many observers contend that our society breeds rapists by socializing males to be socially and sexually dominant.

Psychological Characteristics of Rapists Incarcerated rapists vary in their psychological characteristics. Self-identified sexually aggressive men are more likely than other men to condone rape and violence against women, have traditional gender-role attitudes, be hostile toward

women, engage in sexual activity to express social dominance, be sexually aroused by rape, lack a social conscience, and have peer groups such as fraternities that pressure them into sexual activity. Groth and Birnbaum identified three basic kinds of rape: anger rape, power rape, and sadistic rape.

Adjustment of Rape Survivors Rape survivors are often in a state of crisis afterward. Burgess and Holmstrom identified some common response patterns in rape survivors that they labeled the rape trauma syndrome.

Treatment of Rape Survivors Treatment of rape survivors typically involves helping them through the crisis period following the attack and then helping to foster long-term adjustment.

Rape Prevention Rape prevention involves education of society at large and the taking of a number of precautions that are available to women. Whether or not women take precautions to prevent rape, however, the rapist is always the one responsible for the assault.

Verbal Sexual Coercion

Verbal sexual coercion involves the use of verbal pressure or seduction lines to manipulate a person into having sexual relations.

Sexual Abuse of Children

Like rape, child sexual abuse is greatly underreported.

What Is Child Sexual Abuse? Any form of sexual contact between an adult and a child is abusive, even if force or physical threat is not used, since children are incapable of voluntarily consenting to sexual activity with adults.

Patterns of Abuse Child sexual abuse, like rape and other forms of sexual coercion, cuts across all socioeconomic classes. In most cases, the molesters are close to the children they abuse—relatives, steprelatives, family friends, and neighbors. Genital fondling is the most common type of abuse.

Pedophilia Pedophilia is a type of paraphilia in which adults are sexually attracted to children. Pedophiles are almost exclusively male.

Incest Incest is marriage or sexual relations between people who are so closely related that sex is prohibited and punished by virtue of the kinship tie. Several theories have been expounded to explain the development of the incest taboo, including theories based on the dangers of inbreeding, the role played by the taboo in maintaining stability in the family, and cooperation theory. Father–daughter incest is most likely to be reported and prosecuted, but brother–sister incest is the most common type of incest. Incest frequently occurs within the context of general family disruption.

Effects of Child Sexual Abuse Children who are sexually abused often suffer social and emotional problems that impair their development and persist into adulthood, affecting their self-esteem and their formation of intimate relationships.

Prevention of Child Sexual Abuse In addition to learning to avoid strangers, children need to learn the difference between acceptable touching, such as an affectionate embrace or pat on the head, and unacceptable or "bad" touching. Children who may not be able to prevent abuse may nevertheless be encouraged to tell someone about the experience.

Treatment of Survivors of Child Sexual Abuse Psychotherapy may help adult survivors of child sexual abuse improve their self-esteem and ability to develop intimate relationships. Special programs provide therapeutic services to abused children and adolescents.

Treatment of Rapists and Child Molesters

The effectiveness of prison-based rehabilitation programs and antiandrogen drugs in curbing repeat offenses requires further empirical support.

Sexual Harassment

Sexual Harassment in the Workplace Sexual harassment in the workplace involves "deliberate or repeated unsolicited verbal comments, gestures, or physical contact of a sexual nature that [are] unwelcome [to] the recipient." Sexual harassment may be used as a tactic to keep women "in their place," especially in work settings that are traditional male preserves.

Sexual Harassment on Campus About 25% to 30% of students report at least one incident of sexual harassment in college. Professors may also be harassed by students.

Sexual Harassment in the Schools Sexual harassment at school has become an unwelcome ritual that many junior and senior high school students are forced to endure.

How to Resist Sexual Harassment There is no guaranteed way to put an end to sexual harassment, but some suggestions that have helped many individuals include conveying a professional attitude, avoiding being alone with the harasser, keeping a record of incidents, and seeking legal remedies.

CHAPTER 20

Henri Matisse, *Circus,* Plate 2 from *Jazz.* The Metropolitan Museum of Art, Gift of Lila Acheson Wallace, 1983. © 1996 Succession H. Matisse/Artist Rights Society (ARS), New York. © 1985 by The Metropolitan Museum of Art.

Commercial Sex

Outline

Truth OR Fiction?

_____ Prostitution is illegal throughout the United States.

_____ The massage and escort services advertised in the Yellow Pages are fronts for prostitution.

_____ Most female prostitutes were sexually abused as children.

_____ Typical customers of prostitutes have difficulty forming sexual relationships with other women.

_____ Most prostitutes take precautions to avoid becoming infected by or transmitting the AIDS virus.

_____ Only males are sexually aroused by pornography.

_____ If advertisements are too sexy, consumers may forget what the product was.

I n 1995, England's floppy-haired actor Hugh Grant was caught with a prostitute in a BMW on Hollywood's Sunset Boulevard. Why? His girl-friend was supermodel Elizabeth Hurley, who at the time was promoting the perfume called "Pleasures." Grant exemplified good looks, charm, innocence, and success (Beller, 1995). Still, he sought the sexual services of a woman for hire.

Why, indeed. Why have millions of men (and some women) paid for sex throughout the centuries? In the caverns of Wall Street, brokers and traders sell stocks and other financial instruments that drive the nation's commercial enterprises. On the floor of Chicago's Board of Trade, brokers trade commodities—soybeans, corn, wheat, and other goods. Prices go up, prices go down, responding to the law of supply and demand. On street corners a few short blocks from these financial institutions, another sort of commerce takes place. In New York City and Chicago, as in Hollywood and the nation's smaller towns and villages, prostitutes exchange sex for money or for goods such as drugs.

Sex is also used to sell more legitimate goods and services. "Sex sells" is a common catchphrase that has driven the imaginations of countless copywriters to create advertising campaigns projecting a "sexy" image for products ranging from automobiles to blue jeans, from beer to bread sticks.

The World of Commercial Sex: A Disneyland for Adults

Sex as commerce runs the gamut from adult movie theaters and bookshops to strip shows, sex toy shops, erotic hotels and motels, escort/outcall services, "massage parlors," "900" telephone services, and the use of sex appeal in advertisements for legitimate products. The "world of commercial sex is a kind of X-rated amusement park—Disneyland for Adults" (Edgley, 1989, p. 372).

In this chapter, we discuss three commercial aspects of sexuality: prostitution, pornography, and the use of sex in advertising. Though the streetwalker, the purveyor of "adult" movies, and the Madison Avenue copywriter may otherwise have little else in common, they all have learned to use sex to make a profit. We also compare and contrast the concepts of pornography and obscenity. We shall see that one person's art may be another person's pornography.

Prostitution

Hugh Grant ran afoul of the law because prostitution is illegal in California. **Prostitution** is illegal everywhere in the United States except for some rural counties in Nevada, where it is restricted to state-licensed brothels.

It is not true that prostitution is illegal throughout the United States. It is legal in some counties in the state of Nevada, although it is restricted to regulated, state-licensed brothels. ∎

Soliciting the services of a prostitute is also illegal in many states. Police rarely crack down on customers, or "johns," however. Hugh Grant came to their attention because he was engaging in a "lewd act" in a car parked on a public street. The few who are arrested are usually penalized with a small fine. On occasion, the names of convicted johns are pub-

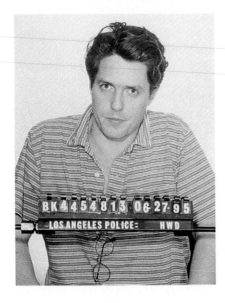

Sex in L.A. Why did British actor Hugh Grant solicit L.A. prostitute Divine Brown for a lewd encounter on Hollywood's Sunset Boulevard? Why did actor Charlie Sheen pay thousands for trysts with the "Hollywood Madam's" call girls?

Prostitution
The sale of sexual activity for money or goods of value, such as drugs. (From the Latin *prostituere*, meaning "to cause to stand in front of." The implication is that one is offering one's body for sale.)

lished in local newspapers, which may deter men who fear publicity. On the other hand, some believe that Hugh Grant's indiscretion boosted receipts for his film *Nine Months*, which opened a few days later. Although prostitutes and their clients can be male or female, most prostitutes are female and virtually all customers are male.

Prostitution is often called "the world's oldest profession," for good reason. It can be traced at least to ancient Mesopotamia, where temple prostitution flourished. The Greek historian Herodotus noted that all women in the city were expected to put in some time at the temple. They would offer their bodies to passing strangers, who would make a "religious" donation.

Prostitution flourished in medieval Europe and during the sexually repressive Victorian period in the nineteenth century. Then, as now, the major motive for prostitution was economic. Many poor women were drawn to prostitution as a means of survival. In Victorian England, prostitution was widely regarded as a necessary outlet for men to satisfy their sexual appetites. It was widely held that women lacked the potential to enjoy sex. Therefore, it was commonly believed that it was better for a man to visit a prostitute than to "soil" his wife with his carnal passions.

In the nineteenth-century United States, married and unmarried men frequented prostitutes regularly. Use of prostitution cut across all economic and social boundaries. Prostitution most often occurred within two contexts, sexual initiation for young males and regular brothel visitation.

Incidence of Prostitution in the United States Today

No one knows how many prostitutes there are in the United States. The little we know of prostitution derives from sex surveys.

Almost two thirds of the White males in Kinsey's sample (Kinsey et al., 1948) reported visiting a prostitute at least once. About 15% to 20% visited them regularly. The use of prostitutes varied with educational level, however. By the age of 20, about 50% of Kinsey's non-college-educated single males, but only 20% of his college-educated males, had visited a prostitute. By the age of 25, the figures swelled to about two thirds for non-college-educated males but only slightly above 25% for college men.

Kinsey's data foreshadowed a falling off of experience with prostitutes that seems linked to the decay of the sexual double standard. Kinsey found that 20% of his college-educated men had been sexually initiated by prostitutes. This figure was more than cut in half among generations who came of age in the 1960s and 1970s (Hunt, 1974). Less than 10% of both college-educated *and* non-college-educated males in the *Playboy* survey (Hunt, 1974) of the 1970s reported being sexually initiated by a prostitute.

Why are young men less likely to visit prostitutes than they were in Kinsey's day? For one thing, young men in recent generations were more likely to become sexually initiated with their girlfriends (see Chapter 13). As Edgley (1989) put it, "An old and hallowed economic principle was at work; those who charge for a service cannot compete with those who give it away" (p. 392). Increased concern about sexually transmitted diseases, especially AIDS, has also limited the use of prostitution. Nevertheless, prostitution continues to flourish.

Types of Female Prostitutes

Female prostitutes—commonly called *hookers, whores, working girls,* or *escorts*—are usually classified according to the settings in which they work. The major types of prostitutes today are streetwalkers; brothel or "house" prostitutes, many of whom work in massage parlors and for "escort services" (many prostitutes today have their customers "let their fingers do the walking through the Yellow Pages"); and call girls. Traditional brothel prostitution is much less common today than before World War II.

Streetwalkers Part of the mystery about Hugh Grant was why he would seek the services of any prostitute. Another part of it was why he would seek out a **streetwalker.**

Streetwalkers

Prostitutes who solicit customers on the streets.

Pimps

Men who serve as agents for prostitutes and live off their earnings. (From the Middle French *pimper,* meaning "to dress smartly.")

Although most prostitutes are streetwalkers, streetwalkers occupy the bottom rung in the hierarchy of prostitutes. They earn the lowest incomes and are usually the least desirable. They also incur the greatest risk of abuse by customers and **pimps.** Streetwalkers tend to come from poverty and to have had unhappy childhoods (Edgley, 1989). Perhaps as many as 80% are survivors of rape, sexual abuse, or incest (Gordon & Snyder, 1989). Many were teenage runaways who turned to prostitution to survive.

Streetwalkers operate in the open. They are thus more likely than other prostitutes to draw attention to themselves and risk arrest. To avoid arrest, streetwalkers may be indirect about their services. They may ask passersby if they are interested in a "good time" or some "fun" rather than sex per se. In many cities, streetwalkers dress in revealing or provocative fashions.

There is the stereotype of the prostitute as a sexually unresponsive woman who feigns sexual arousal with johns while she keeps one eye glued to the clock. Most street prostitutes in a Philadelphia sample, however, reported that some forms of sex with customers were "very satisfying" (Savitz & Rosen, 1988). More than 60% of the prostitutes reported achieving orgasm with customers at least occasionally. Most prostitutes also reported that they had enjoyable sexual relationships in their private lives and were regularly orgasmic. Not surprisingly, they garnered more sexual enjoyment from their personal relationships than from their customers.

Streetwalkers. Streetwalkers earn the lowest wages and have the lowest status among prostitutes. They are also at greatest risk of arrest and abuse by pimps.

In most locales, penalties for prostitution involve small fines or short jail terms. Many police departments, besieged by crimes such as drug peddling and violent crimes, consider prostitution a "minor" or "nuisance" crime (Carvajal, 1995). Many prostitutes find the criminal justice system a revolving door. They pay the fine. They spend a night or two in jail. They return to the streets.

A bar prostitute is a variation of the streetwalker. She approaches men in a bar she frequents, rather than on the streets. Payoffs to bar owners or managers secure their cooperation, although the women are sometimes tolerated because they draw customers. Some streetwalkers work X-rated, or "adult," movie houses and may service their patrons in their seats with manual or oral sex. Payoffs may secure the cooperation of the management.

Many streetwalkers support a pimp. A pimp acts as lover–father–companion–master. He provides streetwalkers with protection, bail, and sometimes room and board, in exchange for a high percentage of their earnings, often more than 90%. As Chris, a street-walker explains, a prostitute cannot expect to survive long on the streets without a pimp:

CHRIS: You can't really work the streets for yourself unless you got a man—not for a long length of time. . . . 'cause the other pimps are not going to like it because you don't have anybody to represent you. They'll rob you, they'll hit you in the head if you don't have nobody to take up for you. Yea, it happens. They give you a hassle. . . . [The men] will say, "Hey baby, what's your name? Where your man at? You got a man?"

INTERVIEWER: So you can't hustle on your own?

CHRIS: Not really, no. You can, you know, but not for long.

(Romenesko & Miller, 1989, pp. 116–117)

Prostitutes are often physically abused by their pimps, who may use threats and beatings as means of control. In a study of young streetwalkers in Boston, Virginia Ann Price (1989) observed that as the relationship progressed, the beatings became more vicious. Kim Romenesko and Eleanor Miller (1989), who studied streetwalkers in Milwaukee, commented, "Clearly, 'men' are the rulers of the underworld" (p. 117).

Streetwalkers do not tend to remain in the business (sometimes referred to as "the life") very long (Edgley, 1989). Some make the transition to a more traditional life or get married. Others die young from drug abuse, disease, suicide, or physical abuse from pimps or customers. Those who survive become less marketable with age.

Streetwalkers who work hotels and conventions generally hold a higher status than those that work the streets or bars. Clients are typically conventioneers or businessmen traveling away from home. The hotel prostitute must be skilled in conveying subtle messages to potential clients without drawing the attention of hotel management or security. They usually provide sexual services in the client's hotel room. Some hotel managers will tolerate known prostitutes (usually for a payoff under the table), so long as the woman conducts herself discreetly.

Brothel Prostitution Many brothel prostitutes occupy a middle status in the hierarchy of prostitutes, between streetwalkers on one end and call girls on the other (Edgley, 1989). They work in a brothel, or, more commonly today, in a massage parlor or for an escort service.

The life of the brothel (or "house") prostitute is usually neither as lucrative as that of the call girl nor as degrading as that of the streetwalker. Some prostitutes in massage

Brothel Prostitutes. In this Nevada brothel, customers typically select their sex partners from women who line up in a central area.

parlors or working for escort services may not consider themselves to be "real prostitutes" because they do not walk the streets and because they work for businesses that present a legitimate front (Edgley, 1989). *Cathouse, bordello, cat wagon, parlor house, whorehouse, joy house, sport house, house of ill repute*—these are but a handful of the names given to houses in which prostitutes work. The heyday of the brothel is all but over in the United States. Formal brothels today are rare, except in Nevada, where they are legal but regulated.

Brothel prostitutes may attempt to maintain a traditional life apart from their prostitution activities. Ricker (1980) tells the story of one dual-world prostitute:

> Jan has been married 15 years and is the mother of three children—her earnings help keep them in a snooty Northern California boarding school. A relative newcomer [at the Chicken Ranch, a licensed Nevada brothel], she tried massage parlors, escort services, and other forms of "the business" [earlier]. Jan got into this line of work because she needed extra money. . . . Jan feels her home relationship has been improved by her job. "Before I went to work, my husband and I were always entertaining, trying to keep up that affluent suburban image. Now, when we're together we just enjoy each other and the children." She also feels her work has made her more interesting to her husband. "I've had to learn to relate to all kinds of different people. And I've learned how to play a variety of roles—I can be nurse, sophisticated companion, psychologist, temptress. . . . " No, Jan doesn't tell her children what she does (p. 282).

Jan, like other brothel prostitutes, splits her fees with the management. In addition to her "split," she receives free room and board. They are on duty three weeks a month and on call 24 hours a day during that time. When a customer arrives, they step into the living room "lineup." After one has been chosen, they wait again, resting, reading, or watching television.

Jan doesn't see herself as having a bad life. Yet some brothel prostitutes lead lives of complete degradation. Many poor Asian women have been recently lured to the United States by promises of the good life. Upon arrival, they have found themselves enslaved in brothels—working for tips and not allowed to leave. Such a brothel was recently closed by police at 208 Bowery in New York City. It housed more than 30 women smuggled from Thailand and came to the attention of police when one woman jumped from a window (Goldberg, 1995).

The Massage Parlor   "Massage parlors" have sprung up from coast to coast to fill the vacuum left by the departure of the brothels. Many massage parlors are legitimate establishments that provide massage, and only massage, to customers. Masseuses and masseurs are licensed in many states, and laws restrict them from offering sexual services. Many localities require that the masseuse or masseur keep certain parts of her or his body clothed and not touch the client's genitals.

Many massage parlors serve as fronts for prostitution, however. Today they are often found in malls in middle-class suburbs, where there is ample parking (Carvajal, 1995). In these establishments, clients typically pay fees for a standard massage and then tip the workers for sexual extras.

Massage parlor prostitutes generally offer to perform manual stimulation of the penis ("a local"), oral sex, or less frequently, coitus. Some massage parlor prostitutes are better educated than streetwalkers and brothel workers and would not work in these other venues.

Escort Services   If Hugh Grant had hired an "escort," we probably would never have learned of it. Conventioneers and businessmen are more likely to turn to the listings for "massage" and "escort services" in the telephone directory or under the personal ads in local newspapers than to seek hotel prostitutes. Services that provide "outcall" send masseuses (or masseurs) or escorts to the hotel room.

Escort services are typically (but not always) fronts for prostitution. Escort services are found in every major American city and present themselves as legitimate business providing escorts for men. Indeed, one will find female companionship for corporate functions and for unattached men traveling away from home under "escort services." Many escort services provide only prostitution, however, and clients of other escort services sometimes negotiate sexual services after formal escort duties are completed—or in their stead.

T r u t h **OR** *Fiction?*
R E V I S I T E D

Not all of the massage and escort services advertised in the Yellow Pages are fronts for prostitution. Legitimate masseuses and masseurs often advertise that they are licensed by their states. ■

Prostitutes who work for escort services often come from middle-class backgrounds and are well educated—so much the better to help prepare them to hold their own in social conversation. Escort services may establish arrangements with legitimate companies to provide "escorts" for visiting customers or potential clients. Escort services also provide female escorts to "entertain" at conventions. Because of her high-society background, Sidney Biddle Barrow, the so-called Mayflower Madam, attracted a great deal of publicity when it was discovered that she ran an exclusive "escort service" in New York City in the 1980s.

Call girls

Prostitutes who arrange for their sexual contacts by telephone. *Call* refers both to telephone calls and to being "on call."

Call Girls   Call girls occupy the highest status on the social ladder of female prostitution. Many of them overlap with escorts. Call girls tend to be the most attractive and well-educated prostitutes and tend to charge more for their services. Many come from middle-class backgrounds (Edgley, 1989). Unlike other types of prostitutes, call girls usually work on their own. Thus, they need not split their income with a pimp, escort service, or massage parlor. Consequently they can afford to lead a luxurious lifestyle when business is good, living in expensive neighborhoods and wearing stylish clothes, and to be more selective about the customers they will accept. Yet they incur expenses for answering services and laundry services, and for payoffs to landlords, doormen, and sometimes to police to maintain their livelihood and avoid arrest.

Call girls often escort their clients to dinner and social functions, and are expected not only to provide sex but also charming and gracious company and conversation (Edgley, 1989). Call girls often give clients the feeling that they are important and attractive. They may effectively simulate pleasure and orgasm and can create the illusion that time does not matter. It does, of course. To the call girl, as to other entrepreneurs, time is money.

Call girls may receive clients in their apartments or make "outcalls" to clients' homes and hotels. Call girls may trade or sell "black books" that list clients and their sexual preferences. To protect themselves from police and abusive clients, call girls may insist on reviewing a client's business card or learning his home telephone number before personal contact is made. They may investigate whether the customer is in fact the person he purports to be.

Characteristics of Female Prostitutes

No single factor explains entry into female prostitution. Yet, poverty and sexual and/or physical abuse figure prominently in the backgrounds of many prostitutes. They often come from conflict-ridden or one-parent homes in poor urban areas or rural farming communities.

For young women of impoverished backgrounds and marginal skills, the life of the prostitute may seem alluring. It is an alternative to the menial and dismal work that is otherwise available. Based on their studies of streetwalkers in Milwaukee, Romensko and Miller (1989) concluded that

> poverty, and the many concomitants of poverty manifest in American society, were the factors pushing these women into the world of illicit work. Conversely, the bright lights, money, and independence that the street seemingly offered—things that were largely absent from these women's lives prior to their entrance into street life—were enticements that drew women to street life. (p. 112)

Researchers also find a high level of psychological disturbance among streetwalkers. In New York, Exner and his colleagues (1977) found that call girls and brothel prostitutes could not be distinguished from nonprostitutes on their psychological characteristics. Streetwalkers and drug-addicted prostitutes showed higher rates of psychological disturbance than comparison groups, however.

Cross-cultural evidence from a study of 41 prostitutes in Belgium showed similar patterns of psychopathology (de Schampheleire, 1990). Compared to a group of nonprostitutes (women flight attendants), streetwalkers in the Belgian study were more fearful, anxious, resentful, and depressed. They also had poorer relationships with their families and were in poorer health. In a study in the United States, teenage female prostitutes were more likely than normal female adolescents or delinquents who did not engage in prostitution to show signs of psychological disturbance and to have been placed in special-education classes in school (Gibson et al., 1988).

Poverty accounts for the entry of young women into prostitution in many countries. In some Third World nations, such as Thailand, rural, impoverished parents may in effect sell daughters to recruiters who place them in brothels in cities (Erlanger, 1991; Goldberg, 1995). Many of the women send home whatever money they can and also work hard to try to pay off the procurers and break free of their financial bonds.

In the United States and Canada, many initiates into prostitution are teenage runaways. The family backgrounds of teenage runaways vary in socioeconomic status (some come from middle-class or affluent homes, whereas others are reared in poverty). However, family discord and dysfunction frequently set the stage for their entry to street life and prostitution (Price, 1989). Many teenage runaways perceive life on the street to be the only possible escape from family strife and conflict, or from the physical, emotional, or sexual abuse they suffer at home. Despite its dangers, life on the streets appears more attractive than remaining in the troubled family environment. A study of teenage prostitutes in Boston found that a majority had come from broken homes and were reared by single parents or in reconstituted families consisting of half siblings and stepsiblings (Price, 1989). Those who came from intact families nevertheless reported high levels of family conflict.

Teenage runaways are at particularly high risk of unsafe sexual practices, such as unprotected sex with multiple partners. The average male teenage runaway in a New York City study reported having had 11 female sexual partners in his lifetime (Rotheram-Borus et al., 1992). Only 8% of the teenage boys reported using condoms consistently.

Teenage runaways with marginal skills and limited means of support may find few alternatives to prostitution. Adolescent prostitution results from the "necessities of street life—it is survival behavior more than it is sexual behavior" (Seng, 1989, p. 674). It is not long before the teenage runaway is approached by a pimp or a john. A study of 149 teenage runaways in Toronto found that 67% of the boys and 82% of the girls who had been away from home for more than a year had been offered money to engage in sexual activity with an adult (Hartman et al., 1987).

Studies of teenage prostitutes in the United States show that perhaps as many as one half to two thirds of female prostitutes had been sexually abused as children (Seng, 1989). One sample of 45 former prostitutes in Canada showed that 73% had been sexually abused in childhood (Bagley & Young, 1987).

Truth **OR** Fiction?
R E V I S I T E D

It appears that the majority of female prostitutes were in fact sexually abused as children. ■

Some teenagers who have endured sexual abuse or incest may have learned how to detach themselves emotionally from sex in order to survive unwanted sexual experiences. The transition to prostitution may represent an extension of this unfortunate learning experience. Though teenage prostitutes may turn to prostitution primarily for money, Price (1989) recognizes that survivors of sexual abuse or incest may also be attracted to prostitution because they have learned that it is through their sexuality that they can obtain attention or love from adults:

> For a lonely adolescent, attention from tricks or a sugar daddy is not all that different from the attention he or she received at home. In fact, it may be preferable, as there may not be any physical abuse involved. (p. 84)

Not all sexually abused children become prostitutes, of course. Only 12% of one sample of predominantly female 16- to 18-year-olds who had been sexually abused became involved in prostitution (Seng, 1989). Abused children who run away from home are much more likely to become involved in prostitution than those who do not (Seng, 1989). Runaways are also more likely to become drug and alcohol abusers.

Nor do all teenage runaways become prostitutes. Though information on prevalences of prostitution among runaways is scarce, a Boston study of homeless street youth in the mid-1980s found that fewer than 20% had engaged in prostitution (Price, 1989). Though most had been approached for prostitution within a few days of living on the streets, the overwhelming majority refused.

In sum, evidence suggests that most female prostitutes are survivors of sexual abuse or incest. Running away from home appears to funnel many survivors of childhood sexual abuse into prostitution, yet not all survivors of sexual abuse, nor all teenage runaways, become prostitutes.

Customers of Female Prostitutes

Hugh Grant was a "john" or a "trick." That is how many prostitutes refer to their customers. Terms such as *patron, meatball, sucker,* and *beefbuyer* are also heard. Men who use female prostitutes come from all walks of life and represent all socioeconomic and racial groups. Many, perhaps most, are married men of middle-class background. A study of the address listings of customers (seized by the local police) of an "escort service" in a southern city showed that most of the clients lived in relatively affluent neighborhoods consisting of a high percentage of well-educated, largely White, and married residents (Adams, 1987).

Most patrons are "occasional johns." Examples include traveling salesmen or military personnel who are stopping over in town and away from their regular sex partners. One study of 30 occasional johns showed that all had regular sex partners. They used prostitutes because they desired novelty or sexual variety, not because they lacked other sexual outlets (Holzman & Pines, 1982).

"Habitual johns" use prostitutes as their major or exclusive sexual outlet. Some habitual johns have never established an intimate sexual relationship. Some wealthy men who wish to avoid intimate relationships habitually patronize call girls.

Whore–madonna complex
A rigid stereotyping of women as either sinners or saints.

"Compulsive johns" feel driven to prostitutes to meet some psychological or sexual need. They may repeatedly resolve to stop using prostitutes but feel unable to control their compulsions. Some compulsive johns engage in acts of fetishism or transvestism with prostitutes but would not inform their wives or girlfriends of their variant interests. Some men who are compulsive users of prostitutes suffer from a **whore–madonna complex.** They see women as either sinners or saints. They can permit themselves to enjoy sex only with prostitutes or would ask only prostitutes to engage in acts such as fellatio. They see marital coitus as a duty or obligation.

Motives for Using Prostitutes   Though the reasons for using prostitutes vary, researchers have identified six of the most common motives (Edgley, 1989; Gagnon, 1977):

1. *Sex without negotiation.* Prostitution may be attractive to men who do not want to spend the time, effort, and money involved in dating and getting to know someone simply to obtain sex. As Edgley comments, the customer "gives [the prostitute] money for sex, she gives sex in return. The entire matter is simple, direct, and sure" (p. 393). Hugh Grant may have been sexually aroused, and his girlfriend was a continent and an ocean away. The streetwalker was willing to supply sex in the absence of a relationship.
2. *Sex without commitment.* Prostitutes require no commitment from the man other than payment for services rendered. The prostitute will not call him at home or expect to be called in return. The relationship is virtually anonymous as well as impersonal.
3. *Sex for eroticism and variety.* Many prostitutes offer "something extra" in the way of novel or kinky sex—for example, use of costumes (e.g., leather attire) and S&M rituals (such as bondage and discipline or spanking). Men may desire such activity but not obtain it with their regular partners. They may even be afraid to mention the idea. Desire for oral sex is a traditional reason for visiting prostitutes. Prostitutes may also be attractive to men who seek additional sex partners for the sake of variety or novelty. Hugh Grant may have acted on some of these motives.

4. *Prostitution as sociability.* In the nineteenth and early twentieth centuries, the brothel served not only as a place to obtain sex, but also as a kind of "stopping off" place between home and work—referred to by some writers as a "third place" (Oldenberg & Brissett, 1980). The local tavern or pool hall are nonsexual examples of "third places." At times, sex was secondary to the companionship and amiable conversation that men would find in brothels, especially in the days of the "bawdy houses" of the pioneer West. Today, however, such brothels are more likely to exist in nostalgia than reality. Sociability is more likely to be found among call girls and escort prostitutes who offer social companionship, with or without sex. The discovery that sex is not always part of the deal may come as a surprise. As Edgley notes, "Sometimes companionship and sociability is all the client wants for his money" (p. 396).

5. *Sex away from home.* The greatest contemporary use of prostitution occurs among men who are away from home, such as businessmen attending conventions and sports fans attending out-of-town sporting events. In these typical all-male preserves, there is often intense peer pressure to engage in sexual adventures.

T r u t h OR *Fiction?*
R E V I S I T E D

It is not true that typical customers of prostitutes have difficulty forming sexual relationships with other women. Many men often turn to prostitutes for sexual variety or because they seek sexual activity when they are away from home. ∎

6. *Problematical sex.* Persons with physical disabilities or disfiguring conditions sometimes seek the services of prostitutes because of difficulty attracting other partners or because of fears of rejection. (One prostitute at a Nevada brothel said that she was a favorite of the management because she accepted johns with cerebral palsy.) Though some prostitutes are selective about the clients they will accept, others will accept any client who is willing to pay. Men with sexual dysfunctions may also turn to prostitutes to help them overcome their problems. Some lonely men who lack sex partners may seek prostitutes as substitutes.

Male Prostitution

Male prostitution includes both male–male and male–female activities. Male prostitutes who service female clients—*gigolos*—are rare. Gigolos' clients are typically older, wealthy, unattached women. Gigolos may serve as escorts or as surrogate sons for the women, and may or may not offer sexual services. Many gigolos are struggling actors or models.

The overwhelming majority of male prostitutes service gay men. Men who engage in male prostitution are called **hustlers.** Their patrons are typically called **scores.** Hustlers average 17 to 18 years of age and become initiated into prostitution at an average age of 14 or so (Coleman, 1989). They typically have less than eleventh-grade educations and few, if any, marketable skills. The majority come from working-class and lower-class backgrounds. Many male prostitutes, like many female prostitutes, come from families troubled by conflict, alcoholism, or abuse (Coleman, 1989). More than 4 of 5 (83%) of a sample of 47 male prostitutes in Seattle, Washington, had been survivors of sexual abuse (Boyer, 1989). Two of three are survivors of rape or attempted rape. In another study, the factor that most clearly distinguished juvenile male prostitutes and male delinquent street youth was the absence of sexual victimization in the histories of the delinquents (Janus et al., 1984).

Hustlers may be gay, bisexual, or heterosexual in orientation. At least half of the male prostitutes surveyed are gay. Seventy percent of the male prostitutes in the Seattle study identified themselves as gay or bisexual. Only 30% identified themselves as heterosexual (Boyer, 1989).

The major motive for male prostitution, like female prostitution, is money. In one study, 69% of male prostitutes cited money as their principal motive (Fisher et al., 1982). Running away from home typically serves as an entry point for male as well as female prostitution. In one study, three of four male prostitutes had run away by an average age of 15 (Weisberg, 1985). Some had run away because of family problems; others, because of a desire for adventure or independence (Coleman, 1989). Some gay male prostitutes are

Hustlers
Men who engage in prostitution with male customers.

Scores
Customers of hustlers.

literally thrown out because their families cannot accept their sexual orientation (Coleman, 1989; Kruks, 1991). Researcher Debra Boyer (1989) comments:

> The responses of families to the [sexual orientation] of their sons ranged from strong condemnation to total rejection, for example "it's disgusting"; "we refuse to accept it"; "we don't want to talk about it"; "that's it, you are leaving." These young men suffered outright rejection from their families and were often literally thrown away as sullied human beings. (pp. 168–169)

For many of these gay "throwaways," prostitution may represent a way of obtaining adult acceptance, albeit within the context of exchanging sex for money. Another distinguishing characteristic of the gay prostitutes in the Seattle study was the lack of a network of gay friends. These young gay males became initiated into the gay subculture in the life of the street. Their only contacts with other gay men were through turning tricks or "hanging out" with other young hustlers. The ability to attract clients and the money they received inflated their self-esteem. As Boyer put it, they were "no longer outcasts, but stars" (p. 177). Many hoped to find companionship or a meaningful relationship through prostitution. Some would fall in love with "tricks," only to be disappointed when the encounter or relationship fizzled.

Heterosexual hustlers may try to psychologically detach themselves from male clients by refusing to kiss or hug them or to perform fellatio. Gagnon (1977) writes that, "As long as the [client's] head is below the [hustler's] belly button and contact is on the penis, it is the other person who is [gay]" (p. 264). To become aroused, heterosexual hustlers may fantasize about women while the "score" is fellating them. Many heterosexual male prostitutes maintain heterosexual relationships in their private lives while "turning tricks" with men to earn money.

Most hustlers are part-timers who continue some form of educational or vocational activity as they support themselves through prostitution. Drug dealing and drug use are also common among hustlers (Coleman, 1989). In one study, about three in four male prostitutes used drugs while they were hustling (Fisher et al., 1982).

Unlike female prostitutes, hustlers typically are not attached to a pimp (Luckenbill, 1985). They generally make contacts with clients in gay bars and social clubs, or by working the streets in areas frequented by gay men. They typically learn to hustle through their interactions with other hustlers and by watching other hustlers ply their trade (Luckenbill, 1985).

Coleman (1989) identifies several types of male prostitutes:

- *Kept boys* have relationships with older, economically secure men who keep them in an affluent lifestyle. The older male, or "sugar daddy," often assumes a parental role.
- *Call boys,* like call girls, may work on their own or through an agency or escort service.
- *Punks* are prison inmates who are used sexually by other inmates and rewarded with protection or goods such as cigarettes or drugs.
- *Drag prostitutes* are transvestites or presurgical male-to-female transsexuals who impersonate female prostitutes and have sex with men who are frequently unaware of their gender. Some drag prostitutes limit themselves to fellatio on their customers to conceal their genders. Others take the passive role in anal sex (Boles & Elifson, 1994).
- *Brothel prostitutes* are rarer than their female counterparts. Fewer houses of male prostitution exist.
- *Bar hustlers* and *street hustlers,* like their female counterparts, occupy the lowest status and ply their trade in gay bars or on streets frequented by gay passersby. Street hustlers are the most common and typically the youngest subtype. They are also the most visible and consequently the ones most likely to draw the attention of the police.

Male prostitutes typically have shorter careers than their female counterparts (Price, 1989). By and large, male prostitution is an adolescent enterprise. The younger the hustler, the higher the fee he can command. The more tricks he can turn. By the time he reaches his mid-20s, he may be forced to engage in sexual activities he might have rejected when younger or to seek clients in sleazier places.

HIV, AIDS, and Prostitution

Concerns about the spread of sexually transmitted diseases by prostitution is nothing new. In the 1960s, two of three prostitutes surveyed by Gebhard (1969) had contracted gonorrhea or syphilis. Though prostitutes are still exposed to a heightened risk of contracting or spreading these and other sexually transmitted diseases, such as chlamydia, today the risk of AIDS poses a more deadly threat. The risk of HIV transmission has been linked to both male and female prostitution (Bloor et al., 1990; Campbell, 1991; Van den Hoek et al., 1990; Yates et al., 1991).

Sex with prostitutes is the most important factor in the male–female transmission of HIV in Africa, where the infection is spread predominantly via male–female sexual intercourse (see Chapter 17). A Florida study showed that regular contact with female street prostitutes was a risk factor in the transmission of HIV in U.S. men (Castro et al., 1988). Prostitutes incur a greater risk of HIV transmission because they have sexual relations with a great many partners, often without protection (Quadagno et al., 1991). Moreover, many prostitutes and their clients and other sex partners inject drugs and share contaminated needles (Bloor et al., 1990; Freund et al., 1989). HIV may be spread by unprotected sex from prostitutes to customers, then to the customers' wives or lovers. Nationwide, about 12% of the prostitutes tested in the late 1980s were seropositive for HIV (Lambert, 1988). In Thailand, the transmission of HIV by prostitution seems even more widespread, as noted in the nearby World of Diversity feature.

Men who frequent male prostitutes may represent a vector, or conduit, for male–female sexual transmission of HIV. The rate of HIV infection is high among male prostitutes, and many, if not most, of their male customers describe themselves as either bisexual or heterosexual (Morse et al., 1992). One study found that the rate of HIV infection was 50% for gay male prostitutes, 36.5% for bisexual male prostitutes, and 18.5% for heterosexual male prostitutes (Boles & Elifson, 1994). Customers of such men may thus be exposing their wives and girlfriends to HIV.

Despite the obvious dangers of HIV transmission, many U.S. prostitutes, like many Thai prostitutes, have not altered either their sexual behavior or their patterns of drug use to any large extent. Only 30% of a sample of 20 street prostitutes in Camden, New Jersey, reported always using condoms (Freund et al., 1989). A study of 72 heroin-addicted female street prostitutes in southern California showed a high level of knowledge and fear about AIDS but a failure to change patterns of sexual behavior or drug use (Bellis, 1990). The prostitutes sampled did nothing to protect themselves or their clients from HIV. Their need for money led them to deny the risks to which they were exposing themselves. Surveys of adolescent prostitutes show a similar pattern of denial, as Price (1989) observes:

> Some [adolescent prostitutes] simply believe it will not happen to them, while others say they are willing to take the risk. Still others do not care whether they live or die, and expect their lives to end shortly anyway. (p. 86)

Some changes in prostitution practices have taken place. Brothel owners in Nevada, for example, now require customers to wear condoms. But prostitutes who are bent on denial or are so filled with despair that they care nothing about their own or clients' lives may be most resistant to change.

Truth **OR** Fiction?

R E V I S I T E D

It is not true that most prostitutes take precautions to avoid becoming infected by or transmitting the AIDS virus. Most street prostitutes in the United States, and many brothel workers in foreign nations, do not take precautions against becoming infected by or transmitting HIV. ■

~ Reflections ~

▢ Agree or disagree with the following statement, and support your answer: Prostitution should be legalized throughout the United States.

▢ What are the connections between prostitution, child sexual abuse, and drug abuse?

▢ Why do you think that an attractive, popular actor like Hugh Grant would turn to a prostitute?

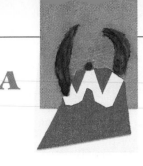 
'TIS A PUZZLEMENT: ON AIDS AND PROSTITUTION IN THAILAND

" 'Tis a puzzlement," sang the king in the Broadway musical *The King and I*. The king of nineteenth-century Thailand was referring to the importation of Western values and culture. Today it could be considered a puzzlement that so many Thais continue high-risk sexual behavior in the face of AIDS, which may be another import from the West.

HIV may have been brought to Thailand by gay Thais who lived for a while in the West (Erlanger, 1991). Through the 1980s, HIV was spread in Thailand mostly via gay male sexual activity and injectable drug use. In the 1990s, however—in a progression that is found in many other nations—the central route of infection has become male-female sexual intercourse.

AIDS may be spiraling out of control in Thailand. In 1991, more than 300,000 of this nation of 56 million were infected. Given the rate of infection, however, the Population and Community Development Association of Thailand estimated that more than 5 million could be infected by the year 2000, with more than a million dead.

The high-risk sexual behavior in question involves prostitution. Whereas only a minority of Westerners visit (or admit to visiting) prostitutes, prostitution is a way of life in Thailand. About 3 in 4 Thai men—at a rate of 450,000 a day—avail themselves of prostitutes. In many brothels in northwest Thailand, such as in the city of Chiang Mai, where the epidemic is most advanced,

80% of the "working women" test positive for HIV antibodies (Erlanger, 1991). In populous Bangkok, the figure now exceeds 20%. Fourteen percent of the male army recruits from the northwest region test positive. HIV is leapfrogging from prostitutes to customers to the customers' wives, lovers, and— through pregnancy, childbirth, or breast-feeding—to their children.

Printed on the glass "showcase" of one brothel in Chiang Mai is the

legend "We welcome only guests using condoms." Yet 59% of Thai men report that they never wear them (and more than 80% do not consider AIDS a threat). Do the prostitutes insist on condoms? As says Daeng, a Bangkok bar girl, "If the man seems clean and healthy, I say, OK. If the man comes to me often and is nice to me, I say, OK. If he offers me more money, I say, OK" (Erlanger, 1991, p. 49).

'Tis a puzzlement.

Prostitution in Thailand. Many prostitutes in Thailand are infected with HIV. It is common for their customers to become infected and to then transmit HIV to their wives.

Pornography and Obscenity

The production and distribution of sexually explicit materials has become a boom industry in the United States. In the United States, 20 million "adult" magazines are sold each month. X-rated or adult movies (also called *porn* movies) have moved from sleazy adult theaters to the living rooms of middle America in the form of videocassette rentals and sales. According to a Gallup poll, X-rated films account for about one in five video sales (Linsley, 1989).

Pornography is indeed popular, but also highly controversial. Many people in our society are opposed to pornography on moral grounds. Feminists oppose pornography on the grounds that it portrays women in degrading and dehumanizing roles, as sexual objects who are subservient to men's sexual wishes, as sexually insatiable nymphomaniacs, or as sexual masochists who enjoy being raped and violated. Moreover, feminists hold that depictions of women in sexually subordinate roles may encourage men to treat them as sex objects and may increase the potential for rape (Scott & Schwalm, 1988).

Yet feminists are split on the issue of legal suppression of pornography. For example, the feminist writer Kate Millett argues that "We're better off hanging tight to the First Amendment so that we have freedom of speech" (Press et al., 1985).

What is pornography? How is it defined? Who uses it? Why? How does it affect users?

What Is Pornographic?

Pornography

Written, visual, or audiotaped material that is sexually explicit and produced for purposes of eliciting or enhancing sexual arousal. (From Greek roots meaning "to write about prostitutes.")

Prurient

Tending to excite lust; lewd. (From the Latin *prurire*, meaning "to itch" in the sense of "to long for.")

Webster's Deluxe Unabridged Dictionary defines **pornography** as "writing, pictures, etc., intended to arouse sexual desire." The inclusion of the word *intended* places the determination of what is pornographic in the mind of the person composing the work. Applying this definition makes it all but impossible to determine what is pornographic. If a filmmaker admits that he or she wanted to arouse the audience sexually, we may judge the work to be pornographic, even if no naked bodies or explicit sex scenes are shown. On the other hand, explicit representations of people engaged in sexual activity would not be pornographic if the work was intended as an artistic expression, rather than created for its **prurient** value. Many works that were once prohibited in this country because of explicit sexual content, such as the novels *Tropic of Cancer* by Henry Miller, *Lady Chatterley's Lover* by D. H. Lawrence, and *Ulysses* by James Joyce, are now generally considered literary works rather than excursions into pornography. Even Mark Twain's *Huckleberry Finn,* John Steinbeck's *The Grapes of Wrath,* and Ernest Hemingway's *For Whom the Bell Tolls* have been banned from place to place because local citizens found them to be offensive, obscene, or morally objectionable (Linsley, 1989).

There is thus a subjective element in the definition of pornography. An erotic statue that sexually arouses viewers may not be considered pornographic if the sculptor's intent was artistic. A grainy photograph of a naked body that was intended to excite sexually may be pornographic. One alternative definition finds material pornographic when it is judged to be offensive by others. This definition, too, relies on the subjective judgment of the person exposed to the material. In other words, one person's pornography is another person's work of art.

Obscenity

That which offends people's feelings or goes beyond prevailing standards of decency or modesty. (From the Latin *caenum*, meaning "filth.")

Legislative bodies usually write laws about **obscenity** rather than pornography. Even the Supreme Court, however, has had a difficult time defining obscenity and determining where, if anywhere, laws against obscenity do not run afoul of the Bill of Rights' guarantee of free speech. In the case of *Miller v. California* (1973), Supreme Court Justice William Brennan wrote that obscenity is "incapable of definition with sufficient clarity to withstand attack on vagueness grounds." Such vagueness did not deter Supreme Court Justice Potter Stewart from quipping that although he could not define obscenity in objective terms, he knew it when he saw it. Recall that *Huckleberry Finn* was once considered obscene, however.

Erotica

Books, pictures, and so on that have to do with sexual love (from the Greek *eros*, meaning "love"). Many contemporary writers use the term *erotica* to refer to sexual material that is artistically produced or motivated by artistic intent.

Let us follow Mosher (1988) and define pornography as written, visual, or audiotaped material that is sexually explicit or graphic and produced for purposes of eliciting or enhancing sexual arousal. **Erotica** may be as sexually explicit as pornography is, but many writers use the term to refer to sexual materials that are artistically produced or motivated. Although some people find any erotic material to be offensive or obscene, it makes little sense to lump together artistic expressions of erotic themes and "hard-core" pornography.

Pornography is often classified as either "hard-core" (X-rated) or "soft-core" (R-rated). Hard-core pornography includes graphic and sexually explicit depictions of sex organs and sexual acts. Soft-core porn, as represented by R-rated films and *Playboy* or *Penthouse* photo spreads, features more stylized nude photos and suggestive (or simulated) rather than explicit sexual acts.

Pornography and the Law

Laws against obscenity provide the legal framework for outlawing the dissemination of pornography. Since the definition of obscenity relies on offending people or running afoul of community standards, that which is deemed obscene may vary from person to person and from culture to culture. Going topless on a public beach may be deemed obscene in some locales but not along beaches on the French Riviera or Rio de Janeiro, where this style of (un)dress is customary and broadly accepted. The word *obscene* extends beyond sexual matters. One could judge TV violence or some beer commercials to be obscene because they are personally offensive or are offensive to women, even if such depictions do not meet legal standards of obscenity.

In the United States, legal prohibition of pornography as a form of obscenity dates to the nineteenth century. In 1873, an antiobscenity bill, the Comstock Act, was passed by Congress. One effect of the bill was to outlaw the dissemination of information about birth control (see Chapter 12). The Comstock Act and similar laws made it a felony to mail obscene books, pamphlets, photographs, drawings, or letters. But what is obscene?

A landmark case in 1957 helped establish the legal basis of obscenity in the United States. In *Roth v. United States,* the U.S. Supreme Court ruled that portrayal of sexual activity was protected under the First Amendment to the Constitution unless its dominant theme dealt with "sex in a manner appealing to prurient interest" (*Roth v. United States,* 1957, p. 487). In a 1973 case, *Miller v. California,* the U.S. Supreme Court held that obscenity is based upon a determination of

> (a) whether the average person, applying contemporary community standards, would find that the work, taken as a whole, appeals to the prurient interest . . . ; (b) whether the work depicts or describes, in a patently offensive way, sexual conduct specifically defined by the applicable state law; and (c) whether the work, taken as a whole, lacks serious literary, artistic, political, or scientific value.
>
> (*Miller v. California,* 1973, p. 24).

Courts have since had to grapple with the *Miller* standard in judging whether material is obscene. *Miller* recognizes that judgments of obscenity may vary with "community standards." As a result, the same material may be considered obscene in one community but not in another. The *Miller* standard raises some obvious and unresolved questions. For example, who is the *average* person who can speak for a community? Many of us live in ethnically, racially, and religiously diverse communities. Can one viewpoint in *any* community truly represent the community? Even in relatively homogeneous communities, a diversity of opinion may exist on particular issues. Moreover, what is a *community?* Is it one's neighborhood, police precinct, municipality, county, or a larger political unit? What does "patently" offensive mean? Who judges "serious" literary, artistic, political, or scientific value? An attempt to clarify this last question was made in a 1987 case, *Pope v. Illinois,* in which the Supreme Court held that

> the proper inquiry is not whether an ordinary member of any given community would find serious literary, artistic, political, or scientific value in allegedly obscene material, but whether a reasonable person would find such value in the material, taken as a whole. (p. 445)

In this ruling, the court held that sexually explicit material could not be declared obscene if many or most people in a particular community held it to lack serious literary, artistic, political, or scientific value, unless a "reasonable" person were to reach the same judgment. Whether the concept of a "reasonable" person will provide the courts with a clearer standard than that of an "average" or "ordinary" person for adjudicating obscenity cases remains to be seen.

Child pornography and violent, degrading, or dehumanizing pornography complicate matters further. People who do not find depictions, however explicit, of consensual sexual activity between adults to be obscene may regard child pornography or violent pornography to be obscene. Child pornography is clearly psychologically harmful to the juvenile actors (Silbert, 1989). Many people also object to sexually explicit material that portrays women as "sex objects" or in a position subordinate to men—one serving no function other than gratifying the sexual appetites of ravenous men.

Some footnotes: The U.S. Supreme Court ruled (in *Stanley v. Georgia,* 1969) that the possession of obscene material in one's home is not a criminal act (Sears, 1989). However, states may make it illegal to possess child pornography (Sears, 1989). Some communities (such as Indianapolis) have sought to ban pornography on the grounds that it discriminates against women. Pornography, that is, damages women's opportunities for equal rights by perpetuating stereotypes of women as subservient to men. The Indianapolis ordinance was overturned by a federal court on the grounds that it represented an unconstitutional infringement of free speech (Lewin, 1992a). However, in a 1992 ruling the Supreme Court of Canada redefined obscenity as involving sexually explicit material containing violence toward women or material that degrades or dehumanizes women (Lewin, 1992a).

Prevalence and Use of Erotica and Pornography

Most of us have been exposed to sexually explicit materials, whether in the form of a novel, an article in *Playboy* or *Playgirl* (purchased, no doubt, for its literary value), or an X-rated film. The NHSLS study found that about one man in four (23%) and one woman in ten (11%) had bought an X-rated movie or video within the past year (Michael et al., 1994). Sixteen percent of the men and 4% of the women had bought sexually explicit magazines or books.

People in the United States are typically introduced to pornography by their high school years, often by peers (Bryant & Brown, 1989). Females are more likely to have been exposed to pornography by their boyfriends than the reverse (Bryant & Brown, 1989).

Pornography is typically used to elicit or enhance sexual arousal, often as a masturbation aid (Michael et al., 1994). Pornographic materials may also be used by couples to enhance sexual arousal during lovemaking. Couples may find that running a soft- or hard-core video on the VCR, or reading an erotic story aloud, enlivens their sexual appetite or suggests novel sexual techniques.

Researchers have found that both men and women are physiologically sexually aroused by pornographic pictures, movies, or audiotaped passages (Goleman, 1995). That is, both men and women respond to pornographic stimuli with vasocongestion of the genitals and myotonia (muscle tension). However, there is a significant difference between physiological response and subjective feelings of arousal in women. Despite what is happening within their bodies, women tend to rate romantic scenes as more sexually arousing than sexually explicit scenes (Laan & Heiman, 1994).

Women are less accepting of sex without emotional involvement (Townsend, 1995). "Women like sex to come from an emotional connection," says marital and sex therapist Lonnie Barbach (1995). "For women there's a predisposition to allowing themselves to become turned on that romance allows. This wouldn't necessarily be measured by genital arousal."

Repeated exposure to the same pornographic materials progressively lessens the sexual response to them. People may become aroused by the familiar materials again if some time is allowed to go by. Novel materials are also likely to reactivate a sexual response (Meuwissen & Over, 1990; Zillmann, 1989).

Truth **OR** *Fiction?*
R E V I S I T E D

It is *not* true that only males are sexually aroused by pornography. Most men *and* women are sexually aroused by erotica, physiologically speaking. As we see in the following section, however, their interest in, and subjective responses to, pornography may differ quite a bit. ∎

Gender Differences in Response to Pornography   Both genders can become physiologically aroused by erotic materials. Yet men and women do not necessarily share the same subjective response to them or level of interest in them. Visual pornography (sexually explicit pictures or films) is actually largely a male preserve (Symons, 1995; Winick, 1985). The majority of erotic visual materials are produced by men for men. Attempts to market visual materials to females have been largely unsuccessful (Symons, 1995). Women may read erotic romance novels, but they show little interest in acquiring erotic pictures, films, or videotapes (Lawrence & Herold, 1988). Women respondents to the

CYBERSEX: FROM COMPUTER PORN TO VIRTUAL SEX

In the computer industry, a "killer app" is a software program or application that makes the hardware appealing to users. Word processing and spreadsheet programs were among the first generation of "killer apps" that popularized the personal computer. In the mid-1990s, however, a potentially new killer app began to appear: CD-ROM disks that play X-rated interactive videos (Tierney, 1994). In some versions, nude female models appear on the computer screen and respond sexually to commands input by the user on a keyboard or by use of a computer mouse. We should not be surprised by this development, as pornography has crept into virtually every other form of popular media, from books and magazines to videotapes. Like other forms of pornography, X-rated CD-ROMs have been criticized for projecting an image of women as sexual objects or playthings who are always readily available to satisfy a man's every sexual whim and fancy (virtually all users of these products are men).

X-rated interactive CD-ROMs may represent the first volleys in a technological revolution that might be limited only by the imaginations and libidos of computer engineers and programmers. Futurists can envision a world of *virtual sex* in which developments in technology will allow people to have simulated sexual encounters even if they are hundreds or thousands of miles apart. In one version of this cybersexual future, people will be able to link their computers electronically and then don wired body suits and virtual reality helmets that allow them to have simulated sexual encounters with one another in a virtual reality environment. The suits may be fitted with miniature tactile detectors coupled to simulators that allow them to experience sounds, sights, and the sensations of touching and being touched. The images projected in this virtual world are conceivably endless, with the participants taking on the appearance of their favorite movie stars or even engaging in gender-bending transformations. These cybersexual encounters might involve rapid scene changes, from a medieval castle to a Roman bath house to the surface of an alien planet. We have only to wonder whether this "brave new world" of virtual sex might one day vie for popularity with "the real thing."

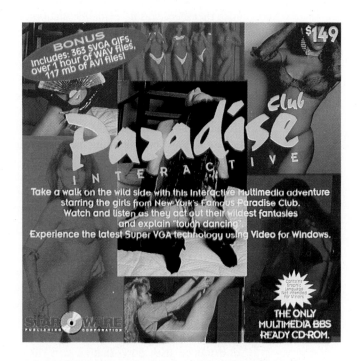

Adults Only: 2001. The VCR has already brought explicit sex from the red-light district into America's living rooms—or bedrooms. Now the home computer is getting involved as people purchase CD-ROM disks that play X-rated interactive videos.

Bryant (1985) survey were twice as likely to be disgusted by their initial exposure to X-rated material as to enjoy it. Men, by contrast, were twice as likely to report a positive response.

The reasons for these gender differences remain unclear (Bryant & Brown, 1989). Women may find erotica a "turn-off" when it portrays women in unflattering roles, as "whorish," as subservient to the sexual demands of men, and as sexually aroused by male domination and coercion. Symons (1979), a sociobiologist, believes that a basic evolutionary process is at work. He argues that ancestral men who were more sexually aroused by the sight of a passing female may have had reproductive advantages over their less arousable peers:

> The male's desire to look at female genitals, especially genitals he has not seen before, and to seek out opportunities to do so, is part of the motivational process that maximizes male reproductive opportunities. (p. 181)

Women, however, have fewer mating opportunities than men and must make the most of any reproductive opportunity by selecting the best possible mate and provider. To be sexually aroused by the sight of male genitalia might encourage random matings, which would undermine their reproductive success.

Pornography and Sexual Coercion

Is pornography a harmless diversion or an impetus to sexual violence or other antisocial acts? Let us consider several sources of evidence in examining these highly charged questions, beginning with the findings of a 1970 government commission impaneled to review the evidence that was available at the time.

The Commission on Obscenity and Pornography   In the 1960s, Congress created the Commission on Obscenity and Pornography to study the effects of pornography. Upon reviewing the existing research, the commission (Abelson et al., 1970) concluded that there was no evidence that pornography led to crimes of violence or sexual offenses such as exhibitionism, voyeurism, or child molestation. Some people were sexually aroused by pornography and increased the frequency of their usual sexual activity, such as masturbation or coitus with regular partners, following exposure. They did not engage in antisocial behavior, however. These results have been replicated many times.

The commission found no causal link between pornography and delinquent behavior or sexual violence against women. The commission noted, for example, that when pornographic materials became widely available in Denmark following its legalization in late 1960s, there was no corresponding increase in the incidence of sex crimes. Finding pornography basically harmless (Edgley, 1989), the commission recommended that "federal, state, and local legislation should not seek to interfere with the right of adults who wish to read, obtain, or view explicit sexual materials" (Abelson et al., 1970, p. 58). Congress and then-president Richard Nixon rejected the commission's findings and recommendation, however, on moral and political—not scientific—grounds.

Pornography and Sex Offenders   Another approach to examining the role of pornography in crimes of sexual violence involves comparing the experience of sex offenders and nonoffenders with pornographic materials. A review of the research literature found little or no difference in the level of exposure to pornography between incarcerated sex offenders and comparison groups of felons who were incarcerated for nonsexual crimes (Marshall, 1989).

Yet evidence also shows that as many as one in three rapists and child molesters use pornography to become sexually aroused immediately preceding, and during the commission of, their crimes (Marshall, 1989). These findings suggest that pornography may stimulate sexually deviant urges in certain subgroups of men who are predisposed to commit crimes of sexual violence (Marshall, 1989).

The Meese Commission Report   In 1985, President Ronald Reagan appointed a committee headed by Attorney General Edwin Meese to reexamine the effects of pornography. In 1986, the U.S. Attorney General's Commission on Pornography, known as the Meese commission, issued a report that reached very different conclusions than the 1970 commission. The Meese commission claimed to find a causal link between sexual violence and exposure to violent pornography (U.S. Department of Justice, 1986). The commission asserted that a substantial increase in the proliferation of violent pornography had occurred since the earlier commission had been convened. Moreover, the report concluded that exposure to pornography that portrayed women in degrading or subservient roles increased acceptability of rape in the minds of viewers. The commission found no evidence linking exposure to nonviolent, nondegrading pornography (consensual sexual activity between partners in equal roles) and sexual violence but noted that only a small fraction of the pornographic materials on the market was of this type.

The commission issued 92 recommendations for tighter enforcement of obscenity laws and greater restrictions on the dissemination of pornography. Some recommendations focused on the enforcement and prosecution of existing child pornography laws. Others encouraged states that had not already done so to make the knowledgeable possession of child pornography a felony.

The commission's findings are controversial. Critics claim that although the Meese commission did not blatantly falsify the data, its conclusions reflected an overgeneralization of laboratory-based findings (Wilcox, 1987). Two researchers in the area, Edward Donnerstein and Daniel Linz (1987), contended that the Meese commission failed to distinguish between the effects of sexually explicit materials per se and the effects of violent materials. Evidence of links between exposure to sexually explicit materials (without violent content) and sexual aggression is lacking. Donnerstein and Linz concluded that violence, not sex, is the obscenity. Nor do researchers confirm the Meese commission's belief in the rising incidence of violent pornography. Evidence does not show depictions of violence in sexually explicit media such as in the magazines *Playboy* and *Hustler,* or in X-rated movies and videos, to have increased in recent years (Scott & Cuvelier, 1993). In fact, X-rated movies and videos contain less violence than do general release movies.

If nothing else, the Meese commission raised awareness about different types of pornography and their potential effects on viewers' behaviors and attitudes. Let us take a look at the scientific evidence on the effects of violent and nonviolent pornography.

Violent Pornography   Laboratory-based studies have shown that men exposed to violent pornography are more likely to become aggressive against females and to show less sensitivity toward women who have been sexually assaulted. In one study (Donnerstein, 1980), 120 college men interacted with a male or female confederate (accomplice) of the experimenter, who treated them in either a neutral or hostile manner. The study participants were then shown neutral, nonviolent pornographic films or violent pornographic films. In the latter, a man forced himself into a woman's home and raped her. Participants were then given the opportunity to deliver electric shock to the male or female confederate, presumably to assist the confederate in learning a task. The measure of aggression was the intensity of the shock chosen. No shock was actually delivered, but participants did not know that the shock apparatus was fake. Unprovoked men who viewed violent pornographic films showed greater aggression toward the women than did unprovoked men who viewed nonviolent films, however. Provoked men who were shown violent pornography selected the highest shock levels of all. The film may have served as a model for retaliation.

In another study, aggression by males against female confederates following exposure to violent pornography (a rape scene) was increased by depictions of the woman being raped as either enjoying the experience or becoming sexually aroused during the rape (Donnerstein & Berkowitz, 1981). These findings suggest that depictions of women enjoying or becoming aroused by their victimization may legitimize violence against women in the viewer's mind, reinforcing the cultural myth that some women need to be dominated and are sexually aroused by an overpowering male.

Other research has shown that exposure to violent pornography leads men to become more accepting of rape, less sensitive to women survivors of rape, and more accepting of the use of violence in interpersonal relationships (Donnerstein & Linz, 1987; Malamuth, 1984).

Yet research suggests that it is the violence in violent pornography, and not sexual explicitness, that hardens men's attitudes toward rape survivors. In one study (Donnerstein & Linz, 1987), college men were exposed to films consisting of either violent pornography, nonviolent pornography (a couple having consensual intercourse), or a violent film that was not sexually explicit. The violent pornographic and nonpornographic films both showed a woman being tied up and slapped at gunpoint, but the nonpornographic version contained no nudity or explicit sexual activity. The men had first been either angered or treated in a neutral manner by a female confederate of the experimenter. The results showed that, in comparison with nonviolent pornography, both violent pornographic films and violent *non*pornographic films produced greater acceptance of rape myths, increased reported willingness to force a woman into sexual activity, and greater reported likelihood of engaging in rape (if the man also knew that he could get away with it). These effects occurred regardless of whether the man was angered by the woman or not.

In another study, Linz and his colleagues (1988) assigned college men, at random, to watch five feature-length films over a two-week period. One group saw X-rated nonviolent films. A second group watched R-rated "slasher-type" violent films such as *Friday the 13th, Part 2.* ("Slasher films" show graphic violence, primarily directed at women, intermingled with mild erotic scenes.) A third group saw R-rated, nonviolent "teenage sex films" such as *Porky's.* Afterwards, the men viewed a videotaped reenactment of a trial in which a woman accused a man of raping her. Men who had watched the R-rated slasher films showed less sensitivity toward the woman complainant than did men who had been exposed to either the R- or the X-rated nonviolent films. Exposure to sexually explicit material *without violence,* whether soft-core (R-rated) or hard-core (X-rated), did not reduce sympathy toward the woman complainant.

Based on a review of the research literature, Linz (1989) concluded that short-term and prolonged exposure to sexual violence, whether sexually explicit or not, lessens sensitivity toward survivors of rape and increases acceptance of the use of force in sexual encounters. "Slasher" films are connected with the strongest antisocial effects. Such films, however, are regularly shown over commercial television, although some of the more gruesome parts may be edited. (They are uncut on pay cable channels.)

Research on the effects of pornography should be interpreted with caution, however. Most of it has employed college students, whose behavior may or may not be typical of people in general or of people with propensities toward sexual violence. On the other hand, research discussed in Chapter 19 shows that a large percentage of college men have engaged in rape, attempted rape, or engaged in some form of sexual coercion. Another issue is that most studies in this area are laboratory-based experiments that involve simulated aggression or judgments of sympathy toward hypothetical women who have been portrayed as rape victims. None measured *actual* violence against women outside the lab. We are still bereft of evidence that normal men have been, or would be, spurred to rape or to sexually violate women because of exposure to violent pornography or other forms of violent media.

Nonviolent Pornography   Nonviolent pornography may not contain scenes of sexual violence, but it typically portrays women in degrading or dehumanizing roles—as sexually promiscuous, insatiable, and subservient. Might such portrayals of women reinforce traditional stereotypes of women as sex objects? Might they lead viewers to condone acts of rape by suggesting that women are essentially promiscuous? Might the depiction of women as readily sexually accessible inspire men to refuse to "take no for an answer" on dates?

Most of the research on the effects of pornography has focused on violent pornography (Linz, 1989), so we cannot respond to these questions with certainty. The evidence nevertheless raises concerns that nonviolent pornography may also affect male sensitivity toward women who are sexually victimized (Zillmann & Weaver, 1989). Zillmann and Bryant (1982, 1984), for example, exposed male and female study participants to six sessions of pornography over six consecutive weeks. Participants were exposed to either a massive dose of pornography, consisting of six nonviolent pornographic films ("Swedish erotica") during each weekly session; to an intermediate dose consisting of three pornographic and three neutral films each session; or to a no-dose control, consisting of six nonsexual films each session. When later tested in a purportedly independent study, both males and females who received extended exposure to pornography, especially those receiving the massive dose, gave more lenient punishments to a rapist who was depicted in a newspaper article. Moreover, males became more callous in their attitudes toward women.

Zillmann and Weaver (1989) argue that making women appear sexually permissive and promiscuous increases men's callousness toward women who have been sexually assaulted. Once men brand women as promiscuous, they lose respect for them and see them as "public property" who have forfeited their rights to exercise choice in sex partners.

Not all researchers, however, find exposure to nonviolent pornography to increase callousness toward women. Some report finding that nonviolent pornography did not reduce the sensitivity of men (Linz et al., 1988) and women (Krafka, 1985) to female victims of sexual assault. Others report that nonviolent pornography did not increase men's aggression toward women in laboratory studies (Malamuth & Ceniti, 1986). Still others did not find repeated exposure to nonviolent pornography to make men adopt more callous attitudes toward women or increase their acceptance of rape myths (Padgett et al., 1989).

Given the inconsistencies in the research findings and the limited amount of research on nonviolent pornography, Linz (1989) concludes that

> . . . the data, *overall,* do not support the contention that exposure to nonviolent pornography has significant adverse effects on attitudes toward rape as a crime or more general evaluations of rape victims. (p. 74)

Moreover, if nonviolent pornography can be connected with negative attitudes toward women, Linz (1989) suggests that such attitudes may result from the demeaning portrayals of women as sexual playthings who are valued only for their physical attributes and sexual availability, rather than from sexual explicitness per se.

Yet another concern is the possible effect of nonviolent pornography on the viewer's sexual and family values. Nonviolent pornography typically features impromptu sexual encounters between new acquaintances. Might repeated exposure to such material alter viewers' attitudes toward traditional sexual and family values? Zillmann (1989) reports intriguing evidence that repeated exposure to this type of nonviolent pornography loosens traditional sexual and family values. When compared to people who viewed nonsexual films, men and women who were exposed to weekly, hour-long sessions involving scenes of explicit sexual encounters between new acquaintances over a six-week period showed attitudinal changes including greater acceptance, in comparison to controls who viewed nonsexual films, of premarital and extramarital sex and of simultaneous sexual relationships with multiple partners. Men and women who viewed such pornography also reported desiring fewer children than people in the control groups and were relatively less committed to marriage as an "essential institution."

Zillmann (1989) argues that nonviolent pornography loosens traditional family values by projecting an image of sexual enjoyment without responsibility or obligations. Prolonged exposure to such pornography may also foster dissatisfaction with the physical appearance and sexual performance of one's intimate partners (Zillmann, 1989).

In sum, research on the effects of nonviolent pornography does not permit definite conclusions. The effects of nonviolent pornography may be more connected with whether or not women are presented in a dehumanizing manner than with sexual explicitness per se. No research has yet linked sexual explicitness itself with undesirable effects. It is of interest to note that only a minority of people in the United States support legislation making sexually explicit materials illegal, yet three out of four favor the criminalization of *violent* pornography (Harris, 1988).

～ *Reflections* ～

- Agree or disagree with the following statement, and support your answer: One person's pornography is another person's art.
- Why do you think that men are more interested in pornography than women are?
- In *Miller v. California,* the U.S. Supreme Court held that obscenity is based on "whether the average person, applying contemporary community standards, would find that the work, taken as a whole, appeals to the prurient interest." What is your "community"? What are its standards? What types of films, photographs, or written stories would an average person in your community consider to be obscene? Why?
- Do you believe that obscenity and pornography are causes of sexual violence and sexual abuse? What does the research evidence show?
- Which do you consider to be the greater danger—the danger of having pornography available or the danger of censorship? Why?

ARE THE OBSCENITIES OF TODAY THE CLASSICS OF TOMORROW? AN ESSAY ON ART, PORNOGRAPHY, AND CENSORSHIP
—Lois Fichner-Rathus

Man's drive for self-expression, which over the centuries has built his monuments, does not stay within set bounds; the creations which yesterday were the detested and the obscene become the classics of today.

(California Supreme Court Justice Matthew Tobriner, in ruling that Henry Miller's *Tropic of Cancer* was not pornographic [*Wall Street Journal.* 1964, February 3])

We are about to delve into some works of art that have been considered to inhabit the gray areas between pornography and art. Given that contemporary Western culture is inundated with images of performers such as Madonna and Michael Jackson engaging in pelvic thrusting in concert (see Figure 20.1), you may chuckle at those who would have censored the first two of them. But you might rather

Figure 20.1.   In Concert.
Madonna and other performers engage in pelvic thrusting on stage. Is their behavior obscene according to contemporary community standards? Should companies use such performers to advertise their wares? Should the government ban them, or would you rather cast your vote by buying— or not buying—tickets, recordings, and the products they promote?

have kept others under wraps yourself. As you wend your way through these works and the commentaries, you will see that I am biased in favor of free expression. The issues surrounding censorship are not always cut and dried, however.

On the one hand, we have been reared to value free speech, which is protected by the U.S. Constitution. Free speech would seem to extend to unfettered expression of artistic impulses. On the other hand, when people are shocked or offended by things that seem obscene to them, they sometimes rethink their devotion to freedom. They may focus, instead, on matters related to the effects of pornography. It is almost impossible to argue that *nothing* is pornographic and that material of this sort is in no way harmful to innocent people. How can we ignore the evidence that violent pornography stimulates many men to behave aggressively toward women?— and violence against women strikes me as obscene. How can we ignore evidence that child pornography is harmful to the actors and, perhaps, other children who might be victimized by people who gather this material?—especially when hurting children, in my eyes, is the ultimate obscenity.

It is also difficult to argue that taxpayers must support the exhibition of artworks or indeed the creative efforts of an artist whom they find obscene or hurtful toward other human beings. Yet because of the history of almost arbitrary censorship, it is difficult to align oneself with the notion that select forms of artistic expression should be censored. But when the ideal of free expression comes into conflict with the demonstrated potential to harm society's most vulnerable people, it is difficult to lightly ignore either value.

It is not my purpose here to arrive at final answers as to where art ends and pornography and obscenity begin. I shall illustrate, however, that many

works in the history of art—from different periods and cultures—have been labeled as obscene or pornographic. You will also see that many artists, art professionals such as gallery directors, and the public have suffered from censorship.

The depictions of genitalia and explicit sex in the visual arts and literature are not recent developments. We find relief carvings depicting acts of sexual intercourse as early as 7,000 B.C. in modern Zaire. Sculptures depicting exaggerated female genitalia can be dated back even further, and similar sculptures, sometimes referred to as "vulva goddesses," are created by modern Nigerians (see Figure 20.2). Grecian urns and cups were often decorated with explicit male–female and male–male sexual activity (see Chapter 1). The Indian sex manual of the third century, the *Kama Sutra*, had graphic illustrations, and statues of idealized men and women in erotic acts grace the facades of many Hindu temples

Figure 20.2.   Nigerian Vulva Goddess.
Artworks have shown human genitalia for thousands of years. Is the exhibition of nudity obscene? Do artists (and other people) have the right to express themselves as they wish? Where, if anywhere, is the line to be drawn between art and obscenity?

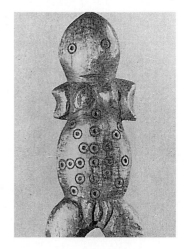

Figure 20.3. *Maya Desnuda.* This oil on canvas painting (37 ³/₈ by 74 ³/₄ inches) was executed in about 1796 by Francisco Goya. (Museo del Prado, Madrid.) Although it may be hard to imagine, given contemporary community standards, paintings such as the nude on the left were once considered obscene. Goya therefore painted the clothed (*vestida*) Maya shown on the right.

(Fichner-Rathus, 1995). Chinese novels of the early seventeenth century contained explicit sexual narratives. Genitalia, often of exaggerated size, were commonly depicted in Japanese art from 1600 through 1900 (Brewer, 1982).

As there have been nude and erotic works in various cultures, so too has there been censorship—and the threat of censorship (Schneemann, 1991). You may have noticed in museums that many later copies of some of the classical sculptures of ancient Greece, a culture that exalted the human body, sport strategically placed fig leaves. In spite of centuries of so-called enlightenment, censorship could not be kept at bay. The Spaniard Francisco Goya (1746–1828) is considered to be one of the greatest painters of the neoclassical and romantic periods (Fichner-Rathus, 1995). Yet at the time of its appearance in about 1796, his *Maya Desnuda* (see Figure 20.3) was quite controversial because of the way the model displayed her nudity and confronted the viewer with her direct gaze. In an article entitled "Burn It, Hide It, Flaunt It," Tomlinson (1991) describes the official Spanish attitude toward nudity at the time:

> In 1762 King Carlos III ordered the First Court Painter, Anton Rafael Mengs, to assemble all the paintings in the royal collection that showed "too much nudity" so that they might be burned. Since these included five paintings by Titian . . . as well as works by Rubens, we may be thankful that Mengs suggested an alternative solution of moving the paintings to his studio. . . . The incendiary passion seems to have been hereditary, for in 1792 Carlos IV sought once again to burn the paintings. (p. 61)

In part because of this oppressive atmosphere, Goya also painted a number of draped Mayas.

The French painter Édouard Manet (1832–1883) was a pivotal figure in the rise of the impressionist movement (Fichner-Rathus, 1995). Manet's work is known for its luminosity; its duplication of natural light; its broad, flat application of pigments; and its capturing of the fleeting moment. Manet's artistic innovations and, in this case, his sassy brush, aroused the ire of the French critics and public alike. His masterpiece *Le Déjeuner sur l'Herbe* (see Figure 20.4), a contemporary reinterpretation of a painted passage by Renaissance master Raphael, aroused the public for more than stylistic reasons:

> What was so alarming to the Parisian spectator, and remains so to this day, is that there is no explanation for the behavior of the picnickers. Why are the men clothed and the women undraped to varying degrees? Why are the men chatting among themselves, seemingly unaware of the women? The public was quite used to the painting of nudes, . . . but they were not prepared to witness one of their fold—an ordinary citizen—displayed so shamefully on such a grand scale [the painting is 7 feet high and almost 9 feet wide]. The painting was further intolerable because the seated woman meets the viewer's stare, as if the viewer had intruded on their gathering in a voyeuristic fashion. (p.)

Today, prudish reactions to the works of Goya and Manet seem unjustified or downright silly. But in their time, these works posed moral dilemmas for their observers.

Today, the issue of where the lines are to be drawn between art and pornography may be most clearly embodied in the photographs of Robert Mapplethorpe, who died of AIDS in 1989. Philadelphia's Institute of Contemporary Art compiled a traveling retrospective exhibition of the artist's

Figure 20.4. *Le Déjeuner sur l'Herbe.* This oil-on-canvas painting (7 feet by 8 feet ten inches) was worked by Édouard Manet in 1863. (Musée d'Orsay, Galerie du Jeu de Paume.) This work aroused the ire of the public and critics alike at a Parisian exhibition.

work from the late 1960s to 1988, just shortly before his death, entitled: "Robert Mapplethorpe: The Perfect Moment." As noted by Judith Tannenbaum (1991), however,

> . . . what started out to be a "normal" exhibition turned into something quite different—a national cause célèbre, the impetus for intense congressional debate about federal funding of the arts, and, ultimately, the focus of an obscenity trial in Cincinnati. (p. 71)

In 1989, the Corcoran Gallery of Art in Washington, DC, canceled its scheduled installation of the exhibition. When shown in Philadelphia and Cincinnati, the exhibition was accompanied by warnings that there were sexually explicit photographs and that the content might be inappropriate for children. The obscenity trial involved Dennis Barrie, the director of the Contemporary Arts Center of Cincinnati, Ohio. He was indicted and subsequently acquitted, in October 1990, on charges of pandering to obscenity and the illegal use of a minor in the exhibition.

The "illegal use of a minor" charge referred to photographs of children that showed frontal nudity. Since nudity itself is hardly ever considered the criterion for obscenity in Western culture these days, it is hard to imagine that these photographs stirred members of the public or government officials. But they did. The reason may be in part because other sections of the exhibition, such as the *X Portfolio*, contained photographs such as *X Portfolio, Patrice* (see Figure 20.5). Though *Patrice* may distress some readers in its barely contained sexual power, other photographs portrayed explicit homoerotic sex acts, such as fisting (see Chapter 10). The nudes of the children, in the larger context, did disturb people at the exhibition. The "larger context," by the way, also included lovely, uncontroversial photographs of flowers and a number of more familiar sorts of adult female nudes.

Treating Dennis Barrie and the works of art by critically acclaimed photographer Robert Mapplethorpe according to the letter of the law as it applies to obscenity and abuse of minors—rather than interpreting the case according to the spirit of the law—raises serious questions. For ex-

Figure 20.5. *X Portfolio, Patrice.* This gelatin silver print (7¾ by 7¾ inches) was created by Robert Mapplethorpe in 1977. (Estate of Robert Mapplethorpe.) Photographs from Mapplethorpe's *X Portfolio* stimulated authorities in Cincinnati, Ohio, to indict a gallery director for "pandering to obscenity." The gallery director was subsequently acquitted, however.

ample, can the government serve as a competent final judge as to what is pornographic or obscene? Can the government serve as art critic and aesthetician? Artists and advocates of free expression have the greatest of fears in the face of these prospects. Their concerns are rooted in ghastly historical events affecting the arts, such as Hitler's denouncing of, and his overt threats to, German expressionists and abstract artists whom he labeled as degenerate.

The artists discussed up to this point have been men. Women artists are no more immune to being consid-

ered pornographers, however, or at least of exceeding the bounds of community standards of decency. Artist Sue Coe was commissioned by *Boston* magazine to illustrate the reportage of a highly publicized rape trial in New Bedford. A group of men were accused of the gang rape of a woman on a pool table in a bar. The result was *Gray Rape* (see Figure 20.6). Carol Jacobsen (1991) reports that Coe discovered that the magazine had printed the drawing *with the bottom half—the part showing the rape—cut off.* This "editing" was carried out without the artist's prior knowledge or permission. Jacobsen (1991) notes that

> more significant is the fact that rape itself—both a national disgrace and a glaring symptom of our misogynist public policies and laws—has so far been addressed in only one major art exhibition: the 1985 show titled "Rape," organized by Stephanie Blackwood at Ohio State University. (1991, p. 49)

Nor are our great U.S. cathedrals of learning—our universities—safe from censorship. In 1987, the Perkison Gallery at Illinois's Millikin University invited a Chicago artists' cooperative to present a group exhibition. The exhibition included Joan Lyons's painting *Seduction III* (see Figure 20.7), which shows some nudes interacting in a suggestively erotic but not sexually explicit manner. As noted by Lyons, the university president removed the painting from the gallery after it had been on display for a week. The president asserted that the painting was "not ap-

Figure 20.6. *Gray Rape.* This 1983 charcoal-on-paper (30 by 40 inches) by Sue Coe was commissioned by a news magazine. The bottom half of the drawing was cut off when it was printed, without the artist's prior knowledge or permission.

Figure 20.7. *Seduction III.*
This acrylic-on-canvas painting (58 by 44 inches) was worked by Joan Lyons in 1984. (Collection of the artist, Glencoe, Illinois.) It was censored by a university president.

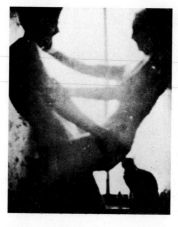

Figure 20.8. *Fuses* **and a Sculpture from Zaire.**
In her 1965 film *Fuses*, artist Carolee Schneemann engaged in sexual activity with a partner to depict her "deepest expressive and responsive life core." Here, Schneemann juxtaposes a film still from *Fuses* with a sculpture on the same theme from Zaire to show that people from many cultures have responded to their sexuality through artistic expression. Judgments as to what is obscene are made within a cultural context.

propriate for a general, nonselective audience" (Lyons, 1991, p. 81). The other artists in the exhibition withdrew their works in protest, and some other artists have since declined offers to have solo exhibitions at the university.

Carolee Schneemann has been creating erotic drawings, paintings, photographs, films, installations, and performances since the 1960s. She may be considered one of the founders of the sexual revolution in the arts. One source of the controversy that has surrounded her work is that she is the artist and the subject of so many of her works. Her film *Fuses*, for example, shows her engaging in explicit sexual activity with a partner (see Figure 20.8). She performed in the nude in *Body Collage* (see Figure 20.9). Schneemann (1991) discusses her motives for creating *Fuses* and considers society's response to it:

> Since my deepest expressive and responsive life core was considered obscene, I thought I had better see what it looked like in my own vision. I had never seen any erotica or pornography that approached what lived sexuality felt like. . . . My film *Fuses* has been subject to constant censorship despite its special awards in Cannes in 1968 and at the Yale Film Festival in 1972. . . .
>
> If my paintings, photographs, film, and enacted works have been judged obscene, the question arises: is this

because I use the body in its actuality—without contrivance, fetishization, displacement? Is this because my photographic works are usually self-shot, without an external, controlling eye? And are these works obscene because I posit my female body as a locus of autonomy, pleasure, desire; and insist that as an artist I can be both image and image maker, merging two aspects of a self deeply fractured in the contemporary imagination? (pp. 31, 33)

What of it? What are the limits? May artists, as Schneemann states,

make any image that they wish? If their "deepest expressive and responsive life core [is] considered obscene," may they nevertheless express themselves without being fettered by the government? Can the U.S. public in the 1990s tolerate the right to free expression and allow—to paraphrase Justice Tobriner—that some of the creations that today are the detested and the obscene may become the classics of tomorrow?

Figure 20.9. *Body Collage* **and an Owl Goddess from New Guinea.** Here artist Carolee Schneemann juxtaposes an image of herself in a 1968 performance with an "owl goddess" from New Guinea that also celebrates the female form.

Sex in Advertising

In the 1980s a coquettish Brooke Shields was featured in a TV commercial that showed her spreading her denim-clad legs, smiling coyly at the camera, and murmuring that nothing came between her and her Calvins (Calvin Klein jeans, that is). The advertising campaign evoked a storm of complaints from viewers who felt that it was vulgar and obscene. Meanwhile, the sales of Calvin Klein jeans went through the roof. In short, sex sells.

Calvin Klein ads keep on "pushing the envelope" in the United States. That is, they keep on challenging the limits of what is acceptable to the public. Critics have accused Klein of engaging in child pornography by using advertisements such as those shown in Figure 20.10. Yet ads such as these remain in place—and sell Calvins.

The use of sexual imagery in advertising ranges from more subtle uses of innuendo and double entendre, such as slogans like "Take it off, take it all off" (for Noxema shave cream) and "*It's* better in the Bahamas," to the use of an attractive woman who says her men wear "English Leather or they wear nothing at all."

Sex in advertising operates according to the principle of association. Advertisers hope that people will link the product with the sexual imagery that is incorporated within the advertisement. Perhaps the use of a sexy ad will make consumers think that the product will make them more sexually alluring or enhance their sexual arousal, which, in turn, will prompt them to purchase the product rather than that of a competitor.

Researchers caution, however, that sexy ads can backfire. Viewers may pay such careful attention to the sexy imagery that they tune out the advertising message or product claims, or even forget what the product is (Edgley, 1989; Severn et al., 1990). Sexy advertising may not only be distracting. It may also turn people off to the advertisement and, by extension, to the product, especially if the sexual image is unrelated to the nature of the product.

Figure 20.10. "Pushing the Envelope." Calvin Klein's ad campaigns have been accused of using child pornography to sell jeans. What do you think? How far is too far?

It is true that sexy ads may cause consumers to focus on the sexual content of the advertisements and thus forget the products. ■

Advertisers may also need to consider the gender of the target audience. Researchers find that men tend to react more positively and women more negatively toward various forms of sexual content in advertising, whether it be sexual innuendos uttered by female models in TV commercials (Bello et al., 1983) or female nudity in print advertising (La-Tour, 1990).

Advertising and Gender-Role Stereotypes

The frequent use of sexy female models in advertisements raises broader concerns about the depiction of women in advertising. As Edgley notes, "Despite years of feminist consciousness-raising about the issue, commercials still tend to depict women in stereotypical ways" (Edgley, 1989). What Komisar said of advertising in 1971 may be as true today as it was then:

> If television commercials are to be believed, most American women go into uncontrollable ecstasies at the sight and smell of tables and cabinets that have been lovingly caressed with long-lasting, satin-finish, lemon-scented, spray-on furniture polish. Or they glow with rapture at the blinding whiteness of their wash—to the green-eyed envy of their neighbors. . . . it is an amazing feat of hocus-pocus worthy of Tom Sawyer and P. T. Barnum to lovingly declare that domestic labor is the true vocation of women wearing wedding bands. (p. 209)

Studies of TV commercials in the United States, Canada, the United Kingdom, and Italy show a consistent pattern: Females are more likely to be portrayed visually on screen, whereas males are more likely to do voice-overs as the "voice of authority" (Ferrante et al., 1988; Furnham & Voli, 1989; Lovdal, 1989). A study of 320 U.S. TV commercials employing voice-overs showed that 91% used male voices. Only 9% used female voices (Lovdal, 1989).

TV commercials also tend to portray men in a wider variety of occupational roles than women (Bretl & Cantor, 1988; Lovdal, 1989). Despite increased awareness of gender-role stereotypes, the image of women in TV commercials has not changed much in recent years (Lovdal, 1989). Women's roles are still generally stereotyped in traditional roles as wives, mothers, brides, waitresses, actresses, and so on. Rarely are they photographers, athletes, or businesswomen. Still, we can report some signs of change, at least with respect to the portrayal of men's roles. Men today are increasingly represented in commercials as spouses and parents (Bretl & Cantor, 1988). Women, however, are still more likely to be seen in domestic settings, advertising products that they can use in the home (Bretl & Cantor, 1988).

Why should we be concerned about how women are portrayed in advertising? For one thing, stereotypical advertising may serve to perpetuate traditional gender-role expectations by portraying women primarily in domestic roles or as sex objects. TV commercials (and programs), for example, may influence viewers' perceptions of acceptable gender-role behaviors (Lovdal, 1989). Girls and young women who are continually exposed to images of women in domestic roles may perceive themselves as having fewer career options than their male counterparts. Not surprisingly, researchers have found that heavier TV viewing is linked to the adoption of more traditional gender-role attitudes among children (Gross & Jeffries-Fox, 1978).

~ *Reflections* ~

▨ Agree or disagree with the following statement, and support your answer: Advertising practices today are contributing to the moral decay of the United States.

- What advertisements in magazines and on television today seem to rely heavily on sex appeal? Have they affected your attitudes toward the products involved? Have they affected your purchasing practices? (Be honest!)
- Agree or disagree with the following statement, and support your answer: Sex in advertising perpetuates traditional gender-role stereotypes.

Summing Up

The World of Commercial Sex: A Disneyland for Adults

Commercial sex runs the gamut from "adult" movie theaters and bookshops to strip shows, sex toy shops, brothels, escort services, massage parlors, "900" telephone services, and the use of sex in advertising.

Prostitution

In the United States, prostitution is illegal everywhere except rural counties in Nevada.

Incidence of Prostitution in the United States Today Fewer young men in the United States use prostitutes than in Kinsey's day, apparently because of the liberalizing trends of the sexual revolution.

Types of Female Prostitutes The major types of female prostitutes are streetwalkers, brothel prostitutes—many of whom work in massage parlors and for "escort services"—and call girls. Streetwalkers often support, and are abused by, pimps.

Characteristics of Female Prostitutes No single factor explains entry into female prostitution, but poverty and sexual and/or physical abuse figure prominently in the backgrounds of many prostitutes. Teenage runaways with marginal skills and limited means of support may find few alternatives to prostitution.

Customers of Female Prostitutes The consumers of prostitutes are often referred to as "johns" or "tricks." Most patrons are "occasional johns" with regular sex partners. Some people use prostitutes habitually or compulsively, however.

Male Prostitution Most male prostitutes are "hustlers" who service male clients. Hustlers typically begin selling sex in their teens and may be gay or heterosexual in orientation.

HIV, AIDS, and Prostitution Prostitutes are at greater risk of transmission of HIV because they have sexual relations with many partners, often without protection. Many prostitutes and their clients and other sex partners also inject drugs and share contaminated needles. HIV may be spread by unprotected sex from prostitutes to customers, then to the customers' wives or lovers. Despite the dangers of HIV transmission, many U.S. prostitutes have not altered either their sexual behavior or their patterns of drug use.

Pornography and Obscenity

What Is Pornographic? Pornography is "writing, pictures, etc., intended to arouse sexual desire." Erotica, by contrast, refers to sexual materials that are artistically produced or motivated. The judgment as to what is pornographic or obscene varies from person to person and culture to culture.

Pornography and the Law In *Miller v. California*, the U.S. Supreme Court held that obscenity is based upon a determination of "whether the average person, applying contemporary community standards, would find that the work . . . appeals to the prurient interest . . . ; whether the work depicts [sexual behavior] in a patently offensive way, [and] whether the work, taken as a whole, lacks serious literary, artistic, political, or scientific value." *Miller* recognizes that judgments of obscenity may vary with "community standards."

Prevalence and Use of Erotica and Pornography People in the United States are typically introduced to pornography by their high school years. Although both genders can become physiologically aroused by erotic materials, men are relatively more interested in sexually explicit pictures and films.

Pornography and Sexual Coercion A 1970 government commission found no harmful effects of pornographic material on normal people. A later government commission, the Meese commission, issued a report in 1986 linking exposure to violent pornography with sexual aggression, and exposure to degrading but nonviolent pornography with increased acceptability of rape in the minds of viewers. Research evidence suggests that exposure to pornography may stimulate sexually deviant urges in some men who are predisposed to commit crimes of sexual violence. Research evidence in laboratory settings also suggests that violent pornography may stimulate college men to act more aggressively toward women. Some researchers argue that it is the violence in violent pornography, and not sexual explicitness per se, that promotes violence against women. The effects of nonviolent pornography on normal populations remain unclear.

Sex in Advertising

Sex in advertising operates according to the principle of association. Advertisers hope that people will link the product with the sexual imagery that is incorporated within the advertisement. Sexy ads can backfire, however, by diverting attention from the product or turning people off to the product.

Advertising and Gender-Role Stereotypes Women in TV commercials are still generally stereotyped as wives, mothers, brides, waitresses, actresses, and so on.

CHAPTER 21

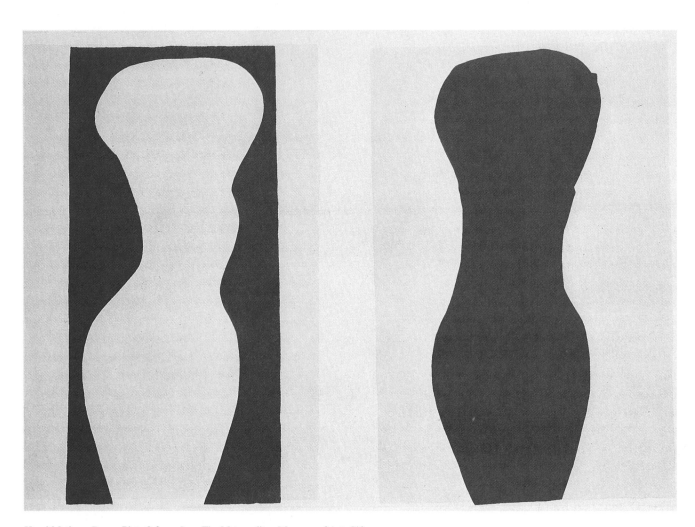

Henri Matisse, *Forms,* Plate 9 from *Jazz.* The Metropolitan Museum of Art, Gift of Lila Acheson Wallace, 1983. © 1996 Succession H. Matisse/Artist Rights Society (ARS), New York. © 1985 by The Metropolitan Museum of Art.

Making Responsible Sexual Decisions—An Epilogue

Outline

Making choices is deeply intertwined with our sexual experience. Although sex is a natural function, the ways in which we express our sexuality are matters of personal choice. We choose how, where, and with whom to become sexually involved. We may face a wide array of sexual decisions: Whom should I date? When should my partner and I become sexually intimate? Should I initiate sexual relations or wait for my partner to approach me? Should my partner and I practice contraception? If so, which method? Should I use a condom to protect against sexually transmitted diseases (or insist that my partner does)? Should I be tested for HIV? Should I insist that my partner be tested for HIV before we engage in sexual relations?

Choices, Information, and Decision Making

We have presented you with information that can help you make responsible sexual decisions. Information alone cannot determine whether the options you consider are morally acceptable to you, however. Many issues raise moral concerns, such as premarital and extramarital sex, contraception, and abortion. Gathering information and weighing the scientific evidence will alert you to what is possible in the contemporary world, but only you can determine which of your options are compatible with your own moral values. We all have unique sets of moral values—as Americans, as members of one of America's hundreds of subcultures, as individuals. No single value system defines us all. Indeed, the world of diversity in which we live is a mosaic of different moral codes and cultural traditions and beliefs.

Conflict

The most difficult decisions involve choices between alternatives that each have positive and negative aspects or that each have compelling negative features.

Consider the issue of deciding whether to obtain screening for cancer. The pluses include freedom from anxiety (when results are negative) and early detection (when cancer is found). The negatives include the costs of screening, inconvenience, discomfort (in some techniques), and hearing results one would rather not hear (if cancer is found) (White et al., 1994).

Consider contraceptive techniques. The pill is effective and does not interfere with sexual spontaneity, but it is costly and has side effects. The condom has no side effects (for the great majority of users), but some people find that it disrupts lovemaking and reduces sexual sensations. It is also not as effective as the pill.

Or consider the plight of Kim, a college student who becomes pregnant as a result of date rape: Should she have an abortion, which may be morally offensive to her, or bear an unwanted child? Then, too, should she report the crime and hope the criminal justice system will successfully prosecute her assailant, or should she try to swallow her bitter feelings and protect her anonymity? Or consider the college student who feels morally committed to remaining a virgin until marriage but fears earning the disapproval of dating partners or having no dates at all.

When we are pulled in different directions at the same time, we experience psychological conflict. Conflict can be extremely stressful, especially if it is prolonged. People in conflict often feel "damned if they do and damned if they don't." They may also vacillate—take tentative steps in one direction and then in the other. Kim, a survivor of date rape, takes a bus to an abortion clinic across town and gets off at the next stop. She checks the telephone number of the police but then hesitates to pick up the telephone. She is obsessed with the question as to what is the right thing to do.

Part of Kim's conflict is over a moral issue. She would very much like to terminate her unwanted pregnancy by having an abortion, but she holds back because she firmly believes that the embryo within is a precious human life. Her conflict over whether or not to report her assailant is in part moral, in part practical. It is morally proper to report him, but what if she is not believed? What if the incident becomes widely known on campus and to her family? Moreover, she realizes that the longer she waits, the more it may appear that she is making up the story.

Decisions, Decisions, Decisions . . .

The way out of conflict is to make decisions. Making decisions involves choosing among various courses of action. The act of not making a formal decision may itself represent a tacit decision. For example, we may vacillate about whether to use a particular form of birth control but continue to engage in unprotected sex. Is this because we have not made a decision or because we have decided to let happen what will happen?

Gathering information helps us to predict the outcomes of the decisions we make. This textbook provides you with a broad data base concerning scientific developments and ways of relating to other people—including people who come from other cultures. By talking to people who have had similar questions or been in similar conflicts, you can also learn which decisions worked for them, which did not, and, perhaps, why. Or you may be able to learn what happens when people do not make decisions but simply hope for the best. You can also talk to your parents, friends, religious counselors, course instructors, psychologists, and other helping professionals. Regarding which contraceptive method to use, you may wish to discuss the information in this book with a physician, nurse, or other health counselor.

Value Systems

Our value systems provide another framework for judging the moral acceptability of sexual options. We often approach sexual decisions by determining whether the choices we face are compatible with our moral values. Our value systems do not necessarily determine the outcomes of all of our sexual decisions, however—any more than laws strictly determine people's behavior. Some of us adhere to stricter moral values. Some people make choices that bend or violate their values but try not to focus on the discrepancies too closely. Many of us also act on impulse, especially sexual impulses, without thinking through the consequences of our actions. Afterward, we may regret our decisions or feel guilty if our behavior was inconsistent with our values.

Our value systems—our sexual standards—have many sources: parents, peers, religious training, ethnic subcultures, the larger culture, and our appraisal of all these influences. Value systems that provide a guiding framework to determine the moral acceptability of sexual choices include legalism, situation ethics, hedonism, asceticism, utilitarianism, and rationalism.

Legalism

The legalistic approach formulates ethical behavior on the basis of a code of moral laws derived from an external source, such as the creed of a particular religion (Knox, 1988). The Bible contains many examples of the moral code of the Jewish and Christian religions. In the Book of Leviticus (20:10–17) in the Old Testament we find many of the biblical prohibitions against adultery, incest, sexual activity with people of one's own gender, and bestiality:

> And the man that committeth adultery with another man's wife, even he that committeth adultery with his neighbor's wife, both the adulterer and the adulteress shall surely be put to death. And the man that lieth with his father's wife . . . both of them shall surely be put

to death; their blood shall be upon them. . . . And if a man lie with mankind, as with womankind, both of them have committed abomination: they shall surely be put to death; . . . And if a man lie with a beast, he shall surely be put to death; and ye shall slay the beast. . . . And if a man shall take his sister, . . . and see her nakedness, and she sees his nakedness: it is a shameful thing; and they shall be cut off in the sight of the children of their people. . . .

Leviticus also proscribes intercourse during menstruation and the forcing of daughters into prostitution.

Throughout the centuries, many Christians and Jews have adhered to religious laws that are intended to promote the solidarity of the family and the community by minimizing interpersonal jealousies and frictions. Adultery, for example, could set neighbor against neighbor. Religious laws have also directed followers to be "fruitful and multiply" so as to ensure that an ample number of progeny would be available to meet the needs for labor and defense of the family and the community of religious followers.

Many religious followers today accept the moral codes of their religions as a matter of faith and commitment, not necessarily because they can logically or rationally derive them from contemporary societal needs. Some people find it reassuring to be informed by religious authorities or scripture that a certain course of action is right or wrong. Others, however, have questioned how closely one must adhere to religious teachings if one is to be ethical. A number of fundamentalist Protestants, conservative Catholics, and orthodox Jews would argue that the Bible is to be followed to the letter, not just "in spirit." They see the Bible, in all its literal details, as the revealed word of God.

Other Christians and Jews take a more liberal view. They say that the Bible was inspired by God but that it was written or transcribed by fallible humans and is subject to various interpretations. They may also assert that the Bible reflects the social setting of the time in which it was written, not just divine inspiration. At a time of burgeoning population growth in many parts of the world, biblical injunctions to be fruitful and multiply may no longer be socially and environmentally sound. Prohibitions, such as that against coitus during menstruation, may have been based on prescientific perceptions of danger. Thus, religious teachings may be viewed as a general framework for decision making rather than as a set of absolute rules.

Situation Ethics

Episcopal theologian Joseph Fletcher (1966, 1967) argued that ethical decision making should be guided by genuine love for others rather than by rigid moral rules. Fletcher advocated that sexual decision making should be based on the context of the particular situation that the person faces. For this reason, his view is termed *situation ethics*. According to Fletcher, a Roman Catholic woman will have been taught that abortion is the taking of a human life. Her situation, however—her love for her existing family and her recognition of her limited resources for providing for another child—might influence her to decide in favor of an abortion.

Fletcher argues that one's rules for conduct should not be inflexible. Rather, they should be general guidelines. "The situationist is prepared in any concrete case to suspend, ignore, or violate any principle if by doing so he can effect more good than by following it" (1966, p. 34).

Note that situation ethics is not an excuse for selfishness. The moral situation ethicist acts in a manner that he or she believes will lead to the greater good. Now and then, such an act may be frustrating, painful, or difficult. Situation ethicists also may find it difficult, as psychologist David Knox (1988) points out, to make sexual decisions on a case-by-case basis:

"I don't know what's right anymore" reflects the uncertainty of a situation ethics view. Once a person decides that mutual love is the context justifying intercourse, how often and how soon should the person fall in love? Can love develop after two hours of conversation? How does one know that her or his own love feelings and those of a partner are genuine? The freedom that situation ethics brings to sexual decision making requires responsibility, maturity, and judgment. In some cases, individuals may deceive themselves by believing they are in love so they will not feel guilty about having intercourse.

(Knox, 1988, p. 97. Reprinted by permission.)

Ethical Relativism

Ethical relativism assumes that diverse values are fundamental to human existence. Ethical relativists reject the idea that there is a single correct moral view. One person may believe that premarital sex is unacceptable under any circumstances, whereas another may hold that "being in love" makes it acceptable. Still another person may believe that premarital sex is morally permissible without an emotional commitment between the partners.

The ethical relativist believes that there is no objective way of justifying one set of moral values over another. In this view, the essence of human morality is to derive one's own principles and apply them according to one's own conscience. From this perspective, whatever a person believes is right is right for him or her. Subscribing to ethical relativism does not free us of the need to develop moral beliefs, however. It challenges us, instead, to take responsibility for our decisions and to live up to them.

Opponents of ethical relativism believe that allowing people free rein to determine what is right or wrong may bring about social chaos and decay.

One form of ethical relativism is cultural relativism. From this perspective, what is right or wrong must be understood in terms of the cultural beliefs that affect sexual decision making. In some cultures, premarital sex is tolerated or even encouraged, whereas in others it is considered immoral. Cultural relativism, like ethical relativism, does not ascribe moral superiority to one cultural tradition over another.

Hedonism

The hedonist is guided by the pursuit of pleasure, not by whether a particular behavior is morally or situationally justified (Knox, 1988). "If it feels good, do it" expresses the hedonistic ethic. The hedonist believes that sexual desires, like hunger or thirst, do not invoke moral considerations.

Of course, one could make the case that there are two kinds of hedonism: short-sighted and long-term hedonism. Basing decisions upon what feels good at the moment may fail to account for the long-term consequences of one's actions. The short-sighted hedonist may risk becoming so driven by the pursuit of pleasure that sex becomes a form of "addiction" in which sexual pleasure overshadows other important aspects of life.

On the other hand, taking a long-term hedonistic view, one can attempt to make responsible sexual decisions that can lead to a lifetime of sexual pleasure. Choosing to do what is necessary to maintain our sexual health, for instance, can help us lead long lives and to enjoy our bodies throughout our span of years.

Asceticism

Religious celibates, such as Roman Catholic priests and nuns, choose asceticism (self-denial of material and sexual desires) in order to devote themselves to spiritual pursuits. Many ascetics in Eastern and Western religions seek to transcend physical and worldly desires.

Utilitarianism

Some people believe that it is necessary to adhere to specific religious principles or teachings if one is to be a moral or ethical person, but others believe that ethical guidelines can be based on principles other than religious ones. The English philosopher John Stuart Mill (1806–1873), for example, proposed an ethical system based on utilitarianism.

The core ethic of utilitarianism is that moral conduct is based on that which will bring about "the greatest good for the greatest number" (Mill, 1863). The utilitarian characterizes behavior as ethical when it does the greatest good and causes the least harm. This is not license. Utilitarians may come down hard in opposition to premarital sex and bearing children out of wedlock, for example, if they believe that these behavior patterns jeopardize a nation's health and social fabric. Mill's ethics generally require that we treat one another justly and honestly, because it serves the greater good for people to be true to their word and just in their dealings with others.

Rationalism

Rationalism involves the use of reason as the means of determining a course of action (Knox, 1988). The rationalist believes that decisions should be based on intellect and reasoning, rather than emotions or strict obedience to a particular faith. The rationalist attempts to assess the facts in a sexual situation and then logically weigh the consequences of each course of action before making a decision. The rationalist shares with the utilitarian the belief that reasoning can lead to a course of ethical behavior. The rationalist is not bound, however, to the utilitarian code that makes choices on the basis of the greatest good for the greatest number. The rationalist may contend that personal needs and desires outweigh the needs of the many.

The utilitarian may decide, for example, to prolong an unhappy marriage because of the belief that the greater good (of the family and the community) is better served by maintaining an unhappy marriage than by dissolving it. The rationalist might decide that the personal consequences of continuing an unhappy marriage outweigh the consequences to the family or the community at large. The religious follower, adopting a legalistic view, might decide that divorce is or is not acceptable, depending on the tenets of the person's religion. The situation ethicist might interpret religious principles in light of how the greater good would be served in a particular situation.

These ethical systems represent general frameworks of moral reasoning or pathways for judging the moral acceptability of sexual and nonsexual behavior. Whereas some of us may adopt one or another of these systems in their purest forms, others adopt a system of moral reasoning that involves some combination or variation of these ethical systems. Some also shift from one ethical system to another from time to time, sometimes reasoning legalistically and sometimes adopting a more flexible situationist approach. Despite these variations, these general guidelines of moral reasoning assist our understanding of how people approach questions of moral acceptability of sexual choices.

∼ Reflections ∼

▪ Do any of the value systems discussed in the chapter seem similar to your own? What role does your sociocultural background play in your value system? Explain.

▪ Agree or disagree with the following statement, and support your answer: There is no objective way of justifying one set of moral values over another.

▪ Agree or disagree with the following statement, and support your answer: Sexual decisions should be based on intellect and reasoning, rather than emotions or strict obedience to a particular faith.

The Balance Sheet for Decision Making

You might use a balance sheet to help weigh the pluses and minuses of alternatives when making decisions. Sheri Oz (1994, 1995) suggests that it is particularly important to weigh the costs of deciding in one direction or another. Oz notes that in making decisions about sex, marriage, and divorce, we frequently weigh costs in self-esteem against costs in terms of the approval of other people—often our intimate partners.

TABLE 21.1. Rosa's balance sheet for deciding whether or not to use birth-control pills

Issues		Positive Anticipations	Negative Anticipations
Experiential gains and losses	For self	Sex would be spontaneous	Possible side effects: nausea, bloating, etc.
	For partner	Sex would be spontaneous	None
Biological gains and losses	For self	High effectiveness	Probably no negative impact on health; (useless against STDs)
	For partner	High effectiveness	None
Financial gains and losses	For self	(Needn't worry about the cost of a child)	Expensive!
	For partner	(Needn't worry about the cost of a child)	(None!)
Ethical gains and losses	For self	Would not risk bearing unwanted child or having to decide whether to have an abortion if became pregnant	Moderate concern about using artificial means of birth control; responsibility for birth control would be all mine
	For partner	Would not have to worry about causing pregnancy	None!
Legal factors	For self		None
	For partner		None

Rosa, a Mexican American student at a California state college, has been involved in a sexual relationship for several weeks and is contemplating going on the pill. Rosa uses the balance sheet to list the projected gains and losses for herself and her partner according to five criteria:

1. *Experiential.* How will it feel? What is its effect on sexual relations? How does it affect sexual sensations and spontaneity?
2. *Biological.* How do contraceptive methods work? What are the side effects of birth-control methods? What are the risks involved? What are its effects on preventing STDs?
3. *Financial.* Can I afford it—literally? For example, how much do pills cost? How much do babies cost?
4. *Ethical.* Is what I am considering consistent with my religious and parental teachings? Is that important to me? Will I experience guilt, anxiety, or shame? Is the course of behavior consistent with my ideas concerning sex roles and who takes the responsibility for the decision? (For example, should the responsibility for birth control be placed on the woman's shoulders only?)
5. *Legal.* Am I contemplating something that is against the law? What could happen to my partner and me?

As shown in Table 21.1, Rosa filled in some of the spaces on the sheet to indicate the following pieces of information:

- Sex can be spontaneous.
- For all practical purposes, the pill can be considered 100% effective (I'm assuming I'll take them as directed).
- I'm 20 years old (young enough and healthy enough not to be too worried about the pill's potential effect on my health).

- The pill is kind of expensive.
- I have some moral concerns about using the pill.
- The pill is legal.

The remaining blank spaces prompted Rosa to consider other issues. For example, she realized that she had forgotten to think about the side effects of the pill and the fact that it is useless against STDs. The information prompted by using the balance sheet is placed in parentheses.

Rosa decided not to go on the pill for several reasons: (1) She was concerned about side effects; (2) she did not want to spend the money; and (3) she felt that by taking the pill, she was assuming all responsibility for birth control and that she would rather share it with her partner. Her periods were regular and she decided (1) to use the rhythm method (to abstain from intercourse for a week in the middle of her cycle) and (2) to have her partner use condoms (and spermicide containing nonoxynol-9) every time they made love. The condoms and spermicide would also afford protection against STDs.

After completing a balance sheet, Rosa might fill out a similar one for the alternative of using the condom before making a decision. The balance sheet does not automatically lead to one "correct" choice. You might, for example, reach a different decision than Rosa if you were faced with the same situation. Rather, it is a means of organizing one's perceptions of the positive and negative features of each alternative for oneself and one's partner. Research has shown that balance sheet users hold fewer regrets about the road not taken and are more likely to stick with their decisions.

~ *Reflections* ~

What decisions are you facing in your own sex life? What sexual decisions are you likely to face in the future? As we return to our worlds of diversity, what value systems will you draw upon in making these decisions?

What kinds of conflicts may emerge if your partner comes from another cultural background and holds different values? How can the information in this book be of help to you?

Will you use the information in this textbook to critically examine stereotypes and folklore, or will you think "Oh, it's just another textbook" and toss it aside at the end of the term?

We have come a long way together, and we wish you well. Perhaps we have helped you to phrase the most important questions and to find some answers. We also hope that we have encouraged you to try to understand other people's sexual beliefs and values in light of their cultural backgrounds. Understanding is an essential stopping point on the pathway to respect, and respect is vital to resolving conflicts and establishing healthy relationships.

Appendix A

Scoring Keys for Self-Scoring Questionnaires

Scoring Key for the Love Attitudes Scale (Chapter 7, p. 198)

First add your scores on the 30 items of the scale to yield a total score.

Write down your total score here: _____

Note that each of the items is keyed so that lower numbered responses represent more romantic responses; higher numbered responses represent more realistic responses. The lower your total score (30 is the lowest possible score), the more you identify with a romantic view of love. The higher your score (150 is the highest possible score), the more realistic you are in your love attitudes. A score of 90 places you at the midpoint on the romantic-realist dimension. You may wish to compare your score with your partner's score to see who is more the romantic or more the realist.

Scoring Key for Sternberg's Triangular Love Scale (Chapter 7, p. 203)

First add your scores for the items on each of the three components—Intimacy, Passion, and Decision/Commitment—and divide each total by 15. This will yield an average rating for each subscale. An average rating of 5 on a particular subscale indicates a moderate level of the component represented by the subscale. A higher rating indicates a greater level. A lower rating indicates a lower level. Examining your ratings on these components will give you an idea of the degree to which you perceive your love relationship to be characterized by these three components of love. For example, you might find that passion is stronger than decision/commitment, a pattern that is common in the early stages of an intense romantic relationship. You might find it interesting to complete the questionnaire a few months or perhaps a year or so from now to see how your feelings about your relationship change over time. You might also ask your partner to complete the scale so that the two of you can compare your respective scores. Comparing your ratings for each component with those of your partner will give you an idea of the degree to which you and your partner see your relationship in a similar way.

Sternberg (1988) reports the results of administering the scale to a sample of 50 men and 51 women (average age of 31 years) from the New Haven (CT) area who were either married or presently involved in a close relationship. Average scores for the three components were 7.39 for intimacy, 6.51 for passion, and 7.20 for commitment. High scores (scores representing approximately the top 15 percent of scores) were 8.6 for intimacy, 8.2 for passion, and 8.7 for commitment. Low scores, representing the bottom 15 percent of scores, were 6.2, 4.9, and 5.7 for the three components, respectively. Since romantic ardor may be more difficult to maintain over time, the lower average scores for passion may reflect the length of the relationships in which the people in the sample were involved, which averaged 6.3 years in length. Although you may want to compare your scores with those from this sample, we caution that the Sternberg sample was small and most likely does not accurately represent the general population.

Scoring Key for Reasoning About Abortion Scale
(Chapter 12, p. 362)

First tally your scores for the following items: 1,3,7,8,9,11,13,14,17,20. This score represents your support for a pro-choice point of view: ___33___.

Now tally your scores for the remaining items: 2,4,5,6,10,12,15,16,18,19. This score represents your support for a pro-life point of view: ___14___.

Now subtract your *pro-choice* score from your *pro-life score*. Write the difference, including the sign, here: ___14___. A positive score indictes agreement with a pro-life philosophy. A negative score indicates agreement with a pro-choice philosophy. The higher your score, the more strongly you agree with the philosophy you endorsed. Scores may range from -40 to +40.

One sample of 230 undergraduate students (115 of each gender) obtained a mean score of -7.48 and a median score of -13.33 (Parsons et al., 1990). This indicates that the students tended to be pro-choice in their attitudes. Another sample of 38 graduate students (31 women and 7 men) obtained mean scores of -11 to -12 and median scores of -17 to -18 on two separate occasions.

Scoring Key for STD Attitude Scale
(Chapter 16, p. 475)

Scores on this scale are interpreted in terms of a predisposition to high-risk sexual behavior. The scale is composed of three subscales, which measure your predisposition to high-risk behavior on the basis of your *beliefs* about STDs (items 1–9), your *feelings* about STDs (items 10–18), and your *intentions* to act (items 19–27). Calculate a total for each subscale and for the total scale by using the point values below.

For items 1, 10–14, 16, 25:

Strongly Agree	= 5 points
Agree	= 4 points
Undecided	= 3 points
Disagree	= 2 points
Strongly Disagree	= 1 point

For items 2–9, 15, 17–24, 26, 27:

Strongly Agree	= 1 point
Agree	= 2 points
Undecided	= 3 points
Disagree	= 4 points
Strongly Disagree	= 5 points

Subtotal for Beliefs subscale (items 1–9): _____
Subtotal for Feelings subscale (items 10–18): _____
Subtotal for Intentions to Act subscale (items 19–27): _____
Total score (based on all items): _____

The higher your subscale and total scores, the greater the likelihood that your attitudes, feelings, and intentions put you at risk of contracting an STD. The lower your scores, the less risk you are likely to incur. Although we have no norms at present, we suggest that subscale scores higher than 27 and total scores higher than 81 indicate that your responses are weighted more toward risky than safe behavior. We suggest that you weigh your particular risk by examining not only your scores but your responses to the individual scale items as well. Ask yourself, " How do my responses to these items increase or decrease my risk of contracting an STD?" Then ask yourself, " How might I change my attitudes to reduce my chances of contracting an STD?"

Appendix B

Additional Readings: Books on Human Sexuality and Related Topics

Asbell, B. (1995). *The pill: A biography of the drug that changed the world.* New York: Random House. Fascinating history of the development of the birth-control pill, and how the pill has affected sexual values and behavior.

Barbach. I. G. (1975). *For yourself: The fulfillment of female sexuality.* Garden City, NY: Doubleday & Co., Inc. A popular self-help book for women who have difficulty achieving orgasm.

Barbach, L. (1984). *For each other.* New York: Signet. Suggestions for enhancing communication and sexual satisfaction in relationships.

Barrett, M. B. (1990). *Invisible lives: The truth about millions of women-loving women.* New York: Morrow. Based upon interviews with 125 lesbians, this book reveals what it is like to be a lesbian in contemporary America and seeks to build a bridge of understanding between lesbians and parents, children, and friends.

Beck, A. (1988). *Love is never enough.* New York: Harper & Row. Aaron Beck, a leading psychiatrist and originator of cognitive therapy, examines the factors that underlie relationship problems and presents specific techniques that couples can use to resolve conflicts and improve their relationships.

Blumstein, P., & Schwartz, P. (1983). *American couples.* New York: Morrow. A major study of relationships in contemporary America, based on a sample of heterosexual and homosexual couples.

Bornoff, N. (1991). *Pink samurai: Love, marriage & sex in contemporary Japan.* New York: Pocket Books. An account of sexual customs and practices in modern Japan.

Boston Women's Health Book Collective (1984). *The new our bodies, ourselves.* New York: Simon & Schuster. A highly popular repository of information concerning women's health care and sexuality.

Bridge, T. P., Mirsky, A. F., & Goodwin, F. K. (Eds.). (1988). *Psychological, neuropsychiatric, and substance abuse aspects of AIDS.* New York: Raven Press. A scholarly compendium of information about the medical, behavioral, and legal aspects of AIDS.

Butler, R. & Lewis, M. (1988). *Love and sex after 60* (rev. ed.). New York: Harper & Row. Practical information about adjusting to sexual changes in later life.

Calderone, M.S., & Johnson, E. W. (1989). *Family book about sexuality* (rev. ed.). New York: Harper & Row. A straightforward and balaced compendium of information and advice about sexual development through the life cycle.

Calderone, M. S., & Ramey, J. (1982). *Talking with your child about sex.* New York: Random House. A practical guide for parents in raising sexually healthy children. Provides parents with answers to questions that children frequently ask about sex.

Cass, V. (1988). *There's more to sex than AIDS: The A to Z guide to safe sex.* Richmond, Victoria, Australia: Greenhouse Publications. A comprehensive guide to safer sexual techniques.

Coles, R., & Stokes, G. (1985). *Sex and the American teenager.* New York: Harper & Row. Findings of a survey of the sexual attitudes and practices of a national sample of 1067 teenagers in the United States.

Cook, E. P. (1985). *Psychological androgyny.* New York: Pergamon. An examination of psychological androgny that compares and contrasts androgyny to traditional masculine and feminine gender roles.

Donnerstein, F., Linz, D., & Penrod, S. (1987). *The question of pornography.* New York: The Free Press. A comprehensive review of scientific knowledge of the effects of exposure to pornography and legal issues in the debate over pornography.

Eisenberg, A., Murkoff, H., & Hathaway, S. E. (1989). *What to expect the first year.* New York: Workman Publishing. A comprehensive guide to infant development during the first year of life.

Ford, C. S., & Beach, F. A. (1951). *Patterns of sexual behavior.* New York: Harper. A classic study of sexuality from a cross-cultural and cross-species perspective.

Gilligan, C. (1982). *In a different voice.* Cambridge, MA: Harvard University Press. An influential book that examines the differences between men and women with respect to issues of autonomy and intimacy.

Grauerholz, E., & Koralewski, M. A. (Eds.). (1991). *Sexual coercion: A sourcebook on its nature, causes, and prevention.* Lexington, MA: D.C. Heath and Company. A number of leading scholars address the nature, causes, and prevention of sexual coercion.

Greenburg, M. (1985). *The birth of a father.* New York: Continuum. A firsthand account of the experience of fatherhood.

Griffin, C., Wirth, M., & Wirth, A. (1986). *Beyond acceptance.* Englewood Cliffs, NJ: Prentice-Hall. Written by parents of gay and lesbian children for parents of gay and lesbian children, this book sensitively discusses issues and conflicts that arise when one discovers one's child is homosexual.

Hatcher, R., et al. (1990). *Contraceptive technology: 1989–1990.* New York: Irvington. The authoritative guide to the most recent developments in contraception.

Hatfield, E., & Sprecher, S. (1986). *Mirror, mirror . . . The importance of looks in everyday life.* Albany, NY: SUNY Press. An examination of the role of physical appearance in interpersonal attraction and relationships.

Heiman, J., & LoPiccolo, J. (1988). *Becoming orgasmic: A sexual and personal growth program for women.* Englewood Cliffs, NJ: Prentice Hall. A self-help guide for women to learn to become orgasmic and enhance their sexual pleasure in masturbation and lovemaking.

Holmes, K. K., et al. (1990). *Sexually transmitted diseases* (2nd ed.). New York: McGraw-Hill Information Services Company. A scholarly, technical resource book on sexually transmitted diseases.

Kaplan, H. (1987). *The illustrated manual of sex therapy.* New York: Brunner/Mazel. A well-illustrated manual that clearly describes the steps involved in sex therapy for various sexual dysfunctions in men and women.

Kaplan, H. S. (1979). *Disorders of sexual desire.* New York: Brunner/Mazel. A leading sex therapist, Helen Singer Kaplan, examines the causes and treatments of sexual desire disorders.

Katz, J. N. (1995). *The invention of heterosexuality.* New York: Dutton. A politically-oriented book that discusses societal reactions to gay male and lesbian sexual orientations.

Kinsey, A. C., Pomeroy, W., & Martin, C. (1948). *Sexual behavior in the human male.* Philadelphia, PA: W. B. Saunders Co.

Kinsey, A. C., Pomeroy, W., Martin, C., & Gebhard, P. (1953). *Sexual behavior in the human female.* Philadelphia, PA: W. B. Saunders Co. The classic "Kinsey reports" contain statistical tales and data describing the sexual behavior patterns of men and women in the United States, based on interviews with nearly 12,000 people.

Kon, I. S. (1995). *The sexual revolution in Russia.* New York: The Free Press. An entertaining look at sex in Russia since *glasnost.* (Take it with a grain of salt mine.)

Langston, D. (1983). *Living with herpes.* Garden City, NY: Doubleday & Co. A sensitive, practical guide that will be useful to people coping with herpes and to their sexual partners.

Laumann, E. O., Gagnon, J. H., Michael, R. T., & Michaels, S. (1994). *The social organization of sexuality: Sexual practices in the United States.* Chicago: University of Chicago Press. A recent scholarly look at sexual behavior in the United States.

Leach, P. (1989). *Your baby & child: From birth to age five* (rev. ed.). New York: Knopf. A comprehensive, clearly presented and well-illustrated guide to child care.

MacFarlane, K., Waterman, J., and others (Eds.). (1986). *Sexual abuse of young children: Evaluation and treatment.* New York: Guildford. This collection of articles features clinical and research findings on the problem of child sexual abuse.

Madaras, L. (1983). *The what's happening to my body? book for girls: A growing up guide for parents and daughters.* New York: Newmarket Press.

Madaras, L. (1984). The what's happening to my body? book for boys: *A growing up guide for parents and sons.* New York: Newmarket Press. Down-to-earth guides about the changes of puberty and adolescence.

Margulis, L., & Sanga, D. (1991). *Mystery dance: On the evolution of human sexuality.* New York: Summit Books. An exploration of the ancestral origins of human sexuality.

Marshall, D., & Suggs, R. (Eds.). (1971). *Human sexual behavior: Variations in the ethnographic spectrum.* Englewood Cliffs, NJ: Prentice-Hall. A splendid compendium of ethnographic accounts of sexual behavior and customs in various cultures around the world.

Master, W., & Johnson, V. (1966). *Human sexual response.* Boston: Little, Brown. An account of the classic scientific studies of sexual arousal and response in men and women by Masters and Johnson. Must reading for students seeking more detailed knowledge of sexual physiology and functioning.

Masters, W. H., & Johnson, V. (1970). *Human sexual inadequacy.* Boston: Little, Brown. This classic book describes the treatment protocol and results of Masters and Johnson's sex therapy program.

McNaught, B. (1988). *On being gay.* New York: St. Martin's Press. The author discusses various aspects of the experience of being gay, including the coming-out process, dealing with conflicts with family members, developing gay relatioships, and confronting the AIDS crisis.

McWhirter, D. P., Sanders, S. A., & Reinisch, J. M. (Eds.). (1990). *Homosexuality/heterosexuality: Concepts of sexual orientation. The Kinsey Institute Series, Volume II.* New York: Oxford University Press. A compendium of scholarly articles on the classification and understanding of sexual orientation.

Michael, R. T., Gagnon, J. H., Laumann, E. O., & Kolata, G. (1994). *Sex in America; A definitive survey.* Boston: Little, Brown. A popularized version of the Laumann (1994) work, *The social organization of sexuality: Sexual practices in the United States.* This book actually contains some interesting information not reported in Laumann.

Millet, K. (1976). *The prostitution papers.* New York: Ballantine Books. A leading feminist examines the role of prostitutes in our society and argues for decriminalization, but not legalization, of prostitution.

Money, J. (1988). *Gay, straight, and in-between: The sexology of erotic orientation.* New York: Oxford University Press. Written by a leading researcher, this is a scholarly treatise on the biological and psychosocial factors that determine gender identity.

Money, J. & Ehrhardt, A. (1972). *Man and woman, boy and girl.* Baltimore: Johns Hopkins University Press. A comprehensive analysis of the biological and psychological factors that determine gender identity.

Nilson, L. (1977). *A child is born.* New York: Dell. Breathtaking pictures of fetal development with accompanying text.

Peters, B. (1988). *Terrific sex in fearful times.* New York: St. Martin's Press. A guide to safer sex in the age of AIDS.

Pomeroy, W., Flax, C., & Wheeler, C. (1982). *Taking a (???) history: Interviewing and recording.* New York: Free Press. The authors review the interviewing methods used in the original Kinsey research and discuss contemporary issues (???) conducting sex surveys.

Reinisch, J. (1990). *The Kinsey Institute new report on sex: What you must know to be sexually literate.* New York: St. Martin's Press. The findings of a national survey of sexual knowledge, along with a comprehensive and well-researched compendium of information on contraception, sexually transmitted diseases, sexual development, sexual health, problems in sexual functioning, and sex with a partner.

Reinisch, J., & Rosenblum, L. (Eds.). (1987). *Masculinity-femininity: Basic perspectives.* New York: Oxford University Press. A compendium of scientific articles that address issues of gender differences from multiple perspectives, including the biological, psychosocial, and developmental perspectives.

Rubin, L. B. (1983). *Intimate strangers: Men and women together.* New York: Harper & Row. A sensitive and probing study of the struggle of men and women, both within themselves and with their partners, to establish intimate relationships.

Samuels, M., & Samuels, N. (1986). *The well pregnancy book.* New York: Harper & Row. A comprehensive and sensitive guide to pregnancy and childbirth.

Sheehy, G. (1995). *New passages: Mapping your life across time.* New York: Random House. An upbeat look at growing older in the United States today. Includes hopeful information about sexuality.

Shilts, R. (1987). *And the band played on: Politics, people, and the AIDS epidemic.* New York: Viking Penguin. A national best-seller by investigative reporter Randy Shilts, who provides a compelling account of the chronology of the AIDS epidemic and the lack of governmental response to the AIDS crisis.

Spark, R. F. (1991). *Male sexual health: A couple's guide.* Mount Vernon, NY: Consumer Reports Books. A concise, up-to-date guide to male sexual problems ranging from infertility to erectile dysfunction.

Starr, B., & Weiner, M. (1981). *The Starr-Weiner report on sex and sexuality in the mature years.* New York: Stein & Day. Findings of a survey of the sexual interests and practices of a sample of more than 800 people from 60 to 91 years of age.

Stephenson, L. (1987). *Give us a child: Coping with the personal crisis of infertility.* New York: Harper & Row. A sensitive guide for couples coping with infertility.

Sternberg, R. J., & Barnes, M. L. (Eds.). (1988). *The psychology of love.* New Haven, CT: Yale University Press. Modern scholars examine the concept of love from a scientific standpoint.

Symons, D. (1979). *The evolution of human sexuality.* New York: Oxford University Press. A provocative exploration of the evolutionary roots of human sexuality.

Tannahill, R. (1980). *Sex in history.* New York: Stein & Day. A highly readable and entertaining account of the history of sexual practices and customs in Western and Eastern societies.

Tannen, D. (1990). *You just don't understand: Women and men in conversation.* New York: Morrow. Written by a linguistics professor, this down-to-earth, best-selling book shows how gender-based differences in conversational styles lead to misunderstandings in relationships between men and women.

Tennov, D. (1979). *Love and limerence*: The experience of being in love. New York: Stein & Day. A clearly written book describing the experience of love.

Thompson, S. (1995). *Going all the way.* New York: Hill & Wang. A look at the sexual behavior of some young people in the United States today.

Warshaw, R. (1988). *I never called it rape.* New York: Harper & Row. A probing review of the problem of acquaintance rape and date rape.

Weitzman, S., Kuter, J., & Pizer, H.F. (1986). *Confronting breast cancer.* A straightforward guide to detecting, treating, and coping with breast cancer.

Zilbergeld, B. (1978). *Male sexuality: A guide to sexual fulfillment.* Boston: Little, Brown. A clearly written guide that deals with the physical and emotional aspects of male sexuality and seeks to debunk sexual myths and unrealistic stereotypes.

Glossary

ABCDE model   Levinger's view, which approaches romantic relationships in terms of five stages: attraction, building, continuation, deterioration, and ending.

Acquaintance rape   Rape by an acquaintance of the person who is assaulted.

Acquired immunodeficiency syndrome (AIDS)   A condition caused by the human immunodeficiency virus (HIV) and characterized by destruction of white blood cells in the immune system so that the body is stripped of its ability to fend off life-threatening diseases.

Activating effects   Those effects of sex hormones that influence the level of the sex drive but not sexual orientation.

Age of viability   The age at which a fetus can sustain independent life.

Amenorrhea   The absence of menstruation.

Amniocentesis   A procedure for drawing off and examining fetal cells in the amniotic fluid to determine the presence of various disorders in the fetus.

Amniotic fluid   Fluid within the amniotic sac that suspends and protects the fetus.

Amniotic sac   The sac containing the fetus.

Ampulla   A sac or dilated part of a tube or canal. The wide segment of a fallopian tube near the ovary. (A Latin word meaning "bottle.")

Analogous   Similar in function.

Analogue   Something that is similar or comparable to something else.

Androgen-insensitivity syndrome   A form of pseudohermaphroditism in which a genetic male is prenatally insensitive to androgens. As a result his genitals do not become normally masculinized.

Androgenital syndrome   A form of pseudohermaphroditism in which a genetic female has internal female sexual structures but masculinized external genitals.

Androgens   Male sex hormones. (From the Greek *andros,* meaning "man" or "males," and *-gene,* meaning "born.")

Anger rape   A vicious, unplanned rape that is triggered by feelings of intense anger and resentment toward women.

Anilingus   Oral stimulation of the anus.

Anorexia nervosa   A potentially life-threatening eating disorder characterized by refusal to maintain a healthy body weight, intense fear of being overweight, a distorted body image, and, in females, lack of menstruation (amenorrhea).

Anorgasmic   Never having reached orgasm. (Literally, "without orgasm.")

Anovulatory   Without ovulation.

Anoxia   Oxygen deprivation.

Anthropomorphism   The attributing of human characteristics to an animal.

Antiandrogen drug   A chemical substance that reduces the sex drive by lowering the level of testosterone in the bloodstream.

Antibodies   Specialized proteins produced by the white blood cells of the immune system in response to disease organisms and other toxic substances. Antibodies attach themselves to foreign substances in the body, inactivating them and marking them for destruction.

Antigen   A protein, toxin, or other substance to which the body reacts by producing antibodies. (Combined word formed from *anti*body *gen*erator.)

Aphrodisiac   Any drug or other agent that is sexually arousing or increases sexual desire. (From *Aphrodite,* the Greek goddess of love and beauty.)

Areola   The dark ring on the breast that encircles the nipple.

Arthritis   A progressive disease that is characterized by inflammation or pain in the joints.

Artificial contraception   A method of contraception that applies a human-made device.

Artificial insemination   The introduction of sperm in the reproductive tract through means other than sexual intercourse.

Asexuals   Bell and Weinberg's term for gay people who live alone and have few sexual contacts.

Asymptomatic   Without symptoms.

Auto-immune response   The production of antibodies that attack naturally occurring substances that are (incorrectly) recognized as being foreign or harmful.

Autonomic nervous system The division of the nervous system that regulates automatic bodily processes, such as heartbeat, pupil dilation, respiration, and digestion. Abbreviated *ANS*.

Aversion therapy A method for terminating undesirable sexual behavior in which the behavior is repeatedly paired with an aversive stimulus, such as electric shock, so that a conditioned aversion develops.

Bacteria Plural of *bacterium*, a class of one-celled microorganisms that have no chlorophyll and can give rise to many illnesses. (From the Greek *baktron*, meaning "stick," referring to the fact that many bacteria are rod-shaped.)

Bacterial vaginosis A form of vaginitis usually caused by the *Gardnerella vaginalis* bacterium.

Bartholin's glands Glands that lie just inside the minor lips and secrete fluid just before orgasm.

Basal body temperature (BBT) method A fertility awareness method of contraception that relies on prediction of ovulation by tracking the woman's temperature during the course of the menstrual cycle.

Behavior therapy The systematic application of the principles of learning to help people modify problem behavior.

Behaviorists Learning theorists who argue that a scientific approach to understanding behavior must refer only to observable and measurable behaviors.

Benign Doing little or no harm.

Bestiality Sexual relations between a person and an animal.

Bisexual Sexually responsive to either gender. (From the Latin *bi-*, meaning "two.")

Bisexuality Erotic attraction to, and interest in developing romantic relationships with, both males and females.

Blastocyst A stage within the germinal stage of prenatal development, in which the embryo is a sphere of cells surrounding a cavity of fluid.

Bondage Ritual restraint, as by shackles, as practiced by many sexual masochists.

Braxton-Hicks contractions So-called false labor contractions that are relatively painless.

Breech presentation Emergence of the baby feet first from the womb.

Bulbourethral glands Another term for *Cowper's glands*.

Butch A lesbian who assumes a traditional masculine gender role.

Calendar method A fertility awareness (rhythm) method of contraception that relies on prediction of ovulation by tracking menstrual cycles, typically for a 10- to 12-month period, and assuming that ovulation occurs 14 days prior to menstruation.

Call girls Prostitutes who arrange for their sexual contacts by telephone. *Call* refers both to telephone calls and to being "on call."

Candidiasis A form of vaginitis caused by a yeastlike fungus, *Candida albicans*.

Case study A carefully drawn, in-depth biography of an individual or a small group of individuals that may be obtained through interviews, questionnaires, and historical records.

Castration anxiety In psychoanalytic theory, a man's fear that his genitals will be removed. Castration anxiety is an element of the Oedipus complex and is implicated in the directionality of erotic interests.

Celibacy Complete sexual abstinence. (Sometimes used to describe the state of being unmarried, especially in the case of people who take vows to remain single.)

Cephalic presentation Emergence of the baby head-first from the womb.

Cephalocaudal From the head downward. (From Latin roots meaning "head" and "tail.")

Cerebellum A part of the hindbrain that governs muscle coordination and balance.

Cerebral cortex The wrinkled surface area (gray matter) of the cerebrum.

Cerebral palsy A muscular disorder that is caused by damage to the central nervous system (usually prior to or during birth) and characterized by spastic paralysis.

Cerebrum The large mass of the forebrain, which consists of two hemispheres.

Cervicitis Inflammation of the cervix.

Cervix The lower end of the uterus. (Latin for "neck.")

Cesarean section A method of childbirth in which the fetus is delivered through a surgical incision in the abdomen.

Chancre A sore or ulcer.

Chancroid An STD caused by the *Hemophilus ducreyi* bacterium. Also called *soft chancre*.

Chattel A movable piece of personal property, such as furniture or livestock. (From the Old French word meaning "cattle.")

Chromosome One of the rodlike structures, found in the nucleus of every living cell, that carries the genetic code in the form of genes.

Cilia Hairlike projections from cells that beat rhythmically to produce locomotion or currents.

Circumcision Surgical removal of the foreskin of the penis. (From the Latin *circumcidere*, meaning "to cut around.")

Climacteric A long-term process, including menopause, that involves the gradual decline in the reproductive capacity of the ovaries.

Clitoridectomy Surgical removal of the clitoris.

Clitoris   A female sex organ consisting of a shaft and glans located above the urethral opening. It is extremely sensitive to sexual sensations.

Cloaca   The cavity in birds, reptiles, and many fish into which the genitourinary and intestinal tracts empty. (From the Latin *cluere,* meaning "to cleanse.")

Clomiphene   A synthetic hormone that is chemically similar to LH and induces ovulation.

Close couples   Bell and Weinberg's term for gay couples whose relationships resemble marriage in their depth of commitment and exclusiveness.

Cohabitation   Living together as though married but without legal sanction.

Coitus interruptus   The practice of withdrawing the penis prior to ejaculation during sexual intercourse.

Coitus   (co-it-us or co-EET-us). Sexual intercourse.

Comarital sex   Swinging; mate-swapping.

Combination pill   A birth-control pill that contains synthetic estrogen and progesterone.

Complete hysterectomy   Surgical removal of the ovaries, fallopian tubes, cervix, and uterus.

Concordance   Agreement.

Concubine   A secondary wife, usually of inferior legal and social status. (From Latin roots meaning "lying with.")

Condom   A sheath made of animal membrane or latex that covers the penis during coitus and serves as a barrier to sperm following ejaculation.

Congenital syphilis   A syphilis infection that is present at birth.

Consensual adultery   Extramarital sex that is engaged in openly with the knowledge and consent of one's spouse.

Control group   A group of study participants who do not receive the experimental treatment. However, other conditions are held comparable to those of individuals in the experimental group.

Conventional adultery   Extramarital sex that is kept clandestine (hidden) from one's spouse.

Coprophilia   A paraphilia in which sexual arousal is attained in connection with feces. (From the Greek *copros,* meaning "dung.")

Copulation   Sexual intercourse. (From the Latin *copulare,* meaning "to unite" or "to couple.")

Corona   The ridge that separates the glans from the body of the penis. (From the Latin for "crown.")

Corpora cavernosa   Masses of spongy tissue in the clitoris and penis that become engorged with blood and stiffen in response to sexual stimulation. (Latin for "cavernous bodies.")

Corpus luteum   The follicle that has released an ovum and then produces copious amounts of progesterone and estrogen during the luteal phase of a woman's cycle. (From Latin roots meaning "yellow body.")

Corpus spongiosum   The spongy body that runs along the bottom of the penis, contains the penile urethra, and enlarges at the tip of the penis to form the glans.

Correlation coefficient   A statistic that expresses the strength and direction (positive or negative) of the relationship between two variables.

Courtesan   A prostitute—especially the mistress of a noble or wealthy man. (From Italian roots meaning "court lady.")

Covert sensitization   A form of aversion therapy in which thoughts of engaging in undesirable behavior are paired repeatedly with imagined aversive stimuli.

Cowper's glands   Structures that lie below the prostate and empty their secretions into the urethra during sexual arousal.

Cremaster muscle   The muscle that raises and lowers the testicle in response to temperature changes and sexual stimulation.

Crisis   A highly stressful situation that can involve shock, loss of self-esteem, and lessened capacity for making decisions.

Critical period of vulnerability   A period of time during which an embryo or fetus is vulnerable to the effects of a teratogen.

Cruising   The name homosexuals give to searching for a sex partner.

Crura   Anatomical structures resembling legs that attach the clitoris to the pubic bone. (Singular: crus. A Latin word meaning "leg" or "shank.")

Cryptorchidism   A condition in which one or two testicles fail to descend from the abdomen into the scrotum. (From roots meaning "hidden testes.")

Culpotomy   A kind of tubal sterilization in which the fallopian tubes are approached through an incision in the back wall of the vagina.

Cunnilingus   A sexual activity involving oral stimulation with the female genitals.

Cystitis   An inflammation of the urinary bladder. (From the Greek *kystis,* meaning "sac.")

Cysts   Saclike structures filled with fluid or diseased material.

D&C   Abbreviation for *dilation and curettage,* an operation in which the cervix is dilated and uterine contents are then gently scraped away.

D&E   Abbreviation for *dilation and evacuation,* an abortion method in which the cervix is dilated prior to vacuum aspiration.

Dartos muscle   The muscle in the middle layer of the scrotum that contracts and relaxes in response to temperature changes.

Debriefing   Information about a completed procedure that helps avert potential harm to participants.

Defense mechanisms   In psychoanalytic theory, automatic processes that protect the ego from anxiety by disguising or ejecting unacceptable ideas and urges.

Defloration   Destruction of the hymen (especially as a cultural ritual).

Demographic   Concerning the vital statistics (density, race, age, etc.) of human populations.

Dependent variables   The measured results of an experiment, which are believed to be a function of the independent variables.

DES   Diethylstilbestrol: an estrogen that was once given to women at risk for miscarriage to help maintain pregnancy.

Diaphragm   A shallow rubber cup or dome, fitted to the contour of a woman's vagina, that is coated with a spermicide and inserted prior to coitus to prevent conception.

Dilate   To open or widen.

Dildo   A penis-shaped object used in sexual activity.

Displacement   In psychoanalytic theory, a defense mechanism that allows one to transfer unacceptable wishes or desires onto more appropriate or less threatening objects.

Dizygotic (DZ) twins   Twins who develop from different fertilized ova; fraternal twins.

DNA   Deoxyribonucleic acid—the chemical substance whose molecules make up genes and chromosomes.

Dominican Republic syndrome   A form of pseudohermaphroditism in which a genetic enzyme disorder prevents testosterone from masculinizing the external genitalia.

Don Juanism   An excessive, insatiable sexual appetite or drive in men. (After the fictional Spanish nobleman who was unable to obtain true sexual gratification despite numerous affairs.)

Donor IVF   A variation of in vitro fertilization in which the ovum is taken from one woman, fertilized, and then injected into the uterus or fallopian tube of another woman.

Douche   To rinse or wash the vaginal canal by inserting a liquid and allowing it to drain out. (From the Italian *doccia,* meaning "shower bath.")

Down syndrome   A chromosomal abnormality that leads to mental retardation, caused by an extra chromosome on the 21st pair.

Dysfunctionals   Bell and Weinberg's term for gay people who live alone and have sexual, social, or psychological problems.

Dysmenorrhea   Pain or discomfort during menstruation.

Dyspareunia   A sexual dysfunction characterized by persistent or recurrent pain during sexual intercourse. (From roots meaning "badly paired.")

Ectoderm   The outermost cell layer of the newly formed embryo, from which the skin and nervous system develop.

Ectoparasites   Parasites that live on the outside of the host's body— as opposed to *endo*parasites, which live within the body. (From the Greek *ektos,* meaning "outside.")

Ectopic pregnancy   A pregnancy in which the fertilized ovum implants outside the uterus, usually in the fallopian tube. (*Ectopic* derives from Greek roots meaning "out of place.")

Efface   To become thin.

Ego   In Freud's theory, the second mental structure to develop, which is characterized by self-awareness, planning, and delay of gratification.

Ejaculatory duct   A duct formed by the convergence of a vas deferens with a seminal vesicle through which sperm pass through the prostate gland and into the urethra.

Elephantiasis   A disease characterized by enlargement of parts of the body, especially the legs and genitals, and by hardening and ulceration of the surrounding skin. (From the Greek *elephas,* meaning "elephant," referring to the resemblance of the affected skin areas to elephant hide.)

Embryo   The stage of prenatal development that begins with implantation of a fertilized ovum in the uterus and concludes with development of the major organ systems at about two months after conception.

Embryonic disk   The platelike inner part of the blastocyst, which differentiates into the ectoderm, mesoderm, and endoderm of the embryo.

Embryonic transfer   A method of conception in which a woman volunteer is artificially inseminated by the male partner of the intended mother, after which the embryo is removed from the volunteer and inserted within the uterus of the intended mother.

Emission stage   The first phase of ejaculation, which involves contractions of the prostate gland, seminal vesicles, and the upper part of the vas deferens.

Empirical   Derived from or based on observation and experimentation.

Endocrine gland   A ductless gland that releases its secretions directly into the bloodstream.

Endoderm   The inner layer of the newly formed embryo, from which the lungs and digestive system develop.

Endometriosis   An abnormal condition in which endometrial tissue is sloughed off into the abdominal cavity rather than out of the body during menstruation. The condition is characterized by abdominal pain and may cause infertility.

Endometrium   The innermost layer of the uterus. (From Latin and Greek roots meaning "within the uterus.")

Epididymis   A tube that lies against the back wall of each testicle and serves as a storage facility for sperm. (From Greek roots meaning "upon testicles.")

Epididymitis   Inflammation of the epididymis.

Episiotomy   A surgical incision in the perineum that widens the birth canal, preventing random vaginal tearing during childbirth. (From the Greek roots *epision*, meaning "pubic region," and *tome*, meaning "cutting.")

Erection   The enlargement and stiffening of the penis as a consequence of engorgement with blood.

Erogenous zones   Parts of the body, including but not limited to the sex organs, that are especially sensitive to tactile sexual stimulation. (*Erogenous* is derived from roots meaning "giving birth to erotic sensations.")

Eros   The kind of love that is closest in meaning to the modern-day concept of passion.

Erotic   Arousing sexual feelings or desires. (From the Greek word for love, *eros*.)

Erotica   Books, pictures, and so on that have to do with sexual love (from the Greek *eros*, meaning "love"). Many contemporary writers use the term *erotica* to refer to sexual material that is artistically produced or motivated by artistic intent.

Estrogen   A generic term for female sex hormones (including estradiol, estriol, estrone, and others) or synthetic compounds that promote the development of female sex characteristics and regulate the menstrual cycle. (From the roots meaning "generating" [-*gen*] and "estrus.")

Estrous cycle   The female reproductive cycle of most mammals (other than primates), which is under hormonal control and includes a period of heat, followed by ovulation.

Estrus   The periodic sexual excitement in which female mammals (other than primates) are most receptive to the sexual advances of males.

Ethnocentric   Adjectival form of the noun *ethnocentrism*, meaning the tendency to view other groups or cultures according to the standards of one's own. (From the Greek *ethnos* meaning "race," "culture," or "people," and *kentric*, meaning "center.")

Ethnography   The branch of anthropology that deals descriptively with specific cultures, especially preliterate societies.

Evolution   The development of a species to its present state, which is believed to involve adaptations to its environment.

Excitement phase   The first phase of the sexual response cycle, which is characterized by erection in the male, vaginal lubrication in the female, and muscle tension and increases in heart rate in both males and females.

Exhibitionism   A paraphilia characterized by persistent, powerful urges and sexual fantasies involving exposing one's genitals to unsuspecting strangers to achieve sexual arousal or gratification.

Experiment   A scientific method that seeks to confirm cause-and-effect relationships by manipulating independent variables and observing their effects on dependent variables.

Experimental group   A group of study participants who receive a treatment.

Expulsion stage   The second stage of ejaculation, during which muscles at the base of the penis and elsewhere contract rhythmically, forcefully expelling semen and providing pleasurable sensations.

Extramarital sex   Sexual relations between a married person and someone other than his or her spouse.

Fallopian tubes   Tubes that extend from the upper uterus toward the ovaries and conduct ova to the uterus. (After the Italian anatomist Gabriel Fallopio, who is credited with their discovery.)

False positive   An erroneous positive test result or clinical finding.

Fellatio   A sexual activity involving oral stimulation of the male genitals.

Female-superior position   A coital position in which the woman is on top.

Femme   A lesbian who assumes a traditional feminine gender role.

Fetal alcohol syndrome   A cluster of symptoms caused by maternal drinking, in which the child shows developmental lags and characteristic facial features such as an underdeveloped upper jaw, flattened nose, and widely spaced eyes.

Fetishism   A paraphilia in which an inanimate object, such as an article of clothing or items made of rubber, leather, or silk, elicits sexual arousal.

Fibroadenoma   A benign, fibrous tumor.

Fimbriae   Projections from a fallopian tube that extend toward an ovary. (Singular: fimbria. Latin for "fiber" or "fringe.")

Fixation   In psychoanalytic theory, arrested development, which includes attachment to objects of an earlier stage of psychosexual development.

Follicle-stimulating hormone (FSH)   A gonadotropin that stimulates development of follicles in the ovaries.

Follicle   A capsule within an ovary that contains an ovum. (From a Latin word meaning "small bag.")

Forcible rape   Sexual intercourse with a nonconsenting person obtained by the use of force or the threat of force.

Foreplay   Physical interactions that are sexually stimulating and set the stage for intercourse.

Foreskin   The loose skin that covers the penile glans. Also referred to as the *prepuce*.

Fornication   Sexual intercourse between people who are not married to one another. (If one of the partners is married, the act may be labeled *adultery*.)

Frenulum   The sensitive strip of tissue that connects the underside of the penile glans to the shaft. (From the Latin *frenum*, meaning "bridle.")

Frequency   The number of times an action is repeated within a given period.

Frotteurism   A paraphilia characterized by recurrent, powerful sexual urges and related fantasies involving rubbing against or touching a nonconsenting person. (From the French *frotter* meaning "to rub.")

Functionals   Bell and Weinberg's term for gay people who live alone, have adapted well to a swinging lifestyle, and are sociable and well adjusted.

Fundus   The uppermost part of the uterus. (*Fundus* is a Latin word meaning "base.")

Gamete intrafallopian transfer (GIFT)   A method of conception in which sperm and ova are inserted into a fallopian tube to encourage conception.

Gay bashing   Violence against homosexuals.

Gay males   Males who are erotically attracted to and desire to form romantic relationships with other males.

Gender   One's personal, social, and legal status as male or female.

Gender assignment   The labeling of a newborn as a male or female.

Gender constancy   The concept that people's genders do not change, even if they alter their dress or behavior.

Gender dysphoria   The subjective experience of incongruity between genital anatomy and gender identity or role.

Gender identity   The psychological sense of being male or female.

Gender roles   Complex clusters of ways in which males and females are expected to behave within a given culture.

Gender schema   A cluster of mental representations about male and female physical qualities, behaviors, and personality traits.

Gender stability   The concept that people retain their genders for a lifetime.

Gender typing   The process by which children acquire behavior that is deemed appropriate to their gender.

General anesthesia   The use of drugs to put people to sleep and eliminate pain, as during childbirth.

General paresis   A progressive form of mental illness caused by neurosyphilis and characterized by gross confusion.

Generalize   To go from the particular to the general.

Genes   The basic units of heredity, which consist of chromosomal segments of DNA.

Genital herpes   An STD caused by the *Herpes simplex* virus type 2 and characterized by painful shallow sores and blisters on the genitals.

Genital warts   An STD that is caused by the human papilloma virus and takes the form of warts that appear around the genitals and anus.

Germ cell   A cell from which a new organism develops. (From the Latin *germen*, meaning "bud" or "sprout.")

Germinal stage   The period of prenatal development prior to implantation in the uterus.

Gonadotropin-releasing hormone (Gn-RH)   A hormone secreted by the hypothalamus that stimulates the pituitary to release gonadotropins.

Gonadotropins   Pituitary hormones that stimulate the gonads. (Literally, "that which 'feeds' the gonads.")

Gonorrhea   An STD caused by the *Neisseria gonorrhoeae* bacterium and characterized by a discharge and burning urination. Left untreated, gonorrhea can give rise to pelvic inflammatory disease (PID) and infertility. (From the Greek *gonos*, meaning "seed," and *rheein*, meaning "to flow," referring to the fact that in ancient times the penile discharge characteristic of the illness was erroneously interpreted as a loss of seminal fluid.)

Grafenberg spot   A part of the anterior wall of the vagina, whose prolonged stimulation is theorized to cause particularly intense orgasms and a female ejaculation. Abbreviated *G-spot*.

Granuloma inguinale   A tropical STD caused by the *Calymmatobacterium granulomatous* bacterium.

Group marriage   A social arrangement in which three or more people share an intimate relationship. Group marriages are illegal in the United States.

Gynecologist   A physician who treats women's diseases, especially of the reproductive tract. (From the Greek *gyne*, meaning "woman.")

Gynecomastia   Overdevelopment of a male's breasts. (From Greek roots meaning "woman" [*gyne*] and "breast" [*mastos*].)

Hegar's sign   Softness of a section of the uterus between the uterine body and the cervix, which indicates that a woman is pregnant.

Hepatitis   An inflammation of the liver. (From the Greek *hepar*, meaning "liver.")

Hermaphrodites   People who possess both ovarian and testicular tissue. (From the names of the male and female Greek gods *Hermes* and *Aphrodite*.)

***Herpes simplex* virus type 2**   The virus that causes genital herpes. Abbreviated *HSV-2*.

Herpes simplex virus type 1 The virus that causes oral herpes, which is characterized by cold sores or fever blisters on the lips or mouth. Abbreviated *HSV-1*.

Heteroerotic Of an erotic nature and involving members of the other gender.

Heterosexual orientation Erotic attraction to, and preference for, developing romantic relationships with members of the other gender.

Homoerotic Of an erotic nature and involving members of one's own gender.

Homogamy The practice of marrying people who are similar in social background and standing. (From Greek roots meaning "same" [*homos*] and "marriage" [*gamos*].)

Homologous Similar in structure; developing from the same embryonic tissue.

Homophobia A cluster of negative attitudes and feelings toward gay people, including intolerance, hatred, and fear. (From Greek roots meaning "fear" [of members of the] "same" [gender].)

Homosexual orientation Erotic attraction to, and preference for, developing romantic relationships with members of one's own gender. (From the Greek *homos*, meaning "same," not the Latin *homo*, which means "man").

Hormone-replacement therapy (HRT) Replacement of naturally occurring estrogen or estrogen and progesterone with synthetic equivalents, following menopause.

Hormone A substance secreted by an endocrine gland that regulates various body functions. (From the Greek *horman*, meaning "to stimulate" or "to excite.")

Human chorionic gonadotropin A hormone produced by women shortly after conception, which stimulates the corpus luteum to continue to produce progesterone. The presence of HCG in a woman's urine indicates that she is pregnant.

Human immunodeficiency virus (HIV) A sexually transmitted virus that destroys white blood cells in the immune system, leaving the body vulnerable to life-threatening diseases.

Human sexuality The ways in which we experience and express ourselves as sexual beings.

Hustlers Men who engage in prostitution with male customers.

Hyaluronidase An enzyme that briefly thins the zona pellucida, enabling one sperm to penetrate. (From roots meaning "substance that breaks down a glasslike fluid.")

Hymen A fold of tissue across the vaginal opening that is usually present at birth and remains at least partly intact until a woman engages in coitus. (Greek for "membrane.")

Hypersexuality An excessive or apparently insatiable sex drive that disrupts the person's ability to concentrate on other needs or leads to self-defeating behavior, such as indiscriminate sexual contacts.

Hypogonadism An endocrine condition marked by abnormally low levels of testosterone production.

Hypothalamus A bundle of neural cell bodies near the center of the brain (below the thalamus) that are involved in regulating body temperature, motivation, and emotion.

Hypothesis A precise prediction about behavior that is tested through research.

Hypoxyphilia A practice in which a person seeks to enhance sexual arousal, usually during masturbation, by becoming deprived of oxygen. (From the Greek root meaning "under" [*hypo-*].)

Hysterectomy Surgical removal of the uterus. (*Not* appropriate as a method of sterilization.)

Hysterosalpingogram A test in which a dye is injected into the reproductive tract and its progress is tracked by X-rays to determine whether or not the fallopian tubes are blocked. (From roots meaning "record of," "uterus," and "fallopian tubes.")

Hysterotomy An abortion method in which the fetus is removed by cesarean section.

Id In Freud's theory, the mental structure that is present at birth, embodies physiological drives, and is fully unconscious.

Identification In psychoanalytic theory, the process of incorporating within ourselves our perceptions of the behaviors, thoughts, and feelings of others.

Immune system A term for the body's complex of mechanisms for protecting itself from disease-causing agents such as pathogens.

Implicit personality theories Our assumptions about the personalities of other people, which we use to predict their behavior.

Impotence Recurrent difficulty in achieving or sustaining an erection sufficient to successfully engage in sexual intercourse. (The term has been replaced by the terms *male erectile disorder* or *erectile dysfunction*, as discussed in Chapter 15.)

In vitro fertilization A method of conception in which mature ova are surgically removed from an ovary and placed in a laboratory dish along with sperm.

Incest taboo The prohibition against intercourse and reproduction among close blood relatives.

Incest Marriage or sexual relations between people who are so closely related (by "blood") that sexual relations are prohibited and punishable by law. (From the Latin *in-*, meaning "not," and *castus*, meaning "chaste.")

Incidence A measure of the occurrence or the degree of occurrence of an event.

Independent variable A condition in a scientific study that is manipulated so that its effects may be observed.

Induced abortion   The purposeful termination of a pregnancy before the embryo or fetus is capable of sustaining independent life. (From the Latin *abortio,* meaning "that which is miscarried.")

Infatuation   A state of intense absorption in or focus on another person, which is usually accompanied by sexual desire, elation, and general physiological arousal or excitement; passion.

Inference   Conclusion or opinion.

Infertility   Inability to conceive a child.

Inflammation   Redness and warmth that develop at the site of an injury, reflecting dilation of blood vessels that permits the expanded flow of leukocytes to the region.

Informed consent   The term used by researchers to indicate that people have agreed to participate in research after receiving information about the purposes and nature of the study, and its potential risks and benefits.

Infundibulum   The outer, funnel-shaped part of a fallopian tube. (A Latin word meaning "funnel.")

Inguinal canal   A fetal canal that connects the scrotum and the testes, allowing their descent. (From the Latin *inguinus,* meaning "near the groin.")

Interstitial cells   Cells that lie between the seminiferous tubules and secrete testosterone. (*Interstitial* means "set between.")

Intimacy   Feelings of closeness and connectedness that are marked by sharing of inmost thoughts and feelings.

Intra-amniotic infusion   An abortion method in which a substance is injected into the amniotic sac to induce premature labor. Also called *instillation.*

Intracytoplasmic injection   A method of conception in which sperm is injected directly into an ovum.

Intrauterine device   A small object that is inserted into the uterus and left in place to prevent conception. Abbreviated *IUD.*

Introitus   The vaginal opening. (From the Latin for "entrance.")

Isthmus   The segment of a fallopian tube closest to the uterus. (A Latin word meaning "narrow passage.")

Jaundice   A yellowish discoloration of the skin and the whites of the eyes. (From the French *jaune,* meaning "yellow.")

Klinefelter's syndrome   A sex-chromosomal disorder caused by an extra X sex chromosome.

Klismaphilia   A paraphilia in which sexual arousal is derived from use of enemas.

Labia majora   Large folds of skin that run downward from the mons along the sides of the vulva. (Latin for "large lips" or "major lips.")

Labia minora   Hairless, light-colored membranes, located between the labia majora. (Latin for "small lips" or "minor lips.")

Lactation   Production of milk by the mammary glands.

Lamaze method   A childbirth method in which women learn about childbirth, learn to relax and to breathe in patterns that conserve energy and lessen pain, and have a coach (usually the father) present at childbirth. Also termed *prepared childbirth.*

Laparoscopy   A medical procedure in which a long, narrow tube (laparoscope) is inserted through an incision in the navel, permitting the visual inspection of organs in the pelvic cavity. Also, sterilization by means of inserting a laparoscope just below the navel and cauterizing, or clamping the fallopian tubes. Sometimes referred to as "belly button surgery." (From the Greek *lapara,* meaning "flank.")

Larynx   A structure of muscle and cartilage at the upper end of the trachea that contains the vocal cords; the voice box.

Lesbians   Females who are erotically attracted to and desire to form romantic relationships with other females. (After *Lesbos,* the Greek island on which, legend has it, female–female sexual activity was idealized.)

Leukocytes   White blood cells that are essential to the body's defenses against infection. (From the Greek *leukos,* meaning "white," and *kytos,* meaning "a hollow," and used in combination with other word forms to mean *cell.*)

Leydig's cells   Another term for *interstitial cells.*

Limbic system   A group of structures active in memory, motivation, and emotion; the structures that are part of this system form a fringe along the inner edge of the cerebrum.

Local anesthesia   Anesthesia that eliminates pain in a specific area of the body, as during childbirth.

Lochia   A reddish vaginal discharge that may persist for a month after delivery. (From the Greek *lochios,* meaning "of childbirth.") **Coitus interruptus**   A method of contraception in which the penis is withdrawan from the vagina prior to ejaculation. Also referred to as the *withdrawal method.*

Lovemap   A representation in the mind and in the brain of the idealized lover and the idealized erotic activity with the lover.

Lumpectomy   Surgical removal of a lump from the breast.

Luteinizing hormone (LH)   A gonadotropin that helps regulate the menstrual cycle by triggering ovulation.

Lymphogranuloma venereum   A tropical STD caused by the *Chlamydia trachomatis* bacterium.

Male erectile disorder   Persistent difficulty achieving or maintaining an erection sufficient to allow the man to engage in or complete sexual intercourse. Also termed *erectile dysfunction.*

Male-superior position   A coital position in which the man is on top.

Malignant   Lethal; causing or likely to cause death.

Mammary glands   Milk-secreting glands. (From the Latin *mamma*, which means both "breast" and "mother.")

Mammography   A special type of X-ray test that detects cancerous lumps in the breast.

Mastalgia   A swelling of the breasts that sometimes causes premenstrual discomfort.

Mastectomy   Surgical removal of the entire breast.

Masturbation   Sexual self-stimulation.

Matching hypothesis   The concept that people tend to develop romantic relationships with people who are similar to themselves in attractiveness.

Mating gradient   The tendency for women to "marry up" (in social or economic status) and for men to "marry down."

Medulla   An oblong area of the hindbrain involved in regulation of heartbeat and respiration.

Menarche   The onset of menstruation; first menstruation. (From Greek roots meaning "month" [*men*] and "beginning" [*arche*].)

Menopause   The cessation of menstruation.

Menstrual phase   The fourth phase of the menstrual cycle, during which the endometrium is sloughed off in the menstrual flow.

Menstruation   The cyclical bleeding that stems from the shedding of the uterine lining (endometrium).

Mesoderm   The central layer of the embryo, from which the bones and muscles develop.

Minilaparotomy   A kind of tubal sterilization in which a small incision is made in the abdomen to provide access to the fallopian tubes.

Minipill   A birth-control pill that contains synthetic progesterone but no estrogen.

Miscarriage   A spontaneous abortion.

Missionary position   The coital position in which the man is on top. Also termed the *male-superior position*.

Mittelschmerz   Pain that occurs during ovulation. (German for "middle pain," reflecting the fact that the pain occurs midway between menstrual periods).

Modeling   Acquiring knowledge and skills by observing others.

Molluscum contagiosum   An STD is caused by a pox virus that causes painless raised lesions to appear on the genitals, buttocks, thighs, or lower abdomen.

Monogamy   The practice of having one spouse. (From the Greek *mono-*, meaning "single" or "alone.")

Monozygotic (MZ) twins   Twins who develop from the same fertilized ovum; identical twins.

Mons veneris   A mound of fatty tissue that covers the joint of the pubic bones in front of the body, below the abdomen and above the clitoris. (The name is a Latin phrase meaning hill or "mount of Venus," the Roman goddess of love. Also known as the *mons pubis*, or simply *mons*.)

Morning sickness   Symptoms of pregnancy, including nausea, aversions to specific foods, and vomiting.

Motility   Self-propulsion. A measure of the viability of sperm cells.

Multiple orgasms   One or more additional orgasms following the first, which occur within a short period of time and before the body has returned to a pre-plateau level of arousal.

Mutations   Random changes in the molecular structure of DNA.

Mutuality   A phase in building a relationship in which members of a couple come to regard themselves as "we," no longer two "I's" who happen to be in the same place at the same time.

Myometrium   The middle, well-muscled layer of the uterus. (*Myo-* stems from the Greek *mys*, meaning "muscle.")

Myotonia   Muscle tension.

Natural childbirth   A method of childbirth in which women use no anesthesia but are given other strategies for coping with discomfort and are educated about childbirth.

Natural selection   The evolutionary process by which adaptive traits enable members of a species to survive to reproductive age and transmit these traits to future generations.

Naturalistic observation   A method in which organisms are observed in their natural environments.

Necrophilia   A paraphilia characterized by desire for sexual activity with corpses. (From the Greek *nekros*, meaning "dead body.")

Neural tube   A hollow area in the blastocyst from which the nervous system will develop.

Neurosyphilis   Syphilitic infection of the central nervous system, which can cause brain damage and death.

Neurotransmitter   A chemical that transmits messages from one brain cell to another.

Nocturnal emission   Involuntary ejaculation of seminal fluid while asleep. Also referred to as a "wet dream," although the individual need not be dreaming about sex, or dreaming at all, at the time.

Nymphomania   An excessive, insatiable sexual appetite or drive in women. (From the Greek roots *nymphe*, meaning "a bride," and *mania*, which means "madness.")

Obscenity   That which offends people's feelings or goes beyond prevailing standards of decency or modesty. (From the Latin *caenum*, meaning "filth.")

Observer effect   A distortion of individuals' behavior caused by the act of observation.

Ocular herpes   A herpes infection of the eye, usually caused by touching an infected area of the body and then touching the eye.

Oedipus complex   In psychoanalytic theory, a conflict of the phallic stage in which the boy wishes to possess his mother sexually and perceives his father as a rival in love. (The analogous conflict for girls is the *Electra complex.*)

Open couples   Bell and Weinberg's term for gay couples who live together but engage in secret affairs.

Open marriage   A marriage that is characterized by the personal privacy of the spouses and the agreed-upon liberty of each spouse to form intimate relationships, which may include sexually intimate relationships, with people other than the spouse.

Operational definition   A definition of a construct or variable in terms of the methods used to measure it.

Ophthalmia neonatorum   A gonorrheal infection of the eyes of newborn children who contract the disease by passing through an infected birth canal. (From the Greek *ophthalmos,* meaning "eye.")

Opportunistic diseases   Diseases that take hold only when the immune system is weakened and unable to fend them off. Kaposi's sarcoma and pneumocystis carinii pneumonia (PCP) are examples of opportunistic diseases found in AIDS patients.

Oral contraceptive   A contraceptive, consisting of sex hormones, which is taken by mouth.

Orgasm   The climax of sexual excitement.

Orgasmic disorders   Sexual dysfunctions in which people persistently or recurrently have difficulty reaching orgasm or reach orgasm more rapidly than they would like, despite attaining a level of sexual stimulation of sufficient intensity to normally result in orgasm.

Orgasmic platform   The thickening of the walls of the outer third of the vagina, due to vasocongestion, that occurs during the plateau phase of the sexual response cycle.

Orgasmic reconditioning   A method for strengthening the connection between sexual arousal and appropriate sexual stimuli (such as fantasies about an adult of the other gender) by repeatedly pairing the desired stimuli with orgasm.

Os   The opening in middle of the cervix. (Latin for "mouth.")

Osteoporosis   A condition caused by estrogen deficiency and characterized by a decline in bone density, such that bones become porous and brittle. (From the Greek *osteon,* meaning "bone," and the Latin *porus,* meaning "pore.")

Outercourse   Forms of sexual expression, such as massage, hugging, caressing, mutual masturbation, and rubbing bodies together, that do not involve the exchange of body fluids. (Contrast with *intercourse.*)

Outing   The revelation of the identities of gay people by other gay people. The method is intended to combat discrimination against gay people by forcing individuals out of the closet and into the fray.

Ova   Egg cells. (Singular: ovum.)

Ovariectomy   Surgical removal of the ovaries.

Ovaries   Almond-shaped organs that produce ova and the hormones estrogen and progesterone.

Ovulation   The release of an ovum from an ovary.

Ovulation method   A fertility awareness method of contraception that relies on prediction of ovulation by tracking the viscosity of the cervical mucus.

Ovulatory phase   The second stage of the menstrual cycle, during which a follicle ruptures and releases a mature ovum.

Oxytocin   A pituitary hormone that stimulates uterine contractions in labor and the ejection of milk during nursing.

Pap test   A test of a sample of cervical cells that screens for cervical cancer and other abnormalities. (Named after the originator of the technique, Dr. Papanicolaou.)

Paraphilia   A diagnostic category used by the American Psychiatric Association to describe atypical patterns of sexual arousal or behavior that become problematic in the eyes of the individual or society, such as fetishism or exhibitionism. The urges are recurrent and are either acted on or are distressing to the individual. (From Greek roots meaning "to the side of" [*para-*] and "loving" [*philos*].)

Paraplegic   A person with sensory and motor paralysis of the lower half of the body.

Parasympathetic   The branch of the ANS most active during processes that restore the body's reserves of energy, such as digestion. The parasympathetic ANS largely controls erection.

Partialism   A paraphilia related to fetishism, in which sexual arousal is exaggeratedly associated with a particular body part, such as feet, breasts, or buttocks.

Participant observation   A method in which observers interact with the people they study as they collect data.

Pathogen   An agent, especially a microorganism, that can cause a disease. (From the Greek *pathos, meaning "suffering" or "disease," and genic,* meaning "forming" or "coming into being."

Patriarchy   A form of social organization in which the father or eldest male runs the group or family; government, rule, or domination by men. (From the Greek *pater,* meaning "father," and *archein,* meaning "to rule.")

Peak days   The days during the menstrual cycle during which a woman is most likely to be fertile.

Pederasty   Sexual love of boys. (From the Greek *paidos,* meaning "boy.")

Pediculosis   A parasitic infestation by pubic lice (*Pthirus pubis*) that causes itching.

Pedophiles   Persons with pedophilia, a paraphilia involving sexual interest in children.

Pedophilia   A type of paraphilia that is defined by sexual attraction to unusual stimuli: children. (From the Greek *paidos*, meaning "child," not the Latin *pedis*, meaning "foot.")

Pelvic inflammatory disease   Inflammation of the pelvic region—possibly including the cervix, uterus, fallopian tubes, abdominal cavity, and ovaries—that can be caused by organisms such as *Neisseria gonorrhoeae*. Its symptoms are abdominal pain, tenderness, nausea, fever, and irregular menstrual cycles. The condition may lead to infertility. Abbreviated *PID*.

Penile strain gauge   A device for measuring sexual arousal in men in terms of changes in the circumference of the penis.

Penis envy   In psychoanalytic theory, the girl's wish to have a penis.

Penis   The male organ of sexual intercourse. (From the Latin for "tail.")

Performance anxiety   Feelings of dread and foreboding experienced in connection with sexual activity (or any other activity that might be judged by another person).

Perimetrium   The outer layer of the uterus. (From roots meaning "around the uterus.")

Perineum   The area between the vulva and the anus. (From Greek roots meaning "around" and "to empty out.")

Period of the ovum   Germinal stage.

Peyronie's disease   An abnormal condition characterized by an excessive curvature of the penis that can make erections painful.

Phallic symbols   Images of the penis.

Phallic worship   Worship of the penis as a symbol of generative power.

Pharyngeal gonorrhea   A gonorrheal infection of the pharynx (the cavity leading from the mouth and nasal passages to the larynx and esophagus) that is characterized by a sore throat.

Pheromones   Chemical substances secreted externally by certain animals, which convey information to, or produce specific responses in, other members of the same species. (From the Greek *pherien*, meaning "to bear [a message]" and *hormone*.)

Philia   (FEEL-yuh) Friendship love, which is based on liking and respect rather than sexual desire.

Phimosis   An abnormal condition in which the foreskin is so tight that it cannot be withdrawn from the glans. (From the Greek *phimos*, meaning "muzzle.")

Pimps   Men who serve as agents for prostitutes and live off their earnings. (From the Middle French *pimper*, meaning "to dress smartly.")

Pituitary gland   The gland that secretes growth hormone, prolactin, oxytocin, and others.

Placenta   An organ connected to the fetus by the umbilical cord. The placenta serves as a relay station between mother and fetus, allowing the exchange of nutrients and wastes.

Plateau phase   The second phase of the sexual response cycle, which is characterized by increases in vasocongestion, muscle tension, heart rate, and blood pressure in preparation for orgasm.

Polyandry   A form of marriage in which a woman has two or more husbands at the same time. (From the Greek *andros*, meaning "man" or "male.")

Polygamy   The practice of having two or more spouses at the same time. (From the Greek roots meaning "many" [*poly-*] and "marriage" [*gamos*].)

Polygyny   A form of marriage in which a man has two or more wives at the same time. (From the Greek *gyne*, meaning "woman.")

Polymorphously perverse   In psychoanalytic theory, being receptive to all forms of sexual stimulation.

Pons   A structure of the hindbrain that regulates respiration, attention, sleep, and dreaming.

Population   A complete group of organisms or events.

Pornography   Written, visual, or audiotaped material that is sexually explicit and produced for purposes of eliciting or enhancing sexual arousal. (From Greek roots meaning "to write about prostitutes.")

Postpartum depression   Persistent and severe mood changes during the postpartum period, involving feelings of despair and apathy and characterized by changes in appetite and sleep, low self-esteem, and difficulty in concentrating.

Postpartum   Following birth.

Posttraumatic stress disorder   A type of stress reaction brought on by a traumatic event and characterized by flashbacks of the experience in the form of disturbing dreams or intrusive recollections, a sense of emotional numbing or restricted range of feelings, and heightened body arousal. Abbreviated *PTSD*.

Power rape   Rape that is motivated by the desire to control and dominate the person assaulted.

Premature ejaculation   A sexual dysfunction in which ejaculation occurs with minimal sexual stimulation and before the couple desires it.

Premenstrual syndrome (PMS)   A combination of physical and psychological symptoms (e.g., anxiety, depression, irritability, weight gain from fluid retention, and abdominal discomfort) that regularly afflicts many women during the four- to six-day interval that precedes their menses each month.

Prepuce The fold of skin covering the glans of the clitoris (or penis). (From Latin roots meaning "before a swelling.")

Preterm Born prior to 37 weeks of gestation.

Primary amenorrhea Lack of menstruation in a woman who has never menstruated.

Primary dysmenorrhea Menstrual pain or discomfort that occurs in the absence of known organic problems.

Primary erogenous zones Erogenous zones that are particularly sensitive because they are richly endowed with nerve endings.

Primary sex characteristics Physical characteristics that differentiate males and females and are directly involved in reproduction, such as the sex organs.

Probability sample A sample in which the probability of inclusion in the sample of any particular member is known.

Prodromal symptoms Warning symptoms that signal the onset or flare-up of a disease. (From the Greek *prodromos*, meaning "forerunner.")

Progesterone A steroid hormone secreted by the corpus luteum or prepared synthetically that stimulates proliferation of the endometrium and is involved in regulation of the menstrual cycle. (From the root *pro-*, meaning "promoting," and the words *gestation, steroid,* and *one.*)

Prolactin A pituitary hormone that stimulates production of milk. (From roots meaning "for milk.")

Proliferative phase The first phase of the menstrual cycle, which begins with the end of menstruation and lasts about 9 or 10 days. During this phase, the endometrium proliferates.

Prophylactic An agent that protects against disease.

Prostaglandins Hormones that cause muscle fibers in the uterine wall to contract, as during labor.

Prostate gland The gland that lies beneath the bladder and secretes prostatic fluid, which gives semen its characteristic odor and texture.

Prostatitis Inflammation of the prostate gland.

Prostitution The sale of sexual activity for money or goods of value, such as drugs. (From the Latin *prostituere*, meaning "to cause to stand in front of." The implication is that one is offering one's body for sale.)

Proximodistal From the central axis of the body outward. (From Latin roots meaning "near" and "far.")

Prurient Tending to excite lust; lewd. (From the Latin *prurire*, meaning "to itch" in the sense of "to long for.")

Pseudohermaphrodites People who possess the gonads of one gender but external genitalia that are ambiguous or typical of the other gender.

Psychoanalysis The theory of personality originated by Sigmund Freud, which proposes that human behavior represents the outcome of clashing inner forces.

Psychological androgyny Possession of stereotypical masculine traits, such as assertiveness and instrumental skills, along with stereotypical feminine traits, such as expressiveness, nurturance, and cooperation.

Psychosexual development In psychoanalytic theory, the process by which sexual feelings shift from one erogenous zone to another as a human being matures.

Puberty The stage of development during which reproduction first becomes possible. Puberty begins with the appearance of *secondary sex characteristics* and ends when the long bones make no further gains in length. (From the Latin *puber,* meaning "of ripe age.")

Pubococcygeus muscle The muscle that encircles the entrance to the vagina.

Pudendum The external female genitals.

Radiotherapy Treatment of a disease by X-rays or by emissions from a radioactive substance.

Random sample A sample in which every member of a population has an equal chance of participating.

Rape trauma syndrome A two-phase reaction to rape that is characterized by disruption of the survivor's lifestyle (the acute phase) and reorganization of the survivor's life (the long-term phase).

Rape Sexual intercourse that takes place as a result of force or threats of force rather than consent. (The legal definition of rape varies from state to state.) See also *forcible rape* and *statutory rape.*

Recessive trait A trait that is not expressed when the gene or genes involved have been paired with dominant genes. Recessive traits are transmitted to future generations, however, and are expressed if they are paired with other recessive genes.

Reciprocity Mutual exchange.

Reflex A simple, unlearned response to a stimulus that is mediated by the spine rather than the brain.

Refractory period A period of time following a response (e.g., orgasm) during which an individual is no longer responsive to stimulation (e.g., sexual stimulation).

Reliability The consistency or accuracy of a measure.

Repression In psychoanalytic theory, the most basic defense mechanism through which threatening ideas and impulses are ejected from conscious awareness.

Resolution phase The fourth phase of the sexual response cycle, during which the body gradually returns to its prearoused state.

Respiratory distress syndrome A cluster of breathing problems, including weak and irregular breathing, to which preterm babies are especially vulnerable.

Reticular activating system A part of the brain active during attention, sleep, and arousal.

Retrograde ejaculation Ejaculation in which the ejaculate empties into the bladder. (From the Latin *retrogradi,* meaning "to go backward.")

Rh incompatibility   A condition in which antibodies produced by a pregnant woman are transmitted to the fetus and may cause brain damage or death.

Root   The base of the penis, which extends into the pelvis.

Rubella   A viral infection that can cause mental retardation and heart disease in an embryo. Also called *German measles*.

Rubin test   A test in which carbon dioxide gas is blown through the cervix and its progress through the reproductive tract is tracked to determine whether or not the fallopian tubes are blocked.

Sacrum   The thick, triangular bone located near the bottom of the spinal column.

Sadism   A paraphilia characterized by the desire or need to inflict pain or humiliation on others to enhance sexual arousal so that gratification is attained. (From the name of the author Marquis de Sade.)

Sadistic rape   A highly ritualized, savage rape in which the person who is attacked is subjected to painful and humiliating experiences and threats.

Sadomasochism   A mutually gratifying sexual interaction between consenting sex partners in which sexual arousal is associated with the infliction and receipt of pain or humiliation. Commonly known as *S&M*.

Sample   Part of a population.

Satyriasis   An excessive, insatiable sexual appetite or drive in men. (After *satyr,* a sexually insatiable, goat-legged creature with pointed ears and short horns in Greek mythology. Satyrs were part man, part beast.)

Scabies   A parasitic infestation caused by a tiny mite (*Sarcoptes scabiei*) that causes itching.

Schema   Concept; way of interpreting experience or processing information.

Scores   Customers of hustlers.

Scrotum   The pouch of loose skin that contains the testes. (From the same linguistic root as the word *shred,* meaning "a long, narrow strip," and probably referring to the long furrows on the scrotal sac.)

Secondary amenorrhea   Lack of menstruation in a woman who has previously menstruated.

Secondary dysmenorrhea   Menstrual pain or discomfort that is caused by identified organic problems.

Secondary erogenous zones   Parts of the body that become erotically sensitized through experience.

Secondary sex characteristics   Physical traits that distinguish the genders but are not directly involved in reproduction.

Secretory phase   The third phase of the menstrual cycle, which follows ovulation. Also referred to as the *luteal phase,* after the *corpus luteum,* which begins to secrete large amounts of progesterone and estrogen following ovulation.

Selection factor   A bias that may operate in research when people are allowed to determine whether or not they will receive a treatment.

Self-disclosure   The revelation of personal, perhaps intimate, information.

Semen   The whitish fluid that constitutes the ejaculate, consisting of sperm and secretions from the seminal vesicles, prostate, and Cowper's glands.

Seminal vesicles   Small glands that lie behind the bladder and secrete fluids that combine with sperm in the ejaculatory ducts.

Seminiferous tubules   Tiny, winding, sperm-producing tubes that are located within the lobes of the testes. (From Latin roots meaning "seed bearing.")

Sensate focus exercises   Exercises in which sex partners take turns giving and receiving pleasurable stimulation in nongenital areas of the body.

Serial monogamy   A pattern of involvement in one exclusive relationship after another, as opposed to engaging in multiple sexual relationships at the same time.

Seronegative   Lacking a pathogen or antibodies to that pathogen in the bloodstream.

Seropositive   Having a pathogen or antibodies to that pathogen in the bloodstream.

Sex flush   A reddish rash that appears on the chest or breasts late in the excitement phase of the sexual response cycle.

Sex skin   Reddening of the labia minora that occurs during the plateau phase.

Sex therapy   A collective term for short-term behavioral models for treatment of sexual dysfunctions.

Sexism   The prejudgment that because of gender, a person will possess negative traits.

Sexologist   A person who engages in the scientific study of sexual behavior.

Sexual arousal disorders   Sexual dysfunctions in which people persistently or recurrently fail to become adequately sexually aroused to engage in or sustain sexual intercourse.

Sexual assault   Any sexual activity that involves the use of force or the threat of force.

Sexual desire disorders   Sexual dysfunctions in which people have persistent or recurrent lack of sexual desire or aversion to sexual contact.

Sexual differentiation   The process by which males and females develop distinct reproductive anatomy.

Sexual dysfunctions   Persistent or recurrent difficulties in becoming sexually aroused or reaching orgasm.

Sexual harassment   Deliberate or repeated unsolicited verbal comments, gestures, or physical contact of a sexual nature that is considered to be unwelcome by the recipient.

Sexual masochism   A paraphilia characterized by the desire or need for pain or humiliation to enhance sexual arousal so that gratification may be attained. (From the name of the author Leopold von Sacher-Masoch.)

Sexual orientation   The directionality of one's sexual interests—toward members of the same gender, the other gender, or both genders.

Sexual pain disorders   Sexual dysfunctions in which people persistently or recurrently experience pain during coitus.

Sexual response cycle   Masters and Johnson's model of sexual response, which consists of four phases.

Sexual sadists   People who become sexually aroused by inflicting pain or humiliation on others.

Sexually transmitted diseases   Diseases that are communicated through sexual contact. Abbreviated STDs.

Shaft   The body of the penis, which expands as a result of vasocongestion.

Shigellosis   An STD caused by the *Shigella* bacterium.

Small talk   A superficial kind of conversation that allows exchange of information but stresses breadth of topic coverage rather than in-depth discussion.

Social desirability   A response bias to a questionnaire or interview in which the person provides a socially acceptable response.

Social skills training   Behavior therapy methods for building social skills that rely on a therapist's coaching and practice.

Social-exchange theory   The view that the development of a relationship reflects the unfolding of social exchanges—that is, the rewards and costs of maintaining the relationship as opposed to ending it.

Social-learning theory   A cognitively oriented learning theory in which observational learning, values, and expectations play key roles in determining behavior.

Socialization   The process of guiding people into socially acceptable behavior patterns by means of information, rewards, and punishments.

Sociobiology   The theory that dispositions toward behavior patterns that enhance reproductive success may be genetically transmitted.

Spectator role   A role, usually taken on because of performance anxiety, in which people observe rather than fully participate in their sexual encounters.

Sperm   The male germ cell. (From a Greek root meaning "seed.")

Spermatic cord   The cord that suspends a testicle within the scrotum and contains a vas deferens, blood vessels, nerves, and the cremaster muscle.

Spermatids   Cells formed by the division of spermatocytes. Each spermatid has 23 chromosomes.

Spermatocyte   An early stage in the development of sperm cells, in which each parent cell has 46 chromosomes, including one X and one Y sex chromosome.

Spermatogenesis   Process by which sperm cells are produced and developed.

Spermatozoa   Mature sperm cells.

Sphincters   Ring-shaped muscles that surround body openings and open or close them by expanding or contracting. (From the Greek for "that which draws close.")

Spontaneous abortion   The sudden, involuntary expulsion of the embryo or fetus from the uterus before it is capable of independent life.

Squeeze technique   A method for treating premature ejaculation whereby the tip of the penis is squeezed temporarily to prevent ejaculation.

Statutory rape   Sexual intercourse with a person who is below the age of consent. Sexual intercourse under such conditions is considered statutory rape even though the person attacked may cooperate.

Stereotype   A fixed, conventional idea about a group of people.

Sterilization   Surgical procedures that render people incapable of reproduction without affecting sexual activity.

Stillbirth   The birth of a dead fetus.

Stranger rape   Rape that is committed by an assailant previously unknown to the person who is assaulted.

Stratified random sample   A random sample in which known subgroups in a population are represented in proportion to their numbers in the population.

Streetwalkers   Prostitutes who solicit customers on the streets.

Superego   In Freud's theory, the third mental structure, which functions as a moral guardian and sets forth high standards for behavior.

Surface contact   A probing phase of building a relationship in which people seek common ground and check out feelings of attraction.

Surfactants   Substances that prevent the walls of the airways from sticking together.

Surrogate mother   A woman who is impregnated through artificial insemination, with the sperm of a prospective father, carries the embryo and fetus to term, and then gives the child to the prospective parents.

Survey   A detailed study of a sample obtained by means such as interviews and questionnaires.

Swinging   A form of consensual adultery in which both spouses share extramarital sexual experiences. Also referred to as *mate-swapping*.

Sympathetic pregnancy   The experiencing of a number of signs of pregnancy by the father.

Sympathetic   The branch of the ANS most active during emotional responses that spend the body's reserves of energy, such as fear and anxiety. The sympathetic ANS largely controls ejaculation.

Syphilis   An STD that is caused by the *Treponema pallidum* bacterium, which may progress through several stages of development—often from a chancre to a skin rash to damage to the cardiovascular or central nervous systems. (From the Greek *siphlos,* meaning "maimed" or "crippled.")

Systematic desensitization   A method for terminating the connection between a stimulus (such as a fetishistic object) and an inappropriate response (such as sexual arousal to the paraphilic stimulus). Muscle relaxation is practiced in connection with each stimulus in a series of increasingly arousing stimuli, so that the person learns to remain relaxed (and not sexually aroused) in their presence.

Tampon   A cylindrical plug of cotton that is inserted into the vagina and left in place to absorb menstrual fluid. (A French word, meaning a gun barrel "plug.")

Telephone scatologia   A paraphilia characterized by the making of obscene telephone calls. (From the Greek *skatos,* meaning "excrement")

Teratogens   Environmental influences or agents that can damage an embryo or fetus. (From the Greek *teras,* meaning "monster.")

Testes   The male sex glands, suspended in the scrotum, that produce sperm cells and male sex hormones. Singular: *testis.*

Testicles   Testes.

Testosterone   The male steroid sex hormone that fosters the development of male sex characteristics and is connected with the sex drive.

Thalamus   An area near the center of the brain involved in the relay of sensory information to the cortex and in the functions of sleep and attention.

Toucherism   A practice related to frotteurism and characterized by the persistent urge to fondle nonconsenting strangers.

Toxemia   A life-threatening condition that is characterized by high blood pressure.

Transition   The process during which the cervix becomes nearly fully dilated and the head of the fetus begins to move into the birth canal.

Transsexual   A person with a gender-identity disorder who feels that he or she is really a member of the other gender and trapped in a body of the wrong gender.

Transverse position   A crosswise birth position.

Transvestism   A paraphilia in which a person repeatedly cross-dresses to achieve sexual arousal or gratification, or is troubled by persistent, recurring urges to cross-dress. (From the Latin roots *trans-,* meaning "cross," and *vestis,* meaning "garment.") Also known as *transvestic fetishism.*

Treatment   In experiments, an intervention that is administered to participants (e.g., a test, a drug, or a sex education program) so that its effects may be observed.

Trichomoniasis   A form of vaginitis caused by the protozoan *Trichomonas vaginalis.*

Trophoblast   The outer part of the blastocyst, from which the amniotic sac, placenta, and umbilical cord develop.

Tubal sterilization   The most common method of female sterilization, in which the fallopian tubes are surgically blocked to prevent the meeting of sperm and ova. Also called *tubal ligation.*

Tumescence   Swelling; erection. (From the Latin *tumere,* meaning "to swell." *Tumor* has the same root.)

Turner syndrome   A sex-chromosomal disorder caused by loss of some X chromosome material.

Umbilical cord   A tube that connects the fetus to the placenta.

Unconscious mind   Those parts or contents of the mind that lie outside of conscious awareness.

Urethral bulb   The small tube that makes up the prostatic part of the urethral tract, which balloons out as muscles close at either end, trapping semen prior to ejaculation.

Urethral opening   The opening through which urine passes from the female's body.

Urethritis   An inflammation of the bladder or urethra.

Urologist   A physician who specializes in the diagnosis and treatment of diseases of the urogenital system.

Urophilia   A paraphilia in which sexual arousal is associated with urine.

Uterus   The hollow, muscular, pear-shaped organ in which a fertilized ovum implants and develops until birth.

Vacuum aspiration   Removal of the uterine contents by suction. An abortion method used early in pregnancy. (From the Latin *aspirare,* meaning "to breathe upon.")

Vagina   The tubular female sex organ that contains the penis during sexual intercourse and through which a baby is born. (Latin for "sheath.")

Vaginal photoplethysmograph   A tampon-shaped probe that is inserted in the vagina and suggests the level of vasocongestion by measuring the light reflected from the vaginal walls.

Vaginismus   A sexual dysfunction characterized by involuntary contraction of the muscles surrounding the vaginal barrel, preventing penile penetration or rendering penetration painful.

Vaginitis   Any type of vaginal infection or inflammation.

Validity   With respect to tests, the degree to which a particular test measures the constructs or traits it purports to measure.

Values   The qualities in life that are deemed important or unimportant, right or wrong, desirable or undesirable.

Variables   Quantities or qualities that vary or may vary.

Vas deferens   A tube that conducts sperm from the testicle to the ejaculatory duct of the penis. (From Latin roots meaning "a vessel" that "carries down.")

Vasectomy   A male sterilization procedure in which the vas deferens is severed, preventing sperm from reaching the ejaculatory duct.

Vasocongestion   Engorgement of blood vessels with blood, which swells the genitals and breasts during sexual arousal. (From the Latin *vas,* meaning "vessel.")

Vasovasotomy   The surgical method of reversing vasectomy in which the cut or cauterized ends of the vas deferens are sewn together.

VDRL   The test named after the Venereal Disease Research Laboratory of the U.S. Public Health Service that tests for the presence of antibodies to *Treponema pallidum* in the blood.

Vestibular bulbs   Cavernous structures that extend downward along the sides of the introitus and swell during sexual arousal.

Viscosity   Stickiness, consistency.

Volunteer bias   A slanting of research data that is caused by the characteristics of individuals who volunteer to participate, such as willingness to discuss intimate behavior.

Voyeurism   A paraphilia characterized by strong, repetitive urges and related sexual fantasies of observing unsuspecting strangers who are naked, disrobing, or engaged in sexual relations. (From the French verb *voir,* meaning "to see.")

Vulva   The external sexual structures of the female.

Whore–madonna complex   A rigid stereotyping of women as either sinners or saints.

Zona pellucida   A gelatinous layer that surrounds an ovum. (From roots meaning "zone that light can shine through.")

Zoophilia   A paraphilia involving persistent or repeated sexual urges and related fantasies involving sexual contact with animals.

Zygote   A fertilized ovum (egg cell).

Zygote intrafallopian transfer (ZIFT)   A method of conception in which an ovum is fertilized in a laboratory dish and then placed in a fallopian tube.

References

ABC News *Nightline* Poll. (1995, February 17). *Most favor sex ed. in schools, believing it changes behavior.* New York: ABC News.

Abel, G. G., et al. (1984). Complications, consent, and cognitions in sex between children and adults. *International Journal of Law and Psychiatry, 7,* 89–103.

Abel, G. G., et al. (1989). The measurement of the cognitive distortions of child molesters. *Annals of Sex Research, 2,* 135–152.

Abelson, H., et al. (1970). Public attitudes toward and experience with erotic materials. In *Technical reports of the commission on obscenity and pornography,* (Vol. 6). Washington, DC: U.S. Government Printing Office.

Abou-David, K. (1967). Epidemiology of carcinoma of the cervix uteri in Lebanese Christians and Moslems. *Cancer, 20,* 1706–1714.

Abramowitz, S. (1986). Psychosocial outcomes of sex reassignment surgery. *Journal of Consulting and Clinical Psychology, 54,* 183–189.

Acker, M., & Davis, M. H. (1992). Intimacy, passion and commitment in adult romantic relationships: A test of the triangular theory of love. *Journal of Social and Personal Relationships, 9,* 21–50.

Ackerman, D. (1990). *A natural history of the senses.* New York: Random House.

Ackerman, D. (1991). *The moon by whale light.* New York: Random House.

Adams, H. E., et al. (1981). Behavior therapy with sexual deviations. In S. M. Turner, et al., (Eds.), *Handbook of clinical behavior therapy* (pp. 318–346). New York: Wiley.

Adams, M. M. (1995). The continuing challenge of preterm delivery. *Journal of the American Medical Association, 273* (9), 739–740.

Adams, R. (1987). The role of prostitution in AIDS and other STDs. *Medical Aspects of Human Sexuality, 21,* 27–33.

Adams, V. (1980, August). Sex therapists in perspective. *Psychology Today,* pp. 35–36.

Adelson, A. (1990, November 19). Study attacks women's roles in TV. *The New York Times,* p. C18.

Ade-Ridder, L. (1985). Quality of marriage: A comparison between golden-wedding couples and couples married less than fifty years. *Lifestyles, 7,* 224–237.

Adler, J. (1993, April 26). Sex in the snoring '90s. *Newsweek,* 55, 57.

Adler, J., et al. (1991, November 18). Living with the virus: When-and-how HIV turns into AIDS. *Newsweek,* 33–34.

Adler, N., et al. (1990, April 6). Psychological responses after abortion. *Science.*

Ahmed, R. A. (1991). Women in Egypt and the Sudan. In L. L. Adler (Ed.), *Women in cross-cultural perspective* (pp. 107–134). New York: Praeger.

AIDS study hints other drugs may be superior to AZT alone. (1995, September 15). *The New York Times,* p. A20.

AIDS update. (1993, July/August). *American Health,* 8.

AIDS without needles or sex. (1993, December 20). *Newsweek,* 106–107.

Aiken, L. S., et al. (1994). Health beliefs and compliance with mammography-screening recommendations in asymptomatic women. *Health Psychology, 13,* 122–129.

Akhtar, S. (1988). Four culture-bound psychiatric syndromes in India. *International Journal of Social Psychiatry, 34,* 70–74.

Alan Guttmacher Institute. (1991). *Facts in brief.* New York: Author.

Alexander, C. J., et al. (1993). Sexual activities, desire, and satisfaction in males pre– and post–spinal cord injury. *Archives of Sexual Behavior, 22,* 217–228.

Allen, J. R., & Setlow, V. P. (1991). Heterosexual transmission of HIV: A view of the future. *Journal of the American Medical Association, 266,* 1695–1696.

Alter-Reid, K., et al. (1986). Sexual abuse of children: A review of the empirical findings. *Clinical Psychology Review, 6,* 249–266.

Althof, S. E. (1994). Paper presented to the annual meeting of the American Urological Association. San Francisco, CA.

Althof, S. E., et al. (1991). Sexual, psychological, and marital impact of self-injection of papaverine and phentolamine: A long-term prospective study [Special issue: The treatment of male erectile disorders]. *Journal of Sex & Marital Therapy, 17,* 101–112.

Alman, L. K. (1996, January 30). 3-drug therapy AIDS shows promise against AIDS. *The New York Times,* p. C5.

Altman, L. K. (1991, April 15). Study challenges federal research on risks of IUD's. *The New York Times,* p. A1.

Altman, L. K. (1992a, April 9). Ashe received a transfusion before blood supply was tested for H.I.V. *The New York Times,* p. B15.

Altman, L. K. (1992b, July 21). Women worldwide nearing higher rate for AIDS than men. *The New York Times,* p. C3.

Altman, L. K. (1993a, February 17). 2 new studies link vasectomy to higher prostate cancer risk. *The New York Times,* p. C12.

Altman, L. K. (1993b, February 21). New caution, and some reassurance, on vasectomy. *The New York Times,* Section 4, p. 2.

Altman, L. K. (1993c, June 8). World health official says AIDS spread could be controlled. *The New York Times,* p. C6

Altman, L. K. (1995a, February 2). Combination of drugs appears to slow AIDS virus, studies say. *The New York Times,* p. A20.

Altman, L. K. (1995b, February 7). Protein in saliva found to block AIDS virus in test tube study. *The New York Times,* p. C3.

Altman, L. K. (1995c, July 7). Drug for treating impotence is ready for sale, F. D. A. says. *The New York Times,* p. A13.

Alzate, H. (1985). Vaginal eroticism: A replication study. *Archives of Sexual Behavior, 14,* 529–537.

Alzate, H., & Londono, M. L. (1984). Vaginal erotic sensitivity. *Journal of Sex and Marital Therapy, 10,* 49–56.

Amaro, H. (1995). Love, sex, and power: Considering women's realities in HIV prevention. *American Psychologist, 50,* 437–447.

Amato, P. R., & Keith, B. (1991). Parental divorce and the well-being of children: A meta-analysis. *Psychological Bulletin, 110,* 26–46.

American Cancer Society. (1990). *For men only: Testicular cancer and how to do TSE* (Rev. ed.). Atlanta: Author.

American Cancer Society. (1991). *Cancer facts and figures.* New York: Author.

American Cancer Society. (1994). *Cancer facts and figures.* Atlanta: Author.

American Cancer Society. (1995a). America Online. Document ID: ACS049.

American Cancer Society. (1995b). America Online. Document ID: ACS050.

American Cancer Society. (1995c). America Online. Document ID: ACS052.

American Cancer Society. (1995d). America Online. Document ID: ACS053.

American Cancer Society. (1995e). America Online. Document ID: ACS058.

American Psychiatric Association. (1994). *Diagnostic and statistical manual of mental disorders* (4th ed.). Washington, DC: Author.

Americans generally well-informed about AIDS, but many lack knowledge about preventive aspects. (1993). *Family Planning Perspectives, 25,* 139–140.

Ames, M. A., & Houston, D. A. (1990). Legal, social, and biological definitions of pedophilia. *Archives of Sexual Behavior, 19,* 333–342.

Anderson, B. J., & Wold, F. M. (1986). Chronic physical illness and sexual behavior. *Journal of Consulting and Clinical Psychology, 54,* 168–175.

Anderson, J. L., et al. (1992). Was the Duchess of Windsor right? A cross-cultural review of the socioecology of ideals of female body shape. *Ethology and Sociobiology, 13,*197–227.

Anderson, P. B., & Aymami, R. (1993). Reports of female initiating of sexual contact: Male and female diferences. *Archives of Sexual Behavior, 22,* 335–343.

Anderson, V. N. (1992). For whom is this world just? Sexual orientation and AIDS. *Journal of Applied Social Psychology, 22,* 248–259.

Angier, N. (1990, July 19). Scientists say gene on Y chromosome makes a man a man. *The New York Times,* pp. A1, 19.

Angier, N. (1991, August 30). Zone of brain linked to men's sexual orientation. *The New York Times,* A1, D18.

Angier, N. (1992, January 30). Odor receptors discovered in sperm cells. *The New York Times,* p. A19.

Angier, N. (1993a). Future of the pill may lie just over the counter. *The New York Times,* Section 4, p. 5.

Ansen, D., et al. (1993, January 18). A lost generation. *Newsweek,* 16–23.

Antill, J. K. (1983). Sex role complementarity versus similarity in married couples. *Journal of Personality and Social Psychology, 52,* 260–267.

Antonarakas, S. E., et al. (1991). Prenatal origin of the extra chromosome in trisomy 21 as indicated by analysis of DNA polymorphisms. *New England Journal of Medicine, 324,* 872–876.

Antoni, M. H., et al. (1990). Psychoneuroimmunology and HIV-1. *Journal of Consulting and Clinical Psychology, 58,* 38–49.

Antoni, M. H., et al. (1991). Cognitive–behavioral stress management intervention buffers distress responses and immunologic changes following notification of HIV-1 seropositivity. *Journal of Consulting and Clinical Psychology, 59,* 906–915.

Appell, R. A. (1986). Importance of the neurological examination in erectile dysfunction. *Medical Aspects of Human Sexuality, 20,* 32–36.

Armsworth, M. W. (1991). Psychological response to abortion. *Journal of Counseling and Development, 69,* 377–379.

Asbell, B. (1995). *The pill: A biography of the drug that changed the world.* New York: Random House.

ASHA takes a stand. (1995). *The PULSE of the American School Health Association, 16* (1), 4.

Assalian, P. (1994). Premature ejaculation: Is it really psychogenic? *Journal of Sex Education and Therapy, 20* (1), 1–4.

Asso, D., & Magos, A. (1992). Psychological and physiological changes in severe premenstrual syndrome. *Biological Psychology, 33,* 115–132.

Astley, S. J., et al. (1992). Analysis of facial shape in children gestationally exposed to marijuana, alcohol, and/or cocaine. *Pediatrics, 89,* 67–77.

Atkeson, B. M., et al. (1989). Victim resistance to rape: The relationship of previous victimization, demographics, and situational factors. *Archives of Sexual Behavior, 18,* 497–507.

Atwater, L. (1982). *The extramarital connection: Sex, intimacy and identity.* New York: Irvington Publishers.

Axinn, W. G. (1991). The influence of interviewer sex on responses to sensitive questions in Nepal. *Social Science Research, 20,* 303–318.

Bach, G. R., & Deutsch, R. M. (1970). *Pairing.* New York: Peter H. Wyden.

Bachu, A. (1991). Cited in Pear, R. (1991, December 4). Larger number of new mothers are unmarried. *The New York Times,* p. A20.

Bagatell, C. J., & Bremner, W. J. (1996). Drug therapy: Androgens in men—Uses and abuses. *New England Journal of Medicine, 334,* 707–714.

Bagley, C., & Young, L. (1987). Juvenile prostitution and child sexual abuse: A controlled study. *Canadian Journal of Community Mental Health, 6,* 5–26.

Bailey, J. M., et al. (1993). Heritable factors influence sexual orientation in women. *Archives of General Psychiatry, 50,* 217–223.

Bailey, J. M., & Zucker, K. J. (1995). Childhood sex-typed behavior and sexual orientation: A conceptual analysis and quantitative review. *Developmental Psychology, 31,* 43–55.

Baker, J. N. (1990, Summer/Fall). Coming out [Special issue]. *Newsweek,* 60–61.

Baker, S., et al. (1988). Parents' behavioral norms as predictors of adolescent sexual activity and contraceptive use. *Adolescence, 23,* 278–281.

Baker, T. C., et al. (1990). Rape victims' concerns about possible exposure to HIV infection. *Journal of Interpersonal Violence, 5,* 49–60.

Baldwin, J. D., & Baldwin, J. I. (1989). The socialization of homosexuality and heterosexuality in a non-Western society. *Archives of Sexual Behavior, 18,* 13–29.

Baldwin, J. D., et al. (1992). The effect of ethnic group on sexual activities related to contraception and STDs. *Journal of Sex Research, 29,* 189–205.

Bancroft, J. (1984). Hormones and human sexual behavior. *Journal of Sex and Marital Therapy, 10,* 3–21.

Bancroft, J. (1990). Commentary: Biological contributions to sexual orientation. In D. P. McWhirter, et al. (Eds.), *Homosexuality/heterosexuality: Concepts of sexual orientation* (pp. 101–111). New York: Oxford University Press.

Bancroft, J., et al. (1983). Mood, sexuality, hormones, and the menstrual cycle. III: Sexuality and the role of androgens. *Psychosomatic Medicine, 45*, 509–516.

Banmen, J., & Vogel, N. (1985). The relationship between marital quality and interpersonal sexual communication. *Family Therapy, 12*, 45–58.

Banning, A. (1989). Mother–son incest: Confronting a prejudice. *Child Abuse and Neglect, 13*, 563–570.

Barbach, L. G. (1975). *For yourself: The fulfillment of female sexuality.* New York: Doubleday.

Barbach, L. G. (1995). Cited in Goleman, D. (1995, June 14). Sex fantasy research said to neglect women. *The New York Times,* p. C14.

Barbaree, H. E., & Marshall, W. L. (1991). The role of male sexual arousal in rape: Six models. *Journal of Consulting and Clinical Psychology, 59*, 621–630.

Barlow, D. H. (1986). Causes of sexual dysfunction: The role of anxiety and cognitive interference. *Journal of Consulting and Clinical Psychology, 54*, 140–148.

Barlow, D. H., & Durand, V. M. (1995). *Abnormal psychology.* Pacific Grove, CA: Brooks/Cole.

Barr, H. M., et al. (1990). Prenatal exposure to alcohol, caffeine, tobacco, and aspirin. *Developmental Psychology, 26*, 339–348.

Barrett, M. B. (1990). *Invisible lives: The truth about millions of women-loving women.* New York: Harper & Row (Perennial Library).

Barringer, F. (1990, August 17). After long decline, teen births are up. *The New York Times,* p. A14.

Barringer, F. (1991, June 7). Changes in family patterns: Solitude and single parents. *The New York Times,* pp. A1, A18.

Barringer, F. (1992a, July 17). Rate of marriage continues decline. *The New York Times,* p. A20.

Barringer, F. (1992b, July 19). More Americans are saying, "I don't." *The New York Times,* p. E2.

Barringer, F. (1993a, April 1). Viral sexual diseases are found in 1 of 5 in U.S. *The New York Times,* pp. A1, B9.

Barringer, F. (1993b, April 15). Sex survey of American men finds 1% are gay. *The New York Times,* p. A1.

Barringer, F. (1993c, June 2). School hallways as gauntlets of sexual taunts. *The New York Times,* p. B7.

Bart, P. B., & O'Brien, P. B. (1985). *Stopping rape: Successful survival strategies.* Elsmford, NY: Pergamon Press.

Bar-Tal, D., & Saxe, L. (1976). Perceptions of similarly and dissimilarly physically attractive couples and individuals. *Journal of Personality and Social Psychology, 33*, 772–781.

Bartell, G. (1970). Group sex among mid-Americans. *Journal of Sex Research, 6*, 113–131.

Bartlett, J. G. (1993). Zidovudine now or later? *New England Journal of Medicine, 329*, 351–352.

Bartoshuk, L. M., & Beauchamp, G. K. (1994). Chemical senses. *Annual Review of Psychology, 45*, 419–449.

Basgara, O., et al. (1993). Alcohol intake increases human immunodeficiency virus type 1 replication in human peripheral blood mononuclear cells. *Journal of Infectious Diseases, 167*, 789–797.

Baumeister, R. F. (1988a). Gender differences in masochistic scripts. *Journal of Sex Research, 25*, 478–499.

Baumeister, R. F. (1988b). Masochism as escape from self. *Journal of Sex Research, 25*, 28–59.

Baxter, D. J., et al. (1986). Sexual responses to consenting and forced sex in a large sample of rapists and nonrapists. *Behaviour Research and Therapy, 17*, 215–222.

Bayer, R., et al. (1995). Testing for HIV infection at home. *New England Journal of Medicine, 332*, 1296–1299.

Beck, A. (1988). *Love is never enough.* New York: Harper & Row.

Beck, J. G. (1993). Vaginismus. In W. O'Donohue & J. H. Geer (Eds.), *Handbook of sexual dysfunctions: Assessment and treatment* (pp. 381–397). Boston: Allyn & Bacon.

Beck, J. G., & Davies, D. K. (1987). Teen contraception: A review of perspectives on compliance. *Archives of Sexual Behavior, 16*, 337–368.

Becker, J. V., et al. (1986). Level of postassault sexual functioning in rape and incest victims. *Archives of Sexual Behavior, 15*, 37–49.

Becker, J. V., et al. (1989). Factors associated with erection in adolescent sex offenders. *Journal of Psychopathology and Behavioral Assessment, 11*, 353–362.

Beitchman, J. H., et al. (1992). A review of the long-term effects of child sexual abuse. *Child Abuse and Neglect, 16*, 101–118.

Belcastro, P. A. (1985). Sexual behavior differences between black and white students. *Journal of Sex Research, 21*, 56–67.

Bell, A. P., & Weinberg, M. S. (1978). *Homosexualities: A study of diversity among men and women.* New York: Simon & Schuster.

Bell, A. P., et al. (1981). *Sexual preference: Its development in men and women.* Bloomington: University of Indiana Press.

Bell, S., et al. (1994). Understanding attributions of blame in stranger rape and date rape situations: An examination of gender, race, identification, and students' social perceptions of rape victims. *Journal of Applied Social Psychology, 24* (19), 1719–1734.

Beller, T. (1995, July 13). Why? Don't ask. *The New York Times,* p. A23.

Bellis, D. J. (1990). Fear of AIDS and risk reduction among heroin-addicted female street prostitutes: Personal interviews with 72 Southern California subjects. *Journal of Alcohol and Drug Education, 35*, 26–37.

Bello, D. C., et al. (1983). The communications effects of controversial sexual content in television programs and commercials. *Journal of Advertising, 12* (3), 32–42.

Bem, S. L. (1974). The measurement of psychological androgyny. *Journal of Consulting and Clinical Psychology, 42*, 151–162.

Bem, S. L. (1975). Sex role adaptability: One consequence of psychological androgyny. *Journal of Personality and Social Psychology, 31*, 634–643.

Bem, S. L. (1981). Gender schema theory: A cognitive account of sex typing. *Psychological Review, 88*, 354–364.

Bem, S. L. (1983). Gender schema theory and its implications for child development: Raising gender-aschematic children in a gender-schematic society. *Signs, 8*, 598–616.

Bem, S. L. (1985). Androgyny and gender schema theory: A conceptual and empirical integration. In T. B. Sonderegger (Ed.), *Nebraska symposium on motivation, 1984: Psychology and gender.* Lincoln: University of Nebraska Press.

Bem, S. L. (1993). *The lenses of gender.* New Haven: Yale University Press.

Bem, S. L., et al. (1976). Sex typing and androgyny: Further explorations of the expressive domain. *Journal of Personality and Social Psychology, 34*, 1016–1023.

Bennett, N. G., et al. (1988). Commitment and the modern union: Assessing the link between premarital cohabitation and subsequent marital stability. *American Sociological Review, 53*, 127–138.

Bentler, P. M. (1976). A typology of transsexualism: Gender identity theory and data. *Archives of Sexual Behavior, 5,* 567–584.

Berlin, F. S. (1983). Sex offenders: A biomedical perspective and a status report of biomedical treatment. In J. G. Greer & I. R. Stuart (Eds.), *The sexual aggressor* (pp. 83–123). New York: Van Nostrand Reinhold.

Berlin, F. S. (1989). The paraphilias and Depo-Provera: Some medical, ethical and legal considerations. *Bulletin of the American Academy of Psychiatry and the Law, 17,* 233–239.

Berliner, D. (1993). Cited in Blakeslee, S. (1993, September 7). Human nose may hold an additional organ for a real sixth sense. *The New York Times,* p. C3.

Bernstein, W. M., et al. (1983). Causal ambiguity and heterosexual affiliation. *Journal of Experimental Social Psychology, 19,* 78–92.

Bernstein, S. J., et al. (1993). The appropriateness of hysterectomy: A comparison of care in seven health plans. *Journal of the American Medical Association, 269,* 2398–2402.

Berscheid, E. (1988). Some comments on love's anatomy: Or, whatever happened to old-fashioned lust? In R. J. Sternberg & M. L. Barnes (Eds.), *The psychology of love* (pp. 359–374). New Haven: Yale University Press.

Berscheid, E., & Walster, E. (1978). *Interpersonal attraction.* Reading, MA: Addison-Wesley.

Beutler, L. E., et al. (1984). Women's satisfaction with partners' penile implant: Inflatable vs. noninflatable prosthesis. *Urology, 24,* 552–558.

Beutler, L. E., et al. (1986). Inflatable and noninflatable penile prostheses: Comparative follow-up evaluation. *Urology, 28,* 136–143.

Bieber, I. (1976). A discussion of "Homosexuality: The ethical challenge." *Journal of Consulting and Clinical Psychology, 44,* 163–166.

Bieber, I., et al. (1962). *Homosexuality.* New York: Basic Books.

Biggar, R. J., & Melbye, M. (1992). Responses to anonymous questionnaires concerning sexual behavior: A method to examine potential biases. *American Journal of Public Health, 82,* 1506–1512.

Billingham, R. E., & Sack, A. R. (1986). Gender differences in college students' willingness to participate in alternative marriage and family relationships. *Family Perspectives, 20,* 37–44.

Billy, J. O. G., et al. (1993). The sexual behavior of men in the United States. *Family Planning Perspectives, 25,* 52–60.

Binion, V. J. (1990). Psychological androgyny: A Black female perspective. *Sex Roles, 22,* 487–507.

Bixler, R. H. (1981). The incest controversy. *Psychological Reports, 49,* 267–283.

Blair, C. D., & Lanyon, R. I. (1981). Exhibitionism: A critical review of the etiology and treatment. *Psychological Bulletin, 89,* 439–463.

Blakeslee, S. (1992, January 22). An epidemic of genital warts raises concern but not alarm. *The New York Times,* p. C12.

Blakeslee, S. (1993a, June 2). New therapies are helping men to overcome impotence. *The New York Times,* p. C12.

Blakeslee, S. (1993b, September 7). Human nose may hold an additional organ for a real sixth sense. *The New York Times,* p. C3.

Blanchard, R. & Bogaert, A. F. (1996). Homosexuality in men and number of older brothers. *American Journal of Psychiatry, 153* (1), 27–31.

Blanchard, R., & Hucker, S. J. (1991). Age, transvestism, bondage, and concurrent paraphilic activities in 117 fatal cases of autoerotic asphyxia. *British Journal of Psychiatry, 159,* 371–377.

Blanchard, R., et al. (1985). Gender dysphoria, gender reorientation, and the clinical management of transsexualism. *Journal of Consulting and Clinical Psychology, 53,* 295–304.

Blenner, J. L. (1992). Stress and mediators: Patients' perceptions of infertility treatment. *Nursing Research, 41,* 92–97.

Blood test's value in early prostate cases. (1993, August 25). *The New York Times,* p. C10.

Bloom, B. J., et al. (1978). Marital disruption as a stressor: A review and analysis. *Psychological Bulletin, 85,* 867–894.

Bloor, M., et al. (1990). An ethnographic study of HIV-related risk practices among Glasgow rent boys and their clients: Report of a pilot study. *AIDS Care, 2,* 17–24.

Blumstein, P., & Schwartz, P. (1983). *American couples: Money, work, sex.* New York: William Morrow.

Blumstein, P. & Schwartz, P. (1990). Intimate relationships and the creation of sexuality. In D. P. McWhirter, et al. (Eds.), *Homosexuality/heterosexuality: Concepts of sexual orientation* (pp. 307–320). New York: Oxford University Press.

Blustein, J. (1995). Medicare coverage, supplemental insurance, and the use of mammography by older women. *New England Journal of Medicine, 332,* 1138–1143.

Boeringer, S. B., et al. (1991). Social contexts and social learning in sexual coercion and aggression: Assessing the contribution of fraternity membership. *Family Relationships, 40,* 58–64.

Bogert, C., et al. (1995, September 25). "Making men listen." Africa: Women bear the brunt of the AIDS crisis. *Newsweek,* 52.

Bohlen, C. (1995, April 4). Almost anything goes in birth science in Italy. *The New York Times,* p. A14.

Boles, J., & Elifson, K. W. (1994). Sexual identity and HIV: The male prostitute. *Journal of Sex Research, 31,* 39–46.

Boodman, S. (1993, April 8). A doctor's story: A firm belief that "What goes around comes around." *The Washington Post,* p. A16.

Bosanko, D. (1995, September). Abortion's slow decline. *American Demographics,* 20–22.

Boskind-White, M., & White, W. C. (1986). Bulmariexia: A historical-sociocultural perspective. In K. D. Brownell & J. P. Foreyt (Eds.), *Handbook of eating disorders: Physiology, psychology, and treatment of obesity, anorexia, and bulimia* (pp. 353–378). New York: Basic Books.

Bostick, R. M., et al. (1994). Predictors of cancer prevention attitudes and participation in cancer screening examinations. *Preventive Medicine: An International Journal Devoted to Practice and Theory, 23* (6), 816–826.

Boston Women's Health Book Collective. (1992). *The new our bodies, ourselves.* New York: Simon & Schuster.

Boswell, J. (1990). Sexual and ethical categories in premodern Europe. In D. P. McWhirter, et al. (Eds.), *Homosexuality/heterosexuality: Concepts of sexual orientation* (pp. 15–31). New York: Oxford University Press.

Both-Orthman, B., et al. (1988). Menstrual cycle phase: Related changes in appetite in patients with premenstrual syndrome and in control subjects. *American Journal of Psychiatry, 145,* 628–631.

Boulton, M., et al. (1992). The sexual behaviour of bisexual men in relation to HIV transmission. *AIDS Care, 4,* 165–175.

Bowie, W. R. (1990). Approach to men with urethritis and urologic complications of sexually transmitted diseases. *Medical Clinics of North America, 74,* 1543–1557.

Bowlby, J. (1969). *Attachment and loss* (Vol. 1). New York: Basic Books.

Boyer, D. (1989). Male prostitution and homosexual identity [Special issue: Gay and lesbian youth: I]. *Journal of Homosexuality, 17,* 151–184.

Bozzette, S. A., et al. (1995). A randomized trial of three anti-pneumocystis agents in patients with advanced human immunodeficiency virus infection. *New England Journal of Medicine, 332,* 693–699.

Brady, E. C., et al. (1991). Date rape: Expectations, avoidance strategies, and attitudes toward victims. *Journal of Social Psychology, 131,* 427–429.

Brandt, A. M. (1985). *No magic bullet: A social history of venereal disease in the United States since 1880.* New York: Oxford University Press.

Breast fears fade. (1993, November). *Prevention,* 19–20.

Brecher, E. M, and the Editors of Consumer Reports Books. (1984). *Love, sex, and aging.* Boston: Little, Brown.

Breslow, N. (1989). Sources of confusion in the study and treatment of sadomasochism. *Journal of Social Behavior and Personality, 4,* 263–274.

Breslow, N., et al. (1985). On the prevalence and roles of females in the sadomasochistic subculture: Report on an empirical study. *Archives of Sexual Behavior, 14,* 303–317.

Breslow, N., et al. (1986). Comparisons among heterosexual, bisexual and homosexual male sadomasochists. *Journal of Homosexuality, 13,* 83–107.

Bretl, D. J., & Cantor, J. (1988). The portrayal of men and women in U.S. television commercials: A recent content analysis and trends over 15 years. *Sex Roles, 18,* 595–609.

Bretschneider, J., & McCoy, N. (1988). Sexual interest and behavior in healthy 80- to 102-year-olds. *Archives of Sexual Behavior, 17,* 109.

Brewer, J. J. (1982). A history of erotic art as illustrated in the collectors of the Institute for Sex Research (the "Kinsey Institute"). In A. Hoch & H. I. Lief (Eds.), *Sexology: Sexual biology, behavior and therapy* (pp. 318–321). Amsterdam: Excerpta Medica.

Briere, J., & Runtz, M. (1987). Post sexual abuse trauma: Data and implications for clinical practice. *Journal of Interpersonal Violence, 2,* 367–379.

Briere, J., & Runtz, M. (1989). University males' sexual interest in children: Predicting potential indices of "pedophilia" in a nonforensic sample. *Child Abuse and Neglect, 13,* 65–75.

Briselden, A. M., & Hillier, S. L. (1990). Longitudinal study of the biotypes of Gardnerella vaginalis. *Journal of Clinical Microbiology, 28,* 2761–2764.

Brody, J. E. (1989a, January 5). How women can begin to cope with premenstrual syndrome, a biological mystery. *The New York Times,* p. B12.

Brody, J. E. (1989b, July 27). Research casts doubt on need for many Caesarean births as their rate soars. *The New York Times,* p. B5.

Brody, J. E. (1990a, January 23). Scientists trace aberrant sexuality. *The New York Times,* pp. C11, C12.

Brody, J. E. (1990b, August 2). In fight against breast cancer, mammograms are a crucial tool, but not foolproof. *The New York Times,* p. B5.

Brody, J. E. (1992a, April 29). How to outwit a rapist: Rehearse. *The New York Times,* p. C13.

Brody, J. E. (1992b, May 20). Alternatives to hormone therapy after menopause. *The New York Times,* p. C14.

Brody, J. E. (1992c, November 11). PMS is a worldwide phenomenon. *The New York Times,* p. C14.

Brody, J. E. (1993a, July 7). Genital herpes drug found safe for daily use. *The New York Times,* p. C11.

Brody, J. E. (1993b, August 4). A new look at an old quest for sexual stimulants. *The New York Times,* p. C12.

Brody, J. E. (1995a, May 3). Breast scans may indeed help women under 50. *The New York Times,* p. C11.

Brody, J. E. (1995b, July 19). Revolution in treating infertile men turns hopelessness to parenthood. *The New York Times,* p. C8.

Brody, J. E. (1995c, August 30). Hormone replacement therapy for men: When does it help? *The New York Times,* p. C8.

Brooke, J. (1993, January 25). In deception and denial, an epidemic looms: AIDS in Latin America. *The New York Times,* pp. A1, A6.

Brooks, V. R. (1982). Sex differences in student dominance behavior in female and male professors' classrooms. *Sex Roles, 8,* 683–690.

Brooks-Gunn, J., & Furstenberg, F. F. (1989). Adolescent sexual behavior. *American Psychologist, 44,* 249–257.

Brooks-Gunn, J., & Matthews, W. S. (1979). *He and she: How children develop their sex-role identity.* Englewood Cliffs, NJ: Spectrum.

Brooks-Gunn, J., et al. (1986). Physical similarity of and disclosure of menarchal status to friends: Effects of grade and pubertal status. *Journal of Early Adolescence, 6,* 3–14.

Broude, G. J., & Greene, S. J. (1976). Cross-cultural codes on twenty sexual attitudes and practices. *Ethnology, 15,* 409–429.

Brown, R. A. (1994). Romantic love and the spouse selection criteria of male and female Korean college students. *Journal of Social Psychology, 134* (2), 183–189.

Brozan, N. (1991, March 7). Rise in anti-gay crimes is reported in New York. *The New York Times,* p. B3.

Bryant, H., & Brasher, P. (1995). Breast implants and breast cancer—reanalysis of a linkage study. *New England Journal of Medicine, 332,* 1535–1539.

Bryant, J., & Brown, D. (1989). Uses of pornography. In D. Zillmann & J. Bryant (Eds.), *Pornography: Research advances and policy considerations* (pp. 25–55). Hillsdale, NJ: Erlbaum.

Bryson, Y. J., et al. (1995). Clearance of HIV infection in a perinatally infected infant. *New England Journal of Medicine, 332,* 833–838.

Buchanan, M., & Robbins, C. (1990). Early adult psychological consequences for males of adolescent pregnancy and its resolution. *Journal of Youth and Adolescence, 19,* 413–424.

Buffum, J. (1985). Pharmacosexology update: Yohimbine and sexual function. *Journal of Psychoactive Drugs, 17,* 131–132.

Buhaug, H., et al. (1990). Should asymptomatic patients be tested for Chlamydia trachomatis in general practice? *British Journal of General Practice, 40,* 142–145.

Buhrich, N., et al. (1979). Plasma testosterone, serum FSH, and serum LH levels in transvestism. *Archives of Sexual Behavior, 8,* 49–54.

Bullough, V. L. (1990). The Kinsey Scale in historical perspective. In D. P. McWhirter, et al. (Eds.), *Homosexuality/heterosexuality: Concepts of sexual orientation* (pp. 3–14). New York: Oxford University Press.

Bullough, V. L. (1991). Transvestism: A reexamination. *Journal of Psychology and Human Sexuality, 4,* 53–67.

Bullough, V. L., & Weinberg, T. S. (1989). Women married to transvestites: Problems and adjustments. *Journal of Psychology & Human Sexuality, 1,* 83–104.

Bumiller, E. (1990, October 25). Japan's abortion agony: In a country that prohibits the pill, reality collides with religion. *The Washington Post.*

Bumpass, L. (1991). Cited in Pear, R. (1991, December 4). Larger number of new mothers are unmarried. *The New York Times,* p. A20.

Bumpass, L. (1995). Cited in Steinhauer, J. (1995, July 6). No marriage, no apologies. *The New York Times,* pp. C1, C7.

Bumpass, L., et al. (1988, August). *Changing patterns of remarriage.* Paper presented at the meeting of the American Sociological Association, Atlanta, GA.

Burden, D. S. (1986). Single parents and the work setting: The impact of multiple job and home-life responsibilities. *Family Relations, 35,* 37–44.

Burgess, A. W., & Hartman, C. R. (1986). *Sexual exploitation of patients by health professionals.* New York: Praeger.

Burgess, A. W., & Holmstrom, L. L. (1974). Rape trauma syndrome. *American Journal of Psychiatry, 131,* 981–986.

Burkhart, B., & Fromuth, M. E. (1991). Individual psychological and social psychological understandings of sexual coercion. In E. Grauerholz & M. A. Koralewski (Eds.), *Sexual coercion: A sourcebook on its nature, causes, and prevention* (pp. 7–89). Lexington, MA: Lexington Books.

Burruss, L. (1988). *The battle of the books: Library censorship in the public schools, 1950–1985.* Metuchen, NJ: Scarecrow Press.

Burt, M. R. (1980). Cultural myths and supports for rape. *Journal of Personality and Social Psychology, 38,* 217–230.

Buss, D. M. (1994). *The evolution of desire: Strategies of human mating.* New York: Basic Books.

Buxton, A. P. (1994). *The other side of the closet.* New York: Wiley.

Byers, E. S., & Lewis, K. (1988). Dating couples' disagreements over the desired level of sexual intimacy. *Journal of Sex Research, 24,* 15–29.

Byrnes, J., & Takahira, S. (1993). Explaining gender differences on SAT-math items. *Developmental Psychology, 29,* 805–810.

Caceres, C. F., & van-Griensven, G. J. P. (1994). Male homosexual transmission of HIV-1. *AIDS, 8* (8), 1051–1061.

Cado, S., & Leitenberg, H. (1990). Guilt reactions to sexual fantasies during intercourse. *Archives of Sexual Behavior, 19,* 49–64.

Calderone, M. S., & Johnson, E. W. (1989). *Family book about sexuality* (rev. ed.). New York: Harper & Row.

Calhoun, K. S., & Atkeson, B. M. (1991). *Treatment of rape victims: Facilitating social adjustment.* New York: Pergamon Press.

Cameron, P., et al. (1986). Child molestation and homosexuality. *Psychological Reports, 58,* 327–337.

Campbell, C. A. (1991). Prostitution, AIDS, and preventive health behavior. *Social Science and Medicine, 32,* 1367–1378.

Campbell, S. B., & Cohn, J. F. (1991). Prevalence and correlates of postpartum depression in first-time mothers. *Journal of Abnormal Psychology, 100,* 594–599.

Cappella, J. N., & Palmer, M. T. (1990). Attitude similarity, relational history, and attraction: The mediating effects of kinesic and vocal behaviors. *Communication Monographs, 5,* 161–183.

Carani, C., et al. (1990). Effects of androgen treatment in impotent men with normal and low levels of free testosterone. *Archives of Sexual Behavior, 19,* 223–234.

Carey, J., et al. (1992). Effectiveness of latex condoms as a barrier to human immunodeficiency virus-sized particles under conditions of simulated use. *Sexually Transmitted Diseases, 19,* 230–234.

Carlson, M. (1990, July 9). Abortion's hardest cases. *Time,* 22–26.

Carmignani, G., et al. (1987). Cavernous artery revascularization in vasculogenic impotence: New simplified technique. *Urology,* 23–26.

Carnes, P. (1983). *The sexual addiction.* Minneapolis: Comp-Care Publications.

Carper, A. (1993, October 19). Questions about safety. *New York Newsday,* p. 15.

Carreran, M. (1981). *Sex: The facts, the acts and your feelings.* New York: Crown.

Carrier, J. M. (1986). Childhood cross-gender behavior and adult homosexuality. *Archives of Sexual Behavior, 15,* 89–93.

Carson, S. (1988). Sex selection: The ultimate in family planning. *Fertility and Sterility, 50,* 16–19.

Cartwright, R. D., et al. (1983). The traditional-liberated woman dimension: Social stereotype and self-concept. *Journal of Personality and Social Psychology, 44,* 581–588.

Carvajal, D. (1995). Oldest profession's newest home. *The New York Times,* pp. L29, L32.

A case of too much candor. (1994, December 19). *U.S. News & World Report,* 31.

Cash, T. F., & Duncan, N. C. (1984). Physical attractiveness stereotyping among black American college students. *Journal of Social Psychology, 122,* 71–77.

Castro, K. G., et al. (1988). Transmission of HIV in Belle Glade, Florida: Lessons for other communities in the United States. *Science, 239,* 193–197.

Castro, J. (1992, January 20). Sexual harassment: A guide. *Time,* 37.

Catalan, J., et al. (1990). Couples referred to a sexual dysfunction clinic: Psychological and physical morbidity. *British Journal of Psychiatry, 156,* 61–67.

Catalona, W. J., et al. (1993). Detection of organ-confined prostate cancer is increased through prostate-specific antigen-based screening. *Journal of the American Medical Association, 270,* 948–954.

Catania, J. A., et al. (1992a). Coping with death anxiety: Help-seeking and social support among gay men with various HIV diagnoses. *AIDS, 6,* 999–1005.

Catania, J. A., et al. (1992b). Prevalence of AIDS-related risk factors and condom use in the United States. *Science, 258,* 1101–1106.

Catania, J. A., et al. (1991). Changes in condom use among homosexual men in San Francisco. *Health Psychology, 10,* 190–199.

Cates, W., Jr., & Stone, K. M. (1992a). Family planning, sexually transmitted diseases, and contraceptive choice: A literature update. *Family Planning Perspectives, 24,* 75–84.

Cates, W., Jr., & Stone, K. M. (1992b). Family planning, sexually transmitted diseases, and contraceptive choice: A literature update—Part II. *Family Planning Perspectives, 24,* 122–127.

Cates, W., Jr., & Wasserheit, J. N. (1991). Genital chlamydial infections: Epidemiology and reproductive sequelae. *American Journal of Obstetrics and Gynecology, 164,* 1171–1181.

CBS News. (1991, May 22). *48 hours: For better or worse.*

Celis, W. (1991, January 2). Students trying to draw line between sex and an assault. *The New York Times,* pp. 1, B8.

Centers for Disease Control. (1985). Chlamydia trachomatis infections. *Morbidity and Mortality Weekly Report, 34,* 53.

Centers for Disease Control. (1988). Leads from the *MMWR/Morbidity and Mortality Weekly Report* (Vol. 37/Nos. 7, 9; 1988): Condoms for prevention of sexually transmitted diseases. *Journal of the American Medical Association, 259,* 1925–1927.

Centers for Disease Control. (1989a). Summaries of identifiable diseases in the United States.

Centers for Disease Control. (1989b). Treatment guidelines for sexually transmitted diseases. *Morbidity and Mortality Weekly Report, 38,* No. S-8.

Centers for Disease Control. (1990a). Progress toward achieving the 1990 objectives for the nation for sexually transmitted diseases. *Morbidity and Mortality Weekly Report 39,* 53–57.

Centers for Disease Control. (1990b). Update: Acquired immunodeficiency syndrome—United States, 1989. *Journal of the American Medical Association, 263,* 1191–1192.

Centers for Disease Control, Division of Sexually Transmitted Diseases/HIV Prevention. (1991b). *Annual Report.* Atlanta: Author.

Centers for Disease Control. (1992, January). *HIV infection and AIDS: Are you at risk?* Atlanta: Author.

Centers for Disease Control. (1993a). Evaluation of surveillance for *Chlamydia trachomatis* infections in the United States, 1987 to 1991. *Mortality and Morbidity Weekly Report, 42* (SS-3), 21–27.

Centers for Disease Control. (1993b). Selected behaviors that increase risk for HIV infection, other sexually transmitted diseases, and unintended pregnancy among high school students—United States, 1991. *Mortality and Morbidity Weekly Report, 41,* 945–950.

Centers for Disease Control. (1993c). Sexual risk behaviors of STD clinic patients before and after Earvin "Magic" Johnson's HIV-infection announcement—Maryland, 1991–1992. *Mortality and Morbidity Weekly Report, 42,* 46–48.

Centers for Disease Control. (1993d). Update: Barrier protection against HIV infection and other sexually transmitted diseases. *Mortality and Morbidity Weekly Report, 42,* 589–591, 597.

Centers for Disease Control. (1993e). Update: Investigations of persons treated by HIV-infected health-care workers—United States. *Mortality and Morbidity Weekly Report, 42,* 329–331, 337.

Centers for Disease Control. (1993f). Update: Mortality attributable to HIV infection/AIDS among persons aged 25–44 years—United States, 1990 and 1991. *Mortality and Morbidity Weekly Report, 42,* 481–486.

Centers for Disease Control and Prevention. (1995). *HIV/AIDS surveillance report: U.S. HIV and AIDS cases reported through December 1994, 6* (2).

Centers for Disease Control. AIDS Hotline Communication. (1996). April 1, 1996.

The cervical cancer virus. (1995, September). *Discover,* 24–26.

Chadda, R. K., & Ahuja, N. (1990). Dhat syndrome: A sex neurosis of the Indian subcontinent. *British Journal of Psychiatry, 156,* 577–579.

Chan, C. (1992). Cultural considerations in counseling Asian American lesbians and gay men. In S. Dworkin & F. Gutierrez (Eds.), *Counseling gay men and lesbians: Journey to the end of the rainbow.* Alexandria, VA: American Association for Counseling and Development.

Chan, D. W. (1990). Sex knowledge, attitudes, and experiences of Chinese medical students in Hong Kong. *Archives of Sexual Behavior, 19,* 73–93.

Chance of breast cancer is figured at 1 in 8. (1992, September 27). *The New York Times,* p. A30.

Charny, I. W., & Parnass, S. (1995). The impact of extramarital relationships on the continuation of marriages. *Journal of Sex and Marital Therapy, 21,* 100–115.

Cheating going out of style but sex is popular as ever. (1993, October 19). *New York Newsday,* p. 2.

Check, J. V. P., & Malamuth, N. M. (1983). Sex-role stereotyping and reactions to depictions of stranger versus acquaintance rape. *Journal of Personality and Social Psychology, 45,* 344–356.

Chideya, F., et al. (1993, August 30). Endangered family. *Newsweek,* pp. 17–27.

Chin, P. (1989). Death discloses Billy Tipton's strange secret: He was a she. *People Weekly, 31,* 95–96.

Chira, S. (1992, February 12). Bias against girls is found rife in schools, with lasting damage. *The New York Times,* pp. A1, A23.

Choi, P. Y. (1992). The psychological benefits of physical exercise: Implications for women and the menstrual cycle. [Special issue: The menstrual cycle]. *Journal of Reproductive and Infant Psychology, 10,* 111–115.

Christensen, C. (1995). Prescribed masturbation in sex therapy: A critique. *Journal of Sex and Marital Therapy, 21* (2), 87–99.

Clapper, R. L., & Lipsitt, L. P. (1991). A retrospective study of risk-taking and alcohol-mediated unprotected intercourse. *Journal of Substance Abuse, 3,* 91–96.

Clark, M. S., et al. (1989). Keeping track of needs and inputs of friends and strangers. *Personality and Social Psychology Bulletin, 15,* 533–542.

Clumeck, N. (1995). Primary prophylaxis against opportunistic infections in patients with AIDS. *New England Journal of Medicine, 332,* 739–740.

Cobb, J. (1996, January). The genes of 1995. *Discover,* 36.

Cobb, M., & Jallon, J. M. (1990). Pheromones, mate recognition and courtship stimulation in the Drosophila melanogaster species sub-group. *Animal Behaviour, 39,* 1058–1067.

Cochran, W. G., et al. (1953). Statistical problems of the Kinsey Report. *Journal of the American Statistical Association, 48,* 673–716.

Cohen, D., et al. (1991). *Journal of Sex Research, 28,* (1), 139–144.

Cohen, J. B. (1990, December 13). *A crosscutting perspective on the epidemiology of HIV infection in women [abstract].* Paper presented at the Women and AIDS Conference, Washington, DC.

Cohen, J. (1993). AIDS research: The mood is uncertain. *Science, 260,* 1254–1255.

Cohn, L. D., et al. (1995). Risk-perception: Differences between adolescents and adults. *Health Psychology, 14,* 217–222.

Colditz, G. A., et al. (1993). Family history, age, and risk of breast cancer: Prospective data from the nurses' health study. *Journal of the American Medical Association, 270,* 338–343.

Colditz, G. A., et al. (1995). The use of estrogens and progestins and the risk of breast cancer in postmenopausal women. *New England Journal of Medicine, 332,* 1589–1593.

Cole, C. J. (1995, August). Cited in "Sex, the single lizard, and the missing parent." *National Geographic.*

Cole, H. M. (Ed.). (1989). Intrauterine devices. *Journal of the American Medical Association, 261,* 2127–2130.

Cole, S. S. (1988). Women's sexuality, and disabilities. *Women and Therapy, 7,* 277–294.

Coleman, E. (1986, July). Sexual compulsion vs. sexual addiction: The debate continues. *SIECUS Report,* 7–10.

Coleman, E. (1989). The development of male prostitution activity among gay and bisexual adolescents [Special issue: Gay and lesbian youth]. *Journal of Homosexuality, 17,* 131–149.

Coleman, M., & Ganong, L. H. (1985). Love and sex role stereotypes: Do macho men and feminine women make better lovers? *Journal of Personality and Social Psychology, 49,* 170–176.

Coles, C. (1994). Critical periods for prenatal alcohol exposure: Evidence from animal and human studies. *Alcohol Health and Research World, 18* (1), 22–29.

Coles, R., & Stokes, G. (1985). *Sex and the American teenager.* New York: Harper & Row.

Collaer, M. L., & Hines, M. (1995). Human behavioral sex differences: A role for gonadal hormones during early development? *Psychological Bulletin, 118,* 55–107.

Collins, G., & Kinder, B. (1984). Adjustment following surgical implantation of a penile prosthesis: A critical overview. *Journal of Sex and Marital Therapy, 10,* 255–271.

Collins, N. L., & Miller, L. C. (1994). Self-disclosure and liking: A meta-analytic review. *Psychological Bulletin, 116,* 457–475.

Comstock, A. (1967). *Traps for the young* (Reprint). R. Bremner, Ed. Cambridge, MA: Belnap Press.

Concorde Coordinating Committee (1994). Concorde: MRC/ANRS randomised double-blind controlled trials of immediate and deferred zidovudine in symptom-free HIV infection. *Lancet, 343,* 871–881.

Condon, J. W., & Crano, W. D. (1988). Inferred evaluation and the relation between attitude similarity and interpersonal attraction. *Journal of Personality and Social Psychology, 54,* 789–797.

Connor, E. M., et al. (1994). Reduction of maternal–infant transmission of human immunodeficiency virus type 1 with zidovudine treatment. *New England Journal of Medicine, 331,* 1173–1180.

Constantine, L., & Constantine, J. (1973). *Group marriage.* New York: Macmillan.

Consumer's Union. (1995, May). Consumer reports: How reliable are condoms? America Online.

Cooper, A. J. (1986). Progestogens in the treatment of male sex offenders: A review. *Canadian Journal of Psychiatry, 31,* 73–79.

Cooper, A. J., et al. (1990). A female sex offender with multiple paraphilias: A psychologic, physiologic (laboratory sexual arousal) and endocrine case study. *Canadian Journal of Psychiatry, 35,* 334–337.

Cooper, D. A., et al. (1993). Zidovudine in persons with asymptomatic HIV infection and CD4 cell counts greater than 400 per cubic millimeter. *New England Journal of Medicine, 329,* 297–303.

Corea, G. (1985). *The mother machine: Reproductive technologies from artificial semination to artificial wombs.* New York: Harper & Row.

Coronel, S., & Roscan, N. (1993). For the boys. *Ms., 4* (3), 10–15.

Cosgray, R. E., et al. (1991). Death from auto-erotic asphyxiation in a long-term psychiatric setting. *Perspectives in Psychiatric Care, 27,* 21–24.

Court, 9–0, makes sex harassment easier to prove. (1993, November 10). *The New York Times,* pp. A1, A22.

Cox, D. J. (1988). Incidence and nature of male genital exposure behavior as reported by college women. *Journal of Sex Research, 24,* 227–234.

Craig, M. E., et al. (1989). Verbal coercive sexual behavior among college students. *Archives of Sexual Behavior, 18,* 421–434.

Crews, D. (1994). Animal sexuality. *Scientific American, 270* (1), 108–114.

Crichton, S. (1993, October 25). Sexual correctness: Has it gone too far? *Newsweek,* 52–56.

Cronin, A. (1993, June 27). Two viewfinders, two views of Gay America. *The New York Times,* Section 4, p. 10.

Crowe, L. C., & George, W. H. (1989). Alcohol and human sexuality: Review and integration. *Psychological Bulletin, 105,* 374–386.

Crum, C., & Ellner, P. (1985). Chlamydia infections: Making the diagnosis. *Contemporary Obstetrics and Gynecology, 25,* 153–159, 163, 165, 168.

Cunningham, F. G., & Levens, J. J. (1995). Childbearing among older women—the message is cautiously optimistic. *New England Journal of Medicine, 333* (15), 1002–1004.

Cunningham, G., et al. (1989). Testosterone replacement with transdermal therapeutic systems. *Journal of the American Medical Association, 261,* 2525–2531.

Cunningham, M. R., et al. (1995). "Their ideas of beauty are, on the whole, the same as ours": Consistency and variability in the cross-cultural perception of female physical attractiveness. *Journal of Personality and Social Psychology, 68* (2), 261–279.

Curtis, R. C., & Miller, K. (1986). Believing another likes or dislikes you: Behavior making the beliefs come true. *Journal of Personality and Social Psychology, 51,* 284–290.

Cutler, W. B., & Preti, G. (1986). Human axillary secretions influence women's menstrual cycles: The role of donor extract from men. *Hormones and Behavior, 20,* 463–473.

Cutrona, C. E. (1983). Causal attributions and perinatal depression. *Journal of Abnormal Psychology, 92,* 161–172.

Dabbs, J. M., Jr., & Morris, R. (1990). Testosterone, social class, and antisocial behavior in a sample of 4,462 men. *Psychological Science, 1,* 1–3.

Dahl, S. (1989). Acute response to rape: A PTSD variant [Special issue: Traumatic stress: Empirical studies from Norway]. *Acta Psychiatrica Scandinavica, 80* (Suppl. 355), 56–62.

Danner, S. A., et al. (1995). A short-term study of the safety, pharmacokinetics, and efficacy of ritonavir, an inhibitor of HIV-1 protease, *New England Journal of Medicine, 333,* 1528–1533.

Darabi, K. F., et al. (1986). Hispanic adolescent fertility. *Hispanic Journal of Behavioral Sciences, 8,* 157–171.

Darling, C. A., & Davidson, J. K., Sr. (1986). Coitally active university students: Sexual behaviors, concerns, and challenges. *Adolescence, 21,* 403–419.

Darling, C. A., et al. (1991). The female sexual response revisited: Understanding the multiorgasmic experience in women. *Archives of Sexual Behavior, 20,* 527–540.

Darling, C. A., et al. (1992). The mystique of first intercourse among college youth: The role of partners, contraceptive practices, and psychological reactions. *Journal of Youth and Adolescence, 21,* 97–117.

DATTA (Diagnostic and Theapeutic Technology Assessment). (1988). Questions and answers: Penile implants for erectile impotence. *Journal of the American Medical Association, 260,* 997–1000.

D'Augelli, A. R. (1992a). Lesbian and gay male undergraduates' experiences of harassment and fear on campus. *Journal of Interpersonal Violence, 7,* 383–395.

D'Augelli, A. R. (1992b). Sexual behavior patterns of gay university men: Implications for preventing HIV infection. *Journal of American College Health, 41,* 25–29.

Davenport, W. (1965). Sexual patterns and their regulation in a society of the Southwest Pacific. In F. A. Beach (Ed.), *Sex and behavior.* New York: Wiley.

Davenport, W. (1977). Sex in cross-cultural perspective. In F. Beach (Ed.), *Human sexuality in four perspectives* (pp. 115–163). Baltimore: Johns Hopkins University Press.

Davidson, J. K., & Hoffman, L. E. (1986). Sexual fantasies and sexual satisfaction: An empirical analysis of erotic thought. *Journal of Sex Research, 22,* 184–205.

Davidson, K. J., et al. (1989). The role of the Grafenberg spot and female ejaculation in the female orgasmic response: An empirical analysis. *Journal of Sex and Marital Therapy, 15,* 102–119.

Davidson, N. E. (1995). Hormone-replacement therapy—breast versus heart versus bone. *New England Journal of Medicine, 332,* 1638–1639.

Davies, P. T., & Cummings, E. M. (1994). Marital conflict and child adjustment. *Psychological Bulletin, 116,* 387–411.

Davis, J. A., & Smith, T. (1987). *General social surveys, 1972–1987: Cumulative data.* Storrs, CT: University of Connecticut, Roper Center for Public Opinion Research.

Davison, G. C. (1977). Elimination of a sadistic fantasy by a client-controlled counterconditioning technique. In J. Fischer & H. Gochios (Eds.), *Handbook of behavior therapy with sexual problems.* New York: Pergamon Press.

Dawes, R. M. (1989). Statistical criteria for establishing a truly false consensus effect. *Journal of Experimental Social Psychology, 25,* 1–17.

Day, N. L., & Richardson, G. A. (1994). Comparative teratogenicity of alcohol and other drugs. *Alcohol Health and Research World, 18* (1), 42–48.

Dean, C. W., & deBruyn-Kops, E. (1982). *The crime and consequences of rape.* Springfield, IL: Thomas.

DeAngelis, T. (1994). Educators reveal keys to success in classroom. *APA Monitor, 25* (1), 39–40.

Deaux, K. (1985). Sex and gender. *Annual Review of Psychology, 36,* 49–81.

Deaux, K., & Lewis, L. L. (1983). Assessment of gender stereotypes: Methodology and components. *Psychological Documents, 13,* 25 (Ms. No. 2583).

Deepening shame: A *Newsweek* investigation into the scandal that is rocking the navy. (1992, August 10). *Newsweek,* 30–36.

Defense dept. suspends its policy on homosexuals. (1993, October 8). *The New York Times,* p. A25.

Dekker, J. (1993). Inhibited male orgasm. In W. O'Donohue & J. H. Geer (Eds.), *Handbook of sexual dysfunctions: Assessment and treatment* (pp. 279–301). Boston: Allyn & Bacon.

Delgado, J. (1969). *Physical control of the mind.* New York: Harper & Row.

Del Priore, G., et al. (1995). Risk of ovarian cancer after treatment for infertility. *New England Journal of Medicine, 332,* 1300.

de Luca, R. V., et al. (1992). Group treatment for child sexual abuse [Special issue: Violence and its aftermath]. *Canadian Psychology, 33,* 168–179.

D'Emilion, J., & Freedman, E. B. (1988). *Intimate matters: A history of sexuality in America.* New York: Harper & Row.

Denny, N., et al. (1984). Sex differences in sexual needs and desires. *Archives of Sexual Behavior, 13,* 233–245.

DeParle, J. (1993, July 14). Big rise in birth outside wedlock. *The New York Times,* pp. A1, A14.

de Raad, B., & Doddema-Winsemius, M. (1992). Factors in the assortment of human mates: Differential preferences in Germany and the Netherlands. *Personality and Individual Differences, 13,* 103–114.

de Schampheleire, D. (1990). MMPI characteristics of professional prostitutes: A cross-cultural replication. *Journal of Personality Assessment, 54,* 343–350.

Desmond, A. M. (1994). Adolescent pregnancy in the United States: Not a minority issue. *Health Care for Women International, 15* (4), 325–331.

Deutsch, F. M., et al. (1987). What is in a smile? *Psychology of Women Quarterly, 11,* 341–352.

DeWitt, K. (1991, October). The evolving concept of sexual harassment. *The New York Times.*

de Young, M. (1982). *The sexual victimization of children.* Jefferson, NC: McFarland & Company.

Diamond, M. (1993). Homosexuality and bisexuality in different populations. *Archives of Sexual Behavior, 22,* 291–310.

DiClemente, R. J. (1992). Epidemiology of AIDS, HIV prevalence, and HIV incidence among adolescents. *Journal of School Health, 62,* 325–330.

Dick-Read, G. (1944). *Childbirth without fear: The principles and practices of natural childbirth.* New York: Harper & Bros.

Dietz, P. E., et al. (1990). The sexually sadistic criminal and his offenses. *Bulletin of the American Academy of Psychiatry and the Law, 18,* 163–178.

Dindia, K., & Allen, M. (1992). Sex differences in self-disclosure: A meta-analysis. *Psychological Bulletin, 112,* 106–124.

Discovery Journal: The Lynchburg Story. (1994, July 2, 9–10 P.M.). *Discovery Channel.*

Disease discovered Europe first? (1992, November 24). *New York Newsday,* p. 49.

Dixon, J. (1991). Feminist reforms of sexual coercion. In E. Grauerholz & M. A. Koralewski (Eds.), *Sexual coercion: A sourcebook on its nature, causes, and prevention* (pp. 161–171). Lexington, MA: Lexington Books.

Doctors tie male mentality to shorter life span. (1995, June 14). *The New York Times,* p. C14.

Donnerstein, E. (1980). Aggressive erotica and violence against women. *Journal of Personality and Social Psychology, 39,* 269–277.

Donnerstein, E., & Berkowitz, L. (1981). Victim reactions in aggressive erotic films as a factor in violence against women. *Journal of Personality and Social Psychology, 41,* 710–724.

Donnerstein, E. I., & Linz, D. G. (1987). *The question of pornography.* New York: The Free Press.

Donoghue, D. (1995, August 20). The politics of homosexuality. *The New York Times Book Review,* pp. 3, 20.

Doorn, C. D., et al. (1994). Cross-gender identity in transvestites and male transsexuals. *Archives of Sexual Behavior, 23* (2), 185–201.

Douglas, J. M., Jr. (1990). Molluscum contagiosum. In K. K. Holmes, et al. (Eds.), *Sexually transmitted diseases* (2nd ed.) (pp. 443–448). New York: McGraw-Hill.

Dow, M. G. T., & Gallagher, J. (1989). A controlled study of combined hormonal and psychological treatment for sexual unresponsiveness in women. *British Journal of Clinical Psychology, 28,* 201–212.

Drapers, P. (1975). !Kung women: Contrasts in sexual egalitarianism in foraging and sedentary contexts. In R. R. Reiter (Ed.), *Toward an anthropology of women* (pp. 77–109). New York: Monthly Review Press.

Dube, R., & Hebert, M. (1988). Sexual abuse of children 12 years of age: A review of 511 cases. *Child Abuse and Neglect, 12,* 321–330.

Dubin, S. C. (1992). *Arresting images: Impolitic art and uncivil actions.* New York: Routledge.

Duffy, S. M., & Rusbult, C. E. (1985/1986). Satisfaction and commitment in homosexual and heterosexual relationships. *Journal of Homosexuality, 12,* 1–24.

Dunlap, D. W. (1994, December 21). *The New York Times,* p. 21.

Dunlap, D. W. (1995, May 1). Support for gay adoptions seems to wane. *The New York Times,* p. A13.

Dunn, M. E., & Trost, J. E. (1989). Male multiple orgasms: A descriptive study. *Archives of Sexual Behavior, 18,* 377–387.

DuRant, R. H., & Sanders, J. M. (1989). Sexual behavior and contraceptive risk taking among sexually active adolescent females. *Journal of Adolescent Health Care, 10,* 1–19.

DuRant, R. H., et al. (1990). Contraceptive behavior among sexually active Hispanic adolescents. *Journal of Adolescent Health Care, 11,* 490–496.

Durfee, M. (1989). Prevention of child sexual abuse. *Psychiatric Clinics of North America, 12,* 445–453.

Dworkin, J., et al. (1991). Concern about AIDS among hospital physicians, nurses and social workers. *Social Science Medicine, 33,* 239–248.

Dwyer, M. (1988). Exhibitionism/voyeurism. *Journal of Social Work and Human Sexuality, 7,* 101–112.

Dziech, B. W., & Weiner, L. (1984). *The lecherous professor: Sexual harassment on campus.* Boston: Beacon Press.

Eckert, E. D., et al. (1986). Homosexuality in monozygotic twins reared apart. *British Journal of Psychiatry, 148,* 421–425.

Edgley, C. (1989). Commercial sex: Pornography, prostitution, and advertising. In K. McKinney & S. Sprecher (Eds.), *Human sexuality: The societal and interpersonal context* (pp. 370–424). Norwood, NJ: Ablex Publishing Corporation.

Edlin, B. R., et al. (1994). Intersecting epidemics: Crack cocaine use and HIV infection among inner-city young adults. *New England Journal of Medicine, 331,* 1422–1427.

Edmonson, B. (1988). Disability and sexual adjustment. In V. B. Van Hasselt, et al. (Eds.), *Handbook of developmental and physical disabilities* (pp. 91–106). New York: Pergamon Press.

Eggert, A. K., & Muller, J. K. (1989). Mating success of pheromone-emitting necrophorus males: Do attracted females discriminate against resource owners? *Behaviour, 110,* 248–257.

Ehrhardt, A. A. (1992). Trends in sexual behavior and the HIV pandemic. *American Journal of Public Health, 82,* 1459–1461.

Eisen, M., & Zellman, G. (1987). Changes in incidence of sexual intercourse of unmarried teenagers following a community-based sex education program. *Journal of Sex Research, 23,* 527–544.

Ellis, A. (1962). *Reason and emotion in psychotherapy.* New York: Lyle Stuart.

Ellis A. (1977). The basic clinical theory of rational–emotive therapy. In A. Ellis & R. Grieger (eds.), *Handbook of rational–emotive therapy.* New York: Springer.

Ellis, B. J., & Symons, D. (1990). Sex differences in sexual fantasy: An evolutionary psychological approach. *Journal of Sex Research, 27,* 527–555.

Ellis, L., & Ames, M. A. (1987). Neurohormonal functioning and sexual orientation: A theory of homosexuality–heterosexuality. *Psychological Bulletin, 101,* 233–258.

Ellis, L., et al. (1987). Sexual orientation as a continuous variable: A comparison between the sexes. *Archives of Sexual Behavior, 16,* 523–529.

Elmer-Dewitt, P. (1991, September 30). Making babies. *Time,* 56–63.

Ember, C. R., & Ember, M. (1990). *Anthropology* (6th ed., instructor's edition). Englewood Cliffs, NJ: Prentice-Hall.

English, P. B., & Eskenazi, B. (1992). Reinterpreting the effects of maternal smoking on infant birthweight and perinatal mortality: A multivariate approach to birthweight standardization. *International Journal of Epidemiology, 21,* 1097–1105.

Erel, O., & Burman, B. (1995). Interrelatedness of marital relations and parent–child relations: A meta-analytic review. *Psychological Bulletin, 118,* 108–132.

Erlanger, S. (1991, July 14). A plague awaits. *The New York Times Magazine,* pp. 24, 26, 49, 53.

Eron, J. J., et al. (1995). Treatment with lamivudine, zidovudine, or both in HIV-positive patients with 200 to 500 CD4+ cells per cubic millimeter. *New England Journal of Medicine, 333,* 1662–1669.

Eskenazi, G. (1990, June 3). The male athlete and sexual assault. *The New York Times,* pp. L1, L4.

Etaugh, C., & Rathus, S. A. (1995). *The world of children.* Fort Worth, TX: Harcourt Brace College Publishers.

Everaerd, W. (1993). Male erectile disorder. In W. O'Donohue & J. H. Geer (Eds.), *Handbook of sexual dysfunctions: Assessment and treatment* (pp. 201–224). Boston: Allyn & Bacon.

Everitt, B. J. (1990). Sexual motivation: A neural and behavioural analysis of the mechanisms underlying appetitive and copulatory responses of male rats. *Neuroscience and Biobehavioral Reviews, 14,* 217–232.

Everson, S. A., et al. (1995). Effects of surgical menopause on psychological characteristics and lipid levels: The healthy women study. *Health Psychology, 14,* 435–443.

Exner, J. E., et al. (1977). Some psychological characteristics of prostitutes. *Journal of Personality Assessment, 41,* 474–485.

Ezzell, C. (1993, July). On borrowed time: Long-term survivors of HIV-1 infection. *Journal of NIH Research,* 77–82.

Faller, K. C. (1989a). The role relationship between victim and perpetrator as a predictor of characteristics of intrafamilial sexual abuse. *Child and Adolescent Social Work Journal, 6,* 217–229.

Faller, K. C. (1989b). Why sexual abuse? An exploration of the intergenerational hypothesis. *Child Abuse and Neglect, 13,* 543–548.

Fallon, A. E., & Rozin, P. (1985). Sex differences in perceptions of desirable body shape. *Journal of Abnormal Psychology, 94,* 102–105.

Faludi, S. (1993, October 25). Whose hype? *Newsweek,* 61.

Farley, A. U., et al. (1990). The syphilis epidemic in Connecticut: Relationship to drug use and prostitution. *Sexually Transmitted Diseases, 17,* 163–168.

Fay, R. E., et al. (1989). Prevalence and patterns of same-gender sexual contact among men. *Science, 243,* 338–348.

Federal Bureau of Investigation. (1991). *Uniform crime reports.* Washington, DC: U.S. Department of Justice.

Federman, D. D. (1994). Life without estrogen. *New England Journal of Medicine, 331,* 1088–1089.

Feingold, A. (1991). Sex differences in the effects of similarity and physical attractiveness on opposite-sex attraction. *Basic and Applied Social Psychology, 12,* 357–367.

Feingold, A. (1994). Gender differences in personality: A meta-analysis. *Psychological Bulletin, 116,* 429–456.

Felsman, D., et al. (1987). Control theory in dealing with adolescent sexuality and pregnancy. *Journal of Sex Education and Therapy, 13,* 15–16.

Feng, T. (1993). Substance abuse in pregnancy. *Current Opinions in Obstetrics and Gynecology, 5,* 16–23.

Fenichel, O. (1945). *The psychoanalytic theory of neurosis.* New York: Norton.

Fensterheimn, H., & Kantor, J. S. (1980). Behavioral approach to sexual disorders. In B. Wolman & J. Money (Eds.), *Handbook of human sexuality.* Englewood Cliffs, NJ: Prentice-Hall.

Ferrante, C. L., et al. (1988). Image of women in television advertising. *Journal of Broadcasting and Electronic Media, 32,* 231–237.

Ferree, M. M. (1991). The gender division of labor in two-earner marriages. *Journal of Family Issues, 12* (2), 158–180.

Fetal heart rate patterns. (1995). Technical bulletin no. 207. Washington, DC: American College of Obstetricians and Gynecologists.

Fichner-Rathus, L. (1995). *Understanding art* (4th ed.). Englewood Cliffs, NJ: Prentice Hall.

Finkelhor, D. (1984). *Child sexual abuse: Theory and research.* New York: The Free Press.

Finkelhor, D. (1990). Early and long-term effects of child sexual abuse: An update. *Professional Psychology: Research and Practice, 21,* 325–330.

Finkelhor, D., & Hotaling, G. T. (1984). Sexual abuse in the National Incidence Study of Child Abuse and Neglect: An appraisal. *Child Abuse and Neglect, 8,* 22–33.

Finkelhor, D., & Russell, D. (1984). Women as perpetrators: Review of the evidence. In D. Finkelhor (Ed.), *Child sexual abuse: Theory and research.* New York: The Free Press.

Finkelhor, D., & Yllo, K. (1982). Rape in marriage: A sociological view. In D. Finkelhor, et al. (Eds.), *The dark side of families: Current family violence research* (pp. 119–130). Beverly Hills, CA: Sage.

Finkelhor, D., et al. (1990). Sexual abuse in a national survey of adult men and women: Prevalence, characteristics, and risk factors. *Child Abuse and Neglect, 14,* 19–28.

Fischl, M. A., et al. (1990). A randomized controlled trial of a reduced daily dose of zidovudine in patients with acquired immunodeficiency syndrome. *New England Journal of Medicine, 323,* 1009–1014.

Fish, L. S., et al. (1994). Structural couple therapy in the treatment of inhibited sexual drive. *American Journal of Family Therapy, 22* (2), 113–125.

Fisher, B., et al. (1982). *Report on adolescent male prostitution.* San Francisco: Urban and Rural Systems Associates.

Fisher, J. (1992, January 11). Boy beaver foils experts. Cited in Associated Press. *The New York Times,* p. 6.

Fisher, J. D., & Misovich, S. J. (1991). *1990 technical report on undergraduate students' AIDS-preventive behavior, AIDS-knowledge, and fear of AIDS.* Storrs, CT: University of Connecticut, Department of Psychology.

Fisher, T. D., & Hall, R. H. (1988). A scale for the comparison of the sexual attittudes of adolescents and their parents. *Journal of Sex Research, 24,* 90–100.

Fisher, W. A., et al. (1995). Understanding and promoting AIDS-preventive behavior: Insights from the theory of reasoned action. *Health Psychology, 14,* 255–264.

Fisher-Thompson, D. (1990). Adult sex typing of children's toys. *Sex Roles, 23,* 291–303.

Fitzgerald, L. F. (1993a). *Sexual harassment in higher education: Concepts and issues.* Washington, DC: National Education Association.

Fitzgerald, L. F. (1993b). Sexual harassment: Violence against women in the workplace. *American Psychologist, 48,* 1070–1076.

Fitzgerald, L. F., et al. (1988). Academic harassment: Sex and denial in scholarly garb. *Psychology of Women Quarterly, 12,* 329–340.

Fletcher, J. (1966). *Situation ethics.* Philadelphia: Westminster Press.

Fletcher, J. (1967). *Moral responsibility: Situation ethics at work.* Philadelphia: Westminster Press.

Fletcher, J. M., et al. (1991). Neurobehavioral outcomes in diseases of childhood: Individual change models for pediatric human immunodeficiency viruses. *American Psychologist, 46,* 1267–1277.

Floyd, R. L., et al. (1993). A review of smoking in pregnancy: Effects on pregnancy outcomes and cessation efforts. *Annual Review of Public Health, 14,* 379–411.

Fogle, S. (1991). The advent of AIDS. *Journal of NIH Research, 3,* 88–91.

For high school girls, Norplant debate hits home. (1993, March 7). *The New York Times,* p. 28.

Ford, C. S., & Beach, F. A. (1951). *Patterns of sexual behavior.* New York: Harper & Row.

Forrest, J. D., & Fordyce, R. R. (1993). Women's contraceptive attitudes and use in 1992. *Family Planning Perspectives, 25,* 175–179.

Forster, P., & King, J. (1994). Fluoxetine for premature ejaculation. *American Journal of Psychiatry, 151* (10), 1523.

Franzoi, S. L., & Herzog, M. E. (1987). Judging physical attractiveness: What body aspects do we use? *Personality and Social Psychology Bulletin, 13,* 19–33.

Fraser, A. M., et al. (1995). Association of young maternal age with adverse reproductive outcomes. *New England Journal of Medicine, 332,* 1113–1117.

Frayser, S. (1985). *Varieties of sexual experience: An anthropological perspective on human sexuality.* New Haven: Human Relations Area Files Press.

Frazier, P. A. (1990). Victim attributions and post-rape trauma. *Journal of Personality and Social Psychology, 59,* 298–304.

Freiberg, P. (1995). Psychologists examine attacks on homosexuals. *APA Monitor, 26* (6), 30–31.

Freud, S. (1922/1959). Analysis of a phobia in a 5-year-old boy. In A. & J. Strachey (Ed. & Trans.), *Collected papers* (Vol. 3). New York: Basic Books. (Original work published 1909.)

Freund, J., & Blanchard, R. (1986). The concept of courtship disorder. *Journal of Sex and Marital Therapy, 12,* 79–92.

Freund, K., et al. (1988). The value of self-reports in the study of voyeurism and exhibitionism. *Annals of Sex Research, 1,* 243–262.

Freund, M., et al. (1989). Sexual behavior of resident street prostitutes with their clients in Camden, New Jersey. *Journal of Sex Research, 26,* 460–478.

Frey, K. S., & Ruble, D. N. (1992). Gender constancy and the "cost" of sex-typed behavior: A test of the conflict hypothesis. *Developmental Psychology, 28,* 714–721.

Friday, N. (1973). *My secret garden.* New York: Trident.

Fried, P. A. (1986). Marijuana use in pregancy. In I. J. Chasnott (Ed.), *Drug use in pregancy: Mother and child.* Boston: MTP Press.

Friedman, L. C., et al. (1994). Dispositional optimism, self-efficacy, and health beliefs as predictors of breast self-examination. *American Journal of Preventive Medicine, 10* (3), 130–135.

Friedman, R. C., & Downey, J. I. (1994). Homosexuality. *New England Journal of Medicine, 331,* 923–930.

Friedrich, E. (1985). Vaginitis. *American Journal of Obstetrics and Gynecology, 152,* 247–251.

Friedrich, W. N., & Gerber, P. N. (1994). Autoerotic asphyxia: The development of a paraphilia. *Journal of the American Academy of Child and Adolescent Psychiatry, 33* (7), 970–974.

Frisch, R. E. (1983). Fatness, puberty and fertility: The effects of nutrition and physical training on menarche and ovulation. In J. Brooks-Gunn & A. C. Petersen (Eds.), *Girls at puberty: Biological and psychosocial aspects.* New York: Plenum.

Frisch, R. E. (1988, March). Fatness and fertility. *Scientific American,* 88–95.

Frodi, A. M., et al. (1977). Are women always less aggressive than men? A review of the experimental literature. *Psychological Bulletin, 84,* 634–660.

Fuchs, C. S., et al. (1995). Alcohol consumption and mortality among women. *New England Journal of Medicine, 332,* 1245–1250.

Fuentes, A. (1993, June 30). AIDS rising among Latinos. *New York Daily News,* p. 21.

Fujimoto, T. (1994). Housework, paid work, and depression among husbands and wives. *Journal of Health and Social Behavior, 35,* 179–191.

Furnham, A., & Voli, V. (1989). Gender stereotypes in Italian television advertisements. *Journal of Broadcasting and Electronic Media, 33,* 175–185.

Furstenberg, F. F., Jr., et al. (1989). Teenaged pregnancy and childbearing. *American Psychologist, 44,* 313–320.

Gabriel, T. (1995a, April 23). When one spouse is gay and a marriage unravels. *The New York Times,* pp. A1, A22.

Gabriel, T. (1995b, June 12). A new generation seems ready to give bisexuality a place in the spectrum. *The New York Times,* p. A12.

Gaddis, A., & Brooks-Gunn, J. (1985). The male experience of pubertal change. *Journal of Youth and Adolescence, 14,* 61.

Gagnon, J. H. (1977). *Human sexualities.* Glenview, IL: Scott, Foresman.

Gagnon, J. H. (1990). Gender preferences in erotic relations: The Kinsey scale and sexual scripts. In D. P. McWhirter, et al. (Eds.), *Homosexuality/heterosexuality: Concepts of sexual orientation* (pp. 177–207). New York: Oxford University Press.

Gagnon, J. H., & Simon, W. (1973). *Sexual conduct: The social origins of human sexuality.* Chicago: Aldine.

Gagnon, J. H., & Simon, W. (1987). The sexual scripting of oral genital contacts. *Archives of Sexual Behavior, 16,* 1–25.

Ganitsch, C. (1992, January 14). Personal communication.

Garber, M. (1995). *Vice versa.* New York: Simon & Schuster.

Gardiner, H. W., & Gardiner, O. S. (1991). Women in Thailand. In L. L. Adler (Ed.), *Women in cross-cultural perspective* (pp. 175–187). New York: Praeger.

Garland, S. M., et al. (1990). Chlamydia trachomatis: Role in tubal infertility. *Australian and New Zealand Journal of Obstetrics and Gynaecology, 30,* 83–86.

Garnets, L., & Kimmel, D. (1991). In J. D. Goodchilds (Ed.). *Psychological perspectives on human diversity in America.* Washington, DC: American Psychological Association.

Garrett, L. (1993a, June 9). Experts: Tailor AIDS treatment: Strains need different tactics. *New York Newsday,* p. 21.

Garrett, L. (1993b, June 15). Why some survive. *New York Newsday,* pp. 61, 66.

Garwood, S. G., et al. (1980). Beauty is only "name deep": The effect of first name in ratings of physical attraction. *Journal of Applied Social Psychology, 10,* 431–435.

Gay colonel kicked out of military is reinstated. (1994, June 2). *Des Moines Register,* p. 3A.

Gay, P. (1984). *The bourgeois experience: Victoria to Freud.* New York: Oxford University Press.

Gayle, J., et al. (1990). Surveillance for AIDS and HIV infection among Black and Hispanic children and women of childbearing age, 1981–1989. *Morbidity and Mortality Weekly Report: Progress in Chronic Disease Prevention, 39,* 23–29. Washington, DC: U.S. Department of Health and Human Services.

Gebhard, P. H. (1969). Misconceptions about female prostitutes. *Medical Aspects of Human Sexuality, 3,* 24–26.

Gebhard, P. H. (1976). The institute. In M. S. Weinberg (Ed.), *Sex research: Studies from the Kinsey Institute.* New York: Oxford University Press.

Gebhard, P. H. (1977). *Memorandum on the incidence of homosexuals in the United States.* Bloomington, IN: Indiana University Institute for Sex Research.

Gebhard, P. H., et al. (1965). *Sex offenders: An analysis of types.* New York: Harper & Row.

Geer, J., et al. (1984). *Human sexuality.* Englewood Cliffs, NJ: Prentice-Hall.

Geiger, R. (1981). Neurophysiology of sexual response in spinal cord injury. In D. Bullard & S. Knight (Eds.), *Sexuality and physical disability: Personal perspectives.* St. Louis: C. V. Mosby.

Gelles, R. J., & Cornell, C. P. (1985). *Intimate violence in families.* Beverly Hills, CA: Sage.

Gelman, D., with P. Kandell. (1993, January 18). Isn't it romantic? *Newsweek,* 60–61.

Genuis, M., et al. (1991, Fall). Male victims of child sexual abuse: A brief overview of pertinent findings [Special issue: Child sexual abuse]. *Journal of Child and Youth-Care,* 1–6.

Geringer, W. M., et al. (1993). Knowledge, attitudes, and behavior related to condom use and STDs in a high risk population. *Journal of Sex Research, 30,* 75–83.

Gerrard, M. (1987). Sex, sex guilt, and contraceptive use revisited: The 1980s. *Journal of Personality and Social Psychology, 52,* 975–980.

Gerrol, R., & Resick, P. A. (1988, November). *Sex differences in social support and recovery from victimization.* Paper presented at the meeting of the Association for Advancement of Behavior Therapy, New York, NY.

Gibbs, N. (1991, June 3). When is it rape? *Time,* 48–54.

Gibson, A. I., et al. (1988). Adolescent female prostitutes. *Archives of Sexual Behavior, 17,* 431–438.

Gidycz, C. A., & Koss, M. P. (1990). A comparison of group and individual sexual assault victims. *Psychology of Women Quarterly, 14,* 325–342.

Gil, V. E. (1990). Sexual fantasy experiences and guilt among conservative Christians: An exploratory study. *Journal of Sex Research, 27,* 527–555.

Gilbert, H. W., & Gingell, J. C. (1991). The results of an intracorporeal papaverine clinic. *Sexual and Marital Therapy, 6,* 49–56.

Gillespie, M. W., et al. (1988). Secular trends in abortion attitudes: 1975–1980–1985. *Journal of Psychology, 122,* 323–341.

Gillis, J. S., & Avis, W. E. (1980). The male-taller norm in mate selection. *Personality and Social Psychology Bulletin, 6,* 396–401.

Gilmartin, B. G. (1975 September). That swinging couple down the block. *Psychology Today, 54.*

Giovannucci, E., et al. (1993a). A prospective cohort study of vasectomy and prostate cancer in U.S. men. *Journal of the American Medical Association, 269,* 873–877.

Giovannucci, E., et al. (1993b). A retrospective cohort study of vasectomy and prostate cancer in U.S. men. *Journal of the American Medical Association, 269,* 878–882.

Gitlin, M. J., & Pasnau, R. O. (1989). Psychiatric syndromes linked to reproductive function in women: A review of current knowledge. *American Journal of Psychiatry, 146,* 1413–1422.

Glass, R. H., & Ericsson, R. (1982). *Getting pregnant in the 1980s.* Berkeley: University of California Press.

Glass, S. P., & Wright, T. L. (1992). Justifications of extramarital relationships: The association between attitudes, behaviors, and gender. *Journal of Sex Research, 29,* 361–387.

Glusker, A. (1995, November/December). The pill: What it's done for us . . . and to us. *Ms.,* 30–32.

Gold, R. S., & Skinner, M. J. (1992). Situational factor and thought processes associated with unprotected intercourse in young gay men. *AIDS, 6,* 1021–1030.

Gold, S. R., & Gold, R. G. (1993). Sexual aversions: A hidden disorder. In W. O'Donohue & J. H. Geer (Eds.), *Handbook of sexual dysfunctions: Assessment and treatment* (pp. 83–102). Boston: Allyn & Bacon.

Goldberg, C. (1995, September 11). Sex slavery, Thailand to New York. *The New York Times,* pp. B1, B6.

Goldberg, L. H., et al. (1993). Longterm suppression of recurrent genital herpes with acyclovir. *Archives of Dermatology, 129,* 582–587.

Goldberg, M. (1987). Understanding hypersexuality in men and women. In G. R. Weeks and Larry Hof (Eds.), *Integrating sex and marital therapy: A clinical guide* (pp. 202–220). New York: Brunner/Mazel.

Goldenberg, R. L., & Klerman, L. V. (1995). Adolescent pregnancy—another look. *New England Journal of Medicine, 332,* 1161–1162.

Golding, J. M., et al. (1989, January). Social support sources following sexual assault. *Journal of Community Psychology, 17* (1), 92–107.

Goldman, J. A., & Harlow, L. L. (1993). Self-perception variables that mediate AIDS-preventive behavior in college students. *Health Psychology, 12,* 489–498.

Goldman, L., & Tosteson, A. N. A. (1991). Uncertainty about postmenopausal estrogen: Time for action, not debate. *New England Journal of Medicine, 325,* 800–802.

Goldstein, A. M., & Clark, J. H. (1990). Treatment of uncomplicated gonococcal urethritis with single-dose ceftriaxone. *Sexually Transmitted Diseases, 17,* 181–183.

Colestein, I. Penile revascularization. *Urologic Clinics of North America, 14,* 805–813.

Goleman, D. (1988, October 18). Chemistry of sexual desire yields its elusive secrets. *The New York Times,* pp. C1, C15.

Goleman, D. (1991, October 22). Sexual harassment: It's about power, not lust. *The New York Times,* pp. C1, C12.

Goleman, D. (1992). Therapies offer hope for sex offenders. *The New York Times,* pp. C1, C11.

Goleman, D. (1993, October 6). Abuse-prevention efforts aid children. *The New York Times,* p. C13.

Goleman, D. (1995, June 14). Sex fantasy research said to neglect women. *The New York Times,* p. C14.

Golombok, S. & Tasker, F. (1996). Do parents influence the sexual orientation of their children? Findings from a longitudinal study of lesbian families. *Developmental Psychology, 32* (1), 3–11.

Gomez, J., & Smith, B. (1990). Taking the home out of homophobia: Black lesbian health. In E. C. White (Ed.), *The Black women's health book: Speaking for ourselves.* Seattle: Seal Press.

Gomez-Schwartz, B., et al. (1990). *Child sexual abuse: The initial effects.* Newbury Park, CA: Sage.

Gonsiorck, J. (1988). Mental health issues of gay and lesbian adolescents. *Journal of Adolescent Health Care, 9,* 114–122.

Goodkin, K., et al. (1992). Life stressors and coping style are associated with immune measures in HIV-1 infection: A preliminary report. *International Journal of Psychiatry in Medicine, 22,* 155–172.

Goodwin, J. M., et al. (1990). Borderline and other severe symptoms in adult survivors of incestuous abuse. *Psychiatric Annals, 20,* 22–32.

Gordon, P. H., & DeMarco, L. J. (1984). Reproductive health services for men: Is there a need? *Family Planning Perspectives, 16,* 44–46.

Gordon, S., & Snyder, C. W. (1989). *Personal issues in human sexuality: A guidebook for better sexual health* (2nd ed.). Boston: Allyn & Bacon.

Gottlieb, M. S. (1991, June 5). AIDS—the second decade: Leadership is lacking. *The New York Times,* p. A29.

Goulart, M., & Madover, S. (1991). An AIDS prevention program for homeless youth. *Journal of Adolescent Health, 12,* 573–575.

Graber, B. (1993). Medical aspects of sexual arousal disorders. In W. O'Donohue & J. H. Geer (Eds.), *Handbook of sexual dysfunctions: Assessment and treatment* (pp. 103–156). Boston: Allyn & Bacon.

Graca, L. M., et al. (1991). Acute effects of maternal cigarette smoking on fetal heart rate and fetal body movements felt by the mother. *Journal of Perinatal Medicine, 19,* 385–390.

Graham, J. M., & Blanco, J. D. (1990). Chlamydial infections. *Primary Care: Clinics in Office Practice, 17,* 85–93.

Graham, S., et al. (1982). Sex patterns and herpes simplex virus type 2 in the epidemiology of cancer of the cervix. *American Journal of Epidemiology, 115,* 729–735.

Grauerholz, E. (1989). Sexual harassment of women professors by students: Exploring the dynamics of power, authority, and gender in a university setting. *Sex Roles, 21,* 789–301.

Gray, J. (1995, December 8). Senators pass ban on form of abortion. *The New York Times,* p. B14.

Green, R. (1978). Sexual identity of 37 children raised by homosexual or transsexual parents. *American Journal of Psychiatry, 135,* 692–697.

Green, R. (1987). *The "sissy boy syndrome" and the development of homosexuality.* New Haven, CT: Yale University Press.

Greenberg, E. R., et al. (1984). Breast cancer in mothers given diethylstilbestrol in pregnancy. *New England Journal of Medicine, 311,* 1393–1398.

Greene, B. (1994). Ethnic-minority lesbians and gay men: Mental health and treatment issues. *Journal of Consulting and Clinical Psychology, 62,* 243–251.

Greenhouse, L. (1992, February 27). Court opens path for student suits in sex-bias cases. *The New York Times,* pp. A1, A16.

Greenwald, E., & Leitenberg, H. (1989). Long-term effects of sexual experiences with siblings and non-siblings during childhood. *Archives of Sexual Behavior, 18,* 389–399.

Griffin, E., & Sparks, G. G. (1990). Friends forever: A longitudinal exploration of intimacy in same-sex friends and platonic pairs. *Journal of Social and Personal Relationships, 7,* 29–46.

Groden, J. (1995). Clearance of HIV—Lessons from newborns. *New England Journal of Medicine, 332,* 883–887.

Grodstein, F., et al. (1993). Relation of tubal infertility to history of sexually transmitted diseases. *American Journal of Epidemiology, 137,* 577–584.

Grogger, J., & Bronars, S. (1993). The socioeconomic consequences of teenage childbearing: Findings from a natural experiment. *Family Planning Perspectives, 25,* 156–161.

Groneman, C. (1994). Nymphomania: The historical construction of female sexuality. *Signs, 19* (2), 337–367.

Gross, J. (1991, February 11). New challenge of youth: Growing up in gay home. *The New York Times,* pp. A1, B7.

Gross, J. (1992, July 13). Suffering in silence no more: Fighting sexual harassment. *The New York Times,* pp. A10, D10.

Gross, J. (1993, September 25). Combating rape on campus in a class on sexual consent. *The New York Times,* pp. 1, 9.

Gross, L., & Jeffries-Fox, S. (1978). What do you want to be when you grow up, little girl? In G. Tuchman, et al. (Eds.), *Hearth and home: Images of women in the mass media.* New York: Oxford University Press.

Grossman, S. (1991, December 22). Cited in "Undergraduates drink heavily, survey discloses." *The New York Times,* p. 46.

Groth, A. N. (1978). Patterns of sexual assault against children and adolescents. In A. W. Burgess, et al. (Eds.), *Sexual assault of children and adolescents.* Toronto: Lexington Books.

Groth, A. N., & Birnbaum, H. J. (1979). *Men who rape: The psychology of the offender.* New York: Plenum.

Groth, A. N., & Burgess, A. W. (1980). Male rape: Offenders and victims. *American Journal of Psychiatry, 137,* 806–810.

Groth, A. N., & Hobson, W. (1983). The dynamics of sexual assault. In L. Schlesinger & E. Revitch (Eds.), *Sexual dynamics of antisocial behavior.* Springfield, IL: Thomas.

Gruber, J. E., & Bjorn, L. (1986). Women's responses to sexual harassment: An analysis of sociocultural, organizational, and personal resource models. *Social Science Quarterly, 67,* 814–826.

Gruber, V. A., & Wildman, B. G. (1987). The impact of dysmenorrhea on daily activities. *Behaviour Research and Therapy, 25,* 123–128.

Grunfeld, C. (1995). What causes wasting in AIDS? *New England Journal of Medicine, 333,* 123–124.

Grych, J. H., & Fincham, F. D. (1993). Children's appraisals of marital conflict. *Child Development, 64,* 215–230.

Guinan, M. E. (1992). Cited in Leary, W. E. (1992, February 1). U.S. panel backs approval of first condom for women. *The New York Times,* p. 7.

Gupta, M. (1994). Sexuality in the Indian subcontinent. *Sexual and Marital Therapy, 9* (1), 57–69.

Haas-Hawkings, G., et al. (1985). A study of relatively immediate adjustment to widowhood in late life. *International Journal of Women's Studies, 8,* 158–165.

Hack, M., & Merkatz, I. (1995). Preterm delivery and low birth weight—a dire legacy. *New England Journal of Medicine, 333* (26), 1772–1774.

Haffner, D. (1993, August). *Sex education: Trends and issues.* Paper presented at the meeting of the American Psychological Association, Toronto, Canada.

Haglund, B., & Cnattingius, S. (1990). Cigarette smoking as a risk factor for sudden infant death syndrome: A population based study. *American Journal of Public Health, 80,* 29–32.

Hall, C. S. (1984). "A ubiquitous sex difference in dreams" revisited. *Journal of Personality and Social Psychology, 46,* 1109–1117.

Hall, G. C. N. (1989). Sexual arousal and arousability in a sexual offender population. *Journal of Abnormal Psychology, 98,* 145–149.

Hall, G. C. N., & Hirschman, R. (1991). Toward a theory of sexual aggression: A quadripartite model. *Journal of Consulting and Clinical Psychology, 59,* 662–669.

Hamer, D. H., et al. (1993, July 16). A linkage between DNA markers on the X chromosome and male sexual orientation. *Science, 261,* 321–327.

Hamilton, J. D., et al. (1992). A controlled trial of early versus late treatment with zidovudine in symptomatic human immunodeficiency virus infection. *New England Journal of Medicine, 326,* 437–443.

Hamilton, M., & Yee, J. (1990). Rape knowledge and propensity to rape. *Journal of Research in Personality, 24,* 111–122.

Hampton, H. L. (1995). Care of the woman who has been raped. New England Journal of Medicine, *332,* 234–237.

Handler, A. (1990). The correlates of the initiation of sexual intercourse among young urban Black females. *Journal of Youth and Adolescence, 19,* 159–170.

Handsfield, H. (1984). Gonorrhea and uncomplicated gonococcal infection. In K. K. Holmes et al. (Eds.), *Sexually transmitted diseases* (pp. 205–220). New York: McGraw-Hill.

Hanrahan, J. P., et al. (1992). The effect of maternal smoking during pregnancy on early infant lung function. *American Review of Respiratory Disease, 145,* 1129–1135.

Hanson, R. K. (1990). The psychological impact of sexual assault on women and children: A review. *Annals of Sex Research, 3,* 187–232.

Hanson, S. L., et al. (1989). The antecedents of teenage fatherhood. *Demography, 26,* 579–596.

Harahap, M., & Siregar, A. (1988). Circumcision: A review and a new technique. *Journal of Dermatology and Surgical Oncology, 14,* 383–386.

Harding, J. J. (1989). Postpartum psychiatric disorders: A review. *Comprehensive Psychiatry, 30,* 109–112.

Hariton, E. B., & Singer, J. L. (1974). Women's fantasies during sexual intercourse: Normative and theoretical implications. *Journal of Consulting and Clinical Psychology, 42,* 313–322.

Harkness, R. (1996, January 22). *Des Moines Register,* p. 3T.

Harney P. A., & Muehlenhard, C. L. (1991). Rape. In E. Grauerholz & M. A. Koralewski (Eds.), *Sexual coercion: A sourcebook on its nature, causes, and prevention* (pp. 3–16). Lexington, MA: Lexington Books.

Harris, L. (1988). *Inside America.* New York: Vintage.

Harris, L., et al. (1995, May 14). Cited in "Mom the Provider." *The New York Times,* p. A14.

Hart, J., et al. (1991). Sexual behavior in pregnancy: A study of 219 women. *Journal of Sex Education and Therapy, 17,* 86–90.

Hartman, C. R., et al. (1987). Pathways and cycles of runaways: A model for understanding repetitive runaway behavior. *Hospital and Community Psychiatry, 38,* 292–299.

Harvey, S. (1987). Female sexual behavior: Fluctuations during the menstrual cycle. *Journal of Psychosomatic Research, 31,* 101–110.

Hass, A. (1979). *Teenage sexuality.* New York: Macmillan.

Hatcher, R. A., et al. (1990). *Contraceptive technology 1990–1992* (15th rev. ed.). New York: Irvington Publishers.

Hatcher, R. A., et al. (1994). *Contraceptive technology 1992–1994* (16th rev. ed.). New York: Irvington Publishers.

Hatfield, E. (1988). Passionate and companionate love. In R. J. Sternberg & M. L. Barnes (Eds.), *The psychology of love* (pp. 191–217). New Haven: Yale University Press.

Hatfield, E., & Sprecher, S. (1986). Measuring passionate love in intimate relationships. *Journal of Adolescence, 9,* 383–410.

Hausknecht, R. U. (1995). Methotrexate and misoprostol to terminate early pregnancy. *New England Journal of Medicine, 333,* 537–540.

Havemann, E., & Lehtinen, M. (1990). *Marriages and families: New problems, new opportunities* (2nd ed.). Englewood Cliffs, NJ: Prentice-Hall.

Haverkos, H. W. (1993). Reported cases of AIDS: An update. *New England Journal of Medicine, 329,* 511.

Hayes, C. D. (Ed.). (1987). *Risking the future* (Vol. 1). Washington, DC: National Academy Press.

Hays, R. B., et al. (1992). Social support, AIDS-related symptoms, and depression among gay men. *Journal of Consulting and Clinical Psychology, 60,* 463–469.

Hazan, C., & Shaver, P. (1987). Love conceptualized as an attachment process. *Journal of Personality and Social Psychology, 52,* 511–524.

Heath, C. B. (1995). Chlamydia trachomatis infection update. *American Family Physician, 52,* 1455–1462.

Heath, R. (1972). Pleasure and brain activity in man. *Journal of Nervous and Mental Disease, 154,* 3–18.

Hechtman, L. (1989). Teenage mothers and their children: Risks and problems: A review. *Canadian Journal of Psychiatry, 34,* 569–575.

Hegeler, S., & Mortensen, M. (1977). Sexual behavior in elderly Danish males. In R. Gemme & C. Wheeler (Eds.), *Progress in sexology* (pp. 285–292). New York: Plenum.

Heiman, J. R., & LoPiccolo, J. (1987). *Becoming orgasmic* (2nd ed.). Englewood Cliffs, NJ: Prentice-Hall.

Hendrick, C., & Hendrick, S. (1986). A theory and method of love. *Journal of Personality and Social Psychology, 50,* 392–402.

Henneberger, M. (with M. Marriott). (1993). For some, rituals of abuse replace youthful courtship. *The New York Times,* pp. A1, A33.

Henry, J. (1963). *Culture against man.* New York: Random House.

Henshaw, S. K., & Silverman, J. (1988). The characteristics and prior contraceptive use of U.S. abortion patients. *Family Planning Perspectives, 20,* 158–168.

Hensley, W. E. (1992). Why does the best-looking person in the room always seem to be surrounded by admirers? *Psychological Reports, 70,* 457–458.

Hensley, W. E. (1994). Height as a basis for interpersonal attraction. *Adolescence, 29,* 469–474.

Herdt, G. H. (1981). *Guardians of the flutes: Idioms of masculinity.* New York: McGraw-Hill.

Herdt, G. H. (1987). *The Sambia: Ritual and gender in New Guinea.* New York: Holt, Rinehart & Winston.

Hernandez, J. T., & Smith, F. J. (1990). Inconsistencies and misperceptions putting college students at risk of HIV infection. *Journal of Adolescent Health Care, 11,* 295–297.

Herzog, L. (1989). Urinary tract infections and circumcision. *American Journal of Diseases of Children, 143,* 348–350.

Hess, B. B., et al. (1993). *Sociology* (4th ed.). New York: Macmillan.

Highsmith, C. (1995, October). Why women are more vulnerable to HIV infection. *RN, 58,* 69.

Hillier, S., & Holmes, K. K. (1990). Bacterial vaginosis. In K. K. Holmes, et al. (Eds.), *Sexually transmitted diseases* (2nd ed.) (pp. 547–560). New York: McGraw-Hill.

Hillier, S. L., et al. (1995). Association between baterial vaginosis and preterm delivery of a low-birth-weight infant. *The New England Journal of Medicine, 333* (26), 1737–1742.

Hilton, E., et al. (1992). Ingestion of yogurt containing *Lactobacillus acidophilus* as prophylaxis for candidal vaginitis. *Annals of Internal Medicine, 116,* 353–357.

Hilts, P. J. (1995, July 26). In a ranking of maternal health, U.S. trails most developed nations. *The New York Times,* p. C8.

Hingson, R. W., et al. (1990). Beliefs about AIDS, use of alcohol and drugs, and unprotected sex among Massachusetts adolescents. *American Journal of Public Health, 80,* 295–298.

Hirsch, M. S., & D'Aquila, R. T. (1993). Therapy for human immunodeficiency virus infection. *New England Journal of Medicine, 328,* 1686–1695.

Hite, S. (1976). *The Hite report.* New York: Macmillan.

Hite, S. (1977). *The Hite report: A nationwide study of female sexuality.* New York: Dell.

Hite, S. (1981). *The Hite report on male sexuality.* New York: Knopf.

H.I.V. clue supports early use of condom. (1992, December 18). *The New York Times,* p.C9.

HIV disease: Mortality rates are higher in women. (1995, June). *RN, 58,* 12.

Ho, D. D. (1995). Time to hit HIV, early and hard. *New England Journal of Medicine, 333,* 450–451.

Hoagwood, K. (1990). Blame and adjustment among women sexually abused as children. *Women and Therapy, 9,* 89–110.

Hobfoll, S. E., et al. (1993). Safer sex knowledge, behavior, and attitudes of inner-city women. *Health Psychology, 12,* 481–488.

Hock, Z. (1983). The G spot. *Journal of Sex and Marital Therapy, 9,* 166–167.

Hodges, B. C., et al. (1992). Gender differences in adolescents' attitudes toward condom use. *Journal of School Health, 62,* 103–106.

Hodgson, R., et al. (1990). Chlamydia trachomatis: The prevalence, trend and importance in initial infertility management.

Australian and New Zealand Journal of Obstetrics and Gynaecology, 30, 251–254

Hodson, D. S., & Skeen, P. (1994). Sexuality and aging: The hammerlock of myths. *Journal of Applied Gerontology, 13* (3), 219–235.

Hofferth, S. L., & Hayes, C. D. (Eds.). (1987). *Risking the future: Adolescent sexuality, pregnancy, and childbearing: Vol. 2. Working papers and statistical reports.* Washington, DC: National Academy Press.

Hoffman, J. (1993, January 10). The morning after pill: A well-kept secret. *The New York Times Sunday Magazine,* p. 12.

Hogan, D. P., & Kitigawa, E. M. (1985). The impact of social status, family structure and neighborhood on the fertility of black adolescents. *Family Planning Perspectives, 17,* 165–169.

Holden, G. W., & Ritchie, K. L. (1991). Linking extreme marital discord, child rearing, and child behavior problems. *Child Development, 62,* 311–327.

Hollinger, L. M., & Buschmann, M. B. (1993). Factors influencing the perception of touch by elderly nursing home residents and their health caregivers. *International Journal of Nursing Studies, 30,* 445–461.

Holtzman, D., et al. (1992). HIV education and health education in the United States: A national survey of local school district policies and practices. *Journal of School Health, 62,* 421–427.

Holzman, H. R., & Pines, S. (1982). Buying sex: The phenomenology of being a john. *Deviant Behavior, 4,* 89–116.

Honey, M. (1994, September 26). Mexico's open secret. *The Nation,* 310–312.

Hornblower, M. (1993, June 21). The skin trade. *Time,* 44+.

Horowitz, R. (1983). *Honor and the American dream: Culture and identity in a Chicano community.* New Brunswick, NJ: Rutgers University Press.

How we got here. (1995, May/June). *Ms.,* 54–57.

How women lawyers fare. (1996). *U.S. News & World Report,* 14.

Howard, J. A., et al. (1987). Social or evolutionary theories: Some observations on preferences in mate selection. *Journal of Personality and Social Psychology, 53,* 194–200.

Howard, M., & McCabe, J. B. (1990). Helping teenagers postpone sexual involvement. *Family Planning Perspectives, 22,* 21–26.

Howard, M. C. (1989). *Contemporary cultural anthropology* (3rd ed.). Glenview, IL: Scott, Foresman.

Howards, S. S. (1995). Current concepts: Treatment of male infertility. *New England Journal of Medicine, 332,* 312–317.

Hsu, B., et al. (1994). Gender differences in sexual fantasy and behavior in a college population: A ten-year replication. *Journal of Sex and Marital Therapy, 20* (2), 103–118.

Hu, S. (1992). Cited in "Immune deficiency vaccine for monkeys succeeds." (1992, January 24). *The New York Times,* p. A17.

Huang, K., & Uba, L. (1992). Premarital sexual behavior among Chinese college students in the United States. *Archives of Sexual Behavior, 21,* 227–240.

Hubbard, R., & Wald, E. (1993). *Exploding the gene myth.* Boston: Beacon Press.

Hucker, S., et al. (1988). A double blind trial of sex drive reducing medication in pedophiles. *Annals of Sex Research, 1,* 227–242.

Huffman, T., et al. (1994). Gender differences and factors related to the disposition toward cohabitation. *Family Therapy, 21* (3), 171–184.

Hunt, M. (1974). *Sexual behavior in the 1970's.* New York: Dell.

Hunt, M. (1979, January 9). Legal rape. *Family Circle.*

Hunter, D. J., et al. (1996). Cohort studies of fat intake and the risk of breast cancer–A pooled analysis. *New England Journal of Medicine, 334,*356–361.

Hursch, C. (1977). *The trouble with rape.* Chicago: Nelson-Hall.

Hyde, J. S., & Linn, M. C. (1988). Gender differences in verbal ability: A meta-analysis. *Psychological Bulletin, 104,* 53–69.

Hyde, J. S., & Plant, E. A. (1995). Magnitude of psychological gender differences: Another side to the story. *American Psychologist, 50,* 159–161.

Hyde, J. S., et al. (1990). Gender differences in mathematics performance: A meta-analysis. *Psychological Bulletin, 107,* 139–155.

Imperato-McGinley, J., et al. (1974). Steroid 5 reductase deficiency in man: An inherited form of male pseudohermaphroditism. *Science, 186,* 1213–1215.

Ingersoll, S. L, & Patton, S. O. (1991). *Treating perpetrators of sexual abuse.* Lexington, MA: Lexington Books.

Ingrassia, M. (1993, October 25). Abused and confused. *Newsweek,* 57–58.

Isay, R. A. (1990). Psychoanalytic theory and the therapy of gay men. In D. P. McWhirter, et al. (Eds.), *Homosexuality/heterosexuality: Concepts of sexual orientation* (pp. 283–303). New York: Oxford University Press.

Isay, R. A. (1993, April 23). Sex survey may say most about society's attitudes to gays [Letter]. *The New York Times,* Section 4, p. 16.

Ison, C. A. (1990). Laboratory methods in genitourinary medicine: Methods of diagnosing gonorrhoea. *Genitourinary Medicine, 66,* 453–459.

Jacklin, C. N., et al. (1984). Sex-typing behavior and sex-typing pressure in child–parent interaction. *Archives of Sexual Behavior, 13,* 413–425.

Jackson, B. B., et al. (1991). How age conditions the relationship between climacteric status and health symptoms in African American women. *Research in Nursing and Health, 14,* 1–9.

Jackson, J., et al. (1990). Young adult women who report childhood intrafamilial sexual abuse: Subsequent adjustment. *Archives of Sexual Behavior, 19,* 211–221.

Jackson, L. A., & Ervin, K. S. (1992). Height stereotypes of women and men: The liabilities of shortness for both sexes. *Journal of Social Psychology, 132,* 433–445.

Jacobsen, C. (1991). Redefining censorship: A feminist view. *Art Journal, 50* (4), 42–55.

Jacobson, J. L., & Jacobson, S. W. (1994). Prenatal alcohol exposure and neurobehavioral development: Where is the threshold? *Alcohol Health and Research World, 18* (1), 30–36.

Jamison, P. L., & Gebhard, P. H. (1988). Penis size increase between flaccid and erect states: An analysis of the Kinsey data. *Journal of Sex Research, 24,* 177–183.

Jankowiak, W. R., & Fischer, E. F. (1992). A cross-cultural perspective on romantic love. *Ethnology, 31,* 149–155.

Janus, M. D., et al. (1984). Youth prostitution. In A. W. Burgess (Ed.), *Sex rings and child pornography.* Lexington, MA: Heath.

Janus, S. S., & Janus, C. L. (1993). *The Janus report on sexual behavior.* New York: Wiley.

Jencks, C., & Mayer, S. E. (1990). Residential segregation, job proximity, and Black job opportunities. In L. E. Lynn and M. McGeary (Eds.), *Inner-city poverty in the United States.* Washington, DC: National Academy Press.

Jenks, R. (1985). Swinging: A replication and test of a theory. *Journal of Sex Research, 21,* 199–210.

Job rights for homosexuals backed in poll. (1992, September 7). *The New York Times,* p. L10.

Johnson, D. (1990, March 8). AIDS clamor at colleges muffling older dangers. *The New York Times,* p. A18.

Johnson, K. A., & Williams, L. (1993). Risk of breast cancer in the nurses' health study: Applying the Gail model. *Journal of the American Medical Association, 270,* 2925–2926.

Jones, A., et al. (1994). Erectile disorder and the elderly: An analysis of the case for funding. *Sexual and Marital Therapy, 9* (1), 9–15.

Jones, E. F., et al. (1985). Teenage pregnancy in developed countries: Determinants and policy implications. *Family Planning Perspectives, 17,* 53–62.

Jones, H. W., & Toner, J. P. (1993). The infertile couple. *New England Journal of Medicine, 329,* 1710–1715.

Jones, J. (1994). Embodied meaning: Menopause and the change of life. [Special issue: Women's health and social work: Feminist perspectives]. *Social Work in Health Care, 19* (3–4), 43–65.

Jones, K. (1995, April 16). Dallas leaders halt an anti-AIDS program they say subsidizes immorality. *The New York Times,* p. 12.

Jorgensen, S. R., et al. (1980). Dyadic and social network influences on adolescent exposure to pregnancy risk. *Journal of Marriage and the Family, 42,* 141–155.

Journal of the American Medical Association. (1993a). Preventing HIV/AIDS among adolescents; Schools as agents of behavior change [Editorial]. *Journal of the American Medical Association, 269,* 760–762.

Judson, F. N. (1990). Gonorrhea. *Medical Clinics of North America, 74,* 1353–1366.

Kagay, M. R. (1991, June 19). Poll finds AIDS causes single people to alter behavior. *The New York Times,* p. C3.

Kalick, S. M. (1988). Physical attractiveness as a status cue. *Journal of Experimental Social Psychology, 24,* 469–489.

Kallmann, F. J. (1952). Comparative twin study on the genetic aspects of male homosexuality. *Journal of Nervous and Mental Disease, 115,* 283–298.

Kammeyer, K. C. W. (1990). *Marriage and family: A foundation for personal decisions* (2nd ed.). Boston: Allyn & Bacon.

Kammeyer, K. C. W., et al. (1990). *Sociology: Experiencing changing societies.* Boston: Allyn & Bacon.

Kang, S. H., et al. (1994). Cancer screening among African-American women: Their use of tests and social support. *American Journal of Public Health, 84* (1), 101–103.

Kanin, E. J. (1985). Date rapists: Differential sexual socialization and relative deprivation. *Archives of Sexual Behavior, 14,* 219–231.

Kantner, J. F., & Zelnik, M. (1972). Sexual experience of young unmarried women in the United States. *Family Planning Perspectives, 4,* 9–18.

Kantrowitz, B. (1990a, Summer/Fall Special Issue). High school homeroom. *Newsweek,* 50–54.

Kantrowitz, B. (1990b, Summer/Fall Special Issue). The push for sex education. *Newsweek,* 52.

Kantrowitz, B. (1992, December 14). A "silver bullet" against teen pregnancies? Baltimore offers Norplant at school. *Newsweek,* 43.

Kaplan, D. (1993, January 18). The incorrigibles. *Newsweek,* 48–50.

Kaplan, H. S. (1974). *The new sex therapy: Active treatment of sexual dysfunctions.* New York: Brunner/Mazel.

Kaplan, H. S. (1979). *Disorders of sexual desire.* New York: Simon & Schuster.

Kaplan, H. S. (1987). *Sexual aversion, sexual phobias, and panic disorder.* New York: Brunner/Mazel.

Kaplan, H. S. (1990). Sex, intimacy, and the aging process. *Journal of the American Academy of Psychoanalysis, 18,* 185–205.

Karney, B. R., & Bradbury, T. N. (1995). The longitudinal course of marital quality and stability: A review of theory, method, and research. *Psychological Bulletin, 118,* 3–34.

Katz, J. N. (1995). *The invention of heterosexuality.* New York: Dutton.

Katz, R. C. (1990). Psychosocial adjustment in adolescent child molesters. *Child Abuse and Neglect, 14,* 567–575.

Kaufman, A., et al. (1980). Male rape victims: Noninstitutionalized assault. *American Journal of Psychiatry, 137,* 221–223.

Kay, D. S. (1992). Masturbation and mental health: Uses and abuses. *Sexual and Marital Therapy, 7,* 97–107.

Kedia, K. (1983). Ejaculation and emission: Normal physiology, dysfunction, and therapy. In R. J. Krane, et al. (Eds.), *Male sexual dysfunction* (pp. 37–54). Boston: Little, Brown.

Keen, S., & Zur, O. (1989). Who is the new ideal man? *Psychology Today, 23* (11), 54–60.

Kegel, A. H. (1952). Sexual functions of the pubococcygeus muscle. *Western Journal of Surgery, 60,* 521–524.

Keith, J. B., et al. (1991). Sexual activity and contraceptive use among low-income urban Black adolescent females. *Adolescence, 26,* 769–785.

Kellerman, J., et al. (1989). Looking and loving: The effects of mutual gaze on feelings of romantic love. *Journal of Research in Personality, 23,* 145–161.

Kelly, M. P., et al. (1990). Attitudinal and experiential correlates of anorgasmia. *Archives of Sexual Behavior, 19,* 165–177.

Kennell, J., et al. (1991). Continuous emotional support during labor in a U.S. hospital: A randomized controlled trial. *Journal of the American Medical Association, 265,* (17), 2197–2201.

Kenney, A. M., et al. (1989). Sex education and AIDS education in the schools. *Family Planning Perspectives, 21,* 56–64.

Kent, M. R. (1991). Women and AIDS. *New England Journal of Medicine, 324,* 1442.

Kerns, J. G., & Fine, M. A. (1994). The relation between gender and negative attitudes toward gay men and lesbians: Do gender role attitudes mediate this relation? *Sex Roles, 31* (5–6), 297–307.

Kessler, R. Cited in Blakeslee, S. (1992, January 9). Chemical a factor in male impotence. *The New York Times,* pp. 1, B10.

Kettl, P., et al. (1991). Female sexuality after spinal cord injury. *Sexuality and Disability, 9,* 287–295.

Kiely, E. A., et al. (1987). Assessment of the immediate and long-term effects of pharmacologically induced penile erections in the treatment of psychogenic and organic impotence. *British Journal of Urology, 59,* 164–169.

Killmann, P. R., & Auerbach, R. (1979). Treatments of premature ejaculation and psychogenic impotence: A critical review of the literature. *Archives of Sexual Behavior, 8,* 81–100.

Killmann, P. R., et al. (1987). The treatment of secondary orgasmic dysfunction II. *Journal of Sex and Marital Therapy, 13,* 93–105.

Kilpatrick, D. G., et al. (1987, January). *Rape in marriage and dating relationships: How bad are they for mental health?* Paper presented at the meeting of the New York Academy of Science, New York, NY.

Kimble, D. P. (1992). *Biological psychology* (2nd ed.). Fort Worth, TX: Harcourt Brace Jovanovich.

Kimlicka, T., et al. (1983). A comparison of androgynous, feminine, masculine, and undifferentiated women on self-esteem, body satisfaction, and sexual satisfaction. *Psychology of Women Quarterly, 1,* 291–294.

Kinard, E., & Reinherz, H. (1987). School aptitude and achievement in children of adolescent mothers. *Journal of Youth and Adolescence, 16,* 69–78.

Kinder, B. N., & Curtiss, G. (1988). Specific components in the etiology, assessment, and treatment of male sexual dysfunctions: Controlled outcome studies. *Journal of Sex and Marital Therapy, 14,* 40–48.

King, L. (1988). Editorial comment in response to Wisell et al., 1987. *Journal of Urology, 139,* 883.

Kinloch–de Loes, S., et al. (1995). A controlled trial of zidovudine in primary human immunodeficiency virus infection. *New England Journal of Medicine, 333,* 408–413.

Kinsey, A. C., et al. (1948). *Sexual behavior in the human male.* Philadelphia: W. B. Saunders Co.

Kinsey, A. C., et al. (1953). *Sexual behavior in the human female.* Philadelphia: W. B. Saunders Co.

Kintsch, W. (1994). Text comprehension, memory, and learning. *American Psychologist, 49,* 294–303.

Kirby, D., et al. (1992). School-based clinics: Their reproductive health services and impact on sexual behavior. *Family Planning Perspectives, 23,* 6–16.

Kirby, D., et al. (1993). The effects of school-based health clinics in St. Paul on school-wide birthrates. *Family Planning Perspectives, 25,* 12–16.

Kite, M. E. (1992). Individual differences in males' reactions to gay males and lesbians. *Journal of Applied Social Psychology, 22,* 1222–1239.

Klepinger, D. H., et al. (1993). Perceptions of AIDS risk and severity and their association with risk-related behavior among U.S. men. *Family Planning Perspectives, 25,* 74–82.

Klüver, H., & Bucy, P. C. (1939). Preliminary analysis of functions of the temporal lobes in monkeys. *Archives of Neurology and Psychiatry, 42,* 979.

Knapp, M. L. (1978). *Social intercourse: A behavioral approach to counseling.* Champaign, IL: Research Press.

Knight, R. A., et al. (1991). *Antisocial personality disorder and Hare assessments of psychopathy among sexual offenders.* Manuscript in preparation.

Knight, S. E. (1989). Sexual concerns of the physically disabled. In B. W. Heller, et al. (Eds.), *Psychosocial interventions with physically disabled persons* (pp. 183–199). New Brunswick, NJ: Rutgers University Press.

Knox, D. (1983). *The love attitudes inventory* (Rev. ed.). Saluda, NC: Family Life Publications.

Knox, D. (1988). *Choices in relationships.* St. Paul: West.

Knudsen, D. D. (1991). Child sexual coercion. In E. Grauerholz & M. A. Koralewski (Eds.), *Sexual coercion: A sourcebook on its nature, causes, and prevention* (pp. 17–28). Lexington, MA: Lexington Books.

Knussman, R., et al. (1986). Relations between sex hormone levels and sexual behavior in men. *Archives of Sexual Behavior, 15,* 429–445.

Kockott, G., & Fahrner, E. (1987). Transsexuals who have not undergone surgery: A follow-up study. *Archives of Sexual Behavior, 16,* 511–522.

Kohlberg, L. (1966). A cognitive–developmental analysis of children's sex-role concepts and attitudes. In E. E. Maccoby (Ed.), *The development of sex differences.* Stanford, CA: Stanford University Press.

Kohn, A. (1987, February). Shattered innocence. *Psychology Today,* 54–58.

Kolata, G. (1996, February 28). Study reports small risk, if any, from breast implants. *The New York Times,* p. A12.

Kolata, G. (1993a, February 26). Studies say mammograms fail to help many women. *The New York Times,* pp. A1, A15.

Kolata, G. (1993b, March 7). Targeting urged in attack on AIDS. *The New York Times,* pp. A1, A26.

Kolata, G. (1993c, December 14). Breast cancer screening under 50: Experts disagree if benefit exists: Statisticians find no proof that screening saves lives. *The New York Times,* pp. C1, C17.

Kolata, G. (1995, May 28). Will the lawyers kill off Norplant? *The New York Times,* pp. F1, F5.

Kolbert, E. (1991, October 11). Sexual harassment at work is pervasive, survey suggests. *The New York Times,* pp. A1, A17.

Kolodny, R. C. (1981). Evaluating sex therapy: Process and outcome at the Masters & Johnson Institute. *Journal of Sex Research, 17,* 301–318.

Komisar, L. (1971). The image of women in advertising. In V. Gornick & B. Moran (Eds.), *Women in sexist society.* New York: Basic Books.

Kon, I. S. (1995). *The sexual revolution in Russia.* New York: The Free Press.

Kontula, O., et al. (1992). Sexual knowledge, attitudes, fears and behaviors of adolescents in Finland (the KISS study). *Health Education Research, 7,* 69–77.

Koop, C. E. (1988). *Understanding AIDS.* HHS Publication No. HHS-88-8404. Washington, DC: U.S. Government Printing Office.

Korb, L. J. (1995, March 19). Asked, told, pursued. *The New York Times,* Section 4, p. 15.

Kornblum, W. J. (1994). *Sociology in a changing world* (3nd ed.). Ft. Worth, TX: Harcourt Brace.

Koss, L. (1989). The papanicolaou test for cervical cancer detection. *Journal of Sex Research, 261,* 737.

Koss, M. P. (1993). Rape: Scope, impact, interventions, and public policy responses. *American Psychologist, 48,* 1062–1069.

Koss, M. P., et al. (1987). The scope of rape: Incidence and prevalence of sexual aggression and victimization in a national sample of higher education students. *Journal of Consulting and Clinical Psychology, 55,* 162–170.

Koutsky, L. A., et al. (1992). A cohort study of the risk of cervical intraepithelial neoplasia Grade 2 or 3 in relation to papillomarvirus infection. *New England Journal of Medicine, 327,* 1272.

Kouzi, A. C., et al. (1992). Contraceptive behavior among intravenous drug users at risk for AIDS. *Psychology of Addictive Behaviors.*

Krafka, C. L. (1985). *Sexually explicit, sexually violent, and violent media: Effects of multiple naturalistic exposures and debriefing on female viewers.* Unpublished doctoral dissertation, University of Wisconsin-Madison.

Kresin, D. (1993). Medical aspects of inhibited sexual desire disorder. In W. O'Donohue & J. H. Geer (Eds.), *Handbook of sexual dysfunctions: Assessment and treatment* (pp. 15–52). Boston: Allyn & Bacon.

Kruesi, M. J. P., et al. (1992). Paraphilias: A double-blind crossover comparison of clomipramine versus desipramine. *Archives of Sexual Behavior, 21,* 587–594.

Kruks, G. (1991). Gay and lesbian homeless/street youth: Special issues and concerns [Special issue: Homeless youth]. *Journal of Adolescent Health, 12,* 515–518.

Ku, L. C., et al. (1992). The association of AIDS education and sex education with sexual behavior and condom use among teenage men. *Family Planning Perspectives, 24,* 100–106.

Kuhn, D., et al. (1978). Sex-role concepts of two- and three-year olds. *Child Development, 49,* 445–451.

Kuiper, B., & Cohen-Kettenis, P. (1988). Sex reassignment surgery: A study of 141 Dutch transsexuals. *Archives of Sexual Behavior, 17,* 439–457.

Kulin, H., et al. (1989). The onset of sperm production in pubertal boys. *American Journal of Diseases of Children, 143,* 190–193.

Kumar, U. (1991). Life stages in the development of the Hindu woman in India. In L. L. Adler (Ed.), *Women in cross-cultural perspective* (pp. 143–158). New York: Praeger.

Kunkel, L. E., & Temple, L. L. (1992). Attitudes towards AIDS and homosexuals: Gender, marital status, and religion. *Journal of Applied Social Psychology, 22,* 1030–1040.

Kurdek, L. A, & Schmitt, J. P. (1986a). Relationship quality of gay men in closed or open relationships. *Journal of Homosexuality, 12* (2), 85–99.

Kurdek, L. A., & Schmitt, J. P. (1986b). Relationship quality of partners in heterosexual married, heterosexual cohabiting, gay, and lesbian relationships. *Journal of Personality and Social Psychology, 51,* 711–720.

Laan, E., & Heiman, J. (1994). *Archives of Sexual Behavior.*

Lacayo, R. (1993, March 22). One doctor down, how many more? *Time,* 47.

Ladas, A. K., et al. (1982). *The G spot and other recent discoveries about human sexuality.* New York: Holt, Rinehart & Winston.

Laird, J. (1994). A male pill? Gender discrepancies in contraceptive commitment. *Feminism and Psychology, 4* (3), 458–468.

Lamaze, F. (1981). *Painless childbirth.* New York: Simon & Schuster.

Lambert, B. (1988, September 20). AIDS among prostitutes not as prevalent as believed, studies show. *The New York Times,* p. B1.

Lamke, L. K. (1982a). Adjustment and sex-role orientation. *Journal of Youth and Adolescence, 11,* 247–259.

Lamke, L. K. (1982b). The impact of sex-role orientation on self-esteem in early adolescence. *Child Development, 53,* 1530–1535.

Lane, K. E., & Gwartney-Gibbs, P. A. (1985). Violence in the context of dating and sex. *Journal of Family Issues, 6,* 45–59.

Lang, A. R. (1985). The social psychology of drinking and human sexuality. *Journal of Drug Issues, 15,* 273–289.

Lang, A. R., et al. (1980). Expectancy, alcohol, and sex guilt as determinants of interest in and reaction to sexual stimuli. *Journal of Abnormal Psychology, 89,* 644–653.

Lang, R. A., et al. (1989). An examination of sex hormones in genital exhibitionists. *Annals of Sex Research, 2,* 67–75.

Langevin, R., et al. (1979). Experimental studies of the etiology of genital exhibitionism. *Archives of Sexual Behavior, 8,* 307–332.

Langevin, R., et al. (1985). Sexual aggression: Constructing a predictive equation. In R. Langevin (Ed.), *Erotic preference, gender identity, and aggression in men: New research studies* (pp. 39–76). Hillsdale, NJ: Erlbaum.

Langevin, R., et al. (1989). Characteristics of sex offenders who were sexually victimized as children. *Annals of Sex Research, 2,* 227–253.

Lansky, D., & Wilson, G. T. (1981). Alcohol, expectations, and sexual arousal in males: An information-processing analysis. *Journal of Abnormal Psychology, 90,* 35–45.

LaTour, M. S. (1990). Female nudity in print advertising: An analysis of gender differences in arousal and ad response. *Psychology and Marketing, 7,* 65–81.

Laumann, E. O., et al. (1994). *The social organization of sexuality: Sexual practices in the United States.* Chicago: University of Chicago Press.

Laviola, M. (1989). Effects of older brother–younger sister incest: A review of four cases. *Journal of Family Violence, 4,* 259–274.

Lavoisier, P., et al. (1995). Clitoral blood flow increases following vaginal pressure stimulation. *Archives of Sexual Behavior, 24,* 37–45.

Lawrence, K., & Herold, E. S. (1988). Women's attitudes toward and experience with sexually explicit materials. *Journal of Sex Research, 24,* 161–169.

Lawson, C. (1993, August 5). Single but mothers by choice: "Who is my daddy?" can be answered in different ways. *The New York Times,* pp. C1, C9.

Leary, W. E. (1990, September 13). New focus on sperm brings fertility successes. *The New York Times,* p. B11.

Leary, W. E. (1992, December 10). Medical panel says most sexual impotence in men can be treated without surgery. *The New York Times,* p. D20.

Leary, W. E. (1993, April 28). Screening of all newborns urged for sickle cell disease. *The New York Times,* p. C11.

Leary, W. E. (1995, May 11). When it comes to giant sperm, this tiny fruit fly is a whale. *The New York Times,* p. A26.

Leavitt, G. C. (1990). Sociobiological explanations of incest avoidance: A critical review of evidential claims. *American Anthropologist, 92,* 971–993.

Ledray, L. E. (1990). Counseling rape victims: The nursing challenge. *Perspectives in Psychiatric Care, 26,* 21–27.

Lee, F. R. (1995, May 9). Anguish in the era of AIDS: Choosing to have babies. *The New York Times,* pp. A1, B6.

Lee, J. A. (1988). Love-styles. In R. J. Sternberg & M. L. Barnes (Eds.), *The psychology of love* (pp. 38–67). New Haven: Yale University Press.

Leiblum, S. R., & Rosen, R. C. (1991). Couples therapy for erectile disorders: Conceptual and clinical considerations [Special issue: The treatment of male erectile disorders]. *Journal of Sex and Marital Therapy, 17,* 147–159.

Leigh, B. C., et al. (1994). Sexual behavior of American adolescents: Results from a U.S. national survey. *Journal of Adolescent Health, 15* (2) 117–125.

Leitenberg, H., & Henning, K. (1995). Sexual fantasy. *Psychological Bulletin, 117,* 469–496.

Leitenberg, H., et al. (1989). The relation between sexual activity among children during preadolescence and/or early adolescence and sexual behavior and sexual adjustment in young adulthood. *Archives of Sexual Behavior, 18,* 299–313.

Leitenberg, H., et al. (1993). Gender differences in masturbation and the relation of masturbation experience in preadolescence and/or early adolescence to sexual behavior and sexual adjustment in young adulthood. *Archives of Sexual Behavior, 22,* 87–98.

Leiter, R. A. (Ed.). (1993). *National survey of state laws.* Detroit, MI: Gale Research.

Leland, N. L., & Barth, R. P. (1992). Gender differences in knowledge, intentions, and behaviors concerning pregnancy and sexually transmitted disease prevention among adolescents. *Journal of Adolescent Health, 13,* 589–599.

Lemon, S. J., & Newbold, J. E. (1990). Viral hepatitis. In K. K. Holmes, et al. (Eds.), *Sexually transmitted diseases* (2nd ed.) (pp. 449–466). New York: McGraw-Hill.

Lenihan, G., et al. (1992). Gender differences in rape supportive attitudes before and after a date rape education intervention. *Journal of College Student Development, 33,* 331–338.

Lesnik-Oberstein, M., & Cohen, L. (1984). Cognitive style, sensation seeking, and assortive mating. *Journal of Personality and Social Pshychology, 46,* 57–66.

Letourneau, E., & O'Donohue, W. (1993). Sexual desire disorders. In W. O'Donohue & J. H. Geer (Eds.), *Handbook of sexual dysfunctions: Assessment and treatment.* (pp. 53–81). Boston: Allyn & Bacon.

LeVay, S. (1991). A difference in hypothalamic structure between heterosexual and homosexual men. *Science, 253,* 1034–1037.

Lever, J., et al. (1992). Behavior patterns and sexual identity of bisexual males. *Journal of Sex Research, 29,* 141–167.

Levine, G. I. (1991). Sexually transmitted parasitic diseases. *Primary Care: Clinics in Office Practice, 18,* 101–128.

Levinger, G. (1980). Toward the analysis of close relationships. *Journal of Experimental Social Psychology, 16,* 510–544.

Levitt, E. E. (1988). Alternative life style and marital satisfaction: A brief report. *Annals of Sex Research, 1,* 455–461.

Levitt, E. E., & Mulcahy, J. J. (1995). The effect of intracavernosal injection of papaverine hydrochloride on orgasm latency. *Journal of Sex and Marital Therapy, 21,* 39–41.

Levy, D. S. (1991, September 16). Why Johnny might grow up violent and sexist. *Time,* 16–19.

Levy, G. D., & Carter, D. B. (1989). Gender schema, gender constancy, and gender-role knowledge: The roles of cognitive factors in preschoolers' gender-role stereotype attributions. *Developmental Psychology, 25,* 444–449.

Levy, J. Right brain, left brain: Fact and fiction. *Pschology Today, 19,* (5), 38–44.

Lewin, T. (1991, February 8). Studies on teen-age sex cloud condom debate. *The New York Times,* p. A14.

Lewin, T. (1992a, February 28). Canada court says pornography harms women. *The New York Times,* p. B7.

Lewin, T. (1992b, May 28). Parental consent to abortion: How enforcement can vary. *The New York Times,* pp. A1, B8.

Lewin, T. (1995). Women are becoming equal providers. *The New York Times,* p. A27.

Lewis, D. K., & Watters, J. K. (1991). Sexual risk behavior among heterosexual intravenous drug users: Ethnic and gender variations. *AIDS, 5,* 77–83.

Lewis, P. H. (1995, August 21). Planet Out: "Gay global village" of cyberspace. *The New York Times,* p. D3.

Libman, E. (1989). Sociocultural and cognitive factors in aging and sexual expression: Conceptual and research issues. *Canadian Psychology, 30,* 560–567.

Libman, E., et al. (1985). The role of therapeutic format in the treatment of sexual dysfunction: A review. *Clinical Psychology Review, 5,* 103–117.

Lief, H. I., & Hubschman, L. (1993). Orgasm in the postoperative transsexual. *Archives of Sexual Behavior, 22* 145–155.

Lindermalm, G., et al. (1986). Long-term follow-up of "sex change" in 134 male to female transsexuals. *Archives of Sexual Behavior, 15,* 187–210.

Lindsey, R. (1988, February 1). Circumcision under criticism as unnecessary to newborn. *The New York Times,* p. A1.

Linsley, W. A. (1989). The case against censorship of pornography. In D. Zillmann & J. Bryant (Eds.), *Pornography: Research advances and policy considerations* (pp. 343–359). Hillsdale, NJ: Erlbaum.

Linz, D. (1989). Exposure to sexually explicit materials and attitudes toward rape: A comparison of study results. *Journal of Sex Research, 26,* 50–84.

Linz, D., et al. (1988). The effects of long-term exposure to violent and sexually degrading depictions of women. *Journal of Personality and Social Psychology, 55,* 758–767.

Lisak, D. (1991). Sexual aggression, masculinity, and fathers. *Signs, 16,* 238–262.

Lisak, D., & Roth, S. (1990). Motives and psychodynamics of self-reported, unincarcerated rapists. *American Journal of Orthopsychiatry, 60,* 268–280.

Liskin, L., et al. (1990). Condoms—now more than ever. *Population Reports, 8,* 1–36.

Lohr, J. (1989). The foreskin and urinary tract infections. *Journal of Pediatrics, 114,* 502–504.

LoPiccolo, J. (1994). The evolution of sex therapy. *Sexual and Marital Therapy, 9* (1), 5–7.

LoPiccolo, J., & Friedman, J. (1988). Broad-spectrum treatment of low sexual desire: Integration of cognitive, behavioral, and systemic therapy. In S. Leiblum & R. Rosen (Eds.), *Sexual desire disorders.* New York: Guilford Press.

LoPiccolo, J., & Stock, W. E. (1986). Treatment of sexual dysfunction. *Journal of Consulting and Clinical Psychology, 54,* 158–167.

Lorch, D. (1993a, February 23). Uganda, scared by AIDS, turns to its youth. *The New York Times,* pp. A1, A10.

Lorch, D. (1993b, December 18). After years of ignoring AIDS epidemic, Kenya has begun facing up to it. *The New York Times,* p. A5.

Lorch, D. (1995, May 15). Wave of rape adds new horror to Rwanda's trail of brutality. *The New York Times,* p. A1.

Lorefice, L. S. (1991). Fluoxetine treatment of a fetish. *Journal of Clinical Psychiatry, 52.*

Lott, B. (1985). The potential enhancement of social/personality psychology through feminist research and vice versa. *American Psychologist, 40,* 155–164.

Lottes, I. L., & Kuriloff, P. J. (1992). The effects of gender, race, religion, and political orientation on the sex role attitudes of college freshmen. *Adolescence, 27,* 675–688.

Lovdal, L. T. (1989). Sex role messages in television commercials: An update. *Sex Roles, 21,* 715–724.

Lown, J., & Dolan, E. (1988). Financial challenges in remarriage. *Lifestyles: Family and Economic Issues, 9,* 73–88.

Lowry, R., et al. (1994). Substance use and HIV-related sexual behaviors among US high school students: Are they related? *American Journal of Public Health, 84* (7) 1116–1120.

Loy, P. H., & Stewart, L. P. (1984). The extent and effects of the sexual harassment of working women. *Sociological Focus, 17,* 31–43.

Lublin, J. S. (1995, September 28). Survey finds more Fortune 500 firms have at least two female directors. *Wall Street Journal,* p. B16.

Luckenbill, D. F. (1985). Entering male prostitution. *Urban Life, 14,* 131–153.

Lundstrom, B., et al. (1984). Outcome of sex reassignment surgery. *Acta Psychiatrica Scandinavica, 70,* 289–294.

Lynxwiler, J., & Gay, D. (1994). Reconsidering race differences in abortion attitudes. *Social Science Quarterly, 75* (1) 67–84.

Lyons, J. (1991). Artistic freedom and the university. *Art Journal, 50* (4), 77–83.

Macallan, D. C., et al. (1995). Energy expenditure and wasting in human immunodeficiency virus infection. *New England Journal of Medicine, 333,* 83–88.

Maccoby, E. E. (1990). Gender and relationships: A developmental account. *American Psychologist, 45,* 513–520.

Maccoby, E. E., & Jacklin, C. N. (1974). *The psychology of sex differences.* Stanford, CA: Stanford University Press.

MacDonald, N. E., et al. (1990). High-risk STD/HIV behavior among college students. *Journal of the American Medical Association, 263,* 3155–3159.

MacLean, P. M. (1976). Brain mechanisms of elemental sexual functions. In B. J. Sadock et al. (Eds.), *The sexual experience.* Baltimore: Williams & Wilkins.

Mahoney, E. R., et al. (1986). Sexual coercion and assault: Male socialization and female risk. *Sexual Coercion and Assault, 1,* 2–8.

Major, B., & Cozzarelli, C. (1992). Psychosocial predictors of adjustment to abortion. *Journal of Social Issues, 48,* 121–142.

Malamuth, N. M. (1981). Rape proclivity among males. *Journal of Social Issues, 37,* 138–157.

Malamuth, N. M. (1984). Aggression against women: Cultural and individual causes. In N. M. Malamuth & E. Donnerstein (Eds.), *Pornography and sexual aggression* (pp. 19–52). Orlando, FL: Academic Press.

Malamuth, N. M., & Ceniti, J. (1986). Repeated exposure to violent and nonviolent pornography: Likelihood of raping ratings and laboratory aggression against women. *Aggressive Behavior, 12,* 129–137.

Male birth control. (1995, August 1). *New York Newsday,* p. B31.

Males, M. A. (1995, July 8). Adult involvement in teenage childbearing and STD. *Lancet, 346,* 64–65.

Maletzky, B. M. (1980). Self-referred vs. court-referred sexually deviant patients: Success with assisted covert sensitization. *Behavior Therapy, 11,* 306–314.

Malinowski, B. (1927). *Sex and repression in savage society.* London: Kegan Paul, Trench, Trubner & Co.

Malinowski, B. (1929). *The sexual life of savages in north-western Melanesia.* New York: Eugenics.

Malloy, M. H., et al. (1992). Sudden infant death syndrome and maternal smoking. *American Journal of Public Health, 82,* 1380–1382.

Mammograms on rise, federal study finds. (1992, April 29). *The New York Times,* p. C13.

Marchbanks, P., et al. (1988). Risk factors for ectopic pregnancy. *Journal of the American Medical Association, 259,* 1823–1827.

Marcus, A. J. (1995). Aspirin as a prophylaxis against colorectal cancer. *New England Journal of Medicine, 333,* 656–658.

Margolin, L., et al. (1989). When a kiss is not just a kiss: Relating violations on consent in kissing to rape myth acceptance. *Sex Roles, 20,* 231–243.

Markowitz, J., et al. (1995). A preliminary study of ritonavir, an inhibitor of HIV-1 protease, to treat HIV-1 infection. *New England Journal of Medicine, 333,* 1534–1539.

Marks, G., et al. (1981). Effect of targets' physical attractiveness on assumption of similarity. *Journal of Personality and Social Psychology, 41,* 198–206.

Marshall, D. (1971). Sexual behavior on Mangaia. In D. Marshall & R. Suggs (Eds.), *Human sexual behavior: Variations in the ethnographic spectrum* (pp. 103–162). New York: Basic Books.

Marshall, W. L. (1989). Pornography and sex offenders. In D. Zillmann & J. Bryant (Eds.), *Pornography: Research advances and policy considerations* (pp. 185–214). Hillsdale, NJ: Erlbaum.

Marshall, W. L., et al. (1991). Treatment outcome with sex offenders. *Clinical Psychology Review, 11,* 465–485.

Marsiglio, W. (1993a). Adolescent males' orientation toward paternity and contraception. *Family Planning Perspectives, 25,* 22–31.

Marsiglio, W. (1993b). Attitudes toward homosexual activity and gays as friends: A national survey of heterosexual 15- to 19-year-old males. *Journal of Sex Research, 30,* 12–17.

Martens, M., & Faro, S. (1989, January). Update on trichomoniasis: Detection and management. *Medical Aspects of Human Sexuality,* 73–79.

Martin, C. L., & Halverson, C. F., Jr. (1981). A schematic processing model of sex typing and stereotyping in children. *Child Development, 54,* 1119–1134.

Martin, C. L., & Halverson, C. F., Jr. (1983). The effects of sex-typing schemas on young children's memory. *Child Development, 54,* 563–574.

Martin, D. H. (1990). Chlamydial infections. *Medical Clinics of North America, 74,* 1367–1387.

Martinez, F. D., et al. (1992). Increased incidence of asthma in children of smoking mothers. *Pediatrics, 89,* 21–26.

Martinson, F. M. (1976). Eroticism in infancy and childhood. *The Journal of Sex Research, 2,* 251–262.

Mason, R. T., et al. (1989). Sex pheromones in snakes. *Science, 245,* 290–293.

Masters, W. H., & Johnson, V. E. (1966). *Human sexual response.* Boston: Little, Brown.

Masters, W. H., & Johnson, V. E. (1970). *Human sexual inadequacy.* Boston: Little, Brown.

Masters, W. H., & Johnson, V. E. (1979). *Homosexuality in perspective.* Boston: Little, Brown.

Masters, W. H., et al. (1989). *Human sexuality* (4th ed.) New York: Harper Collins.

Matek, O. (1988). Obscene phone callers. *Journal of Social Work and Human Sexuality, 7,* 113–130.

Matthews, K. A., et al. (1990). Influences of natural menopause on psychological characteristics and symptoms of middle-aged healthy women. *Journal of Consulting and Clinical Psychology, 58,* 345–351.

Maybach, K. L., & Gold, S. R. (1994). Hyperfemininity and attraction to macho and non-macho men. *Journal of Sex Research, 31* (2), 91–98.

Mayeaux, E. J., Jr. (1995). Noncervical human papilloma virus genial infections. *American Family Physicians, 52,* 1137–1146.

Mayer, J. P., et al. (1990). A randomized evaluation of smoking cessation interventions for pregnant women at a WIC [women, infants, and children] clinic. *American Journal of Public Health, 80,* 76–79.

McArthur, M. J. (1990). Reality therapy with rape victims. *Archives of Psychiatric Nursing, 4,* 360–365.

McCabe, M. P., & Delaney, S. M. (1992). An evaluation of therapeutic programs for the treatment of secondary inorgasmia in women. *Archives of Sexual Behavior, 21,* 69–89.

McCann, K. (1992). The impact of receiving a positive HIV antibody test: Factors associated with the response. *Counseling Psychology Quarterly, 5,* 37–45.

McConaghy, M. J. (1979). Gender performance and the genital basis of gender: Stages in the development of constancy of gender. *Child Development, 50,* 1223–1226.

McConaghy, N. (1987). Heterosexuality/homosexuality: Dichotomy or continuum? *Archives of Sexual Behavior, 16,* 411–424.

McConaghy, N., & Blaszczynski, A. (1980). A pair of monozygotic twins discordant for homosexuality: Sex-dimorphic behavior and penile volume responses. *Archives of Sexual Behavior, 9,* 123–124.

McCormack, W. M. (1990). Overview. *Sexually Transmitted Diseases, 57,* 187–191.

McCusker, J., et al. (1992). Maintenance of behavioral change in a cohort of homosexually active men. *AIDS, 6,* 861–868.

McGuire, R. J., et al. (1965). Sexual deviation as conditioned behavior: A hypothesis. *Behaviour Research and Therapy, 2,* 185–190.

McKeachie, W. (1994). Cited in DeAngelis, T. (1994). Educators reveal keys to success in classroom. *APA Monitor, 25* (1), 39–40.

McKinney, K. (1989). Social factors in contraceptive and abortion attitudes and behaviors. In K. McKinney & S. Sprecher (Eds.), *Human sexuality: The societal and interpersonal context.* Norwood, NJ: Ablex Publishing Corporation.

McKinney, K., & Maroules, N. (1991). Sexual harassment. In E. Grauerholz & M. A. Koralewski (Eds.), *Sexual coercion: A sourcebook on its nature, causes, and prevention* (pp. 29–44). Lexington, MA: Lexington Books.

McKirnan, D. J., et al. (1995). Bisexually active men: Social characteristics and sexual behavior. *Journal of Sex Research, 32,* 65–76.

McLaren, J., & Brown, R. E. (1989). Childhood problems associated with abuse and neglect. *Canada's Mental Health, 37* (3), 1–6.

McLaughlin, F. J., et al. (1992). Randomized trial of comprehensive prenatal care for low-income women: Effect on infant birth weight. *Pediatrics, 89,* 128–132.

Mead, M. (1935). *Sex and temperament in three primitive societies.* New York: Dell.

Mead, M. (1967). *Male and female: A study of the sexes in a changing world.* New York: Morrow.

Meana, M., & Binik, Y. M. (1994). Painful coitus: A review of female dyspareunia. *Journal of Nervous and Mental Disease, 182* (5), 264–272.

Meiselman, K. C. (1978). *Incest: A psychological study of causes and effects with treatment recommendations.* San Francisco: Jossey-Bass.

Meisler, A. W., & Carey, M. P. (1990). A critical reevaluation of nocturnal penile tumescence monitoring in the diagnosis of erectile dysfunction. *Journal of Nervous and Mental Disease, 178,* 78–89.

Mélange. (1994, June 1). *Chronicle of Higher Education,* p. B3.

Melvin, S. Y. (1990). Syphilis: Resurgence of an old disease. *Primary Care: Clinics in Office Practice, 17,* 47–57.

Mertz, G. J. (1990). Genital herpes simplex virus infections. *Medical Clinics of North America, 74,* 1433–1454.

Mertz, G. J., et al. (1992). Risk factors for the sexual transmission of genital herpes. *Annals of Internal Medicine, 116,* 197–202.

Messenger, J. C. (1971). Sex and repression in an Irish folk community. In D. S. Marshall and R. C. Suggs (Eds.), *Human sexual behavior: Variations in the ethnographic spectrum* (pp. 3–37). New York: Basic Books.

Meston, C. M., & Gorzalka, B. B. (1992). Psychoactive drugs and human sexual behavior: The role of serotonergic activity. *Journal of Psychoactive Drugs, 24,* 1–40.

Meuwissen, I., & Over, R. (1990). Habituation and dishabituation of female sexual arousal. *Behaviour Research and Therapy, 28,* 217–226.

Meyer, J. K., & Reter, D. J. (1979). Sex reassignment: Follow-up. *Archives of General Psychiatry, 36,* 1010–1015.

Meyer-Bahlburg, H. F. L., et al. (1995). Prenatal estrogens and the development of homosexual orientation. *Developmental Psychology, 31* (1), 12–21.

Michael, R. T., et al. (1994). *Sex in America: A definitive survey.* Boston: Little, Brown.

Michaels, D., & Levine, C. (1992). Estimates of the number of motherless youth orphaned by AIDS in the United States. *Journal of the American Medical Association, 268,* 3456–3461.

Mill, J. S. (1939). Utilitarianism. In E. A. Burtt (Ed.), *The English philosophers.* New York: Modern Library. (Original work published 1863)

Miller, B. C., & Bingham, C. R. (1989). Family configuration in relation to the sexual behavior of female adolescents. *Journal of Marriage and the Family, 51,* 499–506.

Miller, B. C., et al. (1986). Dating age and stage as correlates of adolescent sexual attitudes and behavior. *Journal of Adolescent Research, 1,* 361–371.

Miller, D. (1995). Personal communication.

Miller, H. G., et al. (Eds.). (1990). *AIDS: The second decade.* Washington, DC: National Academy Press.

Mills, J. L. (1995). Protecting the embryo from X-rated drugs. *New England Journal of Medicine, 333,* 124–125.

Minai, N. (1981). *Women in Islam: Tradition and transition in the Middle East.* London: John Murray.

Minkoff, H. L., et al. (1990). The relationship of cocaine use to syphilis and human immunodeficiency virus infections among inner city parturient women. *American Journal of Obstetrics and Gynecology, 163,* 521–526.

Mirotznik, J. (1991). Genital herpes: A survey of the attitudes, knowledge, and reported behaviors of college students at risk for infection. *Journal of Psychology and Human Sexuality, 4,* 73–99.

Mirotznik, J., et al. (1987). Genital herpes: An investigation of its attitudinal and behavioral correlates. *Journal of Sex Research, 23,* 266–272.

Mishell, D. R., Jr. (1989). Medical progress: Contraception. *New England Journal of Medicine, 320,* 777–787.

MMWR. (1995). Update: AIDS among women—United States, 1994. *Morbidity and Mortality Weekly Report, 44,* 81–84.

Mohr, D. C., & Beutler, L. E. (1990). Erectile dysfunction: A review of diagnostic and treatment procedures. *Clinical Psychology Review, 10,* 123–150.

Moi, H., et al. (1989). Should male consorts of women with bacterial vaginosis be treated? *Genitourinary Medicine, 65,* 263–268.

Molotsky, I. (1995, November 18). Admiral has to quit over his comments on Okinawa rape. *The New York Times,* p. 1+.

Money, J. (1987a). Sin, sickness or status—Homosexual gender identity and psychoneuroendocrinology. *American Psychologist, 42,* 384–399.

Money, J. (1987b). Treatment guidelines: Antiandrogen and counseling of paraphiliac sex offenders. *Journal of Sex and Marital Therapy, 13,* 219–223.

Money, J. (1988). *Gay, straight, and in-between.* New York: Oxford University Press.

Money, J. (1990). Agenda and credenda of the Kinsey Scale. In D. P. McWhirter, et al. (Eds.), *Homosexuality/heterosexuality: Concepts of sexual orientation* (pp. 41–60.). New York: Oxford University Press.

Money, J. (1994). The concept of gender identity disorder in childhood and adolescence after 39 years. *Journal of Sex and Marital Therapy, 20* (3), 163–177.

Money, J., & Ehrhardt, A. (1972). *Man and woman, boy and girl.* Baltimore: Johns Hopkins University Press.

Money, J., & Lamacz, M. (1989). *Vandalized lovemaps.* Buffalo, NY: Prometheus Books.

Money, J., & Wiedeking, C. (1980). Gender identity/role: Normal differntiation and its transpositions. In. B. Wolman & J. Money (Eds.), *Handbook of human sexuality* (pp. 269–284). Englewood Cliffs, NJ: Prentice-Hall.

Money, J., et al. (1984). Micropenis: Adult follow-up and comparison of size against new norms. *Journal of Sex and Marital Therapy, 10,* 105–116.

Mooney, K. M., et al. (1992). Physical distance and AIDS: Too close for comfort? *Journal of Applied Social Psychology, 22,* 1442–1452.

Moore, K. A., & Stief, T. M. (1992). Changes in marriage and fertility behavior: Behavior versus attitudes of young adults. *Youth and Society, 22,* 362–386.

Morales, E. (1992). Latino gays and Latina lesbians. In S. Dworkin & F. Gutierrez (Eds.), *Counseling gay men and lesbians: Journey to the end of the rainbow.* Alexandria, VA: American Association for Counseling and Development.

Moran, J. S., & Zenilman, J. M. (1990). Therapy for gonococcal infections: Options in 1989. *Reviews of Infectious Diseases* (Suppl. 6), S633-S644.

More single mothers. (1993, July 26). *Time,* 16.

Morris, N., et al. (1987). Marital sex frequency and midcycle female testosterone. *Archives of Sexual Behavior, 7,* 157–173.

Morrison, E. S., et al. (1980). *Growing up sexual.* New York: Van Nostrand Reinhold.

Morse, E., et al. (1992). Sexual behavior patterns of customers of male street prostitutes. *Archives of Sexual Behavior, 21,* 347.

Moscarello, R. (1990). Psychological management of victims of sexual assault. *Canadian Journal of Psychiatry, 35,* 25–30.

Mosher, D. L. (1988). Pornography defined: Sexual involvement theory, narrative context, and goodness-of-fit. *Journal of Psychology and Human Sexuality, 1,* 67–85.

Mosher, W. D., & Bachrach, C. A. (1987). First premarital contraceptive use. *Studies in Family Planning, 18,* 83.

Most taking their time tying the knot. (1994, August 26). *The Wall Street Journal,* p. B1.

Ms. (1995, July/August). p. 17.

Muehlenhard, C. L., & Falcon, P. L. (1990). Men's heterosocial skill and attitudes toward women as predictors of verbal sexual coercion and forceful rape. *Sex Roles, 23,* 241–259.

Muehlenhard, C. L., & Linton, M. A. (1987). Date rape and sexual aggression in dating situations: Incidence and risk factors. *Journal of Counseling Psychology, 34,* 186–196.

Mueser, K. T., et al. (1984). You're only as pretty as you feel: Facial expression as a determinant of physical attractiveness. *Journal of Personality and Social Psychology, 46,* 469–478.

Mulry, G., et al. (1994). Substance use and unsafe sex among gay men: Global versus situational use of substances. *Journal of Sex Education and Therapy, 20* (3), 175–184.

Murray, J. B. (1988). Psychopharmacological therapy of deviant sexual behavior. *Journal of General Psychology, 115,* 101–110.

Murstein, B. I. (1988). A taxonomy of love. In R. J. Sternberg & M. L. Barnes (Eds.), *The psychology of love* (pp. 13–37). New Haven: Yale University Press.

Murstein, B., et al. (1991). Love styles in the United States and France: A cross-cultural comparison. *Journal of Social and Clinical Psychology, 10,* 37–46.

Muster, N. J. (1992). Treating the adolescent victim-turned-offender. *Adolescence, 27,* 441–450.

Myers, A. M., & Gonda, G. (1982). Utility of the masculinity–femininity construct: Comparison of traditional and androgyny approaches. *Journal of Personality and Social Psychology, 43,* 514–523.

Myers, M. F. (1989). Men sexually assaulted as adults and sexually abused as boys. *Archives of Sexual Behavior, 18,* 203–215.

Nadeau, R., et al. (1993). Knowledge and beliefs regarding STDs and condoms among students. *Canadian Journal of Public Health, 84,* 181–185.

Nadler, R. D. (1990). Homosexual behavior in nonhuman primates. In D. P. McWhirter, et al. (Eds.) *Homosexuality/heterosexuality: Concepts of sexual orientation* (pp. 138–170). New York: Oxford University Press.

Nakanishi, M. (1986). Perceptions of self-disclosure in initial interaction: A Japanese sample. *Human Communication Research, 13,* 167–190.

National Abortion Rights League. Action Fact Sheet. (1993, July). Washington, DC: Author.

National Academy of Sciences, Institute of Medicine. (1982). *Marijuana and health.* Washington, DC: National Academy Press.

National Academy of Sciences. (1995, September 25). Cited in "A strong endorsement for clean needles." *The New York Times,* p. A14.

National Crime Victimization Survey. (1995). U.S. Bureau of Justice Statistics. Washington, DC: U.S. Department of Justice.

National Research Council. (1993). *Losing generations: Adolescents in high risk settings.* Washington, DC: National Academy Press.

Navarro, M. (1993, February 18). New York needle exchanges called surprisingly effective. *The New York Times,* pp. A.1, B4.

Nelson, R. (1988). Nonoperative management of impotence. *Journal of Urology, 139,* 2–5.

Nevid, J. S. (1983). Exposure to homoerotic stimuli: Effects on attitudes and affects of heterosexual viewers. *Journal of Social Psychology, 119,* 249–255.

Nevid, J. S. (1984). Sex differences in factors of romantic attraction. *Sex Roles, 11,* 401–411.

The new providers. (1995, May22). *Newsweek,* 36–38.

A new use for Prozac. (1995, June 19). *Newsweek,* 85.

Newcomb, P. A., & Storer, B. E. (1995). Postmenopausal hormone use and risk of large-bowel cancer. *Journal of the National Cancer Institute, 87* (14), 1067–1071.

Newcomer, S. F., & Udry, J. R. (1985). Oral sex in an adolescent population. *Archives of Sexual Behavior, 14,* 41–46.

Nichols, M. (1990a). Lesbian relationships: Implications for the study of sexuality and gender. In D. P. McWhirter, et al. (Eds.), *Homosexuality/heterosexuality: Concepts of sexual orientation* (pp. 350–364). New York: Oxford University Press.

1990: The year that was. (1991). *Ms., 1* (4), 14–15.

Nock, S. L. (1995). A comparison of marriages and cohabiting relationships. *Journal of Family Issues, 16* (1) 53–76.

Norman, J., & Harris, M. (1981). *The private life of the American teenager.* New York: Rawson Wade.

The Norplant backlash. (1995, November 27). *Newsweek,* p. 52.

Nosek, M. A., et al. (1994). Wellness models and sexuality among women with physical disabilities. *Journal of Applied Rehabilitation Counseling, 25* (1), 50–58.

Notebook. (1994, June 1). *Chronicle of Higher Education,* p. A31.

Novello, A. C. (1991). Women and HIV infection. *Journal of the American Medical Association, 265,* 1805.

Nyamathi, A., et al. (1995). Psychosocial predictors of AIDS risk behavior and drug use behavior in homeless and drug addicted women of color. *Health Psychology, 14,* 265–273.

Ochs, R. (1993a, December 7). Breast cancer risk: What the numbers mean. *New York Newsday,* pp. 72–75.

Ochs, R. (1993b, December 7). Prostate cancer jolt: 16% increase attributed to wider screening. *New York Newsday,* p. 7.

Ochs, R. (1994, January 11). Cervical cancer comeback. *New York Newsday,* pp. 55, 57.

O'Connell, M. (1991). Cited in Pear, R. (1991, December 4). Larger number of new mothers are unmarried. *The New York Times,* p. A20.

O'Donohue, W., et al. (1993). Premature ejaculation. In W. O'Donohue & J. H. Geer (Eds.), *Handbook of sexual dysfunctions: Assessment and treatment.* (pp. 303–333). Boston: Allyn & Bacon.

O'Hara, M. W., et al. (1984). Prospective study of postpartum depression: Prevalence, course, and predictive factors. *Journal of Abnormal Psychology, 93,* 158–171.

O'Hara, M. W., et al. (1991). Prospective study of postpartum blues: Biological and psychosocial factors. *Archives of General Psychiatry, 48,* 801–806.

Okami, P., & Goldberg, A. (1992). Personality correlates of pedophilia: Are they reliable indicators? *Journal of Sex Research, 29,* 297–328.

Oldenburg, R., & Brissett, D. (1980, April). The essential hangout. *Psychology Today,* pp. 81–84.

Olds, J. (1956). Pleasure centers in the brain. *Scientific American, 193,* 105–116.

Olds, J., & Milner, P. (1954). Positive reinforcement produced by electrical stimulation of the septal area and other regions of the rat brain. *Journal of Comparative and Physiological Psychology, 47,* 419–427.

One true gay life in the navy. (1995, February 6). *U.S. News & World Report,* 60–61.

O'Neill, N., & O'Neill, G. (1972). *Open marriage.* New York: Evans.

Osborne, N. G., & Adelson, M. D. (1990). Herpes simplex and human papillomavirus genital infections: Controversy over obstetric management. *Clinical Obstetrics and Gynecology, 33,* 801–811.

Oswalt, R., & Matsen, K. (1993). Sex, AIDS, and the use of condoms: A survey of compliance in college students. *Psychological Reports, 72,* 764–766.

Overholser, J. C., & Beck, S. (1986). Multimethod assessment of rapists, child molesters, and three control groups on behavioral and psychological measures. *Journal of Consulting and Clinical Psychology, 54,* 682–687.

Oz, S. (1994). Decision making in divorce therapy: Cost–cost comparisons. *Journal of Marital and Family Therapy, 20,* 77–81.

Oz, S. (1995). A modified balance-sheet procedure for decision making in therapy: Cost–cost comparisons. *Professional Psychology: Research and Practice, 26,* 78–81.

Padesky, C. (1988). Attaining and maintaining positive lesbian self-identity: A cognitive therapy approach. *Women and Therapy, 8,* 145–156.

Padgett, V. R., et al. (1989). Pornography, erotica, and attitudes toward women: The effects of repeated exposure. *Journal of Sex Research, 26,* 479–491.

Padian, N. S., et al. (1991). Female-to-male transmission of human immunodeficiency virus. *Journal of the American Medical Association, 266,* 1664–1667.

Padilla, E. R., & O'Grady, K. E. (1987). Sexuality among Mexican Americans: A case of sexual stereotyping. *Journal of Personality and Social Psychology, 52,* 5–10.

Painter, K. (1987, October 27). Poll challenges Hite's figures on fidelity. *USA Today,* p. D1.

Palace, E. M. (1995). Modification of dysfunctional patterns of sexual arousal through autonomic arousal and false physiological feedback. *Journal of Consulting and Clinical Psychology, 63,* 604–615.

Palmore, E. (1981). *Social patterns in normal aging: Findings from the Duke Longitudinal Study.* Durham, NC: Duke University Press.

Palson, C., & Palson, R. (1972). Swinging in wedlock. *Society, 9* (4), 28–37.

Parlee, M. B. (1982, September). New findings: Menstrual cycles and behavior. *Ms.,* 126–128.

Parsons, E. (1991, November 18). Women become top U.S. AIDS risk group. *The New York Times,* p. A14.

Parsons, N. K., et al. (1990). Validation of a scale to measure reasoning about abortion. *Journal of Counseling Psychology, 37,* 107–112.

Patterson, C. J. (1995). Special issue: Sexual orientation and human development. *Developmental Psychology, 31,* 3–140.

Pauly, B., & Edgerton, M. (1986). The gender-identity movement. *Archives of Sexual Behavior, 15,* 315–329.

Pauly, I. B. (1974). Female transsexualism: Part 1. *Archives of Sexual Behavior, 3,* 487–508.

Pear, R. (1991, December 4). Larger number of new mothers are unmarried. *The New York Times,* p. A20.

Pearson, C. A. (1992). Cited in Leary, W. E. (1992, February 1). U.S. panel backs approval of first condom for women. *The New York Times,* p. 7.

Peckham, C., & Gibb, D. (1995). Mother-to-child transmission of the human immunodeficiency virus. *New England Journal of Medicine, 333,* 298–302.

Pelkan, F. (1995, March–April). Voices from a war zone. *The Humanist, 55,* 6–10.

Penn, F. (1993, October 21). Cancer confusion: The risks and realities of human papilloma virus. *Manhattan Spirit,* pp. 14–15.

People. (1995, June 19). 59.

Peplau, L. A., & Cochran, S. D. (1980, September). *Sex differences in values concerning love relationships.* Paper presented at the annual meeting of the American Psychological Association, Montreal, Canada.

Peplau, L. A., & Cochran, S. D. (1990). A relationship perspective on homosexuality. In D. P. McWhirter, et al. (Eds.), *Homosexuality/heterosexuality: Concepts of sexual orientation* (pp. 321–349). New York: Oxford University Press.

Peplau, L., & Gordon, S. L. (1985). Women and men in love: Sex differences in close heterosexual relationships. In V. O'Leary et al. (Eds.), *Women, gender, and social psychology.* Hillsdale, NJ: Erlbaum.

Perduta-Fulginiti, P. S. (1992). Sexual functioning of women with complete spinal cord injury: Nursing implications [Special issue: Nursing roles and perspectives]. *Sexuality and Disability, 10,* 103–118.

Perlman, P., et al. (1993). To the editor [Letter]. *Journal of the American Medical Association, 270,* 706–707.

Perrett, D. I. (1994). *Nature.* Cited in Brody, J. E. (1994, March 21). Notions of beauty transcend culture, new study suggests. *The New York Times,* p. A14.

Perry, D. G., & Bussey, K. (1979). The social learning theory of sex differences: Imitation is alive and well. *Journal of Personality and Social Psychology, 37,* 1699–1712.

Perry, J. D., & Whipple, B. (1981). Pelvic muscle strength of female ejaculation: Evidence in support of a new theory of orgasm. *Journal of Sex Research, 17,* 22–39.

Perry, M. J., et al. (1994). High risk sexual behavior and alcohol consumption among bar-going gay men. *AIDS, 8* (9), 1321–1324.

Persky, H., et al. (1982). The relation of plasma androgen levels to sexual behaviors and attitudes of women. *Psychosomatic Medicine, 44,* 305–309.

Person, E. S., et al. (1989). Gender differences in sexual behaviors and fantasies in a college population. *Journal of Sex and Marital Therapy, 15,* 187–198.

Pfeiffer, N. (1992). Long-term survival and HIV disease: Are there really any secrets? *AIDS Patient Care, 6,* 134–139.

Phillips, K. A., et al. (1995). Potential use of home HIV testing. *New England Journal of Medicine, 332,* 1308–1310.

Pillard, R. C. (1990). The Kinsey Scale: Is it familial? In D. P. McWhirter, et al. (Eds.), *Homosexuality/heterosexuality: Concepts of sexual orientation* (pp. 88–100). New York: Oxford University Press.

Pillard, R. C., & Weinrich, J. D. (1986). Evidence of familial nature of male homosexuality. *Archives of Sexual Behavior, 43,* 808–812.

Pines, A., & Aronson, E. (1983). Antecedents, correlates, and consequences of sexual jealousy. *Journal of Personality, 51,* 108–109.

Pinkerton, S. D., & Abramson, P. R. (1992). Is risky sex rational? *Journal of Sex Research, 29,* 561–568.

Pitnick, S. (1995, May 11). *Nature.*

Plan for wider use of Norplant by girls dividing Baltimore. (1993, Feburary 11). *The New York Times,* p. B16.

Platt, R., et al. (1983). Risk of acquiring gonorrhea and prevalence of abnormal adrenal findings among women recently exposed to gonorrhea. *Journal of the American Medical Association, 250,* 3205–3209.

Platz-Christensen, J., et al. (1989). Detection of bacterial vaginosis in Papanicolaou smears. *American Journal of Obstetrics and Gynecology, 160,* 132–133.

Pliner, A. J., & Yates, S. (1992). Psychological and legal issues in minors' rights to abortion. *Journal of Social Issues, 48,* 203–216.

Podolsky, D. (1991, April 15). Charting premenstrual woes. *U.S. News & World Report,* pp. 68–69.

The politics of nature's nurture. (1995, August). *Governing, 8,* 54.

Polit-O'Hara, D., & Kahn, J. (1985). Communication and adolescent contraceptive practices in adolescent couples. *Adolescence, 20,* 33–43.

Pomeroy, W. B. (1966). Normal vs. abnormal sex. *Sexology, 32,* 436–439.

Population Council. (1995). Cited in Brody, J. E. (1995, August 31). Abortion method using two drugs gains in a study. *The New York Times,* pp. A1, B12.

Porter, N., et al. (1985). Androgyny and leadership in mixed-sex groups. *Journal of Personality and Social Psychology, 49,* 808–823.

Poussaint, A. (1990, September). An honest look at Black gays and lesbians. *Ebony,* 124, 126, 130–131.

Powderly, W. G., et al. (1995). A randomized trial comparing fluconazole with clotrimazole troches for the prevention of fungal infections in patients with advanced human immunodeficiency virus infection. *New England Journal of Medicine, 332,* 700–705.

Powell, E. (1991). *Talking back to sexual pressure.* Minneapolis: CompCare Publications.

Pratt, C., & Schmall, V. (1989). College students' attitudes toward elderly sexual behavior: Implications for family life education. *Family Relations, 38,* 137–141.

Prentky, R. A., & Knight, R. A. (1991). Identifying critical dimensions for discriminating among rapists. *Journal of Consulting and Clinical Psychology, 59,* 643–661.

Prescription for passion. (1995). *Health, 9,* 100–103.

Press, A., et al. (1985, March 18). The war against pornography. *Newsweek,* pp. 58–66.

Preti, G., et al. (1986). Human axillary secretions influence women's menstrual cycles: The role of donor extract of females. *Hormones and Behavior, 20,* 474–482.

Price, V. A. (1989). Characteristics and needs of Boston street youth: One agency's response [Special issue: Runaway, homeless, and shut-out children and youth in Canada, Europe, and the United States]. *Children and Youth Services Review, 11,* 75–90.

Proctor, F., et al. (1974). The differentiation of male and female orgasm: An experimental study. In N. Wagner (Ed.), *Perspectives on human sexuality.* New York: Behavioral Publications.

Pryde, N. A. (1989). Sex therapy in context. *Sexual and Marital Therapy, 4,* 215–227.

Psyched to get married. (1994, August). *Money,* 122–123.

Publicity about Magic Johnson may have led some to reduce their risky behavior, request HIV testing. (1993). *Family Planning Perspectives, 25,* 192–193.

Purdy, M. (1995, November 6). A kind of sexual revolution: At some nursing homes, intimacy is a matter of policy. *The New York Times*, pp. B1, B6.

Purifoy, F. E., et al. (1992). The relationship of sexual daydreaming to sexual activity, sexual drive, and sexual attitudes for women across the life-span. *Archives of Sexual Behavior, 21*, 369–375.

Quadagno, D., et al. (1991). Women at risk for human immunodeficiency virus. *Journal of Psychology and Human Sexuality, 4*, 97–110.

Quam, J. K., & Whitford, G. S. (1992). Adaptation and age-related expectations of older gay and lesbian adults. *Gerontologist, 32*, 367–374.

Quevillon, R. P. (1993). Dyspareunia. In W. O'Donohue & J. H. Geer (Eds.), *Handbook of sexual dysfunctions: Assessment and treatment* (pp. 367–380). Boston: Allyn & Bacon.

Quinn, T. C. (1990). Unique aspects of human immunodeficiency virus and related viruses in developing countries. In K. K. Holmes et al. (Eds.), *Sexually transmitted diseases* (2nd ed.) (pp. 355–369). New York: McGraw-Hill.

Quinsey, V. L., et al. (1984). Sexual arousal to nonsexual violence and sadomasochistic themes among rapists and non-sex-offenders. *Journal of Consulting and Clinical Psychology, 52*, 651–657.

Rachman, S. (1966). Sexual fetishism: An experimental analogue. *Psychological Record, 16*, 293–296.

Radlove, S. (1983). Sexual response and gender roles. In E. R. Allgeier & N. B. McCormick (Eds.), *Changing boundaries: Gender roles and sexual behavior*. Palo Alto, CA: Mayfield.

Rae, S. (1995). A long and happy sex life. *Men's Health, 10*, 62+.

Rajfer, J., et al. (1992). Nitric oxide as a mediator of relaxation of the corpus cavernosum in response to nonadrenergic, noncholinergic neurotransmission. *New England Journal of Medicine, 326*, 90–94.

Ramirez, A. (1990, August 12). The success of sweet smell. *The New York Times*, p. 10F.

Rao, K., et al. (1992). Child sexual abuse of Asians compared with other populations. *Journal of the American Academy of Child and Adolescent Psychiatry, 31*, 880–886.

Rate of births for teen-agers drops again. (1995, September 22). *The New York Times*, p. A18.

Rathus, S. A. (1978). Treatment of recalcitrant ejaculatory incompetence. *Behavior Therapy, 9*, 962.

Rathus, S. A., & Nevid, J. S. (1995). *Adjustment and growth: The challenges of life* (6th ed.). Fort Worth, TX: Harcourt Brace.

Rathus, S. A., & Fichner-Rathus, L. (1994). *Making the most of college* (2nd ed.). Englewood Cliffs, NJ: Prentice-Hall.

Ratican, K. L. (1992). Sexual abuse survivors: Identifying symptoms and special treatment considerations. *Journal of Counseling and Development, 71*, 33–38.

Raychaba, B. (1989). Canadian youth in care: Leaving care to be on our own with no direction from home [Special issue: Runaway, homeless, and shut-out children and youth in Canada, Europe, and the United States]. *Children and Youth Services Review, 11*, 61–73.

Reaby, L. L., et al. (1994). Body image, self-concept, and self-esteem in women who had a mastectomy and either wore an external breast prosthesis or had breast reconstruction and women who had not experienced mastectomy. *Health Care for Women International, 15* (5), 361–375.

Reichart, C. A., et al. (1990). Evaluation of Abbott Testpack Chlamydia for detection of chlamydia trachomatis in patients attending sexually transmitted diseases clinics. *Sexually Transmitted Diseases, 17*, 147–151.

Reid, T. R. (1990, December 24). Snug in their beds for Christmas Eve: In Japan, December 24th has become the hottest night of the year. *The Washington Post*.

Rein, M. F., & Muller, M. (1990). *Trichomonas vaginalis* and trichomoniasis. In K. K. Holmes, et al. (Eds.), *Sexually transmitted diseases* (2nd ed.) (pp. 481–492). New York: McGraw-Hill.

Reinisch, J. M. (1990). *The Kinsey Institute new report on sex: What you must know to be sexually literate*. New York: St. Martin's Press.

Reiss, B. F. (1988, Spring/Summer). The long-lived person and sexuality. *Dynamic Psychotherapy, 6*, 79–86.

Reiss, I. L. (1980). *Family systems in America*. New York: Holt, Rinehart & Winston.

Remafedi, G. (1990). Study group report on the impact of television portrayals of gender roles on youth. *Journal of Adolescent Health Care, 11* (1), 59–61.

Renzetti, C. M., & Curran, D. J. *Women, men, and society: The sociology of gender*. Boston: Allyn & Bacon.

Research panel concludes AIDS has small impact on most of U.S. (February 5, 1993). *The New York Times*, p. A11.

Resick, P. A., & Schnicke, M. K. (1990). Treating symptoms in adult victims of sexual assault. *Journal of Interpersonal Violence, 5*, 488–506.

Rice, M. E., et al. (1990). A follow-up of rapists assessed in a maximum-security psychiatric facility. *Journal of Interpersonal Violence, 5*, 435–448.

Rice, M. E., et al. (1991). Sexual recidivism among child molesters released from a maximum security psychiatric institution. *Journal of Consulting and Clinical Psychology, 59*, 381–386.

Richardson, S. (1996, February). The scent of a man. *Discover,* 26–27.

Riche, M. (1988, November 23–26). Postmarital society. *American Demographics, 60*.

Ricker, A. L. (1980, November). Sex for sale in Las Vegas. *Cosmopolitan*, 280–315.

Riggio, R. E., & Woll, S. B. (1984). The role of nonverbal cues and physical attractiveness in the selection of dating partners. *Journal of Social and Personal Relationships, 1*, 347–357.

Rindfuss, R. R. (1991). Cited in Pear, R. (1991, December 4) Larger number of new mothers are unmarried. *The New York Times*, p. A20.

Roadblock thrown at Internet indecency ban. (1996, February). *Des Moines Register*, p. 7A.

Roberto, L. G. (1983). Issues in diagnosis and treatment of transsexualism. *Archives of Sexual Behavior, 12*, 445–473.

Roehrich, L., & Kinder, B. N. (1991). Alcohol expectancies and male sexuality: Review and implications for sex therapy. *Journal of Sex & Marital Therapy, 17*, 45–54.

Rogan, H. (1984, October 30). Executive women find it difficult to balance demands of job, home. *Wall Street Journal*, pp. 35, 55.

Rogers, A. S., et al. (1993). Investigation of potential HIV _transmission to the patients of an HIV-infected surgeon. *Journal of the American Medical Association, 269*, 1795–1801.

Rogers, S. M. (1991, November). Male–male sexual contact in the U.S.: Findings from five sample surveys, 1970–1990. *Journal of Sex Research, 28*, 491–519.

Roland, B., et al. (1989). MMPI correlates of college women who reported experiencing child/adult sexual contact with father, stepfather, or with other persons. *Psychological Reports, 64*, 1159–1162.

Rolfs, R. T., & Nakashima, A. K. (1990). Epidemiology of primary and secondary syphilis in the United States: 1981 through 1989. *Journal of the American Medical Association, 264*, 1432–1437.

Rolfs, R. T., et al. (1990) Risk factors for syphilis: Cocaine use and prostitution. *American Journal of Public Health, 80,* 853–857.

Rollins, J. (1986). Single men and women: Differences and similarities. *Family Perspective, 20,* 117–124.

Romenesko, K., & Miller, E. M. (1989). The second step in double jeopardy: Appropriating the labor of female street hustlers. *Crime and Delinquency, 35,* 109–135.

Ronald, A. R., & Albritton, W. (1990). Chancroid and *Haemophilus ducreyi.* In K. K. Holmes, et al. (Eds.), *Sexually transmitted diseases* (2nd ed.) (pp. 263–272). New York: McGraw-Hill.

Roper Organization. (1985). *The Virginia Slims American women's poll.* New York: Author.

Rose, R. J. (1995). Genes and human behavior. *Annual Review of Psychology, 46,* 625–654.

Rosen, I. (1967). *Pathology and treatment of sexual deviations.* London: Oxford University Press.

Rosen, R. C., & Beck, J. G. (1988). *Patterns of sexual arousal.* New York: Guilford Press.

Rosen, R. C., et al. (1994) Psychologically based treatment for male erectile disorder: A cognitive–interpersonal model. *Journal of Sex and Marital Therapy, 20* (2), 67–85.

Rosenberg, M. J., & Gollub, E. L. (1992). Commentary: Methods women can use that may prevent sexually transmitted disease, including HIV.

Rosenthal, A. M. (1993, November 12). Female genital torture. *The New York Times,* p. A33.

Rosenthal, A. M. (1994, September 6). A victory in Cairo. *The New York Times,* p. A19.

Rosenthal, A. M. (1995, June 13). The possible dream. *The New York Times,* p. A25.

Rosenthal, D. A., et al. (1992). AIDS, adolescents, and sexual risk taking: A test of the Health Belief Model. *Australian Psychologist, 27,* 166–171.

Rosenthal, E. (1992, July 22). Her image of his ideal, in a faulty mirror. *The New York Times,* p. C12.

Rosman, J. P., & Resnick, P. J. (1989). Sexual attraction to corpses: A psychiatric review of necrophilia. *Bulletin of the American Academy of Psychiatry and the Law, 17,* 153–163.

Ross, M., & Need, J. (1989). Effects of adequacy of gender reassignment surgery on psychological adjustment: A follow-up of fourteen male-to-female patients. *Archives of Sexual Behavior, 18,* 145–153.

Rotheram-Borus, M. J., & Koopman, C. (1991a). HIV and adolescents [Special issue: Preventing the spread of the human immunodeficiency virus]. *Journal of Primary Prevention, 12,* 65–82.

Rotheram-Borus, M. J., & Koopman, C. (1991b). Sexual risk behaviors, AIDS knowledge, and beliefs about AIDS among runaways. *American Journal of Public Health, 81,* 209–211.

Rotheram-Borus, M. J., et al. (1992). Lifetime sexual behaviors among predominantly minority male runaways and gay/bisexual adolescents in New York City. *AIDS Education and Prevention,* (Fall Suppl.), 34–42.

Rothman, B. K. (1991). *In labor: Women and power in the birthplace.* New York: Norton.

Rovet, J., & Ireland, L. (1994). Behavioral phenotype in children with Turner syndrome. *Journal of Pediatric Psychology, 19,* 779–790.

Rozin, P., & Fallon, A. (1988). Body image, attitudes to weight, and misperceptions of figure preferences of the opposite sex: A comparison of men and women in two generations. *Journal of Abnormal Psychology, 97,* 342–345.

Rubin, A., & Adams, J. (1986). Outcomes of sexually open marriages. *Journal of Sex Research, 22,* 311–319.

Rubinow, D. R., & Schmidt, P. J. (1995). The treatment of premenstrual syndrome—forward into the past. *New England Journal of Medicine, 332,* 1574–1575.

Ruble, D. N., & Ruble, T. L. (1982). Sex stereotypes. In A. G. Miller (Ed.), *In the eye of the beholder: Contemporary issues in stereotyping.* New York: Praeger.

Ruefli, T., et al. (1992). Sexual risk taking in smaller cities: The case of Buffalo, New York. *Journal of Sex Research, 29,* 95–108.

Russell, C. (1995, September). Why teen births boom. *American Demographics,* 8.

Russell, D. (1982). *Rape in marriage.* New York: Macmillan.

Russo, N. F., et al. (1992). U.S. abortion in context: Selected characteristics and motivations of women seeking abortions. *Journal of Social Issues, 48,* 183–202.

Sack, W. H., & Mason, R. (1980). Child abuse and conviction of sexual crimes: A preliminary finding. *Law and Human Behavior, 4,* 211–215.

Sadalla, E. K., et al. (1987). Dominance and heterosexual attraction. *Journal of Personality and Social Psychology, 52,* 730–738.

Sadava, S. W., & Matejcic, C. (1987). Generalized and specific loneliness in early marriage. *Canadian Journal of Behavioural Science, 19,* 56–66.

Sadker, M., & Sadker, D. (1994). *How America's schools cheat girls.* New York: Scribners.

Sagan, C., & Dryan, A. (1990, April 22). The question of abortion: A search for answers. *Parade Magazine,* 4–8.

Sagarin, E. (1973). Power to the peephole. *Sexual Behavior, 3,* 2–7.

St. Lawrence, J. S., et al. (1995). Cognitive–behavioral intervention to reduce African American adolescents' risk for HIV infection. *Journal of Consulting and Clinical Psychology, 63,* 221–237.

Sales, E., et al. (1984). Victim readjustment following assault. *Journal of Social Issues, 40,* 117–136.

Saluter, A. F. (1992). Marital status and living arrangements: March 1992. *Current Population Reports,* Series P20–468.

Samuels, M., & Samuels, N. (1986). *The well pregnancy book.* New York: Simon & Schuster.

Sanchez-Guerrero, J., et al. (1995). Silicone breast implants and the risk of connective tissue diseases and symptoms. *New England Journal of Medicine, 332,* 1666–1670.

Sanday, P. R. (1981). The socio-cultural context of rape: A cross-cultural study. *Journal of Social Issues, 37,* 5–27.

Sanders, S. A., et al. (1990). Homosexuality/heterosexuality: An overview. In D. P. McWhirter, et al. (Eds.), *Homosexuality/ heterosexuality: Concepts of sexual orientation* (pp. xix–xxvii). New York: Oxford University Press.

Sandross, R. (1988, December). Sexual harassment in the Fortune 500. *Working Woman,* 69.

Sanger, M. (1938). *Margaret Sanger: An autobiography.* New York: Norton.

Sargent, T. O. (1988). Fetishism. *Journal of Social Work and Human Sexuality, 7,* 27–42.

Sarrel, P., & Masters, W. (1982). Sexual molestation of men by women. *Archives of Sexual Behavior, 11,* 117–131.

Sauer, M. V., et al. (1990). A preliminary report on oocyte donation extending reproductive potential to women over 40. *New England Journal of Medicine, 323,* 1157–1160.

Savitz, L., & Rosen, L. (1988). The sexuality of prostitutes: Sexual enjoyment reported by "streetwalkers." *Journal of Sex Research, 24,* 200–208.

Schachter, J. (1989). Why we need a program for the control of *Chlamydia trachomatis*. *New England Journal of Medicine, 320,* 802–804.

Schafer, R. B., & Keith, P. M. (1990). Matching by weight in married couples: A life cycle perspective. *Journal of Social Psychology, 130,* 657–664.

Schafran, L. H. (1995, August 26). Rape is still underreported. *The New York Times,* p. A19.

Schiavi, R. C., et al. (1990). Healthy aging and male sexual function. *American Journal of Psychiatry, 147,* 766–771.

Schillinger, L. (1995, June 10). More sex please, we're Russian. *The New York Times Book Review,* p. 49.

Schmid, G. P. (1995). Evolving strategies for management of the nongonococcal urethritis syndrome. *Journal of the American Medical Association, 274,* 577–579.

Schmidt, G. (1994). Sex therapy, 1970–1994. *Nordisk-Sexologi, 12* (3), 178–183.

Schmidt, K. W., et al. (1992). Sexual behaviour related to psycho-social factors in a population of Danish homosexual and bisexual men. *Social Science and Medicine, 34,* 1119–1127.

Schneemann, C. (1991). The obscene body/politic. *Art Journal, 50* (4), 28–35.

Schnell, D. J., & O'Reilly, K. R. (1991). Patterns of sexual behavior change among homosexual/bisexual men—selected U.S. sites, 1987–1990. *Mortality and Morbidity Weekly Report, 40, 46,* 792–794.

Schoendorf, K. C., & Kiely, J. L. (1992). Relationship of sudden infant death syndrome to maternal smoking during and after pregnancy. *Pediatrics, 90,* 905–908.

Schork, K. (1990, August 19). The despair of Pakistan's women: Not even Benazir Bhutto could stop the repression. *The Washington Post.*

Schott, R. L. (1995). The childhood and family dynamics of transvestites. *Archives of Sexual Behavior, 24,* 309–327.

Schreiner-Engle, P., & Schiavi, R. (1986). Lifetime psychopathology in individuals with low sexual desire. *Journal of Nervous and Mental Disease, 174,* 646–651.

Schultz, N. R., Jr., & Moore, D. W. (1984). Loneliness: Correlates, attributions, and coping among older adults. *Personality and Social Psychology Bulletin, 10,* 67–77.

Schwartz, I. M. (1993). Affective reactions of American and Swedish women to their first premarital coitus: A cross-cultural comparison. *Journal of Sex Research, 30,* 18–26.

Schwartz, M. F., & Masters, W. H. (1984). The Masters and Johnson treatment program for dissatisfied homosexual men. *American Journal of Psychiatry, 141,* 173–181.

Scott, J., & Schuman, H. (1980). Attitude strength and social action in the abortion dispute. *American Sociological Review, 53,* 785–793.

Scott, J. E., & Cuvelier, S. J. (1993). Violence and sexual violence in pornography: Is it really increasing? *Archives of Sexual Behavior, 22,* 357–371.

Scott, J. E., & Schwalm, L. A. (1988). Rape rates and the circulation rates of adult magazines. *Journal of Sex Research, 24,* 241–250.

Seachrist, L. (1995, September 23). Amount of virus sets cancer risk. *Science News,* p. 197.

Sears, A. E. (1989). The legal case for restricting pornography. In D. Zillmann & J. Bryant (Eds.), *Pornography: Research advances and policy considerations.* Hillsdale, NJ: Erlbaum.

Seattle-King County Department of Public Health. (1991). The AIDS Prevention Project: The Seattle Star: A report to the community on what we're learning from the "Be A Star Study." Seattle: Author.

Seftel, A. D., et al. (1991). Disturbed sexual function in patients with spinal cord disease. *Neurologic Clinics, 9,* 757–778.

Segal, S. J. (1990). Mifeprisone (RU 486). *New England Journal of Medicine, 322,* 691–693.

Segal, Z. V., & Marshall, W. L. (1985). Heterosexual social skills in a population of rapists and child molesters. *Journal of Consulting and Clinical Psychology, 53,* 55–63.

Segraves, R. T. (1988a). Drugs and desire. In S. Leiblum & R. Rosen (Eds.), *Sexual desire disorders.* New York: Guilford Press.

Segraves, R. T. (1988b). Sexual side-effects of psychiatric drugs. *International Journal of Psychiatry in Medicine, 18,* 243–252.

Segraves, R. T., & Segraves, K. B. (1993). Medical aspects of orgasm disorders. In W. O'Donohue & J. H. Geer (Eds.), *Handbook of sexual dysfunctions: Assessment and treatment* (pp. 225–252). Boston: Allyn & Bacon.

Self. (1995, June). 75.

Seligmann, J. (1993, July 26). Husbands no, babies yes. *Newsweek,* 53.

Sell, R. L., et al. (1995). The prevalence of homosexual behavior and attraction in the United States, the United Kingdom, and France: Results of national, population-based samples. *Archives of Sexual Behavior, 24,* 235–248.

Seltzer, R. (1992). The social location of those holding antihomosexual attitudes. *Sex Roles, 26,* 391–398.

Selvin, B. W. (1993, June 1). Transsexuals are coming to terms with themselves and Society. *New York Newsday,* pp. 55, 58, 59.

Semans, J. (1956). Premature ejaculation: A new approach. *Southern Medical Journal, 49,* 353–358.

Seng, M. J. (1989). Child sexual abuse and adolescent prostitution: A comparative analysis. *Adolescence, 24,* 665–675.

Serrill, M. S. (1993, June 21). Defiling the children. *Time,* 52+.

Severn, J., et al. (1990). The effects of sexual and non-sexual advertising appeals and information level on cognitive processing and communication effectiveness. *Journal of Advertising, 19,* 14–22.

Sex has many accents. (1993, May 24). *Time,* 66.

Shafer, M. A., et al. (1993). Evaluation of urine-based screening strategies to detect *Chlamydia trachomatis* among sexually active asymptomatic young men. *Journal of the American Medical Association, 270,* 2065–2070.

Shanteau, J., & Nagy, G. (1979). Probability of acceptance in dating choice. *Journal of Personality and Social Psychology, 37,* 522–533.

Shapiro, J. P. (1992, July 13). The teen pregnancy boom. *U.S. News & World Report,* 38.

Shaver, P., et al. (1988). Love as attachment. In R. J. Sternberg & M. L. Barnes (Eds.), *The psychology of love* (pp. 68–99). New Haven: Yale University Press.

Shaw, J. (1989). The unnecessary penile implant. *Archives of Sexual Behavior, 18,* 455–460.

Sheehy, G. (1995). *New passages: Mapping your life across time.* New York: Random House.

Shenon, P. (1992, November 8). After years of denial, Asia faces scourge of AIDS. *The New York Times,* p. A1.

Shenon, P. (1995, July 15). New Zealand seeks causes of suicides by young. *The New York Times,* p. A3.

Sheppard, J. A., & Strathman, A. J. (1989). Attractiveness and height: The role of stature in dating preference, frequency of dating, and perceptions of attractiveness. *Personality and Social Psychology Bulletin, 15,* 17–627.

Sherman, K. J., et al. (1990). Sexually transmitted diseases and tubal pregnancy. *Sexually Transmitted Diseases, 17,* 115–121.

Sherwin, B. B., et al. (1985). Androgen enhances sexual motivation in females: A prospective, crossover study of sex steroid administration in the surgical menopause. *Psychosomatic Medicine, 47,* 339–351.

Shettles, L. (1982, June). Predetermining children's sex. *Medical Aspects of Human Sexuality, 172.*

Shilts, R. (1987). *And the band played on: Politics, people, and the AIDS epidemic.* New York: Penguin.

Siegel, J. M., et al. (1990). Reactions to sexual assault: A community study. *Journal of Interpersonal Violence, 5,* 229–246.

Siegel, K., et al. (1988). Patterns of change in sexual behavior among gay men in New York City. *Archives of Sexual Behavior, 17,* 481–497.

Siegler, I. C., et al. (1995). Predictors of adoption of mammography in women under age 50. *Health Psychology, 14,* 274–278.

Signorielli, N. (1990). Children, television, and gender roles: Messages and impact. *Journal of Adolescent Health Care, 11* (1), 50–58.

Silber, S. J. (1991). *How to get pregnant with the new technology.* New York: Time Warner.

Silbert, M. H. (1989). The effects on juveniles of being used for pornography and prostitution. In D. Zillmann & J. Bryant (Eds.), *Pornography: Research advances and policy considerations* (pp. 215–234). Hillsdale, NJ: Erlbaum.

Simpson, J. A., et al. (1986). The association between romantic love and marriage: Kephart (1967) twice revisited. *Personality and Social Psychology Bulletin,* 363–372.

Singer, J., & Singer, I. (1972). Types of female orgasm. *Journal of Sex Research, 8,* 255–267.

Singh, D. (1994a). Body fat distribution and perception of desirable female body shape by young Black men and women. *International Journal of Eating Disorders, 16* (3) 289–294.

Singh, D. (1994b). Is thin really beautiful and good? Relationship between waist-to-hip ratio (WHR) and female attractiveness. *Personality and Individual Differences, 16* (1) 123–132.

Singh, G. K., & Yu, S. M. (1995). Cited in Pear, R. (1995, July 10). Infant mortality rate drops but racial disparity grows. *The New York Times,* p. B9.

Sirles, E. A., & Franke, P. J. (1989). Factors influencing mother's reactions to intrafamily sexual abuse. *Child Abuse & Neglect, 13,* 131–139.

Slattery, M. L., & Kerber, R. A. (1993). A comprehensive evaluation of family history and breast cancer risk: The Utah population database. *Journal of the American Medical Association, 270,* 1563–1568.

Slonim-Nevo, V. (1992). First premarital intercourse among Mexican-American and Anglo-American adolescent women: Interpreting ethnic differences. *Journal of Adolescent Research, 7,* 332–351.

Smart, C. R., et al. (1995, April). *Cancer.* Cited in Brody, J. E. (1995a, May 3). Breast scans may indeed help women under 50. *The New York Times,* p. C11.

Smith, E. A., & Udry, J. R. (1985). Coital and non-coital sexual behaviors of white and black adolescents. *American Journal of Public Health, 75,* 1200–1203.

Smith, E. P., et al. (1994). Estrogen resistance caused by a mutation in the estrogen-receptor gene in a man. *The New England Journal of Medicine, 331,* 1056–1061.

Smolowe, J. (1993, June 14). New, improved and ready for battle. *Time,* pp. 48–51.

Smothers, R. (1995, July 25). Required fees for rape test may soon end: Alabama won't ask victims to pay bill. *The New York Times,* p. A8.

Sobel, J. D. (1990). Vaginal infections in adult women. *Medical Clinics of North America, 74,* 1573–1602.

Solano, C. H., et al. (1982). Loneliness and patterns of self-disclosure. *Journal of Personality and Social Psychology, 43,* 524–531.

Sonenstein, F. L., et al. (1989). Sexual activity, condom use and AIDS awareness among adolescent males. *Family Planning Perspectives, 21,* 152–157.

Sorensen, R. C. (1973). *Adolescent sexuality in contemporary America.* New York: World.

Sorrenti-Little, I., et al. (1984). An operational definition of the long-term harmfulness of sexual relations with peers and adults by young children. *Canadian Child, 9,* 46–57.

Sourander, L. B. (1994). Geriatric aspects on estrogen effects and sexuality. *Gerontology, 40* (Suppl. 3), 14–17.

Southerland, D. (1990, May 27). Limited "sexual revolution" seen in China: Nationwide survey shows more liberal attitudes developing in conservative society. *The Washington Post.*

Spark, R. F. (1991). *Male sexual health: A couple's guide.* Mount Vernon, NY: Consumer Reports Books.

Speckens, A. E. M., et al. (1995). Psychosexual functioning of partners of men with presumed non-organic erectile dysfunction: Cause or consequence of the disorder? *Archives of Sexual Behavior, 24,* 157–172.

Speroff, L., et al. (1985). *Clinical gynecologic endocrinology and infertility.* Baltimore: Williams & Wilkins.

Spiro, M. E., (1965). *Children of the kibbutz.* New York: Schocken Books.

Spitz, I. M. (1995, February 6). Antiprogestins: Modulators in reproduction. *Chemistry and Industry,* 89–92.

Spitzer, R. L., et al. (1989). *DSM-III-R casebook.* Washington, DC: American Psychiatric Press.

Spotlight is now on domestic violence. (1994, June 22). *Des Moines Register,* 1A–2A.

Sprecher, S. (1989). Premarital sexual standards for different categories of individuals. *Journal of Sex Research, 26,* 232–248.

Sprecher, S., et al. (1994). Mate selection preferences: Gender differences examined in a national sample. *Journal of Personality and Social Psychology, 66* (6), 1074–1080.

Sprecher, S., et al. (1995). "Was it good for you, too?" Gender differences in first sexual intercourse experiences. *Journal of Sex Research, 32,* 3–15.

Stamm, W. E., & Holmes, K. K. (1990). *Chlamydia trachomatis* infections of the adult. In K. K. Holmes, et al. (Eds.), *Sexually transmitted diseases* (2nd ed.) (pp. 181–194). New York: McGraw-Hill.

Stampfer, M. J., et al. (1988). A prospective study of past use of oral contraceptive agents and risk of cardiovascular diseases. *New England Journal of Medicine, 319,* 1313–1317.

Stampfer, M. J., et al. (1991, June). Ten-year follow-up study of estrogen replacement therapy in relation to cardiovascular disease and mortality. Paper presented at the 24th annual meeting of the Society for Epidemiologic Research, Buffalo, New York.

Stangor, C., & Ruble, D. N. (1989). Differential influences of gender schemata and gender constancy on children's information processing and behavior. *Social Cognition, 7,* 353–372.

Starr, B. D., & Weiner, M. B. (1981). *The Starr-Weiner report on sex and sexuality in the mature years.* New York: Stein & Day.

Starrs, A. (1987). Preventing the tradegy of maternal deaths. Report presented at the International Safe Motherhood Conference, Nairobi, Kenya.

Steele, C. M., & Josephs, R. A. (1990). Alcohol myopia: Its prized and dangerous effects. *American Psychologist, 45,* 21–933.

Steiner, M., et al. (1995). Fluoxetine in the treatment of premenstrual dysphoria. *New England Journal of Medicine, 332,* 1529–1534.

Steinhauer, J. (1995, July 6). No marriage, no apologies. *The New York Times,* pp. C1, C7.

Stephens, T. (1991). AIDS in women reveals health-care deficiencies. *Journal of NIH Research, 3,* 27–30.

Stephens, W. N. (1982). *The family in cross-cultural perspective.* Washington, DC: University Press of America.

Stericker, A., & LeVesconte, S. (1982). Effect of brief training on sex-related differences in visual–spatial skill. *Journal of Personality and Social Psychology, 43,* 1018–1029.

Sternberg, R. J. (1986). A triangular theory of love. *Psychological Review, 93,* 119–135.

Sternberg, R. J. (1987). Liking versus loving: A comparative evaluation of theories. *Psychological Bulletin, 102,* 331–345.

Sternberg, R. J. (1988). *The triangle of love: Intimacy, passion, commitment.* New York: Basic Books.

Sternberg, R. J., & Grajek, S. (1984). The nature of love. *Journal of Personality and Social Psychology, 47,* 312–329.

Sterngold, J. (1992, September 8). Japan confronts sudden rise in AIDS. *The New York Times,* p. L13.

Stewart, F. H. (1992). Cited in Leary, W. E. (1992, February 1). U.S. panel backs approval of first condom for women. *The New York Times,* p. 7.

Still no pill for Japan. (1992, March 22). *The New York Times,* Section 4, p. 7.

Stock, W. E. (1991). Feminist explanations: Male power, hostility, and sexual coercion. In E. Grauerholz & M. A. Koralewski (Eds.), *Sexual coercion: A sourcebook on its nature, causes, and prevention* (pp. 61–73). Lexington, MA: Lexington Books.

Stock, W. E. (1993). Inhibited female orgasm. In W. O'Donohue & J. H. Geer (Eds.), *Handbook of sexual dysfunctions: Assessment and treatment* (pp. 253–301). Boston: Allyn & Bacon.

Stoller, R. J. (1969). Parental influences in male transsexualism. In R. Green & J. Money (Eds.), *Transsexualism and sex reassignment.* Baltimore: Johns Hopkins University Press.

Stoller, R. J. (1977). Sexual deviations. In R. Beach (Ed.), *Human sexuality in four perspectives* (pp. 190–214). Baltimore: Johns Hopkins University Press.

Stoller, R. J., & Herdt, G. H. (1985). Theories of origins of male homosexuality. *Archives of General Psychiatry, 42,* 399–404.

Stone, S. (1989). Assessing oral contraceptive risks. *Medical Aspects of Human Sexuality,* 112–122.

Storms, M. D. (1979). Sexual orientation and self-perception. In P. Pliner et al. (Eds.), *Advances in the study of communication and affect* (Vol. 5). New York: Plenum.

Storms, M. D. (1980). Theories of sexual orientation. *Journal of Personality and Social Psychology, 38,* 783–792.

Stotland, N. (1992, October 21). The myth of the abortion trauma syndrome. *Journal of the American Medical Association.*

Strassberg, D. S., et al. (1990). The role of anxiety in premature ejaculation: A psychophysiological model. *Archives of Sexual Behavior, 19,* 251–257.

Strickland, B. R. (1995). Research on sexual orientation and human development: A commentary. *Developmental Psychology, 31,* 137–140.

Strom, S. (1993, April 18). Human pheromones. *The New York Times,* p. V12.

Struckman-Johnson, C. (1988). Forced sex on dates: It happens to men, too. *Journal of Sex Research, 24,* 234–241.

Sue, D. (1979). Erotic fantasies of college students during coitus. *Journal of Sex Research, 15,* 299–305.

Sue, D., et al. (1981). *Understanding abnormal behavior.* Boston: Houghton Mifflin Co.

Sullivan, A. (1995). *Virtually normal.* New York: Knopf.

Summers, R. J. (1991). Determinants of the acceptance of co-workers with AIDS. *Journal of Social Psychology, 131,* 577–578.

Suppe, F. (1994). Explaining homosexuality: Philosophical issues, and who cares anyhow? *Journal of Homosexuality, 27* (3–4), 223–268.

Swann, W. B., Jr., et al. (1987). Cognitive–affective crossfire: When self-consistency meets self-enhancement. *Journal of Personality and Social Psychology, 52,* 881–889.

Symons, D. (1979). *The evolution of human sexuality.* New York: Oxford University Press.

Symons, D. (1995). Cited in Goleman, D. (1995, June 14). Sex fantasy research said to neglect women. *The New York Times,* p. C14.

Szasz, G., & Carpenter, C. (1989). Clinical observations in vibratory stimulation of the penis of men with spinal cord injury. *Archives of Sexual Behavior, 18,* 461–474.

Taking care to deter child abuse. (1995). *Science News, 147,* 88.

Tanfer, K., et al. (1993). Condom use among U.S. men, 1991. *Family Planning Perspectives, 25,* 61–66.

Tang, C. S., et al. (1995). Sexual aggression and victimization in dating relationships among Chinese college students. *Archives of Sexual Behavior, 24,* 47–53.

Tannahill, R. (1980). *Sex in history.* Briarcliff Manor, NY: Stein & Day.

Tannen, D. (1990). *You just don't understand.* New York: Ballantine.

Tannenbaum, J. (1991). Robert Mapplethorpe: The Philadelphia story. *Art Journal, 50* (4), 71–76.

Tavris, C., & Sadd, S. (1977). *The Redbook report on female sexuality.* New York: Delacorte.

Taylor, R. (1993a, July). Asia now second only to Africa in total HIV infections. *Journal of NIH Research,* 48–50.

Taylor, R. (1993b, July). Dentist-to-patient HIV-1 transmission: More heat, no light. *Journal of NIH Research,* 50.

Taylor, R. (1993c). Sex surveys help map AIDS risk. *Journal of NIH Research, 5,* 31–32.

Tedeschi, C. (1995, January). Snuffing tigers for sex and profit. *Discover,* p. 59.

Tedeschi, J. T., & Felson, R. B. (1994). *Violence, aggression, & coercive actions.* Washington, DC: American Psychological Association.

Telushkin, J. (1991). *Jewish literacy.* New York: Morrow.

Tempest, R. (1993, February 18). Ancient traditions vs. the law. *The Los Angeles Times,* pp. A1, A10.

Teen-agers and aids: The risk worsens. (1992, April 14). *The New York Times,* p. C3.

Tharinger, D. (1990). Impact of child sexual abuse on developing sexuality. *Professional Psychology: Research and Practice, 21,* 331–337.

Thomason, J. L., & Gelbart, S. M. (1989). Trichomonas vaginalis. *Obstetrics and Gynecology, 74,* 536–541.

Thomlison, B., et al. (1991, Fall). Characteristics of Canadian male and female child sexual abuse victims [Special issue: Child sexual abuse]. *Journal of Child and Youth Care,* 65–76.

Thompson, D. S. (Ed.). (1993). *Every woman's health: The complete guide to body and mind.* New York: Simon & Schuster.

Thompson, J. K., & Tantleff, S. (1992). Female and male ratings of upper torso: Actual, ideal, and stereotypical conceptions. *Journal of Social Behavior and Personality, 7,* 345–354.

Thompson, M. E. (1991). Self-defense against sexual coercion: Theory, research, and practice. In E. Grauerholz & M. A. Koralewski (Eds.), *Sexual coercion: A sourcebook on its nature, causes, and prevention* (pp. 111–121). Lexington, MA: Lexington Books.

Thornton, A., & Camburn, D. (1987). The influence of the family on premarital sexual attitudes and behavior. *Demography, 24,* 323–340.

Tierney, J. (1994, January 9). Porn, the low-flung engine of progress. *The New York Times,* Section 2, pp. 1, 18.

Ting, D., & Carter, J. H. (1990). Behavioral change through empowerment: Prevention of AIDS. *Journal of the National Medical Association, 84,* 225–228.

Tobias, S. (1982). Sexist equations. *Psychology Today, 16* (1), pp. 14–17.

Tollison, C. D., & Adams, H. E. (1979). *Sexual disorders: Treatment, theory, and research.* New York: Gardner Press.

Tomlinson, J. A. (1991). Burn it, hide it, flaunt it. *Art Journal, 50* (4), 59–64.

Toner, J. P., et al. (1991). Basal follicle-stimulating hormone level is a better predictor of in vitro fertilization performance than age. *Fertility and Sterility, 55,* 784–791.

Toomey, K. E., & Barnes, R. C. (1990). Treatment of chlamydia trachomatis genital infection. *Reviews of Infectious Diseases* (Suppl. 6), S645-S655.

Toubia, N. (1994). Female circumcision as a public health issue. *New England Journal of Medicine, 331,* 712–716.

Touchette, N. (1991). HIV-1 link prompts circumspection of circumcision. *Journal of NIH Research, 3,* 44–46.

Townsend, J. M. (1995). Sex without emotional involvement: An evolutionary interpretation of sex differences. *Archives of Sexual Behavior, 24,* 173–206.

Trenton State College. (1991, Spring). *Sexual Assault Victim Education and Support Unit (SAVES-U) Newsletter.*

Trieschmann, R. (1989). Psychosocial adjustment to spinal cord injury. In B. W. Heller, et al. (Eds.), *Psychosocial interventions with physically disabled persons* (pp. 117–136). New Brunswick, NJ: Rutgers University Press.

Trinkaus, J., & Chow, M. B. (1990). Misgivings about AIDS transmission: An informal look. *Psychological Reports, 66,* 230–254.

Trovato, F. (1986). The relationship between marital dissolution and suicide: The Canadian case. *Journal of Marriage and the Family, 48,* 341–348.

Trujillo, C. (Ed.). (1991). *Chicana lesbians: The girls our mothers warned us about.* Berkeley, CA: Third Woman Press.

Trussell, J., et al. (1993). Contraceptive efficacy of the diaphragm, the sponge, and the cervical cap. *Family Planning Perspectives, 25,* 100–105.

Tseng, W. et al. (1992). Koro epidemics in Guangdong, China: A questionnaire survey. *Journal of Nervous and Mental Disease, 180,* 117–123.

Turner, C. F., et al. (Eds.). (1989). *AIDS: Sexual behavior and intravenous drug use.* Washington, DC: National Academy Press.

Tutty, L. M. (1992). The ability of elementary school children to learn child sexual abuse prevention concepts. *Child Abuse and Neglect, 16,* 369–384.

Two viewfinders, two views of Gay America. (1993, June 27). *The New York Times,* Section 4, p. 10.

Udry, J. R., & Billy, J. O. G. (1987). Initiation of coitus in early adolescence. *American Sociological Review, 52,* 841–855.

Udry, J. R., et al. (1985). Serum androgenic hormones motivate sexual behavior in adolescent boys. *Fertility and Sterility, 43,* 90–94.

Udry, J. R., et al. (1986). Biosocial foundations for adolescent female sexuality. *Demography, 23* (2), 217–230.

Ulbrich, P. M., et al. (1990) Involuntary childlessness and marital adjustment: His and hers. *Journal of Sex & Marital Therapy, 16,* 147–158.

U.S. Bureau of the Census. (1987). *Statistical abstract of the United States.* Washington, DC: U.S. Government Printing Office.

U.S. Bureau of the Census. (1990a). Marital status and living arrangements: March 1990. *Current Population Reports,* Series P-20, No. 450. Washington, DC: U.S. Government Printing Office.

U.S. Bureau of the Census. (1990b). *Statistical abstract of the United States.* Washington, DC: U.S. Government Printing Office.

U.S. Bureau of the Census. (1991). *Statistical abstract of the United States.* Washington, DC: U.S. Government Printing Office.

U.S. Department of Health and Human Services (USDHHS). (1990a). *The health benefits of smoking cessation: A report of the Surgeon General.* (DHHS Publication No. CDC 90–8416). Rockville, MD: Public Health Service, Centers for Disease Control, Center for Chronic Disease Prevention and Health Promotion, Office on Smoking and Health.

U.S. Department of Health and Human Services (USDHHS). (1991). *Strategies to control tobacco use in the United States: A blueprint for public health action in the 1990's.* (NIH Publication No. 92–3316). Washington, DC: National Cancer Institute, Public Health Service, National Institutes of Health, National Cancer Institute.

U.S. Department of Health and Human Services (USDHHS). (1992a). *Smoking and health in the Americas.* (DHHS Publication No. [CDC] 92–8419). Atlanta: Public Health Service, Centers for Disease Control, National Center for Chronic Disease Prevention and Health Promotion, Office on Smoking and Health.

U.S. Department of Health and Human Services, Public Health Service, Centers for Disease Control, Operational Research Section, Behavioral and Prevention Research Branch, Division of STD/HIV Prevention, Center for Prevention Services. (1992b). *What we have learned from the AIDS Community Demonstration Projects.* Atlanta: Centers for Disease Control.

U.S. Department of Justice. (1986). *Attorney general's commission on pornography: Final report.* Washington, DC: U.S. Government Printing Office.

U.S. finds heavy toll of rapes on young. (1994, June 23). *The New York Times,* p. A13.

U.S. Merit Systems Protection Board. (1981). *Sexual harassment in the federal workplace: Is it a problem?* Washington, DC: Office of Merit Systems Review and Studies.

U.S. says 349,000 caesareans in 1991 were not necessary. (1993, April 23). *The New York Times,* p. A16.

U.S. Senate Committee on the Judiciary. (1991). Violence against women: The increase of rape in America 1990. *Response to the Victimization of Women and Children, 14* (79, No. 2), 20–23.

Utne Reader. (1992, March/April). pp. 46–47.

Vaginal yeast infection can be an HIV warning. (1992, November 24). *New York Newsday,* p. 51.

Van den Hoek, A., et al. (1990). Heterosexual behaviour of intravenous drug users in Amsterdam: Implications for the AIDS epidemic. *AIDS, 4,* 449–453.

Van der Velde, F. W., et al. (1994). Perceiving AIDS-related risk: Accuracy as a function of differences in actual risk. *Health Psychology, 13,* 25–33.

Van Steirteghem, A. C., et al. (1993). High fertilization and implantation rates after intracytoplasmic sperm injection. *Human Reproduction, 8,* 1061–1066.

Vazi, R., et al. (1989). Evaluation of a testicular cancer curriculum for adolescents. *Journal of Pediatrics, 114,* 150–162.

Vinacke, W., et al. (1988). Similarity and complementarity in intimate couples. *Genetic, Social, and General Psychology Monographs, 114,* 51–76.

Voeller, B. (1991). AIDS and heterosexual anal intercourse. *Archives of Sexual Behavior, 20,* 33–276.

Von Krafft-Ebing, R. (1978). *Psychopathia sexualis.* Philadelphia: F. A. Davis. (Original work published 1886)

von Reyn, C. F., et al. (1993). Absence of HIV transmission from an infected orthopedic surgeon: A 13-year look-back study. *Journal of the American Medical Association, 269,* 1807–1811.

Voyer, D., et al. (1995). Magnitude of sex differences in spatial abilities: A meta-analysis and consideration of critical variables. *Psychological Bulletin, 117,* 250–270.

Waigandt, A., et al. (1990). The impact of sexual assault on physical health status. *Journal of Traumatic Stress, 3,* 93–102.

Wald, A., et al. (1995). Virologic characteristics of subclinical and symptomatic genital herpes infections. *New England Journal of Medicine, 333,* 770–775.

Waldinger, M. D., et al. (1994). Paroxetine treatment of premature ejaculation: A double-blind, randomized, placebo-controlled study. *American Journal of Psychiatry, 151* (9), 1377–1379.

Walfish, S., & Myerson, M. (1980). Sex role identity and attitudes toward sexuality. *Archives of Sexual Behavior, 9,* 199–204.

Wallace, H. M., & Vienonen, M. (1989). Teenage pregnancy in Sweden and Finland. *Journal of Adolescent Health Care, 10,* 231–236.

Wallerstein, J. S., & Blakeslee, S. (1989). *Second chances: Women and children a decade after divorce.* New York: Ticknor & Fields.

Wallerstein, J. S., & Kelly, J. B. (1980). *Surviving the breakup: How children and parents cope with divorce.* New York: Basic Books.

Walster, E., & Walster, G. W. (1978). *A new look at love.* Reading, MA: Addison-Wesley.

Walt, V. (1993, July 26). Some 2nd thoughts on Depo. *New York Newsday,* p. 13.

Walter, H. J., & Vaughan, R. D. (1993). AIDS risk reduction among a multiethnic sample of urban high school students. *Journal of the American Medical Association, 270,* 725–730.

Ward, S. K., et al. (1991). Acquaintance rape and the college social scene. *Family Relations, 40* 65–71.

Wardlaw, G. M., & Insel, P. M. (1990). *Perspectives in nutrition.* St. Louis: Times Mirror/Mosby College Publishing.

Warren, C. W., et al. (1990). Assessing the reproductive behavior of on- and off-reservation American Indian females: Characteristics of two groups in Montana. *Social Biology, 37,* 69–83.

Washington, A. C., et al. (1983). Contraceptive practices of teenage mothers. *Journal of the National Medical Association, 75,* 1059–1063.

Waterman, J. (1986). Overview of treatment issues. In K. MacFarlane et al. (Eds.), *Sexual abuse of young children: Evaluation and treatment* (pp. 197–203). New York: Guilford Press.

Waterman, J., & Lusk, R. (1986). Scope of the problem. In K. MacFarlane et al. (Eds.), *Sexual abuse of young children: Evaluation and treatment* (pp. 3–14). New York: Guilford Press.

Waterman, J., et al. (1986). Challenges for the future. In K. MacFarlane et al. (Eds.), *Sexual abuse of young children: Evaluation and treatment* (pp. 315–332). New York: Guilford Press.

Weinberg, M. S., et al. (1984). The social constituents of sadomasochism. *Social Problems, 31,* 379–389.

Weinberg, M. S., et al. (1994). *Dual attraction.* New York: Oxford University Press.

Weinberg, T. S. (1987). Sadomasochism in the United States: A review of recent sociological literature. *Journal of Sex Research, 23,* 50–69.

Weinberg, T. S., & Bullough, V. L. (1986). *Women married to transvestites: Problems and adjustments.* Paper presented at the annual meeting of the Society for the Study of Social Problems, New York, NY.

Weinberg, T. S., & Bullough, V. L. (1988). Alienation, self-image, and the importance of support groups for the wives of transvestites. *Journal of Sex Research, 24,* 262–268.

Weiner, J., et al. (1951). Carcinoma of the cervix in Jewish women. *American Journal of Obstetrics and Gynecology, 61,* 418.

Weingarten, H. (1985). Marital status and well-being: A national study comparing first-married, currently divorced, and remarried adults. *Journal of Marriage and the Family, 47,* 653–662.

Weinstock, H. S., et al. (1993). Factors associated with condom use in a high-risk heterosexual pouplation. *Sexually Transmitted Diseases, 20,* 14–20.

Weis, D. L., & Rabinowitz, B. (1992). Individual changes in sexual attitudes and behavior within college-level human sexuality courses. *Journal of Sex Research, 29,* 43–59.

Weisberg, D. K. (1985). *Children of the night: A study of adolescent prostitution.* Lexington, MA: Heath.

Weiss, D. L. (1983). Affective reactions of women to their initial experience of coitus. *Journal of Sex Research, 19,* 209–237.

Weiss, R. D., & Mirin, S. M. (1987). *Cocaine.* Washington, DC: American Psychiatric Press.

Werner, D., & Cohen, A. (1990). Instructor's edition. In C. R. Ember & M. Ember, *Anthropology.* (6th ed.) (pp. I-1–I-146). Englewood Cliffs, NJ: Prentice-Hall.

Westrom, L. V. (1990). Chlamydia trachomatis—clinical significance and strategies of intervention. *Seminars in Dermatology, 9,* 117–125.

Whalen, R. E., et al. (1990). Models of sexuality. In D. P. McWhirter, et al. (Eds.), *Homosexuality/Hetero-sexuality: Concepts of sexual orientation* (pp. 61–70). New York: Oxford University Press.

Wharton, C., & Blackburn, R. (1988, November). Lower-dose pills. *Population Reports,* Series A, No. 7.

Wheeler, J., & Kilmann, P. R. (1983). Comarital sexual behavior: Individual and relationship variables. *Archives of Sexual Behavior, 12,* 295–306.

Whiffen, V. E. (1992). Is postpartum depression a distinct diagnosis? *Clinical Psychology Review, 12,* 485–508.

Whipple, B., & Komisaruk, B. R. (1988). Analgesia produced in women by genital self-stimulation. *Journal of Sex Research, 24,* 130–140.

Whitam, F. L. (1977). Childhood indicators of male homosexuality. *Archives of Sexual Behavior, 6,* 89–96.

Whitam, F. L., et al. (1993). Homosexual orientation in twins: A report on 61 pairs and three triplet sets. *Archives of Sexual Behavior, 22,* 187–206.

White, G. L. (1981). Some correlates of romantic jealousy. *Journal of Personality, 49,* 129–146.

White, J. W. (1983). Sex and gender issues in aggression research. In R. G. Green & E. I. Donnerstein (Eds.), *Aggression: Theoretical and empirical reviews* (Vol. 2). New York: Academic Press.

White, S. D., & DeBlassie, R. R. (1992). Adolescent sexual behavior. *Adolescence, 27,* 183–191.

White, V. M., et al. (1994). Is the conflict model of decision making applicable to the decision to be screened for cervical cancer? A field study. *Journal of Behavioral Decision Making, 7* (1), 57–72.

Whitley, B. E., Jr. (1983). Sex role orientation and self-esteem: A critical meta-analysis. *Journal of Personality and Social Psychology, 44,* 765–788.

Whitley, B. E., Jr., & Kite, M. E. (1995). Sex differences in attitudes toward homosexuality. *Psychological Bulletin, 117,* 146–154.

Whitley, R., et al. (1991). Predictors of morbidity and mortality in infants with herpes simplex virus infections. *New England Journal of Medicine, 324,* 450–454.

Whittemore, A. S. (1994). The risk of ovarian cancer after treatment for infertility. *New England Journal of Medicine, 331,* 805–806.

Whittemore, A. S., et al. (1992). Characteristics relating to ovarian cancer risk: Collaborative analysis of 12 U.S. case-control studies: II. Invasive ovarian cancers in white women. *American Journal of Epidemiology, 136,* 1184–1203.

WHO (1995). Cited in "Rise in STDs concerns group." (1995, September 12). *Newsday,* p. B27.

Wilcox, A. J. (1995). Fertility in men exposed prenatally to diethylstilbestrol. *New England Journal of Medicine, 332,* 1411–1416.

Wilcox, A. J., et al. (1995). Timing of sexual intercourse in relation to ovulation: Effects on the probability of conception, survival of the pregancy, and sex of the baby. *New England Journal of Medicine, 333,* 1517–1521.

Wilcox, B. L. (1987). Pornography, social science and politics: When research and ideology collide. *American Psychologist, 42,* 941, 943.

Wildman, B. G., & White, P. A. (1986). Assessment of dysmenorrhea using the Menstrual Symptom Questionnaire: Factor structure and validity. *Behaviour Research & Therapy, 24,* 547–551.

Wilford, J. N. (1992, November 17). Clues etched in bone debunk theory of a plague's spread. *The New York Times,* p. C1, C8.

Wille, R., & Beier, K. M. (1989). Castration in Germany. *Annals of Sex Research, 2,* 103–133.

Williams, D. E., & D'Alessandro, J. D. (1994). A comparison of three measures of androgyny and their relationship to psychological adjustment. *Journal of Social Behavior and Personality, 9* (3) 469–480.

Williams, J. G., & Solano, C. H. (1983). The social reality of feeling lonely: Friendship and reciprocation. *Personality and Social Psychology Bulletin, 9,* 237–242.

Williams, S. S., et al. (1992). College students use implicit personality theory instead of safer sex. *Journal of Applied Social Psychology, 22,* 921–933.

Willis, R. J., & Michael, R. T. (1994). Innovation in family formation: Evidence on cohabitation in the United States. In J. Eruisch & K. Ogawa (Eds.), *The family, the market and the state in aging societies.* London: Oxford University Press.

Willoughby, T., et al. (1994). Isolating variables that impact on or detract from the effectiveness of elaboration strategies. *Journal of Educational Research, 86,* 279–289.

Wilson, G., & Cox, D. (1983). Personality of pedophile club members. *Personality and Individual Differences, 4,* 323–329.

Wilson, J. D. (1995). The promiscuous receptor: Prostate cancer comes of age. *New England Journal of Medicine, 332,* 1440–1441.

Wilson, M. R., & Filsinger, E. E. (1986). Religiosity and marital adjustment: Multidimensional interrelationships. *Journal of Marriage and the Family, 48,* 147–151.

Wilson, S. N., & Sanderson, C. A. (1988). The sex report curriculum: Is "just say no" effective? *SIECUS Report, 17,* 10–11.

Wilton, J. M., (1991). Compelled hospitalization and treatment during pregnancy: Mental health status as models for legislation to protect children from prenatal drug and alcohol exposure. *Family Law Quarterly, 25.*

Winick, C. (1985). A content analysis of sexually explicit magazines sold in an adult bookstore. *Journal of Sex Research, 21,* 206–210.

Wise, T. N. (1994). Sertraline as a treatment for premature ejaculation. *Journal of Clinical Psychiatry, 55* (9), 417.

Wisell, T. E., et al. (1987). Declining frequency of circumcision: Implications for changes in the absolute incidence and male to female sex ratio of urinary tract infections in early infancy. *Pediatrics, 79,* 338–342.

Wolman, T. (1985). Drug addiction. In M. Farber (Ed.), *Human sexuality* (pp. 277–285). New York: Macmillan.

Woloshyn, V. E., et al. (1994). Use of elaborative interrogation to help students acquire information consistent with prior knowledge and information inconsistent with prior knowledge. *Journal of Educational Psychology, 86,* 79–89.

Woodard, C. (1993, January 12). Minorities hit harder by AIDS, panel says. *New York Newsday,* p. 4.

Woodman, S. (1995, November/December). On the run from the law. *Ms.,* 38–42.

Wooldridge, W. E. (1991). Syphilis: A new visit from an old enemy. *Postgraduate Medicine, 89,* 199–202.

Wortman, C. B., et al. (1976). Self-disclosure: An attributional perspective. *Journal of Personality and Social Psychology, 33,* 184–191.

WuDunn, S. (1996, January 25). In Japan, a ritual of mourning for abortions. *The New York Times,* A1, A8.

WuDunn, S. (1995, July 9). Many Japanese women are resisting servility. *The New York Times,* p. 10.

Wulfert, E., & Wan, C. K. (1993). Condom use: A self-efficacy model. *Health Psychology, 12,* 346–353.

Wyatt, G. E. (1985). The sexual abuse of Afro-American and white American women in childhood. *Child Abuse and Neglect, 9,* 507–519.

Wyatt, G. E. (1988). The relationship between child sexual abuse and adolescent sexual functioning in Afro-American and white American women. *Annals of the New York Academy of Sciences, 528,* 111–122.

Wyatt, G. E. (1989). Reexamining factors predicting Afro-American and white American women's age at first coitus. *Archives of Sexual Behavior, 18,* 271–298.

Wyatt, G. E., & Newcomb, M. (1990). Internal and external - mediators of women's sexual abuse in childhood. *Journal of Consulting and Clinical Psychology, 58,* 758–767.

Wyatt, G. E., et al. (1988a). Kinsey revisited, Part I: Comparisons of the sexual socialization and sexual behavior of white women over 33 years. *Archives of Sexual Behavior, 17* (3), 201–209.

Wyatt, G. E., et al. (1988b). Kinsey revisited, Part II: Comparisons of the sexual socialization and sexual behavior of black women over 33 years. *Archives of Sexual Behavior, 17* (4), 289–332.

Wyatt, G. E., et al. (1990). Internal and external mediators of women's rape experiences. *Psychology of Women Quarterly, 14,* 153–176.

X chromosome again linked to homosexuality. (1995, November 4). *Science News,* 295.

Yarber, W. L., & Parillo, A. V. (1992). Adolescents and sexually transmitted diseases. *Journal of School Health, 62,* 331–338.

Yarber, W. L., et al. (1989). Development of a three-component sexually transmitted diseases attitude scale. *Journal of Sex Education and Therapy, 15,* 36–49.

Yates, G. L., et al. (1991). A risk profile comparison of homeless youth involved in prostitution and homeless youth not involved [Special issue: Homeless youth]. *Journal of Adolescent Health, 12,* 545–548.

Yorber, B. (1995, July 9). Why couples choose to live together. *The New York Times,* p. 14.

Zarutskie, P. W., et al. (1989). The clinical relevance of sex selection techniques. *Fertility and Sterility, 52,* 891–905.

Zaviacic, M., & Whipple, B. (1993). Update on the female prostate and the phenomenon of female ejaculation. *Journal of Sex Research, 30,* 148–151.

Zaviacic, M., et al. (1988a). Concentrations of fructose in female ejaculate and urine: A comparative biochemical study. *Journal of Sex Research, 24,* 319–325.

Zaviacic, M., et al. (1988b). Female urethral expulsions evoked by local digitial stimulation of the G-spot: Differences in the response patterns. *Journal of Sex Research, 24,* 311–318.

Zavos, M. A. (1995, August). Sexual orientation law in the 1990s. *Trial,* 27–32.

Zeman, N. (1990, Summer/Fall). The new rules of courtship [Special Edition]. *Newsweek,* 24–27.

Zenker, P. N., & Rolfs, R. T. (1990). Treatment of syphilis, 1989. *Reviews of Infectious Diseases* (Suppl. 6), S590-S609.

Zhang, J., & Fried, D. B. (1992). Relationship of maternal smoking during pregnancy to placenta previa. *American Journal of Preventative Medicine, 8,* 278–282.

Zhou, J. (1995, November 2). A sex difference in the human brain and its relation to transsexuality. *Nature,* 68–70.

Zilbergeld, B. (1978). *Male sexuality.* Boston: Little, Brown.

Zilbergeld, B., & Evans, M. (1980). The inadequacy of Masters & Johnson. *Psychology Today, 14,* 29–34, 47–53.

Zillmann, D. (1989). Effects of prolonged consumption of pornography. In D. Zillmann & J. Bryant (Eds.), *Pornography: Research advances and policy considerations* (pp. 127–157). Hillsdale, NJ: Erlbaum.

Zillmann, D., & Bryant, J. (1982, Autumn). Pornography, sexual callousness, and the trivialization of rape. *Journal of Communication,* 10–21.

Zillmann, D., & Bryant, J. (1984). Effects of massive exposure to pornography. In N. M. Malamuth & E. Donnerstein (Eds.), *Pornography and sexual aggression* (pp. 115–138). New York: Academic Press.

Zillmann, D., & Weaver, J. B. (1989). Pornography and men's sexual callousness toward women. In D. Zillmann & J. Bryant (Eds.), *Pornography: Research advances and policy considerations* (pp. 95–125). Hillsdale, NJ: Erlbaum.

Zimmer, D., et al. (1983). Sexual fantasies of sexually distressed and nondistressed men and women: An empirical investigation. *Journal of Sex and Marital Therapy, 9,* 38–50.

Name Index

Boswell, J., 270
Boswell, J., 333
Boulton, M., 525
Bouru, R., 430
Bowie, W., 484
Bowlby, J., 375
Boyer, D., 608
Bozzette, S., 522
Bradbard, 178
Bradbury, T., 208, 215
Brady, E., 570
Brandt, A., 481, 496
Brasher, P., 80
Brecher, E., 429
Bremner, R., 613
Bremner, W., 466
Breslow, N., 547, 548, 553, 554
Bretl, D., 625
Bretschneider, J., 429
Brewer, J., 621
Briere, J., 583, 585
Briselden, A., 486
Brissett, D., 608
Britton, J., 361, 364
Brody, J., 79, 80, 93, 96, 109, 130, 131, 299,
     322, 443, 489, 491, 537, 555, 577, 578
Bronars, S., 394
Brooke, J., 509
Brooks, V., 170
Brooks-Gunn, J., 20, 160, 387, 389, 390, 391,
     392, 393, 397
Broude, G., 25, 244, 270, 376
Brown, D., 614, 615
Brown, L., 300
Brown, R. A., 192
Brown, R. E., 587
Brozan, N., 274
Bryant, H., 80
Bryant, J., 614, 615, 618
Bryson, Y., 510
Buchanan, M., 393
Bucy, P., 136
Buffum, J., 131
Buhaug, H., 497
Buhrich, N., 539
Bullough, V., 266, 269, 539, 541
Bumiller, E., 9
Bumpass, L., 406, 407, 408, 409, 412, 424
Burden, D., 423
Burgess, A., 568, 575
Burkhart, B., 571
Burt, M., 569
Buss, D., 192, 193, 414
Bussey, K., 174, 177
Butler, R., 430
Buxton, A., 285
Byers, E., 577
Byrnes, J., 169

Caceres, C., 511
Cado, S., 254
Caesar, J., 14
Calderone, M., 340, 378, 382, 383, 476
Calhoun, K., 565, 566, 568, 569, 572, 573, 574
Caligula, 14
Calvin, J., 16, 17
Camburn, D., 393

Cameron, P., 586
Cammermeyer, M., 287
Campbell, C., 610
Campbell, S., 326
Cantor, E., 222
Cantor, J., 625
Cappella, J., 195
Carani, C., 138, 443, 466
Carey, M., 448, 449
Carlson, M., 364
Carmignani, G., 466
Carnes, P., 550
Carpenter, C., 434
Carper, A., 367
Carrier, J., 282
Carroll, L., 208
Carson, S., 297
Carter, D., 178
Carter, J., 526
Cartwright, R., 165
Carvajal, D., 602, 604
Casanova, G., 333
Castro, J., 593, 610
Catalan, J., 453, 464
Catalona, W., 115
Catania, J., 287, 523, 524
Cates, W., 344, 350, 484
Celis, W., 567, 577
Ceniti, J., 619
Chadda, R., 452
Champman, 527
Chan, C., 392
Chan, D., 272
Charny, I., 421
Chaucer, G., 613
Chideya, F., 413
Chin, P., 163
Chira, S., 175, 594
Choi, P., 98
Chow, M., 514
Christensen, C., 465
Chubbuck, K., 508
Churchill, W., 426
Clark, J., 480
Clark, M., 168, 196
Clinton, H., 168
Clinton, W., 288, 379, 616
Clumeck, N., 522
Cnattingius, S., 315
Coates, 524
Cobb, M., 128
Cochran, S., 283, 289
Cochran, W., 44
Coe, S., 622
Cohen, A., 173, 425
Cohen, D., 496
Cohen, J., 521
Cohen, L., 414
Cohen-Kettenis, P., 164
Cohn, J., 326
Cohn, L., 527
Colditz, G., 79, 92
Cole, C., 298
Cole, H., 344
Cole, S., 432, 434
Coleman, E., 608, 609
Coleman, M., 181

Coleman, S., 369
Coles, R., 43, 314, 381, 382, 386–387, 388,
     390, 393, 394, 395, 397, 398
Collaer, M., 161, 173, 278
Collins, G., 466
Collins, N., 211
Columbus, C., 481
Comstock, A., 333, 613
Condon, J., 196
Connolly, M., 130
Connor, E., 522
Constantine, J., 425
Constantine, L., 425
Cooper, A., 558, 584
Cooper, D., 521
Corea, G., 326
Cornell, C., 272
Coronel, S., 604
Cosgray, R., 546
Cox, D., 541, 585
Cozzarelli, C., 369
Craig, M., 579
Crano, W., 196
Crawford, C., 194
Cronin, A., 267, 283
Crowe, L., 132
Cummings, E., 422, 424
Cunningham, F., 315
Cunningham, G., 190
Cunningham, M., 138
Curie, M., 170
Curran, D., 571, 573
Curtis, R., 196
Curtiss, G., 455, 465
Cutler, W., 127
Cutrona, C., 326
Cuvelier, S., 617

Dabbs, J., 139
D'Acquila, R., 521
Dahl, S., 575
D'Alessandro, J., 180
Dante, 197
Darabi, K., 392
Darling, C., 146, 343, 394, 395
Darwin, C., 22, 190
D'Augelli, A., 274, 525
Davenport, W., 8, 25, 270
Davidson, J., 242, 253, 254
Davidson, J., Sr., 394
Davidson, K., 149, 150
Davidson, N., 92, 93
Davies, D., 397, 398
Davies, P., 422, 424
Davis, J., 272
Davis, M., 204
Davison, G., 557
Dawes, R., 195
Day, N., 315
de Bruyn-Kops, E., 571
de Luca, R., 589
de Raad, B., 192
de Schampheleire, D., 606
de Young, M., 585
Dean, C., 571
DeAngelis, T., 6
Deaux, K., 165, 170

Goldenberg, R., 395
Golding, J., 574
Goldman, J., 528
Goldman, L., 92
Goldstein, A., 480
Goldstein, I., 466
Goleman, D., 138, 588, 590, 592, 614
Gollub, E., 473, 496
Golombok, S., 272
Gomez, J., 273
Gomez-Schwartz, B., 587
Gonda, G., 165
Gonsiorck, J., 273
Goodkin, K., 522
Goodwin, J., 587
Goodyear, C., 333
Gordon, P., 398
Gordon, S., 199, 219, 272, 364, 414, 428, 570, 576, 602
Gorzalka, B., 131
Gottlieb, M., 502, 503
Goulart, M., 526
Goya, F., 621
Graber, B., 445
Graca, L., 315
Grafenberg, E., 149
Graham, J., 483
Graham, S., 18, 235, 236, 490
Grajek, S., 199
Grant, H., 600, 601, 602, 604, 607
Grauerholz, E., 594
Gray, J., 365
Green, R., 272, 281
Green, S., 244, 270, 376
Greenberg, E., 313
Greene, B., 272, 273
Greene, S., 25
Greenhouse, L., 593
Greenwald, E., 586, 588
Greer, G., 77
Gregory III, 270
Gresh, 390, 395, 519, 525, 527, 528
Griffin, E., 195
Griffin, M., 364
Groden, J., 510
Grogger, J., 394
Groneman, C., 551
Gross, J., 262, 568
Gross, L., 625
Grossman, S., 132
Groth, A., 563, 568, 571, 572
Gruber, J., 591
Gruber, V., 96
Grunfeld, C., 510
Guinan, M., 358
Gunn, D., 364
Gupta, M., 15
Guskin, A., 568
Gwartney-Gibbs, P., 579

Haas-Hawkings, G., 431
Hack, M., 326
Haffner, D., 380, 388
Haglund, B., 315
Hall, C., 170
Hall, E., 221
Hall, G., 571, 572

Hall, R., 377
Halverson, C., 177, 178
Hamada, Y., 171
Hamer, D., 267, 277
Hamilton, J., 521
Hamilton, M., 577
Hammer, J., 508
Hampton, H., 574
Handler, A., 397
Handsfield, H., 480
Hanrahan, J., 315
Hanson, R., 574
Harahap, M., 105
Harding, J., 326
Haring, K., 504
Hariton, E., 254, 255
Harkness, R., 313
Harlow, L., 528
Harney, P., 571, 572
Harris, L., 168, 266, 619
Harris, M., 380
Hart, J., 210, 304
Hartman, C., 606
Harvey, S., 89
Hass, A., 387
Hatcher, R., 298, 339, 340, 341, 342, 343, 344, 345, 347, 348, 351, 352, 354, 356, 357, 358, 359, 514
Hatfield, E., 187, 199
Hausknecht, R., 312, 367
Havemann, E., 50, 173, 221, 422, 425
Haverkos, H., 512
Hawthorne, N., 17
Hawton, 464
Hayashi, H., 407
Hayes, C., 390, 399
Hays, R., 522
Hazan, C., 196
Heath, C., 136
Hebert, M., 583
Hechtman, L., 395, 396
Hegeler, S., 429
Heilbron, F., 430
Heiman, J., 243, 460, 496, 614
Hemingway, E., 102, 612
Hendrick, C., 200
Hendrick, S., 200
Henneberger, M., 594
Henning, K., 241, 242, 243
Henry III, king, 539
Henshaw, S., 360
Hensley, W., 187, 188
Herdt, G., 173, 270
Hernandez, J., 526
Herodotus, 549, 601
Herold, E., 614
Herzog, L., 105
Herzog, M., 188
Hess, B., 394, 396
Highsmith, C., 515
Hill, A., 562
Hill, P., 361, 364
Hillier, S., 486, 487
Hillingdon, A., 18
Hilton, E., 487
Hines, M., 161, 173, 278
Hingson, R., 526

Hippocrates, 476
Hirsch, M., 521
Hirschman, R., 572
Hite, S., 46, 239, 240, 241, 248
Hitler, A., 622
Ho, D., 520, 521
Hoagwood, K., 588
Hoberman, E., 431
Hobfoll, S., 528
Hobson, W., 572
Hock, Z., 150
Hodges, B., 527
Hodgson, R., 484
Hodson, D., 429
Hofferth, S., 390
Hoffman, J., 341
Hoffman, L., 242, 254
Hogan, D., 393
Holmes, D., 431
Holmes, K., 484, 486, 487
Holmstrom, L., 575
Holzman, H., 607
Homer, 13
Honey, M., 360
Horowitz, R., 392
Houston, D., 584, 585
Howard, J., 192
Howard, M., 400
Howard, M. C., 24
Howards, S., 298, 299, 301
Hsu, B., 242
Hu, S., 520
Huang, K., 392
Hubbard, R., 316
Hubschman, L., 164
Hucker, S., 546, 590
Hudson, R., 502, 504
Huffman, T., 407
Hunt, M., 41, 43, 43, 45–46, 47, 49, 242, 247, 388, 415, 416, 417, 420, 422, 569, 602
Hunter, D., 79
Hurley, E., 600
Hyde, J., 169, 170

Imperato-McGinley, J., 159
Ingersoll, S., 590
Insel, P., 327
Ireland, L., 157
Isay, R., 267, 280, 281, 284, 285
Ison, C., 480

Jacklin, C., 169, 170, 174, 175, 176
Jackson, B., 92
Jackson, J., 588
Jackson, L., 188
Jackson, M., 620
Jacobsen, C., 622
Jacobson, J., 314
Jacobson, S., 314
Jallon, J., 128
Jamison, P., 106
Jankowiak, W., 196
Janus, C., 42, 43, 196, 197, 267, 389, 582
Janus, M., 608
Janus, S., 42, 43, 196, 197, 267, 389, 582
Javier, R., 167
Jeffries-Fox, S., 625

Jencks, C., 396
Jenks, R., 422
Johnson, D., 526, 528
Johnson, E. (M.), 502
Johnson, E. W., 340, 378, 382, 383, 476
Johnson, K., 79
Johnson, S., 333
Johnson, V., 51–52, 95, 105, 121, 128, 140,
    145–148, 239, 245, 246, 264, 284, 287, 288,
    304, 416, 446, 447, 449, 456–457, 458, 459,
    463–465
Jones, E., 396
Jones, H., 298
Jones, J., 92, 429
Jones, K., 529
Jorgensen, C., 161
Jorgensen, S., 397, 398
Josephs, R., 133
Joyce, J., 612
Judson, F., 480

Kagay, M., 524
Kahn, J., 397
Kalick, S., 194
Kallmann, F., 276
Kammeyer, K., 8, 219, 409, 429
Kang, S., 83
Kantner, J., 388
Kantor, J., 556
Kantor, S., 431
Kantrowitz, B., 391, 394, 399, 400
Kaplan, D., 67, 590
Kaplan, H., 145, 429, 446, 454, 455, 457, 458,
    462
Karney, B., 208, 215
Katz, J., 267, 271, 273
Kaufman, A., 568
Kay, D., 236
Kedia, K., 446, 449
Keen, S., 213
Kegel, A., 70
Keith, B., 424
Keith, J., 390
Keith, P., 194, 414
Kellermann, J., 221
Kellogg, J., 234, 236
Kelly, J., 424
Kelly, M., 238, 452
Kennell, J., 323
Kenney, A., 380, 400
Kent, M., 517
Kerber, R., 79
Kerns, J., 273, 274
Kessler, R., 449
Kettl, P., 434
Kiely, E., 467
Kiely, J., 315
Killmann, P., 457, 462, 465
Kilmann, P., 421
Kilpatrick, D., 569
Kimble, D., 135, 138
Kimlicka, T., 181
Kimmel, D., 272
Kinard, E., 395
Kinder, B., 132, 455, 465, 466
King, J., 465
King, L., 105

Kinloch-de-Loes, S., 521
Kinsey, A., 19, 43, 44–45, 47, 48, 129, 146,
    236, 238, 240, 241, 245, 247, 249, 264, 265,
    266, 268, 288, 375, 380, 388, 415, 416,
    417–418, 456, 545, 546, 553, 549, 601–602
Kintsch, W., 6
Kirby, D., 399
Kite, M., 274
Kitigawa, E., 393
Klein, C., 624
Klepinger, D., 524
Klerman, L., 395
Klungess, L., 414
Kl ver, H., 136
Knapp, M., 210
Knight, R., 432, 433, 434, 435, 571
Knox, D., 198, 368, 411, 425, 429, 586, 631,
    632–633, 634
Knudsen, D., 582, 583
Kockott, G., 163, 164
Kohlberg, L., 176, 177
Kohn, A., 582
Kolata, G., 45, 80, 341, 419, 529
Kolodny, R., 463, 464
Komisar, L., 625
Komisaruk, B., 149
Kon, I., 8, 9
Koocher, G., 588
Koop, C., 496
Koopman, C., 524
Korb, L., 288
Kornblum, W., 404
Koss, M., 564, 565, 568, 573, 575, 577
Koutsky, L., 493
Kouzi, A., 525
Krafft-Ebing, R., 19, 236, 263
Krafka, 619
Kresin, D., 89, 442
Kruesi, M., 557
Kruks, G., 609
Ku, L., 526
Kuhn, D., 174
Kuiper, B., 164
Kulin, H., 385
Kumar, U., 387
Kuntz, T., 361
Kurdek, L., 283
Kuriloff, P., 274

Laan, E., 614
Lacayo, R., 365
Ladas, A., 150
Laird, J., 359
Lamacz, M., 555
Lamaze, F., 322
Lambert, B., 610
Lamke, L., 181
Landon, A., 41
Lane, K., 579
Lang, A., 132
Lang, R., 552
Langevin, R., 542, 544, 552
Lansky, D., 132
Lanyon, R., 542, 554
LaTour, M., 625
Laumann, E., 29, 30t, 43, 45, 46, 48, 195, 237,
    242, 247, 249, 258, 267, 269, 271, 407, 408,

    414, 416, 418, 419, 420, 422, 429, 440, 442,
    447, 531, 564, 565
Laviola, M., 586
Lavoisier, P., 148
Lawrence, D., 19, 416, 612
Lawrence, K., 614
Lawson, C., 413
Leary, W., 108, 111, 299, 316, 445, 449
Leavitt, G., 585
Ledray, L., 576
Lee, F., 518, 520
Lee, J., 196, 197
Lehtinen, M., 50, 173, 221, 422, 425
Leiblum, S., 443, 453, 454, 457
Leigh, B., 389
Leitenberg, H., 236, 238, 241, 242, 243, 254,
    380, 387, 586
Leiter, R., 364
Leland, N., 397
Lemon, S., 492
Lenihan, G., 570
Lesnik-Oberstein, M., 414
Letourneau, E., 442, 443
LeVay, S., 278
Levens, J., 315
Lever, J., 264
LeVesconte, S., 170
Levine, C., 506
Levine, G., 487, 495
Levinger, G., 208
Levitt, E., 421, 467
Levy, D., 571
Levy, G., 178
Levy, J., 173
Lewin, T., 168, 256, 364, 399, 524, 525, 614
Lewis, D., 525
Lewis, K., 577
Lewis, L., 165
Lewis, P., 286
Lewis, R., 495
Lewis, S., 196
Liberace, 504
Libman, E., 429, 457
Lief, H., 164
Lindermalm, G., 164
Lindsey, R., 105
Lininger, 447
Linn, M., 169
Linsley, W., 611, 612
Linton, M., 566
Linz, D., 617, 618, 619
Lisak, D., 570
Liskin, L., 496
Liu, D., 48, 49
Lohr, J., 105
Londono, M., 150
LoPiccolo, J., 243, 447, 456, 457, 460, 462,
    463, 465, 466, 496
Lorch, D., 508, 516, 570
Lorefice, L., 557
Lott, B., 180
Lottes, I., 274
Lovdal, L., 625
Lowe, J., 431
Lown, J., 424
Lowry, R., 474, 513
Loy, P., 591, 592

Lublin, J., 31
Luckenbill, D., 609
Lundstrom, B., 164
Lusk, R., 582, 583, 586, 587, 588
Luther, M., 16
Lynxweiler, J., 365
Lyons, J., 622, 623

Macallan, D., 510
Maccoby, E., 169, 170, 176
MacDonald, N., 526
Macke, R., 608
MacLean, P., 136
Madonna, 16, 620
Madover, S., 526
Magos, A., 96
Major, B., 369
Malamuth, N., 570, 619
Males, M., 397
Maletzky, B., 557
Malinowski, B., 24, 51, 585
Malloy, M., 315
Manet, E., 621
Mapplethorpe, R., 504, 621–622
Marchbanks, P., 74
Marcou, A., 82
Marcus, A., 344
Margolin, L., 570
Marier, R., 169
Marks, G., 195
Maroules, N., 592
Marshall, D., 451
Marshall, W., 558, 571, 572, 616
Marsiglio, W., 271, 273, 274, 397
Martens, M., 487
Martin, C., 177, 178
Martin, D., 483, 484
Martinez, F., 315
Martinson, F., 374
Mason, R., 128, 571
Masters, W., 51–52, 95, 105, 121, 128, 140,
    145–148, 150, 239, 245, 246, 264, 284, 287,
    288, 304, 416, 446, 447, 449, 456–457, 458,
    459, 463–465, 569
Matejcic, C., 216
Matek, O., 543
Mathis, J., 130
Matlin, 387
Matsen, K., 526, 527
Matthews, K., 92, 584
Matthews, W., 160
Maybach, K., 191
Mayer, J., 314
Mayer, S., 396
McArthur, M., 574
McCabe, J., 400
McCabe, M., 465
McCann, K., 522
McConaghy, M., 158
McConaghy, N., 276, 281, 282
McCormack, K., 334
McCoy, N., 429
McCusker, J., 525
McGuire, R., 553
McIntyre, 390, 395, 519, 525, 527, 528
McKeachie, W., 6
McKinney, K., 364, 592, 593

McKirnan, D., 524
McLaren, J., 587
McLaughlin, F., 325
Mead, M., 24, 51, 170, 173, 193
Meana, M., 447
Meese, E., 616
Meiselman, K., 586
Meisler, A., 448, 449
Melbye, M., 41
Meltzer, G., 431
Melvin, S., 481
Mendel, G., 22
Mercury, F., 504
Merkatz, I., 326
Mertz, G., 489
Messenger, J., 450
Meston, C., 131
Meuwissen, I., 614
Meyer, 512
Meyer, J., 163
Meyer-Bahlburg, H., 277, 524
Michael, R., 30t, 45, 194, 195, 209, 236, 389,
    390, 406, 409, 414, 416, 418, 419, 565, 614
Michaels, D., 506
Michaels, S., 30t, 45, 419, 565
Michelangelo, 548
Miedzian, M., 571
Mill, J. S., 634
Miller, B., 387, 390, 391, 393
Miller, D., 557
Miller, E., 603, 605
Miller, H., 415, 612, 620
Miller, H. G., 526
Miller, K., 196
Miller, L., 211
Mills, J., 313
Milner, P., 136
Minai, N., 15
Minkoff, H., 481, 516
Mirin, S., 134, 449
Mirotznik, J., 491
Mishell, D., 338, 339, 340, 342, 344, 348
Misovich, S., 526
Mohr, D., 448, 449, 457, 466, 467
Moi, H., 486
Molotsky, I., 608
Money, J., 159, 160, 161, 162, 163, 165, 173,
    106, 138, 139, 270, 277, 282, 537, 538, 555,
    558
Mooney, K., 514
Moore, 527
Moore, D., 590, 591
Moore, D. W., 216
Moore, K., 394, 412
Morales, E., 272
Morokoff, 445, 453
Morris, N., 139
Morris, R., 139
Morrison, E., 67, 77, 377, 378, 379, 387, 394
Morse, E., 610
Mortensen, M., 429
Moscarello, R., 575
Mosher, C., 18
Mosher, D., 612
Mosher, W., 397
Muehlenhard, C., 566, 570, 571, 572
Mueser, K., 191

Muhammad, 15
Mulcahy, J., 467
Muller, J., 128
Muller, M., 487
Mulry, G., 513
Murray, J., 558
Muster, N., 584
Myers, A., 165
Myers, M., 568
Myerson, M., 181

Nadeau, R., 527
Nadler, R., 271
Nakamura, R., 278
Nash, O., 133
Navarro, M., 506, 518
Need, J., 164
Neisser, A., 476
Nelson, R., 449
Nevid, J., 192, 274, 424, 515
Newbold, J., 492
Newcomb, M., 588
Newcomb, P., 93
Newcomer, S., 388, 393
Newman, L., 288
Nichols, M., 451
Nock, S., 408
Norman, J., 380
Nosek, M., 432
Novello, A., 512
Nureyev, R., 504
Nyamathi, A., 515, 516

O'Brien, P., 577
Ochs, R., 79, 114, 493
O'Connell, M., 412, 413
O'Donohue, W., 442, 443, 455, 464
O'Grady, K., 392
O'Hara, M., 326
Okami, P., 585
Oldenberg, R., 608
Olds, J., 136
O'Neill, G., 425
O'Neill, N., 425
O'Reilly, K., 524
Orwell, G., 613
Osborne, N., 490
Osgood, C., 405
Osterhout, 390, 395, 519, 525, 527, 528
Oswalt, R., 526, 527
Over, R., 614
Overholser, J., 571, 585
Oz, S., 634

Packwood, R., 562, 563f
Padesky, C., 286
Padgett, V., 619
Padian, N., 516
Padilla, E., 392
Palace, E., 133
Palmer, M., 195
Palmore, E., 429
Palson, C., 51
Palson, R., 51
Papanicolau, G., 73
Parillo, A., 474, 483
Parks, G., 613

Subject Index

Numbers followed by the letter *f* refer to figures; numbers followed by the letter *t* refer to tables.

Down syndrome, 294, 315
    detection of, 318
    maternal age and, 317t
Doxycycline, 485
Drag prostitutes, 609
Droit de seigneur, 69
Drosophila bifurca, 111
Drugs
    abortion-inducing, 367
    affecting sexual performance, 448, 449–450
    effect on fetus, 313
Ductus deferens, 110
Dysfunctionals, 290
Dysmenorrhea, 94
Dyspareunia, 441, 447
    treatment of, 463

Eclampsia, 312
Ectoderm, 309
Ectoparasitic diseases, 479t, 494–495
Ectopic pregnancy, 74, 312
Education
    and sexuality, 29, 31
    of women, 17
Efface, defined, 319
Ego, defined, 26
Egypt, ancient
    bathing in, 127
    sexual attitudes in, 11
Ejaculation, 121
    premature, 446, 459f, 465–467
    retrograde, 122
Ejaculatory ducts, 110, 111
Ejaculatory incompetence, 445
Elavil, 131
Electra complex, 174, 279
    defined, 28
Elephantiasis, 485
ELISA, 517
Elmer Gantry, 196
Embryo, 308f, 309
    defined, 154
Embryonic disk, 307
Embryonic stage, of prenatal development, 308–309
Embryonic transfer, 301
Emission stage, 121
Emotions, affecting sexual performance, 453
Empathy training, 590
Emphysema, affecting sexual performance, 449
Empirical, defined, 36
Empty love, 202, 202t
Ending a relationship, 215–216
Endocrine glands
    defined, 84
    locations of, 85f
Endocrine problems, affecting sexual performance, 448
Endoderm, 309
Endometriosis, 73, 300
Endometritis, 483
Endometrium, 73
Enzyme-linked immunosorbent assay, 517
Epididymis, 110
Epididymitis, 480, 483
Epidural block, 322
Episiotomy, 69, 321

Equal Opportunity Commission, 592
Erectile disorder, 133
Erectile dysfunction, 443–445
Erection, 116–117
Erogenous zones, 27, 128
    defined, 28
Eros, 196, 197, 200
Erotic, defined, 5
Erotica, defined, 612
ERT (estrogen replacement therapy), 139
Erythroblastosis, fetal, 313
Erythromycin, 485
Escort services, 604–605
Estimation, faulty, 47
Estrogen, 74, 75, 139
    effects of, 340
    role in puberty, 383
Estrogen replacement therapy, 139
Estrous cycle, 84
Estrus, 84, 139
Ethical relativism, 634
Ethics, in sex research, 56–58
Ethnocentric, defined, 26
Ethnographic-observation method, 51
Ethnography, defined, 51
Evolution, defined, 22
Evolution of Human Sexuality, 552
Exaggeration, as source of survey inaccuracy, 50
Excitement phase, 141
Exercise, benefits of, 131
Exhibitionism, 541–542
    coping with, 543
    learning theorists on, 553–554
    treatment for, 556–557
Experiment, defined, 54
Experimental group, defined, 55
Experimental method, 54–55
    limitations of, 56
Expulsion stage, 121
External sex organs
    differentiation of, 156f
    female, 62–71
    male, 102–107
    structures underlying, 69–70
Extramarital sex, 420–421
Eyes, in communication, 221

Faggot, origin of term, 274
Fallopian tubes, 74
False positive, defined, 484
Family, and premarital intercourse, 393
Family Planning in Japanese Society, 369
Family Planning Perspectives, 360
Fantasies, 129
Fantasy, sexual, 241–243
    during coitus, 253–254, 258f
    homosexual, 267–268
FAS, 314, 315
Fatigue, affecting sexual performance, 448
Fatuous love, 202, 202t, 204
Feedback loop, 108
Fellatio, 14, 246
    techniques of, 247
Female condom, 358
Female genitals, dream symbols for, 28t
Female orgasmic disorder, 446
    treatment of, 459–461, 460f

Female sexual arousal disorder, 445
Female-superior position, 178, 252, 253f, 461f
Femme, defined, 276
Fertility awareness methods, 352–355
Fertility problems
    in females, 299–301
    in males, 298–299
Fertilization, in vitro, 21
Fetal alcohol syndrome, 314, 315
Fetal erythroblastosis, 313
Fetal stage, of prenatal development, 310
Fetishism, 537, 538
    learning theorists on, 553
    psychoanalytic view of, 552
Fetus, 308f, 310
    movements of, 310
Fibroadenoma, 79
Fidelity, cultural attitudes towards, 8
Field study, 50
Fijian people, sexual attitudes of, 421
Film, depiction of sexuality in, 19, 20, 623
Fimbriae, 74
Fisting, 287, 496
Fixation, 27
    defined, 28
Flagyl, 486, 488
Flashing, 541
Fluoxetine, 131
    retarding ejaculation, 465
    to treat paraphilias, 557
Follicle, 75
Follicle-stimulating hormone (FSH), 85, 108
Follicular phase, 86
For Whom the Bell Tolls, 612
Forcible rape, 563
Foreplay, 244–245
    cross-species perspective on, 21–22, 244
    defined, 5
    duration and techniques of, 416
    techniques of, 245–246
Foreskin, 104
Forever, 613
Fornication, defined, 14
France
    attitudes toward menstruation in, 90
    unwed motherhood in, 397
Frenulum, of penis, 104
Frequency, defined, 44
Freudian theory, 26–27
    on homosexuality, 278–279
    on sexual performance, 454
Friendship, 200
Frotteurism, 548
Fruit fly, 111
FSH (follicle-stimulating hormone), 85, 108
Fulani people, attitudes toward menstruation among, 90
Functionals, 290
Fundus, 73
Fuses, 623

Game-playing love, 200
Gamete intrafallopian transfer, 300, 301
Gang rape, 568
Gardnerella vaginalis, 477t, 486
Gay activism, 275

Lateral-entry position, 252, 254f
Latin America, AIDS in, 509
L-dopa, 131
Learning theories, 28–29
    on homosexuality, 281
Learning Tree, 613
Legalism, 631–632
Lesbians
    adjustment of, 282–283
    defined, 262
    as parents, 272
    sexual techniques of, 289
    therapy for, 283–284
Lesu people, sexual attitudes of, 376
Leukocytes, defined, 506
Leydig's cells, 107, 109
LGV, 485
LH (luteinizing hormone), 85, 108
LH-releasing hormone (LH-RH), 108
Librium, effect on fetus, 314
Lifelong erectile disorder, 444
Lifelong sexual dysfunctions, 441
Liking, 201, 202t
Limbic system, 135, 135f, 136
Lindane, 494, 495
Listening, 223
    active, 224
    in communication, 223–224
Lizards, parthenogenetic, 298
Local anesthesia, 322
Lochia, 327
Logical love, 200
Loneliness, 216
    causes of, 216
    coping with, 216–217
Lotrimin, 487
Love
    arousal and, 199–200
    history of, 196–197
    modern view of, 197, 199
    rating attitudes on, 198
    realistic, 198
    romantic, 197, 199
    styles of, 200
    theories of, 199–205
Love bites, 545, 547
Lovemap, 555
Low birthweight babies, 314–315, 324
Low sperm count, 298
LSD
    effect on fetus, 314
    sexual effects of, 133
Lubrication, inadequate, 447
Ludus, 200
Lumpectomy, 80
Luteal phase, 88
Luteinizing hormone (LH), 85, 108
    predicting ovulation, 296, 354
Lymphogranuloma venereum, 485
Lytta vesicatoria, 130

Macbeth, 132
Machismo, 166–167
Maja Desnuda, 621
Male, sexual function in, 116–122
Male erectile disorder, 443–445
    treatment of, 459f

Male genitals, dream symbols for, 28t
Male orgasmic disorder, 445–446
Male pill, 359
Male prostitution, 608
Male rape, 568
Male-superior position, 178, 251–252, 252f
Malignant, defined, 79
Malnutrition, effect on fetus, 310
Mammary glands, 77
Mammography, 78, 80, 83
Man-on-top position, 251–252
Mangaia, sexuality in, 451
Mania, 200
Manopause, 109
Marianismo, 166–167
Marijuana
    effect on fetus, 313, 314
    sexual effects of, 133
Marital rape, 568–569
Marriage, 409
    alternative, 425–426
    dissolution of, 422–424
    group, 425–426
    historical perspectives on, 410–411
    mate selection for, 414–415
    open, 425
    reasons for, 411–412
    sexual satisfaction in, 419t
    sexuality in, 415–420
    traditional vs. modern, 411t
    types of, 413–414
Marshall Islanders, sexual attitudes of, 421
Mashing, 548
Masochism, 545–546
    learning-theory view of, 554
    psychoanalytic view of, 552
Massage parlors, 604
Mastalgia, 95
Mastectomy, 80
    psychological effects of, 82
Master gland, 85
Masturbation
    in adolescence, 386–387
    attitudes towards, 25
    in childhood, 377
    defined, 5
    fantasies in, 243
    healthy attitudes toward, 378
    historical views on, 234–236
    in infancy, 375
    modern attitudes toward, 236–238
    and orgasmic potential, 238–239, 461
    reasons for, 235t
    sociocultural factors in, 237t
    techniques of, 239–241
Matching hypothesis, 193–195
Mate preferences, 191–192, 193t
    cultural aspects of, 194
    race and, 194
Mate-swapping, 51, 421
Maternal depression, 326
Math skills, gender differences in, 169, 175
Mating gradient, 414
Mattachine Society, 275
Measles, effect on fetus, 311
Meatus, 103
Media, sexism in, 175

Medroxyprogesterone acetate, 359
    to treat paraphilias, 558, 590
Medulla, 134
Meese Commission, 616–617
Meeting, methods of, 209f
Men
    aging in, 427t, 428
    attractiveness in, 189
    desirable traits in, 213
    external sex organs of, 102–107
    internal sex organs of, 107–112
    masturbation techniques, 239–240
    reproductive system of, 103f
    romanticism of, 414
    sexual fantasies among, 242, 243
    sexual response cycle in, 143f
    stereotypes of sexuality of, 179
Menarche, 84, 381–382, 386f
Menopause
    defined, 90
    described, 90–91
    hormone therapy for, 92–93
    myths about, 92–93
Menstrual cycle, 83–84
    changes occurring in, 87f
    phases of, 86–89
    regulation of, 84–85
    synchrony in, 127
Menstrual phase, 88
Menstruation, 88–89
    attitudes towards, 90–91
    coitus during, 89
    coping with, 96–98
    defined, 83
    problems of, 94–95
Mental retardation, and sexuality, 435
Mescaline, sexual effects of, 133
Mesoderm, 309
Mesopotamia, prostitution in, 601
Methadone, effect on fetus, 314
Methotrexate, 367
Metronidazole, 486, 488
Mexico, AIDS in, 509
Miconazole, 487
Microsoft Network, Planet Out, 286
Middle Ages, sexual attitudes in, 16
Mifepristone, 367, 368
Migraine, 95
Miller v. California, 612, 613
Minilaparotomy, 356
Minipill, 337
Miscarriage, 304
Misoprostol, 367
Missionary position, 251
Mittelschmerz, 88
Modeling, defined, 29
Molluscum contagiosum, 493–494
Mongolism, 315
Moniliasis, 478t, 486
Monistat, 487
Monogamy, 413
    defined, 12
    incidence of, 25
    serial, 405
Monozygotic twins, 276
Mons veneris, 62, 63
Mormon church, 25

Morning sickness, 304
Morning-after pill, 341
Morphine, affecting sexual performance, 449
Motility, 298
M llerian ducts, 155, 156
M llerian inhibiting substance, 155
Multiphasic pill, 337
Multiple orgasms, 146–147
Multiple sclerosis, affecting sexual performance, 448, 449
Mumps, effect on fetus, 311
Mundugumor people, gender roles of, 173
Muria Gond people, sexual attitudes of, 376
Muscular dystrophy, detection of, 318
Mutations, defined, 22
Mutuality, 213–214
My Fair Lady, 164
My Hamburger, 613
My Left Foot, 432
My Secret Garden, 244
Mycelex, 487
Myometrium, 73
Myotonia, 140, 144

Nagele's rule, 306
Nama people, perspectives on beauty, 187
Name, importance of, 191
Narcotics
    affecting sexual performance, 449
    effect on fetus, 314
National Gay and Lesbian Task Force, 286
National Health and Social Life Survey (NHSLS), 45, 48
Native Americans
    sexual attitudes among, 25, 30t
    surveys of, 48–49
Natural birth control, 352–355
Natural childbirth, 322
Natural selection, defined, 22
Naturalistic observation, 50
Navajo culture, attitudes toward menstruation in, 90
Necrophilia, 549
Negative feedback, 108
Negotiating differences, 228–229
Neisseria gonorrhoeae, 476
Neural tube, 309
Neural tube defects, detection of, 318
Neurosyphilis, 482
Neurotransmitters, role in ejaculation, 465
New Guinea
    erotic art from, 623
    gender roles in, 173
    sexual attitudes in, 270
NGU, 477t, 483
NHSLS study, 45, 48
Nicotine, sexual effects of, 132
Nigeria, erotic art of, 620
1984, 613
Nitric oxide, 449
Nocturnal emission, 385
Nocturnal penile tumescence, 449
Nongonococcal urethritis, 477t, 483
Nonlove, 202t
Nonoxynol-9, 351, 531–532
Nonspecific treatment factor, defined, 55

Nonverbal communication, 220–221
    cues, 225
Norplant, 341–342
    use in adolescence, 399
Nymphomania, 551, 552

Oberlin College, 17
Obesity, attitudes toward, 189, 191
Obscene phone calls, 542–544
Obscenity, 612, 613
Observational methods, 42
Observer effect, 52
Occasional johns, 607
Ocular herpes, 490
Oedipus complex, 27, 174, 278–279
    defined, 28
Of Mice and Men, 613
Onanism, 234, 235
Open couples, 290
Open marriage, 425
Opening lines, 209–210
Operational definition, defined, 39, 40
Ophthalmia neonatorum, 476, 480
Opportunistic diseases, 510
Oral contraceptives, 336–341
Oral herpes, 478t
    transmission of, 489–490
Oral-genital stimulation, 246–249
    abstaining from, 249–250
    in adolescence, 388
    socioeconomic factors in, 247, 248–249, 248t
    and STDs, 130
OraSure, 517
Organizing effects, of hormones, 137
Orgasm, 21, 418–419
    controversies about, 146–150
    defined, 120
    and ejaculation, 120–121
    fantasies and, 129
    multiple, 146–147
    phases of, 140–145
    subjective experience of, 144
    types of, 147–149
Orgasmic disorders, 441
    treatment of, 459–463
    types of, 445–446
Orgasmic phase, 142–144
Orgasmic platform, 142
Orgasmic reconditioning, 557
Os, 72
Osteoporosis, 91
Our Bodies, Ourselves, 613
Outercourse, 531
Outing, defined, 275
Ova, 62, 75f
Ovarian cycle, 307f
Ovariectomy, 139
Ovaries, 74–75
    cancer of, 75
    development of, 156–157
    endocrine function of, 84
Ovulation, 84
Ovulation method, of contraception, 353
Ovulation-prediction kits, 354
Ovulatory mucus, 354
Ovulatory phase, 86

Oxytocin, 85
    and childbirth, 319
    and lactation, 327

Pain, as ethical concern in research, 56–57
Painful intercourse, 447, 448
Pakistan, sexual attitudes in, 8
Panic, sexual, 443
Pap test, 73, 76
Papaverine, 466, 467
Paralysis, 433
Paraphilias, 537–538
    as addictive behavior, 550
    behavior therapy for, 556–557
    biological perspectives on, 550, 552
    drug therapy for, 556–557
    learning theories on, 553–554
    psychoanalytic perspectives on, 552
    psychotherapy for, 556
    sociological perspectives on, 554–555
    theories about, 550–555
    treatment of, 555–558
    types of, 538–549
Paraphrasing, 224
Paraplegia, 433
Paraplegic, defined, 120
Parasympathetic nervous system, 119
Parents, as role models, 442, 451
Parents and Friends of Lesbians and Gays, 286
Parous introitus, 68, 68f
Paroxetine, retarding ejaculation, 465
Partialism, 538
Participant observation, 51
Passion, as component of love, 200
Pathogen, defined, 506
Patriarchy, 410
Peak days, defined, 354
Pederasty, defined, 13
Pediculosis, 479t, 494–495
Pedophilia, 538, 584–585
    defined, 557, 584
    treatment of, 556–557
Peeping Toms, 544
Peer harassment, 593
Pelvic examination, 75
Pelvic inflammatory disease, 344, 480, 483
Pelvic thrusting, in infancy, 375
Penile implants, 466
Penile injection, 466
Penile strain gauge, 39
Penis, 102–104
    anatomy of, 103f
    compared with clitoris, 64
    damage to, 449
    size of, 105–106
    stimulation of, 246
Penis envy, 279
Pentothal sodium, use in childbirth, 322
Performance anxiety, 116, 443, 444, 455
Pergonal, 300
Perimetrium, 73, 74
Perineum, 69, 321
Period of the ovum, 307
Personality, gender and, 170–171, 173
Peru, attitudes toward menstruation in, 90
Petting, 388
    as communication, 225

Peyronie's disease, 120
Phallic symbols, 11, 102
Phallic worship, 11
Pharaonic circumcision, 66
Pharyngeal gonorrhea, 476, 480
Phenobarbital, effect on fetus, 314
Pheromones, 128
Philia, 196, 197, 200
Phimosis, 105
Phobia, sexual, 443
Photoplethysmograph, vaginal, 39, 40
Phthirius pubis, 479t, 494
Physical attraction, 187–191
   cultural aspects of, 190
Physical disability, and sexuality, 432–434
PID, 344, 480, 483
Pill, the, 336–341
   male, 359
Pimps, 602
Piperonyl butoxide, 494
Pituitary, hormone secretion by, 84, 85, 137
Placenta, 309
Planet Out, 286
Plateau phase, 141–142
Play, gender and, 175
Play It Again, Sam, 208
Playboy Foundation Survey, 45–46
Pleasure centers, 136
PMS (premenstrual syndrome), 95–96
   tracking, 97
Pneumocystis carinii pneumonia, 502, 510
Polyandry, 25, 413, 414
   cross-species view of, 23
Polygamy, 413
   defined, 12
Polygyny, 25, 413
Polymorphously perverse, defined, 278
Polynesia, sexuality in, 451
Pons, 134
Pope v. Illinois, 613
Poppers, 131
Population, defined, 40
Pornography, 611–612
   vs. art, 620–623
   computerized, 615
   defined, 612
   vs. erotica, 612
   gender differences in response to, 614–616
   legal issues in, 613–614
   prevalence of, 614–616
   violent, 617
Possessing the Secret of Joy, 66, 67
Possessive love, 200
POSSLQ, 405
Postpartum depression, 326
Posttraumatic stress disorder, 575
Potassium nitrate, 131
Power rape, 572
Pragma, 200
Preadolescence, sexuality in, 379–381
Prediction, based on theory, 38
Preeclampsia, 312
Pregnancy, 301
   AIDS in, 518
   ectopic, 74, 312
   effects of, 304

failed, 304
pros and cons of, 302–303
psychological changes in, 305
risk in, 336
sex during, 304–305
signs of, 302
teenage, 391–397
tests for, 303–304
Premarital sex, 388–389
   in China, 9
   factors in, 390–391
   motives for, 389–390
Premature ejaculation, 105, 446
   treatment of, 459f, 465–467
Premenstrual syndrome (PMS), 95–96
   tracking, 97
Prenatal development, 305–306
   embryonic stage of, 308–309
   environmental influences on, 310–315
   fetal stage of, 310
   germinal stage of, 307–308
Preorgasmic, defined, 446
Preovulatory phase, 86
Prepared childbirth, 322
Prepuce, 64, 104
Preterm, defined, 324
Priapism, 467
Primal scene, 552
Primary amenorrhea, 95
Primary dysmenorrhea, 94
Primary erogenous zones, 128
Primary sex characteristics, defined, 381
Primary sexual dysfunction, 444
Primary syphilis, 482
Probability sample, 41
Prodromal symptoms, 490
Progesterone, 74, 75, 139
Progestin
   effects of, 340
   effects on fetus, 313
Projection, defined, 27t
Prolactin, 85
   and lactation, 327
Proliferative phase, 86
Prostaglandins, 95
   and childbirth, 319
Prostate gland, 111–112
   cancer of, 114–115
   enlargement of, 113–114
   inflammation of, 115
   removal of, affecting sexual performance, 448
Prostatitis, 115
Prostitutes
   characteristics of, 605–606
   types of, 602–605
Prostitution, 600–601
   customers of, 607–608
   HIV and, 610, 611
   incidence of, 601–602
   legal issues in, 600–601
   male, 608–609
   in Victorian era, 18
Protease inhibitors, 521
Protestantism
   attitudes toward abortion, 365
   sexual attitudes in, 16–17
Proxemics, 221

Proximodistal development, 308
Prozac, 96, 131
   retarding ejaculation, 466
   to treat paraphilias, 557
Prurient, defined, 612
PSA (prostate-specific antigen), 115
Pseudohermaphroditism, 158, 159–161
Psychoactive drugs, sexual effects of, 132
Psychoanalysis, defined, 26
Psychoanalytic theory, 26–27
   dream symbols in, 28t
   on paraphilias, 552
Psychodynamic theory, on gender roles, 174
Psychological androgyny, 180
   advantages of, 180–181
   model of, 180f
   and sexual behavior, 181
Psychological disability, and sexuality, 435
Psychopathia Sexualis, 19, 236, 263
Psychosexual development, 27
   defined, 28
Psychosexual therapy, 457
PTSD, 575
Puberty
   defined, 381
   female, 382–384
   male, 384–386
Pubic lice, 479t, 494
Pubococcygeus muscle, 70, 461
Pudendal block, 322
Pudendum, 62
Pullo people, perspectives on beauty, 190
Punks, 609
Puritans, 17
Pyrethrins, 494

Quadriplegia, 433
Questions, in communication, 224, 228

Race, and mate preference, 194
Radioimmunoassay, 303
Radiotherapy, defined, 73
Random assignment, 55
Random sample, 41
Rape, 562–564
   blaming the victim, 8
   incidence of, 564–565
   myths about, 569–570
   prevention of, 576–579
   psychological disorders from, 575
   psychology of, 571–572
   sociocultural factors in, 570–571
   surviving, 572–576
   treatment of perpetrators of, 589–590
   treatment of victims of, 576
   types of, 565–569
   by women, 569
Rape trauma syndrome, 575
Rapid orgasm, 446
Rapists
   motives of, 572
   psychological characteristics of, 571–572
   treatment of, 589–590
Rationalism, 634
Rationalization, defined, 27t
Reaction formation, defined, 27t
Realistic love, 198

Rear-entry position, 252–253, 255f
Recessive traits, 316
Reciprocity, 195–196
Recreational sex, 416
Rectovaginal examination, 76
Reflection, defined, 6
Reflex
    defined, 117
    described, 118f
Reflex arc, 117
Reformation, Protestant, 16–17
Refractory period, 144
Relationship
    affecting sexual performance, 453
    traits important for, 191–192, 193t
Reliability, defined, 44
Religion, and sexuality, 31
Repression, 26
    defined, 27t, 28, 279
Requests, making, 226–227
Research
    ethics in, 56–58
    goals and methods in, 37–40
    sampling methods for, 40–42
    scientific method in, 36–37
    types of, 42–56
Resolution phase, 144–145
Respiratory distress syndrome, 324
Retardation, and sexuality, 435
Retarded ejaculation, 445
Reticular activating system (RAS),
    134
Retrograde ejaculation, 122
Retroverted, defined, 73
Reverse transcriptase, 507
Rh incompatibility, 312
Rhythm method, 352–355
RIA, 303
Rimming, 496
Roe v. Wade, 334, 363
Romantic love, 197, 199, 200, 202,
    202t
    ABCDE model of, 208–216
Rome, ancient
    attitudes toward menstruation in,
        90
    marriage in, 410
    sexual attitudes in, 11, 14
Romeo and Juliet, 196
Root, of penis, 104
Roth v. United States, 613
RU-486, 367, 368
Rubella, effect on fetus, 312
Rubin test, 300
Russia, sexual attitudes in, 8–9

S&M, 546–548
Sacrum, 118
Sadism, 14, 545, 546–548
    psychoanalytic view of, 552
Sadistic rape, 572
Sadomasochism, 546–548
    social context of, 554–555
Saltpeter, 131
Sambian people
    gender roles of, 173
    sexual attitudes of, 270, 271

Sample
    defined, 40
    of convenience, 42
    methods of choosing, 41–42
Sandpipers, polyandry among, 23
Sarcoptes scabei, 479t, 495
Satyriasis, 551, 552
Scabies, 479t, 495
Scarlet Letter, The, 17
Schema, defined, 176
School
    contraceptive distribution in, 398–400
    gender typing in, 175
    sexual harassment at, 594
Scientific method, 36–37
Scores, defined, 608
Scrotum, 107
Secondary amenorrhea, 95
Secondary dysmenorrhea, 94
Secondary erogenous zones, 128
Secondary sex characteristics, 77, 108,
    137
    defined, 381
Secondary sexual dysfunction, 444
Secondary syphilis, 482
Secretory phase, 88
Sedatives, effect on fetus, 314
Seduction III, 622–623
Seduction lines, 579
Selection factor, defined, 55
Self-defense, 578–579
Self-disclosure, 210–211
    cross-cultural views of, 212
    gender differences in, 212–213
    in intimacy, 224–225
Self-esteem, in intimacy, 218
Self-massage, 461
Selfless love, 200
Semantics, 50
Semen, contents of, 112
Seminal vesicles, 110, 111
Seminiferous tubules, 108, 110
Seniang people, sexual attitudes of, 376
Sensate focus exercises, 456
Sensory disabilities, and sexuality, 434
Septate hymen, 68f
Septum, 134, 136
Serial monogamy, 405
Seronegative, defined, 517
Seropositive, defined, 517
Serotonin, retarding ejaculation, 465
Sertraline, retarding ejaculation, 465
Serving in Silence, 287
Sex
    defined, 4
Sex and Temperament in Three Primitive Societies, 24
Sex characteristics, defined, 381
Sex chromosomes, 108, 154–155
    abnormalities of, 157
    talk about, 222
Sex education, 380–381
Sex flush, 141
Sex in America: A definitive survey, 45
Sex organs, defined, 5
Sex partners, number of, 30t
Sex skin, 142

Sex therapy, 456
    evaluation of, 463–465
    outcomes of, 464t
    seeking, 467–468
Sex-linked abnormalities, 316
Sexism, 166–167, 169
    in schools, 175
Sexology, 19
Sexual Addiction, The, 550
Sexual arousal disorders, 441
    treatment of, 458–459
    types of, 443–445
Sexual assault, 563–564
    aftermath of, 574–575, 574t
Sexual aversion disorder, 443
Sexual behavior
    in adolescence, 387–391
    androgyny and, 181
    in childhood, 378–379
    defined, 5
    deviant, 536–558
    gender roles and, 178–179
    hormones and, 137–140
    in preadolescence, 380
Sexual Behavior in the Human Female, 19, 553
Sexual Behavior in the Human Male, 19
Sexual Behavior in the 1970s, 45
Sexual coercion
    of children, 582–589
    harassment, 590–596
    pornography and, 616–619
    rape, 562–579
    verbal, 579–582
Sexual competency, importance of, 454–455
Sexual contact
    anal intercourse, 255–259
    breast stimulation, 246
    foreplay, 244–245
    intercourse, 250–255
    kissing, 245
    oral-genital stimulation, 246–250
    touching, 245–246
Sexual desire disorders, 441
    treatment of, 457–458
    types of, 442–443
Sexual differentiation
    of brain, 157
    of gonads, 155f
    hormones and, 155–156
    prenatal, 154–155
    stages of, 156–157
Sexual dysfunctions, 440
    organic causes of, 448–450
    origins of, 448–456
    psychosocial issues in, 450–455
    sociocultural aspects of, 448t
    treatment of, 456–468
    types of, 441–448
Sexual fantasy, 241–243
    during coitus, 253–254, 258f
    homosexual, 267–268
Sexual harassment, 590
    on campus, 593–594
    defined, 591
    resisting, 594–596
    in school, 594
    in the workplace, 592–593

Sexual orientation, 262–263
    affecting sexual performance, 453
    biological perspectives on, 276–278
    brain and, 278
    classification of, 263–268
    cross-cultural perspectives on, 270–271
    cross-species perspectives on, 271
    ethnicity and, 272
    and gender identity, 263
    genetics and, 276–277
    hormones and, 277–278
    legal issues in, 274–275
    modern attitudes toward, 271–276
    nonconforming, 281–284
    psychological perspectives on, 278–281
Sexual pain disorders, 441
    treatment of, 463
    types of, 447–448
Sexual panic state, 443
Sexual phobia, 443
Sexual response cycle, 140–145
Sexual revolution, 19–20, 415–416
Sexual satisfaction, and frequency of inter-
    course, 54f
Sexual techniques, affecting sexual perfor-
    mance, 453
Sexuality
    in adolescence, 381–391
    biological perspective on, 21
    in childhood, 377–379
    communicating with children about, 382–383
    critical thinking about, 7–10
    cross-cultural perspective on, 23–26
    cross-species perspective on, 21–23
    defined, 5
    disabilities and, 432–435
    historical perspectives on, 10–20
    in infancy, 374–377
    in marriage, 415–419
    in old age, 429–431
    in preadolescence, 379–381
    psychological perspective on, 26–29
    scientific approach to, 36–40
    sociocultural perspectives on, 29–31
    study of, 5, 18–19
    and values, 6–7
Sexually-transmitted diseases. See STDs
Shaft, of penis, 104
Shigella, 485
Sickle cell anemia, 315–316
    detection of, 318
Side-entry position, 252
Signaling, 226
Silent rape reaction, 575–576
Simple kissing, 245
Singlehood, 404–405
Siriono people, foreplay among, 245
Situation ethics, 632–633
Situational sexual dysfunctions, 441
Sixty-nine, 248–249, 250f
Skene's glands, 149
Skepticism, 7
Skin, role in sexual arousal, 127–129
Small talk, 209
Smegma, 447
Smell, role in sexual arousal, 126–127
Smoking, effect on fetus, 314–315

Snappers, 131
Social desirability, defined, 47, 50
Social Desirability Scale, 50
Social Organization of Sexuality, The, 45
Social skills training, 557
Social-exchange theory, 208
Social-learning theory
    defined, 29
    on gender roles, 174–176
Socialization, defined, 174
Sociobiology, 23
    on gender typing, 172
Sodomy, 256, 269
    laws against, 274–275
Soixante-neuf, 248–249, 250f
Somatic nervous system, 119
South America, sexual attitudes in, 8, 9
Spanish fly, 130
Spectator role, 446
Spectinomycin, 480
Speculum, 76
Sperm, 107, 108, 110
Spermatic cord, 107
Spermatids, 108, 110
Spermatocytes, 108, 110
Spermatozoa, 108, 110
    passage of, 111f
Spermicides, 347–348
Sphincters, 69
Spina bifida, detection of, 318
Spinal block, 322
Spinal cord, and sexual function, 118, 433–434
Spinal cord injury, affecting sexual perfor-
    mance, 448
Spine, and sexual function, 117
Spirochete, 481
Spontaneous abortion, 294, 304
Squeeze technique, 462–463
Stanley v. Georgia, 614
Staphylococcus aureus, 89
Staring, as communication, 221
Statutory rape, 563
STDs
    anal intercourse and, 259
    attitudes towards, 475
    bacterial, 476, 477t, 480–485
    communicating about, 474
    ectoparasitic, 479t, 494–495
    health care for, 488
    hotlines for, 498
    incidence of, 473–474
    oral-genital transmission of, 130
    prevention of, 495–497
    vaginal infections, 477t-478t, 485–488
    viral, 478t-479t, 489–494
Stereotypes, 10, 165
    advertising and, 625
Sterilization
    advantages and disadvantages of, 357–358
    female, 356–357
    male, 355–356
Stillbirth, 312
Stone Age, sexual attitudes in, 11
Stonewall Inn, 275
Stop-start method, 463
Storge, 196, 200
Stranger rape, 565

Stratified random sample, 41
Street hustlers, 609
Streetwalkers, 602–603
Stress, as ethical concern in research, 56–57
Studies in the Psychology of Sex, 18", 236
Sublimation, defined, 27t
Successive approximations, 211
Suffrage, women, 17
Superego, 26
    defined, 27
Surface contact, 209
Surfactants, 324
Surgery, for erectile disorder, 466
Surrogate mother, 301
Survey
    defined, 43
    of specific population, 46–47
Survey method, 43–50
    limitations of, 47
Survival of the fittest, 22
Swan people, sexual attitudes of, 270
Sweden, unwed motherhood in, 397, 413
Swinging, 51, 420, 421
Sympathetic nervous system, 119
Sympathetic pregnancy, 305
Syndrome, defined, 510
Syphilis, 477t
    affecting sexual performance, 449
    chancre of, 482
    diagnosis and treatment of, 483
    effect on fetus, 311, 312
    incidence of, 481–482
    origin of, 481
    stages of, 482
    symptoms of, 482–483
    transmission of, 482
Systematic desensitization, 556

Tacoma, Washington, 529
Tailhook scandal, 562
Tampons, 89
Taoism, sexual attitudes in, 15
Taste, role in sexual arousal, 129
Tay-Sachs disease, 315, 316
    detection of, 318
Tchambuli people, gender roles of, 173
Teenage pregnancy
    consequences of, 394–395
    incidence of, 391
    rates of, 395–397
    resolution of, 392–393
    schools and, 398–400
Telephone scatalogia, 542–544
Teratogens, effect on fetus, 311
Terazol, 487
Terconazole, 487
Tertiary syphilis, 482
Testes, 84, 102
    cancer of, 113
    development of, 156–157
    endocrine function of, 84
    hormonal control of, 108f
    self-examination of, 114f
    sexual function of, 107–110
Testicles. See Testes

Photo Credits: *(continued from page ii)* **Chapter 9:** p. 242, Laurie Platt Winfrey, Inc.; p. 249, Costa Manos/Magnum Photos. **Chapter 10:** p. 263, Donna Binder/Impact Visuals; p. 273, Catherine Noren/Stock, Boston; p. 276, Rick Reinhard/Impact Visuals; p. 280, Stephen Marks; p. 283, Donna Binder/Impact Visuals; p. 287, Jacques Chenet/Woodfin Camp & Associates. **Chapter 11:** p. 295, Francis LeRoy/Bio Cosmos/Photo Researchers Science Source; p. 305, J. Koontz/The Picture Cube; p. 306 (all), Petit Format/Nestle/Photo Researchers/Science Source; p. 318, Will & Demi McIntyre/Photo Researchers; p. 319 (all), SIU/Photo Researchers; p. 325, Willia J. Hill, Jr./The Image Works. **Chapter 12:** p. 333, Courtesy of Planned Parenthood of New York City; p. 337, Courtesy of Cable News Network; p. 342, Courtesy of Wyeth Ayerst Laboratories; p. 343, Custom Medical Stock Photo; p. 358, Courtesy of Wisconsin Pharmaceutical Co.; p. 361, Reuters/Steve Mawyer-POOL/Archive Photos; p. 363, Robert Harbison; p. 368, D. H. Hessell/Stock, Boston. **Chapter 13:** p. 375, Robert Harbison; p. 378, Rick Smolan/Stock, Boston; p. 386, Dan Habib/Impact Visuals; p. 392, Lawrence Migdale/Stock, Boston; p. 396, Gale Zucker/Stock, Boston; p. 400, Jeff Lowenthal/Woodfin Camp & Associates. **Chapter 14:** p. 405, David Wells/The Image Works; p. 407, Stephanie Maze/Woodfin Camp & Associates; p. 410 (left), Nancy Sheehan/The Picture Cube; p. 410 (right), Esbin-Anderson/The Image Works; p. 418, Lou Jones; p. 427, Paul Fusco/Magnum Photos; p. 432, Christopher Springman/The Stock Market. **Chapter 15:** p. 442, Shackman/Monkmeyer; p. 450, Nicholas DeVore III/Photographers Aspen; p. 454, Roy Morsch/The Stock Market; p. 466, G. Thomas Bishop/Custom Medical Stock Photo. **Chapter 16:** p. 473, Dan Budnik/Woodfin Camp & Associates; p. 476, Courtesy of Dr. Nicholas J. Fiumara; p. 481, Custom Medical Stock Photo/CMSP/NIAID/NIH; p. 482, C. James Webb/Phototake NYC; p. 489, Phototake/CNRI; p. 492, Bio Photo Assoc/Photo Researchers; p. 494, E. Gray/Photo Researchers Science Photo Library. **Chapter 17:** p. 507, Bill Longcone/Photo Researchers Science Source; p. 509, Betty Press/Woodfin Camp & Associates; p. 512, UPI/Corbis-Bettmann; p. 514, AP/Wide World Photos; p. 521, Alon Reininger/Woodfin Camp & Associates; p. 523, Alon Reininger/WoodfinCamp & Associates; p. 531, James D. Wilson/Woodfin Camp & Associates. **Chapter 18:** p. 538, Alon Reininger/Contact/Woodfin Camp & Associates; p. 539, Donna Binder/Impact Visuals; p. 551, North Wind Picture Archives. **Chapter 19:** p. 563, AP/Wide World Photos; p. 564, Michael Nichols/Magnum Photos; p. 566, Steve McCurry/Magnum Photos; p. 572, Bob Daemmrich/Stock, Boston; p. 577, Rob Crandall/Stock, Boston; p. 579, Clark Jones/Impact Visuals; p. 583, Courtesy of LaPorte County Child Abuse Prevention Council; p. 588, Courtesy of Western Psychological Services; p. 591, Archive Photos/Fotos International; p. 593, John Coletti. **Chapter 20:** p. 601 (both), AFP/Corbis-Bettmann; p. 602, Tony O'Brien/JB Pictures; p. 603, Mike Yamashita/Woodfin Camp & Associates; p. 611, Paul Chesley/Photographers Aspen; p. 615, Courtesy of Star Ware Publishing; p. 620 (left), AP/Wide World Photos; p. 620 (right), Carolee Schneemann; p. 621 (all), Art Resource; p. 622 (bottom), Sue Coe, *Bedford Rape*, Copyright © 1983 Sue Coe, Courtesy of Galerie St. Etienne, New York; p. 623 (top left), Joan Lyon; p. 623 (top middle and right), Carolee Schneemann; p. 623 (bottom both), Carolee Schneemann; p. 624, J. Kirk Condyles/Impact Visuals.